Current Law STATUTES 1996

VOLUME THREE

AUSTRALIA
The Law Book Company
Brisbane • Sydney • Melbourne • Perth

CANADA
Carswell
Ottawa • Toronto • Calgary • Montreal • Vancouver

Agents:
Steimatzky's Agency Ltd., Tel Aviv;
N. M. Tripathi (Private) Ltd., Bombay;
Eastern Law House (Private) Ltd., Calcutta;
M.P.P. House, Bangalore;
Universal Book Traders, Delhi;
Aditya Books, Delhi;
MacMillan Shuppan KK, Tokyo;
Pakistan Law House, Karachi

Current Law
STATUTES

1996

VOLUME THREE

SWEET & MAXWELL EDITORIAL TEAM

SARAH ANDREWS
SHIRLEY ARCHER
RACHAEL ARMITAGE
MELANIE BHAGAT
HANNAH CASEY
CAROL LOCKE
CERI PICKERING
JANICE SAYER
MELISSA TEMPLE
SUZANNE WARREN

W. GREEN EDITORIAL TEAM

STEPHEN HARVEY
PETER NICHOLSON
JANIE BRASH

LONDON

SWEET & MAXWELL

EDINBURGH

W. GREEN

1997

Published by
SWEET & MAXWELL LIMITED
of 100 Avenue Road, London,
and W. GREEN LIMITED
of Alva Street, Edinburgh,
Typeset by MFK Information Services Limited, Hitchin, Herts.
and printed in Great Britain
by The Bath Press

ISBN This Volume only : 0 421 56590 X
As a set : 0 421 56610 8

CONTENTS

CHRONOLOGICAL TABLE

VOLUME THREE

Annotators' names are in italic

VOLUME THREE

ALPHABETICAL INDEX OF SHORT TITLES

STATUTES 1996

(References are to chapter numbers of 1996)

HOUSING GRANTS, CONSTRUCTION AND REGENERATION ACT 1996*

(1996 c. 53)

ARRANGEMENT OF SECTIONS

PART I

GRANTS, &C. FOR RENEWAL OF PRIVATE SECTOR HOUSING

CHAPTER I

THE MAIN GRANTS

Introductory

*Annotations by Andrew Arden Q.C., LL.B., Caroline Hunter, B.A., Barrister, Lecturer in Law, University of Nottingham, Charles Gardner, Partner at Reynolds Porter Chamberlain, Rudi Klein of the Specialist Engineering Contractors' Group.

CHAPTER III

HOME REPAIR ASSISTANCE

CHAPTER IV

DEFERRED ACTION NOTICES, &C.

Deferred action notices

Power to improve enforcement procedures

Power to charge for enforcement action

Supplementary provisions

CHAPTER V

SUPPLEMENTARY PROVISIONS

Contributions by Secretary of State

Consent of the Secretary of State

Parsonages, charities, &c.

Interpretation

Transitional and consequential provisions

PART II

CONSTRUCTION CONTRACTS

Introductory provisions

An Act to make provision for grants and other assistance for housing purposes and about action in relation to unfit housing; to amend the law relating to construction contracts and architects; to provide grants and other assistance for regeneration and development and in connection with clearance areas; to amend the provisions relating to home energy efficiency schemes; to make provision in connection with the dissolution of urban development corporations, housing action trusts and the Commission for the New Towns; and for connected purposes. [24th July 1996]

PARLIAMENTARY DEBATES

Hansard, H.L. Vol. 568, col. 1558; Vol. 569, cols. 976, 1004, 1459; Vol. 570, cols. 1576, 1650, 1836, 1905; Vol. 571, cols. 11, 37, 87, 795, 856, 901, 971, 1419; Vol. 574, col. 1316. H.C. Vol. 277, col. 45; Vol. 281, col. 21.

INTRODUCTION

This Act makes provision, *inter alia*, with regard to grants for renewal of private sector housing, including group repair schemes and home repair assistance and deferred action notices. The Act also makes provision as regards construction contracts, entitling a party to such a contract to payment by instalments, stage payments or other periodic payments for any work under the contract, except in certain circumstances. The Act also amends the law relating to architects.

PART I

GRANTS, &C. FOR RENEWAL OF PRIVATE SECTOR HOUSING

INTRODUCTION AND GENERAL NOTE

The principal purpose of this Part is to downgrade grant assistance for housing which is unfit or otherwise in need of works, from mandatory (so far as it has been such) to discretionary aid. Mandatory grants for property falling below a defined standard of acceptability have been available since the House Purchase and Housing Act 1959 (c. 33); the principal structure of grant-aid as it has been known over recent years was introduced by the Housing Act 1974 (c. 44), subsequently consolidated into the Housing Act 1985 (c. 68), and then replaced by Pt. VIII of the Local Government and Housing Act 1989 (c. 42), the latter of which introduced "means-testing". Under that Act, grants for works to prevent or remedy unfitness for human habitation or serious disrepair, were—broadly—mandatory. Under this Act, the only mandatory grants will be "disabled facilities grants" (see s.24).

The problem is one of money. *The Future of Private Housing Renewal Programmes, A Consultation Document* issued by the D.O.E. in June 1993, foreshadowed the change: "For 1994/95 onwards, expenditure is projected to grow above planned provision ... It is clear that this will give rise to unsustainable financial pressure ... The domination of mandatory grants has contributed to a number of unintended consequences. It has become increasingly difficult for authorities to act strategically and, where appropriate, on an area basis ... The current system of mandatory grants, requiring authorities to deal with valid applications within 6 months, tends to encourage pepper-potting of assistance whether or not this is the most appropriate course. The build up of financial pressures exacerbates this effect" (paras. 3.3, 3.4).

The White Paper, *Our Future Homes*, June 1995, Cm. 2901, which preceded both this Act and its sister legislation, the Housing Act 1996 (c. 52), considered grant-aid in its Chapter Two, on Promoting Sustainable Home Ownership. Describing us as a "nation of home improvers", it states that since 1990, almost 350,000 house renovation, disabled facilities and minor works assistance grants had been given, totalling more than £1 billion (p.16). None the less, "Further change is needed. Some authorities have been unable to meet the demand for mandatory renovation grants and disabled facilities grants within their available budgets. The case for help to private owners needs to be considered alongside other local housing priorities ... The present grant provisions give local authorities little scope for making the best use of resources. In many areas a strategic approach—which aims at the renewal of a whole area or which focuses on special problems—is likely to be more cost-effective than meeting individual needs as they arise" (p.17).

Accordingly, renovation grants for owner occupied property would become discretionary, while assistance for landlords—which would likewise only be discretionary—would be confined to renewal areas (under the Local Government and Housing Act 1989). This was developed in the linked Explanatory Paper, *The Future of Private Housing Renewal Programmes*, June 1995: "Although only a small minority of privately owned homes are both unfit and owned by people who cannot afford essential repairs, the problem can only be tackled over a period of years. Both cost and logistics preclude the immediate repair of all unfit houses" (para. 2.2). "... The present right to mandatory renovation grants has created unrealistic expectations. The demand for grants has greatly exceeded the resources available for the purpose at a time of general expenditure constraint..." (para. 2.3, or "the lion's share of resources", *per* Minister of State, Department of the Environment (Earl Ferrers), *Hansard* (H.L.), Second Reading, February 20, 1996, col. 981). In substance, the future is to lie with strategic activity, developed in authorities' Housing Investment Programmes (para. 2.5).

Landlords were to meet costs as an overhead of the business, although discretionary grants in renewal areas were to be available so as not to frustrate local authority policies (para. 3.2): these additional restrictions have not, however, (yet) moved forward into legislation (see *Hansard* (H.L.), Second Reading, February 20, 1996, col. 981, and see the reserve power in s.31, below). All grants were still to be means-tested or otherwise to have regard to applicants' resources (para. 3.3). Transitional provisions would preserve the right to mandatory grants under the 1989 Act which were not decided before commencement of this Part: see now s.102, below. The Explanatory Paper added:

> "Local authorities will need to consider the implications of the changes to those who have made enquiries about the availability of grant but have not submitted formal applications. In particular authorities will wish to consider what steps they should take to ensure that those enquirers having a reasonable expectation of a mandatory grant are fully aware of the proposal" (para. 3.6).

This last conceals direct reference to one of the means to which authorities without sufficient resources were obliged to resort, waiting lists for application forms. Once an application under the 1989 Act was made, it had to be determined within six months; many authorities, however, were reported to have maintained a waiting-list for application forms, to prevent time beginning to run. (This attracted particular attention in Birmingham during 1995, but that authority was far from the only authority to rely on patience, and/or ignorance, in order to meet what the government had come to accept was a burden that authorities simply could not meet. The legality of maintaining waiting lists was never tested in court, perhaps reflecting a growing awareness of their dubious standing and a preference for quiet concession over dramatic defeat.)

Local authorities also exercise functions in relation to unfitness under the Housing Act 1985 (c. 68), which requires them to take one of three courses of action in relation to a property that is unfit for human habitation as defined in s.604 of that Act (as amended by the 1989 Act): to require it to be repaired, or to close it to human habitation, or to cause it to be demolished. Where repairs were required, an owner could seek a mandatory grant:

> "With the abolition of mandatory grants ... [l]ocal authorities will ... be given an additional 'deferred action' option under which they may decide that, while there is unfitness that requires repair, dealing with it is not essential or does not have priority. ... The authority will also be required to review its decision after 12 months" (para. 6.2; see now Chapter IV, below).

One other aspect of grant-aid to which attention has been paid and may be drawn is the changes designed to "reduce the opportunities for abuse. Grant is primarily intended to help people remain in their own homes. To further this objective only people who have both owned and lived in a property for three years will normally qualify for grant" (paras. 8.1, 8.2), although this would not apply in renewal areas, or for disabled facilities grants, or the home repairs grants introduced by Chap. III, below (but which are expected to be confined to an amount of £2,000 in any one year, and £4,000 in any three year period: see para. 5.3, and s.36, below). The claw-back provisions have likewise been tightened to prevent "windfall gain from grant assistance" (para. 8.3), and to encourage enforcement local authorities will have to repay subsidy to the D.O.E. "where grant has been or *could have been* recovered" (para. 8.4, emphasis added).

Relocation grants, designed to "help to keep local communities together by assisting people" (*Hansard* (H.L.), Second Reading, February 20, 1996, Minister of State, Department of the Environment (Earl Ferrers), col. 982, see also *The Future of Private Housing Renewal Programmes*, s.7), are governed by Pt. IV of this Act.

The length of this Act, and in particular of this Part (*cf.* the 1989 Act, Pt. VIII, which was only 38 sections long) reflects what appears to be a new approach to drafting legislation, with two key aspects: first, provisions are generally broken down into smaller, more digestible sections; secondly, "because it has been drafted largely to include and to restate previous legislation rather than simply to amend it. It therefore avoids the maddening consequence of having to read the Bill and having constantly to refer in cross-reference to existing statutes" (*Hansard* (H.L.), Second Reading, February 20, 1996, col. 977, Minister of State, Department of the Environment (Earl Ferrers)).

Note

Although, therefore there is much that is familiar, if not identical, to earlier grant law, and although as such it is certain that some if not many of the earlier subordinate instruments filling out much of the detail of how this Part will operate in practice will be restated under this Part, the temptation to use such materials—and guidance under the previous law—in explanation or elaboration of this Part has been resisted, as (until the new details are available) these notes will quickly be not merely out of date in that respect but actively tend to mislead (and, in the *interregnum*, may subsequently prove guilty of having raised false expectations). With very few exceptions (where earlier guidance or instrument is the only practicable way to explain an otherwise elliptical statutory expression), these notes (as those in the Housing Act 1996) are accordingly confined to the policy statements or publications already available, and the statutory provisions themselves.

CHAPTER I

THE MAIN GRANTS

Introductory

Grants for improvements and repairs, &c.

1.—(1) Grants are available from local housing authorities in accordance with this Chapter towards the cost of works required for—

(a) the improvement or repair of dwellings, houses in multiple occupation or the common parts of buildings containing one or more flats,

(b) the provision of dwellings or houses in multiple occupation by the conversion of a house or other building, and

(c) the provision of facilities for disabled persons in dwellings and in the common parts of buildings containing one or more flats.

(2) A grant relating to—

(a) the improvement or repair of a dwelling, or

(b) the provision of dwellings by the conversion of a house or other building,

is referred to as a "renovation grant".

(3) A grant relating to the improvement or repair of the common parts of a building is referred to as a "common parts grant".

(4) A grant for the provision of facilities for a disabled person—

(a) in a dwelling, or

(b) in the common parts of a building containing one or more flats, is referred to as a "disabled facilities grant".

(5) A grant for—

(a) the improvement or repair of a house in multiple occupation, or

(b) the provision of a house in multiple occupation by the conversion of a house or other building,

is referred to as an "HMO grant".

(6) In the following provisions of this Chapter the expression "grant", without more, means any of these types of grant.

DEFINITIONS

"common parts": s.58.
"disabled persons": s.100.
"dwelling": s.101.
"flat": s.58.
"house in multiple occupation": s.101.
"improvement": s.101.
"local housing authority": s.101.

GENERAL NOTE

This Part introduces a new system of grant-aid for private housing to replace that contained in the Local Government and Housing Act 1989, Pt. VIII. Applications under the 1989 Act not approved before this Part comes into force are governed by s.102, below.

Under the Housing Act 1985, Pt. XV, which was replaced by the 1989 Act, Pt. VIII, there were five main grants: the *improvement* grant, for the conversion of premises into dwellings, or for "major" works of improvement; the *intermediate* grant for the improvement of dwellings lacking standard amenities; the *repairs* grant, for works of repair or replacement not associated with conversion, major improvement or the provision of standard amenities; the *special* grant for works to a house in multiple occupation; and the *common parts* grant for the repair or improvement of common parts of a building containing one or more flats.

The 1989 Act replaced these five with four new principal grants: a *renovation* grant for the improvement or repair of a dwelling, or provision of dwellings by conversion; a *common parts* grant for the improvement or repair of the common parts of a building; a *disabled facilities* grant for the provision of facilities for a disabled person; and *HMO* grant for the improvement or repair of a house in multiple occupation ("HMO") or for the provision of an HMO by conversion. The 1989 Act, s.131, introduced what was effectively a fifth grant—for minor works, including thermal insulation, to a dwelling.

This Act retains the four principal grants available under the 1989 Act, and replaces the minor works grant with a new category of "home repair assistance" under Chap. III, below. Reduction of number of grants was not the purpose, so much as reduction in their status from mandatory to discretionary: see Introduction to Pt. I, above.

Local housing authorities

These are district councils, London borough councils, the Common Council of the City of London, Welsh county councils or county borough councils and the Council of the Isles of Scilly, and those unitary authorities on which housing has devolved under the Local Government Act 1992 (c. 19): see s.1 of the Housing Act 1985.

Improvement or Repair

Although there has been much case-law in recent years on the distinction between improvement and repair, as the expression used in this Act is inclusive of both, nothing turns on that distinction in this context. Indeed, as "improvement" includes alteration and enlargement (s.101), there is (as there long has been in this area) no room for substantive argument: on the face of it, any works that are not mere routine maintenance would qualify, even, *e.g.* major works of planned maintenance that in their own right can also be considered repairs and even improvement—*cf. R. v. Hackney L.B.C., ex p. Secretary of State for the Environment* (1989) 88 L.G.R. 96, Q.B.D.

Rather than case-law, therefore, what governs the phrase are the purposes and other provisions of the legislation (see, *e.g.* ss.4 [more than 10 years old], 12 [purposes for which grant may be given, including compliance with s.189 or s.190 of the Housing Act 1985, unfitness or disrepair notice, insulation and heating, internal arrangement, means of escape from fire], 45 [recalculation or withholding of grant because not completed to satisfaction of authority]), and the explicit directions as to work excluded from grant by the Secretary of State under s.5, and as to construction standards and otherwise required by the Secretary of State under s.12(1)(g)–(i).

Conversion

In *R. v. Bristol City Council, ex p. Naqvi* (1994) 26 H.L.R. 640, Q.B.D., the applicant owned a shop with a flat above. In November 1991, planning permission was granted for change of use of the ground floor from shop to residential use, and to combine it with the flat to make one dwelling. Although it was held in that case that the true nature of the scheme was one for the provision of a dwelling by conversion (see below, s.4), it was also noted that works of improvement or repair can include the conversion of some accommodation provided that the dwelling as a whole still retained its identity and that the overall nature of the proposal remained one of improvement and repair.

Although the section refers to the provision of dwelling*s* (in the plural), this means one or more dwellings: see s.12(2), below.

Dwelling

Dwelling is defined by s.101 as "a building or part of a building occupied or intended to be occupied as a separate dwelling, together with any yard, garden, outhouses and appurtenances belonging to it or usually enjoyed with it". The dwelling, to be "separate", must contain all the facilities for normal living activity, *e.g.* a kitchen (see, *e.g. Neale v. Del Soto* [1945] K.B. 144, C.A.; *Winters v. Dance* [1949] L.J.R. 165, C.A.), although not necessarily its own bathroom/lavatory (see, *e.g. Cole v. Harris* [1945] K.B. H.L.; *Marsh v. Cooper* [1969] 1 W.L.R. 803, C.A.). The latter could, however, be amongst the services or amenities specified by the Secretary of State under s.12(1)(h), below.

Appurtenances. This extended definition dates back to the Artizans' and Labourers' Dwellings Act 1868 (c. 130), and has been maintained since (see, *e.g.* Housing of the Working Classes Act 1890 (c. 70), s.29, Housing Act 1925 (c. 14), s.135, Housing Act 1936 (c. 51), s.188, Housing Act 1957 (c. 56), s.189, Housing Act 1985 (c. 68), s.56). In *Trim v. Sturminster R.D.C.* [1938] 2 K.B. 508, under the 1936 Act, 10 acres of grassland were let together with a cottage. On the question whether they were appurtenant to the cottage, it was held that the expression "appurtenances" meant only such matters as outhouses, yards and gardens, but not the land itself: how much of the land could be included in this definition depended on the facts, but would certainly be less than the whole of the 10 acres that had been thus let.

In *Clymo v. Shell-Mex & B.P.* (1963) 10 R.R.C. 85, C.A., under the Rating and Valuation Act 1925 (c. 90), it was held that open land surrounded by depot buildings was appurtenant to the buildings, on the basis that had there been a conveyance or demise the land would have passed without any need specifically to mention it. In *Methuen-Cambell v. Walters* [1979] Q.B. 525, under the Leasehold Reform Act 1967 (c. 88), it was held that land cannot ordinarily be appurtenant to land, although the ordinary and strict meaning of the word appurtenant could yield to a wider meaning if the context so requires.

In *Hansford v. Jago* [1921] 1 Ch. 322, a right of way was held to come within the word appurtenance. In *Sovmots Investments v. Secretary of State for the Environment* [1979] A.C. 144, H.L., however, it was held that appurtenances could not include rights of way and other ancillary rights not yet defined or in some cases even in existence (though specifically over-turned by the Local Government (Miscellaneous Provisions) Act 1976 (c. 57), s.13, so far as concerns compulsory purchase by local authorities). In *R. v. Lambeth L.B.C., ex p. Clayhope* at first instance ((1986) 18 H.L.R. 541), it was held that the common parts and the roof of a block of flats were not appurtenant to each and every flat (this was not considered in the Court of Appeal—above—as it did not arise in the light of the finding that the flats were not houses).

In *F.F.F. Estates v. Hackney L.B.C.* [1981] Q.B. 503, 3 H.L.R. 107, C.A., however, the court, considering the meaning of dwelling in connection with improvement notices under Pt. VII of the Housing Act 1985, said that the case-law on rights passing on a conveyance was not of "any real help".

Common Parts

This includes, by s.58, "the structure and exterior of the building and common facilities provided, whether in the building or elsewhere, for persons who include the occupiers of one or more dwellings in the building". The facilities do not, accordingly, have to be exclusive to occupiers of the dwellings.

The words "structure and exterior" have been held to include the partition wall between a house and the adjoining house (*Green v. Eales* (1841) 2 Q.B. 225), windows (*Quick v. Taff Ely B.C.* [1986] Q.B. 809, C.A., see also *Ball v. Plummer, The Times*, June 17, 1879, and *Boswell v. Crucible Steel Co* [1925] 1 K.B. 119, but *cf. Holiday Fellowship v. Hereford* [1959] 1 W.L.R. 221), and essential means of access to a house (*Brown v. Liverpool Corporation* [1969] 3 All E.R.

1345; 13 H.L.R. 1, C.A.), although not a back yard (*Hopwood v. Cannock Chase D.C.* [1975] 1 W.L.R. 373, 13 H.L.R. 31, C.A., and *King v. South Northamptonshire D.C.* (1991) 24 H.L.R. 284, C.A.). The latter (or its equivalent, *e.g.* common gardens, car-parks) will, however, be brought in by the reference to facilities "whether in the building or elsewhere".

A roof will invariably form a part of the structure and exterior, and, thus, the common parts, even if it may also be considered a part of the top floor flat, and/or if the tenant of the top floor flat has liability for its maintenance: consider *Douglas-Scott v. Scorgie* [1984] 1 W.L.R. 716, 13 H.L.R. 97, C.A.

In the context of reduction of rateable value under the Housing Act 1974 (c. 44), Sched. 8, for the purposes of the Leasehold Reform Act 1967 (c. 88), the Court of Appeal adopted a wide view of what was meant by structural:

> "It is something appertaining to the fabric of the building so as to be part of the complete whole. A house is a complete unity. Structure implies concern with the constituent or material parts of that unity. That involves more than the load bearing elements, such as walls, roof and foundations. Rather it is that which pertains to basic fabric and parts, as distinguished from decoration and fittings" (*Pearlman v. Keepers & Governors of Harrow School* [1979] 1 Q.B. 56, C.A.).

House in Multiple Occupation

House in multiple occupation—or HMO—is defined by s.100 applying the definition to be found in Pt. VII of the Local Government and Housing Act 1989, which in turn (s.101) incorporates the definition to be found in the Housing Act 1985, Pt. XI, *save* that it excludes those parts of the HMO occupied as a separate dwelling by persons forming a single household. A house in multiple occupation is (1985 Act, s.345, as amended by the 1989 Act, Sched. 9, para. 44) "a house which is occupied by persons who do not form a single household", defining "house" to include "any part of a building which (a) apart from this subsection would not be regarded as a house; and (b) was originally constructed or subsequently adapted for occupation by a single household".

The definition therefore has three elements: "house", "occupied" and "by persons who do not form a single household".

House. The extended definition statutorily incorporates the decisions in *R. v. London Borough of Southwark, ex p. Lewis Levy* (1983) 8 H.L.R. 1; *R. v. Camden L.B.C., ex p. Rowton (Camden Town)* (1983) 10 H.L.R. 28, in which the term "house" was held—for the purposes of HMO legislation—to apply to a hostel or building used for multiple-occupation or as a lodging-house. Similarly, a large house operating as a holiday home for children has been held to be a house: *Reed v. Hastings Corporation* [1964] L.G.R. 588. In that case Lord Harman said " ... 'house' means what it obviously is, namely, a place fitted and used and adapted for human habitation". The decision was followed in *R. v. Hackney L.B.C., ex p. Evenbray* (1987) 19 H.L.R. 557, where it was held that a part of a hotel occupied by homeless families was a house, since it was a building constructed and used for human habitation.

Occupied. In order to show that the house is occupied it is not necessary to show any particular legal arrangement: *Minford Properties v. Hammersmith L.B.C.* (1978) 247 E.G. 561. The word broadly means "lived in": *Silbers v. Southwark L.B.C.* (1977) 76 L.G.R. 421. This is wide enough to cover a bed and breakfast hotel occupied by homeless families placed there by local authorities in pursuance of their duties to the homeless under Pt. III of the 1985 Act or Pt. VII of the Housing Act 1996 (c. 52): *Thrasyvoulou v. Hackney L.B.C.* (1986) 18 H.L.R. 370.

Single household. There is no statutory definition of single household. It has been said that "both the expression 'household' and membership of it is a question of fact and degree, there being no certain indicia the presence or absence of which is by itself conclusive..." (*per* Lord Hailsham, *Simmons v. Pizzey* [1979] A.C. 37, H.L.). In that case, some 75 women were in occupation of a women's refuge. None of the occupants intended to live there indefinitely. No occupant had any special part of the house to herself, so that there was no concept of separate households. Rather, the women organised the business of the house collectively, eating and undertaking the arrangements of the house together. It was held that this could not, however, amount to occupation as a single household.

More recently, in *Barnes v. Sheffield City Council* (1995) 27 H.L.R. 719, the Court of Appeal considered whether a group of students living in a shared house were a single household. The Court said that although it would be wrong to suggest that there was a litmus test which could be applied to the question whether there were separate households, the following factors were helpful indicators:

(a) whether the persons living in the house came to it as a single group or whether they were independently recruited;

(b) what facilities were shared;
(c) whether the occupiers were responsible for the whole house or just their particular rooms;
(d) whether individual tenants were able to, or did, lock other occupiers out of their rooms;
(e) whose responsibility it was to recruit new occupiers when individuals left;
(f) who allocated rooms;
(g) the size of the property;
(h) how stable the group composition was;
(i) whether the mode of living was communal.

The decision of the county court judge that the house was not an HMO because the group of students occupying it were a single household, was upheld.

See also *Silbers v. Southwark L.B.C.*, above; *cf. Hackney L.B.C. v. Ezedinma* [1981] 3 All E.R. 438.

Disabled Persons

This is defined in s.100 and means a person whose sight, hearing or speech is substantially impaired, who has a mental disorder or impairment of any kind, or which is physically substantially disabled by illness, injury, impairment present since birth, or otherwise: s.100(1).

Persons aged 18 or more are taken to be disabled if registered under s.29 of the National Assistance Act 1948 (c. 29), or if a person for whom welfare arrangements *have* been made under that section, or for whom such arrangements *might be* made (in the opinion of the social services authority): s.100(2).

Persons under 18 are taken to be disabled if registered under the Children Act 1989 (c. 41), Sched. 2, para. 2, or if the social services authority consider them to be a disabled child within the 1989 Act, Pt. III: s.100(3).

The social services authority are the authority having responsibility under the Local Authority Social Services Act 1970 (c. 42), which means a London borough council or the Common Council of the City of London or the Council of the Isles of Scilly, in England, in the area of a unitary authority that authority, and otherwise, in a metropolitan county the district council, and in a non-metropolitan county the county council and in Wales the county or county borough: Local Government Acts 1972 (c. 70) and 1992 (c. 19); 1970 Act, s.1 (as amended)—s.100(4).

Applications for grants

2.—(1) No grant shall be paid unless an application for it is made to the local housing authority in accordance with the provisions of this Chapter and is approved by them.

(2) An application for a grant shall be in writing and shall specify the premises to which it relates and contain—

(a) particulars of the works in respect of which the grant is sought (in this Chapter referred to as the "relevant works");
(b) unless the local housing authority otherwise direct in any particular case, at least two estimates from different contractors of the cost of carrying out the relevant works;
(c) particulars of any preliminary or ancillary services and charges in respect of the cost of which the grant is also sought; and
(d) such other particulars as may be prescribed.

(3) In this Chapter "preliminary or ancillary services and charges", in relation to an application for a grant, means services and charges which—

(a) relate to the application and the preparation for and the carrying out of works, and
(b) are specified for the purposes of this subsection by order of the Secretary of State.

(4) The Secretary of State may by regulations prescribe a form of application for a grant and an application for a grant to which any such regulations apply is not validly made unless it is in the prescribed form.

Definitions

"grant": s.1(6).
"local housing authority": s.101.

General Note

All applications for all categories of grant must be made to the local housing authority in writing and must contain:

(i) particulars of the works for which the grant is sought (the relevant works);
(ii) two estimates from different contractors of the costs of carrying out the works (the authority may dispense with this requirement for a particular case);
(iii) particulars of any preliminary or ancillary services and charges, if a grant is sought for these costs;
(iv) other prescribed particulars.

Only those charges and services as specified by the Secretary of State which relate to the application and the preparation and carrying out of works may be claimed for (subs. (3)).

The Secretary of State has reserved the power to prescribe the use of a particular application form: subs. (4). Without the exercise of such power, the authority cannot impose their own requirements (as under the 1985 Act, although many authorities have nonetheless claimed the right to treat as invalid applications not received on their own forms. The point is not academic, as levels of grant-aid may be affected by whether an application has been "made" or not).

Preliminary conditions

Ineligible applicants

3.—(1) No grant is payable under this Chapter unless the applicant is aged 18 or over on the date of the application.

In the case of a joint application, any applicant under the age of 18 years on the date of the application shall be left out of account.

(2) No grant is payable under this Chapter if the person who would otherwise qualify as the applicant for the grant is—

(a) a local authority;
(b) a new town corporation;
(c) an urban development corporation;
(d) a housing action trust;
(e) the Development Board for Rural Wales;
(f) a health authority, special health authority or NHS trust;
(g) a police authority established under section 3 of the Police Act 1964;
(h) a joint authority established by Part IV of the Local Government Act 1985;
(i) a residuary body established by Part VII of that Act; or
(j) an authority established under section 10(1) of that Act (waste disposal).

(3) No grant is payable under this Chapter if the applicant is of a description excluded from entitlement to grant aid by regulations made by the Secretary of State.

(4) Regulations under subsection (3) may proceed wholly or in part by reference to the provisions relating to entitlement to housing benefit, or any other form of assistance, as they have effect from time to time.

DEFINITIONS

"grant": s.1(6).
"housing action trust": s.101.
"local authority": s.101.
"new town corporation": s.101.
"urban development corporation": s.101.

GENERAL NOTE

There are three categories of person who may not apply for a grant:

(i) *Persons under 18.* If there is a joint application, and one of the applicants is a minor, *i.e.* under 18 (see the Family Law Reform Act 1969 (c. 46), s.12), he or she is to be disregarded. The exclusion of persons under 18 is not effected by the requirements for legal interest to be found in ss.8, 9, below, on the basis that a minor cannot hold a legal estate in land (Law of Property Act 1925 (c. 20), s.1(6)), as a person under 18 can enjoy rights in equity, and can propose to become an owner on achievement of majority. Indeed, a conveyance to a minor of a legal estate takes effect as a contract to convey the estate or interest to him on his majority (*ibid.*, s.19(1)). Likewise, a conveyance to two persons, one of whom is a minor, takes effect as a conveyance to the adult, on trust for himself and the minor (*ibid.*, s.19(2)).

In addition, it must be considered unlikely that a mentally handicapped person could apply (even for a disabled facilities grant), unless he can understand the implications of the application, and his responsibilities thereunder: *cf. R. v. Oldham M.B.C., ex p. Garlick*; *R. v. Bexley L.B.C., ex p. Bentum*; *R. v. Tower Hamlets L.B.C., ex p. Begum* [1993] A.C. 509, 25 H.L.R. 319, H.L., under Pt. III of the Housing Act 1985 (homelessness), in which it was held that there was only a duty to offer accommodation to those applicants who could decide whether or not to accept, not including persons so disabled that they have neither the capacity themselves to apply nor to authorise an agent on their behalf. There must be the capacity to understand and respond to the offer, and to undertake its responsibilities; whether or not a person so qualifies is a matter for the authority.

(ii) *Public bodies.* The list of public bodies excluded from the grant system is not confined to housing authorities, but includes authorities with a wider remit which are likely to hold housing, and some bodies (see subparas. (f)–(h)) which have inherited specific responsibilities from local authorities, and either with them acquired some extent of housing stock, or have acquired stock on their own part incidental to their principal functions, either for employees, or else when exercising compulsory purchase powers.

"local authority" means a county, district or London borough council, the Common Council of the City of London, a Welsh county council or county borough, or the council of the Isles of Scilly (see s.101 and the Housing Act 1985, s.4);

"new town corporation" means a development corporation of the Commission for New Towns (see s.101 and the Housing Act 1985, s.4);

"urban development corporation" means an urban development corporation established under Pt. XVI of the Local Government, Planning and Land Act 1980 (c. 65) (see s.101 and the Housing Act 1985, s.4); and,

"housing action trust" means a housing action trust established under Pt. III of the Housing Act 1988.

(iii) *Prescribed applicants.* The Secretary of State has reserved power to add to the class of person who may not apply, including by relying on regulations governing housing benefit or other welfare assistance as they may be amended from time to time. What is in mind here is the exclusion of immigrants with limited leave to remain who are disqualified from recourse to public funds (*Hansard* (H.C.), Report, July 8, 1996, col. 35, Parliamentary Under-Secretary-for State for the Environment (Mr Clappison)).

The age of the property

4.—(1) A local housing authority shall not entertain an application for a grant in respect of premises provided (by construction or conversion) less than ten years before the date of the application, unless—

(a) the application is for a disabled facilities grant, or

(b) the application is for an HMO grant in respect of a house in multiple occupation provided by conversion.

(2) The Secretary of State may by order amend subsection (1) so as to substitute another period for that specified.

DEFINITIONS

"disabled facilities grant": s.1.

"HMO grant": s.1.

"local housing authority": s.101.

GENERAL NOTE

In broad terms, grants are not intended for new properties. However, HMOs provided by conversion form "a special case" (*Hansard* (H.C.), Report, July 8, 1996, col. 21, Parliamentary Under-Secretary of State for the Environment (Mr Clappison)). Likewise, application for a disabled facilities grant may be justified regardless of the age of the property. Other grants, however, may not be awarded unless premises are provided—by construction or conversion—at least 10 years before application, although the Secretary of State may prescribe a different period.

In *R. v. Bristol City Council, ex p. Naqvi* (1994) 26 H.L.R. 640, Q.B.D., the applicant owned a shop with a flat above. In November 1991, planning permission was granted for change of use of the ground floor from shop to residential use, and to combine it with the flat to make one dwelling. Application for grant was refused on the basis that the dwelling (that would be produced) had been provided for less than 10 years and did not fulfil the pre-condition in the analogous provisions of the 1989 Act (s.103).

The application failed on the provisions of the 1989 Act distinguishing mandatory and discretionary grants. It was held, however, that the scheme was one for the provision of a dwelling by conversion, so that the 10-year rule applied to the *building* out of which the dwelling was to be provided, not the dwelling itself (see also notes to s.1, above).

Excluded descriptions of works

5.—(1) No grant is payable in respect of works of a description excluded from grant aid under this Chapter by regulations made by the Secretary of State.

(2) Regulations may be made with respect to local housing authorities generally or to a particular local housing authority and may be made with respect to particular areas.

(3) Regulations may specify descriptions of works for which grant aid is not to be available without the Secretary of State's consent, which may be given—

(a) to local housing authorities generally or to a particular local housing authority,
(b) with respect to particular areas, or
(c) with respect to applications generally or to a particular description of application.

Definitions
"local housing authority": s.101.

General Note
This section allows the Secretary of State to override local policies by excluding categories of work nationally or locally from the availability of grant-aid. So far as the power is without any procedural preconditions, it is exercisable subject only to the conventional constraints of public law: see also notes to s.13, below.

It may be thought, however, that the general duty of fairness would require *some* (however informal) extent of consultation if the Secretary of State were to plan to use this power in relation to an authority whose policies would be affected by it: the courts are willing to supplement statutory procedures where it is necessary to do so in order to ensure the achievement of fairness (*Wiseman v. Boreman* [1971] A.C. 297, H.L.; *R. v. Hull Prison Visitors, ex p. St. Germain* [1979] 1 W.L.R. 1401; *Lloyd v. McMahon* [1987] A.C. 625, see also most recently *R. v. R.B. Kensington & Chelsea, ex p. Grillo* (1995) 28 H.L.R. 94, C.A., on the duty—or want of duty—to give reasons [see below, notes to s.34], which is itself imported by the requirement of fairness [see, *e.g. R. v. Higher Education Funding Council, ex p. Institute of Dental Surgery* [1994] 1 W.L.R. 242]. See also *R. v. Bristol C.C., ex p. Bailey* (1994) 27 H.L.R. 307, Q.B.D., on the want of duty to give reasons for the refusal of a grant: see s.34, below).

Defective dwellings

6.—(1) No grant is payable if—

(a) the dwelling, house or building is or forms part of a building of a class designated under section 528 or 559 of the Housing Act 1985 (defective dwellings),
(b) the applicant is eligible for assistance under Part XVI of that Act in respect of a defective dwelling which is or forms part of the dwelling, house or building concerned, and
(c) the relevant works are, within the meaning of that Part, works required to reinstate that defective dwelling.

(2) If the local housing authority consider that the relevant works include works for which assistance is available under Part XVI of the Housing Act 1985 (assistance for owners of defective housing), they shall treat the application as if the relevant works did not include those works.

Definitions
"dwelling": s.101.
"local housing authority": s.101.
"relevant works": s.2.

GENERAL NOTE

Part XVI of the Housing Act 1985 contains provisions initially enacted in the Housing Defects Act 1984 (c. 50), which are concerned with system-built housing which has, by reason of construction or design, proved defective to the point that some of it has at times—and, sometimes, merely in some areas—become unsaleable. Pt. XVI contains a framework for assistance by way of *either* reinstatement grant, *or* repurchase, available in respect of those properties designated for the purpose by the Secretary of State (1985 Act, s.528), or within a local (discretionary) designation (1985 Act, s.559). The form of assistance is chosen by the authority, with a presumption in favour of reinstatement (if the property is likely to provide satisfactory housing for a period of 30 years and it is likely that a would-be buyer could obtain a mortgage), having regard to cost of works and value of property once repaired: the 1985 Act, s.538.

This section means that the provisions of Pt. XVI and of this Act are mutually exclusive so far as concerns the works the subject of the application for grant (see s.2(2), above): if relevant works (within the Act) *are* works required to reinstate the defective dwelling (within the 1985 Act, Pt. XVI), no grant is available (subs. (1)); if they merely *include* reinstatement works, then those works are automatically excluded from the grant application (subs. (2)).

Renovation grants

Renovation grants: owner's applications and tenant's applications

7.—(1) A local housing authority shall not entertain an application for a renovation grant unless they are satisfied—

(a) that the applicant has, or proposes to acquire, an owner's interest in every parcel of land on which the relevant works are to be carried out, or

(b) in the case of an application other than a conversion application, that the applicant is a qualifying tenant of the dwelling (alone or jointly with others) but does not have, or propose to acquire, an owner's interest in the dwelling.

(2) References in this Chapter to an "owner's application" or a "tenant's application", in relation to a renovation grant, shall be construed accordingly.

(3) In accordance with directions given by the Secretary of State, a local housing authority may treat the condition in subsection (1)(a) as met by a person who has, or proposes to acquire, an owner's interest in only part of the land concerned.

(4) References in this Chapter to "a qualifying owner's interest", in relation to an application for a renovation grant, are to an owner's interest meeting the condition in subsection (1)(a) or treated by virtue of subsection (3) as meeting that condition.

(5) In this Chapter a "qualifying tenant", in relation to an application for a renovation grant, means a person who (alone or jointly with others) is a tenant of the premises to which the application relates—

(a) who is required by the terms of his tenancy to carry out the relevant works and whose tenancy is not of a description excluded from this subsection by order of the Secretary of State, or

(b) whose tenancy is of a description specified for the purposes of this subsection by order of the Secretary of State.

(6) In subsection (5) "tenant" includes a person having a licence to occupy the premises concerned which satisfies such conditions as may be specified by order of the Secretary of State.

References in this Chapter to tenants and other expressions relating to tenancies, in the context of a tenant's application for a renovation grant, shall be construed accordingly.

DEFINITIONS

"common parts": s.58.

"conversion application": s.58.

"dwelling": s.101.
"house in multiple occupation": s.101.
"local housing authority": s.101.
"owner's interest": s.101.
"relevant works": s.2.
"renovation grant": s.1.
"tenancy": s.101.

General Note

An applicant for a renovation grant, accordingly, either for improvement or repair, or else for the provision of dwellings by conversion (s.2(2), above), must either already have—or be intending to have—an appropriate interest in the property, unless the application falls within the exemption in s.95 (applications relating to certain church lands and applications made by charities).

There are two classes of application: owner's applications and tenant's applications.

Owner's application. An owner has to have—or be proposing to acquire—an owner's interest in every parcel of land on which the relevant works are to be carried out: subs. (1)(a). This may, however, be reduced to an interest in only part, on a direction from the Secretary of State: subs. (3). "Owner's interest" means a freehold interest, or a leasehold interest with at least five years unexpired, which the applicant holds solely or jointly: s.101, below. Where the application is from a prospective owner, approval of the grant must await acquisition of the relevant interest: s.13(3).

"Land" includes "buildings and other structures, land covered by water, any estate, interest, easement, servitude or right in or over land": Interpretation Act 1978 (c. 30), Sched. 1.

Tenant's application. Tenants may only apply for a renovation grant if it is *not* a "conversion grant", which means an application for a grant within s.2(2)(b), *i.e.* the provision of a dwelling by conversion, see s.58, below. The tenant must not have or be proposing to acquire an owner's interest in the dwelling or parts to which work is to be carried out (subs. (1)(b)). The tenancy may be sole or joint, and one only of the joint tenants may apply (*ibid.*).

"Tenancy" includes sub-tenancy, and an agreement for a tenancy or sub-tenancy: s.101. This means a legally enforceable contract. All contracts entered into since September 27, 1989, for the sale or other disposition of land—therefore, including grant of lease—must have been made in writing, and by including all of the terms in one document (or, where contracts are exchanged, in each of them): Law of Property (Miscellaneous Provisions) Act 1989 (c. 34), s.2. The terms need not be set out in the document, however: they can be incorporated by cross-reference to another document. The document must be signed by or on behalf of each of the parties, save in the case of exchange, where each document must be signed by at least one: *ibid.*, s.2(3).

These requirements do not apply to leases within s.54(2) of the Law of Property Act 1925 (*ibid.*, s.2(5)(a)), which means "the creation by parol of leases taking effect in possession for a term not exceeding three years ... at the best rent which can be reasonably obtained without taking a fine", which includes a periodic tenancy). It was *formerly* the case that a contract for a tenancy had to be in writing, even if the grant itself would not require to be in writing: Law of Property Act 1925, s.40 (and see *Botting v. Martin* (1808) Camp. 317; *Crago v. Julian* [1992] 1 W.L.R. 372, C.A.). Section 40 was, however, replaced by s.2 of the 1989 Act (*ibid.*, s.2(8)).

A tenant's application must also fall within one of the following categories:

(i) the tenant is required under the terms of his tenancy to carry out the relevant works, and the tenancy is not of a class disqualified by the Secretary of State. It is unlikely that tenants under short leases (those with five or more years remaining will have an owner's interest, see s.101) will have any obligation to repair or improve. In all leases of less than seven years, the Landlord and Tenant Act 1985, s.11, imposes a repairing obligation on the landlord as to the structure and exterior of the dwelling and services (though this may be contracted out with leave of the county court, under the Landlord and Tenant Act 1985, s.12); or

(ii) the tenancy is one of a type specified by the Secretary of State.

A tenant's application also requires a certificate of intended letting (unless the authority decides that it is unreasonable to require it) from the tenant's landlord: see s.9(3).

It is not only tenants who may apply, but also licensees provided the licence satisfies specified conditions: subs. (6). As to the distinction between tenancy and licence, see generally *Street v. Mountford* [1985] A.C. 809, 17 H.L.R. 402, H.L.; *Eastleigh B.C. v. Walsh* [1985] 1 W.L.R. 525, 17 H.L.R. 392, H.L.; *A.G. Securities v. Vaughan* [1990] 1 A.C. 417, (1989) 21 H.L.R. 79, H.L. In short, where residential accommodation is granted for a term at a rent with exclusive possession, the grantor providing neither attendance nor services, the legal consequence will normally be the creation of a tenancy.

In *Burrows v. Brent L.B.C.* (1995) 27 H.L.R. 748, C.A., a *post*-possession order agreement for the tenant to remain on terms (including payment off the arrears) was held to have created a new agreement, which was either tenancy or licence. However, in *Greenwich L.B.C. v. Regan* (1996) 28 H.L.R. 469, C.A., the court, distinguishing *Burrows*, held that it was a question of fact in every case whether what had taken place was the variation of an existing relationship, or the creation of a new tenancy or licence; where the variation was of payment off arrears, it was likely to be referable to the court's powers to modify a suspended order (and, thus, to a modification of the relationship).

The mere acceptance of use and occupation charges does not create a licence (not even if a rent rebate is awarded): *Westminster C.C. v. Basson* (1990) 23 H.L.R. 225, C.A. However, a distinction must be drawn between a case where an occupier seeks to take advantage of bureaucratic incompetence in order to build up an argument in favour of authorised occupation amounting to a licence, and a case such as *Tower Hamlets L.B.C. v. Ayinde* (1994) 26 H.L.R. 631, C.A., where the occupation was wholly above board, numerous requests were made for the transfer of a tenancy into the occupier's name, and payment was being made, which could only lead to one conclusion, that a tenancy had been created. See also *Vaughan-Armatrading v. Sarsah* (1995) 27 H.L.R. 631, C.A.

Subs. (1)

The test is the subjective one, which prohibits approval unless the authority "are satisfied" as to the conditions: see General Note to s.13, below, as to the powers of the court to intervene.

Renovation grants: certificates required in case of owner's application

8.—(1) A local housing authority shall not entertain an owner's application for a renovation grant unless it is accompanied by an owner-occupation certificate or a certificate of intended letting in respect of the dwelling to which the application relates or, in the case of a conversion application, in respect of each of the dwellings to be provided.

(2) An "owner-occupation certificate" certifies that the applicant—

(a) has or proposes to acquire a qualifying owner's interest, and

(b) intends that throughout the grant condition period he or a member of his family will live in the dwelling as his (or that member's) only or main residence.

(3) A "certificate of intended letting" certifies that the applicant—

(a) has or proposes to acquire a qualifying owner's interest, and

(b) intends that throughout the grant condition period the dwelling will be let or available for letting as a residence (and not for a holiday) to a person who is not connected with the owner for the time being of the dwelling.

In paragraph (b) "letting" does not include a letting on a long tenancy.

(4) In subsection (3) references to letting include the grant of a licence to occupy premises.

References in this Chapter to tenants and other expressions relating to tenancies, in the context of a certificate of intended letting, shall be construed accordingly.

(5) Where section 10 applies (prior qualifying period in certain cases) a local housing authority shall not entertain an owner's application for a renovation grant unless it is also accompanied by a certificate specifying how the requirements of that section are met.

DEFINITIONS

"conversion application": s.58.
"dwelling": s.101.
"grant condition period": s.44.
"local housing authority": s.101.
"long tenancy": s.101.
"member of family": s.97.
"owner's interest": s.101.
"qualifying owner's interest": s.7.
"renovation grant": s.1.

General Note

This section sets out the "occupation" preconditions to consideration of applications for a renovation grant by an owner. Unless these preconditions are fulfilled, no grant may be entertained. See also ss.9, 10, below.

Apart from certifying the current interest of the applicant in the property, the certificates are concerned with future intentions at the time of the application, and may be distinguished from conditions as to future occupation, and breach of such conditions, see ss.48 and 49. Under the corresponding former provisions of the 1989 Act, this meant that non-compliance with the intentions set out in this section did not also *necessarily* amount to breach of conditions as set out in those sections or entitle the authority to recover on disposal: the grant conditions have now, however, largely been harmonised with the certificates in order to prevent abuse (see Introduction to Pt. I, above): see ss.48, 49, below.

Where the application is a conversion application, the preconditions have to be fulfilled in respect of each of the dwellings to be provided: subs. (1). The occupation preconditions are not applicable to applications in respect of certain church lands and applications made by charities: s.95, below.

There are two categories of application, and accompanying conditions:

(i) Owner-occupation certificate, together (where the requirement is not excluded by s.10(3)) with proof of prior qualification; *or*

(ii) Certificate of intended letting.

Owner-occupation certificate. This certifies that the applicant has or that he proposes to acquire a qualifying owner's interest (as defined by ss.7(4) and 101) in the dwelling and that he or a member of his family intends to occupy the dwelling within the building as his only or main residence for at least 12 months from the certified date: subs. (1). There are accordingly two sub-criteria:

(a) Only or main residence. The phrase "only or main residence" is to be found in the Leasehold Reform Act 1967, s.1(2), where it has been held that a tenant who occupies part but sublets the remainder of his home qualifies: *Harris v. Swick Securities* [1969] 1 W.L.R. 1604, C.A. In *Poland v. Cadogan* [1980] 3 All E.R. 544, C.A. it was held that while long absence may not prevent residential occupation, a long absence abroad with the premises sublet may indicate a lack of intention to occupy, sufficient to defeat the meaning in that Act. In *Powell v. Radford* (1970) 21 P. & C.R. 99, C.A., a claim under the 1967 Act by a husband and wife each to be occupying a different house as the main home was upheld, although considered unusual. Because of the different nature of the rights, these decisions, too, must be treated with caution, and can be distinguished by the statutory context.

Under the Housing Acts 1985 and 1988, the phrase used is "only or principal home". This probably bears no different meaning. In *Crawley B.C. v. Sawyer* (1988) 20 H.L.R. 98, C.A., it was expressly held that there was no material difference between this phrase and occupation as a residence under the Rent Acts, as that phrase had been interpreted, although this must be treated with some caution as many of the cases under the Rent Acts were concerned with people who had two homes, and the substantive issue was whether—in the light of the second home—the first was still in use as "a" home: see *Bevington v. Crawford* (1974) 232 E.G. 191, C.A.; *Gofor Investments v. Roberts* (1975) 119 Sol. Jo. 320, C.A.; see also *Langford Property Co. v. Tureman* [1949] 1 K.B. 29, C.A., and *Beck v. Scholtz* [1953] 1 Q.B. 570, C.A., for two cases usefully illustrating where the line is drawn.

Under the Housing Act 1985, it is clear that occupation must be as an "only or principal home", but subject to this *caveat* occupation—as a home or as a residence—under the two codes of security of tenure (Housing Act and Rent Act) has the same general meaning ("a substantial degree of regular personal occupation … of an essentially residential nature": *Herbert v. Byrne* [1946] 1 W.L.R. 519, C.A.).

Accordingly, it is not necessary to show actual or continuous physical occupation of the home, so long as the property is still in use as a home, to demonstrate which it will usually be necessary to show some physical or tangible signs of continued such use, coupled with an intention to resume physical occupation (see *Brown v. Brash* [1948] 2 K.B. 247, C.A.): see, *e.g.*, *Roland House Gardens v. Cravitz* (1974) 29 P. & C.R. 432, C.A.; *Hampstead Way Investments v. Lewis-Weare* [1985] 1 W.L.R. 164, 17 H.L.R. 152, H.L.; *Brickfield Properties v. Hughes* (1980) 20 H.L.R. 108, C.A. Absence in hospital will not affect residence: *Tomkins v. Rowley* [1949] E.G.D. 314, C.A.

In *Sawyer* (above), the tenant left his secure tenancy to live with his girlfriend. The gas and electricity to the premises the subject of the secure tenancy were subsequently cut off and the following year he informed the local authority that he was living with his girlfriend and that they intended to purchase her home. The authority instituted possession proceedings but by the time of the hearing, the tenant and his girlfriend had separated and he was again living at the premises. He gave evidence that he had not abandoned the premises and had every intention of returning to them and the judge found that they were at all times his principal home, a decision upheld by the Court of Appeal.

See also *Regalian Securities v. Scheuer* (1982) 5 H.L.R. 48, C.A., and *Richards v. Green* (1984) 11 H.L.R. 1, C.A. A tenancy may go in and out of security, depending on whether the occupation requirement is fulfilled (see, *e.g. Hussey v. Camden L.B.C.* (1994) 27 H.L.R. 5, C.A.). If the reason for the finding of non-occupation is subletting or parting with possession of the whole of the premises, however, then under Housing Act 1985, s.93 security will be lost and cannot be recovered. A distinction must be drawn, however, between subletting and a mere sharing arrangement where one of the occupiers alone holds the tenancy, and another lives or shares the property with him, from which the normal or natural inference will be that the sharer is no more than a lodger or licensee of the tenant: see *Monmouth B.C. v. Marlog* (1994) 27 H.L.R. 30, C.A.

(b) Member of the family. See notes to s.98, below.

Certificate of Intended Letting. This certifies that the applicant has, or intends to acquire, a qualifying owner's interest (as defined by ss.7(4) and 101) *and* intends that throughout the period of the grant condition the dwelling will be let—or available for letting—as a residence, for a period of not less than five years on a tenancy, which is *not* a long tenancy, to someone other than a member of his family. There are two elements to which attention may be drawn:

(a) "Long tenancy" has the meaning given it by Housing Act 1985, s.115, *i.e.* a tenancy granted for a fixed term exceeding 21 years, a tenancy for a term fixed by law under a grant with a covenant or obligation for perpetual renewal, except a tenancy by sub-demise from a tenancy which is not itself a long tenancy, and any tenancy granted in pursuance of the right to buy under Pt. V of the 1985 Act. A tenancy determinable by notice after death is expressly not a long lease, unless the lease constitutes a shared ownership tenancy: 1985 Act, s.115(2).

(b) "Holiday" is not a defined expression. There has been a number of cases on whether or not premises are let for the purposes of a holiday, which arose under the exemption from security of tenure conferred by the Rent Act 1977 (c. 42), s.9. A second alleged holiday letting must be a dubious entity, and any knowledge that the owner acquires during the first letting will be admissible as to the purpose of the second: *R. v. Rent Officer for Camden L.B.C., ex p. Plant* (1981) 7 H.L.R. 17, Q.B.D. A person believed by the owner to be on holiday, but not actually so, would probably not contravene the intention (or, as it translates into breach, see s.49, below), for the purpose would remain holiday whatever the tenant's own plans: *Buchmann v. May* [1978] 2 All E.R. 993, 7 H.L.R. 1, C.A.

To prove want of intention, or a breach, it would be necessary to show that the owner knew—actually or constructively, *e.g.* through an agent—that the tenant was not on holiday: *ex p. Plant.* A working holiday may well be a holiday for this purpose: *Buchmann*; see also *McHale v. Daneham* (1979) 249 E.G. 969, C. C.

Subs. (4)

As to licences, see notes to s.7, above.

Subs. (5)

See notes to s.10, below.

Renovation grants: certificates required in case of tenant's application

9.—(1) A local housing authority shall not entertain a tenant's application for a renovation grant unless it is accompanied by a tenant's certificate.

(2) A "tenant's certificate" certifies—

(a) that the applicant is a qualifying tenant of the dwelling, and

(b) that he or a member of his family intends to live in the dwelling as his (or that member's) only or main residence.

(3) Except where the authority consider it unreasonable in the circumstances to require such a certificate, they shall not entertain a tenant's application for a renovation grant unless it is also accompanied by a certificate of intended letting (see section 8(3)) by the person who at the time of the application is the landlord under the tenancy.

(4) Where section 10 applies (prior qualifying period in certain cases) a local housing authority shall not entertain a tenant's application for a reno-

vation grant unless it is also accompanied by a certificate specifying how the requirements of that section are met.

DEFINITIONS

"dwelling": s.101.
"local housing authority": s.101.
"member of family": s.98.
"qualifying tenant": s.7.
"tenant": s.101.

GENERAL NOTE

This section governs the preconditions when the application for a renovation grant is by a tenant. Such a renovation grant application cannot be a conversion application: see s.7(1)(b). The tenant's certificate must certify (i) that the tenant is a qualifying tenant (as to which, see s.7(5), above), and (ii) that the tenant or a member of his family (as to which, see notes to s.98, below) intends to live in the dwelling as his only or main residence (as to which, also see notes to s.8, above): subs. (2). A tenant must also present a certificate of intended letting (again, see notes to s.8, above) from his landlord, unless the authority consider it unreasonable to require one: subs. (3).

Subs. (3)

The test is whether the authority consider it unreasonable to require a certificate: see General Note to s.13, below, as to the powers of the court to intervene.

Subs. (4)

See notes to s.10, below.

Renovation grants: prior qualifying period

10.—(1) Subject to subsection (3), a local housing authority shall not entertain an application to which this section applies unless they are satisfied—

(a) that the ownership or tenancy condition (see section 11) was met throughout the qualifying period, and
(b) in the case of an application accompanied by an owner-occupation certificate or a tenant's certificate, that the applicant lived in the dwelling as his only or main residence throughout that period.

In the case of a joint application it is sufficient if those conditions are met by any of the applicants.

(2) The qualifying period for the purposes of this section is the period of three years, or such other period as may be specified by order of the Secretary of State, ending with the date of the application.

(3) A local housing authority may dispense with compliance with either or both of the conditions in subsection (1), and may do so either generally or in relation to particular cases or descriptions of case.

(4) Subject to subsection (5), this section applies to every application for a renovation grant, other than—

(a) a conversion application,
(b) an application in respect of a dwelling in a renewal area,
(c) an application in respect of works to provide means of escape in case of fire or other fire precautions, or
(d) an application of any other description excepted from this section by order of the Secretary of State.

(5) This section does not apply to a landlord's application unless the Secretary of State by order so provides, which he may do with respect to all landlord's applications or any description of landlord's application.

Any such order may provide that this section applies to a landlord's application notwithstanding that it is of a kind mentioned in paragraphs (a) to (d) of subsection (4).

(6) A "landlord's application" for a renovation grant means an owner's application which is accompanied by a certificate of intended letting.

A conversion application for the provision of two or more dwellings shall not be treated as a landlord's application if any of the certificates accompanying the application is an owner-occupation certificate.

DEFINITIONS

"local housing authority": s.101.
"owner-occupation certificate": s.8.
"renewal area": s.101.
"tenant's certificate": s.9.

GENERAL NOTE

The purpose of this section is to prevent "carpet-bagging". That is to say, people moving into accommodation—*e.g.* in the area of an authority which is presently in funds for the award of discretionary grants—in order to renovate with the assistance of grant-aid, and sell as soon as the period for the application of grant conditions has expired (see ss.44, 45, 48 and 49). See also Introduction to Pt. I, above. Accordingly, an applicant (or if more than one of them, at least one of them) is now required to satisfy the authority:

(i) that "the ownership or tenancy condition" was met, throughout a qualifying period of three years (or such other period as may be specified by the Secretary of State: subs. (2)), ending with the date of the application, and

(ii) *save* in the case of an owner's application accompanied by a certificate of intended letting (as to which, see s.8, above), which is known as a landlord's application (see subs. (5)), that the applicant—be he owner or tenant—has lived in the dwelling the subject of the application throughout that period, as his only or main residence (as to which, see notes to s.8, above).

Accordingly, and on the face of it, *all* applicants must show that they have enjoyed the relevant interest for the qualifying period, while those who are applying in respect of their own homes must *also* show residence over that period. This will permit authorities to adopt policies, *e.g.* preferring owner-occupiers or tenants, without correspondingly encouraging abuse, *e.g.* "to help speculative purchasers increase their profits on the sale of the property or to enable an applicant to move up market by buying an unfit property and then improving it with the benefit of a renovation grant" (*Hansard* (H.L.), Committee (First Day), March 26, 1996, col. 1609, Minister of State, Department of the Environment (Earl Ferrers)).

The authority may, however, disapply the condition in its entirety: subs. (3). Further, the requirement so far as it applies to a landlord's application is inapplicable unless and until the Secretary of State brings it back into play: see subs. (4).

The ownership or tenancy condition is, essentially, no more than that the owner or tenant has had the qualifying owner's or qualifying tenant's interest (see s.7) for the qualifying period, but this is subject to provisions which "deem" compliance, *i.e.* inheritance, age and ill-health, domestic breakdown: see s.11, below.

There are five categories of application which are in practice exempt from the requirements:

(a) application for a renovation grant to provide dwellings by conversion (see s.2(2)(b)), treating an application for conversion any one dwelling of which it is intended that the landlord shall occupy as *not* being a conversion application for this purpose (subs. (5)), so that the requirements will continue to apply in the normal way;

(b) application in respect of a dwelling in a renewal area, meaning an area of unsatisfactory living conditions declared by the authority under Pt. VII of the Local Government and Housing Act 1989, replacing the housing action and general improvement area policies of the Housing Act 1985;

(c) application in respect of works to provide means of escape in case of fire, or other fire precautions;

(d) applications within a description specified for this purpose by the Secretary of State; and

(e) "landlord's applications" (unless the Secretary of State orders that all or some such applications should be brought within the requirement).

A landlord's application is an owner's application accompanied by a certificate of letting, *i.e.* the same category of applicant as is identified by subs. (1)(b); the effect is to disapply subs. (1)(a)—ownership throughout the qualifying period—unless and until it is re-applied by order.

Subs. (1)

The test is the subjective one, which prohibits approval unless the authority "are satisfied" as to the conditions: see General Note to s.13, below, as to the powers of the court to intervene.

Prior qualifying period: the ownership or tenancy condition

11.—(1) The "ownership or tenancy condition" for the purposes of section 10 is that the applicant had a qualifying owner's interest in, or was a qualifying tenant of, the dwelling.

That condition shall be treated as having been met in the following circumstances.

(2) Where the applicant took his owner's interest or became a qualifying tenant under the will or on the intestacy of a member of his family, the ownership or tenancy condition shall be treated as having been met—

(a) during any period when the deceased both held a qualifying owner's interest in or was a qualifying tenant of the dwelling and lived in the dwelling as his only or main residence, and

(b) if immediately before his death the deceased both—

(i) held such an interest or was such a tenant, and

(ii) lived in the dwelling as his only or main residence,

during any period not exceeding one year when his personal representatives, or the Public Trustee under section 9 of the Administration of Estates Act 1925, held such an interest or was such a tenant.

(3) The local housing authority may treat a person as continuing to meet the residence requirement in subsection (2)(a) or (b)(ii) for up to a year after he has, by reason of age or infirmity—

(a) gone to live with and be cared for by a member of his family, or

(b) gone to live in a hospital, hospice, sheltered housing, residential care home or similar institution.

(4) Where the applicant took his owner's interest or became a qualifying tenant by virtue of a disposal made by a member of his family, and the authority are satisfied—

(a) that the person making the disposal was elderly or infirm, and

(b) that he made the disposal with the intention of—

(i) going to live with and be cared for by a member of his family, or

(ii) going to live in a hospital, hospice, sheltered housing, residential care home or similar institution as his only or main residence,

the ownership or tenancy condition shall be treated as having been met during any period ending on the date of the disposal when the person making the disposal held a qualifying owner's interest in or was a qualifying tenant of the dwelling.

(5) Where the applicant took his owner's interest or became a qualifying tenant by virtue of a disposal made by his spouse, and the authority are satisfied that the disposal was made as a result of arrangements in relation to divorce, judicial separation or declaration of nullity of marriage, the ownership or tenancy condition shall be treated as having been met during any period ending on the date of the disposal when the spouse held a qualifying owner's interest in or was a qualifying tenant of the dwelling.

(6) The references in subsection (5) to the spouse of the applicant—

(a) in the case of divorce, include his former spouse, and

(b) in the case of a declaration of nullity, shall be construed as references to the other party to the marriage.

DEFINITIONS

"dwelling": s.101.
"member of family": s.98.
"qualifying owner's interest": s.7.
"qualifying tenant": s.7.

GENERAL NOTE

The purpose of this section is to create certain exceptions to the otherwise rigid requirement that the qualifying interest (owner's or tenant's—see s.7, above) has been held by the applicant for three years before the application (see s.10(1)). This section requires the authority to treat it as fulfilled in the following cases.

(i) *Inheritance.* The interest—ownership or tenancy—will be treated as having been held if the applicant took it under the will or on the intestacy of a member of his family (as to which, see notes to s.98, below), for such period as the deceased held that interest and occupied the property as his only or principal residence (as to which, also see notes to s.8, above), *together with* (assuming the deceased so qualified immediately before his death) a period of up to one year when the interest was held by person representatives or the Public Trustee, *i.e.* if so qualifying at death, the period can be extended for a year while probate is undertaken (subs. (2)), disregarding (at the authority's discretion—see notes to s.13, below) a period of a year during which the deceased had gone to live with a member of his family (not necessarily the applicant) or else had moved into a hospital, residential care home or the like, by reason of age or infirmity (subs. (3)).

Accordingly, on inheritance there is not only taken into account the deceased's former occupation, but also a period of up to a year after death—for probate—and a period of up to a year before death—for ill health.

(ii) *Age and health disposals.* The authority are also obliged to treat the qualifying interest—ownership or tenancy—as having been held for the three year period if the applicant took it from a member of his family (as to which, see notes to s.98, below) because the person from whom he took it was elderly or infirm, and disposed of his interest in it either to go and be cared for by a member of the family (not necessarily the applicant), or else had moved into a hospital, residential care home or the like, to live in it as his only or principal residence (as to which, also see notes to s.8) (subs. (4)).

"Residential care home" has a technical meaning for the purposes of the Registered Homes Act 1984 (c. 23): "any establishment which provides or is intended to provide, whether for reward or not, residential accommodation with both board and personal care for persons in need of personal care by reason of old age, disablement, past or present dependence on alcohol or drugs, or past or present mental disordered"—s.1. This definition is not imported into this Act, and the expression "or similar institution" means that it is unnecessary to rely on it, although it is undoubtedly such establishments which, *inter alia*, are in mind.

(iii) *Domestic breakdown.* Subsection (5) is designed to cater for transfers of interest—ownership or tenancy—whether by the court or by agreement, which are related to divorce, judicial separation or nullity, without loss of the right to apply for grant (without a new period of qualification).

Renovation grants: purposes for which grant may be given

12.—(1) The purposes for which an application for a renovation grant, other than a conversion application, may be approved are the following—

(a) to comply with a notice under section 189 of the Housing Act 1985 (repair notice in respect of unfit premises) or otherwise to render the dwelling fit for human habitation;

(b) to comply with a notice under section 190 of that Act (repair notice in respect of premises not unfit but in need of substantial repair) or otherwise to put the dwelling in reasonable repair;

(c) to provide adequate thermal insulation;

(d) to provide adequate facilities for space heating;

(e) to provide satisfactory internal arrangements;

(f) to provide means of escape in case of fire or other fire precautions, not being precautions required under or by virtue of any enactment (whenever passed);

(g) to ensure that the dwelling complies with such requirements with respect to construction or physical condition as may be specified by the Secretary of State;

(h) to ensure that there is compliance with such requirements with respect to the provision or condition of services and amenities to or within the dwelling as are so specified;

(i) any other purpose for the time being specified for the purposes of this section by order of the Secretary of State.

(2) The purpose for which a conversion application may be approved is to provide one or more dwellings by the conversion of a house or other building.

(3) If in the opinion of the authority the relevant works are more or less extensive than is necessary to achieve any of the purposes set out in subsection (1) or (2), they may, with the consent of the applicant, treat the application as varied so that the relevant works are limited to or, as the case may be, include such works as seem to the authority to be necessary for that purpose.

(4) The reference in paragraph (f) of subsection (1) to precautions required under or by virtue of an enactment does not include precautions required to comply with a notice under section 352 of the Housing Act 1985 (notice requiring execution of works to render house in multiple occupation fit for number of occupants) so far as it relates to premises which are not part of a house in multiple occupation for the purposes of this Part.

(5) In exercise of the powers conferred by paragraphs (g) and (h) of subsection (1) the Secretary of State may specify requirements generally or for particular cases, and may specify different requirements for different areas.

Definitions

"conversion application": s.58.
"dwelling": s.101.
"reasonable repair": s.96.
"renovation grant": s.1.

General Note

This section comprises a major part of the concept of the renovation grant, by identifying those purposes for which (alone) the application may (see s.13, below) be approved. They are as follows:

(i) *Housing Act notices*. Notices may be served under the Housing Act 1985, s.189, to carry out works to remedy unfitness (as defined *ibid.*, s.604—see below, s.97), or s.190 to put into reasonable repair (as defined in s.96, below) property which, though not unfit, requires substantial repairs or is in such a state of disrepair as to interfere materially with the personal comfort of an occupying tenant (see further, note below);

(ii) *Heat and energy*. To provide thermal insulation, and to provide adequate facilities for space heating—the two will commonly be related;

(iii) *Internal arrangement*. Internal arrangement probably means such matters as narrow, steep or winding staircases, want of handrails, inadequate landings, ill-defined changes in floor level, one bedroom entered only through another (see Ministry of Housing and Local Government Circular 68/69, App., para. 23). It used to be one of the key *indicia* of unfitness, under the Housing Act 1985, s.604 (and back to 1954), for the purposes of local authority action, and it remains one of the criteria under the Landlord and Tenant Act 1985, s.10, but the Local Government and Housing Act 1989, Sched. 9, para. 83, substituted a new s.604 in the 1985 Act (see notes to s.98, below), from which internal arrangement was omitted. It remains a purpose of renovation, however.

(iv) *Fire precautions*. Renovation grants are available for fire escapes and other precautions, *not* including those required under or by statute, *e.g.* not including those required under Building Acts and/or Regulations over the years, nor those required by a local authority in relation to a house in multiple occupation under the Housing Act 1985, s.352, *cf.* below, s.17. There is, however, one category of fire precaution which will qualify, by subs. (4): that is, precautions which are required to comply with a notice under the 1985 Act, s.352, so far—and only so far—as they relate to premises which are *not* part of an HMO, *i.e.* fire precaution works in self-contained units within houses in multiple occupation", (*Hansard* (H.C.), May 21, 1996, Standing Committee F, Third Sitting, col. 110, Parliamentary Under-Secretary of State for the Environment (Mr Clappison)).

(v) *Secretary of State's requirements*. The Secretary of State has power to prescribe construction standards, or requirements as to physical conditions, and with respect to the provision or condition of services and amenities to or in the dwelling.

(vi) *Secretary of State's added purposes*. The Secretary of State likewise has power to prescribe further purposes.

Housing Act 1985 Notices

Section 189. (as amended—see words in single square brackets—by the Housing Act 1988, Sched. 15, para. 1, and—see words in double square brackets—by the Local Government and Housing Act 1989, Sched. 9, para. 1):

"(1) [Subject to subsection (lA)] where the local housing authority are satisfied that a [dwelling house] [[or house in multiple occupation]] is unfit for human habitation, they shall serve a repair notice on the person having control of the [dwelling-house] [[or house in multiple occupation if they are satisfied, in accordance with section 604A, that serving a notice under this subsection is the most satisfactory course of action.]].

. . .

"(2) A repair notice under this section shall—

(a) require the person on whom it is served to execute the works specified in the notice [[(which may be works of repair or improvement or both)]] [and to begin those works not later than such reasonable date, being not earlier than the [[twenty-eighth day after the notice is served]] as is specified in the notice and to complete those works within such reasonable time as is so specified, and]

(b) state that in the opinion of the authority the works specified in the notice will render the [dwelling-house] [[or, as the case may be, house in multiple occupation]] fit for human habitation."

For the meaning of unfitness, see notes to s.97, below. For the persons who may be served, see notes to s.82, below.

Section 190. (as amended—see words in single square brackets—by the Housing Act 1988, Sched. 15, para. 2, and—see words in double square brackets—by the Local Government and Housing Act 1989, Sched. 9, para. 2):

"(1) [[Subject to subsection (1B)]] where the local authority—

(a) are satisfied that a [dwelling-house] [[or house in multiple occupation]] is in such a state of disrepair that, although not unfit for human habitation, substantial repairs are necessary to bring it up to a reasonable standard, having regard to its age, character and locality, or

(b) are satisfied [whether] on a representation made by an occupying tenant [or otherwise] that a [dwelling-house] [[or house in multiple occupation]] is in such a state of disrepair that, although not unfit for human habitation, its condition is such as to interfere materially with the personal comfort of the occupying tenant [[or, in the case of a house in multiple occupation, the persons occupying it (whether as tenants or licensees)]],

they may serve a repair notice on the person having control of the [dwelling-house] [[or house in multiple occupation]].

. . .

"(2) A repair notice under this section shall require the person on whom it is served, [to execute the works specified in the notice, not being works of internal decorative repair, and—

(a) to begin those works not later than such reasonable date, being not earlier than the [[twenty-eight day after the notice is served]] as is specified in the notice; and

(b) to complete those works within such reasonable time as is so specified].

As to "age, character and locality", see notes to s.96, below. For the persons who may be served, see notes to s.82, below.

Appeals. There are provisions for appeal against both classes of notice: see also 1985 Act, s.191. See also s.83, below.

Most satisfactory course of action. This is not statutorily defined, but by 1985 Act, s.604A, the Secretary of State has power to issue guidance to which the authority are bound to have regard. Authorities are not bound to follow the guidance blindly; and they may depart from its provisions so long as they have first had regard to them—*De Falco, Silvestri v. Crawley B.C.* [1980] Q.B. 460, C.A., *Miller v. Wandsworth L.B.C.*, *The Times*, March 19, 1980, *Lambert v. Ealing L.B.C.* [1982] 1 W.L.R. 550, 2 H.L.R. 58, C.A. As Parliament has required authorities to have regard to it, however, deviation may amount to a *prima facie* case that it has not been taken into account, sufficient at least (in practice) to call for an explanation from the authority: *cf. Padfield v. Minister of Agriculture, Fisheries & Food* [1968] A.C. 997, H.L. The Act is, of course, the governing instrument and if there is a conflict between a provision of the Act and of the guidance, the Act takes precedence: *R. v. Waveney D.C., ex p. Bowers* [1983] Q.B. 238, 4 H.L.R. 118, C.A.

The current guidance under s.604A is to be found in DOE Circular [6]/90, Local Government and Housing Act 1989, Area Renewal, Unfitness, Slum Clearance and Enforcement Action, Annex F. This guidance is to be treated as guidance on the most satisfactory course of action under this Act: s.98(2), below.

Subs. (3)

With the consent of an applicant, the authority can treat an application for works which are more extensive than needed to achieve any of the statutory purposes of a renovation grant as reduced to those which are so necessary, alternatively to increase the works the subject of an application which would otherwise not achieve the purposes: without such consent and corresponding variation, the application will not be one which the authority enjoy power to approve—see s.13(2), below.

Renovation grants: approval of application

13.—(1) The local housing authority may approve an application for a renovation grant if they think fit, subject to the following provisions.

(2) The authority shall not approve an application for a renovation grant unless they are satisfied that the works are necessary for one or more of the purposes set out in section 12(1) or (2).

(3) Where an authority entertain an owner's application for a renovation grant made by a person who proposes to acquire a qualifying owner's interest, they shall not approve the application until they are satisfied that he has done so.

(4) An authority proposing to approve an application for a renovation grant shall consider whether the premises to which it relates are fit for human habitation.

(5) If it appears to the authority that the premises are not fit for human habitation, they shall not approve the application unless they are satisfied—

(a) that on completion of the relevant works, together with any other works proposed to be carried out, the premises will be fit for human habitation,

(b) that there are satisfactory financial and other arrangements for carrying out those works, and

(c) that the carrying out of the works is the most satisfactory course of action.

(6) In considering whether to approve an application for a renovation grant the authority shall have regard to the expected life of the building (taking account, where appropriate, of the effect of carrying out the works).

Definitions

"fit for human habitation": s.97.
"local housing authority": s.101.
"owner's application": s.101.
"qualifying owner's interest": s.7.
"relevant works": s.2.
"renovation grant": s.1.

General Note

This the last of the series of the sections creating an entitlement to apply for, and a discretion to approve, renovation grants; it contains the residual limitations:

(i) *Purposes.* The authority cannot approve the grant unless the works are needed for one or more of the s.12 purposes;

(ii) *Owner's interest.* Application may be made by a person planning to acquire an owner's interest (see s.7(1)), but may not be approved until it has been acquired;

(iii) *Fitness for human habitation.* No grant may be approved unless on completion of the works the subject of the application (the relevant works—see s.2) together with other works which may be proposed, *i.e.* unaided (for a variation under s.12(3) would vary what comprised the relevant works themselves), the property will be fit for human habitation (as to which, see notes to s.97, below), and that there are satisfactory financial arrangements and other arrangements (*e.g.* temporary rehousing of tenants) for carrying out the works, and that carrying out the works is "the most satisfactory course of action" (also see notes to s.97, below).

In addition, the authority are obliged to "have regard to" the expected life of the building after the works have been done: subs. (6).

The amount of the grant is governed by ss.30, 31, 33, below.

Discretion and public law

Introduction. Although it was a major part of the purpose of this Act (see Introduction to Pt. I, above) that grant-aid should be reduced from mandatory status to discretionary, there is no such thing as a "pure" discretion; all decisions of public bodies are ultimately reviewable by the courts, usually by judicial review, under R.S.C. Ord. 53, in the Crown Office list of the High Court, if their decision-making procedures are defective, so that the decision that follows will be considered *ultra vires*.

Literature. Judicial review, and the corresponding principles of administrative law, is a growth area of legal activity and has generated both a substantial body of case-law, and of legal literature. New editions of the two leading text-books in the area have both recently been issued: *Administrative Law*, Wade & Forsyth, 7th. ed. (1994), and *Judicial Review of Administrative Action*, de Smith, Woolf & Jowell, 5th. ed. (1995). Recourse may also usefully be had to *Judicial Remedies in Public Law*, Lewis (1992), and, for the increasing reliance on E.C. law, its companion volume, *Remedies and the Enforcement of European Community Law*, Lewis (1996). Introductory texts are to be found in *Judicial Review Proceedings*, Manning (1995), and *Judicial Review: Law and Procedure*, 2nd ed., Gordon (1996).

Ultra Vires. What the principles invariably involve is that authorities should always approach their decisions in a lawful manner. If it can be shown that a public body such as a local authority have approached their decision unlawfully, the decision will be void and the courts will not give effect to it. A decision improperly reached is *ultra vires*, *i.e.* outside the authority's powers, and without effect in law, whether it is because on the face of the statute there was no authority to engage in the action at all, or because the statute has been misconstrued, or because the authority have misapplied the statute in another sense, *e.g.* by failing to use the powers to implement the purpose of the statute, or by reaching a decision under the statute by reference to something which is irrelevant, or in ignorance of something which is relevant, to the way the power under the statute is intended to be operated (see, most recently, *Crédit Suisse v. Allerdale M.B.C.*, *Crédit Suisse v. Waltham Forest L.B.C.*, *The Times,* May 20, 1996, C.A.).

Wednesbury. It is always important to bear in mind that the court does not act as an appeal tribunal from the authority's decision; instead, it is undertaking an investigation into the way in which the decision has been reached: *Associated Provincial Picture Houses v. Wednesbury Corporation* [1948] 1 K.B. 223, C.A. Lord Greene M.R. said:

> "What, then, is the power of the courts? They can only interfere with an act of executive authority if it be shown that the authority has contravened the law. It is for those who assert that the local authority has contravened the law to establish that proposition ... It is not to be assumed *prima facie* that responsible bodies like the local authority in this case will exceed their powers; but the court, whenever it is alleged that the local authority have contravened the law, must not substitute itself for that authority ... When an executive discretion is entrusted by Parliament to a body such as the local authority in this case, what appears to be an exercise of that discretion can only be challenged in the courts in a strictly limited class of case. ... When discretion of this kind is granted the law recognises certain principles upon which that discretion must be exercised, but within the four corners of those principles the discretion ... is an absolute one and cannot be questioned in any court of law. What then are those principles? They are well understood. They are principles which the court looks to in considering any question of discretion of this kind. The exercise of such a discretion must be a real exercise of the discretion. If, in the statute conferring the discretion, there is to be found expressly or by implication matters which the authority exercising the discretion ought to have regard to, then in exercising the discretion it must have regard to those matters. Conversely, if the nature of the subject-matter and the general interpretation of the Act make it clear that certain matters would not be germane to the matter in question, the authority must disregard those irrelevant collateral matters" (p.228).
>
> "There have been in the cases expressions used relating to the sort of things that authorities must not do ... I am not sure myself whether the permissible grounds of attack cannot be defined under a single head.... Bad faith, dishonesty—those of course, stand by themselves—unreasonableness, attention given to extraneous circumstances, disregard of public policy and things like that have all been referred to, according to the facts of individual cases, as being matters which are relevant to the question. If they cannot all be confined under one head, they at any rate ... overlap to a very great extent. For instance, we have heard in this case a great deal about the meaning of the word 'unreasonable'.
>
> "It is true the discretion must be exercised reasonably. Now what does that mean? ... It has frequently been used and is frequently used as a general description of the things that must not be done.... A person entrusted with a discretion must ... direct himself properly in law. He must call his own attention to the matters which he is bound to consider. He must exclude from his consideration matters which are irrelevant to what he has to consider. If he does not obey those rules, he may truly be said, and often is said, to be acting 'unreasonably'. Similarly, there may be something so absurd that no sensible person could ever dream that it lay within the powers of the authority. Warrington L. J. in *Short v. Poole Corporation* [1926] Ch. 66 gave the example of the red-haired teacher, dismissed because she had red hair. That is unreasonable

in one sense. In another sense it is taking into consideration extraneous matters. It is so unreasonable that it might almost be described as being done in bad faith; and, in fact, all these things run into one another ..." (p.229).

"It is true to say that, if a decision on a competent matter is so unreasonable that no reasonable authority could ever have come to it, then the courts can interfere... But to prove a case of that kind would require something overwhelming ... [The] proposition that the decision of the local authority can be upset if it is proved to be unreasonable, really meant that it must be proved to be unreasonable in the sense that the court considers it to be a decision that no reasonable body could have come to. It is not what the court considers unreasonable, a different thing altogether... The effect of the legislation is not to set up the court as an arbiter of the correctness of one view over another. It is the local authority that are set in that position and, provided they act, as they have acted, within the four corners of their jurisdiction, this court... cannot interfere ..." (pp.230–231).

"The court is entitled to investigate the action of the local authority with a view to seeing whether they have taken into account matters which they ought not to take into account, or, conversely, have refused to take into account or neglected to take into account matters which they ought to take into account. Once that question is answered in favour of the local authority, it may still be possible to say that, although the local authority have kept within the four corners of the matters which they ought to consider, they have nevertheless come to a conclusion so unreasonable that no reasonable authority could ever have come to it. In such a case, again, I think the court can interfere. The power of the court to interfere in each case is not as an appellate authority to override a decision of the local authority, but as a judicial authority which is concerned, and concerned only, to see whether the local authority have contravened the law by acting in excess of the powers which Parliament has confided in them" (pp.233–234).

Modern Re-classification. The principles of administrative law may be expressed, and classified, in a number of different ways. In *Council of Civil Service Unions v. Minister for the Civil Service* [1985] 1 A.C. 374, H.L., Lord Diplock re-classified them under three headings: "illegality", "irrationality" and "procedural impropriety".

"By 'illegality' as a ground of judicial review I mean that the decision-maker must understand correctly the law that regulates his decision-making power and must give effect to it. Whether he has or not is par excellence a justiciable question to be decided, in the event of dispute, by those persons, the judges, by whom the judicial power of the state is exercisable.

"By 'irrationality' I mean what can by now be succinctly referred to as 'Wednesbury unreasonableness'... It applies to a decision which is so outrageous in its defiance of logic or of accepted moral standards that no sensible person who had applied his mind to the question to be decided could have arrived at it. Whether a decision falls within this category is a question that judges by their training and experience should be well equipped to answer, or else there would be something badly wrong with our judicial system ... 'Irrationality' by now can stand upon its own feet as an accepted ground on which a decision may be attacked by judicial review. I have described the third head as 'procedural impropriety' rather than failure to observe basic rules of natural justice or failure to act with procedural fairness towards the person who will be affected by the decision. This is because susceptibility to judicial review under this head covers also failure by an administrative tribunal to observe procedural rules that are expressly laid down in the legislative instrument by which its jurisdiction is conferred, even where such failure does not involve any denial of natural justice ...".

This statement has been described as "a valuable, and already 'classical'" statement (though, again, "certainly not exhaustive" (*per* Lord Scarman in *Nottinghamshire County Council v. Secretary of State for the Environment* [1986] 1 A.C. 240, H.L. at p.249).

It may be noted that in *C.C.S.U.* Lord Diplock raised—but did not answer—the question whether or not the principle of "proportionality" might yet be imported into domestic administrative law from Europe (at p.410), although it is considered (see *R. v. Secretary of State for the Home Department, ex p. Brind* [1991] 1 A.C. 696, H.L.) that it does not enjoy any standing independently of conventional unreasonableness. Proportionality is the doctrine that there has to be a reasonable relationship between the governmental (including local) action under review, and its purpose in a given context.

Practical classification. In practice, the principles tend to overlap with one another. They may be considered under one or more of the following sub-headings:

(i) A statutory authority must take into account all the relevant factors before making their decision, and must disregard the irrelevant: *Wednesbury.* See also *Bristol District Council v. Clark* [1975] 1 W.L.R. 1443, C.A. It is sufficient to void a decision on the basis that an irrelevant factor has been taken into account if the factor is significant, or potentially of influence, meaning that if it had not been taken into account, the decision may have been different: see also *Hanks v. Ministry of Housing and Local Government* [1963] 1 Q.B. 999, *R. v. Lewisham L.B.C., ex p. Shell (UK)* [1988] 1 All E.R. 938, C.A.

(ii) The decision must be based on the facts; a decision totally at variance with the facts or for which there is no factual basis cannot be sustained:

"If a judgment requires, before it can be made, the existence of some facts, then although the evaluation of those facts is for the Secretary of State alone, the courts must enquire whether those facts exist, and have been taken into account, whether the judgment has been made on a proper self-direction as to those facts, whether the judgment has not been made on other facts which ought not to have been taken into account..." (*per* Lord Wilberforce, *Secretary of State for Education and Science v. Metropolitan Borough of Tameside* [1977] A.C. 1014, H.L., at p.1047).

(iii) The authority must not act in bad faith or dishonestly: *Wednesbury.*

(iv) The authority must direct themselves properly in law, so that a decision based on a misunderstanding or misapplication of the law will not have been reached properly: *ibid.* This is the point in *Wednesbury* that is restated as "illegality" in *C.C.S.U.* See also *Anisminic v. Foreign Compensation Commission* [1969] 2 A.C. 147, H.L.

(v) The authority must act so as to promote, and not to defeat, the objects or policy of the Act in question: *Padfield v. Minister of Agriculture, Fisheries & Food* [1968] A.C. 997, H.L.; see also *Meade v. Haringey L.B.C.* [1979] 1 W.L.R. 1, C.A. Powers conferred for public purposes must be used in a way that Parliament can be presumed to have intended: *R. v. Tower Hamlets L.B.C., ex p. Chetnick Developments* [1988] A.C. 858, H.L.

(vi) The decision must not be one to which no reasonable authority could have come: this is conclusive evidence that the decision is improper: *Wednesbury*; see also *C.C.S.U.* and *Nottinghamshire.*

(vii) The authority must reach their own decision on each individual case; they must not fetter their discretion by approaching a decision with a predetermined policy as to how they will deal with any case falling within a particular class. The leading case on this is now probably *British Oxygen Co. v. Minister of Technology* [1971] A.C. 610, H.L. See also *R. v. Secretary of State for the Environment, ex p. Brent L.B.C.* [1982] Q.B. 593.

While a public authority can adopt a policy or limiting rule in order to guide the future exercise of their discretion if they think good administration requires it, they must consider its application individually in every case where it is sought to make an exception: *Stringer v. Minister of Housing and Local Government* [1970] 1 W.L.R. 1281, C.A.; *Cummings v. Birkenhead Corporation* [1972] Ch. 12, C.A.; *Elliott v. Brighton B.C.* (1981) 79 L.G.R. 506, C.A. *British Oxygen* was adopted and applied by the House of Lords in *In Re Betts* [1983] 2 A.C. 613, 10 H.L.R. 97, H.L. Even the "guideline" approach was disapproved by Templeman L.J. in *Att.-Gen., ex rel. Tilley v. Wandsworth L.B.C.* [1981] 1 W.L.R. 854, C.A., but the other two judges expressly reserved their positions on this and, of course, *British Oxygen* is the superior authority. See further note, below, on Policies.

(viii) It is the authority who are entrusted with the decision-making power and must make the decision. They cannot avoid their duties by adopting the decision of another body: *Lavender & Sons v. Minister of Housing and Local Government* [1970] 1 W.L.R. 1231. See also *R. v. Bolsover District Council and the Rent Officer for the Derbyshire Registration Area, ex p. East Midlands Development, and Denis Rye* (1995) 28 H.L.R. 329, Q.B.D., where the authority could not lawfully delegate to a rent officer their function of determining a notional increase in rental value (for grant aid purposes: see s.31, below), even though statutorily entitled to take his advice into account. (However, in the absence of any evidence to contradict the basis on which a rent officer had proceeded, it was considered unrealistic to expect them to adopt any other figure.)

(ix) As the full authority are *prima facie* entrusted with the decision-making power, the full authority must reach the decision unless they have, as they are empowered to do under Local Government Act 1972, s.101, delegated this power to a sub-committee or to an officer. It is they who must execute it: it cannot be transferred to another (even by the court), see *Gardner v. London Chatham and Dover Railway (No. 1)* (1867) L.R. 2 Ch. App. 201; *Marshall v. South Staffordshire Tramways* [1895] 2 Ch. 36 and, most recently, *Parker v. Camden L.B.C.* [1986] 1 Ch. 162, C.A.

There can be no delegation to a single member, as there cannot be a committee or sub-committee of one: *R. v. Secretary of State for the Environment, ex p. Hillingdon L.B.C.* [1986] 1 W.L.R. 807, C.A. (However, there can be delegation to an officer, to be exercised in consultation with a member, so long as the member does not play the dominant role to the extent that the officer cannot be said to have reached the decision himself: *R. v. Port Talbot B.C., ex p. Jones* [1988] 2 All E.R. 207, Q.B.D.). There can be no delegation to a person or body outside the authority, even a company formed by the authority: *Crédit Suisse v. Allerdale M.B.C., Crédit Suisse v. Waltham Forest L.B.C., The Times,* May 20, 1996, C.A.

(x) In all cases, an authority must act fairly, or in accordance with natural justice: *Re HK* [1967] 2 Q.B. 617, C.A.; see also *Sevenoaks D.C. v. Emmott* (1979) 39 P. & C.R. 404, C.A. The extent of this duty will depend upon circumstances, and the nature of the decision.

Variations on a theme. These propositions or principles are all, by and large, variations upon a theme. In *R. v. Greater London Council, ex p. Bromley L.B.C.* [1983] 1 A.C. 768, H.L., the arguments in the House of Lords were described as different ways of saying the same thing. Lack of natural justice or administrative fairness will usually mean that a public body have also failed to take something relevant into account, *i.e.* the views of the person affected, and what they might have told the authority. Similarly, the policy of an Act is a relevant consideration, and so also are the correct meaning of the law, and the correct facts. Bad faith or dishonesty would indicate consideration of irrelevant matters. Improper delegation, and the application of policy where an individual decision is required, both amount to a failure to consider the question (in the particular case) at all, which necessarily means that there has been a failure to take all that is relevant into account. (See also *Wednesbury*, above.)

Burden of proof. Whenever the decision of a public body is challenged on these principles, the burden of proof lies upon the person seeking to show that the decision is void: *Wednesbury, Cannock Chase D.C. v. Kelly* [1978] 1 W.L.R. 1, C.A. The allegations must be both substantiated, and particularised: *ibid.* For example, it is never enough to say simply that the applicant is a homeless person and in priority need, because this would not be enough to raise the inference of a duty: the duty arises only when the authority are satisfied, or have reason to believe, or consider that the fact or state of affairs is as it is claimed to be. It must be alleged that they have refused or failed to reach a decision, or that such decision as has been reached must be treated by the courts as void, for want of compliance with specified principles, and the factual basis for this allegation must be set out.

Policies

It is the application of "policies" which is most likely to lead authorities into error. On the one hand, the very purpose of the legislation is to liberate authorities' discretion to select and target their own renewal policies (see Introduction to Pt. I, above); on the other, it is trite public law that a policy cannot be applied so rigidly that no exceptions are made, or so that each individual case—or, in context, renovation grant application—is not decided on its own merits. See the cases cited above, para. (vii).

In *R. v. Bristol C.C., ex p. Bailey* (1994) 27 H.L.R. 307, Q.B.D., the authority declined to pay a discretionary renovation grant on the basis that it was the policy of the authority only to pay such grants where properties were unfit. This decision could be, and was, appealed to the authority's Housing (Special Purposes) Sub-committee, which confirmed the refusal in "all the circumstances relevant to this case", which was later explained by the authority's solicitor as meaning that the committee considered that officers had correctly determined that the property was not unfit. This was challenged as constituting a fetter on the authority's discretion to award renovation grants, even when there was no unfitness. The authority gave evidence that they had made realistic provision for discretionary grants in appropriate cases. It was held that they were entitled to formulate a policy for the allocation of grants, and that they had not fettered their discretion to depart from it.

In *R. v. Sunderland C.C., ex p. Redezeus* (1994) 27 H.L.R. 477, Q.B.D., however, the authority's "policy" was to award grant at a lower level than provided for by statute, so that, even though there was a clause permitting higher levels in exceptional cases, the policy could not stand as it was outside their statutory powers.

Expected life. The authority are bound to "have regard to" the expected life of the property. See note on *Most Satisfactory Course of Action* in notes to s.12, above. The requirement does not and cannot bind the authority to a particular result. So long as the authority have regard to the expected life, they may decide to issue a grant notwithstanding the limited period that will be added, and alternatively would err in law if they declined all grants that did not produce a certain, minimum further life (although they could adopt such a guideline, provided on occasion it would be possible to depart from it).

Common parts grants

Common parts grants: occupation of flats by occupying tenants

14.—(1) A local housing authority shall not entertain an application for a common parts grant unless they are satisfied that at the date of the application at least the required proportion of the flats in the building concerned is occupied by occupying tenants.

(2) In this Chapter an "occupying tenant", in relation to a flat in a building, means a person who has in relation to the flat (alone or jointly with others)—

(a) a tenancy to which section 1 of the Landlord and Tenant Act 1954 or Schedule 10 to the Local Government and Housing Act 1989 applies (long tenancies at low rents),

(b) an assured tenancy, a protected tenancy, a secure tenancy or a statutory tenancy,

(c) a protected occupancy under the Rent (Agriculture) Act 1976 or an assured agricultural occupancy within the meaning of Part I of the Housing Act 1988, or

(d) a tenancy or licence which satisfies such conditions as may be specified by order of the Secretary of State,

and who occupies the flat as his only or main residence.

References in this Chapter to other expressions relating to tenancies, in the context of an application for a common parts grant, shall be construed accordingly.

(3) The "required proportion" mentioned in subsection (1) is three-quarters or such other proportion as may be—

(a) specified for the purposes of this section by an order of the Secretary of State, or

(b) approved by him, in relation to a particular case or description of case, on application made by the local housing authority concerned.

Definitions

"common parts grant": s.1.
"flat": s.58.
"local housing authority": s.101.

General Note

This section sets out the first of the conditions which must be satisfied in the case of a common parts grant. See also ss.15, 16, below.

The authority must be satisfied that, at the date of the application, the required proportion (*i.e.* 75 per cent or such other proportion as is prescribed by the Secretary of State: subs. (3)) of the flats in the building are occupied by "occupying tenants": subs. (1).

An occupying tenant is one who:
(i) has one of the interests set out in para. (a) to (d) of subs. (2); and
(ii) who occupies the flat as his only or main residence: see notes to s.8, above.

Long tenancy at low rent. On what would be the termination of long tenancies at a low rent which were granted before the commencement of the Housing Act 1988 (January 15, 1989), there is provision under s.1 of the Landlord and Tenant Act 1954 for the lease to continue contractually, until determined in accordance with Pt. I of the 1954 Act, following which the tenancy will become a statutory tenancy under the Rent Act 1977 (see further, note below). Under the Local Government and Housing Act 1989, s.186 and Sched. 10, analogous provision is made for the treatment of long tenancies at a low rent in substance to become assured tenancies under the Housing Act 1988 (which means that they will subsist contractually until a court orders possession: see further, note below). Transitional provisions serve to substitute the latter regime for some long leases which would otherwise have fallen within the former (1989 Act, s.186(3)).

In each case, the protection is available to long leaseholders at low rents, whose tenancies would have been within the principal security Act but for the low rent (see notes below): 1954 Act, s.2; 1989 Act, s.186 and Sched. 10, para. 1. For each purpose, long lease means a tenancy granted for a term certain of more than 21 years: 1954 Act, s.2(4); 1989 Act, Sched. 10, para. 2(3). Time runs from the date of the grant, not from the date of commencement of the lease: *Roberts v. Church Commissioners for England* [1972] 1 Q.B. 278, C.A. (decided under the Leasehold Reform Act 1967). "Low rent" is defined, prior to April 1, 1990, by reference to rateable values, and subsequently by reference under the 1954 Act to fixed amounts and by reference under the 1989 Act to the premium paid as against the term granted: 1954 Act, s.2(5), 1989 Act, Sched. 10, para. 1(2A), as amended by the References to Rating (Housing) Regulations 1990 (S.I. 1990 No. 434).

Assured tenancy. Since the coming into force of the Housing Act 1988 (January 15, 1989), assured tenancies have been the usual form of letting in the wholly private sector, and by housing associations, replacing (i) Rent Act security for most private tenants, and (ii) Housing Act 1985 security for most housing association tenants (and in each case, Rent Act control of rents). There are exceptions (see the Housing Act 1988, ss.34, 35), but these are confined to (transitional) cases where there is what might be called some "prior element", *e.g.* grants of new tenancies to tenants within the previous regime, in the same or other property.

There is a number of exceptions to status as an assured tenant or assured agricultural occupancy: see Sched. 1 to the Housing Act 1988. Assured *shorthold* tenancies do not, however, form an exception: while there are special provisions which govern them, they are none the less assured tenancies as it were in their own right (see 1988 Act, s.20(1): "... an assured shorthold tenancy is an assured tenancy which ..." complies with stated conditions). Accordingly, a letting of an assured shorthold tenancy is a letting of an assured tenancy, and within this section.

Subject to exceptions and transitional provisions, an assured tenancy is one:

(i) granted after the commencement of the Housing Act 1988 (January 15, 1989),

(ii) which is of a dwelling-house (which may be a house or part of a house: Housing Act 1988, s.45),

(iii) let (which means on a tenancy rather than on a licence, see notes to s.7, above),

(iv) as (which imports consideration of the purpose of the letting),

(v) a separate dwelling (see notes to s.1, above),

(vi) under which the tenant is an individual (rather than corporate body)—or if joint tenants, at least one of the tenants is an individual,

(vii) who uses the dwelling as his only or principal home (see notes to s.8, above).

The exceptions, briefly described, are (1988 Act, Sched. 1):

(a) Tenancies entered into before commencement (this exception is omitted when considering whether a long tenancy falls within the continuation provisions of the Local Government and Housing Act 1989, Sched. 10, see note above);

(b) High rateable value lettings;

(c) Low rent tenancies (see also note above on long tenancy);

(d) Business tenancies within the Landlord and Tenant Act 1954, Pt. II;

(e) Licensed premises;

(f) Agricultural land;

(g) Agricultural holdings;

(h) Lettings to students;

(i) Holiday lettings;

(j) Resident landlords;

(k) Crown tenancies; and,

(l) Public sector tenancies (including local authorities, Commission for the New Towns, new town development corporations, Development Board for Rural Wales, urban development corporation, housing action trust—see generally notes to s.3, above).

Assured tenancies cannot be brought to an end by the landlord, except by obtaining an order of the court: 1988 Act, s.5. This abolishes the distinction which had prevailed in the private sector before the 1988 Act of the distinction between contractual, and statutory, tenancies: see next note. Court orders for possession can only be made on certain grounds: *ibid.*, s.7 and Sched. 2.

Protected and statutory tenancy. Until the Housing Act 1988 came into force (January 15, 1989), Rent Act protection was the normal form of security of tenure for private sector tenants, and comprised the code of rent control applicable both to private sector tenants and housing association tenants (whose security, however, was governed by the Housing Act 1985). A protected tenant is a tenant within the Rent Act 1977, whose contractual tenancy has not yet been determined. A statutory tenant is a former protected tenant who enjoys the right to remain in occupation conferred by the 1977 Act, s.2. Save under the transitional provisions of the Housing Act 1988, new protected tenancies could not be granted after January 15, 1989.

Subject to exceptions provisions, a protected or statutory tenancy is:

(i) the letting of a dwelling-house (which may be a house or part of a house: the Rent Act 1977, s.1),

(ii) let (which means on a tenancy rather than on a licence, see notes to s.7, above),

(iii) as (which imports consideration of the purpose of the letting),

(iv) a separate dwelling (see notes to s.1, above),

(v) under which security of tenure pursuant to the statutory tenancy is only available to an individual (rather than corporate body),

(vi) who continues to occupy the dwelling as a residence (see notes to s.8, above): the Rent Act 1977, s.2.

The exceptions, briefly described, are:

(a) High rateable value lettings (1977 Act, s.4);

(b) Low rent tenancies (see also note above on long tenancy) (1977 Act, s.5);

(c) Lettings together with other land (as distinct from land let with the dwelling-house) (1977 Act, s.6);

(d) Lettings with board or attendance (1977 Act, s.7);
(e) Lettings to students (1977 Act, s.8);
(f) Holiday lettings (1977 Act, s.9);
(g) Agricultural holdings (1977 Act, s.10);
(h) Licensed premises (1977 Act, s.11);
(i) Resident landlords (1977 Act, s.12);
(j) Crown lettings (1977 Act, s.13);
(k) Public sector lettings (including local authorities, Commission for the New Towns, new town development corporations, Development Board for Rural Wales, urban development corporation, housing action trust—see generally notes to s.3, above) (1977 Act, s.14);
(l) Housing association lettings (1977 Act, s.15);
(m) Housing co-operative lettings (1977 Act, s.16);
(n) Business tenancies within the Landlord and Tenant Act 1954, Pt. II (1977 Act, s.24).

A contractual tenancy within the Rent Act is determined in the normal way; a statutory tenancy is determined by a possession order, which, like the assured tenancy, can only be made on specified grounds (1977 Act, s.98 and Sched. 15).

Protected and assured occupancy. In the case of workers in agriculture and forestry, living in tied accommodation, security of tenure was conferred by the Rent (Agriculture) Act 1976 (c. 80), largely to correspond to security of tenure under (what was to become) the Rent Act 1977 (c. 42). Analogous replacement provisions, governing workers in agriculture, were contained in the Housing Act 1988 (c. 50), and similarly confer a code of security corresponding to that available to assured tenants under that Act.

Secure Tenancy. This is the regime applicable to—primarily—local authority tenancies. It was formerly also applicable to housing association tenancies, but save under the transitional provisions of the Housing Act 1988, new housing association tenancies could not be granted after January 15, 1989.

A secure tenancy is:
(i) the letting (on a tenancy or on a licence—Housing Act 1985, s.79(3), *cf.* notes to s.7, above),
(ii) of a dwelling-house (which may be a house or part of a house: 1985 Act, s.112),
(iii) by a public sector landlord (meaning local authority, new town corporation, housing action trust, urban development corporation, Development Board for Rural Wales, or a housing co-operative to which the section applied—1985 Act, s.80, see generally notes to s.3, above),
(iv) as (which imports consideration of the purpose of the letting),
(v) a separate dwelling (see notes to s.1, above),
(vi) under which the tenant is an individual (rather than corporate body)—or if joint tenants, at least one of the tenants is an individual,
(vii) who uses the dwelling as his only or principal home (see notes to s.8, above).

The exceptions, briefly described, are (1985 Act, Sched. 1):
(a) Long tenancies (*i.e.* term certain exceeding 21 years—1985 Act, s.115);
(b) Certain categories of accommodation related to employment;
(c) Land acquired for development;
(d) Accommodation for homeless persons;
(e) Temporary accommodation for persons taking up employment, *i.e.* to encourage job mobility;
(f) Private sector, sub-leasing schemes;
(g) Temporary accommodation during works;
(h) Agricultural holdings;
(i) Licensed premises;
(j) Student lettings;
(k) Business tenancies within Landlord and Tenant Act 1954, Pt. II;
(l) Almshouses.

In addition, the Housing Act 1996 introduces a new and optional exception to secure tenancy, which is the "introductory tenancy" which provides for re-possession merely by following a specified procedure, without more, *i.e.* it does not need specific grounds for possession.

Secure tenancies cannot be brought to an end by the landlord, except by obtaining an order of the court: 1985 Act, s.82. Court orders for possession can only be made on certain grounds: *ibid.*, s.84 and Sched. 2.

Tenancy or licence. Licensees (see note to s.7, above) may qualify, if within conditions specified by the Secretary of State, as may any other tenant so specified, who is not within the classes identified above.

Common parts grants: landlord's and tenants' applications

15.—(1) A local housing authority shall not entertain an application for a common parts grant unless they are satisfied—

(a) that the applicant has an owner's interest in the building and has a duty or power to carry out the relevant works, or

(b) that the application is made by at least three-quarters of the occupying tenants of the building who under their tenancies have a duty to carry out, or to make a contribution in respect of the carrying out of, some or all of the relevant works.

(2) References in this Chapter to a "landlord's application" and a "tenants' application", in relation to a common parts grant, shall be construed accordingly.

(3) In deciding whether the requirement in subsection (1)(b) is met—

(a) where a tenancy is held by two or more persons jointly, those persons shall be regarded as a single occupying tenant; and

(b) a tenant whose tenancy is of a description specified for the purposes of that paragraph by order of the Secretary of State shall be treated as an occupying tenant falling within that paragraph.

(4) A person who has an owner's interest in the building and who has a duty or power to carry out any of the relevant works may also join in a tenants' application for a common parts grant; and where such a person does join in an application, he is in this Chapter referred to as a "participating landlord".

DEFINITIONS

"common parts grant": s.1.
"local housing authority": s.101.
"occupying tenants": s.14.
"owner's interest": s.101.
"relevant works": s.2.

GENERAL NOTE

This is the second of the conditions which must be satisfied in the case of a common parts grant. See also s.14, above, and s.16, below. The second condition is that the application must qualify:

either as an application by someone with (a) an owner's interest (see s.101, see also note to s.7, above), and (b) a duty or power to carry out the works the subject of the application (a landlord's application—subs. (2)),

or as an application made by at least three-quarters of those occupying tenants (see s.14, above), under whose tenancies there is either a duty to carry out some or all of the works the subject of the application, or else an obligation to make a contribution in respect of them (a tenants' application—subs. (2)).

Landlords. Whether or not a landlord has a duty or a power to carry out the works the subject of the application will normally be a matter of construing the terms of tenancies and leases and comparing them to the works in question. The meaning of "common parts" has been discussed in the notes to s.1, above: see also s.58, below—"'common parts' in relation to a building, includes the structure and exterior of the building and common facilities provided, whether in the building or elsewhere, for persons who include the occupiers of one or more flats").

In some cases, the term may be that implied by s.11(1), as extended by s.11(1A), (1B) of the Landlord and Tenant Act 1985, added by the Housing Act 1988, s.116, applicable to leases and tenancies granted after January 15, 1989:

"(1) In a lease to which this section applies ... there is implied a covenant by the lessor—

(a) to keep in repair the structure and exterior of the dwelling-house (including drains, gutters and external pipes),

(b) to keep in repair and proper working order the installations in the dwelling-house (including basins, sinks, baths and sanitary conveniences, but not other fixtures, fittings and appliances for making use of the supply of water, gas or electricity), and

(c) to keep in repair and proper working order the installations in the dwelling-house for space heating and heating water.

"(1A) If a lease to which this section applies is a lease of a dwelling-house which forms part only of a building, then, subject to subsection (1B), the covenant implied by subsection (1) shall have effect as if—

(a) the reference in paragraph (a) of that subsection to the dwelling-house included a reference to any part of the building in which the lessor has an estate or interest; and

(b) any reference in paragraphs (b) and (c) of that subsection to an installation in the dwelling-house included a reference to an installation which, directly or indirectly, serves the dwelling-house and which either:

(i) forms part of any part of a building in which the lessor has an estate or interest; or

(ii) is owned by the lessor or under his control.

"(1B) Nothing in subsection (1A) shall be construed as requiring the lessor to carry out any works or repairs unless the disrepair (or failure to maintain in working order) is such as to affect the lessee's enjoyment of the dwelling-house or of any common parts, as defined in section 60(1) of the Landlord and Tenant Act 1987, which the lessee, as such, is entitled to use".

("'Common parts', in relation to any building or part of a building, includes the structure and exterior of that building or part and any common facilities within it": s.60, 1987 Act, *i.e.* it is in the same terms as s.58 of this Act without the extension to facilities provided in another building, which can, however, be within the landlord's repairing obligation under s.11(1A)(b)).

A landlord's duty to carry out works may be implied by the terms of the lease, or by the absence of any express liability, *e.g.* where maintenance of means of access was implied as necessary, as in *Liverpool C.C. v. Irwin* [1977] A.C. 239, H.L., or where the tenant's obligations to maintain the interior would have been meaningless without a corresponding obligation in respect of the exterior on the part of the landlord, as in *Barrett v. Lounova (1982)* (1988) 20 H.L.R. 584, C.A.

Even if the landlord cannot be said to be under a *duty*, if the leases are silent then a landlord will normally be considered to have *power* to carry out works of repair or maintenance, and certainly so if the works in question, even not within his express responsibilities, fall within the terms of what he can recover by way of service charge.

A landlord (within this definition) may also join in with a tenants' application, in which case he is known as a "participating landlord": subs. (4).

Tenants. The application must be by three-quarters of the occupying tenants of the building who have a duty to do the works in question, or to contribute to their cost. Note that this quotient is not of the flats as a whole (three-quarters of which must be occupied by occupying tenants under s.14, above), but of the occupying tenants (thus, *prima facie*, three-quarters of three-quarters). Even so, it is only a quotient of three-quarters of those occupying tenants who have a duty to do some or all of the works in question (which could include a roof or windows), or to contribute to their cost (which will be much more common), which must be fulfilled for a tenants' application to be made.

Subs. (3)

This makes two ancillary provisions: (a) that a joint tenancy counts as a sole tenancy for the purpose of determining whether the quotient of tenants has been met, and (b) to allow the Secretary of State to prescribe occupying tenants for this purpose, independently of the power to prescribe additional occupying tenants generally under s.14, *i.e.* if he wishes to apply provisions differentially.

Common parts grants: certificate required to accompany application

16.—(1) A local housing authority shall not entertain a landlord's application for a common parts grant unless it is accompanied by a certificate signed by the applicant which—

(a) specifies the interest of the applicant in the building, and

(b) certifies that the required proportion of the flats in the building is occupied by occupying tenants.

(2) A local housing authority shall not entertain a tenants' application for a common parts grant unless it is accompanied by a certificate signed by each of the applicants which—

(a) specifies the interest of each of the applicants in each flat in the building, and

(b) certifies that the required proportion of the flats in the building is occupied by occupying tenants.

DEFINITIONS

"common parts grant": s.1.
"flat": s.58.
"local housing authority": s.101.

GENERAL NOTE

This is the third of the conditions which must be satisfied in the case of a common parts grant. See also ss.14, 15, above. The third condition is that the application must be accompanied by either a landlord's certificate or a tenants' certificate, the first of which must specify the interest of the applicant in the building, and the second of which must specify the interest of each applicant in their flats, and both of which must certify that the required proportion of flats in the building (above, s.14) is occupied by occupying tenants.

Common parts grants: purposes for which grant may be given

17.—(1) The purposes for which an application for a common parts grant may be approved are—

(a) to comply with a notice under section 189 of the Housing Act 1985 (repair notice in respect of unfit premises) or otherwise to cause the building to meet the requirements in section 604(2) of that Act;
(b) to comply with a notice under section 190 of that Act (repair notice in respect of premises not unfit but in need of substantial repair) or otherwise to put the building in reasonable repair;
(c) to comply with a notice under section 352 of that Act (notice requiring works to render premises fit for the number of occupants) or otherwise to enable the house to meet one or more of the requirements in subsection (1A) of that section;
(d) to provide adequate thermal insulation;
(e) to provide adequate facilities for space heating;
(f) to provide satisfactory internal arrangements;
(g) to provide means of escape in case of fire or other fire precautions, not being precautions required under or by virtue of any enactment (whenever passed);
(h) to ensure that the building complies with such requirements with respect to construction or physical condition as may be specified by the Secretary of State;
(i) to ensure that there is compliance with such requirements with respect to the provision or condition of services and amenities to or within the building as are so specified;
(j) any other purpose for the time being specified for the purposes of this section by order of the Secretary of State.

(2) If in the opinion of the local housing authority the relevant works are more or less extensive than is necessary to achieve any of the purposes set out in subsection (1), they may, with the consent of the applicant, treat the application as varied so that the relevant works are limited to or, as the case may be, include such works as seem to the authority to be necessary for that purpose.

(3) In exercise of the powers conferred by paragraphs (h) and (i) of subsection (1) the Secretary of State may specify requirements generally or for particular cases, and may specify different requirements for different areas.

DEFINITIONS

"common parts grant": s.1.
"local housing authority": s.101.

GENERAL NOTE

See notes to s.12, above, to which this is identical in all respects, save
(i) for the omission of reference to conversion grant (see s.12(2)); and,

(ii) for the inclusion as a purpose of the common parts grant of compliance with a notice under s.352 of the Housing Act 1985.

Note that, in addition to these purposes, a disabled facilities grant application may qualify as a common parts application (*n.b. not* "common parts *grant* application"), if it is for works designed to facilitate access to accommodation or facilities: see s.23, below.

Housing Act 1985, section 352. This section is concerned with houses in multiple occupation (as to which, see notes to s.1, above). A house in multiple occupation could, however, be the subject of an application for a common parts grant, if the occupancy conditions of s.14 were fulfilled. If not, then it could still be the subject of application for an HMO grant.

Section 352(1) empowers the authority to serve notice—

"where [in the opinion of the authority, a house in multiple occupation fails to meet one or more of the requirements in paragraphs (a) to (e) of subsection (1A) and, having regard to the number of individuals or households or both for the time being accommodated on the premises, by reason of that failure the premises are not reasonably suitable for occupation by those individuals or households.

"(1A) The requirements in respect of a house in multiple occupation referred to in subsection (1) are the following, that is to say,—

(a) there are satisfactory facilities for the storage, preparation and cooking of food including an adequate number of sinks with a satisfactory supply of hot and cold water;

(b) it has an adequate number of suitably located water-closets for the exclusive use of the occupants;

(c) it has, for the exclusive use of the occupants, an adequate number of suitably located fixed baths or showers and wash-hand basins each of which is provided with a satisfactory supply of hot and cold water;

(d) subject to section 365, there are adequate means of escape from fire; and

(e) there are adequate other fire precautions.]

(2) [Subject to subsection (2A)] the notice shall specify the works which in the opinion of the authority are required for rendering the premises reasonably suitable—

(a) for occupation by the individuals or households for the time being accommodated there, or

(b) for a smaller number of individuals or households, or both, which, in the opinion of the authority, the [house] could reasonably accommodate if the works were carried out [but the notice shall not specify any works to any premises outside the house].

[(2A) Where the authority have exercised or propose to exercise their powers under section 368 to secure that part of the house is not used for human habitation, they may specify in the notice such work only as in their opinion is required to meet such of the requirements in subsection (1A) as may be applicable if that part is not so used.]"

(As amended—see words in square brackets—by the Local Government and Housing Act 1989, Sched. 9).

Section 365—so far as here relevant—obliges an authority in certain circumstances to consult with the local fire authority before serving a notice in respect of means of escape from fire and, since amendment, other fire precautions: 1985, s.365(3), as to be amended by the Housing Act 1996, s.75. For the persons who may be served, see notes to s.82, below. There is provision for appeal against a s.352 notice (1985, s.353); see also notes to s.83, below.

The power to include means of escape from fire, and other fire precautions, in a notice under s.352 overrides the limitation in subs. (1)(g), that the provision of means of escape in case of fire, and other fire precautions, are not within the purposes of a grant if they are required under or by virtue of an enactment: if required under s.352, they will be.

Common parts grants: approval of application

18.—(1) The local housing authority may approve an application for a common parts grant if they think fit, subject to the following provisions.

(2) The authority shall not approve an application for a common parts grant unless they are satisfied that the works are necessary for one or more of the purposes set out in section 17(1).

(3) An authority proposing to approve an application for a common parts grant shall consider whether the building to which the application relates meets the requirements mentioned in paragraphs (a) to (e) of section 604(2) of the Housing Act 1985.

(4) If it appears to the authority that the building does not meet those requirements, they shall not approve the application unless they are satisfied—

(a) that on completion of the relevant works, together with any other works proposed to be carried out, the building will meet those requirements,

(b) that there are satisfactory financial and other arrangements for carrying out those works, and

(c) that the carrying out of the works is the most satisfactory course of action.

(5) In considering whether to approve an application for a common parts grant the local housing authority shall have regard to the expected life of the building (taking account, where appropriate, of the effect of carrying out the works).

DEFINITIONS

"common parts grant": s.1.

"local housing authority": s.101.

GENERAL NOTE

See notes to s.13, above, to which this section corresponds save in the following respects: it is the building which must meet the specified fitness criteria of s.604 of the Housing Act 1985, rather than the premises which are intended to achieve fitness. The relevant criteria are structural stability, freedom from serious disrepair, freedom from dampness, adequate provision for ventilation, and an effective system for the draining of foul, waste and surface water. See notes to s.97, below.

The amount of the grant is governed by ss.31–33, below.

Disabled facilities grants

Disabled facilities grants: owner's and tenant's applications

19.—(1) A local housing authority shall not entertain an application for a disabled facilities grant unless they are satisfied—

(a) that the applicant has, or proposes to acquire, an owner's interest in every parcel of land on which the relevant works are to be carried out, or

(b) that the applicant is a tenant (alone or jointly with others)—

(i) in the case of an application in respect of works to a dwelling, of the dwelling, or

(ii) in the case of a common parts application, of a flat in the building,

and, in either case, does not have or propose to acquire such an owner's interest as is mentioned in paragraph (a).

(2) References in this Chapter to an "owner's application" or a "tenant's application", in relation to a disabled facilities grant, shall be construed accordingly.

(3) In accordance with directions given by the Secretary of State, a local housing authority may treat the condition in subsection (1)(a) as met by a person who has, or proposes to acquire, an owner's interest in only part of the land concerned.

(4) In this Chapter, in relation to an application for a disabled facilities grant—

"qualifying owner's interest" means an owner's interest meeting the condition in subsection (1)(a) or treated by virtue of subsection (3) as meeting that condition; and

"qualifying tenant" means a tenant who meets the conditions in subsection (1)(b).

(5) In this Chapter "tenant", in relation to a disabled facilities grant, includes—

(a) a secure tenant, introductory tenant or statutory tenant,

(b) a protected occupier under the Rent (Agriculture) Act 1976 or a person in occupation under an assured agricultural occupancy within the meaning of Part I of the Housing Act 1988,

(c) an employee (whether full-time or part-time) who occupies the dwelling or flat concerned for the better performance of his duties, and
(d) a person having a licence to occupy the dwelling or flat concerned which satisfies such conditions as may be specified by order of the Secretary of State;

and other expressions relating to tenancies, in the context of an application for disabled facilities grant, shall be construed accordingly.

DEFINITIONS

"dwelling": s.101.
"disabled facilities grant": s.1.
"flat": s.58.
"local housing authority": s.101.
"owner's interest": s.101.

GENERAL NOTE

This section begins the series which culminates in the sole remaining mandatory grant (see Introduction to Pt. I, above), the disabled facilities grant (see s.24, below). Application may be made by—

(i) Someone who has, or proposes to acquire, an owner's interest—see notes to s.7, above (an owner's application—subs. (2)); or
(ii) A tenant (or one of joint tenants) of the dwelling (a tenant's application—subs. (2)); or
(iii) A tenant (or one of joint tenants) of a flat in a building, where the application is a "common parts application" (to be distinguished from "common parts *grant* application"—see ss.14, *et seq.*, above) (a tenant's application—subs. (2)).

In the case of either category of tenant's application, the tenant must not also have, or propose to acquire, an owner's interest.

In the case of an application based on proposed ownership, the authority will not be able to approve the grant until the interest has been acquired: see s.24(2).

Subs. (5)

All tenants are included: the purpose of this subsection is to *extend* the meaning of tenant (see notes to s.7, above) to include occupiers who are deemed to be tenants under other provisions (*e.g.*, licensees who are secure tenants or introductory tenants—see notes to s.14, above) or are put in an analogous position (as with statutory tenants, who have a "personal right" or "right of irremovability" rather than a true tenancy in the sense of being an interest in land—see *Keaves v. Dean* [1924] 1 K.B. 685, *Jessamine Investments v. Schwartz* [1978] Q.B. 264, and protected and assured occupiers—see notes to s.14, above). The Secretary of State has the power to specify further categories of qualifying licence.

Reflecting the desirability of helping the disabled into, or to keep, work, also included here are employees (full or part-time) occupying premises for the better performance of their duties, and who, as such, are likely to be licensees.

The phrase—better performance of duties—is one derived from the case-law distinguishing service tenancy and service occupation. The former creates a true tenancy and refers merely to someone whose landlord and employer is the same: see *Redbank Schools v. Abdullahzadeh* (1995) 28 H.L.R. 431, C.A.

The latter, on the other hand, amounts to no more than a license and refers to someone who needs to occupy accommodation in order to perform his employment duties: see *Smith v. Seghill Overseers* (1875) L.R. 10 Q.B. 422—approved in *Street v. Mountford* [1985] A.C. 809, 17 H.L.R. 402, H.L.; *Hirst v. Sargent* (1967) 65 L.G.R. 127; *Chapman v. Freeman* [1978] 1 W.L.R. 1298; *Royal Philanthropic Society v. County* (1985) 18 H.L.R. 83, C.A.—all adopting or tending towards a test of necessity rather than mere convenience, *cf. Fox v. Dalby* (1874) L.R. 10 C.P. 285 and *Glasgow Corporation v. Johnstone* [1965] A.C. 609, H.L., where it seemed that a slightly more lax or subjective test, on the part of the employer, might suffice.

The cases should be distinguished from those where what is under consideration is a contractual obligation to reside in particular premises, for some other purpose, *e.g.* exclusion from security under the Housing Act 1985, Sched. 1, para. 2, *cf. Hughes v. Greenwich L.B.C.* [1994] 1 A.C. 170, 26 H.L.R. 99, H.L.

Disabled facilities grants: the disabled occupant

20. In this Chapter the "disabled occupant", in relation to an application for disabled facilities grant, means the disabled person for whose benefit it is proposed to carry out any of the relevant works.

DEFINITIONS
"disabled facilities grant": s.1.
"disabled person": s.100.

GENERAL NOTE
The disabled person for whose benefit works are to be undertaken need not be the owner or tenant himself.

Disabled facilities grants: certificate required in case of owner's application

21.—(1) A local housing authority shall not entertain an owner's application for a disabled facilities grant unless it is accompanied by an owner's certificate in respect of the dwelling to which the application relates or, in the case of a common parts application, in respect of each flat in the building occupied or proposed to be occupied by a disabled occupant.

(2) An "owner's certificate", for the purposes of an application for a disabled facilities grant, certifies that the applicant—

(a) has or proposes to acquire a qualifying owner's interest, and
(b) intends that the disabled occupant will live in the dwelling or flat as his only or main residence throughout the grant condition period or for such shorter period as his health and other relevant circumstances permit.

DEFINITIONS
"disabled facilities grant": s.1.
"dwelling": s.101.
"flat": s.58.
"grant condition period": s.44.
"local housing authority": s.101.
"owner's application": s.19.

GENERAL NOTE
An owner's application must be accompanied by an owner's certificate. If the application is for a dwelling, then it must be in respect of the dwelling; if the application is a common parts application for a disabled facilities grant, then it must be in respect of each flat which is or is proposed to be occupied by a disabled occupier. The certificate must confirm that the applicant has, or proposes to acquire, an owner's certificate; the certificate must also confirm that it is intended that throughout the grant condition period (normally five years—s.44(3), below)—or for such shorter period as health and other relevant circumstances (*e.g.* availability of home care) will permit—the disabled occupant will live in the relevant property as his only or main residence (as to which, see notes to s.8, above).

This requirement is not applicable to applications in respect of certain church lands and applications made by charities: s.95, below.

Disabled facilities grants: certificates required in case of tenant's application

22.—(1) A local housing authority shall not entertain a tenant's application for a disabled facilities grant unless it is accompanied by a tenant's certificate.

(2) A "tenant's certificate", for the purposes of an application for a disabled facilities grant, certifies—

(a) that the application is a tenant's application, and
(b) that the applicant intends that he (if he is the disabled occupant) or the disabled occupant will live in the dwelling or flat as his only or main residence throughout the grant condition period or for such shorter period as his health and other relevant circumstances permit.

(3) Except where the authority consider it unreasonable in the circumstances to require such a certificate, they shall not entertain a tenant's application for a disabled facilities grant unless it is also accompanied by an

owner's certificate from the person who at the time of the application is the landlord under the tenancy.

DEFINITIONS

"disabled facilities grant": s.1.
"disabled occupant": ss.20, 100.
"dwelling": s.101.
"flat": s.58.
"grant condition period": s.44.
"local housing authority": s.101.
"owner's certificate": s.21.

GENERAL NOTE

This section makes provision corresponding to the last, where the application is a tenant's application, confirming the intended residence of the disabled occupant. An owner's certificate under s.21 is *also* required, unless the authority consider it unreasonable to require it.

This requirement is not applicable to applications in respect of certain church lands and applications made by charities: s.95, below.

Disabled facilities grants: purposes for which grant must or may be given

23.—(1) The purposes for which an application for a disabled facilities grant must be approved, subject to the provisions of this Chapter, are the following—

(a) facilitating access by the disabled occupant to and from the dwelling or the building in which the dwelling or, as the case may be, flat is situated;
(b) making the dwelling or building safe for the disabled occupant and other persons residing with him;
(c) facilitating access by the disabled occupant to a room used or usable as the principal family room;
(d) facilitating access by the disabled occupant to, or providing for the disabled occupant, a room used or usable for sleeping;
(e) facilitating access by the disabled occupant to, or providing for the disabled occupant, a room in which there is a lavatory, or facilitating the use by the disabled occupant of such a facility;
(f) facilitating access by the disabled occupant to, or providing for the disabled occupant, a room in which there is a bath or shower (or both), or facilitating the use by the disabled occupant of such a facility;
(g) facilitating access by the disabled occupant to, or providing for the disabled occupant, a room in which there is a washhand basin, or facilitating the use by the disabled occupant of such a facility;
(h) facilitating the preparation and cooking of food by the disabled occupant;
(i) improving any heating system in the dwelling to meet the needs of the disabled occupant or, if there is no existing heating system in the dwelling or any such system is unsuitable for use by the disabled occupant, providing a heating system suitable to meet his needs;
(j) facilitating the use by the disabled occupant of a source of power, light or heat by altering the position of one or more means of access to or control of that source or by providing additional means of control;
(k) facilitating access and movement by the disabled occupant around the dwelling in order to enable him to care for a person who is normally resident in the dwelling and is in need of such care;
(l) such other purposes as may be specified by order of the Secretary of State.

(2) An application for a disabled facilities grant may be approved, subject to the provisions of this Chapter, for the purpose of making the dwelling or building suitable for the accommodation, welfare or employment of the disabled occupant in any other respect.

(3) If in the opinion of the local housing authority the relevant works are more or less extensive than is necessary to achieve any of the purposes set out in subsection (1) or the purpose mentioned in subsection (2), they may, with the consent of the applicant, treat the application as varied so that the relevant works are limited to or, as the case may be, include such works as seem to the authority to be necessary for that purpose.

Definitions

"disabled facilities grant": s.1.
"disabled occupant": ss.20, 100.
"dwelling": s.101.
"flat": s.58.
"local housing authority": s.101.

General Note

This section sets out precisely for what purposes a disabled facilities grant *must* be approved (and see s.24(1)(a), below), in terms of facilitating access by the disabled person for whose benefit the works are proposed to the dwelling in question, or a flat in a building, the principal family room, a bedroom, and facilitating access to and use of a lavatory, a room with a hand-basin, a room with a bath and/or shower, a room for cooking, as well as the introduction of a usable (or any) heating system, facilitating switches, sockets and other means of using power, light and heat, and facilitating the access and movement of a disabled person to allow him to care for someone else normally resident in the property and who is in need of care, *i.e.* himself to act as the carer not merely or necessarily the cared for. The Secretary of State may prescribe other purposes.

Subsection (1)(b) is designed "to be sufficiently flexible to give grant to provide a special safe room or rooms for a disabled person who suffers from behavioural difficulties and for those who live with him, and also to provide safety measures for disabled people generally where these are necessary" (*Hansard* (H.L.), Report, April 18, 1996, col. 833, [Government Whip] [Lord Lucas]).

In addition, a disabled facilities grant *may* also be approved in order to make the dwelling or building suitable for the accommodation, welfare *or employment* of the disabled occupant, in any respect additional to the mandatory purposes (see also s.24(1)(b), below).

Subs. (3)

See note to s.12(3), above.

Disabled facilities grants: approval of application

24.—(1) The local housing authority—
(a) shall approve an application for a disabled facilities grant for purposes within section 23(1), and
(b) may if they think fit approve an application for a disabled facilities grant not for a purpose within that provision but for the purpose specified in section 23(2),
subject to the following provisions.

(2) Where an authority entertain an owner's application for a disabled facilities grant made by a person who proposes to acquire a qualifying owner's interest, they shall not approve the application until they are satisfied that he has done so.

(3) A local housing authority shall not approve an application for a disabled facilities grant unless they are satisfied—
(a) that the relevant works are necessary and appropriate to meet the needs of the disabled occupant, and
(b) that it is reasonable and practicable to carry out the relevant works having regard to the age and condition of the dwelling or building.

In considering the matters mentioned in paragraph (a) a local housing authority which is not itself a social services authority shall consult the social services authority.

(4) An authority proposing to approve an application for a disabled facilities grant shall consider—

(a) in the case of an application in respect of works to a dwelling, whether the dwelling is fit for human habitation;

(b) in the case of a common parts application, whether the building meets the requirements in section 604(2) of the Housing Act 1985,

and the authority shall take that into account in deciding whether it is reasonable and practicable to carry out the relevant works.

(5) A local housing authority shall not approve a common parts application for a disabled facilities grant unless they are satisfied that the applicant has a power or is under a duty to carry out the relevant works.

DEFINITIONS

"disabled facilities grant": s.1.
"disabled occupant": ss.20, 100.
"fit for human habitation": s.97.
"local housing authority": s.101.
"owner's application": s.19.
"relevant works": s.2.
"social services authority": s.100.

GENERAL NOTE

This section mirrors the last, dividing disabled facilities grants into two types: mandatory if within s.23(1), and discretionary if within s.23(2). As to the exercise of discretion, and policies, see notes to s.13, above.

If an owner's application was based on proposed ownership (see s.19, above), the authority cannot approve the grant until the interest has been acquired: subs. (2).

The authority shall not approve a grant unless satisfied that the works the subject of the application are "necessary and appropriate to meet the needs of the disabled occupant", to assess which, if not themselves a social services authority (as to which, see notes to s.100, below, *i.e.* if the housing authority are a non-unitary, district council in a non-metropolitan county), the authority must consult the social services authority (the non-metropolitan county council): subs. (3). The decision on whether it is reasonable and practicable to carry out the works having regard to age and condition of dwelling or building is, however, one for the housing authority themselves: *ibid.*

The amount of the grant is governed by ss.30, 31, 33, below.

Subs. (4)

See notes to ss.13 and 18, above, and 97 below. The authority are not, however, prohibited from approving a grant merely because the dwelling will still be unfit, or fail to meet the relevant and corresponding conditions for a building, but are merely required to take it into account.

Subs. (5)

See notes to s.15, above.

HMO grants

HMO grants: the interest of the applicant in the property

25.—(1) A local housing authority shall not entertain an application for an HMO grant unless they are satisfied that the applicant has or proposes to acquire an owner's interest in every parcel of land on which the relevant works are to be carried out.

(2) In accordance with directions given by the Secretary of State, a local housing authority may treat the condition in subsection (1) as fulfilled by a person who has, or proposes to acquire, an owner's interest in only part of the land concerned.

(3) References in this Chapter to "a qualifying owner's interest", in relation to an application for an HMO grant, are to an owner's interest meet-

ing the condition in subsection (1) or treated by virtue of subsection (2) as meeting that condition.

DEFINITIONS
"HMO grant": s.1.
"local housing authority": s.101.
"owner's interest": s.101.
"relevant works": s.2.

GENERAL NOTE

Only owners can apply for an HMO grant. There is a minor discretion available to the authority—acting only in accordance with directions given by the Secretary of State—whereby the overriding requirement of ownership of all the land on which the works the subject of the application are to be carried can be waived if there is ownership of part of that land. An owner's application can be made on the basis of a proposed acquisition of interest, but in that case there can be no approval of the grant until the interest has been acquired: s.28(3).

For HMO purposes (see s.101, below), owner has the same meaning as under Pt. XI of the Housing Act 1985, where it—

"(a) means a person (other than a mortgagee not in possession) who is for the time being entitled to dispose of the fee simple of the premises whether in possession or in reversion, and
(b) includes also a person holding or entitled to the rents and profits the premises under a lease having an unexpired term exceeding three years" (1985 Act, s.398(3)).

HMO grants: certificate required to accompany application

26.—(1) A local housing authority shall not entertain an application for an HMO grant unless it is accompanied by a certificate of future occupation.

(2) A "certificate of future occupation" certifies that the applicant—

(a) has or proposes to acquire a qualifying owner's interest in the house, and

(b) intends that throughout the grant condition period the house or a part of it (specified in the certificate) will be residentially occupied, or available for residential occupation, under tenancies or licences by persons who are not connected with the owner for the time being of the house.

In paragraph (b) "residential occupation" does not include occupation for a holiday, and "tenancies" does not include a long tenancy.

DEFINITIONS
"connected with the owner": s.98.
"grant condition period": s.44.
"HMO grant": s.1.
"local housing authority": s.101.
"long tenancy": s.101.
"owner's interest": s.101.
"tenancy": s.101.

GENERAL NOTE

An application for an HMO grant may not be entertained unless it is accompanied by a certificate stating—

(i) that the applicant has or proposes to acquire an owner's interest in the house in question, and
(ii) that he intends that throughout the grant condition period (normally five years—see s.44(3), below) the house, or such part of it as may be identified in the certificate, will be "residentially occupied" under tenancies or licences by persons who are "not connected with the owner for the time being of the house".

Residential occupation. There is no magic about this phrase, to which the case-law on occupation as a residence or as an only or main or principal home may have some relevance: see notes to s.8, above. The term is introduced here expressly to exclude holiday lettings: also see notes to s.8, above.

Tenancy or licence. Excluded from tenancy for this purpose is a long tenancy, which has the meaning given it by the Housing Act 1985, s.115, *i.e.* normally a tenancy granted for a fixed term exceeding 21 years (see notes to s.8, above). Such tenancies will procure a capital payment and as such are more akin to owner-occupation than tenancy popularly so-called.

As to the distinction between tenancy and licence, see notes to s.7, above. The inclusion of premises licensed by the owner will cover those cases where no occupier has been granted exclusive possession of any part of the house, and there is no joint tenancy of the whole of the house, see *A.G. Securities v. Vaughan, Antoniades v. Villiers* [1990] A.C. 417, 21 H.L.R. 79, H.L., distinguishing between a genuine such arrangement and a mere pretense.

Connected with the owner. A person is connected with the owner (see notes to s.25, above) if property is held by personal representatives or trustees, and he is someone who is beneficially entitled to an interest in, or to the proceeds of sale of, the property, *i.e.* the requirement to keep an HMO available for letting is not met by a "letting" between trustee and beneficiary.

A person is *also* connected with the owner if he is a member of the owner's family: see s.98, applying s.113 of the Housing Act 1985, to the expression "member of family"; see notes thereto, below.

HMO grants: purposes for which grant may be given

27.—(1) The purposes for which an application for an HMO grant (other than a conversion application) may be approved are—

(a) to comply with a notice under section 189 of the Housing Act 1985 (repair notice in respect of unfit premises) or otherwise to render the house fit for human habitation;

(b) to comply with a notice under section 190 of that Act (repair notice in respect of premises not unfit but in need of substantial repair) or otherwise to put the building in reasonable repair;

(c) to comply with a notice under section 352 of that Act (notice requiring works to render premises fit for the number of occupants) or otherwise to enable the house to meet one or more of the requirements in subsection (1A) of that section;

(d) to provide adequate thermal insulation;

(e) to provide adequate facilities for space heating;

(f) to provide satisfactory internal arrangements;

(g) to provide means of escape in case of fire or other fire precautions, not being precautions required under or by virtue of any enactment (whenever passed);

(h) to ensure that the house complies with such requirements with respect to construction or physical condition as may be specified by the Secretary of State;

(i) to ensure that there is compliance with such requirements with respect to the provision or condition of services and amenities to or within the house as are so specified;

(j) any other purpose for the time being specified for the purposes of this section by order of the Secretary of State.

(2) The purpose for which a conversion application may be approved is to provide a house in multiple occupation by the conversion of a house or other building.

(3) If in the opinion of the authority the relevant works are more or less extensive than is necessary to achieve any of the purposes set out in subsection (1) or (2), they may, with the consent of the applicant, treat the application as varied so that the relevant works are limited to or, as the case may be, include such works as seem to the authority to be necessary for that purpose.

(4) In exercise of the powers conferred by paragraphs (h) and (i) of subsection (1) the Secretary of State may specify requirements generally or for particular cases, and may specify different requirements for different areas.

DEFINITIONS

"HMO grant": s.1.

"house in multiple occupation": s.101.

GENERAL NOTE

This section specifies the purposes for which an HMO grant may be approved, and is identical to s.17, above (see also s.12, above), save that it provides in subs. (2) for a conversion HMO grant, *i.e.* for the provision of an HMO by conversion of a house or other building, under s.1(5)(b).

HMO grants: approval of application

28.—(1) The local housing authority may approve an application for an HMO grant if they think fit, subject to the following provisions.

(2) The authority shall not approve an application for an HMO grant unless they are satisfied that the works are necessary for one or more of the purposes set out in section 27(1) or (2).

(3) Where an authority entertain an application for an HMO grant made by a person who proposes to acquire a qualifying owner's interest, they shall not approve the application until they are satisfied that he has done so.

(4) An authority proposing to approve an application for an HMO grant shall consider whether the house to which the application relates is fit for human habitation and meets the requirements in section 352(1A) of the Housing Act 1985.

(5) If it appears to the authority that the house is not fit for human habitation or does not meet those requirements, they shall not approve the application unless they are satisfied—

(a) that on completion of the relevant works, together with any other works proposed to be carried out, the house will be fit for human habitation and meet those requirements,

(b) that there are satisfactory financial and other arrangements for carrying out those works, and

(c) that the carrying out of the works is the most satisfactory course of action.

(6) In considering whether to approve an application for an HMO grant the local housing authority shall have regard to the expected life of the house (taking account, where appropriate, of the effect of carrying out the works).

DEFINITIONS

"fit for human habitation": s.97.
"HMO grant": s.1.
"local housing authority": s.101.
"qualifying owner's interest": s.25.
"relevant works": s.2.

GENERAL NOTE

This section makes provision parallel to that to be found in ss.13, 18, above—see in particular notes to s.13 on the exercise of discretion, and policies. Note, too, that under this section the authority must consider both the requirements in the Housing Act 1985, s.352(1A) (as to which, see notes to s.17, above), as well as fitness for human habitation (see notes to s.97, below).

No approval can be given to an application on the basis of a proposed acquisition of interest, until the interest has been acquired: subs. (3).

The amount of the grant is governed by ss.31, 33, below.

Restrictions on grant aid

Restriction on grants for works already begun

29.—(1) Subject as follows, a local housing authority shall not approve an application for a grant if the relevant works have been begun before the application is approved.

(2) Where the relevant works have been begun but have not been completed, the authority may approve the application for a grant if they are satisfied that there were good reasons for beginning the works before the application was approved.

(3) Where an authority decide to approve an application in accordance with subsection (2), they may, with the consent of the applicant, treat the application as varied so that the relevant works do not include any that are completed.

But in determining for the purposes of the application the physical condition of the dwelling, common parts or house or other building concerned, they shall consider the condition of the premises at the date of the application.

(4) Subject as follows, a local housing authority shall not approve an application for a grant if the relevant works have been completed.

(5) Nothing in this section applies to an application for a grant in respect of works necessary—

(a) to render a dwelling fit for human habitation or to comply with a notice under section 189 or 190 of the Housing Act 1985 (repair notices), or

(b) to enable a house in multiple occupation to meet one or more of the requirements in section 352(1A) of that Act (fitness for the number of occupants) or to comply with a notice under that section.

(6) If the local housing authority consider that the relevant works include works in addition to those necessary for the purposes mentioned in subsection (5)(a) or (b), they shall treat the application as an application to which this section applies so far as it relates to those additional works.

DEFINITIONS

"common parts": s.58.
"local housing authority": s.101.
"relevant works": s.2.

GENERAL NOTE

The starting-point of this section seems at odds with what follows. In substance, a local authority *may* approve an application for a grant (but need not do so, even if otherwise mandatory) where the works the subject of the application have been *commenced but not completed* prior to approval, if satisfied that there were good reasons for beginning the works without awaiting approval, *e.g.* urgency (subs. (2)): as to discretion and policy, see notes to s.13, above. They cannot do so if the works have been completed (subs. (4)).

These prohibitions do not apply, however, if the works were necessary to achieve fitness for human habitation or to comply with a notice under the Housing Act 1985, ss.189, 192 (above, notes to s.12), or to enable an HMO to meet the requirements of s.352(1A) or to comply with a notice under that section (above, notes to s.17). Works additional to those necessary for such purposes are treated in accordance with the residual "good reason" discretion (subs. (5)).

One route the authority can take is to decide to vary the works (with the agreement of the applicant) to exclude those which have been begun before approval, *cf.* ss.12(3), 17(2), 23(3) and 27(3): in reaching their decision on a grant, however, the authority are bound to consider the physical condition of the property, under a number of headings (to achieve the stated purposes under ss.12, 17, 23 and 27, to consider fitness and condition after the works under ss.13, 18, 24 and 28, and to consider expected life under ss.13, 18 and 28). In determining "the physical condition" of the dwelling, for the purpose of deciding whether or not to vary the works to exclude those begun before approval, subs. (3) requires the authority to consider the condition of the premises at the date of application, *i.e.* to disregard intervening, pre-approval works; this appears to mean that the authority cannot refuse the grant because what works remain are not, on their own, necessary to the objectives, although would have been so considered when taken with those which have already been executed.

These provisions apply where the authority know about the works prior to approval: where they subsequently discover that works were started before approval, they may refuse to pay the grant, or any further instalment, or reduce the grant or demand repayment: see s.42, below.

Means testing in case of application by owner-occupier or tenant

30.—(1) This section applies—

(a) to an application for a renovation grant which is—

(i) an owner's application accompanied by an owner-occupation certificate, or

(ii) a tenant's application; and

(b) to any application for a disabled facilities grant.

(2) An owner's application for a renovation grant shall be treated as falling within this section if it is a conversion application for the provision of two or more dwellings and any of the certificates accompanying the application is an owner-occupation certificate.

(3) If in the case of an application for a renovation grant to which this section applies the financial resources of the applicant exceed the applicable amount, the amount of any grant which may be paid shall, in accordance with regulations, be reduced from what it would otherwise have been.

(4) If in the case of an application for a disabled facilities grant the financial resources of any person of a description specified by regulations exceed the applicable amount, the amount of any grant which may be paid shall, in accordance with regulations, be reduced from what it would otherwise have been.

(5) Provision may be made by regulations—

(a) for the determination of the amount which is to be taken to be the financial resources of any person,

(b) for the determination of the applicable amount referred to in subsection (3) or (4), and

(c) as to circumstances in which the financial resources of a person are to be assumed (by reason of his receiving a prescribed benefit or otherwise) not to exceed the applicable amount.

(6) Regulations may, in particular—

(a) make provision for account to be taken of the income, assets, needs and outgoings not only of the person himself but also of his spouse, any person living with him or intending to live with him and any person on whom he is dependent or who is dependent on him;

(b) make provision for amounts specified in or determined under the regulations to be taken into account for particular purposes.

(7) Regulations may apply for the purposes of this section, subject to such modifications as may be prescribed, any other statutory means-testing regime as it has effect from time to time.

(8) Regulations may make provision requiring any information or evidence needed for the determination of any matter under this section to be furnished by such person as may be prescribed.

(9) In this section "regulations" means regulations made by the Secretary of State with the consent of the Treasury.

DEFINITIONS

"conversion application": s.58.
"disabled facilities grant": s.1.
"owner's application": s.7.
"owner occupation certificate": s.8.
"renovation grant": s.1.
"tenant's application": s.7.

GENERAL NOTE

This section provides for means-testing applicants for renovation grants who are owner-occupiers or tenants, and applicants for a disabled facilities grant: excluded are landlord's applications, applications for common parts grants, and applications for HMO grants. These are dealt with, by way of the authority's discretion, under s.31, below. Application for a renovation grant to provide *two* or more dwellings by conversion is treated as an owner's application if the applicant provides an owner-occupation certificate in respect of one of them (see s.8, above, *i.e.* intends to live in one of them; *cf.* s.58, below: a conversion grant may be to provide only one dwelling by conversion, but in such a case it would be "either/or" [landlord's application or owner-occupation certificate] without the need for this express provision)—subs. (2).

Means-testing is carried out by comparison of financial resources and applicable amount, according to a formula or method to be dictated by regulations: subss. (3)–(9).

Amount of grant. Subject to means-testing, and to grant maxima specified under s.33, below, and having regard to the express discretion in s.31 and to the wording of subss. (3), (4) ("what [the grant] would otherwise have been") and that of s.32(5) ("the grants that would be payable ... under section 33"), it does seem that—even though most grants are discretionary—there is no residual discretion to approve a grant, but at a lower amount: see *R. v. Sunderland C.C., ex p. Redezeus* (1994) 27 H.L.R. 477, Q.B.D.

Determination of amount of grant in case of landlord's application

31.—(1) This section applies to—

(a) an owner's application for a renovation grant which is accompanied by a certificate of intended letting (not being an application which falls within section 30: see subsection (2) of that section),

(b) a landlord's application for a common parts grant,

(c) a landlord's application for a disabled facilities grant, and

(d) any application for an HMO grant.

(2) The reference in subsection (1)(c) to a landlord's application for a disabled facilities grant is to an owner's application in respect of works to a dwelling which is or is intended to be let, or to the common parts of a building in which a flat is or is intended to be let.

(3) The amount of the grant (if any) shall be determined by the local housing authority, having regard to—

(a) the extent to which the landlord is able to charge a higher rent for the premises because of the works, and

(b) such other matters as the Secretary of State may direct.

(4) The authority may, if they think it appropriate, seek and act upon the advice of rent officers as to any matter.

(5) The Secretary of State may by regulations make provision requiring any information or evidence needed for the determination of any matter under this section to be furnished by such person as may be prescribed.

DEFINITIONS

"certificate of intended letting": s.8.
"common parts grant": s.1.
"disabled facilities grant": s.1.
"HMO grant": s.1.
"landlord's application": ss.10, 15.
"local housing authority": s.101.
"owner's application": s.7.
"renovation grant": s.1.
"statutory tenancy": s.101.

GENERAL NOTE

This section, in contrast to the last, deals with what are essentially landlord's applications, whether so-called in relation to common parts and disabled facilities (see subs. (1)(b), (c)) or not so called in relation to renovation grant in subs. (1)(a) (yet could have been—see s.10(5)), or necessarily so in relation to an HMO grant. The authority have discretion to determine the amount of the grant, subject (a) to having "regard to" both the possibility of higher rent attributable to the works, and to such matters as the Secretary of State may direct, and (b) as always, the requirements of administrative law (as to which, see notes to s.13, above).

The phrase "have regard to" has been considered in the notes to s.12, above, in relation to the determination of the most satisfactory course of action in the context of unfitness. Authorities will not be bound to follow the Secretary of State's directions as to matters to be taken into account blindly and will be able to depart from them so long as they have first had regard to them—*De Falco, Silvestri v. Crawley B.C.* [1980] Q.B. 460, C.A.; *Miller v. Wandsworth L.B.C.*, *The Times*, March 19, 1980; *Lambert v. Ealing L.B.C.* [1982] 1 W.L.R. 550, 2 H.L.R. 58, C.A. As Parliament has required authorities to have regard to them, however, deviation may amount to a *prima facie* case that they have not been taken into account, sufficient at least (in practice) to call for an explanation from the authority: *cf. Padfield v. Minister of Agriculture, Fisheries & Food* [1968] A.C. 997, H.L.

The sort of matters which are likely to be the subject of directions, as under the 1989 Act, include cost of works, capital values and loan charges. In order to determine subsequent levels of rent, the authority may choose to seek and act on the advice of rent officers: subs. (4). The power of the rent officer to undertake this task is to be found in the Housing Act 1988, s.12, as amended by Sched. 1, para. 13, below.

Subs. (4)

The authority cannot lawfully delegate to the rent officer their function of determining the notional increase in rental value, even though they may take his advice and, in the absence of any evidence to contradict the basis on which a rent officer has proceeded, it may be unrealistic to expect them to adopt any other figure: *R. v. Bolsover D.C. and the Rent Officer for the Derbyshire Registration Area, ex p. East Midlands Development, and Denis Rye* (1995) 28 H.L.R. 329, Q.B.D.

Apportionment in case of tenants' application for common parts grant

32.—(1) This section applies where a local housing authority approve a tenants' application for a common parts grant.

(2) The local housing authority shall decide how much of the cost of the relevant works is attributable to the applicants ("the attributable cost").

(3) For the purposes of this section the attributable cost is an amount equal to the following proportion of the cost of the relevant works—

(a) if it can be ascertained, the proportion that the aggregate of the respective liabilities of each of the applicants to carry out or contribute to the carrying out of the relevant works bears to the aggregate of all such liabilities on the part of all persons (including the applicants) so liable; or

(b) if the proportion mentioned in paragraph (a) cannot be ascertained, the proportion that the number of applicants bears to the number of persons (including the applicants) liable to carry out or contribute to the carrying out of works to the building.

(4) The local housing authority shall then apportion the attributable cost to each of the applicants—

(a) in a case where the attributable cost is calculated by reference to the proportion mentioned in subsection (3)(a), according to the proportion that his liabilities to carry out or contribute to the carrying out of the relevant works bears to the aggregate of the applicants' liabilities mentioned in that paragraph; or

(b) in a case where the attributable cost is calculated by reference to the proportion mentioned in subsection (3)(b), equally.

(5) The amount of the grant payable shall be the aggregate of the grants that would be payable to each of the applicants under section 30 or, in the case of a participating landlord, under section 31 if each of the applicants was an individual applicant in respect of his portion of the attributable cost.

(6) Where the interest of an occupying tenant is held jointly by two or more persons, those persons shall be regarded as a single person for the purposes of this section.

DEFINITIONS

"common parts grant": s.1.
"local housing authority": s.101.
"relevant works": s.2.

GENERAL NOTE

Where the application is by tenants for a common parts grant, the authority must first establish how much of the cost of the relevant works is attributable to the applicants—"the attributable cost": subs. (2). This is achieved by applying one of two formulae: subs. (3).

If it is ascertainable, then the attributable cost is the aggregate of the individual proportions of the applicants' responsibility, *e.g.* under service charge provisions in a lease, as against the total cost of the relevant works. Thus, if 10 flats and five applicants (each bearing a one-fifth liability), the attributable cost would be 50 per cent; or, if service charges are allocated according to a different formula, such as floor area, four applicants may have liability between them for—say, purely for the sake of example 60 per cent of the service charge (or relevant element of service charges), in which case the attributable cost would be 60 per cent: subs. (3)(a).

If this approach is not workable, then a strictly numerical apportionment is adopted: subs. (3)(b). Thus, seven applicants, 20 contributors to costs, attributable cost 35 per cent.

Once the attributable cost has been ascertained, it is then apportioned to each of the applicants individually, either on the basis of a similar "proportionate" test, or else strictly numerically, depending on which approach has been used in calculating the attributable cost itself: subs. (4). Section 33 is then applied to determine the grant as if each one of the applicants had applied individually for that amount of grant (and, if one of the applicant's is a participating landlord—see notes to s.15, above—section 34 is likewise brought into play on the same basis).

Power to specify maximum amount of grant

33.—(1) The Secretary of State may, if he thinks fit, by order specify a maximum amount or a formula for calculating a maximum amount of grant which a local housing authority may pay in respect of an application for a grant.

(2) An order under this section may make different provision for different types of grant, or for the same type of grant in different circumstances.

(3) In relation to an application for a grant in respect of works for any of the purposes in section 23(1) (mandatory disabled facilities grant), the order may—

(a) provide for a maximum amount of grant to be paid if the application is approved, and

(b) authorise the local housing authority, if they think fit, to pay a further amount in excess of that maximum but subject to such other maximum (if any) as may be specified in or determined in accordance with the order.

(4) An authority may not, except as mentioned in subsection (3), pay an amount of grant in excess of a specified maximum amount.

DEFINITIONS

"disabled facilities grant": s.1.

"local housing authority": s.101.

GENERAL NOTE

Short, central and to the point: the ultimate limit on grants payable is set by the Secretary of State; save as may be permitted in relation to disabled facilities grants under subs. (3), authorities have no discretion to exceed the maxima set—see subs. (4).

Decision and notification

Decision and notification

34.—(1) A local housing authority shall by notice in writing notify an applicant for a grant as soon as reasonably practicable, and, in any event, not later than six months after the date of the application concerned, whether the application is approved or refused.

(2) Where an authority decide to approve an application for a grant, they shall determine—

(a) which of the relevant works are eligible for grant (in this Chapter referred to as "the eligible works"),

(b) the amount of the expenses which in their opinion are properly to be incurred in the execution of the eligible works,

(c) the amount of the costs which in their opinion have been properly incurred, or are properly to be incurred, with respect to preliminary or ancillary services and charges, and

(d) the amount of grant they have decided to pay, taking into account all the relevant provisions of this Chapter.

The total of the amounts referred to in paragraphs (b) and (c) is referred to in this Chapter as "the estimated expense".

(3) If the authority notify the applicant under subsection (1) that the application is approved, they shall specify in the notice—

(a) the eligible works,
(b) the amounts referred to in subsection (2)(b) and (c), and how those amounts have been calculated, and
(c) the amount of the grant.

(4) If the authority notify the applicant under subsection (1) that the application is refused, they shall at the same time notify him of the reasons for the refusal.

(5) If after an application for a grant has been approved the authority are satisfied that owing to circumstances beyond the control of the applicant—
(a) the eligible works cannot be, or could not have been, carried out on the basis of the amount of expenses referred to in subsection (2)(b),
(b) the amount of the costs which have been or are to be incurred as mentioned in subsection (2)(c) has increased, or
(c) the eligible works cannot be, or could not have been, carried out without carrying out additional works which could not have been reasonably foreseen at the time the application was made,

the authority may re-determine the estimated expense and the amount of the grant.

(6) Where an application for a grant is approved, the local housing authority may not impose any condition in relation to the approval or payment of the grant, except—
(a) as provided by the following provisions of this Chapter, or
(b) with the consent of the Secretary of State;

and this applies whether the condition purports to operate as a condition, a personal covenant or otherwise.

DEFINITIONS

"local housing authority": s.101.
"preliminary or ancillary services and charges": s.2.
"relevant works": s.2.

GENERAL NOTE

The authority are bound to issue their decision on an application as soon as reasonably practicable, and in any event within six months, in writing, stating the constituent financial elements of the grant payable (if approved) (subs. (3)), or the reasons for a refusal (subs. (4)). This permits the applicant to challenge *both* a refusal *and* a lower grant than he believes he is entitled to.

Financial elements. So far as concerns the constituent financial elements, this means:

(i) The relevant works (*i.e.* the works the subject of the application—see notes to s.2, above) which are eligible for grant (*i.e.* under ss.12, 17, 23 and 27, having regard to the duty under ss.13, 18, 14 and 28 not to pay grant on more works than are needed to achieve the objectives)—the eligible works (these may later be revised to include added, unforeseeable works arising in circumstances beyond the control of the applicant—see subs. (4));

(ii) The amount of expenses properly incurred in relation to these eligible works—see notes to s.2, above: the eligible expense (this may later be revised to include added cost arising in circumstances beyond the control of the applicant—see subs. (4));

(iii) The amount of costs involved in the application and preparing for and carrying out of the works (see notes to s.2, above); and,

(iv) The amount of grant (which will include means-testing under s.30, landlord's discretionary amounts under s.31, allocation between applicants under s.32 and maxima under s.33).

Reasons. "I hold the view that good local authorities already do what the amendments would require, but there is merit in converting good practice into a general rule," (*Hansard* (H.L.), Report, April 18, 1996, col. 858, [Government Whip] [Lord Lucas]).

There is no general legal duty to give reasons for administrative decision, save although such a duty can on occasion be implied by law "in appropriate circumstances": *R. v. Secretary of State for the Home Department, ex p. Doody* [1994] 1 A.C. 531, H.L. *per* Lord Mustill (see also *R. v. Civil Service Appeal Board, ex p. Cunningham* [1991] 4 All E.R. 310, where there is something in a decision which "cries out for some explanation", and where the absence of any explanation will support the inference that the reasoning is flawed or aberrant).

In *R. v. Bristol C.C. ex p. Bailey* (1994) 27 H.L.R. 307, Q.B.D., a duty to give reasons for refusing a grant application under the 1989 Act had been expressly disclaimed, although this may have been a more particular than general decision, as there had been an appeal hearing, in which all facts and matters were put before a sub-committee, and the issue (whether or not property unfit) was a simple one, *i.e.* the reasons were clear. See further *R. v. Higher Education Funding Council, ex p. Institute of Dental Surgery* [1994] 1 W.L.R. 242, Q.B.D., and *R. v. Kensington & Chelsea R.B.C., ex p. Grillo* (1995) 28 H.L.R. 94, C.A. In *R. v. Corporation of the City of London, ex p. Matson, The Times*, October 20, 1995, C.A., fairness and justice required the Court of Aldermen of the City of London to give reasons when deciding not to ratify the election of an alderman.

The duty is, however, now clear. It is similar to the duty to give notification of decision and reasons under Pt. III of the Housing Act 1985, in respect of applications for accommodation by the homeless. It has been held that the purpose of the requirement to give reasons is to enable the recipient to see whether they might be challengeable in law: see (originally) *Thornton v. Kirklees M.B.C.* [1979] Q.B. 626, C.A. (a judicial summary of counsel's submission, rather than a judicial observation in its own right), see also *R. v. Tynedale D.C., ex p. Shield* (1987) 22 H.L.R. 144, and *R. v. Northampton B.C., ex p. Carpenter* (1992) 25 H.L.R. 349, in which the decision letter was said to be "manifestly defective" because it failed to address the reasons the applicant had left his previous accommodation and accordingly defeated the purpose of the section which was "to enable someone who is entitled to a decision to see what the reasons are for that decision and to challenge those reasons if they are apparently inadequate.".

In *R. v. Croydon L.B.C., ex p. Graham* (1993) 26 H.L.R. 286, C.A., Sir Thomas Bingham M.R. said:

"I readily accept that these difficult decisions are decisions for the housing authority and certainly a pedantic exegesis of letters of this kind would be inappropriate. There is, nonetheless, an obligation under the Act to give reasons and that must impose on the council a duty to give reasons which are intelligible and which convey to the applicant the reasons why the application has been rejected in such a way that if they disclose an error of reasoning the applicant may take such steps as may be indicated."

This quotation was cited with approval in *R. v. Islington L.B.C., ex p. Hinds* (1995) 28 H.L.R. 302, C.A., where the duty to give reasons was found to be complied with as the reasons stated in the decision letter were intelligible and conveyed clearly to the applicant the reason why his application had been rejected.

Save in exceptional circumstances, the courts will not permit the reasons given in the notification to be supplemented by affidavit on a challenge: see *R. v. Croydon L.B.C., ex p. Graham* (1993) 26 H.L.R. 286, C.A., and *R. v. Westminster C.C., ex p. Ermakov* (1995) 8 Admin.L.R. 381; 28 H.L.R. forthcoming, C.A., see also *R. v. Southwark L.B.C., ex p. Dagou* (1995) 28 H.L.R. 72; *cf. R. v. Cardiff C.C., ex p. John* (1982) 9 H.L.R. 56, where the court had held that the fact that the decision letter did not itself disclose the proper reasons for the decision did not prevent the authority from relying on proper reasons and justifying their decision accordingly, and *Hobbs v. Sutton L.B.C.* (1993) 26 H.L.R. 286, C.A., where the Court of Appeal accepted affidavit evidence amplifying and explaining earlier evidence as to reasons).

In *R. v. Westminster C.C., ex p. Augustin* (1993) 25 H.L.R. 281, C.A., however, it was held that a later letter could serve to rectify the shortcomings of an earlier notification (which, however, was not considered defective albeit "sparse"—*per* Auld J. in the court below—or "cryptic" [and brief]—*per* Glidewell L.J. in the Court of Appeal: it was considered to give the applicant the information she needed).

Furthermore, the courts have not always held authorities to the words of their reasons when decisions are challenged: see *De Falco, Silvestri v. Crawley B.C.* [1980] Q.B. 460, C.A.; *R. v. Hillingdon L.B.C., ex p. Islam* [1983] 1 A.C. 688, 1 H.L.R. 107, H.L.; *R. v. Westminster C.C., ex p. Chambers* (1982) 6 H.L.R. 15. It has been held that authorities are entitled to give their reasons quite simply: "their decision and their reasons are not to be analysed in minute detail. They are not to be gone through as it were with a toothcomb. They are not to be criticised by saying: 'They have not mentioned this or that'": *Tickner v. Mole Valley D.C.* [1980] 2 April, C.A. Transcript. In *Kelly v. Monklands D.C.*, July 12, 1985, Ct. of Session (O.H.), a mere recital of the words of the Act was even held sufficient on this point.

The nature and extent of reasons must, however, relate to the substantive issues raised by an applicant or, perhaps, by an applicant's adviser: see, *Re Poyser & Mills Arbitration* [1964] 2 Q.B. 467, approved by the House of Lords in *Westminster C.C. v. Great Portland Estates* [1985] A.C. 661, and again in *Save Britain's Heritage v. Secretary of State for the Environment* [1991] 1 W.L.R. 153: "the reasons that are set out must be reasons which will not only be intelligible, but which deal with the substantial points that have been raised," *per* Megaw J. in *Poyser*, and "The three criteria suggested in the *dictum* of Megaw J. are that the reasons should be proper, intelligible and adequate," *per* Lord Bridge in *Save Britain's Heritage*. See also *Givaudan v. Minister of Housing and Local Government* [1967] 1 W.L.R. 250, *Mountview Court Properties v. Devlin* (1970) 21 P. & C.R. 689. In *Edwin H. Bradley & Sons v. Secretary of State for the*

Environment (1982) 266 E.G. 264, 926, Glidewell J. added to the *dictum* of Megaw J. that reasons can be briefly stated (also approved in *Great Portland Street*).

In *R. v. Hillingdon L.B.C., ex p. H* (1988) 20 H.L.R. 559, it was held that while the authority were entitled to express themselves quite simply, and could not be criticised for not having gone into great detail, it was none the less incumbent on them to say what was the deliberate act or omission in consequence of which it had been concluded that the applicant had ceased to occupy accommodation available for his occupation and which it would have been reasonable for him to continue to occupy (definition of intentional homeless, s.60, 1985 Act). In the context of the case, this had required more than a statement that he could have continued to occupy his council tenancy in Northern Ireland.

See also *R. v. Tower Hamlets L.B.C., ex p. Monaf* (1988) 20 H.L.R. 529, C.A.; *R. v. Southwark L.B.C., ex p. Davies* (1993) 26 H.L.R. 677, and *R. v. Slough B.C., ex p. Khan* (1995) 27 H.L.R. 492, in the latter of which a decision letter which addressed only one of a number of grounds on which a local connection was claimed was held to be defective. In *R. v. Brent L.B.C., ex p. Baruwa* (1995) 28 H.L.R. 361, it was impossible to work out from the decision letter any reasoning process, or the primary underlying reasoning, which had led the authority to conclude that the applicant was deliberately declining to pay rent which she could afford.

See also the cases on reasons for the decisions of Housing Benefit Review Boards: *R. v. Housing Benefit Review Board, ex p. Thomas* (1991) 25 H.L.R. 1, Q.B.D.; *R. v. Housing Benefit Review Board for East Devon D.C., ex p. Gibson* (1993) 25 H.L.R. 487 C.A.; *R. v. Sefton M.B.C., ex p. Cunningham* (1991) 23 H.L.R. 534; *R. v. Solihull M.B.C. Housing Benefit Review Board, ex p. Simpson* (1994) 27 H.L.R. 41, C.A.; *R. v. Sutton L.B.C., ex p. Partridge* (1994) 28 H.L.R. 315, Q.B.D.

See notes to s.13, above, for a general statement on what is—and is not—a proper approach to decision generally by local authorities, on which (additional to or independently of challenge based on misinterpretation of the provisions of this Act) a challenge may be made, potentially based on what has been disclosed by the notification.

Subs. (5)

This subsection enables re-determination of grant in the event of additional or unforeseeable expenditure, works or costs.

Subs. (6)

Grant *conditions* are only those for which provision is made in the following sections, or that are attached with the consent of the Secretary of State. For example, without such consent, the authority could not agree a landlord's conversion application on the basis of a nomination right to some or all of the flats produced.

Payment of grants

Payment of grants: general

35.—(1) Where the local housing authority have approved an application for a grant, they shall pay the grant, subject to the following provisions of this Chapter.

(2) The grant may be paid—

(a) in whole after the completion of the eligible works, or

(b) in part by instalments as the works progress and the balance after completion of the works.

(3) Where a grant is paid by instalments, the aggregate of the instalments paid before the completion of the eligible works shall not at any time exceed nine-tenths of the amount of the grant.

DEFINITIONS

"eligible works": s.34.

"local housing authority": s.101.

GENERAL NOTE

Grants may be paid after the completion of the eligible works (as to the meaning of which, see s.34, above) or in stage payments ("as the works progress", which seems to imply no *earlier* than commencement and execution of *some* works), but to a maximum of 90 per cent of the total grant due. See notes to s.13, above, on Discretion and Policy. See also s.39, below, as to grant made payable to contractor. See also ss.40–44 for circumstances where payment may not be forthcoming.

See also next section where a mandatory disabled facilities grant is payable.

Delayed payment of mandatory grant

36.—(1) Where the local housing authority are obliged to approve an application for a grant under section 24(1)(a) (mandatory disabled facilities grant), they may do so on terms that payment of the grant, or part of it, will not be made before a date specified in the notification of their decision on the application.

(2) That date shall not be more than twelve months, or such other period as may be specified by order of the Secretary of State, after the date of the application.

DEFINITIONS

"disabled facilities grant": s.1.

"local housing authority": s.101.

GENERAL NOTE

This section is designed to allow an authority to budget where mandatory grants are in issue; it follows a number of incidents over the years in which authorities have complained of inability to pay mandatory grants, partly because of government spending constraints, but on occasion because of difficulty managing the budgetary process. "... Authorities have little scope to manage their financial resources by prioritising cases where mandatory grant is an issue ... We believe that our proposals will help authorities in their financial management by giving them the discretion to withhold payment of mandatory disabled facilities grants for up to 12 months after the date of the application ... We envisage that authorities should only need to use the measure sparingly and in exceptional cases ... " (*Hansard* (H.L.), Committee, April 18, 1996, col. 1667 (Government Whip) (Lord Lucas)).

Use of the section is discretionary: on the one hand, it permits an authority to *defer* commencement of payment of a mandatory disabled facilities grant (see s.24, above), insofar as approval must be no later than six months after application (see s.34, above), and stage payments *could* commence almost as soon as works have begun (see notes to last section); on the other hand—if used—it limits the start of payments to a date that is no later than 12 months after the date of the application (unless another date is specified by the Secretary of State), by which time it is unlikely that all works would be completed (see notes to s.37, below), so that—in this sense—its use may positively benefit the applicant. Put another way, the latter effect is the price for the element of discretion.

The payment may be all or part only of the grant: the section does not appear to be in conflict with the previous section, save as to discretion, and it is accordingly submitted that the 90 per cent limit in s.35, above, is applicable.

Payment of grants: conditions as to carrying out of the works

37.—(1) It is a condition of payment of every grant that the eligible works are carried out within twelve months from—

(a) the date of approval of the application concerned, or

(b) where section 36 applies (delayed payment of mandatory grant), the date specified in the notification of the authority's decision,

or, in either case, such further period as the local housing authority may allow.

(2) The authority may, in particular, allow further time where they are satisfied that the eligible works cannot be, or could not have been, carried out without carrying out other works which could not have been reasonably foreseen at the time the application was made.

(3) In approving an application for a grant a local housing authority may require as a condition of payment of the grant that the eligible works are carried out in accordance with such specifications as they determine.

(4) The payment of a grant, or part of a grant, is conditional upon—

(a) the eligible works or the corresponding part of the works being executed to the satisfaction of the authority, and

(b) the authority being provided with an acceptable invoice, demand or receipt for payment for the works and any preliminary or ancillary services or charges in respect of which the grant or part of the grant is to be paid.

For this purpose an invoice, demand or receipt is acceptable if it satisfies the authority and is not given by the applicant or a member of his family.

DEFINITIONS

"eligible works": s.34.
"local housing authority": s.101.
"member of family": s.98.

GENERAL NOTE

This section contains some important, if discrete, elements of the grant process:

(i) *Completion.* All works must be completed within 12 months of approval of application (save if a mandatory disabled facilities grant is deferred, in which case 12 months from the date to which first payment has been deferred: see s.36, above), unless a further period is allowed by the authority, in particular where the works have been prolonged because of added, unforeseeable works—subss. (1), (2).

(ii) *Specifications.* The authority *may* impose a grant condition that the eligible works are carried out in accordance with a specification determined by them, *e.g.* no substitution of different methods or materials—subs. (3).

(iii) *Satisfactory Works.* The authority must be satisfied that the works—or, if a stage payment, the relevant part of the works—have been executed to their satisfaction—subs. (4)(a). (This duty is imposed for the protection of the public purse, and does not create any duty of care on the part of the authority towards the recipient, such as would found an action in tort if the works have not been carried out satisfactorily: see *Curran v. Northern Ireland Co-Ownership Housing Association* [1987] 1 A.C. 718; 19 H.L.R. 318, H.L.)

(iv) *Proof of expenditure.* The authority must be satisfied with the invoices, demands or receipts for payments in respect of which the grant—or part—is payable, which cannot include ones issued by the applicant himself or a member of his family (as to which see notes to s.98, below). See also s.39, below, for grant made payable to contractor.

Payment of grants: conditions as to contractors employed

38.—(1) It is a condition of payment of every grant, unless the local housing authority direct otherwise in any particular case, that the eligible works are carried out by the contractor whose estimate accompanied the application or, where two or more estimates were submitted, by one of those contractors.

(2) The Secretary of State may by regulations make provision as to the establishing and maintaining by local housing authorities of lists of contractors approved by them for the purpose of carrying out grant-aided works.

(3) The regulations may provide that it shall be a condition of payment of every grant by a local housing authority by whom such a list is maintained that, except in such cases as may be prescribed and unless the local housing authority direct otherwise in any particular case, the eligible works are carried out by a contractor who is on the authority's list of approved contractors.

DEFINITIONS

"local housing authority": s.101.

GENERAL NOTE

Grant applications have to be accompanied by estimates from two different contractors: s.2(2)(b). Unless the authority *direct* otherwise, it is a condition of payment that one of those who has provided the original estimate (not necessarily the lowest estimate, or that on which the authority have based the grant) carries out the works. The "direction" power would be available where the authority have (or, since application, have acquired) cause to be dissatisfied with the workmanship or efficiency of a contractor, *e.g.* in relation to completion of works, or other such circumstances.

Where the Secretary of State has used his power to permit authorities to draw up and maintain "approved lists" of grant contractors (subs. (2)), and provided that—absent a direction from the authority to the contrary in a particular case—the works can only be carried out by a contractor on the approved list, it does not seem to be so much a case of the authority "directing" the applicant not to use an estimating (but non-approved) contractor, for unless the applicant does not do so, he will not get his grant by reason of subs. (3); on the other hand, unless the authority do so direct, he will not get his grant for reason of subs. (1). Presumably the confusion will be resolved by the authority directing the applicant to get an additional estimate, from an approved contractor, under s.2(2)(b).

Payment of grant to contractor

39.—(1) The local housing authority may pay a grant or part of a grant—

(a) by payment direct to the contractor, or

(b) by delivering to the applicant an instrument of payment in a form made payable to the contractor.

They shall not do so unless the applicant was informed before the grant application was approved that this would or might be the method of payment.

(2) Where an amount of grant is payable, but the works in question have not been executed to the satisfaction of the applicant, the local housing authority may at the applicant's request and if they consider it appropriate to do so withhold payment from the contractor.

If they do so, they may make the payment to the applicant instead.

DEFINITIONS

"local housing authority": s.101.

GENERAL NOTE

If the applicant was so informed of the possibility before approval, the authority can pay grant directly to the contractor, or else by issuing a cheque or other money instrument payable to the contractor: subs. (1). If the applicant asks the authority not to pay direct, because he is dissatisfied with the works, he may ask the authority to withhold payment and the authority *may* do so and *may* instead make the payment direct to the applicant.

If the authority *decline* to comply with the request, at least so far as it concerns withholding payment from the contractor, they may find themselves joined to any subsequent litigation, and the foundation or parameters of the decision in *Curran v. Northern Ireland Co-Ownership Housing Association* [1987] 1 A.C. 718; 19 H.L.R. 318, H.L. (see note to s.37, above) may be in some doubt.

Applicant ceasing to be entitled before payment of grant

40.—(1) This section applies where an application for a grant is approved but before the certified date the applicant ceases to be a person entitled to a grant of that description.

In the case of a joint application this section does not apply unless all the applicants cease to be so entitled.

(2) Where this section applies—

(a) in the case of a renovation grant, disabled facilities grant or HMO grant, no grant shall be paid or, as the case may be, no further instalments shall be paid, and

(b) in the case of a common parts grant approved on a landlord's application, the local housing authority may refuse to pay the grant or any further instalment,

and the authority may demand that any instalment of the grant which has been paid be repaid forthwith, together with interest from the date on which it was paid until repayment, at such reasonable rate as the authority may determine.

(3) For the purposes of this section an applicant ceases to be a person entitled to a renovation grant—

(a) in the case of an owner's application—

(i) if he ceases to have a qualifying owner's interest, or

(ii) if he ceases to have the intention specified in the owner-occupation certificate or certificate of intended letting which accompanied the application;

(b) in the case of a tenant's application—
(i) if he ceases to be a qualifying tenant of the dwelling, or
(ii) if the application was accompanied by a certificate of intended letting and the landlord ceases to have the intention specified in the certificate; or

(c) if the application was approved under section 13(5) (approval of grant in respect of works to unfit premises) and the authority cease to be satisfied of the matters mentioned in that provision.

(4) For the purposes of this section an applicant ceases to be a person entitled to a disabled facilities grant—

(a) in the case of an owner's application—
(i) if he ceases to have a qualifying owner's interest, or
(ii) if he ceases to have the intention specified in the owner's certificate which accompanied the application;

(b) in the case of a tenant's application—
(i) if he ceases to be a qualifying tenant of the dwelling, or
(ii) if the application was accompanied by an owner's certificate and the landlord ceases to have the intention specified in the certificate.

But if the case falls within section 41 (change of circumstances affecting disabled occupant), the authority shall act under that section.

(5) For the purposes of this section an applicant ceases to be a person entitled to an HMO grant—

(a) if he ceases to have a qualifying owner's interest in the house;
(b) if he ceases to have the intention specified in the certificate of future occupation which accompanied the application; or
(c) if the application was approved under section 28(5) (approval of grant in respect of works to unfit premises) and the authority cease to be satisfied of the matters mentioned in that provision.

(6) For the purposes of this section an applicant whose application is a landlord's application for a common parts grant ceases to be a person entitled to a grant—

(a) if he ceases to have an owner's interest in the building;
(b) if he ceases to have a duty or power to carry out the relevant works; or
(c) if the application was approved under section 18(4) (approval of grant in respect of works to unfit premises) and the authority cease to be satisfied of the matters mentioned in that provision.

(7) This section has effect subject to section 56 (provisions relating to death of applicant).

DEFINITIONS

"certified date": s.44.
"common parts grant": s.1.
"disabled facilities grant": s.1.
"disabled occupant": ss.20, 100.
"HMO grant": s.1.
"local housing authority": s.101.
"owner's application": s.7.
"renovation grant": s.1.

GENERAL NOTE

This section governs changes of circumstances between approval and final payment of grant: it matches the pre-conditions for various grants under ss.7–11, 14–16, 19–22 and 25–26, above, and the circumstances in which grant paid may be repayable (see ss.45–50, below). It is part of the general process of tightening up against abuse: see Introduction to Pt. I, above. See also—

(i) s.41, below, which governs disabled facilities grants when there is a change affecting the disabled occupant (which section, if applicable, takes priority over the provisions of this: see subs. (4)),

(ii) s.42, where grants may be recalculated, withheld or repayable as a result of factors relating to the works as distinct from the factors relating to the applicant,

(iii) s.43, where the applicant—unknown to the authority—was not entitled to the grant at all, and

(iv) s.56, which governs the position on the death of the applicant (in priority to this section: see subs. (7)).

Subs. (1)

The section applies where an applicant ceases to be a person entitled to the relevant grant, between approval and the "certified date", which means the date certified by the authority as that on which execution of the works was completed to their satisfaction under s.44(3), below. Where there is a joint application, all of the applicants must so cease before the section can come into play.

Subs. (2)

Where the section applies, no grant is payable, or no further instalments are payable, and the authority may demand repayment of grant, together with interest at such reasonable rate as they may determine: subs. (2). The restriction in subs. (2)(b) means that only cessation of qualification by a landlord will lead to these consequences in relation to a common parts grant (reflecting the unfairness to the landlord if payment stopped, or a demand for repayment was made, as a result of a change in the numbers of relevant occupiers under ss.15(1)(b) and 16(1)(b), as well as the difficulties that would arise were grant to be withheld, or demand to be made for repayment, from—for example—one of a number of occupier-applicants, *i.e.* recalculation of grants for the *other* or *remaining* occupier-applicants, possibly to the point that some might claim that they would not have taken on the responsibility if the consequential figures had been known at the outset).

Subs. (3)

See s.8(2) and (3) as to the original conditions which would not have been met had these changes occurred before approval; the reference to s.13(5) involves satisfaction as to fitness on completion, satisfactory financial and other arrangements for carrying out the works, and that execution of the works is the most satisfactory course of action.

Subs. (4)

This subsection concerns disabled facilities grant. If the change of circumstance is one that falls within the next section, then it is to be applied in place of the provisions of this section.

See s.21 and s.22 as to the original conditions which would not have been met had these changes occurred before approval.

Subs. (5)

See s.25 and s.26 as to the original conditions which would not have been met had these changes occurred before approval; the reference to s.28(5) involves satisfaction as to conditions on completion, satisfactory financial and other arrangements for carrying out the works, and that execution of the works is the most satisfactory course of action.

Subs. (6)

See s.15(1)(a) and s.16(1)(a) as to the original conditions which would not have been met had these changes occurred before approval; the reference to s.14(4) involves satisfaction as to conditions on completion, satisfactory financial and other arrangements for carrying out the works, and that execution of the works is the most satisfactory course of action.

Change of circumstances affecting disabled occupant

41.—(1) This section applies where an application for a disabled facilities grant has been approved and before the certified date—

(a) the works cease to be necessary or appropriate to meet the needs of the disabled occupant, or

(b) the disabled occupant ceases to occupy the dwelling or flat concerned or it ceases to be the intention that he should occupy it, or

(c) the disabled occupant dies.

Where the application related to more than one disabled occupant, this section applies if any of paragraphs (a) to (c) applies in relation to any of them.

(2) This section applies whether or not the disabled occupant (or any of them) is the applicant (or one of them).

(3) Where this section applies the local housing authority may take such action as appears to them appropriate and may decide—

(a) that no grant shall be paid or, as the case may be, no further instalments shall be paid,
(b) that the relevant works or some of them should be completed and the grant or an appropriate proportion of it paid, or
(c) that the application should be redetermined in the light of the new circumstances.

(4) In making their decision the authority shall have regard to all the circumstances of the case.

(5) If the authority decide that no grant shall be paid or that no further instalments shall be paid, they may demand that any instalment of the grant which has been paid be repaid forthwith, together with interest from the date on which it was paid until repayment, at such reasonable rate as the authority may determine.

DEFINITIONS

"certified date": s.44.
"disabled facilities grant": s.1.
"disabled occupant": ss.20, 100.
"dwelling": s.101.
"flat": s.58.
"local housing authority": s.101.

GENERAL NOTE

Where there is a change of circumstances between grant approval and the "certified date", which means the date certified by the authority as that on which the execution of the works had been completed to their satisfaction under s.44(3), below, which if it had taken place before approval would have meant that no grant would have been available, s.40, above, will normally determine what steps the authority may take to prevent further, or recover, payments of grant. Where the change is one of those identified in subs. (1) (and, if more than one disabled occupant, if the change applies to any one of them—subs. (2)), however, they have a much broader discretion as to what to do in the circumstances, which *may* involve cessation of payments or even demand for repayment (*e.g.* if it is thought that the change may or should have been anticipated by applicant), but equally may involve continuation with grant process in its entirety: see subs. (3). As to Discretion and Policy, see notes to s.13, above.

Subs. (5)

The entitlement to interest continues until payment and does not end with (by merger in) the judgment: see *Ealing L.B.C. v. El Isaac* [1980] 1 W.L.R. 932, C.A.

Cases in which grants may be re-calculated, withheld or repaid

42.—(1) This section applies where an application for a grant has been approved by the local housing authority and—
(a) the authority ascertain that the amount was determined under section 30 or 31 on the basis of inaccurate or incomplete information and exceeds that to which the applicant was entitled;
(b) the authority ascertain that without their knowledge the eligible works were started before the application was approved;
(c) the eligible works are not completed to the satisfaction of the authority within the period specified under section 37(1), or such extended period as they may allow under that provision;
(d) the authority ascertain that the aggregate of the cost of completing the eligible works and the costs incurred with respect to preliminary or ancillary services and charges, is or is likely to be lower than the estimated expense; or
(e) the authority ascertain that without their knowledge the eligible works were carried out otherwise than as required by section 38 (conditions as to contractors employed).

(2) Where this section applies, the authority may—
(a) refuse to pay the grant or any further instalment of grant which remains to be paid, or

(b) make a reduction in the grant which, in a case falling within subsection (1)(d), is to be a reduction proportionate to the reduction in the estimated expense;

and they may demand repayment by the applicant forthwith, in whole or part, of the grant or any instalment of the grant paid, together with interest at such reasonable rate as the authority may determine from the date of payment until repayment.

DEFINITIONS

"eligible works": s.34.
"local housing authority": s.101.
"preliminary or ancillary services and charges": s.2.

GENERAL NOTE

This section identifies a number of circumstances, in the main relating to the property and to the works rather than to the applicant, but including a case where it is ascertained that more grant was awarded than the applicant was entitled to "on the basis of inaccurate or incomplete information", which (a) would clearly cover erroneous assessment by way of means-testing under s.30, landlord's grant under s.31 or allocation of common parts grant under s.32, and (b) is equally clearly not confined to (but will comprise) fraudulent or wilful deception or omission. See also next section where it appears to an authority *post*-approval that the applicant was not entitled to grant at all. The section is another part of the general process of tightening up against abuse: see Introduction to Pt. I, above.

There is also a range of reactions on the part of the authority, in particular to refuse further payment, reduce grant or demand repayment, with interest at such reasonable rate as they may determine: subs. (2). Where the change is that the costs are to be lower than estimated, there is an express obligation to confine any reduction in the grant to an amount that is proportionate to the reduced expenditure: subs. (2)(b). This should not be read as automatically meaning that lower costs will mean no more than reduced grant: lower costs *could* reflect "inaccurate or incomplete information", in which case either there may be somewhat more than reduction, or else the reduction may be under subs. (1)(a). (There is no corresponding limitation on a reduction arising under subs. (1)(a), which supports proposition (b) in the last paragraph.)

Subs. (2)

See notes to s.41(5), above.

Repayment where applicant not entitled to grant

43.—(1) This section applies where an application for a grant is approved but it subsequently appears to the local housing authority that the applicant (or, in the case of a joint application, any of the applicants) was not, at the time the application was approved, entitled to a grant of that description.

(2) Where this section applies—

(a) in the case of a renovation grant, disabled facilities grant or HMO grant, no grant shall be paid or, as the case may be, no further instalments shall be paid, and

(b) in the case of a common parts grant approved on a landlord's application, the local housing authority may refuse to pay the grant or any further instalment,

and the authority may demand that any grant which has been paid be repaid forthwith, together with interest from the date on which it was paid until repayment, at such reasonable rate as the authority may determine.

(3) For the purposes of this section an applicant is not entitled to a renovation grant—

(a) in the case of an owner's application if—

(i) he does not have a qualifying owner's interest, or

(ii) he does not have the intention specified in the owner-occupation certificate or certificate of intended letting which accompanied the application; or

(b) in the case of a tenant's application if—

(i) he is not a qualifying tenant of the dwelling, or

(ii) if the application was accompanied by a certificate of intended letting and the landlord does not have the intention specified in the certificate.

(4) For the purposes of this section an applicant is not entitled to a disabled facilities grant—

(a) in the case of an owner's application—

(i) if he does not have a qualifying owner's interest, or

(ii) if he does not have the intention specified in the owner's certificate which accompanied the application; or

(b) in the case of a tenant's application—

(i) if he is not a qualifying tenant of the dwelling, or

(ii) if the application was accompanied by an owner's certificate and the landlord does not have the intention specified in the certificate.

(5) For the purposes of this section an applicant is not entitled to an HMO grant—

(a) if he does not have a qualifying owner's interest in the house; or

(b) if he does not have the intention specified in the certificate of future occupation which accompanied the application.

(6) For the purposes of this section an applicant whose application is a landlord's application for a common parts grant is not entitled to a grant—

(a) if he does not have an owner's interest in the building; or

(b) if he does not have a duty or power to carry out the relevant works.

DEFINITIONS

"common parts grant": s.1.
"disabled facilities grant": s.1.
"H.M.O. grant": s.1.
"local housing authority": s.101.
"renovation grant": s.1.

GENERAL NOTE

This section is a further part of the general process of tightening up against abuse: see Introduction to Pt. I, above. In the past, there was a mismatch between the intentions declared in the course of applying for a grant, and the circumstances in which grant could be recovered. Where the latter did not apply, but there was a suspicion that an applicant was not entitled to grant in the first place, *i.e.* has lied about his intentions, the remedies open to the authority were few and only occasionally available:

(i) in a particularly blatant case, to invite investigation and possible prosecution by the police, (see, for example, *R. v. Parker* (1993) 26 H.L.R. 508, C.A.) and/or

(ii) to take civil action for recovery for the tort of deceit. Action for deceit can be founded on a statement of intentions. "The state of a man's mind is as much a fact as the state of his digestion. It is true that it is very difficult to prove what the state of a man's mind at a particular time is, but if it can be ascertained it is as much a fact as anything else": *Edgington v. Fitzmorris* (1885) 29 Ch.D. 459.

It is now not necessary to prove dishonesty—or perhaps recklessness—because if it comes to appear to the authority that there was no entitlement to the grant that has been awarded (meaning the grant itself, as distinct from an amount of it, which would fall within s.42, above), then the grant is to cease and so far as any of it has been paid, the authority may demand repayment, together with interest at such reasonable rate as they may determine: subs. (2). The entitlement to interest continues until payment and does not end with (by merger in) the judgment: see *Ealing L.B.C. v. El Isaac* [1980] 1 W.L.R. 932, C.A.

While the provision is couched in the subjective form ("The section is framed in a 'subjective' form . . . This form of section is quite well-known and at first sight might seem to exclude judicial review . . . " *per* Lord Wilberforce, *Secretary of State for Education and Science v. Tameside M.B.C.* [1977] A.C. 1014, H.L. at p.1047), the decision must none the less be based on the facts:

"If a judgment requires, before it can be made, the existence of some facts, then although the evaluation of those facts is for the Secretary of State alone, the courts must enquire whether those facts exist, and have been taken into account, whether the judgment has been made on a proper self-direction as to those facts, whether the judgment has not been made on other facts which ought not to have been taken into account . . ." (*per* Lord Wilberforce, *ibid.).*

See generally notes to s.13, above.

Subs. (2)

See note to s.40(2), above, with particular reference to the distinct position of a common parts grant.

Subs. (3)

See s.8(2) and (3) as to the original conditions which would not have been met had these changes occurred before approval.

Subs. (4)

See s.21 and s.22 as to the original conditions which would not have been met had these changes occurred before approval.

Subs. (5)

See s.25 and s.26 as to the original conditions which would not have been met had these changes occurred before approval.

Subs. (6)

See s.15(1)(a) and s.16(1)(a) as to the original conditions which would not have been met had these changes occurred before approval.

Grant conditions and repayment

Grant conditions: introductory

44.—(1) The following sections have effect with respect to the conditions to be observed where an application for a grant has been approved by a local housing authority.

In this Chapter a "grant condition" means a condition having effect in accordance with any of those sections.

(2) Except as otherwise provided—

(a) the grant conditions as to repayment on disposal (sections 45 to 47) have effect from the date on which the application is approved until the end of the grant condition period;

(b) the grant conditions as to occupation (sections 48 to 50) have effect from the certified date until the end of the grant condition period; and

(c) a grant condition imposed under section 52 (power to impose other conditions with consent of Secretary of State) has effect for such period as may be specified in, or in accordance with, the Secretary of State's consent.

(3) In this Chapter—

(a) the "grant condition period" means the period of five years, or such other period as the Secretary of State may by order specify or as may be imposed by the local housing authority with the consent of the Secretary of State, beginning with the certified date; and

(b) the "certified date" means the date certified by the local housing authority as the date on which the execution of the eligible works is completed to their satisfaction.

(4) A local housing authority may not impose any condition requiring a grant to be repaid except in accordance with the following sections.

This applies whether the condition purports to operate as a condition of the grant, as a personal covenant or otherwise.

DEFINITIONS

"local housing authority": s.101.

GENERAL NOTE

This section introduces the grant conditions—and the only conditions—which an authority are entitled to enforce by means of repayment: subs. (4) (*cf.* s.34(5) on conditions generally, which are limited to those already considered in the preceding sections, and those in the following sections, and can be extended with the consent of the Secretary of State. The apparent exclusion—even with such consent—of a condition requiring repayment, is mitigated by the qualification that the authority may do so as permitted or provided for by the following sections, which includes s.52, below, empowering just such added conditions, albeit with consent).

Grant conditions involving repayment on disposal last from the *date of approval* of grant until the end of the grant period, which is five years *from the certified date* (*or* such other period as the Secretary of State may prescribe, *or* such other period as the authority may impose but only with the consent of the Secretary of State): the certified date is the date certified by the authority as that on which the works are completed to their satisfaction (but *n.b. Curran v. Northern Ireland Co-Ownership Housing Association* [1987] 1 A.C. 718; 19 H.L.R. 318, H.L. in notes to s.37, above). The date to be certified is the date on which the works were physically completed to that standard, not the date when the local authority have inspected the finished works and approved them: see *R. v. Westminster C.C., ex p. Hazan* (1988) 20 H.L.R. 205, C.A.

Accordingly, the full period may be as much as six and a half years, or even more (six months from application to approval, s.34; 12 months from approval to completion, s.37; five years from certification, this section, but in the case of completion there could be an extension granted by the authority, and of course certification will itself take some period of time, *e.g.* a few days or even weeks).

Grant conditions involving repayment on change of occupation last *from the certified date* (as above) until the end of the grant condition period, *i.e.* five years or such other period as may be prescribed or permitted by the Secretary of State.

Grant conditions on repayment. Owners and others can "redeem" the condition by repayment of the grant to the authority under s.55, below; conditions also cease when repayment is activated under ss.45–50, below, or if the authority determine not to demand repayment for breach of grant condition under those parts of those sections which allow them a discretion.

Condition for repayment on disposal: renovation grants

45.—(1) It is a condition of a renovation grant that if an owner of the premises to which the application relates makes a relevant disposal (other than an exempt disposal)—

(a) of the whole or part of the premises to which the application relates,
(b) after any instalment of grant has been paid, and
(c) before the certified date,

he shall repay to the local housing authority on demand the amount of grant that has been paid.

(2) It is a condition of a renovation grant that if an owner of the dwelling to which the application relates or, in the case of a conversion application, any dwelling provided by the relevant works, makes a relevant disposal (other than an exempt disposal)—

(a) of the whole or part of the dwelling,
(b) on or after the certified date, and
(c) before the end of the grant condition period,

he shall repay to the local housing authority on demand the amount of grant that has been paid.

In the case of a conversion application the grant shall be treated for this purpose as apportioned equally between the dwellings provided.

(3) A condition under this section is a local land charge and is binding on any person who is for the time being an owner of the premises concerned.

(4) Where the authority have the right to demand repayment of an amount as mentioned in subsection (1) or (2), they may—

(a) if the case falls within subsection (5), or
(b) in any other case, with the consent of the Secretary of State,

determine not to demand payment or to demand a lesser amount.

(5) The cases referred to in subsection (4)(a) are where the authority are satisfied that the owner of the dwelling—

(a) is elderly or infirm and is making the disposal with the intention—
   (i) of going to live in a hospital, hospice, sheltered housing, residential care home or similar institution as his only or main residence, or

(ii) of moving to somewhere where care will be provided by any person; or

(b) is making the disposal with the intention of going to live with and care for an elderly or infirm member of his family or his partner's family.

(6) Any condition under this section shall cease to be in force with respect to any premises if there is a relevant disposal of the premises that is an exempt disposal, other than—

(a) a disposal within section 54(1)(a) (disposal to associates of person making disposal), or

(b) a disposal within section 54(1)(b) (vesting under will or on intestacy).

DEFINITIONS

"certified date": s.44.
"conversion application": s.58.
"dwelling": s.101.
"exempt disposal": s.54.
"grant condition period": s.44.
"member of family": s.98.
"owner": s.99.
"partner": s.101.
"relevant disposal": s.53.
"renovation grant": s.1.

GENERAL NOTE

The cornerstone of this section—and those following—is the concept of "the relevant disposal" which is not an "exempt disposal", a concept introduced by the Housing Act 1980 (c. 51) (subsequently, the Housing Act 1985) to govern claw-back of discount on right to buy (and now in use, *inter alia*, in the Housing Act 1996 to govern a new right to buy scheme for the tenants of registered social landlords), albeit not in identical terms. See ss.53, 54, below. Under this Act, as under the 1989 Act, repayment is triggered by a relevant disposal which is not an exempt disposal. In view of the wording of subss. (4), (5), and of ss.46(4), 47(4), 48(4), 49(4), 50(5), 51(5) and 52(4), there is no doubt that the authority have no other discretion not to reclaim the payments of grant in full. There is no discount for "complete years", as in right to buy.

The circumstances governed by this section concern renovation grants: if any owner of premises makes a non-exempt relevant disposal of the whole or part of the premises, after payment of any instalment of grant but before the certified date (see notes to s.44, above), the grant is repayable; likewise, if the owner of a dwelling make such a disposal, on or after the certified date but before the end of the grant condition period (see notes to s.44, above), the grant is repayable, with grant apportioned equally according to the number of dwellings provided by conversion. The distinction between premises and dwellings covers conversion grants, which may start with buildings which are not dwellings.

Owner. For this purpose (*cf.* above, s.25, below, s.47, on H.M.O. grants), owner is defined in s.99 and means the person entitled to receive from a lessee a rent of not less than two-thirds of the net annual value of the dwelling, or who would be so entitled if the dwelling were so let, but excluding someone who is only the lessee of the dwelling or of property including the dwelling, and who is bound to pay such a rent to a superior landlord, in which case it is the superior landlord who will be the owner (see also *White v. Barnet L.B.C.* (1989) 21 H.L.R. 346). Thus an owner-occupier will be an owner, even though the premises are not actually let. In a block of flats, it will normally be leaseholders who are on rents lower than the two-thirds criterion, or such leaseholders plus the landlord in respect of flats let on rents at or above the two-thirds criterion, who will qualify as the owner of the block: *Pollway v. Croydon L.B.C.* [1987] A.C. 79, 18 H.L.R. 443, H.L.

The reference to net annual value reflects the replacement of former (and long-standing) references to rents as a proportion of rateable value. Net annual value means the rent at which the dwelling might reasonably be expected to be let if the tenant undertook to pay the usual tenant's rates and taxes and to bear the cost of repair and insurance and other expenses to maintain the dwelling in a state to command such a rent: s.99(2). This definition is modelled on that used for rateable values: see the Local Government Finance Act 1988, Sched. 6, para. 2(1) and see further *Ryde on Rating and Council Tax*, Chaps. E3 and E4. The fact that statute may constrain the recoverable rent will not affect the issue: that which is a statutory will limit what can reasonably be expected—*Rawlance v. Croydon Corporation* [1952] 2 Q.B. 803, C.A. A dispute as to net annual value is referable to the District Valuer: s.97(3).

See also notes to s.82, below.

Subs. (3)

Local land charge. So long as the grant condition is in force, it binds any owner for the time being. Such a condition creates an incumbrance or burden on the property, binding successive owners, and it is for this reason that it requires to be registered as a local land charge: see *Rignall Developments Ltd. v. Halil* (1988) 20 H.L.R. 7, Ch.D. It should be noted that failure to register the condition as a local land charge does not affect its enforceability against subsequent purchasers (Local Land Charges Act 1975 (c. 76), s.10(1)) but where there has been a failure to register the charge, the local authority operating the register in which the land is situated will be liable to pay compensation for any loss caused: *ibid.*

Subss. (4), (5)

These subsections contain the only and limited discretion to *not* recover the grant or all of the grant, which is exercisable *either* with the consent of the Secretary of State, *or* on the authority's own motion because the owner is elderly or infirm and is making the disposal in order to go to live in a hospital, hospice, sheltered housing or residential care home or similar institution (see notes to s.11, above), as his only or main residence (see notes to s.8, above), or of moving somewhere where care will be provided, or else is disposing in order to go and live with and care for an elderly or infirm member of his family, or his partner's family. "Partner" means spouse, or a person with whom the owner lives as husband and wife (see s.101, below).

Subs. (6)

Even though it will not cause repayment, the condition ceases to be in force when there is an exempt disposal, other than of the two classes identified, *i.e.* such disposals keep the condition alive (but, because they are exempt, do not activate repayment).

Condition for repayment on disposal: common parts grants

46.—(1) It is a condition of a common parts grant approved on a landlord's application that if the applicant makes a relevant disposal (other than an exempt disposal)—

(a) of the whole or part of the building,
(b) after any instalment of grant has been paid, and
(c) before the certified date,

he shall repay to the local housing authority on demand the amount of grant that has been paid.

(2) It is a condition of a common parts grant approved on a landlord's application that if the applicant makes a relevant disposal (other than an exempt disposal)—

(a) of the whole or part of the building,
(b) on or after the certified date, and
(c) before the end of the grant condition period,

he shall repay to the local housing authority on demand the amount of grant that has been paid.

(3) A condition under this section is a local land charge and is binding on any person who is for the time being a successor in title to the interest in the building by virtue of which the applicant made his application.

(4) Where the authority have the right to demand repayment of an amount as mentioned in subsection (1) or (2), they may, with the consent of the Secretary of State, determine not to demand payment or to demand a lesser amount.

(5) Any condition under this section shall cease to be in force with respect to any premises if there is a relevant disposal of the premises that is an exempt disposal.

Definitions

"certified date": s.44.
"common parts grant": s.1.
"exempt disposal": s.54.
"grant conditions period": s.44.
"landlord's application": s.15.
"local housing authority": s.101.
"relevant disposal": s.53.

GENERAL NOTE

This section makes provision analogous to the last, governing a landlord's application for common parts grant (see also notes to s.40, above, on the difficulties with recovery of common parts grant where individual leaseholders sell or let their own flats), in two stages, as between approval and certified date, and between certified date and end of grant condition period (see notes to s.44, above).

Subs. (4)

Cf. above, s.45(4), (5), and General Note on the limited discretion *not* to recover, which here is only exercisable with the consent of the Secretary of State.

Subs. (5)

Cf. above, s.45(6): the condition does not survive an exempt disposal.

Condition for repayment on disposal: HMO grants

47.—(1) It is a condition of an HMO grant that if an owner of the house makes a relevant disposal (other than an exempt disposal)—

(a) of the whole or part of the house,

(b) after any instalment of grant has been paid, and

(c) before the certified date,

he shall repay to the local housing authority on demand the amount of grant that has been paid.

(2) It is a condition of an HMO grant that if an owner of the house makes a relevant disposal (other than an exempt disposal)—

(a) of the whole or part of the house,

(b) on or after the certified date, and

(c) before the end of the grant condition period,

he shall repay to the local housing authority on demand the amount of grant that has been paid.

(3) A condition under this section is a local land charge and is binding on any person (other than a local housing authority or registered social landlord) who is for the time being an owner of the house.

(4) Where the authority have the right to demand repayment of an amount as mentioned in subsection (1) or (2), they may, with the consent of the Secretary of State, determine not to demand payment or to demand a lesser amount.

(5) Any condition under this section shall cease to be in force with respect to any premises if there is a relevant disposal of the premises that is an exempt disposal.

DEFINITIONS

"exempt disposal": s.54.
"HMO grant": s.1.
"local housing authority": s.101.
"owner": ss.99, 101.
"registered social landlord": s.101.
"relevant disposal": s.53.

GENERAL NOTE

This section makes provision analogous to the last two, governing an HMO grant, in two stages, as between approval and certified date, and between certified date and end of grant condition period (see notes to s.44, above).

Owner. For HMO purposes, see notes to s.15, above. There can, accordingly, be more than one "owner" for this purpose (*cf.* above, s.45, note on Owner for renovation grant purposes), who may breach the condition.

Subs. (3)

The local land charge is *not* binding on either the local housing authority themselves, or another housing authority, or a "registered social landlord", which is the concept introduced by Pt. I of the Housing Act 1996, to replace registered housing associations, but (a) which still requires registration with the Housing Corporation, and (b) which will include all currently registered housing associations.

Subs. (4)

Cf. above, s.45(4), (5), and General Note on the limited discretion *not* to recover, which here is only exercisable with the consent of the Secretary of State.

Subs. (5)

Cf. above, s.45(6): the condition does not survive an exempt disposal.

Condition as to owner-occupation: renovation grants

48.—(1) Where an application for a renovation grant was accompanied by an owner-occupation certificate in respect of any dwelling (see section 8(2)), it is a condition of the grant that throughout the grant condition period the dwelling is occupied in accordance with the intention stated in the certificate.

(2) It is also a condition of the grant that if at any time when that condition is in force the authority serve notice on the owner of the dwelling requiring him to do so, he will within the period of 21 days beginning with the date on which the notice was served furnish to the authority a statement showing how that condition is being fulfilled.

(3) A condition under this section is a local land charge and is binding on any person who is for the time being an owner of the dwelling.

(4) In the event of a breach of a condition under this section, the owner for the time being of the dwelling shall on demand repay to the local housing authority the amount of the grant, together with compound interest on that amount as from the certified date, calculated at such reasonable rate as the authority may determine and with yearly rests.

(5) The local housing authority may determine not to make such a demand or to demand a lesser amount.

(6) Any condition under this section shall cease to be in force with respect to the dwelling if there is a relevant disposal of the dwelling that is an exempt disposal, other than—

(a) a disposal within section 54(1)(a) (disposal to associates of person making disposal), or

(b) a disposal within section 54(1)(b) (vesting under will or on intestacy).

Definitions

"dwelling": s.101.
"exempt disposal": s.53.
"grant condition period": s.44.
"local housing authority": s.101.
"owner": s.99.
"owner-occupation certificate": s.8.
"relevant disposal": s.53.
"renovation grant": s.1.

General Note

This is the first of the "occupation conditions" (*cf.* above, s.44) and is applicable to renovation grants. It contains two elements. The first is that the intention stated in the owner-occupation certificate (see notes to s.8, above), as applied (in the case of a conversion grant) to any dwelling provided (see s.8(1)), is fulfilled throughout the grant condition period, *i.e.* that he or a member of his family will occupy the dwelling as an only or main residence: subs. (1). The second element is that on demand by the authority, the owner of the dwelling (as to which, see s.99, and also General Note to s.45, above) will within 21 days furnish the authority with a statement showing how the condition is being fulfilled: subs. (2).

Subss. (4), (5)

The "penalty" for breach of *either* condition is repayment of grant, together with *compound* interest (at yearly rests) at such reasonable rate as the authority may determine; however, the authority *do* enjoy a discretion not to recover the full or any amount (*cf.* above, ss.45(4), 46(4), 47(4)). The entitlement to interest continues until payment and does not end with (by merger in) the judgment: see *Ealing L.B.C. v. El Isaac* [1980] 1 W.L.R. 932, C.A.

Subs. (6)

Even though it will not cause repayment, the conditions cease to be in force when there is an exempt disposal, other than of the two classes identified, *i.e.* such disposals keep the condition alive (but, because they are exempt, do not activate repayment).

Condition as to availability for letting: renovation grants

49.—(1) Where an application for a renovation grant was accompanied by a certificate of intended letting in respect of any dwelling (see section 8(3)), it is a condition of the grant that throughout the grant condition period the dwelling is let or available for letting in accordance with the intention stated in the certificate.

(2) It is also a condition of the grant that if at any time within the grant condition period the local housing authority by whom the grant was paid serve notice on the owner of the dwelling requiring him to do so, he will within the period of 21 days beginning on the date on which the notice was served furnish to the authority a statement showing how the condition in subsection (1) is being fulfilled.

(3) A condition under this section is a local land charge and is binding on any person (other than a local housing authority or registered social landlord) who is for the time being the owner of the dwelling.

(4) In the event of a breach of a condition under this section, the owner for the time being of the dwelling shall on demand repay to the local housing authority the amount of the grant, together with compound interest on that amount as from the certified date, calculated at such reasonable rate as the authority may determine and with yearly rests.

(5) The local housing authority may determine not to make such a demand or to demand a lesser amount.

(6) The terms of any tenancy of the dwelling (or any part of it, or any property including the dwelling or part of it) shall be deemed to include a duty on the part of the tenant, if required to do so by the owner of the dwelling, to furnish him with such information as he may reasonably require to enable him to comply with a notice under subsection (2).

DEFINITIONS

"certificate of intended letting": s.8.
"dwelling": s.101.
"grant condition period": s.44.
"local housing authority": s.101.
"owner": s.99.
"renovation grant": s.1.
"tenant": s.101.

GENERAL NOTE

This section makes analogous provision to the last, including the two elements—

(i) compliance with the intention stated in the certificate of intended letting (see notes to s.8, above), as applied (in the case of a conversion grant) to any dwelling provided (see s.8(1)), throughout the grant condition period, *i.e.* let or available for letting (and not for a holiday) to a tenant who is not connected with the landlord (subs. (1)), and

(ii) on demand by the authority to furnish the authority with a statement showing how the condition is being fulfilled (subs. (2)(a)).

Corresponding to the second condition, it is to be an implied term of any tenancy of (or of part of) the dwelling that the tenant will provide the owner (as to which, see s.99, and also General Note to s.45, above) with such information as he reasonably requires to comply with the authority's notice: subs. (6).

Subs. (3)

Cf. note to s.47(3), above.

Subss. (4), (5)

See note to s.48(4), (5), above.

Conditions as to occupation: HMO grants

50.—(1) It is a condition of an HMO grant that throughout the grant condition period—

(a) the house is occupied or available for residential occupation in accordance with the intention stated in the certificate of future occupation that accompanied the application (see section 26(2)); and

(b) that the house is not so occupied as to cause

(i) a breach of the duty under section 353A of the Housing Act 1985 (duty to keep premises fit for number of occupants), or

(ii) a breach of any direction given by the local housing authority under section 354 of that Act (power to limit number of occupants of house).

(2) It is also a condition of the grant that if at any time within the grant condition period the local housing authority by whom the grant was paid serve notice on the owner of the house requiring him to do so, he will within the period of 21 days beginning with the date on which the notice was served furnish to the authority a statement showing how the condition in subsection (1)(a) is being fulfilled.

(3) A condition under this section is a local land charge and is binding on any person (other than a local housing authority or registered social landlord) who is for the time being an owner of the house.

(4) In the event of a breach of a condition under this section, the owner for the time being of the dwelling shall on demand pay to the local housing authority the amount of the grant, together with compound interest on that amount as from the certified date, calculated at such reasonable rate as the authority may determine and with yearly rests.

(5) The local housing authority may determine not to make such a demand or to demand a lesser amount.

(6) The terms of any tenancy of any part of the house shall be deemed to include a duty on the part of the tenant, if required to do so by the owner of the house, to furnish him with such information as he may reasonably require to enable him to comply with a notice under subsection (2).

DEFINITIONS

"certificate of future occupation": s.26.
"HMO grant": s.1.
"local housing authority": s.101.
"owner": ss.99, 101.

GENERAL NOTE

This section makes analogous provision to the last two, including the two elements—

(i) compliance with the intention stated in the certificate of future occupation (see notes to s.26, above), throughout the grant condition period, *i.e.* residential occupation under tenancy or licence by persons who are not connected with the landlord (subs. (1)(a)), and

(ii) on demand by the authority to furnish the authority with a statement showing how the condition is being fulfilled (subs. (2)(a)).

Corresponding to the second condition, it is to be an implied term of any tenancy of (or of part of) the dwelling that the tenant will provide the owner (as to which, see s.101, see General Note to s.47, above) with such information as he reasonably requires to comply with the authority's notice: subs. (6).

The *first* condition is also subject to extension in relation to an HMO grant: that the house is not occupied so as to cause a breach of duty under s.353A, Housing Act 1985, to keep the premises fit for the number of occupants, or so as to cause a breach of direction by the local housing authority under *ibid.* s.354 to limit the number of occupants.

Housing Act 1985, s.353A (added by the Housing Act 1996, s.73):

"(1) It is the duty of the person having control of a house in multiple occupation, and of the person managing it, to take such steps as are reasonably practicable to prevent the occurrence of a state of affairs calling for the service of a notice or further notice under section 352 (notice requiring execution of works to render a house fit for number of occupants).

(2) A breach of duty is actionable in damages at the suit of any tenant or other occupant of the premises, or any other person who suffers loss, damage or personal injury in consequence of the breach.

(3) A person who fails to comply with the duty imposed on him by subsection (1) commits a summary offence and is liable on conviction to a fine not exceeding level 5 on the standard scale".

For the relevant provisions of s.352, see notes to s.17 above.

Housing Act 1985, s.354 (as amended—see words in square brackets—by the Local Government and Housing Act 1988, Sched. 9, para. 52):

"(1) The local housing authority may, for the purpose of preventing the occurrence of, or remedying, a state of affairs calling for the service of a notice or further notice under section 352 ... —

(a) fix as a limit for the house what is in their opinion the highest number of individuals or households, or both, who should, having regard to the [requirements set out in subsection (1A)] of that section, occupy the house in its existing conditions, and

(b) give a direction applying that limit to the house.

(2) The authority may also exercise the powers conferred by subsection (1) in relation to a part of a house; and the authority shall have regard to the desirability of applying separate limits where different parts of a house are, or are likely to be, occupied by different persons".

For the relevant provisions of s.352, see notes to s.17, above.

Subs. (3)

Cf. note to s.47(3), above.

Subss. (4), (5)

See note to s.48(4), (5), above.

Conditions as to repayment in case of other compensation, &c

51.—(1) Where a local housing authority approve an application for a grant they may, with the consent of the Secretary of State, impose a condition requiring the applicant to take reasonable steps to pursue any relevant claim to which this section applies and to repay the grant, so far as appropriate, out of the proceeds of such a claim.

(2) The claims to which this section applies are—

(a) an insurance claim, or a legal claim against another person, in respect of damage to the premises to which the grant relates, or

(b) a legal claim for damages in which the cost of the works to premises to which the grant relates is part of the claim;

and a claim is a relevant claim to the extent that works to make good the damage mentioned in paragraph (a), or the cost of which is claimed as mentioned in paragraph (b), are works to which the grant relates.

(3) In the event of a breach of a condition under this section, the applicant shall on demand pay to the local housing authority the amount of the grant so far as relating to any such works, together with compound interest as from such date as may be prescribed by or determined in accordance with the regulations, calculated at such reasonable rate as the authority may determine and with yearly rests.

(4) The local housing authority may determine not to make such a demand or to demand a lesser amount.

DEFINITIONS

"local housing authority": s.101.

GENERAL NOTE

A new concept, this section permits the local authority—with the consent of the Secretary of State—to impose a condition on a grant approval which requires the applicant to take steps to pursue claims out of which the grant, or part of it, may be repaid, *i.e.* insurance or legal claim, where the works to which the grant relates are or include works to make good the damage the subject of the claim (see subs. (2)).

"... The new clause will enable the local authority to give grant for essential works in the knowledge that the grant, or the relevant part of it, can be recovered from the applicant if the claim is successfully resolved. That is not possible under current legislation. While the condition will require the consent of the Secretary of State, we envisage there being a general consent, under [s.94, below], covering house insurance and claims for damages to property and to the individual." *Hansard* (H.C.), June 6, 1996, Standing Committee F, Fifth Sitting, col. 199, Parliamentary Under-Secretary of State for the Environment (Mr Clappison).

Subs. (3)

The compound interest provision is the same—deliberately penal—provision which governs breach of occupation conditions (as distinct from repayment without interest on a decision to dispose).

Subs. (5)

The authority have discretion to waive a claim, or to claim less than the whole of the amount recouped that relates to grant-aided works.

Power to impose other conditions with consent of Secretary of State

52.—(1) Where a local housing authority approve an application for a grant they may, with the consent of the Secretary of State, impose such conditions as they think fit—

(a) relating to things done or omitted before the certified date and requiring the repayment to the local housing authority on demand of any instalments of grant paid, or

(b) relating to things done or omitted on or after that date and requiring the payment to the local housing authority on demand of a sum equal to the amount of the grant paid;

and, in either case, that amount may be required to be paid together with compound interest on that amount as from the date of payment, calculated at such reasonable rate as the authority may determine and with yearly rests.

(2) A condition under this section is a local land charge and is binding on—

(a) any person who is for the time being an owner of the dwelling, house or building, and

(b) such other persons (if any) as the authority may, with the consent of the Secretary of State, specify.

(3) The reference in subsection (2)(a) to the owner of the building shall be construed—

(a) in the case of a grant condition imposed on a landlord's application for a common parts grant, as a reference to the applicant or any successor in title to the interest in the building by virtue of which the applicant made his application;

(b) in the case of a grant condition imposed on an application for an HMO grant, as excluding a local housing authority or registered social landlord.

(4) Where the authority have the right to demand repayment of an amount as mentioned in subsection (1), they may determine not to demand payment or to demand a lesser amount.

(5) Any conditions imposed under this section are in addition to the conditions provided for by sections 45 to 51.

DEFINITIONS

"certified date": s.44.
"common parts grant": s.1.
"HMO grant": s.1.
"landlord's application": s.15.
"local housing authority": s.101.
"owner": ss.99, 101.

GENERAL NOTE

Further conditions (*cf.* subs. (5)) may be imposed on approval, with the consent of the Secretary of State, relating to things done or omitted either before or after the certified date (subs. (1)), which can require repayment of instalment, or of grant, with compound interest at yearly rests, but subject to a discretion on the part of the authority to recoup no, or a lesser, amount (subs. (4)). Examples given were nomination rights, recovery of specialised equipment, insurance and maintenance: *Hansard* (H.C.), June 6, 1996, Standing Committee F, Fifth Sitting, col. 202, Parliamentary Under-Secretary of State for the Environment (Mr Clappison).

Meaning of relevant disposal

53.—(1) A disposal is a relevant disposal for the purposes of the provisions of this Chapter relating to grant conditions if it is—

(a) a conveyance of the freehold or an assignment of the lease, or
(b) the grant of a lease (other than a mortgage term) for a term of more than 21 years otherwise than at a rack rent.

(2) For the purposes of subsection (1)(b) it shall be assumed—

(a) that any option to renew or extend a lease or sub-lease, whether or not forming part of a series of options, is exercised, and
(b) that any option to terminate a lease or sub-lease is not exercised.

(3) The grant of an option enabling a person to call for a relevant disposal shall be treated as such a disposal made to him.

GENERAL NOTE

This section is modelled on the Housing Act 1985, s.159.

A conveyance is "an instrument that transfers property from one person to another" (*Eastbourne Corporation v. A.G.* [1904] A.C. 155, H.L.). An instrument which does not pass a legal estate will not qualify as a conveyance, even if it is sufficient to amount to an enforceable contract for the conveyance and so pass an equitable interest in the property under the rule in *Walsh v. Lonsdale* (1882) 21 Ch.D. 9: see *Rodger v. Harrison* (1893) 1 Q.B. 161; *I.R.C. v. Angus* (1889) 23 Q.B.D. 579.

A sub-letting for the whole of the remainder of a term will take effect as an assignment: *Milmo v. Carreras* [1946] K.B. 306. The fact that there is a right of re-entry or forfeiture will not prevent a lease being for more than 21 years: *Quinlan v. Avis* (1933) 149 L.T. 214.

The term "rack-rent" means a rent of, or near to, the full annual value of a property (*Re Sawyer and Withall* [1919] 2 Ch. 333) determined as at the date of the grant (*London Corporation v. Cusack-Smith* [1955] A.C. 337, H.L.; *cf.*, above, notes to s.45, on net annual value) or the maximum rent which is permitted by law: *Compton Group v. Estates Gazette* (1978) 36 P. & C.R. 148, C.A. "The former meaning is its primary meaning in legal language, although the meaning of the expression may vary according to the context in which it is used": *Woodfall, Landlord and Tenant Law*, para. 7.013, citing *Compton.*

Meaning of exempt disposal

54.—(1) A disposal is an exempt disposal for the purposes of the provisions of this Chapter relating to grant conditions if it is a disposal of the whole or part of the premises to which the application relates of any of the following descriptions—

(a) a conveyance of the freehold or an assignment of the lease where the person, or each of the persons, to whom it is made is a qualifying person (as defined in subsection (2));
(b) a vesting in a person taking under a will or on an intestacy;
(c) a disposal in pursuance of any such order as is mentioned in subsection (3);
(d) a compulsory disposal (see subsection (4));
(e) a disposal of property consisting of land included in the dwelling by virtue of section 184 of the Housing Act 1985 (land let with or used for the purposes of the dwelling-house);
(f) a disposal under which the interest of a person entitled to assistance by way of repurchase under Part XVI of that Act (assistance for owners of defective housing) is acquired in accordance with Schedule 20 to that Act;

(g) a disposal by way of enfranchisement or lease extension under Part I of the Leasehold Reform Act 1967;

(h) a disposal in pursuance of an obligation arising under Chapter I or II of Part I of the Leasehold Reform, Housing and Urban Development Act 1993;

(i) a disposal on the exercise of a right of first refusal under Part I of the Landlord and Tenant Act 1987 or in accordance with an acquisition order under Part III of that Act;

(j) a disposal on the exercise of—

(i) the right to buy under Part V of the Housing Act 1985, or

(ii) the right conferred by section 16 of the Housing Act 1996 (right of tenant of registered social landlord to acquire dwelling);

(k) a conveyance of the freehold or an assignment of the lease where—

(i) the person making the disposal is aged at least 70,

(ii) the disposal is to provide an annuity income, and

(iii) the person concerned is entitled to continue to occupy the premises as his only or main residence;

(l) a disposal of any other description specified by order of the Secretary of State for the purposes of this section.

(2) A person is a qualifying person for the purposes of subsection (1)(a) if—

(a) in the case of an individual, he is—

(i) the person, or one of the persons, by whom the disposal is made;

(ii) the spouse, or former spouse, of that person or one of those persons; or

(iii) a member of the family of that person or one of those persons; or

(b) in the case of a company, it is an associated company of the company by whom the disposal is made.

Section 416 of the Income and Corporation Taxes Act 1988 (meaning of associated company) applies in determining whether a company is an associated company of another for the purposes of paragraph (b).

(3) The orders referred to in subsection (1)(c) are orders under—

(a) section 24 or 24A of the Matrimonial Causes Act 1973 (property adjustment orders or orders for the sale of property in connection with matrimonial proceedings);

(b) section 2 of the Inheritance (Provision for Family and Dependants) Act 1975 (orders as to financial provision to be made from estate);

(c) section 17 of the Matrimonial and Family Proceedings Act 1984 (property adjustment orders or orders for the sale of property after overseas divorce, etc.); or

(d) paragraph 1 of Schedule 1 to the Children Act 1989 (orders for financial relief against parents).

(4) For the purposes of subsection (1)(d) a compulsory disposal is a disposal of property which is acquired compulsorily, or is acquired by a person who has made or would have made, or for whom another person has made or would have made, a compulsory purchase order authorising its compulsory purchase for the purposes for which it is acquired.

(5) The grant of an option enabling a person to call for an exempt disposal shall be treated as such a disposal made to him.

DEFINITIONS

"member of the family": s.98.

GENERAL NOTE

This section defines the exempt disposals, which in some cases (see ss.45(6), 46(5), 47(5), 48(6)) have the incidental effect of bringing a grant condition to a premature end *without* requiring repayment. These disposals are:

(i) *Voluntary re-arrangements*. Disposals by or to oneself together with others, or to one's own spouse, former spouse, or family member, or that of one of the co-disponors, and in the case of a company to an associated company. Note, however, that these disposals, while exempt and so not activating repayment, do not terminate the repayment condition under ss.45 or 48.
(ii) *Death*. Likewise, the vesting in a person under a will or intestacy, while exempt and so not activating repayment, does not terminate the repayment condition under ss.45 or 48.
(iii) *Court ordered transfer*. Orders under the provisions identified in subs. (3) do not activate repayment and do terminate the repayment condition. A property sale under s.24A, Matrimonial Causes Act 1973 (c. 18), is now within the exemption, whereas it would not have been within the analogous provisions of the previous legislation (although see s.141, below), *cf. R. v. Rushmore B.C., ex p. Barrett* (1988) 20 H.L.R. 366, C.A. (under the right to buy provisions of the Housing Act 1985).
(iv) *Compulsory purchase*. This includes a sale by agreement to a person who has made, or could have made, a compulsory purchase order, or for whom another (such as a local authority or the Housing Corporation) could make such an order authorising compulsory purchase: see subs. (4).
(v) *Added land*. Land let together with a dwelling house is treated as part of the dwelling house for the purposes of right to buy, under the Housing Act 1985, s.184(1), unless it is agricultural land exceeding two acres; also, land not within s.184(1) may be added at the request of the purchasing tenant, if it is reasonable to do so and it is land which is or has been used for the purposes of the dwelling—see s.184(2). Such added lands may be disposed of, without activating repayment.
(vi) *Defective dwellings*. Repurchase under Pt. XVI of the Housing Act 1985, see notes to s.6, above.
(vii) *Leaseholders*. Under the Leasehold Reform Act 1967 (c. 88), long leaseholders of houses may be able to require the extension of their leases by 50 years, or their enfranchisement (purchase of freehold); likewise, there are powers for leaseholders of flats to acquire the freeholds of their blocks, under both the Landlord and Tenant Act 1987 (c. 31), and the Leasehold Reform, Housing and Urban Development Act 1993 (c. 28). Any of these disposals—compulsory against the freeholder or person with a superior interest—could mean that a freeholder or person with a superior interest, who has received a grant, finds himself making a disposal he has not initiated and which is against his will, for which reason the disposal is exempt, and the condition comes to an end.
(viii) *Right to buy*. The right to buy under the Housing Act 1985 can in some circumstances be exercisable as against bodies other than local authorities, and the analogous right under the Housing Act 1996, if passed, will be a right against registered social landlords who are not excluded from grant by s.2, above, for which reason these landlords are in the same position as the last, *i.e.* Leaseholders.
(ix) *Annuity disposals*. Some elderly people sell their homes, with the right to continue to reside in them until death, in exchange for an annuity: such disposals are likewise exempt, and the repayment condition ceases to apply.
(x) *Reserve powers*. The Secretary of State has reserve powers to specify additional exempt disposals.

Cessation of conditions on repayment of grant, &c

55.—(1) If at any time while a grant condition remains in force with respect to a dwelling, house or building—

(a) the owner of the dwelling, house or building to which the condition relates pays the amount of the grant to the local housing authority by whom the grant was made,
(b) a mortgagee of the interest of the owner in that dwelling, house or building being a mortgagee entitled to exercise a power of sale, makes such a payment,
(c) the local housing authority determine not to demand repayment on the breach of a grant condition, or
(d) the authority demand repayment in whole or in part on the breach of a grant condition and that demand is satisfied,

that grant condition and any other grant conditions shall cease to be in force with respect to that dwelling, house or building.

(2) In the case of a grant condition imposed on a landlord's application for a common parts grant the references in subsection (1)(a) and (b) to the owner of the building are to the applicant or any such successor in title as is referred to in section 46(3).

(3) An amount paid by a mortgagee under subsection (1)(b) above shall be treated as part of the sums secured by the mortgage and may be discharged accordingly.

(4) The purposes authorised for the application of capital money by—

(a) section 73 of the Settled Land Act 1925,

(b) that section as applied by section 28 of the Law of Property Act 1925 in relation to trusts for sale, and

(c) section 26 of the Universities and College Estates Act 1925,

include the making of payments under this section.

DEFINITIONS

"common parts grant": s.1.
"dwelling": s.101.
"landlord's application": s.15.
"local housing authority": s.101.
"owner": ss.99, 101.

GENERAL NOTE

This section permits an owner voluntarily to repay a grant in order to free himself from all of the conditions attached to it: note that, as with repayment on disposal under ss.45–47, no interest is payable on reimbursement.

An applicant may find that he has effectively or in practice traded away his right to use this right. In *R. v. Hackney L.B.C., ex p. Gransils Investments* (1988) 20 H.L.R. 313, Q.B.D., the landlord had agreed that—in return for the local authority not enforcing a compulsory purchase order—he would convert the property into three flats with assistance by way of grant-aid (under Pt. XV of the Housing Act 1985), subject to certificates of availability for letting (see now the certificate of intended letting under s.8(3)). On completion of the works the landlord sought to repay the grant and sell the flats. The authority responded by seeking to implement the compulsory purchase order, which the court held that they were entitled to do.

The right is available not only to an owner, but also to a mortgagee who is entitled to exercise the power of sale, in which case the amount so repaid is treated as part of the sum secured by the mortgage, *i.e.* may be repaid out of the proceeds of sale: subss. (3), (4).

The section also provides that if the authority determine not to enforce a repayment entitlement, at all or in full, the grant conditions will come to an end, just as if they do so demand and the demand is met. Where an authority make an incorrect determination of the amount owing that is smaller than the amount due, it is arguable that the authority would be estopped from seeking the larger sum, where the applicant has acted in reliance, and to his detriment, on the demand: see *Lombard North Central v. Stobart* [1990] C.C.L.R. 53, C.A.

Supplementary provisions

Provisions relating to death of applicant

56.—(1) References in this Chapter to the applicant, in relation to a grant or an application for a grant, shall be construed in relation to any time after his death as a reference to his personal representatives.

(2) Where the applicant dies after liability has been incurred for any preliminary or ancillary services or charges, the local housing authority may, if they think fit, pay grant in respect of some or all of those matters.

(3) Where the applicant dies after the relevant works have been begun and before the certified date, the local housing authority may, if they think fit, pay grant in respect of some or all of the works already carried out and other relevant works covered by the application.

(4) Nothing in this section shall be construed as preventing the provisions as to grant conditions applying in relation to any payment of grant under subsection (2) or (3).

DEFINITIONS

"local housing authority": s.101.
"preliminary or ancillary services or charges": s.2.
"relevant works": s.2.

General Note

If an applicant dies, the provisions of this Chapter apply to his personal representatives, so that if the grant condition period (see notes to s.44) is still running, they will be bound by it, but so also that if, before approval, they would not in their own right qualify for the grant (whether by reason of means-testing or otherwise, *e.g.* non-compliance with residence intentions), no grant will be available (subs. (1)). However, the authority *may* none the less pay grant in respect of costs incurred before the death, whether in making the application, or preparing for the works, or indeed on relevant works (subss. (2), (3)), in which case the grant conditions will apply to such sums in the same way as if the full grant had been paid (subs. (4)).

Power of local housing authority to carry out works which would attract grant

57.—(1) A local housing authority may by agreement with a person having the requisite interest execute at his expense—

(a) any works towards the cost of which a grant under this Chapter is payable or might be paid on an application duly made and approved, and

(b) any further works which it is in their opinion necessary or desirable to execute together with the works mentioned in paragraph (a).

(2) Except in the case of a common parts grant, the "requisite interest" means a qualifying owner's interest for the purposes of a renovation grant, or an owner's interest for the purposes of a disabled facilities grant or HMO grant, as the case may be.

(3) In the case of a common parts grant, the reference in subsection (1) to a person having the requisite interest is a reference to the person who has—

(a) an owner's interest in the building, or

(b) such an interest in a flat in the building as is mentioned in section 14(2)(a) to (d) (occupying tenants),

and has a power or duty to carry out the relevant works.

Definitions

"common parts grant": s.1.
"H.M.O. grant": s.1.
"local housing authority": s.101.
"qualifying owner's interest": ss.7, 19, 25.
"renovation grant": s.1.

General Note

This section permits "agency agreements", under which the authority may carry out grant-aided works, or works which could have been grant-aided if an application had been duly paid and approved, and any additional works they consider desirable to carry out together with such works: subs. (1). The person for whom the authority carry out the works must have a "requisite interest" as defined in subss. (2) and (3). A tenant's application under s.9 may still lead to agency works provided the person with whom the arrangement is made has a requisite interest, for the works will still be grant-aided or grant-aidable.

"Execution" is wide enough to cover not only the authority doing the works themselves, *e.g.* by a Direct Labour Organisation, but also commissioning and supervising works: "Many owners have been deterred from improving their homes because they do not know how to set about it, or because they do not relish making detailed arrangements ... The local authority would be in a position to supervise the improvement works: and to make sure that the work was well done at reasonable cost ... " (DoE Circular 63/69, para. 9, of the analogous power in the Local Government and Housing Act 1989, s.135).

Minor definitions: Chapter I

58. In this Chapter—

"common parts", in relation to a building, includes the structure and exterior of the building and common facilities provided, whether in the building or elsewhere, for persons who include the occupiers of one or more flats in the building;

"common parts application", in relation to an application for a disabled facilities grant, means an application in respect of works to the common parts of a building containing one or more flats;

"conversion application"—

(a) in relation to an application for a renovation grant, means an application in respect of works required for the provision of one or more dwellings by the conversion of a house or other building, and

(b) in relation to an application for an HMO grant, means an application for a grant in respect of works for the provision of a house in multiple occupation by the conversion of a house or other building;

"flat" means a dwelling which is a separate set of premises, whether or not on the same floor, divided horizontally from some other part of the building.

General Note

See notes to s.1, above.

Index of defined expressions: Chapter I

59. In this Chapter the expressions listed below are defined by or otherwise fall to be construed in accordance with the provisions indicated—

certificate of future occupation (in relation to an application for an HMO grant)	section 26(2)
certificate of intended letting (in relation to an application for a renovation grant)	section 8(3)
certified date	section 44(3)(b)
common parts	section 58
common parts application (in relation to a disabled facilities grant)	section 58
common parts grant	section 1(3)
connected (with the owner of a dwelling)	section 98(2)
conversion application	section 58
disabled facilities grant	section 1(4)
disabled occupant	section 20
disabled person	section 100(1) to (3)
dwelling	section 101
elderly	section 101
eligible works	section 34(2)(a)
estimated expense	section 34(2)
exempt disposal	section 54
fit for human habitation	section 97(1)
flat	section 58
grant (without more)	section 1(6)
grant condition	section 44(1)
grant condition period	section 44(3)(a)
HMO grant	section 1(5)
house in multiple occupation	section 101
housing action trust	section 101
improvement	section 101
introductory tenant	section 101
landlord's application	
—in relation to a renovation grant	section 10(6)
—in relation to a common parts grant	section 15(1) and (2)
local authority	section 101
local housing authority	section 101
long tenancy	section 101
member of family	section 98(1)
new town corporation	section 101

occupying tenant (in relation to an application for a common parts grant)	section 14(2)
owner	sections 99 and 101
owner-occupation certificate (in relation to an application for a renovation grant)	section 8(2)
owner's application	
—in relation to a renovation grant	section 7(1) and (2)
—in relation to a disabled facilities grant	section 19(1) and (2)
owner's certificate (in relation to an application for a disabled facilities grant)	section 21(2)
owner's interest	section 101
participating landlord (in relation to a tenants' application for a common parts grant)	section 15(4)
partner	section 101
preliminary or ancillary services and charges	section 2(3)
prescribed	section 101
qualifying owner's interest	
—in relation to an application for a renovation grant	section 7(4)
—in relation to an application for a disabled facilities grant	section 19(4)
—in relation to an application for an HMO grant	section 25(3)
qualifying tenant	
—in relation to an application for a renovation grant	section 7(5)
—in relation to an application for a disabled facilities grant	section 19(4)
reasonable repair	section 96
registered social landlord	section 101
relevant disposal	section 53
relevant works (in relation to a grant application)	section 2(2)(a)
renewal area	section 101
renovation grant	section 1(2)
secure tenancy and secure tenant	section 101
social services authority	section 100(4)
statutory tenancy and statutory tenant	section 101
tenancy and tenant (generally)	section 101
tenant (and expressions relating to tenancies)	
—in the context of a tenant's application for a renovation grant	section 7(6)
—in the context of a certificate of intended letting	section 8(4)
—in the context of an application for a common parts grant	section 14(2)
—in the context of an application for disabled facilities grant	section 19(5)
tenant's application	
—in relation to a renovation grant	section 7(1) and (2)
—in relation to a disabled facilities grant	section 19(1) and (2)
tenants' application (in relation to a common parts grant)	section 15(1) and (2)
tenant's certificate	
—for the purposes of an application for a renovation grant	section 9(2)
—for the purposes of an application for a disabled facilities grant	section 22(2)
urban development corporation	section 101

CHAPTER II

GROUP REPAIR SCHEMES

Introductory

Group repair schemes

60.—(1) A local housing authority may prepare a scheme (a "group repair scheme") for the carrying out of works—

(a) to put in reasonable repair the exterior of the buildings to which the scheme relates, or

(b) to render the buildings to which the scheme relates structurally stable,

or for both those purposes.

(2) For the purposes of this Chapter "building" includes the whole or part of a terrace of houses or other units.

(3) The scheme must satisfy the requirements of sections 61 and 62 as to the buildings to which it relates and the works specified in it.

DEFINITIONS

"exterior": s.62.
"local housing authority": s.101.
"reasonable repair": s.96.
"structural stability": s.62.

GENERAL NOTE

"Enveloping is the renovation of the external fabric and curtilage of dwellings which have deteriorated beyond the scope of routine maintenance. ... It includes such items as repair or renewal of roof and chimneys, rainwater goods, work to external walls, repair or replacement of doors and windows and improvements to the curtilages. Whole terraces or blocks are dealt with simultaneously ...": DoE Circular 29/82.

The practice of enveloping used only to be possible where the authority declared a housing action area or general improvement area, and consequently had the power to carry out works to the housing within the area. The cost of the works was not generally sought from the owners of the properties concerned. Enveloping works can still be carried out in a renewal area, under Pt. VII of the Local Government and Housing Act 1989 (particularly, s.93). In addition, they can be carried out—not only in renewal areas (but *cf.* below, s.67(4)(a), for lower contributions in a renewal area)—by way of grant-aided group repair scheme, a concept first introduced by that Act, Pt. VIII, and repeated here, subject to some amendment.

Group repair schemes require the approval of the Secretary of State if they are to lead to any activity: see s.63, below.

Subs. (1)

Works extend both to putting the building into reasonable repair (which would have included works necessary thereto which amounted to works of structural stability), and those merely intended to achieve structural stability (*Hansard* (H.C.), Report, July 8, 1996, col. 64, Parliamentary Under-Secretary for State for the Environment (Mr Clappison)). See also s.62, below.

Subs. (2)

The group repair scheme is concerned with "buildings", defined to include "the whole or part of a terrace of houses or other units": this definition is intended to extend the natural meaning of building, to include terrace, rather than to confine the operation of the grant to what is or originally was built as what might be considered a house. While one of the buildings must still be a primary building, within s.61(3), below, that definition is now left to regulations, and no longer includes the former requirement (1989 Act, s.128(2)), that, as constructed, it contained no less than four separate houses.

The definition is clearly used to render unnecessary recourse to the extensive case-law on the meaning of the word "house", although insofar as regulations on the meaning of primary and qualifying buildings may yet rely on the word house, and insofar as the historical genesis of a concept is never irrelevant to statutory interpretation (either to show what it means or, sometimes, to show what it does *not* mean), it is still useful to summarise it here. (See also, on purpose-built HMOs treated as "houses", notes to s.1, above).

The word "house" has in any event never had any very precise meaning (*Quilotex Co. v. Minister of Housing and Local Government* [1966] 1 Q.B. 704, C.A.), being a mixed question of law (involving construction of the Act in question) and fact (*In Re Butler, Camberwell (Wingfield Mews) No. 2 Clearance Order 1936* [1939] 1 K.B. 570, C.A.) to be left in the first instance to the decision-maker, with whose decision the courts can only interfere on conventional (administrative law) grounds (*cf.* notes to s.13, above): *Re South Shields (D'Arcy Street) Compulsory Purchase Order 1937* [1939] 1 All E.R. 419, C.A.; *Ashbridge Investments v. Minister of Housing and Local Government* [1965] 1 W.L.R. 1320, C.A.

A house is a "building for human habitation": *Reed v. Hastings Corporation* (1964) 62 L.G.R. 588, C.A., or a "building constructed or adapted for use as or for the purposes of a dwelling" (*Ashbridge Investments*, above). A garage or workshop with a dwelling above was held to be a house in *In Re Butler* (above)—see also *Re Hammersmith (Bergham Mews) Clearance Order 1936* [1937] 3 All E.R. 539. Where a building is used partly for residential purposes, and partly for others, it has to be looked at as a whole to ascertain whether, as a question of degree, it can properly be described as a house: *Annicola Investments v. Minister of Housing and Local Government* [1968] 1 Q.B. 631, C.A. It need not be shown that all the rooms in a building are in residential use: *Premier Garage Co. v. Ilkeston Corporation* (1933) 97 J.P. 786.

Although original construction is important (*In Re Butler*, above), use at the time the question falls to be determined is also relevant (*ibid.*, see also *Grosvenor v. Hampstead Junction Railway* [1957] L.J. Ch. 731; an unfinished house may qualify as a house—*Alexander v. Crystal Palace Railway* (1862) 30 Beav. 556; a building constructed as a house but used for other purposes has been considered to remain a house—*Howard v. Ministry of Housing and Local Government* (1967) 65 L.G.R. 257.

A building subdivided into flats can remain a house, whether or not so constructed: *Annicola* (above), *Quilotex* (above), *Benabo v. Wood Green B.C.* [1946] 1 K.B. 38, *Critchell v. Lambeth L.B.C.* [1957] 2 Q.B. 535, C.A., *Okereke v. Brent L.B.C.* [1967] 1 Q.B. 42, C.A. A flat itself however, is not a house, nor for like reasons a building (*R. v. Lambeth L.B.C., ex p. Clayhope* (1987) 19 H.L.R. 426, C.A.), even although for most housing purposes it is not so treated, and it clearly is a dwelling, or can be premises. In *Lake v. Bennett* [1970] 1 Q.B. 663, C.A., under the Leasehold Reform Act 1967, Lord Denning M.R. doubted whether a tower block could *ever* reasonably be called a house, but Salmon L.J. emphasised that the decision did not necessarily affect the Housing Acts, and the wording of the 1967 Act does refer to a house "reasonably so-called".

It has commonly been noted that care must be taken when applying case-law that is derived from other legislation, and even from other parts of the Housing Acts: see *Quilotex* (above), *Annicola* (above), *R. v. Cardiff C.C., ex p. Cross* (1981) 1 H.L.R. 54, Q.B.D. (upheld on appeal at (1982) 6 H.L.R. 1, C.A.); in view of the definition of building, there will be no such difficulties in relation to group repair schemes.

Qualifying buildings

61.—(1) The buildings to which a group repair scheme relates must be qualifying buildings.

(2) A building is a qualifying building if at the time the scheme is prepared it satisfies the conditions prescribed for qualifying buildings in relation to a group repair scheme.

(3) A group repair scheme must relate to at least one qualifying building which at the time the scheme is prepared satisfies the conditions prescribed for a primary building in relation to a group repair scheme.

(4) Each of the other qualifying buildings to which a group repair scheme relates must satisfy the conditions prescribed for an additional building in relation to a group repair scheme.

DEFINITIONS

"building": s.60.

GENERAL NOTE

A group repair scheme concerns (a) a primary building, and (b) other qualifying buildings (additional buildings). The conditions for each of these concepts is to be defined in regulations. By virtue of the definition of building in s.60(2), above, the primary building itself may be the whole or part of a terrace of houses (or other units, *e.g.*, former offices or warehousing converted into housing, or shops with flats above which might or more not, in their own rights, have fallen to be considered houses—see notes to s.60(2), above).

Scheme works

62.—(1) The works specified in a group repair scheme ("scheme works") must be works of the following descriptions.

(2) In the case of works to put in reasonable repair the exterior of the buildings to which the scheme relates, the works must be—

(a) works to the exterior of the buildings to which the scheme relates, or

(b) so far only as may be necessary to give satisfactory effect to such works, additional works to other parts of the buildings,

and must be such that on completion of the works the exterior of the buildings will be in reasonable repair.

(3) In the case of works to render the buildings to which the scheme relates structurally stable, the works must be—

(a) works to the structure or to the foundations of the buildings to which the scheme relates, or

(b) other works necessary to give satisfactory effect to such works,

and must be such that on completion of the works the buildings will be structurally stable.

(4) For the purposes of this Chapter the exterior of a building means—

(a) any part of the building which is exposed to the elements of wind and rain or otherwise faces into the open air (including, in particular, roofs, chimneys, walls, doors, windows, rainwater goods and external pipework), and

(b) the curtilage of the building, including any wall within the curtilage which is constructed as a retaining wall or otherwise to protect the structure of the building.

(5) In relation to works to the curtilage of a building the reference in subsection (2)(b) to additional works to other parts of the building includes additional works on land outside the curtilage.

(6) For the purposes of this Chapter the exterior of a building shall not be regarded as in reasonable repair unless it is substantially free from rising or penetrating damp.

DEFINITIONS

"building": s.60.
"group repair scheme": s.60.

GENERAL NOTE

The works in a group repair scheme must either be—

(a) to put the "exterior of the buildings" in reasonable repair (save so far as additional works are necessary to give satisfactory effect to external works), and they must be such that on completion, the exterior of the buildings will be in reasonable repair (see notes to s.96, below), which has an expanded definition for the purposes of such schemes, that a building will not be regarded as in reasonable repair unless on completion of the works it is "substantially free from rising or penetrating damp" (subs. (6)); or

(b) to render the building itself structurally stable, meaning works to the foundations (save so far as additional works are necessary to give satisfactory effect to works to the foundation).

Subs. (4)

Curtilage. The meaning of "curtilage" was considered in *Dyer v. Dorset C.C.* [1989] Q.B. 346, 20 H.L.R. 490, C.A., in relation to the exemption from the right to buy in what is now Sched. 5, para. 5, to the Housing Act 1985, where it was held to involve some small and necessary extension to the property to which the word is attached. An area of land could not properly be described as a curtilage unless it formed part and parcel of the house or building which it contains or to which it is attached. See also *Barwick v. Kent C.C.* (1992) 24 H.L.R. 341, C.A.

Exterior. See also cases on "structure and exterior" in notes to s.1, above, although this statutory definition is relatively comprehensive and comprises all that would be so defined.

Approval of scheme by Secretary of State

63.—(1) If a group repair scheme prepared by a local housing authority is approved by the Secretary of State, the authority may, with the consent of the persons participating in the scheme, enter into agreements to secure the carrying out of the works specified in the scheme.

(2) The approval of the Secretary of State may be given either to a specific scheme or generally to schemes which fulfil such criteria as he may from time to time specify.

(3) Different criteria may be specified for different types of scheme and for different areas.

(4) The approval of a scheme may be made conditional upon compliance with requirements specified by the Secretary of State.

DEFINITIONS

"group repair scheme": s.60.
"local housing authority": s.101.
"persons participating in the scheme": s.64.

GENERAL NOTE

This section requires the approval of the Secretary of State to a group repair scheme, without which there can be no agreements to effect the works.

Participation in group repair scheme

Persons eligible to participate in group repair scheme

64.—(1) A person is eligible to participate in a group repair scheme if at the date of the approval of the scheme—

(a) he has an owner's interest in a dwelling or other premises comprised in a building to which the scheme relates, and

(b) as respects the dwelling or other premises in which he has an owner's interest he either—

(i) is able to give possession of any part of the building to which scheme works are proposed to be carried out, or

(ii) has the consent of the occupier of that part to the carrying out of those works.

In the case of a scheme not submitted for specific approval, the date of approval shall be taken to be the date on which the authority decide that the scheme fulfils the criteria for general approval.

(2) A person eligible to participate in a group repair scheme may participate as an assisted participant—

(a) if the owner's interest which he has is an interest in a dwelling and he gives an owner-occupation certificate or a certificate of intended letting, or

(b) if the owner's interest which he has is an interest in a house in multiple occupation and he gives a certificate of future occupation.

This is subject to the exceptions specified in subsection (7) or by order under that subsection.

(3) An "owner-occupation certificate" certifies that the person concerned—

(a) has an owner's interest in the dwelling, and

(b) intends that throughout the protected period he, or a member of his family, will live in the dwelling, as his (or that member's) only or main residence.

(4) A "certificate of intended letting" certifies that the person concerned—

(a) has an owner's interest in the dwelling, and

(b) intends that throughout the protected period the dwelling will be let or available for letting as a residence and not for a holiday to someone other than a member of his family.

In paragraph (b) "letting" does not include a letting on a long tenancy.

(5) In subsection (4) references to letting include the grant of a licence to occupy premises.

References in this Chapter to tenants, and other expressions relating to tenancies, in the context of a certificate of intended letting, shall be construed accordingly.

(6) A "certificate of future occupation" certifies that the person concerned—

(a) has an owner's interest in the house, and
(b) intends that throughout the protected period the house or a part of it (specified in the certificate) will be residentially occupied, or available for residential occupation, under tenancies or licences by persons who are not connected with the owner for the time being of the house.

In paragraph (b) "residential occupation" does not include occupation for a holiday, and "tenancies" does not include a long tenancy.

(7) The following may not participate in a group repair scheme as an assisted participant—

(a) a local authority;
(b) a new town corporation;
(c) the Development Board for Rural Wales;
(d) a health authority, special health authority or NHS trust;
(e) a police authority established under section 3 of the Police Act 1964;
(f) a housing action trust;
(g) a registered social landlord;
(h) any other authority, body or other person excluded by order of the Secretary of State.

(8) An order under subsection (7)(h) may proceed wholly or in part by reference to the provisions relating to entitlement to housing benefit, or any other form of assistance, as they have effect from time to time.

(9) A person eligible to participate in a group repair scheme who is unable to participate as an assisted participant may participate as an unassisted participant.

DEFINITIONS

"building": s.60.
"dwelling": s.101.
"group repair scheme": s.60.
"house in multiple occupation": s.101.
"housing action trust": s.101.
"local authority": s.101.
"long tenancy": s.101.
"new town corporation": s.101.
"member of family": s.98.
"owner's interest": s.101.
"registered social landlord": s.101.

GENERAL NOTE

This section defines the participants eligible to participate in an approved group repair scheme. Participation is by the consent (s.65(1)) of eligible participants, whether or not assisted participants, but the contribution of an assisted participant is at a lower level than that (100 per cent) of an unassisted participant: s.67. See s.68, below, for variation of schemes, including as to participation. See also ss.69 *et seq.*, for conditions attached to reduced contributions.

Participants. The applicant must have an owner's interest in *a* dwelling (therefore, including the owner of a flat or something less than the whole of a building—see notes to s.1, above) or other premises to which the scheme relates (subs. (1)(a)): see notes to s.7, above. He must be able to give up sufficient possession of the premises to enable the works to be carried out, or else have the consent of the occupier: subs. (1)(b). These qualifications have to be established as at the date of approval or—if the scheme is not subject to specific approval, but instead to a general approval under s.63, above—on the date when the authority decide that the scheme so qualifies.

(Or, in the case of a scheme that is varied to allow new participants, at the date of the variation specific approval, or qualification under a general approval: see s.68(3), below). Even if the participant does not qualify as an assisted participant, he can still participate as an *un*assisted participant: subs. (7).

Assisted Participants. A participant can only be an *assisted* participant (*i.e.* enjoy the benefit of grant assistance under ss.67 *et seq*., below), if (subs. (2)):

(i) he is not one of the public or quasi-public landlords identified in or prescribed under subs. (6), and

(ii) (a) *either* he has an owner's interest in a dwelling, *i.e.* not merely in a property which has dwellings within it or other property to be dealt with under the scheme, (b) *or* he has an owner's interest in an HMO (as to the meaning of which, see notes to s.1, above), and

(iii) he gives one of the two classes of certificate—for an owner of a dwelling, an owner-occupation certificate or a certificate of intended letting; for an owner of an HMO, a certificate of future occupation.

Owner-Occupation certificate. See notes to s.8, above—but a certificate of *proposed* acquisition will not here qualify.

Certificate of intended letting. See notes to s.8, above—again, a certificate of *proposed* acquisition will not here qualify.

Certificate of future occupation. See notes to s.26, above—with the same exception for certificate of *proposed* acquisition.

Scheme consent and restriction on works

65.—(1) The persons who are eligible to participate in a group repair scheme do so by signifying consent ("scheme consent"), in accordance with the terms of the scheme, to the proposals to carry out the works specified in the scheme.

(2) No scheme works shall be carried out to a part of a building which consists of premises in respect of which no person eligible to participate has signified scheme consent, except as mentioned below.

(3) The restriction in subsection (2) does not apply to works carried out to premises in respect of which there is no person (or no ascertainable person) eligible to participate in the scheme.

(4) The restriction in subsection (2) does not apply to works—

(a) which are carried out to premises in respect of which the person eligible to participate consents to their being carried out but has not signified scheme consent (and, accordingly, is not liable to contribute), and

(b) which it is necessary to carry out in order satisfactorily to carry out any works specified in the scheme to another part of the same building in respect of which a person eligible to participate has signified scheme consent.

DEFINITIONS

"eligible to participate": s.64.
"group repair scheme": s.60.
"scheme works": s.62.

GENERAL NOTE

The burden of participation is contribution: s.67. Contribution is confined to those who are eligible participants (s.64) who consent to the scheme works: subs. (1). Scheme works cannot normally be carried out to parts of a building which consist of premises in respect of which there is no eligible participant who has signified his consent: subs. (2). This restriction is lifted where there is *no one* (or no ascertainable person) who is eligible to participate (*i.e.* eligible, but declines consent, so that he will not become a contributor): subs. (3).

The restriction also does not apply where there is an eligible participant (in respect of part of a building) who declines consent (and, therefore, cannot be a contributor), where it is *necessary* to carry out works satisfactorily to another part of that building which is within the scheme (because someone who is eligible in respect of that part has consented and is therefore participating): subs. (4).

Certificate of completion date

66.—(1) When the works specified in a group repair scheme are completed, the local housing authority shall send to each assisted participant a certificate specifying the date on which the works were completed to the authority's satisfaction.

(2) In this Chapter that date is referred to as "the completion date".

DEFINITIONS

"assisted participant": s.64.
"group repair scheme": s.60.
"local housing authority": s.101.

GENERAL NOTE

Once the works have been completed to their satisfaction (*cf.* notes to s.44, above), the authority are to notify each assisted participant (see notes to s.64, above) specifying the date on which the works were so completed (*i.e.* the date on which the works were physically completed to that standard, not the date when the local authority have inspected the finished works and approved them: *R. v. Westminster C.C., ex p. Hazan* (1988) 20 H.L.R. 205, C.A.). This date is the completion date: subs. (2).

Contributions by participants

67.—(1) The participants in a group repair scheme are liable to contribute to the cost, as notified to them under the scheme, of scheme works relating to the premises in which they have an interest, at a rate determined in accordance with this section.

(2) The cost of the works shall be apportioned between the several buildings and premises in such way as may be agreed between the participants with owner's interests in them or, in default of agreement, equally.

(3) In the case of an unassisted participant, the rate of contribution is 100 per cent.

(4) In the case of an assisted participant whose owner's interest is in premises other than a dwelling or house in multiple occupation, the rate of contribution is—

(a) 25 per cent. where the building is in a renewal area, and
(b) 50 per cent. in any other case.

The Secretary of State may by order amend paragraph (a) or (b) so as to specify a different percentage.

(5) In the case of any other assisted participant, the rate of contribution is a percentage determined by the local housing authority not exceeding that which would apply under subsection (4).

(6) In making their determination the authority shall have regard to the way in which—

(a) section 30 (means-testing in case of application by owner-occupier or tenant), or
(b) section 31 (determination of amount of grant in case of landlord's application),

would apply if he were an applicant for a renovation grant or, as the case may require, an HMO grant.

(7) They shall also have regard to any guidance given by the Secretary of State for the purposes of this section.

Different guidance may be given for different cases, different descriptions of cases and different areas and, in particular, with respect to different local housing authorities or descriptions of authority (including a description framed by reference to authorities in a particular area).

DEFINITIONS

"assisted participant": s.64.
"group repair scheme": s.60.
"house in multiple occupation": s.101.
"participants": s.64.
"owner's interest": s.101.
"renewal area": s.101.
"scheme works": s.62.
"unassisted participant": s.64.

GENERAL NOTE

Consent to the scheme (s.65) means paying a contribution to the costs, the level of which depends on the considerations set out in this section: subs. (1). See also ss.69 *et seq.*, for conditions attached to reduced contributions.

The cost is apportioned by agreement between all those having owner's interests (see s.64), or otherwise equally between all the buildings and premises.

Premises would normally seem to be capable of including flats: yet the requirement for equal division between buildings and premises (in default of agreement) cannot here mean, *e.g.* an equal amount for a building and a flat, and if it did so it would encourage refusal to agree an apportionment—the omission of the word "dwelling" suggests therefore that it is buildings as a whole which are in mind at this stage, although this leaves aside division between owners of flats in buildings: subs. (2). (The provisions of subss. (4), (5), assist in determining level of contribution to apportionment, and not only does not resolve this problem but supports the risk that it will occur.)

An unassisted participant must pay a contribution of 100 per cent (subs. (3)). Assisted participants pay different contributions as follows:

(i) Owner's contribution *not* in a dwelling or an HMO, 25 per cent in a renewal area and 50 per cent otherwise (subs. (4)—but *n.b.* power of Secretary of State to prescribe different percentage (*ibid.*);

(ii) Owner's contribution in a dwelling or an HMO, of *no more than* 25 per cent or 50 per cent or other prescribed percentage (as above), but otherwise calculated having regard to the calculation of renovation grant under s.30 or landlord's grant under s.31 (subss. (5), (6)).

The authority are not *bound* to pay in accordance with ss.30, 31 (see notes to s.31, above, on the obligation "to have regard", but if less is offered, it would seem to require explanation—see *ibid.*; see also notes to s.13, above, on Discretion and Policy). The authority are also bound to have regard to guidance issued for the purposes of the section by the Secretary of State (subs. (7)).

Variation of group repair scheme

Variation of group repair scheme

68.—(1) A group repair scheme may be varied at any time before the completion date.

The variation may relate to the participants in the scheme, the buildings to which the scheme relates, the scheme works or any other matter.

(2) A variation is not effective unless approved by the Secretary of State.

The provisions of section 63(2) to (4) (supplementary provisions as to approval of scheme) apply to approval of a variation.

(3) Where a scheme is varied to enable other persons to participate section 64 (persons eligible to participate) applies in relation to new participants with the substitution for the reference to the date of approval of the scheme of a reference to the date of approval of the variation.

In the case of a variation not submitted for specific approval, the date of approval shall be taken to be the date on which the authority decide that the variation fulfils the criteria for general approval.

(4) Before varying a group repair scheme the local housing authority shall consult the existing participants and consider any representations made by them.

(5) Fresh scheme consent is required in the case of an existing participant as to whom the authority are satisfied that his interests are adversely affected by the variation.

In any other case the existing scheme consent shall be treated as extended to the scheme as varied.

DEFINITIONS

"completion date": s.66(2).
"group repair scheme": s.60.
"participants": s.64.

GENERAL NOTE

This section is intended to "allow late participants to join an approved scheme once it has been approved thus creating greater facility. The amendments contain safeguards for existing participants, and enable schemes to be varied": *Hansard* (H.C.), June 11, 1996, Standing Committee F, Sixth Sitting, col. 213, Parliamentary Under-Secretary of State for the Environment (Mr Clappison).

The basic power is to vary a scheme at any time until the completion date (under s.66, above): subs. (1). The variation may be to participants, property or works: *ibid*. The variation requires the consent of the Secretary of State: subs. (2). (Consent may be specific or general, and may be subject to different criteria for different schemes or areas, and may be conditional: see s.63(2)-(4), above, applied to this section by subs. (3)). Participation qualification is on the same terms as under s.64, but with the substitution of the date of approval of variation, or date when the authority consider that the variation qualifies within a variation general approval: subs. (3).

Subs. (4)
Consultation.

"... [T]he essence of consultation is the communication of a genuine invitation to give advice and a genuine consideration of that advice ... To achieve consultation sufficient information must be supplied by the consulting to the consulted party to enable it to tender helpful advice. Sufficient time must be given by the consulting to the consulted party. Sufficient, in that context, does not mean ample, but at least enough to enable the relevant purpose to be fulfilled. By helpful advice, in this context, I mean sufficiently informed and considered information or advice about aspects of the form or substance of the proposals, or their implications for the consulted party, being aspects material to the implementation of the proposal as to which the party consulted might have relevant information nor advice to offer." (*per* Webster J., *R. v. Secretary of State for Social Services, ex p. Association of Metropolitan Authorities* [1986] 1 W.L.R. 1 at p.4).

See also *R. v. Brent L.B.C., ex p. Gunning* (1985) 84 L.G.R. 168, *R. v. Warwickshire D.C., ex p. Bailey* [1991] C.O.D. 284.

Conditions of participation

Conditions of participation: general

69.—(1) The following sections have effect with respect to the conditions of participation in a group repair scheme as an assisted participant.

(2) Except as otherwise provided those conditions have effect for the period of five years, or such other period as may be prescribed, beginning with the completion date.

That period is referred to in this Chapter as "the protected period".

(3) For the purposes of those conditions the "balance of the cost" is the difference between—

(a) the cost as notified to the participant under the scheme of such of the works specified in the scheme as relate to the premises in which his owner's interest subsisted, and
(b) the amount of the contribution in respect of that cost paid by him by virtue of section 67.

DEFINITIONS

"assisted participant": s.64.
"completion date": s.66.
"group repair scheme": s.60.

General Note

A reduced contribution is analogous to a grant: see s.67(5), (6), above. Accordingly, conditions analogous to grant conditions are applied to assisted participants for the "protected period" of five years or such other period as may be prescribed, commencing with the completion date defined by s.66 (subs. (2)). The amount to which they are applied is the "balance of the cost", meaning the difference between the amount of the cost of the scheme as whole, notified under s.67(1), as apportioned under s.67(2), and the amount of the contribution that the applicant will have paid under s.67(5), (6). The grant conditions operate as conditions of participation in the scheme (ss.70(1), 71(1)).

Condition as to payment of balance of cost on disposal

70.—(1) It is a condition of participation in a group repair scheme as an assisted participant that if, at any time after signifying scheme consent and before the end of the protected period, he makes a relevant disposal (other than an exempt disposal) of the premises in which he had an owner's interest at the date of the approval of the scheme, he shall pay to the local housing authority on demand the balance of the cost.

(2) The condition under this section is a local land charge and is binding on any person who is for the time being an owner of the premises concerned.

(3) Where the authority have the right to demand payment of an amount as mentioned in subsection (1), they may determine not to demand payment or to demand a lesser amount.

(4) The condition under this section shall cease to be in force with respect to any premises if there is a relevant disposal of the premises that is an exempt disposal, other than—

(a) a disposal within section 54(1)(a) (disposal to associates of person making disposal), or

(b) a disposal within section 54(1)(b) (vesting under will or on intestacy).

Definitions

"assisted participant": s.64.
"exempt disposal": s.72.
"group repair scheme": s.60.
"owner's interest": s.101.
"protected period": s.69.
"relevant disposal": s.72.
"scheme consent": s.65.

General Note

This section identifies the first condition of participation (see also s.71, below), which corresponds to the grant conditions under ss.44 *et seq.*, above. As with those conditions, it operates in relation to a "relevant disposal" which is not an "exempt disposal" (defined in s.72, below by cross reference): see notes to ss.53, 54, above. The condition comprises (subs. (1)) an obligation to pay (on demand by the authority) the balance of the cost (as defined in s.69(3), above), if such a disposal of the premises in which he had an owner's interest (above, s.64) takes place between (a) the date when he signified consent to the scheme under s.65(1), above, and (b) the end of the protected period, *i.e.* five years (or other prescribed period) from completion date (under s.66): see s.69(2)).

Repayment is at the discretion of the authority: subs. (3). "... We recognise the concern among local authorities that the requirement to pay the balance of the cost might deter some people from joining a group repair scheme if they were uncertain as to whether they could meet the conditions. We want to encourage authorities to take a strategic approach to renewal. [The amendments] will help to increase the flexibility of group repair by giving local authorities full discretion in determining the amount, if any, to be recovered from participants if the property is disposed of during the five-year protected period ... Although we would still expect authorities to demand payment where the owner can clearly afford it, they will be able to waive or abate payments where payment in full would cause hardship ..." (*Hansard* (H.L.), Report, April 18, 1996, col. 881, Government Whip, (Lord Lucas)).

See the discussion of Discretion and Policy in notes to s.13, above.

Subs. (2)

See notes to s.45(3), above.

Subs. (4)

The condition remains in force only until the relevant disposal which is not an exempt disposal, *save* that in two classes the condition remains in force even if there is such a disposal, in which case it will continue to bind under subs. (2). See notes to s.45(6), above. See also notes to s.54, above.

Conditions as to occupation

71.—(1) It is a condition of participation in a group repair scheme as an assisted participant—

(a) where the participant gave an owner-occupation certificate, that throughout the protected period the dwelling is occupied in accordance with the intention stated in the certificate;

(b) where the participant gave a certificate of intended letting, that throughout the protected period the dwelling is let or available for letting in accordance with the intention stated in the certificate; and

(c) where the participant gave a certificate of future occupation, that throughout the protected period the house is residentially occupied, or available for residential occupation, in accordance with the intention stated in the certificate.

(2) It is also a condition of participation as an assisted participant that if at any time when any of the above conditions is in force the authority serve notice on the owner of the dwelling or house requiring him to do so, he will within the period of 21 days beginning with the date on which the notice was served furnish to the authority a statement showing how that condition is being fulfilled.

(3) A condition under this section is a local land charge and is binding on any person who is for the time being an owner of the dwelling or house.

(4) In the event of a breach of a condition under this section, the owner for the time being of the dwelling or house shall pay to the local housing authority on demand the balance of the cost.

(5) The local housing authority may determine not to make such a demand or may demand a lesser amount.

(6) Any condition under this section shall cease to be in force with respect to any premises if there is a relevant disposal of the premises which is an exempt disposal other than a disposal within section 54(1)(a) (disposal to associates of person making disposal).

DEFINITIONS

"assisted participant": s.64.
"balance of cost": s.69.
"certificate of intended letting": s.64.
"dwelling": s.101.
"group repair scheme": s.60.
"local housing authority": s.101.
"owner": ss.99, 101.
"owner occupation certificate": s.64.
"protected period": s.69.

GENERAL NOTE

This is the second condition on participation: see notes to s.70, above. The condition is to pay the authority on demand the balance of the cost (see s.69, above), if the intentions in the relevant occupation certificate (see notes to s.64, above) are breached as specified in subs. (1) (as to which, see notes to ss.48(1), 49(1), 50(1), above, to which the conditions in this section correspond). There is also a condition requiring the owner to provide the authority with a statement showing how the occupation requirement is being fulfilled, within 21 days of a demand to do so by the authority: subs. (2): this corresponds to ss.48(2), 49(2)(a) and 50(2)(a), above, but there is no provision requiring a tenant or occupier to comply with a request from the owner for information, corresponding to ss.49(2)(b) and 50(2)(b).

The demand is at the authority's discretion: subs. (5). See the discussion of Discretion and Policy in notes to s.13, above.

Meaning of relevant disposal and exempt disposal

72. Sections 53 and 54 (meaning of "relevant disposal" and "exempt disposal") apply for the purposes of this Chapter.

Payment of balance of cost, &c: cessation of conditions

73.—(1) If at any time while a condition of participation under section 70 or 71 remains in force—

(a) the assisted participant pays the balance of the cost to the local housing authority,

(b) a mortgagee of the interest of the assisted participant in the premises being a mortgagee entitled to exercise a power of sale, makes such a payment,

(c) the authority determine not to demand payment on the breach of a condition of participation, or

(d) the authority demand payment in whole or in part on the breach of a condition of participation and that demand is satisfied,

that condition and any other conditions of participation shall cease to be in force with respect to the premises of that assisted participant.

(2) An amount paid by a mortgagee under subsection (1)(b) above shall be treated as part of the sums secured by the mortgage and may be discharged accordingly.

(3) The purposes authorised for the application of capital money by—

(a) section 73 of the Settled Land Act 1925,

(b) that section as applied by section 28 of the Law of Property Act 1925 in relation to trusts for sale, and

(c) section 26 of the Universities and College Estates Act 1925,

include the making of payments under this section.

Definitions

"assisted participant": s.64.

"local housing authority": s.101.

General Note

This makes provision corresponding to s.55, above.

Supplementary provisions

Power of Secretary of State to modify operation of Chapter

74.—(1) If the Secretary of State so directs in the case of any scheme or any description of scheme, such of the preceding provisions of this Chapter as are specified in the direction shall not apply in relation to that scheme or, as the case may be, in relation to a scheme of that description.

(2) The power under this section to give directions may be so exercised as to make different provision with respect to different local housing authorities or descriptions of authority (including a description framed by reference to authorities in a particular area).

Definition

"local housing authority": s.101.

General Note

The Secretary of State has power to disapply any of the provisions of this Chapter to any particular scheme or description of scheme, including as to categories of authority or parts of the country.

Index of defined expressions: Chapter II

75. In this Chapter the expressions listed below are defined by or otherwise fall to be construed in accordance with the provisions indicated—

assisted participant	section 64(2) and (7)
balance of the cost (in relation to conditions of participation)	section 69(3)
building	section 60(2)
certificate of future occupation	section 64(6)
certificate of intended letting	section 64(4)
completion date	section 66(2)
connected (with the owner of a dwelling)	section 98(2)
dwelling	section 101
eligible to participate	section 64(1)
exempt disposal	section 72 (and section 54)
group repair scheme	section 60(1)
house in multiple occupation	section 101
housing action trust	section 101
local authority	section 101
local housing authority	section 101
long tenancy	section 101
member of family	section 98(1)
new town occupation	section 101
owner	sections 99 and 101
owner-occupation certificate	section 64(3)
owner's interest	section 101
prescribed	section 101
protected period (in relation to conditions of participation)	section 69(2)
reasonable repair	section 96
registered social landlord	section 101
relevant disposal	section 72 (and section 53)
renewal area	section 101
scheme consent	section 65(1)
scheme works	section 62
tenancy and tenant (generally)	section 101
tenant and related expressions (in the context of a certificate of intended letting)	section 64(5)
unassisted participant	section 64(9)

Chapter III

Home repair assistance

Home repair assistance

76.—(1) A local housing authority may, on application being made to them, give assistance under this Chapter ("home repair assistance") in the form of a grant or the provision of materials for the carrying out of works of repair, improvement or adaptation to a dwelling.

(2) The Secretary of State may by order make provision as to the total amount or value of home repair assistance that may be given—

(a) on any one application, or

(b) in respect of the same dwelling in any period of three years.

(3) Home repair assistance shall not be given in respect of works—

(a) for which a grant under Chapter I has been approved or in respect of which an application for a grant is pending, or

(b) which are specified in a group repair scheme approved under Chapter II or prepared and awaiting the approval of the Secretary of State.

Definitions

"dwelling": s.101.

"local housing authority": s.101.

General Note

The home repair grant replaces the minor works grant under the Local Government and Housing Act 1989. It is a discretionary grant, an alternative (not supplement) to grant aid under Chap. I or group repair under Chap. II (see subs. (3)), and is expected to be (see subs. (2)) at a level of £2,000 in any one year, and £4,000 in any three year period: *The Future of Private Housing Renewal Programmes, Explanatory Paper* linked to the White Paper "*Our Future Homes*", June 1995, s.5.

Entitlement to home repair assistance

77.—(1) Subject to the following provisions of this section, a local housing authority shall not entertain an application for home repair assistance unless they are satisfied—

(a) that the applicant is aged 18 or over on the date of the application,
(b) that he lives in the dwelling as his only or main residence,
(c) that he has an owner's interest in the dwelling, or is a tenant of the dwelling, alone or jointly with others,
(d) that he has a duty or power to carry out the works in question, and
(e) that he or his partner is in receipt of income support, family credit, housing benefit, council tax benefit or disability working allowance.

(2) In the case of an application in respect of works to adapt a dwelling to enable an elderly, disabled or infirm person to be cared for, the condition in subsection (1)(b) shall be treated as met if the elderly, disabled or infirm person (whether or not the applicant) lives or proposes to live in the dwelling as his only or main residence.

(3) For the purposes of the condition in subsection (1)(c) "tenant" includes—

(a) a secure tenant or statutory tenant,
(b) a protected occupier under the Rent (Agriculture) Act 1976 or a person in occupation under an assured agricultural occupancy within the meaning of Part I of the Housing Act 1988, and
(c) an employee (whether full-time or part-time) who occupies the dwelling or flat concerned for the better performance of his duties;

but does not include a tenant of an authority or body mentioned in section 3(2) (authorities and bodies not eligible to apply for grants under Chapter I).

(4) An application may be made by a person who does not satisfy the condition in subsection (1)(c) but who occupies the dwelling under a right of exclusive occupation granted for his life or for a period of more than five years.

But except in the case of—

(a) works to adapt a dwelling to enable an elderly, disabled or infirm person, who lives or proposes to live in the dwelling as his only or main residence, to be cared for,
(b) works relating to means of escape from fire or other fire precautions, or
(c) any works to a dwelling in a renewal area,

the local housing authority shall not entertain an application made by virtue of this subsection unless they are satisfied that the applicant has occupied the dwelling as his only or main residence for a period of at least three years immediately preceding the date of the application.

(5) The condition in subsection (1)(e) does not apply—

(a) to an applicant who is elderly, disabled or infirm, or
(b) to an application in respect of works to adapt a dwelling to enable an elderly, disabled or infirm person, who lives or proposes to live in the dwelling, to be cared for.

Definitions

"disabled person": s.100.
"dwelling": s.101.
"elderly person": s.101.

"owner's interest": s.101.
"partner": s.101.
"secure tenant": s.101.
"statutory tenant": s.101.

General Note

This section contains the limitations on availability of home repair assistance. There are five principal conditions which must be fulfilled by an applicant.

(i) The applicant must be aged 18 or more on the date of the application—see notes to s.3, above.

(ii) The applicant must live in the dwelling as his only or main residence—see notes to s.8, above; in the case of an application to adapt a dwelling for an elderly, disabled or infirm person, this condition may be fulfilled by intended occupation (subs. (2)).

(iii) The applicant must either have an owner's interest in the dwelling (see notes to s.7, above) or be a tenant (in either case, alone or jointly with another); tenants include secure and statutory tenants, protected and assured agricultural occupiers, and service occupiers (see notes to s.19, above), including someone with a right to occupy for life (see notes to s.19, above) or for more than three years (subss. (3), (4)), but *not* if the tenancy is held from one of the public bodies disqualified from the principal, Chap. I grants by s.3 above (see notes thereto) (subs. (3)); the applicant must normally have occupied the dwelling (as an only or main residence) for a period of at least three years before the application (see s.10, above), *save*

(a) in the case of works to adapt a dwelling for an elderly, disabled or infirm person, or

(b) in the case of works relating to means of escape from fire or other fire precautions (see s.12, above), or

(c) in the case of works to a dwelling in a renewal area (see notes to s.10, above) (subs. (4)).

(Note the extension to occupiers of houseboats and mobile homes, below, s.78.)

(iv) The applicant has a duty or power to carry out the works (*cf.* notes to s.15, above).

(v) *Either* the applicant or his partner is in receipt of one of the identified social security benefits, *or* the applicant is elderly, disabled or infirm, *or* the application is for works to adapt a dwelling for an elderly, disabled or infirm person who lives or proposes to live in the dwelling (subs. (5)).

Assistance in respect of house-boats and mobile homes

78.—(1) Subject to the following provisions of this section, sections 76 and 77 (home repair assistance) apply in relation to a house-boat or mobile home as in relation to a dwelling.

(2) For the purposes of those sections as they apply in relation to a house-boat or mobile home, any person lawfully in occupation of the house-boat or mobile home shall be treated as a person with an owner's interest in or a tenant of a dwelling.

But except in the case of—

(a) works to adapt a house-boat or mobile home to enable an elderly, disabled or infirm person, who lives or proposes to live there as his only or main residence, to be cared for, or

(b) works relating to means of escape from fire or other fire precautions,

the local housing authority shall not entertain an application for home repair assistance unless the residence requirement is met.

(3) The residence requirement in the case of a house-boat is that the local housing authority are satisfied that—

(a) the applicant has occupied the boat as his only or main residence for a period of at least three years immediately preceding the date of the application;

(b) the boat has for that period had its only or main mooring in the same locality on an inland waterway or in marine waters within the boundary of the authority; and

(c) the applicant had a right to moor his boat there.

(4) The residence requirement in the case of a mobile home is that the local housing authority are satisfied that—

(a) the applicant has occupied the mobile home as his only or main residence for a period of at least three years immediately preceding the date of the application;

(b) the mobile home has for that period been on land forming part of the same protected site within the meaning of the Mobile Homes Act 1983; and

(c) the applicant occupied it under an agreement to which that Act applies or under a gratuitous licence.

(5) In this section—

"house-boat" means a boat or similar structure designed or adapted for use as a place of permanent habitation, and

"mobile home" means a caravan within the meaning of Part I of the Caravan Sites and Control of Development Act 1960 (disregarding the amendment made by section 13(2) of the Caravan Sites Act 1968),

which is a dwelling for the purposes of Part I of the Local Government Finance Act 1992 (council tax).

DEFINITIONS

"disabled person": s.100.
"elderly person": s.101.
"local housing authority": s.101.

GENERAL NOTE

This section extends home repair assistance to the occupiers of house-boats and mobile homes (as defined), in which cases "any person lawfully in occupation" is treated as fulfilling the condition in s.77(1)(c), above, that he has an owner's interest in or is a tenant of the house-boat or mobile home.

The applicant must have occupied the house-boat or mobile home as his only or main residence (see notes to s.8, above) for at least three years preceding the application, unless the works are either to adapt the property for an elderly, disabled or infirm person who lives in the house-boat or mobile home or who intends to do so, or for works relating to means of escape from fire or other fire precautions (see s.77(4), above): subss. (2)–(4).

In addition, however, and if this residence requirement requires to be fulfilled (*i.e.* not if the works are for an elderly, etc., person or fire-related),

(i) in the case of a houseboat, the applicant must have had the right to a mooring, which has been its only or main mooring for the same period, but whether or not the same mooring throughout, within the authority's boundaries, and

(ii) in the case of a mobile home, the applicant must have had an agreement in relation to a protected site within the meaning of the Mobile Homes Act 1983 (c. 34), or a free licence to occupy such a site (subss. (3), (4)).

Houseboat. The houseboat—a boat or similar structure designed or adapted for use as a place of permanent habitation (subs. (5))—must qualify as a dwelling for the council tax purposes of Pt. I of the Local Government Finance Act 1992 (c. 14), *i.e.* "any property" which *would have been* a hereditament for rating purposes under the General Rate Act 1967 (c. 9) if that Act had remained in force, and is *not* on a non-domestic rating list, and is *not* exempt from local non-domestic rating, *nor* is a yard, garden, outhouse or other appurtenance, or a private garage, or private storage premises, forming part of a larger property which is a dwelling—1992, s.3.

Mobile home. This means a caravan which is a dwelling within Pt. I of the Local Government Finance Act 1992 (see last note), and which is within the meaning of Pt. I of the Caravan Sites and Control of Development Act 1960 (c. 62), *i.e.* a structure designed or adapted for human habitation and capable of being moved from one place to another, and any motor vehicle so designed, but not including railway rolling-stock or a tent—1960, s.29. Thus, a large van used, but neither designed nor adapted, for human habitation was not a caravan in *Backer v. Secretary of State for the Environment* [1983] J.P.L. 602.

Protected site. This means (Mobile Homes Act 1983, s.5) a site requiring a licence for use as a caravan site under s.1, Caravan Sites Act 1968 (c. 52) (see *Balthazar v. Mullane* (1985) 17 H.L.R. 561, C.A.; *Adams v. Watkins* (1990) 22 H.L.R. 107, C.A.).

Power to make further provision by regulations

79.—(1) The Secretary of State may by regulations make provision as to—

(a) the manner of making an application for home repair assistance and the contents of such an application;

(b) the procedure for dealing with applications for home repair assistance and for ensuring that works are carried out to any standard specified in the regulations;

(c) the way in which the amount of home repair assistance to be given on any application is to be determined; and

(d) the taking into account (in such manner and to such extent as may be prescribed) of the financial circumstances of the applicant.

(2) The Secretary of State may by regulations make provision extending or restricting the availability of home repair assistance, by reference to such description of persons, circumstances or other factors as the Secretary of State thinks fit.

(3) Regulations under subsection (2) may proceed wholly or in part by reference to the provisions relating to entitlement to housing benefit, or any other form of assistance, as they have effect from time to time.

GENERAL NOTE

The bulk of the provisions—including how to apply for home repair assistance, approval and determination procedure and means-testing—will be governed by regulations made by the Secretary of State, which regulations may also extend or limit those who may apply for such assistance, or otherwise extend or limit the assistance, *e.g.* to particular categories of work.

Index of defined expressions: Chapter III

80. In this Chapter the expressions listed below are defined by or otherwise fall to be construed in accordance with the provisions indicated—

disabled person	section 100(1) to (3)
dwelling	section 101
elderly	section 101
home repair assistance	section 76(1)
improvement	section 101
local housing authority	section 101
owner's interest	section 101
partner	section 101
prescribed	section 101
renewal area	section 101
secure tenant	section 101
statutory tenant	section 101
tenancy and tenant (generally)	section 101

CHAPTER IV

DEFERRED ACTION NOTICES, &C.

Deferred action notices

Deferred action notices

81.—(1) If the local housing authority are satisfied that a dwelling-house or house in multiple occupation is unfit for human habitation, but are satisfied that serving a deferred action notice is the most satisfactory course of action, they shall serve such a notice.

(2) A deferred action notice is a notice—

(a) stating that the premises are unfit for human habitation,

(b) specifying the works which, in the opinion of the authority, are required to make the premises fit for human habitation, and

(c) stating the other courses of action which are available to the authority if the premises remain unfit for human habitation.

(3) The notice becomes operative, if no appeal is brought, on the expiry of 21 days from the date of the service of the notice and is final and conclusive as to matters which could have been raised on an appeal.

(4) A deferred action notice which has become operative is a local land charge so long as it remains operative.

(5) The fact that a deferred action notice has been served does not prevent the local housing authority from taking any other course of action in relation to the premises at any time.

DEFINITIONS

"dwelling-house": s.90.
"house in multiple occupation": s.90.
"local housing authority": s.101.
"unfit for human habitation": s.97.

GENERAL NOTE

Introduction. This Chapter is in a different category to those which have gone before: it creates no grant entitlement; it is in substance amendment of other legislation; it is related to the earlier Chapters, but only in practice, not in theory. What the first group of sections (ss.81–85, see also ss.86–98 which have a wider application) in this Chapter does—on the demise of the mandatory grant to remedy or prevent unfitness and serious disrepair—is to empower the local authority to serve a "deferred action notice" where currently they would be *obliged* to serve notice under s.189 of the Housing Act 1985, whether the property is a house, a dwelling-house (therefore, including a flat), or a house in multiple occupation, which is unfit (*unless* not satisfied that to do so would be the most satisfactory course of action, in which case they would be obliged to take the alternative action of closing the property to human habitation or even demolishing it under *ibid.*, Pt. IX).

The notice. The deferred action notice is, in substance, an early warning notice that the authority consider the premises unfit, identifying the works which the authority consider are required to make the premises fit, and identifying the courses of action other than deferred action (therefore, repair notice, or closing or demolition order) which are available to the authority if the premises remain unfit: subs. (2). The deferred action notice is without prejudice to recourse to their other powers, at any time: subs. (5).

It may be that the courts would consider that service of a deferred action notice has created a legitimate expectation that there will be no recourse to other powers, at least without forewarning and/or other than in changed circumstances, although highly unlikely—in the light of subs. (5)—to go further than this in limiting by case-law what Parliament has expressly left unlimited. Further, s.86 provides the Secretary of State with express power to impose procedural requirements, including by way of forewarning, on the service of notices under the relevant provisions of the Housing Act 1985 (and indeed on the service of a deferred action notice: see s.86(1)(a)). While the existence of or failure to use these powers cannot be fatal to a claim based on legitimate expectation, they must also serve to make it less likely.

Most satisfactory course of action. The notice may only be served if the authority are satisfied that to do so is the most satisfactory course of action (subs. (1)): in reaching this decision, the authority are to have regard to such guidance as may from time to time be given by the Secretary of State (prepared in accordance with the requirements of the Housing Act 1985, s.604A(2)–(4), which, *inter alia*, require that the guidance be laid in draft before Parliament)—see s.85, below. As to the duty imported by the expression "have regard to", see notes to ss.12, 31, above.

Appeal and challenge. Unless there is an appeal against the notice (under s.83, below), the notice becomes operative 21 days from date of service of notice, and is final and conclusive as to matters which could have been raised on appeal (subs. (3)). Matters which go to the *vires* of the authority in serving the notice *can* be raised on an appeal: see *Wandsworth L.B.C. v. Winder* [1985] A.C. 461, 17 H.L.R. 196, H.L.; *Elliott v. Brighton B.C.* (1980) 258 E.G. 441, C.A., and *Nolan v. Leeds C.C.* (1990) 23 H.L.R. 135, C.A.; see also *R. v. Hackney L.B.C., ex p. Teepee Estates (1956)*, (1967) 19 P. & C.R. 87, D.C.; *Minford Properties v. Hammersmith L.B.C.* (1978) 247 E.G. 561, D.C.

It may be arguable, therefore, that as they *can* so be raised, they cannot be raised by way of judicial review, although the opposite is also arguable: compare *Smith v. East Elloe R.D.C.* [1956] A.C. 736, H.L., applied in *R. v. Secretary of State for the Environment, ex p. Ostler* [1977] Q.B. 122, C.A., distinguishing *Anisminic v. Foreign Compensation Commission* [1969] 2 A.C. 147, H.L., on the side of "final and conclusive", and *Pearlman v. Keepers & Governors of Harrow School* [1979] Q.B. 56, C.A., and *Meade v. Haringey L.B.C.* [1979] 1 W.L.R. 637, C.A., on the side of recourse to judicial review notwithstanding the "final and conclusive" clause.

Dwelling-house. See s.90, below. It includes any yard, garden, outhouses and appurtenances belonging to the dwelling-house: the Housing Act 1985, s.207(2)—see notes to s.1, above. A flat can be a dwelling-house: see 1985 Act, ss.189(2), 207(2). Where a building is divided horizontally, the horizontal divisions are flats: 1985 Act, ss.207(2), s.183. Where a building is not structurally detached, and any material part of it overlaps or underlaps another part of the structure, it is also a flat: *ibid*.

House in multiple occupation. See s.90, below. It means a house which is occupied by persons who do not form a single household: the Housing Act 1985, s.345—see notes to s.1, above. For this purpose, it includes a part of a building which would not in its own right be considered a house, and which was constructed or has been adapted for occupation by a single household: s.345(2). A flat in multiple occupation is a reference to any part of a building—whether as a result of this extended definition or not—which is itself occupied by persons who do not form a single household: *ibid*.

Unfit for human habitation. See notes to s.97, below.

Subs. (4)

See notes to s.45(3), above.

The notice remains operative until *either* there is a successful appeal (under s.83—in itself or as applied by s.84(4), below), *or* on a s.84 review the authority cease to be satisfied that it is the most satisfactory course of action, *or* the authority take action within s.84(6), below.

Service of deferred action notices

82.—(1) The local housing authority shall serve a deferred action notice—

(a) in the case of a notice relating to a dwelling-house, on the person having control of the dwelling-house as defined in section 207 of the Housing Act 1985;

(b) in the case of a notice relating to a house in multiple occupation, on the person having control of the house as defined in section 398 of that Act.

(2) Where the authority are satisfied that a dwelling-house which is a flat, or a flat in multiple occupation, is unfit for human habitation by virtue of section 604(2) of the Housing Act 1985, they shall also serve the notice on the person having control (as defined in section 207 of that Act) of the building or part of the building in question.

(3) In the case of a house in multiple occupation, the authority may serve the notice on the person managing the house instead of the person having control of the house.

(4) Where the authority serve a notice under subsection (1), (2) or (3)—

(a) they shall also serve a copy of the notice on any other person having an interest in the premises concerned, whether as freeholder, mortgagee or lessee (within the meaning of Part VI of the Housing Act 1985), and

(b) they may serve a copy of the notice on any person having a licence to occupy the premises.

(5) Section 617 of the Housing Act 1985 (service of notices) applies for the purpose of this section as it applies for the purpose of that Act.

DEFINITIONS

"deferred action notice": s.81.
"dwelling-house": s.90.
"flat": s.90.
"flat in multiple occupation": s.90.
"house in multiple occupation": s.90.
"local housing authority": s.101.
"owner": s.90.
"unfit for human habitation": s.97.

GENERAL NOTE

The deferred action notice is served on the person having control of the house, meaning as defined in s.207 of the Housing Act 1985 in the case of a dwelling-house, and *ibid*., s.398, in the case of an HMO. The authority *must* also serve the notice on the person having control of a building or part of a building, where satisfied that a flat or a flat in multiple occupation is unfit (subs. (2)). The authority *may* also serve the notice of the manager of an HMO instead of the person having control (subs. (3)): see notes to s.90, below. The authority *must* also serve a copy of the notice on any other person having an interest in either dwelling-house or HMO, as freeholder, mortgage or lessee, and *may* serve a copy on a licensee (see notes to s.7, above): subs. (4). A notice served on entirely the wrong person may simply be ignored, and does not become final and conclusive under s.80, above: *Pollway Nominees v. Croydon L.B.C.* [1987] A.C. 79, 18 H.L.R. 443, H.L.

Person having control. This is the person who receives the rack-rent of the premises, meaning a rent that is not less than two-thirds of the net annual value, whether on his own account or as agent or trustee for another, or who would so receive it if it were so let: 1985 Act, ss.207, 398. The freeholder of a block of flats is not the person having control of it as, although the common parts may be said to remain in his possession in the sense that he could let them out, he could not let out the block: only the individual leaseholders, who were occupying on leases at less than a rack-rent, could let out their individual flats, so that the person in control would seem to be all of the long leaseholders, plus the freeholder in respect of (a) common parts, and (b) any flats let out at a rack-rent: *Pollway.*

The fact that there may be rent controls is unlikely to affect what comprises the net annual value: *Rawlance v. Croydon Corporation* [1952] 2 Q.B. 803, C.A. The question is to be determined at the date of the letting, so that a subsequent variation in value will not affect the matter: *London Corporation v. Cusack-Smith* [1955] A.C. 337, H.L. If there is a letting at a rack-rent, there is no need to look further and see whether someone else might in some circumstances be able (also) to let at a rack-rent: *Kensington B.C. v. Allen* [1926] 1 K.B. 576. Where there is a chain of lettings at less than a rack-rent, only the person in possession will be in a position to let *at* a rack-rent: *Truman, Hanbury, Buxton & Co. v. Kerslake* [1894] 2 Q.B. 774; *Pollway.*

Subs. (5)

Under the Housing Act 1985, s.617, the authority must take reasonable steps to identify anyone who may be a person having control, or managing, or having an estate or interest in premises: s.617(1). Persons merely having an estate or interest can serve notice of their interest on the authority, who are bound to record it: s.617(2). If not reasonably practicable to ascertain the name or address of a person to be served, it may be served by addressing it to the person having control of (the address in question), and delivering it to some person on the premises or, if no such, by fixing it to some conspicuous part of the premises: s.617(3). Where there is more than one person who qualifies to be served, more than one of them may be served: s.617(4).

Appeals against deferred action notices

83.—(1) A person aggrieved by a deferred action notice may within 21 days after the service of the notice appeal to the county court.

(2) Without prejudice to the generality of subsection (1), it is a ground of appeal that serving a notice under section 189 of the Housing Act 1985, or making a closing order under section 264 of that Act or a demolition order under section 265 of that Act, is a more satisfactory course of action.

(3) Where the grounds on which an appeal is brought are or include that specified in subsection (2), the court, on the hearing of the appeal, shall have regard to any guidance given to the local housing authority under section 604A of the Housing Act 1985 or section 85 of this Act.

(4) On an appeal the court may make such order either confirming, quashing or varying the notice as it thinks fit.

(5) Where the appeal is allowed and the reason or one of the reasons for allowing the appeal is that serving a notice under section 189 of that Act or making a closing order under section 264 of that Act or a demolition order under section 265 of that Act is a more satisfactory course of action, the judge shall, if requested to do so by the appellant or the local housing authority, include in his judgment a finding to that effect.

(6) If an appeal is brought, the deferred action notice does not become operative until—

(a) a decision on the appeal confirming the notice (with or without variation) is given and the period within which an appeal to the Court of Appeal may be brought expires without any such appeal having been brought, or

(b) if a further appeal to the Court of Appeal is brought, a decision on that appeal is given confirming the notice (with or without variation);

and for this purpose the withdrawal of an appeal has the same effect as a decision confirming the notice or decision appealed against.

DEFINITIONS

"deferred action notice": s.81.

"local housing authority": s.21.

GENERAL NOTE

Appeal. Within 21 days of service (not including the day of service itself: *Goldsmith's Co. v. West Metropolitan Ry. Co.* [1904] 1 K.B. 1, C.A.), a person aggrieved (*i.e.* some deprived of a legal entitlement, or subject to a legal burden, but not necessarily a pecuniary grievance—*Ex p. Sidebotham* (1880) 14 Ch.D. 458; *R. v. London Quarter Sessions, ex p. Westminster Corporation* [1951] 2 K.B. 508) may appeal to the county court (subs. (1)), in which case the deferred action notice does not become operative until a final decision of the court below or at the Court of Appeal confirming the notice (with or without variation), or withdrawal of an appeal: subs. (6).

Leave for further appeal. It does not seem that leave is needed to appeal to the Court of Appeal, because the court would not seem here to be sitting in an appellate capacity within County Courts Appeals Order 1991, art. 2(1)(b), which applies where the court is sitting at second instance, *i.e.* on appeal from the District Judge: see the commentary in the Supreme Court Practice, at para. 59/1/34; see also *Sherred & Tarling v. Dover D.C.*, September 26, 1995, Mr Registrar Adams, Transcript.

Grounds. The grounds for appeal are not specified, nor are they confined by subs. (2) (see also *Elliott v. Brighton B.C.* (1980) 258 E.G. 441, C.A., and *Nolan v. Leeds C.C.* (1990) 23 H.L.R. 135, C.A.; see generally note on Appeal and Challenge, notes to s.81, above).

Powers of court. When determining what is the most satisfactory course of action, both under s.81 (see notes thereto), and under the relevant provisions of the Housing Act 1985, the authority are bound to have regard to (see notes to s.85, below) guidance issued by the Secretary of State: s.81(1), above and s.85, below; 1985 Act, ss.189(1), (2), 264(1), 265(2) and 604A(1). So also must the court: subs. (3). The court may make an order confirming, quashing or varying the notice: subs. (4).

Subs. (5)

If the authority omit to ask the judge to make a finding, it will not be possible to return at a later date for this purpose: *Victoria Square Property Co. v. Southwark L.B.C.* [1978] 1 W.L.R. 463, C.A.

Review of deferred action notices

84.—(1) The local housing authority may at any time review any deferred action notice served by them, and they shall do so not later than two years after the notice becomes operative and at intervals of not more than two years thereafter.

The Secretary of State may by order amend this subsection so as to specify such other period or periods as he considers appropriate.

(2) The authority shall for the purposes of any such review inspect the premises concerned.

For this purpose sections 197 (powers of entry) and 198 (penalty for obstruction) of the Housing Act 1985 apply as they apply for the purposes of Part VI of that Act.

(3) If the authority are satisfied that the deferred action notice remains the most satisfactory course of action, they shall renew the notice and serve notice of their decision.

(4) The provisions of section 82 (service of deferred action notice) and section 83(1) to (5) (appeals against deferred action notices) apply in relation to the authority's decision to renew a deferred action notice as in relation to the original notice.

(5) If an appeal is brought against the decision to renew a deferred action notice, the notice remains operative until any decision on the appeal, or any further appeal, quashing or varying the notice.

(6) If the authority take action in relation to the premises under any of the provisions listed in section 604A(1) of the Housing Act 1985, the deferred

action notice shall cease to be operative on the relevant notice, order or declaration becoming operative.

DEFINITIONS

"deferred action notice": s.81.

"local housing authority": s.101.

GENERAL NOTE

Review and inspection. The deferred action notice may be reviewed at any time, but no later than two years (or such other period as the Secretary of State may specify by amendment by order) after it became operative, *i.e.* 21 days after service if no appeal (s.81(3), above), or on the final determination or withdrawal of appeal under s.83(6), above: subs. (1). A review involves a mandatory inspection: subs. (2). (See s.87, below, for the costs of inspection). If satisfied that deferred action remains the most satisfactory course of action, the authority renew it and serve notice of their decision (subs. (3)), in which case the provisions as to service (s.82) and appeal (s.83) apply to the notice of renewal in like manner as they applied to the initial notice: subs. (4). In this case, however, the deferred action notice *remains* operative pending the final outcome of the appeal: subs. (5).

Alternative courses of action. The notice ceases to be operative, independently of review, if the authority take action within subs. (6):

(i) Under s.189(1) or (1A) of the Housing Act 1985 (see notes to s.12, above);

(ii) Under *ibid.*, s.264(1) or (2), ordering a dwelling-house, HMO or the whole or part of a building containing unfit flats to be closed to human habitation;

(iii) Under *ibid.*, s.265(1) or (2), ordering a dwelling-house which is not a flat, or an HMO which is not a flat in multiple occupation (in each case, see notes to s.89, below), or the whole or part of a building containing unfit flats to be demolished; or

(iv) Declaring a clearance area over land which includes the dwelling-house, HMO or building under *ibid.*, s.289.

Subs. (2)

For the purpose of inspection, the provisions of 1985 Act, ss.197 and 198 are applied. The former permits a person authorised in writing by the local authority, on seven days' notice to the occupier, and to the owner if known, to enter at any reasonable time; the written authorisation must be produced for inspection on demand by the occupier (or someone acting on his behalf). The latter makes it a summary offence, punishable by a fine not exceeding level 3 on the standard scale, to obstruct an officer of the authority, or person authorised by the authority to enter, in the performance of the function for which he was authorised to enter.

Guidance by Secretary of State

85.—In deciding for the purposes of section 81 (deferred action notices) or section 84 (review of deferred action notices) what is the most satisfactory course of action in relation to any premises, the local housing authority shall have regard to such guidance as may from time to time be given by the Secretary of State.

(2) The provisions of section 604A(2) to (4) of the Housing Act 1985 (supplementary provisions as to guidance) apply in relation to such guidance.

GENERAL NOTE

See notes to ss.12, 31, above.

Power to improve enforcement procedures

Unfitness for human habitation etc.: power to improve enforcement procedures

86.—(1) The Secretary of State may by order provide that a local housing authority shall act as specified in the order before taking action of any of the following kinds—

(a) serving a deferred action notice under section 81 or renewing such a notice under section 84;

(b) serving a notice under section 189 of the Housing Act 1985 (repair notice in respect of house which unfit for human habitation);

(c) serving a notice under section 190 of that Act (repair notice in respect of house in state of disrepair but not unfit for human habitation);
(d) making a closing order under section 264 of that Act;
(e) making a demolition order under section 265 of that Act.

(2) An order under this section may provide that the authority—
(a) shall as soon as practicable give to the person against whom action is intended a written notice which satisfies the requirements of subsection (3); and
(b) shall not take any action against him until after the end of such period beginning with the giving of the notice as may be determined by or under the order.

(3) A notice satisfies the requirements of this subsection if it—
(a) states the nature of the remedial action which in the authority's opinion should be taken, and explains why and within what period;
(b) explains the grounds on which it appears to the authority that action might be taken as mentioned in subsection (1); and
(c) states the nature of the action which could be taken and states whether there is a right to make representations before, or a right of appeal against, the taking of such action.

(4) An order under this section may also provide that, before the authority takes any action against any person, they—
(a) shall give to that person a written notice stating—
(i) that they are considering taking the action and the reasons why they are considering it; and
(ii) that the person may, within a period specified in the notice, make written representations to them or, if the person so requests, make oral representations to them in the presence of a person determined by or under the order; and
(b) shall consider any representations which are duly made and not withdrawn.

(5) An order under this section may in particular—
(a) make provision as to the consequences of any failure to comply with a provision made by the order;
(b) contain provisions (including provisions modifying enactments relating to the periods within which proceedings must be brought) which are consequential upon, or supplemental or incidental to, the provisions made by the order.

(6) Nothing in any order made under this section shall—
(a) preclude a local housing authority from taking immediate action against any person, or from requiring any person to take immediate remedial action to avoid action being taken against him, in any case where it appears to them to be necessary to take such action or impose such a requirement; or
(b) require such an authority to disclose any information the disclosure of which would be contrary to the public interest.

DEFINITIONS
"deferred action notice": s.81.
"local housing authority": s.101.
"unfit for human habitation": s.97.

GENERAL NOTE
Introduction. There is in general no requirement to give any warning before action is taken under housing enforcement procedures such as a repairs notice (ss.189, 190 of the Housing Act 1985—see notes to s.12, above), closing order under *ibid.*, s.264 or demolition order under *ibid.*, s.265, although in the last two cases, such action formerly only followed a "time and place" procedure at which the future of the property would be discussed and an undertaking to repair could be accepted—see 1985 Act, s.264, as enacted (before it was replaced under the Local Government and Housing Act 1989, Sched. 9, para. 14). While informal procedures may be

available, many authorities do not in practice use them, for a number of reasons, *e.g.* they rarely lead to works and commonly lead to waste of time, there is no recoupment of the cost of the informal procedures (but see now s.87, below), there is a risk of abuse by officers (and a probably greater risk of accusation of such abuse).

Pre-notice procedures. This section empowers the Secretary of State by order to introduce a code of forewarning in relation to the actions specified in subs. (1), including the deferred action notice itself (subs. (2)), which, *inter alia*, will provide the person served with the opportunity to take pre-emptive voluntary action, and may also provide him with the right to make representations (subs. (3)), in which case the authority must serve notice of their reasons for considering action and give the person served a period in which to make representations, and indeed must take those representations into account (subs. (4)). The provisions take effect subject to the subs. (6) "necessity" override.

Reasons: see notes to s.34, above.

Subs. (6)

Where the authority consider it *necessary* to take immediate action, or to require immediate action to be taken, the requirements of an order need not cause them to delay. Nor, in the context of the requirement to give reasons in subs. (4)(a)(i) does the duty require the disclosure of information contrary to the public interest.

Power to charge for enforcement action

Unfitness for human habitation, etc.: power to charge for enforcement action

87.—(1) A local housing authority may make such reasonable charge as they consider appropriate as a means of recovering certain administrative and other expenses incurred by them in taking action of any of the following kinds—

(a) serving a deferred action notice under section 81 or deciding to renew such a notice under section 84;
(b) serving a notice under section 189 of the Housing Act 1985 (repair notice in respect of house which unfit for human habitation);
(c) serving a notice under section 190 of that Act (repair notice in respect of house in state of disrepair but not unfit for human habitation);
(d) making a closing order under section 264 of that Act;
(e) making a demolition order under section 265 of that Act.

(2) The expenses are, in the case of the service of a notice under section 81 of this Act or section 189 or 190 of the Housing Act 1985, the expenses incurred in—

(a) determining whether to serve the notice,
(b) identifying the works to be specified in the notice, and
(c) serving the notice.

(3) The expenses are, in the case of a decision to renew a notice under section 84 of this Act, the expenses incurred in—

(a) deciding whether to renew the notice, and
(b) serving notice of the authority's decision.

(4) The expenses are, in the case of a closing order under section 264 of the Housing Act 1985 or a demolition order under section 265 of that Act, the expenses incurred in—

(a) determining whether to make the order, and
(b) serving notice of the order.

(5) The amount of the charge shall not exceed such amount as is specified by order of the Secretary of State.

(6) Where a court allows an appeal against the underlying notice, decision or order mentioned in subsection (1), it may make such order as it thinks fit reducing, quashing or requiring the repayment of any charge under this section made in respect of the notice, decision or order.

DEFINITIONS

"local housing authority": s.101.
"unfit for human habitation": s.97.

GENERAL NOTE

Introduction. Local authorities' powers to charge were considered in *McCarthy & Stone v. Richmond L.B.C.* [1992] 2 A.C. 48, H.L., in relation to charges for "pre-application" planning inquiries (for which *applications* scale fees were set), which were held to be *ultra vires*. Where a statute provides its own comprehensive code of powers, there is no room for the implication of further powers (of the order governed by the code) under s.111 of the Local Government Act 1972: *ibid.*; see also *Hazell v. Hammersmith L.B.C.* [1992] 2 A.C. 1, H.L.; see further *Crédit Suisse v. Allerdale B.C., Same v. Waltham Forest L.B.C., The Times*, May 20, 1996, C.A.

Whatever the position may be in other cases, the express power to execute works in default of compliance with a repairs notice under the Housing Act 1985, ss.189, 190, to be found in *ibid.*, s.193, backed by the right to recover their expenses of so doing (under *ibid.* Sched. 10), and other analogous provisions (see, *e.g.*, ss.271–272, 288), suggested that any attempt to seek to recover any *other* costs associated with these functions would be doomed to failure.

The Local Government and Housing Act 1989 does, however, contain power for the Secretary of State to prescribe circumstances in which authorities may make charges: s.150.

Chargeable functions. The new power is to make reasonable charges in order to recover their administrative and other expenses incurred in taking action to serve or renew a deferred action notice, or to serve a repairs notice under ss.189, 190 of the Housing Act 1985, or to make a closing order under *ibid.*, s.264 or a demolition order under *ibid.*, s.265: subs. (1). In the case of a deferred action or repairs notice, the expenses in question are those incurred in deciding whether or not to serve the notice, identifying the works and actually serving the notice (subs. (2)). In the case of the renewal of a deferred action notice, the expenses are those incurred in deciding whether to renew, and serving notice of renewal (the inspection function already being a statutory part of the decision-making process, by s.84(2), above): subs. (3). In the case of a closing or demolition order, the expenses are likewise those of deciding whether or not to make—and of serving—the order: subs. (4).

Interestingly, there is no express inclusion of charging for compliance with any requirements under s.86, above. However, if these are statutorily required pre-conditions of the decision-making process, there would seem to be no reason why they should not be comprised within the expression "determining whether to" serve or renew the notice, or make the order.

Expenses incurred. Expenditure is incurred when the payer comes under a liability to make a payment, rather than when the payment itself is made, but not a loss or expenditure which is no more than impending, threatened or anticipated: see, *e.g.*, *Capital and Counties Freehold Equity Trust v. B.L.* [1987] 2 E.G.L.R. 49, *West Ham Corporation v. Grant* (1888) 40 Ch.D. 331, *Law v. Coburn* [1972] 1 W.L.R. 1238; see also *New Zealand Flax Investments v. Federal Commissioner* (1938) 61 C.L.R. 179 at p.207, *Federal Commissioner for Taxation v. James Flood Pty.* (1953) 88 C.L.R. 492, *King v. Commissioner of Inland Revenue* [1974] 2 N.Z.L.R. 190.

Amount of charge. The Secretary of State may set a maximum charge: subs. (5). Subject thereto, the amount must be (a) reasonable, and (b) *as a means of* recovering administrative and other expenses incurred in following the course of action in question: see, generally, discussion of administrative law in notes to s.13, above. The Secretary of State has power to prescribe both a form for a demand for a charge (under s.88(3)), *and* the particulars to be contained in it: s.89, below.

Appeal. On an appeal under s.84, the court has jurisdiction to make such order as it thinks fit in respect of any charge made under this section.

Recovery. See following section.

Recovery of charge for enforcement action

88.—(1) The following provisions have effect with respect to the recovery of a charge under section 87.

(2) The charge may be recovered by the authority concerned from—

(a) in the case of a notice under section 81 of this Act, or section 189 or 190 of the Housing Act 1985, any person on whom the notice is served;

(b) in the case of a renewal of a notice under section 84 of this Act, any person on whom notice of the decision to renew the notice is served;

(c) in the case of an order under section 264 or 265 of the Housing Act 1985, any person on whom notice of the order is served as an owner of the premises.

(3) A demand for payment of the charge shall be served on the person from whom the authority seeks to recover it.

(4) The demand becomes operative, if no appeal is brought against the underlying notice, decision or order, on the expiry of the period of 21 days from the service of the demand.

(5) The sum recoverable by the authority is, until recovered, a charge on the premises concerned; and—

(a) the charge takes effect when the demand becomes operative,
(b) the authority have for the purpose of enforcing the charge the same powers and remedies under the Law of Property Act 1925 and otherwise as if they were mortgagees by deed having powers of sale and lease, of accepting surrenders of leases and of appointing a receiver, and
(c) the power of appointing a receiver is exercisable at any time after the expiration of one month from the date when the charge takes effect.

GENERAL NOTE

This section governs from whom the administration charge in s.87, above, may be recovered. The demand becomes operative on the expiry of 21 days from service, unless an appeal is brought: subs. (4). If such an appeal is brought, then the powers of the court are those to be found in s.87(6), above.

Supplementary provisions

Power to prescribe forms

89.—The Secretary of State may by regulations prescribe the form of and the particulars to be contained in—

(a) a deferred action notice, or a notice of an authority's decision to renew a deferred action notice, or
(b) a demand for payment of any charge under section 87 (power to charge for enforcement action).

GENERAL NOTE

Deferred action notices—or notices of their renewal—may need to be in prescribed form, if the Secretary of State so provides; the same may be true of a demand for payment of a charge.

Minor definitions: Chapter IV

90. In this Chapter—

(a) "dwelling-house", "flat" and references to the owner of a dwelling-house or flat, have the same meaning as in Part VI of the Housing Act 1985 (repair notices); and
(b) "house in multiple occupation", "flat in multiple occupation" and references to the owner of or person managing such a house or flat, have the same meaning as in Part XI of that Act.

GENERAL NOTE

Dwelling-house. This includes any yard, garden, outhouses and appurtenances belonging to the dwelling-house: Housing Act 1985, s.207(2)—see notes to s.1, above. A flat can be a dwelling-house: see 1985 Act, ss.189(2), 207(2). Where a building is divided horizontally, the horizontal divisions are flats: 1985 Act, ss.207(2), 183. Where a building is not structurally detached, and any material part of it overlaps or underlaps another part of the structure, it is also a flat: *ibid.*

The owner of a dwelling-house means a person (other than a mortgagee not in possession) entitled to dispose of the fee simple of the premises, and includes a person holding or entitled to the rents and profits under a lease of which there is at least three years unexpired: 1985 Act, s.207.

House in multiple occupation. This means a house which is occupied by persons who do not form a single household: the Housing Act 1985, s.345—see notes to s.1, above. For this purpose, it includes a part of a building which would not in its own right be considered a house, and which was constructed or has been adapted for occupation by a single household: s.345(2). A flat in multiple occupation is a reference to any part of a building—whether as a result of this extended definition or not—which is itself occupied by persons who do not form a single household: *ibid.*

"Owner" of a house in multiple occupation has the same meaning as of a dwelling-house: 1985 Act, s.398(3). "Person managing" a house in multiple occupation means an owner or lessee (including a statutory tenant: 1985 Act, s.398(2)) who, directly or through an agent or trustee, receives rents or other payments from tenants or lodgers of parts of the premises or would so receive those rents or other payments but for having entered into an arrangement (whether pursuant to a court order or otherwise) with another person, who is not an owner or lessee of the premises, by virtue of which that other person receives the rents or other payments: 1985 Act, s.398(6), as to be amended by the Housing Act 1996, s.79(2). If received through an agent or trustee, the agent or trustee is also a person managing the HMO: *ibid.*

Index of defined expressions: Chapter IV

91. In this Chapter the expressions listed below are defined by or otherwise fall to be construed in accordance with the provisions indicated—

deferred action notice	section 81
dwelling-house	section 90(a)
flat	section 90(a)
flat in multiple occupation	section 90(b)
house in multiple occupation	section 90(b)
local housing authority	section 101
owner	
–in relation to a dwelling-house or flat	section 90(a)
–in relation to a house or flat in multiple occupation	section 90(b)
person managing (a house or flat in multiple occupation)	section 90(b)
prescribed	section 101
unfit for human habitation	section 97

Chapter V

Supplementary Provisions

Contributions by Secretary of State

Contributions by the Secretary of State

92.—(1) The Secretary of State may pay contributions to local housing authorities towards such expenditure incurred by them under this Part as he may determine.

(2) The rate or rates of the contributions, the calculation of the expenditure to which they relate and the manner of their payment shall be such as may be determined by the Secretary of State with the consent of the Treasury.

(3) A determination under subsection (1) or (2)—

(a) may be made generally or with respect to a particular local housing authority or description of authority, including a description framed by reference to authorities in a particular area, and

(b) may make different provision in relation to different cases or descriptions of case.

(4) Contributions under this section shall be payable subject to such conditions as to records, certificates, audit or otherwise as the Secretary of State may, with the approval of the Treasury, impose.

(5) If, before the declaration of a renewal area, a local housing authority are satisfied that the rate of contributions which, in accordance with a determination under subsection (2), would otherwise be applicable to the authority will not be adequate, bearing in mind the action they propose to take with regard to the area, they may, before making the declaration, apply to the Secretary of State for contributions at a higher rate in respect of that area.

(6) An application under subsection (5) shall be made in such form and shall contain such particulars as the Secretary of State may determine; and, if

such an application is made, the authority shall not declare the area concerned to be a renewal area until the application is approved, refused or withdrawn.

(7) If an application under subsection (5) is approved, the Secretary of State may pay contributions under subsection (1) in respect of the area concerned at such higher rate as he may determine under subsection (2).

DEFINITIONS

"local housing authority": s.101.
"renewal area": s.101.

GENERAL NOTE

This section provides for central government subsidy to be provided by the Secretary of State, with the consent of the Treasury, which may be general, specific or differential between types of scheme, or different categories of authority, including by reference to parts of the country. The express power for authorities to apply for a higher level of subsidy in respect of a renewal area (pending the outcome of which the renewal area is not to be declared: subs. (6)), to be found in subs. (5), corresponds to the provision made by s.99 of the Local Government and Housing Act 1989, governing subsidy for renewal areas generally.

Recovery of contributions

93.—(1) Where the Secretary of State has paid contributions under section 92 to a local housing authority, he may recover from the authority such amount as he determines to be appropriate in respect of repayments of grant under this Part.

(2) For the purposes of this section—

(a) a "grant" includes the cost of scheme works for a group repair scheme (see section 62(1)), and
(b) "repayment of grant" includes the payment to the authority of the balance of the cost (see section 69(3)) by assisted participants in such a scheme.

(3) The amount shall be calculated by reference to the amount appearing to the Secretary of State to represent his contribution to—

(a) grants in respect of which repayments have been made to the authority, or
(b) grants in respect of which repayments could have been recovered if reasonable steps had been taken by the authority,

together with an appropriate percentage of any interest received by the authority, or which would have been received if reasonable steps had been taken by the authority.

(4) The question what steps it would have been reasonable for the authority to take shall be determined by the Secretary of State.

In determining whether the authority took reasonable steps, the Secretary of State may consider whether the authority properly exercised its discretion not to demand repayment of grant or to demand payment of a lesser sum.

DEFINITIONS

"local housing authority": s.101.

GENERAL NOTE

This is a new power, designed to encourage enforcement of grant conditions (defined to include reduced contributions to group repair schemes under Chap. II—see subs. (2)): see the *Explanatory Paper*, *The Future of Private Housing Renewal Programmes*, June 1995, linked to the White Paper, *Our Future Housing*—see Introduction to Pt. I, above. It empowers the Secretary of State to recover subsidy under s.92 where grants have been or could have been recovered by an authority, for breach of condition (see ss.45–52, and 70 and 71, above): subs. (2). The recoupment may be together with the interest which has been received or could have been charged by the authority: *ibid*.

The question of what steps it would have been reasonable for the authority to take, when deciding recoupment on the ground of repayment and interest which an authority have not, but could have, claimed, is described (subs. (3)) as one for the Secretary of State, which may be considered to pre-empt challenge that it is extremely unlikely would in any event have been successful, but will still have to be determined properly, within the usual principles of administrative law, including the requirements of fairness, *i.e.* to give the authority forewarning of what he is minded to consider reasonable and an opportunity to comment (see notes to ss.5, 13, 34, above).

This power is independent of the right of the Secretary of State to recoup any overpayment of subsidy on other grounds, *e.g.* error of law or mistake of fact: see *R. v. Secretary of State for the Environment, ex p. Camden L.B.C.* (1995) 28 H.L.R. 321, Q.B.D. In such a case, which will be based on the principle of restitution (unjust enrichment), the Secretary of State may deduct the amount from a subsequent payment of subsidy (*Auckland Harbour Board v. R.* [1924] A.C. 318, P.C.), although the defence of "change of position" may be available: *Lipkin Gorman v. Karpnale* [1991] 2 A.C. 548, H.L. If it is raised as a defence to a recoupment by way of deduction, it is a matter for the Secretary of State whether or not he accepts it; *he* is not obliged to refer it to a court to be tested, although the authority could still do so (see *Camden*).

Consent of the Secretary of State

Consent of the Secretary of State

94. The consent of the Secretary of State for the purposes of—

(a) section 45(4)(b), 46(4) or 47(4) (consent to waiver of liability to repay renovation grant, common parts grant or HMO grant on disposal), or

(b) section 34(6)(b), 44(3)(a), 51 or 52 (conditions imposed with consent of Secretary of State),

may be given either generally or in relation to any one or more specified authorities or descriptions of authority or in relation to particular cases or descriptions of case.

Parsonages, charities, etc.

Parsonages, charities, etc.

95.—(1) The provisions of Chapter I (main grants) mentioned below do not apply to—

(a) an application for a grant in respect of glebe land or the residence house of an ecclesiastical benefice, or

(b) an application for a grant made by a charity or on behalf of a charity by the charity trustees of the charity.

(2) Those provisions are—

(a) sections 7 to 11 (conditions for application for renovation grant);

(b) sections 19, 21 and 22 (conditions for application for disabled facilities grant);

(c) sections 25 and 26 (conditions for application for HMO grant).

(3) In considering under section 31 the amount (if any) of the grant where the applicant is a charity or the application is in respect of glebe land, the local housing authority shall have regard, in addition to the matters mentioned in that section, to any obligation or practice on the part of the applicant to let dwellings at a rent less than that which could be obtained on the open market.

(4) In Chapter II (group repair schemes), in section 64(2) (persons eligible to participate in group repair scheme as assisted participants), the requirement in paragraph (a) that a person give an owner-occupation certificate or a certificate of intended letting does not apply if—

(a) the person concerned is a charity or the trustee of a charity, or

(b) the dwelling is the residence house of an ecclesiastical benefice;

and the requirement in paragraph (b) that a person give a certificate of future occupation does not apply if the person concerned is a charity or the trustee of a charity.

(5) In Chapter III (home repair assistance), section 77(1)(c) (condition that applicant have owner's interest or tenancy) does not apply to an application by an individual in respect of glebe land or the residence house of an ecclesiastical benefice.

(6) In this section "charity" does not include a registered social landlord but otherwise has the same meaning as in the Charities Act 1993.

GENERAL NOTE

This section disapplies occupation certificates and conditions in the stated cases.

"Charity" does not include a registered social landlord under Pt. I of the Housing Act 1996. It means any institution—corporate or not—established for charitable purposes, and which is subject to the control of the High Court (in the exercise of its jurisdiction over charities); Charities Act 1993 (c. 10), s.96(1). Of the four principal categories of charity (*Income Tax Special Purposes Commissioners v. Pemsel* [1891] A.C. 531, H.L.)—for the relief of poverty, for the advancement of education, for the advancement of religion, and for other purposes beneficial to the community—it is the last, and in some circumstances the first, which will be most likely to be relevant under this Act.

Interpretation

Meaning of "reasonable repair"

96. In determining for the purposes of this Part what is "reasonable repair", in relation to a dwelling, house or building, a local housing authority—

(a) shall have regard to the age and character of the dwelling, house or building and the locality in which it is situated, and

(b) shall disregard the state of internal decorative repair.

DEFINITIONS

"dwelling": s.101.

"local housing authority": s.101.

GENERAL NOTE

The definition of reasonable repair by reference to the "age and character of the dwelling, house or building and the locality in which it is situated" is drawn from the case-law on the meaning of "good tenantable repair" in a lease: see *Proudfoot v. Hart* (1890) 25 Q.B.D. 42, see also *Jaquin v. Holland* [1960] 1 W.L.R. 258. There has not been much judicial consideration of what the words actually mean, beyond the oft-cited observation in *Proudfoot* that different standards will apply by reference to "the occupation of a reasonable minded tenant of the class who would be likely to take" a property, so that different standards were to be expected in Grosvenor Square than in Spitalfields.

Fitness for human habitation

97.—(1) Section 604 of the Housing Act 1985 (fitness for human habitation) applies for the purposes of this Part as it applies for the purposes of that Act.

(2) In deciding whether they are satisfied that the carrying out of the relevant works is the most satisfactory course of action in a case where the house or dwelling concerned is unfit for human habitation, the local housing authority shall have regard to any guidance given under section 604A of the Housing Act 1985 and section 85 of this Act.

For that purpose the authority shall treat any guidance given in respect of the serving of a repair notice under section 189(1) of the Housing Act 1985 as guidance given in respect of the completion of the relevant works.

DEFINITIONS

"local housing authority": s.101.

"relevant works": s.2.

GENERAL NOTE

By Housing Act 1985, s.604(1), as substituted by the Local Government and Housing Act 1989, Sched. 9, para. 83, a house is unfit for human habitation if in the opinion of the authority it fails to meet one or more of the following requirements, and by reason of that failure, it is not reasonably suitable for occupation:

"(a) it is structurally stable;
(b) it is free from serious disrepair;
(c) it is free from dampness prejudicial to the health of the occupants (if any);
(d) it has adequate provision for lighting, heating and ventilation;
(e) it has an adequate supply of wholesome water;
(f) there are satisfactory facilities in the dwelling-house for the preparation and cooking of food, including a sink with a satisfactory supply of hot and cold water;
(g) it has a suitably located water-closet for the exclusive use of the occupants (if any);
(h) it has, for the exclusive use of the occupants (if any), a suitably located fixed bath or shower and wash-hand basin each of which is provided with a satisfactory supply of hot and cold water; and
(i) it has an effective system for the draining of foul, waste and surface water".

By *ibid.*, s.604(2), even if a dwelling which is a flat satisfies the foregoing definition, it will still be unfit for human habitation if the building or some part of the building outside of the flat fails to meet one of the following requirements and, by reason of that failure, the flat is not reasonably suitable for occupation:

"(a) the building or part is structurally stable;
(b) it is free from serious disrepair;
(c) it is free from dampness;
(d) it has adequate provision for ventilation; and
(e) it has an effective system for the draining of foul, waste and surface water".

By *ibid.*, s.604(3), s.604(1) applies to a house in multiple occupation by reference to the house itself.

By s.8 of the Landlord and Tenant Act 1985, there is a statutorily implied term that a property will be both put into a state of fitness for human habitation at the commencement of, and kept in such a state during, the tenancy. This, however, applies to lettings at extremely low rents (at their *highest*, £80 p.a. in London and £52 p.a. elsewhere, for lettings from July 6, 1957), and it does not apply at all to a letting for three years or more which is on terms that the tenant put the premises into a condition reasonably fit for human habitation. Unfitness for the purposes of this covenant has the same meaning as it originally had under the Housing Act 1985, s.604, before it was amended by the 1989 Act (Landlord and Tenant Act 1985, s.10):

"In determining for the purposes of this Act whether a house is unfit for human habitation, regard shall be had to its condition in respect of the following matters—

repair,
stability,
freedom from damp,
internal arrangement,
natural lighting,
ventilation,
water supply,
drainage and sanitary conveniences,
facilities for preparation and cooking of food and for the disposal of waste water;

and the house shall be regarded as unfit for human habitation if, and only if, it is so far defective in one or more of those matters that it is not reasonably suitable for occupation in that condition".

Most satisfactory course of action. See notes to s.12, above.

Members of a person's family and connected persons

98.—(1) Section 113 of the Housing Act 1985 (meaning of "members of a person's family") applies in determining whether a person is a member of another's family for the purposes of this Part.

(2) For the purposes of this Part a person is connected with the owner for the time being of a dwelling if—

(a) in a case where personal representatives or trustees are the owner, he is a person who under the will or intestacy or, as the case may be, under the terms of the trust concerned is beneficially entitled to an interest in the dwelling or to the proceeds of sale of the dwelling;
(b) in any other case, he is a member of the family of the owner.

General Note

Section 113 of the Housing Act 1985, defines "member of the family" in term of spouses, persons living together as husband and wife, parents, grandparents, children, grandchildren, siblings, aunts, uncles, nephews and nieces, treating relationships by marriage as if by blood, half blood and whole blood, step-relationships as real and illegitimacy as legitimacy (although this last is a reference otiose in the light of the Family Law Reform Act 1987 (c. 42)).

Cohabitation. It is self-evident that cohabitants can be living together as husband and wife, but that does not mean that every cohabitation so qualifies (nor does homosexual cohabitation so qualify: see *Harrogate B.C. v. Simpson* (1984) 17 H.L.R. 205, C.A.).

Sexual relations are not determinative. In *Adeoso v. Adeoso* [1980] 1 W.L.R. 1535, C.A., it was held that a couple living in a two-room flat (*i.e.* one bedroom and a living room) had to be considered to be living in the same household "as husband and wife", albeit that for months they had not spoken, had communicated only by notes, that each slept in one of the rooms and kept the doors locked, but shared the rent and electricity charge. (This was for the purposes of Domestic Violence and Matrimonial Proceedings Act 1976 (c. 50), s.1(2) and, as such, should be treated with some caution insofar as words must always be read in context).

Whether or not persons are living together as husband and wife is in part a question of intention: in *City of Westminster v. Peart* (1992) 24 H.L.R. 389, C.A., a couple who had reconciled were held not to be living together as husband and wife, on the particular facts of the case including particularly that the defendant had retained another flat.

Under the Rent Acts, it was initially held that a cohabitant could not succeed as a member of the family of a deceased tenant: see *Brock v. Wollams* [1949] 2 K.B. 388, C.A., *Gammans v. Ekins* [1950] 2 K.B. 328, C.A. In *Hawes v. Evenden* [1953] 1 W.L.R. 1169, C.A., however, a woman who had lived with a man for 12 years without taking his name, and who had two children by him, was held to be a member of his family. In *Dyson Holdings v. Fox* [1976] 1 Q.B. 503, C.A., a stable, 20-year period of cohabitation without marriage, but in which the woman had taken the man's name, was held to be a family relationship, having regard to changing popular meaning of the word "family".

This last approach was rejected in *Helby v. Rafferty* [1979] 1 W.L.R. 13, C.A., wherein was held that the word family should have the meaning applicable when first used by Parliament; a man, accordingly, was unable to succeed to the tenancy of a woman with whom he had lived for approximately five years, as her lover, sharing expenses, caring for her while she was dying, but neither having taken the other's name. In *Watson v. Lucas* [1980] 1 W.L.R. 1493, C.A., conversely, and considering themselves bound by *Dyson*, the Court of Appeal held that a man who had lived with a woman for nearly 20 years, even although he had never divorced his lawful wife, was a member of her family.

Children. It is unclear whether a *de facto*—but not *de jure*—adopted child can fall within the definition: see *Brock v. Wollams* (above), where this was allowed under the Rent Acts, even though by the time the question arose the child had achieved his majority. As there can be no *de jure* adoption between adults, there can accordingly be no *de facto* such adoption: see *Carega Properties S.A. v. Sharratt* [1979] 1 W.L.R. 928, H.L.

Meaning of "owner" of dwelling

99.—(1) In this Part "owner", in relation to a dwelling, means the person who—

(a) is for the time being entitled to receive from a lessee of the dwelling (or would be so entitled if the dwelling were let) a rent at an annual rate of not less than two-thirds of the net annual value of the dwelling; and

(b) is not himself liable as lessee of the dwelling, or of property which includes the dwelling, to pay such a rent to a superior landlord.

(2) For this purpose the net annual value of a dwelling means the rent at which the dwelling might reasonably be expected to be let from year to year if the tenant undertook to pay all usual tenant's rates and taxes and to bear the cost of repair and insurance and the other expenses, if any, necessary to maintain the dwelling in a state to command that rent.

(3) Any dispute arising as to the net annual value of a dwelling shall be referred in writing for decision by the district valuer.

In this subsection "district valuer" has the same meaning as in the Housing Act 1985.

General Note

See General Note to s.45, above.

Disabled persons

100.—(1) For the purposes of this Part a person is disabled if—

(a) his sight, hearing or speech is substantially impaired,

(b) he has a mental disorder or impairment of any kind, or

(c) he is physically substantially disabled by illness, injury, impairment present since birth, or otherwise.

(2) A person aged eighteen or over shall be taken for the purposes of this Part to be disabled if—

(a) he is registered in pursuance of any arrangements made under section 29(1) of the National Assistance Act 1948 (disabled persons' welfare), or

(b) he is a person for whose welfare arrangements have been made under that provision or, in the opinion of the social services authority, might be made under it.

(3) A person under the age of eighteen shall be taken for the purposes of this Part to be disabled if—

(a) he is registered in a register of disabled children maintained under paragraph 2 of Schedule 2 to the Children Act 1989, or

(b) he is in the opinion of the social services authority a disabled child as defined for the purposes of Part III of the Children Act 1989 (local authority support for children and their families).

(4) In this Part the "social services authority" means the council which is the local authority for the purposes of the Local Authority Social Services Act 1970 for the area in which the dwelling or building is situated.

(5) Nothing in subsection (1) above shall be construed as affecting the persons who are to be regarded as disabled under section 29(1) of the National Assistance Act 1948 or section 17(11) of the Children Act 1989 (which define disabled persons for the purposes of the statutory provisions mentioned in subsections (2) to (4) above).

General Note

The social services authority are the authority having responsibility under the Local Authority Social Services Act 1970 (c. 42), which means a London borough council or the Common Council of the City of London or the Council of the Isles of Scilly, in England, in the area of a unitary authority that authority, and otherwise, in a metropolitan county the district council, and in a non-metropolitan county the county council and, in Wales the county or county borough council: the Local Government Acts 1972 and 1992; 1970 Act (as amended), s.1—s.98(4).

Minor definitions: Part I

101. In this Part—

"dwelling" means a building or part of a building occupied or intended to be occupied as a separate dwelling, together with any yard, garden, outhouses and appurtenances belonging to it or usually enjoyed with it;

"elderly" means aged 60 years or over;

"house in multiple occupation" has the same meaning as in Part VII of the Local Government and Housing Act 1989;

"housing action trust" means a housing action trust established under Part III of the Housing Act 1988 and includes any body established by order under section 88 of the Housing Act 1988;

"improvement" includes alteration and enlargement;

"introductory tenancy" and "introductory tenant" have the same meaning as in Chapter I of Part V of the Housing Act 1996;

"local authority" and "local housing authority" have the same meaning as in the Housing Act 1985;
"long tenancy" has the meaning assigned by section 115 of that Act;
"new town corporation" has the same meaning as in the Housing Act 1985 and includes any body established by order under paragraph 7 of Schedule 9 to the New Towns Act 1981;
"owner", in relation to a dwelling, has the meaning given by section 99, and, in relation to a house in multiple occupation, has the same meaning as in Part XI of the Housing Act 1985;
"owner's interest", in relation to any premises, means—
(a) an estate in fee simple absolute in possession, or
(b) a term of years absolute of which not less than five years remain unexpired at the date of the application,
whether held by the applicant alone or jointly with others;
"partner", in relation to a person, means that person's spouse or a person other than a spouse with whom he or she lives as husband or wife;
"prescribed" means prescribed by regulations made by the Secretary of State;
"registered social landlord" has the same meaning as in Part I of the Housing Act 1996;
"renewal area" has the same meaning as in Part VII of the Local Government and Housing Act 1989;
"secure tenancy" and "secure tenant" have the same meaning as in Part IV of the Housing Act 1985;
"statutory tenancy" and "statutory tenant" mean a statutory tenancy or statutory tenant within the meaning of the Rent Act 1977 or the Rent (Agriculture) Act 1976;
"tenancy" includes a sub-tenancy and an agreement for a tenancy or sub-tenancy;
"tenant" includes a sub-tenant and any person deriving title under the original tenant or sub-tenant;
"urban development corporation" has the same meaning as in the Housing Act 1985 and includes any body established by order under section 165B of the Local Government, Planning and Land Act 1980.

GENERAL NOTE

For the main definitions, see as follows:
Notes to s.1, above—dwelling, house in multiple occupation, improvement, local housing authority;
Notes to s.3, above—housing action trust, local authority, new town corporation, urban development corporation;
Notes to s.7, above—owner's interest, tenancy, tenant;
Notes to s.8, above—long tenancy;
Notes to s.10, above—renewal area;
Notes to s.14, above—statutory tenancy;
Notes to s.25, above—owner of HMO;
Notes to s.45, above—owner;
Notes to s.47, above—registered social landlord;
Notes to s.98, above—living together as husband and wife.

Transitional and consequential provisions

Transitional provisions

102.—(1) The provisions of Chapters I to III of this Part have effect in place of Part VIII of the Local Government and Housing Act 1989 (grants towards cost of improvements and repairs, etc.).

(2) Subject as follows, the provisions of that Part continue to apply to applications for grant of the descriptions mentioned in section 101 of that Act made before the commencement of this Part.

(3) Sections 112 and 113 of that Act (which require a local housing authority to approve certain grant applications) do not apply to an application under that Part made after 2nd February 1996 which has not been approved or refused before the commencement of this Part, unless—

(a) the six month period under section 116(1) of that Act (period within which applicant to be notified of decision) has elapsed before commencement, or

(b) the works were begun on or before 2nd February 1996—

(i) in an emergency, or

(ii) in order to comply with a notice under section 189, 190 or 352 of the Housing Act 1985.

(4) An application to which section 112 or 113 of the Local Government and Housing Act 1989 would have applied but for subsection (3) above shall be dealt with after the commencement of this Part as if those sections were omitted from Part VIII of that Act.

(5) The above provisions do not affect the power conferred by section 150(4) to make transitional provision and savings in relation to the commencement of this Part, including provision supplementary or incidental to the above provisions.

Supplementary and incidental provision may, in particular, be made adapting the provisions of Part VIII of that Act in the case of applications to which section 112 or 113 would have applied but for the above provisions.

General Note

This section contains the transitional provisions which effectively terminate rights to grants under Pt. VIII of the Local Government and Housing Act 1989—including the broader range of mandatory grants available thereunder. The provisions of this Part are expected to be brought into force "about 2 months after Royal Assent" (D.o.E. letter to Chief Executives of local authorities and the Town Clerk of the City of London, February 2, 1996). The former provisions will, however, continue to apply *if either*

(i) the application was made before February 2, 1996 (when the original Bill was introduced), *or*

(ii) the application was made after February 2, 1996 (but before the commencement of this Part), and this Part is brought into force after August 2, 1996, and the application had not been determined, in accordance with the six month requirement under s.116 of the 1989 Act, corresponding to s.34(1), above, *or*

(iii) the application was made after February 2, 1996, (but before the commencement of this Part), but the works were commenced on or before February 2, 1996 (*i.e. pre*-application, *cf.* above, s.29) because of an emergency, or in order to comply with a notice under ss.189, 190 of the Housing Act 1985 (see notes to s.12, above) or under *ibid.*, s.352 (see notes to s.17, above).

Where an application not thus permitted to continue *post*-commencement has not been determined by the time this Part commences, it continues subject to the conditions of Pt. VIII of the 1989 Act *without* the benefit of ss.112 and 113, *i.e.* those provisions which render some applications mandatory. Such applications will be treated as discretionary applications instead (see DOE letter, above). The letter continued:

"Local authorities should inform grant applicants of the detail and timescale of the proposed changes making clear that they are subject to Parliament's approval. It is for authorities to decide how to ensure those who have already received initial enquiry forms and other information on the current regime are notified of the possible changes. For example an authority may take the view that it is sufficient to outline the changes as a Public Notice in two or more local newspapers. Another approach might be for an authority that has been in correspondence with people seeking grant assistance to write to notify them of the possible changes".

This (understandably) begs the questions which may well yet arise, in relation to applicants under the 1989 Act for mandatory grants, as to any entitlement to damages either for non-compliance with this suggestion or for other action which may have been taken in the past which may be construable as designed to deter applicants (in extreme cases, even to mislead them as to entitlement, albeit almost certainly only by omission), so that they at no time came within

Pt. VIII of the 1989 Act, or, of definition, within these transitional provisions. (See also Introduction to Pt. I, above.)

The former omission is unlikely to lead to redress—amounting to no more than a non-statutory suggestion in relation to prospective legislation (at a later rather than earlier stage in the life of a Parliament, so that some may legitimately and reasonably have considered that it was unlikely to complete its passage). Omission at an earlier time, when only the 1989 Act fell to be considered (without the prospect of this legislation), is also unlikely to lead to redress, reflecting no breach of statutory duty (*e.g.* to publicise or promote grants, *cf.* Social Security and Housing Benefits Act 1982, s.31—the only relevant duty was under the Housing Act 1985, s.605, at least annually to *consider* what action to take under Pt. VIII of the 1989 Act, as, now the duty extends to grants under this Part [see Sched. 1, para. 10, below]. The position *may* also be different in a renewal area, under Pt. VII of the 1989 Act, where the authority have a duty to provide an information and advice service to residents and owners of property in the area "who wish to carry out works to housing accommodation": 1989 Act, s.91).

Communications with individual applicants which were somewhat more active in their intentions to deter (if any), however, *may* be in a somewhat different category (*cf. X v. Bedfordshire C.C.* [1995] 2 A.C. 633, H.L. The decision in *Curran v. Northern Ireland Co-Ownership Housing Association* [1987] 1 A.C. 817; 19 H.L.R. 318, H.L.—see notes to ss.37, 44, above—would not seem to have any bearing on this question).

Consequential amendments: Part I

103. The enactments mentioned in Schedule 1 have effect with the amendments specified there which are consequential on the provisions of this Part.

PART II

CONSTRUCTION CONTRACTS

INTRODUCTION

Part II of this Act stemmed from the Final Report produced by Sir Michael Latham in July 1994 entitled "*Constructing the Team*" (H.M.S.O. publication). This was a joint government and industry review of procurement and contractual arrangements in the U.K. construction industry. Sir Michael Latham had commenced work on the Review in September 1993. The terms of reference for the Review involved a consideration of:

(i) Current procurement and contractual arrangements; and
(ii) Current roles, responsibilities and performance of the participants, including the client.

A principle recommendation of the Report was that the industry should only use standard form contracts. Latham specifically recommended the use of the *New Engineering Contract* (NEC) published by Thomas Telford Services Ltd for the Institution of Civil Engineers (now in its second edition and renamed, the *Engineering and Construction Contract*) but recognised the need for the continuance of the standard forms of contract published by the Joint Contracts Tribunal (JCT) and its civil engineering counterpart, the Conditions of Contract Standing Joint Committee (CCSJC), provided that they were amended in accordance with the principles of a modern contract listed in Chap. 5.18 of the Report. These included matters such as adjudication; "secure trust fund routes of payment"; assessment of interim payments by methods other than monthly valuations; and incentives for exceptional performance. If the standard forms were amended in accordance with these principles, it was the Reviewer's opinion that the use of standard forms would increase. However, he went further:

> "All parties in the construction process should then be encouraged to use those Standard Forms without amendment. To aid confidence and promote the use of such forms, their central provisions should be underpinned by legislation. This might best be done by a 'Construction Contracts Bill' which extended, *inter alia*, unfair contracts legislation".

Where one of the standard forms (including sub-contracts) is used (i.e. NEC, JCT and CCSJC contracts), the Reviewer recommended that the legislation should declare unfair or invalid certain actions. These included:

(i) Attempts to amend/delete sections relating to times and conditions of payment including a right of interest for late payment;
(ii) Denial or frustration of the right of immediate adjudication where it had been requested by a party;
(iii) Refusal to implement an adjudicator's decision;
(iv) The exercise of rights of set-off without advance notification and without giving specific reasons for the proposed deduction(s) and not being prepared to go to adjudication and accept the result thereof;

(v) Setting-off monies in respect of any contract other than the one in progress.

Recognising that the industry would continue to use bespoke forms, the Reviewer further recommended that the legislation should be extended to all construction contracts. Furthermore, clauses in bespoke forms which have the "*effect of introducing pay-when-paid conditions should be expressly declared unfair and invalid*" (Chap 8.10).

Insolvency Protection

The Reviewer also strongly recommended that "*mandatory trust funds for payment*" should apply to all construction work governed by "*formal conditions of contract*". This would require both public and private sector clients to deposit monies in a trust fund at the beginning of each payment period. In the event of insolvency of the main contractor, payments would be made out of the trust fund directly to sub-contractors. Similarly, if the client failed, payments would be made out of the fund to the contractor. The same arrangement would also cover retention monies.

In this context, the Reviewer advocated the reversal of the House of Lords' decision in *British Eagle International Airlines v. Compagnie Nationale Air France* [1975] 1 W.L.R. 758. Although this case was concerned with the operation of a clearing-house scheme for airline ticket sales, it has been generally assumed that its effect is to rule out direct payments from clients to sub-contractors in the event of the insolvency of a main contractor (*Joo Yee Construction Pte (in liquidation) v. Diethelm Industries Pte* (1991) 7 Const. L.J. 53; In *Re Right Time Construction Co. (in liquidation)* (1990) 52 B.L.R. 117; *B. Mullan & Sons (Contractors) v. John Ross and Malcolm London* (1996) C.I.L.L. 1149; but see *Glow Heating v. Eastern Health Board* (1992) 8 Const. L.J. 56).

Construction Liability

The Reviewer finally recommended for inclusion in a Construction Contracts Bill a package of measures to reform the law on liability in the construction industry including the introduction of compulsory latent defects insurance. These included;

(i) Introduction of a system of proportionate liability in place of joint and several liability;

(ii) A single limitation period of 10 years to commence from the date of practical completion or "*effective occupation*".

(iii) The transfer of a client's contractual rights where all or any part of a project is transferred by the client to a purchaser or tenant.

The Reviewer proposed that the liability period should be underwritten by compulsory latent defects insurance for 10 years from completion of the works. This would apply to all new commercial, retail and industrial building work.

The Government's Position

The Department of the Environment (DoE) launched a consultation exercise in mid-1995 to gauge reaction to its proposals for incorporating Latham's recommendations in legislation. In its consultation paper, "Fair Construction Contracts", the DoE stated: "The reform of current contractual relations is ... central to the competitiveness of the industry in both the short and long term".

In the consultation paper, the DoE concluded that the industry's standard forms of contract (or packages of standard forms) could be given statutory recognition after taking into account, "the presence, fairness and adequacy" of the terms dealing with:

(i) dispute resolution
(ii) right of set-off
(iii) prompt payment
(iv) protection against insolvency.

The DoE was of the view that little could be done to curb the use of bespoke contracts.

Furthermore, the Government was prepared to legislate only in respect of those matters on which there was a broad industry consensus and for which there was a workable and practical legislative solution.

Part II was drafted following the responses to the DoE's consultation exercise and further consultation with industry representative organisations.

During this process it was generally recognised that statutory approval for certain standard forms could have the opposite effect by encouraging the use of bespoke contracts. Therefore, any statutory requirements would have to apply to all forms of contract. This would necessitate a statutory mechanism for ensuring that such requirements were part of all contracts in the event of non-compliance with the statute. The result was the Secretary of State's Scheme for Construction Contracts (see below).

What is Omitted from Part II of the Act?

Construction Liability

The recommendations in relation to statutory reform of liability law for construction and compulsory latent defects insurance were not included in Pt. II. Concerns about the implications for ring-fencing construction (as far as the reform of liability law was concerned) proved a formidable obstacle to the inclusion of the Reviewer's recommendations in legislation.

A consultation paper issued by the Department of Trade and Industry in early 1996: "*Feasibility Investigation of Joint and Several Liability*" (carried out by the Law Commission), concluded that the rule on joint and several liability should be retained. The DTI will be issuing a further paper following responses to its consultation paper.

The Law Commission is currently undertaking a comprehensive review of the law relating to limitation periods with a view to its simplification and rationalisation (item 3 in the Law Commission's 6th programme of law reform). A consultation paper is likely to be published in the early part of 1997. Also the Law Commission has recently published its Report, "*Privity of Contract: Contracts for the Benefit of Third Parties*" (Law Commission Paper No.242, Cmd 3329). The Report includes a draft Bill which may go some way towards enabling third parties (such as purchasers or tenants) to acquire rights under construction contracts or professional terms of engagement.

In the absence of any statutory ring-fencing for construction liability, the proposal for compulsory latent defects insurance fell by the wayside, but, in any event, there was considerable reluctance to give statutory legitimacy to existing policies which, in the opinion of some industry bodies, were very limited in scope.

Trust Funds

A failure on the part of construction industry representative bodies to agree on a suitable statutory framework for setting up trust funds was a barrier to the Government's preparedness to legislate on trust funds. But there was also reluctance by the Government to embrace trust funds primarily because of its unwillingness to disturb the well-established rules relating to the distribution of an insolvent's assets. It was also for this reason that the Government refused to legislate to overturn the perceived effect of the *British Eagle* decision so far as the construction industry was concerned. This was in spite of the fact that there already exists a statutory precedent in s.159 of the Companies Act 1989 (c. 40) for exempting the rules of distribution of an insolvent's assets. The exemption applies to schemes operated by investment exchanges and finance clearing houses in relation to the settlement of debts arising under market contracts.

> "The concept of trust funds is contentious in the construction industry ... There are several problems. The first is that trust funds may fundamentally alter the cash flow of contractors in that sums of money will have to be set aside regularly to maintain and to replenish the fund, and they will therefore be unusable while they are in the fund. That is a prospect which is attractive neither to clients nor to most contractors simply because it is expensive to have considerable sums of money lying idle. The construction industry always has considerable cash flow difficulties and if one locks away a certain slice of cash into a trust fund that may exacerbate the difficulties with which businesses have to deal.
>
> The Government are not convinced that trust funds are consistent with well established practice in respect of insolvency. Parliament has agreed an order of creditors if a company is liquidated under the Insolvency Acts. Trust funds would change that order by ring-fencing payments owed on construction contracts from the main assets of the insolvent company. That may be very convenient for the unsecured creditors who are on construction contracts but it would be very much less acceptable to secured creditors who are claiming on a depleted stock of assets." (*per* Earl Ferrers, Government spokesman, H.L. Committee Stage: *Hansard*, H.C. Vol. 570, col. 1921 1–2).

Interest on Late Payment

Although there was industry agreement on the inclusion of a right of interest for late payment, the Government—reflecting the views of the Confederation of British Industry—has always refrained from making this compulsory for any sector of British industry.

Cross-Contract Set-off

Cross-contract set-off is not expressly forbidden by Pt. II of the Act—again, this reflects the fact that there was no industry agreement on this point. The Government was, no doubt, also concerned about losing Crown set-off rights by which a Government Department is enabled to set-off monies against a contractor in respect of outstanding claims against that contractor from other Departments.

Synopsis of the Act

Scope

The Act applies to construction contracts involving the carrying out of "construction operations". Much of the core of construction activity is included within the definition section—s.105—but some construction activity is excluded and some is not included at all. The main express exclusions are:

(i) Extraction of oil, natural gas and minerals and any works incidental thereto;
(ii) Supply and installation of plant for the process industries, e.g. plant for the processing of chemicals, pharmaceuticals, oil, gas, food and drink, etc.;
(iii) Off-site fabrication or manufacture of building/engineering components/equipment, etc.; and of components for systems of heating, power supply, ventilation, communications etc.;
(iv) Making, installation and repair of artistic works, e.g. sculptures.

Construction of dwellings which the other contracting party occupies or intends to occupy is specifically excluded. It was never the intention to include such work but the exclusion does not extend to the construction of speculative housing developments.

The Act applies only where the agreement for construction operations is in writing but this requirement is widely defined. Thus, if the parties orally agree on work to be done and the agreement incorporates one of the industry's standard forms of contract, this would be sufficient to satisfy the Act.

Payment

There are seven elements to the payment provisions:

(i) A statutory right to payment by instalments;
(ii) Contracts to have an "*adequate mechanism*" for determining what and when payments become due;
(iii) Contracts to specify period for discharge of due payments;
(iv) Contracts to provide for giving of notice specifying the amount of the instalment payment and the basis of the calculation;
(v) Statutory restrictions on rights to withhold monies;
(vi) Statutory right of suspension for non-payment;
(vii) Restrictions on use of pay-when-paid provisions.

Dispute Resolution

The adjudication provisions in Pt. II of the Act were the subject of intense debate during the Bill's passage through Parliament. Under s.108 a party has a "*right to refer a dispute arising under the contract*" to an adjudicator in accordance with the procedure in s.108(2). Much of that debate arose because the Government and the industry were at cross-purposes as to the meaning of "adjudication". Initially, the Government seemed to regard it as a form of "fast-track" arbitration with the adjudicator having the power to issue a final award. The industry regarded it a "stop-gap" procedure for dealing with disputes quickly and cheaply without a forensic inquiry involving legal representation and the paraphernalia associated with arbitral or court proceedings. Adjudicators' decisions should reflect soundly-rooted commercial commonsense rather than any detailed application of technical legal principle.

It remains to be seen whether the courts will adopt a similar view rather than being over-anxious to overturn an adjudicator's decision on the grounds that he has erred in applying the law. The statutory procedure for adjudication only provides a very basic framework. Contracts should be drafted to steer the courts in the direction desired by the parties.

"Where parties have agreed on machinery ... for the resolution of disputes, it is not for the court to intervene and replace its own process for the contractual machinery agreed by the parties" (*per* Dunn L.J. in *Northern Regional Health Authority v. Derek Crouch Construction Co.* ([1984] Q.B. 644).

Lord Ackner's contribution to the debate at Report Stage in the House of Lords, no doubt, reflected the construction industry's view of adjudication:

"What I have always understood to be required by the adjudication process was a quick, enforceable interim decision which lasted until practical completion when, if not acceptable, it would be the subject matter of arbitration or litigation. That was a highly satisfactory process. It came under the rubric of 'pay now argue later', which was a sensible way of dealing expeditiously and relatively inexpensively with disputes which might hold up the completion of important contracts" (*Hansard*, H.L. Vol. 571, cols. 989, 990).

In fact, precedents already exist in the standard forms of building sub-contract used with the main contract forms published by the Joint Contracts Tribunal. Adjudication in these sub-contracts is confined to set-off disputes but other standard forms of contract in the industry have made provision for adjudication on a wider variety of matters. These include the Supplementary Provisions to the Standard Form of Building Contract with Contractors' Design (1981) published by the Joint Contracts Tribunal, forms published by the Association of Consulting Architects and, also, the *Engineering and Construction Contract*.

Prior to the Committee Stage in the House of Lords, the Government issued draft proposals for the *Scheme for Construction Contracts*. The Scheme is a default mechanism to be incorporated in the contract if there was no contractual procedure to adjudicate disputes. Unfortunately, these proposals generated more heat than light since they tended to confuse adjudication with arbitration. Thus it was stated that, "an adjudicator's award, unless expressly provisional, shall be final and binding". Matters were not helped by the reference in the Bill (now s.108(6) of the Act) to the possibility that the Scheme would apply the provisions of the Arbitration Act 1996 (c. 23) (albeit "with such adaptations and modifications as appear to the Minister making the scheme to be appropriate").

The essential difference between adjudication and arbitration is that the former does not involve a final disposal of the dispute between the parties. In *A Cameron v. John Mowlem and Co.* (1990) 25 Con L.R. 11, the Court of Appeal had to deal with a dispute over the enforceability of an adjudicator's award under the set-off provisions of DOM/1 (the standard domestic sub-contract for use with the Standard Form of Building Contract 1980 published by the Joint Contracts Tribunal). The Court had to consider an application under s.26 of the Arbitration Act 1950 (c. 27) for leave to enforce the decision of an adjudicator in the same manner as a judgment of the court. Section 26 allows enforcement only of an "award on an arbitration agreement". The Court rejected the application and upheld the first instance decision of H.H. Judge Esyr Lewis Q.C. that, "the adjudicator ... does not perform an arbitral function and does not make any final award definitive of the parties' rights". Since the sub-contract provided that the adjudicator's decision was binding until final determination of the dispute by an arbitrator, the Court held that, "The decision has an ephemeral and subordinate character which, in our view, makes it impossible for the decision to be described as an award on an arbitration agreement. The structure of the sub-contract is against that conclusion" (*per* Mann L.J. at p.25).

However, in Ord. 14 proceedings, the courts have been prepared to enforce the award of an adjudicator even though it is of "an ephemeral and subordinate character" (see, e.g. *Drake & Scull Engineering v. McLaughlin and Harvey* (1992) 60 B.L.R. 102; *Mellowes PPG v. M Fitzpatrick & Sons* (1991) (unreported)).

Following intense industry lobbying, the Bill underwent substantial surgery. The original wording of the Bill referred to "resolution" by an adjudicator. The use of the word "resolution" could have been construed as giving finality to the process but the word was removed from the Bill during its passage in the Commons. The matter is now put beyond doubt by s.108(3) which was inserted as a Government amendment. This makes clear that an adjudicator's decision is of temporary effect until finally resolved by agreement of the parties, by arbitration or by the courts. The parties remain free to accept that the adjudicator's decision is final.

As already mentioned, the contractual adjudication procedure required by Pt. II of the Act is fairly minimal; it envisages the adjudicator reaching a decision within 28 days of referral of a dispute although the period can be extended. The contract must provide a timetable to enable an adjudicator to be appointed and disputes to be referred to him within seven days of notification of a dispute. Other provisions in the Act deal with the immunity of the adjudicator and the need for him to act impartially.

The effect of adjudication (as is, no doubt, intended by s.108) will be to substantially reduce the number of disputes going to arbitration, the standard dispute resolution procedure in the industry. Therefore, the decision of an adjudicator will often amount to a final disposal of the dispute in question. The downside is that parties may resort to the courts to overturn an adjudicator's decision probably on unmeritorious procedural or technical grounds—to avoid the waiting for arbitration.

Scheme For Construction Contracts

Both the payment and adjudication provisions (with the exception of ss.111(1) and 112) have a requirement that, in the event that contracts do not conform to the legislation, the Secretary of State's Scheme for Construction Contracts shall apply. As already explained, the proposals for such a Scheme were published for consideration by the House of Lords at Committee Stage but were withdrawn after considerable criticism. A draft Scheme is likely to be published in October 1996 for full industry-wide consultation.

Conclusion

In introducing the legislation at Second Reading in the House of Commons, Robert Jones, the Minister for Construction, Planning & Energy Efficiency, said: "Our aim is to encourage the industry to get its contracts right" (*Hansard*, H.C. Vol. 277, col. 53).

Part II may help to establish benchmarks for commercial activity and shape the culture of the industry particularly at site level where prevailing attitudes often lead to unnecessary conflict and disputes. Sir Michael Latham's conclusion was that standards of commercial dealing in the industry would have to improve so that every participant would have a real stake in the process, thereby promoting teamwork. The Act, whilst implementing a key recommendation in "Constructing the Team", also represents part of a finely-balanced package which has as its primary objective the reduction of construction costs by 30 per cent by the turn of the century.

In the meantime, the Government has undertaken to monitor the legislation to ensure that it is working in practice.

> "Clearly, as time goes on, we shall be able to monitor the success of this legislation. In an industry where contracts are frequently very long, it might take us quite a while to be sure whether or not we have got matters right. If events show that we have missed the mark in significant ways, we will revisit the issue of fair contracts legislation and make the appropriate changes.
>
> However, legislation should not be seen as an end in itself. The Bill is meant only to be a stepping-stone in the drive to build better relationships within the construction industry and to work towards the wider aims outlined by Sir Michael Latham in Constructing the Team" (*per* Lord Lucas, Government spokesman, during final stage of the Bill in the House of Lords: *Hansard*, H.L. Vol. 574, col. 1350).

Commencement

Part II will not be implemented until the Scheme for Construction Contracts has been settled following industry-wide consultation. Therefore, implementation is unlikely to be before May 1, 1997.

Part II will be brought into force on a day appointed by order of the Secretary of State (s.150(3)). The Secretary of State is likely to lay two orders simultaneously before Parliament to vary the definition of "Construction Operations" in s.105 (see s.105(3) and s.106(1)(b)) and to introduce the *Scheme for Construction Contracts* under s.114(1). For technical reasons, it is likely that both orders will have to be approved under the affirmative resolution procedure of each House before Pt. II can come into force. The date of the commencement order for Scotland will not necessarily coincide with that for England and Wales.

Introductory provisions

Construction contracts

104.—(1) In this Part a "construction contract" means an agreement with a person for any of the following—

(a) the carrying out of construction operations;

(b) arranging for the carrying out of construction operations by others, whether under sub-contract to him or otherwise;

(c) providing his own labour, or the labour of others, for the carrying out of construction operations.

(2) References in this Part to a construction contract include an agreement—

(a) to do architectural, design, or surveying work, or

(b) to provide advice on building, engineering, interior or exterior decoration or on the laying-out of landscape,

in relation to construction operations.

(3) References in this Part to a construction contract do not include a contract of employment (within the meaning of the Employment Rights Act 1996).

(4) The Secretary of State may by order add to, amend or repeal any of the provisions of subsection (1), (2) or (3) as to the agreements which are construction contracts for the purposes of this Part or are to be taken or not to be taken as included in references to such contracts.

No such order shall be made unless a draft of it has been laid before and approved by a resolution of each of House of Parliament.

(5) Where an agreement relates to construction operations and other matters, this Part applies to it only so far as it relates to construction operations.

An agreement relates to construction operations so far as it makes provision of any kind within subsection (1) or (2).

(6) This Part applies only to construction contracts which—

(a) are entered into after the commencement of this Part, and

(b) relate to the carrying out of construction operations in England, Wales or Scotland.

(7) This Part applies whether or not the law of England and Wales or Scotland is otherwise the applicable law in relation to the contract.

Definitions

"construction contract": subss. (1), (2) and (3).

General Note

Subs. (1)

A construction contract is a contract for the provision of work and materials but the definition of construction contract has been considerably extended by this Act to include agreements for professional services; for the provision of surveys and reports or the giving of advice as long as they are all related to "construction operations" as defined in s.105.

It is not clear why there is a need for both subss. (1)(b) and 1(c). The essence of both is that it is immaterial that the "construction operations" are procured from others in the contractual chain including, for example, sub-sub-contractors and labour-only contractors. However, subs. (1)(c) is couched in fairly wide terms; it could, for example, apply to employment agencies supplying labour to contractors and sub-contractors.

Subs. (2)

This makes clear that services provided by contractors such as design and advice are within the definition of "construction operations"; in the original draft of the Bill there was some doubt as to whether this was the position.

Subs. (3)

As already indicated, construction contracts will include labour only sub-contracts (where they involve the carrying out of "construction operations"). However, to the chagrin of the Inland Revenue and Contributions Agency, many labour-only sub-contractors are, in fact, engaged under a contract of service rather than for services. Therefore, subs. (3) ensures that employed people are not within the scope of the legislation.

Subs. (4)

The Secretary of State is likely to make an order prior to the commencement date of the Act which will exclude from the definition of "construction contract", contracts entered into under Private Finance Initiative arrangements. It is understood that certain types of private sector agreements will also be excluded. These are likely to include loan agreements for financing "construction operations" and joint venture or partnership agreements for the carrying out of "construction operations" for a third party.

Subs. (5)

It would have been much "cleaner" if the whole agreement was made subject to the Act in the event that only part of it was within the scope of the Act. Where there are disputes it could be difficult to disentangle the subject-matter of a dispute where an element of the work is outside the scope of the Act. For example, a steelwork fabricator enters into an agreement to manufacture off-site certain steelwork. In the same agreement he also provides a design service in relation to the fixing of the steelwork (which is to be carried out by a third party). His design service will be within scope but the off-site fabrication will be outwith the Act (see s.105(2)(d)). In the event of any dispute about the steelwork, it could be difficult to separate issues concerning the design input from those relating to the fabrication and fixing processes.

Subs. (6)

In relation to subs. (6)(a) it should be noted that the Act is likely to apply to works which have started prior to the commencement of Pt. II although the contract is not executed until after Pt. II has taken effect. Normally express or implied acceptance of a bid or tender would create a contract, even though execution of the documentation is much later. It is a matter of construction whether the execution of a formal contract is a necessary pre-requisite to contractual liability.

"It appears to be well settled by the authorities that if the documents or letters relied on as constituting a contract contemplate the execution of a further contract between the parties, it is a question of construction whether the execution of the further contract is a condition of terms of the bargain or whether it is a mere expression of the desire of the parties as to the manner in which the transaction already agreed to will in fact go through. In the former case there is no enforceable contract either because the condition is unfulfilled or because the law does not recognise a contract to enter into a contract. In the latter case there is a binding contract and the reference to the more formal document may be ignored" (*per* Parker J. in *Von Hatzfeldt-Wildenburg v. Alexander* [1912] I Ch 284 at pp.28 8–9; see also *Chillingworth v. Esche* [1924] 1 Ch 978).

Where there is a chain of contracts and sub-contracts, the Act may apply to agreements lower down the chain but not to agreements higher up the chain if they were entered into prior to the date of commencement.

The Act will be extended to Northern Ireland by Order in Council (s.149).

Meaning of "construction operations"

105.—(1) In this Part "construction operations" means, subject as follows, operations of any of the following descriptions—

(a) construction, alteration, repair, maintenance, extension, demolition or dismantling of buildings, or structures forming, or to form, part of the land (whether permanent or not);

(b) construction, alteration, repair, maintenance, extension, demolition or dismantling of any works forming, or to form, part of the land, including (without prejudice to the foregoing) walls, roadworks, power-lines, telecommunication apparatus, aircraft runways, docks and harbours, railways, inland waterways, pipe-lines, reservoirs, water-mains, wells, sewers, industrial plant and installations for purposes of land drainage, coast protection or defence;

(c) installation in any building or structure of fittings forming part of the land, including (without prejudice to the foregoing) systems of heating, lighting, air-conditioning, ventilation, power supply, drainage, sanitation, water supply or fire protection, or security or communications systems;

(d) external or internal cleaning of buildings and structures, so far as carried out in the course of their construction, alteration, repair, extension or restoration;

(e) operations which form an integral part of, or are preparatory to, or are for rendering complete, such operations as are previously described in this subsection, including site clearance, earthmoving, excavation, tunnelling and boring, laying of foundations, erection, maintenance or dismantling of scaffolding, site restoration, landscaping and the provision of roadways and other access works;

(f) painting or decorating the internal or external surfaces of any building or structure.

(2) The following operations are not construction operations within the meaning of this Part—

(a) drilling for, or extraction of, oil or natural gas;

(b) extraction (whether by underground or surface working) of minerals; tunnelling or boring, or construction of underground works, for this purpose;

(c) assembly, installation or demolition of plant or machinery, or erection or demolition of steelwork for the purposes of supporting or providing access to plant or machinery, on a site where the primary activity is—

(i) nuclear processing, power generation, or water or effluent treatment, or

(ii) the production, transmission, processing or bulk storage (other than warehousing) of chemicals, pharmaceuticals, oil, gas, steel or food and drink;

(d) manufacture or delivery to site of—

(i) building or engineering components or equipment,

(ii) materials, plant or machinery, or

(iii) components for systems of heating, lighting, air-conditioning, ventilation, power supply, drainage, sanitation, water supply or fire protection, or for security or communications systems,

except under a contract which also provides for their installation;

(e) the making, installation and repair of artistic works, being sculptures, murals and other works which are wholly artistic in nature.

(3) The Secretary of State may by order add to, amend or repeal any of the provisions of subsection (1) or (2) as to the operations and work to be treated as construction operations for the purposes of this Part.

(4) No such order shall be made unless a draft of it has been laid before and approved by a resolution of each House of Parliament.

DEFINITIONS

"construction operations": subss. (1)(a) to (1)(f).

GENERAL NOTE

Subs. (1)

The base definition of "construction operations" was taken from s.567 of the Income and Corporation Taxes Act 1988 (c. 1). However, a definition which might be appropriate for one piece of legislation is not necessarily appropriate to advance the objectives of another. Since the Act is designed to encourage sound contractual practice, its ambit should, arguably, extend towards a more liberal definition of construction such as that found in *Reg. 2, Construction (Design and Management) Regulations 1994* (S.I. 1994 No. 3140).

Definitional disputes often result in litigation (see, e.g. the volume of litigation over the definition of "factory" in the Factories Act 1961 (c. 34)) but it is to be hoped that the courts will place greater emphasis on overcoming the mischief addressed by the Act rather than being too astute in finding gaps in the definition.

The major change to the definition of "construction operations" in the draft Bill was the inclusion of maintenance which generated much of the debate at Committee Stage in the Commons on subs. (1). The Government was concerned that the inclusion of maintenance would unnecessarily widen the scope of the Act so that it would apply to general maintenance work. Since repair was already included, the Government felt this was sufficient.

The Opposition view was that the exclusion of maintenance would remove a substantial slice of construction activity from the scope of the legislation and could also encourage unnecessary disputes. As the Opposition spokesman for construction, Nick Raynsford, said in Committee, "When does maintenance cease to be maintenance and become a repair?" (House of Commons, Official Report—Standing Committee F: June 13, 1996, col. 279). However, the Act is now likely to apply to contracts such as facilities management contracts where there is an element of building maintenance.

The reference to "fittings forming part of the land" in subs. (1)(c) includes: "Control systems, fire alarms, close circuit television systems, lifts and other such objects ..." (*per* Robert Jones, Minister for Construction, etc., House of Commons, Official Report—Standing Committee F: June 13, 1996, col. 288). In considering whether "fittings" have become a "part of the land", the courts are likely to draw on the wealth of precedent relating to the distinction between fixtures and chattels.

> "materials worked by one into the property of another become part of that property. This is equally true whether it be fixed or moveable property. Bricks built into a wall become part of the house, thread stitched into a coat which is under repair, or planks and nails and pitch worked into a ship under repair, become part of the coat or the ship" (*per* Blackburn J. in *Appleby v. Myers* [1867] L.R. 2 C.D. 651 at p.659).

Subsection (1)(e) is extremely wide: it could include, for example, anything from geotechnical surveys to fitting-out or finishing work. At Committee Stage in the Commons, the Construction Minister opined that subs. (1)(e) would include dredging, exploration work and the provision and relaying of services by utilities although some of the latter work could be regarded as work forming part of the land in subs. (1)(b).

Subs. (2)

Subsection (2) was the most contentious part of s.105 since it excludes matters which, within the industry, are normally considered to be construction activities.

Subsection (2)(c) is an illogical exemption which was achieved through persistent lobbying by an organisation using the unfortunate acronym PILG—Process Industries Latham Group. This body represented the interests of clients in the process industries who maintained that they were not affected by the ills associated with the rest of the construction industry; therefore, the legislation was not relevant to their needs.

During the passage of the Bill the scope of the process plant exemption was significantly reduced.

"I want to make it clear that we do not intend all work on a process engineering site to be excluded from fair contracts provision. We want to exclude only work on the machinery and plant that is highly specific to the process industry, together with work on steelwork that is so intimately associated with that plant and machinery that it could not possibly be reasonably considered apart. To that end, we have made it clear that the steelwork mentioned in the exclusion is only that which relates to support and access ... I repeat that all normal construction activities on a process engineering site will be subject to the provisions of the Bill. That includes building roads, erecting fences, laying foundations, and building offices or factories—even if they are made of steel" (*per* Robert Jones, M.P., Minister for Construction etc., at Committee Stage in the Commons, House of Commons, Official Report—Standing Committee F: June 13, 1996, cols. 301–2).

However, in some instances such as sewerage and power generation plant, the distinction between that which constitutes plant and construction can become fairly blurred. This distinction has been considered by the courts in connection with the legislation relating to capital allowances (now the Capital Allowances Act 1990 (c. 1)). Thus, for example, it has been held that expenditure on an underground sub-station for transforming electricity was not expenditure on plant (*Bradley (Inspector of Taxes) v. London Electricity*, *The Times*, August 1, 1996). The test appears to be whether the structure in question is performing a "plant-like function" (*per* Blackburne J.; see also, e.g., *Schofield v. R & H Hall* (1974) 49 TC 538 where a grain silo was held to be plant).

Rather more surprising is the exclusion of components and materials manufactured off-site in subs. (2)(d) (unless the contract for their supply also provides for their fixing). A substantial amount of construction work is now carried out off-site as a way of reducing construction costs. In fact, much off-site fabrication (not involving a fixing element) is carried out under forms of construction contract/sub-contract generally in use within the industry. The Government's position was that it would be extremely difficult to include bespoke off-site work since there was a risk that this could let in supply contracts for items such as bricks, nails, etc. which were for general use. Nevertheless, the Act will apply to a supply-only contract to the extent that the supplier is also engaged in a "construction operation". For example, if a supplier of a boiler also agrees as part of his contract to test and commission it on installation, this would be for "rendering complete [a construction operation]".

Subss. (3) & (4)

It is likely that the Secretary of State will closely monitor the operation of subss. (1) and (2) to ensure that any significant anomalies or omissions are dealt with fairly speedily (see commentary on s.104(4)).

Provisions not applicable to contract with residential occupier

106.—(1) This Part does not apply—

(a) to a construction contract with a residential occupier (see below), or

(b) to any other description of construction contract excluded from the operation of this Part by order of the Secretary of State.

(2) A construction contract with a residential occupier means a construction contract which principally relates to operations on a dwelling which one of the parties to the contract occupies, or intends to occupy, as his residence.

In this subsection "dwelling" means a dwelling-house or a flat; and for this purpose—

"dwelling-house" does not include a building containing a flat; and

"flat" means separate and self-contained premises constructed or adapted for use for residential purposes and forming part of a building from some other part of which the premises are divided horizontally.

(3) The Secretary of State may by order amend subsection (2).

(4) No order under this section shall be made unless a draft of it has been laid before and approved by a resolution of each House of Parliament.

DEFINITIONS

"dwelling": subs. (2).
"dwelling-house": subs. (2).
"flat": subs. (2).

GENERAL NOTE

Subs. (1)

The Latham Report specifically excluded work on residential premises from the recommendation for legislation on contracts and this was accepted by both Government and the bodies representing the industry. The Act will, however, apply to sub-contracts (e.g. for plumbing, electrical work) sub-let under the main contract with the residential occupier (with regard to subs. (1)(b), see commentary on s.105(3) and 105(4)).

Subs. (2)

In the original draft of the Bill this residential exemption applied where the dwelling "the whole or any part of which is the subject of operations to which the [construction] contract relates" (clause 103(1)). The Government recognised that there was some ambiguity in these words since a party could seek to avoid the legislation by making use of the so-called "penthouse loophole". Thus, for example, if the contract is for an office block with a penthouse on the roof it could be exempt from the Act if the client intends to reside in the penthouse (which was "the subject of operations" under the contract). Such loophole would appear to be closed by the requirement that the construction contract must "principally" relate to operations on a dwelling.

But, there remains a difficulty with the wording of subs. (2). It is a matter of fact whether the residential occupier is in occupation of the dwelling but the difficulty arises from the use of the word "intends". This could mean, for example, that a party could contract for building or structure stating that he intends to use it as a dwelling on completion but subsequently changes his mind and uses it for a commercial purpose.

Provisions applicable only to agreements in writing

107.—(1) The provisions of this Part apply only where the construction contract is in writing, and any other agreement between the parties as to any matter is effective for the purposes of this Part only if in writing.

The expressions "agreement", "agree" and "agreed" shall be construed accordingly.

(2) There is an agreement in writing—

(a) if the agreement is made in writing (whether or not it is signed by the parties),

(b) if the agreement is made by exchange of communications in writing, or

(c) if the agreement is evidenced in writing.

(3) Where parties agree otherwise than in writing by reference to terms which are in writing, they make an agreement in writing.

(4) An agreement is evidenced in writing if an agreement made otherwise than in writing is recorded by one of the parties, or by a third party, with the authority of the parties to the agreement.

(5) An exchange of written submissions in adjudication proceedings or in arbitral or legal proceedings in which the existence of an agreement otherwise than in writing is alleged by one party against another party and not denied by the other party in his response constitutes as between those parties an agreement in writing to the effect alleged.

(6) References in this Part to anything being written or in writing include its being recorded by any means.

General Note

Subs. (1)

Apart from the words "construction contract" in subs. (1) and "adjudication proceedings" in subs. (5), s.107 is the same as s.5 of the Arbitration Act 1996. Under s.5 of the Arbitration Act 1996, Pt. I of that Act only applies where the arbitration agreement is in writing. However, "writing" is defined extremely widely.

The purpose of this section is rather different to that of s.5 of the Arbitration Act 1996. This Act was not intended to catch the myriad informal arrangements entered into between builders, plumbers, electricians, etc., and individual consumers or householders. By contrast s.5 of the Arbitration Act 1996 provides a liberal definition of writing to ensure that as many arbitration agreements as possible are brought within scope so that they are adequately underpinned by the statutory framework.

It is likely that s.107 may catch transactions for which the Act was not intended but an all-embracing definition of writing was probably required in order to reduce the opportunities for avoidance.

Prima facie, contracts partly in writing and partly oral are excluded, since subs. (1) states that the Act applies "only where the construction contract is in writing" (but see notes to subs. (3)).

Subs. (2)

Often construction contracts/sub-contracts are executed after the commencement of the work but they may have retrospective effect (see, *e.g. Trollope & Colls v. Atomic Power Constructions* [1963] 1 W.L.R. 333; *City of Box Hill v. E.W. Tauschke* [1974] V.R. 39).

In any event, subs. (2) does not appear to place any temporal limit on when the written agreement must come into existence. The following exchange took place at Committee Stage in the Commons:

"Mr Raynsford: ... where there is a verbal agreement, work has begun on the site and the written confirmation comes 24 hours later—would the written confirmation be within the terms of clause 106(2)(c) [now s.107(2)(c)]?

Mr. Jones: In the interests of brevity, the answer is yes" (House of Commons Official Report, Standing Committee F, June 18, 1996, col. 318).

Initially, there may be some uncertainty about whether the Act will apply pending the issue of the necessary documentation and acceptance of it by the other party. If work has already commenced on the basis of a letter of intent, such letter may not constitute a contract for the works, in which case the Act will not apply at all (see, e.g. *British Steel Corporation v. Cleveland Bridge and Engineering* [1984] 1 All E.R. 504; *Monk Construction v. Norwich Union Life Assurance Society* (1992) 62 B.L.R. 107).

For the most part, subs. (2) will apply to fairly informal arrangements such as an exchange of letters or a written acceptance of a quote.

Subs. (3)

Thus, if in an oral agreement the parties refer to, for example, the terms of a written quote or to JCT 80 (the Standard Form of Building Contract published by the Joint Contracts Tribunal), this will be sufficient to satisfy the requirement for writing. There is no requirement that the terms of the oral agreement must be found exclusively in the written terms referred to; therefore, the Act may apply to partly oral and partly written contracts.

Furthermore, the written terms may be found in more than one document.

Subs. (4)

Subsection (4) amplifies subs. (2)(c). For example, if the parties reach agreement over the telephone and, with the approval of the other party, the conversation is subsequently noted by one of the parties or by an employee, such note would bring the agreement within the Act. Presumably, if the note did not accurately reflect the agreement, it would not constitute evidence of that agreement but, until this issue is decided, the note would attract the provisions of the Act (provided that the other party had given his authority for the agreement to be recorded).

Subs. (5)

This is a rather more controversial extension of s.107. The effect of subs. (5) is that an oral agreement will be converted into a written agreement if one party alleges an oral agreement (which is not denied by the other) in written submissions in adjudication, arbitral and legal proceedings. It is more likely that such result would only arise in arbitral or legal proceedings rather than adjudication proceedings (unless the parties had orally agreed to have their disputes dealt with by an adjudicatory process similar to that provided for in s.108).

In practice, difficulties could arise here. If the oral agreement has not reflected (as is likely) the requirements of the Act, the Scheme will operate retrospectively with the result that one of the parties might have been in breach of his contract. Consequently, it would be in the interests of both parties to avoid disputes if they wish to preserve their oral agreement. Alternatively, the parties would need to ensure that their oral agreement reflects the requirements of the Act even though it was never intended that the Act would apply to such agreements.

Subs. (6)

The concept of "writing" is further extended to include, for example, oral communications recorded on audio tape (such as that contained in a telephone answering machine) or video tape.

Adjudication

Right to refer disputes to adjudication

108.—(1) A party to a construction contract has the right to refer a dispute arising under the contract for adjudication under a procedure complying with this section.

For this purpose "dispute" includes any difference.

(2) The contract shall—

(a) enable a party to give notice at any time of his intention to refer a dispute to adjudication;

(b) provide a timetable with the object of securing the appointment of the adjudicator and referral of the dispute to him within 7 days of such notice;

(c) require the adjudicator to reach a decision within 28 days of referral or such longer period as is agreed by the parties after the dispute has been referred;

(d) allow the adjudicator to extend the period of 28 days by up to 14 days, with the consent of the party by whom the dispute was referred;

(e) impose a duty on the adjudicator to act impartially; and

(f) enable the adjudicator to take the initiative in ascertaining the facts and the law.

(3) The contract shall provide that the decision of the adjudicator is binding until the dispute is finally determined by legal proceedings, by arbitration (if the contract provides for arbitration or the parties otherwise agree to arbitration) or by agreement.

The parties may agree to accept the decision of the adjudicator as finally determining the dispute.

(4) The contract shall also provide that the adjudicator is not liable for anything done or omitted in the discharge or purported discharge of his functions as adjudicator unless the act or omission is in bad faith, and that any employee or agent of the adjudicator is similarly protected from liability.

(5) If the contract does not comply with the requirements of subsections (1) to (4), the adjudication provisions of the Scheme for Construction Contracts apply.

(6) For England and Wales, the Scheme may apply the provisions of the Arbitration Act 1996 with such adaptations and modifications as appear to the Minister making the scheme to be appropriate.

For Scotland, the Scheme may include provision conferring powers on courts in relation to adjudication and provision relating to the enforcement of the adjudicator's decision.

General Note

Subs. (1)

The most significant aspect of this section is that there is not a mandatory requirement for the parties to refer their disputes to adjudication; rather a party has a statutory right to refer disputes to adjudication. The parties are, therefore, free to use alternative methods of dispute resolution. Another possibility is for the parties to resort to adjudication only for certain types of disputes. A difficult question is whether the statutory right can, by contract, be excluded or waived. Reference should be made to the commentary to s.112 but, in any event, s.108(5) would appear to militate against such exclusion or waiver. If a contract does not conform to the procedure required by s.108(1) (as set out in s.108(2)) or the requirements of ss.108(3) and 108(4), the Scheme will apply. If the statutory right was excluded or waived, the Scheme could not operate and therefore, the implication must be that contracts cannot override the statutory right.

A further difficulty arises when the parties have commenced arbitral or legal proceedings without referring the dispute to adjudication. If one party then decides to exercise his statutory right of adjudication it would appear that the arbitrator or the court would have little choice but to stay the proceedings pending the outcome of the adjudication. The party requesting the adjudication may, however, be penalised in costs for not having made the request before the commencement of the proceedings.

It would have been helpful if s.108 had included a similar provision to s.40 of the Arbitration Act 1996 which requires that: "The parties shall do all things necessary for the proper and expeditious conduct of the arbitral proceedings". Assuming that the adjudication provision in the contract conforms to the requirements of s.108, it may be necessary for contracts to include a similar provision. Without such provision there is a risk that a party could frustrate the procedure by delaying tactics or by simply ignoring it. If there is such a provision, failure by a party to adhere to the procedure would be a breach of contract which could, possibly, be remedied by mandatory injunction to force compliance. But, seeking the aid of the court will have meant that the party practising the non-cooperation will have achieved his aim of delaying matters.

If, on the other hand, an adjudicator decides to act without the involvement of the other party, would that party be bound by his decision? Since adjudication is a statutory right, it would be surprising if a court allowed a party to frustrate the exercise of the right by the simple expedient of pretending that it didn't exist. Again, by way of contrast, s.41(4) of the Arbitration Act 1996 specifically enables the arbitrator to make an award in the absence of any evidence or submissions from one of the parties.

This issue was the subject of an amendment in the House of Lords but the response of the Government spokesman, Lord Lucas, was not entirely convincing:

"If an adjudication procedure is not intended to resolve the disputes which are referred to it and does not require parties to submit to the process and act upon its outcome, it will be defective under the terms of that clause" (*Hansard*, H.L. Vol. 570, col. 1885).

The adjudicator is empowered to deal with disputes "arising under the contract". Therefore, pre-contract matters are likely to be outside his jurisdiction. The following has received judicial consideration within the context of arbitration agreements:

"There is, I suggest, a broad distinction which may be drawn between those clauses which refer to arbitration only, those disputes which may arise regarding the rights and obligations which are created by the contract itself, and other clauses which show an intention to refer some wider class or classes of disputes. This distinction is obviously clear and justified as a matter of law. It may also be one which would be recognised by the parties whose contract it is, for at the very least, by making the contract, they demonstrate their agreement to create a new category of legal rights and obligations, legally enforceable between themselves. Disputes regarding this category may well be described, as a matter of language, as ones arising "under" the contract, and this meaning of that phrase has been authoritatively recognised and established, *e.g.* by the House of Lords in *Heyman v. Darwins* ([1942] 1 All E.R. 337, [1942] A.C. 356) and by the Court of Appeal in *Ashville.* Conversely, if the parties agree to refer disputes arising "in relation to" or "in connection with" their contract, *a fortiori* if the clause covers disputes arising "during the execution of this contract" (*Astro Vencedor Cia Naviera SA v. Mabanaft GmbH, The Damianos* [1971] 2 All E.R. 1301, [1971] 2 Q.B. 588) or in relation to "the work to be carried out hereunder", a common form in construction contracts, then both as a matter of language and of authority, some wider category may be intended". (*per* Evans J. in *Overseas Union Insurance v. A A Mutual International Insurance* [1988] 2 Lloyd's Rep 63 at p.67).

In *Ashville Investments v. Elmer Contractors* (1987) 10 Con L.R. 72, Balcombe L.J. said (at p.93):

"Such a dispute (about mistake leading to rectification) is not as to any matter or thing ... arising *under* the contract ... Similarly, a dispute between the parties as to whether an innocent misrepresentation, or negligent mis-statement, which led Ashville to enter into the contract ... [is not] a dispute as to any matter arising *under* the contract."

In *Fillite (Runcorn) v. Aqua-Lift* (1989) 26 Con L.R. 66, the Court of Appeal held that the words "arising under these heads of agreement" were not wide enough to include claims for negligent mis-statement, negligent misrepresentation under the Misrepresentation Act 1967 (c. 7) or claims arising under a collateral contract. "In my judgment, on the ordinary and natural meaning of words, the phrase 'disputes arising under a contract' is not wide enough to include disputes which do not concern obligations created by or incorporated in that contract" (*per* Slade L.J. at p.76).

It is, of course, up to the parties whether they would wish to extend the adjudicator's jurisdiction to include matters such as mistake, rectification and misrepresentation by expressly including disputes arising in connection with the contract. This was the substance of an Opposition amendment in the House of Commons but it failed to attract the support of the Government. The Government's view was that an extension of the adjudicator's jurisdiction to disputes arising in connection with the contract would cloth the adjudicator with the powers of an arbitrator.

The reference to "difference" in subs. (1) helps to avoid possible delaying tactics by one side, for example, claiming that he is not in dispute because he has not had time to check the veracity or strength of a claim made by the other party. Therefore, to the extent that he has not acceded to the claim, there exists a difference between the parties.

Standard forms of contract in the construction industry generally reserve power to the arbitrator to open up, review and revise architect's or engineer's certificates. It was stated obiter in *Northern Regional Health Authority v. Derek Crouch Construction Co.* [1984] Q.B. 644, that the courts do not have the same power as the arbitrator in this regard (but see *Tarmac Construction v. Esso Petroleum Co.* (1996, (unreported)).

> "Despite the fact that the architect is subject to a duty to act fairly, these powers might be regarded as Draconian and unacceptable if they were not subject to review and revision by a more independent individual. That process is provided for by the arbitration clause. It is, however, a rather special clause. Arbitration is usually no more and no less than litigation in the private sector. The arbitrator is called upon to find the facts, apply the law and grant relief to one or other or both of the parties. Under a JCT arbitration clause (cl. 35), the arbitrator has these powers but he also has power to 'open up, review and revise any certificate, opinion, decision, requirement or notice'. This goes far further than merely entitling him to treat the architect's certificates, opinions, decisions, requirements and notices as inconclusive in determining the rights of the parties. It enables, and in appropriate cases requires, him to vary them and so create new rights, obligations and liabilities in the parties. This is not a power which is normally possessed by any court and again it has a strong element of personal judgment by an individual nominated in accordance with the agreement of the parties" (*per* Sir John Donaldson M.R. at p.670).

Section 43A of the Supreme Court Act 1981 (c. 54) (inserted by s.100 of the Courts and Legal Services Act 1990 (c. 41)) allows the courts to take on the powers of the arbitrator under the arbitration agreement provided both parties consent. The issue is whether an adjudicator would also be able to exercise the power to open-up, review and revise certificates. Whilst it is clear that disputes over certificates are disputes arising under the contract, there may be some doubt whether an adjudicator would be able to substitute his own judgment for that of the certifier; it would make the adjudication procedure devoid of substance if the adjudicator was not able to open-up, review and revise certificates. This problem could also arise where one party had reserved to himself those decisions which would otherwise have been the preserve of a third party certifier (see *Balfour Beatty Civil Engineering v. Docklands Light Railway* (1996) C.I.L.L. 1143).

Many disputes in the industry arise because of dissatisfaction with the certified amounts. If the adjudicator was not able to substitute his decision for that of the certifier, his only role would be to examine whether the certifier had acted honestly, fairly and reasonably (see *Balfour Beatty Civil Engineering v. Docklands Light Railway* (1996) C.I.L.L.; 1143; *John Barker Construction v. London Portman Hotel* (1996) C.I.L.L. 1152). For the avoidance of doubt, (and provided that the parties are so agreed) contracts should be expressed to confer upon the adjudicator the power to open-up, review and revise certificates. There may be some resistance to this from certifiers (and, no doubt, their insurers) since their traditional powers will be fettered by adjudicators' decisions.

Subs. (2)(a)

Subsection (2) lays down fairly minimal procedural requirements which all contracts must contain. Each party has an unrestricted right to give notice that he intends to refer a dispute to the adjudicator; there is no temporal limitation on the exercise of the right to refer a dispute to adjudication. Thus, such right could be exercised during the progress of the works, after completion or abandonment of the works. But, where a contract has been discharged by breach, the adjudicator is unlikely to have jurisdiction to deal with any disputes since they would not be "arising under the contract"—it is discharged. This would also apply if the contract is discharged following the exercise of any express rights of termination or determination. However, many of the standard forms in use in the industry only provide for the determination of the contractor's 'employment' and, therefore, the contract is preserved.

There is always the danger that one party may "store up" a dispute in order to secure adequate time by which to fully develop his case or to refer it to an adjudicator at a time which is most disadvantageous to the other party. The content of such notice, to whom it must be issued and the means of service are matters for the contract. Where there is no agreement on the "manner of service", ss.115(3) and 115(4) will apply.

Subs. (2)(b)

The period of seven days is an extremely short time in which to secure the appointment of the adjudicator and for referral of the dispute to him. Therefore, it would be prudent for the identity of the adjudicator to be agreed upon at the outset of the contract and for the party giving notice of his intention to refer a dispute to the adjudicator (under subs. (2)(a)), to provide with that, notice of the submissions which he intends to rely upon in support of his case. This should allow the party receiving such notice sufficient time in which to forward his own response (see s.116 for how periods of time are reckoned). However, the response time may have to "eat into" the period of 28 days (subs. (2)(c)) to enable the respondent to deal adequately with the case against him which the other party may have prepared over a number of weeks or even months.

Again, in order to streamline the procedure, a copy of the notice in subs. (2)(a) (together with accompanying submissions) could be used for the purpose of referring the dispute to the adjudicator.

It should be noted that the timetable of seven days for appointment of and referral of the dispute to the adjudicator is expressed as an objective and, is not mandatory. Contracts may have to extend the timetable to cater for death, illness or unavailability of the adjudicator or even for delays in securing the appointment of an adjudicator in the first place.

Subs. (2)(c)

There is nothing in the Act which forbids the contract from restricting the scope of the decision which the adjudicator might make. Thus, for example, a contractual provision which requires the adjudicator to limit his decision on money claims to £x may not offend the Act. On the other hand, if the limit is extremely low in relation to the contract value, the statutory right to refer disputes to adjudication will have been frustrated. Unfortunately, this could provide some scope for litigation.

Another way in which limits could be placed on the adjudicator's decision making power is by requiring that the adjudicator shall not make a decision which is in excess of that already given by an adjudicator under another contract. For example, an adjudicator under a sub-contract could be restrained from awarding an extension of time which is in excess of that previously awarded by the adjudicator under the main contract (assuming that both the main contract and sub-contract adjudications related to the same factual circumstances).

Given the complexity of disputes that could be referred to the adjudicator, it is understandable that the parties should have the right to extend the 28 day limit. There is no limit on the time by which the statutory period can be extended. There may be an opportunity here for stronger parties to pressurise the weaker into accepting an unreasonable extension.

Subs. (2)(d)

If the adjudicator requires an extension of time, it would normally be in the interest of the party referring the dispute to grant it. It should be noted that the period can be extended by any number of days up to the full 14 days.

Subs. (2)(e)

All the matters listed in subss. 2(c) to 2(f) should be included in a tripartite agreement between the parties and the adjudicator so that the adjudicator is also contractually bound. Such agreement would require the adjudicator to act impartially which means that, at least, he should apply the rules of natural justice. Therefore, he should declare any interests which could mean that he has a bias towards one of the parties. He should ensure that each party has an adequate opportunity to present his case and deal with that submitted by the other within the time constraints allowed by the statute. Reference should be made to the wealth of precedent concerning the impartiality (or lack of it) of arbitrators stemming from applications to remove them for misconduct (now embodied in s.24 of the Arbitration Act 1996).

Subs. (2)(f)

This gives the adjudicator power to seek legal advice and make his own inquiries as to the facts. Thus, for example, he may wish to visit the site to inspect work which is the subject of the dispute and ask questions of relevant personnel. In fact, subject to his duty to act impartially, the adjudicator should be "master in his own house". Procedures which are detailed and prescriptive would undermine the adjudicatory process by providing endless opportunities for jurisdictional disputes arising from procedural lapses by the adjudicator. This was, no doubt, in the mind of Lord Lucas (the Government spokesman) at Committee Stage in the House of Lords.

"An adjudicator should have access to legal or other expert advice and should not have to rely solely on the evidence offered to him by the parties if better evidence is available within the time available to him. There is no need to specify that the adjudicator should restrict himself to the 'relevant' facts. We should leave it to the expert to decide what is relevant and what is not; to do otherwise could be a recipe for wrangling and delays" (*Hansard*, H.L. Vol. 570, col. 1880).

Subs. (3)

In the majority of cases, the parties are likely to reserve their right to have disputes considered afresh in arbitration or by the court. In practice, it is likely that the adjudicator's decision will hold sway or, alternatively, the parties will reach a settlement based upon that decision. Indeed, subs. (3) makes clear that the parties may agree to accept the adjudicator's decision as final. It should be noted that there is no requirement that the agreement is to be in writing. There is also the possibility that such agreement could be implied, if it transpires that the parties have conducted their relationship on the assumption that the adjudicator's decision is final.

Subs. (4)

Again, this should be included as part of a tripartite agreement between the parties and the adjudicator. If this was only in the contract between the parties to the construction contract, it is possible that one party would not enforce the contract in this regard, if the other decided to sue the adjudicator. It should be noted that the adjudicator does not have statutory immunity as does an arbitrator under s.29 of the Arbitration Act 1996. Therefore, the adjudicator could, for example, face actions in negligence brought by third parties. There may be scope for such actions against the adjudicator under the so-called "reliance cases" (see e.g. *White v. Jones* [1995] 2 W.L.R. 187; *Henderson v. Merrett Syndicates* [1994] 3 W.L.R. 761).

Subs. (5)

Contracts draftsmen should faithfully reflect all the requirements in subss. (1) to (4) if they wish to ensure that the Scheme does not apply. The Scheme will, no doubt, have to address the substantive and procedural issues raised in the commentaries on the previous subsections.

Subs. (6)

Apart from being a "belt and braces" provision, it is difficult to understand why subs. (6) is required, when s.114(4) states that the Scheme is to take effect as "implied terms of the contract". This would give a sufficient signal to the courts on the extent to which they can intervene in disputes arising out of the application of the Scheme. Nonetheless, the Government has decided to "draw down" the powers of the courts in relation to the Arbitration Act 1996 and extend them to adjudication (in so far as appropriate to adjudication). Since, in Scotland, there is no statutory arbitration law the Scheme will have to give certain powers to the courts. Apart from enforcing decisions of the adjudicator and intervening in jurisdictional issues (preferably substantive rather than procedural), it is difficult to envisage a greater role for the courts in the adjudicatory process. After all, the statutory right of adjudication is designed to obviate the need for litigation. With the very short time span allowed for the adjudication procedure to be completed and, in view of the fact that the adjudicator's decision is only of a temporary nature, the outcome of many applications to the courts is likely to be academic.

Section 24 of the Arbitration Act 1996 gives the courts power to remove an arbitrator on certain grounds such as lack of impartiality, non-possession of qualifications required by the arbitration agreement or failure to conduct the proceedings with all reasonable dispatch. Such powers are required since arbitrators are issuing final awards.

The Scheme will need to provide for an adjudication procedure which "fleshes out" the provisions of s.108. Therefore, the Scheme will have to include matters such as the appointment of the adjudicator, procedures governing the way in which each party is to present its case to the adjudicator, and the time in which the decision is to be implemented. Baring in mind the nature of adjudication and the procedural time limits, there should not be any scope for oral hearings with legal representation.

Payment

Entitlement to stage payments

109.—(1) A party to a construction contract is entitled to payment by instalments, stage payments or other periodic payments for any work under the contract unless—

(a) it is specified in the contract that the duration of the work is to be less than 45 days, or

(b) it is agreed between the parties that the duration of the work is estimated to be less than 45 days.

(2) The parties are free to agree the amounts of the payments and the intervals at which, or circumstances in which, they become due.

(3) In the absence of such agreement, the relevant provisions of the Scheme for Construction Contracts apply.

(4) References in the following sections to a payment under the contract include a payment by virtue of this section.

GENERAL NOTE

Subs. (1)

Most forms of construction contract (both standard and non-standard forms) either provide for periodic payments (usually monthly) or stage payments. In the absence of any express provision for interim payments the presumption is that the contract is an entire one—completion of the works is a condition precedent to payment (see, *e.g. Sumpter v. Hedges* [1898] 1 Q.B. 673; *Ibmac v. Marshall (Homes)* (1968) 208 E.G. 851). At common law there is some authority which suggests that interim payments can be implied in construction contracts. In *D.R. Bradley (Cable Jointing) v. Jefco Mechanical Services* (1989) (6 Construction Law Digest—7–21), Mr Recorder Rich Q.C., sitting as an Official Referee had to consider a dispute concerning non-payment by a main contractor under a sub-contract which had no express provisions as to time or method of payment:

> "Having heard their evidence as to the custom of the industry, I concluded that it was an implied term of a contract that application could be made for payment not more frequently than monthly. Payment would then be due within a reasonable period of such application, for the work done and any unused material on site, valued in each case in accordance with the contract between the parties. I announced in the course of the hearing my intention to hold that I construed a reasonable time in all the circumstances as 30 days with a period of grace to allow 42 days in all, and I now hold that 42 days was a reasonable time for payment".

It is not clear what "stage payments" or "periodic payments" in subs. (1) add to the statutory right to "payment by instalments" other than being illustrative. The industry's standard forms of contract generally provide for monthly periodic payments based upon the valuation of the total works carried out to the date of the instant payment less the total of the amounts already received by way of interim payments and any cash retention. In "Constructing the Team", Sir Michael Latham recommended that: "The eventual aim should be to phase out the traditional system of monthly measurement or remeasurement ..." Instead, he recommended: "Express provision for assessing interim payments by methods other than monthly valuation *i.e.* mile stones, activity schedules or payment schedules".

Stage payments are different from periodic payments in that completion of a stage is a condition of precedent to payment. Therefore, if, for whatever reason, the stage is not completed, the obligation to make payment does not arise—this simply reflects the rule relating to "entire contracts" which has already been referred to above.

The right to payment by instalments extends to "any work under the contract". Thus, it would seem that off-site work including any design is included in addition to on-site work.

The statutory right to instalment payments will, first, arise if the contract states that the work will last less than 45 days even if the actual number of days stated is wholly unrealistic. Furthermore, there is no requirement that the figure actually stated must reflect continuous working. Thus, for example, the work may, in fact, last 30 days in total but those days may be spread over six months.

Subsection (1)(b) provides an alternative where there is no stipulation in the contract as to the period for the duration of work. The parties can agree that the work is likely to last less than 45 days; which agreement should be obtained before commencement of the works (although there is no requirement that this should be so).

Subs. (2)

Subsection (2) confirms that, in practice, the effect of s.109 is likely to be minimal. Thus, for example, a contract lasting 12 months could provide that the bulk of the price will be paid on completion and that nominal amounts of £5 as advances on the price will be paid at four monthly intervals.

Subs. (3)

It is likely that the Scheme will reflect the norm in the industry which is monthly periodic payments based upon measurement and valuation of all the work carried out prior to the making of each interim payment.

Dates for payment

110.—(1) Every construction contract shall—

(a) provide an adequate mechanism for determining what payments become due under the contract, and when, and

(b) provide for a final date for payment in relation to any sum which becomes due.

The parties are free to agree how long the period is to be between the date on which a sum becomes due and the final date for payment.

(2) Every construction contract shall provide for the giving of notice by a party not later than five days after the date on which a payment becomes due from him under the contract, or would have become due if—

(a) the other party had carried out his obligations under the contract, and

(b) no set-off or abatement was permitted by reference to any sum claimed to be due under one or more other contracts,

specifying the amount (if any) of the payment made or proposed to be made, and the basis on which that amount was calculated.

(3) If or to the extent that a contract does not contain such provision as is mentioned in subsection (1) or (2), the relevant provisions of the Scheme for Construction Contracts apply.

General Note

Subs. (1)

There is no definition of "adequate mechanism" in subs. (1)(a). Lord Lucas, on behalf of the Government, sought to justify this omission at Second Reading in the House of Lords:

"The industry covers thousands of different operations and dozens of different types of contract. Payment is already determined in far too many ways for us to come up with a single definition. This legislation requires that payment should be defined in terms of amount and date. That will be a big improvement on what happens at the moment". (*Hansard*, H.L. Vol. 569, col. 1027).

Traditional payment arrangements in the industry (other than at the level of domestic subcontracts) provide for a process of measurement, valuation and certification often by a third party—an architect or engineer. This determines what payments become due. Once a certificate is issued it gives rise to a debt subject to opening-up, review or revision in a subsequent arbitration or, possibly, by a court where the parties are so agreed (see *Lubenham Fidelities and Investment Co. v. South Pembrokeshire D.C.* (1986) 33 B.L.R. 39).

Subject to any contractual provisions to the contrary, it was once assumed that certificated amounts had to be paid in full, irrespective of any set-off or counterclaim (*Dawnays v. M.G. Minter* [1971] 1 W.L.R. 1205). The matter was finally resolved by the House of Lords in *Modern Engineering (Bristol) v. Gilbert Ash (Northern)* [1974] A.C. 689 which held that very clear express terms were required in the contract to deny the right of the payer to set-off or raise a defence to justify a refusal to pay certificated amounts. The sanctity of certificates (if it ever existed) was further undermined in *R.M. Douglas Construction v. Bass Leisure* (1990) 25 Con L.R. 38. The Court held that the payer could resist an application for summary judgment under Ord. 14: "Where ... in good faith and on reasonable material [he] raises an arguable contention that a certificate is open to challenge" (*per* H.H. Judge Bowsher Q.C. at p.48).

The requirement for an "adequate mechanism" is intended, firstly, to identify "what payments become due". The fact that the payer discharges a certificate by paying less than the due amount on account of a set-off or for any other reason is unlikely to offend against subs. (1)(a).

However, the payment machinery in consultants' agreements and in the vast majority of subcontracts (except, for example, the nominated sub-contract documentation published by the Joint Contracts Tribunal) will not involve certification. Nevertheless, excluding work carried out under the various consultants' agreements, the process of measurement and valuation based upon the contract pricing documents (*e.g.* bills of quantities, schedules of rates, contract sum analyses) is likely to suffice for the purposes of subs. (1)(a).

Alternatively, if other methods of payments such as stage payments, activity schedules or payment milestones are used, then as long as there is an apportionment of the contract sum to each stage, milestone or activity this should also suffice. For consultants' agreements, a similar approach may be necessary so that instalments of the consultant's fee is apportioned to the work stages completed.

Where measure and value is the basis of payment, it suggested that contracts should make clear which party has the responsibility for carrying out the valuation in order to produce an authoritative statement of what is due. In some of the industry standard form contracts such as the domestic sub-contracts linked to JCT main forms, it is unclear who has the responsibility for carrying out valuations.

The "adequate mechanism" must also serve to determine when payments become due. To some extent this overlaps with s.109 since it would be expected that on the expiry of the payment period or completion of a stage of work, payment would become due. Nevertheless, subs. (1)(a) would seem to require that contracts clearly identify the event which qualifies as the due date. Thus if interim payments are made dependent upon the issue of certificates, the date of issue of the certificate will need to be identified as the "due date".

Finally, subs. (1)(b) requires the insertion of a further date following the due date by which payment must be discharged. Such requirement tends to be reflected in most of the standard forms of contract use in the industry.

Subs. (2)

It should be noted that the requirement for the notice is contractual rather than statutory. The form of notice, how it is to be served and upon whom, are matters for the contract (but if the manner of service is not agreed, ss.115(3) and 115(4) apply). The requirement that the notice shall state the basis upon which the amount was calculated will be of immense help to the payee in deciding whether or not to dispute that amount before the adjudicator. In fact, valuation disputes are likely to provide a substantial slice of an adjudicator's workload.

The contractual notice requirements must apply even if payment would have been due but for:

(i) Failure by the payee to comply with his contract, *e.g.* the works were not in accordance with the contractual specification (see *Acsim (Southern) v. Dancom Danish Contracting and Development Co.* (1989) 47 B.L.R. 59) and/or;

(ii) The exercise by the payer of a right of "set-off or abatement (sic) ... under one or more contracts" (subs. (2)(b)).

It is unclear why "set-off" and "abatement" were used in this context. If the payer wishes to exercise set-off rights under another contract they would, in any event, have to be exercised against any sums due under the extant contract since, strictly, set-off negates or reduces the obligation to discharge any *due* payment.

Furthermore, abatement results in the diminution or extinction of the contract price on the ground that it has not been earned because the relevant work has not been carried out or, if it has, it does not comply with the contract. It is generally not possible to abate the price under the extant contract because of deficiencies in the work under another contract. In fact, it would have made for much simpler drafting if the trigger for the giving of the notice had been left at the date on which payment becomes due—which would, in any event, have taken account of any abatement. The fact that payment might not have actually been made between that date and the "final date for payment" because of a set-off is immaterial. (This is further discussed in the commentary on s.111.)

If the "payment made or proposed to be made" is nil because the payer has abated the price or exercised a right of set-off, such notice would be acceptable under s.111(1) provided that it has complied with s.111(2).

Subs. (3)

It is unlikely that, the Scheme (in making provision for an "adequate mechanism") would deviate too far from the industry norm of determining payment on a measure and value basis or on the basis of each complete work stage.

Notice of intention to withhold payment

111.—(1) A party to a construction contract may not withhold payment after the final date for payment of a sum due under the contract unless he has given an effective notice of intention to withhold payment.

The notice mentioned in section 110(2) may suffice as a notice of intention to withhold payment if it complies with the requirements of this section.

(2) To be effective such a notice must specify—

(a) the amount proposed to be withheld and the ground for withholding payment, or

(b) if there is more than one ground, each ground and the amount attributable to it,

and must be given not later than the prescribed period before the final date for payment.

(3) The parties are free to agree what that prescribed period is to be.

In the absence of such agreement, the period shall be that provided by the Scheme for Construction Contracts.

(4) Where an effective notice of intention to withhold payment is given, but on the matter being referred to adjudication it is decided that the whole or part of the amount should be paid, the decision shall be construed as requiring payment not later than—

(a) seven days from the date of the decision, or

(b) the date which apart from the notice would have been the final date for payment,

whichever is the later.

General Note

Subs. (1)

Section 111 is primarily designed to reduce the incidence of set-off abuse by formalising the process by which the payer claims to be entitled to pay less than that expected by the payee. The payer is entitled to refuse to discharge payments on the ground that the payee has failed to comply with his contractual obligations in some respect. In equity such set-off is regarded as a self-help remedy and is a substantive defence to a claim for non-payment. The set-off may be for an unliquidated amount but must arise out of the same or a closely connected transaction.

By contrast, a legal or statutory set-off (compensation in Scotland) can only be raised as a defence in legal proceedings. This avoids the need for a multiplicity of actions where there may be claims and counterclaims arising out of different or unconnected transactions.

Legal or statutory set-off originated in the Statutes of Set-Off in 1729 and 1739 which were repealed by s.2 of the Civil Procedure Acts Repeal 1879 (c. 59) and are now, by virtue of the Supreme Court Act 1981 (c. 54) embodied in rules of court. The Statutes of Set-Off applied to mutual debts but now R.S.C. Ord. 18, r.17 permits a defendant to raise claims in legal proceedings, "whether of an ascertained amount or not".

In *The Nanfri*, Lord Denning M.R. in the Court of Appeal ([1978] 3 All E.R. 1066) explained the nature of equitable set-off in the context of time charters:

"When the ship owner is guilty of a breach of contract which deprives the time charterer of part of the consideration for which the hire has been paid in advance, the charterer can deduct an equivalent amount out of the hire falling due for the next month ... In my opinion, therefore, in a time charter, if the shipowner wrongly and in breach of contract deprives the charterer for a time of the use of the vessel, the charterer can deduct a sum equivalent to the hire for the time so lost".

Furthermore, "when the debtor has a true [equitable] set-off it goes in reduction of the sums owing to the creditor" (at p.1077).

Therefore, unlike legal or statutory set-off, equitable set-off will amount to a discharge of sums due or owing (see also *Laroque v. Beauchemin* [1897] A.C. 358).

Where the contract is silent upon the issue of set-off, "one starts with the presumption that neither party intends to abandon any remedies for its breach arising by operation of law, and clear express words must be used in order to rebut this presumption" (*per* Lord Diplock in *Modern Engineering v. Gilbert-Ash* [1994] A.C. 689 at p.717: see also *Redpath Dorman Long v. Cummins Engine Co.* 1981 S.C. 370). This view has held sway in spite of the statement by Lord Cross in *Mottram Consultants v. Bernard Sunley* [1975] 2 Lloyd's Rep. 197 who said (at p.205): "one should approach each case without any *parti pris* in favour or against the existence of a right of set-off, though one must bear in mind the principle established in *Mondel v. Steel*".

The standard forms of sub-contract for use with the forms of main contract published by the Joint Contracts Tribunal provide the exclusive machinery for the exercise of set-off rights. Non-standard forms of contract/sub-contract tend to extend set-off rights (often expressed—incorrectly—as common law set-off) to include set-off across contracts.

Technically, there is a distinction between set-off and common law abatement which was clearly explained in the classic case of *Mondel v. Steel* [1841] 8 M. & W. 858 where Park B. said at pp.871–2;

"It must however be considered, that in all these cases of goods sold and delivered with a warranty ... the rule which has been found so convenient is established; and that it is competent for the defendant ... not to set-off by a proceeding in the nature of a cross-action, the amount of damages which he has sustained by breach of the contract, but simply to defend himself by showing how much less of the subject-matter of the action is worth, by reason of the breach of contract; and to the extent that he obtains, or is capable of obtaining, an abatement of price on that account, he must be considered as having received satisfaction for the breach of contract, and is precluded from recovering in another action to that extent; but no more".

Mondel v. Steel was concerned with defects in a ship delivered under a ship-building contract. For reasons which are not apparently clear, abatement only applies to contracts for the sale of goods and contracts for work and materials. It has the effect, not of discharging payment, but of preventing the obligation to make payment arising in the first place. Since the work is defective (or has not been completed according to the contract) payment has not been earned.

In practice, the distinction between abatement and set-off is of not great consequence—courts sometimes use the terms interchangeably. However, the distinction may be significant where the particular contract expressly excludes rights of set-off or limits the exercise of those rights. This was illustrated by *Acsim (Southern Ltd) v. Dancom Danish Contracting and Development Co.* (1989) 47 B.L.R. 59. The Court of Appeal had to consider the set-off provisions in the "blue" form of domestic sub-contract for use with the 1963 Edition of the Standard Form of Building Contract published by the Joint Contracts Tribunal. The main contractor's entitlement to set-off against sums owing to the sub-contractor were fully set out in the contract. The contractor had failed to give the requisite notice when seeking to exercise his right of set-off on the ground that the work was either not done or it was defective. The Court of Appeal applied *Mondel v. Steel.* The Court held that the contractor had the right to defend a claim for interim payment by showing that the sum claimed had not been earned by reason of the breach of contract. Such defence amounted to common law abatement rather than set-off. (A useful potted history of the evolution of set-off and abatement is given in the judgment by Morris L.J. in *Hanak v. Green* [1958] 2 All E.R. 141 at pp.145–51.)

The Concise Oxford Dictionary (7th Ed.) states that "withhold" means "hold back" but (as has already been discussed), as a matter of strict law, abatement or set-off is not a holding back although, in common parlance it would be regarded as so. Thus, the effect of common law abatement is to deny that monies are due or owing whereas equitable set-off has the effect of discharging monies due or owing.

The question is whether courts will be prepared to approach subs. (1) in a purposive way to deal with the "mischief" which s.111 is seeking to address rather than being too preoccupied with technical considerations. An argument could, of course, be made out that s.111 would otherwise be devoid of any content; it has to refer something. In such a situation the court is able to consider the Parliamentary history of the legislation or *Hansard* to discover the "mischief" (see *Pepper v. Hart* [1993] 1 All E.R. 42). Nonetheless, it is a pity that the parliamentary draftsman did not provide a statutory definition of "withhold" to include "set-off and abatement". However, since the notice in s.110(2) can also serve as a "notice of intention to withhold payment" the draftsman must have contemplated that set-off or abatement was included, since s.110(2) still requires a notice if payment is not made because of failure to perform the contract or a set-off or abatement under other contracts.

Subs. (2)

The payer may wish to safeguard his position in the event that the amount(s) stated in the notice or the ground(s) to which it is linked are, subsequently, found to be inaccurate as new information comes to light. There is nothing in s.111 which would prevent the payer from reserving his right to amend the amount(s) withheld and/or the ground(s) for such withholding in the event of any subsequent adjudication, arbitration or litigation.

Subs. (3)

Since the s.110(2) notice for specifying payments to be made must be issued within 5 days of the date when payment becomes due, and, since such notice can also qualify as a notice under s.111(1), it would be sensible to relate the "prescribed period" to the 5 days required by s.110(2). In any event, this may be provided by the Scheme.

Subs. (4)

If there is a failure to comply with the adjudicator's decision within the stipulated time, the payee could exercise his statutory right of suspension under s.112 or seek to recover the adjudicator's award in debt recovery proceedings.

It should be noted that the obligation to issue an "effective notice" is statutory. The Scheme will not supply such provision where it is not included in the contract. It is unlikely that the obligation can, by contract, be waived or excluded (see commentary on s.108(1) and s.112(1)). In particular the reference in subs. (3) to the Scheme stipulating the "prescribed period" presumes the existence of the statutory obligation.

Right to suspend performance for non-payment

112.—(1) Where a sum due under a construction contract is not paid in full by the final date for payment and no effective notice to withhold payment has been given, the person to whom the sum is due has the right (without prejudice to any other right or remedy) to suspend performance of his obligations under the contract to the party by whom payment ought to have been made ("the party in default").

(2) The right may not be exercised without first giving to the party in default at least seven days' notice of intention to suspend performance, stating the ground or grounds on which it is intended to suspend performance.

(3) The right to suspend performance ceases when the party in default makes payment in full of the amount due.

(4) Any period during which performance is suspended in pursuance of the right conferred by this section shall be disregarded in computing for the purposes of any contractual time limit the time taken, by the party exercising the right or by a third party, to complete any work directly or indirectly affected by the exercise of the right.

Where the contractual time limit is set by reference to a date rather than a period, the date shall be adjusted accordingly.

GENERAL NOTE

Subs. (1)

At common law there is no right to suspend the works for non-payment or late payment:

"Apart from suing for interim payments, or requiring arbitration where that is provided for, the remedy—and apparently the only remedy—which the contractor is recognised as having at common law is rescission if a sufficiently serious breach has occurred. If he chooses not to rescind, his own obligations continue. He is bound to go on with the work. All the available English and Commonwealth text books on building contracts state the law consistently with this view..." (*per* Cooke & Woodhouse JJ. in *Canterbury Pipelines v. Christ Church Drainage* [1979] 2 N.Z.L.R. 347 at p.351).

This view was reinforced by Staughton L.J. in *Eurotunnel v. TML* [1992] C.I.L.L. 754;

"It is well established that if one party is in serious breach, the other can treat the contract as altogether at an end; but there is not yet any established doctrine of English law that the other party may suspend performance, keeping the contract alive".

In fact, apart from making the timing of payment of the essence, it is only in very limited circumstances that the payee can regard late or non-payment as going to the root of the contract allowing him to treat the contract as discharged for breach.

"The case would have been quite different if the defendants' breaches had been such as reasonably to shatter the plaintiffs' confidence in the defendants' ability to pay for the goods with which the plaintiffs supplied them. I think that, in such circumstances, the consequences of the breach could properly have been regarded as most serious, indeed fundamental, and going to the root of the contract so that the plaintiffs would have been entitled to refuse to continue doing business with the defendants." (*per* Salmon L.J. in *Decro-Wall v. Practitioners in Marketing* [1971] 2 All E.R. 216 at p.222; applied in *D.R. Bradley (Cable Jointing) v. Jefco Mechanical Services* (1989) 6-CLD-07-21).

A right of suspension for non-payment is expressly provided in the standard sub-contracts for use with the main contracts published by the Joint Contracts Tribunal.

The right to suspend provided by subs. (1) is a statutory right but there is no bar on contractual waiver or exclusion of such right. Furthermore, s.112 does not provide for the right to be included in the Scheme if it does not appear in the contract.

"Although there is a general principle that a person may waive any right conferred on him by statute (*quilibet protest renunciare juri pro se introducto*) difficulties arise in determining whether the right is exclusively personal or is designed to serve other more broad public purposes. In the latter situation, public policy would require that the right be treated as mandatory and not be waivable by the party for whose benefit it operates. Whether a statutory right is waivable depends on the overall purpose of the statute and whether this purpose would be frustrated by permitting waiver. Thus in *Johnson v. Moreton* [1980] A.C. 37 the House of Lords held that a tenant could not contract out of the protection afforded by s.24 of the Agricultural Holdings Act 1948 (c. 63) as this would undermine the overall purpose of the Act in prompting efficient farming in the national interest" (Chitty on Contracts, 27th Ed. at p.782).

In *Johnson v. Moreton, Lord Simon of Glaisdale* at p.69 said:
"The principle which, in my view, emerges ... is as follows. Where it appears that the mischief which Parliament is seeking to remedy is that a situation exists in which the relations of parties cannot properly be left to private contractual regulation, a party cannot contract out of such statutory regulation (albeit exclusively in its own favour) because so to permit would be to reinstate the mischief which the statute was designed to remedy and to render the statutory provision a dead letter".

The broad public purpose of the Act could be said to be the improvement in the efficiency of the construction industry by stimulating cash flow, improving disputes resolution machinery and reducing the incidence of insolvency. Although, on its own, the exercise of the right of suspension might not be considered as being for the public good, it should be viewed as an integral part of the statutory package.

An Opposition amendment at Report Stage in the House of Commons sought to ensure that all the provisions in the Act would have effect notwithstanding any agreement to set aside the provisions. The amendment was withdrawn after the Government had given an assurance that the parties would not be able to sign away their rights in advance.

Before the right of suspension can be exercised the payee must ensure:

(i) A sum is due; and

(ii) Payment has not been made in *full* by the final date for payment, *i.e.* the expiry of the period of discharge; and

(iii) An effective notice to withhold payment has not been given.

Where the contract provides for certificated payments, the issue of a certificate is a condition precedent to a sum becoming due (see *Lubenham Fidelities and Investment Co. v. South Pembrokeshire D.C.* (1986) 33 B.L.R. 39).

Therefore the exercise of the statutory right of suspension in the absence of a certificate would be rather foolhardy. On the other hand, if a certificate represents a substantial under-valuation the payee may suspend work if he considers that the certifier has not acted honestly, fairly and reasonably (*Northern Regional Health Authority v. Derek Crouch Construction Co.* [1984] Q.B. 644; *Balfour Beatty Civil Engineering v. Docklands Light Railway* (1996) C.I.L.L. 1143).

While doubts remain about whether abatement or set-off rights are, technically, a withholding of payment, there will remain some uncertainty associated with the exercise of the statutory right of suspension which will affect both payer and payee. Thus, for example, if the payer claims that a sum is not due on account of poor workmanship, but has not issued an "effective notice" to withhold payment, he could face severe disruption to the progress of his work. It would not be surprising if this issue was litigated sooner rather than later.

The exercise of the right of suspension is without prejudice to other rights or remedies so that the payee is free to exercise any contractual rights of determination for non-payment or, indeed, to sue for the outstanding sum as a debt.

Subs. (2)

A condition precedent to the exercise of the right of suspension is the giving of seven day's notice of intention to suspend but the form and content, manner of service and upon whom it is to be served are matters for the contract (although if manner of service is not agreed, ss.115(3) and 115(4) will apply). It is thought that the ground for exercising the right of suspension would normally be failure by the payer to make payment in accordance with the notice issued under s.110(2) or the balance of the amount stated in such notice after taking into account any sums withheld in any further notice issued under s.111(1).

Subs. (3)

It would appear that, in theory, the right of suspension remains even where the parties have compromised the debt since the reference is to "payment in full of the amount due" under the contract. To avoid any ambiguity, contracts should make clear that amounts due include any such amount which has been revised following a compromise or settlement.

Subs. (4)

The drafting is tortuous but, in essence, any overrun over the contract period or date for completion will not constitute a breach of contract by the party suspending performance of the works. This protection is also available to a third party such as a sub-contractor who is unable to continue work as a result of suspension by a main contractor.

On the other hand, suspension is not necessarily a convenient excuse for justifying any delay in the works since the delay in question must be traced back to work which was "directly or indirectly" affected by the suspension. If the suspension has occurred on a critical path in the programme, the extent of work indirectly affected by the suspension could be fairly substantial.

It should be noted that there is no express statutory provision for the recovery of any loss or expense incurred by the payee during the period of suspension; this is a matter which should be addressed in the contract.

Prohibition of conditional payment provisions

113.—(1) A provision making payment under a construction contract conditional on the payer receiving payment from a third person is ineffective, unless that third person, or any other person payment by whom is under the contract (directly or indirectly) a condition of payment by that third person, is insolvent.

(2) For the purposes of this section a company becomes insolvent—

(a) on the making of an administration order against it under Part II of the Insolvency Act 1986,

(b) on the appointment of an administrative receiver or a receiver or manager of its property under Chapter I of Part III of that Act, or the appointment of a receiver under Chapter II of that Part,

(c) on the passing of a resolution for voluntary winding-up without a declaration of solvency under section 89 of that Act, or

(d) on the making of a winding-up order under Part IV or V of that Act.

(3) For the purposes of this section a partnership becomes insolvent—

(a) on the making of a winding-up order against it under any provision of the Insolvency Act 1986 as applied by an order under section 420 of that Act, or

(b) when sequestration is awarded on the estate of the partnership under section 12 of the Bankruptcy (Scotland) Act 1985 or the partnership grants a trust deed for its creditors.

(4) For the purposes of this section an individual becomes insolvent—

(a) on the making of a bankruptcy order against him under Part IX of the Insolvency Act 1986, or

(b) on the sequestration of his estate under the Bankruptcy (Scotland) Act 1985 or when he grants a trust deed for his creditors.

(5) A company, partnership or individual shall also be treated as insolvent on the occurrence of any event corresponding to those specified in subsection (2), (3) or (4) under the law of Northern Ireland or of a country outside the United Kingdom.

(6) Where a provision is rendered ineffective by subsection (1), the parties are free to agree other terms for payment.

In the absence of such agreement, the relevant provisions of the Scheme for Construction Contracts apply.

GENERAL NOTE

Subs. (1)

Subsection (1) aims to curb the widespread use of pay when paid arrangements which are generally found in bespoke sub-contracts or amended standard forms of sub-contracts. They also tend to spread down the contractual chain to sub-sub-contracts. If the third party (usually the client or building owner) does not make payment, sub-contractors, generally do not have any rights of recourse against the third party for non-payment or late payment.

There is an inherent ambiguity in the term "pay when paid". It can be construed as relating to:

(i) *Timing* so that payment to the payee is made *when* payment is received by the payer from the third party;

(ii) Entitlement to payment so that payment is only made *if* payment has been received by the payer from the third party.

If the pay when paid clause is construed as only relating to the timing of payment, it would seem that, in principle, the courts would enforce such provision. (See, *e.g. Schindler Lifts (Hong Kong) v. Shui On Construction Co.* [1985] HKLR 118; *Brightside Mechanical & Electrical Services Group v. Hyundai Engineering & Construction Co.* (1988) 41 B.L.R. 110).

However, a number of cases decided in the United States, Australia and New Zealand suggest that the courts are reluctant to accept that payment entitlement can be wholly dependent upon receipt of payment from a third party unless very clear words to that effect are used. In effect, a pay-if-paid clause requires the payee to act as the insurer of the payer following non-payment by the third party. (See, *e.g. Pace Construction Corporation v. OBS Co Inc.* (1988) Fla App 531 So 2d 737 (Florida District Court of Appeal); *Smith & Smith Glass v. Winston Architectural Cladding Systems* [1992] 2 NZLR 473; *Iezzi Constructions Pty v. Currumbin Crest Development Pty* (1994) 10 B.C.L. 408; "*Are 'pay when paid' clauses in construction sub-contracts; conditions precedent or terms of payment?*" by Harold J. Murphy [1989] 61 C.L.R. 196). Furthermore, a pay when paid condition is unlikely to apply if a contract has been brought to an end by some breach on the part of the payer (See, *Scobie & McIntosh v. Clayton Bowmore* (1990) 49 B.L.R. 119).

There is no English precedent on pay when paid clauses but there are probably three fairly slim grounds on which they could be attacked:

(i) If the payer contends that clause in question is a pay if paid arrangement, the courts are likely to construe it *contra proferentum* if there is any ambiguity concerning the purport of the clause.

(ii) Failure by the payer to bring to the payee's notice a particularly onerous requirement; there is some doubt about whether this would apply if the contract in question had been executed by the payee (See *Interfoto Picture Library v. Stiletto Visual Programmes* [1989] 1 Q.B. 433).

(iii) A paid when paid clause could be unreasonable under s.3 of the Unfair Contract Terms Act 1977 (c. 50). Thus, where the payee deals on the payer's "written standard terms of business", the payer cannot "by reference to any contract term [unless such term satisfies the requirement of reasonableness] claim to be entitled in respect of the whole or any part of his contractual obligations to render no performance at all". But, if the pay when paid clause is clearly drafted so that no obligation to make payment arises until and unless payment is received from the third party (*i.e.* receipt of payment from the third party is a condition precedent to payment by the payer), s.3 is unlikely to have any application since there is no contractual obligation to make payment in the first place.

In spite of the note in the margin referring to "Prohibition of conditional payment provisions", such provisions are only ineffective and not all conditional payment arrangements are covered. Thus, for example, it may be possible to re-introduce pay when paid arrangements by the "back door" by inserting other conditions such as making payment dependent upon receipt by the payer of a certificate (which includes the relevant payment) issued by the architect or engineer engaged by the third party—the client or building owner (see *Dunlop & Ranken v. Hendall Steel Structures* [1957] 1 W.L.R. 1102).

At Committee Stage in the Commons, an amendment was passed that "clauses having the effect of pay when paid" should be ineffective. However, this was overturned by the Government at Report Stage ostensibly on the ground that it was too wide and could interfere with the process of issuing certificates for payment which is common in the construction industry.

In the draft of the Bill the word "void" was used instead of "ineffective" which was adopted at Committee Stage in the House of Lords, supposedly to cater for certain, undefined, legal sensitivities in Scotland. "Void" is generally accepted in our legal lexicon as meaning that the contract or clause in question should be regarded as having never existed at all; the change of wording was probably necessary to meet the conceptual difficulty of pronouncing pay-when-paid clauses "void" while resurrecting them again on the insolvency of the third party.

If there exists a pay when paid clause in the sense defined in subs. (1), it may be resurrected where the third person is insolvent. This seems to be the purport of subs. (1) but the drafting is not entirely clear as to *when* the insolvency of the third person must have occurred. Must the third person be insolvent at the time that the payer and payee enter into the contract? The ambiguity seems to stem from the fact that subs. (1) is expressed in the present tense: "*A provision making payment.... conditional on the payer receiving payment from a third party is ineffective, unless that third person ... is insolvent*".

Furthermore subs. (6) enables the parties to agree alternative payment provisions. The effect of any such agreement would be to remove the pay when paid clause from the contract altogether unless its resurrection (on the occurrence of the third person's insolvency) was expressly reserved.

A pay-when-paid arrangement can also be resurrected where the third person was also dependent upon payment (directly or indirectly) by another and that other party has gone into insolvency. However, such further dependency would have to be written into the contract or sub-contract between the payer and payee.

It is unclear what the position is where the contract states that payment will not be made if the third person has set-off monies against the payer with the result that the payer has not received the relevant monies. Arguably, the set-off could mean that payment to the payer has been discharged although he has not actually received the cash (see, commentary on s.111). It would have been better if the condition in subs. (1) was expressed as "discharge of payment" to the payer from the third person rather than "receiving payment". (See *Larocque v. Beauchemin* [1897] A.C. 358; *Brightside Mechanical & Electrical Services Group v. Hyundai Engineering & Construction Co.* (1988) 41 B.L.R. 110).

Subss. (2)–(5)

It would seem that there is no reason why a payee cannot still challenge the validity of a pay if paid arrangement and, if successful, obtain a "*quantum meruit*" for the work executed up to the time the third party became insolvent.

It would appear that the definition of insolvency as including, for example, administration orders and administrative receivership is rather too wide. In the case of administration, it is contemplated that the insolvent company will carry on business and therefore payments would continue along the contractual chain. This is also the case where the "third person" is in administrative receivership since the receiver may decide to continue the contract in question and continue payment.

Subs. (6)

There may, of course, be resistance to the suggestion that the pay when paid clause is ineffective under the legislation in which case the dispute will have to be referred to the adjudicator as required by s.108. Assuming that this first hurdle is overcome (or does not exist), the agreement must establish a payment procedure which complies with the Act so that:

(i) payments are made on an instalment basis;
(ii) there is an adequate mechanism for determining what and when payments are due;
(iii) the period of grace in which payment has to be made following the due date is stated;
(iv) there is a requirement that the payer issues a notice within 5 days of the due payment date indicating the amount due and justifying the calculation.
(v) there is stated the period for the giving of notice for withholding payment under s.111(2).

In practice, it is likely that some parties will reach agreement by expressly incorporating the provisions of the Scheme or, as is more likely, the Scheme's provisions will apply because of the failure of the parties to reach an agreement.

If the Scheme applies, there is no provision for what is to happen when a pay when paid clause is resurrected because of the insolvency of the "third person". Presumably, the Scheme would include a provision that it will cease to apply on the insolvency of the third person (provided that there already exists a pay when paid provision in the contract).

Supplementary provisions

The Scheme for Construction Contracts

114.—(1) The Minister shall by regulations make a scheme ("the Scheme for Construction Contracts") containing provision about the matters referred to in the preceding provisions of this Part.

(2) Before making any regulations under this section the Minister shall consult such persons as he thinks fit.

(3) In this section "the Minister" means—

(a) for England and Wales, the Secretary of State, and

(b) for Scotland, the Lord Advocate.

(4) Where any provisions of the Scheme for Construction Contracts apply by virtue of this Part in default of contractual provision agreed by the parties, they have effect as implied terms of the contract concerned.

(5) Regulations under this section shall not be made unless a draft of them has been approved by resolution of each House of Parliament.

DEFINITIONS

"Minister; the": subss. (3)(a), 3(b).

GENERAL NOTE

The Scheme for Construction Contracts—the default scheme—will be introduced as a statutory instrument to be passed by affirmative resolution in both Houses of Parliament. The Government has committed itself to the widest possible consultation.

The Scheme will provide the following:

(i) An adjudication procedure.
(ii) The intervals or circumstances when payments become due.

(iii) An adequate mechanism for determining what and when payments become due; a final date for payment in respect of due sums, and a requirement for a notice setting out the amount which was due to be paid and basis of calculation.
(iv) The period in which notice of withholding payment must be given.
(v) Failure of parties to agree payment terms where a paid when paid clause is "ineffective".

Where the provisions of the Scheme apply, they are to take effect as "implied terms" of the contract. Normally terms are implied (whether under statute or at law) to the extent that there isn't anything expressed in the contract to the contrary. In this context, the function of the Scheme is not only to fill in the gaps when the contract is silent but to override the terms of the contract where it includes provisions which do not reflect the statutory requirements.

Service of notices, &c.

115.—(1) The parties are free to agree on the manner of service of any notice or other document required or authorised to be served in pursuance of the construction contract or for any of the purposes of this Part.

(2) If or to the extent that there is no such agreement the following provisions apply.

(3) A notice or other document may be served on a person by any effective means.

(4) If a notice or other document is addressed, pre-paid and delivered by post—

(a) to the addressee's last known principal residence or, if he is or has been carrying on a trade, profession or business, his last known principal business address, or

(b) where the addressee is a body corporate, to the body's registered or principal office,

it shall be treated as effectively served.

(5) This section does not apply to the service of documents for the purposes of legal proceedings, for which provision is made by rules of court.

(6) References in this Part to a notice or other document include any form of communication in writing and references to service shall be construed accordingly.

General Note

Notice procedures generally underpin most of the requirements in Pt. II and, as already stated in some of the commentaries, contracts will have to determine the form and content of the requisite notices, mode of service and upon whom they are to be served. Section 115 deals with only one aspect of notice procedure—the manner of service. Although service can be carried out by "any effective means", subs. (4) makes clear that where service is carried out in accordance with its provisions, there is effective service whether or not express provisions are included in the contract on this matter.

In subs. (6), as a minimum requirement, notices (and service thereof) can "include any form of communication in writing". It will, no doubt, be in the interests of one of the parties to have more onerous notice requirements in relation to matters such as suspension but, in other matters, where that party is required to issue a notice, it may wish to make the procedure as informal as possible.

Reckoning periods of time

116.—(1) For the purposes of this Part periods of time shall be reckoned as follows.

(2) Where an act is required to be done within a specified period after or from a specified date, the period begins immediately after that date.

(3) Where the period would include Christmas Day, Good Friday or a day which under the Banking and Financial Dealings Act 1971 is a bank holiday in England and Wales or, as the case may be, in Scotland, that day shall be excluded.

General Note

There was an attempt at Committee Stage in the House of Lords to extend subs. (3) to include "days forming part of a customary holiday period within the industry in question". This was rejected by the Government in no uncertain terms. Earl Ferrers, leading for the Government, said: "It seems unreasonable to tell people who are expecting money, and may be expecting some money on, say, 15th August, that everyone has gone on holiday for two weeks and they have to wait for two weeks for their money. After all, this is a case of making payments when payments are known to be expected and payments are due. I should have thought that it is perfectly reasonable to say in those circumstances that only the statutory holidays should be taken into account". (*Hansard*, H.L. Vol. 571, col. 39).

Crown application

117.—(1) This Part applies to a construction contract entered into by or on behalf of the Crown otherwise than by or on behalf of Her Majesty in her private capacity.

(2) This Part applies to a construction contract entered into on behalf of the Duchy of Cornwall notwithstanding any Crown interest.

(3) Where a construction contract is entered into by or on behalf of Her Majesty in right of the Duchy of Lancaster, Her Majesty shall be represented, for the purposes of any adjudication or other proceedings arising out of the contract by virtue of this Part, by the Chancellor of the Duchy or such person as he may appoint.

(4) Where a construction contract is entered into on behalf of the Duchy of Cornwall, the Duke of Cornwall or the possessor for the time being of the Duchy shall be represented, for the purposes of any adjudication or other proceedings arising out of the contract by virtue of this Part, by such person as he may appoint.

General Note

Prior to publication of the Bill there was some doubt about whether contracts entered into with the Crown would be encompassed by the legislation but the Government's acceptance of Sir Michael Latham's recommendation in "Constructing the Team" that it should be a *best practice* client would have "rung" rather hollow if the Crown had been exempted.

Part III

Architects

Introduction

This part of the Act revises the law relating to the registration of Architects by amending the Architects (Registration) Act 1931 (c. 33) and the Architects Registration Act 1938 (c. 54) and by repealing the Architects Registration (Amendment) Act 1969 (c. 42). The principle of protecting the use of the word "Architect" is preserved but there are changes to the management of the registration of Architects, the regulation of professional conduct and there is provision for a new code of professional practice. The Board of Architectural Education, the Admission Committee and the Discipline Committee, which were established under the 1931 Act, are abolished and their functions are taken over by the Architects Registration Board and the Register of Architects. The Architects Registration Board also takes over the remaining functions of the Architects Registration Council of the U.K., which was established under the 1931 Act.

Commencement

The changes introduced by the Act will come into force in accordance with the provisions of s.150(3) upon such day as may be appointed by the Secretary of State. Different days may be appointed for different areas and different purposes. The Secretary of State also has the power to make transitional provisions and savings as appear to him to be appropriate (s.150(4)).

Abbreviations

"1931 Act" : Architects (Registration) Act 1931.
"Board; the": Architects Registration Board.

The Architects Registration Board

The Board and its committees

118.—(1) The Architects' Registration Council of the United Kingdom established under the Architects (Registration) Act 1931 ("the 1931 Act") shall be known as the Architects Registration Board.

(2) The Board of Architectural Education, the Admission Committee and the Discipline Committee constituted under the 1931 Act are abolished.

(3) In section 3 of the 1931 Act (constitution and functions of Architects' Registration Council), after subsection (2) insert—

"(2A) Part I of the First Schedule to this Act makes provision about the constitution and proceedings of the Board.

(2B) There shall be a Professional Conduct Committee of the Board and Part II of that Schedule makes provision about its constitution and proceedings.

(2C) Part III of that Schedule gives to the Board power to establish other committees and makes provision about their constitution and proceedings.

(2D) Part IV of that Schedule makes general provision about the Board and its committees.".

(4) For the First Schedule to the 1931 Act (constitution of Council) substitute the Schedule set out in Part I of Schedule 2.

DEFINITIONS

"Architects Registration Board": s.118(1).

"Board; the": s.118(1), Sched. 2, Pt. II, para. 2(2).

"Professional Conduct Committee": s.118(3) and Sched. 2, Pt. I (new First Schedule as inserted in the 1931 Act at Pt. II).

GENERAL NOTE

This section renames the Architects Registration Council of the U.K. ("ARCUK") as the Architects Registration Board ("ARB"). The Government changed its mind at least twice on this issue, initially taking the view that ARCUK should be abolished and that other arrangements should be made to secure the continued integrity of the architectural profession (see *Hansard*, H.L. Vol. 569, col. 980). The Government ultimately decided that the Council should be reformed in order to make it more efficient. Unfortunately, the Act does not repeal all the earlier legislation but amends by adding sections to previous enactments with consequential amendments and repeals. In consequence, the Act must be read together with the 1931 and 1938 Acts.

Under Sched. 2, Pt. 1, provision is made for the ARB to consist of a total of 15 members, seven of whom shall be elected and eight shall be appointed. The elected members will represent bodies who are deemed to be representative of Architects in accordance with a scheme to be prepared by the ARB and approved by the Privy Council. The appointed members will represent consumer and public interests and will be appointed by the Privy Council. The innovation is that the majority of the members (eight) will be lay members and they will not be Architects. The profession is therefore no longer self-regulating. This is unusual, as in most professions the governing or disciplinary body is constituted of members of the profession itself. The aim of the reforms would seem to be to strike a balance between the interests of Architects generally and those of the general public.

This section also abolishes the Board of Architectural Education, the Admission Committee and the Discipline Committee, which were established under the 1931 Act. The powers and duties of those bodies are conferred upon the ARB (subs. (1)), which is also given power to establish other committees (subs. (3)(2C)), including specifically a Professional Conduct Committee (subs. (3)(2B)). The constitution and regulation of the Professional Conduct Committee is set out in the new 1931 Schedule (see clauses 11–15). The ARB is not expected to spawn several new large or expensive committees. Though Members of any additional committees need not be members of the ARB, the majority must be ARB members (cl. 17 of the new First Schedule and the ARB can only discharge its statutory functions through its own members (cl. 18) (see *Hansard*, H.L. Vol. 571, col. 45). This aim should be ensured by the reduction of members from ARCUK's 73 to ARB's 15 and ensure a minimalist organisation.

Registrar and staff

119. For section 4 of the 1931 Act substitute—

"**The Registrar**

4.—(1) The Board shall appoint a person to be known as the Registrar of Architects.

(2) The Board shall determine the period for which, and the terms on which, the Registrar is appointed.

(3) The Registrar shall have the functions provided by or by virtue of this Act and any other functions which the Board directs.

(4) The Board may, in addition to paying to the Registrar a salary or fees—

(a) pay pensions to or in respect of him or make contributions to the payment of such pensions; and
(b) pay him allowances, expenses and gratuities.

Staff

4A.—(1) The Board may appoint staff.

(2) The Board shall determine the period for which, and the terms on which, its staff are appointed.

(3) Staff appointed by the Board shall have the duties which the Board directs.

(4) The Board may, in addition to paying salaries to its staff—

(a) pay pensions to or in respect of them or make contributions to the payment of such pensions; and
(b) pay them allowances, expenses and gratuities.".

DEFINITIONS

"Board; the": s.118(1) and Sched. 2, Pt. II, para. 2(2).
"Registrar of Architects": s.119 (new s.4(1) as inserted in the 1931 Act).
"Registrar; the": Sched. 2, Pt. II, para. 2(b) and s.119.

GENERAL NOTE

This section creates a new post of Registrar of Architects, who shall be appointed and paid by the ARB and whose function shall be to exercise the responsibilities set out in ss.120 and 121 of the Act, together with such other functions as the ARB may decide. The ARB also has power to appoint other paid staff for such periods and to carry out such duties as the ARB may decide.

Registration and discipline

Registration

120.—(1) Before section 6 of the 1931 Act insert—

"**The Register**

5A.—(1) The Registrar shall maintain the Register of Architects in which there shall be entered the name of every person entitled to be registered under this Act.

(2) The Register shall show the regular business address of each registered person.

(3) The Registrar shall make any necessary alterations to the Register and, in particular, shall remove from the Register the name of any registered person who has died or has applied in the prescribed manner requesting the removal of his name.

(4) The Board shall publish annually the current version of the Register and a copy of the most recently published version of the Register

shall be provided to any person who requests one on payment of a reasonable charge determined by the Board.

(5) A copy of the Register purporting to be published by the Board shall be evidence (and, in Scotland, sufficient evidence) of any matter mentioned in it.

(6) A certificate purporting to be signed by the Registrar which states that a person—

(a) is registered;

(b) is not registered;

(c) was registered on a specified date or during a specified period;

(d) was not registered on a specified date or during a specified period; or

(e) has never been registered,

shall be evidence (and, in Scotland, sufficient evidence) of any matter stated.".

(2) For section 6 of the 1931 Act substitute—

"Entitlement to registration

6.—(1) A person who has applied to the Registrar in the prescribed manner for registration in pursuance of this section is entitled to be registered if—

(a) he holds such qualifications and has gained such practical experience as may be prescribed; or

(b) he has a standard of competence which, in the opinion of the Board, is equivalent to that demonstrated by satisfying paragraph (a).

(2) The Board may require a person who applies for registration on the ground that he satisfies subsection (1)(b) to pass a prescribed examination in architecture.

(3) Before prescribing—

(a) qualifications or practical experience for the purposes of subsection (1)(a); or

(b) any examination for the purposes of subsection (2),

the Board shall consult the bodies representative of architects which are incorporated by royal charter and such other professional and educational bodies as it thinks appropriate.

(4) The Board may require—

(a) an applicant for registration in pursuance of this section; and

(b) a candidate for any examination under subsection (2),

to pay a fee of a prescribed amount.

(5) The Board may by rules prescribe the information and evidence to be furnished to the Registrar in connection with an application for registration in pursuance of this section.

(6) Where a person has duly applied for registration in pursuance of this section—

(a) if the Registrar is satisfied that the person is entitled to be registered, he shall enter his name in the Register; but

(b) if the Registrar is not so satisfied, he shall refer the application to the Board.

(7) The Registrar shall not consider an application for registration in pursuance of this section in any case in which it is inappropriate for him to do so (for instance because he is in any way connected with the applicant) but in such a case he shall refer the application to the Board.

(8) Where a person's application is referred to the Board under subsection (6) or (7), the Board shall direct the Registrar to enter the person's name in the Register if the Board is satisfied that the person is entitled to be registered.

(9) The Registrar shall serve on an applicant for registration in pursuance of this section written notice of the decision on his application—

(a) where the application is made on the ground that he satisfies subsection (1)(a), within three months of his application being duly made; and

(b) where the application is made on the ground that he satisfies subsection (1)(b), within six months of his application being duly made.".

(3) After section 6A of the 1931 Act insert—

"Retention of name in Register

6B.—(1) The Board may require a registered person to pay a fee (in this section referred to as a "retention fee") of a prescribed amount if he wishes his name to be retained in the Register in any calendar year after that in which it was entered.

(2) Where, after the Registrar has sent a registered person who is liable to pay a retention fee a written demand for the payment of the fee, the person fails to pay the fee within the prescribed period, the Registrar may remove the person's name from the Register.

(3) Where a person whose name has been removed from the Register under subsection (2) pays the retention fee, together with any further prescribed fee, before the end of the calendar year for which the retention fee is payable or such longer period as the Board may allow—

(a) his name shall be re-entered in the Register (without his having to make an application under section 6 or 6A); and

(b) if the Board so directs, it shall be treated as having been re-entered on the date on which it was removed.

Registration: additional requirements

6C.—(1) Where the Board is not satisfied that a person who—

(a) applies for registration in pursuance of section 6 or 6A;

(b) wishes his name to be retained or re-entered in the Register under section 6B; or

(c) applies for his name to be re-entered in the Register under section 7ZD,

has gained such recent practical experience as rules made by the Board require a person to have gained before he is entitled to have his name entered, retained or re-entered in the Register, his name shall not be so entered or re-entered, or shall be removed, unless he satisfies the Board of his competence to practise.

(2) Where the Board decides that the name of a person to whom paragraph (b) of subsection (1) applies is by virtue of that subsection to be removed from, or not to be re-entered in, the Register, the Registrar shall serve on him written notice of the decision within the prescribed period after the date of the decision.".

DEFINITIONS

"Board; the": Sched. 2, Pt. II, para. 2(2) and s.118(1).

"Register of Architects": s.120(1) (new s.5A(1) as inserted into the 1931 Act).

"Register; the": Sched. 2, Pt. II, para. 2(5) and s.120(1) (new s.5A(1) as inserted into the 1931 Act).

"registered person": Sched. 2, pt. II, para. 2(3) and s.2 of the 1931 Act.

"retention fee": subs.(3) (new s.6B(1) as inserted into the 1931 Act).

GENERAL NOTE

This section adds a new s.5A to the 1931 Act and requires the Registrar of Architects to maintain a Register of Architects, containing the name of every person entitled to be registered and showing the regular business address of each such registered person. The Registrar of Architects is required to make the necessary alterations to the Register in order to keep it up-to-date and also to publish it annually and provide it to anyone requiring a copy, on payment of a reasonable fee which shall be determined by the ARB. A copy of the Register or a Certificate extracted from the Register and purporting to be signed by the Registrar of Architects shall be evidence (Evidence Act 1845 (c. 113), s.1) (or in Scotland, sufficient evidence).

Subs. (2)

A new s.6 of the 1931 Act is added and sets out the requirements for registration. An Architect is entitled to be registered, providing he holds such qualifications and practical experience as the ARB shall prescribe, or has satisfied the ARB that he has achieved an equivalent standard of competence. The requirements for either any examination or any alternative qualification will be set by the ARB after consultation with relevant professional and educational bodies. In this context, the Board must now consult the chartered bodies, that is to say the Royal Institute of British Architects and its equivalents in Scotland and Northern Ireland, but may also consult such other professional and educational bodies as it thinks appropriate.

Power is also given to the ARB under a new s.6(4) of the 1931 Act to require an applicant for registration or for examination to pay fees and to provide the information and evidence required in connection with the application for registration. The Registrar himself is entitled to enter the applicant's name on the Register (subs. (6)(a)), if he is properly satisfied that the person is entitled to be registered but otherwise shall refer the application to the ARB (subs. (6)(b)). The Registrar must do so if he is in any way connected with the applicant (subs. 7). All decisions on applications must be made within three months of the application (subs. (9)(a)) and shall be notified to the applicant, save where the applicant is not applying on the grounds of established qualifications and practical experience, when the period shall be six months (subs. 9(b)).

Subs. (3)

This sub-section provides a new s.6B to the 1931 Act. Under new 6B(1) a retention fee may be annually charged to any registered person who wishes to retain his name on the Register and provision is made for demands for payment of such fee (s.6B(2)) and for the removal of a registered person's name for failure to pay.

Discipline

121. For section 7 of the 1931 Act substitute—

"**Unacceptable professional conduct and serious professional incompetence**

7.—(1) Where an allegation is made that a registered person is guilty of—

(a) unacceptable professional conduct (that is, conduct which falls short of the standard required of a registered person); or

(b) serious professional incompetence,

or it appears to the Registrar that a registered person may be so guilty, the case shall be investigated by persons appointed in accordance with rules made by the Board.

(2) Where persons investigating a case under subsection (1) find that a registered person has a case to answer they shall report their finding to the Professional Conduct Committee.

(3) Where the Professional Conduct Committee receives a report under subsection (2) in relation to a registered person, the Committee shall consider whether he is guilty of unacceptable professional conduct or serious professional incompetence.

(4) Before considering whether a registered person is guilty of unacceptable professional conduct or serious professional incompetence the Professional Conduct Committee shall—

(a) serve on him written notice outlining the case against him; and

(b) give him the opportunity to appear before the Committee to argue his case.

(5) At any such hearing the registered person is entitled to be legally represented.

(6) The Board may make rules as to the procedure to be followed by the Professional Conduct Committee in any proceedings under this section.

(7) If the Board does not make rules for the appointment of persons to investigate whether registered persons have been guilty of unacceptable professional conduct or serious professional incompetence, the Professional Conduct Committee shall consider such questions without any prior investigation.

Disciplinary orders

7ZA.—(1) The Professional Conduct Committee may make a disciplinary order in relation to a registered person if—

(a) it is satisfied, after considering his case, that he is guilty of unacceptable professional conduct or serious professional incompetence; or

(b) he has been convicted of a criminal offence other than an offence which has no material relevance to his fitness to practise as an architect.

(2) In this Act "disciplinary order" means—

(a) a reprimand;

(b) a penalty order;

(c) a suspension order; or

(d) an erasure order.

(3) Where the Professional Conduct Committee makes a disciplinary order in relation to a person, the Registrar shall serve written notice of the order on the person as soon as is reasonably practicable.

(4) The Professional Conduct Committee shall, at appropriate intervals and in such manner as it considers appropriate, publish—

(a) the names of persons whom it has found guilty of unacceptable professional conduct or serious professional incompetence or in relation to whom it has made a disciplinary order under subsection (1)(b); and

(b) in the case of each person a description of the conduct, incompetence or offence concerned and the nature of any disciplinary order made.

(5) Where, after considering the case of a registered person, the Professional Conduct Committee is not satisfied that he is guilty of unacceptable professional conduct or serious professional incompetence, it shall, if he so requests, publish a statement of that fact in such manner as it considers appropriate.

Penalty orders

7ZB.—(1) Where a penalty order is made in relation to a registered person, he shall pay to the Board the sum specified in the order.

(2) A penalty order may not specify a sum exceeding the amount which, at the relevant time, is the amount specified as level 4 on the standard scale of fines for summary offences.

In this subsection "the relevant time" means—

(a) in a case within subsection (1)(a) of section 7ZA, the time of the conduct or incompetence of which the registered person is found guilty; and

(b) in a case within subsection (1)(b) of that section, the time when he committed the criminal offence of which he has been convicted.

(3) A penalty order shall specify the period within which the sum specified in it is to be paid.

(4) If the person in relation to whom a penalty order is made does not pay the sum specified in the order within the period so specified, the Professional Conduct Committee may make a suspension order or an erasure order in relation to him.

(5) The Board shall pay into the Consolidated Fund any sum paid under a penalty order.

Suspension orders

7ZC. Where a suspension order is made in relation to a registered person, the Registrar shall remove his name from the Register but shall re-enter it in the Register at the end of such period not exceeding two years as is specified in the order.

Erasure orders

7ZD.—(1) Where an erasure order is made in relation to a registered person, the Registrar shall remove his name from the Register and it shall not be re-entered in the Register unless the Board so directs.

(2) No application shall be made for the name of a person in relation to whom an erasure order has been made to be re-entered in the Register—

(a) before the end of the period of two years beginning with the date of the erasure order or such longer period specified in the erasure order as the Professional Conduct Committee considers appropriate in a particular case; or

(b) where he has made a previous application for his name to be re-entered in the Register, before the end of the prescribed period beginning with the date of the decision of the Board on that application.

(3) The Registrar shall serve on a person who applies for his name to be re-entered in the Register under this section written notice of the decision on his application within the prescribed period after the date of the decision.

(4) The Board may require a person whose name is re-entered in the Register under this section to pay a fee of a prescribed amount.".

DEFINITIONS

"Professional Conduct Committee": s.118(3) (new 2B as inserted into the 1931 Act).

"relevant time; the": s.121 (new s.7ZB(2) as inserted into the 1931 Act).

GENERAL NOTE

This section replaces s.7 to the 1931 Act. The powers and obligations of the new Professional Conduct Committee are more extensive than those of the old Discipline Committee which it replaces.

Whereas under the previous law a registered person was liable to be removed from the Register if he had been guilty of disgraceful conduct, the new provisions in this section provide a different basis for disciplinary action which is defined as "unacceptable professional conduct" or "serious professional incompetence".

The provision in old s.7 of the 1931 Act which subjected a registered person to removal from the Register if he had been convicted of a criminal offence is modified. Only those criminal offences which have a material relevance to his fitness to practice as an architect will now be taken into account (new s.7ZA(1)(b)). Concern that professional incompetence alone might lead to some Architects being unjustly penalised, led to a late amendment to the Act requiring that the professional incompetence must be serious. Judicial interpretation of this word may give rise to problems, since it is likely to be wholly a matter of subjective opinion.

The Registrar of Architects is of his own volition entitled to refer a registered person for investigation (new s.7(1)) and, if it is found that a registered Architect has a case to answer, the Professional Conduct Committee must consider the issue. It should be noted that the new s.7(3) requires the Professional Conduct Committee to consider any case where there has been an allegation of either of the two kinds of offences and, since the Committee has no option but to pursue the matter, this may well lead to an increase in its administrative activities and may impair its efficiency.

The Professional Conduct Committee will have a wide range of penalties which it may impose if it is satisfied that a registered person is guilty. The old s.7 only provided for the removal from the Register of a registered person but the Professional Conduct Committee now has discretionary power to make a disciplinary order (s.7ZA(2)) which may be either a reprimand or may impose financial penalties (s.7ZB(5)) or may impose suspension (s.72C) or erasure from the Register of Architects (s.7ZD). The period of suspension which may be imposed by the Professional Conduct Committee may not exceed a period of two years, after which the Registrar must reinstate the architect (s.7ZC) whereas the 1931 Act provided only that there was a discretionary limit upon any period of disqualification from registration. This represents an extension of the equivalent powers provided under the 1931 Act, which were limited to either suspension or erasure. The Professional Conduct Committee is also entitled to publish the names of persons against whom it has made a disciplinary order (s.7ZA(4)), together with a description of the person's conduct giving rise to the offence and the nature of the disciplinary order that may be made. If a person is not found guilty of a disciplinary offence, he may require a statement to be published to that purpose (s.7ZA(5)).

Code of practice

122. After section 7ZD of the 1931 Act insert—

"**Code of practice**

7ZE.—(1) The Board shall issue a code laying down standards of professional conduct and practice expected of registered persons.

(2) The Board shall keep the code under review and vary its provisions whenever it considers it appropriate to do so.

(3) Before issuing or varying the code, the Board shall—

(a) consult such professional bodies and such other persons with an interest in architecture as it considers appropriate; and

(b) publish in such manner as it considers appropriate notice that it proposes to issue or vary the code, stating where copies of the proposals can be obtained.

(4) Failure by a registered person to comply with the provisions of the code—

(a) shall not be taken of itself to constitute unacceptable professional conduct or serious professional incompetence on his part; but

(b) shall be taken into account in any proceedings against him under section 7.

(5) The Board shall provide a copy of the code to any person who requests one on payment of a reasonable charge determined by the Board (and may provide a copy free of charge whenever it considers appropriate).".

General Note

This section which inserts s.7ZE into the 1931 Act creates a new statutory obligation which is imposed upon the ARB to lay down a code of professional conduct and practice, setting the standards to be expected of registered persons. The code will be kept under continuous review and will be produced after consultation with such professional bodies and such other persons with an interest in architecture as it considers appropriate (s.7ZE(3)). The object of the code appears to be to provide guidelines by which registered persons may avoid unacceptable acts which may lead to disciplinary proceedings under the new s.7 disciplinary provisions. Copies of the code will be available upon request.

Miscellaneous

Offence of practising while not registered

123.—(1) In section 1 (prohibition on practising or carrying on business under title of architect by person who is not registered) of the Architects Registration Act 1938 ("the 1938 Act"), after subsection (1) insert—

"(1A) In this Act (and in section 17 of the principal Act) "business" includes any undertaking which is carried on for gain or reward or in the course of which services are provided otherwise than free of charge.".

(2) In section 3 of the 1938 Act (offence of practising while not registered), for the words from "to a fine" to "therefor:" substitute "to a fine not exceeding level 4 on the standard scale:".

(3) Re-number that section as subsection (1) of that section and after that subsection as so renumbered insert—

"(2) In relation to an offence under subsection (1)—

(a) section 127(1) of the Magistrates' Courts Act 1980 (information to be laid within six months of offence);

(b) Article 19(1) of the Magistrates' Courts (Northern Ireland) Order 1981 (complaint to be made within that time); and

(c) section 136(1) of the Criminal Procedure (Scotland) Act 1995 (proceedings to be commenced within that time),

shall have effect as if for the references in them to six months there were substituted references to two years.".

(4) Re-number section 17 of the 1931 Act (defence for certain bodies corporate, firms and partnerships) as subsection (1) of that section and after that subsection as so renumbered insert—

"(2) The Board may by rules provide that subsection (1) shall not apply in relation to a body corporate, firm or partnership unless it has provided to the Board such information necessary for determining whether that subsection applies as may be prescribed.".

DEFINITIONS

"Board; the": Sched. 2, Pt. II, para. 2(2) and s.118(1).

GENERAL NOTE

This clarifies the offence of practising whilst not registered, which was introduced by s.1 of the Architects Registration Act 1938. It is now confirmed that the offence arises also when practising or carrying on the business of an architect under any name, style or title containing the word "architect". As a consequence, since any person using the title "architect" has to be registered, the general public should not be misled by those who might seek to offer themselves as architects in any commercial venture or in any undertaking where architectural services are provided for a consideration and are not free. The maximum penalty for practising whilst not registered is now applicable in Northern Ireland upon the same basis as for the rest of the U.K. The offence is penalised by a fine not exceeding level 4 on the standard scale (currently £2,500, s.143 of the Magistrates' Courts Act 1980 as amended).

The Education Fund

124.—(1) No fees received under the 1931 Act shall be credited to the Architects' Registration Council Education Fund ("the Fund") constituted under the Architects Registration (Amendment) Act 1969 ("the 1969 Act").

(2) The Board may transfer the assets of the Fund to such person and on such terms as may be approved by the Secretary of State.

(3) A person to whom the assets of the Fund are transferred under subsection (2) shall apply the assets, and all income arising from the assets, for the purposes authorised in subsection (4) of section 1 of the 1969 Act (assuming for this purpose that the reference in that subsection to the Council were a reference to the person to whom the assets of the Fund are transferred).

DEFINITIONS

"Board; the": Sched. 2, Pt. II, para. 2(2) and s.118(1).

"Fund; the": ss.(1).

GENERAL NOTE

This provides for the cessation of income to the old Architects Registration Council Education Fund and makes arrangements for it to be wound up and empowers the ARB to transfer the assets of the Fund to such person on such terms as may be approved by the Secretary of State.

Supplementary

125.—(1) The amendments made by Part II of Schedule 2, and the transitional provisions and savings in Part III of that Schedule, shall have effect.

(2) In this Part—

"the 1931 Act" means the Architects (Registration) Act 1931,

"the 1938 Act" means the Architects Registration Act 1938, and

"the 1969 Act" means the Architects Registration (Amendment) Act 1969.

(3) In this Part "the Fund" means the Architects' Registration Council Education Fund.

(4) The 1931 Act, the 1938 Act and this Part may be cited together as the Architects Acts 1931 to 1996.

General Note

This brings into effect the new First Schedule to the 1931 Act and the detailed and consequential amendments required to the 1931 and 1938 Acts and other relevant enactments.

Subs. (1)

This subsection brings into effect Pt. I of Sched. 2 to the Act which sets out a replacement first Schedule to the 1931 Act. Part I of this new first Schedule contains the provisions for the constitution of the new ARB, the appointment of its members, its chairmen and their terms of office as well as the filling of casual vacancies on the ARB and its procedures. Part II sets out the provisions governing the appointment of members of the Professional Conduct Committee and that Committee's procedures. Part IV gives power to the Secretary of State after consultation with the ARB and any other persons or bodies which he considers appropriate to amend these provisions though such amendments are subject to annulment by resolution of either House of Parliament.

Part IV

Grants &c. for regeneration, development and relocation

Introduction

This Part contains two discrete elements: that relating to the single regeneration budget, and that relating to relocation grants.

Single Regeneration Budget

The single regeneration budget (SRB) was introduced in April 1994, to combine 20 previously separate programmes, ranging from housing schemes such as Estate Action, through the Urban Programme, to employment schemes such as Business Start-Up and TEC (Training and Enterprise Councils) Challenge. SRB "aims to promote sustainable regeneration, economic development and competitiveness at local level": Environment Committee, First Report, Single Regeneration Budget, Vol. II Memorandum by the Department of Environment, para. 1.

The SRB has built on the experience of City Challenge (which involved urban areas competing for funds) and bids have likewise been allocated on the basis of competitive bidding. During the first round of bids, 469 applications were received of which 201 were successful. Although a budget of £1.4 billion was made available for the year 1995/96, to be used over a timescale of from one to seven years, a large part of it was already committed to the existing projects; accordingly, only £125 million was available for new projects during the 1995–96 first round of bidding. Further bidding took place during 1995 for the second round, for which a further £40 million was made available, and the SRB has now entered into its third round.

Given the wide range of existing funding schemes from which the SRB was drawn, with five different government departments involved, the Government decided that it was more sensible to have one single statutory framework (*per* Lord Lucas (Government Whip), *Hansard*, H.L., Second Reading, February 20, 1996, col. 1029). Sections 126 to 129 constitute this framework, although it may be noted that the SRB is not directly referred to in the legislation, which is drawn broadly enough to be applied to future variations.

Relocation Grant

Although major slum clearance programmes are now relatively few, where they do take place they are hugely disruptive of local communities. The new relocation grant, which authorities may introduce in clearance areas, *if* they have adequate resources, "will help people whose homes are in clearance areas and who wish to acquire a replacement home in the same local area. .... This grant will help to keep local communities together by assisting people. It will help to bridge the gap between the cost of a replacement home in the locality and the amount of money which the applicant can reasonably afford, taking into account any compensation which he may receive for the loss of his home" (*per* Lord Ferrers (Minister for the Environment and Countryside), Second Reading, *Hansard*, H.L., February 20, 1996, Vol. 569, cols. 981, 982).

The scheme is based on a pilot project conducted by the DoE and Birmingham City Council in the South Saltley area of Birmingham: The future of Private Housing Renewal Programmes, Explanatory Paper linked to the Housing White Paper, DoE, para. 7.1.

Financial assistance for regeneration and development

Power of Secretary of State to give financial assistance for regeneration and development

126.—(1) The Secretary of State may, with the consent of the Treasury, give financial assistance to any person in respect of expenditure incurred in connection with activities which contribute to the regeneration or development of an area.

(2) Activities which contribute to the regeneration or development of an area include, in particular—

(a) securing that land and buildings are brought into effective use;
(b) contributing to, or encouraging, economic development;
(c) creating an attractive and safe environment;
(d) preventing crime or reducing the fear of crime;
(e) providing or improving housing or social and recreational facilities, for the purpose of encouraging people to live or work in the area or of benefiting people who live there;
(f) providing employment for local people;
(g) providing or improving training, educational facilities or health services for local people;
(h) assisting local people to make use of opportunities for education, training or employment;
(i) benefiting local people who have special needs because of disability or because of their sex or the racial group to which they belong.

(3) In subsection (2)—

"local people", in relation to an area, means people who live or work in the area; and

"racial group" has the same meaning as in the Race Relations Act 1976.

DEFINITIONS

"financial assistance": s.127.

GENERAL NOTE

See notes to Introduction, above.

Subs. (1)

This subsection contains the broad power for the Secretary of State to give financial assistance (as defined in s.128, below) in connection with activities which contribute to the regeneration or development of an area. The financial assistance may be given to "any person". Thus it is not limited to local authorities: "It could be a person; it could be a company; it could be a non-statutory body" (*per* Lord Ferrers (Minister for the Environment and Countryside), Committee, *Hansard*, H.L., April 1, 1996, Vol. 571, col. 102). Although in the first round of bidding for the Single Regeneration Budget, local authorities were involved in 85 per cent of the bids, and the lead partner in just over half, Training and Enterprise Councils (TECs) also play an important role, being the lead bidder in just under a quarter of bids: Environment Committee, First Report, Single Regeneration Budget, Vol. II, Memorandum by the Department of Environment, para. 15.

Subs. (2)

The activities for which assistance may be given is not confined to those listed. They are in any event broadly framed: "We have tried deliberately to propose broad categories of activities so as to ensure that we can accommodate a very wide range of regeneration and development activities" (*per* Lord Ferrers (Minister for the Environment and Countryside), Committee, *Hansard*, H.L., April 1, 1996, Vol. 571, col. 90).

Subs. (3)

"Racial group" means "a group of persons defined by reference to colour, race, nationality or ethnic or national origins": Race Relations Act 1976 (c. 74), s.3(1). This has been broadly interpreted to include Sikhs (*Mandla v. Lee* [1983] 2 A.C. 548, H.L.) and gypsies (*Commission for Racial Equality v. Dutton* [1989] 1 All E.R. 306, C.A.) but does not include Rastafarians (*Crown Suppliers (PSA) v. Dawkins* [1993] I.R.L.R. 284, C.A.).

Regeneration and development: forms of assistance

127.—(1) Financial assistance under section 126 (powers of Secretary of State to give financial assistance) may be given in any form.

(2) Assistance may, in particular, be given by way of—

(a) grants,

(b) loans,

(c) guarantees, or

(d) incurring expenditure for the benefit of the person assisted.

(3) The Secretary of State must not, in giving financial assistance under section 126, purchase loan or share capital in a company.

GENERAL NOTE

This section prescribes the forms in which financial assistance may be given by the Secretary of State. Assistance under the Single Regeneration Budget (SRB) has been provided thus far in the form of grants, but under subs. (2) financial assistance may also take the form of loans, guarantees and the incurring of expenditure, but not (subs. (3)) the purchase of loan or share capital in a company. Some of the schemes which were brought into the SRB had been funded by way of credit approvals to local authorities (under Pt. IV of the Local Government and Housing Act 1989 (c. 42)), but the Government has specifically excluded this form of assistance for the SRB, preferring "a form of support that provided maximum flexibility and was of benefit to everyone", and which could fund revenue as well as capital projects (*per* Lord Ferrers (Minister for the Environment and Countryside), Committee, *Hansard*, H.L., April 1, 1996, Vol. 571, col. 106).

Regeneration and development: terms on which assistance is given

128.—(1) Financial assistance under section 126 may be given on such terms as the Secretary of State, with the consent of the Treasury, considers appropriate.

(2) The terms may, in particular, include provision as to—

(a) circumstances in which the assistance is to be repaid, or otherwise made good, to the Secretary of State, and the manner in which that is to be done; or

(b) circumstances in which the Secretary of State is entitled to recover the proceeds or part of the proceeds of any disposal of land or buildings in respect of which assistance was provided.

(3) The person receiving assistance must comply with the terms on which it is given, and compliance may be enforced by the Secretary of State.

DEFINITIONS

"financial assistance": s.127.

GENERAL NOTE

As with all Government funding, it may be given on terms which may be enforced by the Secretary of State.

Regeneration and development: consequential amendment

129. In section 175(2)(b) of the Leasehold Reform, Housing and Urban Development Act 1993, for the words from "sections 27 to 29" to the end, substitute "sections 126 to 128 of the Housing Grants, Construction and Regeneration Act 1996 (financial assistance for regeneration and development)".

GENERAL NOTE

The Urban Regeneration Agency (known as English Partnerships) was created by the Leasehold Reform, Housing and Urban Development Act 1993 (c. 28). By s.175 of that Act, the agency may be appointed to act as agent for the Secretary of State for certain purposes. These included Urban Development Grant (UDG), one of the constituent elements of the SRB, under s.27 of the Housing and Planning Act 1986 (c. 63). As the provisions relating to UDG are now being repealed and superseded (see Sched. 3, Pt. III), this section makes a consequential amendment to the 1993 Act which permits the Secretary of State to appoint English Partnerships as agent for the purposes of the SRB. It should be noted, however, that at the present time the SRB has been administered by the Government Offices for the Regions.

Regeneration and development: Welsh Development Agency

130.—(1) In the Welsh Development Agency Act 1975, after section 10 insert—

"**Financial assistance for regeneration and development**

10A.—(1) The Secretary of State may appoint the Agency to act as his agent in connection with such of his functions mentioned in subsection (2) below as he may specify.

(2) The functions are—

(a) functions under sections 126 to 128 of the Housing Grants, Construction and Regeneration Act 1996 (financial assistance for regeneration and development), so far as they relate to—

(i) financial assistance which the Agency has power to give apart from this section; or

(ii) financial assistance given under that Act in pursuance of an agreement entered into by the Secretary of State for Wales before the coming into force of this section, or

(b) functions of the Secretary of State in relation to financial assistance given by the Secretary of State for Wales under sections 27 to 29 of the Housing and Planning Act 1986.

(3) An appointment under this section shall be on such terms as the Secretary of State, with the approval of the Treasury, may specify; and the Agency shall act under the appointment in accordance with those terms.

(4) The Agency's powers in relation to functions under an appointment under this section include the powers it has in relation to functions under subsection (3) of section 1 by virtue of subsections (6) and (7) of that section."

(2) In section 2(8) of that Act, after "declared that" insert ", except as provided by section 10A below,".

GENERAL NOTE

In England, the administration of the SRB has been devolved to the 10 Government Offices for the Regions, providing a single point of contact (although see notes to s.129, above). In Wales, the Secretary of State will have power to delegate the operation of the SRB to the Welsh Development Agency.

Relocation grants in clearance areas

Resolution by local housing authority to pay relocation grants

131.—(1) Before deciding whether to declare an area to be a clearance area under section 289 of the Housing Act 1985, a local housing authority shall—

(a) consider whether their resources are sufficient for the purpose of carrying into effect a resolution declaring the power to pay relocation grants to be exercisable as regards that area; and

(b) in deciding that question, have regard to such guidance as may from time to time be given by the Secretary of State.

(2) Where a local housing authority decide that their resources are sufficient for that purpose, they shall—

(a) consider whether to pass such a resolution; and

(b) notify every person on whom notice is required to be served under subsection (2B)(a) of section 289 of the Housing Act 1985 that they are so considering and invite him to make representations.

(3) In deciding whether to pass such a resolution, a local housing authority shall—

(a) have regard to such guidance as may from time to time be given by the Secretary of State; and

(b) take account of any representations made by persons notified under subsection (2)(b).

(4) Where a local housing authority pass such a resolution, they shall transmit a copy of it to the Secretary of State at the same time as they transmit to him a copy of the resolution under section 289 of the Housing Act 1985.

(5) Subsections (2) to (4) of section 604A of the Housing Act 1985 (duty to consider guidance before taking enforcement action) shall apply in relation to guidance under subsection (1)(b) or (3)(a) as they apply in relation to guidance under subsection (1) of that section.

DEFINITIONS

"clearance area": H.A. 1985, s.289.

"local housing authority": s.140; H.A. 1985, s.1.

GENERAL NOTE

A clearance area is "an area which is to be cleared of all buildings ...": Housing Act 1985 (c. 68), s.289(1). By s.289(2) (as amended) a local authority must declare a clearance area if they are satisfied:

"(a) that the buildings in the area which are dwelling-houses or houses in multiple occupation or contain one or more flats (... referred to as 'residential buildings') are unfit for human habitation or are by reason of their bad arrangement, or the narrowness or bad arrangement of the streets, dangerous or injurious to the health of the inhabitants of the area, and

(b) that the other buildings, if any, in the area are for a like reason dangerous or injurious to the health of the inhabitants of the area and

in accordance with section 604A [of the Housing Act 1985] that the most satisfactory course of action is the demolition of all the buildings in the area."

Before deciding to declare such an area, the local housing authority must consider whether they have sufficient resources to pay relocation grants in the area: subs. (1)(a). This requirement to consider sufficiency of resources also arises prior to deciding whether to declare a clearance area at all (H.A. 1985, s.289(4)(b)). In that context, it has been held that the authority are not bound to consider specific figures, but that a general satisfaction may be sufficient: *Goddard v. Minister of Housing and Local Government* [1958] 1 W.L.R. 1151. In reaching the decision as to whether they have sufficient resources, authorities will have to have regard to the guidance issued by the Secretary of State (see further note to subs. (5) below).

Subss. (2), (3)

Having made the decision that resources are adequate, the authority must then consider whether to pass a resolution instituting a relocation grant scheme for the clearance area, and must consult prior to making this decision. Under s.289(2B)(a) of the 1985 Act, authorities are required to serve a notice on every person who has an interest in the building (whether as freeholder, lessee or mortgagee), and in the case of a residential building (as defined in s.289(2)(a), see above note), with everyone who has such an interest in any flat within the building. These people must also be consulted regarding the relocation grant scheme: subs. (2)(b).

Having considered the Secretary of State's Guidance and the results of the consultation exercise, the authority may then decide whether or not to implement a relocation grant scheme.

Subs. (5)

The Housing Act 1985, s.604A(2) permits the Secretary of State to give guidance generally or to different descriptions of authorities or to authorities in different areas. It also permits him to give guidance in particular in respect of financial and social considerations to be taken into account by authorities. Section 604A(3) and (4) require the draft guidance to be laid on the table in Parliament.

Relocation grants: applications and payments

132.—(1) Where a local housing authority have passed a resolution declaring the power to pay relocation grants to be exercisable as regards a clearance area, they may pay such grants for the purpose of enabling qualifying persons to acquire qualifying dwellings (see section 133).

(2) No relocation grant shall be paid unless—

(a) an application for it is made to the authority by a qualifying person in accordance with the provisions of this section and is approved by them;

(b) the application is accompanied by a certificate falling within subsection (5) in respect of the qualifying dwelling to which the application relates; and

(c) such other conditions (whether as to the dwelling or the interest to be acquired or otherwise) as may be prescribed are fulfilled,

and regulations made under paragraph (c) may provide for particular questions arising under the regulations to be determined by the authority.

(3) An application for a relocation grant shall be in writing and shall specify the qualifying dwelling to which it relates and contain such particulars as may be prescribed.

(4) The Secretary of State may by regulations prescribe a form of application for a relocation grant and an application to which any such regulations apply shall not be validly made unless it is in the prescribed form.

(5) A certificate under this subsection certifies—

(a) that the applicant proposes to acquire an owner's interest in the qualifying dwelling to which the application relates; and

(b) that he, or a member of his family, intends to live in that dwelling as his (or that member's) only or main residence throughout the grant condition period.

(6) A relocation grant shall be paid in such manner and at such time as the authority may determine having regard to the purpose for which it is paid.

(7) Nothing in section 25 of the Local Government Act 1988 (consent required for provision of financial assistance) shall apply in relation to any exercise of the power to pay relocation grants.

DEFINITIONS

"clearance area": H.A. 1985, s.289.
"dwelling": s.140.
"local housing authority": s.140; H.A. 1985, s.1.
"member of family": s.140.
"owner's interest": s.140.
"qualifying dwelling": s.133(2).
"qualifying person": s.133(1).

GENERAL NOTE

Subs. (1)

Payment of relocation grants is permitted only to "qualifying persons", to enable them to purchase "qualifying dwellings". Both these terms are defined in s.133, see notes thereto.

Subss. (2), (3), (4)

All applications for a relocation grant must be made in writing by a "qualifying person" and be accompanied by the requisite certificate (see notes to subs. (5)). The Secretary of State may also prescribe other conditions for payment of a relocation grant, and these are likely to include conditions as to the size and physical state of the property (*per* Lord Lucas (Government Whip), Report, *Hansard*, H.L., April 22, 1996, Vol. 571, col. 1004). The application must specify the "qualifying dwelling", and the Secretary of State has reserved the power to prescribe the use of a particular application form.

Subs. (5)

The certificate required in the case of a relocation grant is the same as the "owner-occupation certificate" for a renovation grant, save that in all cases of a relocation grant the applicant certifies that he is proposing to acquire the interest, rather than that he has already acquired it. See further notes to s.7 ("owner's interest"); s.8 ("only or main residence") and s.98 ("member of the family").

Subs. (6)

The manner and timing of payment of the grant is at the discretion of the authority. It is likely that authorities will wish to make the payment at the time of completion of purchase of the qualifying dwelling. They may also make payments directly to the client account of the applicant's solicitors.

Subs. (7)

Under s.24 of the Local Government Act 1988 (c. 9), local authorities may provide financial assistance in connection with, *inter alia*, the acquisition of any property which is or is intended to be privately let as housing accommodation. Such assistance is subject to the condition in s.25 of the 1988 Act, that consent is required from the Secretary of State. In so far as relocation grants could be caught by this provision (*e.g.* where the new property is to be part let), the requirements of s.25 are disapplied.

Relocation grants: qualifying persons and qualifying dwellings

133.—(1) A person is a qualifying person for the purposes of section 132 (relocation grants: applications and payments) if—

(a) an interest of his in a dwelling in the clearance area ("the original dwelling") has been, or is to be, acquired by the local housing authority under section 290 of the Housing Act 1985 or section 154 of the Town and Country Planning Act 1990;

(b) that interest on the acquisition date was greater than a tenancy for a year or from year to year; and

(c) the original dwelling was his only or main residence both on the declaration date and throughout the period of 12 months ending with the acquisition date.

(2) A dwelling is a qualifying dwelling for the purposes of section 132 if it is—

(a) in the clearance area; or

(b) in an area designated by the local housing authority as an area for the relocation of persons displaced by the clearance;

and any area so designated may be in or outside the authority's area.

(3) In making a designation under subsection (2) a local housing authority shall have regard to such guidance as may from time to time be given by the Secretary of State.

(4) Subsections (2) to (4) of section 604A of the Housing Act 1985 (duty to consider guidance before taking enforcement action) shall apply in relation to guidance under subsection (3) as they apply in relation to guidance under subsection (1) of that section.

(5) Any reference in the preceding provisions of this section to the clearance area includes a reference to any land surrounded by or adjoining the clearance area which has been, or is to be, acquired by the local housing authority under section 290 of the Housing Act 1985 or section 154 of the Town and Country Planning Act 1990.

(6) In this section—

"the acquisition date", in relation to an acquisition under section 290 of the Housing Act 1985, means the date of—

(a) the notice to treat under section 5 of the Compulsory Purchase Act 1965;

(b) the general vesting declaration under section 4 of the Compulsory Purchase (Vesting Declarations) Act 1981; or

(c) the agreement between the local housing authority and the applicant,

in pursuance of which the interest in the original dwelling was, or is to be, acquired by the authority;

"the acquisition date", in relation to an acquisition under section 154 of the Town and Country Planning Act 1990 (effect of valid blight notice), means the date mentioned in subsection (3) of that section;

"the declaration date" means the date on which the clearance area was declared by the authority.

DEFINITIONS

"clearance area": H.A. 1985, s.289.
"dwelling": s.140.
"local housing authority": s.140; H.A. 1985, s.1.

GENERAL NOTE

This section defines the two key qualifying concepts for relocation grants: "qualifying person" and "qualifying dwelling".

Qualifying person

A "qualifying person" must (subss. (1), (5), (6)):

(a) have an interest on the acquisition date (see below) which was greater than a tenancy for a year or from year to year (thus excluding periodic tenants and fixed term tenants of a year or less);

(b) in a dwelling (see s.139, below) that was his only or main residence (see notes to s.8, above) both on the date on which the clearance area was declared and throughout the period of 12 months ending with the acquisition date;

(c) in a clearance area (see notes to s.130, above) or land surrounded or adjoining a clearance area (see below);

(d) which has been or is to be acquired by the local housing authority under the Housing Act 1985, s.290 or the Town and Country Planning Act 1990, s.154.

The interest of the qualifying person may be acquired under either the Housing Act 1985, s.290 or the Town and Country Planning Act 1990 (c. 8), s.154. Under s.290, once a clearance area has been declared, the authority must proceed to "secure the clearance area ... by purchasing the land comprised in the area ...". The authority may also purchase land surrounded by the clearance area where it is reasonably necessary for the purpose of securing a cleared area of convenient shape and dimensions and adjoining land which is reasonably necessary for the satisfactory development or use of the cleared area: s.290(2). The land may be acquired compulsorily or by agreement: s.290(3). Where purchased by agreement, the acquisition date is the date of the agreement to purchase; where compulsorily, it is either the date of the notice to treat under the Compulsory Purchase Act 1965 (c. 56), s.5 or the general vesting declaration under the Compulsory Purchase (Vesting Declarations) Act 1981 (c. 66), s.4: subs. (6).

Where a local authority propose re-development, such as clearance, it may "blight" surrounding properties. In those circumstances the owner of the property may, under the Town and Country Planning Act 1990, s.154 serve a notice on the authority requiring them to purchase the property. The purchase then takes the form of a conventional compulsory purchase, from which the authority are not permitted to withdraw: s.154. In such a case, the acquisition date means two months after the service of the blight notice, unless the notice is appealed to the Lands Tribunal, in which case it is the date specified by the Lands Tribunal in its directions issued following rejection of the appeal: subs. (6), applying 1990 Act, s.154(3).

"Qualifying dwelling"

A qualifying dwelling must be either inside the clearance area itself or in an area designated by the authority: subs. (2). For these purposes, "clearance area" includes surrounded or adjoining land acquired under the Housing Act 1985, s.290(2) or the Town and Country Planning Act 1990, s.154: subs. (5). In deciding to designate areas outside the clearance area, authorities must have regard to guidance issued by the Secretary of State under the Housing Act 1985, s.604A: subss. (3), (4) (see notes to s.131(5), above).

Relocation grants: amount

134.—(1) Subject to subsections (2) to (4), the amount of any relocation grant shall be such amount as the local housing authority may determine.

(2) The amount of any relocation grant shall not exceed such amount as may be prescribed.

(3) The amount of any relocation grant shall not exceed the difference between—

(a) the cost of acquiring the qualifying dwelling to which the application relates; and
(b) such part as may be prescribed of the amount which has been, or is to be, paid by the authority in respect of the acquisition of the applicant's interest in the original dwelling.

(4) If the financial resources of the applicant exceed the applicable amount, the amount of any grant which may be paid shall, in accordance with regulations, be reduced from what it would otherwise have been.

(5) For the purposes of subsection (3), the cost of acquiring the qualifying dwelling shall be taken to be whichever of the following is the lesser amount, namely—
(a) the actual cost (including reasonable incidental expenses) of acquiring the dwelling; and
(b) the amount which the authority considers to be the reasonable cost (including such expenses) of acquiring a comparable dwelling in the same area.

(6) Provision may be made by regulations—
(a) for the determination of the amount which is to be taken to be the financial resources of an applicant,
(b) for the determination of the applicable amount referred to in subsection (4), and
(c) as to circumstances in which the financial resources of an applicant are to be assumed (by reason of his receiving a prescribed benefit or otherwise) not to exceed the applicable amount.

(7) Regulations may, in particular—
(a) make provision for account to be taken of the income, assets, needs and outgoings not only of the applicant himself but also of his spouse, any person living with him or intending to live with him and any person on whom he is dependent or who is dependent on him;
(b) make provision for amounts specified in or determined under the regulations to be taken into account for particular purposes.

(8) Regulations may apply, subject to such modifications as may be prescribed by the regulations, any other statutory means-testing regime as it has effect from time to time.

(9) Regulations may make provision requiring any information or evidence needed for the determination of any matter under this section to be furnished by such person as may be prescribed.

(10) In this section—
"the original dwelling" has the same meaning as in section 133;
"regulations" means regulations made by the Secretary of State with the consent of the Treasury.

DEFINITIONS

"local housing authority": s.140; H.A. 1985, s.1.
"qualifying dwelling": s.133(2).
"relocation grant": s.132.

GENERAL NOTE

The amount of grant is to be determined by the authority (subs. (1)) but is subject to two limits:
(a) an amount prescribed by the Secretary of State (subs. (2)); and,
(b) the difference between the cost of acquiring the new dwelling and the prescribed part of the compensation paid to the applicant in respect of acquiring the original dwelling. This requires an applicant to put the compensation he receives for the loss of his old home towards the cost of buying the new one: subs. (3). The cost of acquiring the new dwelling may be limited to the amount that the authority consider to be the reasonable cost of acquiring the dwelling, if this is less than the actual cost: subs. (5).

Payment of grant is also subject to a means test to be carried out by comparison of financial resources and applicable amount, according to a formula or method to be dictated by regulations: subss. (4), (6)–(8).

Relocation grants: condition for repayment on disposal

135.—(1) It is a condition of a relocation grant that, if an owner of the qualifying dwelling makes a relevant disposal (other than an exempt disposal) of the dwelling within the grant condition period, he shall repay to the local housing authority on demand the amount of the grant.

(2) A condition under this section is binding on any person who is for the time being an owner of the qualifying dwelling.

(3) Where the authority have the right to demand repayment of an amount as mentioned in subsection (1), they may—

(a) if the case falls within subsection (4), or

(b) in any other case, with the consent of the Secretary of State,

determine not to demand payment or to demand a lesser amount.

(4) The cases referred to in subsection (3)(a) are where the authority are satisfied that the owner of the dwelling—

(a) is elderly or infirm and is making the disposal with the intention—

(i) of going to live in a hospital, hospice, sheltered housing, residential care home or similar institution as his only or main residence, or

(ii) of moving to somewhere where care will be provided by any person; or

(b) is making the disposal with the intention of going to live with and care for an elderly or infirm member of his family or his partner's family.

(5) The consent of the Secretary of State for the purposes of subsection (3)(b) may be given either generally or in relation to any one or more specified authorities or descriptions of authority or in relation to particular cases or descriptions of case.

(6) A condition under this section shall cease to be in force with respect to a dwelling if there is a relevant disposal of the dwelling that is an exempt disposal, other than—

(a) a disposal within section 54(1)(a) (disposal to associates of person making disposal), or

(b) a disposal within section 54(1)(b) (vesting under will or on intestacy) to a person who resided with the deceased in the dwelling as his only or main residence throughout the period of twelve months ending with the date of the deceased's death.

(7) Any disposal which—

(a) by virtue of section 53 (meaning of relevant disposal), is a relevant disposal; or

(b) by virtue of section 54 (meaning of exempt disposal), is an exempt disposal,

for the purposes of the provisions of Part I of this Act (relating to grant conditions) is also such a disposal for the purposes of this section.

DEFINITIONS

"grant condition period": s.140.
"local housing authority": s.140; H.A. 1985, s.1.
"owner": s.140.
"qualifying dwelling": s.133(2).
"relocation grant": s.131.

GENERAL NOTE

This section introduces a grant condition similar to that under s.45, above, requiring repayment on a "relevant disposal", which is not otherwise "exempt". The condition applies during the grant condition period, *i.e.* five years from the date of purchase of the dwelling, or such other period as the Secretary of State may prescribe: s.140. See notes to ss.53 and 54 above as to relevant disposal and exempt disposal, which have the same meaning under this section: subs. (7).

For the definition of "owner", see s.140 and notes to s.45, above.

Subs. (2)
Unlike under the equivalent s.45(3), the condition is not a local land charge, since the duty to repay takes effect as a charge on the premises: see s.138 below.

Subss. (3), (4), (5)
These subsections contain the only and limited discretion to not recover the grant, in the same terms as are contained in s.45(4), (5), see notes thereto.

Subs. (6)
Even though it will not cause repayment, the condition ceases when there is an exempt disposal, other than in the two classes identified, *i.e.* such other disposals keep the condition alive (but, because they are exempt, do not activate repayment).

Relocation grants: conditions as to owner-occupation

136.—(1) It is a condition of a relocation grant that throughout the grant condition period the qualifying dwelling is occupied in accordance with the intention stated in the certificate under section 132(5)(b).

(2) It is also a condition of the grant that if at any time when that condition is in force the local housing authority serve notice on the owner of the qualifying dwelling requiring him to do so, he will within the period of 21 days beginning with the date on which the notice was served furnish to the authority a statement showing how that condition is being fulfilled.

(3) A condition under this section is binding on any person who is for the time being an owner of the dwelling.

(4) In the event of a breach of a condition under this section, the owner for the time being of the dwelling shall on demand repay to the local housing authority the amount of the grant, together with compound interest on that amount as from the beginning of the grant condition period, calculated at such reasonable rate as the authority may determine and with yearly rests.

(5) The local housing authority may determine not to make such a demand or to demand a lesser amount.

(6) Subsections (6) and (7) of section 135 apply for the purposes of this section as they apply for the purposes of that section.

DEFINITIONS
"dwelling": s.140.
"local housing authority": s.140; H.A. 1985, s.1.
"owner": s.140.
"qualifying dwelling": s.133(2).
"relocation grant": s.131.

GENERAL NOTE
This section introduces an "occupation condition" equivalent to that for owner-occupiers in receipt of renovation grant: see notes to s.48, above.

Relocation grants: cessation of conditions on repayment of grant, &c.

137.—(1) If at any time while a condition under section 135 or 136 (a "grant condition") remains in force with respect to a qualifying dwelling—

(a) the owner of the dwelling to which the condition relates pays the amount of the grant to the local housing authority by whom the grant was made, or
(b) a mortgagee of the interest of the owner in that dwelling being a mortgagee entitled to exercise a power of sale, makes such a payment, or
(c) the local housing authority determine not to demand repayment on the breach of a grant condition, or
(d) the authority demand repayment in whole or in part on the breach of a grant condition and that demand is satisfied,

the grant condition and any other grant conditions shall cease to be in force with respect to that dwelling.

(2) An amount paid by a mortgagee under subsection (1)(b) shall be treated as part of the sums secured by the mortgage and may be discharged accordingly.

DEFINITIONS

"local housing authority": s.140; H.A. 1985, s.1.
"owner": s.140.
"qualifying dwelling": s.133(2).

GENERAL NOTE

This section permits an owner voluntarily to repay a grant in order to free himself from all of the conditions attached to it: see further notes to s.55, above.

Relocation grants: liability to repay is a charge on dwelling

138.—(1) The liability that may arise under a condition under section 135, or under section 136(4), is a charge on the qualifying dwelling, taking effect as if it had been created by deed expressed to be by way of legal mortgage.

(2) The charge has priority immediately after any legal charge securing an amount—

(a) advanced to the applicant by an approved lending institution for the purpose of enabling him to acquire the dwelling, or
(b) further advanced to him by that institution;

but the local housing authority may at any time by written notice served on an approved lending institution postpone the charge taking effect by virtue of this section to a legal charge securing an amount advanced or further advanced to the applicant by that institution.

(3) A charge taking effect by virtue of this section is a land charge for the purposes of section 59 of the Land Registration Act 1925 notwithstanding subsection (5) of that section (exclusion of mortgages), and subsection (2) of that section applies accordingly with respect to its protection and realisation.

(4) A condition under section 135 or 136 does not, by virtue of its binding any person who is for the time being an owner of the dwelling, bind a person exercising rights under a charge having priority over the charge taking effect by virtue of this section, or a person deriving title under him.

(5) The approved lending institutions for the purposes of section 156 of the Housing Act 1985 (right to buy: liability to repay discount is a charge on premises) are also approved lending institutions for the purposes of this section.

DEFINITIONS

"local housing authority": s.140; H.A. 1985, s.1.
"qualifying dwelling": s.133(2).

GENERAL NOTE

This section does not have an equivalent in Pt. I, Chap. I. It makes repayment liabilities arising under s.135 and s.136(4) a charge on the dwelling which has been purchased with the relocation grant. The charge is to take effect as if it had been created by deed expressed to be by way of mortgage, and it will have priority immediately following the priority of the mortgage with which the dwelling is itself purchased, or a further advance from the body which gave that initial mortgage (providing that the body is an approved lending institution within subs. (5)). A purchase effected with a loan by someone other than one of the bodies specified, will accordingly mean that the lender's charge on the property takes priority behind the repayment covenant.

The mortgage is registrable as a land charge under the Land Registration Act 1925 (c. 21), s.59 and thus may be protected against subsequent dealings in the dwelling by entry of a notice or caution.

Subs. (5)

Under the Housing Act 1985, s.156(4), the Housing Corporation, Housing for Wales, building societies, banks, trustee savings banks, insurance companies and friendly societies are all approved lending institutions. The Secretary of State also has power to specify other institutions and has done so in a number of statutory instruments listing institutions similar to those automatically approved. For an up-to-date list see the *Encyclopedia of Housing Law and Practice,* Vol. 1.

Relocation grants: contributions by the Secretary of State

139.—(1) The Secretary of State may pay contributions to local housing authorities towards such expenditure incurred by them under section 132 (payment of relocation grants) as he may determine.

(2) The rate or rates of the contributions, the calculation of the expenditure to which they relate and the manner of their payment shall be such as may be determined by the Secretary of State.

(3) Any determination under subsection (1) or (2) may be made generally, or with respect to a particular local housing authority or description of authority, including a description framed by reference to authorities in a particular area.

(4) Contributions under this section shall be payable subject to such conditions as to repayment, and such conditions as to records, certificates, audit or otherwise, as the Secretary of State may impose.

DEFINITIONS

"local housing authority": s.140; H.A. 1985, s.1.

GENERAL NOTE

This section provides for the subsidy to be provided by the Secretary of State, which may be general, or specific to particular authorities or categories of authorities, including by reference to parts of the country. The government have indicated that they expect to pay subsidy at the same rate as for slum clearance subsidy, *i.e.* 60 per cent (see Annex J, to DoE Circular 6/90, as amended), *per* Lord Lucas (Government Whip), Committee, *Hansard*, H.L., April 1, 1996, Vol. 571, col. 116.

Minor definitions relating to relocation grants

140.—(1) In sections 131 to 139 (provisions as to relocation grants)—

"dwelling" means a building or part of a building occupied or intended to be occupied as a separate dwelling, together with any yard, garden, outhouses and appurtenances belonging to it or usually enjoyed with it;

"grant condition period" means the period of five years, or such other period as the Secretary of State may by order specify, beginning with the date of the acquisition of the owner's interest in the qualifying dwelling;

"local housing authority" has the same meaning as in the Housing Act 1985;

"owner", in relation to a dwelling, means the person who—

(a) is for the time being entitled to receive from a lessee of the dwelling (or would be so entitled if the dwelling were let) a rent of not less than two-thirds of the net annual value of the dwelling; and

(b) is not himself liable as lessee of the dwelling, or of property which includes the dwelling, to pay such a rent to a superior landlord;

"owner's interest", in relation to any premises, means—

(a) an estate in fee simple absolute in possession, or

(b) a term of years absolute of which not less than five years remain unexpired at the date of the application,

whether held by the applicant alone or jointly with others;

"prescribed" means prescribed by regulations made by the Secretary of State;

"qualifying dwelling" has the meaning given by section 133(2);

"qualifying person" has the meaning given by section 133(1);

"relocation grant" means a grant under section 132.

(2) For the purposes of the definition of "owner" in subsection (1), the net annual value of a dwelling means the rent at which the dwelling might reasonably be expected to be let from year to year if the tenant undertook to pay all usual tenant's rates and taxes and to bear the cost of repair and insurance and the other expenses, if any, necessary to maintain the dwelling in a state to command that rent.

(3) Any dispute arising as to the net annual value of a dwelling shall be referred in writing for decision by the district valuer.

In this subsection "district valuer" has the same meaning as in the Housing Act 1985.

(4) Section 113 of the Housing Act 1985 (meaning of "members of a person's family") applies in determining whether a person is a member of another's family for the purposes of sections 132 and 135.

General Note

For the main definitions, see as follows:
Notes to s.1, above—dwelling, local housing authority.
Notes to s.7 above—owner's interest.
Notes to s.45 above—owner.

Subs. (4)

See notes to s.98, above.

Part V

Miscellaneous and general provisions

Miscellaneous provisions

Existing housing grants: meaning of exempt disposal

141.—(1) Section 124 of the Local Government and Housing Act 1989 (relevant and exempt disposals for purposes of housing grants) is amended as follows.

(2) In subsection (3) (exempt disposals), for paragraph (c) substitute—

"(c) a disposal of the whole of the dwelling in pursuance of any such order as is mentioned in subsection (4A) below;".

(3) After subsection (4) insert—

"(4A) The orders referred to in subsection (3)(c) above are orders under—

(a) section 24 or 24A of the Matrimonial Causes Act 1973 (property adjustment orders or orders for the sale of property in connection with matrimonial proceedings),

(b) section 2 of the Inheritance (Provision for Family and Dependants) Act 1975 (orders as to financial provision to be made from estate),

(c) section 17 of the Matrimonial and Family Proceedings Act 1984 (property adjustment orders or orders for the sale of property after overseas divorce, &c.), or

(d) paragraph 1 of Schedule 1 to the Children Act 1989 (orders for financial relief against parents);".

General Note

This section makes an equivalent extension to the definition of "exempt disposal", to the existing grants regime under the Local Government and Housing Act 1989, as is made under s.54 above (see notes thereto) to overturn the decision in *R. v. Rushmoor B.C., ex p. Barrett* (1988) 20 H.L.R. 366, C.A., and also to add orders under the Matrimonial and Family Proceedings Act 1984 (c. 42) and the Children Act 1989 (c. 41).

Home energy efficiency schemes

142.—(1) In section 15 of the Social Security Act 1990 (grants for the improvement of energy efficiency in certain dwellings, &c.) for subsection (1) (power to make grants) substitute—

"(1) The Secretary of State may make or arrange for the making of grants—

(a) towards the cost of carrying out work for the purpose of—

(i) improving the thermal insulation of dwellings, or

(ii) otherwise reducing or preventing the wastage of energy in dwellings (whether in connection with space or water heating, lighting, the use of domestic appliances or otherwise), and

(b) where any such work is, or is to be, carried out, towards the cost of providing persons with advice on reducing or preventing the wastage of energy in dwellings;

but no grants shall be made under this section except in accordance with regulations made by the Secretary of State.".

(2) In subsection (10) of that section, after the definition of "functions", insert—

" "materials" includes space and water heating systems;".

General Note

This section makes minor amendments to the home energy grant scheme contained in the Social Security Act 1990 (c. 27), s.15, reflecting the fact that technology has moved on: Robert Jones (Minister for Construction, Planning and Energy Efficiency), *Hansard*, H.C., 11th sitting, Standing Committee F, June 20, 1996, col. 413. In particular, the scheme is extended to include grants for the reduction or prevention of wastage of energy in dwellings, not just through space and water heating but also through lighting, the use of domestic appliances or otherwise.

Urban development corporations: pre-dissolution transfers

143.—(1) After section 165A of the Local Government, Planning and Land Act 1980 insert—

"**Transfer of property, rights and liabilities to statutory bodies**

165B.—(1) Subject to this section, the Secretary of State may at any time by order transfer to a statutory body, upon such terms as he thinks fit, any property, rights or liabilities which—

(a) are for the time being vested in an urban development corporation, and

(b) are not proposed to be transferred under section 165 or 165A above.

(2) An order under this section may terminate—

(a) any appointment of the corporation under subsection (1) of section 177 of the Leasehold Reform, Housing and Urban Development Act 1993 (power of corporations to act as agents of the Urban Regeneration Agency); and

(b) any arrangements made by the corporation under subsection (2) of that section.

(3) An order under this section may—

(a) establish new bodies corporate to receive any property, rights or liabilities to be transferred by an order under this section;

(b) amend, repeal or otherwise modify any enactment for the purpose of enabling any body established under any enactment to receive such property, rights or liabilities.

(4) An order under this section—

(a) may contain such incidental, consequential, transitional or supplementary provision as the Secretary of State thinks necessary or expedient (including provisions amending, repealing or otherwise modifying any enactment); and

(b) shall be made by statutory instrument which shall be subject to annulment in pursuance of a resolution of either House of Parliament.

(5) Before making an order under this section, the Secretary of State shall consult each local authority in whose area all or part of the urban development area is situated.

(6) In this section—

"enactment" includes any instrument made under any enactment;

"statutory body" means any body established under this section or any other enactment.".

(2) In consequence of the above amendment, the Local Government, Planning and Land Act 1980 is amended as follows.

(3) In section 165(9) (meaning of local authority) for "sections 165A and 166" substitute "sections 165A to 166".

(4) In section 165A(1) (power of Secretary of State to transfer property &c. to himself) for paragraph (b) substitute—

"(b) are not proposed to be transferred under section 165 above or 165B below.".

(5) In section 166(5) (dissolution of corporations) after "section 165A" insert "or 165B".

General Note

This and the following two sections make provision for the transfer of property, rights or liabilities vested in an urban development corporation (this section), a housing action trust (s.144), or the Commission for New Towns (s.145), to a residuary body or bodies. In the case of urban development corporations and housing action trusts, the government intends to create a new body based on a reformed Commission for the New Towns, and in the final case it plans simply to reform that body: Robert Jones (Minister for Construction, Planning and Energy Efficiency), *Hansard*, H.C., 11th sitting, Standing Committee F, June 20, 1996, col. 415.

Housing action trusts: orders for dissolution

144.—(1) Section 88 of the Housing Act 1988 (dissolution of housing action trusts) is amended as follows.

(2) In subsection (4) (contents of dissolution orders) after paragraph (a) insert—

"(aa) where it provides for any such disposal or transfer as is mentioned in subsection (2)(b) above, may contain provisions—

(i) establishing new bodies corporate to receive the disposal or transfer; or

(ii) amending, repealing or otherwise modifying any enactment for the purpose of enabling any body established under any enactment to receive the disposal or transfer;".

(3) In paragraph (b) of that subsection (supplementary and transitional provisions) for the words from "any enactment", where it first appears, to "order" substitute ", repealing or otherwise modifying any enactment".

(4) After that subsection insert—

"(5) In this section "enactment" includes any instrument made under any enactment.".

General Note

See notes to s.143 above.

The Commission for the New Towns: orders for dissolution

145.—(1) In Schedule 9 to the New Towns Act 1981 (additional provisions as to the Commission for the New Towns) paragraph 7 (power to dissolve Commission) is amended as follows.

(2) After sub-paragraph (2) insert—

"(2A) Any order under this paragraph may—

(a) establish new bodies corporate to receive any property, rights, liabilities or obligations vested by an order under this paragraph;

(b) amend, repeal or otherwise modify any enactment for the purpose of enabling any body established under any enactment to receive such property, rights, liabilities or obligations.".

(3) In sub-paragraph (3) (incidental, supplemental, consequential or transitional provision) for the words from "amendments" to the end substitute "provisions amending, repealing or otherwise modifying any enactment.".

(4) For sub-paragraph (7) (interpretation) substitute—

"(7) In this paragraph—

"accountable public authority" means a body established under this paragraph or any other enactment;

"enactment" includes any instrument made under any enactment.".

General Note

See notes to s.143 above.

General provisions

Orders, regulations and directions

146.—(1) Orders, regulations and directions under this Act may make different provision for different cases or descriptions of case, including different provision for different areas.

(2) Orders and regulations under this Act may contain such incidental, supplementary or transitional provisions and savings as the Secretary of State considers appropriate.

(3) Orders and regulations under this Act shall be made by statutory instrument which, except for—

(a) orders and regulations subject to affirmative resolution procedure (see sections 104(4), 105(4), 106(4) and 114(5)),

(b) orders under section 150(3), or

(c) regulations which only prescribe forms or particulars to be contained in forms,

shall be subject to annulment in pursuance of a resolution of either House of Parliament.

Repeals and revocations

147. The enactments specified in Schedule 3 are repealed or revoked to the extent specified.

Extent

148.—(1) The provisions of this Act extend to England and Wales.

(2) The following provisions of this Act extend to Scotland—

Part II (construction contracts),

Part III (architects),

sections 126 to 128 (financial assistance for regeneration and development), and

Part V (miscellaneous and general provisions), except—

(i) sections 141, 144 and 145 (which amend provisions which do not extend to Scotland), and

(ii) Part I of Schedule 3 (repeals consequential on provisions not extending to Scotland).

(3) The following provisions of this Act extend to Northern Ireland—

Part III (architects), and

Part V (miscellaneous and general provisions), except—
(i) sections 142 to 145 (home energy efficiency schemes and residuary bodies), and
(ii) Parts I and III of Schedule 3 (repeals consequential on provisions not extending to Northern Ireland).

(4) Except as otherwise provided, any amendment or repeal by this Act of an enactment has the same extent as the enactment amended or repealed.

Corresponding provision for Northern Ireland

149. An Order in Council under paragraph 1(1)(b) of Schedule 1 to the Northern Ireland Act 1974 (legislation for Northern Ireland in the interim period) which states that it is made only for purposes corresponding to those of Part II (construction contracts) or section 142 (home energy efficiency schemes)—
(a) shall not be subject to paragraph 1(4) and (5) of that Schedule (affirmative resolution of both Houses of Parliament), but
(b) shall be subject to annulment in pursuance of a resolution of either House of Parliament.

Commencement

150.—(1) The following provisions of this Act come into force on Royal Assent—
section 146 (orders, regulations and directions),
sections 148 to 151 (extent, commencement and other general provisions).

(2) The following provisions of this Act come into force at the end of the period of two months beginning with the date on which this Act is passed—
sections 126 to 130 (financial assistance for regeneration and development),
section 141 (existing housing grants: meaning of exempt disposal),
section 142 (home energy efficiency schemes),
sections 143 to 145 (residuary bodies),
Part III of Schedule 3 (repeals consequential on Part IV) and section 147 so far as relating to that Part.

(3) The other provisions of this Act come into force on a day appointed by order of the Secretary of State, and different days may be appointed for different areas and different purposes.

(4) The Secretary of State may by order under subsection (3) make such transitional provision and savings as appear to him to be appropriate in connection with the coming into force of any provision of this Act.

Short title

151. This Act may be cited as the Housing Grants, Construction and Regeneration Act 1996.

SCHEDULES

Section 103

SCHEDULE 1

PRIVATE SECTOR RENEWAL: CONSEQUENTIAL AMENDMENTS

Rent Act 1977 (c.42)

1.—(1) Section 116 of the Rent Act 1977 (court order where tenant unwilling to consent to works) is amended as follows.

(2) In subsection (2), omit "any of paragraphs (a) to (c) of".

(3) For subsection (3) substitute—

"(3) The condition is that the works were specified in an application for a renovation grant, a common parts grant, a disabled facilities grant or an HMO grant under Chapter I of

Part I of the Housing Grants, Construction and Regeneration Act 1996 and the application has been approved.".

(4) In subsection (5), for the words from "under section 512(2)" to the end, substitute "under section 37 of the Housing Grants, Construction and Regeneration Act 1996.".

Housing Act 1985 (c.68)

2. In section 47(4) of the Housing Act 1985 (limitation of service charges: deduct amount of grant), for the words from "Part XV" to "or conversion)" substitute "section 523 of the Housing Act 1985 (assistance for provision of separate service pipe for water supply) or any provision of Part I of the Housing Grants, Construction and Regeneration Act 1996 (grants, &c. for renewal of private sector housing) or any corresponding earlier enactment".

3. In section 48(3A) of the Housing Act 1985 (information as to relevant costs: grant), for the words from "Part XV" to the end substitute "section 523 of the Housing Act 1985 (assistance for provision of separate service pipe for water supply) or any provision of Chapter I of Part I of the Housing Grants, Construction and Regeneration Act 1996 (grants for renewal of private sector housing) or any corresponding earlier enactment".

4.—(1) In section 100(2) of the Housing Act 1985 (power to reimburse cost of tenant's improvements; grant), for "improvement grant" to "Part XV" substitute "renovation grant or common parts grant under Chapter I of Part I of the Housing Grants, Construction and Regeneration Act 1996 (grants for renewal of private sector housing)".

(2) In that section, omit subsection (2A).

5.—(1) In section 101(1) of the Housing Act 1985 (rent not to be increased on account of tenant's improvements: grant), for "improvement grant" to the end substitute "renovation grant or common parts grant under Chapter I of Part I of the Housing Grants, Construction and Regeneration Act 1996 (grants for renewal of private sector housing).".

(2) In that section, omit subsection (1A).

6. In section 190A of the Housing Act 1985 (repair notices and group repair schemes)—

(a) in subsection (2), for "subsection 130(1)" to the end substitute "subsection 66(1) of the Housing Grants, Construction and Regeneration Act 1996).".

(b) in subsection (5), for "Part VIII" to the end substitute "Chapter II of Part I of the Housing Grants, Construction and Regeneration Act 1996 (group repair schemes).".

7.—(1) In section 244 of the Housing Act 1985 (environmental works: no assistance where grant made), for subsection (3) substitute—

"(3) No such assistance shall be given towards works in respect of which an application for renovation grant or common parts grant under Chapter I of Part I of the Housing Grants, Construction and Regeneration Act 1996 (grants for renewal of private sector housing) has been approved.".

(2) In that section, omit subsection (3A).

8.—(1) In subsection (2)(b) of section 255 of the Housing Act 1985 (general powers of local housing authority not to include making grants), for "an improvement grant" to the end substitute "a renovation grant or common parts grant might be made under Chapter I of Part I of the Housing Grants, Construction and Regeneration Act 1996 (grants for renewal of private sector housing).".

(2) In that section, omit subsection (3).

9. In section 535(1)(a) of the Housing Act 1985 (exclusion of assistance under Part XV of that Act where grant application pending or approved), for the words from "an improvement grant" to "Part XV" substitute "renovation grant or common parts grant under Chapter I of Part I of the Housing Grants, Construction and Regeneration Act 1996 (grants for renewal of private sector housing).".

10. In section 605 of the Housing Act 1985 (consideration by local housing authority of housing conditions in their district), for subsection (1)(e) substitute—

"(e) Part I of the Housing Grants, Construction and Regeneration Act 1996 (grants, &c. for renewal of private sector housing).".

Landlord and Tenant Act 1985 (c.70)

11.—(1) In subsection (1) of section 20A of the Landlord and Tenant Act 1985 (limitation of service charges: grant-aided works), for the words from "Part XV" to "conversion)" substitute "section 523 of the Housing Act 1985 (assistance for provision of separate service pipe for water supply) or any provision of Part I of the Housing Grants, Construction and Regeneration Act 1996 (grants, &c. for renewal of private sector housing) or any corresponding earlier enactment".

(2) In subsection (2) of that section—

(a) for "Part VIII of the Local Government and Housing Act 1989" substitute "Part I of the Housing Grants, Construction and Regeneration Act 1996"; and

(b) for "the outstanding balance determined in accordance with subsections (3) and (4) of section 130 of that Act" substitute "the balance of the cost determined in accordance with section 69(3) of the Housing Grants, Construction and Regeneration Act 1996".

12. In section 21 of the Landlord and Tenant Act 1985 (request for summary of relevant costs)—

(a) in subsection (5), for the words from "Part XV" to "conversion)" substitute "section 523 of the Housing Act 1985 (assistance for provision of separate service pipe for water supply) or any provision of Part I of the Housing Grants, Construction and Regeneration Act 1996 (grants, &c. for renewal of private sector housing) or any corresponding earlier enactment"; and

(b) in subsection (5B) for "Part VIII of the Local Government and Housing Act 1989" substitute "Chapter II of Part I of the Housing Grants, Construction and Regeneration Act 1996 or any corresponding earlier enactment".

Housing Act 1988 (c.50)

13. In section 121(1) of the Housing Act 1988 (rent officers' functions), for "section 110" to the end substitute "section 31 of the Housing Grants, Construction and Regeneration Act 1996 applies.".

Local Government and Housing Act 1989 (c.42)

14. In section 93(5) of the Local Government and Housing Act 1989 (general powers of local housing authority: works in renewal area), for "Part VIII of this Act" substitute "Part I of the Housing Grants, Construction and Regeneration Act 1996".

15.—(1) Section 169 of the Local Government and Housing Act 1989 (power of local authority and Secretary of State to provide professional, &c. services in relation to works) is amended as follows.

(2) In subsection (2)(b), for "section 114(3) or (4) above" substitute "section 23 of the Housing Grants, Construction and Regeneration Act 1996 (disabled facilities grants: purposes)".

(3) In subsection (2)(c), for "section 115(3) above" substitute "or under section 12 or 27 of the Housing Grants, Construction and Regeneration Act 1996 (renovation grants or HMO grants: purposes)".

(4) For subsection (2)(d) substitute—

"(d) works in relation to home repair assistance under sections 76 to 79 of the Housing Grants, Construction and Regeneration Act 1996.".

Sections 118 and 125

SCHEDULE 2

ARCHITECTS

PART I

NEW FIRST SCHEDULE TO THE 1931 ACT

1. This is the Schedule to be substituted for the First Schedule to the 1931 Act—

"**Section 3**

FIRST SCHEDULE

THE BOARD AND ITS COMMITTEES

PART I

THE BOARD

Membership

1. The Board shall consist of—

(a) seven elected members; and

(b) eight appointed members.

Elected members

2.—(1) The elected members shall be elected in accordance with an electoral scheme made by the Board, with the approval of the Privy Council, after consultation with such bodies as appear to the Board to be representative of architects.

(2) An electoral scheme under sub-paragraph (1) may be amended by the Board with the approval of the Privy Council and after consultation with such bodies as are mentioned in that sub-paragraph.

(3) The persons qualified—

(a) to elect the elected members; and

(b) to be elected as elected members,

are all those who are registered persons when the election is held.

Appointed members

3.—(1) The appointed members shall be appointed by the Privy Council, after consultation with the Secretary of State and such other persons or bodies as the Privy Council think fit, to represent the interests of users of architectural services and the general public.

(2) No registered person shall be eligible for appointment as an appointed member.

Term of office

4.—(1) Subject to sub-paragraphs (2) and (3), the term of office of a member of the Board is three years.

(2) A member may resign at any time by notice in writing addressed to the Registrar.

(3) The Board may by rules prescribe grounds (such as repeated absence from meetings or unacceptable professional conduct) on which any member may be removed from office and the procedure for removal.

5. A person who has held office as a member of the Board for a continuous period of six years may not be elected or appointed as a member until at least three years have elapsed since he last held office.

Casual vacancies

6.—(1) Where a vacancy occurs among the members of the Board otherwise than by the expiry of a member's term of office—

(a) if the vacancy is among the elected members, the Board shall appoint a registered person to fill it; and

(b) if the vacancy is among the appointed members, the Privy Council shall appoint a person to fill it.

(2) Subject to paragraph 4(2) and (3), a person appointed under sub-paragraph (1) to fill a vacancy holds office until the date on which the term of office of the member whose vacancy he fills would have expired.

(3) A person appointed under sub-paragraph (1)(a) shall be regarded as an elected member and a person appointed under sub-paragraph (1)(b) shall be regarded as an appointed member.

Chairman

7.—(1) The members of the Board shall elect a chairman from among themselves.

(2) The chairman—

(a) may resign by notice in writing addressed to the Registrar; and

(b) may be removed by a majority vote of the other members of the Board.

(3) Rules made by the Board may make provision for the appointment of a person to act as chairman in the event of a vacancy in the office of chairman or in such other circumstances as may be prescribed.

8. In the event of a tie in any vote of the Board the chairman shall have an additional casting vote.

Procedure

9. The quorum of the Board shall be nine, of whom at least four shall be elected members and at least four shall be appointed members.

10. The Board may make rules governing its meetings and procedure.

PART II

THE PROFESSIONAL CONDUCT COMMITTEE

11. The Professional Conduct Committee shall consist of—

(a) four elected members of the Board, including at least one whose address in the Register is in Scotland, or (if there is no elected member whose address in the Register is in Scotland or no such elected member who is willing to act) three elected members and one registered person whose address in the Register is in Scotland;

(b) three appointed members of the Board; and

(c) two persons nominated by the President of the Law Society.

12.—(1) The members of the Professional Conduct Committee shall elect a chairman from among themselves.

(2) The chairman—

(a) may resign by notice in writing addressed to the Registrar; and

(b) may be removed by a majority vote of the other members of the Professional Conduct Committee.

(3) Rules made by the Board may make provision for the appointment of a person to act as chairman in the event of a vacancy in the office of chairman or in such other circumstances as may be prescribed.

13.—(1) The quorum of the Professional Conduct Committee shall be one elected member of the Board, one appointed member of the Board and one person nominated by the President of the Law Society.

(2) Where the Committee is considering the case of a person whose address in the Register is in Scotland, the Committee is not quorate unless there is present a member of the Committee who is a registered person and whose address in the Register is in Scotland.

14. In the event of a tie in any vote of the Professional Conduct Committee the chairman shall have an additional casting vote; and in any proceedings relating to a registered person the additional vote shall be cast in favour of that person.

15. The Board may make rules governing the selection and term of office of members of the Professional Conduct Committee (including casual vacancies).

PART III

OTHER COMMITTEES

16. The Board may establish such committees as it considers appropriate to discharge any of its functions under this Act other than—

(a) prescribing fees under section 6(4), 6A(1A), 6B(1) or (3) or 7ZD(4); or

(b) acting under section 6(1), (2) or (5), 6A(1) or (1B), 6C(1) or 7ZE(1), (2) or (3),

or to assist the Board in the discharge by the Board of any of its functions.

17.—(1) Any committee established by the Board may include persons who are not members of the Board; but if a committee is established to discharge any function of the Board, the majority of the members of the committee must be members of the Board.

(2) Subject to that, the membership of any committee established by the Board shall be determined by the Board.

18. No vote of any committee established by the Board for the discharge of any of its functions shall be valid unless the majority of those voting are members of the Board.

19. The Board may make rules governing the term of office of members of any committee established by the Board (including casual vacancies) and the meetings and procedure (including chairmanship and quorum) of any committee established by the Board.

PART IV

GENERAL

20.—(1) The Board, the Professional Conduct Committee and any committee established by the Board may exercise its functions even though there is a vacancy among its members.

(2) No proceedings of the Board, the Professional Conduct Committee or any committee established by the Board are invalidated by any defect in the election or appointment of a member.

21. The Board may by rules provide for the payment to members of the Board, the Professional Conduct Committee or any committee established by the Board of—

(a) fees for attendance at meetings of the Board or committee; and

(b) travelling and subsistence allowances in respect of attendance at such meetings or the conduct of business of the Board or committee.

22.—(1) The Secretary of State may, after consultation with the Board and such other persons or bodies as he thinks fit, by order amend the provisions of this Schedule.

(2) An order under sub-paragraph (1) shall be made by statutory instrument which shall be subject to annulment in pursuance of a resolution of either House of Parliament.".

PART II

OTHER AMENDMENTS

The 1931 Act

2.—(1) Section 2 of the 1931 Act (interpretation) is amended as follows.

(2) For the definition of "the Council" substitute—

"The expression "the Board" means the Architects Registration Board.".

(3) In the definition of "registered person", for "registered under this Act" substitute "whose name is in the Register".

(4) In the definition of "prescribed", for "regulations made by the Council" substitute "rules made by the Board".

(5) In the definition of "the Register", for "kept in pursuance of this Act" substitute "of Architects".

(6) After that definition insert—

"The expression "the Registrar" means the Registrar of Architects appointed by the Board under section 4.

The expressions "penalty order", "suspension order" and "erasure order" shall be construed in accordance with sections 7ZB, 7ZC and 7ZD.

The expression "disciplinary order" has the meaning given by section 7ZA.".

3.—(1) Section 3 of the 1931 Act (constitution and functions of Architects' Registration Council) is amended as follows.

(2) In subsection (1), for the words from the beginning to "name," substitute "The Architects Registration Board shall be a body corporate".

(3) In subsection (2)—

(a) omit the first sentence, and

(b) in the second sentence, for "Council" (in both places) substitute "Board".

(4) For the sidenote substitute "The Board and its committees.".

4.—(1) Section 6A of the 1931 Act (European qualifications) is amended as follows.

(2) In subsection (1), for the words from "shall" to the end substitute "and has applied to the Registrar in the prescribed manner for registration in pursuance of this section is entitled to be registered.".

(3) After that subsection insert—

"(1A) The Board may require an applicant for registration in pursuance of this section to pay a fee of a prescribed amount.

(1B) The Board may by rules prescribe the information and evidence to be furnished to the Registrar in connection with an application for registration in pursuance of this section.".

(4) In subsection (7), for the words from "The Council" to "aware that" substitute "An application by a person for registration in pursuance of this section may be refused if".

(5) In subsection (8), for the words from "Council" to "applicant" substitute "Registrar shall serve on an applicant for registration in pursuance of this section written notice of the decision on his application".

(6) In subsection (9)—

(a) for "Council consult" substitute "Board consults", and

(b) for "Council of" substitute "Board of".

5.—(1) Section 7A of the 1931 Act (removal of name from Register: disqualification in another member State) is amended as follows.

(2) In subsection (1)—

(a) for "Council were" substitute "Board was",

(b) for "Council, on" substitute "Board, on", and

(c) for "cause his name to be removed" substitute "order the Registrar to remove his name".

(3) In subsection (2), for "7 of this Act" substitute "7ZA(1)".

(4) After that subsection insert—

"(3) Where the Board orders the Registrar to remove a person's name from the Register under this section, the Registrar shall serve written notice of the removal on the person as soon as is reasonably practicable.".

6.—(1) Section 9 of the 1931 Act (right of appeal against removal from Register) is amended as follows.

(2) For the words "by the removal" onwards substitute "by—

(a) his name not being re-entered in, or being removed from, the Register by virtue of section 6C(1);

(b) the making of a disciplinary order in relation to him; or

(c) the Board ordering the Registrar to remove his name from the Register under section 7A,

may appeal to the High Court or the Court of Session within three months from the date on which notice of the decision or order concerned is served on him; and on an appeal under this section the Court may make any order which appears appropriate, and no appeal shall lie from any decision of the Court on such an appeal.".

(3) For the sidenote substitute "Appeals.".

7. In section 11 of the 1931 Act (removal of name from Register for failure to notify change of address), for "Council" (in each place) substitute "Registrar".

8. In section 12 of the 1931 Act (penalty for obtaining registration by false representation), for "wilfully" substitute "intentionally".

9. For section 13 of the 1931 Act (regulations) substitute—

"**Rules**

13.—(1) The Board may make rules generally for carrying out or facilitating the purposes of this Act.

(2) The Board shall, before making any rules under this Act, publish a draft of the rules and give those to whom the rules would be applicable an opportunity of making representations to the Board.".

10.—(1) Section 15 of the 1931 Act (supply of regulations and forms) is amended as follows.

(2) For "Council" substitute "Registrar".

(3) For "regulations" (in each place, including the sidenote) substitute "rules".

11.—(1) Section 16 of the 1931 Act (service of documents) is amended as follows.

(2) In subsection (1), for "to be sent" substitute "to be served".

(3) In subsection (2), for "to the removal from the Register of the name of any registered person" substitute "required to be served by section 6C(2), 7(4)(a), 7ZA(3) or 7A(3)".

12.—(1) Section 17 of the 1931 Act (defence for certain bodies corporate, firms and partnerships) is amended as follows.

(2) In paragraph (a), for "superintendent who is a registered person and" substitute "registered person".

(3) In paragraph (b), for the words from "and" to "who is" substitute "it is carried on by or under the supervision of".

(4) For the sidenote substitute "Defence for business under control and management of registered person.".

13. For section 18(2) of the 1931 Act (application to Northern Ireland) substitute—

"(2) This Act extends to Northern Ireland.".

The 1938 Act

14.—(1) Section 1A of the 1938 Act (visiting EC architects) is amended as follows.

(2) In subsections (2), (3) and (4), for "Council" (in each place) substitute "Registrar".

(3) In subsection (3), for "they consider" substitute "the Registrar considers".

(4) In subsection (6), for the words from "when" to the end substitute "when—

(a) he is subject to a disqualifying decision in another member State;

(b) his name has been removed from the Register pursuant to a suspension order or an erasure order and has not been re-entered; or

(c) he is required under section 6C(1) of the principal Act to satisfy the Board of his competence to practise but has not done so.".

(5) In subsection (8), for the words from the beginning to "the regulation of" substitute "The provisions of, and of rules under, the principal Act relating to".

15. In section 3 of the 1938 Act (offence of practising while not registered), in the proviso—

(a) in paragraph (a), omit "of the Council" and "subsection (2) of section six of", and

(b) for paragraphs (b) and (c) substitute—

"(b) in a case where the contravention is occasioned by the removal of the defendant's name from the Register in circumstances in which notice is required to be served on him—

(i) that the notice had not been duly served before that date,

(ii) that the time for bringing an appeal against the removal had not expired at that date, or

(iii) that such an appeal had been duly brought, but had not been determined, before that date.".

16. In section 5 of the 1938 Act (construction and citation), in subsection (2), for the words from "Acts 1931 and" to the end substitute "Act 1931".

17. For section 6(1) of the 1938 Act (application to Northern Ireland) substitute—

"(1) This Act extends to Northern Ireland.".

Other enactments

18. In section 6 of the Inspection of Churches Measure 1955 (interpretation), in the definition of "qualified person", for "Architects Registration Acts 1931 to 1969" substitute "Architects Acts 1931 to 1996".

19. In section 52(1) of the Cathedrals Measure 1963 (interpretation), in the definition of "architect", for "Architects (Registration) Acts 1931 to 1938" substitute "Architects Acts 1931 to 1996".

20. In section 20(1) of the Care of Cathedrals Measure 1990 (interpretation), in the definition of "architect", for "Architects Registration Acts 1931 to 1969" substitute "Architects Acts 1931 to 1996".

Part III

Transitional provisions and savings

First elections and appointments to the Board

21.—(1) Part I of the First Schedule to the 1931 Act as substituted by Part I of this Schedule shall have effect before the appointed day so far as is necessary to enable the election and appointment of members of the Board to take office on that day.

(2) Until the appointed day references to the Board in paragraph 2 of that Schedule shall have effect as references to the Council.

(3) Where persons elected or appointed as members of the Board by virtue of this paragraph attend meetings before the appointed day in preparation for the conduct of business of the Board on or after that day, the Council may pay to them any such fees or travelling or subsistence allowances in respect of their attendance as appear appropriate.

(4) The term of office of the members of the Board appointed by the Privy Council (by virtue of this paragraph) to take office on the appointed day—

(a) is one year beginning with that day in the case of three of those members,

(b) is two years beginning with that day in the case of another three of those members, and

(c) is three years beginning with that day in the case of the remaining two members.

Registration

22. Where before the appointed day a person has duly applied for registration under the 1931 Act but no decision on the application has been made, the application shall be dealt with on and after the appointed day in the same way as an application duly made on or after that day (except that no further fee may be required to be paid).

23. Examinations in architecture which immediately before the appointed day were recognised by the Council for the purposes of subsection (1)(c) of section 6 of the 1931 Act (as it has effect before the substitution made by section 120 of this Act) shall (subject to rules made by the Board) be treated on and after that day as qualifications prescribed under subsection (1)(a) of that section (as it has effect after that substitution).

24. Section 6B of the 1931 Act shall have effect as if the reference in subsection (3) of that section to a person whose name has been removed from the Register under subsection (2) of that section included a reference to a person whose name was removed from the Register under section 13(5) of the 1931 Act before the appointed day.

25. The first reference to the Board in section 7A(1) of the 1931 Act shall be construed, in relation to the entry of a name in the Register at a time before the appointed day, as a reference to the Council.

Discipline

26. Where before the appointed day—

(a) the Discipline Committee has begun an inquiry into a case in which it is alleged that a registered person has been guilty of conduct disgraceful to him in his capacity as an architect, but

(b) the Council has not decided whether to remove his name from the Register,

the case shall be referred to the Professional Conduct Committee which shall consider whether he is guilty of unacceptable professional conduct or serious professional incompetence.

27.—(1) Subject to sub-paragraph (2), the provisions substituted by section 121 of this Act for section 7 of the 1931 Act have effect in relation to anything done or omitted to be done before the appointed day as in relation to anything done or omitted to be done after that day.

(2) The Professional Conduct Committee—

(a) may only make a disciplinary order in respect of anything done, or omitted to be done, by a person before the appointed day if the Council could have removed his name from the

Register under section 7 of the 1931 Act (as it had effect before the substitution made by section 121 of this Act), and

(b) may not make a reprimand or penalty order in respect of anything so done or omitted to be so done.

Pre-commencement removals and disqualifications

28.—(1) Where a person's name has been removed from the Register under section 7 of the 1931 Act before the appointed day, he may at any time on or after that day apply to the Board for his name to be re-entered in the Register.

(2) If he does so, the Board may direct that his name shall be re-entered in the Register.

(3) The Registrar shall serve on a person who applies for his name to be re-entered in the Register under this paragraph written notice of the decision on his application within the prescribed period after the date of the decision.

(4) The Board may require a person whose name is re-entered in the Register under this paragraph to pay a fee of such amount, not exceeding the fee then payable by an applicant for registration in pursuance of section 6 of the 1931 Act, as may be prescribed.

29. A person may appeal under section 9 of the 1931 Act against—

(a) the removal of his name from the Register before the appointed day, or

(b) a determination of the Council before the appointed day that he be disqualified for registration during any period,

within three months from the date on which notice of the removal or determination was served on him.

30. Section 1A(6)(b) of the 1938 Act shall have effect as if it included a reference to a period of disqualification imposed by the Council.

Offence of practising while not registered

31. The amendments made in sections 1 and 3 of the 1938 Act and section 17 of the 1931 Act by section 123(1), (3) and (4) of this Act do not apply in relation to an offence committed before the appointed day.

32. The repeal made in section 3 of the 1938 Act by section 123(2) of this Act applies in relation to an offence committed before the appointed day (as well as in relation to one committed on or after that day).

Transfer of Fund

33. If the transfer of the assets of the Fund takes place after the appointed day, the repeal by this Act of sections 1(1) and (4) to (6), 3 and 4 of the 1969 Act shall not come into force until the transfer is made; and during the period beginning with the appointed day and ending with the transfer references in those provisions to the Council shall have effect as references to the Board.

Supplementary

34.—(1) In this Part of this Schedule—

(a) "the Board" means the Architects Registration Board, and

(b) other expressions used in the 1931 Act have the same meanings as in that Act.

(2) In this Part of this Schedule "appointed day" means the day appointed by the Secretary of State for the coming into force of this Part of this Act.

35. Nothing in this Schedule prejudices the operation of section 16 or 17 (effect of repeals) of the Interpretation Act 1978.

Section 147

SCHEDULE 3

Repeals and Revocations

Part I

Grants, &c for renewal of private sector housing

Chapter	Short title	Extent of repeal
1977 c. 42.	Rent Act 1977.	In section 116(2), the words "any of paragraphs (a) to (c) of".
1985 c. 68.	Housing Act 1985.	Section 100(2A). Section 101(1A). Section 244(3A). Section 255(3).
1989 c. 42.	Local Government and Housing Act 1989.	Part VIII. In Schedule 11, paragraph 52, paragraph 63, and paragraphs 66 to 69.
1993 c. 10.	Charities Act 1993.	In Schedule 6, paragraph 30, the words "The Local Government and Housing Act 1989 section 138(1)".
1994 c. 19.	Local Government (Wales) Act 1994.	In Schedule 8, paragraph 10(1) and (2).
1994 c. 29.	Police and Magistrates' Courts Act 1994.	In Schedule 4, paragraph 40.

Part II

Architects

Chapter	Short title	Extent of repeal
21 & 22 Geo. 5 c. 33.	Architects (Registration) Act 1931.	In section 3, in subsection (2), the first sentence and subsections (3) and (4). Section 5. In section 6A(1), the words "Subject to the provisions of this Act,". In section 7A(1), the words "of this Act". Section 8. The Second Schedule. The Third Schedule.
1 & 2 Geo. 6 c. 54.	Architects Registration Act 1938.	In section 1(3), the words "the words "Registered Architects" in subsection (3) of section three of the principal Act, and for", "respectively" and "the word "Architects" and". In section 3, the words "of the Council" and "subsection (2) of section six of".
1969 c. 42.	Architects Registration (Amendment) Act 1969.	The whole Act.
1977 c. 45.	Criminal Law Act 1977.	In Schedule 6, the entry relating to the Architects Registration Act 1938.
S.I. 1987/1824.	Architects' Qualifications (EEC Recognition) Order 1987.	Article 4.
1995 c. 40.	Criminal Procedure (Consequential Provisions) (Scotland) Act 1995.	In Schedule 2, in Part II, the entry relating to the Architects Registration Act 1938.

PART III

FINANCIAL ASSISTANCE FOR REGENERATION AND DEVELOPMENT

Chapter	Short title	Extent of repeal
1986 c. 63.	Housing and Planning Act 1986.	Part III. In section 58(1) and (2), the words "Part III (financial assistance for urban regeneration);".
1993 c. 28.	Leasehold Reform, Housing and Urban Development Act 1993.	Section 174. In section 188(6), the words "174,".

INDEX

References are to sections and Schedules

STATUTORY INSTRUMENTS (PRODUCTION AND SALE) ACT 1996

(1996 c. 54)

An Act to make provision (with retrospective effect) for the printing and sale of statutory instruments under the authority of the Queen's printer, for their issue under the authority of Her Majesty's Stationery Office and for the reception in evidence of lists of such instruments which do not bear the imprint of the Queen's printer. [24th July 1996]

PARLIAMENTARY DEBATES

Hansard, H.C. Vol. 280, col. 984, H.L. Vol. 573, col. 1690; Vol. 574, cols. 813, 1356, 1381.

INTRODUCTION

This Act provides that the Statutory Instruments Act 1946 (c. 36) shall be amended so as to provide, *inter alia*, for the printing and sale of statutory instruments under the authority of the Queen's printer.

Instruments etc. produced and sold under authority

1.—(1) The Statutory Instruments Act 1946 shall have effect and be taken always to have had effect—

(a) with the insertion of "or under the authority of" after "sold by" and "issued by" in each place, and

(b) with the omission of "purporting to bear the imprint of the King's printer" in section 3(1).

(2) Subsection (1) does not affect the operation of section 3(2) of that Act in relation to proceedings commenced before 21st June 1996.

Short title and extent

2.—(1) This Act may be cited as the Statutory Instruments (Production and Sale) Act 1996.

(2) This Act has the same extent as the Statutory Instruments Act 1946.

INDEX

References are to sections

BROADCASTING ACT 1996*

(1996 c. 55)

ARRANGEMENT OF SECTIONS

PART I

DIGITAL TERRESTRIAL TELEVISION BROADCASTING

Introductory

---

* Annotations by Thomas Gibbons, Senior Lecturer in Law, The University of Manchester.

An Act to make new provision about the broadcasting in digital form of television and sound programme services and the broadcasting in that form on television or radio frequencies of other services; to amend the Broadcasting Act 1990; to make provision about rights to televise sporting or other events of national interest; to amend in other respects the law relating to the provision of television and sound programme services; to provide for the establishment and functions of a Broadcasting Standards Commission and for the dissolution of the Broadcasting Complaints Commission and the Broadcasting Standards Council; to make provision for the transfer to other persons of property, rights and liabilities of the British Broadcasting Corporation relating to their transmission network; and for connected purposes. [24th July 1996]

PARLIAMENTARY DEBATES

Hansard, H.L. Vol. 567, col. 1376; Vol. 568, cols. 468, 1128; Vol. 569, cols. 122, 514, 588, 741, 803, 1144; Vol. 570, cols. 155, 235, 418, 495, 1155, 1243; Vol. 574, cols. 743, 1004. H.C. Vol. 275, col. 537; Vol. 280, cols. 553, 729; Vol. 282, col. 249.

INTRODUCTION AND GENERAL NOTE

This Act supplements and modifies the Broadcasting Act 1990 (c. 42) (hereafter referred to as the 1990 Act). First, in Pts. I and II, it establishes the framework for facilitating and regulating what is anticipated to be a new era of digital terrestrial broadcasting. Secondly, in Sched. 2, it revises the rules about media ownership, incorporating an approach based on market share as a surrogate for owners' influence on audiences and readerships. Thirdly, in Pt. V, it provides for the merger of the Broadcasting Complaints Commission with the Broadcasting Standards Council. It also makes new provision for listed events, in Pt. IV, and for the privatisation of the

BBC's transmission system, in Pt. VI. Finally, it makes a number of changes to the 1990 Act in the light of experience with the regulatory scheme which that Act introduced. In respect of digital broadcasting, the underlying policy was set out in the consultation paper, *Digital Terrestrial Broadcasting* (1995) Cm. 2946. The basic approach to ownership was floated in *Media Ownership: The Government's Proposals* (1995) Cm. 2872. Other influences on the legislation were the White Paper, *The Future of the BBC: Serving the Nation, Competing World-Wide* (1994) Cm. 2621, and the report of the National Heritage Committee, *The Future of the BBC, Second Report*, (1993–94) H.C. 77-I.

The Act must be read in conjunction with the Broadcasting Act 1990. This Act amends the 1990 Act generally, especially in Pt. III and Sched. 10, and supplements its provisions. Furthermore, by s.147(1), both Acts are substantially to be construed together.

The Act refers generally to the Independent Television Commission which was established by s.1 of the Broadcasting Act 1990, the Radio Authority established by s.83 of that Act, and the Channel Four Television Corporation established by s.23 of that Act. The Welsh Authority is Channel 4's Welsh counterpart, Sianel Pedwar Cymru (S4C), and it was established by s.56(1) of the 1990 Act.

PART I

DIGITAL TERRESTRIAL TELEVISION BROADCASTING

GENERAL NOTE

Digital broadcasting enables the provision of programming to be separated from transmission. A particular frequency no longer need be associated with a particular television or radio channel. Instead, by converting images and sound into binary digits and coding their relationship to each other, it is possible to send together the basis of many programmes and sources of information along a single frequency. At the receiving end, the code can be deciphered and the appropriate bits of information can be reassembled to provide separate programmes. This process of compressing and combining digital signals for transmission is known as multiplexing. Digital compression enables a relatively small amount of data to be sent when pictures are of low quality or almost still (only the changes from frame to frame need be transmitted), and enables more enhanced data to be sent to provide high-definition or wide-screen programming. There is considerable flexibility, therefore, as to the way that the frequency can be allocated to particular types of programme.

Introductory

Multiplex services and digital programme services

1.—(1) In this Part "multiplex service" means a service provided by any person which consists in the broadcasting for general reception of two or more services specified in subsection (3) by combining the relevant information in digital form, together with any broadcasting in digital form of digital additional services (as defined by section 24(1)).

(2) A service in respect of which a licence under section 7 is in force is not prevented from being a multiplex service at a particular time merely because only one service specified in subsection (3) is being broadcast in digital form at that time.

(3) The services referred to in subsections (1) and (2) are—

(a) a digital programme service (as defined by subsection (4)), or

(b) a qualifying service (as defined by section 2(2)).

(4) In this Part "digital programme service" means a service consisting in the provision by any person of television programmes (together with any ancillary services, as defined by section 24(2)) with a view to their being broadcast in digital form for general reception, whether by him or by some other person, but does not include—

(a) a qualifying service,

(b) a teletext service, or

(c) any service in the case of which the visual images to be broadcast do not consist wholly or mainly of images capable of being seen as moving pictures, except, in the case of a service falling within paragraph (b) or (c), to the extent that it is an ancillary service.

(5) The Secretary of State may, if having regard to developments in broadcasting technology he considers it appropriate to do so, by order amend the definition of "digital programme service" in subsection (4).

(6) No order under subsection (5) shall be made unless a draft of the order has been laid before and approved by a resolution of each House of Parliament.

(7) In this section—

"broadcast" means broadcast otherwise than—

(a) by satellite, or

(b) in the provision of a local delivery service (as defined by section 72(1) of the 1990 Act), and

"for general reception" means for general reception in, or in any area in, the United Kingdom.

DEFINITIONS

"ancillary service": s.24(2); s.39(1).
"digital additional service": s.24(1); s.39(1).
"qualifying service": s.2(2); s.39(1).
"1990 Act; the": s.147(1).

GENERAL NOTE

This section defines the main components of the scheme for regulating digital television. The multiplex service will be licensed to co-ordinate and manage the broadcasting of programmes and information in digital form. It includes both the marketing and the technical aspects of such broadcasting. In respect of marketing, it is anticipated that a package of services will be brought together to meet the needs of the various audiences which will be able to access the frequency. A range of programme types and data services may be offered in differing permutations, possibly by reference to particular themes or "bouquets". From the technical perspective, it is the use of digital compression which enables so many services to share the same frequency and the multiplex service will consist of allocating the use of available capacity to ensure that the flows of bits, or packets, of electronic information are directed to the appropriate recipients as efficiently as possible and without confusion. The multiplex service is not the same as transmission, although transmission is one element of digital broadcasting that the multiplex operator will have to organise. Nor does the multiplex service consist in providing the raw material that is to be broadcast.

In theory, all these functions could be undertaken by one operator but the Government's policy was to separate them to encourage investment, especially by non-media sources, and competition generally. This section therefore distinguishes programme provision from the multiplex services which will disseminate it. The concept of a digital programme service, which will require a separate licence, is intended to cover programming (other than that provided by the BBC) whose only dissemination by terrestrial means is in digital form. That does not preclude material that has been or will be disseminated also by cable or satellite (under the separate licensing regime under the 1990 Act). However, digital programming which is also provided in analogue form, on Channels 3, 4 (including S4C) and 5, is defined as a qualifying service, under s.2, and does not constitute a digital programme service. Furthermore, digitally broadcast additional services, such as teletext or data services, are regulated separately under ss.24–27.

Subs. (2)

It is expected that multiplex services will cater for a number of digital programme services or qualifying services. This subsection allows some flexibility, however, by enabling a licence to exist even where only one programme provider is using the multiplex. This may occur at the start of digital terrestrial broadcasting, or it may happen that all but one provider withdraws from using the multiplex, whether for technical or financial reasons. In such circumstances, the multiplex can continue to function while new providers are attracted to it.

Subs. (4)

The definition is contrived to allow different kinds of broadcast material to be licensed in different ways. Qualifying services are excluded because their content has already been licensed, as analogue programmes under the 1990 Act, and because the policy of the Act, manifested in s.28, is to encourage analogue broadcasters to lead the transition to digital broadcasting by giving them an entitlement to capacity on multiplex frequencies. Teletext and data services are excluded because they are licensed separately as digital additional services. But where such services are ancillary to the content of conventional television programmes, such as subtitling for the deaf or programme listings, that material will be licensed with the substantive digital programme.

Subss. (5) and (6)

Since it is only possible to speculate about the likely development of the digital terrestrial broadcasting industry, at this stage, the Secretary of State is given some flexibility to respond to change. The affirmative resolution procedure is adopted, however, because an alteration to the definition of digital programme service would affect the whole licensing regime and would be one of policy rather than fine-tuning to reflect technological advances.

Subs. (7)

By s.147(2), this section is to be interpreted as if it were contained in the 1990 Act and, by s.202 of that Act, "broadcast" means broadcast by wireless telegraphy.

Although it is not a logical requirement of the technology, the effect of this subsection is to keep the regulation of digital terrestrial television broadcasting separate from other forms of delivery which can also exploit digital technology. Satellite is distinguishable, at least, because the spectrum is not confined to the frequencies controlled by the U.K. Local delivery services are a separately established market where broadcasting may be used as (generally) an incidental method of conveying programmes; this subsection makes it clear that such services do not need to obtain multiplex licences.

Meaning of "independent analogue broadcaster" and "qualifying service"

2.—(1) In this Part "independent analogue broadcaster" means—

(a) the Channel Four Television Corporation,

(b) the Welsh Authority,

(c) any person who holds a Channel 3 licence or a Channel 5 licence, or

(d) the public teletext provider.

(2) Subject to subsections (4) and (5), in this Part "qualifying service" means any service which—

(a) is provided by an independent analogue broadcaster falling within paragraph (a) or (c) of subsection (1) who has notified the Commission, within the period of one month beginning with the commencement of this section, of his intention to provide a service specified in subsection (3) ("the corresponding analogue service") for broadcasting in digital form, and

(b) as respects the programmes included in the service and the times at which they are broadcast, is identical with the corresponding analogue service.

(3) The services referred to in subsection (2) are—

(a) Channel 4, and

(b) any Channel 3 service or Channel 5.

(4) If the Welsh Authority notify the Commission, within the period of one month beginning with the commencement of this section, of their intention to provide S4C Digital, S4C Digital shall be a qualifying service for the purposes of this Part.

(5) If—

(a) the public teletext provider notifies the Commission, within the period of one month beginning with the commencement of this section, of his intention to provide a teletext service for broadcasting in digital form, and

(b) the Commission consent under section 30 to his provision of that service,

that service (in this Part referred to as "the qualifying teletext service") shall be a qualifying service for the purposes of this Part.

(6) In this Part "public teletext provider" means the person who holds the additional services licence (within the meaning of Part I of the 1990 Act) which relates to the teletext service referred to in section 49(2) of that Act.

(7) In subsection (2) "programme" does not include an advertisement.

DEFINITIONS
"Channel 3 licence": s.39(1); s.71(1) of the Broadcasting Act 1990.
"Channel 3 service": s.39(1); s.71(1) of the Broadcasting Act 1990.
"Channel 4": s.39(1); s.71(1) of the Broadcasting Act 1990.
"Channel 5": s.39(1); s.71(1) of the Broadcasting Act 1990.
"Channel 5 licence": s.39(1); s.71(1) of the Broadcasting Act 1990.
"Commission; the": s.39(1).
"S4C Digital": s.39(1); s.57(1A)(a) of the Broadcasting Act 1990.

GENERAL NOTE

This section defines the independent analogue broadcasters and the qualifying services which they are anticipated to provide. The section should be read in conjunction with s.28 which entitles the independent analogue broadcasters to capacity on multiplex frequencies provided that they provide qualifying services. Essentially, existing independent broadcasters are being offered reserved capacity in return for broadcasting their existing analogue programming in digital, but otherwise identical, form. Special arrangements are made for the Welsh language S4C, however, because the Welsh Authority broadcasts Channel 4 programmes at the times of the day when S4C is not scheduled. Subsection (4) has the effect of requiring the Welsh Authority to simulcast only that Welsh language service and not duplicate Channel 4 provision which is likely to be available to Welsh viewers through Channel 4's own multiplex.

Subs. (7)

By s.147(2), this section is to be interpreted as if it were contained in the 1990 Act and, by s.202 of that Act, "programme" includes an advertisment. This subsection makes an exception in respect of qualifying services. The reason is to enable independent analogue broadcasters to secure separate advertising revenue for their digital programming.

General provisions about licences

Licences under Part I

3.—(1) Any licence granted by the Independent Television Commission (in this Part referred to as "the Commission") under this Part shall be in writing and (subject to the provisions of this Part) shall continue in force for such period as is provided, in relation to a licence of the kind in question, by the relevant provision of this Part.

(2) A licence may be so granted for the provision of such a service as is specified in the licence or for the provision of a service of such a description as is so specified.

(3) The Commission—

(a) shall not grant a licence to any person unless they are satisfied that he is a fit and proper person to hold it, and

(b) shall do all that they can to secure that, if they cease to be so satisfied in the case of any person holding a licence, that person does not remain the holder of the licence;

and nothing in this Part shall be construed as affecting the operation of this subsection or of section 5(1) or (2)(b) or (c).

(4) The Commission may vary a licence by a notice served on the licence holder if—

(a) in the case of a variation of the period for which a licence having effect for a specified period is to continue in force, the licence holder consents, or

(b) in the case of any other variation, the licence holder has been given a reasonable opportunity of making representations to the Commission about the variation.

(5) Paragraph (a) of subsection (4) does not affect the operation of section 17(1)(b); and that subsection shall not authorise the variation of any conditions included in a licence in pursuance of section 13(1).

(6) A licence granted to any person under this Part shall not be transferable to any other person without the previous consent in writing of the Commission.

(7) Without prejudice to the generality of subsection (6), the Commission shall not give their consent for the purposes of that subsection unless they are satisfied that any such other person would be in a position to comply with all of the conditions included in the licence which would have effect during the period for which it is to be in force.

(8) The holding by any person of a licence to provide any service shall not relieve him of any requirement to hold a licence under section 1 of the Wireless Telegraphy Act 1949 or section 7 of the Telecommunications Act 1984 in connection with the provision of that service.

DEFINITIONS

"Commission; the": s.39(1).
"licence": s.39(1).

GENERAL NOTE

Subs. (3)

The Commission have a broad discretion to satisfy themselves who is "a fit and proper person" for the purposes of holding a licence, but they will have to reach the conclusion on a rational basis, under the principle in *Associated Picture Houses v. Wednesbury Corporation* [1948] 1 K.B. 223. A fit and proper person will be one who has the ability to comply with the terms of the licence. There is also an element of public interest implied in the expression, however, and it may be that persons who are or have been engaged in unlawful or dishonest activities could justifiably be regarded as undesirable by the Commission.

The Commission must also "do all that they can to secure" that, if they cease to be satisfied about someone's suitability, that person does not remain a licence holder. The Commission has a continuing duty, therefore, and an overriding one, compared to other restrictions on the holding of licences, under the final clause. It is phrased in this way because the means of achieving the objectives in question are beyond the direct control of the Commission. The duty is, however, a stronger version of the "best endeavours" obligation that exists where there is "a duty to satisfy": see *R. v. Independent Broadcasting Authority, ex p. Whitehouse, The Times*, April 4, 1985; the Commission must establish methods of working or some system, therefore, that will assess the continued suitability of licence holders. As part of the all embracing nature of the duty, the Commission will be expected to use informal methods, perhaps correspondence or meetings, as well as the formal conditions of the licence.

Subss. (4) and (5)

The power to vary the duration of the licence, in subs. (4)(a), is constrained by the requirement of consent in order to provide some certainty for the investment involved in the service. It is most likely to be used where a licensee becomes unable to comply with the licence conditions and wishes to limit the extent of his obligations but it could also be used as a negotiated sanction in place of the middle-range penalty of shortening a licence period that may be imposed upon a defaulting multiplex operator, under s.17(1). By subs. (5), however, the power does not affect the use of that penalty. In addition, the consensual shortening of a licence does not affect any conditions relating to the payment of the additional payments ("the levy") for multiplex licences under s.13(1).

Other variations may be imposed by the Commission without consent, provided that the licence holder has been given a reasonable opportunity to make representations.

Subss. (6) and (7)

The Commission cannot prevent takeovers and other changes of ownership in companies holding licences but these subsections enable them to ensure that a transfer of responsibility for the licence will only occur if the new licence holder is in a position to comply with all the requirements of the original licence and is a fit and proper person. Effectively, prospective transferees will have to apply to the Commission for approval.

Subs. (8)

Insofar as the provision of digital services entails broadcasting transmission and the use of telecommunications systems, separate licences, in addition to those issued by the Commission, are required from the Radiocommunications Agency and OFTEL, respectively.

General licence conditions

4.—(1) A licence may include—

(a) such conditions as appear to the Commission to be appropriate having regard to any duties which are or may be imposed on them, or on the licence holder, by or under the 1990 Act or this Act;

(b) conditions requiring the payment by the licence holder to the Commission (whether on the grant of the licence or at such times thereafter as may be determined by or under the licence, or both) of a fee or fees of an amount or amounts so determined;

(c) conditions requiring the licence holder to provide the Commission, in such manner and at such times as they may reasonably require, with such information as they may require for the purpose of exercising the functions assigned to them by or under the 1990 Act or this Act;

(d) conditions providing for such incidental and supplemental matters as appear to the Commission to be appropriate.

(2) A licence may in particular include conditions requiring the licence holder—

(a) to comply with any direction given by the Commission as to such matters as are specified in the licence or are of a description so specified, or

(b) (except to the extent that the Commission consent to his doing or not doing them) not to do or to do such things as are specified in the licence or are of a description so specified.

(3) The fees required to be paid to the Commission by virtue of subsection (1)(b) shall be in accordance with such tariff as may from time to time be fixed by the Commission; and the amount of any fee which is to be so paid by the holder of a licence of a particular class or description shall be such as to represent what appears to the Commission to be the appropriate contribution of the holder of such a licence towards meeting the sums which the Commission regard as necessary in order to discharge their duty under paragraph 12(1) of Schedule 1 to the 1990 Act.

(4) A tariff fixed under subsection (3) may specify different fees in relation to different cases or circumstances; and the Commission shall publish every such tariff in such manner as they consider appropriate.

(5) Where the holder of any licence—

(a) is required by virtue of any condition imposed under this Part to provide the Commission with any information, and

(b) in purported compliance with that condition provides them with information which is false in a material particular,

he shall be taken for the purposes of sections 17, 23 and 27 of this Act and section 42 of the 1990 Act to have failed to comply with that condition.

(6) Nothing in this Part which authorises or requires the inclusion in a licence of conditions relating to any particular matter or having effect for any particular purpose shall be taken as derogating from the generality of subsection (1).

DEFINITIONS

"Commission; the": s.39(1).
"licence": s.39(1).
"1990 Act; the": s.147(1).

GENERAL NOTE

The licence is the mechanism that enables the Commission to implement the objectives that they have a duty to secure under this Act and their broader functions under the 1990 Act. Examples are, that disqualified persons should not become licence holders, that good taste and decency must be observed and that the decisions of the Broadcasting Standards Commission are publicised. The licence is also the means whereby the promises and understandings that formed the basis of the licensee's application, and resulted in the grant of the licence, may be enforced by being incorporated into the licence as conditions. This section provides the Commission with broad powers to draw up licences for the purpose of exercising their various statutory functions.

It includes the power to impose conditions about the provision of relevant information and it will be a breach of those conditions, attracting sanctions of financial penalties or revocation, to supply information that is false in a material particular. To supplement those powers, there is also power to issue directions in respect of matters specified in the licence. This allows some flexibility in determining the way that the licence is to be enforced and enables the Commission to respond quickly to new and unanticipated circumstances. The Commission are not empowered to make directions that go beyond the scope of their general powers but if they became aware of a likely breach of the regulatory scheme, they could request information, under subs. (5), and instruct a licensee not to take an unacceptable course of action on pain of the sanctions available to them.

The fees that are charged by the Commission provide an important source of their income. While subs. (3) allows them to charge differential rates, the "appropriate" amount for each licence is to be determined by reference to the costs of regulating the particular service in question. Under subs. (1)(b), fees may be payable after the licence has been issued but before it has come into force.

Restrictions on holding of licences under Part I

5.—(1) The Commission shall do all that they can to secure—

(a) that a person does not become or remain the holder of a licence if he is a person who is a disqualified person in relation to that licence by virtue of Part II of Schedule 2 to the 1990 Act (as amended by this Act); and

(b) that any requirements imposed by or under Parts III to V of that Schedule (as so amended) are complied with by or in relation to persons holding licences in relation to which those requirements apply.

(2) The Commission may accordingly—

(a) require any applicant for a licence to provide them with such information as they may reasonably require for the purpose of determining—

(i) whether he is such a disqualified person as is mentioned in subsection (1)(a),

(ii) whether any such requirements as are mentioned in subsection (1)(b) would preclude them from granting a licence to him, and

(iii) if so, what steps would be required to be taken by or in relation to him in order for any such requirements to be complied with;

(b) revoke the award of a licence to a body where a relevant change takes place after the award, but before the grant, of the licence;

(c) make the grant of a licence to any person conditional on the taking of any specified steps that appear to them to be required to be taken as mentioned in paragraph (a)(iii);

(d) impose conditions in any licence enabling them to require the licence holder, if a body corporate, to give to them advance notice of proposals affecting—

(i) shareholdings in the body, or

(ii) the directors of the body,

where such proposals are known to the body;

(e) impose conditions in any licence enabling them to give the licence holder directions requiring him to take, or arrange for the taking of, any specified steps appearing to them to be required to be taken in order for any such requirements as are mentioned in subsection (1)(b) to be complied with.

(3) Where the Commission—

(a) revoke the award of any licence in pursuance of subsection (2)(b), or

(b) determine that any condition imposed by them in relation to any licence in pursuance of subsection (2)(c) has not been satisfied,

any provisions of this Part relating to the awarding of licences of the kind in question shall (subject to subsection (4)) have effect as if the person to whom the licence was awarded or granted had not made an application for it.

(4) Those provisions shall not so have effect if the Commission decide that it would be desirable to publish a fresh notice under this Part in respect of the grant of a licence, or (as the case may be) a further licence, to provide the service in question.

(5) Every licence shall include such conditions as the Commission consider necessary or expedient to ensure that where—

(a) the holder of the licence is a body, and

(b) a relevant change takes place after the grant of the licence,

the Commission may revoke the licence by notice served on the holder of the licence and taking effect forthwith or on a date specified in the notice.

(6) The Commission shall not serve any such notice on the licence holder unless—

(a) they have notified him of the matters complained of and given him a reasonable opportunity of making representations to them about those matters, and

(b) in a case where the relevant change is one falling within subsection (7)—

(i) they have also given him an opportunity of complying with Parts III and IV of Schedule 2 to the 1990 Act within a period specified in the notification, and

(ii) the period specified in the notification has elapsed.

(7) A relevant change falls within this subsection if it consists only in one or more of the following—

(a) a change in the percentage of total audience time attributable to one or more services for the purposes of paragraph 2 of Part III of Schedule 2 to the 1990 Act,

(b) a change in the national market share (within the meaning of Part IV of that Schedule) of one or more national newspapers (within the meaning of that Part of that Schedule), or

(c) a change in the local market share (within the meaning of that Part of that Schedule) in a particular area of one or more local newspapers (within the meaning of that Part of that Schedule).

(8) In this section "relevant change", in relation to a body to which a licence has been awarded or granted, means—

(a) any change affecting the nature or characteristics of the body,

(b) any change in the persons having control over or interests in the body, or

(c) any other change giving rise to a failure to comply with any requirement imposed by or under Schedule 2 to the 1990 Act,

being (in any case) a change which is such that, if it fell to the Commission to determine whether to award the licence to the body in the new circumstances of the case, they would be induced by the change to refrain from so awarding it.

DEFINITIONS

"Commission; the": s.39(1).
"licence": s.39(1).
"1990 Act; the": s.147(1).

Multiplex services

Assignment of frequencies by Secretary of State

6.—(1) The Secretary of State may by notice assign to the Commission, for the purpose of the provision of multiplex services falling to be licensed by them under this Part, such frequencies as he may determine; and any frequency so assigned shall be taken to be so assigned for the purpose only of being used for the provision of one or more of those services.

(2) Any frequency assigned by the Secretary of State under subsection (1) may be so assigned for use only in such area or areas as may be specified by the Secretary of State when making the assignment.

(3) The Secretary of State may by notice revoke the assignment under subsection (1) of any frequency specified in the notice, whether or not the frequency is for the time being one on which there is being provided a multiplex service licensed under this Part.

DEFINITIONS
"Commission; the": s.39(1).
"licensed": s.39(1).
"multiplex service": s.1(1); s.39(1).

Multiplex licences

7.—(1) Where the Commission propose to grant a licence to provide a multiplex service (in this Part referred to as a "multiplex licence") they shall publish, in such manner as they consider appropriate, a notice—

(a) stating that they propose to grant such a licence,
(b) specifying the frequency or frequencies on which the service is to be provided,
(c) specifying, in such manner as the Commission consider appropriate, the area or areas in the United Kingdom within which the frequency or frequencies is or are to be available,
(d) inviting applications for the licence and specifying the closing date for such applications,
(e) specifying the fee payable on any application, and
(f) stating whether any percentage of multiplex revenue for each accounting period would be payable by an applicant in pursuance of section 13 if he were granted the licence and, if so, specifying that percentage.

(2) Unless an order under section 13(2) is in force—

(a) the consent of the Secretary of State shall be required for so much of the notice as relates to the matters specified in subsection (1)(f), and
(b) the Commission may if they think fit (with that consent) specify under subsection (1)(f)—
 (i) different percentages in relation to different accounting periods falling within the period for which the licence would be in force, and
 (ii) a nil percentage in relation to any accounting period so falling.

(3) When publishing a notice under subsection (1), the Commission—

(a) shall publish with the notice general guidance as to requirements to be met by proposals as to the matters referred to in subsection (4)(b)(i) and (ii) and (f), and
(b) may publish with the notice such other general guidance as they consider appropriate.

(4) An application made in pursuance of a notice under subsection (1) must be in writing and accompanied by—

(a) the fee specified in the notice under subsection (1)(e),
(b) a technical plan relating to the service which the applicant proposes to provide and indicating—
 (i) the parts of the area specified under subsection (1)(c) which would be within the coverage area of the service,
 (ii) the timetable in accordance with which that coverage would be achieved, and
 (iii) the technical means by which it would be achieved,

(c) the applicant's proposals as to the number of digital programme services to be broadcast, as to the characteristics of each of those services and as to the areas in which they would be provided,
(d) the applicant's proposals as to the timetable in accordance with which the broadcasting of each of those services would begin,
(e) the applicant's proposals as to the broadcasting of digital additional services,
(f) the applicant's proposals for promoting or assisting the acquisition, by persons in the proposed coverage area of the service, of equipment capable of receiving all the multiplex services available in that area,
(g) such information as the Commission may reasonably require as to the applicant's present financial position and his projected financial position during the period for which the licence would be in force, and
(h) such other information as the Commission may reasonably require for the purpose of considering the application.

(5) In subsection (4)(f) "acquisition" includes acquisition on hire or loan.

(6) At any time after receiving such an application and before determining it, the Commission may require the applicant to furnish additional information under any of paragraphs (b) to (h) of subsection (4).

(7) Any information to be furnished to the Commission under this section shall, if they so require, be in such form or verified in such manner as they may specify.

(8) The Commission shall, as soon as reasonably practicable after the date specified in a notice under subsection (1) as the closing date for applications, publish in such manner as they consider appropriate—

(a) the following matters, namely—
   (i) the name of every person who has made an application to them in pursuance of the notice,
   (ii) the proposals submitted by him under subsection (4)(c), and
   (iii) such other information connected with his application as the Commission consider appropriate; and
(b) a notice—
   (i) inviting representations to be made to them with respect to any of the applications, and
   (ii) specifying the manner in which, and the time by which, any such representations are to be so made.

DEFINITIONS

"Commission; the": s.39(1).
"digital additional service": s.24(1); s.39(1).
"digital programme service": s.1(4); s.39(1).
"licence": s.39(1).
"multiplex service": s.1(1); s.39(1).

GENERAL NOTE

The Act introduces a "light touch" regulatory scheme for awarding multiplex licences. The policy is to encourage the development of digital terrestrial broadcasting and to make it accessible and economical for as many viewers as possible. The requirements of this section, together with the criteria for awarding licences in s.8, are intended to further those aims.

The White Paper, *Digital Terrestrial Broadcasting*, proposed that, initially, six multiplex frequencies will be made available, with differential coverage of the U.K. At April 1996, the ITC expected multiplexes one, two and three to have 90 per cent coverage, the fourth 85 per cent, the fifth 75 per cent and the sixth 70 per cent (Standing Committee, col. 153). The most extensive frequency will be allocated to the BBC and the Commission have the responsibility for awarding the other five.

Subsections (1) to (3) deal with the Commission giving notice of their proposal to grant a multiplex licence. Their main function is to set the timetable for applications, the frequencies and coverage available having been determined already by the Secretary of State's assignment to them under s.6. The amount, if any, of additional payments (the "levy"), under subs. (1)(f), are subject to the Secretary of State's consent. By s.13(2), he may make an order requiring that no percentage be specified under subs. (1)(f). Initially, in order to encourage the development of the new services, and in recognition of the high levels of investment that will be required, there will be no levy stipulated.

Subsections (4) to (7) deal with the procedure to be followed by applicants. The main components of the application are the technical plan, the proposals for programming and other services, the proposals for access to the services by viewers and the business plan. In each case, the applicants will have to anticipate the criteria for awarding licences which are set out in s.8. The technical plan covers the extent of coverage and the timetable for achieving it, together with proposals for transmission and digitalisation. By subs. (3)(a), the Commission must publish guidance about such matters. The programming proposals are required to give details of the various digital programme services and digital additional services which are envisaged. The access proposals are required to indicate what kinds of decoding equipment will be needed by viewers to receive the programmes and what kinds of incentives, perhaps financial, may be offered to viewers to buy receiving equipment. From the consumer's perspective, there are obvious attractions in having available a single set-top box which can provide access and decryption for all multiplex services in the area. Multiplex licence applicants will have to consider, therefore, the relationship between their and others' proposed systems and the Commission will be able to take their plans into account when awarding a licence. Furthermore, they may be able to encourage the development of an industry standard, by means of the requirement in subs. (3)(a) that they should publish guidance about such equipment, although that may conflict with the obligation to promote fair competition, in s.8. Finally, the applicant's business plan must demonstrate that the service can be maintained throughout the licence period, initially 12 years, by s.16.

Subsection (8) provides for some public consultation on the applications. Provision for the results of that consultation to be taken into account in awarding licences is made in s.8(1).

Award of multiplex licences

8.—(1) Where the Commission have published a notice under section 7(1), they shall in determining whether, or to whom, to award the multiplex licence in question, have regard to the extent to which, taking into account the matters specified in subsection (2) and any representations made to them in pursuance of section 7(8)(b) with respect to those matters, the award of the licence to each applicant would be calculated to promote the development of digital television broadcasting in the United Kingdom otherwise than by satellite.

(2) The matters referred to in subsection (1) are—

(a) the extent of the coverage area proposed to be achieved by the applicant as indicated in the technical plan submitted by him under section 7(4)(b),

(b) the timetables proposed by the applicant under section 7(4)(b)(ii) and (d),

(c) the ability of the applicant to establish the proposed service and to maintain it throughout the period for which the licence will be in force,

(d) the capacity of the digital programme services proposed to be included in the service to appeal to a variety of tastes and interests,

(e) any proposals by the applicant for promoting or assisting the acquisition, by persons in the proposed coverage area of the service, of equipment capable of receiving all the multiplex services available in that area, and

(f) whether, in contracting or offering to contract with persons providing digital programme services or digital additional services, the applicant has acted in a manner calculated to ensure fair and effective competition in the provision of such services.

(3) In subsection (2)(e) "acquisition" includes acquisition on hire or loan.

(4) Where the Commission have awarded a multiplex licence to any person in accordance with this section, they shall, as soon as reasonably practicable after awarding the licence—

(a) publish in such manner as they consider appropriate—
(i) the name of the person to whom the licence has been awarded, and
(ii) such other information as the Commission consider appropriate, and
(b) grant the licence to that person.

DEFINITIONS

"Commission; the": s.39(1).
"digital additional service": s.24(1); s.39(1).
"digital programme service": s.1(4); s.39(1).
"licence": s.39(1).
"multiplex licence": s.39(1).
"multiplex service": s.1(1); s.39(1).

GENERAL NOTE

In awarding multiplex licences, the Commission's dominant criterion is the one set out in subs. (1), "the development of digital television broadcasting in the United Kingdom otherwise than by satellite". It is in the light of that broad objective that the representations made under s.7(8)(b) and the supplementary criteria in subs. (2) have to be considered. Thus, other factors being equal, technical plans which provide for wider coverage are likely to be preferred to those with less. Similarly, faster timetables for implementation will be preferred. However, the plans must be financially viable and the services provided must appeal to a variety of tastes and interests. In addition, the Commission must take into account the extent to which the applicant intends to encourage the sales of digital receivers. Exactly what weight is to be given to this criterion is not clear, however, because it may conflict with the criterion in subs. (2)(f). The latter seeks to promote fair and effective competition in the provision of programmes and additional services. A problem may arise where the encouragement of a single standard for decoders creates a barrier to entry for programme providers who wish to use a different system.

One criterion which is noticeable by its absence is any reference to the quality of the multiplex service and the programming it offers. The Government strongly resisted any attempts to introduce such a requirement into the Act. It considered that there was no danger that programming quality would be inferior because of the presence of qualifying services on the larger multiplexes and the opportunities for independent analogue broadcasters to continue their existing practices when developing the additional capacity which will be reserved for them. However, the Act does not prohibit a multiplex from providing a diet of low-quality material – provided it appeals to a variety of tastes and interests. It was pointed out, in debate, that the Commission has a general responsibility to promote quality, under the 1990 Act. But that responsibility would not allow the Commission to refuse a multiplex application on grounds of quality alone. By Sched. 10, para. 1(1), the duty in s.2(2) of the 1990 Act, to ensure the provision of high quality services, is extended to digital services. However, that duty refers to all television services, taken as a whole. Since the existence of Channels 3, 4 and 5 would operate as a counterweight to any poor quality digital programming which might be produced, s.2(2) of the 1990 Act does not have an indirect, let alone direct, effect on the award of licences under s.7 of this Act.

Power to require two or more multiplex licences to be granted to one person

9.—(1) The Commission may, before publishing a notice under section 7(1), determine that two or more multiplex licences are on that occasion to be granted to one person.

(2) Where the Commission have so determined, they shall publish a single notice under section 7(1) in relation to the licences.

(3) In relation to any application made in pursuance of such a notice—
(a) references in section 7(4) to the proposed service shall have effect as references to each of the proposed services,
(b) the reference in section 8(1) to the multiplex licence shall have effect as a reference to all the licences concerned,
(c) in section 8(2), the reference in paragraph (d) to the proposed service shall have effect as a reference to all the proposed services considered together, and other references to the proposed service shall have

effect as references either to each of the proposed services or to all of them considered together, as the Commission consider appropriate.

(4) Nothing in this section applies in relation to the renewal of a multiplex licence.

DEFINITIONS
"Commission; the": s.39(1).
"licence": s.39(1).
"multiplex licence": s.39(1).

GENERAL NOTE
This section enables the Commission to award multiple licences. It is not clear as to what extent such a power is necessary. In debate on the Bill, however, the Government maintained that it could facilitate economies of scale, in respect of transmission facilities and marketing. If so, it is possible that multiple licences will be made available for the smaller multiplexes, the fifth and sixth, which will have only 60–70 per cent, albeit not identical, national coverage each. In any event, by Sched. 2, para. 5(1), no more than three multiplex licences may be held by one person.

Award of multiplex licence subject to conditions

10.—(1) The Commission may, when awarding a multiplex licence to any person, make the grant of the licence to him conditional on his compliance before the grant with such specified requirements relating to the financing of the service as appear to them to be appropriate, having regard to—

(a) any duties which are or may be imposed on them, or on the licence holder, by or under the 1990 Act or this Act, and
(b) any information provided to them under section 7(4)(g) by the person to whom the licence is awarded as to his projected financial position during the period for which the licence would be in force.

(2) Where the Commission determine that any condition imposed by them in relation to a multiplex licence in pursuance of subsection (1) has not been satisfied, section 8 shall (subject to subsection (3)) have effect as if the person to whom the licence was awarded had not made an application for it.

(3) Section 8 shall not so have effect if the Commission decide that it would be desirable to publish a fresh notice under section 7(1) in respect of the grant of the licence.

DEFINITIONS
"Commission; the": s.39(1).
"licence": s.39(1).
"multiplex licence": s.39(1).
"1990 Act; the": s.147(1).

GENERAL NOTE
Under this section, the Commission are empowered to set financial conditions on the granting of a licence. They will be concerned to ensure that the person awarded the licence has sufficient guarantees or sources of finance to maintain the service for the licence period. If the awardee fails to meet the conditions, the grant of the licence may be cancelled and awarded to the next applicant without having to start the application process afresh, if the Commission so desire.

Failure to begin providing licensed service and financial penalties on revocation of licence

11.—(1) Subject to subsection (2), subsection (3) applies where at any time after a multiplex licence has been granted to any person but before the licence has come into force—

(a) that person indicates to the Commission that he does not intend to provide the service in question, or

(b) the Commission for any other reason have reasonable grounds for believing that that person will not provide that service once the licence has come into force.

(2) Subsection (3) shall not apply in the case of any person by virtue of paragraph (b) of subsection (1) unless the Commission have served on him a notice stating their grounds for believing that he will not provide the service in question once his licence has come into force; and they shall not serve such a notice on him unless they have given him a reasonable opportunity of making representations to them about the matters complained of.

(3) Where this subsection applies—

(a) the Commission shall serve on the person to whom the licence has been granted a notice revoking the licence as from the time the notice is served on him, and

(b) section 8 shall (subject to subsection (4)) have effect as if he had not made an application for the licence.

(4) Section 8 shall not have effect as mentioned in subsection (3) if the Commission decide that it would be desirable to publish a fresh notice under section 7(1) in respect of the grant of the licence.

(5) Where the Commission revoke a multiplex licence under this section or under any other provision of this Part, they shall serve on the licence holder a notice requiring him to pay to them, within a specified period, a specified financial penalty not exceeding whichever is the greater of—

(a) £50,000, or

(b) the prescribed amount.

(6) In subsection (5) "the prescribed amount" means—

(a) where—

(i) the licence is revoked under this section, or

(ii) the first complete accounting period of the licence holder falling within the period for which the licence is in force has not yet ended,

7 per cent. of the amount which the Commission estimate would have been the multiplex revenue for that accounting period (as determined in accordance with section 14), and

(b) in any other case, 7 per cent. of the multiplex revenue for the last complete accounting period of the licence holder so falling (as so determined).

(7) Any financial penalty payable by any body by virtue of subsection (5) shall, in addition to being recoverable from that body as provided by section 38(4), be recoverable by the Commission as a debt due to them from any person who controls that body.

DEFINITIONS

"Commission; the": s.39(1).
"licence": s.39(1).
"multiplex licence": s.39(1).
"1990 Act; the": s.147(1).

GENERAL NOTE

This section provides for a licence to be revoked after it has been awarded and granted but before it has come into force. By s.147(2) and s.202(4) of the 1990 Act, a licence is in force when the service for which it has been granted is authorised to be provided. The licensee must be given a reasonable opportunity to make representations. Once revoked, the licence may be awarded to the next applicant, if the Commission so desire. In such circumstances, however, the failure to deliver the service has greater repercussions than an earlier withdrawal of service, so provision is made for terminal penalties as a disincentive to licensees to renege on their commitments. The section also makes provision, generally, for such penalties to be imposed in any other case of a licence being revoked. Under subs. (5), the Commission have a discretion to impose a fine not exceeding the greater of £50,000 or seven per cent of estimated or actual multiplex revenue. The fine may be recovered as a civil debt, by subs. (7). By s.36, the figure of £50,000 may be varied, by order.

Conditions attached to multiplex licence

12.—(1) A multiplex licence shall include such conditions as appear to the Commission to be appropriate for securing—

(a) that the licensed service is established by the licence holder in accordance with the timetable and other proposals indicated in the technical plan submitted under section 7(4)(b),

(b) the implementation of any proposals submitted by the licence holder under section 7(4)(c), (d), (e) or (f),

(c) that all digital programme services broadcast under the licence are provided by the holder of a licence under section 18,

(d) that all digital additional services broadcast under the licence are provided by the holder of a licence under section 25,

(e) that in the terms on which the licence holder contracts, or offers to contract, for the broadcasting of digital programme services or digital additional services, he does not show undue discrimination either against or in favour of a particular person providing such a service or a class of such persons,

(f) that the licence holder does not, in any agreement with a person providing a digital programme service or digital additional services which entitles that person to use a specified amount of digital capacity on the frequency or frequencies to which the licence relates, restrict that person's freedom to make arrangements with some other person as to the use of any of that digital capacity (except to the extent that the restriction is reasonably required for the purpose of ensuring the technical quality of the broadcasts or for the purpose of securing compliance with any other condition of the licence),

(g) that the signals carrying the multiplex service attain high standards in terms of technical quality and reliability throughout so much of the area for which the service is provided as is for the time being reasonably practicable, and

(h) that, while the licence is in force, at least 90 per cent. of digital capacity on the frequency or frequencies to which the licence relates is available for the broadcasting of digital programme services, qualifying services, programme-related services or relevant technical services.

(2) Any conditions imposed in pursuance of subsection (1)(a) or (b) may be varied by the Commission with the consent of the licence holder (and section 3(4)(b) shall accordingly not apply to any such variation).

(3) Where the licence holder applies to the Commission for the variation of any condition imposed in pursuance of subsection (1)(b) and relating to the characteristics of any of the digital programme services to be broadcast under the licence, the Commission shall vary the condition accordingly unless it appears to them that, if the application were granted, the capacity of the digital programme services broadcast under the licence to appeal to a variety of tastes and interests would be unacceptably diminished.

(4) In subsection (1)(h)—

(a) "qualifying service" does not include the qualifying teletext service,

(b) "programme-related service" means any digital additional service consisting in the provision of services (apart from advertising) which—

(i) are ancillary to the programmes included in one or more television programme services (within the meaning of Part I of the 1990 Act) and are directly related to the contents of those programmes, or

(ii) relate to the promotion or listing of such programmes, and

(c) "relevant technical service" means any technical service which relates to one or more digital programme services.

(5) The Secretary of State may by order amend subsection (1)(h) by substituting for the percentage for the time being specified there a different percentage specified in the order.

(6) No order under subsection (5) shall be made unless a draft of the order has been laid before and approved by a resolution of each House of Parliament.

(7) Section 10 of the 1990 Act (Government control over licensed services) shall apply in relation to a multiplex service licensed under this Part as it applies in relation to a service licensed under Part I of that Act.

DEFINITIONS

"ancillary service": s.24(2); s.39(1).
"Commission; the": s.39(1).
"digital additional service": s.24(1); s.39(1).
"digital programme service": s.1(4); s.39(1).
"licence": s.39(1).
"licensed": s.39(1).
"multiplex licence": s.39(1).
"multiplex service": s.1(1); s.39(1).
"qualifying service": s.2(2); s.39(1).
"qualifying teletext service": s.39(1).
"technical service": s.24(3); s.39(1).
"1990 Act; the": s.147(1).

GENERAL NOTE

This section supplements the general provisions of s.3 by requiring the Commission to include a number of specific conditions in multiplex licences. It clarifies that applicants undertakings will be incorporated into their licence. Subsection (1)(a) deals with the technical plan and subs. (1)(b) deals with the programme proposals and the proposals for viewer access. By subs. (2), such conditions may be varied by the Commission with the licence holder's consent, in which case the fair hearing requirement for variations under s.3(4)(b) does not apply. The intention here is to provide flexibility in regulating the new industry. In respect of programming characteristics, there is further provision for variation, in subs. (3). Here, the Commission must accede to the licence holder's request, unless the change would unacceptably diminish (in the Commission's view) the diversity of digital programme services on the multiplex. The business plan is covered by s.10.

Subsections (1)(c) and (1)(d) require the multiplex operator to ensure that his broadcasts are licensed as digital programme services or digital additional programme services respectively.

Subsection (1)(e) reflects the fair and effective competition criterion in s.8(2)(f) by requiring no undue discrimination in contracting for digital services. It is not clear exactly what "undue" discrimination might be; the favouring of a particular type of decoding system may be acceptable whereas racial or sexual or disability discrimination would not.

By subs. (1)(f), multiplex providers are not allowed to restrict the potential that digital broadcasting allows to vary the amount of frequency made available for different kinds of broadcasting. It may be desirable, for example, for a programme provider to buy extra capacity, to show a high-definition film, from a news provider, at a time when he is conducting a studio interview which has less demands on picture quality. Programme providers cannot insist on making contractual arrangements that interfere with the very basis of the multiplex service itself, however.

Subsection (1)(g) imposes requirements as to technical quality. The Act does not contain provisions which regulate conditional access to broadcasting services, however. The Government was reluctant to stipulate a particular technology, believing that an industry standard will emerge. Whether or not that happens, access provision for digital transmissions will, in any event, be required to comply with the European Directive on Television Signals and provision is made for that in s.142. In addition, some regulation of conditional access will be implemented through OFTEL's powers to license the telecommunications services which multiplex operators will need to use.

Subsection (1)(h), in conjunction with subs. (4), deals with the relationship between programming services and data services. The total amount of the latter, digital additional services, cannot take up more than 10 per cent of capacity where they are not related to programming (such as subtitling or programme listing) or technical support (such as coding or encryption). In practice, it may be that they will use much less, at least initially. For the purposes of this paragraph, by subs. (4)(a), the public teletext service, presently provided by Teletext Ltd., does not count as a qualifying service; this means that its digital capacity is provided from the 10 per cent allocated to digital additional services. Within that 10 per cent, the Government presently proposes to guarantee it three per cent of capacity on the second multiplex, as an independent analogue broadcaster, and if it should want to expand its services, it will have to negotiate for a further portion of the 10 per cent with the multiplex operator.

Subs. (10)

This is a significant provision, somewhat buried in this section, extending existing government control over broadcasting to multiplex services.

Additional payments to be made in respect of multiplex licences

13.—(1) Where a multiplex licence is granted in pursuance of a notice under subsection (1) of section 7 which specified a percentage of multiplex revenue under paragraph (f) of that subsection, the licence shall include conditions requiring the licence holder to pay to the Commission (in addition to any fees required to be so paid by virtue of section 4(1)(b)) in respect of each accounting period of his falling within the period for which the licence is in force, an amount representing such percentage of the multiplex revenue for that accounting period (determined under section 14) as was specified in the notice.

(2) The Secretary of State may by order provide that, in relation to any notice under subsection (1) of section 7 published while the order is in force, no percentage shall be specified under paragraph (f) of that subsection.

(3) Any order under subsection (2) shall be subject to annulment in pursuance of a resolution of either House of Parliament.

(4) A multiplex licence may include conditions—

(a) enabling the Commission to estimate before the beginning of an accounting period the amount due for that period by virtue of subsection (1), and

(b) requiring the licence holder to pay the estimated amount by monthly instalments throughout that period.

(5) Such a licence may in particular include conditions—

(a) authorising the Commission to revise any estimate on one or more occasions, and to adjust the instalments payable by the licence holder to take account of the revised estimate;

(b) providing for the adjustment of any overpayment or underpayment.

(6) Where—

(a) the first complete accounting period of the licence holder falling within the period for which the licence is in force ("the licence period") does not begin at the same time as that period, or

(b) the last complete accounting period of his falling within the licence period does not end at the same time as that period,

any reference in subsection (1) to an accounting period of his shall include a reference to such part of the accounting period preceding that first complete accounting period, or (as the case may be) following that last complete accounting period, as falls within the licence period; and other references to accounting periods in this Part shall be construed accordingly.

DEFINITIONS

"Commission; the": s.39(1).
"licence": s.39(1).
"multiplex licence": s.39(1).

GENERAL NOTE

The purpose of this section is to enable a levy to be imposed on the profits made by digital terrestrial broadcasters. For the first licence period of 12 years, however, the Government has indicated that the percentage of multiplex revenue will be set at zero. This is intended to encourage investment in the new services. Thereafter, the provisions of this section may be invoked to gear additional payments to the anticipated income and profit for each multiplex licence. The model for such a differential and flexible approach is found in the 1990 Act where the levy on Channel 3 licensees is substantial in many cases but where the levy on local delivery services has typically been set at zero as the infrastructure is being installed during the beginning of the licence period.

Multiplex revenue

14.—(1) For the purposes of section 13(1) the multiplex revenue for each accounting period of the holder of a multiplex licence shall consist of—

(a) all payments received or to be received by him or any person connected with him from a person other than a programme provider or an additional services provider—

(i) in consideration of the inclusion in that period, in any digital programme service or digital additional service broadcast by means of the multiplex service to which the licence relates, of advertisements or other programmes, or

(ii) in respect of charges made in that period for the reception of programmes included in any such digital programme service or digital additional service,

(b) all payments received or to be received by him or any person connected with him in respect of the broadcasting of any qualifying service by means of the multiplex service,

(c) all payments received or to be received by any programme provider or any person connected with him from a person other than the holder of the multiplex licence, an additional services provider or another programme provider—

(i) in consideration of the inclusion in that period, in any digital programme service provided by him for broadcasting by means of the multiplex service, of advertisements or other programmes, or

(ii) in respect of charges made in that period for the reception of programmes included in any such digital programme service, and

(d) all payments received or to be received by any additional services provider or any person connected with him from a person other than the holder of the multiplex licence, a programme provider or another additional services provider—

(i) in consideration of the inclusion in that period, in any digital additional service provided by him for broadcasting by means of the multiplex service, of advertisements or other programmes, or

(ii) in respect of charges made in that period for the reception of programmes included in any such digital additional service.

(2) If, in connection with the inclusion of any advertisements or other programmes whose inclusion is paid for by payments falling within subsection (1)(a)(i), any payments are made to the holder of the multiplex licence or any connected person to meet any payments payable by the licence holder by virtue of section 13(1), those payments shall be regarded as made in consideration of the inclusion of the programmes in question.

(3) In the case of an advertisement included as mentioned in subsection (1)(a)(i), (c)(i) or (d)(i) under arrangements made between—

(a) the holder of the multiplex licence, a programme provider or an additional services provider or any person connected with any of them, and

(b) a person acting as an advertising agent,

the amount of any receipt by the licence holder, programme provider or additional services provider or any connected person that represents a payment by the advertiser from which the advertising agent has deducted any amount by way of commission shall, except in a case falling within subsection

(4), be the amount of the payment by the advertiser after the deduction of the commission.

(4) If the amount deducted by way of commission as mentioned in subsection (3) exceeds 15 per cent. of the payment by the advertiser, the amount of the receipt in question shall be taken to be the amount of the payment less 15 per cent.

(5) If, in any accounting period of the holder of the multiplex licence, a programme provider or an additional services provider or a person connected with any of them derives, in relation to any programme to be included in the relevant service, any financial benefit (whether direct or indirect) from payments made by any person other than the licence holder, by way of sponsorship, for the purpose of defraying or contributing towards costs incurred or to be incurred in connection with that programme, the relevant payments shall be taken to include the amount of the financial benefit so derived by the licence holder or the connected person, as the case may be.

(6) In subsection (5)—

(a) "the relevant service" means—

(i) in relation to a programme provider or a person connected with him, any digital programme service provided as mentioned in subsection (1)(c)(i), and

(ii) in relation to an additional services provider or a person connected with him, any digital additional service provided as mentioned in subsection (1)(d)(i), and

(b) "relevant payments" means—

(i) in relation to a programme provider, the payments referred to in subsection (1)(c), and

(ii) in relation to an additional services provider, the payments referred to in subsection (1)(d).

(7) Where, in any accounting period of the holder of the multiplex licence—

(a) the licence holder provides a digital programme service or digital additional service for broadcasting by means of the multiplex service,

(b) the licence holder is engaged in any activity which, if engaged in by another person, would result in payments falling within subsection (1)(a) being made to the licence holder,

(c) a programme provider is engaged in any activity which, if engaged in by another person, would result in payments falling within subsection (1)(c) being made to the programme provider, or

(d) an additional services provider is engaged in any activity which, if engaged in by another person, would result in payments falling within subsection (1)(d) being made to the additional services provider,

the Commission may, if they consider that the amount which would (apart from this subsection) be the multiplex revenue for that accounting period is less than it would have been if the digital programme service or digital additional service had been provided, or the activity engaged in, by another person at arm's length, treat the multiplex revenue as increased by the amount of the difference.

(8) Where, in any accounting period of the holder of the multiplex licence, the licence holder or a programme provider or additional services provider receives payments falling within subsection (1)(a), (b), (c) or (d) from a person connected with him and it appears to the Commission that the amount which (apart from this subsection) would be the multiplex revenue for that accounting period is less than it would have been if the arrangements between him and the connected person were such as might be expected between parties at arm's length, the Commission may treat the multiplex revenue as increased by the amount of the difference.

(9) In this section—

"additional services provider", in relation to a multiplex licence, means any person who provides any digital additional service for broadcasting by means of the multiplex service to which the licence relates;

"programme provider", in relation to a multiplex licence, means any person who provides a digital programme service for broadcasting by means of the multiplex service to which the licence relates.

DEFINITIONS

"advertising agent": s.147(2); s.202(1) of the Broadcasting Act 1990.
"connected": s.147(2); s.202(1) of the Broadcasting Act 1990.
"Commission; the": s.39(1).
"digital additional service": s.24(1); s.39(1).
"digital programme service": s.1(4); s.39(1).
"licence": s.39(1).
"multiplex licence": s.39(1).
"multiplex service": s.1(1); s.39(1).
"qualifying service": s.2(2); s.39(1).

GENERAL NOTE

This section defines multiplex revenue for the purpose of levying additional payments. Essentially, it requires the computation of all advertising, sponsorship and subscription income related to the multiplex service, together with payments in respect of qualifying services. Advertising agents' commission is excluded, below a ceiling of 15 per cent. By subss. (7) and (8), the Commission have power to circumvent collusive arrangements. Further provision for computing multiplex revenue is made in Sched. 1, Pt. 1, by s.37.

Attribution of multiplex revenue to licence holder and others

15.—(1) For the purposes of section 17(3), the share of multiplex revenue attributable to the holder of a multiplex licence in respect of any accounting period of his shall be—

(a) the aggregate of—

(i) payments falling within paragraphs (a) or (b) of section 14(1), and

(ii) payments received or to be received by him from programme providers and additional services providers in respect of the provision of multiplex services in that period,

less

(b) the amount of any payments made or to be made to programme providers or additional service providers which would fall within paragraph (c) or (d) of section 14(1) but for the fact that they are received from the holder of the multiplex licence.

(2) For the purposes of section 23(3) or section 27(3), the share of multiplex revenue attributable to a programme provider or additional services provider in relation to a multiplex service in respect of any accounting period of the holder of the multiplex licence shall be—

(a) the aggregate of—

(i) payments falling within paragraph (c) or (d) of section 14(1), and

(ii) payments received or to be received from the holder of the multiplex licence which would fall within one of those paragraphs but for the fact that they are received from the holder of the multiplex licence,

less

(b) the amount of any payments made or to be made to the holder of the multiplex licence in respect of the provision of multiplex services in that period.

(3) In a case falling within subsection (7) or (8) of section 14, the Commission may treat the share of multiplex revenue attributable to any person for the accounting period of the holder of the multiplex licence as increased

by such amount as they consider appropriate to take account of the circumstances mentioned in that subsection.

(4) In this section "additional services provider" and "programme provider", in relation to a multiplex licence, have the same meaning as in section 14.

DEFINITIONS

"additional services provider": s.14(9).
"multiplex licence": s.39(1).
"multiplex service": s.1(1); s.39(1).
"programme provider": s.14(9).

GENERAL NOTE

For the purpose of enforcement of licences, the multiplex revenue aggregated in s.14 is disaggregated in this section, so as to distinguish the amounts attributable to multiplex operators (against whom enforcement will take place) and programme providers. It was described in Committee as "an astonishingly complicated process" (col. 156).

Duration and renewal of multiplex licences

16.—(1) A multiplex licence shall (subject to the provisions of this Part and to section 42 of the 1990 Act as applied by section 17(6)) continue in force for a period of twelve years.

(2) A multiplex licence granted within six years of the commencement of this section may be renewed on one occasion in accordance with this section for a period of twelve years beginning with the date on which it would otherwise expire.

(3) An application for the renewal of a multiplex licence under subsection (2) may be made by the licence holder not earlier than four years before the date on which it would otherwise cease to be in force and not later than the relevant date.

(4) At any time before determining the application, the Commission may—

(a) require the applicant to furnish—

(i) a technical plan which supplements that submitted by the licence holder under section 7(4)(b), and

(ii) proposals which supplement any proposals submitted by the licence holder under section 7(4)(f), and

(b) notify the applicant of requirements which must be met by that supplementary technical plan or those supplementary proposals and relate to the matters referred to in section 7(4)(b)(i) and (ii) and (f).

(5) The consent of the Secretary of State shall be required for any exercise by the Commission of their powers under subsection (4) and for any decision by the Commission not to exercise those powers; and in deciding whether to give his consent the Secretary of State shall have regard to any report made to him under subsection (1)(b) of section 33 and to any representations received by him on consultation under subsection (4) of that section.

(6) Where any such application is made before the relevant date, the Commission may postpone consideration of it by them for as long as they think appropriate having regard to subsection (10).

(7) Where an application for the renewal of a multiplex licence has been duly made to the Commission they may refuse the application only if—

(a) it appears to them that the applicant has failed to comply with any of the conditions included in his licence,

(b) any supplementary technical plan or supplementary proposals submitted under subsection (4)(a) fail to meet requirements notified to the applicant under subsection (4)(b), or

(c) they are not satisfied that the applicant would, if his licence were renewed, provide a service which complied with the conditions to be included in the licence as renewed.

(8) Subject to subsection (9), on the grant of any such application the Commission may with the consent of the Secretary of State, and shall if so required by him—

(a) specify a percentage different from that specified under section 7(1)(f) as the percentage of multiplex revenue for each accounting period of his that will be payable by the applicant in pursuance of section 13(1) during the period for which the licence is to be renewed, or

(b) specify such a percentage where none was specified under section 7(1)(f);

and the Commission may specify under paragraph (a) or (b) either of the things mentioned in section 7(2)(b).

(9) Where an order under section 13(2) is in force on the relevant date, no percentage of multiplex revenue shall be payable as mentioned in subsection (8)(a) during the period for which the licence is to be renewed.

(10) Where the Commission have granted a person's application under this section, they shall formally renew his licence from the date on which it would otherwise expire; and they shall not so renew his licence unless they have notified him of any percentage specified by them under subsection (8) and he has, within such period as is specified in that notification, notified them that he consents to the licence being renewed on those terms.

(11) Where a multiplex licence has been renewed under this section, the licence as renewed shall include such further conditions as appear to the Commission to be appropriate for securing the implementation of any supplementary technical plan and supplementary proposals submitted under subsection (4)(a).

(12) In this section "the relevant date", in relation to a multiplex licence, means the date which the Commission determine to be that by which they would need to publish a notice under section 7(1) if they were to grant, as from the date on which that licence would expire if not renewed, a fresh licence to provide the service formerly provided under that licence.

(13) Nothing in this section prevents the holder of a multiplex licence from applying for a new licence on one or more occasions in pursuance of a notice under section 7(1).

Definitions

"Commission; the": s.39(1).
"licence": s.39(1).
"multiplex licence": s.39(1).
"1990 Act; the": s.147(1).

General Note

Subject to revocation, under s.17(6), a multiplex licence lasts for 12 years. It may be renewed once, for a further period of 12 years, provided it has been granted within six years of the commencement of this section. The application for renewal may be made not more than four years before its expiry but before the date which the Commission will have set for a fresh round of multiplex applications. By subs. (7), renewal will occur as of right, provided that the multiplex operator has complied with his existing licence conditions and can meet any supplementary requirements and conditions imposed by the Commission. Such requirements will be imposed with the consent of the Secretary of State, taking into account the review of digital services which is required by s.33. Essentially, the requirements will reflect the targets which are anticipated to be set for the complete transition from analogue to digital broadcasting.

At the same time, a framework is established for the renewed application to contain revised percentages in respect of additional payments (the levy), and such percentages may include different amounts for different accounting periods. The imposition of the levy depends on the lapse of the order specifying a zero percentage, under s.13(2), however. If the decision is made that the industry is sufficiently profitable for the levy to take effect, due notice must be given to the licensee, and his consent obtained, before renewal can take place. In any event, however, the multiplex operator is free to apply for new licences, as and when they are advertised, by subs. (13).

Enforcement of multiplex licences

17.—(1) If the Commission are satisfied that the holder of a multiplex licence has failed to comply with any condition of the licence or with any direction given by the Commission under or by virtue of any provision of this Part, they may (subject to the following provisions of this section) serve on him—

(a) a notice requiring him to pay, within a specified period, a specified financial penalty to the Commission, or

(b) a notice reducing the period for which the licence is to be in force by a specified period not exceeding two years.

(2) The amount of any financial penalty imposed on any person in pursuance of subsection (1)(a) shall not exceed whichever is the greater of—

(a) £50,000, or

(b) the amount determined under subsection (3).

(3) The amount referred to in subsection (2)(b) is—

(a) in a case where a penalty under this section has not previously been imposed on the holder of the multiplex licence during any period for which his licence has been in force ("the relevant period"), 3 per cent. of the share of multiplex revenue attributable to him for his last complete accounting period (as determined in accordance with section 15), and

(b) in any other case, 5 per cent. of the share of multiplex revenue attributable to him for that accounting period (as so determined),

and in relation to a person whose first complete accounting period falling within the relevant period has not yet ended, paragraphs (a) and (b) above shall be construed as referring to 3, or (as the case may be) 5, per cent. of the amount which the Commission estimate to be the share of multiplex revenue attributable to him for that accounting period (as so determined).

(4) The Commission shall not serve on any person such a notice as is mentioned in subsection (1)(a) or (b) unless they have given him a reasonable opportunity of making representations to them about the matters complained of.

(5) Where a licence is due to expire on a particular date by virtue of a notice served on any person under subsection (1)(b), the Commission may, on the application of that person, revoke that notice by a further notice served on him at any time before that date, if they are satisfied that, since the date of the earlier notice, his conduct in relation to the operation of the licensed service has been such as to justify the revocation of that notice.

(6) Section 42 of the 1990 Act (power to revoke Channel 3 or 5 licence) shall have effect in relation to a multiplex licence as it has effect in relation to a Channel 3 licence, but as if the reference in subsection (1)(a) of that section to Part I of the 1990 Act were a reference to this Part.

DEFINITIONS

"Channel 3 licence": s.39(1); s.71(1) of the Broadcasting Act 1990.
"Channel 5 licence": s.39(1); s.71(1) of the Broadcasting Act 1990.
"Commission; the": s.39(1).
"licence": s.39(1).
"licensed": s.39(1).
"multiplex licence": s.39(1).
"1990 Act; the": s.147(1).

GENERAL NOTE

This section contains sanctions that have a financial impact on the licensee. They apply to failures to comply with both conditions and directions issued by the Commission. Where such failures occur, the Commission have the power to serve a notice imposing a financial penalty within a specified period. There is a ceiling of £50,000, or of three per cent of the multiplex revenue for the first offence and five per cent for the subsequent offences, whichever is the greater. The maximum period of shortening is two years, but the penalty is conditional and may be revoked if performance improves before the shortened licence expires. For provisions as to notices, including requirements to publish them, see s.199 of the 1990 Act. By s.38(4), the fine may be recoverable by the Commission as a debt. By s.36, the figure of £50,000 may be varied, by order.

Digital programme services

Licensing of digital programme services

18.—(1) An application for a licence to provide digital programme services (in this Part referred to as a "digital programme licence") shall—

(a) be made in such manner as the Commission may determine, and

(b) be accompanied by such fee (if any) as they may determine.

(2) At any time after receiving such an application and before determining it, the Commission may require the applicant to furnish such additional information as they may consider necessary for the purpose of considering the application.

(3) Any information to be furnished to the Commission under this section shall, if they so require, be in such form or verified in such manner as they may specify.

(4) Where an application for a digital programme licence is made to the Commission in accordance with the provisions of this section, they shall grant the licence unless precluded from doing so by section 3(3)(a) or 5(1).

(5) Subject to subsection (6), sections 6 to 12 of the 1990 Act (general provisions relating to services licensed under Part I of that Act) shall apply in relation to a digital programme service licensed under this Part as they apply in relation to a service licensed under that Part of that Act.

(6) In its application in relation to a digital programme service—

(a) section 6 of the 1990 Act shall have effect with the omission of subsection (8), and

(b) section 12(1)(b) of that Act shall have effect as if the reference to the Commission's functions under Chapter II of Part I of that Act included a reference to their functions under this Part.

DEFINITIONS

"Commission; the": s.39(1).
"digital programme service": s.1(4); s.39(1).
"licence": s.39(1).
"1990 Act; the": s.147(1).

GENERAL NOTE

The procedure for licensing digital programme services is relatively informal. By subs. (4), licences will be issued, essentially, on demand. The only limitation on issue is that the licensee is a fit and proper person, under s.3(3)(a), and is not restricted from holding licences, under s.5(1). The Commission's powers to request information, under subss. (2) and (3), must be interpreted in that context. Having obtained the licence, however, the licensee will be required to comply with a number of conditions. By subss. (5) and (6), the general provisions about licensed services in the 1990 Act are applied to digital programme services and their ancillary services. These comprise general requirements, such as the ensuring of taste and decency, accurate and impartial news, due impartiality on controversial matters and the absence of subliminal images, together with the absence of political or discriminatory advertising. They also include the application of the Programme Standards and Advertising Codes. In addition, the Commission's duty to monitor programming and to conduct audience research applies to digital programme services. Other conditions relating to digital programme services are contained in the following ss.19 to 21.

Duration and conditions of digital programme licence

19.—(1) Subject to the provisions of this Part and to section 42 of the 1990 Act as applied by section 23(8), a digital programme licence shall continue in force until it is surrendered by its holder.

(2) A digital programme licence shall include such conditions as the Commission consider necessary or appropriate to secure in relation to each service provided under the licence—

(a) that a proper proportion of the matter included in the programmes provided by the service is of European origin, and

(b) that in each year not less than 10 per cent. of the total amount of time allocated to the broadcasting of qualifying programmes included in the service is allocated to the broadcasting of a range and diversity of independent productions.

(3) A digital programme licence shall also include such conditions as appear to the Commission to be appropriate for requiring the holder of the licence—

(a) on entering into any agreement with the holder of a multiplex licence for the provision of a digital programme service to be broadcast by means of a multiplex service, to notify the Commission—

(i) of the identity of the multiplex service,

(ii) of the characteristics of the digital programme service to which the agreement relates,

(iii) of the period during which it will be provided, and

(iv) where under the agreement the holder of the digital programme licence will be entitled to the use of a specified amount of digital capacity, of that amount,

(b) when any such agreement is varied so far as it relates to any of the matters mentioned in paragraph (a)(i), (ii), (iii) or (iv), to notify the Commission of the variation so far as relating to those matters, and

(c) where he is providing a digital programme service to the holder of a multiplex licence in accordance with such an agreement as is mentioned in paragraph (a) but intends to cease doing so, to notify the Commission of that fact.

(4) A digital programme licence shall also include such conditions as appear to the Commission to be appropriate for requiring the holder of the licence, on entering into any such agreement as is mentioned in subsection (3)(a), to submit to the Commission proposals for training or retraining persons employed or to be employed by him in order to help fit them for employment in, or in connection with, the making of programmes to be included in his service, together with his proposals for encouraging the training or retraining of persons employed or to be employed by persons providing programmes for inclusion in that service.

(5) Where the holder of a digital programme licence has submitted proposals to the Commission in accordance with a condition included in the licence by virtue of subsection (4) or has failed to comply with such a condition, the Commission may, after consulting him, vary the licence so as to include in the licence such further conditions as they consider appropriate in relation to the matters referred to in that subsection.

(6) In framing any condition in pursuance of subsection (2)(a), the Commission shall have regard to such of the international obligations of United Kingdom as the Secretary of State may notify to them for the purposes of this subsection.

(7) In subsection (2)(b)—

(a) "independent productions" and "qualifying programmes" have the same meaning as in section 16(2)(h) of the 1990 Act, and

(b) the reference to a range of independent productions is a reference to a range of such productions in terms of cost of acquisition as well as in terms of the types of programme involved.

(8) The Secretary of State may by order amend subsection (2)(b) by substituting a different percentage for the percentage for the time being specified there.

(9) Before making an order under subsection (8) the Secretary of State shall consult the Commission; and no such order shall be made unless a draft of it has been laid before and approved by a resolution of each House of Parliament.

(10) In this section "programme" does not include an advertisement.

DEFINITIONS

"digital programme licence": s.39(1).
"digital programme service": s.1(4); s.39(1).
"licence": s.39(1).
"multiplex licence": s.39(1).
"multiplex service": s.1(1); s.39(1).
"1990 Act; the": s.147(1).

GENERAL NOTE

Subs. (1)

A licence for a digital programme service has an indefinite duration, continuing in force until surrendered. This does not imply that the holder must provide a continuous stream of programming and it may be that the licensee provides only a limited amount of specialised material on an intermittent basis.

Subs. (2)

The conditions in this subsection are governed by the European Community's Broadcasting Directive of 1989. The Directive is currently being revised but the present requirement for programmes of European origin is that they should comprise "a majority" of the broadcaster's output. The figure for independent productions is set at 10 per cent and it is that minimum proportion which has been adopted here, contrasting with the higher figure of 25 per cent which has been set for analogue programmes under the 1990 Act. In applying the European quota, the Commission are given responsibility for implementing the European Directive, under subs. (6), but it is the Secretary of State who must do the same when setting the independent productions quota, under subss. (8) and (9).

Subs. (10)

In this section, a programme does not include an advertisement. This reflects the position under the European Directive.

Code relating to provision for deaf and visually impaired

20.—(1) The Commission shall draw up, and from time to time review, a code giving guidance as to—

(a) the extent to which digital programme services and qualifying services should promote the understanding and enjoyment by—
  (i) persons who are deaf or hard of hearing, and
  (ii) persons who are blind or partially-sighted,
  of the programmes to be included in such services, and
(b) the means by which such understanding and enjoyment should be promoted.

(2) In this section "assistance" means assistance of any of the following three kinds, namely—

(a) subtitling for the deaf,
(b) audio-description for the blind, and
(c) presentation in, or translation into, sign language.

(3) The code must require that, as from the tenth anniversary of the date of the commencement of the provision of any digital programme service, in each week—

(a) at least 50 per cent. of so much of the service as consists of programmes which are not excluded programmes in relation to subtitling for the deaf is to be accompanied by such subtitling, and
(b) at least 10 per cent. of so much of the service as consists of programmes which are not excluded programmes in relation to audio-description for the blind is to be accompanied by such audio-description.

(4) The code must specify—

(a) in relation to subtitling for the deaf, those classes of programmes in relation to which the Commission consider that it would be inappropriate for the requirement in paragraph (a) of subsection (3) to apply, and

(b) in relation to audio-description for the blind, those classes of programmes in relation to which the Commission consider that it would be inappropriate for the requirement in paragraph (b) of that subsection to apply.

(5) If an order under section 21(1)(b) is in force, the code must also specify, in relation to presentation in, or translation into, sign language, those classes of programmes in relation to which the Commission consider that it would be inappropriate for the requirements specified in the order to apply.

(6) In determining under subsection (4) or (5) whether it is appropriate for a particular requirement to apply to any class of programmes, the Commission shall have regard, in particular, to the benefit which the assistance would be likely to confer on the persons for whom it is intended and to the technical difficulty of providing it.

(7) In this section "excluded programme", in relation to assistance of a particular kind, means a programme falling within a class specified under subsection (4) or (5) in relation to assistance of that kind.

(8) Without prejudice to the generality of subsection (1), the code may—

(a) require persons providing digital programme services, at any time or times before the anniversary referred to in subsection (3), to meet specified targets in relation to subtitling for the deaf or audio-description for the blind,

(b) require a specified percentage of so much of any digital programme service as consists of programmes which are not excluded programmes in relation to presentation in, or translation into, sign language, to be so presented or translated, and

(c) require, in relation to assistance of any kind, a specified percentage of so much of any digital programme service as consists of excluded programmes falling within a specified class to be accompanied by assistance of that kind.

(9) In subsection (8) "specified" means specified in, or determined by the Commission under, the code.

(10) Subsections (3) and (8), so far as relating to audio-description for the blind or presentation in, or translation into, sign language, shall have effect as if any reference to a digital programme service included a reference to a qualifying service.

(11) The Commission may determine that, for the purposes of any provision included in the code in pursuance of subsection (3), a digital programme service provided by any person is to be treated as a continuation of a digital programme service previously provided by him.

(12) Before drawing up the code or reviewing it in pursuance of this section the Commission shall consult such bodies or persons appearing to them to represent the interests of the persons referred to in subsection (1)(a) as the Commission think fit.

(13) The Commission shall publish the code drawn up under this section, and every revision of it, in such manner as they consider appropriate; and in determining the manner of publication, the Commission shall have regard to the need to make the code or revision accessible to persons who are blind or partially sighted and persons who are deaf or hard of hearing.

(14) In this section—

"programme" does not include an advertisement;

"qualifying service" does not include the qualifying teletext service.

DEFINITIONS
"Commission; the": s.39(1).
"digital programme service": s.1(4); s.39(1).
"qualifying service": s.2(2); s.39(1).
"qualifying teletext service": s.39(1).

GENERAL NOTE
This section, which should be read together with s.21, requires the Commission to draw up a code of practice for assisting the deaf, through subtitling and sign language, and the blind, through audio-description. In subs. (3), there are specific targets which must be incorporated into the code. The relevant percentages, 50 per cent for subtitling and 10 per cent for audio-description, may be amended by order, under s.21(1). Targets for sign language may also be incorporated into the code, under s.21(3). Changes to the targets can be made only after consultation with the Commission and they, in turn, are required to consult with representative parties, under subs. (12).

The Commission are given discretion to determine which digital programmes will be suitable for such assistance and those which are not ("excluded programmes") and to set intermediate targets where appropriate. Advertisements are not included, by subs. (14) and nor are qualifying teletext services. Although other qualifying services already have commitments to provide assistance under s.35 of the 1990 Act, they will be required to enhance their assistance in digital form under the provisions of the code, by subs. (10).

Powers of Secretary of State in relation to code under section 20

21.—(1) The Secretary of State may by order—

(a) amend subsection (3) of section 20 by substituting for any percentage specified there a percentage specified in the order, and
(b) require the Commission to include in the code maintained under that section the requirement that in each week, at least a percentage specified in the order of so much of any digital programme service or qualifying service as consists of programmes which are not excluded programmes for the purposes of that section in relation to presentation in, or translation into, sign language is to be so presented or translated.

(2) In subsection (1) "qualifying service" does not include the qualifying teletext service.

(3) Before making an order under subsection (1), the Secretary of State shall consult the Commission.

(4) No order under subsection (1) shall be made unless a draft of the order has been laid before and approved by a resolution of each House of Parliament.

DEFINITIONS
"Commission; the": s.39(1).
"digital programme service": s.1(4); s.39(1).
"qualifying service": s.2(2); s.39(1).
"qualifying teletext service": s.39(1).

Compliance with code under section 20

22.—(1) The Commission shall do all that they can to secure that the provisions of the code maintained by them under section 20 are observed in the provision of digital programme services and qualifying services.

(2) Without prejudice to the generality of subsection (1), a digital programme licence shall include such conditions as appear to the Commission to be appropriate for requiring the holder of the licence, on entering into any such agreement as is mentioned in section 19(3)(a), to submit to the Commission proposals for ensuring that the code is complied with in relation to the provision of the digital programme service.

(3) Where the holder of a digital programme licence has submitted proposals to the Commission in accordance with a condition included in the licence by virtue of subsection (2) or has failed to comply with such a condition, the Commission shall, after consulting him, vary the licence so as to

include in the licence such further conditions as they consider appropriate for the purpose of securing compliance with the code in the provision of the digital programme service in question.

DEFINITIONS

"Commission; the": s.39(1).
"digital programme licence": s.39(1).
"digital programme service": s.1(4); s.39(1).
"licence": s.39(1).
"qualifying service": s.2(2); s.39(1).

GENERAL NOTE

Compliance with the code for assisting the deaf and the blind will be secured by incorporating its requirements into the digital programme licence which may be enforced under s.23.

Enforcement of digital programme licences

23.—(1) If the Commission are satisfied that the holder of a digital programme licence has failed to comply with any condition of the licence or with any direction given by the Commission under or by virtue of any provision of this Part, they may (subject to the following provisions of this section) serve on him—

(a) a notice requiring him to pay, within a specified period, a specified financial penalty to the Commission, or
(b) a notice providing that the licence is to expire on a specified date, which shall be at least one year from the date of service of the notice.

(2) The amount of any financial penalty imposed on any person in pursuance of subsection (1)(a) shall not exceed whichever is the greater of—

(a) £50,000, or
(b) the amount determined under subsection (3).

(3) The amount referred to in subsection (2)(b) is—

(a) in a case where a penalty under this section has not previously been imposed on the holder of the digital programme licence during any period for which his licence has been in force, 3 per cent. of the aggregate amount of the shares of multiplex revenue attributable to him in relation to multiplex services in respect of relevant accounting periods (as determined in accordance with section 15), and
(b) in any other case, 5 per cent. of the aggregate amount of those shares of multiplex revenue (as so determined).

(4) In subsection (3)(a) "relevant accounting period", in relation to a multiplex service, means the last accounting period of the holder of the multiplex licence.

(5) Where, in the case of any multiplex service, the first accounting period of the holder of the multiplex licence throughout which the holder of the digital programme licence provides a digital programme service for broadcasting by means of the multiplex service ("the first period") has not yet ended, then for the purposes of subsection (3) the share of multiplex revenue attributable to the holder of the digital programme licence in relation to that multiplex service for the relevant accounting period shall be taken to be the amount which the Commission estimate to be the share of multiplex revenue attributable to him for the first period.

(6) The Commission shall not serve on any person such a notice as is mentioned in subsection (1)(a) or (b) unless they have given him a reasonable opportunity of making representations to them about the matters complained of.

(7) Where a licence is due to expire on a particular date by virtue of a notice served on any person under subsection (1)(b), the Commission may, on the application of that person, revoke that notice by a further notice

served on him at any time before that date, if they are satisfied that, since the date of the earlier notice, his conduct in relation to the operation of the licensed service has been such as to justify the revocation of that notice.

(8) Subject to subsection (9), section 40(1) to (4) (power to direct licensee to broadcast correction or apology or not to repeat programme) and section 42 (power to revoke Channel 3 or 5 licence) of the 1990 Act shall apply in relation to a digital programme licence as they apply in relation to a Channel 3 licence.

(9) In its application in relation to a digital programme licence, section 42 of the 1990 Act shall have effect—

(a) with the substitution for the reference in subsection (1)(a) to Part I of that Act of a reference to this Part, and

(b) with the omission of subsection (4) and of the reference to that subsection in subsection (6).

(10) It is hereby declared that any exercise by the Commission of their powers under subsection (1) in respect of any failure to comply with any condition of a digital programme licence shall not preclude the exercise by them of their powers under section 40 of the 1990 Act in respect of that failure.

DEFINITIONS

"Channel 3 licence": s.39(1); s.71(1) of the Broadcasting Act 1990.
"Channel 5 licence": s.39(1); s.71(1) of the Broadcasting Act 1990.
"Commission; the": s.39(1).
"digital programme licence": s.39(1).
"digital programme service": s.1(4); s.39(1).
"licence": s.39(1).
"licensed": s.39(1).
"multiplex licence": s.39(1).
"multiplex service": s.1(1); s.39(1).
"1990 Act; the": s.147(1).

GENERAL NOTE

This section incorporates three levels of sanction against a recalcitrant digital programme licensee. The most lenient, and directed at programme content, is the power to direct the licensee to broadcast a correction or apology or not to repeat the programme, under subss. (8) and (10). The power to direct an apology or correction is not intended to be used for individual complaints of unfairness or invasions of privacy; those are dealt with by the Broadcasting Standards Commission under Pt. V. Rather, the sanction, which applies only to breaches of licence conditions, enables the Commission to require the licensee to admit publicly that the service has fallen below standard and undertake not to let that happen again. Where the fault can be remedied by the provision of further information, a correction will be appropriate. If the problem is contained within a particular programme, the licensee may be directed not to repeat it.

The next level of sanction is the financial penalty, for which provision is made in subss. (1) to (7). It applies to failures to comply with both conditions and directions issued by the Commission. Where such failures occur, the Commission have the power to serve a notice imposing a financial penalty within a specified period. There is a ceiling of three per cent of the multiplex revenue for the first offence and five per cent for the subsequent offences, or £50,000, whichever is the greater. In addition, there is a power to serve a notice to shorten the licence period, which could have a severe financial impact on the licensee. There is no maximum period by which the licence may be shortened but it cannot take effect before one year after service of the notice. The penalty is conditional, however, and may be revoked if performance improves before the shortened licence expires. For provisions as to notices, including requirements to publish them, see s.199 of the 1990 Act. Both types of sanction may be combined with the power to direct an apology or correction. There is no appeal against "sentence" but it is submitted that some degree of proportionality between the offence and the level of fine or degree of shortening would be required under *Wednesbury* reasonableness. By s.38(4), the fine may be recoverable by the Commission as a debt. By s.36, the figure of £50,000 may be varied, by order.

The most severe sanction is revocation, for which provision is made in subss. (8) and (9), applying s.42 of the 1990 Act. Revocation might be expected to be used in only the most serious cases. By s.42(1)–(3), there must have been a failure to comply with a licence condition or a direction from the Commission. It must be a failure that would justify revocation if it were not remedied, by s.42(1)(b); this is a requirement that the penalty must be related to the seriousness of the offence. Before a notice of revocation is issued, however, the licensee must be given an opportunity, by notice, to remedy the failure within a specified period. Only if that also fails to occur, and it is necessary in the public interest to do so, may the Commission revoke the licence. For provisions as to notices, including requirements to publish them, see s.199 of the 1990 Act. This section also applies the power to revoke, under s.42(5) of the 1990 Act, where false or misleading information has been provided.

Digital additional services provided on television broadcasting frequencies

Digital additional services

24.—(1) In this Part "digital additional service" means any service which—

(a) is provided by any person with a view to its being broadcast in digital form by means of a multiplex service, whether by him or by some other person, but

(b) is not a digital programme service, a qualifying service, an ancillary service or a technical service.

(2) In this Part "ancillary service" means any service which is provided by the holder of a digital programme licence or by an independent analogue broadcaster and consists in the provision of—

(a) subtitling for the deaf in connection with programmes included in a digital programme service or qualifying service provided by him, or

(b) other services (apart from advertising) which—

(i) are ancillary to such programmes and directly related to their contents, or

(ii) relate to the promotion or listing of such programmes.

(3) In this Part "technical service" means a service which—

(a) is provided for technical purposes connected with the encryption or decryption of one or more digital programme services or digital additional services, and

(b) is of a description specified in an order made by the Secretary of State.

(4) An order under subsection (3) shall be subject to annulment in pursuance of a resolution of either House of Parliament.

DEFINITIONS

"digital additional service": s.24(1); s.39(1).
"digital programme service": s.1(4); s.39(1).
"multiplex service": s.1(1); s.39(1).
"qualifying service": s.2(2); s.39(1).

GENERAL NOTE

Digital additional services are defined negatively in this section, being services which are not digital programme services or qualifying services (analogous to familiar television programming), ancillary services (such as subtitling which is directly related to the content of a programme) or technical services (such as encoding and decoding signals). In effect, the services which are covered are data services or (possibly) interactive services. Examples include "super-teletext", business or finance information and, possibly, home shopping. By s.12(1)(h), digital additional services may not use more than 10 per cent of the capacity of a multiplex.

Licensing of digital additional services

25.—(1) An application for a licence to provide digital additional services (in this Part referred to as a "digital additional services licence") shall—

(a) be made in such manner as the Commission may determine, and

(b) be accompanied by such fee (if any) as they may determine.

(2) At any time after receiving such an application and before determining it, the Commission may require the applicant to furnish such additional

information as they may consider necessary for the purpose of considering the application.

(3) Any information to be furnished to the Commission under this section shall, if they so require, be in such form or verified in such manner as they may specify.

(4) Where an application for a digital additional services licence is made to the Commission in accordance with the provisions of this section, they shall grant the licence unless precluded from doing so by section 3(3)(a) or 5(1).

(5) Subject to subsection (6), sections 6 to 12 of the 1990 Act (general provisions relating to services licensed under Part I of that Act) shall apply in relation to any digital additional service which is licensed under this Part of this Act and is broadcast for general reception in, or in any area in, the United Kingdom as they apply in relation to services licensed under Part I of the 1990 Act.

(6) In its application in relation to a digital additional service—

(a) section 6 of the 1990 Act shall have effect with the omission of subsection (8), and

(b) section 12(1)(b) of the 1990 Act shall have effect as if the reference to the Commission's functions under Chapter II of Part I of that Act included a reference to their functions under this Part.

DEFINITIONS

"Commission; the": s.39(1).
"digital additional service": s.24(1); s.39(1).
"licence": s.39(1).
"licensed": s.39(1).
"1990 Act; the": s.147(1).

GENERAL NOTE

See the note to s.18, to which this section corresponds. It is notable, however, that the "consumer protection" requirements of the 1990 Act do apply to digital additional services, unlike their analogue counterparts, the additional services.

Duration and conditions of digital additional services licence

26.—(1) Subject to the provisions of this Part and to section 42 of the 1990 Act as applied by section 27(8), a digital additional services licence shall continue in force until it is surrendered by its holder.

(2) A digital additional services licence shall include such conditions as appear to the Commission to be appropriate for requiring the holder of the licence—

(a) on entering into any agreement with the holder of a multiplex licence for the broadcasting of digital additional services by means of a multiplex service, to notify the Commission—

(i) of the identity of the multiplex service,

(ii) of the period during which the services will be provided,

(iii) where under the agreement the holder of the digital additional services licence will be entitled to the use of a specified amount of digital capacity, of that amount,

(b) when any such agreement is varied so far as it relates to any of the matters mentioned in paragraph (a)(i), (ii) or (iii), to notify the Commission of the variation so far as relating to those matters, and

(c) where he is providing digital additional services to the holder of a multiplex licence in accordance with such an agreement as is mentioned in paragraph (a) but intends to cease doing so, to notify the Commission of that fact.

DEFINITIONS

"digital additional services licence": s.39(1).
"multiplex licence": s.39(1).

"multiplex service": s.1(1); s.39(1).
"1990 Act; the": s.147(1).

GENERAL NOTE

This section corresponds to s.19. The conditions relating to digital additional services differ from those relating to digital programme services, however. There is no European programme or independent productions quota. Nor is there any requirement to provide training for the industry. In addition, there is no obligation, in subs. (2)(a) which corresponds to s.19(3)(a), on the licensee to provide the Commission with details of the characteristics of the service agreed with the multiplex operator.

Enforcement of digital additional services licences

27.—(1) If the Commission are satisfied that the holder of a digital additional services licence has failed to comply with any condition of the licence or with any direction given by the Commission under or by virtue of any provision of this Part, they may (subject to the following provisions of this section) serve on him—

(a) a notice requiring him to pay, within a specified period, a specified financial penalty to the Commission, or
(b) a notice providing that the licence is to expire on a specified date, which shall be at least one year from the date of service of the notice.

(2) The amount of any financial penalty imposed on any person in pursuance of subsection (1)(a) shall not exceed whichever is the greater of—

(a) £50,000, or
(b) the amount determined under subsection (3).

(3) The amount referred to in subsection (2)(b) is—

(a) in a case where a penalty under this section has not previously been imposed on the holder of the digital additional services licence during any period for which his licence has been in force, 3 per cent. of the aggregate amount of the shares of multiplex revenue attributable to him in relation to multiplex services in respect of relevant accounting periods (as determined in accordance with section 15), and
(b) in any other case, 5 per cent. of the aggregate amount of those shares of multiplex revenue (as so determined).

(4) In subsection (3)(a) "relevant accounting period", in relation to a multiplex service, means the last accounting period of the holder of the multiplex licence.

(5) Where, in the case of any multiplex service, the first accounting period of the holder of the multiplex licence throughout which the holder of the digital additional services licence provides a digital additional service for broadcasting by means of the multiplex service ("the first period") has not yet ended, then for the purposes of subsection (3) the share of multiplex revenue attributable to the holder of the digital additional services licence in relation to that multiplex service for the relevant accounting period shall be taken to be the amount which the Commission estimate to be the share of multiplex revenue attributable to him for the first period.

(6) The Commission shall not serve on any person such a notice as is mentioned in subsection (1)(a) or (b) unless they have given him a reasonable opportunity of making representations to them about the matters complained of.

(7) Where a licence is due to expire on a particular date by virtue of a notice served on any person under subsection (1)(b), the Commission may, on the application of that person, revoke that notice by a further notice served on him at any time before that date, if they are satisfied that, since the date of the earlier notice, his conduct in relation to the operation of the licensed service has been such as to justify the revocation of that notice.

(8) Subject to subsection (9), sections 40(1) to (4) and section 42 of the 1990 Act shall apply in relation to a digital additional services licence as they apply in relation to a Channel 3 licence.

(9) In its application in relation to a digital additional services licence, section 42 of the 1990 Act shall have effect—

(a) with the substitution for the reference in subsection (1)(a) to Part I of that Act of a reference to this Part, and

(b) with the omission of subsection (4) and of the reference to that subsection in subsection (6).

(10) It is hereby declared that any exercise by the Commission of their powers under subsection (1) in respect of any failure to comply with any condition of a digital additional services licence shall not preclude the exercise by them of their powers under section 40 of the 1990 Act in respect of that failure.

DEFINITIONS

"Channel 3 licence": s.39(1); s.71(1) of the Broadcasting Act 1990.
"Commission; the": s.39(1).
"digital additional services licence": s.39(1).
"licence": s.39(1).
"licensed": s.39(1).
"multiplex licence": s.39(1).
"multiplex service": s.1(1); s.39(1).
"1990 Act; the": s.147(1).

GENERAL NOTE

See the note to s.23, to which this section corresponds. By s.36, the figure of £50,000 in subs. (2)(a) may be varied, by order.

Digital broadcasting of services provided by independent analogue broadcasters

Provision for broadcasting of services provided by independent analogue broadcasters

28.—(1) The Secretary of State shall exercise his powers under this section for the purposes of—

(a) facilitating the broadcasting of qualifying services by means of multiplex services licensed under this Part, and

(b) entitling any independent analogue broadcaster who in accordance with this section provides a qualifying service for broadcasting in digital form on a frequency to the use of digital capacity on that frequency.

(2) The Secretary of State shall, in assigning frequencies to the Commission under section 6, by direction to the Commission—

(a) designate one or two frequencies as frequencies to which this section applies, and

(b) specify in relation to each frequency so designated—

(i) the independent analogue broadcasters for whom digital capacity is to be reserved in accordance with this section,

(ii) the amount of digital capacity to be so reserved for each of them,

(iii) the times of day between which or days of the week on which such capacity is to be so reserved,

(iv) the area in the United Kingdom in which each of them is to be permitted to provide services, and

(v) the qualifying services which, subject to the provisions of this section, are intended to be broadcast on that frequency.

(3) The Secretary of State may by order—

(a) provide, in relation to any frequency to which this section applies—

(i) that any or all of the provisions of sections 7 to 16 and sections 18 and 19 are not to apply, or are to apply with specified modifications, and

(ii) that provisions of the order are to have effect in place of any or all of those provisions,

(b) provide for the Commission to include in any multiplex licence granted in respect of any such frequency such conditions as may be specified in, or determined by them under, the order, including conditions for securing the result specified in subsection (4),

(c) provide for the Commission to vary any licence under which the service specified in section 2(3) corresponding to the qualifying service ("the corresponding analogue service") is provided so as to include such conditions relating to the broadcasting of the qualifying service as may be specified in, or determined by the Commission under, the order and to include those conditions in any other licence under which the corresponding analogue service is subsequently provided, and

(d) make such other provision for either of the purposes specified in subsection (1) as he considers appropriate.

(4) The result referred to in subsection (3)(b) is that, in consideration of the making, by any independent analogue broadcaster specified under subsection (2)(b)(i) in relation to the frequency concerned, of such payments as are from time to time agreed between him and the holder of the multiplex licence or (in default of agreement) determined by the Commission under the order, the holder of that licence will use the digital capacity specified under subsection (2)(b)(ii) for the broadcasting of services provided by that broadcaster.

(5) Where under subsection (2)(b) digital capacity is reserved only between particular times, on particular days or in a particular area, the reference in subsection (4) to broadcasting is a reference to broadcasting between those times, on those days or in that area.

(6) Without prejudice to the generality of section 200(2)(a) of the 1990 Act (which provides that orders may make different provision for different cases), an order under this section may make different provision for different frequencies.

(7) Any order under this section shall be subject to annulment in pursuance of a resolution of either House of Parliament.

DEFINITIONS

"Commission; the": s.39(1).
"independent analogue broadcaster": s.2(1); s.39(1).
"licence": s.39(1).
"licensed": s.39(1).
"multiplex licence": s.39(1).
"multiplex service": s.1(1); s.39(1).
"qualifying service": s.2(2); s.39(1).
"1990 Act; the": s.147(1).

GENERAL NOTE

This section makes provision for the Secretary of State to modify the general pattern for regulating digital terrestrial television, so as to allow existing analogue broadcasters the opportunity to secure favourable positions in developing the new technology. The Government's policy was explained in Standing Committee, at cols. 206–210. The BBC will be allocated the first of the six multiplexes. The second will be reserved for Teletext (three per cent), the Channel 3 companies (48.5 per cent) and Channel 4 (48.5 per cent). If those channels indicate their intention to use the multiplex, in return for providing qualified services, the Commission will not advertise the licence but will settle its terms with the broadcasters or any multiplex operating company that they may set up for the purpose. The third multiplex will be reserved for Channel 5 (one half) and, S4C (the other half in Wales only). This multiplex will be advertised in accordance with ss.7 to 17, but subject to the licensee's obligation to provide the reserved capacity; the opportunities for new digital services on this multiplex will obviously be less. The remaining multiplexes will be licensed in accordance with ss.7 to 17. The fact that the independent analogue broadcasters will have capacity reserved for them does not prevent them, however, from buying further capacity to develop their digital programming and services.

The S4C digital service

29.—(1) If the Welsh Authority provide S4C Digital, it shall be their duty—

(a) to provide it as a public service for disseminating information, education and entertainment,

(b) to ensure that all the programmes in Welsh which are broadcast on S4C are broadcast on S4C Digital at the same time, and

(c) to ensure that the programmes which are broadcast on S4C Digital but not on S4C maintain—

(i) a high general standard in all respects (and, in particular, in respect of their content and quality), and

(ii) a wide range in their subject matter, having regard both to the programmes as a whole and also to the days of the week on which, and the times of the day at which, the programmes are broadcast.

(2) Sections 57(4), 58(5), 59, 60 and 64 of the 1990 Act shall apply in relation to S4C Digital as they apply in relation to S4C.

(3) No payment shall be required by the BBC in respect of the broadcasting pursuant to subsection (1)(b) of programmes provided by them under section 58(1) of the 1990 Act.

(4) In this section "programme" does not include an advertisement.

DEFINITIONS

"BBC; the": s.147(1).
"S4C": s.39(1); s.71(1) of the Broadcasting Act 1990.
"S4C Digital": s.39(1); s.57(1A)(a) of the Broadcasting Act 1990.
"1990 Act; the": s.147(1).

GENERAL NOTE

This section establishes S4C Digital as a completely separate service to be offered by the Welsh Authority. It establishes a public service remit for the digital service, which will be in addition to the analogue service, S4C, which is regulated under the 1990 Act. Furthermore, the effect is to sever the relationship between S4C and Channel 4, in respect of digital services. Under s.2(4), S4C Digital is a qualifying service but its obligation to simulcast Welsh S4C programmes is contained in subs. (1)(b). The authority for the Welsh Authority to extend its operations, in this way, is found in s.84(2), amending s.57 of the 1990 Act.

The qualifying teletext service

30.—(1) If the public teletext provider has notified the Commission under section 2(5) of his intention to provide a teletext service for broadcasting in digital form as a qualifying service, he shall submit to the Commission his proposals for providing that service in compliance with the requirements specified in subsection (3).

(2) The Commission shall give their consent to the provision of the service unless it appears to them that the proposed service would not comply with the requirements specified in subsection (3).

(3) The requirements referred to in subsections (1) and (2) are—

(a) that the service includes a sufficient amount of news items which are of high quality and deal with both national and international matters,

(b) that the service includes a sufficient amount of information which is of particular interest to persons living within different areas for which the service is provided, and

(c) that (taken as whole) the service includes a sufficient amount of information (other than news) which is calculated to appeal to a wide variety of tastes and interests.

(4) Where the Commission have given their consent under subsection (2), they shall vary the relevant licence held by the public teletext provider so as to include such conditions as appear to them to be appropriate—

(a) for imposing on the public teletext provider, in specified circumstances, an obligation to provide the qualifying teletext service, and

(b) for securing that the qualifying teletext service, if provided, accords with the proposals submitted under subsection (1);

and they may include those conditions in any other licence under which the analogue service is subsequently provided.

(5) Sections 6 to 12 of the 1990 Act (general provisions relating to services licensed under Part I of that Act) shall apply in relation to the qualifying teletext service as they apply in relation to the analogue service, but as if the reference in section 12(1)(b) of the 1990 Act to the Commission's functions under Chapter II of Part I of that Act included a reference to their functions under this Part.

(6) In this section—

"the analogue service" means the service referred to in section 49(2) of the 1990 Act;

"the relevant licence" means the additional services licence (within the meaning of Part I of the 1990 Act) under which the analogue service is provided.

DEFINITIONS

"Commission; the": s.39(1).
"public teletext provider": s.2(6); s.39(1).
"qualifying service": s.2(2); s.39(1).
"1990 Act; the": s.147(1).

GENERAL NOTE

The public teletext provider, currently Teletext Ltd., will not be obliged to simulcast its analogue service on its reserved multiplex capacity. Under this section, however, its new digital service, a qualifying service under s.2(5), will be subject to public service requirements. This section applies limited positive obligations, in subs. (2), and the "consumer protection" requirements of the 1990 Act, in subs. (5).

Advertisements included in qualifying services

31. Where an independent analogue broadcaster other than the Welsh Authority or the public teletext provider includes in a qualifying service advertisements which are not included in the corresponding analogue service (within the meaning of section 2(2)), sections 8 and 9 of the 1990 Act shall have effect as if the provision of the advertisements constituted the provision of a service licensed under Part I of the 1990 Act.

DEFINITIONS

"independent analogue broadcaster": s.2(1); s.39(1).
"public teletext provider": s.2(6); s.39(1).
"qualifying service": s.2(2); s.39(1).
"1990 Act; the": s.147(1).

Miscellaneous and supplemental

Digital broadcasting of Gaelic programmes

32.—(1) The Secretary of State may by order provide for the Commission to include in any multiplex licence granted in respect of one frequency to which section 28 applies such conditions relating to the broadcasting of programmes in Gaelic for reception wholly or mainly in Scotland as may be specified in, or determined by them under, the order.

(2) The Secretary of State may by order require the holder of a multiplex licence ("the holder"), in complying with any such conditions, to broadcast programmes in Gaelic supplied by each of the persons mentioned in subsection (4) ("the suppliers") amounting to such minimum number of hours (if

any) of transmission time per year as may be specified in the order in relation to that supplier.

(3) For the purpose of enabling the holder to comply with any such conditions and any obligation imposed by virtue of subsection (2), it shall be the duty of each supplier to provide the holder, free of charge, with such programmes in Gaelic which have been broadcast by the supplier as the holder may request.

(4) The suppliers are—

(a) the BBC,

(b) the Channel Four Television Corporation,

(c) any holder of a Channel 3 licence to provide a regional Channel 3 service (within the meaning of Part I of the 1990 Act) for reception wholly in Scotland, and

(d) such other persons providing television broadcasting services as may be specified by order by the Secretary of State.

(5) Subsection (3) shall not apply in relation to any programme first broadcast by the supplier concerned—

(a) before 1st January 1993, or

(b) in the period beginning on 1st January 1993 and ending on 31st March 1997, if the supplier has no right to broadcast it again or has such a right but is not entitled to transfer it to the holder.

(6) The holder may broadcast any programme supplied by virtue of subsection (3) on one occasion only.

(7) The holder shall consult Comataidh Craolaidh Gaidhlig and the suppliers about—

(a) the quantity of programmes likely to be requested by the holder from each supplier by virtue of subsection (3), and

(b) the schedules proposed for the broadcast by the holder of programmes supplied by virtue of that subsection,

and shall have regard to any comments made as a result of such consultation.

(8) Any order under this section shall be subject to annulment in pursuance of a resolution of either House of Parliament.

(9) In this section "Gaelic" means the Gaelic language as spoken in Scotland.

DEFINITIONS

"BBC; the": s.147(1).
"Channel 3 licence": s.39(1); s.71(1) of the Broadcasting Act 1990.
"Commission; the": s.39(1).
"multiplex licence": s.39(1).
"regional Channel 3 service": s.39(1); s.71(1) of the Broadcasting Act 1990.
"1990 Act; the": s.147(1).

GENERAL NOTE

Provision for analogue Gaelic broadcasting is made in ss.183 and 184 of the 1990 Act. This section enables an increase in Gaelic programming through digital broadcasting. The Government's intention is to oblige the Commission to require the third multiplex operator, who will be responsible for broadcasting Channel 5 and S4C Digital, to include, in Scotland, a minimum of 30 minutes of Gaelic programming at peak times. Such programming will have been transmitted by the providers in analogue form and must be supplied to the multiplex operator free of charge.

Review of digital television broadcasting

33.—(1) For the purpose of considering for how long it would be appropriate for television broadcasting services to continue to be provided in analogue form, the Secretary of State—

(a) shall keep under review the extent of—

(i) the provision in the United Kingdom of multiplex services,

(ii) the availability in the United Kingdom in digital form of the services specified in section 2(3), S4C Digital, the qualifying teletext service, and the television broadcasting services of the BBC, and

(iii) the ownership or possession in the United Kingdom of equipment capable of receiving the services referred to in sub-paragraph (ii) when broadcast or transmitted in digital form,

and the likely future extent of such provision, such availability and such ownership or possession, and

(b) shall, on or before the fourth anniversary of the day on which the first multiplex licence is granted under section 8, and at such time or times thereafter as he thinks fit, require the Commission and the BBC to report to him on the matters referred to in paragraph (a).

(2) If the Commission or the BBC are required to submit a report under subsection (1)(b), they shall submit the report within twelve months of the date of the requirement.

(3) Before making any report under subsection (1)(b), the Commission shall consult—

(a) the holders of all multiplex licences,
(b) the holders of digital programme licences who are providing digital programme services which are being broadcast,
(c) such other persons providing services licensed by the Commission under this Part or Part I or II of the 1990 Act as the Commission think fit, and
(d) the Welsh Authority;

and the Commission shall include in their report a summary of representations made to them by the persons consulted.

(4) For the purpose mentioned in subsection (1), the Secretary of State shall, on requiring reports under subsection (1)(b), consult—

(a) such persons appearing to him to represent viewers as he thinks fit, and
(b) such other persons as he thinks fit,

in connection with the matters referred to in subsection (1)(a) and also, if the Secretary of State thinks fit, as to the likely effects on viewers of any television broadcasting service ceasing to be broadcast in analogue form.

(5) In this section "television broadcasting service" has the same meaning as in Part I of the 1990 Act.

DEFINITIONS

"BBC; the": s.147(1).
"Commission; the": s.39(1).
"digital programme licence": s.39(1).
"digital programme service": s.1(4); s.39(1).
"multiplex licence": s.39(1).
"multiplex service": s.1(1); s.39(1).
"qualifying teletext service": s.39(1).
"S4C Digital": s.39(1); s.57(1A)(a) of the Broadcasting Act 1990.
"1990 Act; the": s.147(1).

GENERAL NOTE

In the medium term, it is expected that digital broadcasting will replace analogue broadcasting. This section requires the Secretary of State to keep under review the progress of the digital industry in order to assess the prospects for switching off the analogue service. That event will only occur once the vast majority of the audience has changed to digital reception. The review must first take place, in effect, within five years of the grant of the first multiplex licence under open competition.

Promotion of equal opportunities and fair treatment

34.—(1) Any multiplex licence or digital programme licence shall include conditions requiring the licence holder—

(a) to make arrangements for promoting, in relation to employment by him, equality of opportunity between men and women and between persons of different racial groups,
(b) to make arrangements for promoting, in relation to employment by him, the fair treatment of disabled persons, and
(c) to review those arrangements from time to time.

(2) In subsection (1) "racial group" has the same meaning as in the Race Relations Act 1976, and "disabled person" has the same meaning as in the Disability Discrimination Act 1995.

DEFINITIONS
"digital programme licence": s.39(1).
"multiplex licence": s.39(1).

Enforcement of licences held by BBC companies

35. Where the Commission—
(a) give a direction to a BBC company under section 40(1) of the 1990 Act as applied by section 23(8) or 27(8),
(b) serve a notice on a BBC company under any provision of section 17, 23 or 27, or
(c) receive any representations from a BBC company under section 17(4), 23(6) or 27(6) or under section 42 of the 1990 Act as so applied,

the Commission shall send a copy of the direction, notice or representations to the Secretary of State.

DEFINITIONS
"BBC; the": s.147(1).
"Commission; the": s.39(1).

Power to vary amount of financial penalties

36.—(1) The Secretary of State may by order amend any of the provisions specified in subsection (2) by substituting a different sum for the sum for the time being specified there.

(2) The provisions referred to in subsection (1) are—
section 11(5)(a);
section 17(2)(a);
section 23(2)(a); and
section 27(2)(a).

(3) An order under subsection (1) shall be subject to annulment in pursuance of a resolution of either House of Parliament.

Computation of multiplex revenue

37. Part I of Schedule 1 (which contains provisions relating to the computation of multiplex revenue for the purposes of this Part) shall have effect.

Certain receipts of Commission to be paid into Consolidated Fund

38.—(1) Where, in respect of any licence granted under this Part, the Commission receive any of the amounts specified in subsection (2), that amount shall not form part of the revenues of the Commission but shall—
(a) if the licence is for the provision of a service for any area in Great Britain, be paid into the Consolidated Fund of the United Kingdom,
(b) if the licence is for the provision of a service for any area in Northern Ireland, be paid into the Consolidated Fund of Northern Ireland, or
(c) in any other case, be paid into whichever of those Funds the Commission consider appropriate or into both of those Funds in such proportions as the Commission consider appropriate.

(2) The amounts referred to in subsection (1) are amounts payable to the Commission by virtue of any of the following provisions—

section 11(5);
section 13(1);
section 17(1);
section 23(1);
section 27(1).

(3) Subsection (1) shall not be construed as applying to any amount which is required by the Commission for the making of an adjustment in respect of an overpayment made by any person.

(4) Any amount payable by any person to the Commission under or by virtue of this Part shall be recoverable by them as a debt due to them from that person; and, where any amount is so payable by a person as the holder of a licence granted under this Part, his liability to pay it shall not be affected by his licence ceasing (for any reason) to be in force.

(5) The Commission shall, in respect of each financial year, prepare an account showing—

(a) all such amounts falling within subsection (1) as have been received by them, and

(b) the sums paid into the Consolidated Funds of the United Kingdom and Northern Ireland respectively under that subsection in respect of those amounts,

and shall send that account to the Comptroller and Auditor General not later than the end of the month of November following the financial year to which it relates; and the Comptroller and Auditor General shall examine, certify and report on the account and lay copies of it, together with his report, before each House of Parliament.

DEFINITIONS

"Commission; the": s.39(1).
"licence": s.39(1).

Interpretation of Part I

39.—(1) In this Part—

"ancillary service" has the meaning given by section 24(2);

"a Channel 3 licence" has the same meaning as in Part I of the 1990 Act and "a Channel 3 service" means a regional or national Channel 3 service (within the meaning of that Part);

"Channel 4", "Channel 5" and "a Channel 5 licence" have the same meaning as in Part I of the 1990 Act;

"the Commission" means the Independent Television Commission;

"digital additional service" has the meaning given by section 24(1), and "digital additional services licence" means a licence to provide such services;

"digital programme service" has the meaning given by section 1(4), and "digital programme licence" means a licence to provide such services;

"independent analogue broadcaster" has the meaning given by section 2(1);

"licence" means a licence under this Part, and "licensed" shall be construed accordingly;

"multiplex service" has the meaning given by section 1(1), and "multiplex licence" means a licence to provide such a service;

"public teletext provider" has the meaning given by section 2(6);

"qualifying service" has the meaning given by section 2(2);

"qualifying teletext service" means the public teletext service provided by the public teletext provider for broadcasting in digital form as a qualifying service;

"S4C" and "on S4C" have the same meaning as in Part I of the 1990 Act;

"S4C Digital" means the service referred to in section 57(1A)(a) of the 1990 Act, and "on S4C Digital" means in that service;

"technical service" has the meaning given by section 24(3).

(2) Where the person who is for the time being the holder of any licence ("the present licence holder") is not the person to whom the licence was originally granted, any reference in this Part (however expressed) to the holder of the licence shall be construed, in relation to any time falling before the date when the present licence holder became the holder of it, as including a reference to a person who was previously the holder of the licence.

Part II

Digital Terrestrial Sound Broadcasting

Introductory

Radio multiplex services

40.—(1) In this Part "radio multiplex service" means a service provided by any person which consists in the broadcasting for general reception of two or more services specified in subsection (3) by combining the relevant information in digital form, together with any broadcasting in digital form of digital additional services (as defined by section 63(1)).

(2) A service in respect of which a licence under section 46 or 50 is in force is not prevented from being a radio multiplex service at a particular time merely because only one service specified in subsection (3) is being broadcast in digital form at that time.

(3) The services referred to in subsections (1) and (2) are—

(a) a digital sound programme service (as defined by subsection (5)), or

(b) a simulcast radio service (as defined by section 41(2)).

(4) A radio multiplex service provided on a frequency or frequencies assigned to the Authority under section 45(1) may be either—

(a) provided for a particular area or locality in the United Kingdom (a "local radio multiplex service"), or

(b) provided without any restriction by virtue of this Act to a particular area or locality in the United Kingdom (a "national radio multiplex service").

(5) In this Part "digital sound programme service" means a service consisting in the provision by any person of programmes consisting wholly of sound (together with any ancillary services, as defined by section 63(2)) with a view to their being broadcast in digital form for general reception, whether by him or by some other person, but does not include—

(a) a simulcast radio service (as defined by section 41(2)), or

(b) a service where the sounds are to be received through the use of coded reference to pre-defined phonetic elements of sounds.

(6) The Secretary of State may, if having regard to developments in broadcasting technology he considers it appropriate to do so, by order amend the definition of "digital sound programme service" in subsection (5).

(7) No order under subsection (6) shall be made unless a draft of the order has been laid before and approved by a resolution of each House of Parliament.

(8) In this section—

"broadcast" means broadcast otherwise than—

(a) by satellite, or

(b) in the provision of a local delivery service (as defined by section 72(1) of the 1990 Act), and

"for general reception" means for general reception in, or in any area in, the United Kingdom.

DEFINITIONS
"area": s.72(2).
"Authority; the": s.72(1).
"locality": s.72(2).

GENERAL NOTE

Digital terrestrial sound broadcasting, or digital audio broadcasting (DAB), will be regulated similarly to digital terrestrial television. There is less opportunity for expanding DAB, however. The Government proposes to allocate two multiplexes for national radio, one to the BBC and the other for independent broadcasters' national radio. There will be a further five multiplexes allocated for local radio services. Existing independent national radio licensees under the 1990 Act will be given reserved capacity on the second national multiplex. However, since the available frequencies are limited compared to television, there will be pressure on that reserved space in developing new programming, so they will not be required to provide a fully simultaneous broadcast of their analogue programming, under s.2.

As with s.1, the definitions of digital sound programme service, simulcast radio service and digital sound programme service are contrived to distinguish differing licensing arrangements. See generally, the note to s.1.

Meaning of "independent national broadcaster" and "simulcast radio service"

41.—(1) In this Part "independent national broadcaster" means any person who is the holder of a national licence (within the meaning of Part III of the 1990 Act).

(2) In this Part a "simulcast radio service" means any service provided for broadcasting in digital form—

(a) which is provided by an independent national broadcaster who has notified the Authority, within the period of one month beginning with the commencement of this section, of his intention to provide a service for broadcasting in that form which corresponds to a national service (within the meaning of Part III of the 1990 Act) provided by him otherwise than in that form, and

(b) which corresponds to that national service.

(3) For the purposes of this Part a service provided for broadcasting in digital form corresponds to a national service (within the meaning of Part III of the 1990 Act) if, and only if, in every calendar month—

(a) at least 80 per cent. of so much of the national service as consists of programmes, consists of programmes which are also included in the digital service in that month, and

(b) at least 50 per cent. of so much of the national service as consists of such programmes is broadcast at the same time on both services.

(4) The Secretary of State may by order amend subsection (3)(a) or (b) by substituting for the percentage for the time being specified there a different percentage specified in the order.

(5) Before making an order under subsection (4) the Secretary of State shall consult such persons appearing to him to represent listeners as he thinks fit.

(6) An order under subsection (4) shall be subject to annulment in pursuance of a resolution of either House of Parliament.

(7) In subsection (3) "programme" does not include an advertisement.

DEFINITIONS
"Authority; the": s.72(1).
"1990 Act; the": s.147(1).

GENERAL NOTE

A simulcast radio service is analogous to a qualifying service in digital television. It differs, however, in applying only to national radio and in providing what is actually less simulcasting. As in the case of television, the willingness of the independent national broadcaster to provide a simulcast radio service will result in digital capacity being reserved on the second national multiplex, under s.48. The degree of simulcasting of the analogue service is specified in subs. (3): at least 80 per cent of the content must be identical and at least 50 per cent of that content must be broadcast at the same time. There is provision for the Secretary of State to amend those proportions to take account of consumers switching over to digital receivers.

General provisions about licences

Licences under Part II

42.—(1) Any licence granted by the Radio Authority (in this Part referred to as "the Authority") under this Part shall be in writing and (subject to the provisions of this Part) shall continue in force for such period as is provided, in relation to a licence of the kind in question, by the relevant provision of this Part.

(2) The Authority—

(a) shall not grant a licence to any person unless they are satisfied that he is a fit and proper person to hold it, and

(b) shall do all that they can to secure that, if they cease to be so satisfied in the case of any person holding a licence, that person does not remain the holder of the licence;

and nothing in this Part shall be construed as affecting the operation of this subsection or of section 44(1) or (2)(b) or (c).

(3) The Authority may vary a licence by a notice served on the licence holder if—

(a) in the case of a variation of the period for which a licence having effect for a specified period is to continue in force, the licence holder consents, or

(b) in the case of any other variation, the licence holder has been given a reasonable opportunity of making representations to the Authority about the variation.

(4) Paragraph (a) of subsection (3) does not affect the operation of section 59(1)(b); and that subsection shall not authorise the variation of any condition included in a licence in pursuance of section 55(1).

(5) A licence granted to any person under this Part shall not be transferable to any other person without the previous consent in writing of the Authority.

(6) Without prejudice to the generality of subsection (5), the Authority shall not give their consent for the purposes of that subsection unless they are satisfied that any such other person would be in a position to comply with all of the conditions included in the licence which would have effect during the period for which it is to be in force.

(7) The holding by any person of a licence to provide any service shall not relieve him of any requirement to hold a licence under section 1 of the Wireless Telegraphy Act 1949 or section 7 of the Telecommunications Act 1984 in connection with the provision of that service.

DEFINITIONS

"licence": s.72(1).

"licence holder": s.72(3).

GENERAL NOTE

See the note to s.3, to which this section corresponds with the exception of s.3(2).

General licence conditions

43.—(1) A licence may include—

(a) such conditions as appear to the Authority to be appropriate having regard to any duties which are or may be imposed on them, or on the licence holder, by or under the 1990 Act or this Act;

(b) conditions enabling the Authority to supervise and enforce technical standards in connection with the provision of the licensed service;

(c) conditions requiring the payment by the licence holder to the Authority (whether on the grant of the licence or at such times thereafter as may be determined by or under the licence, or both) of a fee or fees of an amount or amounts so determined;

(d) conditions requiring the licence holder to furnish the Authority, in such manner and at such times as they may reasonably require, with such information as they may require for the purpose of exercising the functions assigned to them by or under this Act;

(e) conditions requiring the licence holder, if found by the Authority to be in breach of any condition of his licence, to reimburse to the Authority, in such circumstances as are specified in any conditions, any costs reasonably incurred by them in connection with the breach of that condition;

(f) conditions providing for such incidental and supplemental matters as appear to the Authority to be appropriate.

(2) A licence may in particular include—

(a) conditions requiring the licence holder—

(i) to comply with any direction given by the Authority as to such matters as are specified in the licence or are of a description so specified, or

(ii) (except to the extent that the Authority consent to his doing or not doing them) not to do or to do such things as are specified in the licence or are of a description so specified; and

(b) conditions requiring the licence holder to permit—

(i) any employee of, or person authorised by, the Authority, or

(ii) any officer of, or person authorised by, the Secretary of State,

to enter any premises which are used in connection with the broadcasting of the licensed service and to inspect, examine, operate or test any equipment on the premises which is used in that connection.

(3) The fees required to be paid to the Authority by virtue of subsection (1)(c) shall be in accordance with such tariff as may from time to time be fixed by the Authority; and the amount of any fee which is to be so paid by the holder of a licence of a particular class or description shall be such as to represent what appears to the Authority to be the appropriate contribution of the holder of such a licence towards meeting the sums which the Authority regard as necessary in order to discharge their duty under paragraph 12(1) of Schedule 8 to the 1990 Act.

(4) A tariff fixed under subsection (3) may specify different fees in relation to different cases or circumstances; and the Authority shall publish every such tariff in such manner as they consider appropriate.

(5) Where the holder of any licence—

(a) is required by virtue of any condition imposed under this Part to provide the Authority with any information, and

(b) in purported compliance with that condition provides them with any information which is false in a material particular,

he shall be taken for the purposes of sections 59, 62 and 66 of this Act and section 111 of the 1990 Act to have failed to comply with that condition.

(6) Nothing in this Act which authorises or requires the inclusion in a licence of conditions relating to any particular matter or having effect for any particular purpose shall be taken as derogating from the generality of subsection (1).

DEFINITIONS

"Authority; the": s.72(1).
"licence": s.72(1).
"licensed": s.72(1).
"licence holder": s.72(3).
"1990 Act; the": s.147(1).

General Note

See the note to s.4, to which this section corresponds with the following exceptions. Additional conditions may be inserted in radio licences to deal with the supervision of technical standards, by subs. (1)(b), the reimbursing of the Authority, by subs. (1)(e), and the inspection of premises, by subs. (2)(b). These will reflect the Authority's closer support and supervision of local stations.

Restrictions on holding of licences under Part II

44.—(1) The Authority shall do all that they can to secure—

(a) that a person does not become or remain the holder of a licence if he is a person who is a disqualified person in relation to that licence by virtue of Part II of Schedule 2 to the 1990 Act (as amended by this Act); and

(b) that any requirements imposed by or under Parts III to V of that Schedule (as so amended) are complied with by or in relation to persons holding licences in relation to which those requirements apply.

(2) The Authority may accordingly—

(a) require any applicant for a licence to provide them with such information as they may reasonably require for the purpose of determining—

(i) whether he is such a disqualified person as is mentioned in subsection (1)(a),

(ii) whether any such requirements as are mentioned in subsection (1)(b) would preclude them from granting a licence to him, and

(iii) if so, what steps would be required to be taken by or in relation to him in order for any such requirements to be complied with;

(b) revoke the award of a licence to a body where a relevant change takes place after the award, but before the grant, of the licence;

(c) make the grant of a licence to any person conditional on the taking of any specified steps that appear to them to be required to be taken as mentioned in paragraph (a)(iii);

(d) impose conditions in any licence enabling them to require the licence holder, if a body corporate, to give to them advance notice of proposals affecting—

(i) shareholdings in the body, or

(ii) the directors of the body,

where such proposals are known to the body;

(e) impose conditions in any licence enabling them to give the licence holder directions requiring him to take, or arrange for the taking of, any specified steps appearing to them to be required to be taken in order for any such requirements as are mentioned in subsection (1)(b) to be complied with.

(3) Where the Authority—

(a) revoke the award of any licence in pursuance of subsection (2)(b), or

(b) determine that any condition imposed by them in relation to any licence in pursuance of subsection (2)(c) has not been satisfied,

any provisions of this Part relating to the awarding of licences of the kind in question shall (subject to subsection (4)) have effect as if the person to whom the licence was awarded or granted had not made an application for it.

(4) Those provisions shall not so have effect if the Authority decide that it would be desirable to publish a fresh notice under this Part in respect of the grant of a licence, or (as the case may be) a further licence, to provide the service in question.

(5) Every licence shall include such conditions as the Authority consider necessary or expedient to ensure that where—

(a) the holder of the licence is a body, and

(b) a relevant change takes place after the grant of the licence, the Authority may revoke the licence by notice served on the holder of the licence and taking effect forthwith or on a date specified in the notice.

(6) The Authority shall not serve any such notice on the licence holder unless—

(a) the Authority have notified him of the matters complained of and given him a reasonable opportunity of making representations to them about those matters, and

(b) in a case where the relevant change is one falling within subsection (7)—

(i) they have also given him an opportunity of complying with Parts III and IV of Schedule 2 to the 1990 Act within a period specified in the notification, and

(ii) the period specified in the notification has elapsed.

(7) A relevant change falls within this subsection if it consists only in one or more of the following—

(a) a reduction in the total number of points, calculated in accordance with paragraph 9 of Part III of Schedule 2 to the 1990 Act, attributable to all the services referred to in paragraph 8(1) or (2)(a) or (b) of that Part of that Schedule,

(b) a change in the national market share (within the meaning of Part IV of that Schedule) of one or more national newspapers (within the meaning of that Part of that Schedule), or

(c) a change in the local market share (within the meaning of that Part of that Schedule) in a particular area of one or more local newspapers (within the meaning of that Part of that Schedule).

(8) In this section "relevant change", in relation to a body to which a licence has been awarded or granted, means—

(a) any change affecting the nature or characteristics of the body,

(b) any change in the persons having control over or interests in the body, or

(c) any other change giving rise to a failure to comply with any requirement imposed by or under Schedule 2 to the 1990 Act,

being (in any case) a change which is such that, if it fell to the Authority to determine whether to award the licence to the body in the new circumstances of the case, they would be induced by the change to refrain from so awarding it.

DEFINITIONS

"Authority; the": s.72(1).
"licence": s.72(1).
"licence holder": s.72(3).
"1990 Act; the": s.147(1).

GENERAL NOTE

See the note to s.5, to which this section corresponds.

Radio multiplex services

Assignment of frequencies by Secretary of State

45.—(1) The Secretary of State may by notice assign to the Authority, for the purpose of the provision of radio multiplex services falling to be licensed by them under this Part, such frequencies as he may determine.

(2) Any frequency assigned by the Secretary of State under subsection (1) may be so assigned for use only in such area or areas as may be specified by the Secretary of State when making the assignment.

(3) When assigning a frequency under subsection (1), the Secretary of State shall specify whether the frequency is to be assigned for the purpose of

the provision of a national radio multiplex service or for the purpose of the provision of a local radio multiplex service; and any frequency assigned under that subsection shall be taken to be so assigned only for that purpose.

(4) When assigning a frequency under subsection (1) for the purpose of the provision of a national radio multiplex service, the Secretary of State may also direct the Authority to secure that the holder of the licence to provide that service is required—

(a) to broadcast one or more digital sound programme services of a particular character, or

(b) not to broadcast more than a specified number of digital sound programme services of a particular character.

(5) References in subsection (4) to digital sound programme services of a particular character include references to digital sound programme services catering for the tastes and interests of persons living within a specified area or locality.

(6) The Secretary of State may by notice revoke the assignment under subsection (1) of any frequency specified in the notice, and may do so whether or not that frequency is for the time being one on which a radio multiplex service is being provided.

DEFINITIONS

"area": s.72(2).
"Authority; the": s.72(1).
"digital sound programme service": s.40(5); s.72(1).
"licence": s.72(1).
"licence holder": s.72(3).
"licensed": s.72(1).
"locality": s.72(2).
"local radio multiplex service": s.40(4); s.72(1).
"national radio multiplex service": s.40(4); s.72(1).
"radio multiplex service": s.40(1); s.72(1).

GENERAL NOTE

This section is analogous to s.6. It differs in enabling the Authority, on the direction of the Secretary of State, under subs. (4), to prescribe particular characteristics to digital sound programme services. The Government's intention (see Standing Committee, col. 292) is that the second national multiplex should be required to carry a non-pop service and a talk service. In addition, no more than two services on the multiplex should be aimed at predominantly the same sections of the listening audience. This reflects the existing approach to analogue services, where pop, classical music and talk programming is distinguished. In digital broadcasting, there is greater opportunity to differentiate programming strands.

National radio multiplex licences

46.—(1) Where the Authority propose to grant a licence to provide a national radio multiplex service, they shall publish, in such manner as they consider appropriate, a notice—

(a) stating that they propose to grant such a licence,

(b) specifying the frequency on which the service is to be provided,

(c) specifying, in such manner as the Authority consider appropriate, the area of the United Kingdom in which the frequency is to be available,

(d) where digital capacity on the frequency is reserved in pursuance of a direction under section 48 for the broadcasting of a simulcast radio service, stating that fact and specifying the capacity reserved and the identity of the national service or services concerned,

(e) where the frequency is one in respect of which a direction under section 45(4) has been given, setting out the terms of the direction,

(f) inviting applications for the licence and specifying the closing date for such applications,

(g) specifying the fee payable on any application made in pursuance of the notice, and

(h) stating whether any percentage of multiplex revenue for each accounting period would be payable by an applicant in pursuance of section 55 if he were granted the licence and, if so, specifying that percentage.

(2) Unless an order under section 55(2) is in force—

(a) the consent of the Secretary of State shall be required for so much of the notice as relates to the matters specified in subsection (1)(h), and

(b) the Authority may if they think fit (with that consent) specify under subsection (1)(h)—

(i) different percentages in relation to different accounting periods falling within the period for which the licence would be in force, and

(ii) a nil percentage in relation to any accounting period so falling.

(3) When publishing a notice under subsection (1), the Authority—

(a) shall publish with the notice general guidance as to requirements to be met by proposals as to the matters referred to in subsection (4)(b)(i) and (ii) and (f), and

(b) may publish with the notice such other general guidance as they consider appropriate.

(4) Any application made in pursuance of a notice under subsection (1) must be in writing and accompanied by—

(a) the fee specified in the notice under subsection (1)(g),

(b) a technical plan relating to the service which the applicant proposes to provide and indicating—

(i) the parts of the area specified under subsection (1)(c) which would be within the coverage area of the service,

(ii) the timetable in accordance with which that coverage would be achieved, and

(iii) the technical means by which it would be achieved,

(c) the applicant's proposals as to the number of digital sound programme services to be broadcast and as to the characteristics of each of those services,

(d) the applicant's proposals as to the timetable in accordance with which the broadcasting of each of those services would begin,

(e) the applicant's proposals as to the broadcasting of digital additional services,

(f) the applicant's proposals for promoting or assisting the acquisition, by persons in the proposed coverage area of the service, of equipment capable of receiving the service,

(g) such information as the Authority may reasonably require as to the applicant's present financial position and his projected financial position during the period for which the licence would be in force, and

(h) such other information as the Authority may reasonably require for the purpose of considering the application.

(5) In subsection (4)(f) "acquisition" includes acquisition on hire or loan.

(6) At any time after receiving such an application and before determining it, the Authority may require the applicant to furnish additional information under any of paragraphs (b) to (h) of subsection (4).

(7) Any information to be furnished to the Authority under this section shall, if they so require, be in such form or verified in such manner as they may specify.

(8) The Authority shall, as soon as reasonably practicable after the date specified in a notice under subsection (1) as the closing date for applications, publish in such manner as they consider appropriate—

(a) the following matters, namely—

(i) the name of every person who has made an application to them in pursuance of the notice,

(ii) the proposals submitted by him under subsection (4)(c), and

(iii) such other information connected with his application as the Authority consider appropriate; and

(b) a notice—

(i) inviting representations to be made to them with respect to any of the applications, and

(ii) specifying the manner in which, and the time by which, any such representations are to be so made.

DEFINITIONS

"area": s.72(2).
"Authority; the": s.72(1).
"digital additional service": s.63(1); s.72(1).
"digital sound programme service": s.40(5); s.72(1).
"licence": s.72(1).
"national radio multiplex service": s.40(4); s.72(1).
"simulcast radio service": s.41(2); s.72(1).

GENERAL NOTE

See the note to s.7, to which this section corresponds subject to the following differences. The notice of intention to award a licence must specify details of the digital capacity reserved for simulcast radio programmes, by subs. (1)(d), and of any directions as to the characteristics of the services to be broadcast, by subs. (1)(e). Under subs. (4)(c), it is not necessary for the applicant to specify the areas in which digital sound programme services will be provided. In subs. (4)(f), the proposals for promoting the acquisition of receiving equipment are restricted to the applicant's own proposed coverage area, and not to all multiplex areas generally.

Award of national radio multiplex licences

47.—(1) Where the Authority have published a notice under section 46(1), they shall in determining whether, or to whom, to award the national radio multiplex licence in question, have regard to the extent to which, taking into account the matters specified in subsection (2) and any representations received by them in pursuance of section 46(8)(b) with respect to those matters, the award of the licence to each applicant would be calculated to promote the development of digital sound broadcasting in the United Kingdom otherwise than by satellite.

(2) The matters referred to in subsection (1) are—

(a) the extent of the coverage area (within the area specified in the notice under section 46(1)(c)) proposed to be achieved by the applicant as indicated in the technical plan submitted by him under section 46(4)(b),

(b) the timetables proposed by the applicant under section 46(4)(b)(ii) and (d),

(c) the ability of the applicant to establish the proposed service and to maintain it throughout the period for which the licence will be in force,

(d) the capacity of the digital sound programme services proposed to be included in the service to appeal to a variety of tastes and interests,

(e) any proposals by the applicant for promoting or assisting the acquisition, by persons in the proposed coverage area of the service, of equipment capable of receiving the service, and

(f) whether, in contracting or offering to contract with persons providing digital sound programme services or digital additional services, the applicant has acted in a manner calculated to ensure fair and effective competition in the provision of such services.

(3) In subsection (2)(e) "acquisition" includes acquisition on hire or loan.

(4) Where a direction under section 45(4) has effect in relation to any frequency, the Authority shall not award a national radio multiplex licence in relation to that frequency unless they are satisfied that the proposals submitted by the applicant under section 46(4)(c) comply with the direction.

(5) Where the Authority have awarded a national radio multiplex licence to any person in accordance with this section, they shall, as soon as reasonably practicable after awarding the licence—

(a) publish in such manner as they consider appropriate—

(i) the name of the person to whom the licence has been awarded, and

(ii) such other information as the Authority consider appropriate, and

(b) grant the licence to that person.

DEFINITIONS

"area": s.72(2).
"Authority; the": s.72(1).
"digital additional service": s.63(1); s.72(1).
"digital sound programme service": s.40(5); s.72(1).
"licence": s.72(1).
"national radio multiplex licence": s.72(1).

GENERAL NOTE

See the note to s.8, to which this section generally corresponds. The overriding criterion for the Authority to apply is whether the award of licence would "promote the development of digital sound broadcasting in the United Kingdom other than by satellite". However, the access to services criterion, in subs. (2)(f), is limited to the applicant's own proposed coverage area. There is also an addition criterion, in subs. (4), that the applicant must be able to comply with a direction as to the characteristics of the services to be provided, where appropriate.

Reservation of capacity for independent national broadcasters

48.—(1) The Secretary of State may, in assigning a frequency to the Authority under section 45 for the purpose of the provision of a national radio multiplex service, direct the Authority that, in relation to each independent national broadcaster specified in the direction, an amount of digital capacity specified in the direction is to be reserved, subject to the provisions of this Part, for the broadcasting of a simulcast radio service.

(2) Before giving a direction under subsection (1) in relation to any simulcast radio service, the Secretary of State shall consult the Authority as to the amount of digital capacity which the Authority consider appropriate in all the circumstances for the broadcasting of that service.

(3) Where a direction under subsection (1) has been given in relation to a frequency—

(a) the Authority shall include in any national radio multiplex licence granted in respect of that frequency such conditions as appear to them to be appropriate for securing that, in consideration of the making by any independent national broadcaster in relation to whom capacity is reserved of such payments as are from time to time agreed between him and the licence holder or (in default of agreement) determined under this section, the licence holder uses such digital capacity not exceeding the amount reserved under subsection (1) as may from time to time be requested by the independent national broadcaster for the broadcasting of services provided by that broadcaster, and

(b) the Authority shall vary the licence under which the national service is provided to include such conditions relating to the broadcasting of the simulcast radio service as they may determine.

(4) Where the holder of a national radio multiplex licence and an independent national broadcaster fail to agree as to the payments to be made under a condition included in the licence in accordance with subsection (3)(a), either of them may refer the matter to the Authority for their determination.

(5) Before making a determination under subsection (4), the Authority shall give the licence holder and the independent national broadcaster an opportunity of making representations to the Authority about the matter.

(6) In making any determination under subsection (4), the Authority shall have regard to—

(a) the expenses incurred, or likely to be incurred, by the licence holder in providing the national radio multiplex service and in broadcasting the simulcast radio service in question, and

(b) the terms on which persons providing national radio multiplex services contract with persons providing national digital sound programme services for the broadcasting of those services.

DEFINITIONS

"Authority; the": s.72(1).
"independent national broadcaster": s.41(1); s.72(1).
"licence": s.72(1).
"licence holder": s.72(3).
"national digital sound programme service": s.60(1); s.72(1).
"national radio multiplex licence": s.72(1).
"national radio multiplex service": s.40(4); s.72(1).
"simulcast radio service": s.41(2); s.72(1).

GENERAL NOTE

This section makes provision for digital capacity to be reserved for independent national broadcasters in order for their simulcast radio services to be broadcast. The exact amount of capacity will be determined in the light of the broadcasters' needs and the amount of frequency available. In debate on the Bill, it was anticipated that the three independent national broadcasters would be allocated, between them, about one sixth of the capacity available on the second multiplex. Unlike the case with digital television, the existing national radio broadcasters will not be offered capacity in excess of that required for the simulcast radio service. But the opportunity for them to develop new digital services is provided by the fact that the analogue service need not be reproduced in its entirety.

The section also enables the Authority to supervise the commercial terms under which the multiplex operator provides capacity to the independent national broadcasters.

Duty of Authority to reserve digital capacity for certain purposes of BBC

49.—(1) In exercising their powers to grant local radio multiplex licences, the Authority shall reserve to the BBC such digital capacity as the Authority consider appropriate in all the circumstances with a view to enabling every BBC local radio service and every BBC radio service for Wales, Scotland or Northern Ireland to be received in digital form within a coverage area which, so far as reasonably practicable, corresponds with the coverage area for that service as provided otherwise than in digital form.

(2) The circumstances to which the Authority may have regard in performing their duty under subsection (1) include the likely demand for digital capacity by persons providing or proposing to provide local digital sound programme services.

(3) Where the Authority propose to grant a licence to provide a local radio multiplex service, they shall notify the BBC of the Authority's proposals for reserving to the BBC digital capacity on the frequency in respect of which the licence is to be granted in respect of the area or locality in which it is to be granted.

(4) If the BBC do not give their consent to the proposals within such period as the Authority may specify in their notice under subsection (3), the Authority shall refer the proposals to the Secretary of State, who may determine—

(a) whether any digital capacity is to be reserved to the BBC on the grant of the licence, and

(b) if so, the amount of that capacity.

(5) Before making any determination under subsection (4), the Secretary of State shall give the Authority and the BBC an opportunity of making representations to him about the Authority's proposals.

(6) Where a local radio multiplex licence is granted in respect of a frequency and area or locality in respect of which digital capacity is reserved in

pursuance of this section, the licence shall include such conditions as appear to the Authority to be appropriate for the purpose of securing that, in consideration of the making by the BBC of such payments as are from time to time agreed between the holder of the licence and the BBC, the holder of the licence uses such digital capacity as may from time to time be requested by the BBC (not exceeding the amount so reserved) for the broadcasting of services provided by the BBC.

DEFINITIONS

"area": s.72(2).
"Authority; the": s.72(1).
"BBC; the": s.147(1).
"licence holder": s.72(3).
"local digital sound programme service": s.60(1); s.72(1).
"local radio multiplex licence": s.72(1).
"locality": s.72(2).

GENERAL NOTE

Although the BBC will be allocated the first national radio multiplex for its national digital services, its local services will have to be provided on frequencies shared with independent local radio services. This section provides for the Radio Authority to negotiate, in effect, with the BBC as to their allocations. The decision will be made in the broad context of existing local radio provision which is characterised by a multiplicity of services catering for local needs and interests. At the local level, digital radio is unlikely to replace analogue radio but will be provided alongside it for the foreseeable future. Since digital coverage will be larger than analogue coverage, not all the existing stations can have a realistic chance of becoming digital and there is no reserved capacity for local services. The Authority's task, therefore, will be to balance the various demands at the local level, including those of the BBC, and produce a flexible response. Nevertheless, subs. (1) requires the Authority to facilitate digital coverage for the BBC that corresponds with their analogue coverage, so far as reasonably practicable. In practice, a discrepancy might arise where a BBC local radio station's area does not coincide with a radio multiplex area.

Local radio multiplex licences

50.—(1) Where—
(a) the BBC have given their consent to proposals made to them under subsection (3) of section 49, or
(b) the Secretary of State has made a determination under subsection (4) of that section,

the Authority shall publish, in such manner as they consider appropriate, a notice under subsection (2).

(2) A notice under this subsection is a notice—
(a) stating that the Authority propose to grant a local radio multiplex licence,
(b) specifying the frequency on which the service is to be provided,
(c) specifying, in such manner as the Authority consider appropriate, the area or locality in the United Kingdom in which it is to be available,
(d) stating whether in pursuance of a direction under section 49 any digital capacity on the frequency in that area or locality is to be reserved for the broadcasting in digital form of one or more BBC radio services and, if so, specifying the capacity reserved and the identity of the BBC radio services concerned,
(e) inviting applications for the licence and specifying the closing date for such applications, and
(f) specifying the fee payable on any application made in pursuance of the notice.

(3) When publishing a notice under subsection (2), the Authority—
(a) shall publish with the notice general guidance as to requirements to be met by proposals as to the matters referred to in subsection (4)(b)(i) and (ii), and

(b) may publish with the notice such other general guidance as they consider appropriate.

(4) Any application made in pursuance of a notice under subsection (2) must be in writing and accompanied by—

(a) the fee specified in the notice under subsection (2)(f),

(b) a technical plan relating to the service which the applicant proposes to provide and indicating—

(i) the parts of the area or locality specified under subsection (2)(c) which would be within the coverage area of the service,

(ii) the timetable in accordance with which that coverage would be achieved, and

(iii) the technical means by which it would be achieved,

(c) the applicant's proposals as to the number of digital sound programme services (other than BBC services) to be broadcast and as to the characteristics of each of those services,

(d) the applicant's proposals as to the timetable in accordance with which the broadcasting of each of those services would begin,

(e) the applicant's proposals as to the broadcasting of digital additional services,

(f) such information as the Authority may reasonably require as to the applicant's present financial position and his projected financial position during the period for which the licence would be in force, and

(g) such other information as the Authority may reasonably require for the purpose of considering the application.

(5) At any time after receiving such an application and before determining it the Authority may require the applicant to furnish additional information under any of paragraphs (b) to (g) of subsection (4).

(6) Any information to be furnished to the Authority under this section shall, if they so require, be in such form or verified in such manner as they may specify.

(7) The Authority shall, as soon as reasonably practicable after the date specified in a notice under subsection (2) as the closing date for applications, publish in such manner as they consider appropriate—

(a) the following matters, namely—

(i) the name of every person who has made an application to them in pursuance of the notice,

(ii) the proposals submitted by him under subsection (4)(c), and

(iii) such other information connected with his application as the Authority consider appropriate; and

(b) a notice—

(i) inviting representations to be made to them with respect to any of the applications, and

(ii) specifying the manner in which, and the time by which, any such representations are to be so made.

DEFINITIONS

"area": s.72(2).
"Authority; the": s.72(1).
"BBC; the": s.147(1).
"digital additional services licence": s.72(1).
"digital sound programme service": s.40(5); s.72(1).
"licence": s.72(1).
"locality": s.72(2).
"local radio multiplex licence": s.72(1).

GENERAL NOTE

See the note to s.46, to which this section corresponds with the following differences. In subs. (1), the notice of intention to award a licence can take place only after a settlement with the BBC has been reached, and, under subs. (2)(d), the details of the BBC's reserved capacity must be specified. There is no provision for imposing a levy on local radio multiplex services; it is recognised that the market is precarious, with little scope for excessive profit. Consistently, there is no provision for requiring local multiplex applicants to make proposals about promoting receiving equipment.

Award of local radio multiplex licences

51.—(1) Where the Authority have published a notice under section 50(2), they shall in determining whether, or to whom, to award the local radio multiplex licence in question, have regard (in relation to each applicant) to the matters specified in subsection (2).

(2) The matters referred to in subsection (1) are—

(a) the extent of the coverage area (within the area or locality specified in the notice under section 50(2)(c)) proposed to be achieved by the applicant as indicated in the technical plan submitted by him under section 50(4)(b),

(b) the timetables proposed by the applicant under section 50(4)(b)(ii) and (d),

(c) the ability of the applicant to establish the proposed service and to maintain it throughout the period for which the licence will be in force,

(d) the extent to which the digital sound programme services (other than BBC services) proposed to be included in the service would cater for the tastes and interests of persons living in the area or locality for which the service is to be provided and, where it is proposed to cater for any particular tastes and interests of such persons, the extent to which those services would cater for those tastes and interests,

(e) the extent to which any such digital sound programme services would broaden the range of programmes available by way of local digital sound programme services to persons living in the area or locality for which it is to be provided and, in particular, the extent to which they would cater for tastes and interests different from those already catered for by local digital sound programme services provided for that area or locality,

(f) the extent to which the application is supported by persons living in that area or locality, and

(g) whether, in contracting or offering to contract with persons providing digital sound programme services or digital additional services, the applicant has acted in a manner calculated to ensure fair and effective competition in the provision of those services.

(3) In considering the matters referred to in subsection (2), the Authority shall take into account any representations made to them in pursuance of section 50(7)(b) with respect to those matters.

(4) Where the Authority have awarded a local radio multiplex licence to any person in accordance with this section, they shall, as soon as reasonably practicable after awarding the licence—

(a) publish in such manner as they consider appropriate—

(i) the name of the person to whom the licence has been awarded, and

(ii) such other information as the Authority consider appropriate, and

(b) grant the licence to that person.

DEFINITIONS

"area": s.72(2).
"Authority; the": s.72(1).
"BBC; the": s.147(1).
"digital additional services licence": s.72(1).
"digital sound programme service": s.40(5); s.72(1).
"licence": s.72(1).
"locality": s.72(2).
"local radio multiplex licence": s.72(1).

GENERAL NOTE

The criteria for awarding local radio multiplex services differ from those for national services by emphasising a sensitivity to the needs and interests of local audiences. The development of digital sound broadcasting in general, as in s.47(1), is not mentioned. Subsections (2)(d) to (2)(f) refer to the tastes and interests of local persons, the broadening of the range of programmes available to them and the extent of local support for the application.

Power to require two or more local radio multiplex licences to be granted to one person

52.—(1) The Authority may, before publishing a notice under section 50(2), determine that two or more local radio multiplex licences are on that occasion to be granted to one person.

(2) Where the Authority have so determined, they shall publish a single notice under section 50(2) in relation to the licences.

(3) In relation to any application made in pursuance of such a notice—

(a) references in section 50(4) and 51(2) to the proposed service shall have effect as references to each of the proposed services, and

(b) the reference in section 51(1) to the local radio multiplex licence shall have effect as a reference to all the licences concerned.

(4) Nothing in this section applies in relation to the renewal of a local radio multiplex licence.

DEFINITIONS

"Authority; the": s.72(1).

"local radio multiplex licence": s.72(1).

GENERAL NOTE

This section corresponds to s.9 but, since only one national radio multiplex is available for licensing by the Authority, it applies only to local radio multiplexes.

Failure to begin providing licensed service and financial penalties on revocation of licence

53.—(1) Subject to subsection (2), subsection (3) applies where at any time after a radio multiplex licence has been granted to any person but before the licence has come into force—

(a) that person indicates to the Authority that he does not intend to provide the service in question, or

(b) the Authority for any other reason have reasonable grounds for believing that that person will not provide that service once the licence has come into force.

(2) Subsection (3) shall not apply in the case of any person by virtue of paragraph (b) of subsection (1) unless the Authority have served on him a notice stating their grounds for believing that he will not provide the service in question once his licence has come into force, and they shall not serve such a notice on him unless they have given him a reasonable opportunity of making representations to them about the matters complained of.

(3) Where this subsection applies—

(a) the Authority shall serve on the person to whom the licence has been granted a notice revoking the licence as from the time the notice is served on him, and

(b) section 47 or 51 shall (subject to subsection (4)) have effect as if he had not made an application for the licence.

(4) Section 47 or 51 shall not have effect as mentioned in subsection (3) if the Authority decide that it would be desirable to publish a fresh notice under section 46(1) or 50(2) in respect of the grant of the licence.

(5) Where the Authority revoke a radio multiplex licence under this section or under any other provision of this Part, they shall serve on the licence

holder a notice requiring him to pay to them, within a specified period, a specified financial penalty not exceeding—

(a) in the case of a local radio multiplex licence, £50,000, or

(b) in the case of a national radio multiplex licence, whichever is the greater of—

(i) £50,000, or

(ii) the prescribed amount.

(6) In subsection (5)(b)(ii) "the prescribed amount" means—

(a) where—

(i) the licence is revoked under this section, or

(ii) the first complete accounting period of the licence holder falling within the period for which the licence is in force has not yet ended,

7 per cent. of the amount which the Authority estimate would have been the multiplex revenue for that accounting period (as determined in accordance with section 56), and

(b) in any other case, 7 per cent. of the multiplex revenue for the last complete accounting period of the licence holder so falling (as so determined).

(7) Any financial penalty payable by any body by virtue of subsection (5) shall, in addition to being recoverable from that body as provided by section 71(4), be recoverable by the Authority as a debt due to them from any person who controls that body.

DEFINITIONS

"Authority; the": s.72(1).
"licence": s.72(1).
"licence holder": s.72(3).
"local radio multiplex licence": s.72(1).
"national radio multiplex licence": s.72(1).

GENERAL NOTE

See the note to s.11, to which this section corresponds, with the exception that the maximum fine in respect of a local multiplex licence is £50,000. This sum may be varied by order, under s.69(1).

Conditions attached to national or local radio multiplex licence

54.—(1) A radio multiplex licence shall include such conditions as appear to the Authority to be appropriate for securing—

(a) that the licensed service is established by the licence holder in accordance with the timetable and other proposals indicated in the technical plan submitted under section 46(4)(b) or 50(4)(b),

(b) the implementation of any proposals submitted by the licence holder under section 46(4)(c) to (f) or 50(4)(c) to (e),

(c) that all digital sound programme services broadcast under the licence are provided—

(i) in the case of a national radio multiplex licence, by the holder of a national digital sound programme licence under section 60, and

(ii) in the case of a local radio multiplex licence, by the BBC or the holder of a local digital sound programme licence under that section,

(d) that all digital additional services broadcast under the licence are provided by the holder of a licence under section 64,

(e) that in the terms on which the holder of the licence contracts, or offers to contract, for the broadcasting of digital sound programme services or digital additional services, he does not show undue discrimination either against or in favour of a particular person providing such a service or a class of such persons,

(f) that the holder of the licence does not, in any agreement with a person providing a digital sound programme service or digital additional services which entitles that person to use a specified amount of digital capacity on the frequency or frequencies to which the licence relates, restrict that person's freedom to make arrangements with some other person as to the use of any of that digital capacity (except to the extent that the restriction is reasonably required for the purpose of ensuring the technical quality of the broadcasts or for the purpose of securing compliance with any other condition of the licence),

(g) that the signals carrying the radio multiplex service attain high standards in terms of technical quality and reliability throughout so much of the area or locality for which the service is provided as is for the time being reasonably practicable, and

(h) that, while the licence is in force, at least 90 per cent. of digital capacity on the frequency or frequencies to which the licence relates is available for the broadcasting of digital sound programme services, simulcast radio services, programme-related services or relevant technical services.

(2) In paragraph (1)(h)—

(a) "programme-related service" means any digital additional service consisting in the provision of services (apart from advertising) which—

(i) are ancillary to the programmes included in one or more digital sound programme services, simulcast radio services or local or national services (within the meaning of Part I of the 1990 Act) and are directly related to the contents of those programmes, or

(ii) relate to the promotion or listing of such programmes, and

(b) "relevant technical service" means any technical service which relates to one or more digital sound programme services.

(3) The Secretary of State may, after consulting the Authority, by order amend subsection (1) by substituting a different percentage for the percentage for the time being specified in paragraph (h) of that subsection.

(4) No order under subsection (3) shall be made unless a draft of the order has been laid before and approved by a resolution of each House of Parliament.

(5) Any conditions imposed in pursuance of subsection (1)(a) or (b) may be varied by the Authority with the consent of the licence holder (and section 42(3)(b) shall accordingly not apply to any such variation).

(6) Where the licence holder applies to the Authority for the variation of any condition imposed in pursuance of subsection (1)(b) and relating to the characteristics of any of the digital sound programme services to be broadcast under the licence, the Authority shall vary the condition accordingly unless—

(a) it appears to the Authority that, if the application were granted, the capacity of the digital sound programme services broadcast under the licence to appeal to a variety of tastes and interests would be unacceptably diminished, or

(b) in the case of a national radio multiplex licence in relation to which a direction under section 45(4) has effect, the Authority are not satisfied that the proposed variation complies with that direction.

(7) Section 94 of the 1990 Act (Government control over licensed services) shall apply in relation to a radio multiplex service licensed under this Part as it applies in relation to a service licensed under Part III of that Act.

DEFINITIONS

"ancillary service": s.63(2); s.72(1).
"area": s.72(2).
"Authority; the": s.72(1).

"digital additional service": s.63(1); s.72(1).
"digital sound programme service": s.40(5); s.72(1).
"licence": s.72(1).
"licence holder": s.72(3).
"licensed": s.72(1).
"local digital sound programme licence": s.72(1).
"local radio multiplex licence": s.72(1).
"locality": s.72(2).
"national digital sound programme licence": s.72(1).
"national radio multiplex licence": s.72(1).
"radio multiplex service": s.40(1); s.72(1).
"simulcast radio service": s.41(2); s.72(1).
"technical service": s.63(3); s.72(1).
"1990 Act; the": s.147(1).

General Note

See the note to s.12, to which this section corresponds in essence.

Additional payments to be made in respect of national radio multiplex licences

55.—(1) Where a national radio multiplex licence is granted in pursuance of a notice under subsection (1) of section 46 which specified a percentage of multiplex revenue under paragraph (h) of that subsection, the licence shall include conditions requiring the licence holder to pay to the Authority (in addition to any fees required to be so paid by virtue of section 43(1)(c)) in respect of each accounting period of his falling within the period for which the licence is in force, an amount representing such percentage of the multiplex revenue for that accounting period (determined under section 56) as was specified in the notice.

(2) The Secretary of State may by order provide that, in relation to any notice under subsection (1) of section 46 published while the order is in force, no percentage shall be specified under paragraph (h) of that subsection.

(3) Any order under subsection (2) shall be subject to annulment in pursuance of a resolution of either House of Parliament.

(4) A national radio multiplex licence may include conditions—

(a) enabling the Authority to estimate before the beginning of an accounting period the amount due for that period by virtue of subsection (1), and

(b) requiring the licence holder to pay the estimated amount by monthly instalments throughout that period.

(5) Such a licence may in particular include conditions—

(a) authorising the Authority to revise any estimate on one or more occasions, and to adjust the instalments payable by the licence holder to take account of the revised estimate;

(b) providing for the adjustment of any overpayment or underpayment.

(6) Where—

(a) the first complete accounting period of the licence holder falling within the period for which the licence is in force ("the licence period") does not begin at the same time as that period, or

(b) the last complete accounting period of his falling within the licence period does not end at the same time as that period,

any reference in subsection (1) to an accounting period of his shall include a reference to such part of the accounting period preceding that first complete accounting period, or (as the case may be) following that last complete accounting period, as falls within the licence period; and other references to accounting periods in this Part shall be construed accordingly.

Definitions

"licence": s.72(1).
"licence holder": s.72(3).
"national radio multiplex licence": s.72(1).

GENERAL NOTE

See the note to s.13, to which this section corresponds. Note that additional payments cannot be levied in respect of local radio multiplexes.

Multiplex revenue

56.—(1) For the purposes of section 55(1) the multiplex revenue for each accounting period of the holder of a national radio multiplex licence shall consist of—

(a) all payments received or to be received by him or any person connected with him from a person other than a programme provider or an additional services provider—

(i) in consideration of the inclusion in that period, in any digital sound programme service or digital additional service broadcast by means of the national radio multiplex service to which the licence relates, of advertisements or other programmes, or

(ii) in respect of charges made in that period for the reception of programmes included in any such digital sound programme service or digital additional service,

(b) all payments received or to be received by him or any person connected with him in respect of the broadcasting of any simulcast radio service by means of the national radio multiplex service,

(c) all payments received or to be received by any programme provider or any person connected with him from a person other than the holder of the radio multiplex licence, an additional service provider or another programme provider—

(i) in consideration of the inclusion in that period, in any digital sound programme service provided by him for broadcasting by means of the national radio multiplex service, of advertisements or other programmes, or

(ii) in respect of charges made in that period for the reception of programmes included in any such digital sound programme service, and

(d) all payments received or to be received by any additional services provider or any person connected with him from a person other than the holder of the radio multiplex licence, a programme provider or another additional services provider—

(i) in consideration of the inclusion in that period, in any digital additional service provided by him for broadcasting by means of the national radio multiplex service, of advertisements or other programmes, or

(ii) in respect of charges made in that period for the reception of programmes included in any such digital additional service.

(2) If, in connection with the inclusion of any advertisements or other programmes whose inclusion is paid for by payments falling within subsection (1)(a)(i), any payments are made to the holder of the radio multiplex licence or any person connected with him to meet any payments payable by the licence holder by virtue of section 55(1), those payments shall be regarded as made in consideration of the inclusion of the programmes in question.

(3) In the case of an advertisement included as mentioned in subsection (1)(a)(i), (c)(i) or (d)(i) under arrangements made between—

(a) the holder of the radio multiplex licence, a programme provider or an additional services provider or any person connected with any of them, and

(b) a person acting as an advertising agent,

the amount of any receipt by the licence holder, programme provider or additional services provider or any connected person that represents a payment by the advertiser from which the advertising agent has deducted any amount by way of commission shall, except in a case falling within subsection (4), be the amount of the payment by the advertiser after the deduction of the commission.

(4) If the amount deducted by way of commission as mentioned in subsection (3) exceeds 15 per cent. of the payment by the advertiser, the amount of the receipt in question shall be taken to be the amount of the payment less 15 per cent.

(5) If, in any accounting period of the holder of the radio multiplex licence, a programme provider or an additional services provider or a person connected with any of them derives, in relation to any programme to be included in the relevant service, any financial benefit (whether direct or indirect) from payments made by any person other than the licence holder, by way of sponsorship, for the purpose of defraying or contributing towards costs incurred or to be incurred in connection with that programme, the relevant payments shall be taken to include the amount of the financial benefit so derived by the licence holder or the connected person, as the case may be.

(6) In subsection (5)—

(a) "the relevant service" means—

(i) in relation to a programme provider or a person connected with him, any digital sound programme service provided as mentioned in subsection (1)(c)(i), and

(ii) in relation to an additional services provider or a person connected with him, any digital additional service provided as mentioned in subsection (1)(d)(i), and

(b) "relevant payments" means—

(i) in relation to a programme provider, the payments referred to in subsection (1)(c), and

(ii) in relation to an additional services provider, the payments referred to in subsection (1)(d).

(7) Where, in any accounting period of the holder of the radio multiplex licence—

(a) the licence holder provides a digital sound programme service or digital additional service for broadcasting by means of the multiplex service,

(b) the licence holder is engaged in any activity which, if engaged in by another person, would result in payments falling within subsection (1)(a) being made to the licence holder,

(c) a programme provider is engaged in any activity which, if engaged in by another person, would result in payments falling within subsection (1)(c) being made to the programme provider, or

(d) an additional services provider is engaged in any activity which, if engaged in by another person, would result in payments falling within subsection (1)(d) being made to the additional services provider,

the Authority may, if they consider that the amount which would (apart from this subsection) be the multiplex revenue for that accounting period is less than it would have been if the digital sound programme service or digital additional service had been provided, or the activity engaged in, by another person at arm's length, treat the multiplex revenue as increased by the amount of the difference.

(8) Where, in any accounting period of the holder of the multiplex licence, the licence holder or a programme provider or additional services provider receives payments falling within subsection (1)(a), (b), (c) or (d) from a person connected with him and it appears to the Authority that the amount which (apart from this subsection) would be the multiplex revenue for that accounting period is less than it would have been if the arrangements between him and the connected person were such as might be expected

between parties at arm's length, the Authority may treat the multiplex revenue as increased by the amount of the difference.

(9) In this section—

"additional services provider", in relation to a national radio multiplex licence, means any person who provides any digital additional service for broadcasting by means of the radio multiplex service to which the licence relates;

"programme provider", in relation to a national radio multiplex licence, means any person who provides a digital sound programme service for broadcasting by means of the radio multiplex service to which the licence relates.

DEFINITIONS

"advertising agent": s.147(2); s.202(1) of the Broadcasting Act 1990.
"Authority; the": s.72(1).
"connected": s.147(2); s.202(1) of the Broadcasting Act 1990.
"digital additional service": s.63(1); s.72(1).
"digital sound programme service": s.40(5); s.72(1).
"licence holder": s.72(3).
"national radio multiplex licence": s.72(1).
"national radio multiplex service": s.40(4); s.72(1).
"simulcast radio service": s.41(2); s.72(1).

GENERAL NOTE

See the note to s.14, to which this section corresponds. Further provision for computing multiplex revenue is made in Sched. 1, Pt. II, by s.70.

Attribution of multiplex revenue to licence holder and others

57.—(1) For the purposes of section 59(3), the share of multiplex revenue attributable to the holder of a national radio multiplex licence in respect of any accounting period of his shall be—

(a) the aggregate of—

(i) payments falling within paragraph (a) or (b) of section 56(1), and

(ii) payments received or to be received by him from programme providers and additional services providers in respect of the provision of radio multiplex services in that period,

less

(b) the amount of any payments made or to be made to programme providers or additional service providers which would fall within paragraph (c) or (d) of section 56(1) but for the fact that they are received from the holder of the national radio multiplex licence.

(2) For the purposes of section 62(3) or section 66(3), the share of multiplex revenue attributable to a programme provider or additional services provider in relation to a national radio multiplex service in respect of any accounting period of the holder of the radio multiplex licence shall be—

(a) the aggregate of—

(i) payments falling within paragraph (c) or (d) of section 56(1), and

(ii) payments received or to be received from the holder of the radio multiplex licence which would fall within one of those paragraphs but for the fact that they are received from the holder of the radio multiplex licence,

less

(b) the amount of any payments made or to be made to the holder of the radio multiplex licence in respect of the provision of radio multiplex services in that period.

(3) In a case falling within subsection (7) or (8) of section 56, the Authority may treat the share of multiplex revenue attributable to any person for the

accounting period of the holder of the national radio multiplex licence as increased by such amount as they consider appropriate to take account of the circumstances mentioned in that subsection.

(4) In this section "additional services provider" and "programme provider", in relation to a national radio multiplex licence, have the same meaning as in section 56.

DEFINITIONS

"Authority; the": s.72(1).
"licence": s.72(1).
"licence holder": s.72(3).
"national radio multiplex licence": s.72(1).

GENERAL NOTE

See the note to s.15, to which this section corresponds.

Duration and renewal of national or local radio multiplex licences

58.—(1) A radio multiplex licence shall (subject to the provisions of this Part and to section 111 of the 1990 Act as applied by section 59(8)) continue in force for a period of twelve years.

(2) A radio multiplex licence which is granted within six years of the commencement of this section may be renewed on one occasion in accordance with this section for a period of twelve years beginning with the date on which it would otherwise expire.

(3) An application for the renewal of a radio multiplex licence under subsection (2) may be made by the licence holder not earlier than four years before the date on which it would otherwise cease to be in force and not later than the relevant date.

(4) At any time before determining the application, the Authority may—

(a) require the applicant to furnish—

(i) a technical plan which supplements that submitted by the licence holder under section 46(4)(b) or 50(4)(b), and

(ii) in the case of a national radio multiplex licence, proposals which supplement that submitted by the licence holder under section 46(4)(f), and

(b) notify the applicant of requirements which must be met by that supplementary technical plan or those supplementary proposals and relate to the matters referred to in section 46(4)(b)(i) and (ii) or 50(4)(b)(i) and (ii).

(5) The consent of the Secretary of State shall be required for any exercise by the Authority of their powers under subsection (4) and for any decision by the Authority not to exercise those powers; and in deciding whether to give his consent the Secretary of State shall have regard to any report made to him under subsection (1)(b) of section 67 and to any representations received by him on consultation under subsection (4) of that section.

(6) Where any such application is made before the relevant date, the Authority may postpone consideration of it by them for as long as they think appropriate having regard to subsection (10).

(7) Where an application for the renewal of a radio multiplex licence has been duly made to the Authority, they may refuse the application only if—

(a) it appears to them that the applicant has failed to comply with any of the conditions included in his licence,

(b) any supplementary technical plan or supplementary proposals submitted under subsection (4)(a) fail to meet requirements notified to the applicant under subsection (4)(b), or

(c) they are not satisfied that the applicant would, if his licence were renewed, provide a service which complied with the conditions to be included in the licence as renewed.

(8) Subject to subsection (9), on the grant of any such application the Authority may with the consent of the Secretary of State, and shall if so required by him—

(a) specify a percentage different from that specified under section 46(1)(h) as the percentage of multiplex revenue for each accounting period of his that will be payable by the applicant in pursuance of section 55(1) during the period for which the licence is to be renewed, or
(b) specify such a percentage where none was specified under section 46(1)(h);

and the Authority may specify under paragraph (a) or (b) either of the things mentioned in section 46(2)(b).

(9) Where an order under section 55(2) is in force on the relevant date, no percentage of multiplex revenue shall be payable as mentioned in subsection (8)(a) during the period for which the licence is to be renewed.

(10) Where the Authority have granted a person's application under this section, they shall formally renew his licence from the date on which it would otherwise expire; but in the case of a national multiplex licence they shall not so renew his licence unless they have notified him of any percentage specified by them under subsection (8) and he has, within such period as is specified in that notification, notified them that he consents to the licence being renewed on those terms.

(11) Where a radio multiplex licence has been renewed under this section, the licence as renewed shall include such further conditions as appear to the Authority to be appropriate for securing the implementation of any supplementary technical plan and supplementary proposals submitted under subsection (4)(a).

(12) In this section "the relevant date", in relation to a radio multiplex licence, means the date which the Authority determine to be that by which they would need to publish a notice under section 46(1) or 50(2) if they were to grant, as from the date on which that licence would expire if not renewed, a fresh licence to provide the service formerly provided under that licence.

(13) Nothing in this section prevents the holder of a radio multiplex licence from applying for a new licence on one or more occasions in pursuance of a notice under section 46(1) or 50(2).

DEFINITIONS

"Authority; the": s.72(1).
"licence": s.72(1).
"licence holder": s.72(3).
"national radio multiplex licence": s.72(1).
"1990 Act; the": s.147(1).

GENERAL NOTE

See the note to s.16, to which this section corresponds. Most of its provisions apply to national and local radio multiplexes but subss. (8) to (10) apply to national radio multiplexes only. In subs. (10) the reference to a national multiplex licence is, in the context, a reference to a radio multiplex.

Enforcement of national or local radio multiplex licences

59.—(1) If the Authority are satisfied that the holder of a radio multiplex licence has failed to comply with any condition of the licence or with any direction given by the Authority under or by virtue of any provision of this Part, they may (subject to the following provisions of this section) serve on him—

(a) a notice requiring him to pay, within a specified period, a specified financial penalty to the Authority, or
(b) a notice reducing the period for which the licence is to be in force by a specified period not exceeding two years.

(2) The amount of any financial penalty imposed in pursuance of subsection (1)(a) on the holder of a national radio multiplex licence shall not exceed whichever is the greater of—

(a) £50,000, or

(b) the amount determined under subsection (3).

(3) The amount referred to in subsection (2)(b) is—

(a) in a case where a penalty under this section has not previously been imposed on the holder of the radio multiplex licence during any period for which his licence has been in force ("the relevant period"), 3 per cent. of the share of multiplex revenue attributable to him for his last complete accounting period (as determined in accordance with section 57), and

(b) in any other case, 5 per cent. of the share of multiplex revenue attributable to him for that accounting period (as so determined),

and in relation to a person whose first complete accounting period falling within the relevant period has not yet ended, paragraphs (a) and (b) above shall be construed as referring to 3, or (as the case may be) 5, per cent. of the amount which the Authority estimate to be the share of multiplex revenue attributable to him for that accounting period (as so determined).

(4) The amount of any financial penalty imposed in pursuance of subsection (1)(a) on the holder of a local radio multiplex licence shall not exceed £50,000.

(5) The Authority shall not serve on any person any notice under subsection (1) unless they have given him a reasonable opportunity of making representations to them about the matters complained of.

(6) Where a licence is due to expire on a particular date by virtue of a notice served on any person under subsection (1)(b), the Authority may, on the application of that person, revoke that notice by a further notice served on him at any time before that date, if they are satisfied that, since the date of the earlier notice, his conduct in relation to the operation of the licensed service has been such as to justify the revocation of that notice.

(7) Where the Authority serve a notice on a BBC company under any provision of this section, they shall send a copy of the notice to the Secretary of State.

(8) Subject to subsection (9), section 111 of the 1990 Act (power to revoke licence granted under Chapter II of Part III of the 1990 Act) shall have effect in relation to a radio multiplex licence as it has effect in relation to a licence under Chapter II of Part III of the 1990 Act.

(9) In its application in relation to a radio multiplex licence, section 111 of the 1990 Act shall have effect—

(a) with the substitution in subsection (1)(a) for the reference to Part III of the 1990 Act of a reference to this Part, and

(b) with the omission of subsection (4) and the reference to that subsection in subsection (6).

DEFINITIONS

"Authority; the": s.72(1).
"licence": s.72(1).
"licence holder": s.72(3).
"local radio multiplex licence": s.72(1).
"national radio multiplex licence": s.72(1).
"1990 Act; the": s.147(1).

GENERAL NOTE

See the note to s.17, to which this section corresponds, with the following exceptions. The maximum fine which can be imposed on local radio multiplex operators is £50,000, by subs. (4). This sum may be varied by order, under s.69(1). A copy of a notice sent to a BBC company must be sent to the Secretary of State, by subs. (7). The references to the 1990 Act are to the provisions for revoking radio licences which, in that Act, correspond to those for television services which, in turn, are reflected in s.17 of this Act.

Digital sound programme services

Licensing of digital sound programme services

60.—(1) For the purposes of this Part a digital sound programme service is—

(a) a "national digital sound programme service" if it is provided for broadcasting by means of a national radio multiplex service, and

(b) a "local digital sound programme service" if it is provided for broadcasting by means of a local radio multiplex service.

(2) A licence to provide digital sound programme services (in this Part referred to as a "digital sound programme licence") may be either—

(a) a licence to provide national digital sound programme services (in this Part referred to as a "national digital sound programme licence"), or

(b) a licence to provide local digital sound programme services (in this Part referred to as a "local digital sound programme licence").

(3) An application for a digital sound programme licence shall—

(a) be made in such manner as the Authority may determine, and

(b) be accompanied by such fee (if any) as they may determine.

(4) At any time after receiving such an application and before determining it, the Authority may require the applicant to furnish such additional information as they may consider necessary for the purpose of considering the application.

(5) Any information to be furnished to the Authority under this section shall, if they so require, be in such form or verified in such manner as they may specify.

(6) Where an application for a digital sound programme licence is made to the Authority in accordance with the provisions of this section they shall grant the licence unless precluded from doing so by section 42(2)(a) or 44(1).

(7) Subject to subsection (8), section 90 of the 1990 Act (general provisions relating to services licensed under Part III of that Act) shall apply in relation to a digital sound programme service licensed under this Part of this Act as it applies in relation to a national or local service (within the meaning of Part III of the 1990 Act).

(8) In its application in relation to a digital sound programme service licensed under this Part, section 90 of the 1990 Act shall have effect with the omission of subsection (7) and with the substitution for subsections (3) and (4) of the following—

"(3) The appropriate requirement referred to in subsection (2)(a) is—

(a) in the case of a national digital sound programme service, that due impartiality is preserved on the part of the person providing the service as respects matters of political or industrial controversy or relating to current public policy;

(b) in the case of a local digital sound programme service, that undue prominence is not given in its programmes to the views and opinions of particular persons or bodies on such matters.

(4) In applying subsection (3)(a) to a national digital sound programme service a series of programmes may be considered as a whole; and in applying subsection (3)(b) to a local digital sound programme service the programmes included in that service shall be taken as a whole."

(9) Subject to subsection (10), sections 91 to 96 of the 1990 Act (general provisions relating to services licensed under Part III of that Act) shall apply in relation to a digital sound programme service licensed under this Part as

they apply in relation to a licensed service (within the meaning of Part III of the 1990 Act).

(10) In its application in relation to a digital sound programme service, section 96(1)(b) shall have effect as if the reference to the Authority's functions under Chapter II of Part III of the 1990 Act included a reference to their functions under this Part.

DEFINITIONS

"Authority; the": s.72(1).
"digital sound programme licence": s.72(1).
"digital sound programme service": s.40(5); s.72(1).
"licensed": s.72(1).
"local radio multiplex service": s.40(4); s.72(1).
"national radio multiplex service": s.40(4); s.72(1).
"1990 Act; the": s.147(1).

GENERAL NOTE

See the note to s.18, to which this section corresponds, with the exception that national and local digital sound programme services are distinguished for the purposes of the treatment of controversial matters. The difference of approach in this respect is reflected in s.90 of the 1990 Act and subs. (8) provides a more felicitous way of applying it to digital radio.

Duration and conditions of digital sound programme licence

61.—(1) Subject to the provisions of this Part and to section 111 of the 1990 Act as applied by section 62(10), a digital sound programme licence shall continue in force until it is surrendered by its holder.

(2) A digital sound programme licence shall include such conditions as appear to the Authority to be appropriate for requiring the holder of the licence—

(a) on entering into any agreement with the holder of a radio multiplex licence for the provision of a digital sound programme service to be broadcast by means of a radio multiplex service, to notify the Authority—

(i) of the identity of the radio multiplex service,

(ii) of the characteristics of the digital sound programme service to which the agreement relates, and

(iii) of the period during which it will be provided,

(b) when any such agreement is varied so far as it relates to any of the matters mentioned in paragraph (a)(i), (ii) or (iii), to notify the Authority of the variation so far as relating to those matters, and

(c) where he is providing a digital sound programme service to the holder of a radio multiplex licence in accordance with such an agreement as is mentioned in paragraph (a) but intends to cease doing so, to notify the Authority of that fact.

(3) A digital sound programme licence shall also include such conditions as appear to the Authority to be appropriate for requiring the holder of the licence, on entering into any such agreement as is mentioned in subsection (2)(a), to submit to the Authority proposals for training or retraining persons employed or to be employed by him in order to help fit them for employment in, or in connection with, the making of programmes to be included in his service.

(4) Where the holder of a digital sound programme licence has submitted proposals to the Authority in accordance with a condition included in the licence by virtue of subsection (3) or has failed to comply with such a condition, the Authority may, after consulting him, vary the licence so as to include in the licence such further conditions as they consider appropriate in relation to the matters referred to in that subsection.

DEFINITIONS
"Authority; the": s.72(1).
"digital sound programme licence": s.72(1).
"digital sound programme service": s.40(5); s.72(1).
"licence holder": s.72(3).
"radio multiplex service": s.40(1); s.72(1).
"1990 Act; the": s.147(1).

GENERAL NOTE

This section corresponds, in essence, to s.19, the note to which should be consulted. But there are no requirements in repect of European programme or independent producer quotas (there being no such European requirements). In addition, it is not necessary, under subs. (2), to specify the digital capacity to be used. Further, in subs. (3), the requirements as to retraining apply to the licensee's own business and not to the industry as a whole.

Enforcement of digital sound programme licences

62.—(1) If the Authority are satisfied that the holder of a digital sound programme licence has failed to comply with any condition of the licence or with any direction given by the Authority under or by virtue of any provision of this Part, they may (subject to the following provisions of this section) serve on him—

(a) a notice requiring him to pay, within a specified period, a specified financial penalty to the Authority,

(b) a notice providing that the licence is to expire on a specified date, which shall be at least one year from the date of service of the notice, and

(c) a notice suspending the licence for a specified period not exceeding six months.

(2) The amount of any financial penalty imposed in pursuance of subsection (1)(a) on the holder of a national digital sound programme licence shall not exceed whichever is the greater of—

(a) £50,000, and

(b) the amount determined under subsection (3).

(3) The amount referred to in subsection (2)(b) is—

(a) in a case where a penalty under this section has not previously been imposed on the holder of the digital sound programme licence during any period for which his licence has been in force, 3 per cent. of the aggregate amount of the shares of multiplex revenue attributable to him in relation to national radio multiplex services in respect of relevant accounting periods (as determined in accordance with section 57), and

(b) in any other case, 5 per cent. of the aggregate amount of those shares of multiplex revenue (as so determined).

(4) In subsection (3) "relevant accounting period", in relation to a national radio multiplex service, means the last accounting period of the holder of the national radio multiplex licence.

(5) Where, in the case of any national radio multiplex service, the first accounting period of the holder of the national radio multiplex licence throughout which the holder of the digital sound programme licence provides a digital sound programme service for broadcasting by means of the radio multiplex service ("the first period") has not yet ended, then for the purposes of subsection (3) the share of multiplex revenue attributable to the holder of the digital sound programme licence in relation to that radio multiplex service for the relevant accounting period shall be taken to be the amount which the Authority estimate to be the share of multiplex revenue attributable to him for the first period.

(6) The amount of any financial penalty imposed in pursuance of subsection (1)(a) on the holder of a local digital sound programme licence shall not exceed £50,000.

(7) The Authority shall not serve on any person any notice under subsection (1) unless they have given him a reasonable opportunity of making representations to them about the matters complained of.

(8) Where a licence is due to expire on a particular date by virtue of a notice served on any person under subsection (1)(b), the Authority may, on the application of that person, revoke that notice by a further notice served on him at any time before that date, if they are satisfied that, since the date of the earlier notice, his conduct in relation to the operation of the licensed service has been such as to justify the revocation of that notice.

(9) Where the Authority serve a notice on a BBC company under any provision of this section, they shall send a copy of the notice to the Secretary of State.

(10) Subject to subsections (11) and (12), section 109 (power to require scripts etc. or broadcasting of correction or apology or not to repeat programme) and section 111 (power to revoke licences) of the 1990 Act shall apply in relation to a digital sound programme licence as they apply in relation to a licence under Chapter II of Part III of the 1990 Act.

(11) In its application in relation to a digital sound programme licence, section 109(1) of the 1990 Act shall have effect with the substitution for the reference to a direction under Part III of that Act of a reference to a direction under this Part.

(12) In its application in relation to a digital sound programme licence, section 111 of the 1990 Act shall have effect—

(a) with the substitution for the reference in subsection (1)(a) to Part III of that Act of a reference to this Part, and

(b) with the omission of subsection (4) and of the reference to that subsection in subsection (6).

(13) It is hereby declared that any exercise by the Authority of their powers under subsection (1) in respect of any failure to comply with any condition of a digital sound programme licence shall not preclude any exercise by the Authority of their powers under section 109 of the 1990 Act in respect of that failure.

Definitions

"Authority; the": s.72(1).
"BBC; the": s.147(1).
"digital sound programme licence": s.72(1).
"digital sound programme service": s.40(5); s.72(1).
"licence": s.72(1).
"licence holder": s.72(3).
"local digital sound programme licence": s.72(1).
"national digital sound programme service": s.60(1); s.72(1).
"national radio multiplex licence": s.72(1).
"national radio multiplex service": s.40(4); s.72(1).
"1990 Act; the": s.147(1).

General Note

See the note to s.23, to which this section corresponds, with the following exceptions. Subsection (1)(c) provides for an additional penalty, the suspension of the digital sound programme licence for a period not exceeding six months. The maximum fine which can be imposed on a local digital sound programme licensee is £50,000, by subs. (6). This sum may be varied by order, under s.69(1). Further, the Authority must send the Secretary of State a copy of any notice served on a BBC company, under subs. (9).

Digital additional services provided on sound broadcasting frequencies

Digital additional services

63.—(1) In this Part "digital additional service" means any service which—

(a) is provided by any person with a view to its being broadcast in digital form by means of a radio multiplex service, whether by him or by some other person, but

(b) is not a digital sound programme service, a simulcast radio service, an ancillary service or a technical service.

(2) In this Part "ancillary service" means any service which is provided by the holder of a digital sound programme licence or by an independent national broadcaster and consists in the provision of any service (other than advertising) which—

(a) is ancillary to programmes included in a digital sound programme service or simulcast radio service provided by him and is directly related to their contents, or

(b) relates to the promotion or listing of such programmes.

(3) In this Part "technical service" means a service which—

(a) is provided for technical purposes connected with the encryption or decryption of one or more digital sound programme services or digital additional services, and

(b) is of a description specified in an order made by the Secretary of State.

(4) An order under subsection (3) shall be subject to annulment in pursuance of a resolution of either House of Parliament.

DEFINITIONS

"digital sound programme licence": s.72(1).
"digital sound programme service": s.40(5); s.72(1).
"independent national broadcaster": s.41(1); s.72(1).
"radio multiplex service": s.40(1); s.72(1).
"simulcast radio service": s.41(2); s.72(1).

GENERAL NOTE

See the note to s.24, to which this section corresponds.

Licensing of digital additional services

64.—(1) An application for a licence to provide digital additional services (in this Part referred to as a "digital additional services licence") shall—

(a) be made in such manner as the Authority may determine, and

(b) be accompanied by such fee (if any) as they may determine.

(2) At any time after receiving such an application and before determining it, the Authority may require the applicant to furnish such additional information as they may consider necessary for the purpose of considering the application.

(3) Any information to be furnished to the Authority under this section shall, if they so require, be in such form or verified in such manner as they may specify.

(4) Where an application for a digital additional services licence is made to the Authority in accordance with the provisions of this section, they shall grant the licence unless precluded from doing so by section 42(2)(a) or 44(1).

DEFINITIONS

"Authority; the": s.72(1).
"digital additional service": s.63(1); s.72(1).

GENERAL NOTE

See the note to s.25, to which this section corresponds, except that the requirements for "consumer protection" in the 1990 Act are not applied to digital additional services for sound.

Duration and conditions of digital additional services licence

65.—(1) Subject to the provisions of this Part and to section 111 of the 1990 Act as applied by section 66(10), a digital additional services licence shall continue in force until it is surrendered by its holder.

(2) A digital additional services licence shall include such conditions as appear to the Authority to be appropriate for requiring the holder of the licence—

(a) on entering into any agreement with the holder of a radio multiplex licence for the provision of digital additional services to be broadcast by means of a radio multiplex service, to notify the Authority—

(i) of the identity of the radio multiplex service,

(ii) of the period during which the services will be provided, and

(iii) where under the agreement the holder of the digital additional services licence will be entitled to the use of a specified amount of digital capacity, of that amount,

(b) when any such agreement is varied so far as it relates to any of the matters mentioned in paragraph (a)(i), (ii) or (iii) to notify the Authority of the variation so far as relating to those matters, and

(c) where he is providing digital additional services to the holder of a radio multiplex licence in accordance with such an agreement as is mentioned in paragraph (a) but intends to cease doing so, to notify the Authority of that fact.

DEFINITIONS

"Authority; the": s.72(1).
"digital additional services licence": s.72(1).
"licence holder": s.72(3).
"radio multiplex service": s.40(1); s.72(1).
"1990 Act; the": s.147(1).

GENERAL NOTE

See the note to s.27, to which this section corresponds.

Enforcement of digital additional services licences

66.—(1) If the Authority are satisfied that the holder of a digital additional services licence has failed to comply with any condition of the licence or with any direction given by the Authority under or by virtue of any provision of this Part, they may (subject to the following provisions of this section) serve on him—

(a) a notice requiring him to pay, within a specified period, a specified financial penalty to the Authority,

(b) a notice providing that the licence is to expire on a specified date, which shall be at least one year from the date of service of the notice, or

(c) a notice suspending the licence for a specified period not exceeding six months.

(2) Subject to subsection (4), the amount of any financial penalty imposed in pursuance of subsection (1)(a) on the holder of a digital additional services licence shall not exceed whichever is the greater of—

(a) £50,000, and

(b) the amount determined under subsection (3).

(3) The amount referred to in subsection (2)(b) is—

(a) in a case where a penalty under this section has not previously been imposed on the holder of the digital additional services licence during any period for which his licence has been in force, 3 per cent. of the aggregate amount of the shares of multiplex revenue attributable to him in relation to national radio multiplex services in respect of relevant accounting periods (as determined in accordance with section 57), and

(b) in any other case, 5 per cent. of the aggregate amount of those shares of multiplex revenue (as so determined).

(4) Where the holder of a digital additional services licence has not provided any digital additional services for broadcasting by means of a national radio multiplex service, the amount of any penalty imposed on him under subsection (1)(a) shall not exceed £50,000.

(5) In subsection (3) "relevant accounting period", in relation to a national radio multiplex service, means the last accounting period of the holder of the national radio multiplex licence.

(6) Where, in the case of any national radio multiplex service, the first accounting period of the holder of the national radio multiplex licence throughout which the holder of the digital additional services licence provides a digital additional service for broadcasting by means of the radio multiplex service ("the first period") has not yet ended, then for the purposes of subsection (3) the share of multiplex revenue attributable to the holder of the digital additional services licence in relation to that radio multiplex service for the relevant accounting period shall be taken to be the amount which the Authority estimate to be the share of multiplex revenue attributable to him for the first period.

(7) The Authority shall not serve on any person any notice under subsection (1) unless they have given him a reasonable opportunity of making representations to them about the matters complained of.

(8) Where a licence is due to expire on a particular date by virtue of a notice served on any person under subsection (1)(b), the Authority may, on the application of that person, revoke that notice by a further notice served on him at any time before that date, if they are satisfied that, since the date of the earlier notice, his conduct in relation to the operation of the licensed service has been such as to justify the revocation of that notice.

(9) Where the Authority serve a notice on a BBC company under any provision of this section, they shall send a copy of the notice to the Secretary of State.

(10) Subject to subsections (11) and (12), section 109 (power to require scripts etc. or broadcasting of correction or apology or not to repeat programme) and section 111 (power to revoke licences) of the 1990 Act shall apply in relation to a digital additional services licence as they apply in relation to a licence under Chapter II of Part III of the 1990 Act.

(11) In its application in relation to a digital additional services licence, section 109(1) of the 1990 Act shall have effect with the substitution for the reference to a direction under Part III of that Act of a reference to a direction under this Part.

(12) In its application in relation to a digital additional services licence section 111 of the 1990 Act shall have effect—

(a) with the substitution for the reference in subsection (1)(a) to Part III of that Act of a reference to this Part, and

(b) with the omission of subsection (4) and of the reference to that subsection in subsection (6).

(13) It is hereby declared that any exercise by the Authority of their powers under subsection (1) in respect of any failure to comply with any condition of a digital additional services licence shall not preclude any exercise by the Authority of their powers under section 109 of the 1990 Act in respect of that failure.

DEFINITIONS

"Authority; the": s.72(1).
"BBC; the": s.147(1).
"digital additional services licence": s.72(1).
"licence": s.72(1).
"licence holder": s.72(3).
"national radio multiplex licence": s.72(1).
"national radio multiplex service": s.40(4); s.72(1).
"1990 Act; the": s.147(1).

GENERAL NOTE

See the note to s.62, to which this section corresponds.

Miscellaneous and supplemental

Review of digital radio broadcasting

67.—(1) For the purpose of considering for how long it would be appropriate for sound broadcasting services to continue to be provided in analogue form, the Secretary of State—

(a) shall keep under review the extent of—

(i) the provision in the United Kingdom of radio multiplex services,

(ii) the availability in the United Kingdom of digital sound programme services and the availability there in digital form of national services (within the meaning of Part III of the 1990 Act) and the sound broadcasting services of the BBC, and

(iii) the ownership or possession in the United Kingdom of equipment capable of receiving the services referred to in sub-paragraph (ii) when broadcast or transmitted in digital form,

and the likely future extent of such provision, such availability and such ownership or possession, and

(b) shall, on or before the fourth anniversary of the day on which the first national radio multiplex licence is granted under section 47, and at such time or times thereafter as he thinks fit, require the Authority and the BBC to report to him on the matters referred to in paragraph (a).

(2) If the Authority or the BBC are required to submit a report under subsection (1)(b), they shall submit the report within twelve months of the date of the requirement.

(3) Before making any report under this subsection (1)(b), the Authority shall consult—

(a) the holders of all radio multiplex licences,

(b) the holders of digital sound programme licences who are providing digital sound programme services which are being broadcast, and

(c) such other persons providing services licensed by the Authority under this Part or Part III of the 1990 Act as the Authority think fit,

and the Authority shall include in their report a summary of representations made to them by the persons consulted.

(4) For the purpose mentioned in subsection (1), the Secretary of State shall, on requiring reports under subsection (1)(b), consult—

(a) such persons appearing to him to represent listeners as he thinks fit, and

(b) such other persons as he thinks fit,

in connection with the matters referred to in subsection (1)(a) and also, if the Secretary of State thinks fit, as to the likely effects on listeners of any sound broadcasting service ceasing to be broadcast in analogue form.

(5) In this section "sound broadcasting service" has the same meaning as in Part III of the 1990 Act.

DEFINITIONS

"Authority; the": s.72(1).
"BBC; the": s.147(1).
"digital sound programme licence": s.72(1).
"digital sound programme service": s.40(5); s.72(1).
"national radio multiplex licence": s.72(1).
"radio multiplex service": s.40(1); s.72(1).
"1990 Act; the": s.147(1).

General Note

See the note to s.33 to which this section corresponds.

Promotion of equal opportunities and fair treatment

68.—(1) Any national radio multiplex licence or national digital sound programme licence shall include conditions requiring the licence holder—

(a) to make arrangements for promoting, in relation to employment by him, equality of opportunity between men and women and between persons of different racial groups,

(b) to make arrangements for promoting, in relation to employment by him, the fair treatment of disabled persons, and

(c) to review those arrangements from time to time.

(2) In subsection (1) "racial group" has the same meaning as in the Race Relations Act 1976, and "disabled person" has the same meaning as in the Disability Discrimination Act 1995.

Definitions

"licence holder": s.72(3).
"national digital sound programme licence": s.72(1).
"national radio multiplex licence": s.72(1).

General Note

See the note to s.34, to which this section corresponds.

Power to vary amount of financial penalties

69.—(1) The Secretary of State may by order amend any of the provisions specified in subsection (2) by substituting a different sum for the sum for the time being specified there.

(2) The provisions referred to in subsection (1) are—
section 53(5)(a) and (b)(i);
section 59(2)(a) and (4);
section 62(2)(a) and (6); and
section 66(2)(a) and (4).

(3) An order under subsection (1) shall be subject to annulment in pursuance of a resolution of either House of Parliament.

Computation of multiplex revenue

70. Part II of Schedule 1 (which contains provisions relating to the computation of multiplex revenue for the purposes of this Part) shall have effect.

Certain receipts of Authority to be paid into Consolidated Fund

71.—(1) Where the Authority receive in respect of any licence any of the amounts specified in subsection (2), that amount shall not form part of the revenues of the Authority but shall—

(a) if the licence is for the provision of a service for any area or locality in Great Britain, be paid into the Consolidated Fund of the United Kingdom,

(b) if the licence is for the provision of a service for any area or locality in Northern Ireland, be paid into the Consolidated Fund of Northern Ireland, or

(c) in any other case, be paid into whichever of those Funds the Authority consider appropriate or into both of those Funds in such proportions as the Authority consider appropriate.

(2) The amounts referred to in subsection (1) are amounts payable by virtue of any of the following provisions—
section 53(5);
section 55(1);

section 59(1);
section 62(1);
section 66(1).

(3) Subsection (1) shall not be construed as applying to any amount which is required by the Authority for the making of an adjustment in respect of an overpayment made by any person.

(4) Any amount payable by any person to the Authority under or by virtue of this Part shall be recoverable by them as a debt due to them from that person; and, where any amount is so payable by a person as the holder of any licence under this Part, his liability to pay it shall not be affected by his licence ceasing (for any reason) to be in force.

(5) The Authority shall, in respect of each financial year, prepare an account showing—

(a) all such amounts falling within subsection (1) as have been received by them, and

(b) the sums paid into the Consolidated Funds of the United Kingdom and Northern Ireland respectively under that subsection in respect of those amounts,

and shall send that account to the Comptroller and Auditor General not later than the end of the month of November following the financial year to which it relates; and the Comptroller and Auditor General shall examine, certify and report on the account and lay copies of it, together with his report, before each House of Parliament.

DEFINITIONS

"Authority; the": s.72(1).
"licence": s.72(1).
"licence holder": s.72(3).

Interpretation of Part II

72.—(1) In this Part (unless the context otherwise requires)—

"ancillary service" has the meaning given by section 63(2);

"the Authority" means the Radio Authority;

"digital additional service" has the meaning given by section 63(1), and "digital additional services licence" means a licence to provide such services;

"digital sound programme service" has the meaning given by section 40(5), and "digital sound programme licence" means a licence to provide such services;

"independent national broadcaster" has the meaning given by section 41(1);

"licence" means a licence under this Part, and "licensed" shall be construed accordingly;

"local digital sound programme service" and "national digital sound programme service" shall be construed in accordance with section 60(1) and "local digital sound programme licence" and "national digital sound programme licence" mean a licence to provide local digital sound programme services and a licence to provide national digital sound programme services respectively;

"local radio multiplex service" and "national radio multiplex service" shall be construed in accordance with section 40(4), and "local radio multiplex licence" and "national radio multiplex licence" mean a licence to provide a local radio multiplex service and a licence to provide a national radio multiplex service respectively;

"radio multiplex service" has the meaning given by section 40(1);

"simulcast radio service" has the meaning given by section 41(2);

"technical service" has the meaning given by section 63(3).

(2) Any reference in this Part to an area in the United Kingdom does not include an area which comprises or includes the whole of England; and nothing in this Part shall be read as precluding a local radio multiplex service from being provided for an area or locality that is to any extent comprised in the area or locality for which another local radio multiplex service is to be provided.

(3) Where the person who is for the time being the holder of any licence ("the present licence holder") is not the person to whom the licence was originally granted, any reference in this Part (however expressed) to the holder of the licence shall be construed, in relation to any time falling before the date when the present licence holder became the holder of it, as including a reference to a person who was previously the holder of the licence.

Part III

Amendments of the Broadcasting Act 1990

Restrictions on holding of licences

Restrictions on holding of licences

73. Schedule 2 (which makes amendments of the 1990 Act relating to restrictions on the holding of licences under that Act or under Part I or II) shall have effect.

Definitions

"1990 Act; the": s.147(1).

General Note

This note is a commentary on Sched. 2 which takes effect under this section and amends Sched. 2 of the 1990 Act.

Definitions and Disqualifications

Part I of the Schedule amends a number of interpretative provisions of Sched. 2 of the 1990 Act. The intention is to close loopholes which the Commission and the Authority identified to the Government. The main problem, which is a likely consequence of the detail drafting style of the Schedule, is that various arrangements have been devised to avoid its provisions. "Warehousing" arrangements have been set up, whereby interests are held in excess of what might legally be held by one company by creating corporate structures that are technically acceptable. In addition, "deadlocked" shareholding, whereby equal holdings mean that no one body, or a small third body, appears to be in control of a company, have enabled evasion of the spirit, if not the letter, of the law. In addition, despite complex provisions to allow the regulators to search behind corporate veils, arrangements have continued to be made to enable the extent of particular bodies' control to be concealed.

The principal amendments are as follows. By para. 1(3), an associate of a body corporate is now defined in terms of control generally, rather than company group. By para. 1(4), the definition of control is extended to include indirect means, such as contractual arrangements or editorial control. The result is to allow the regulators to look through technical arrangements and attribute control to the person who effectively determines corporate policy and decisions, that is, "to achieve the result that the affairs of the body are conducted in accordance with his wishes". The new para. 1(3)(a) incorporates the idea of a controlling interest, found in the old para. 1(3). The new para. 1(3)(b) now makes provision for *de facto* control by direct or indirect means. The new para. 1(3)(c) covers deadlocking agreements. By para. 1(3), the meaning of "connected" is now defined by reference to control rather than by the holding of particular types of licence. By para. 1(6), provision is now made for a participant to be defined in terms of different percentages of share ownership. By para. 2(3), the absence of control is elaborated.

Part II of the Schedule, in paras. 6 to 9, amends the rules as to disqualification to take account of the new digital services and the commercial activities of the public service broadcasters. It may be noted that there are no nationality restrictions on the ownership of the new digital services.

In ss.144 to 146, below, there are provisions for criminal proceedings, resulting in imprisonment, fine or disqualification, to be taken against persons who supply false information connected with the disqualification provisions of Sched. 2.

Accumulations of Interests

The schedule implements, in principle, the ideas set out in the consultation paper, *Media Ownership: The Government's Proposals* (1995) Cm. 2872. The details are altered, however, and aspects of the previous ownership regime have been incorporated into the new. The legislation has been implemented in advance of the conclusions of the European Commission's deliberations on media ownership and the draft E.C. directive which is expected during 1996. In addition, the approach which has been adopted is based on some controversial assumptions. The basic idea is to ascribe media ownership to the share of the market that the media reaches. In the consultation paper, the notion of an exchange rate between different types of media, to reflect the relative ownership of the total media market, was discussed but without full consideration of the way markets might be defined and the relationship between markets and media influence. To quantify market share, however, the measurement of audience share was preferred to that of calculating total revenue and that is the basis of the changes introduced by the schedule. Many of the details of the new rules, such as the 15 per cent threshold, or the decision to include public service broadcasters in the market share, have a certain arbitrariness; however, because there is little experience of this type of regulation and the relevant academic debate suggests its effects are unpredictable and its desirability questionable. The rules have to be made to work by the regulators, of course, and the general effect will be to liberalise the market, reducing restrictions on media ownership on the assumption that large conglomerations in the U.K. are needed to provide adequate competition against foreign, especially North American, companies. At the same time, the Government's policy was to enhance diversity and plurality in the media and to prevent concentrations of ownership which might be considered against the public interest. In theory, the market share approach should have resulted in a schedule that was much less complex than the one it replaces, because the need to "cascade" different percentage interests in different media services is eliminated. In practice, the schedule combines audience share with various fixed limits on ownership relations and, for some purposes, combines cascading with audience share.

The more significant changes are as follows. By para. 11 of the schedule, a new Pt. III of the Schedule to the 1990 Act is substituted. In the substituted schedule, para. 2 sets out the new rules for television services. Basically, no person with more than a 15 per cent share of total audience time may hold two or more licences for Channels 3 and 5, domestic satellite, non-domestic satellite, licensable programme or digital programme services; or have more than a 20 per cent interest in two or more licensees for such services; or hold a licence and have a 20 per cent interest in such a licensee; or provide a foreign (that is, other than non-domestic) satellite service and hold such a licence or have a 20 per cent interest in such a licence; or hold a digital programme services licence providing two or more of those services. For these purposes, and to prevent accretion of interests, half the audience time which counts for a service in which a person has a 20 per cent interest is attributed to his primary audience share. (This approach is similar to that already adopted in respect of radio licences.) The Government's intention, in relation to Channel 3, however, is to alter the threshold, by order, so that the secondary audience time will be attributed on a 15 per cent interest. Audience time will be attributed on a twelve month basis and will be calculated in accordance with para. 3 of the substituted schedule; it will be based on figures supplied by the Broadcasting Audience Research Board. Note that the audiences of public service broadcasters will be included in the total when attributing audience share to commercial licensees. By para. 4 of the substituted schedule, there are absolute limits on the holding of a Channel 3 licence (no national licence to be held with a Channel 5 licence, and no overlapping regional licences) and, by para. 5(1), on multiplex services (no more than three). Restrictions on overlapping digital and analogue services are provided in para. 6 of the substituted schedule and a points system is introduced in respect of digital programme services, in para. 7. Provision for radio services is made in paras. 8 to 10 of Pt. III of the substituted schedule. Again, the 15 per cent threshold is adopted but in conjunction with the points system that has been established for radio audiences. An absolute limit is placed on holding a national radio service (only one) or providing a national digital sound programme service (only one). Restrictions on holding overlapping local radio licences are found in para. 12; the new provisions are liberalising, in allowing three licences (being no more than two FM or AM) to be held, but they are subject to the public interest test in para. 12(4). In para. 15 of the substituted schedule, there are restrictions on cross-ownership of national broadcasting licences (a national Channel 3 or Channel 5 licensee cannot control a national radio licensee and *vice versa*).

Restrictions on cross-holdings between newspapers and television and/or radio services are contained in Pt. IV of the substituted Schedule, by para. 11 of Sched. 2 of this Act. Market share for newspapers is calculated, in para. 2, by reference to newspaper circulation on a rolling six month basis, with national and local levels being distinguished. The regulators have power to determine whether they treat newspapers as national or local. Note that freely distributed papers are included in the total newspaper market. By the substituted para. 4, a national newspaper proprietor with a market share of 20 per cent or more may not hold a Channel 3 or 5 licence or a national or local radio licence, and a local newspaper proprietor with a local share of more than 20 per cent may not hold a corresponding regional Channel 3 licence. Restrictions on participating interests, of 20 per cent, are found in para. 5. The effect is to remove many of the former upper limits on cross-ownership. Local cross-holdings are provided for in para. 6; a local radio licence may not be held by a person with a local market share of 50 per cent or more unless the service is shared and he does not hold another such licence. Generally, and most importantly, paras. 9 to 14 of the substituted schedule provide for a public interest test to be applied, on a one-off basis, whenever cross-holdings become established. The criteria for operating the public interest test are found in para. 13: the desirability of promoting plurality and diversity; the economic benefits of concentration; and the effect of the holding of the licence on the operation of the market.

As a result of these amendments to Sched. 2, the Broadcasting (Restrictions on the Holding of Licences etc.) Order 1991 is almost wholly revoked and the Broadcasting (Restrictions on the Holding of Licences etc.) Orders 1993 and 1995 are entirely revoked. Note that Pt. V of the schedule, dealing with public telecommunications operators, has not been amended and Pt. V of the 1991 Order remains in force.

Note also that Pt. V of Sched. 2 of this Act makes consequential amendments to ss.5 and 88 of the 1990 Act, dealing with revocations following changes in ownership. But revocation is not possible once the new public interest test for cross-ownership has been applied and simply because the regulators' view of the public interest has altered in the meantime.

Regional Channel 3 services

Provision of news programmes by holders of regional Channel 3 licences

74.—(1) With respect to the broadcasting of news programmes on and after 1st January 1998, section 31 of the 1990 Act (provision of news on Channels 3 and 5) is amended as follows.

(2) In subsection (2)—

(a) at the beginning there is inserted "For the purpose of securing the nationwide broadcast, by holders of regional Channel 3 licences (taken together), of news programmes which are able to compete effectively with other news programmes broadcast nationwide in the United Kingdom,",

(b) for "a nominated news provider" there is substituted "the appointed news provider", and

(c) in paragraph (b), for "the same nominated" there is substituted "the appointed".

(3) For subsection (3) there is substituted—

"(3) In subsection (2) "appointed news provider" means, subject to subsection (4), the body corporate for the time being appointed for the purposes of subsection (2), from among the bodies corporate nominated by the Commission under section 32, in accordance with conditions included by virtue of section 31A in regional Channel 3 licences.

(4) A body corporate ceases by virtue of this subsection to be the appointed news provider if its nomination is terminated by the Commission under any provision of section 32."

Definition

"1990 Act; the": s.147(1).

General Note

This section should be read together with ss.75, 76 and 77 to which this note also refers. The effect of these sections is to limit the full effects of s.32 of the 1990 Act which was intended to promote diversity in news provision in the independent sector. Under that Act, it was possible for more than one news provider to be nominated by the Commission, with the possibility that news on Channel 3 could be provided by different companies. That did not occur prior to this Act but the position is now altered so that news provision on Channel 3 will henceforth be restricted to a single provider. It was considered that such a single provider would be needed to supply a weighty counterbalance in competition with the BBC's news provision. The single "appointed news provider" will not be chosen by the Commission directly, however. Instead, they will invite applications for nomination to a pool of qualifying providers and the Channel 3 companies will be required to choose one of them. However, the position of the current nominated news provider, ITN, will not be affected during the period of its existing contract with the Channel 3 companies. Channel 3 licences will be amended to take account of these changes. Since the Channel 3 companies' collective choice of news provider will, *prima facie*, be a restrictive trade practice, provision is made in s.77 for the agreement to be exempted under the Restrictive Trade Practices Act 1976 (c. 34). The conditions are that the agreement will have only an insignificant, or no greater than is necessary, effect on competition.

Appointment of news provider by holders of regional Channel 3 licences

75.—(1) After section 31 of the 1990 Act there is inserted—

"**Appointment of news provider by holders of regional Channel 3 licences**

31A. A regional Channel 3 licence shall include conditions requiring the holder of the licence to do all that he can to ensure—

(a) that arrangements are made between all holders of regional Channel 3 licences ("the relevant licence holders") for the appointment by them, from among the bodies corporate nominated by the Commission under section 32, and on such terms as the relevant licence holders may agree, of a single body corporate to be the appointed news provider for the purposes of section 31(2), and

(b) that, so long as he provides his licensed service, an appointment for the purposes of section 31(2) is in force."

(2) The Independent Television Commission may not include in pursuance of section 31A of the 1990 Act any condition in a regional Channel 3 licence (within the meaning of Part I of the 1990 Act) which would require an appointment for the purposes of section 31(2) of that Act (as amended by this Act) to take effect before 1st January 1998.

DEFINITION

"1990 Act; the": s.147(1).

Nomination by Commission for purposes of section 31(2) of Broadcasting Act 1990

76.—(1) Section 32 of the 1990 Act (nomination of bodies to provide news for regional Channel 3 services) is amended in accordance with subsections (2) to (5).

(2) For subsections (1) to (6) there is substituted—

"(1) With a view to enabling them to nominate bodies corporate as eligible for appointment for the purposes of section 31(2), the Commission shall invite bodies appearing to them to be qualified for nomination to make applications to be so nominated.

(2) Where a body corporate—

(a) applies to the Commission (whether in pursuance of any such invitation or not) to be nominated under this section as a nominated news provider, and

(b) appears to the Commission to be qualified for nomination,

the Commission shall so nominate that body.

(3) Subject to subsection (5), any nomination made by the Commission under this section shall remain in force for a period of ten years, and at the end of that period may be renewed by the Commission for a further period of ten years.

(4) Where the Commission are notified by the holders of licences to provide regional Channel 3 services that the appointment of the appointed news provider is due to expire, or to be renewed or terminated in accordance with the terms of the appointment, the Commission shall review the qualification for nomination of all nominated news providers (including the appointed news provider).

(5) If on any such review it appears to the Commission that a body is no longer qualified for nomination they shall (subject to subsection (6)) by notice terminate that body's nomination.

(6) The Commission shall not terminate a body's nomination under subsection (5) unless they have given the body a reasonable opportunity of making representations to them about the proposed termination."

(3) In subsection (9), paragraph (b) is omitted.

(4) In subsection (12), for the words from "appearing", where second occurring, onwards there is substituted "which—

(a) in their opinion is or, if appointed, would be effectively equipped and adequately financed to provide high quality news programmes for broadcasting in regional Channel 3 services; and

(b) appears to them not to be disqualified for being nominated under this section by virtue of this subsection."

(5) In subsection (13)—

(a) in paragraph (b), after "section", where second occurring, there is inserted "as eligible for appointment", and

(b) after paragraph (b) there is inserted—

"and

(c) references to the appointed news provider are references to the person for the time being appointed for the purposes of section 31(2) under the arrangements referred to in section 31 A(a)."

(6) Subsections (2), (4) and (5) do not affect the application of section 32 of the 1990 Act before 1st January 1998 in relation to nomination for the purposes of section 31(2) of that Act as originally enacted.

DEFINITION

"1990 Act; the": s.147(1).

GENERAL NOTE

See generally, the note to s.74.

Subs. (3)

The effect of this amendment to s.32 of the 1990 Act is to end the 50 per cent limit on the collective shareholdings by Channel 3 companies in a nominated news provider. However, the 20 per cent limit on individual companies' shareholdings, in s.32(9)(a), is not altered.

Modification of Restrictive Trade Practices Act 1976 in its application to agreements relating to Channel 3 news provision

77.—(1) After section 194 of the 1990 Act there is inserted—

"**Modification of Restrictive Trade Practices Act 1976 in its application to agreements relating to Channel 3 news provision**

194A.—(1) In this section a "relevant agreement" means an agreement—

(a) which is made between all holders of regional Channel 3 licences for securing the appointment by them, in accordance with conditions included in their licences by virtue of section 31A(a), of a single body corporate to be the appointed news provider for the purposes of section 31(2), or

(b) which is made between them and the body corporate appointed to be the appointed news provider for the purposes of section 31(2) for purposes connected with the appointment.

(2) If a relevant agreement is registered under the Restrictive Trade Practices Act 1976 ("the 1976 Act"), the Director General of Fair Trading shall report to the Secretary of State as to whether it appears to the Director that the agreement falls within subsection (4).

(3) If, on receiving a report under subsection (2), it appears to the Secretary of State that the agreement falls within subsection (4), he may give a direction to the Director requiring him not to make an application to the Restrictive Practices Court under Part I of the 1976 Act in respect of the relevant agreement.

(4) A relevant agreement falls within this subsection if—

(a) those provisions of the agreement by virtue of which the 1976 Act applies to the agreement do not have, and are not intended or likely to have, to any significant extent the effect of restricting, distorting or preventing competition, or

(b) all or any of those provisions have, or are intended or likely to have, that effect to a significant extent, but that the effect is not greater than is necessary—

(i) in the case of a relevant agreement falling within subsection (1)(a), for securing the appointment by holders of regional Channel 3 licences of a single body corporate to be the appointed news provider for the purposes of section 31(2), or

(ii) in the case of a relevant agreement falling within subsection (1)(b), for compliance by them with conditions included in their licences by virtue of section 31(1) and (2).

(5) The Secretary of State may vary or revoke any direction given under subsection (3) above if he satisfied that there has been a material change of circumstances such that—

(a) the grounds for the direction have ceased to exist, or

(b) there are grounds for giving a different direction;

and where the Secretary of State so varies or revokes any direction, he shall give notice of the variation or revocation to the Director.

(6) In this section—

(a) "agreement" and "Director" have the same meaning as in the 1976 Act, and

(b) "regional Channel 3 licence" has the same meaning as in Part I."

(2) Subsection (1) shall not apply in relation to any agreement (within the meaning of the Restrictive Trade Practices Act 1976) made for the purposes of the provision of news programmes by a nominated news provider under section 31(2) of the 1990 Act as originally enacted.

DEFINITION

"1990 Act; the": s.147(1).

Variation of regional Channel 3 licence following change of control

78.—(1) After section 21 of the 1990 Act there is inserted—

"**Variation of regional Channel 3 licence following change of control**

21A.—(1) Any regional Channel 3 licence granted to a body corporate after the commencement of this section shall include—

(a) a condition requiring the body to give the Commission advance notice of any proposals known to the body that may give rise to a relevant change of control, and

(b) a condition requiring the licence holder to provide the Commission, in such manner and at such times as they may reasonably require, with such information as they may require for the purposes of exercising their functions under this section.

(2) Subsections (3) and (4) have effect where—

(a) in pursuance of a condition in a regional Channel 3 licence the Commission receive notice of any proposals that may give rise to a relevant change of control, or

(b) a relevant change of control takes place in relation to a body corporate which holds a regional Channel 3 licence (whether or not that change has been previously notified to the Commission).

(3) If it appears to the Commission that the relevant change of control is or would be prejudicial to one or more of the following matters, namely—

(a) the quality or range of regional programmes included in the service,

(b) the quality or range of other programmes included in the service which contribute to the regional character of the service, or

(c) the quality or range of the programmes made available by the licence holder for the purposes of inclusion in the nationwide system of services referred to in section 14(1),

then, with a view to ensuring that the relevant change of control is not prejudicial to any of those matters, the Commission shall vary the licence, by a notice served on the licence holder, so as to include in the licence such conditions relating to any of those matters as they consider appropriate.

(4) If it appears to the Commission that, having regard to the effect, or likely effect, of the relevant change of control on—

(a) the time given, in the programmes included in the service—

(i) to regional programmes, or

(ii) to programmes of the kind mentioned in subsection (3)(b),

(b) the proportion of regional programmes included in the service which are made within the area for which the service is provided,

(c) the extent of the use in connection with the service—

(i) of offices or studios situated within the area for which the service is provided, or

(ii) of the services of persons employed (whether by the licence holder or any other person) within that area, or

(d) the extent to which managerial or editorial decisions relating to programmes to be included in the service are taken by persons so employed within that area,

the relevant change of control is or would be prejudicial to the regional character of the service, the Commission may vary the licence, by a notice served on the licence holder, so as to include in the licence such conditions relating to any of the matters specified in paragraphs (a), (b), (c) and (d) as they consider appropriate.

(5) Subject to subsection (6), any new or varied condition imposed under subsection (3) or (4) in relation to any matter specified in that subsection may be more onerous than any existing conditions relating to that matter; and in this subsection "existing condition" means a condition of the licence as it has effect, or had effect, before the relevant change of control.

(6) The Commission may not under subsection (3) or (4) include any new or varied condition in a licence unless the new condition or the condition as varied is one which (with any necessary modifications) would have been satisfied by the licence holder—

(a) during the three months immediately before the relevant date, or

(b) if the Commission consider that the performance of the licence holder during that period is not typical of its performance during the twelve months before the relevant date, during such other period of three months during those twelve months as they may notify in writing to the licence holder;

and for the purposes of this subsection "the relevant date" is the date of the relevant change of control or, if earlier, the date on which the Commission exercise their powers under subsection (3) or (4).

(7) The Commission shall not serve a notice on any body under subsection (3) or (4) unless they have given it a reasonable opportunity of making representations to them about the variation.

(8) Where, in a case falling within subsection (2)(a), a notice under subsection (3) or (4) varying a licence is served before the change to which it relates takes place, the variation shall not take effect until the change takes place.

(9) In this section—

"regional programme", in relation to any regional Channel 3 service, means any programme (including a news programme) which is of particular interest—

(a) to persons living within the area for which the service is provided,

(b) to persons living within any part of that area, or
(c) to particular communities living within that area;

"relevant change of control" means a change in the persons having control over—

(a) the body holding the licence, or
(b) any body which is connected with that body and appears to the Commission to be, or to be likely to be, involved to any extent in the provision of programmes for inclusion in the licensed service."

(2) Any regional Channel 3 licence (within the meaning of Part I of the 1990 Act) granted before the commencement of this section shall, as from that commencement, be taken to include the conditions referred to in section 21A(1)(a) and (b) of the 1990 Act.

DEFINITION

"1990 Act; the": s.147(1).

GENERAL NOTE

This section adds a new section to the 1990 Act to deal with the perceived impact on regional television of changes of ownership of Channel 3 companies. The basic Channel 3 structure is based on regionalism but the trend to greater concentrations of media ownership has been identified as a threat to its continuing. As an important context for this trend, it must be recognised that the round of bidding for the current Channel 3 licences resulted in a higher standard of services than is strictly required by the 1990 Act. Although new owners are bound by the conditions of the licence which was held by the previous owners, they may be prepared to apply them more stringently. The Commission have been concerned to preserve those levels of service which were originally undertaken by the first licensees and the new s.21A of the 1990 Act gives them powers to do so in relation to the quality or range of regional programmes. In s.21A(3), the Commission must alter a licence on change of control where a subjective test as to prejudice to such programming is satisfied. In s.21A(4), they have discretion to alter the licence in the light of more objective criteria. By s.21A(6), however, the Commission may not use this procedure to enhance existing regional provision.

Powers of Commission in relation to modification or replacement of networking arrangements

79.—(1) Section 39 of the 1990 Act (networking arrangements between holders of regional Channel 3 licences) is amended as follows.

(2) After subsection (9) there is inserted—

"(9A) The matters to which the Commission shall have regard in deciding whether to approve any arrangements or modification under subsection (4) or (8) include the likely effect of the arrangements in question, or (as the case may be) those arrangements as proposed to be modified, on the ability of the holders of regional Channel 3 licences to maintain the quality and range—

(a) of the regional programmes (as defined by section 21A(9)) included in each regional Channel 3 service, and
(b) of the other programmes included in each service which contribute to the regional character of the service."

(3) For subsection (10) there is substituted—

"(10) Without prejudice to the generality of their power to refuse to approve any arrangements or modification under subsection (4) or (8), the Commission shall refuse to do so if—

(a) they are not satisfied that the arrangements in question, or (as the case may be) those arrangements as proposed to be modified, would be appropriate for the purpose mentioned in subsection (1), or
(b) it appears to them that the arrangements in question, or (as the case may be) those arrangements as proposed to be modified, would be likely to prejudice the ability of the holder of any regional Channel 3 licence to comply with—

(i) any condition imposed in pursuance of section 33(1), for the purpose of securing the implementation of proposals relating to the matters specified in section 16(2)(c), or

(ii) any condition imposed in pursuance of subsection (3) of section 21A in relation to the matters specified in paragraph (a) of that subsection."

DEFINITION
"1990 Act; the": s.147(1).

GENERAL NOTE
Consistently with s.78, this section amends the Commission's powers to supervise the Channel 3 networking agreement by requiring them to examine, when deciding whether to approve proposed changes to the agreement, the effect on regional programming. In addition, the ability of individual licence holders to meet their regional programming commitments must not be prejudiced.

Channel 4 and S4C

Funding of Sianel Pedwar Cymru

80.—(1) For section 61 of the 1990 Act there is substituted—

"**Funding of Welsh Authority**

61.—(1) The Secretary of State shall, in the year 1998 and in each subsequent year, pay to the Welsh Authority the prescribed amount as increased by the appropriate percentage.

(2) In this section "the prescribed amount" means the 1997 amount or such amount as may from time to time be prescribed under subsection (4).

(3) In this section "the 1997 amount" means the amount paid by the Secretary of State to the Welsh Authority by way of interim payment for the year 1997 (under this section as originally enacted).

(4) The Secretary of State may, if he is satisfied that it is appropriate to do so having regard to the cost to the Welsh Authority of transmitting S4C and the service referred to in section 57(1A)(a), by order provide that the prescribed amount is to be an amount which is greater than the 1997 amount and is specified in the order.

(5) Before making an order under subsection (4) the Secretary of State shall consult the Welsh Authority.

(6) In this section "the appropriate percentage", in relation to any year ("the relevant year"), means the percentage which corresponds to the percentage increase between—

(a) the retail prices index for November 1996, and
(b) the retail prices index for the month of November in the year preceding the relevant year;

and for this purpose "the retail prices index" has the same meaning as in section 19(10).

(7) Any sums required by the Secretary of State under this section shall be paid out of money provided by Parliament.

(8) An order shall not be made under subsection (4) unless a draft of the order has been laid before and approved by a resolution of each House of Parliament."

(2) In section 62 of the 1990 Act for "sections 26 and 61" there is substituted "section 26".

(3) Subsections (1) and (2) shall not have effect in relation to payments for any year before 1998.

(4) No payment shall be made to or by the Welsh Authority under subsection (3) or (4) of section 61 of the 1990 Act (as originally enacted) for the year 1997; and in this subsection "the Welsh Authority" has the same meaning as in the 1990 Act.

DEFINITION
"1990 Act; the": s.147(1).

GENERAL NOTE
The new s.61 of the 1990 Act will place the funding of the Welsh Authority on a similar basis to that of the BBC. Instead of tying its income to national television revenue, the funding which will be due at the beginning of 1997 will be used as a starting point for future payments. They will consist of that amount, uprated annually by reference to the Retail Price Index.

Public service fund of Sianel Pedwar Cymru

81.—(1) After section 61 of the 1990 Act there is inserted—

"**Welsh Authority public service fund**

61A.—(1) The Welsh Authority shall not exercise their powers under section 57(1A)(b) before such date (in this section referred to as "the notified date") as they may notify to the Secretary of State for the purposes of this section.

(2) All amounts received by the Welsh Authority under section 61 on or after the notified date shall be kept by the Authority in a separate fund (in this section referred to as "the public service fund") which may be applied only for the purposes of their functions under section 57(1) or (1A)(a).

(3) No S4C company shall receive any direct or indirect subsidy from the public service fund.

(4) The Welsh Authority shall secure that no television programme which has been wholly or partly financed out of the public service fund is included in a television programme service provided by an S4C company before it is first broadcast on S4C or in the service referred to in section 57(1A)(a).

(5) On the notified date—

(a) all the assets then held by the Welsh Authority other than cash, together with the appropriate proportion of any cash then held by them, shall be taken to be comprised in the public service fund, and

(b) the remainder of any cash then held by the Authority shall be taken to be comprised in a general fund.

(6) In subsection (5)(a) "the appropriate proportion" means the proportion which, in the last financial year in respect of which a statement of accounts has been prepared under paragraph 12(1) of Schedule 6 before the notified date, the total amount received by the Welsh Authority under section 61 bears to the total amount of its income from all sources."

(2) In paragraph 12 of Schedule 6 of the 1990 Act (accounts and audit) after sub-paragraph (1) there is inserted—

"(1A) The statement of accounts must deal separately with the public service fund referred to in section 61A of this Act and with the general fund referred to in subsection (5)(b) of that section.".

DEFINITION
"1990 Act; the": s.147(1).

GENERAL NOTE
The Welsh Authority has been empowered to engage in commercial ventures under the new s.57(1A) of the 1990 Act, introduced by s.84(3), and the new s.61A of the 1990 Act is intended to ensure that no cross-subsidy occurs between public and commercial funds.

Multiplex revenue to be taken into account in connection with funding of Channel Four Television Corporation

82.—(1) Section 26 of the 1990 Act (revenue deficits of Channel Four Television Corporation to be funded by Channel 3 licensees) is amended as follows.

(2) For subsection (2) there is substituted—

"(2) For the purposes of this section the Corporation's prescribed minimum income for any year shall be 14 per cent. of the total television revenues for that year.

(2A) For the purposes of this section "total television revenues" means, in relation to any year, the aggregate of—

(a) the qualifying revenues for that year of the following, namely—
(i) all holders of Channel 3 or Channel 5 licences;
(ii) the Welsh Authority; and
(iii) the Corporation itself; and

(b) the multiplex revenues for that year in respect of all holders of multiplex licences (within the meaning of Part I of the Broadcasting Act 1996)."

(3) After subsection (9) there is inserted—

"(9A) Sections 13(4) to (6) and 14 of, and Schedule 1 to, the Broadcasting Act 1996 shall have effect, with any necessary modifications, for the purpose of enabling the Commission to estimate or determine the multiplex revenue in respect of any person for any year for the purposes of this section."

Definition
"1990 Act; the": s.147(1).

Application of excess revenues of Channel Four Television Corporation

83.—(1) Section 27 of the 1990 Act (application of excess revenues of Channel Four Television Corporation) is amended as follows.

(2) In subsection (1)—

(a) in paragraph (a), for "one half" there is substituted "50 per cent.", and

(b) in paragraph (b), for "the other half" there is substituted "the remainder of the excess".

(3) In subsection (3)—

(a) in paragraph (a), for "half" there is substituted "50 per cent.", and

(b) in paragraph (b), for "the other half" there is substituted "the remainder of that amount".

(4) After subsection (6) there is inserted—

"(7) The Secretary of State may by order—

(a) amend subsection (1)(a) by substituting for the percentage for the time being specified there a percentage specified in the order, which may be nil but must not be more than 50 per cent., and

(b) amend subsection (3)(a) by substituting for the percentage for the time being specified there a percentage specified in the order, which may be nil.

(8) An order shall not be made under subsection (7) unless a draft of it has been laid before and approved by a resolution of each House of Parliament."

Definition
"1990 Act; the": s.147(1).

General Note

The amendment to s.27 of the 1990 Act reflects a vigorous debate about the current funding formula for Channel 4. At present, the Government does not propose to alter the basic arrangement but the amendment gives it greater flexibility to do so and it will be possible, by order, to vary the percentages payable by Channel 4 or the Channel 3 companies to each other. It will also be possible to alter the amount of Channel 4 revenue which is paid into the statutory reserve fund. The Government's intention is to cap that reserve fund at what it considers an appropriate amount and, while it remains at that level, to allow Channel 4 to retain the relevant income.

Extension of powers of Channel Four Television Corporation and Sianel Pedwar Cymru

84.—(1) In section 24 of the 1990 Act (Channel 4 to be provided as licensed service) after subsection (4) there is inserted—

"(5) The Corporation shall also have power—

(a) (subject to and in accordance with Part I of the Broadcasting Act 1996) to arrange for the broadcasting of Channel 4 in digital form in any part of the United Kingdom as a qualifying service (within the meaning of that Part), and

(b) to establish qualifying companies, to purchase or otherwise acquire shares, stocks or other securities of qualifying companies and to assist any qualifying company.

(6) In subsection (5)(b) "qualifying company" means any company (whether incorporated under the law of the United Kingdom or of any other country) which is or will be wholly or mainly engaged in one or more of the following activities—

(a) the provision of one or more services which are licensed by the Commission or by the Radio Authority or which, if provided in the United Kingdom, would be required to be so licensed,

(b) activities incidental to such provision, and

(c) the holding of shares in any other company which is wholly or mainly engaged in such provision or in activities incidental to such provision."

(2) In paragraph 1 of Schedule 3 to the 1990 Act (status and capacity of Channel Four Television Corporation) after sub-paragraph (3) there is inserted—

"(4) Section 24(5)(b) of this Act shall not be taken to limit the Corporation's power by virtue of sub-paragraph (3) to do such things and enter into such transactions as are incidental or conducive to the discharge of their functions under section 24(1) or (5)(a)."

(3) In section 57 of the 1990 Act (functions and duties of Welsh Authority) after subsection (1) there is inserted—

"(1A) The Welsh Authority shall also have power—

(a) (subject to and in accordance with Part I of the Broadcasting Act 1996) to provide a further service as a qualifying service (within the meaning of that Part), and to arrange for the broadcasting of that service in digital form, and

(b) to establish qualifying companies, to purchase or otherwise acquire shares, stocks or other securities of qualifying companies and to assist any qualifying company.

(1B) In subsection (1A)(b) "qualifying company" means any company (whether incorporated under the law of the United Kingdom or of any other country) which is or will be wholly or mainly engaged in one or more of the following activities—

(a) the provision of one or more services which are licensed by the Commission or by the Radio Authority or which, if provided in the United Kingdom, would be required to be so licensed,

(b) activities incidental to such provision, and

(c) the holding of shares in any other company which is wholly or mainly engaged in such provision or in activities incidental to such provision."

(4) In paragraph 1 of Schedule 6 to the 1990 Act (status and capacity of Welsh Authority) after sub-paragraph (2) there is inserted—

"(3) Section 57(1A)(b) of this Act shall not be taken to limit the Authority's power by virtue of sub-paragraph (2) to do such things and enter into such transactions as are incidental or conducive to the discharge of their functions under section 57(1) or (1A)(a)."

DEFINITION

"1990 Act; the": s.147(1).

Miscellaneous amendments relating to television broadcasting

Restricted television services

85. After section 42 of the 1990 Act there is inserted—

"CHAPTER IIA

RESTRICTED SERVICES

Restricted services

42A. In this Part "restricted service" means a service which—

(a) consists in the broadcasting of television programmes for a particular establishment or other defined location, or a particular event, in the United Kingdom, and

(b) is provided on a frequency or frequencies assigned to the Commission under section 65.

Licensing etc. of restricted services

42B.—(1) An application for a licence to provide a restricted service shall be made in such manner as the Commission may determine, and shall be accompanied by such fee (if any) as the Commission may determine.

(2) Subject to subsections (3) and (4), sections 40 to 42 shall apply in relation to such a licence as they apply in relation to a licence to provide a Channel 3 service.

(3) In its application to a licence to provide a restricted service, section 41 shall have effect with the omission of subsection (2); and the maximum amount which the holder of such a licence may be required to pay by way of a financial penalty imposed in pursuance of subsection (1)(a) of that section shall not exceed whichever is the greater of—

(a) £50,000, and

(b) the amount determined under subsection (4).

(4) The amount referred to in subsection (3)(b) is—

(a) in a case where a penalty under section 41(1)(a) has not previously been imposed on the holder of the licence during any period for which his licence has been in force ("the relevant period"), 3 per cent. of the qualifying revenue for his last complete accounting period (as determined in accordance with section 19(2) to (6)); and

(b) in any other case, 5 per cent. of the qualifying revenue for that accounting period (as so determined);

and in relation to a person whose first complete accounting period falling within the relevant period has not yet ended, paragraphs (a) and (b) above shall be construed as referring to 3, or (as the case may be) 5, per cent. of the amount which the Commission estimate to be the qualifying revenue for that accounting period (as so determined)."

DEFINITION

"1990 Act; the": s.147(1).

GENERAL NOTE

This section introduces provision for restricted television services similar to those which are already established for radio. They are intended to apply to community services or special events.

Award of certain licences subject to conditions

86.—(1) After section 17 of the 1990 Act there is inserted—

"**Award of Channel 3 licence subject to conditions**

17A.—(1) The Commission may, when awarding a Channel 3 licence to any person, make the grant of the licence to him conditional on his compliance before the grant with such specified requirements relating to the financing of the service as appear to them to be appropriate, having regard to—

(a) any duties which are or may be imposed on them, or on the licence holder, by or under this Act, and

(b) any information provided to them under section 15(3)(g) by the person to whom the licence is awarded as to his projected financial position during the period for which the licence would be in force.

(2) Where the Commission determine that any condition imposed by them in relation to a Channel 3 licence in pursuance of subsection (1) has not been satisfied, section 17 shall (subject to subsection (3)) have effect as if the person to whom the licence was awarded had not made an application for it.

(3) Section 17 shall not so have effect if the Commission decide that it would be desirable to publish a fresh notice under section 15(1) in respect of the grant of the licence."

(2) In section 51 of the 1990 Act (procedure to be followed by Commission in connection with consideration of applications for, and awarding of, licences to provide additional services), in subsection (3)—

(a) for "section 17" there is substituted "sections 17 and 17A", and

(b) for "it applies" there is substituted "they apply".

(3) After section 76 of the 1990 Act there is inserted—

"**Award of local delivery licence subject to conditions**

76A.—(1) The Commission may, when awarding a local delivery licence to any person, make the grant of the licence to him conditional on his compliance before the grant with such specified requirements relating to the financing of the service as appear to them to be appropriate, having regard to—

(a) any duties which are or may be imposed on them, or on the licence holder, by or under this Act, and

(b) any information provided to them under section 74(3)(d) by the person to whom the licence is awarded as to his projected financial position during the period for which the licence would be in force.

(2) Where the Commission determine that any condition imposed by them in relation to a local delivery licence in pursuance of subsection (1) has not been satisfied, section 76 shall (subject to subsection (3)) have effect as if the person to whom the licence was awarded had not made an application for it.

(3) Section 76 shall not so have effect if the Commission decide that it would be desirable to publish a fresh notice under section 74(1) in respect of the grant of the licence."

DEFINITION

"1990 Act; the": s.147(1).

GENERAL NOTE

See the note to s.10. The new ss.17A and 76A of the 1990 Act make similar provision in respect of Channel 3 and local delivery service licences.

Ancillary services

87. Section 48 of the 1990 Act (additional services) is amended in paragraph (c) of subsection (3) by the addition after the words "their contents" of the words "or relate to the promotion or listing of such programmes".

DEFINITION

"1990 Act; the": s.147(1).

GENERAL NOTE

This amendment allows fuller programmes listings to be included in existing teletext services and enables further information and delivery control to be offered more generally.

Enforcement of licences to provide non-domestic satellite services

88.—(1) Section 45 of the 1990 Act (licensing etc. of non-domestic satellite services) is amended as follows.

(2) In subsection (5), for "and" there is substituted "to".

(3) In subsection (6), for "shall instead be £50,000" there is substituted—

"shall not exceed whichever is the greater of—

(a) £50,000, and

(b) the amount determined under subsection (6A).

(6A) The amount referred to in subsection (6)(b) is—

(a) in a case where a penalty under section 41(1)(a) has not previously been imposed on the holder of the licence during any period for which his licence has been in force ("the relevant period"), 3 per cent. of the qualifying revenue for his last complete accounting period (as determined in accordance with section 19(2) to (6)); and

(b) in any other case, 5 per cent. of the qualifying revenue for that accounting period (as so determined);

and in relation to a person whose first complete accounting period falling within the relevant period has not yet ended, paragraphs (a) and (b) above shall be construed as referring to 3, or (as the case may be) 5, per cent. of the amount which the Commission estimate to be the qualifying revenue for that accounting period (as so determined)."

(4) Subsections (8) and (9) are omitted.

DEFINITION

"1990 Act; the": s.147(1).

Power of Independent Television Commission to suspend licence to provide non-domestic satellite service

89. After section 45 of the 1990 Act there is inserted—

"**Special power of revocation and suspension on certain grounds in case of licence to provide non-domestic satellite service**

45A.—(1) If the Commission are satisfied—

(a) that the holder of a licence to provide a non-domestic satellite service has included in the service one or more programmes containing material likely to encourage or incite to crime or to lead to disorder,

(b) that he has thereby failed to comply with a condition included in the licence in pursuance of section 6(1)(a), and

(c) that the failure is such as to justify the revocation of the licence,

they shall serve on the holder of the licence a notice under subsection (2).

(2) A notice under this subsection is a notice—

(a) stating that the Commission are satisfied as mentioned in subsection (1),

(b) specifying the respects in which, in their opinion, the licence holder has failed to comply with the condition mentioned in paragraph (b) of that subsection,

(c) stating that the Commission may revoke his licence after the end of the period of twenty-one days beginning with the date on which the notice is served on the licence holder,

(d) informing the licence holder of his right to make representations to the Commission within that period about the matters complained of, and

(e) suspending the licence as from the time when the notice is served on the licence holder until the revocation takes effect or the Commission decide not to revoke the licence.

(3) If the Commission, having considered any representations about the matters complained of made to them within the period referred to in subsection (2)(c) by the licence holder, are satisfied that it is necessary in the public interest to revoke the licence in question, they shall serve on the licence holder a notice revoking the licence.

(4) A notice under subsection (3) shall not take effect until the end of the period of twenty-eight days beginning with the day on which that notice was served on the licence holder.

(5) Section 42 (as applied by section 45(5)) shall not have effect in relation to the revocation of a licence in pursuance of a notice under subsection (1)."

DEFINITION

"1990 Act; the": s.147(1).

GENERAL NOTE

The special power of revocation contained in this section provides more immediate and effective control over non-domestic satellite services which breach s.6(1)(a) of the 1990 Act. It differs from the power in s.42 of that Act by allowing an immediate suspension of the offending service, prior to representations, rather than threatening the licensee with revocation unless the failure is remedied.

Enforcement of licences to provide licensable programme services

90.—(1) Section 47 of the 1990 Act (licensing etc. of licensable programme services) is amended as follows.

(2) In subsection (8), for "and" there is substituted "to".

(3) In subsection (9), for "shall instead be £50,000" there is substituted—

"shall not exceed whichever is the greater of—

(a) £50,000, and

(b) the amount determined under subsection (9A).

(9A) The amount referred to in subsection (9)(b) is—

(a) in a case where a penalty under section 41(1)(a) has not previously been imposed on the holder of the licence during any period for which his licence has been in force ("the relevant period"), 3 per cent. of the qualifying revenue for his last complete accounting period (as determined in accordance with section 19(2) to (6)); and

(b) in any other case, 5 per cent. of the qualifying revenue for that accounting period (as so determined);

and in relation to a person whose first complete accounting period falling within the relevant period has not yet ended, paragraphs (a) and (b) above shall be construed as referring to 3, or (as the case may be) 5, per cent. of the amount which the Commission estimate to be the qualifying revenue for that accounting period (as so determined)."

(4) Subsections (11) and (12) are omitted.

DEFINITION
"1990 Act; the": s.147(1).

Certain delivery services to carry certain broadcasts

91.—(1) After section 78 of the 1990 Act there is inserted—

"Inclusion of certain services in local delivery service provided by digital means

78A.—(1) Where the Commission are satisfied, in the case of a local delivery service by means of which one or more of the services specified in section 72(2) is delivered in digital form, that it would be appropriate, having regard to the extent of the use and proposed use of digital technology in the provision of the service, for the service to be treated as a digital local delivery service for the purposes of this section, they shall serve a notice to that effect on the holder of the licence to provide the service.

(2) The Commission shall do all that they can to secure that, subject to subsection (3) and to any exceptions for which the Secretary of State, after consultation with the Commission, the BBC and the Welsh Authority, may by order provide, every digital local delivery service provided by any person in any area includes, by the reception and immediate re-transmission of the broadcasts—

(a) the programmes included in each relevant service, and

(b) if the area for which the local delivery service is provided falls wholly or partly in Wales, the programmes included in the appropriate Welsh service.

(3) The Commission may exempt any digital local delivery service from the requirement to include any service ("the broadcast service") if it appears to the Commission that, at the place where the holder of the licence to provide the local delivery service receives or would receive the broadcast service, the broadcast service is not capable of being received at a level satisfying such technical standards as the Commission may from time to time determine.

(4) Where a relevant service provided for reception in an area for which a digital local delivery service is provided consists in the broadcasting for simultaneous reception of programmes contained in two or more programme schedules, then, so far as relating to that relevant service, the duty in subsection (2) shall be subject to the limitation in whichever of subsections (5) and (6) is appropriate.

(5) Where the programmes contained in one of the programme schedules are broadcast for reception in a greater part of the area than the programmes contained in the other schedule or any of the other schedules, the duty in subsection (2) so far as so relating shall extend only to the programmes contained in the first-mentioned schedule.

(6) Where subsection (5) does not apply, the duty in subsection (2) so far as so relating shall extend only to the programmes contained in such one of the programme schedules as the relevant broadcasting body may determine.

(7) For the purposes of this section Channel 3 shall be taken to be a single service consisting in the broadcasting for simultaneous reception of programmes contained in several programme schedules.

(8) Each broadcaster shall provide any person providing a digital local delivery service with such assistance as he may reasonably require in relation to the technical arrangements for the re-transmission in pursuance of this section of the broadcasts of that broadcaster.

(9) In this section—

"the appropriate Welsh service" means the service referred to in section 57(1A)(a) or, if no such service is being broadcast, S4C;

"broadcaster" means the Welsh Authority or any person providing a relevant service;

"digital local delivery service" means any local delivery service in respect of which the Commission have given a notice under subsection (1);

"the relevant broadcasting body" means—

(a) in relation to any service provided by the BBC, the BBC, and

(b) in relation to any service licensed by the Commission, the Commission;

"relevant service" means any of the following services—

(a) Channel 3, Channel 4 and Channel 5,

(b) the teletext service referred to in section 49(2), and

(c) the television broadcasting services and teletext service provided by the BBC.

(10) Expressions used in subsections (7) and (9) and in Part I of this Act have the same meaning in those provisions as in that Part.

(11) An order under subsection (2) shall be subject to annulment in pursuance of a resolution of either House of Parliament."

(2) In Part III of Schedule 12 to the 1990 Act (transitional provisions relating to existing cable services), for paragraph 4 there is substituted—

"4.—(1) The Commission shall do all that they can to secure that, subject to sub-paragraph (2) and to any exceptions for which the Secretary of State, after consultation with the Commission, the BBC and the Welsh Authority, may by order provide, every diffusion service provided by any person in any area under a relevant licence includes, by the reception and immediate re-transmission of the broadcasts, the programmes included in each relevant service provided for reception in that area.

(2) The Commission may exempt any diffusion service from the requirement to include any relevant service if it appears to the Commission that, at the place where the holder of the licence to provide the diffusion service receives or would receive the relevant service, the relevant service is not capable of being received at a level satisfying such technical standards as the Commission may from time to time determine.

(3) Where a relevant service provided for reception in an area for which a diffusion service is provided consists in the broadcasting for simultaneous reception of programmes contained in two or more programme schedules, then, so far as relating to that relevant service, the duty in sub-paragraph (1) shall be subject to the limitation in whichever of sub-paragraphs (4) and (5) is appropriate.

(4) Where the programmes contained in one of the programme schedules are broadcast for reception in a greater part of the area than the programmes contained in the other schedule or any of the other schedules, the duty in sub-paragraph (1) so far as so relating shall extend only to the programmes contained in the first-mentioned schedule.

(5) Where sub-paragraph (4) does not apply, the duty in sub-paragraph (1) so far as so relating shall extend only to the programmes contained in such one of the programme schedules as the relevant broadcasting body may determine.

(6) For the purposes of this paragraph Channel 3 shall be taken to be a single service consisting in the broadcasting for simultaneous reception of programmes contained in several programme schedules.

(7) Each person providing a relevant service ("the broadcaster") shall provide any person providing a diffusion service with such assistance as he may reasonably require in relation to the technical arrangements for the re-transmission in pursuance of this paragraph of the broadcasts of that broadcaster.

(8) In this paragraph—

"the relevant broadcasting body" means—

(a) in relation to any service provided by the BBC, the BBC, and

(b) in relation to any service licensed by the Commission, the Commission;

"relevant service" means any of the following services—

(a) Channel 3, Channel 4 and S4C,

(b) the teletext service referred to in section 49(2) of this Act, and

(c) the two television broadcasting services provided by the BBC on the passing of the Broadcasting Act 1996 and the teletext service provided by the BBC at that time.

(9) Expressions used in sub-paragraphs (6) and (8) and in Part I of this Act have the same meaning in those sub-paragraphs as in that Part.

(10) An order under sub-paragraph (1) shall be subject to annulment in pursuance of a resolution of either House of Parliament.

4A.—(1) Where the Commission are satisfied, in the case of any diffusion service which is provided under a relevant licence and by means of which one or more of the services specified in section 72(2) of this Act is delivered in digital form, that it would be appropriate, having regard to the extent of the use and proposed use of digital technology in the provision of the service, for the service to be treated as a digital diffusion service for the purposes of this paragraph, they shall serve a notice to that effect on the holder of the licence to provide the service; and in this paragraph "digital diffusion service" means a diffusion service in respect of which such a notice has been served.

(2) Subsections (2) to (8) of section 78A of this Act shall have effect in relation to a digital diffusion service as they have effect in relation to a digital local delivery service (within the meaning of that section); and nothing in paragraph 4 shall have effect in relation to a digital diffusion service."

DEFINITION

"1990 Act; the": s.147(1).

GENERAL NOTE

The new s.71A of the 1990 Act introduces a "must carry" requirement for digital local delivery services. They will have to carry BBC1, BBC2, Channels 3 and 5 and, where practicable, Channel 5. In Wales, S4C Digital must also be included. The section also makes provision for existing diffusion services by enabling the Commission to determine which programmes fall within their "must carry" obligations. The intention is not to require them to include Channel 5 or any of the new digital services. In Sched. 9, which takes effect under s.138, provision is made for the copyright implications of the obligation.

Sound broadcasting

Renewal of licences to provide national radio services

92. After section 103 of the 1990 Act there is inserted—

"**Renewal of national licences**

103A.—(1) A national licence may (subject to the following provisions of this section) be renewed on one occasion for a period of eight years beginning with the date of renewal.

(2) An application for the renewal of a national licence under subsection (1) may be made by the licence holder not earlier than three years before the date on which it would otherwise cease to be in force and not later than the relevant date.

(3) Where any such application is made before the relevant date—

(a) if no simulcast radio service provided by the applicant is being broadcast in digital form when the application is made, the Authority shall postpone the consideration of the application until the relevant date or, if earlier, the date on which the broadcasting of such a service in that form begins, and

(b) in any other case, the Authority may postpone the consideration of the application for so long as they think appropriate having regard to subsection (8).

(4) Where an application for the renewal of a national licence has been duly made to the Authority, they shall (subject to subsection (5)) grant the application if, but only if—

(a) the Authority are satisfied that the applicant would, if his licence were renewed, provide a national service which complied with the conditions included in the licence in pursuance of section 106 (whether as originally imposed or as varied under that section),

(b) the applicant has given notice to the Authority under section 41(2)(a) of the Broadcasting Act 1996 of his intention to provide a service for broadcasting in digital form, and

(c) a simulcast radio service provided by the applicant is being broadcast in digital form or the Authority are satisfied that by the relevant date the applicant has done all that it would in the circumstances be reasonable to expect him to do by that date to procure the broadcasting of such a service within such time as the Authority consider reasonable.

(5) Section 100(4) to (6) shall apply in relation to an applicant for the renewal of a national licence as those provisions apply in relation to such an applicant as is mentioned in section 100(4), but as if any reference to the awarding of such a licence to the applicant were a reference to the renewal of the applicant's licence under this section.

(6) On the grant of any application under this section the Authority—

(a) may, in a case where a simulcast radio service provided by the applicant is not yet being broadcast in digital form on the relevant date, determine a date by which the broadcasting of such a service in that form must begin;

(b) shall determine an amount which is to be payable to the Authority by the applicant in respect of the first complete calendar year falling within the period for which the licence is to be renewed; and

(c) may specify a different percentage from that specified under section 98(1)(d)(ii) as the percentage of qualifying revenue for each accounting period of his that will be payable by the applicant in pursuance of section 102(1)(c) during the period for which the licence is to be renewed.

(7) The amount determined by the Authority under subsection (6)(b) in connection with the renewal of a licence shall be such amount as would, in their opinion, be payable to them by virtue of section 102(1)(a) if they were granting a fresh licence to provide the national service in question.

(8) Where the Authority have granted a person's application under this section they shall formally renew his licence not later than the relevant date or, if that is not reasonably practicable (whether because subsection (3)(a) precluded the consideration of the application before that date or for any other reason), as soon after that date as is reasonably practicable; and they shall not so renew his licence unless they have notified him of—

(a) any date determined by them under subsection (6)(a),
(b) the amount determined by them under subsection (6)(b), and
(c) any percentage specified by them under subsection (6)(c),
and he has, within such period as is specified in that notification, notified them that he consents to the licence being renewed on those terms.

(9) Where a national licence has been renewed under this section
(a) any conditions included in it in pursuance of section 102 shall have effect during the period for which the licence has been renewed—
(i) as if the amount determined by the Authority under subsection (6)(b) were an amount specified in a cash bid submitted by the licence holder, and
(ii) subject to any determination made under subsection (6)(c);
(b) (subject to paragraph (a)) that section shall have effect in relation to the period for which the licence has been renewed as it has effect in relation to the period for which a national licence is originally in force;
(c) where the Authority have determined a date under subsection (6)(a), they shall include in the licence as renewed a condition requiring a simulcast radio service to be broadcast in digital form throughout the period beginning with the date determined under subsection (6)(a) and ending with the date on which the licence (as renewed) is to expire; and
(d) the reference in section 111(4) to the end of the period for which a national licence is to continue in force shall, in relation to the licence, be construed as a reference to the end of the period for which it has been renewed.

(10) Subsections (6)(a) and (9)(c) do not prejudice the generality of section 48(3)(b) of the Broadcasting Act 1996 (power to vary national licence to include conditions relating to digital broadcasting).

(11) In this section—
"simulcast radio service" has the same meaning as in Part II of the Broadcasting Act 1996;
"the relevant date", in relation to a national licence, means the date which the Authority determine to be that by which they would need to publish a notice under section 98(1) if they were to grant, as from the date on which that licence would expire if not renewed, a fresh licence to provide the national service formerly provided under that licence."

DEFINITION
"1990 Act; the": s.147(1).

GENERAL NOTE
In return for investing in digital technology, the existing holders of national radio licences are to be offered the opportunity to renew, for which this section makes provision.

Variation of local radio licence following change of control

93. After section 106 of the 1990 Act there is inserted—

"**Variation of local licence following change of control**

106A.—(1) Any local licence granted to a body corporate before the commencement of this section shall be taken to include—

(a) a condition requiring the body to give the Authority advance notice of any proposals known to the body that may give rise to a relevant change of control, and

(b) a condition requiring the body to provide the Authority, in such manner and at such times as they may reasonably require, with such information as they may require for the purposes of exercising their functions under subsection (3).

(2) Subsection (3) applies in relation to any local licence which—

(a) was granted before the commencement of this section,

(b) is held by a body corporate, and

(c) has not previously been varied under that subsection.

(3) Where, in relation to any local licence to which this subsection applies—

(a) the Authority receive notice, in pursuance of a condition imposed under subsection (1) or section 88(2)(d), of any proposals that may give rise to a relevant change of control, or

(b) a relevant change of control takes place (whether or not that change has been previously notified to the Authority),

the Authority may vary the licence, by a notice served on the licence holder, so as to include in the licence such conditions as they consider appropriate for the purpose of ensuring that the character of the local service is maintained after the relevant change of control.

(4) Subject to subsection (5), any new or varied condition imposed under subsection (3) in relation to any matter may be more onerous than any existing condition imposed under section 106(1) in relation to that matter; and in this subsection "existing condition" means a condition of the licence as it has effect, or had effect, before the relevant change of control.

(5) The Authority may not under subsection (3) include any new or varied condition in a licence unless the new condition or the condition as varied is one which (with any necessary modifications) would have been satisfied by the licence holder—

(a) during the three months immediately before the relevant date, or

(b) if the Authority consider that the performance of the licence holder during that period is not typical of its performance during the twelve months before the relevant date, during such other period of three months during those twelve months as they may notify in writing to the licence holder;

and for the purposes of this subsection "the relevant date" is the date of the relevant change of control or, if earlier, the date on which the Authority exercise their powers under subsection (3).

(6) The Authority shall not serve a notice on any body under subsection (3) unless they have given it a reasonable opportunity of making representations to them about the variation.

(7) Where, in any case falling within paragraph (a) of subsection (3), a notice under that subsection is served before the change to which it relates takes place, the variation shall not take effect until the change to which it relates takes place.

(8) The power in subsection (1) of section 106 to vary conditions imposed under that subsection includes power to vary conditions imposed under subsection (3).

(9) In this section "relevant change of control" means a change in the persons having control over the body holding the licence."

DEFINITION

"1990 Act; the": s.147(1).

GENERAL NOTE

This section is similar to s.78 but, being directed to local radio, the Authority is empowered to intervene where a change of ownership has a likely or actual effect on the local character of the service.

Renewal of licences to provide local radio services

94.—(1) After section 104 of the 1990 Act there is inserted—

"**Renewal of local licences**

104A.—(1) A local licence may (subject to the following provisions of this section) be renewed on one occasion for a period of eight years beginning with the date of renewal.

(2) No application for the renewal of a local licence under subsection (1) may be made before the Authority first publish a notice pursuant to section 50(2) of the Broadcasting Act 1996 inviting applications for a licence to provide a relevant local radio multiplex service.

(3) Subject to subsection (2), an application for the renewal of a local licence under subsection (1) may be made by the licence holder not earlier than three years before the date on which it would otherwise cease to be in force and not later than the relevant date.

(4) The applicant must, in his application or at any time before the consideration of his application, nominate—

(a) a local digital sound programme service provided or to be provided by him, and

(b) a relevant local radio multiplex service,

but may not nominate together a local digital sound programme service and a local radio multiplex service if another local licence held by him includes a condition in pursuance of subsection (12) relating to the broadcasting of that local digital sound programme service by that local radio multiplex service.

(5) Where an application for the renewal of a local licence has been duly made to the Authority, they shall grant the application if—

(a) they are satisfied that the applicant would, if his licence were renewed, provide a local service which complied with the conditions included in the licence in pursuance of section 106 (whether as originally imposed or as varied under that section), and

(b) the nominated local digital sound programme service provided by the applicant is being broadcast by means of the nominated local radio multiplex service.

(6) Where the condition specified in subsection (5)(a) is satisfied, the Authority may grant the application even though the condition specified in subsection (5)(b) is not satisfied if—

(a) the applicant holds a licence to provide local digital sound programme services,

(b) a licence to provide the nominated local radio multiplex service has been awarded, and

(c) it appears to the Authority that, under a contract between the applicant and the person to whom that licence has been awarded, the applicant is obliged to provide the nominated local digital sound programme service for broadcasting by means of the nominated local radio multiplex service.

(7) The Authority may in any case postpone consideration of the application until the relevant date.

(8) If, at the relevant date, the condition specified in subsection (5)(b) is not satisfied, and any of the conditions specified in subsection (6) is not satisfied, the Authority may postpone consideration of the application for such period not exceeding twelve months as they think appropriate.

(9) Where the Authority postpone consideration of an application under this section for any period beyond the relevant date (the "postponement period"), they shall extend the period for which the licence is in force by a period equal to the postponement period; and section 86(3) shall not limit the powers of the Authority under this subsection.

(10) On the grant of any application under this section the Authority shall—

(a) where the nominated local digital sound programme service provided by the applicant is not being broadcast by means of the nominated local radio multiplex service, determine a date by which that service must have begun to be so broadcast; and

(b) specify a fee payable to the Authority in respect of the renewal.

(11) Where the Authority have granted a person's application under this section they shall formally renew his licence as soon afterwards as is reasonably practicable; and they shall not so renew his licence unless they have notified him of—

(a) any date determined by them under subsection (10)(a), and

(b) the renewal fee specified by them under subsection (10)(b),

and he has, within such period as is specified in that notification, notified them that he consents to the licence being renewed on those terms.

(12) Where the Authority renew a licence under this section they shall include in the licence as renewed a condition requiring the licence holder to do all that he can to ensure that the nominated local digital sound programme service is broadcast by means of the nominated local radio multiplex service throughout the period beginning with whichever is the later of—

(a) the date on which the licence would expire if not renewed, and

(b) any date determined by them under subsection (10)(a),

and ending with the date on which the licence (as renewed) is to expire.

(13) In this section—

(a) "local digital sound programme service" has the same meaning as in Part II of the Broadcasting Act 1996;

(b) "nominated" means nominated by the applicant under subsection (4);

(c) "relevant date", in relation to a local licence, means the date which the Authority determine to be that by which they would need to publish a notice under section 104(1) if they were to grant, as from the date on which that licence would expire if not renewed, a fresh licence to provide the local service formerly provided under that licence; and

(d) "relevant local radio multiplex service", in relation to a local licence, means a local radio multiplex service (within the meaning of Part II of the Broadcasting Act 1996) with a coverage area which to a significant extent includes the coverage area of the local service provided under the local licence; and for this purpose "coverage area", in relation to a service, has the meaning given by paragraph 3A of Part I of Schedule 2.

Special application procedure for local licences

104B.—(1) Where—

(a) a local licence is due to expire (otherwise than by virtue of section 110),
(b) the local service provided under the licence falls within category B, C or D of the Table in paragraph 9 of Part III of Schedule 2, and
(c) the Authority propose to grant a further licence to provide the service in question,

the Authority may if they think fit publish a notice under subsection (2) instead of a notice under section 104(1).

(2) A notice under this subsection is a notice—
(a) stating that the Authority propose to grant a further licence to provide a specified local service,
(b) specifying the area or locality in the United Kingdom for which the service is to be provided,
(c) inviting declarations of intent to apply for a licence to provide the service,
(d) specifying the closing date for such declarations, and
(e) specifying—
(i) the application fee payable on any declaration made in pursuance of the notice, and
(ii) a deposit of such amount as the Authority may think fit.

(3) A declaration of intent made in pursuance of a notice under subsection (2) must be in writing and accompanied by the application fee and deposit specified under subsection (2)(e)(i) and (ii).

(4) Where the Authority receive a declaration of intent in accordance with the provisions of this section from a person other than the licence holder in relation to the service in question, they shall—
(a) publish a notice under section 104(1),
(b) specify—
(i) in relation to persons who have made a declaration of intent in accordance with the provisions of this section, no further application fee, and
(ii) in relation to all other applicants, an application fee of the same amount as the fee referred to in subsection (2)(e)(i), and
(c) repay the deposit referred to in subsection (2)(e)(ii) to every person—
(i) who has made a declaration of intent in accordance with the provisions of this section, and
(ii) who duly submits an application in pursuance of the notice referred to in paragraph (a).

(5) Where the Authority receive a declaration of intent in accordance with the provisions of this section from the licence holder in relation to the service in question, and no such declaration from any other person, they shall—
(a) invite the licence holder to apply for the licence in such manner as they may determine (but without requiring any further application fee), and
(b) on receiving an application duly made by him, repay to him the deposit referred to in subsection (2)(e)(ii).

(6) The Secretary of State may by order amend subsection (1) by removing any of the categories of local service for the time being specified in that subsection, or by substituting for any of such categories any one or more categories of local service set out in the Table in paragraph 9 of Part III of Schedule 2.

(7) Any order under subsection (6) shall be subject to annulment in pursuance of a resolution of either House of Parliament."

(2) In section 104 of the 1990 Act (applications for licences other than national licences), subsections (5) and (6)(a) shall cease to have effect.

DEFINITION
"1990 Act; the": s.147(1).

GENERAL NOTE
As with national radio, under s.92, there is provision for preferential renewal of local licences in return for investment in digital services. This section also introduces a special procedure for enabling the Authority to gauge interest in the continuance of local radio licences prior to re-advertisement.

Financing of Gaelic sound programmes

95.—(1) Section 183 of the 1990 Act (financing of television programmes in Gaelic out of Gaelic Television Fund) is amended as mentioned in subsections (2) to (6).

(2) In subsection (2), for "Gaelic Television Fund" there is substituted "Gaelic Broadcasting Fund".

(3) In subsection (3), for "Comataidh Telebhisein Gaidhlig (the Gaelic Television Committee)" there is substituted "Comataidh Craolaidh Gaidhlig (the Gaelic Broadcasting Committee)".

(4) After subsection (3) there is inserted—

"(3A) Before making any appointment under subsection (3) the Commission shall consult the Radio Authority.".

(5) In subsection (4), in each of paragraphs (a)(i) and (b), after "television" there is inserted "and sound".

(6) In subsection (6)—

(a) after "will" there is inserted "—
(a)"; and

(b) for "but" there is substituted—
"(b) widen the range and improve the quality of sound programmes in Gaelic that are broadcast for reception in Scotland;
but".

(7) In Part II of Schedule 1 to the House of Commons Disqualification Act 1975 (bodies of which all members are disqualified) there is inserted at the appropriate place—
"Comataidh Craolaidh Gaidhlig".

DEFINITION
"1990 Act; the": s.147(1).

GENERAL NOTE
This section renames the Gaelic Television Fund the "Gaelic Broadcasting Fund" and extends its scope to include the financing of radio programmes in Gaelic.

Power of Radio Authority to suspend licence to provide satellite service

96. After section 111A of the 1990 Act there is inserted—

"**Power to suspend licence to provide satellite service**

111B.—(1) If the Authority are satisfied—

(a) that the holder of a licence to provide a satellite service has included in the service one or more programmes containing material likely to encourage or incite to crime or to lead to disorder,

(b) that he has thereby failed to comply with the condition included in the licence in pursuance of section 90(1)(a), and

(c) that the failure is such as to justify the revocation of the licence,

they shall serve on the holder of the licence a notice under subsection (2).

(2) A notice under this subsection is a notice—

(a) stating that the Authority are satisfied as mentioned in subsection (1),

(b) specifying the respects in which, in their opinion, the licence holder has failed to comply with the condition mentioned in paragraph (b) of that subsection,

(c) stating that the Authority may revoke his licence after the end of the period of twenty-one days beginning with the date on which the notice is served on the licence holder,

(d) informing the licence holder of his right to make representations to the Authority within that period about the matters complained of, and

(e) suspending the licence as from the time when the notice is served on the licence holder until the revocation takes effect or the Authority decide not to revoke the licence.

(3) If the Authority, having considered any representations about the matters complained of made to them within the period referred to in subsection (2)(c) by the licence holder, are satisfied that it is necessary in the public interest to revoke the licence in question, they shall serve on the licence holder a notice revoking the licence.

(4) A notice under subsection (3) shall not take effect until the end of the period of twenty-eight days beginning with the day on which that notice was served on the licence holder.

(5) Section 111 shall not have effect in relation to the revocation of a licence in pursuance of a notice under subsection (1)."

DEFINITION

"1990 Act; the": s.147(1).

GENERAL NOTE

See the note to s.89, to which this section corresponds.

PART IV

SPORTING AND OTHER EVENTS OF NATIONAL INTEREST

Listed events

97.—(1) For the purposes of this Part, a listed event is a sporting or other event of national interest which is for the time being included in a list drawn up by the Secretary of State for the purposes of this Part.

(2) The Secretary of State shall not at any time draw up, revise or cease to maintain such a list as is mentioned in subsection (1) unless he has first consulted—

(a) the BBC,

(b) the Welsh Authority,

(c) the Commission, and

(d) in relation to a relevant event, the person from whom the rights to televise that event may be acquired;

and for the purposes of this subsection a relevant event is a sporting or other event of national interest which the Secretary of State proposes to include in, or omit from, the list.

(3) As soon as he has drawn up or revised such a list as is mentioned in subsection (1), the Secretary of State shall publish the list in such manner as he considers appropriate for bringing it to the attention of—

(a) the persons mentioned in subsection (2), and

(b) every person who is the holder of a licence granted by the Commission under Part I of the 1990 Act or a digital programme licence granted by them under Part I of this Act.

(4) In this section "national interest" includes interest within England, Scotland, Wales or Northern Ireland.

(5) The addition of any relevant event to such a list as is mentioned in subsection (1) shall not affect—

(a) the validity of any contract entered into before the date on which the Secretary of State consulted the persons mentioned in subsection (2) in relation to the proposed addition, or

(b) the exercise of any rights acquired under such a contract.

(6) The list drawn up by the Secretary of State for the purposes of section 182 of the 1990 Act, as that list is in force immediately before the commence-

ment of this section, shall be taken to have been drawn up for the purposes of this Part.

DEFINITIONS
"BBC; the": s.147(1).
"Commission; the": s.105(1).
"digital programme licence": s.39(1).
"1990 Act; the": s.147(1).

GENERAL NOTE
The provisions in this section and the remainder of this Part of the Act replace those in the repealed s.182 of the 1990 Act. The aim is to enable live coverage of sporting and other events of national interest by the public service terrestrial broadcasters, notwithstanding the increasing number of arrangements between sporting and events organisers and cable or satellite channels, whereby the latter acquire exclusive rights to show certain events on a subscription basis. Initially, the listed events will continue to be those listed for the purposes of the 1990 Act; they include, for example, the FA Cup Final, the Wimbledon tennis finals and the Derby.

Categories of service

98.—(1) For the purposes of this Part television programme services shall be divided into two categories as follows—

(a) such of the services specified in subsection (2) as are provided without any charge being made for the reception of programmes included in the service, and

(b) all television programme services not for the time being falling within paragraph (a).

(2) The services referred to in subsection (1)(a) are—

(a) regional and national Channel 3 services,

(b) Channel 4, and

(c) the television broadcasting services provided by the BBC.

(3) The Secretary of State may by order amend subsection (2) so as to remove any service from, or add any service to, the services specified in it.

(4) An order under subsection (3) shall be subject to annulment in pursuance of a resolution of either House of Parliament.

DEFINITIONS
"BBC; the": s.147(1).
"Channel 4": s.105(1).
"national Channel 3 service": s.105(1).
"regional Channel 3 service": s.105(1).
"television broadcasting service": s.105(1); s.71(1) of the Broadcasting Act 1990.
"television programme service": s.105(1); s.71(1) of the Broadcasting Act 1990.

GENERAL NOTE
The two categories of service, created in this section, provide the basis for subsequent sections which prohibit any one category from having exclusive access to a listed event. The first category, in subs. (1)(a), refers to programme providers with universal reach. The second category, in subs. (1)(b), refers to the remainder who include cable and satellite programme providers but also Channel 5 which will, initially at least, cover only 70 per cent of the U.K.

Contract for exclusive right to televise listed event to be void

99.—(1) Any contract entered into after the commencement of this section under which a television programme provider acquires rights to televise the whole or any part of a listed event live for reception in the United Kingdom, or in any area of the United Kingdom, shall be void so far as it purports, in relation to the whole or any part of the event or in relation to reception in the United Kingdom or any area of the United Kingdom, to grant those rights exclusively to any one television programme provider.

(2) In this Part "television programme provider" means the BBC, the Welsh Authority or any person who is the holder of any licence under Part I of the 1990 Act or a digital programme licence under Part I of this Act.

(3) For the purposes of this section rights to televise the whole or any part of an event live for reception in any area granted to a television programme provider are granted exclusively if the person granting them—

(a) has not granted any such right to any other television programme provider, and

(b) is precluded by the terms of the contract from doing so.

DEFINITIONS

"digital programme licence": s.39(1).
"listed event": s.97(1); s.105(1).
"live": s.105(1).

GENERAL NOTE

This section prevents a television programme provider from obtaining an exclusive right to televise a listed event live.

Contract for televising listed event must specify category of service

100.—(1) Any contract entered into after the commencement of this section shall be void so far as it purports to grant to a television programme provider rights to televise the whole or any part of a listed event live for reception in the United Kingdom, or any area of the United Kingdom, unless the contract complies with subsection (2).

(2) A contract complies with this subsection if the terms of the contract allow the television programme provider to include the live coverage of the listed event—

(a) only in a television programme service falling within paragraph (a) of subsection (1) of section 98, or

(b) only in a television programme service falling within paragraph (b) of that subsection.

DEFINITIONS

"listed event": s.97(1); s.105(1).
"live": s.105(1).
"television programme provider": s.99(2); s.105(1).
"television programme service": s.105(1); s.71(1) of the Broadcasting Act 1990.

GENERAL NOTE

This section requires all contracts, for the rights to televise listed events live, to specify to which category of service the rights attach. Where an event organiser wishes to sell rights for coverage on both public service and subscription channels, the rights must be agreed separately. The section further lays the basis for s.101, which prohibits a programme provider in one category from including live coverage of a listed event in its programmes, unless a programme provider in the other category has also acquired the rights to that live coverage.

Restriction on televising of listed event

101.—(1) A person providing a service falling within either of the categories set out in subsection (1) of section 98 ("the first service") for reception in the United Kingdom or in any area of the United Kingdom shall not, without the previous consent of the Commission, include in that service live coverage of the whole or any part of a listed event unless—

(a) another person, who is providing a service falling within the other category set out in that subsection ("the second service"), has acquired the right to include in the second service live coverage of the whole of the event or of that part of the event, and

(b) the area for which the second service is provided consists of or includes the whole, or substantially the whole, of the area for which the first service is provided.

(2) The Commission may revoke any consent given by them under subsection (1).

(3) Failure to comply with subsection (1) shall not affect the validity of any contract.

(4) Subsection (1) shall not have effect where the television programme provider providing the first service is exercising rights acquired before the commencement of this section.

DEFINITIONS

"Commission; the": s.105(1).
"listed event": s.97(1); s.105(1).
"live": s.105(1).
"television programme provider": s.99(2); s.105(1).

GENERAL NOTE

Generally, live coverage of a listed event must be provided by both categories of service, provided that the coverage area for each service substantially coincides with the other. However, the Commission are effectively given the power to supervise the arrangements because they may approve broadcasting by only one category of service. If a programme provider from only one category is interested in acquiring the rights to show the event live, permission is likely to be given. But if the failure to acquire the rights is the result of inability to agree a reasonable price, the Commission may refuse permission and thereby negate the value of the rights acquired by the programme provider in the other category. Guidance, as to the way in which the Commission's decisions will be made in such circumstances, will be provided in the code to be drawn up under s.104. This section does not apply to pre-existing rights, by subs. (4).

Power of Commission to impose penalty

102.—(1) If the Commission—

(a) are satisfied that the holder of a licence under Part I of the 1990 Act or a digital programme licence under Part I of this Act has failed to comply with subsection (1) of section 101, and

(b) are not satisfied that in all the circumstances it would be unreasonable to expect him to have complied with that subsection,

they may require him to pay, within a specified period, a specified financial penalty to the Commission.

(2) If the Commission are satisfied that, in connection with an application for consent under subsection (1) of section 101, the holder of a licence under Part I of the 1990 Act or a digital programme licence under Part I of this Act has—

(a) provided them with information which was false in a material particular, or

(b) withheld any material information with the intention of causing the Commission to be misled,

they may require him to pay, within a specified period, a specified financial penalty to the Commission.

(3) The amount of any financial penalty imposed on any person under subsection (1) or (2) shall not exceed the amount produced by multiplying the relevant consideration by the prescribed multiplier.

(4) In subsection (3)—

(a) "the relevant consideration" means an amount determined by the Commission as representing so much of any consideration paid by the person on whom the penalty is being imposed as is attributable to the acquisition of the rights to televise the event in question, and

(b) "the prescribed multiplier" means such number as the Secretary of State may from time to time by order prescribe.

(5) An order under subsection (4)(b) shall be subject to annulment in pursuance of a resolution of either House of Parliament.

(6) Where the Commission receive any amount payable to them by virtue of subsection (1) or (2), that amount shall not form part of the revenues of the Commission but shall be paid into the Consolidated Fund.

(7) Any amount payable by any person to the Commission by virtue of subsection (1) or (2) shall be recoverable by them as a debt due to them from that person.

DEFINITIONS
"Commission; the": s.105(1).
"digital programme licence": s.39(1).
"1990 Act; the": s.147(1).

Report to Secretary of State

103.—(1) If the Commission—

(a) are satisfied that a broadcasting body has failed to comply with subsection (1) of section 101, and

(b) are not satisfied that in all the circumstances it would be unreasonable to expect the body to have complied with that subsection,

they shall make a report on the matter to the Secretary of State.

(2) If the Commission are satisfied that, in connection with an application for consent under subsection (1) of section 101, a broadcasting body has—

(a) provided them with information which was false in a material particular, or

(b) withheld any material information with the intention of causing the Commission to be misled,

they shall make a report on the matter to the Secretary of State.

(3) In this section "broadcasting body" means the BBC or the Welsh Authority.

DEFINITIONS
"BBC; the": s.147(1).
"Commission; the": s.105(1).

Code of guidance

104.—(1) The Commission shall draw up, and may from time to time review, a code—

(a) specifying the circumstances in which the televising of listed events generally, or of a particular listed event, is, or is not, to be treated as live for the purposes of this Part, and

(b) giving guidance as to the matters which they will take into account in determining—

(i) whether to give or revoke their consent under section 101(1), or

(ii) for the purposes of section 102(1) or 103(1), whether in all the circumstances it is unreasonable to expect a television programme provider to comply with section 101(1).

(2) In exercising their powers under this Part, the Commission shall have regard to the provisions of the code.

(3) Before drawing up or revising the code the Commission shall consult such persons as appear to the Commission to be appropriate.

(4) As soon as the Commission have drawn up or revised such a code, the Commission shall publish the code in such manner as they consider appropriate for bringing it to the attention of—

(a) the BBC,

(b) the Welsh Authority,

(c) every person from whom the rights to televise a listed event may be acquired, and

(d) every person who is the holder of a licence granted by the Commission under Part I of the 1990 Act or a digital programme licence granted by them under Part I of this Act.

DEFINITIONS
"Commission; the": s.105(1).
"digital programme licence": s.39(1).
"listed event": s.97(1); s.105(1).
"live": s.105(1).
"television programme provider": s.99(2); s.105(1).

GENERAL NOTE
The code will deal with two matters: the question of what counts as live and the reasonableness of arrangements for obtaining rights to show listed events live. There is provision for widespread consultation and, in practice, the code is likely to reflect many features of the existing voluntary code.

Interpretation of Part IV and supplementary provisions

105.—(1) In this Part (unless the context otherwise requires)—
"Channel 4" has the same meaning as in Part I of the 1990 Act;
"the Commission" means the Independent Television Commission;
"listed event" has the meaning given by section 97(1);
"live" shall be construed in accordance with the code drawn up under section 104;
"national Channel 3 service" and "regional Channel 3 service" have the same meaning as in Part I of the 1990 Act;
"television broadcasting service" has the same meaning as in Part I of the 1990 Act;
"television programme provider" has the meaning given by section 99(2);
"television programme service" has the same meaning as in Part I of the 1990 Act.

(2) Section 182 of the 1990 Act (certain events not to be shown on pay-per-view terms) shall cease to have effect.

PART V

THE BROADCASTING STANDARDS COMMISSION

Establishment of Broadcasting Standards Commission

The Broadcasting Standards Commission

106.—(1) There shall be a commission, to be known as the Broadcasting Standards Commission (in this Part referred to as "the BSC").

(2) The BSC shall consist of—
(a) a chairman appointed by the Secretary of State,
(b) a deputy chairman or two deputy chairmen so appointed, and
(c) such number of other members appointed by the Secretary of State as he may from time to time determine,

but so that the total number of members does not exceed fifteen.

(3) Schedule 3 shall have effect with respect to the BSC.

GENERAL NOTE
This section establishes a new Broadcasting Standards Commission which constitutes a merger of the former Broadcasting Complaints Commission (hereinafter referred to as the BCC) and the Broadcasting Standards Council (hereinafter referred to as the Council). The merger was prompted by criticism about the perceived weakness of the BCC and general public confusion about the roles of the two agencies (see: Department of National Heritage, *The Future of the BBC: Serving the Nation, Competing World-Wide* (1994) Cm. 2621 (White Paper), chap. 7; National Heritage Committee, *The Future of the BBC, Second Report*, (1993–94) H.C. 77-I, paras. 41–45). The Government accepted, however, that the BCC's complaints functions were distinct from those of the Council and the consideration of fairness and privacy, separate from standards of decency, is retained in this Act. The Council's former function is retained and has not been extended to that of protecting more general consumer interests in programming.

Unjust or unfair treatment or unwarranted infringement of privacy

Preparation by BSC of code relating to avoidance of unjust or unfair treatment or interference with privacy

107.—(1) It shall be the duty of the BSC to draw up, and from time to time review, a code giving guidance as to principles to be observed, and practices to be followed, in connection with the avoidance of—

(a) unjust or unfair treatment in programmes to which this section applies, or

(b) unwarranted infringement of privacy in, or in connection with the obtaining of material included in, such programmes.

(2) It shall be the duty of each broadcasting or regulatory body, when drawing up or revising any code relating to principles and practice in connection with programmes, or in connection with the obtaining of material to be included in programmes, to reflect the general effect of so much of the code referred to in subsection (1) (as for the time being in force) as is relevant to the programmes in question.

(3) The BSC shall from time to time publish the code (as for the time being in force).

(4) Before drawing up or revising the code. the BSC shall consult—

(a) each broadcasting or regulatory body, and

(b) such other persons as appear to the BSC to be appropriate.

(5) This section applies to—

(a) any programme broadcast by the BBC,

(b) any programme broadcast by the Welsh Authority or included in the service referred to in section 57(1A)(a) of the 1990 Act, and

(c) any programme included in a licensed service.

DEFINITIONS

"BBC; the": s.147(1).
"broadcasting body": s.130(1).
"BSC; the": s.130(1).
"licensed service": s.130(1).
"programme": s.130(1).
"unjust or unfair treatment": s.130(1).
"1990 Act; the": s.147(1).

GENERAL NOTE

This section is based on the former duty to publish a code in respect of programme standards, in the former s.152 of the 1990 Act but, for the first time, applies it to matters of fairness and privacy. This requirement will offer some means of remedying one of the principal defects of the BCC's practice, that it did not properly articulate the principles on which its adjudications were based. It may be expected, however, that the new code on fairness and privacy will incorporate much of the BCC's general approach, which could be gleaned from its annual reports.

Portrayal of violence or sexual conduct etc.

Preparation by BSC of code relating to broadcasting standards generally

108.—(1) It shall be the duty of the BSC to draw up, and from time to time review, a code giving guidance as to—

(a) practices to be followed in connection with the portrayal of violence in programmes to which this section applies,

(b) practices to be followed in connection with the portrayal of sexual conduct in such programmes, and

(c) standards of taste and decency for such programmes generally.

(2) It shall be the duty of each broadcasting or regulatory body, when drawing up or revising any code relating to standards and practice for programmes, to reflect the general effect of so much of the code referred to in subsection (1) (as for the time being in force) as is relevant to the programmes in question.

(3) The BSC shall from time to time publish the code referred to in subsection (1) (as for the time being in force).

(4) Before drawing up or revising the code the BSC shall consult—

(a) each broadcasting or regulatory body, and

(b) such other persons as appear to the BSC to be appropriate.

(5) This section applies to—

(a) any programme broadcast by the BBC,

(b) any programme broadcast by the Welsh Authority or included in the service referred to in section 57(1A)(a) of the 1990 Act,

(c) any programme included in a licensed service, and

(d) any programme included in so much of a local delivery service licensed under Part II of the 1990 Act as is, by virtue of section 79(2) or (4) of that Act, treated for certain purposes as the provision of a service licensed under Part I of that Act.

(6) The code drawn up by the Broadcasting Standards Council under section 152 of the 1990 Act, as that code is in force immediately before the commencement of this section, shall be taken to have been drawn up by the BSC under this section.

Definitions

"BBC; the": s.147(1).
"broadcasting body": s.130(1).
"BSC; the": s.130(1).
"local delivery service": s.130(1); s.72 of the Broadcasting Act 1990.
"licensed service": s.130(1).
"programme": s.130(1).
"regulatory body": s.130(1).
"sexual conduct": s.130(1).
"1990 Act; the": s.147(1).

General Note

This section reenacts the former s.152 of the 1990 Act. The reference in subs. (5)(d) is to foreign satellite services.

Monitoring by BSC of broadcasting standards

109.—(1) It shall be the duty of the BSC to monitor programmes to which section 108 applies with a view to enabling the BSC to make reports on the portrayal of violence and sexual conduct in, and the standards of taste and decency attained by, such programmes generally.

(2) Subject to section 125(2), the BSC may make reports on the matters specified in subsection (1) on such occasions as they think fit; and any such report may include an assessment of either or both of the following, namely—

(a) the attitudes of the public at large towards the portrayal of violence or sexual conduct in, or towards the standards of taste and decency attained by, programmes to which section 108 applies, and

(b) any effects or potential effects on the attitudes or behaviour of particular categories of persons of the portrayal of violence or sexual conduct in such programmes or of any failure on the part of such programmes to attain standards of taste and decency.

(3) The BSC may publish any report made by them in pursuance of subsection (1).

(4) The BSC shall have the further duty of monitoring, so far as is reasonably practicable, all television and sound programmes which are transmitted or sent from outside the United Kingdom but are capable of being received there, with a view to ascertaining—

(a) how violence and sexual conduct are portrayed in those programmes, and

(b) the extent to which those programmes meet standards of taste and decency.

DEFINITIONS

"BSC; the": s.130(1).
"programme": s.130(1).
"programmes to which section 108 applies": s.130(2)(b).
"sexual conduct": s.130(1).

GENERAL NOTE

This section reenacts the former s.153 of the 1990 Act, with two exceptions. One is s.153(5) whose provisions are now found in s.126 of this Act. The other is the omission of the power, given to the Council in the former s.153(1)(b) of the 1990 Act, to start the complaints procedure of its own motion.

Complaints

General functions of BSC in relation to complaints

110.—(1) Subject to the provisions of this Part, it shall be the duty of the BSC to consider and adjudicate on complaints which are made to them in accordance with sections 111 and 114 and relate—

(a) to unjust or unfair treatment in programmes to which section 107 applies, or
(b) to unwarranted infringement of privacy in, or in connection with the obtaining of material included in, such programmes.

(2) Subject to those provisions, it shall also be the duty of the BSC to consider, and make findings on, complaints which are made to them in accordance with sections 113 and 114 and relate—

(a) to the portrayal of violence or sexual conduct in programmes to which section 108 applies, or
(b) to alleged failures on the part of such programmes to attain standards of taste and decency.

(3) In exercising their functions under subsection (1), the BSC shall take into account any relevant provisions of the code maintained by them under section 107; and in exercising their functions under subsection (2) they shall take into account any relevant provisions of the code maintained by them under section 108.

(4) In this Part—

"a fairness complaint" means a complaint to the BSC in respect of any of the matters referred to in subsection (1)(a) and (b), and

"a standards complaint" means a complaint to the BSC in respect of any of the matters referred to in subsection (2)(a) and (b).

DEFINITIONS

"BSC; the": s.130(1).
"programme": s.130(1).
"programmes to which section 107 applies": s.130(2)(a).
"programmes to which section 108 applies": s.130(2)(b).
"sexual conduct": s.130(1).
"unjust or unfair treatment": s.130(1).

GENERAL NOTE

Elements of the former ss.145 and 154 are combined in this section. Subsection (3) is new but clarifies what was the Council's practice in any event.

Subs. (1)(b)

In *R. v. BCC, ex p. Lloyd, The Times*, October 16, 1992, it was held that the BCC's function was to hear complaints about invasions of privacy during the preparation of programmes, regardless of whether the material was subsequently broadcast.

In *R. v. BCC, ex p. Granada Television, The Times*, December 14, 1994 (the Wade and Sandiford case), the Court of Appeal held that the BCC had been given a wide latitude to determine what constitutes privacy. Thus, the BCC's view, that the resurrection of material which had previously been in the public domain and which referred to the complainant's family, could be an infringement of privacy, was found to be not unreasonable.

Complaints of unfair treatment etc.

111.—(1) A fairness complaint may be made by an individual or by a body of persons, whether incorporated or not, but, subject to subsection (2), shall not be entertained by the BSC unless made by the person affected or by a person authorised by him to make the complaint for him.

(2) Where the person affected is an individual who has died, a fairness complaint may be made by his personal representative or by a member of the family of the person affected, or by some other person or body closely connected with him (whether as his employer, or as a body of which he was at his death a member, or in any other way).

(3) Where the person affected is an individual who is for any reason both unable to make a complaint himself and unable to authorise another person to do so for him, a fairness complaint may be made by a member of the family of the person affected, or by some other person or body closely connected with him (whether as his employer, or as a body of which he is a member, or in any other way).

(4) The BSC shall not entertain, or proceed with the consideration of, a fairness complaint if it appears to them that the complaint relates to the broadcasting of the relevant programme, or to its inclusion in a licensed service, on an occasion more than five years after the death of the person affected, unless it appears to them that in the particular circumstances it is appropriate to do so.

(5) The BSC may refuse to entertain a fairness complaint if it appears to them not to have been made within a reasonable time after the last occasion on which the relevant programme was broadcast or, as the case may be, included in a licensed service.

(6) Where, in the case of a fairness complaint, the relevant programme was broadcast or included in a licensed service after the death of the person affected, subsection (5) shall apply as if at the end there were added "within five years (or such longer period as may be allowed by the BSC in the particular case under subsection (4)) after the death of the person affected".

(7) The BSC may refuse to entertain—

(a) a fairness complaint which is a complaint of unjust or unfair treatment if the person named as the person affected was not himself the subject of the treatment complained of and it appears to the BSC that he did not have a sufficiently direct interest in the subject-matter of that treatment to justify the making of a complaint with him as the person affected, or

(b) a complaint made under subsection (2) or (3) by a person other than the person affected or a person authorised by him, if it appears to the BSC that the complainant's connection with the person affected is not sufficiently close to justify the making of the complaint by him.

DEFINITIONS

"BSC; the": s.130(1).
"fairness complaint": s.110(4); s.130(1).
"licensed service": s.130(1).
"person affected; the": s.130(1).
"programme": s.130(1).
"relevant programme; the": s.130(1).

GENERAL NOTE

This section re-enacts the provisions from the former s.144(1) to (4) of the 1990 Act, with the exception of certain jurisdictional limitations which are now found in s.114.

Subs. (7)

The complainant must have a direct interest in what was actually broadcast and cannot use the complaints procedure to gain a right of access to the media: see *R. v. BCC, ex p. BBC, The Times*, May 26, 1994 (the Howard case). Consistently, where an organisation, with a broad political agenda to pursue, has only a collateral concern with a programme which affects an individual whose interests it broadly represents, that will not constitute a direct interest of the organisation: see *R. v. BCC, ex p. BBC, The Times*, February 24 and 27, 1995 (the National Council for One-Parent Families case).

Committee to consider fairness complaints

112. The BSC shall appoint a committee, consisting of members of the BSC, to discharge the functions of the BSC in relation to the consideration of fairness complaints.

DEFINITIONS

"BSC; the": s.130(1).
"fairness complaint": s.110(4); s.130(1).

Complaints relating to taste and decency, etc.

113.—(1) The BSC shall not entertain a standards complaint which is made—

(a) where the relevant programme is a television programme, more than two months after the relevant date, or
(b) where the relevant programme is a sound programme, more than three weeks after that date,

unless it appears to them that in the particular circumstances it is appropriate for them to do so.

(2) In subsection (1) "the relevant date" means—

(a) the date on which the relevant programme was broadcast by a broadcasting body or included in a licensed service, or
(b) where it has been so broadcast or included on more than one occasion, the date on which it was last so broadcast or included.

(3) Where, apart from this subsection, there would fall to be considered by the BSC two or more standards complaints which appear to them to raise the same, or substantially the same, issue or issues in relation to a particular programme, the BSC may determine that those complaints shall be treated for the purposes of this Part as constituting a single complaint.

DEFINITIONS

"broadcasting body": s.130(1).
"BSC; the": s.130(1).
"licensed service": s.130(1).
"programme": s.130(1).
"relevant programme; the": s.130(1).
"standards complaint": s.110(4); s.130(1).

GENERAL NOTE

This section re-enacts element of the former s.154 of the 1990 Act, with the exception of the jurisdictional limitations which are now found in s.114, together with the former power to issue complaints of their own motion, which has not been renewed.

On the general question of jurisdiction, the purpose of the fairness complaints procedure has always been to provide a remedy for individual grievances. This was accepted in *R. v. Broadcasting Complaints Commission, ex p. Owen* [1985] Q.B. 1153, although the Divisional Court held that the words of the statute (in identical terms to the present Act) could apply to a complaint that broadcasters had not been politically impartial. Nevertheless, the Court went on to hold that the BCC had acted reasonably, in the *Wednesbury* sense, in declining jurisdiction on other grounds available to it, that it was inappropriate for it to hear the complaint because of its political implications. That other ground, and more general aspects of jurisdiction, is now found in s.114, which can be expected to be interpreted in the same way.

Supplementary provisions as to making of complaints of either kind

114.—(1) A fairness complaint or a standards complaint must be in writing, or in such other form as the BSC may allow, and must give particulars of the matters complained of.

(2) The BSC shall not entertain, or proceed with the consideration of, a fairness complaint or a standards complaint if it appears to them—

(a) that the matter complained of is the subject of proceedings in a court of law in the United Kingdom, or

(b) that the matter complained of is a matter in respect of which the complainant or, in the case of a fairness complaint, the person affected has a remedy by way of proceedings in a court of law in the United Kingdom, and that in the particular circumstances it is not appropriate for the BSC to consider a complaint about it, or

(c) that the complaint is frivolous, or

(d) that for any other reason it is inappropriate for them to entertain, or proceed with the consideration of, the complaint.

DEFINITIONS

"BSC; the": s.130(1).
"fairness complaint": s.110(4); s.130(1).
"person affected; the": s.130(1).
"standards complaint": s.110(4); s.130(1).

GENERAL NOTE

See the note to s.113, below.

Consideration of fairness complaints

115.—(1) Subject to the provisions of sections 111 and 114, every fairness complaint made to the BSC shall be considered by them either at a hearing or, if they think fit, without a hearing.

(2) Hearings under this section shall be held in private; and where such a hearing is held in respect of a fairness complaint, each of the following persons shall be given an opportunity to attend and be heard, namely—

(a) the complainant,

(b) the relevant person,

(c) where the relevant programme was included in a licensed service, the appropriate regulatory body,

(d) any person not falling within any of paragraphs (a) to (c) who appears to the BSC to have been responsible for the making or provision of that programme, and

(e) any other person who the BSC consider might be able to assist at the hearing.

(3) Before the BSC proceed to consider a fairness complaint they shall send a copy of it—

(a) to the relevant person, and

(b) where the relevant programme was included in a licensed service, to the appropriate regulatory body.

(4) Where the relevant person receives from the BSC a copy of the complaint, it shall be the duty of that person, if so required by the BSC—

(a) to provide the BSC with a visual or sound recording of the relevant programme or of any specified part of it, if and so far as the relevant person has such a recording in his possession;

(b) to make suitable arrangements for enabling the complainant to view or hear the relevant programme, or any specified part of it, if and so far as the relevant person has in his possession a visual or sound recording of it;

(c) to provide the BSC and the complainant with a transcript of so much of the relevant programme, or of any specified part of it, as consisted of speech, if and so far as the relevant person is able to do so;

(d) to provide the BSC and the complainant with copies of any documents in the possession of the relevant person, being the originals or copies of any correspondence between that person and the person affected or the complainant in connection with the complaint;

(e) to furnish to the BSC and the complainant a written statement in answer to the complaint.

(5) Where the relevant person receives from the BSC a copy of a fairness complaint, it shall also be the duty of that person, if so required by the BSC—

(a) where the relevant person is a broadcasting body, to arrange for one or more of the governors, members or employees of the body to attend the BSC and assist them in their consideration of the complaint, or

(b) where the relevant person is a body other than a broadcasting body, to arrange for one or more of the following, namely—

(i) the persons who take part in the management or control of the body, or

(ii) the employees of the body,

to attend the BSC and assist them in their consideration of the complaint, or

(c) where the relevant person is an individual, to attend, or to arrange for one or more of his employees to attend, the BSC and assist them in their consideration of the complaint.

(6) Where the relevant person receives from the BSC a copy of a fairness complaint and, in connection with the complaint, the BSC make to any other person a request to which this subsection applies, it shall be the duty of the relevant person to take such steps as he reasonably can to ensure that the request is complied with.

(7) Subsection (6) applies to the following requests by the BSC to any such other person as is there mentioned, namely—

(a) a request to make suitable arrangements for enabling the complainant and any member or employee of the BSC to view or hear the relevant programme, or any specified part of it, if and so far as the person requested has in his possession a visual or sound recording of it;

(b) a request to provide the BSC and the complainant with a transcript of so much of the relevant programme, or of any specified part of it, as consisted of speech, if and so far as the person requested is able to do so;

(c) a request to provide the BSC and the complainant with copies of any documents in the possession of the person requested, being the originals or copies of any correspondence between that person and the person affected or the complainant in connection with the complaint;

(d) a request to furnish to the BSC and the complainant a written statement in answer to the complaint;

(e) a request to attend, or (where the person requested is not an individual) to arrange for a representative to attend, the BSC and assist them in their consideration of the complaint.

(8) Where the BSC have adjudicated on a fairness complaint, they shall send a statement of their findings to the complainant.

(9) In this section "the relevant person" means—

(a) in a case where the relevant programme was broadcast by a broadcasting body, that body, and

(b) in a case where the relevant programme was included in a licensed service, the licence holder providing the service.

DEFINITIONS
"appropriate regulatory body; the": s.130(1).
"broadcasting body": s.130(1).
"BSC; the": s.130(1).
"fairness complaint": s.110(4); s.130(1).
"licensed service": s.130(1).
"person affected; the": s.130(1).
"programme": s.130(1).
"relevant programme; the": s.130(1).

GENERAL NOTE
The former s.145 of the 1990 Act is re-enacted in this section, except that provision for the payment of expenses is now found in s.118 of this Act.

Consideration of standards complaints

116.—(1) Subject to the provisions of sections 113 and 114, every standards complaint made to the BSC shall be considered by them either without a hearing or, if they think fit, at a hearing (and any such hearing shall be held in private unless the BSC decide otherwise).

(2) Where a hearing is held in respect of a standards complaint, each of the following persons shall be given an opportunity to attend and be heard, namely—
(a) the complainant,
(b) the relevant person,
(c) where the relevant programme was included in a licensed service, the appropriate regulatory body,
(d) any person not within any of paragraphs (a) to (c) who appears to the BSC to have been responsible for the making or provision of that programme, and
(e) any other person who the BSC consider might be able to assist at the hearing.

(3) In a case where the BSC have made a determination in respect of any complaints under subsection (3) of section 113, subsection (2)(a) shall be construed as referring to such one or more of the persons who made those complaints as the BSC may determine.

(4) Before the BSC proceed to consider a standards complaint they shall send a copy of it—
(a) to the relevant person, and
(b) where the relevant programme was included in a licensed service, to the appropriate regulatory body.

(5) Where the relevant person receives from the BSC a copy of the complaint, it shall be the duty of that person, if so required by the BSC—
(a) to provide the BSC with a visual or sound recording of the relevant programme or any specified part of it, if and so far as he has such a recording in his possession;
(b) to provide the BSC with a transcript of so much of the relevant programme, or of any specified part of it, as consisted of speech, if and so far as he is able to do so;
(c) to provide the BSC with copies of any documents in his possession, being the originals or copies of any correspondence between him and the complainant in connection with the complaint;
(d) to furnish to the BSC a written statement in answer to the complaint.

(6) In this section—
"licensed service" includes so much of a local delivery service licensed under Part II of the 1990 Act as is, by virtue of section 79(2) or (4) of that Act, treated for certain purposes as the provision of a service licensed under Part I of that Act, and
"the relevant person" means—

(a) in a case where the relevant programme was broadcast by a broadcasting body, that body, and

(b) in a case where the relevant programme was included in a licensed service, the licence holder providing that service.

DEFINITIONS

"appropriate regulatory body; the": s.130(1).
"broadcasting body": s.130(1).
"BSC; the": s.130(1).
"licensed service": s.130(1).
"local delivery service": s.130(1); s.72 of the Broadcasting Act 1990.
"programme": s.130(1).
"relevant programme; the": s.130(1).
"standards complaint": s.110(4); s.130(1).
"1990 Act; the": s.147(1).

GENERAL NOTE

This section re-enacts the substance of the former s.155 of the 1990 Act. The reference in subs. (6) is to foreign satellite services.

Duty to retain recordings

117. For the purposes of sections 115 and 116 of this Act and of section 167 of the 1990 Act (power to make copies of recordings in connection with certain offences) it shall be the duty of each broadcasting body to retain a recording of every television or sound programme which is broadcast by that body—

(a) where it is of a television programme, during the period of 90 days beginning with the day of the broadcast, and

(b) where it is of a sound programme, during the period of 42 days beginning with the day of the broadcast.

DEFINITIONS

"broadcasting body": s.130(1).
"programme": s.130(1).
"1990 Act; the": s.147(1).

GENERAL NOTE

This section re-enacts the duty in the former s.145(5) of the 1990 Act.

Power to pay allowances to persons attending hearings

118. The BSC may, if they think fit, make to any person who attends them in connection with a fairness complaint or a standards complaint such payments as they think fit by way of travelling allowance or subsistence allowance where expenditure on travelling or, as the case may be, on subsistence is necessarily incurred by him for the purpose of enabling him so to attend.

DEFINITIONS

"BSC; the": s.130(1).
"fairness complaint": s.110(4); s.130(1).
"standards complaint": s.110(4); s.130(1).

Publication of BSC's findings

119.—(1) Where the BSC have—

(a) considered and adjudicated upon a fairness complaint, or

(b) considered and made their findings on a standards complaint,

they may give directions of the kind specified in subsection (2).

(2) Those directions are—

(a) where the relevant programme was broadcast by a broadcasting body, directions requiring that body to publish the matters mentioned in subsection (3) in such manner, and within such period, as may be specified in the directions, and

(b) where the relevant programme was included in a licensed service, directions requiring the appropriate regulatory body to direct the licence holder to publish those matters in such manner, and within such period, as may be so specified.

(3) Those matters are—

(a) a summary of the complaint;

(b) the BSC's findings on the complaint or a summary of them;

(c) in the case of a standards complaint, any observations by the BSC on the complaint or a summary of any such observations.

(4) References in subsection (2) to the publication of any matter are references to the publication of that matter without its being accompanied by any observations made by a person other than the BSC and relating to the complaint.

(5) The form and content of any such summary as is mentioned in subsection (3)(a), (b) or (c) shall be such as may be approved by the BSC.

(6) A broadcasting or regulatory body shall comply with any directions given to them under this section.

(7) Any licence to provide a licensed service which is granted by a regulatory body under this Act shall include conditions requiring the licence holder to comply with such directions as may be given to him by that body for the purpose of enabling them to comply with any directions given to them under this section.

(8) The BSC shall publish, monthly or at such other intervals as they think fit and in such manner as they think fit, reports each containing, as regards every fairness complaint or standards complaint which falls within this subsection and has been dealt with by them in the period covered by the report—

(a) a summary of the complaint and the action taken by them on it,

(b) where they have adjudicated on it, a summary of—

(i) their findings,

(ii) any direction given under subsection (1), or other action taken by them, in relation to the complaint, and

(c) where a direction has been given under subsection (1) in relation to the complaint, a summary of any action taken by a broadcasting body, a regulatory body or the holder of a licence to provide a licensed service in pursuance of the direction.

(9) A fairness complaint or standards complaint made to the BSC falls within subsection (8) unless it is one which under section 111(1), (4) or (5), 113(1) or 114(2) they have refused to entertain.

(10) The BSC may, if they think fit, omit from any summary which is included in a report under subsection (8) and relates to a fairness complaint any information which could lead to the disclosure of the identity of any person connected with the complaint in question other than—

(a) a broadcasting or regulatory body, or

(b) a person providing a licensed service.

(11) The references in subsections (3)(b) and (8)(b) to the BSC's findings on a complaint shall be construed, in relation to a fairness complaint which has been considered by them in two or more parts, as references to their findings on each part of the complaint.

(12) In this section "licensed service", in relation to a programme to which a standards complaint relates, has the extended meaning given by section 116(6).

DEFINITIONS

"appropriate regulatory body; the": s.130(1).
"broadcasting body": s.130(1).
"BSC; the": s.130(1).

"fairness complaint": s.110(4); s.130(1).
"licensed service": s.130(1).
"regulatory body": s.130(1).
"programme": s.130(1).
"relevant programme; the": s.130(1).
"standards complaint": s.110(4); s.130(1).

General Note

The elements of the former ss.146 and 156 of the 1990 Act are re-enacted in this section. Subsection (8) extends the duty to publish monthly reports to fairness and privacy complaints. Subsection (8)(c) refers to the new requirement, in s.120, for programmers to report back to the BSC on the action they have taken to respond to the BSC's adjudications.

The BSC's sanction is publicity for their adjudications. They cannot insist on an apology or the correction of a false impression, or provide financial redress. Subsection (4) makes it clear that it is only the BSC's observations on a complaint that must be published. Formerly, the exception to the restrictions on editorialising, in ss.6(4) and 90(2)(a) of the 1990 Act, relating to programming matters, meant that broadcasters were not prevented from publishing adjudications without comment (as the BBC did in relation to the NCOPF case: see the note to s.111). This could have the effect of undermining the legitimacy of the BSC's findings and could neutralise their already limited effectiveness, so its use is no longer allowed.

Reports on action taken voluntarily in response to findings on complaints

120.—(1) This section applies where the BSC have given a direction under section 119(1) in relation to a fairness complaint or a standards complaint.

(2) Where the relevant programme was included in a licensed service, the appropriate regulatory body shall send to the BSC a report of any supplementary action taken by—

(a) the regulatory body,
(b) the licence holder, or
(c) any other person appearing to the regulatory body to be responsible for the making or provision of the relevant programme.

(3) Where the relevant programme was broadcast by a broadcasting body, that body shall send to the BSC a report of any supplementary action taken by—

(a) the broadcasting body, or
(b) any other person appearing to that body to be responsible for the making or provision of the relevant programme.

(4) The BSC may include, in any report under section 119(8), a summary of any report received by them under subsection (2) or (3) in relation to the complaint.

(5) In this section "supplementary action", in relation to a complaint, means action which, although not taken in pursuance of a direction under section 119(1), is taken in consequence of the findings of the BSC on the complaint.

Definitions

"appropriate regulatory body; the": s.130(1).
"broadcasting body": s.130(1).
"BSC; the": s.130(1).
"fairness complaint": s.110(4); s.130(1).
"licensed service": s.130(1).
"programme": s.130(1).
"regulatory body": s.130(1).
"relevant programme; the": s.130(1).
"standards complaint": s.110(4); s.130(1).

General Note

The effectiveness of the BSC depends on the strength of the moral criticism which they can bring to bear on the programmers, since they do not have direct power to intervene in editorial decisions. This section is intended to prevent programmers from ignoring the BSC's decisions by forcing them to justify their actions subsequent to an adverse adjudication. Whether it will force them to change their practices depends on the moral authority that the BSC is able to command.

Certain statements etc. protected by qualified privilege for purposes of defamation

121.—(1) For the purposes of the law relating to defamation—

(a) publication of any statement in the course of the consideration by the BSC of, and their adjudication on, a fairness complaint,

(b) publication by the BSC of directions under section 119(1) relating to a fairness complaint, or

(c) publication of a report of the BSC, so far as the report relates to fairness complaints,

is privileged unless the publication is shown to be made with malice.

(2) Nothing in subsection (1) shall be construed as limiting any privilege subsisting apart from that subsection.

DEFINITIONS

"BSC; the": s.130(1).
"fairness complaint": s.110(4); s.130(1).

Miscellaneous and general

Power of BSC to commission research

122.—(1) The BSC may make arrangements for the undertaking of research into matters related to or connected with—

(a) the avoidance of unjust or unfair treatment in programmes to which section 107 applies and of unwarranted infringement of privacy in, or in connection with the obtaining of material included in, such programmes,

(b) the portrayal of violence or sexual conduct in programmes to which section 108 applies, or

(c) standards of taste and decency for such programmes generally.

(2) The matters into which research may be undertaken in pursuance of subsection (1) include, in particular, matters falling within section 109(2)(a) and (b).

(3) Arrangements made under subsection (1) shall secure that, so far as is reasonably practicable, any research undertaken in pursuance of the arrangements is undertaken by persons who are neither members nor employees of the BSC.

(4) The BSC may publish the results of any research undertaken in pursuance of subsection (1).

DEFINITIONS

"BSC; the": s.130(1).
"programme": s.130(1).
"programmes to which section 107 applies": s.130(2)(a).
"programmes to which section 108 applies": s.130(2)(b).
"sexual conduct": s.130(1).
"unjust or unfair treatment": s.130(1).

GENERAL NOTE

In this section, the former Council's power to commission research into matters relating to standards is extended to matters relating to fairness and privacy.

International representation by BSC of Government interests

123. The functions of the BSC shall include representing Her Majesty's Government in the United Kingdom, at the request of the Secretary of State, on international bodies concerned with setting standards for television programmes.

DEFINITION
"BSC; the": s.130(1).

Duty to publicise BSC

124.—(1) It shall be the duty of each broadcasting or regulatory body to arrange for the publication (by means of broadcasts or otherwise) of regular announcements publicising the BSC.

(2) Any such announcements may contain a statement of the difference between fairness complaints and standards complaints.

(3) Any licence to provide a licensed service which is granted by a regulatory body under the 1990 Act or under this Act shall include conditions requiring the licence holder to comply with such directions as may be given to him by that body in connection with the performance by them of their duty under subsection (1).

(4) In this section "licensed service" has the extended meaning given by section 116(6).

DEFINITIONS
"broadcasting body": s.130(1).
"BSC; the": s.130(1).
"fairness complaint": s.110(4); s.130(1).
"licensed service": s.130(1).
"regulatory body": s.130(1).
"standards complaint": s.110(4); s.130(1).
"1990 Act; the": s.147(1).

Annual reports

125.—(1) As soon as possible after the end of every financial year the BSC shall prepare a report of their proceedings during that year, and transmit it to the Secretary of State who shall lay copies of it before each House of Parliament.

(2) The report shall include a report by the BSC on the matters specified in section 109(1).

(3) If the Secretary of State so directs, the report shall also include such further information relating to the BSC as he may specify in the direction.

(4) The report may also include a report on any issues of the kind referred to in section 126.

(5) The BSC shall send a copy of the report, together with a copy of the statement of accounts for the year and of the report of the Comptroller and Auditor General on that statement—

(a) to each broadcasting or regulatory body, and
(b) if so requested by any person providing a licensed service, to that person.

(6) In this section "licensed service" has the extended meaning given by section 116(6).

DEFINITIONS
"broadcasting body": s.130(1).
"BSC; the": s.130(1).
"licensed service": s.130(1).
"regulatory body": s.130(1).

Reports to Secretary of State

126. The BSC may from time to time make a report to the Secretary of State on any issues identified by them in the course of carrying out their functions under this Part and appearing to them to raise questions of general broadcasting policy.

DEFINITION
"BSC; the": s.130(1).

Contributions towards cost of BSC

127.—(1) For the financial year which includes the commencement of this section and each subsequent financial year the Secretary of State shall, subject to subsection (2), notify—

(a) to each regulatory body the sum which he considers to be the appropriate contribution of that body, in respect of persons providing licensed services under licences granted by that body, towards the expenses of the BSC; and

(b) to the Welsh Authority the sum which he considers to be the appropriate contribution of that body towards such expenses.

(2) The total of the sums notified under subsection (1) for any financial year must be such that the aggregate of—

(a) that total, and

(b) the amount of any contribution towards the expenses of the BSC for that year which is received, or to be received, by the Secretary of State from the BBC,

represents one half of those expenses.

(3) Each regulatory body and the Welsh Authority shall pay to the Secretary of State any sum notified to them under subsection (1).

DEFINITIONS
"BBC; the": s.147(1).
"BSC; the": s.130(1).
"financial year": s.130(1).
"licensed service": s.130(1).
"regulatory body": s.130(1).

GENERAL NOTE
This section re-enacts the substance of the former s.149 of the 1990 Act, relating to the BCC, for which there was no comparable provision relating to the Council, and extends its provisions to the wider functions of the new BSC.

Transfer of assets of Broadcasting Complaints Commission and Broadcasting Standards Council to BSC and dissolution of those bodies

128.—(1) In this section "the existing boards" means the Broadcasting Complaints Commission and the Broadcasting Standards Council.

(2) On such day as the Secretary of State may by order appoint as the transfer date all the property, rights and liabilities to which either of the existing boards were entitled or subject immediately before that date shall become property, rights and liabilities of the BSC, and Schedule 4 shall have effect for the purpose of supplementing this and the following provisions of this section.

(3) Each of the existing boards shall continue in existence after the transfer date until such time as they are respectively dissolved by order made by the Secretary of State.

(4) On the transfer date the chairman and members of the existing boards shall cease to hold office; and as from that date each of the existing boards—

(a) shall consist only of a chairman appointed by the Secretary of State and, if the Secretary of State thinks fit, such one or more other persons as the Secretary of State may appoint as members, and

(b) shall have only the functions which fall to be carried out by them under or by virtue of Schedule 4.

(5) If requested to do so by the chairman appointed under subsection (4)(a) to either of the existing boards, the BSC shall furnish that existing board with any assistance required by them for the purposes of carrying out any of those functions.

(6) The Secretary of State shall not make an order under subsection (3) in relation to either of the existing boards unless he is satisfied, after consultation with that existing board and the BSC, that nothing further remains to be done by that existing board under or by virtue of Schedule 4.

(7) References in this section and Schedule 4 to property, rights and liabilities of either of the existing boards include references to property, rights and liabilities which are not capable of being transferred or assigned by them.

DEFINITION

"BSC; the": s.130(1).

Transitional provisions relating to complaints

129.—(1) This Part shall have effect in relation to—

(a) any complaint to the Broadcasting Complaints Commission under section 144 of the 1990 Act made but not disposed of by them before the transfer date, or

(b) any complaint to the Broadcasting Standards Council under section 154 of that Act made but not disposed of by them before that date,

as if the complaint had been made to the BSC under this Part, and anything done by the Broadcasting Complaints Commission or, as the case requires, the Broadcasting Standards Council in relation to the complaint before the transfer date had been done by the BSC.

(2) In subsection (1) "the transfer date" means the date appointed under section 128(2).

DEFINITIONS

"BSC; the": s.130(1).
"1990 Act; the": s.147(1).

Interpretation of Part V

130.—(1) In this Part (unless the context otherwise requires)—

"the appropriate regulatory body", in relation to a programme included in a licensed service, means the regulatory body by whom that service is licensed;

"broadcasting body" means the BBC or the Welsh Authority;

"the BSC" means the Broadcasting Standards Commission;

"fairness complaint" has the meaning given by section 110(4);

"financial year" means the twelve months ending with 31st March;

"licensed service" means, subject to sections 116(6), 119(12), 124(4) and 125(6),—

(a) any television programme service (within the meaning of Part I of the 1990 Act) which is licensed under that Part,

(b) any independent radio service (within the meaning of Part III of the 1990 Act) which is licensed under that Part,

(c) any additional service (within the meaning of Part I or III of the 1990 Act) which is licensed under that Part and is for general reception in, or in any area in, the United Kingdom,

(d) any digital programme service (within the meaning of Part I of this Act) which is licensed under that Part,

(e) any qualifying service (within the meaning of Part I of this Act) provided by a person other than the Welsh Authority,

(f) any digital sound programme service (within the meaning of Part II of this Act) which is licensed under that Part,

(g) any simulcast radio service (within the meaning of Part II of this Act), and

(h) any digital additional service (within the meaning of Part I or II of this Act) which is licensed under that Part;

"local delivery service" has the meaning given by section 72 of the 1990 Act;

"participant", in relation to a programme, means a person who appeared, or whose voice was heard, in the programme;

"the person affected"—

(a) in relation to any such unjust or unfair treatment as is mentioned in section 110(1), means a participant in the programme in question who was the subject of that treatment or a person who, whether such a participant or not, had a direct interest in the subject–matter of that treatment, and

(b) in relation to any such unwarranted infringement of privacy as is so mentioned, means a person whose privacy was infringed;

"programme" includes an advertisement and a teletext transmission and, in relation to a service, includes any item included in that service;

"regulatory body" means the Independent Television Commission or the Radio Authority;

"the relevant programme", in relation to a complaint, means the programme to which the complaint relates;

"sexual conduct" means any form of sexual activity or other sexual behaviour;

"standards complaint" has the meaning given by section 110(4);

"unjust or unfair treatment" includes treatment which is unjust or unfair because of the way in which material included in a programme has been selected or arranged.

(2) In this Part—

(a) any reference to programmes to which section 107 applies shall be construed in accordance with section 107(5), and

(b) any reference to programmes to which section 108 applies shall be construed in accordance with section 108(5).

PART VI

THE BRITISH BROADCASTING CORPORATION

Transfer of property, rights and liabilities relating to BBC transmission network

Power of BBC to make transfer schemes relating to its transmission network

131.—(1) The BBC may make a scheme or schemes providing for the transfer to any person or persons of such property, rights and liabilities of the BBC as are specified in, or determined in accordance with the scheme, being property, rights and liabilities which, immediately before the day on which the scheme comes into force, subsist for the purposes of or in connection with or are otherwise attributable to the BBC transmission network.

(2) In subsection (1) "the BBC transmission network" means so much of the undertaking of the BBC as is concerned with the provision of broadcasting transmission services or services related to those services.

(3) In this Part "transfer scheme" means a scheme made under subsection (1).

(4) Schedule 5 shall have effect with respect to transfer schemes.

DEFINITION
"BBC; the": s.147(1).

Powers of Secretary of State in relation to transfer schemes

132.—(1) A transfer scheme shall not take effect unless it is approved by the Secretary of State; and where such a scheme is submitted to the Secretary of State for his approval, he may modify the scheme before approving it.

(2) Subject to subsection (3), the Secretary of State shall not approve a transfer scheme containing any provision in accordance with which any person other than a wholly-owned subsidiary of the BBC becomes entitled or subject to any property, rights and liabilities unless it appears to the Secretary of State that the person has consented to the provisions of the scheme so far as they relate to him.

(3) Subsection (2) shall not require the consent of any person to so much of a transfer scheme as—

(a) relates to property, rights or liabilities to which that person is already entitled or subject, and
(b) appears to the Secretary of State to be made for purposes that are no more than supplemental or incidental to the other provisions of the scheme.

(4) Before—

(a) declining to approve a transfer scheme, or
(b) modifying such a scheme,

the Secretary of State shall consult the BBC and every person who is a transferee under the scheme.

(5) It shall be the duty of the BBC and every person who is a transferee under a transfer scheme to provide the Secretary of State with all such information and other assistance as he may reasonably require for the purposes of, or in connection with, the exercise of any power conferred on him by this paragraph.

(6) In this section "wholly-owned subsidiary" has the meaning given by section 736 of the Companies Act 1985.

DEFINITION
"BBC; the": s.147(1).

Agreements with respect to transfer schemes

133.—(1) The BBC may enter into any such agreement with another person as they think fit for the purpose of accepting or imposing contractual obligations with respect to, or to anything connected with, the manner in which their powers by virtue of section 131 are to be exercised.

(2) Any agreement may, in particular, provide for the making of payments, or the issue of shares or securities, to the BBC (by way of consideration or otherwise) in respect of anything created or transferred in accordance with a transfer scheme.

(3) The consent of the Secretary of State shall be required for the making by the BBC of an agreement under this section.

DEFINITION
"BBC; the": s.147(1).

Transfer schemes: successor companies

134. Schedule 6 (which makes provision about the accounts etc. of wholly-owned subsidiaries of the BBC to which any property, rights or liabilities are transferred in accordance with a transfer scheme) shall have effect.

DEFINITION
"BBC; the": s.147(1).

Taxation provisions with respect to transfer schemes

135. Schedule 7 (which makes provision about tax in connection with transfer schemes) shall have effect.

Services provided by BBC companies

Services provided by BBC companies

136. Schedule 8 (which makes amendments of the 1990 Act relating to the regulation by the Independent Television Commission and the Radio Authority of services provided by bodies corporate in which the BBC have an interest) shall have effect.

DEFINITIONS
"BBC; the": s.147(1).
"1990 Act; the": s.147(1).

PART VII

COPYRIGHT AND RELATED MATTERS

Avoidance of certain terms relating to use for purpose of news reporting of visual images from broadcast or cable programme

137.—(1) Any provision in an agreement is void in so far as it purports to prohibit or restrict relevant dealing with a broadcast or cable programme in any circumstances where by virtue of section 30(2) of the Copyright Designs and Patents Act 1988 (fair dealing for the purpose of reporting current events) copyright in the broadcast or cable programme is not infringed.

(2) In subsection (1)—

(a) "relevant dealing", in relation to a broadcast or cable programme, means dealing by including visual images taken from it in another broadcast or cable programme, and

(b) "broadcast" and "cable programme" have the same meaning as in Part I of the Copyright, Designs and Patents Act 1988.

GENERAL NOTE

This amendment to the 1988 Act was introduced in conjunction with the provisions on Listed Events in Pt. IV. It is intended to ensure that short extracts of sporting events should continue to be available for new-reporting purposes, whatever the source of the programme. Exactly what is fair in any circumstances, for example, if a news report reproduces the climax of a short sporting event, may need to be resolved by the courts if the broadcasters were to fail to agree on the matter. There is a voluntary code of practice on sports broadcasting rights, however, which is intended to resolve such difficulties.

Amendments of Copyright, Designs and Patents Act 1988 relating to cable programme services

138. Schedule 9 (which contains amendments of the Copyright, Designs and Patents Act 1988 relating to broadcasts included in cable programme services) shall have effect.

GENERAL NOTE

Schedule 9 introduces amendments to the Copyright, Designs and Patents Act 1988 (c. 48) to take account of the must-carry provisions which were introduced by s.91 of this Act.

Copyright licensing

139.—(1) After section 135G of the Copyright, Designs and Patents Act 1988 there is inserted—

"**Power to amend sections 135A to 135G**

135H.—(1) The Secretary of State may by order, subject to such transitional provision as appears to him to be appropriate, amend sections 135A to 135G so as—

(a) to include in any reference to sound recordings any works of a description specified in the order; or

(b) to exclude from any reference to a broadcast or cable programme service any broadcast or cable programme service of a description so specified.

(2) An order shall be made by statutory instrument; and no order shall be made unless a draft of it has been laid before and approved by resolution of each House of Parliament."

(2) After section 151 of that Act there is inserted—

"**Award of interest**

151A.—(1) Any of the following, namely—

(a) a direction under section 123(3) so far as relating to a licence for broadcasting a work or including a work in a cable programme service;

(b) a direction under section 128(3) so far as so relating;

(c) an order under section 135D(1); and

(d) an order under section 135F confirming or varying an order under section 135D(1),

may award simple interest at such rate and for such period, beginning not earlier than the relevant date and ending not later than the date of the order, as the Copyright Tribunal thinks reasonable in the circumstances.

(2) In this section "the relevant date" means—

(a) in relation to a direction under section 123(3), the date on which the reference was made;

(b) in relation to a direction under section 128(3), the date on which the reference or application was made;

(c) in relation to an order section 135D(1), the date on which the first payment under section 135C(2) became due; and

(d) in relation to an order under section 135F, the date on which the application was made."

(3) Subsection (2) does not apply in any case where the reference or application to the Copyright Tribunal was or is made before the commencement of this section.

GENERAL NOTE

This section makes provision for varying the requirements of statutory licences relating to broadcasting and cable. The power is anticipatory, since the Government does not presently appear to intend to use the power. There is also provision made for the Copyright Tribunal to exercise discretion to award interest when deciding disputes about monies to be paid under statutory licences. This latter amendment does not extend to licences other than those relating to broadcasting and cable, however.

Unauthorised decoders

140.—(1) In section 297A of the Copyright, Designs and Patents Act 1988 (unauthorised decoders), for subsection (1) there is substituted—

"(1) A person who makes, imports, sells or lets for hire, offers or exposes for sale or hire, or advertises for sale or hire, any unauthorised decoder shall be guilty of an offence and liable—

(a) on summary conviction, to a fine not exceeding the statutory maximum;

(b) on conviction on indictment, to imprisonment for a term not exceeding two years, or to a fine, or to both."

(2) The amendment made by subsection (1) shall not apply to any offence committed before the commencement of this section.

GENERAL NOTE

This section extends the offence of piracy by means of an unauthorised decoder to include the advertising of such decoders as well as their sale. In addition, the maximum penalties for committing such offences are increased.

Apparatus, etc. for unauthorised reception of transmissions

141. In section 298 of the Copyright, Designs and Patents Act 1988 (apparatus, &c for unauthorised reception of transmissions), in subsection (2)(a), after "hire" there is inserted ", offers or exposes for sale or hire, or advertises for sale or hire,".

GENERAL NOTE

This section extends the remedy for infringements against persons who enable unauthorised receptions of transmissions to include persons who offer or advertise relevant equipment as well as supply it.

PART VIII

MISCELLANEOUS AND GENERAL

Standards for transmission systems

Standards for transmission systems

142.—(1) The Independent Television Commission (in this section referred to as "the Commission") shall do all that they can to secure that every licensed service uses a transmission system complying with Article 2 of Council Directive 95/47/EC on the use of standards for the transmission of television signals ("the Directive").

(2) In this section "Community digital standard" means any of the alternatives permitted within the mandatory parts of the standards to be met by a transmission system for the purpose of complying with Article 2(c) of the Directive (which relates to television services that are fully digital).

(3) The Commission may, after consultation with the persons specified in subsection (6), specify particular Community digital standards to be met in the provision of licensed services which are fully digital.

(4) In deciding whether, and if so how, to exercise their powers under subsection (3), the Commission shall, in particular—

(a) have regard to the desirability of promoting—

(i) mutual technical compatibility between digital television services, and

(ii) the development of digital television broadcasting, and

(b) consider whether it would be reasonably practicable for persons providing licensed services which are fully digital to use transmission systems meeting the Community digital standards in question.

(5) Where the Commission have exercised their powers under subsection (3), they shall—

(a) publish notice of their determination in such manner as they think fit, and

(b) do all that they can to secure that any licensed service which is fully digital uses a transmission system meeting the Community digital standards specified under that subsection.

(6) The persons referred to in subsection (3) are—

(a) every person providing a licensed service,

(b) the BBC,

(c) the Welsh Authority,

(d) the Secretary of State,

(e) the Director General of Telecommunications,
(f) the Director General of Fair Trading,
(g) such persons appearing to them to represent manufacturers of television broadcasting or receiving equipment as they think fit,
(h) such persons appearing to them to represent viewers as they think fit, and
(i) such other persons as they think fit.

(7) In this section—

"licensed service" means any service licensed by the Commission under Part I of this Act or Part I or II of the 1990 Act or provided under a relevant cable licence, but does not include any service which is only broadcast or transmitted for reception outside the European Economic Area;

"relevant cable licence" means a relevant licence within the meaning of Part III of Schedule 12 to the 1990 Act (transitional provisions relating to existing cable services).

DEFINITIONS

"BBC; the": s.147(1).
"1990 Act; the": s.147(1).

Disqualification on grounds relating to political objects

Duties of Independent Television Commission and Radio Authority in cases involving disqualification on grounds related to political objects

143.—(1) If it appears to the Independent Television Commission that there are grounds for suspecting that any person who is an applicant for a licence under Part I or II of the 1990 Act or Part I of this Act is by virtue of any of the provisions specified in subsection (5) a disqualified person in relation to that licence, the Commission shall be regarded as failing to discharge their duty under section 5(1) of the 1990 Act, or as the case may be section 5(1) of this Act, if they grant the licence to that person without being provided with information which satisfies them that he is not on those grounds a disqualified person by virtue of that provision.

(2) If it appears to the Independent Television Commission that there are grounds for suspecting that any person who is the holder of a licence under Parts I or II of the 1990 Act or Part I of this Act is by virtue of any of the provisions specified in subsection (5) a disqualified person in relation to that licence, the Commission shall be regarded as failing to discharge their duty under section 5(1) of the 1990 Act, or as the case may be section 5(1) of this Act, unless—

(a) they require him to provide them with information for the purpose of determining whether he is on those grounds a disqualified person by virtue of that provision, and
(b) if they are satisfied that he is a disqualified person, they revoke the licence.

(3) If it appears to the Radio Authority that there are grounds for suspecting that any person who is an applicant for a licence under Part III of the 1990 Act or Part II of this Act is by virtue of any of the provisions specified in subsection (5) a disqualified person in relation to that licence, the Authority shall be regarded as failing to discharge their duty under section 88(1) of the 1990 Act, or as the case may be section 44(1) of this Act, if they grant the licence to that person without being provided with information which satisfies them that he is not on those grounds a disqualified person by virtue of that provision.

(4) If it appears to the Radio Authority that there are grounds for suspecting that any person who is the holder of a licence under Part III of the 1990 Act or Part II of this Act is by virtue of any of the provisions specified in subsection (5) a disqualified person in relation to that licence, the Authority shall be regarded as failing to discharge their duty under section 88(1) of the 1990 Act, or as the case may be section 44(1) of this Act, unless—

(a) they require him to provide them with information for the purpose of determining whether he is a disqualified person on those grounds by virtue of that provision, and

(b) if they are satisfied that he is a disqualified person, they revoke the licence.

(5) The provisions referred to in subsections (1) to (4) are the following provisions of paragraph 1(1) of Part II of Schedule 2 to the 1990 Act—

(a) paragraphs (d) to (g),

(b) paragraph (h) so far as relating to participation by bodies falling within paragraph (d), (e) or (g),

(c) paragraph (hh) so far as relating to a body corporate controlled by a body corporate in which a body falling within paragraph (d), (e) or (g) is a participant with more than a 5 per cent interest,

(d) paragraph (i) so far as relating to control by a person falling within any of paragraphs (d) to (g) or by two or more such persons, and

(e) paragraph (j) so far as relating to participation by a body corporate which is controlled by a person falling within any of paragraphs (d) to (g) or by two or more such persons.

(6) Nothing in subsections (1) to (5) shall be taken to limit the generality of—

(a) the duty imposed on the Independent Television Commission by section 5(1) of the 1990 Act or section 5(1) of this Act, or

(b) the duty imposed on the Radio Authority by section 88(1) of the 1990 Act or section 44(1) of this Act.

DEFINITION

"1990 Act; the": s.147(1).

GENERAL NOTE

This section makes it clear that the regulatory bodies cannot go ahead and issue licences if they have grounds to suspect disqualification on political grounds, but no firm evidence. In effect, the burden of showing that a licence applicant is not disqualified is passed to the applicant, who cannot disingenuously ask the regulators to justify their refusal to grant a licence on those grounds.

Provision of false information, etc.

Offence of providing false information in certain circumstances

144.—(1) A person who, in connection with an application by him for, or his continued holding of, a licence under the 1990 Act or this Act—

(a) makes to the relevant authority a statement which he knows to be false in a material particular, or

(b) recklessly makes to the relevant authority a statement which is false in a material particular,

is guilty of an offence if the statement relates to a matter which would be relevant in determining whether he is by virtue of any of the provisions specified in subsection (3) a disqualified person, and he is by virtue of any of those provisions a disqualified person in relation to that licence.

(2) A person who, in connection with an application by him for, or his continued holding of, a licence under the 1990 Act or this Act, withholds any information with the intention of causing the relevant authority to be misled is guilty of an offence if—

(a) the information would be relevant in determining whether he is by virtue of any of the provisions specified in subsection (3) a disqualified person, and

(b) he is by virtue of any of those provisions a disqualified person in relation to that licence.

(3) The provisions referred to in subsections (1) and (2) are the following provisions of paragraph 1(1) of Part II of Schedule 2 to the 1990 Act—

(a) paragraphs (d) to (g),

(b) paragraph (h) so far as relating to participation by bodies falling within paragraph (d), (e) or (g),
(c) paragraph (hh) so far as relating to a body corporate controlled by a body corporate in which a body falling within paragraph (d), (e) or (g) is a participant with more than a 5 per cent interest,
(d) paragraph (i) so far as relating to control by a person falling within any of paragraphs (d) to (g) or by two or more such persons, and
(e) paragraph (j) so far as relating to participation by a body corporate which is controlled by a person falling within any of paragraphs (d) to (g) or by two or more such persons.

(4) A person guilty of an offence under this section is liable on summary conviction to imprisonment for a term not exceeding three months or to a fine not exceeding level 5 on the standard scale or to both.

(5) In this section "the relevant authority" means—
(a) in relation to any licence under Part I or II of the 1990 Act or Part I of this Act, the Independent Television Commission, and
(b) in relation to any licence under Part III of the 1990 Act or Part II of this Act, the Radio Authority.

DEFINITION
"1990 Act; the": s.147(1).

Disqualification for offence of supplying false information, etc.

145.—(1) Where a person is convicted of an offence under section 144 the court by which he is convicted may make an order (in this section referred to as a "disqualification order") disqualifying him from holding a licence during a period specified in the order.

(2) The period specified in a disqualification order shall not exceed five years beginning with the date on which the order takes effect.

(3) Where an individual is disqualified from holding a licence by virtue of a disqualification order, any body corporate—
(a) of which he is a director, or
(b) in the management of which he is directly or indirectly concerned,
is also disqualified from holding a licence.

(4) Where the holder of a licence is disqualified by virtue of a disqualification order, the licence shall be treated as being revoked with effect from the time when the order takes effect.

(5) For the purposes of any of the provisions specified in subsection (6) (which relate to the imposition of a financial penalty on the revocation of a licence), a licence which is revoked by virtue of subsection (4) shall be taken to have been revoked by the relevant authority as mentioned in that provision.

(6) The provisions referred to in subsection (5) are as follows—
(a) section 18(3) of the 1990 Act,
(b) section 101(3) of the 1990 Act,
(c) section 11(5), and
(d) section 53(5).

(7) In sections 5(1)(a) and 88(1)(a) of the 1990 Act and sections 5(1)(a) and 44(1)(a) of this Act, the reference to a person who is a disqualified person by virtue of Part II of Schedule 2 to the 1990 Act includes a reference to a person who is disqualified by virtue of a disqualification order.

(8) In this section—
"licence" means any licence granted by the Independent Television Commission or the Radio Authority under the 1990 Act or this Act;
"the relevant authority" has the same meaning as in section 144.

DEFINITION
"1990 Act; the": s.147(1).

Supplementary provisions as to disqualification orders

146.—(1) A person disqualified by a disqualification order may appeal against the order in the same manner as against a conviction.

(2) A disqualification order made by a court in England and Wales or Northern Ireland—

(a) shall not take effect until the end of the period within which the person on whose conviction the order was made can appeal against the order, and

(b) if he so appeals, shall not take effect until the appeal has been determined or abandoned.

(3) A disqualification order made by a court in Scotland—

(a) shall not take effect until the end of the period within which the person on whose conviction the order was made can appeal against the order, and

(b) if an appeal against the order or the conviction is taken within that period, shall not take effect until the date when that appeal is determined or abandoned or deemed to have been abandoned.

(4) In this section "disqualification order" means an order under section 145.

General

General interpretation

147.—(1) In this Act—

"the 1990 Act" means the Broadcasting Act 1990;

"the BBC" means the British Broadcasting Corporation.

(2) The 1990 Act and the following provisions of this Act—

(a) Parts I and II and Schedule 1,

(b) Part IV,

(c) Part V and Schedules 3 and 4, and

(d) sections 142 to 146,

shall be construed as if those provisions were contained in that Act.

Minor and consequential amendments, repeals and revocations

148.—(1) Schedule 10 (which makes minor and consequential amendments) shall have effect.

(2) The enactments and instruments mentioned in Schedule 11 are hereby repealed or, as the case may be, revoked to the extent specified in the third column of that Schedule.

Commencement and transitional provisions

149.—(1) The following provisions of this Act—

(a) paragraphs 7 to 9 of Schedule 2 so far as relating to BBC companies (as defined by section 202(1) of the 1990 Act), and section 73 so far as relating to those paragraphs in their application to such companies,

(b) sections 74 to 78,

(c) section 80,

(d) section 83,

(e) sections 88, 90 and 92,

(f) Part VI (and Schedules 5 to 8),

(g) section 147(1),

(h) paragraphs 15 and 19 of Schedule 10 so far as relating to BBC companies (as defined by section 202(1) of the 1990 Act), and section 148(1) so far as relating to those paragraphs in their application to such companies,

(i) the entries in Schedule 11 relating to sections 32(9), 45(8) and (9) and 47(11) and (12) of the 1990 Act, and section 148(2) so far as relating to those entries, and

(j) this section and section 150,

shall come into force on the passing of this Act.

(2) The other provisions of this Act shall come into force on such day as the Secretary of State may by order made by statutory instrument appoint; and different days may be appointed for different purposes.

(3) The power to make an order under this section includes power to make such transitional provisions and savings as the Secretary of State considers appropriate.

Short title and extent

150.—(1) This Act may be cited as the Broadcasting Act 1996.

(2) This Act, except paragraph 27 of Schedule 10, extends to Northern Ireland.

(3) Section 204(6) of the 1990 Act (power to extend to Isle of Man and Channel Islands) applies to the provisions of this Act amending that Act.

(4) Her Majesty may by Order in Council direct that any of the other provisions of this Act shall extend to the Isle of Man or any of the Channel Islands with such modifications, if any, as appear to Her Majesty to be appropriate.

SCHEDULES

Sections 37, 70

SCHEDULE 1

MULTIPLEX REVENUE: SUPPLEMENTARY PROVISIONS

PART I

MULTIPLEX REVENUE FOR PURPOSES OF PART I OF THIS ACT

Computation of multiplex revenue

1.—(1) It shall be the duty of the Commission to draw up, and from time to time review, a statement setting out the principles to be followed in ascertaining—

(a) the multiplex revenue in relation to a licence holder for the purposes of section 14 for any accounting period, and

(b) the share of multiplex revenue attributable to a person in relation to any multiplex service for the purposes of any provision of Part I of this Act—

(i) for any accounting period of the holder of the multiplex licence, or

(ii) for any year.

(2) A statement under this paragraph may set out different principles for persons holding different kinds of licences.

(3) Before drawing up or revising a statement under this paragraph the Commission shall consult the Secretary of State and the Treasury.

(4) The Commission shall—

(a) publish the statement drawn up under this paragraph and every revision of that statement; and

(b) transmit a copy of that statement, and every revision of it, to the Secretary of State;

and the Secretary of State shall lay copies of the statement and of every such revision before each House of Parliament.

Disputes

2.—(1) For the purposes of any provision of Part I of this Act—

(a) the amount of the multiplex revenue in relation to any holder of a multiplex licence for any accounting period of his, or (as the case may be) for any year, or

(b) the amount of any payment to be made to the Commission by any person in respect of any such revenue, or of an instalment of any such payment,

shall, in the event of a disagreement between the Commission and that person, be the amount determined by the Commission.

(2) For the purposes of any provision of Part I of this Act the share of multiplex revenue attributable to any person in relation to a multiplex service for any accounting period or (as the case may be) for any year shall, in the event of a disagreement between the Commission and that person, be the amount determined by the Commission.

(3) No determination of the Commission under this paragraph shall be called in question in any court of law, or be the subject of any arbitration, but nothing in this sub-paragraph shall prevent the bringing of proceedings for judicial review.

PART II

MULTIPLEX REVENUE FOR PURPOSES OF PART II OF THIS ACT

Computation of multiplex revenue

3.—(1) It shall be the duty of the Authority to draw up, and from time to time review, a statement setting out the principles to be followed in ascertaining—

(a) the multiplex revenue in relation to a licence holder for the purposes of section 56 for any accounting period, and

(b) the share of multiplex revenue attributable to a person in relation to any national radio multiplex service for the purposes of any provision of Part II of this Act—

(i) for any accounting period of the holder of the national radio multiplex licence, or

(ii) for any year.

(2) A statement under this paragraph may set out different principles for persons holding different kinds of licences.

(3) Before drawing up or revising a statement under this paragraph the Authority shall consult the Secretary of State and the Treasury.

(4) The Authority shall—

(a) publish the statement drawn up under this paragraph and every revision of that statement; and

(b) transmit a copy of that statement, and every revision of it, to the Secretary of State;

and the Secretary of State shall lay copies of the statement and of every such revision before each House of Parliament.

Disputes

4.—(1) For the purposes of any provision of Part II of this Act—

(a) the amount of the multiplex revenue in relation to any holder of a national radio multiplex licence for any accounting period of his, or (as the case may be) for any year, or

(b) the amount of any payment to be made to the Authority by any person in respect of any such revenue, or of an instalment of any such payment,

shall, in the event of a disagreement between the Authority and that person, be the amount determined by the Authority.

(2) For the purposes of any provision of Part II of this Act the share of multiplex revenue attributable to any person in relation to any national radio multiplex service for any accounting period or (as the case may be) for any year shall, in the event of a disagreement between the Authority and that person, be the amount determined by the Authority.

(3) No determination of the Authority under this paragraph shall be called in question in any court of law, or be the subject of any arbitration; but nothing in this sub-paragraph shall prevent the bringing of proceedings for judicial review.

Section 73

SCHEDULE 2

AMENDMENTS OF BROADCASTING ACT 1990 RELATING TO RESTRICTIONS ON HOLDING OF LICENCES

PART I

AMENDMENTS OF PART I OF SCHEDULE 2

1.—(1) In Part I of Schedule 2, paragraph 1 (which contains interpretative provisions) is amended as follows.

(2) In sub-paragraph (1)—

(a) before the definition of "advertising agency" there is inserted—

" "the 1996 Act" means the Broadcasting Act 1996;",

(b) for paragraph (a) of the definition of "associate" there is substituted—

"(a) in relation to a body corporate, shall be construed in accordance with paragraph (1A), and",

(c) in paragraph (b) of the definition of "control" for "by virtue of the rules regulating that or any other body" there is substituted "by whatever means and whether directly or indirectly",

(d) after the definition of "control" there is inserted—

" "coverage area", in relation to a service, shall be construed in accordance with paragraph 3A;

"digital programme service" has the same meaning as in Part I of the 1996 Act;",

(e) after the definition of "local delivery service" there is inserted—

" "local digital sound programme service" and "national digital sound programme service" have the same meaning as in Part II of the 1996 Act;

"local radio multiplex service" and "national radio multiplex service" have the same meaning as in Part II of the 1996 Act;", and

(f) at the end there is inserted—

" "television multiplex service" means a multiplex service within the meaning of Part I of the 1996 Act.".

(3) After sub-paragraph (1) there is inserted—

"(1A) For the purpose of determining the persons who are the associates of a body corporate for the purposes of this Schedule—

(a) an individual shall be regarded as an associate of a body corporate if he is a director of that body corporate, and

(b) a body corporate and another body corporate shall be regarded as associates of each other if one controls the other or if the same person controls both."

(4) For sub-paragraph (3) there is substituted—

"(3) For the purposes of this Schedule a person controls a body corporate if—

(a) he holds, or is beneficially entitled to, more than 50 per cent of the equity share capital in the body, or possesses more than 50 per cent of the voting power in it, or

(b) although he does not have such an interest in the body, it is reasonable, having regard to all the circumstances, to expect that he will be able, by whatever means and whether directly or indirectly, to achieve the result that the affairs of the body are conducted in accordance with his wishes; or

(c) he holds, or is beneficially entitled to, 50 per cent of the equity share capital in that body, or possesses 50 per cent of the voting power in it, and an arrangement exists between him and any other participant in the body as to the manner in which any voting power in the body possessed by either of them is to be exercised, or as to the omission by either of them to exercise such voting power.

(3A) For the purposes of sub-paragraph (3)(c)—

(a) "arrangement" includes any agreement or arrangement, whether or not it is, or is intended to be, legally enforceable, and

(b) a person shall be treated—

(i) as holding, or being beneficially entitled to, any equity share capital which is held by a body corporate which he controls or to which such a body corporate is beneficially entitled, and

(ii) as possessing any voting power possessed by such a body corporate."

(5) Sub-paragraph (4) is omitted.

(6) For sub-paragraph (6) there is substituted—

"(6) In this Schedule any reference to a participant with more than a 20 per cent interest in a body corporate is a reference to a person who—

(a) holds or is beneficially entitled to more than 20 per cent of the shares in that body, or

(b) possesses more than 20 per cent of the voting power in that body.

(7) Sub-paragraph (6) shall have effect subject to the necessary modifications in relation to other references in this Schedule—

(a) to an interest of more than a specified percentage in a body corporate, or

(b) to an interest of a specified percentage or more in a body corporate.

(8) Any reference in this Schedule to a person who is over a particular age is a reference to a person who has attained that age."

2.—(1) Paragraph 2 of Part I of Schedule 2 is amended as follows.

(2) At the beginning of sub-paragraph (1) there is inserted "Subject to sub-paragraph (1A)".

(3) After sub-paragraph (1) there is inserted—

"(1A) For the purposes of this Schedule, a person's holding of shares, or possession of voting power, in a body corporate shall be disregarded if, or to the extent that—

(a) he holds the shares concerned—

(i) as a nominee,

(ii) as a custodian (whether under a trust or by a contract), or

(iii) under an arrangement pursuant to which he has issued, or is to issue, depositary receipts, as defined by section 220(1) of the Companies Act 1985, in respect of the shares concerned, and

(b) he is not entitled to exercise or control the exercise of voting rights in respect of the shares concerned.

(1B) For the purposes of sub-paragraph (1A)(b)—

(a) a person is not entitled to exercise or control the exercise of voting rights in respect of shares if he is bound (whether by contract or otherwise) not to exercise the voting rights, or not to exercise them otherwise than in accordance with the instructions of another, and

(b) voting rights which a person is entitled to exercise or of which he is entitled to control the exercise only in certain circumstances shall be taken into account only when those circumstances have arisen and for as long as they continue to obtain."

3. For paragraph 3 of Part I of Schedule 2 there is substituted—

"3. For the purposes of this Schedule the following persons shall be treated as connected with a particular person—

(a) a person who controls that person,

(b) an associate of that person or of a person falling within paragraph (a), and

(c) a body which is controlled by that person or by an associate of that person."

4. After paragraph 3 of Part I of Schedule 2 there is inserted—

"3A.—(1) In this Schedule "coverage area"—

(a) in relation to any service licensed by the Commission under Part I of this Act or a television multiplex service licensed by them under Part I of the 1996 Act, means the area of the United Kingdom from time to time determined by the Commission as that within which the service is capable of being received at a level satisfying such technical standards as they may from time to time determine,

(b) in relation to any digital programme service which is broadcast by means of a television multiplex service, means the area of the United Kingdom from time to time determined by the Commission as that within which the digital programme service as so broadcast is capable of being received at such a level,

(c) in relation to any service licensed by the Authority under Part III of this Act, means the area of the United Kingdom from time to time determined by the Authority as that within which the service is capable of being received at a level satisfying such technical standards as they may from time to time determine, and

(d) in relation to any local radio multiplex service licensed by the Authority under Part II of the 1996 Act or any local digital sound programme service which is broadcast by means of such a local radio multiplex service, means the area of the United Kingdom from time to time determined by the Authority as that within which the local radio multiplex service is capable of being received at such a level.

(2) Where the Commission or the Authority make any determination under this paragraph, they shall—

(a) publish the determination in such manner as they think fit, and

(b) send a copy of it to such persons holding licences granted by them as appear to them to be affected by the determination.

3B.—(1) For the purposes of this Schedule—

(a) person who holds a licence to provide digital programme services shall be taken to provide a digital programme service if, under a contract between him and a person who holds a licence to provide a television multiplex service, that person is obliged to broadcast the digital programme service by means of the television multiplex service;

(b) a person who holds a licence to provide national digital sound programme services shall be taken to provide a national digital sound programme service if, under a contract between him and a person who holds a licence to provide a national radio multiplex service, that person is obliged to broadcast the national digital sound programme service by means of the national radio multiplex service;

(c) a person who holds a licence to provide local digital sound programme services shall be taken to provide a local digital sound programme service if, under a contract between him and a person who holds a licence to provide a local radio multiplex service, that person is obliged to broadcast the local digital sound programme service by means of the local radio multiplex service.

(2) For the purposes of this Schedule a person who holds a licence to provide digital programme services, national digital sound programme services or local digital sound programme services shall also be taken to provide a digital programme service, a national digital sound programme service or a local digital sound programme service (as the case may be) if he also holds a relevant multiplex licence and is broadcasting that service under that licence.

(3) In sub-paragraph (2), "relevant multiplex licence" means—

(a) in relation to digital programme services, a licence to provide a television multiplex service,
(b) in relation to national digital sound programme services, a licence to provide a national radio multiplex service, and
(c) in relation to local digital sound programme services, a licence to provide a local radio multiplex service."

5. In paragraph 4 of Part I of Schedule 2 (affirmative resolution procedure), for "this Schedule" there is substituted "any provision of this Schedule other than paragraph 7 in Part III".

PART II

AMENDMENTS OF PART II OF SCHEDULE 2

6.—(1) In Part II of Schedule 2, paragraph 1 (general disqualification of non-EEA nationals and bodies having political connections) is amended as follows.

(2) In sub-paragraph (1), after paragraph (h) there is inserted—

"(hh) a body corporate which is controlled by a body corporate falling within paragraph (h);".

(3) In sub-paragraph (2), the "or" at the end of paragraph (e) is omitted and after paragraph (f) there is inserted—

"(g) a licence to provide a television multiplex service, a national radio multiplex service or a local radio multiplex service,
(h) a licence to provide digital additional services (within the meaning of Part I or II of the 1996 Act),
(i) a licence to provide digital programme services, or
(j) a licence to provide national or local digital sound programme services."

7. In paragraph 3 of Part II of Schedule 2 (disqualification of publicly-funded bodies for radio service licences), in sub-paragraph (1)(a) for "(other than a local authority)" there is substituted "(other than a local authority, the Welsh Authority or the BBC)".

8. In paragraph 5 of Part II of Schedule 2 (general disqualification of broadcasting bodies), paragraphs (c) and (d) are omitted.

9. After paragraph 5 of Part II of Schedule 2 there is inserted—

"*Disqualification of certain companies for certain licences*

5A.—(1) A BBC company, a Channel 4 company or an S4C company is a disqualified person in relation to—

(a) any licence granted by the Commission to provide regional or national Channel 3 services or Channel 5, and
(b) any licence granted by the Commission to provide a local delivery service.

(2) A BBC company is also a disqualified person in relation to any licence granted by the Authority to provide a national, local or restricted service within the meaning of Part III of this Act.

(3) The Secretary of State may by order provide that sub-paragraph (1)(b) shall not have effect in relation to any local delivery service of a description specified in the order."

PART III

PROVISIONS SUBSTITUTED FOR PART III OF SCHEDULE 2

10. For Part III of Schedule 2 there is substituted—

"PART III

RESTRICTIONS TO PREVENT ACCUMULATIONS OF INTERESTS IN LICENSED SERVICES

1.—(1) In this Part of this Schedule "relevant services" means any such services as are mentioned in sub-paragraphs (2) and (3) and, for the purposes of this Part, relevant services shall (subject to paragraph 9) be divided into the seventeen categories specified in those sub-paragraphs.

(2) In the case of services licensed by the Commission, the categories are—

(a) regional and national Channel 3 services and Channel 5;
(b) restricted services (within the meaning of Part I of this Act);
(c) domestic satellite services;

(d) non-domestic satellite services;
(e) licensable programme services;
(f) additional services (within the meaning of Part I of this Act);
(g) television multiplex services;
(h) digital programme services; and
(i) digital additional services (within the meaning of Part I of the 1996 Act).

(3) In the case of services licensed by the Authority, the categories are—
(a) national radio services;
(b) local radio services;
(c) satellite radio services;
(d) licensable sound programme services;
(e) additional services (within the meaning of Part III of this Act);
(f) national or local radio multiplex services;
(g) national or local digital sound programme services; and
(h) digital additional services (within the meaning of Part II of the 1996 Act).

(4) References in this Part to national, local, restricted or satellite radio services are references to national, local, restricted or satellite services within the meaning of Part III of this Act.

General limit on the holding of licences to provide television services or interests in bodies corporate holding such licences

2.—(1) No one person may, at any time when his audience time in respect of the period of twelve months ending with the last day of the preceding calendar month exceeds 15 per cent of total audience time in respect of that period—
(a) hold two or more licences to provide relevant services falling within one or more of the categories specified in paragraph 1(2)(a), (c), (d), (e) or (h),
(b) be a participant with a qualifying interest in two or more bodies corporate each of which holds a licence, or two or more licences to provide services falling within one or more of those categories,
(c) hold any licence to provide a relevant service falling within any of those categories and be a participant with a qualifying interest in any body corporate which holds such a licence or two or more such licences,
(d) provide a foreign satellite service and either hold any licence to provide a relevant service falling within any of those categories or be a participant with a qualifying interest in a body corporate which holds such a licence or two or more such licences, or
(e) hold a licence to provide relevant services falling within the category specified in paragraph 1(2)(h) and provide two or more such services.

(2) For the purposes of sub-paragraph (1) a person's audience time at any time ("the relevant time") in respect of any period is the aggregate of—
(a) the audience time attributable in respect of that period to each relevant service falling within any of the categories specified in paragraph 1(2)(a), (c), (d), (e) or (h) provided under a licence held by him at the relevant time,
(b) one half of the audience time attributable in respect of that period to any relevant service falling within any of the categories specified in paragraph 1(2)(a), (c), (d), (e) or (h) provided under a licence held by a body corporate which he does not control, but in which he is at the relevant time a participant with a qualifying interest, and
(c) the audience time attributable in respect of that period to any foreign satellite service provided by him at the relevant time.

(3) In this paragraph "foreign satellite service" means any service (other than a non-domestic satellite service) which consists in the transmission of television programmes by satellite, is provided on a frequency other than one allocated to the United Kingdom for broadcasting by satellite and either—
(a) appears to the Commission to be intended for general reception in the United Kingdom (whether or not it appears to them to be also intended for general reception elsewhere), or
(b) is (to any extent) relayed by a local delivery service.

(4) References in this paragraph—
(a) to the audience time attributable to any service in respect of any period, or
(b) to total audience time in respect of any period,
shall be construed in accordance with paragraph 3.

(5) In this paragraph "qualifying interest" means an interest of more than 20 per cent

(6) The Secretary of State may by order amend sub-paragraph (5)—

(a) by substituting a different percentage for any percentage for the time being specified there, and
(b) so as to specify different percentages in relation to licences to provide different services.

(7) The Secretary of State may by order amend sub-paragraphs (1)(a), (2)(a) and (b) by adding a reference to relevant services falling within the category specified in paragraph 1(2)(b).

Audience time and total audience time for purposes of paragraph 2

3.—(1) For the purposes of paragraph 2—
(a) the audience time attributable to a service in respect of any period is an estimate by the Commission of the number of hours that would be produced by—
(i) ascertaining, in relation to every person who in that period watched any programme included in that service, the total amount of time he spent in that period watching programmes so included, and
(ii) adding together all the amounts of time so ascertained, and
(b) total audience time in respect of any period is the total of all the audience times attributable to services specified in sub-paragraph (2) in respect of that period.

(2) The services referred to in sub-paragraph (1)(b) are—
(a) every television programme service capable of being received in the British Islands, and
(b) every other service which consists wholly or mainly in the broadcasting, or transmission by satellite, from a place outside the British Islands of television programmes which are capable of being received in the British Islands.

(3) For the purposes of this paragraph the Commission may disregard—
(a) watching in such circumstances, or by persons of such description, as the Commission may from time to time determine,
(b) periods of watching whose duration does not exceed such length of time as they may so determine, and
(c) the watching of recordings of television programmes to such extent as they may so determine.

(4) Any estimate required for the purposes of this paragraph may be made by the Commission in such manner, or by reference to such surveys conducted or statistics prepared by any one or more other persons, as they think fit.

(5) Any determination made by the Commission under sub-paragraph (4) shall be published by them in such manner as they think fit.

(6) In this paragraph—
(a) "programme" includes part of a programme, and
(b) references to watching a programme do not include references to watching it outside the British Islands.

(7) If it appears to the Secretary of State that there has been a significant change in the audience measurement practices prevailing in the television industry, the Secretary of State may, after consulting the Commission, make such amendments of sub-paragraphs (1), (3) and (6) as he considers appropriate for the purpose of taking account of that change.

Restrictions on holding of licences to provide Channel 3 services or Channel 5

4.—(1) No one person may at any time hold a licence to provide a national Channel 3 service and a licence to provide Channel 5.

(2) A person who holds a licence to provide a regional Channel 3 service for a particular area may not also hold any other licence to provide a regional Channel 3 service for that area.

Limit on the holding of licences to provide television multiplex services

5.—(1) No one person may at any time hold more than three licences to provide television multiplex services.

(2) For the purposes of sub-paragraph (1), a person who is a participant with more than a 20 per cent interest in a body corporate which holds a licence to provide a television multiplex service but does not control that body shall be treated as holding the licence held by that body.

(3) No one person may at any time, in relation to each of five or more licences to provide television multiplex services, be either the holder of the licence or a participant with more than a 10 per cent interest in a body corporate which holds the licence.

(4) In relation to any person who, under any arrangement with the BBC, provides a television multiplex service for the BBC (on a frequency which is not assigned to the Commission under section 6(1) of the 1996 Act)—

(a) sub-paragraph (1) shall have effect as if the reference to three licences were a reference to two licences, and

(b) sub-paragraph (3) shall have effect as if the reference to five licences were a reference to four licences.

(5) The Secretary of State may by order—

(a) amend sub-paragraphs (1) to (4) by substituting a different numerical limit or percentage for any numerical limit or percentage for the time being specified there,

(b) designate any television multiplex service as a regional multiplex service for the purposes of this sub-paragraph, and

(c) prescribe restrictions on the holding by any one person of two or more licences to provide regional multiplex services whose coverage areas are to a significant extent the same.

(6) The Secretary of State shall not designate any television multiplex service as a regional television multiplex service for the purposes of sub-paragraph (5) unless less than half of the population of the United Kingdom is resident within the proposed coverage area of the service.

Limits on the holding, by persons providing digital programme services, of licences to provide other categories of service

6.—(1) The Secretary of State may by order prescribe restrictions on the holding, by a person who is providing a digital programme service by means of a television multiplex service designated by order under paragraph 5(5)(b) as a regional multiplex service, of a licence to provide any service specified in sub-paragraph (2) whose coverage area is to a significant extent the same as that of the digital programme service.

(2) The services referred to in sub-paragraph (1) are—

(a) a regional Channel 3 service,

(b) a local radio service, and

(c) a local radio multiplex service.

(3) The Secretary of State may also by order prescribe restrictions on the provision by any one person at any time of both—

(a) a digital programme service by means of a television multiplex service which is designated by order under paragraph 5(5)(b) as a regional multiplex service, and

(b) a digital sound programme service whose coverage area is to a significant extent the same as that of the digital programme service.

Limit in relation to provision of digital programme services

7.—(1) No person holding a licence to provide digital programme services may, at any time before such day as the Secretary of State may by order appoint for the purposes of this paragraph, provide digital programme services by means of two or more television multiplex services if the number of points attributable to those digital programme services (calculated in accordance with this paragraph) exceeds the permitted maximum.

(2) Subject to sub-paragraphs (3) to (5), the number of points attributable to any digital programme service is two.

(3) Where—

(a) the population within the coverage area of a digital programme service is less than half of the population within the coverage area of the television multiplex service by means of which it is provided, or

(b) a digital programme service is provided by means of a television multiplex service designated by the Secretary of State by order under paragraph 5(5)(b) as a regional multiplex service, or

(c) average weekly air time in relation to a digital programme service is at least 12 hours but less than 50 hours, or

(d) in the case of a digital programme service which was first provided after the beginning of the relevant period, the applicant has notified the Commission of his intention to provide a service in relation to which average weekly air time will be at least 12 hours but less than 50 hours,

the number of points attributable to that digital programme service is one.

(4) Subject to sub-paragraph (5), where—

(a) average weekly air time in relation to a digital programme service is less than 12 hours, or

(b) in the case of a digital programme service which was first provided after the beginning of the relevant period, the applicant has notified the Commission of his intention to provide a service in relation to which average weekly air time will be less than 12 hours,

no points are attributable to that digital programme service.

(5) Where the average weekly air time in relation to each of two or more digital programme services ("the relevant services") provided by any one holder of a licence to provide digital programme services is less than 12 hours, the relevant services shall be treated for the purposes of this paragraph as if they were one service with an average weekly air time equal to the aggregate of the average weekly air times in relation to the relevant services.

(6) For the purposes of sub-paragraphs (3) to (5), as they have effect in relation to the operation of sub-paragraph (1) at any time—

(a) "the relevant period" means the period of 13 weeks ending with the last week falling wholly within the previous calendar month, and

(b) "average weekly air time", in relation to a digital programme service, means the average number of hours per week for which the service has been broadcast during the relevant period;

and in this sub-paragraph "week" means a week ending with Saturday.

(7) The permitted maximum shall be determined by reference to the total number of points attributable to all digital programme services being provided by the holders of licences to provide such services, as follows—

(a) where the total number of points is not more than 10, the permitted maximum is 2,

(b) where the total number of points is more than 10 but less than 24, the permitted maximum is 4, and

(c) where the total number of points is 24 or more, the permitted maximum is one quarter of that total.

(8) For the purposes of this paragraph a person who holds a licence to provide digital programme services and is a participant with more than a 20 per cent interest in a body corporate which also holds such a licence, but who does not control that body, shall be taken to provide any digital programme services provided by that body.

(9) The Secretary of State may by order amend this paragraph—

(a) by altering the number of points for the time being attributable to digital programme services falling within sub-paragraph (2), (3) or (4),

(b) by substituting a different number of hours for the number for the time being specified in sub-paragraph (3), (4) or (5),

(c) by substituting different numbers for any numbers for the time being specified in sub-paragraph (7), and

(d) by substituting a different percentage for the percentage for the time being specified in sub-paragraph (8).

(10) An order under this paragraph shall be subject to annulment in pursuance of a resolution of either House of Parliament.

Limits in relation to licences to provide radio services

8.—(1) No one person may, at any time before such day as the Secretary of State may by order appoint for the purposes of this paragraph (in this paragraph referred to as "the appointed day") hold two or more licences to provide services falling within one or more of the categories specified in paragraph 1(3)(a) or (b) such that the total number of points attributable to those services, calculated in accordance with paragraph 9, exceeds 15 per cent of the total number of points so calculated attributable to all such services in respect of which licences are in force or have been awarded.

(2) No one person may, at any time on or after the appointed day—

(a) hold two or more licences to provide services falling within one or more of the categories specified in paragraph 1(3)(a), (b) or (g) such that the total number of points attributable to those services, calculated in accordance with paragraph 9, exceeds 15 per cent of the total number of points so calculated attributable to—

(i) all national or local radio services in respect of which licences are in force or have been awarded, and

(ii) all national or local digital sound programme services which are being provided, or

(b) hold a licence to provide services falling within the category specified in paragraph 1(3)(g) and provide two or more services falling within that category such that the total number of points attributable to those services, calculated in accordance with paragraph 9, exceeds 15 per cent of the total number of points so calculated attributable to all the services referred to in paragraph (a)(i) or (ii).

(3) Before making an order appointing a day for the purposes of this paragraph, the Secretary of State shall consult the Authority.

Calculation of points for purposes of paragraph 8

9.—(1) For the purposes of paragraph 8, to the categories of national or local radio services and national or local digital sound programme services set out in the Table below there shall be attributed points according to that Table.

TABLE

Category of service	*Points*
National radio service or national digital sound programme service	25
Category A local radio service or Category A local digital sound programme service	15
Category B local radio service or Category B local digital sound programme service	8
Category C local radio service or Category C local digital sound programme service	3
Category D local radio service or Category D local digital sound programme service	1

(2) For the purposes of the Table a local radio service or local digital sound programme service falls—

(a) into category A if the number of persons over the age of 15 resident in the coverage area of that service exceeds 4.5 million;

(b) into category B if the number of such persons exceeds 1 million but does not exceed 4.5 million;

(c) into category C if the number of such persons exceeds 400,000 but does not exceed 1 million; and

(d) into category D if the number of such persons does not exceed 400,000.

(3) No points shall be attributed to a national or local digital sound programme service unless the service is being provided.

(4) In the case of a national or local radio service provided on an amplitude modulated (AM) frequency the relevant number of points attributable to the service by virtue of the Table shall be reduced by one third.

(5) A service which, on the day on which the licence to provide it is granted, falls into a particular category for the purposes of the Table shall continue to be regarded as falling into that category so long as any increase or decrease in the relevant number of persons over the age of 15 (which would otherwise take the service outside that category) does not exceed 10 per cent

(6) A person who is a participant with more than a 20 per cent interest in a body corporate which is the holder of a licence to provide a national or local radio service, but who does not control that body, shall for the purposes of paragraph 8 be treated as the holder of a licence to provide a national or local service to which one half of the points which would otherwise be attributable to such a service are attributed.

(7) A person who is a participant with more than a 20 per cent interest in a body corporate which provides a national or local digital sound programme service, but who does not control that body, shall for the purposes of paragraph 8 be treated as providing a national or local digital sound programme service to which one half of the points which would otherwise be attributable to such a service are attributed.

Power to amend paragraphs 8 and 9

10.—(1) The Secretary of State may by order make such amendments of paragraphs 8 and 9 as he thinks fit for the purposes of including restricted radio services among the services referred to in any provision of paragraph 8 and of providing for the calculation of the points to be attributed to any such service, or any category of such service.

(2) The Secretary of State may by order amend paragraph 9—

(a) by substituting different categories for the categories for the time being set out in the Table in sub-paragraph (1) and in sub-paragraph (2) or adding further categories.

(b) by substituting a different number of points for the number of points for the time being attributed to each category,
(c) by substituting different population figures for those for the time being specified in sub-paragraph (2),
(d) by substituting a different age for the age for the time being specified in sub-paragraph (2)(a) and (5),
(e) by substituting a different fraction for the fraction for the time being specified in sub-paragraph (4) or repealing that sub-paragraph, or
(f) by substituting a different percentage for the percentage for the time being specified in sub-paragraphs (6) and (7) in relation to an interest in a body corporate or a different fraction for the fraction for the time being specified in those sub-paragraphs in relation to the points to be attributed to a person falling within either of those sub-paragraphs.

Limits in relation to licences to provide national radio services, radio multiplex services or digital sound programme services

11.—(1) No one person may at any time hold more than one licence to provide a national radio service.

(2) No one person may at any time—
(a) hold more than one licence to provide a national radio multiplex service, or
(b) hold a licence to provide national digital sound programme services and provide more than one national digital sound programme service.

(3) For the purposes of sub-paragraph (2)(a) a person who is a participant with more than a 20 per cent interest in a body corporate which holds a licence to provide a radio multiplex service but does not control that body shall be treated as holding the licence held by that body.

(4) No one person may at any time—
(a) hold a licence to provide a radio multiplex service and be a participant with more than a 10 per cent interest in more than one body corporate which holds any other such licence, or
(b) be a participant with more than a 10 per cent interest in each of three or more bodies corporate which hold such licences.

(5) The Secretary of State may by order—
(a) amend sub-paragraph (1), (2) or (4) by substituting a different numerical limit for any numerical limit for the time being specified there, and
(b) amend sub-paragraph (3) or (4) by substituting a different percentage for any percentage for the time being specified there.

Limits in relation to licences to provide local radio services in overlapping areas

12.—(1) No one person may at any time hold any two licences to provide local radio services which share a potential audience unless either—
(a) one of the licences is an AM licence and the other is an FM licence, or
(b) the Authority have determined that in all the circumstances, having regard to the matters specified in sub-paragraph (4), the holding by that person of the licences in question could not be expected to operate against the public interest within the area concerned.

(2) No one person may at any time hold any three licences to provide local radio services any of which shares a potential audience with each of the other two services unless—
(a) the licences include both an AM licence and an FM licence, and
(b) the Authority have determined that in all the circumstances, having regard to the matters specified in sub-paragraph (4), the holding by that person of the licences in question could not be expected to operate against the public interest within the area concerned.

(3) No one person may at any time hold any four or more licences to provide local radio services any of which shares a potential audience with each of the other services.

(4) The matters referred to in sub-paragraphs (1) and (2) are—
(a) any reduction in plurality of ownership of local radio services within the area concerned that would result from a decision to allow the licences to be held together, and
(b) the likely effect of such a decision on—

(i) the range of programmes available by way of independent radio services to persons living in the area concerned, and

(ii) diversity in the sources of information available to the public in the area concerned and in the opinions expressed on local radio services received in that area.

(5) For the purposes of this paragraph two local radio services share a potential audience if, but only if, the potential audience of one service includes more than half of the potential audience of the other service.

(6) This paragraph has effect subject to paragraph 13.

(7) In this paragraph—

"AM licence" means a licence to provide a local radio service on an amplitude modulated frequency,

"FM licence" means a licence to provide such a service on a frequency modulated frequency, and

"potential audience", in relation to a local radio service means the persons over the age referred to in paragraph 9(2)(a) who reside in the coverage area of that service.

Power by order to impose different restrictions in place of paragraph 12

13. The Secretary of State may by order provide that, where a digital sound programme service is provided in any area, the holding by any one person of two or more licences to provide in that area local radio services which for the purposes of paragraph 12 share a potential audience with each other or with each of the others shall, instead of being subject to the restrictions specified in paragraph 12, be subject to other restrictions specified in the order.

Limits in relation to provision of local digital sound programme services

14.—(1) Subject to sub-paragraph (2), no one person holding a licence to provide local digital sound programme services may at any time provide more than one non-simulcast service by means of a particular local radio multiplex service.

(2) Where—

(a) the coverage area of the local radio multiplex service is to a significant extent the same as that of another local radio multiplex service, and

(b) the person concerned is not providing any non-simulcast service, by means of that other local radio multiplex service,

sub-paragraph (1) shall have effect as if the reference to one non-simulcast service were a reference to two such services.

(3) In this paragraph "non-simulcast service" means any local digital sound programme service other than one which—

(a) is provided by a person who holds a licence to provide a local radio service, and

(b) corresponds to that local radio service.

(4) For the purposes of sub-paragraph (3)(b) a local digital sound programme service corresponds to a local radio service if, and only if, in every calendar month—

(a) at least 80 per cent of so much of the local radio service as consists of programmes, consists of programmes which are also included in the local digital sound programme service in that month, and

(b) at least 50 per cent of so much of the local radio service as consists of such programmes is broadcast at the same time on both services.

(5) The Secretary of State may by order—

(a) amend sub-paragraphs (1) and (2) by substituting a different numerical limit for any numerical limit for the time being specified there, and

(b) amend sub-paragraph (4)(a) or (b) by substituting a different percentage for any percentage for the time being specified there.

(6) In subsection (4) "programme" does not include an advertisement.

Further restrictions on holding of licences of different descriptions

15.—(1) No one person may at any time hold—

(a) a licence to provide a national Channel 3 service or Channel 5, and

(b) a licence to provide a national radio service.

(2) No one person may at any time hold—

(a) a licence to provide a local radio service or local digital sound programme services, and

(b) a licence to provide a regional Channel 3 service whose coverage area is to a significant extent the same as that the local radio service or of any local digital sound programme service provided by him.

Power to impose additional limits in relation to licences to provide television or radio services

16.—(1) The Secretary of State may, in the case of—

(a) any category of relevant services specified in paragraph 1(2)(b), (c), (d) or (f), or
(b) any category of relevant services specified in paragraph 1(3)(c) or (e).

by order prescribe the maximum number of licences which may at any time be held by any one person to provide relevant services falling within that category.

(2) The Secretary of State may by order impose, in relation to any category of relevant services specified in paragraph 1(2)(a) or (b) or paragraph 1(3)(a), (b) or (f) or under sub-paragraph (1), limits on the holding of licences to provide relevant services falling within that category which are additional to the limits specified in paragraphs 2 to 15 or under that sub-paragraph and are framed—

(a) by reference to any specified circumstances relating to the holders of the licences in question or to the services to be provided under them, or
(b) (in the case of licences granted by the Commission) by reference to matters determined by them under the order.

(3) Without prejudice to the generality of sub-paragraph (2), an order made under that sub-paragraph may impose on the holder of a licence to provide any specified category of relevant services specified in paragraph 1(3) limits framed (directly or indirectly) by reference to either or both of the following matters, namely—

(a) the number of licences of any one or more specified descriptions which are held by him or by any body controlled by him; and
(b) his participation, to any specified extent, in any body corporate which is the holder of any licence or licences of any one or more such descriptions.

(4) Where a person holds—

(a) a licence to provide a domestic satellite service,
(b) a licence to provide a non-domestic satellite service, or
(c) a licence to provide a satellite radio service,

which, in accordance with section 44(2), 45(3) or 86(2), authorises the provision of a multichannel service, he shall be treated for the purposes of any order under sub-paragraph (1) as holding such number of licences to provide domestic satellite services, non-domestic satellite services or (as the case may be) satellite radio services as corresponds to the number of channels on which the service may be provided.

(5) In sub-paragraph (4)—

(a) "multichannel service" means a service which to any extent consists in the simultaneous transmission of different programmes on different frequencies; and
(b) any reference to the number of channels on which such a service may be provided is a reference to the number of different frequencies involved.

(6) Where a person who holds a licence to provide any of the services specified in sub-paragraph (4)(a), (b) or (c) provides that service by broadcasting two or more programmes simultaneously in digital form on a single frequency, he shall be treated for the purposes of any order under sub-paragraph (1) as holding such number of licences as corresponds to the number of programmes that are simultaneously transmitted.

Connected persons

17.—(1) Subject to sub-paragraph (2), for the purposes of—

(a) paragraphs 2 to 15, and
(b) any order under paragraph 13 or 16(1) or (2),

a person shall be treated as holding a licence if the licence is held by a person connected with him and shall be treated as providing a service if the service is provided by a person connected with him.

(2) For the purposes of paragraph 12 and any order under paragraph 13, a person shall not be treated as holding a licence to provide a local radio service merely because he is a director of a body corporate which holds the licence.

(3) Any provision of paragraphs 2 to 14 which refers to a person's participation in a body corporate shall have effect as if he and every person connected with him were one person."

PART IV

PROVISIONS SUBSTITUTED FOR PART IV OF SCHEDULE 2

11. For Part IV of Schedule 2 there is substituted—

"PART IV

RESTRICTIONS ON CONTROLLING INTERESTS IN BOTH NEWSPAPERS AND LICENSED SERVICES

Meaning of "relevant authority"

1. In this Part of this Schedule "the relevant authority"—

(a) in relation to any restriction having effect in relation to any licence which has been or may be granted by the Commission, means the Commission, and

(b) in relation to any restriction having effect in relation to any licence which has been or may be granted by the Authority, means the Authority.

National and local newspapers and their respective national and local market shares

2.—(1) In this Part of this Schedule references to a national or local newspaper are (subject to sub-paragraph (3)) references to a national or local newspaper circulating wholly or mainly in the United Kingdom or in a part of the United Kingdom.

(2) Where a newspaper is published in different regional editions on the same day, the relevant authority may determine, having regard to all the circumstances, whether those regional editions are to be treated for the purposes of this Part of this Schedule as constituting one national newspaper, two or more local newspapers or one national newspaper and one or more local newspapers.

(3) The relevant authority may determine that a newspaper which would otherwise be neither a national nor a local newspaper for the purposes of this Part of this Schedule shall be treated as a national or (as the case may be) a local newspaper for the purposes of any particular restriction imposed by or under this Part of this Schedule if it appears to them to be appropriate for the newspaper to be so treated having regard to its circulation or influence in the United Kingdom or (as the case may be) in a part of the United Kingdom.

(4) For the purposes of this Part of this Schedule, the "national market share" of any national newspaper at any time in a calendar month is the total number of copies of that newspaper sold in the United Kingdom in the six months ending with the last day of the previous month, expressed as a percentage of the total number of copies of all national newspapers sold in the United Kingdom in those six months.

(5) For the purposes of this Part of this Schedule, the "local market share" of any local newspaper in any area at any time in a calendar month is the total number of copies of that newspaper sold in that area in the six months ending with the last day of the previous month, expressed as a percentage of the total number of copies of all local newspapers sold in that area in those six months.

(6) For the purposes of sub-paragraphs (4) and (5), the relevant authority may estimate the numbers of copies of any newspaper sold in the United Kingdom, or in any area, during any period in such manner, or by reference to such statistics prepared by any other person, as they think fit.

(7) In relation to any newspaper which is distributed free of charge rather than being sold, references in sub-paragraphs (4) to (6) to the number of copies sold shall have effect as references to the number of copies distributed.

Other interpretative provisions

3.—(1) For the purposes of this Part of this Schedule a person runs a national or local newspaper if—

(a) he is the proprietor of the newspaper, or

(b) he controls a body which is the proprietor of the newspaper.

(2) Paragraph 1(4) in Part III of this Schedule shall have effect for the purposes of this Part of this Schedule as it has effect for the purposes of Part III.

Restrictions on common control etc.

4.—(1) No person who runs a national newspaper which for the time being has, or national newspapers which for the time being together have, a national market share of 20 per cent or more may hold a licence to provide—

(a) a regional or national Channel 3 service or Channel 5, or
(b) a national or local radio service.

(2) A licence to provide a regional Channel 3 service may not be held by a person who runs a local newspaper which for the time being has, or local newspapers which for the time being together have, a local market share of 20 per cent or more in the coverage area of the service.

(3) A licence to provide digital programme services may not be held by a person who runs a local newspaper which for the time being has, or local newspapers which for the time being together have, a local market share of 20 per cent or more in the coverage area of any digital programme service provided under the licence.

(4) For the purposes of this paragraph a person shall be treated as holding a licence if the licence is held by a person connected with him.

Restrictions on participation

5.—(1) No proprietor of a national newspaper which for the time being has, or of national newspapers which for the time being together have, a national market share of 20 per cent or more shall be a participant with more than a 20 per cent interest in a body corporate which is the holder of a licence to provide any of the services specified in sub-paragraph (4).

(2) No person who is the holder of a licence to provide any of the services specified in sub-paragraph (4) shall be a participant with more than a 20 per cent interest in a body corporate which runs a national newspaper which has, or two or more national newspapers which together have, a national market share of 20 per cent or more.

(3) No body corporate in which a person who runs a national newspaper which has, or national newspapers which together have, a national market share of 20 per cent or more is a participant with more than a 20 per cent interest, shall be a participant with more than a 20 per cent interest in a body corporate which holds a licence to provide any of the services specified in sub-paragraph (4).

(4) The services referred to in sub-paragraphs (1), (2) and (3) are—
(a) a regional or national Channel 3 service or Channel 5, and
(b) national or local radio services.

(5) The Secretary of State may by order amend sub-paragraph (1), (2) or (3) by substituting a different percentage interest in a body corporate for the percentage for the time being specified there.

(6) Any restriction imposed by this paragraph on participation in a body corporate which is the holder of a particular kind of licence shall apply equally to participation in a body corporate which controls the holder of such a licence.

(7) Any restriction on participation imposed by this paragraph—
(a) on the proprietor of any newspaper, or
(b) on the holder of any licence,
shall apply as if he and every person connected with him were one person.

Holding of local radio licence by person running local newspapers with at least 50 per cent local market share

6.—(1) A licence to provide a local radio service may not be held by a person who runs a local newspaper which has, or local newspapers which for the time being together have, a local market share of 50 per cent or more in the coverage area of the service unless—
(a) the service in question shares a potential audience with another local radio service, but
(b) he does not hold any other licence to provide a local radio service whose coverage area is to any extent the same as the coverage area of the service in question.

(2) The reference in sub-paragraph (1) to sharing a potential audience shall be construed in accordance with paragraph 12(5) in Part III of this Schedule.

(3) For the purposes of this paragraph a person shall be treated as holding a licence if the licence is held by a person connected with him.

Further restrictions on holding of local radio licences by a person who runs a local newspaper

7.—(1) No person who runs a local newspaper which for the time being has, or local newspapers which for the time being together have, a local market share of 20 per cent or more in each of the relevant areas may hold any three licences to provide local radio services any of which shares a potential audience with each of the other services.

(2) No person who runs a local newspaper which for the time being has, or local newspapers which for the time being together have, a local market share of 20 per cent or more in both the relevant areas may hold any two licences to provide local radio services which

share a potential audience, unless one of the licences is an AM licence and the other is an FM licence.

(3) In sub-paragraphs (1) and (2)—

(a) "the relevant areas" means the coverage areas of the local radio services in question,

(b) references to sharing a potential audience shall be construed in accordance with sub-paragraph (5) of paragraph 12 in Part III of this Schedule, and

(c) "AM licence" and "FM licence" have the same meaning as in that paragraph.

(4) For the purposes of this paragraph a person shall be treated as holding a licence if the licence is held by a person connected with him.

(5) This paragraph has effect subject to paragraph 8.

Power by order to impose different restrictions in place of paragraph 7

8.—(1) The Secretary of State may by order provide that, where a digital sound programme service is provided in any area, the holding, by a person who runs a local newspaper or local newspapers as mentioned in paragraph 7(1), of two or more licences to provide in that area local radio services which for the purposes of paragraph 7 share a potential audience with each other or with each of the others shall, instead of being subject to the restrictions specified in paragraph 7, be subject to other restrictions specified in the order.

(2) For the purposes of any order under sub-paragraph (1), a person shall be treated as holding a licence if the licence is held by a person connected with him.

Additional restrictions applying where control of or by newspaper proprietor may operate against public interest

9.—(1) A licence to provide any of the services specified in sub-paragraph (4) may not be granted to a body corporate which is, or is connected with, the proprietor of a national or local newspaper if the relevant authority determine that in all the circumstances the holding of the licence by that body corporate could be expected to operate against the public interest.

(2) Subject to sub-paragraph (3), a body corporate which holds a licence to provide any of the services specified in sub-paragraph (4) shall not become, or become connected with, the proprietor of a national or local newspaper and continue to hold the licence if the relevant authority determine within the permitted period that in all the circumstances the continued holding of the licence by that body corporate operates, or could be expected to operate, against the public interest.

(3) Sub-paragraph (2) does not apply in any case where the body corporate holding the licence—

(a) is already the proprietor of some other national or local newspaper, or is already connected with such a proprietor, and

(b) does not become connected with any other person who holds a licence to provide any of the services specified in sub-paragraph (4)

(4) The services referred to in sub-paragraphs (1) to (3) are—

(a) a national Channel 3 service or Channel 5,

(b) a national radio service, and

(c) national digital sound programme services.

(5) Subject to sub-paragraph (6), in this paragraph "the permitted period" means a period beginning with the day on which the licence holder becomes, or becomes connected with, the proprietor of the national or local newspaper ("the relevant day") and ending—

(a) in a case where the licence holder has, before the relevant day, notified the relevant authority that he will become, or become connected with, the proprietor of that national or local newspaper on that day, at the end of the period of three months beginning with the relevant day, or

(b) in any other case, at the end of the period of three months beginning with the day on which the licence holder notifies the relevant authority that he has become, or has become connected with, the proprietor of that national or local newspaper.

(6) The relevant authority may in a particular case, after consultation with the licence holder, notify him, before the time when the permitted period would (apart from this sub-paragraph) have ended, that the permitted period in that case is to be calculated as if the references in sub-paragraph (5) to three months were references to such longer period specified in the notification as the relevant authority reasonably consider necessary in the circumstances.

(7) Nothing in any of the preceding provisions of this Schedule shall be construed as affecting the operation of this paragraph or paragraph 10 or 11.

10.—(1) A licence to provide a regional Channel 3 service or a local radio service may not be granted to a body corporate which is, or is connected with, the proprietor of a national newspaper or a relevant local newspaper if the relevant authority determine that in all the circumstances the holding of the licence by that body corporate could be expected to operate against the public interest.

(2) Subject to sub-paragraph (3), a body corporate which holds a licence to provide a regional Channel 3 service or a local radio service shall not become, or become connected with, the proprietor of a national newspaper and continue to hold the licence if the relevant authority determine within the permitted period that in all the circumstances the continued holding of the licence by that body corporate operates, or could be expected to operate, against the public interest.

(3) Sub-paragraph (2) does not apply in any case where the body corporate holding the licence—

(a) is already the proprietor of some other national newspaper or is already connected with such a proprietor, and

(b) does not become connected with—

(i) any other person who holds a licence to provide a regional Channel 3 service or a local radio service, or

(ii) any person who holds a licence to provide digital programme services and is providing a service under that licence.

(4) Subject to sub-paragraph (5), a body corporate which holds a licence to provide a regional Channel 3 service or a local radio service shall not become, or become connected with, the proprietor of a relevant local newspaper and continue to hold the licence if the relevant authority determine within the permitted period that in all the circumstances the continued holding of the licence by that body corporate operates, or could be expected to operate, against the public interest.

(5) Sub-paragraph (4) does not apply in any case where the body corporate which holds the licence—

(a) is already the proprietor of some other local newspaper which is a relevant local newspaper in relation to the service referred to in that sub-paragraph, or is already connected with such a proprietor, and

(b) does not become connected with—

(i) any other person who holds a licence to provide a regional Channel 3 service or local radio service in relation to which that other local newspaper is also a relevant local newspaper, or

(ii) any person who holds a licence to provide digital programme services and is providing a service under that licence in relation to which that other local newspaper is also a relevant local newspaper.

(6) For the purposes of this paragraph a local newspaper is a "relevant local newspaper", in relation to any service, if it serves an area which is to a significant extent the same as the coverage area of the service.

(7) In this paragraph "the permitted period" has the meaning given by paragraph 9(5) and (6).

11.—(1) A body corporate which holds a licence to provide digital programme services and is, or is connected with, the proprietor of a national newspaper or a relevant local newspaper, shall not begin to provide a digital programme service if the Commission determine before the end of the period specified in sub-paragraph (2) that in all the circumstances the provision of that service by that body corporate could be expected to operate against the public interest.

(2) The period referred to in sub-paragraph (1) is the period of three months beginning with the day on which the Commission are notified pursuant to section 19(3) of the 1996 Act of an agreement to provide the digital programme service, or such longer period beginning with that day as the Commission may in a particular case, after consultation with the licence holder, notify him during those three months as being the period which they reasonably consider necessary in the circumstances.

(3) Subject to sub-paragraph (4), a body corporate which is providing a digital programme service shall not become, or become connected with, the proprietor of a national newspaper and continue to provide the service if the Commission determine within the permitted period that in all the circumstances the continued provision of the service by that body corporate operates, or could be expected to operate, against the public interest.

(4) Sub-paragraph (3) does not apply in any case where the body corporate which is providing the digital programme service—

(a) is already the proprietor of some other national newspaper or is already connected with such a proprietor, and

(b) does not become connected with—

(i) the holder of a licence to provide a regional Channel 3 service or a local radio service, or

(ii) the holder of another licence to provide digital programme services who is providing a service under that licence.

(5) Subject to sub-paragraph (6), a body corporate which is providing a digital programme service shall not become, or become connected with, the proprietor of a relevant local newspaper and continue to provide the service if the Commission determine within the permitted period that in all the circumstances the continued provision of the service by that body corporate operates, or could be expected to operate, against the public interest.

(6) Sub-paragraph (5) does not apply in any case where the body corporate which is providing the digital programme service—

(a) is already the proprietor of some other local newspaper which is a relevant local newspaper in relation to the service referred to in that sub-paragraph, or is already connected with such a proprietor, and

(b) does not become connected with—

(i) the holder of a licence to provide a regional Channel 3 service or local radio service in relation to which that other local newspaper is also a relevant local newspaper, or

(ii) the holder of another licence to provide digital programme services who is providing a service under that licence in relation to which that other local newspaper is also a relevant local newspaper.

(7) In this paragraph—

(a) references to a relevant local newspaper shall be construed in accordance with paragraph 10(6), and

(b) "the permitted period" has the meaning given by paragraph 9(5) and (6).

12.—(1) Notice may be given to the relevant authority in accordance with this paragraph of proposed arrangements which might result—

(a) in the application of paragraph 9(2) to a body corporate which holds a licence to provide any of the services specified in paragraph 9(4),

(b) in the application of paragraph 10(2) or (4) to a body corporate which holds a licence to provide a regional Channel 3 service or a local radio service, or

(c) in the application of paragraph 11(1), (3) or (5) to a body corporate which holds a licence to provide digital programme services.

(2) A notice under sub-paragraph (1)—

(a) may be given by the licence holder or any other person appearing to the relevant authority to be concerned,

(b) shall state that the existence of the proposal has been made pubic, and

(c) shall be in such form as the relevant authority may require.

(3) The relevant authority may, at any time before making a determination under this paragraph, require the person who gave the notice to provide them with such further information with respect to the notified arrangements as they think fit.

(4) The relevant authority shall, as soon as reasonably practicable, determine whether in all the circumstances if the notified arrangements were carried into effect, the continued holding of the licence by the body corporate could be expected to operate against the public interest.

(5) If—

(a) the relevant authority determine, in relation to any notified arrangements, that the fact referred to in sub-paragraph (4) could not be expected to operate against the public interest, and

(b) the notified arrangements are carried into effect within the period of 12 months beginning with the date of the determination,

the relevant authority may not make any determination under paragraph 9(2), 10(2) or (4) or 11(1), (3) or (5) arising out of the carrying into effect of the notified arrangements.

(6) Sub-paragraph (5) does not prevent any determination under paragraph 9(2), 10(2) or (4) or 11(1), (3) or (5) being made if—

(a) any information given to the relevant authority in respect of the notified arrangements by the person who gave the notice is in any material respect false or misleading, or

(b) since the making of the determination there has been a material change of circumstances (other than such a change of which notice was given to the relevant authority under sub-paragraph (3) before the making of the determination).

(7) In this paragraph "the notified arrangements" means the arrangements mentioned in the notice under sub-paragraph (1) or arrangements not differing from them in any material respect.

13.—(1) The matters to which the relevant authority shall have regard in determining, for the purposes of paragraph 9, 10, 11 or 12, whether the holding of a licence by a body corporate which is, or is connected with, the proprietor of a newspaper operates, or could be expected to operate, against the public interest include—

(a) the desirability of promoting—

(i) plurality of ownership in the broadcasting and newspaper industries, and

(ii) diversity in the sources of information available to the public and in the opinions expressed on television or radio or in newspapers,

(b) any economic benefits (such as, for example, technical development or an increase in employment or in the value of goods or services exported) that might be expected to result from the holding of the licence by that body but could not be expected to result from the holding of the licence by a body corporate which was not, and was not connected with, the proprietor of a newspaper, and

(c) the effect of the holding of the licence by that body on the proper operation of the market within the broadcasting and newspaper industries or any section of them.

(2) References in paragraphs 9, 10, 11 and 12 to the public interest include references to the public interest within any area of the United Kingdom.

14. In relation to any determination under paragraph 11(1), (3) or (5), references in paragraphs 12 and 13 to the holding of the licence shall have effect as references to the provision of the service.

Restricted television services

15.—(1) The Secretary of State may by order—

(a) prescribe restrictions on the holding of one or more licences to provide restricted television services by a person who runs a national or local newspaper, and

(b) apply any of the provisions of paragraphs 9 to 13, with such modifications as may be specified in the order, in relation to the holding of a licence to provide a restricted television service.

(2) Any order under sub-paragraph (1) may provide that, for the purposes of any provision of the order, a person is to be treated as holding a licence if the licence is held by a person connected with him.

(3) In this paragraph "restricted television service" means a restricted service within the meaning of Part I of this Act."

Part V

Amendments of other provisions of 1990 Act

12.—(1) Section 5 of the 1990 Act (restrictions on the holding of licences) is amended as follows.

(2) For subsection (6) there is substituted—

"(6) The Commission shall not serve any such notice on the licence holder unless—

(a) the Commission have notified him of the matters complained of and given him a reasonable opportunity of making representations to them about those matters, and

(b) in a case where the relevant change is one falling within subsection (6A)—

(i) they have also given him an opportunity of complying with Parts III and IV of Schedule 2 within a period specified in the notification, and

(ii) the period specified in the notification has elapsed.

(6A) A relevant change falls within this subsection if it consists only in one or more of the following—

(a) a change in the percentage of total audience time attributable to one or more services for the purposes of paragraph 2 of Part III of Schedule 2;

(b) a change in the national market share (within the meaning of Part IV of that Schedule) of one or more national newspapers (within the meaning of that Part of that Schedule);

(c) a change in the local market share (within the meaning of that Part of that Schedule) in a particular area of one or more local newspapers (within the meaning of that Part of that Schedule).

(6B) Where a licence has been granted in a case where the Commission could have made a determination under paragraph 9(1) or 10(1) of Part IV of Schedule 2 (if satisfied that the fact mentioned in that provision could have been expected to operate against the public interest), subsection (5) does not enable the licence to be revoked merely because a change is such that the Commission would have made such a determination in the new circumstances of the case."

(3) In subsection (7)—

(a) after paragraph (b) there is inserted—

"or

(c) any other change giving rise to a failure to comply with any requirement imposed by or under Schedule 2,", and

(b) for "(in either case) ' there is substituted "(in any case)".

13.—(1) Section 88 of the 1990 Act (restrictions on the holding of licences) is amended as follows.

(2) For subsection (6) there is substituted—

"(6) The Authority shall not serve any such notice on the licence holder unless—

(a) the Authority have notified him of the matters complained of and given him a reasonable opportunity of making representations to them about those matters, and

(b) in a case where the relevant change is one falling within subsection (6A)—

(i) they have also given him an opportunity of complying with Parts III and IV of Schedule 2 within a period specified in the notification, and

(ii) the period specified in the notification has elapsed.

(6A) A relevant change falls within this subsection if it consists only in one or more of the following—

(a) a reduction in the total number of points, calculated in accordance with paragraph 9 of Part III of Schedule 2, attributable to all the services referred to in paragraph 8(1) or (2)(a) or (b) of that Part of that Schedule;

(b) a change in the national market share (within the meaning of Part IV of that Schedule) of one or more national newspapers (within the meaning of that Part of that Schedule);

(c) a change in the local market share (within the meaning of that Part of that Schedule) in a particular area of one or more local newspapers (within the meaning of that Part of that Schedule).

(6B) Where a licence has been granted in a case where the Authority could have made a determination under paragraph 9(1) or 10(1) of Part IV of Schedule 2 (if satisfied that the fact mentioned in that provision could have been expected to operate against the public interest), subsection (5) does not enable the licence to be revoked merely because a change is such that the Authority would have made such a determination in the new circumstances of the case."

(3) In subsection (7)—

(a) after paragraph (b) there is inserted—

"or

(c) any other change giving rise to a failure to comply with any requirement imposed by or under Schedule 2,", and

(b) for "(in either case)" there is substituted "(in any case)".

Section 106(3)

SCHEDULE 3

BROADCASTING STANDARDS COMMISSION: SUPPLEMENTARY PROVISIONS

Interpretation

1. In this Schedule—

(a) "pension scheme" means a scheme for the payment of pensions, allowances or gratuities,

(b) any reference to the payment of pensions, allowances or gratuities includes a reference to like benefits to be given on death or retirement, and

(c) any reference to the payment of pensions. allowances or gratuities to or in respect of any persons includes a reference to the making of payments towards provision for the payment of pensions, allowances or gratuities to or in respect of those persons.

Status and capacity

2.—(1) The BSC shall be a body corporate.

(2) The BSC shall not be treated for the purposes of the enactments and rules of law relating to the privileges of the Crown as a body exercising functions on behalf of the Crown.

(3) It shall be within the capacity of the BSC as a statutory corporation to do such things and enter into such transactions as are incidental or conducive to the discharge of their functions under this Act.

Appointment of members

3.—(1) A person shall be disqualified for being a member of the BSC so long as he is—

(a) a governor or employee of the BBC,

(b) a member or employee of the Independent Television Commission,

(c) a member or employee of the Radio Authority,

(d) a member or employee of the Channel Four Television Corporation,

(e) a member or employee of the Welsh Authority, or

(f) a person who does not fall within any of the preceding paragraphs but who appears to the Secretary of State to be concerned with, or to have an interest in—

(i) the preparation or provision of programmes for broadcasting by the BBC or the Welsh Authority, or

(ii) the provision of a licensed service or the preparation or provision of programmes for inclusion in such a service.

(2) Before appointing a person to be a member of the BSC the Secretary of State shall satisfy himself that that person will have no such financial or other interest as is likely to affect prejudicially the discharge by him of his functions as a member of the BSC; and the Secretary of State shall also satisfy himself from time to time with respect to every member of the BSC that he has no such interest.

(3) Any person who is, or whom the Secretary of State proposes to appoint to be, a member of the BSC shall, whenever requested by the Secretary of State to do so, furnish him with such information as the Secretary of State considers necessary for the performance by him of his duties under sub-paragraph (2).

Tenure of office

4.—(1) Subject to the following provisions of this paragraph, each member of the BSC shall hold and vacate office in accordance with the terms of his appointment.

(2) A person shall not be appointed to be a member of the BSC for more than five years at a time.

(3) Any member of the BSC may at any time resign his office by notice in writing to the Secretary of State.

Remuneration and pensions of members

5.—(1) The BSC may pay to each member such remuneration and allowances as the Secretary of State may determine.

(2) The BSC may pay or make provision for paying to or in respect of any member such sums by way of pensions, allowances or gratuities as the Secretary of State may determine.

(3) Where a person ceases to be a member otherwise than on the expiry of his term of office and it appears to the Secretary of State that there are special circumstances which make it right for him to receive compensation, the BSC may make a payment to him of such amount as the Secretary of State may determine.

Disqualification of members of BSC for House of Commons and Northern Ireland Assembly

6. In Part II of Schedule 1 to the House of Commons Disqualification Act 1975 (bodies of which all members are disqualified) there shall be inserted at the appropriate place—

"The Broadcasting Standards Commission";

and a corresponding amendment shall be made in Part II of Schedule 1 to the Northern Ireland Assembly Disqualification Act 1975.

Proceedings

7.—(1) Subject to paragraph 8 and to the provisions of Part V of this Act, the quorum of the BSC and the arrangements relating to their meetings shall be such as the BSC may determine.

(2) Subject to section 112, the arrangements may provide for the discharge, under the general direction of the BSC, of any of the BSC's functions by a committee or by one or more of the members or employees of the BSC.

8.—(1) A member who is in any way directly or indirectly interested in any matter that is brought up for consideration at a meeting of the BSC shall disclose the nature of his interest to the meeting; and, where such a disclosure is made—

(a) the disclosure shall be recorded in the minutes of the meeting, and

(b) (subject to sub-paragraph (2)) the member shall not take any part in any deliberation or decision of the BSC, or of any of their committees, with respect to that matter.

(2) Sub-paragraph (1)(b) shall not apply in relation to any meeting of the BSC at which all of the other members present resolve that the member's interest should be disregarded for the purposes of that provision.

(3) For the purposes of sub-paragraph (1), a general notification given at a meeting of the BSC by a member to the effect that he is a member of a specified company or firm and is to be regarded as interested in any matter involving that company or firm shall be regarded as a sufficient disclosure of his interest in relation to any such matter.

(4) A member need not attend in person at a meeting of the BSC in order to make a disclosure which he is required to make under this paragraph if he takes reasonable steps to secure that the disclosure is made by a notice which is taken into consideration and read at the meeting.

(5) In this paragraph references to a meeting of the BSC include references to a meeting of any of their committees.

9. The validity of any proceedings of the BSC shall not be affected by any vacancy among the members or by any defect in the appointment of a member or by any failure to comply with the requirements of paragraph 8 or of section 112.

Employees of the BSC

10.—(1) The BSC may appoint such number of employees as they may determine.

(2) The remuneration and other conditions of service of the persons appointed under this paragraph shall be determined by the BSC.

(3) If the BSC determine to do so in the case of any of their employees, the BSC shall pay to or in respect of those employees such pensions, allowances or gratuities, or provide and maintain for them such pension schemes (whether contributory or not), as the BSC may determine.

(4) Any determination under sub-paragraph (1), (2) or (3) shall require the approval of the Secretary of State.

(5) If any employee of the BSC—

(a) is a participant in any pension scheme applicable to his employment, and

(b) becomes a member of the BSC,

he may, if the Secretary of State so determines, be treated for the purposes of the pension scheme as if his service as a member of the BSC were service as an employee of the BSC.

(6) The Employers' Liability (Compulsory Insurance) Act 1969 shall not require insurance to be effected by the BSC.

Financial provisions

11.—(1) The Secretary of State shall pay to the BSC—

(a) any expenses incurred or to be incurred by the BSC by virtue of paragraph 5 or 10, and

(b) with the consent of the Treasury, such sums as he thinks fit for enabling the BSC to meet other expenses.

(2) Any sums required by the Secretary of State for making payments under sub-paragraph (1) shall be paid out of money provided by Parliament.

Authentication of seal of BSC

12.—(1) The application of the seal of the BSC shall be authenticated by the signature of the chairman or of some other person authorised for the purpose.

(2) Sub-paragraph (1) does not apply in relation to any document which is or is to be signed in accordance with the law of Scotland.

Presumption of authenticity of documents issued by BSC

13. Any document purporting to be an instrument issued by the BSC and to be duly executed under the seal of the BSC or to be signed on behalf of the BSC shall be received in evidence and shall be deemed to be such an instrument unless the contrary is shown.

Accounts and audit

14.—(1) The BSC shall keep proper accounts and proper records in relation to the accounts, and shall prepare in respect of each financial year a statement of accounts in such form as the Secretary of State may direct with the approval of the Treasury.

(2) The BSC shall send a copy of the statement of accounts to the Secretary of State and to the Comptroller and Auditor General within such period after the end of the financial year to which the statement relates as the Secretary of State may direct.

(3) The Comptroller and Auditor General shall—

(a) examine, certify and report on the statement of accounts, and
(b) lay a copy of the statement of accounts and of his report before each House of Parliament.

Section 128

SCHEDULE 4

SUPPLEMENTARY PROVISIONS RELATION TO DISSOLUTION OF BROADCASTING COMPLAINTS COMMISSION AND BROADCASTING STANDARDS COUNCIL

Meaning of "the existing boards"

1. In this Schedule "the existing boards" has the same meaning as in section 128.

Provisions as to vesting of property etc. of existing boards

2.—(1) Sub-paragraph (2) shall have effect for the purposes of, or in connection with, the vesting in the BSC by virtue of section 128(2) of property, rights or liabilities of the existing boards.

(2) Any agreement made, transaction effected or other thing done by or in relation to either of the existing boards which is in force or effective immediately before the transfer date shall have effect as from that date as if made, effected or done by or in relation to the BSC, in all respects as if the BSC were the same person, in law, as that existing board; and accordingly references to either of the existing boards—

(a) in any agreement (whether or not in writing) and in any deed, bond or instrument,
(b) in any process or other document issued, prepared or employed for the purpose of any proceeding before any court or other tribunal or authority, and
(c) in any other document whatever (other than an enactment),

shall be taken as from the transfer date as referring to the BSC.

3.—(1) Where immediately before the transfer date there is in force an agreement which—

(a) confers or imposes on either of the existing boards any rights or liabilities which vest in the BSC by virtue of section 128(2), and
(b) refers (in whatever terms and whether expressly or by implication) to a member or officer of that existing board,

the agreement shall have effect, in relation to anything falling to be done on or after the transfer date, as if for that reference there were substituted a reference to such person as the BSC may appoint or, in default of appointment, to the member or employee of the BSC who corresponds as nearly as possible to the member or officer of that existing board.

(2) References in this paragraph to an agreement include references to a deed, bond or other instrument.

Pensions

4.—(1) It is hereby declared for the avoidance of doubt that section 128(2) is effective to vest the rights and liabilities of either of the existing boards under any agreement or arrangement for the payment of pensions, allowances or gratuities in the BSC along with all other rights and liabilities of the existing boards.

(2) Accordingly, for the purposes of any such agreement or arrangement as it has effect as from the transfer date, any period of employment with either of the existing boards shall count as employment with the BSC.

Final accounts and annual report of existing bodies

5.—(1) The Broadcasting Complaints Commission shall, as soon as possible after the transfer date, prepare such a statement of accounts as is mentioned in paragraph 12 of Schedule 13 to the 1990 Act (accounts and audit) in respect of the period between—

(a) the end of the financial year for which the last such statement of accounts was prepared by them under that paragraph, and
(b) the transfer date,

whether that period is a financial year or not; and that paragraph shall continue to apply on and after that date in relation to the auditing of accounts kept in accordance with that paragraph in respect of that period.

(2) The Broadcasting Complaints Commission shall, as soon as possible after the transfer date, prepare and submit to the Secretary of State, in accordance with section 148 of the 1990 Act (annual reports), such a report as is mentioned in subsection (1) of that section in respect of the period between—

(a) the end of the financial year for which the last such report was prepared by them under that section, and

(b) the transfer date,

whether that period is a financial year or not.

(3) Subsection (2) of that section shall apply to any such report as if the reference to the statement of accounts for the year in question included references to the statement of accounts prepared in accordance with sub-paragraph (1).

6.—(1) The Broadcasting Standards Council shall, as soon as possible after the transfer date, prepare such a statement of accounts as is mentioned in paragraph 13 of Schedule 14 to the 1990 Act (accounts and audit) in respect of the period between—

(a) the end of the financial year for which the last such statement of accounts was prepared by them under that paragraph, and

(b) the transfer date,

whether that period is a financial year or not; and that paragraph shall continue to apply on and after that date in relation to the auditing of accounts kept in accordance with that paragraph in respect of that period.

(2) The Broadcasting Standards Council shall, as soon as possible after the transfer date, prepare and submit to the Secretary of State, in accordance with section 160 of the 1990 Act (annual reports), such a report as is mentioned in subsection (1) of that section in respect of the period between—

(a) the end of the financial year for which the last such report was prepared by them under that section, and

(b) the transfer date,

whether that period is a financial year or not.

(3) Subsection (2) of that section shall apply to any such report as if the reference to the statement of accounts for the year in question included references to the statement of accounts prepared in accordance with sub-paragraph (1).

7.—(1) The Secretary of State shall lay copies of any such report as is mentioned in paragraph 5(2) or 6(2) before each House of Parliament.

(2) Any expenses incurred by the Broadcasting Complaints Commission under paragraph 5 or by the Broadcasting Standards Council under paragraph 6 shall be met by the BSC.

Final contributions towards cost of Broadcasting Complaints Commission

8.—(1) For the period referred to in paragraph 5(1), the Secretary of State shall notify—

(a) to each regulatory body the sum which he considers to be the appropriate contribution of that body, in respect of persons providing licensed services under licences granted by that body, towards the expenses of the Broadcasting Complaints Commission, and

(b) to the Welsh Authority the sum which he considers to be the appropriate contribution of that body towards such expenses.

(2) Each regulatory body and the Welsh Authority shall pay to the Secretary of State any sum notified to them under sub-paragraph (1).

Section 131(4)

SCHEDULE 5

TRANSFER SCHEMES RELATING TO BBC TRANSMISSION NETWORK: SUPPLEMENTARY PROVISIONS

Contents and elect of scheme

1.—(1) A transfer scheme may define the property, rights and liabilities to be transferred to a particular person—

(a) by specifying or describing the property, rights and liabilities in question,

(b) by referring to all (or all but so much as may be excepted) of the property, rights and liabilities comprised in a specified part of the BBC's undertaking, or

(c) partly in one way and partly in the other.

(2) A transfer scheme shall appoint the day on which it is to come into force.

(3) This Act shall have effect, in relation to any provision of a transfer scheme for the transfer of any property, rights or liabilities, so as to transfer the property, rights or liabilities, at the beginning of the day appointed for the coming into force of the scheme, and without further assurance, from the BBC to the person to whom they are allocated under the scheme and to vest them in that person; and the provisions of that scheme in relation to that transfer shall have effect from that time accordingly.

(4) This Act shall have effect, in relation to any provision of a transfer scheme for the creation, by virtue of paragraph 2, of any interest or right, so as to create the specified interests and rights, at the beginning of the day appointed for the coming into force of the scheme and without further assurance.

(5) The preceding provisions of this paragraph shall have effect subject to so much of a transfer scheme as provides for—

(a) the transfer of any of the property, rights or liabilities to be transferred in accordance with the scheme, or

(b) the creation of any of the rights or interests to be created in accordance with the scheme,

to be effected by or under any agreement or instrument entered into or executed in pursuance of an obligation imposed by virtue of paragraph 2(1)(g).

(6) In their application to Scotland, sub-paragraphs (3) and (4) shall have effect with the omission of the words "and without further assurance".

Division of BBC's undertaking by scheme

2.—(1) For the purposes of making any such division as the BBC consider appropriate of any of the property, rights and liabilities of the BBC between two or more persons (including any division between the BBC and any one or more other persons), a transfer scheme may contain provision—

(a) for the creation in favour of the BBC of an interest or right in or in relation to property transferred in accordance with that scheme to any person,

(b) for the creation, in favour of a person to whom any transfer is made, of an interest or right in or in relation to property so transferred to another,

(c) for giving effect to a transfer to any person by the creation, in favour of that person, of an interest or right in or in relation to property retained by the BBC,

(d) for rights and liabilities to be transferred so as to be enforceable by or against more than one transferee or by or against both one or more transferees and the BBC,

(e) for rights and liabilities enforceable by or against more than one person in accordance with any provision falling within paragraph (d) to be enforceable in different or modified respects by or against each or any of them,

(f) for the creation of new rights and liabilities as between different transferees and as between any transferee and the BBC, and

(g) without prejudice to paragraph (f), for imposing on any transferee or the BBC an obligation—

(i) to enter into such written agreements with any other person on whom any corresponding obligation is, could be or has been imposed by virtue of this paragraph of this Schedule (whether in the same or a different scheme), or

(ii) to execute such instruments in favour of any such person,

as may be specified or described in the scheme.

(2) A transfer scheme may contain such supplemental and incidental provision with respect to the interests, rights and liabilities of third parties in relation to anything to which the scheme relates as the BBC consider to be necessary or expedient for the purposes of any such division as is mentioned in sub-paragraph (1), or in connection with anything contained in the scheme by virtue of that sub-paragraph.

(3) The provision that may be contained in a transfer scheme by virtue of sub-paragraph (2) shall include provision for interests, rights or liabilities to which any third party is entitled or subject in relation to anything to which the scheme relates to be modified in such respects or in such manner as may be specified or determined under the scheme.

(4) An obligation imposed on any person by virtue of sub-paragraph (1)(g) shall be enforceable by the bringing, by any person with or in favour of whom the agreement or instrument is to be entered into or executed, of civil proceedings for an injunction or for interdict or for other appropriate relief.

(5) In this paragraph—

(a) references, in relation to a transfer scheme, to a transferee include references to any person in whose favour any interest or right is created in accordance with the scheme, and

(b) the reference, in relation to such a scheme, to a third party is a reference to a person other than—

(i) the BBC, or

(ii) any person who (apart from any provision made by virtue of sub-paragraph (1)(e) or (2)) is a transferee.

(6) Sub-paragraphs (2) and (3) shall be without prejudice to the generality of paragraph 4(1).

Property to which a scheme may relate

3.—(1) The property, rights and liabilities that shall be capable of being transferred in accordance with a transfer scheme shall include—

(a) property, rights and liabilities that would not otherwise be capable of being transferred or assigned by the BBC,

(b) rights and liabilities of the BBC under any agreement or arrangement for the payment of pensions, allowances and gratuities,

(c) property acquired at a time after the making of the scheme and before it comes into force, and rights and liabilities which arise or may arise in respect of anything occurring after the making of the scheme,

(d) property situated anywhere in the United Kingdom or elsewhere and rights and liabilities under the law of any part of the United Kingdom or of any country or territory outside the United Kingdom, and

(e) rights and liabilities under enactments.

(2) The transfers authorised by sub-paragraph (1)(a), and the interests and rights that may be created in accordance with a transfer scheme, include transfers, interests and rights which are to take effect as if there were—

(a) no such requirement to obtain any person's consent or concurrence,

(b) no such liability in respect of a contravention of any other requirement, and

(c) no such interference with any interest or right,

as there would be, in the case of any transaction apart from this Act, by reason of provisions having effect (whether under any enactment or agreement or otherwise) in relation to the terms on which the BBC are entitled or subject to any property, right or liability.

(3) Where apart from this sub-paragraph any person would have an entitlement, in consequence of anything done or likely to be done by or under this Act, to terminate, modify, acquire or claim an interest or right which is vested in the BBC at the passing of this Act or acquired by the BBC after that time, or to treat any such interest or right as modified or terminated, then—

(a) for the purposes of the transfer of the interest or right in accordance with a transfer scheme, that entitlement shall not be enforceable in relation to that interest or right until after its transfer in accordance with such a scheme, and

(b) without prejudice to the preceding provisions of this paragraph or to paragraph 4(2)(a), that entitlement shall be enforceable in relation to the interest or right after its transfer only in so far as the scheme contains provision for it to be transferred subject to the provisions conferring that entitlement.

(4) Subject to sub-paragraphs (5) and (6), nothing in sub-paragraph (1) or (2) shall enable—

(a) any agreement or instrument entered into or executed in pursuance of an obligation imposed by virtue of paragraph 2(1)(g), or

(b) anything done under any such agreement,

to give effect to any transfer, or to create any interest or right, which could not apart from this paragraph have been made by or under that agreement or instrument.

(5) A transfer scheme may provide for—

(a) the transfers to which effect is to be given by or under any agreement or instrument entered into or executed in accordance with the scheme, or

(b) the interests or rights that are to be created by or under any such agreement or instrument,

to include, to such extent as may be specified in the scheme, any such transfer, interest or right as is mentioned in sub-paragraph (2).

(6) A transfer scheme may provide that sub-paragraph (3) shall apply in relation to the provisions of any agreement or instrument which is to be entered into or executed in accordance with the scheme, and in relation to any proposal for such an agreement or for the execution of such an instrument, as if the reference in sub-paragraph (3)(b) to provision contained in the scheme included a reference to provision contained, in accordance with the scheme, in the agreement or instrument.

Supplemental provisions of schemes

4.—(1) A transfer scheme may contain supplemental, incidental, consequential and transitional provision for the purposes of, or in connection with, any transfer of property, rights or liabilities for which the scheme provides or in connection with any other provisions contained in the scheme; and any such provision may include different provision for different cases or different purposes.

(2) A transfer scheme may, in relation to transfers in accordance with the scheme, make provision, either generally or for such purposes as may be specified in the scheme—

(a) for the transferee to be treated as the same person in law as the BBC,

(b) for agreements made, transactions effected or other things done by or in relation to the BBC to be treated, so far as may be necessary for the purposes of or in connection with the transfers, as made, effected or done by or in relation to the transferee,

(c) for references in any agreement (whether or not in writing) or in any deed, bond, instrument or other document to, or to any member or officer of, the BBC to have effect, so far as may be necessary for the purposes of or in connection with any of the transfers, with such modifications as are specified in the scheme,

(d) for proceedings commenced by or against the BBC to be continued by or against the transferee, and

(e) for any such disputes as to the effect of the scheme as arise between different transferees, or between any transferee on the one hand and the BBC on the other, to be referred to such arbitration as may be specified in or determined under the scheme.

(3) Where any person is entitled, in consequence of any transfer made in accordance with a transfer scheme or in pursuance of any provision made under this paragraph, to possession of a document relating in part to the title to, or to the management of, any land or other property in England and Wales or Northern Ireland—

(a) the scheme may contain provision for treating that person as having given another person an acknowledgment in writing of the right of that other person to production of the document and to delivery of copies of the document, and

(b) section 64 of the Law of Property Act 1925 (production and safe custody of documents) or section 9 of the Conveyancing Act 1881 (the corresponding provision for Northern Ireland) shall have effect accordingly, and on the basis that the acknowledgment did not contain any such expression of contrary intention as is mentioned in that section.

(4) Where any person is entitled, in consequence of any transfer made in accordance with a transfer scheme or in pursuance of any provision made under this paragraph, to possession of a document relating in part to the title to, or to the management of, any land or other property in Scotland transferred in accordance with a transfer scheme, subsections (1) and (2) of section 16 of the Land Registration (Scotland) 1979 (omission of certain clauses in deeds) shall have effect in relation to the transfer as if the transfer had been effected by deed and as if from each of those subsections the words "unless specially qualified" were omitted.

(5) In this paragraph—

(a) references to a transfer include references to the creation in any person's favour of any interest or right, and references to a transferee shall be construed accordingly, and

(b) references to a person who is entitled, in consequence of any transfer, to possession of a document include references to the BBC in a case where the BBC are entitled to retain possession of any document following any transfer.

(6) Sub-paragraphs (2) to (4) shall be without prejudice to the generality of sub-paragraph (1).

Certificate of Secretary of State as to vesting of property etc.

5. A certificate issued by the Secretary of State to the effect that any property, right or liability of the BBC vested at a particular time in accordance with a transfer scheme in a person specified in the certificate shall be conclusive evidence of the matters stated in the certificate.

Duties in relation to foreign property etc.

6.—(1) It shall be the duty of the BBC and of any person to whom any foreign property, right or liability is transferred to take all such steps as may be requisite to secure that the vesting in the transferee, in accordance with the scheme, of the foreign property, right or liability is effective under the relevant foreign law.

(2) Until the vesting in the transferee in accordance with the scheme of any foreign property, right or liability is effective under the relevant foreign law, it shall be the duty of the BBC to hold that property or right for the benefit of, or to discharge that liability on behalf of, the transferee.

(3) Nothing in sub-paragraphs (1) and (2) shall be taken as prejudicing the effect under the law of any part of the United Kingdom of the vesting in the transferee in accordance with the scheme of any foreign property, right or liability.

(4) The BBC shall have all such powers as may be requisite for the performance of their duties under this paragraph, but it shall be the duty of a person to whom a transfer is made in accordance with a transfer scheme to act on behalf of the BBC (so far as possible) in performing the duties imposed on them by this paragraph.

(5) Where—

(a) any foreign property, rights or liabilities are acquired or incurred by the BBC in respect of any other property, rights or liabilities, and

(b) by virtue of this paragraph the BBC hold the other property or rights for the benefit of another person or discharge the liability on behalf of another person,

the property, rights or liabilities acquired or incurred are immediately to become property, rights or liabilities of that other person; and the preceding provisions of this paragraph shall have effect accordingly in relation to the property, rights or liabilities acquired or incurred.

(6) References in this paragraph to any foreign property, right or liability are references to any property, right or liability as respects which any issue arising in any proceedings would have to be determined (in accordance with the rules of private international law) by reference to the law of a country or territory outside the United Kingdom.

(7) Any expenses incurred by the BBC under this paragraph shall be met by the person to whom the transfer in question is made.

(8) Any obligation imposed under this paragraph shall be enforceable as if contained in a contract between the BBC and the person to whom the transfer in question is made.

Modification of scheme by agreement

7.—(1) This paragraph applies where any person to whom anything has been transferred in accordance with a transfer scheme agrees in writing with the BBC or another person to whom anything has been transferred in accordance with that or any other transfer scheme that, for the purpose of modifying the effect of the scheme or, as the case may be, of modifying the effect of either or both of the schemes—

(a) any of the property, rights or liabilities transferred in accordance with the scheme or either of them, and

(b) any or all of the property, rights or liabilities acquired or incurred since the transfer in respect of the transferred property, rights or liabilities,

should be transferred from one to the other as from a date appointed by the agreement.

(2) If—

(a) the agreement is entered into within the period of twelve months after the time when a transfer in accordance with a transfer scheme of property, rights or liabilities to any of its parties comes into force, and

(b) the Secretary of State has given his approval to the transfer for which the agreement provides and to its terms and conditions,

then the transfer for which the agreement provides shall take effect on the date appointed by the agreement in the like manner as a transfer for which provision is made by a transfer scheme.

(3) Subject to the approval of the Secretary of State and to sub-paragraph (4), the provisions that may be contained in a modification agreement shall include any such provision in relation to any transfer for which it provides as may be contained, in relation to any transfer for which a transfer scheme provides, in that scheme.

(4) Nothing in any modification agreement shall provide for any interests or rights to be created, as opposed to transferred, except as between persons who are parties to the agreement.

(5) Before—

(a) refusing his approval for the purposes of this paragraph, or

(b) giving his approval for those purposes in a case where the BBC are not a party to the proposed agreement,

the Secretary of State shall consult the BBC.

(6) In this paragraph references to a transfer in accordance with a transfer scheme include references to the creation of any interest, right or liability in accordance with such a scheme.

(7) In this paragraph and paragraphs 8 and 9 "modification agreement" means any agreement providing for a transfer which is to take effect in accordance with sub-paragraph (2).

Compensation

8.—(1) Where, in consequence of any provisions included in a transfer scheme for the purposes of any such division as is mentioned in paragraph 2(1), the interests, rights or liabilities of a third party are modified as mentioned in sub-paragraph (2), the third party shall be entitled to such compensation as may be just in respect of—

(a) any diminution attributable to that modification in the value of any of his interests or rights, or

(b) any increase attributable to that modification in the burden of his liabilities.

(2) The modifications mentioned in sub-paragraph (1) are modifications by virtue of which—

(a) an interest of the third party in any property is transformed into, or replaced by—

(i) an interest in only part of that property, or

(ii) separate interests in different parts of that property,

(b) a right of the third party against the BBC is transformed into, or replaced by, two or more rights which do not include a right which, on its own, is equivalent (disregarding the person against whom it is enforceable) to the right against the BBC, or

(c) a liability of the third party to the BBC is transformed into, or replaced by, two or more separate liabilities at least one of which is a liability enforceable by a person other than the BBC.

(3) Where—

(a) a third party would, apart from any provisions of a transfer scheme or paragraph 3(3), have become entitled to, or to exercise, any interest or right arising or exercisable in respect of the transfer or creation in accordance with such a scheme of any property, rights or liabilities, and

(b) the provisions of that scheme or of paragraph 3(3) have the effect of preventing that person's entitlement to, or to exercise, that interest or right from arising on any occasion in respect of anything mentioned in paragraph (a), and

(c) provision is not made by a transfer scheme for securing that an entitlement to, or to exercise, that interest or right or an equivalent interest or right, is preserved or created so as to arise in respect of the first occasion when corresponding circumstances next occur after the coming into force of the transfers for which the scheme provides,

the third party shall be entitled to such compensation as may be just in respect of the extinguishment of the interest or right.

(4) A liability to pay compensation under this paragraph shall fall on the persons not being themselves third parties who, as the case may be—

(a) have interests in the whole or any part of the property affected by the modification in question,

(b) are subject to the rights of the person to be compensated which are affected by the modification in question,

(c) are entitled to enforce the liabilities of the person to be compensated which are affected by that modification, or

(d) benefit from the extinguishment of the entitlement mentioned in sub-paragraph (3),

and that liability shall be apportioned between those persons in such manner as may be appropriate having regard to the extent of their respective rights or liabilities or the extent of the benefit they respectively obtain from the extinguishment.

(5) Where any liability falls by virtue of sub-paragraph (4) on the BBC, that sub-paragraph shall have effect subject to so much of any transfer scheme (including the one which gives rise to the liability) as makes provision for the transfer of that liability to any other person.

(6) Any dispute as to whether, or as to the person by whom, any compensation is to be paid under this paragraph, and any dispute as to the amount of any compensation to be paid by any person, shall be referred to and determined—

(a) where the claimant requires the matter to be determined in England and Wales or in Northern Ireland, by an arbitrator appointed by the Lord Chancellor, or

(b) where the claimant requires the matter to be determined in Scotland, by an arbiter appointed by the Lord President of the Court of Session.

(7) This paragraph shall have effect in relation to the provisions of any agreement or instrument entered into or executed in pursuance of an obligation imposed by virtue of paragraph 2(1)(g), and to any modification agreement, as it has effect in relation to the provisions of a transfer scheme.

(8) In this paragraph "third party", in relation to provisions capable of giving rise to compensation under this paragraph, means any person other than—

(a) the BBC or any of their wholly-owned subsidiaries (as defined by section 736 of the Companies Act 1985),

(b) the Secretary of State, or

(c) any person whose consent to those provisions has been given for the purposes of section 132(2) or who has agreed to those provisions by virtue of being a party to a modification agreement.

Notice to persons affected by scheme

9.—(1) It shall be the duty of the BBC, where it appears to them in the case of any transfer scheme or modification agreement that there are persons whose property, rights or liabilities are affected in a manner that may give rise to an entitlement to compensation under paragraph 8, to give notice under this paragraph to every such person.

(2) A notice to be given by the BBC under this paragraph shall be given as soon as reasonably practicable after they make the scheme or agreement.

(3) A notice under this paragraph shall set out the general effect of the scheme or, as the case may be, of the agreement and shall describe the respects in which it appears to the BBC that the property, rights or liabilities of the person to whom it is given are affected.

(4) Where it is not reasonably practicable for the notice under this paragraph to any person to be given to that person, the BBC shall, instead, take such steps for publishing the contents of the notice as they may consider appropriate for the purpose of bringing the matters to which the notice relates to the attention of that person.

Consideration for transfer etc.

10.—(1) A transfer in accordance with a transfer scheme may be made for consideration or for no consideration and, if it is made for consideration, the consideration may, in particular, take the form of the issue of shares or securities.

(2) In sub-paragraph (1), "transfer" has the meaning given by paragraph 1(1) of Schedule 7.

Section 134

SCHEDULE 6

TRANSFER SCHEMES RELATING TO BBC TRANSMISSION NETWORK: SUCCESSOR COMPANIES

Interpretation

1.—(1) In this Schedule—

"the Charter" means the Royal Charter of 1st May 1996 for the continuance of the British Broadcasting Corporation;

"preparatory scheme" means a transfer scheme whose main purpose is to provide for a transfer of property, rights or liabilities from the BBC to a wholly-owned subsidiary of the BBC;

"successor company" means a company to which property, rights at liabilities are transferred in accordance with a preparatory scheme at a time when the company is a wholly-owned subsidiary of the BBC;

"transfer" includes—

(a) any transfer effected by or under an agreement or instrument entered into or executed in pursuance of an obligation imposed by a provision contained in a preparatory scheme by virtue of paragraph 2(1)(g) of Schedule 5;

(b) the creation of interests, rights or liabilities by or under any such agreement or instrument; and

(c) the creation of interests, rights or liabilities by virtue of any provision contained in a preparatory scheme by virtue of paragraph 2 of Schedule 5;

and references to a transfer in accordance with a preparatory scheme shall be construed accordingly;

"wholly-owned subsidiary" has the meaning given by section 736 of the Companies Act 1985.

(2) Any reference in this Schedule to vesting in accordance with a preparatory scheme or vesting effected by a preparatory scheme shall be construed as a reference to vesting as a result of a transfer in accordance with a preparatory scheme.

Statutory accounts

2.—(1) The following provisions of this paragraph shall have effect for the purposes of any statutory accounts of a successor company.

(2) The vesting in the company effected by any preparatory scheme shall be taken—

(a) to have been effected immediately after the end of the last financial year of the BBC to end before the coming into force of the scheme, and

(b) to have been a vesting of such property, rights and liabilities as are determined by or under the scheme.

(3) The value of any asset and the amount of any liability which is taken by virtue of sub-paragraph (2) to have been vested in the company shall be taken to have been—

(a) in the case where the value or amount is determined by or under the preparatory scheme, that value or amount, and

(b) in any other case, the value or amount assigned to the asset or liability for the purposes of the Account or Accounts prepared by the BBC for the purposes of Article 18(2) of the Charter in respect of their last financial year to end before the day on which the preparatory scheme comes into force.

(4) If an Account or Accounts are prepared by the BBC for the purposes of Article 18(2) of the Charter in respect of the residual part of a financial year, that residual part shall be treated as a financial year of the BBC for the purposes of sub-paragraph (3).

(5) In this paragraph "statutory accounts", in relation to a company, means any accounts of that company prepared for the purposes of any provision of the Companies Act 1985 (including group accounts).

Distributable reserves

3.—(1) Where statutory accounts of a successor company prepared as at any time would show the company as having net assets in excess of the aggregate of—

(a) its called-up share capital, and

(b) the amount, apart from any property, rights and liabilities transferred to it in accordance with any preparatory scheme, of its undistributable reserves,

then, for the purposes of section 263 of the Companies Act 1985 (profits available for distribution) and of the preparation as at that time of any statutory accounts of the company, that excess shall be treated, except so far as the Secretary of State may otherwise direct, as representing an excess of the company's accumulated realised profits over its accumulated realised losses.

(2) For the purposes of section 264 of the Companies Act 1985 (restriction on distribution of assets) so much of any excess of a company's net assets as falls, in accordance with a direction under this paragraph, to be treated otherwise than as representing an excess of the company's accumulated realised profits over its accumulated realised losses shall be treated (subject to any modification of that direction by a subsequent direction under this paragraph) as comprised in the company's undistributable reserves.

(3) A direction under this paragraph may provide, in relation to any amount to which it applies, that, on the realisation (whether before or after the company in question ceases to be a wholly-owned subsidiary of the BBC) of such profits and losses as may be specified or described in the direction, so much of that amount as may be determined in accordance with the direction is to cease to be treated as mentioned in sub-paragraph (2) and is to fall to be treated as comprised in the company's accumulated realised profits.

(4) The Secretary of State shall not give a direction under this paragraph in relation to a successor company at any time after the company has ceased to be a wholly-owned subsidiary of the BBC.

(5) The consent of the Treasury shall be required for the giving of a direction under this paragraph.

(6) In this paragraph—

"called-up share capital" has the same meaning as in the Companies Act 1985;

"net assets" has the meaning given by subsection (2) of section 264 of that Act;

"undistributable reserves" has the meaning given by subsection (3) of that section;

and references in this paragraph, in relation to a company, to statutory accounts are references to accounts of that company prepared in respect of any period in accordance with the requirements of that Act, or with those requirements applied with such modifications as are necessary where that period is not an accounting reference period.

Dividends

4.—(1) Where a distribution is proposed to be declared during any accounting reference period of a successor company which includes a transfer date or before any accounts are laid or filed in respect of such a period, sections 270 to 276 of the Companies Act 1985 (accounts relevant for determining whether a distribution may be made by a company) shall have effect as if—

(a) references in section 270 to the company's accounts or to accounts relevant under that section, and

(b) references in section 273 to initial accounts,

included references to such accounts as, on the assumptions stated in sub-paragraph (2), would have been prepared under section 226 of that Act in respect of the relevant year (in this paragraph referred to as "the relevant accounts").

(2) Those assumptions are—

(a) that the relevant year had been a financial year of the successor company,

(b) that the vesting in accordance with the preparatory scheme had been a vesting of all the property, rights and liabilities transferred to the company in accordance with that scheme and had been effected immediately after the beginning of that year,

(c) that the value of any asset and the amount of any liability of the BBC vested in the successor company in accordance with the preparatory scheme had been the value or (as the case may be) amount determined by or under the scheme or (if there is no such determination) the value or amount assigned to the asset or liability for the purposes of the Account or Accounts prepared by the BBC for the purposes of Article 18(2) of the Charter in respect of their financial year immediately preceding the relevant year,

(d) that any securities of the successor company issued or allotted before the declaration of the distribution had been issued or allotted before the end of the relevant year, and

(e) such other assumptions (if any) as may appear to the directors of the successor company to be necessary or expedient for the purposes of this paragraph.

(3) If an Account or Accounts are prepared by the BBC for the purposes of Article 18(2) of the Charter in respect of the residual part of a financial year, that residual part shall be treated as a financial year of the BBC for the purposes of sub-paragraph (2)(c).

(4) The relevant accounts shall not be regarded as statutory accounts for the purposes of paragraph 2.

(5) In this paragraph—

"accounting reference period" has the meaning given by section 224 of the Companies Act 1985;

"complete financial year" means a financial year ending with 31st March;

"the relevant year", in relation to any transfer date, means the last complete financial year ending before that date;

"a transfer date", in relation to a successor company, means the date of the coming into force of any preparatory scheme in accordance with which property, rights or liabilities are transferred to that company.

Application of the Trustee Investments Act 1961

5.—(1) For the purpose of applying paragraph 3(b) of Part IV of Schedule 1 to the Trustee Investments Act 1961 (which provides that shares and debentures of a company shall not count as wider-range and narrower-range investments respectively within the meaning of that Act unless the company has paid dividends in each of the five years immediately preceding that in which the investment is made) in relation to investment in shares or debentures of a successor company during the calendar year in which the transfer date falls ("the first investment year") or during any year following that year, the successor company shall be deemed to have paid a dividend as there mentioned—

(a) in every year preceding the first investment year which is included in the relevant five years, and

(b) in the first investment year, if that year is included in the relevant five years and the successor company does not in fact pay such a dividend in that year.

(2) In sub-paragraph (1)—

"the relevant five years" means the five years immediately preceding the year in which the investment in question is made or proposed to be made;

"the transfer date", in relation to a successor company, means the first date on which any preparatory scheme in accordance with which property, rights or liabilities are transferred to that company comes into force.

Section 135 SCHEDULE 7

TRANSFER SCHEMES RELATING TO BBC TRANSMISSION NETWORK: TAXATION PROVISIONS

Interpretation

1.—(1) In this Schedule, unless the context otherwise requires—

"the Allowances Act" means the Capital Allowances Act 1990;

"the BBC transmission network" has the meaning given by section 131(2);

"the Capital Allowances Acts" has the meaning given by section 832(1) of the Taxes Act 1988;

"direct disposal scheme" means a transfer scheme which is not a preparatory scheme;

"direct disposal transfer" means a transfer in accordance with a direct disposal scheme;

"the documents regulating the BBC" includes—

(a) the Royal Charter of 1st May 1996 for the continuance of the British Broadcasting Corporation; and

(b) the Agreement dated 25th January 1996 between Her Majesty's Secretary of State for National Heritage and the British Broadcasting Corporation;

"the Gains Act" means the Taxation of Chargeable Gains Act 1992;

"modification agreement" has the meaning given by paragraph 7(7) of Schedule 5;

"preparatory scheme" means a transfer scheme whose main purpose is to provide for a transfer of property, rights or liabilities from the BBC to a wholly-owned subsidiary of the BBC;

"preparatory transfer" means a transfer in accordance with a preparatory scheme;

"relevant transfer" means a transfer in accordance with a transfer scheme;

"successor company" means a company to which property, rights or liabilities are transferred in accordance with a preparatory scheme at a time when the company is a wholly-owned subsidiary of the BBC;

"the Taxes Act 1988" means the Income and Corporation Taxes Act 1988;

"transfer", except for the purposes of paragraphs 13 to 18, includes—

(a) any transfer effected by or under an agreement or instrument entered into or executed in pursuance of an obligation imposed by a provision contained in a transfer scheme by virtue of paragraph 2(1)(g) of Schedule 5;

(b) the creation of interests, rights or liabilities by or under any such agreement or instrument; and

(c) the creation of interests, rights or liabilities by virtue of any provision contained in a transfer scheme by virtue of paragraph 2 of Schedule 5;

and references to a transfer in accordance with a transfer scheme (or any description of transfer scheme) shall be construed accordingly;

"transferee"—

(a) in relation to a transfer scheme, means a person to whom property, rights or liabilities are transferred in accordance with the transfer scheme; and

(b) in relation to a relevant transfer, means the person to whom the property, rights or liabilities in question are transferred in accordance with the transfer scheme in question;

"wholly-owned subsidiary" has the meaning given by section 736 of the Companies Act 1985.

(2) In any provision of this Schedule "the prescribed amount", in relation to any transferee under a transfer scheme, means such amount as may be specified by the Secretary of State by order for the purposes of that provision in its application to that transferee.

(3) This Schedule—

(a) so far as it relates to corporation tax, shall be construed as one with the Corporation Tax Acts, and

(b) so far as it relates to capital allowances, shall be construed as one with the Capital Allowances Acts.

Chargeable gains: preparatory transfers etc to be without gain or loss

2.—(1) For the purposes of corporation tax on chargeable gains, the disposal of property, rights or liabilities which is constituted by a preparatory transfer shall, subject to the following provisions of this Schedule, be taken in relation to both—

(a) the person to whom the disposal is made, and

(b) the person making the disposal,

to be effected for a consideration such that no gain or loss accrues to the person making the disposal.

(2) Section 171(1) of the Gains Act (which makes provision in relation to the disposal of assets from one member of a group of companies to another member of the group) shall not apply where the disposal in question is a preparatory transfer.

Chargeable gains: amendment of section 35(3)(d) of the Gains Act

3. In section 35(3)(d) of the Gains Act (list of provisions for transfers without gain or loss for purposes of provisions applying to assets held on 31st March 1982) after sub-paragraph (xi) there shall be inserted—

"(xii) paragraph 2(1) of Schedule 7 to the Broadcasting Act 1996;".

Chargeable gains: section 41 of the Gains Act

4. Subsection (1) of section 174 of the Gains Act (which applies section 41 of that Act to cases where assets have been acquired without gain or loss) shall have effect, without prejudice to paragraph 2, where there has been a preparatory transfer as if the asset to which the preparatory transfer relates had thereby been transferred and acquired in relevant circumstances, within the meaning of that subsection.

Chargeable gains: assets held before 6th April 1965

5. Schedule 2 to the Gains Act (assets held on 6th April 1965) shall have effect in relation to any assets which are transferred to a successor company in accordance with a preparatory scheme as if—

(a) the BBC and the successor company were the same person; and

(b) those assets, to the extent that they were in fact acquired or provided by the BBC, were acquired or, as the case may be, provided by the successor company.

Chargeable gains: sale of successor company: group transactions

6.—(1) For the purposes of section 179 of the Gains Act (company ceasing to be a member of a group), where any company ("the degrouped company") ceases, by virtue of a qualifying transaction, to be a member of a group of companies, the degrouped company shall not, by virtue of that qualifying transaction, be treated under that section as having sold, and immediately reacquired, any asset acquired from a company which falls to be regarded for the purposes of subsection (1) of that section as having been at the time of acquisition a member of that group.

(2) Where, disregarding any preparatory transactions, a company would be regarded for the purposes of section 179 of the Gains Act (and, accordingly, of this paragraph) as ceasing to be a member of a group of companies by virtue of a qualifying transaction, it shall be regarded for

those purposes as so doing by virtue of the qualifying transaction and not by virtue of any preparatory transactions.

(3) In this paragraph—

"preparatory transaction", in the case of any qualifying transaction, means anything done for the purpose of initiating, advancing or facilitating the qualifying transaction;

"qualifying transaction" means the disposal by the BBC of any shares or securities of a successor company.

(4) Expressions used in this paragraph and in section 179 of the Gains Act have the same meaning in this paragraph as they have in that section.

Chargeable gains: sale or exchange of shares or securities of successor company

7.—(1) Where a company issues shares or debentures to the BBC in exchange for shares in or debentures of a successor company which have not, before that exchange, been disposed of by the BBC—

(a) sections 127 to 131 of the Gains Act (reorganisation or reduction of share capital) shall not apply by virtue of subsection (3) of section 135 of that Act (exchange of securities) in relation to that exchange, and

(b) section 116 of that Act (reorganisations, conversions and reconstructions) accordingly does not have effect in relation to that transaction,

and the following provisions of this paragraph shall apply accordingly.

(2) The following provisions of this paragraph apply in any case where—

(a) there is a preparatory transfer to a successor company;

(b) the BBC disposes of any shares or securities of the successor company for a consideration in money or money's worth; and

(c) those shares or securities are shares or securities which were—

(i) held by or on behalf of the BBC immediately before the preparatory transfer takes effect, or

(ii) issued to or for the BBC at a time when the successor company is a wholly-owned subsidiary of the BBC,

and which have not previously been disposed of by the BBC.

(3) For the purposes of corporation tax on chargeable gains, neither a chargeable gain nor an allowable loss shall be regarded as arising to the BBC on the disposal mentioned in sub-paragraph (2)(b).

(4) If the consideration for the disposal mentioned in sub-paragraph (2)(b) consists of or includes a right to any variable deferred consideration, then, for the purposes of corporation tax on chargeable gains, neither a chargeable gain nor an allowable loss shall be regarded as arising to the BBC on the disposal of the right to the variable deferred consideration.

(5) In this paragraph "variable deferred consideration" means any consideration—

(a) which is not to be given until after the disposal mentioned in sub-paragraph (2)(b); and

(b) whose amount or value, as at the time when it is to be given, is not ascertainable at the time of that disposal.

No chargeable gain or allowable loss to arise on any disposal constituted by a direct disposal transfer

8.—(1) For the purposes of corporation tax on chargeable gains, neither a chargeable gain nor an allowable loss shall be regarded as arising to the BBC on any disposal constituted by a direct disposal transfer.

(2) If the consideration for a direct disposal transfer consists of or includes a right to any variable deferred consideration, then, for the purposes of corporation tax on chargeable gains, neither a chargeable gain nor an allowable loss shall be regarded as arising to the BBC on the disposal of the right to the variable deferred consideration.

(3) In this paragraph "variable deferred consideration", in the case of any direct disposal transfer, means any consideration—

(a) which is not to be given until after the direct disposal transfer; and

(b) whose amount or value, as at the time when it is to be given, is not ascertainable at the time of the disposal constituted by that transfer.

Chargeable gains: value shifting

9.—(1) Nothing in Part VI of this Act, and no instrument or agreement made, or other thing done, under or by virtue of that Part or for the purpose of initiating, advancing or facilitating the disposal by the BBC of—

(a) the whole or any part of the BBC transmission network, or

(b) any shares or securities of a successor company which are shares or securities which were—

(i) held by or on behalf of the BBC immediately before a preparatory transfer to the successor company takes effect, or

(ii) issued to or for the BBC at a time when the successor company is a wholly-owned subsidiary of the BBC,

and which have not previously been disposed of by the BBC,

shall be regarded as a scheme or arrangement for the purposes of section 30 of the Gains Act (value-shifting).

(2) In any case where—

(a) an asset which is the subject of a preparatory transfer has previously been the subject of a scheme or arrangements falling within subsection (1) of section 30 of the Gains Act,

(b) in consequence, subsection (5) of that section (consideration on disposal to be treated as increased for certain purposes) would, apart from sub-paragraph (3), have had effect in relation to the consideration for the preparatory transfer, and

(c) the consideration for the preparatory transfer falls to be determined, for the purposes of corporation tax on chargeable gains, under paragraph 2,

sub-paragraph (3) shall apply.

(3) Where this sub-paragraph applies—

(a) subsection (5) of section 30 of the Gains Act shall not have effect in relation to the consideration for the preparatory transfer; but

(b) on the first subsequent disposal of the asset which is neither a preparatory transfer nor a group disposal—

(i) that subsection shall have effect in relation to the consideration for that disposal (whether or not it would otherwise have done so); and

(ii) the increase that falls to be made under that subsection shall be so calculated as to include any increase which would, but for paragraph (a) above, have fallen to be made in relation to the preparatory transfer.

(4) In this paragraph "group disposal" means a disposal which falls to be treated by virtue of section 171(1) of the Gains Act as made for a consideration such that no gain or loss accrues to the person making the disposal.

Chargeable gains: receipt of compensation or insurance money

10.—(1) Subsection (4) of section 23 of the Gains Act (adjustments where compensation or insurance money used for purchase of replacement asset) shall have effect in accordance with sub-paragraph (3) in any case where—

(a) there is a relevant transfer such that—

(i) a capital sum received by the BBC by way of compensation for the loss or destruction of an asset, or under a policy of insurance of the risk of the loss or destruction of an asset, becomes available to the transferee; or

(ii) a right of the BBC to receive such a sum is transferred to the transferee, and the transferee receives that sum; and

(b) the transferee acquires an asset in circumstances where—

(i) had there been no such relevant transfer, and

(ii) had the BBC acquired the asset by the application of that sum,

the BBC would be treated for the purposes of that subsection as having so acquired the asset in replacement for the asset lost or destroyed.

(2) Subsection (5) of that section (adjustments where a part of any compensation or insurance money is used for the purchase of a replacement asset) shall have effect in accordance with sub-paragraph (3) in any case where—

(a) there is a relevant transfer such that—

(i) a capital sum received by the BBC by way of compensation for the loss or destruction of an asset, or under a policy of insurance of the risk of the loss or destruction of an asset, becomes available to the transferee; or

(ii) a right of the BBC to receive such a sum is transferred to the transferee, and the transferee receives that sum; and

(b) the transferee acquires an asset in circumstances where—

(i) had there been no such relevant transfer, and

(ii) had the BBC acquired the asset by the application of all of that sum except for a part which was less than the amount of the gain (whether all chargeable gain or not) accruing on the disposal of the asset lost or destroyed,

the BBC would be treated for the purposes of that subsection as having so acquired the asset in replacement for the asset lost or destroyed.

(3) In a case falling within sub-paragraph (1) or (2) of this paragraph, subsection (4) or, as the case may be, subsection (5) of section 23 of the Gains Act shall have effect as if the transferee and the BBC were the same person, except that—

(a) in a case falling within sub-paragraph (1)(a)(i) or (2)(a)(i)—

(i) any claim under the subsection in question must be made by the BBC and the transferee; and

(ii) any adjustment to be made in consequence of paragraph (a) of that subsection shall be made for the purposes only of the taxation of the BBC; and

(b) in a case falling within sub-paragraph (1)(a)(ii) or (2)(a)(ii)—

(i) any claim under the subsection in question must be made by the transferee; and

(ii) any adjustment to be made in consequence of paragraph (a) of that subsection shall be made for the purposes only of the taxation of the transferee.

Loan relationships: disposal of securities by BBC

11.—(1) This paragraph applies in any case where—

(a) there is a preparatory transfer to a successor company;

(b) the BBC disposes of any securities of the successor company for a consideration in money or money's worth; and

(c) those securities are securities issued to or for the BBC in consideration for the preparatory transfer.

(2) Where this paragraph applies, any debits or credits which, by reason of the disposal mentioned in sub-paragraph (1)(b), would, apart from this sub-paragraph, be given by Chapter II of Part IV of the Finance Act 1996 (loan relationships) in respect of a loan relationship for an accounting period of the BBC shall not be brought into account for the purposes of that Chapter as respects the BBC.

Transfer of trade: loss relief and capital allowances

12.—(1) This paragraph applies in any case where, as a result of a relevant transfer,—

(a) the BBC ceases to carry on a trade; and

(b) the transferee begins to carry on that trade.

(2) Where this paragraph applies, section 343 of the Taxes Act 1988 (company reconstructions without change of ownership) shall not have effect in relation to the event described in sub-paragraph (1).

(3) Where this paragraph applies, the trade mentioned in sub-paragraph (1) shall not be treated as permanently discontinued nor a new trade as set up and commenced for the purpose of the allowances and charges provided for by the Capital Allowances Acts; but—

(a) there shall be made to or on the transferee in accordance with those Acts all such allowances and charges as would, if the BBC had continued to carry on the trade, have fallen to be made to or on it; and

(b) the amount of any such allowance or charge shall be computed as if—

(i) the transferee had been carrying on the trade since the BBC began to do so; and

(ii) everything done to or by the BBC had been done to or by the transferee (but so that no sale or transfer which on the transfer of the trade is made to the transferee by the BBC of any assets in use for the purpose of the trade shall be treated as giving rise to any such allowance or charge).

(4) For the purposes of this paragraph—

(a) where, on the BBC ceasing to carry on a trade, a company begins to carry on the activities of the trade as part of its trade, then that part of the trade carried on by the company shall be treated as a separate trade, if the effect of so treating it is that this paragraph applies by virtue of sub-paragraph (1) on that event in relation to that separate trade; and

(b) where, on the BBC ceasing to carry on part of a trade, a company begins to carry on the activities of that part as its trade or part of its trade, the BBC shall be treated as having carried on that part of its trade as a separate trade if the effect of so treating it is that this paragraph applies by virtue of sub-paragraph (1) on that event in relation to that separate trade.

Capital allowances: industrial buildings and structures

13.—(1) This paragraph applies in any case where there is a relevant transfer of property which is, for the purposes of Part I of the Allowances Act (industrial buildings and structures), the relevant interest in relation to any expenditure incurred on the construction of a building or structure.

(2) Where this paragraph applies, the Secretary of State may by order make provision specifying, as respects the transferee,—

(a) the amount which is to be taken for the purposes of Part I of the Allowances Act to be the amount of the capital expenditure incurred on the construction of the building or structure; and

(b) the date which is to be taken for the purposes of that Part as the date on which the building or structure was first used.

(3) This paragraph shall not have effect in relation to any property if paragraph 12(3) has effect in relation to it.

Capital allowances: machinery and plant

14.—(1) For the purposes of Part II of the Allowances Act (capital allowances in respect of machinery and plant) property which is transferred to a successor company in accordance with a preparatory scheme shall be treated as if—

(a) it had been acquired by the successor company, for the purposes for which it is used by that company on and after the date on which the transfer of the property in accordance with the scheme takes effect, on that date; and

(b) capital expenditure of the prescribed amount had been incurred on that date by the successor company on the acquisition of the property for the purposes mentioned in paragraph (a).

(2) This paragraph shall not have effect in relation to any property if paragraph 12(3) has effect in relation to it.

Capital allowances: leased fixtures

15.—(1) This paragraph applies to any lease which is granted in pursuance of an obligation imposed by a provision contained in a preparatory scheme by virtue of paragraph 2(1)(g) of Schedule 5.

(2) Where the conditions in paragraphs (a) and (b) of subsection (1) of section 55 of the Allowances Act (expenditure incurred by incoming lessee: transfer of allowances) are fulfilled in relation to a lease to which this paragraph applies—

(a) the lessee shall be deemed for the purposes of Part II of that Act to have given as consideration for the lease a capital sum which falls to be treated for the purposes of that Part as expenditure on the provision of the fixture concerned;

(b) the amount of that capital sum shall be the prescribed amount; and

(c) subsection (4)(a) of that section shall be disregarded.

(3) Where the conditions in paragraphs (a), (c) and (d) of section 56 of the Allowances Act (expenditure incurred by incoming lessee: lessor not entitled to allowances) are fulfilled in relation to a lease to which this paragraph applies—

(a) the lessee shall be deemed for the purposes of Part II of that Act to have given as consideration for the lease a capital sum which falls to be treated for the purposes of that Part as expenditure on the provision of the fixture concerned; and

(b) the amount of that capital sum shall be the prescribed amount.

Capital allowances: connected persons

16. In Part II of the Allowances Act (machinery and plant) references to a transaction (however described) between connected persons within the meaning of section 839 of the Taxes Act 1988 shall not include references to a preparatory transfer.

Capital allowances: agricultural buildings

17.—(1) This paragraph applies in any case where there is a relevant transfer of property which is the relevant interest in relation to any expenditure for which the BBC would be entitled to an allowance under Part V of the Allowances Act (agricultural buildings etc.) apart from section 128 of that Act (balancing allowances and charges).

(2) Where this paragraph applies—

(a) the acquisition of the relevant interest by the transferee shall, as respects the transferee, be treated for the purposes of Part V of the Allowances Act as a balancing event falling within subsection (1)(a) of section 129 of that Act (so that, in particular, subsection (3) of that section applies by reason of its occurrence); and

(b) it shall accordingly be assumed, as respects the transferee, that an election has been made under subsection (2) of that section (acquisition of relevant interest by another not to be a balancing event without an election under that subsection) with respect to the acquisition of the relevant interest by the transferee.

(3) Where this paragraph applies, subsection (3) of section 129 of the Allowances Act (entitlement of the new owner to allowances) shall, as respects the transferee, have effect with the following modifications, that is to say—

(a) the period which, by virtue of paragraph (a) of that subsection, is to be treated as if it were itself the writing-down period in which the allowances in respect of the expenditure in question were to be made shall be such period as the Secretary of State may by order specify; and

(b) the expenditure which, by virtue of paragraph (b) of that subsection, is to be treated as the expenditure in respect of which the transferee (as being the new owner, within the meaning of that section) is entitled to the allowances mentioned in that paragraph shall be equal to the prescribed amount (without any reduction or addition under that paragraph).

(4) This paragraph shall not have effect in relation to any property if paragraph 12(3) has effect in relation to it.

Corporation tax: BBC and successor company to be treated as one for certain purposes

18.—(1) If any property, rights or liabilities are transferred to a successor company in accordance with a preparatory scheme, then, subject to sub-paragraph (2), the following provisions shall apply for the purposes of the Corporation Tax Acts in their application in respect of any accounting period ending on or after the date on which the transfer takes effect, namely—

(a) any trade or part of a trade carried on by the BBC which is transferred in accordance with the preparatory scheme to the successor company shall be treated as having been, at the time of its commencement and at all times since that time, a separate trade carried on by that company;

(b) the trade or trades carried on by the successor company on and after the date on which the transfer takes effect shall be treated as the same trade or trades as that which, by virtue of paragraph (a), is treated as carried on before that date;

(c) all property, rights and liabilities of the BBC which are transferred in accordance with the scheme to the successor company shall be treated as having been, at the time when they became vested in the BBC and at all times since that time, property, rights and liabilities of that company; and

(d) anything done by the BBC in relation to property, rights and liabilities which are transferred to the successor company in accordance with the preparatory scheme shall be treated as having been done by that company.

(2) Sub-paragraph (1) shall not apply for the purposes of—

(a) corporation tax on chargeable gains,

(b) capital allowances, or

(c) relief for losses incurred in carrying on a trade,

and no provision included in a scheme by virtue of paragraph 4(2)(a) of Schedule 5 shall have effect for those purposes.

Corporation tax: no profit or loss under Case I of Schedule D by reason of a direct disposal transfer

19. In determining for the purposes of Case I of Schedule D the profits or gains or losses arising or accruing to the BBC, it shall be assumed that no profits or gains, and no losses, arise or accrue to the BBC by reason of a direct disposal transfer of—

(a) any trading stock, within the meaning of section 100 of the Taxes Act 1988, belonging to a trade carried on by the BBC;

(b) any right of the BBC to receive an amount which is for the purposes of corporation tax—

(i) an amount brought into account as a trading receipt of the BBC for any accounting period ending before the time when the transfer takes effect; or

(ii) an amount falling to be so brought into account if it is assumed, where it is not the case, that the accounting period of the BBC current on the day before the transfer takes effect ends immediately before that time; or

(c) the whole or any part of the amount of a liability which falls for the purposes of corporation tax—

(i) to be brought into account as deductible in computing the profits of any trade carried on by the BBC for any accounting period ending before the time when the transfer takes effect; or

(ii) to be so brought into account if it is assumed, where it is not the case, that the accounting period of the BBC current on the day before the transfer takes effect ends immediately before that time.

Corporation tax: group relief

20.—(1) None of the following, namely—

(a) the existence of the powers of any Minister of the Crown or the BBC under Part VI of this Act or under the documents regulating the BBC,

(b) any direction given by a Minister of the Crown under that Part or those documents, so far as that direction relates to a transfer scheme or (in a case where there is a preparatory scheme) to the sale of shares or securities issued by the successor company, or

(c) any arrangements (of any kind, whether in writing or not) so far as relating to a transfer scheme or any such sale,

shall be regarded as constituting arrangements falling within subsection (1) or (2) of section 410 of the Taxes Act 1988 (arrangements for the transfer of a company to another group or consortium).

(2) Neither—

(a) the existence of the powers of any Minister of the Crown or the BBC under Part VI of this Act or under the documents regulating the BBC, nor

(b) any direction given as mentioned in sub-paragraph (1)(b),

shall be regarded as constituting option arrangements for the purposes of paragraph 5B of Schedule 18 to the Taxes Act 1988.

(3) Any reference in sub-paragraph (1) or (2) to the documents regulating the BBC is a reference to those documents only so far as they have effect in relation to a disposal by the BBC of—

(a) the whole or any part of the BBC transmission network, or

(b) any shares or securities of a successor company,

or the initiating, advancing or facilitating of any such disposal.

(4) In this paragraph "Minister of the Crown" has the same meaning as in the Ministers of the Crown Act 1975.

Corporation tax: leases at an undervalue

21.—(1) Section 35 of the Taxes Act 1988 (charge on lease granted at an undervalue) shall not apply in the case of any lease which, in accordance with a transfer scheme, is granted—

(a) to a company which is a transferee under that or any other transfer scheme, or

(b) by such a company to the BBC.

(2) Section 87 of the Taxes Act 1988 (taxable premiums) shall not apply where there is an amount which would have become chargeable in relation to any land but for sub-paragraph (1); and, accordingly, references to any such amount shall not be included in references in that section to the amount chargeable.

(3) In this paragraph "lease" has the same meaning as in Part II of the Taxes Act 1988.

Corporation tax: sale and lease-back

22.—(1) Section 779 of the Taxes Act 1988 (sale and lease-back: limitation on tax reliefs) shall not apply where the liability of the transferor or of the person associated with that transferor is as a result of—

(a) the creation, in accordance with a transfer scheme, of any interest or right in favour of a transferee or the BBC;

(b) any other transaction for which a transfer scheme provides; or

(c) the grant by a company which is a transferee under a transfer scheme ("the relevant company") to the BBC or to another company which is a transferee (whether under that or any other transfer scheme) of any interest or right, at a time when the relevant company remains a wholly-owned subsidiary of the BBC, in a case where the ability of the relevant company to grant that interest or right derives from the transfer to the company in accordance with a transfer scheme of an estate or interest in land.

(2) In this paragraph "transferor" has the same meaning as in section 779 of the Taxes Act 1988 and "associated" shall be construed in accordance with that section.

Corporation tax: sale of lease of land

23.—(1) Section 780 of the Taxes Act 1988 (sale and lease-back: taxation of consideration) shall not apply where—

(a) the assignment of the original lease, and

(b) the grant or assignment of the new lease,

each fall within sub-paragraph (2).

(2) The assignment of the original lease, or the grant or assignment of the new lease, falls within this sub-paragraph if—

(a) it is a relevant transfer; or

(b) it takes place between the BBC and a successor company at a time when the successor company remains a wholly-owned subsidiary of the BBC; or

(c) it takes place between two successor companies at a time when both remain wholly-owned subsidiaries of the BBC.

(3) The reference in sub-paragraph (1) to the assignment of the original lease and the grant or assignment of the new lease shall be construed in accordance with section 780 of the Taxes Act 1988 and sub-paragraph (2) shall be construed accordingly.

Corporation tax: leased assets

24.—(1) For the purposes of section 781 of the Taxes Act 1988 (assets leased to traders and others) where the interest of the lessor or the lessee under a lease, or any other interest in an asset, is transferred in accordance with a transfer scheme to the BBC or a transferee, the transfer shall be treated as being effected without any capital sum having been obtained in respect of that interest by the BBC or the transferee.

(2) Section 782 of the Taxes Act 1988 (deduction of payment under leases: special cases) shall not apply to any payments made by the BBC or a company which is a transferee under a transfer scheme if the payments are made—

(a) under any lease created in favour of the BBC or such a company by virtue of, or in pursuance of an obligation imposed by, a provision contained in a transfer scheme by virtue of paragraph 2 of Schedule 5; or

(b) under any lease—

(i) which is granted to or by a successor company at a time when it remains a wholly-owned subsidiary of the BBC; and

(ii) which is a lease of an asset which at any time before the creation of the lease was used by the BBC for the purposes of a trade carried on by the BBC and which was, when so used, owned by the BBC.

(3) In this paragraph "lease" and "asset" have the meaning given by section 785 of the Taxes Act 1988.

Stamp duty

25.—(1) Stamp duty shall not be chargeable on any agreement or instrument to the extent that it is certified by the Secretary of State to the Commissioners of Inland Revenue as being—

(a) a restructuring scheme,

(b) a restructuring scheme modification agreement, or

(c) an instrument giving effect to a restructuring scheme modification agreement,

or as having been made in accordance with, or in pursuance of an obligation imposed by, a restructuring scheme.

(2) No agreement or instrument which is certified as mentioned in sub-paragraph (1) shall be taken to be duly stamped unless—

(a) it is stamped with the duty to which it would be liable, apart from that sub-paragraph; or

(b) it has, in accordance with section 12 of the Stamp Act 1891, been stamped with a particular stamp denoting that it is not chargeable with that duty or that it is duly stamped.

(3) Section 12 of the Finance Act 1895 (collection of stamp duty in cases of property vested by Act or purchased under statutory power) shall not operate to require—

(a) the delivery to the Commissioners of Inland Revenue of a copy of this Act, or

(b) the payment of stamp duty under that section on any copy of this Act,

and shall not apply in relation to any instrument on which, by virtue of the preceding provisions of this paragraph, stamp duty is not chargeable.

(4) In this paragraph—

"restructuring scheme modification agreement" means a modification agreement, so far as relating to a restructuring scheme;

"restructuring scheme" means a preparatory scheme, so far as it provides for the transfer of property, rights or liabilities in accordance with the scheme—

(a) from the BBC to a wholly-owned subsidiary of the BBC;

(b) to the BBC from a wholly-owned subsidiary of the BBC; or

(c) from one wholly-owned subsidiary of the BBC to another.

Stamp duty reserve tax

26.—(1) An agreement to transfer chargeable securities, as defined in section 99 of the Finance Act 1986, from the BBC to a wholly-owned subsidiary of the BBC shall not give rise to a charge to stamp duty reserve tax if the agreement is made for the purposes of, or for purposes connected with, a restructuring scheme.

(2) An agreement shall not give rise to a charge to stamp duty reserve tax if the agreement is a restructuring scheme modification agreement.

(3) In this paragraph "restructuring scheme" and "restructuring scheme modification agreement" have the same meaning as in paragraph 25.

Modifications of transfer schemes

27.—(1) If the effect of any transfer scheme is modified in pursuance of a modification agreement, then the Corporation Tax Acts and this Schedule, other than paragraphs 25 and 26, shall have effect as if—

(a) the scheme originally made had been the scheme as modified; and

(b) anything done by or in relation to the person who without the modification became entitled or subject in accordance with the scheme to any property, rights or liabilities had, so far as relating to the property, rights or liabilities to which another person becomes entitled or subject in consequence of the modification, been done by or in relation to that other person.

(2) If, in a case falling within sub-paragraph (1), the transfer scheme, as originally made, was a preparatory scheme, the scheme as modified shall be taken to be a preparatory scheme, whether or not any company which was a wholly-owned subsidiary of the BBC at the time when the preparatory scheme took effect remains a wholly-owned subsidiary of the BBC at the time when the modification takes effect.

Orders

28.—(1) The Secretary of State shall not make an order under this Schedule in relation to any transferee under a transfer scheme except—

(a) with the consent of the Treasury;

(b) after consultation with the BBC; and

(c) if the transferee is not a wholly-owned subsidiary of the BBC, after consultation with the transferee.

(2) Any power of the Secretary of State to make an order under this Part of this Schedule—

(a) shall be exercisable by statutory instrument; and

(b) shall include power to make different provision for different cases, including different provision in relation to different assets or descriptions of assets.

Section 136

SCHEDULE 8

Amendments of Broadcasting Act 1990 relating to services provided by BBC companies

Television services

1. In section 3 of the 1990 Act (licences under Part I) after subsection (3) there is inserted—

"(3A) Where the Commission are not satisfied that a BBC company which has applied for a licence is a fit and proper person to hold it, they shall, before refusing the application, notify the Secretary of State that they are not so satisfied."

2.—(1) Section 5 of that Act (restrictions on the holding of licences) is amended as follows.

(2) After subsection (2) there is inserted—

"(2A) Before revoking in pursuance of subsection (2)(b) the award of a licence to a BBC company, the Commission shall give the Secretary of State notice of their intention to do so, specifying the relevant change."

(3) After subsection (6B) there is inserted—

"(6C) The Commission shall not serve any such notice as is mentioned in subsection (5) on a BBC company unless they have given the Secretary of State notice of their intention to do so, specifying the relevant change.

(6D) Where the Commission receive any written representations from a BBC company under subsection (6), they shall send a copy of the representations to the Secretary of State."

3. After section 66 of that Act there is inserted—

"Enforcement of licences held by BBC companies

66A.—(1) Where the Commission—

(a) give a direction to a BBC company under section 40(1),

(b) serve a notice on a BBC company under any provision of section 41 or 42, or

(c) receive any written representations from a BBC company under section 40(2), 41(3) or 42(8),

the Commission shall send a copy of the direction, notice or representations to the Secretary of State.

(2) References in subsection (1) to any of the provisions of sections 40 to 42 are references to that provision as applied—

(a) by section 42B(2), in relation to a licence to provide a restricted service,
(b) by section 44(3), in relation to a licence to provide a domestic satellite service,
(c) by section 45(5), in relation to a licence to provide a non-domestic satellite service,
(d) by section 47(8), in relation to a licence to provide a licensable programme service, or
(e) by section 55(4), in relation to an additional services licence."

4. In section 81 of that Act (enforcement of local delivery service licences), after subsection (2) there is inserted—

"(2A) Where the Commission—

(a) serve a notice on a BBC company under any provision of section 41 or 42 (as applied by subsection (1)), or
(b) receive any representations from a BBC company under section 40(2), 41(3) or 42(8) (as so applied),

the Commission shall send a copy of the notice or representations to the Secretary of State."

Radio services

5. In section 86 of that Act (licences under Part III) after subsection (4) there is inserted—

"(4A) Where the Authority are not satisfied that a BBC company which has applied for a licence is a fit and proper person to hold it, they shall, before refusing the application, notify the Secretary of State that they are not so satisfied."

6.—(1) Section 88 of that Act (restrictions on the holding of licences) is amended as follows.

(2) After subsection (2) there is inserted—

"(2A) Before revoking in pursuance of subsection (2)(b) the award of a licence to a BBC company, the Authority shall give the Secretary of State notice of their intention to do so, specifying the relevant change."

(3) After subsection (6B) there is inserted—

"(6C) The Authority shall not serve any such notice as is mentioned in subsection (5) on a BBC company unless they have given the Secretary of State notice of their intention to do so, specifying the relevant change.

(6D) Where the Authority receive any written representations from a BBC company under subsection (6), they shall send a copy of the representations to the Secretary of State."

7. After section 111 of that Act there is inserted—

"Enforcement of licences held by BBC companies

111A. Where the Authority—

(a) serve a notice on a BBC company under any provision of section 109, 110 or 111, or
(b) receive any written representations from a BBC company under section 109(4), 110(4) or 111(8),

the Authority shall send a copy of the direction, notice or representations to the Secretary of State."

Meaning of "BBC company" for purposes of Broadcasting Act 1990

8. In section 202 of that Act (interpretation), after the definition of "the BBC" there is inserted—

" "a BBC company" means—

(a) any body corporate which is controlled by the BBC, or
(b) any body corporate in which the BBC or any body corporate falling within paragraph (a) above is (to any extent) a participant (as defined in paragraph 1(1) of Part I of Schedule 2);".

Section 138

SCHEDULE 9

Amendments of Copyright, Designs and Patents Act 1988 relating to cable programme services

1. For section 73 of the Copyright, Designs and Patents Act 1988 there is substituted—

"Reception and re-transmission of broadcast in cable programme service

73.—(1) This section applies where a broadcast made from a place in the United Kingdom is, by reception and immediate re-transmission, included in a cable programme service.

(2) The copyright in the broadcast is not infringed—

(a) if the inclusion is in pursuance of a relevant requirement, or

(b) if and to the extent that the broadcast is made for reception in the area in which the cable programme service is provided and forms part of a qualifying service.

(3) The copyright in any work included in the broadcast is not infringed if and to the extent that the broadcast is made for reception in the area in which the cable programme service is provided; but where the making of the broadcast was an infringement of the copyright in the work, the fact that the broadcast was re-transmitted as a programme in a cable programme service shall be taken into account in assessing the damages for that infringement.

(4) Where—

(a) the inclusion is in pursuance of a relevant requirement, but

(b) to any extent, the area in which the cable programme service is provided ("the cable area") falls outside the area for reception in which the broadcast is made ("the broadcast area"),

the inclusion in the cable programme service (to the extent that it is provided for so much of the cable area as falls outside the broadcast area) of any work included in the broadcast shall, subject to subsection (5), be treated as licensed by the owner of the copyright in the work, subject only to the payment to him by the person making the broadcast of such reasonable royalty or other payment in respect of the inclusion of the broadcast in the cable programme service as may be agreed or determined in default of agreement by the Copyright Tribunal.

(5) Subsection (4) does not apply if, or to the extent that, the inclusion of the work in the cable programme service is (apart from that subsection) licensed by the owner of the copyright in the work.

(6) In this section "qualifying service" means, subject to subsection (8), any of the following services—

(a) a regional or national Channel 3 service,

(b) Channel 4, Channel 5 and S4C,

(c) the teletext service referred to in section 49(2) of the Broadcasting Act 1990,

(d) the service referred to in section 57(1A)(a) of that Act (power of S4C to provide digital service), and

(e) the television broadcasting services and teletext service of the British Broadcasting Corporation;

and expressions used in this subsection have the same meaning as in Part I of the Broadcasting Act 1990.

(7) In this section "relevant requirement" means a requirement imposed under—

(a) section 78A of the Broadcasting Act 1990 (inclusion of certain services in local delivery services provided by digital means), or

(b) paragraph 4 of Part III of Schedule 12 to that Act (inclusion of certain services in diffusion services originally licensed under the Cable and Broadcasting Act 1984).

(8) The Secretary of State may by order amend subsection (6) so as to add any service to, or remove any service from, the definition of "qualifying service".

(9) The Secretary of State may also by order—

(a) provide that in specified cases subsection (3) is to apply in relation to broadcasts of a specified description which are not made as mentioned in that subsection, or

(b) exclude the application of that subsection in relation to broadcasts of a specified description made as mentioned in that subsection.

(10) Where the Secretary of State exercises the power conferred by subsection (9)(b) in relation to broadcasts of any description, the order may also provide for subsection (4) to apply, subject to such modifications as may be specified in the order, in relation to broadcasts of that description.

(11) An order under this section may contain such transitional provision as appears to the Secretary of State to be appropriate.

(12) An order under this section shall be made by statutory instrument which shall be subject to annulment in pursuance of a resolution of either House of Parliament.

Royalty or other sum payable in pursuance of section 73(4)

73A.—(1) An application to settle the royalty or other sum payable in pursuance of subsection (4) of section 73 (reception and re-transmission of broadcast in cable programme service) may be made to the Copyright Tribunal by the copyright owner or the person making the broadcast.

(2) The Tribunal shall consider the matter and make such order as it may determine to be reasonable in the circumstances.

(3) Either party may subsequently apply to the Tribunal to vary the order, and the Tribunal shall consider the matter and make such order confirming or varying the original order as it may determine to be reasonable in the circumstances.

(4) An application under subsection (3) shall not, except with the special leave of the Tribunal, be made within twelve months from the date of the original order or of the order on a previous application under that subsection.

(5) An order under subsection (3) has effect from the date on which it is made or such later date as may be specified by the Tribunal."

2.—(1) Section 134 of that Act (licences in respect of works included in re-transmissions) is amended as follows.

(2) At the beginning of subsection (1) there is inserted "Subject to subsection (3A)".

(3) After subsection (3) there is inserted—

"(3A) This section does not apply in relation to any application under section 73A (royalty or other sum payable in pursuance of section 73(4))."

3. In section 149 of that Act (jurisdiction of Copyright Tribunal), before paragraph (a) there is inserted—

"(za) section 73 (determination of royalty or other remuneration to be paid with respect to re-transmission of broadcast including work);".

4. In section 205B of that Act (jurisdiction of Copyright Tribunal under Part II), after paragraph (c) there is inserted—

"(cc) paragraph 19 of Schedule 2 (determination of royalty or other remuneration to be paid with respect to re-transmission of broadcast including performance or recording);".

5. For paragraph 19 of Schedule 2 to that Act there is substituted—

"Reception and re-transmission of broadcast in cable programme service

19.—(1) This paragraph applies where a broadcast made from a place in the United Kingdom is, by reception and immediate re-transmission, included in a cable programme service.

(2) The rights conferred by Part II in relation to a performance or recording included in the broadcast are not infringed if and to the extent that the broadcast is made for reception in the area in which the cable programme service is provided; but where the making of the broadcast was an infringement of those rights, the fact that the broadcast was re-transmitted as a programme in a cable programme service shall be taken into account in assessing the damages for that infringement.

(3) Where—

(a) the inclusion is in pursuance of a relevant requirement, but

(b) to any extent, the area in which the cable programme service is provided ("the cable area") falls outside the area for reception in which the broadcast is made ("the broadcast area"),

the inclusion in the cable programme service (to the extent that it is provided for so much of the cable area as falls outside the broadcast area) of any performance or recording included in the broadcast shall, subject to sub-paragraph (4), be treated as licensed by the owner of the rights conferred by Part II in relation to the performance or recording, subject only to the payment to him by the person making the broadcast of such reasonable royalty or other payment in respect of the inclusion of the broadcast in the cable programme service as may be agreed or determined in default of agreement by the Copyright Tribunal.

(4) Sub-paragraph (3) does not apply if, or to the extent that, the inclusion of the work in the cable programme service is (apart from that sub-paragraph) licensed by the owner of the rights conferred by Part II in relation to the performance or recording.

(5) The Secretary of State may by order—

(a) provide that in specified cases sub-paragraph (2) is to apply in relation to broadcasts of a specified description which are not made as mentioned in that sub-paragraph, or

(b) exclude the application of that sub-paragraph in relation to broadcasts of a specified description made as mentioned in that sub-paragraph.

(6) Where the Secretary of State exercises the power conferred by sub-paragraph (5)(b) in relation to broadcasts of any description, the order may also provide for sub-paragraph (3) to apply, subject to such modifications as may be specified in the order, in relation to broadcasts of that description.

(7) An order under this paragraph may contain such transitional provision as appears to the Secretary of State to be appropriate.

(8) An order under this paragraph shall be made by statutory instrument which shall be subject to annulment in pursuance of a resolution of either House of Parliament.

(9) Expressions used in this paragraph have the same meaning as in section 73."

6. After paragraph 19 of Schedule 2 to that Act there is inserted—

"19A.—(1) An application to settle the royalty or other sum payable in pursuance of sub-paragraph (3) of paragraph 19 may be made to the Copyright Tribunal by the owner of the rights conferred by Part II or the person making the broadcast.

(2) The Tribunal shall consider the matter and make such order as it may determine to be reasonable in the circumstances.

(3) Either party may subsequently apply to the Tribunal to vary the order, and the Tribunal shall consider the matter and make such order confirming or varying the original order as it may determine to be reasonable in the circumstances.

(4) An application under sub-paragraph (3) shall not, except with the special leave of the Tribunal, be made within twelve months from the date of the original order or of the order on a previous application under that sub-paragraph.

(5) An order under sub-paragraph (3) has effect from the date on which it is made or such later date as may be specified by the Tribunal."

Section 148(1)

SCHEDULE 10

MINOR AND CONSEQUENTIAL AMENDMENTS

PART I

AMENDMENTS OF BROADCASTING ACT 1990 RELATING TO DIGITAL TERRESTRIAL BROADCASTING

1.—(1) Section 2 of the 1990 Act (regulation by Commission of provision of television services) is amended as follows.

(2) In subsection (1)—

(a) after "this Part" there is inserted "and Part I of the Broadcasting Act 1996", and

(b) after paragraph (b) there is inserted—

"(c) multiplex services (as defined by section 1(1) of the Broadcasting Act 1996) which are provided from places in the United Kingdom by persons other than the BBC, and

(d) digital additional services (as defined by section 24(1) of the Broadcasting Act 1996) which are provided from places in the United Kingdom by persons other than the BBC".

(3) In subsection (2)—

(a) in paragraph (a) after "Part II" there is inserted "and under Part I of the Broadcasting Act 1996", and

(b) in paragraph (b)—

(i) after "this Part" there is inserted "and Part I of the Broadcasting Act 1996",

(ii) after "television programme services" there is inserted "and multiplex services (as defined by section 1(1) of that Act)", and

(iii) for "such services" there is substituted "television programme services."

(4) In subsection (4), in the definition of "television programme service", after paragraph (c) there is inserted—

"or

(d) a digital programme service (as defined by section 1(4) of the Broadcasting Act 1996)."

(5) At the end of subsection (5) there is inserted "but not including a restricted service (as defined by section 42A) or a multiplex service (as defined by section 1(1) of the Broadcasting Act 1996)".

2. In section 13 of the 1990 Act (prohibition on providing television services without a licence), in subsection (1)—

(a) for "or (b)" there is substituted ",(b), (c) or (d)", and

(b) after "this Part" there is inserted "or Part I of the Broadcasting Act 1996".

3. In section 69 of the 1990 Act (frequency planning and development), in subsection (4), after "Part II" there is inserted "or Part I of the Broadcasting Act 1996".

4. In section 72 of the 1990 Act (local delivery services), in subsection (2)—

(a) after paragraph (c) there is inserted—

"(cc) any digital programme service (as defined by section 1(4) of the Broadcasting Act 1996);", and

(b) at the end there is inserted "and

(f) any digital sound programme service (as defined by section 40(5) of the Broadcasting Act 1996)."

5. In section 84 of the 1990 Act (regulation by Authority of independent radio services), in subsection (1)—

(a) after "this Part" there is inserted "and Part II of the Broadcasting Act 1996", and
(b) after paragraph (c) there is inserted—
"(d) radio multiplex services (as defined by section 40(1) of the Broadcasting Act 1996) which are provided from places in the United Kingdom by persons other than the BBC;
(e) digital sound programme services (as defined by section 40(5) of that Act) which are provided from places in the United Kingdom by persons other than the BBC; and
(f) digital additional services (as defined by section 63(1) of that Act) which are provided from places in the United Kingdom by persons other than the BBC;".

6. In section 85 of the 1990 Act (licensing functions of Authority), in subsection (3)—
(a) after "independent radio services" there is inserted "and services falling within section 84(1)(d), (e) and (f)", and
(b) in paragraph (a) after "licensed services" there is inserted "(including digital sound programme services licensed under Part II of the Broadcasting Act 1996)".

7. In section 97 of the 1990 Act (prohibition on providing independent radio services without a licence), in subsection (1)—
(a) after "independent radio service" there is inserted "or any service falling within section 84(1)(d), (e) or (f)", and
(b) after "this Part" there is inserted "or Part II of the Broadcasting Act 1996".

8. In section 112 of the 1990 Act (licensable sound programme services), in subsection (2)(a), after "sound broadcasting service" there is inserted "or a radio multiplex service (as defined by section 40(1) of the Broadcasting Act 1996)".

9. In section 126 of the 1990 Act (interpretation of Part III), at the end of the definition of "sound broadcasting service" there is inserted "but does not include a radio multiplex service (as defined by section 40(1) of the Broadcasting Act 1996)".

10. In section 176 of the 1990 Act (duty to provide advance information about programmes), in subsection (7), in the first column of the table—
(a) after "Welsh Authority" there is inserted "and the service referred to in section 57(1A)(a)", and
(b) after "Radio Authority" there is inserted ", any simulcast radio service (within the meaning of Part II of the Broadcasting Act 1996), and any national digital sound programme service (within the meaning of that Part of that Act) subject to regulation by the Radio Authority".

11. In section 201 of the 1990 Act (meaning of "programme service"), after paragraph (b) there is inserted—
"(bb) any digital sound programme service (within the meaning of Part II of the Broadcasting Act 1996)".

PART II

OTHER AMENDMENTS OF BROADCASTING ACT 1990

12. In section 2 of the 1990 Act (regulation by Commission of provision of television services), in subsection (4), in the definition of "television programme service", after paragraph (a) there is inserted—
"(aa) a restricted service (as defined by section 42A);".

13. In section 6 of the 1990 Act (general requirements as to licensed services) in subsection (8), for "the teletext service referred to in section 49(2)" there is substituted "a teletext service".

14. In section 33 of the 1990 Act (conditions requiring holder of Channel 3 or Channel 5 licence to deliver licensed service), in subsection (3), after "subsection (1)" there is inserted "or section 21A(3) or (4)".

15.—(1) Section 43 of the 1990 Act (domestic and non-domestic satellite services) is amended as follows.

(2) In subsection (3), after "shall", where first occurring, there is inserted "subject to subsection (3A)".

(3) After that subsection there is inserted—

"(3A) For the purposes of this Part, any non-domestic satellite service which is composed by, and transmitted for, a BBC company, a Channel 4 company or an S4C company—
(a) shall be regarded as provided by that company and not by the relevant broadcasting body (even if the relevant broadcasting body is in a position to determine what is to be included in the service), and

(b) shall be regarded as provided from a place in the United Kingdom."

(4) At the end of subsection (4) there is inserted—

" "relevant broadcasting body" means—

(a) in relation to a BBC company, the BBC,

(b) in relation to a Channel 4 company, the Channel Four Television Corporation, and

(c) in relation to an S4C company, the Welsh Authority."

16. In section 46 of the 1990 Act (licensable programme services), in subsection (2)(a), after "television broadcasting service" there is inserted "a multiplex service (as defined by section 1(1) of the Broadcasting Act 1996), a restricted service".

17. In section 71 of the 1990 Act (interpretation of Part I), after the definition of "regional Channel 3 service" there is inserted—

" "restricted service" has the meaning given by section 42A;".

18. In section 72 of the 1990 Act (local delivery services), in subsection (2) after paragraph (a) there is inserted—

"(aa) any restricted service (within the meaning of that Part);".

19.—(1) Section 84 of the 1990 Act (regulation by Radio Authority of independent radio services) is amended as follows.

(2) In subsection (3), after "shall", where first occurring, there is inserted "subject to subsection (3A)".

(3) After that subsection there is inserted—

"(3A) For the purposes of this Part, any satellite service which is composed by, and transmitted for, a BBC company, a Channel 4 company or an S4C company—

(a) shall be regarded as provided by that company and not by the relevant broadcasting body (even if the relevant broadcasting body is in a position to determine what is to be included in the service), and

(b) shall be regarded as provided from a place in the United Kingdom.

(3B) In subsection (3A) "relevant broadcasting body" means—

(a) in relation to a BBC company, the BBC,

(b) in relation to a Channel 4 company, the Channel Four Television Corporation, and

(c) in relation to an S4C company, the Welsh Authority."

20. In section 188 of the 1990 Act (power to give broadcasting bodies etc. directions relating to international obligations), in subsection (2)(e), for "Broadcasting Standards Council" there is substituted "Broadcasting Standards Commission".

21. In section 202(1) of the 1990 Act (interpretation)—

(a) after the definition of "broadcast" there is inserted—

" "a Channel 4 company" means—

(a) any body corporate which is controlled by the Channel Four Television Corporation, or

(b) any body corporate in which the Corporation or any body corporate falling within paragraph (a) above is (to any extent) a participant (as defined in paragraph 1(1) of Part I of Schedule 2);"

(b) in the definition of "connected", for "licence" there is substituted "person", and

(c) after the definition of "programme" there is inserted—

" "an S4C company" means—

(a) any body corporate which is controlled by the Welsh Authority, or

(b) any body corporate in which the Welsh Authority or any body corporate falling within paragraph (a) above is (to any extent) a participant (as defined in paragraph 1(1) of Part I of Schedule 2);".

22. In paragraph 2(1) of Schedule 1 to the 1990 Act (persons disqualified for membership of the Independent Television Commission), for paragraphs (c) and (d) there is substituted—

"or

(c) a member or employee of the Broadcasting Standards Commission."

23. In paragraph 2(1) of Schedule 3 to the 1990 Act (persons disqualified for membership of the Channel Four Television Corporation), for paragraphs (d) and (e) there is substituted—

"or

(d) a member or employee of the Broadcasting Standards Commission."

24. In paragraph 2(1) of Schedule 6 to the 1990 Act (persons disqualified for membership of the Welsh Authority), for paragraphs (b) and (c) there is substituted—

"or

(b) a member or employee of the Broadcasting Standards Commission."

25. In paragraph 2(1) of Schedule 8 to the 1990 Act (persons disqualified for membership of the Radio Authority), for paragraphs (d) and (e) there is substituted—

"or

(d) a member or employee of the Broadcasting Standards Commission."

26. In Schedule 19 to the 1990 Act (the Gaelic Broadcasting Committee: supplementary provisions)—

(a) in paragraph 8—

(i) for "Gaelic Television Fund" there is substituted "Gaelic Broadcasting Fund"; and

(ii) in sub-paragraph (c), after "Commission" there is inserted "and (where the expenses relate to the Commission's functions in connection with sound programmes) the Radio Authority"; and

(b) in paragraph 11(4)—

(i) after "Commission" there is inserted "or the Radio Authority"; and

(ii) for "them", where it first occurs, there is substituted "the Commission or, as the case may be, the Authority".

Part III

Amendments of other enactments

The Welsh Development Agency Act 1975 (c. 70)

27. In section 19 of the Welsh Development Agency Act 1975 (the Agency and the media), in subsection (11)—

(a) in the definition of "the appropriate authority"—

(i) in paragraph (a), after "Act 1990" there is inserted "or Part I of the Broadcasting Act 1996", and

(ii) in paragraph (b), for "that Act" there is substituted "the Broadcasting Act 1990 or Part II of the Broadcasting Act 1996", and

(b) in the definition of "relevant licence" for "(as the case may be) Part III of that Act" there is substituted "III of the Broadcasting Act 1990 or Part I or II of the Broadcasting Act 1996.

The Representation of the People Act 1983 (c. 2)

28. In section 75 of the Representation of the People Act 1983 (prohibition of expenses not authorised by election agent), in subsection (1)(i), after "Broadcasting Act 1990" there is inserted "or Part I or II of the Broadcasting Act 1996".

29. In section 93 of the Representation of the People Act 1983 (broadcasting during elections), in subsection (1), for the paragraphs (a) and (b) inserted by paragraph 35(4)(a) of Schedule 20 to the 1990 Act there is substituted—

"(i) broadcast by the British Broadcasting Corporation or Sianel Pedwar Cymru, or

(ii) included in any service licensed under Part I or III of the Broadcasting Act 1990 or Part I or II of the Broadcasting Act 1996".

30. Without prejudice to the generality of section 20(2) of the Interpretation Act 1978, any reference in paragraph 28 or 29 to a provision of the Representation of the People Act 1983 includes a reference to that provision as applied by any regulations made under paragraph 2 of Schedule 1 to the European Parliamentary Elections Act 1978.

The Copyright, Designs and Patents Act 1988 (c. 48)

31. In section 69 of the Copyright, Designs and Patents Act 1988 (recording for purposes of supervision and control of broadcasts and cable programmes), for subsections (2) and (3) there is substituted—

"(2) Copyright is not infringed by anything done in pursuance of—

(a) section 11(1), 95(1) or 167(1) of the Broadcasting Act 1990 or section 115(4) or (6), 116(5) or 117 of the Broadcasting Act 1996;

(b) a condition which, by virtue of section 11(2) or 95(2) of the Broadcasting Act 1990, is included in a licence granted under Part I or III of that Act or Part I or II of the Broadcasting Act 1996; or

(c) a direction given under section 109(2) of the Broadcasting Act 1990 (power of Radio Authority to require production of recordings etc).

(3) Copyright is not infringed by—

(a) the use by the Independent Television Commission or the Radio Authority, in connection with the performance of any of their functions under the Broadcasting Act 1990 or the Broadcasting Act 1996, of any recording, script or transcript which is provided to them under or by virtue of any provision of those Acts; or

(b) the use by the Broadcasting Standards Commission, in connection with any complaint made to them under the Broadcasting Act 1996, of any recording or transcript requested or required to be provided to them, and so provided, under section 115(4) or (6) or 116(5) of that Act."

32. In Schedule 2 to the Copyright, Designs and Patents Act 1988 (rights in performances: permitted acts), in paragraph 17, for sub-paragraphs (2) and (3) there is substituted—

"(2) The rights conferred by Part II are not infringed by anything done in pursuance of—

(a) section 11 (1), 95(1) or 167(1) of the Broadcasting Act 1990 or section 115(4) or (6), 116(5) or 117 of the Broadcasting Act 1996;

(b) a condition which, by virtue of section 11(2) or 95(2) of the Broadcasting Act 1990, is included in a licence granted under Part I or III of that Act or Part I or II of the Broadcasting Act 1996; or

(c) a direction given under section 109(2) of the Broadcasting Act 1990 (power of Radio Authority to require production of recordings etc).

(3) The rights conferred by Part II are not infringed by—

(a) the use by the Independent Television Commission or the Radio Authority, in connection with the performance of any of their functions under the Broadcasting Act 1990 or the Broadcasting Act 1996, of any recording, script or transcript which is provided to them under or by virtue of any provision of those Acts; or

(b) the use by the Broadcasting Standards Commission, in connection with any complaint made to them under the Broadcasting Act 1996, of any recording or transcript requested or required to be provided to them, and so provided, under section 115(4) or (6) or 116(5) of that Act."

Section 148(2)

SCHEDULE 11

REPEALS AND REVOCATIONS

PART I

ENACTMENTS REPEALED

Chapter	*Short title*	*Extent of repeal*
1975 c. 24.	The House of Commons Disqualification Act 1975.	In Schedule 1, in Part II, the entries relating to the Broadcasting Complaints Commission, the Broadcasting Standards Council and Comataidh Telebhisein Gaidhlig.
1975 c. 25.	The Northern Ireland Assembly Disqualification Act 1975.	In Schedule 1, in Part II, the entries relating to the Broadcasting Complaints Commission and the Broadcasting Standards Council.
1990 c. 42.	The Broadcasting Act 1990.	In section 2, in subsection (1)(a), the second "and" and, in subsection (4), in paragraph (b) of the definition of "television programme service", the word "or". In section 32, in subsection (9), paragraph (b) and the word "and" immediately preceding it, in subsection (10) the words from "and for this purpose" onwards and in subsection (13)(a), the word "and". Section 45(8) and (9). Section 47(11) and (12). In section 72(2)(d), the word "and". In section 84(1)(b), the word "and". Section 104(5) and (6)(a). Sections 142 to 161. Section 182. In section 202(2), paragraph (a) and, in paragraph (b), the words "13,14".

Chapter	*Short title*	*Extent of repeal*
		In Schedule 2, in Part I, paragraphs 1(4) and 2(2) and (3) and, in Part II, in paragraph 1(2)(e), the word "or" and paragraph 5(c) and (d). Schedules 13 and 14. In Schedule 19, paragraph 3. In Schedule 20, paragraph 50.

PART II

SUBORDINATE LEGISLATION REVOKED

Number	*Title*	*Extent of revocation*
S.I. 1991/1176.	The Broadcasting (Restrictions on the Holding of Licences) Order 1991.	Article 2, and Parts II, III and IV.
S.I. 1991/1246.	The Cable (Excepted Programmes) Order 1991.	The whole order.
S.I. 1993/3199.	The Broadcasting (Restrictions on the Holding of Licences) (Amendment) Order 1993.	The whole order.
S.I. 1995/1924.	The Broadcasting (Restrictions on the Holding of Licences) (Amendment) Order 1995.	The whole order.

INDEX

References are to sections and Schedules

EDUCATION ACT 1996*

(1996 c.56)

[A Table showing the derivation of the provisions of this Consolidation Act will be found at the end of the Act. The Table has no official status.]

ARRANGEMENT OF SECTIONS

PART I

GENERAL

CHAPTER I

THE STATUTORY SYSTEM OF EDUCATION

General

SECT.

Educational institutions

Compulsory education

Education in accordance with parental wishes

CHAPTER II

FUNCTIONS OF THE SECRETARY OF STATE

CHAPTER III

LOCAL EDUCATION AUTHORITIES

The authorities

General functions

Establishment etc. of schools

Other arrangements for provision of education

---

* Annotations by Neville S. Harris, LL.M., Ph.D., Barrister, Professor of Law, Liverpool John Moores University.

Governors

Powers

Schools acquiring grant-maintained status: determination etc. of initial governors

New grant-maintained schools: determination etc. of initial governors

General and supplementary

CHAPTER VI

FUNDING OF GRANT-MAINTAINED SCHOOLS

Grants: general

Grants: Wales (until establishment of the SFCW)

Loans

Recovery from local funds

CHAPTER VII

ALTERATION ETC. OF GRANT-MAINTAINED SCHOOLS

CHAPTER VIII

DISCONTINUANCE OF GRANT-MAINTAINED SCHOOLS

Proposals for discontinuance

Withdrawal of grant

Winding up and disposal of property

CHAPTER IX

GROUPS OF GRANT-MAINTAINED SCHOOLS

CHAPTER X

GENERAL AND MISCELLANEOUS

Middle schools

Nursery education

Further education

Teacher training

Provision of benefits and services by local education authority

Transfer and disposal of premises

Modification of instruments

Religious opinions etc. of staff

Exclusion of pupils

Appeal committees

Supplementary

Interpretation

PART IV

SPECIAL EDUCATIONAL NEEDS

CHAPTER I

CHILDREN WITH SPECIAL EDUCATIONAL NEEDS

Introductory

Code of Practice

Special educational provision: general

Identification and assessment of children with special educational needs

Admission numbers for county and voluntary schools

New county and voluntary schools

Admissions appeals relating to county and voluntary schools

Nursery and special schools, etc.

Admission arrangements for grant-maintained schools

Admission numbers for grant-maintained schools

Admissions appeals relating to grant-maintained schools

Co-ordinated arrangements for admissions

Power to direct admission of child to school

Time for admission of pupils

Registration of pupils

Withdrawal of pupils from primary school for secondary education

Supplementary

CHAPTER II

SCHOOL ATTENDANCE

School attendance orders

Control of potentially harmful materials and apparatus

Nuisance or disturbance on school premises

CHAPTER II

CORPORAL PUNISHMENT

CHAPTER III

OTHER PROVISIONS ABOUT SCHOOLS

Duration of school day etc.

Single-sex schools

Educational trusts

Religious educational trusts

CHAPTER IV

EMPLOYMENT OF CHILDREN AND YOUNG PERSONS

CHAPTER V

PERSONS NOT COVERED BY ACT

CHAPTER VI

GENERAL

Documents and evidence

Stamp duty

Orders, regulations and directions

Guidance

Service of documents

Construction

Final provisions

SCHEDULES:

An Act to consolidate the Education Act 1944 and certain other enactments relating to education, with amendments to give effect to recommendations of the Law Commission. [24th July 1996]

PARLIAMENTARY DEBATES

Hansard, H.L. Vol. 572, cols. 209, 657; Vol. 573, col. 1024; Vol. 574, col. 834. H.C. Vol. 282, col. 368.

INTRODUCTION AND GENERAL NOTE

This Act (the EA 1996) consolidates a number of disparate and yet inter-connected measures concerned with education in England and Wales—including the Education Act 1944 (c. 31), the Education Act 1980 (c. 20), the Education (No.2) Act 1986 (c. 61), the Education Reform Act 1988 (c. 40) and the Education Act 1993 (c. 35), together with a number of other shorter statutes. The length of the Act, some 583 sections and 40 Schedules, demonstrates the considerable volume of education statute law which was in force and why this consolidation was necessary. Even so, the 1996 Act does not incorporate all of the statute law in this field. For one thing, its scope is limited to the schools sector: as the Lord Chancellor explained during the Bill's second reading in the House of Lords, "in order to keep the proportions of the Bill within manageable bounds it does not otherwise (*i.e.* apart from containing the general duties of the Secretary of State and local education authorities) deal with further or higher education" (*Hansard*, H.L. Vol. 572, col. 657, May 20, 1996, *per* Lord Mackay of Clashfern). Furthermore, the statutory regime governing the inspection of schools, established by the Education (Schools) Act 1992 (c. 38) and further developed via the Education Act 1993—in particular through the powers to deal with schools which fail to provide an acceptable standard of education—has been separately consolidated, in the School Inspections Act 1996 (c. 57). The Education Act 1994 (c. 30), which establishes the Teacher Training Agency and makes provision regarding initial teacher training, has not been consolidated into the EA 1996. It should also be noted that contemporaneous with the period of passage of the EA 1996 was the consideration, by Parliament, of the Bill which was enacted as the Nursery Education and Grant-Maintained Schools Act 1996 (c. 50); the provisions of that Act are not, therefore, consolidated in the EA 1996, although some of them are amended by it.

The Act contains some improvements to the previous statutory provisions, as recommended by the Law Commission (Law Com No.240, *Education Bill; School Inspections Bill: Report on the Consolidation of Certain Enactments Relating to Education*, Cm 3251 (1996)), many of which rectify minor omissions or clarify the application of certain provisions. For example, s.157 of the Act, which has replaced s.23 of the Education (No.2) Act 1986, makes new provision for informing a pupil aged 18 or over of a decision which makes an exclusion which was for a fixed period into a permanent exclusion and of his and his parents' right to make representations on the matter to the governing body and local education authority (LEA). Another omission dealt with relates to the definition of a school. Pupil referral units may provide part-time or full-time education, but although they were within the definition of "school" (in s.14(5) of the Further and Higher Education Act 1992 (c. 13)) if they provided full-time education, they were not if they provided only part-time education. This gap is met by s.4(2) of this Act.

There was widespread consultation over the Consolidation Bill and, because the Bill was not politically contentious, the Government had the unusual experience of steering an education measure through Parliament without demurral on any side. The Act received the Royal Assent on July 24, 1996, only two months after its second reading.

The legislation consolidated: a brief history

All of the legislation regulating the provision of education by schools or by LEAs outside schools has been incorporated into the EA 1996. What follows is an outline of the major Acts which have been affected, in historical order, describing the main provisions concerned.

The Education Act 1944

Despite the large number of legislative changes after 1979, the basic structure of the education system of England and Wales, based on the notion of a "national service, locally administered", was, immediately before the EA 1996, still that which was laid down by the Education Act 1944—often referred to as the "Butler Act", after R.A. Butler, the Minister of Education responsible for ensuring its passage through Parliament. By 1996 there still survived, in amended form, *inter alia*, the definition and establishment of LEAs and their general responsibility to ensure the provision of "sufficient" schools in their area and to provide school transport in prescribed cases; the defined categories of schools and of the three principal stages of education; provision for discontinuance of voluntary schools; provisions as to the use of school premises and decisions over the school day and holidays; the Secretary of State's general default powers (in ss.68 and 99) to issue directions to LEAs or governors if, for example, they were acting unreasonably or in default of their duties; the duty of parents to ensure that their children received an "efficient education", whether at school "or otherwise" (s.36); the duty to ensure that children were educated "in accordance with the wishes of their parents", provided it would be "compatible with the provision of efficient instruction and the avoidance of unreasonable public expenditure"; the regulation of independent schools; medical examination of pupils and cleanliness provisions; the establishment of conferences to determine an "agreed syllabus" for religious education in schools in the LEA's area; and a whole range of definitions used throughout the Education Acts, including "parent", "pupil" and "sex education" (the last one of several to be added via subsequent amendments).

Over the years, provisions dealing with, for example, the secular curriculum, instruments and articles of government of schools, the enforcement of school attendance, and various grants, were incrementally replaced. Furthermore, legislative changes progressively weakened the partnership between central and local government which the 1944 Act created, by diminishing the role of LEAs (see below).

The Education Act 1980

This Act was known as the Parent's Charter because it not only introduced a requirement that most governing bodies should have parent governors (subsequently replaced, in much amended form, by the Education (No.2) Act 1986) but, more particularly, provided for a right for parents to express a preference for a school for their child, specified that parental preference should be granted save in prescribed circumstances (s.6), gave parents a right of appeal to a local appeal committee if their choice was denied (s.7) (see EA 1996, ss.411 and 423) and imposed duties on LEAs and governing bodies concerning the publication of information about schools (s.8) (see EA 1996, s.414). Parental choice was also enhanced by the availability, under the Act, of financial support for academically able children to attend independent schools—under the "assisted places" scheme. On the other hand, it limited the power to provide free school meals, milk and other refreshments. Some new provisions on school closures and changes of character were also introduced: as amended, these provisions are now in the EA 1996 (Pt. II, Chaps. II and VII).

The Education (No.2) Act 1986

This Act was preceded by a White Paper entitled *Better Schools* (Cmnd 6469, 1985). The means of achieving improvements to the schools system, according to this Act, were to strengthen considerably the powers and role of governing bodies—for example, over staff appointments and the school curriculum—and reform their constitution (the number of parent governors increased, at the expense of LEA-appointed governors); to make provision for the training of governors; and to provide a new legal framework for school discipline, sex education and the political content of education (political bias was in effect outlawed). The changes made by the Act meant that schools required new instruments and articles of government.

The Education Reform Act 1988

The process of reducing the power and influence of LEAs continued with the Education Reform Act 1988 (ERA), most particularly through its provision for grant-maintained (GM) schools and city technology colleges (lying outside LEA control and funded directly by central government, in the case of the former, or by a combination of central government funds and private industry support, in the case of the latter) and for financial delegation of budgets to schools themselves, apart from a small percentage of funds to be retained by the LEA to cover central services, contingencies and a few other matters. The ERA not only continued the process of empowering school governing bodies. Power at the centre was also increased. The Secretary of State not only gained greater controls over further and higher education (which lie outside the scope of the EA 1996), but was also granted power to determine the content of the secular curriculum. The National Curriculum comprised three core subjects—English, mathematics and science—and 10 foundation subjects (plus Welsh in Welsh language schools in Wales) laid down in the ERA itself; but the content of each subject—in other words its attainment targets, programmes of study and assessment arrangements—were to be prescribed via orders made by the Secretary of State. Advice for the Secretary of State on the curriculum and assessment were to be provided by new statutory bodies, such as the National Curriculum Council and the School Examinations and Assessment Authority in England (subsequently replaced by a unitary body—the School Curriculum and Assessment Authority—under the EA 1993). Among other provisions on the curriculum introduced via the ERA 1988 were those on charging for educational provision, a set of broad curricular aims (the curriculum should be "broadly based" and help to prepare pupils for the "opportunities and experiences of adult life") and a requirement that collective worship in county schools should be "broadly Christian" in character. Schools and LEAs were required to operate a procedure for dealing with complaints concerning the manner in which they exercised their responsibilities concerning the curriculum and the provision of information.

The theme of parental choice continued. Not only did parents have a collective say over whether a school should become GM, but there were also further powers on the provision of information (building on those introduced under the 1980 Act, above) and an important change to the legal basis on limits to the number of children who could be admitted to a school in response to parental choice. So far as admissions were concerned, the change was to more "open enrolment". LEAs could not set artificially low admissions limits for schools in their area—as some had done previously in order to spread pupil numbers around the authority's schools and thereby ensure that less popular community schools continued to be viable. Under the ERA, it ceased to be possible to apply the rule that a school place could be denied because the admission of the child would prejudice efficient education or the efficient use of resources, if the school concerned had surplus capacity.

The ERA 1988 also made individual London boroughs responsible for education in their own areas. It also gave considerable control to the Secretary of State in the transition period during which power and authority were transferred from the Inner London Education Authority (ILEA) to the boroughs. Provision had to be made for the transfer of functions, but also personnel and property. These transfers were regulated via statutory instrument. The ILEA itself was abolished by statutory instrument on April 1, 1990.

Subsequent legislation has either left intact, or built upon, these reforms introduced under the ERA. For example, the opportunities for schools to acquire GM status were significantly enhanced by the EA 1993 (see below), which consolidated the ERA's provisions on GM schools as well as reforming this area of provision.

The Education Act 1993

The 1993 Act took away from the ERA the record for the longest education statute in British Parliamentary history, with over 300 sections and nearly 30 Schedules. Based around reforms set out in a White Paper, *Choice and Diversity* (Cm 2021, 1992), the 1993 Act made important changes in the following areas: the role of the Secretary of State; GM schools; the curriculum; school government; special educational needs (see discussion of the 1981 Act above); quality assurance and "failing" schools; and a whole range of miscellaneous measures, including school discipline.

Taking first the area of school discipline, the Act removed the power to exclude pupils indefinitely from school, provided financial disincentives to exclusion (by withdrawing the funding for a pupil from a school once the pupil had been excluded), and limited the number of days for which a pupil could be subjected to a fixed term exclusion in any term. The lawfulness of corporal punishment administered in private schools became dependent on it not being "inhuman or degrading". Part IV of the Act tightened up on the enforcement of school attendance (most of the 1944 Act provisions on attendance were replaced) and put LEAs under a duty to provide alternative arrangements for excluded children and others unable to attend school (with a discretion in respect of those beyond compulsory school age); pupil referral units were put on a proper legal footing. A new power was introduced to direct a school to admit a pupil who had been excluded from another school or who had been refused admission to a school.

In the area of quality assurance, the 1993 Act built on the Education (Schools) Act 1992. The law in this area is now, as noted above, contained in the School Inspections Act 1996.

The Act had a particularly centralising element to it. New funding agencies (one for England and one for Wales) were established, with members to be appointed by the Secretary of State. The agencies' role was not only to administer funds to GM schools. They could also take over from LEAs, or share with them, the duty (then in s.8 of the 1944 Act) to ensure the provision of "sufficient" schools in an area. Such a partial or complete transfer of responsibility could take place in either primary or secondary sectors, or both, once a certain proportion of pupils in state schools in the area were attending GM schools. The agencies were also empowered to propose the establishment of new schools as GM schools and to propose changes to existing GM schools once such a partial or complete transfer of power had taken place. The Secretary of State was also given a power to direct LEAs and others to publish proposals for rationalisation of provision in an area which was considered "excessive". The Secretary of State was given a new general duty not merely to "promote" education (previously in s.1 of the 1944 Act, now in s.10 of the 1996 Act) but also to exercise her/his powers of regulation of educational provision with "a view, amongst other things, to improving standards, encouraging diversity and increasing opportunities for choice" (see now s.11 of the 1996 Act).

The opportunities for schools to acquire GM status were extended (for example, schools could acquire it in groups, and special schools could become GM special schools—a separate category) and the procedure was streamlined (for example, the governing body no longer had to pass a second resolution before instituting a ballot of parents). LEAs' scope for campaigning locally against opting out was restricted. Schools could apply for a change of character at the same time as applying for GM status. New schools, in the form of GM schools, could be proposed by promoters or, once a power transfer had taken place in the area (see above), the funding agency. Both GM schools and voluntary aided schools were able to have sponsor governors. The Act also made provision for co-ordinated admission arrangements as between GM schools, LEAs and voluntary schools.

In the area of special educational needs, Pt. III built upon reforms introduced via the Education Act 1981. The chief components of the 1981 Act were definitions of special educational needs and provision, provision for formal assessment of needs, statements of special educational needs, integration of statemented children into mainstream schools wherever possible, and parental rights, including rights of appeal. The 1993 Act introduced a Code of Practice on the identification and assessment of special educational needs, improved assessment and statementing procedures, and strengthened parental rights, with extended grounds of appeal and the Special Educational Needs Tribunal in place of the existing arrangements.

In the area of the curriculum, there was a new duty on secondary schools to provide sex education (with a right of parents to withdraw their child from it, apart from the biological aspects covered within the National Curriculum). There were also changes to the composition of standing advisory councils and conferences on religious education (RE) (and a duty to reconsider all RE syllabuses not revised since the ERA came into force). The School Curriculum and Assessment Authority was introduced in place of the National Curriculum Council and School Examinations and Assessment Council. Charges for music tuition in groups of up to four could be made (previously only *individual* music tuition could be charged for).

Among the miscellaneous changes was provision for independent ("lay") members of admissions appeal committees and incorporation of school governing bodies (bringing LEA-maintained schools into line with GM schools in this respect).

The 1996 Act

It can be seen from the review of the previous legislation, that the case for consolidation was overwhelming. Education law was a tangle of disparate provisions deriving from an extremely diverse range of statutes dating back to 1944. The 1996 Act incorporates the previous law in its 10 parts.

Pt. I—General

Chapter I sets out the statutory system of education in England and Wales, with its division into three separate stages (primary, secondary and further education). It defines the various categories of school (primary, secondary, middle, nursery and special) in which education takes place in the state sector. "School" is defined in s.4. The provisions on compulsory schooling, previously in s.36 of the 1944 Act and s.277 of the 1993 Act, are contained in this Part (ss.7 and 8, respectively). The general duty to educate children in accordance with the wishes of their parents (previously in s.76 of the 1944 Act) is in s.9.

Chapter II sets out the general functions of the Secretary of State (previously in ss.1 and 2 of the 1993 Act). Chapter III defines LEAs and sets out their general functions (ss.12–14, for example, replace ss.6–8 of the 1944 Act). Provision of education in pupil referral units (previously in s.298 of the 1993 Act) is made here (in s.19 and Sched. 1). Chapter IV prescribes the funding authorities (the Funding Agency for Schools and the Schools Funding Council for Wales) and defines their functions (see also Scheds. 2 and 3). The whole of Chap. V comprises one section (s.27, which replaces s.12 of the 1993 Act); it makes provision for the complete or partial transfer of responsibility for ensuring sufficient school places in an area from an LEA to the relevant funding agency (see also Sched. 4, which replaces Sched. 2 to the 1993 Act).

Pt. II—Schools maintained by local education authorities

Chapters I and II of this Part define the various categories of LEA-maintained schools and make provision for the establishment, alteration, change of site and closure of schools, replacing provisions of the 1944 and 1980 Acts (see also Sched. 5, which replaces Sched. 3 to the 1944 Act). Chapter III contains the arrangements, previously in the 1944 Act, as amended by the 1993 Act, and the Education Act 1946 (c. 50), for the funding of voluntary schools and the provision of sites, etc. for them (see also Sched. 6 on transfer of premises).

Government of LEA-maintained schools (here referring to county, voluntary and maintained special schools) is the subject of Chap. IV (see also Sched. 8), which replicates the relevant parts of the 1986 (No.2) Act in making provision for an instrument of government, the composition of governing bodies, the appointment or election of governors, the grouping of schools under a single governing body and the government of new schools (see also Scheds. 9 and 10). Chapter V, on the other hand, replaces the provisions of the ERA on financial delegation (see also Scheds. 11 and 12).

The conduct and staffing of LEA-maintained schools are covered by Chap. VI. The 1986 (No.2) Act is replaced so far as the duty to have articles of government, the enforcement of discipline at a school (including exclusion and the procedure to be followed: see also Scheds. 15 and 16 on reinstatement and appeals), the general responsibility of the governing body for the conduct of the school and staffing in schools which do not have delegated budgets, are concerned (see also Sched. 13). The 1988 Act is replaced in respect of staffing in schools with delegated budgets (see also Sched. 14). Amongst other important provisions incorporated here are those concerning responsibility for determining school term and holiday dates and session times, control of school premises, governors' annual reports (and see also Sched. 17 (replacing ss.30 and 31 of the 1986 (No.2) Act: see ss.161 and 162)) and their annual meetings with parents (see further Sched. 18), and the conduct and staffing of new schools (s.166 and Sched. 19).

Chapter VII makes provision (previously in s.12 of the 1980 Act and s.273 of the 1993 Act) for the discontinuance of LEA maintained schools. The restrictions on the power of the governing body of a voluntary school to discontinue it and the procedure to be followed (previously in s.14 of the 1944 Act) are also set out here (see ss.173 and 174). Chapter VIII contains miscellaneous and supplementary provisions, including the power of a school to provide further education (s.176, previously in s.16A of the 1986 (No.2) Act) and the modification of enactments relating to employment (so that, irrespective of who has the actual power to hire and fire staff, the LEA may be the body taken to an industrial tribunal and the employer: s.178, previously s.222 of the ERA).

Pt. III—Grant-maintained schools

This replicates, almost exactly, Pt. II of the 1993 Act, in making provision for the establishment (either via a change of status or the creation of a new school), funding, government and discontinuance of GM schools and the transfer of property and staff to them when an LEA-maintained school acquires GM status (see also Scheds. 20–25). Many of the provisions will apply to a GM special school established under Chap. II of Pt. IV (see below).

Chapter I defines GM schools. Chapter II sets out the eligibility for GM status and prescribes the procedure for its acquisition. Chapter III makes provision for the transfer of staff and property from the LEA to a school which is acquiring GM status, including the restrictions on disposal by the LEA. Chapter IV contains the provisions, previously set out in ss.48 *et seq* of the 1993 Act, on the establishment of new schools as GM schools. The government and conduct of GM schools, and the associated powers of governing bodies of such schools, are the subject of Chap. V (see also Sched. 28), which also makes provision as to the constitution of the governing body, the appointment of election of governors and the instrument and articles of government.

Chapter VI makes provision for the funding of GM schools via maintenance, special purpose and capital grants and through loans. Chapter VII deals with alteration of GM schools and Chap. VIII with their discontinuance, including winding up and disposal of property. Provision is made by Chap. IX as to the government of groups of GM schools, and by Chap. X on miscellaneous matters including restrictions on the power of exclusion and the provision of further education and nursery education in GM schools.

Pt. IV—Special Educational Needs

Part IV replaces Pt. III of the 1993 Act. Unlike the latter, however, it is divided into two separate chapters. Chapter I contains the key definitions, the duties on schools, teachers and LEAs regarding identification, assessment, statementing, integration and information, the grounds of appeal, and the constitution of the Special Educational Needs Tribunal and appointment and remuneration of its members. Schedules 26 and 27 to the Act are linked to this part and replace Scheds. 9 and 10, respectively, of the 1993 Act.

Chapter II is concerned with special schools. It defines them (in s.337) and makes provision for their establishment (either as maintained or grant-maintained special schools) and for the required approval, either before or after its establishment, of a non-maintained school which is specially organised to make special educational provision for pupils with special educational needs (s.342, replacing s.188 of the 1993 Act). Provision is also made for, amongst other things, government of special schools, the acquisition of GM special school status by an LEA-maintained school, grouping of GM special schools and approval of independent schools as suitable for the admission of statemented children (s.347, which replaces s.189 of the 1993 Act).

Pt. V—The curriculum

Chapter I of Pt. V replaces Pt. I of the ERA as regards the basic curriculum of schools and Chap. II covers the provision, control and development of, and exemption from, the National Curriculum (see also Scheds. 29 and 30) Chapter III replaces the provisions of the ERA (especially ss.6 and 7 and 9–12 of that Act) and the 1944 Act (s.26) on religious education and collective worship (see also Sched. 31). Chapter IV contains miscellaneous and supplementary provisions, including those on entry of pupils for public examinations, the content of, and withdrawal from, sex education, political indoctrination, provision of information and (replacing s.23 of the ERA) complaints about the carrying out of duties and the exercise of powers concerning the curriculum and provision of information.

Pt. VI—School admissions, attendance and charges

Chapter I replaces: (i) the 1980 Act on parental preference and the right of appeal (ss.6 and 7 of that Act are replaced by ss.411 and 423 of this Act: see also Sched. 33); (ii) the ERA on school admissions numbers (see also Sched. 32); and (iii) the 1993 Act on admission to GM schools, on co-ordinated admissions arrangements (referred to above) and the power to direct the admission of a child to a school (ss.431 and 432, replacing ss.13 and 14 of the 1993 Act). Various other disparate provisions are incorporated here, such as the duties concerning registration of pupils (s.434), previously in s.80 of the 1944 Act.

Chapter I replaces the school attendance enforcement provisions previously in Pt. IV of the 1993 Act and Chap. III replaces the provisions of the 1944 Act and, more particularly, the 1988

Act, on charges in connection with education at LEA-maintained or GM schools.

Pt. VII—Independent schools

Part VII (see also Sched. 34) deals with the definition and regulation of independent schools, replacing (in Chaps. I and II) the relevant parts of the 1944 Act, as amended, and (in Chap. III, see also Sched. 35) the provisions of the 1980 Act relating to the assisted places scheme. Chapter IV sensibly incorporates the statutory basis of city technology colleges; they are defined as independent schools but were previously dealt with under a separate statute (the ERA) to other such schools.

Pt. VIII—Grants and other matters

This Part brings together a number of previously widely dispersed provisions on grants, payment of fees and expenses and recoupment (see the Table of Derivations in respect of ss.484–494).

Pt. IX—Ancillary functions

This Part is an amalgam of numerous disparate powers and duties resting with the Secretary of State (Chap. I), LEAs (Chap. II), and governing bodies (Chaps. III and IV).

Chapter I prescribes the functions of the Secretary of State regarding the determination of disputes (s.495, previously s.67 of the 1944 Act) and his important default powers (ss.496 and 497, previously ss.68 and 99 of the 1944 Act). It also sets out, amongst other things, his powers concerning rationalisation of school places (previously contained in Pt. VI of the 1993 Act).

Chapter II covers LEAs' duties and/or powers on a range of matters (many derived from the 1944 Act). The matters which are covered include provision of school transport (s.509 replaces the well-known and heavily litigated s.55 of the 1944 Act), clothing and meals, payment of allowances to governors, medical inspection and treatment of pupils, enforcement of the cleanliness of pupils and appointment of a chief education officer.

The remainder of Pt. IX deals with provision by governing bodies of various services (Chap. III) and information (Chap. IV) (including the duties previously laid down in s.16 of the Education (Schools) Act 1992).

Pt. X—Miscellaneous and general

As might be expected, the final part of the Act, which covers miscellaneous matters and general provisions (including, in s.580, a general index), is lengthy (at over 40 sections).

Chapter I makes provision as to school premises and buildings standards and also contains (in s.547) the offence (previously in s.40 of the Local Government (Miscellaneous Provisions) Act 1982 (c. 30)) of causing a nuisance or disturbance on school premises.

Chapter II contains three sections (ss.548–550, replacing s.47 of the 1944 Act) which proscribe the provision of corporal punishment (which is defined) in respect of the majority of pupils (including all pupils in maintained schools).

Chapter III deals with other provisions about schools, including religious and educational trusts (see also Sched. 36).

Chapter IV replaces parts of the 1944 Act and the Education (Work Experience) Act 1973 (c. 23) on the employment of children and young persons.

Chapter V excludes persons in the service of the Crown or detained under an order of a court from the scope of the remainder of the Act.

Chapter VI is concerned with various general matters, including certain definitions.

Schedules

Most of the Schedules were referred to above in relation to the various Parts to which they relate. The remaining Scheds. 37–40, relate to consequential amendments, repeals and revocations, transitional arrangements and transitory provisions, and are self-explanatory.

Commencement

Almost all of the provisions of the Act, and thus repeals of the legislation being consolidated, occurred on November 1, 1996, as provided by the Act (s.583(2)). The remaining provisions come into effect by order of the Secretary of State. At the time of writing there has been one such order, bringing s.317(6) into force: the Education Act 1996 (Commencement No.1) Order 1996 (S.I. 1996 No. 2904).

Part I

General

Chapter I

The statutory system of education

General

The stages of education

1.—(1) The statutory system of public education consists of three progressive stages: primary education, secondary education and further education.

(2) This Part—

(a) confers functions on the Secretary of State and local education authorities with respect to primary, secondary and further education; and

(b) provides for functions with respect to primary and secondary education to be conferred on the funding authorities constituted under Chapter IV.

(3) Part I of the Further and Higher Education Act 1992 confers functions with respect to further education on the further education funding councils established under section 1 of that Act.

Apart from section 10 (general duty of Secretary of State), nothing in this Act confers any functions with respect to higher education.

Definition of primary, secondary and further education

2.—(1) In this Act "primary education" means—

(a) full-time education suitable to the requirements of junior pupils who have not attained the age of 10 years and six months; and

(b) full-time education suitable to the requirements of junior pupils who have attained that age and whom it is expedient to educate together with junior pupils within paragraph (a).

(2) In this Act "secondary education" means—

(a) full-time education suitable to the requirements of pupils of compulsory school age who are either—

(i) senior pupils, or

(ii) junior pupils who have attained the age of 10 years and six months and whom it is expedient to educate together with senior pupils of compulsory school age; and

(b) (subject to subsection (5)) full-time education suitable to the requirements of pupils who are over compulsory school age but under the age of 19 which is provided at a school at which education within paragraph (a) is also provided.

(3) Subject to subsection (5), in this Act "further education" means—

(a) full-time and part-time education suitable to the requirements of persons who are over compulsory school age (including vocational, social, physical and recreational training), and

(b) organised leisure-time occupation provided in connection with the provision of such education,

except that it does not include secondary education or (in accordance with subsection (7)) higher education.

(4) Accordingly, unless it is education within subsection (2)(b), full-time education suitable to the requirements of persons over compulsory school age who have not attained the age of 19 is further education for the purposes of this Act and not secondary education.

(5) For the purposes of this Act education provided for persons who have

attained the age of 19 is further education not secondary education; but where a person—

(a) has begun a particular course of secondary education before attaining the age of 18, and

(b) continues to attend that course,

the education does not cease to be secondary education by reason of his having attained the age of 19.

(6) In subsection (3)(b) "organised leisure-time occupation" means leisure-time occupation, in such organised cultural training and recreative activities as are suited to their requirements, for any persons over compulsory school age who are able and willing to profit by facilities provided for that purpose.

(7) References in this section to education do not include references to higher education.

Definition of pupil etc.

3.—(1) In this Act "pupil" means a person for whom education is being provided at a school, other than—

(a) a person who has attained the age of 19 for whom further education is being provided, or

(b) a person for whom part-time education suitable to the requirements of persons of any age over compulsory school age is being provided.

(2) In this Act—

"junior pupil" means a child who has not attained the age of 12; and

"senior pupil" means a person who has attained the age of 12 but not the age of 19.

(3) The definition of "pupil" in subsection (1) also applies (unless the context otherwise requires) for the purposes of any instrument made or having effect as if made under the Education Acts.

Educational institutions

Schools: general

4.—(1) In this Act "school" means an educational institution which is outside the further education sector and the higher education sector and is an institution for providing any one or more of the following—

(a) primary education,

(b) education which is secondary education by virtue of section 2(2)(a), or

(c) full-time education suitable to the requirements of persons who are over compulsory school age but under the age of 19,

whether or not the institution also provides part-time education suitable to the requirements of junior pupils, further education or secondary education not within paragraph (b).

(2) For the purposes of this Act an educational institution that would fall within subsection (1) but for the fact that it provides part-time rather than full-time education shall nevertheless be treated as a school if that part-time education is provided under arrangements made under section 19(1) (pupil referral units).

(3) For the purposes of this Act an institution is outside the further education sector if it is not—

(a) an institution conducted by a further education corporation established under section 15 or 16 of the Further and Higher Education Act 1992, or

(b) a designated institution for the purposes of Part I of that Act (defined in section 28(4) of that Act);

and references to institutions within that sector shall be construed accordingly.

(4) For the purposes of this Act an institution is outside the higher education sector if it is not—

(a) a university receiving financial support under section 65 of that Act,
(b) an institution conducted by a higher education corporation within the meaning of that Act, or
(c) a designated institution for the purposes of Part II of that Act (defined in section 72(3) of that Act);

and references to institutions within that sector shall be construed accordingly.

Primary schools, secondary schools and middle schools

5.—(1) In this Act "primary school" means (subject to regulations under subsection (4)) a school for providing primary education, whether or not it also provides part-time education suitable to the requirements of junior pupils or further education.

(2) In this Act "secondary school" means (subject to regulations under subsection (4)) a school for providing secondary education, whether or not it also provides further education.

(3) In this Act "middle school" means a school in respect of which proposals authorised by section 49, 198(6) or 291 are implemented (that is, a school providing full-time education suitable to the requirements of pupils who have attained a specified age below 10 years and six months and are under a specified age above 12 years).

(4) The Secretary of State shall make regulations for determining, or enabling him to determine, whether a middle school is to be treated for the purposes of this Act and the other enactments relating to education as a primary school or as a secondary school.

(5) The powers conferred by sections 49, 198(6) and 291 and subsection (4) above are exercisable—

(a) notwithstanding anything in this Act (and in particular section 1); but
(b) without prejudice to the exercise of any other power conferred by this Act.

Nursery schools and special schools

6.—(1) A primary school is a nursery school if it is used mainly for the purpose of providing education for children who have attained the age of two but are under the age of five.

(2) A school is a special school if it is specially organised, and for the time being approved, as mentioned in section 337(1).

Compulsory education

Duty of parents to secure education of children of compulsory school age

7. The parent of every child of compulsory school age shall cause him to receive efficient full-time education suitable—

(a) to his age, ability and aptitude, and
(b) to any special educational needs he may have,

either by regular attendance at school or otherwise.

Compulsory school age

8.—(1) Subsections (2) and (3) apply to determine for the purposes of any enactment whether a person is of compulsory school age.

(2) A person begins to be of compulsory school age when he attains the age of five.

(3) A person ceases to be of compulsory school age at the end of the day which is the school leaving date for any calendar year—

(a) if he attains the age of 16 after that day but before the beginning of the school year next following,
(b) if he attains that age on that day, or
(c) (unless paragraph (a) applies) if that day is the school leaving date next following his attaining that age.

(4) The Secretary of State may by order determine the day in any calendar year which is to be the school leaving date for that year.

Education in accordance with parental wishes

Pupils to be educated in accordance with parents' wishes

9. In exercising or performing all their respective powers and duties under the Education Acts, the Secretary of State, local education authorities and the funding authorities shall have regard to the general principle that pupils are to be educated in accordance with the wishes of their parents, so far as that is compatible with the provision of efficient instruction and training and the avoidance of unreasonable public expenditure.

CHAPTER II

FUNCTIONS OF THE SECRETARY OF STATE

General duty of Secretary of State

10. The Secretary of State shall promote the education of the people of England and Wales.

Duty in the case of primary, secondary and further education

11.—(1) The Secretary of State shall exercise his powers in respect of those bodies in receipt of public funds which—

(a) carry responsibility for securing that the required provision for primary, secondary or further education is made—
  (i) in schools, or
  (ii) in institutions within the further education sector,
 in or in any area of England or Wales, or
(b) conduct schools or institutions within the further education sector in England and Wales,

for the purpose of promoting primary, secondary and further education in England and Wales.

(2) The Secretary of State shall, in the case of his powers to regulate the provision made in schools and institutions within the further education sector in England and Wales, exercise his powers with a view to (among other things) improving standards, encouraging diversity and increasing opportunities for choice.

CHAPTER III

LOCAL EDUCATION AUTHORITIES

The authorities

Local education authorities and their areas

12.—(1) The local education authority for a county in England having a county council is the county council.

(2) The local education authority for a district in England which is not in a county having a county council is the district council.

(3) The local education authority for a London borough is the borough

council.

(4) The local education authority for the City of London (which for the purposes of this Act shall be treated as including the Inner Temple and the Middle Temple) is the Common Council of the City of London (in their capacity as a local authority).

(5) As respects Wales—

(a) the local education authority for a county is the county council; and

(b) the local education authority for a county borough is the county borough council.

(6) Any reference in this Act to the area of a local education authority shall be construed in accordance with the preceding provisions of this section.

General functions

General responsibility for education

13.—(1) A local education authority shall (so far as their powers enable them to do so) contribute towards the spiritual, moral, mental and physical development of the community by securing that efficient primary education, secondary education and further education are available to meet the needs of the population of their area.

(2) The duty imposed by subsection (1) does not extend to matters in respect of which any duty is imposed on—

(a) the further education funding councils established under section 1 of the Further and Higher Education Act 1992, or

(b) the higher education funding councils established under section 62 of that Act.

Functions in respect of provision of primary and secondary schools

14.—(1) A local education authority shall secure that sufficient schools for providing—

(a) primary education, and

(b) education that is secondary education by virtue of section 2(2)(a),

are available for their area.

(2) The schools available for an area shall not be regarded as sufficient for the purposes of subsection (1) unless they are sufficient in number, character and equipment to provide for all pupils the opportunity of appropriate education.

(3) In subsection (2) "appropriate education" means education which offers such variety of instruction and training as may be desirable in view of—

(a) the pupils' different ages, abilities and aptitudes, and

(b) the different periods for which they may be expected to remain at school,

including practical instruction and training appropriate to their different needs.

(4) A local education authority is not by virtue of subsection (1)(a) under any duty in respect of children under the age of five.

(5) A local education authority may secure the provision for their area of full-time education suitable to the requirements of persons over compulsory school age who have not attained the age of 19, including provision for persons from other areas.

(6) In exercising their functions under this section, a local education authority shall in particular have regard to—

(a) the need for securing that primary and secondary education are provided in separate schools;

(b) the need for securing that special educational provision is made for pupils who have special educational needs; and

(c) the expediency of securing the provision of boarding accommodation (in boarding schools or otherwise) for pupils for whom education as boarders is considered by their parents and the authority to be desirable.

(7) The duty imposed by subsection (6)(a) does not apply in relation to middle schools or special schools.

Functions in respect of provision of further education

15.—(1) A local education authority shall secure the provision for their area of adequate facilities for further education.

(2) The duty imposed by subsection (1) does not apply in relation to—

(a) education to which section 2(1) of the Further and Higher Education Act 1992 applies (that is, full-time education suitable to the requirements of persons who are over compulsory school age and under the age of 19); or

(b) education to which section 3(1) of that Act applies (that is—

(i) part-time education suitable to the requirements of persons of any age over compulsory school age, and

(ii) full-time education suitable to the requirements of persons who have attained the age of 19,

where the education is provided by means of a course of a description mentioned in Schedule 2 to that Act).

(3) However, in respect of further education falling within subsection (2)(b), a local education authority may secure the provision for their area of such facilities as appear to them to be appropriate for meeting the needs of the population of their area.

(4) A local education authority may secure the provision of further education for persons from other areas.

(5) In exercising their functions under this section a local education authority shall have regard to—

(a) any educational facilities provided—

(i) by institutions within the higher education sector or the further education sector, and

(ii) by other bodies,

which are provided for, or available for use by persons in, their area, and

(b) the requirements of persons over compulsory school age who have learning difficulties.

(6) Subject to subsection (7), a person has a "learning difficulty" for the purposes of subsection (5) if—

(a) he has a significantly greater difficulty in learning than the majority of persons of his age, or

(b) he has a disability which either prevents or hinders him from making use of facilities of a kind generally provided in pursuance of the duty under subsection (1) for persons of his age.

(7) A person is not to be taken as having a learning difficulty solely because the language (or form of the language) in which he is, or will be, taught is different from a language (or form of a language) which has at any time been spoken in his home.

(8) A local education authority may do anything which appears to them to be necessary or expedient for the purposes of or in connection with the exercise of their functions under this section.

Establishment etc. of schools

Power to establish, maintain and assist primary and secondary schools

16.—(1) For the purpose of fulfilling their functions under this Act, a local education authority may—

(a) establish primary schools and secondary schools;
(b) maintain primary and secondary schools, whether established by them or not; and
(c) assist any primary or secondary school which is not maintained by them.

(2) A local education authority may under subsection (1) establish, maintain and assist schools outside as well as inside their area.

(3) A local education authority may not under subsection (1) establish a school to provide—
(a) part-time education suitable to the requirements of persons of any age over compulsory school age; or
(b) full-time education suitable to the requirements of persons who have attained the age of 19.

Powers in respect of nursery education

17.—(1) A local education authority may—
(a) establish nursery schools:
(b) maintain nursery schools established by them or by an authority which was a local education authority within the meaning of any enactment repealed by the Education Act 1944 or an earlier Act; and
(c) assist any nursery school not so established.

(2) Section 14(4) does not affect a local education authority's power under section 16(1) to establish, maintain and assist schools at which education is provided both for children under the age of five and for older pupils (including schools at which there are nursery classes for children under the age of five).

Other arrangements for provision of education

Power to arrange provision of education at non-maintained schools

18. A local education authority may make arrangements for the provision of primary and secondary education for pupils at schools not maintained by them or another local education authority.

Exceptional provision of education in pupil referral units or elsewhere

19.—(1) Each local education authority shall make arrangements for the provision of suitable full-time or part-time education at school or otherwise than at school for those children of compulsory school age who, by reason of illness, exclusion from school or otherwise, may not for any period receive suitable education unless such arrangements are made for them.

(2) Any school established (whether before or after the commencement of this Act) and maintained by a local education authority which—
(a) is specially organised to provide education for such children, and is not a county school or a special school,

shall be known as a "pupil referral unit".

(3) A local education authority may secure the provision of boarding accommodation at any pupil referral unit.

(4) A local education authority may make arrangements for the provision of suitable full-time or part-time education otherwise than at school for those young persons who, by reason of illness, exclusion from school or otherwise, may not for any period receive suitable education unless such arrangements are made for them.

(5) Any child for whom education is provided otherwise than at school in pursuance of this section, and any young person for whom full-time education is so provided in pursuance of this section, shall be treated for the purposes of this Act as a pupil.

(6) In this section "suitable education", in relation to a child or young per-

son, means efficient education suitable to his age, ability and aptitude and to any special educational needs he may have.

(7) Schedule 1 has effect in relation to pupil referral units.

CHAPTER IV

THE FUNDING AUTHORITIES

The Authorities

The Funding Agency for Schools

20.—(1) The Funding Agency for Schools shall continue in existence as a body corporate exercising in relation to England the functions conferred on them.

(2) The agency shall consist of not less than 10 nor more than 15 members appointed by the Secretary of State, one of whom shall be so appointed as chairman.

(3) In appointing the members of the agency the Secretary of State shall have regard to the desirability of including—

(a) persons who appear to him to have experience of, and to have shown capacity in, the provision of primary or secondary education or to have held, and to have shown capacity in, any position carrying responsibility for the provision of such education;

(b) persons who appear to him to have experience of, and to have shown capacity in, the provision of education in voluntary schools, or in grant-maintained schools having foundation governors;

(c) persons who appear to him to have experience of, and to have shown capacity in, industrial, commercial or financial matters or the practice of any profession; and

(d) persons who appear to him to have experience of, and to have shown capacity in, providing for children with special educational needs.

(4) Before appointing any member of the agency the Secretary of State shall consult—

(a) a body appearing to him to be representative of the Church of England, and

(b) a body appearing to him to be representative of the Roman Catholic Church,

in matters relating to the provision of education in voluntary schools, or in grant-maintained schools having foundation governors.

(5) Schedule 2 has effect in relation to the agency.

The Schools Funding Council for Wales

21.—(1) The Secretary of State may by order make provision for the establishment of a body corporate to be known as the Schools Funding Council for Wales to exercise in relation to Wales, as from such date as may be specified in the order, the functions conferred on them.

(2) The council shall consist of not less than eight nor more than 12 members appointed by the Secretary of State, one of whom shall be so appointed as chairman.

(3) In appointing the members of the council the Secretary of State shall have regard to the desirability of including—

(a) persons who appear to him to have experience of, and to have shown capacity in, the provision of primary or secondary education or to have held, and to have shown capacity in, any position carrying responsibility for the provision of such education;

(b) persons who appear to him to have experience of, and to have shown capacity in, industrial, commercial or financial matters or the practice of any profession; and

(c) persons who appear to him to have experience of, and to have shown capacity in, providing for children with special educational needs.

(4) Schedule 2 has effect in relation to the council.

Functions

Functions of funding authorities

22.—(1) The functions which are or may be exercisable by a funding authority include in particular those which are or may be so exercisable by virtue of—

(a) section 23 (value-for-money studies of grant-maintained schools);

(b) section 27 (responsibility for provision of school places to be held together with, or to the exclusion of, local education authority); and

(c) Chapter VI of Part III (funding of grant-maintained schools).

(2) Schedule 3 enables the Secretary of State to transfer to a funding authority certain functions of his with respect to education.

Value-for-money studies of grant-maintained schools

23.—(1) Each funding authority shall make arrangements for carrying out such value-for-money studies of grant-maintained schools in England or, as the case may be, Wales as in their opinion are required or as the Secretary of State may direct.

(2) The authority shall, in particular—

(a) in forming an opinion as to whether any value-for-money study is required to be carried out in pursuance of this section, have regard to the desirability of value-for-money studies being carried out at regular intervals, and

(b) in determining the scope of any value-for-money study to be carried out in pursuance of this section otherwise than on the direction of the Secretary of State, have regard to the scope of any value-for-money study which is being or has recently been carried out.

(3) In this section "value-for-money study", in relation to any grant-maintained school, means—

(a) any examination into the economy, efficiency and effectiveness with which the governing body of the school have, in discharging their functions, used grant made by the authority, and

(b) any study designed to improve economy, efficiency and effectiveness in the management or operations of the school.

Supervision of funding authorities by the Secretary of State

24.—(1) In exercising their functions each funding authority shall comply with any directions contained in an order made by the Secretary of State.

(2) In respect of the exercise by the funding authority of functions in respect of any grant-maintained school, such directions may relate to grant-maintained schools generally or to any class or description of such schools.

(3) Before making an order under this section, the Secretary of State shall consult the funding authority unless, for reasons of urgency, it is not in his opinion reasonably practicable for him to do so.

(4) Sections 496 and 497 (powers of Secretary of State where local education authority etc. are acting unreasonably or are in default) shall apply in relation to a funding authority and the functions conferred on them by or under the Education Acts as they apply in relation to local education authorities and the functions conferred on them by or under this Act.

(5) Subsection (4) does not prejudice the generality of subsection (1).

Supplemental

Grants to funding authorities

25. The Secretary of State may make grants to a funding authority of such amounts and subject to such terms and conditions as he may determine.

Meaning of "funding authority"

26.—(1) Any reference in this Act to a funding authority—
(a) in relation to schools, or local education authority areas, in England is to the Funding Agency for Schools, and
(b) in relation to schools, or local education authority areas, in Wales is, subject to subsection (2), to the Schools Funding Council for Wales,
and in any other context is to the agency or the council.

(2) Before the Schools Funding Council for Wales begin to exercise their functions, any reference in this Act (other than this Part) to a funding authority in relation to schools, or local education authority areas, in Wales is to be read as a reference to the Secretary of State.

CHAPTER V

ALLOCATION OF RESPONSIBILITY FOR EDUCATION AT SCHOOL BETWEEN LEA AND FUNDING AUTHORITY

Responsibility for providing sufficient school places

27.—(1) In respect of the area of any local education authority, the Secretary of State may—
(a) where he wishes responsibility for providing sufficient school places to be held by the funding authority as well as the local education authority, make an order under this paragraph, and
(b) where he wishes that responsibility to be held by the funding authority alone, make an order under this paragraph;
and such an order may relate to primary education, to secondary education or to both.

(2) An order under subsection (1) shall state—
(a) the local education authority area to which the order applies;
(b) whether the order is made under paragraph (a) or (b) of that subsection;
(c) the kind (that is primary or secondary) or kinds of education to which the order relates; and
(d) the date as from which the order is to have effect.

(3) No order may be made in respect of any area under subsection (1) unless—
(a) in the case of an order under subsection (1)(a) or (b), it appears to the Secretary of State that subsection (4) is, or has at any time been, satisfied, or
(b) in the case of an order under subsection (1)(b), the local education authority have at any time requested the Secretary of State to make the order and subsection (4) is, or has at any time been, satisfied,
in relation to the kind of education to which the order relates or, as the case may be, each of the kinds of education to which the order relates.

(4) This subsection is satisfied—
(a) for the purposes of—
(i) subsection (3)(a) in its application to an order under subsection (1)(a), or
(ii) subsection (3)(b),

if not less than 10 per cent. of the pupils for whom education is provided in county, voluntary and grant-maintained schools in the area are registered pupils at grant-maintained schools;

(b) for the purposes of subsection (3)(a) in its application to an order under subsection (1)(b), if not less than 75 per cent. of the pupils for whom education is provided in county, voluntary and grant-maintained schools in the area are registered pupils at grant-maintained schools.

(5) For the purposes of subsection (3) the kind of education to which an order relates—

(a) where an order is expressed to relate only to primary education, includes any secondary education provided in a primary school and excludes any primary education provided in a secondary school, and

(b) where an order is expressed to relate only to secondary education, includes any primary education provided in a secondary school and excludes any secondary education provided in a primary school.

(6) The effect of an order under this section is set out in Schedule 4.

(7) The kind or kinds of education to which an order under subsection (1)(a) or (b) relates are referred to in this Act, in relation to such an order, as "relevant education".

CHAPTER VI

SUPPLEMENTAL

Allocation of functions

Resolution of disputes as to allocation of functions

28. Any dispute as to whether any functions are exercisable by a funding authority or a local education authority shall be determined by the Secretary of State.

Provision of information

Provision of information by local education authorities

29.—(1) A local education authority shall—

(a) make such reports and returns to the Secretary of State, and

(b) give to the Secretary of State such information,

as he may require for the purpose of the exercise of his functions under this Act.

(2) A local education authority shall—

(a) make such reports and returns to the funding authority, and

(b) give to the funding authority such information,

as the funding authority may require for the purpose of the exercise of their functions.

(3) A local education authority shall—

(a) compile such information, and

(b) make such provision for conducting, or assisting the conduct of, research,

as may be required for the purpose of providing the Secretary of State and the funding authority, in such form and at such times as may be prescribed, with such information relating to the provision of primary or secondary education in the area of the local education authority as may be prescribed.

(4) The Secretary of State shall exercise his powers under subsection (3) so as to secure, in particular, the provision of information relating to the provision of education for children with special educational needs.

(5) A local education authority shall, at such time or times and in such

manner as may be required by regulations, publish such information as may be so required with respect to their policy and arrangements in respect of any matter relating to primary or secondary education.

(6) Nothing in subsection (5) applies in relation to—

(a) nursery schools, or

(b) children who will be under the age of five at the time of their proposed admission.

Provision of information by funding authorities

30.—(1) A funding authority—

(a) shall provide the Secretary of State with such information or advice in connection with any function of his relating to the provision of education as he may from time to time require; and

(b) may provide the Secretary of State with such information or advice relating to such provision as they think fit.

(2) The information and advice provided under subsection (1) shall be provided in such manner as the Secretary of State may from time to time determine.

(3) A funding authority shall—

(a) make such reports and returns to any local education authority, and

(b) give to any local education authority such information,

as the local education authority may require for the purpose of the exercise of their functions.

(4) A funding authority shall—

(a) compile such information, and

(b) make such provision for conducting, or assisting the conduct of, research,

as may be required for the purpose of providing the Secretary of State and local education authorities, in such form and at such times as may be prescribed, with such information relating to the provision of education in any area to which an order under section 27 applies as may be prescribed.

(5) The Secretary of State shall exercise his powers under subsection (4) so as to secure, in particular, the provision of information relating to the provision of education for children with special educational needs.

Part II

Schools maintained by local education authorities

Chapter I

Preliminary

County schools and voluntary schools

31.—(1) A primary or secondary school which is maintained by a local education authority is a county school if—

(a) it was established by a local education authority, or

(b) it was not so established but—

(i) it has been maintained as a county school since before the commencement of this Act, or

(ii) it is maintained as a county school in pursuance of proposals under section 35(1)(b), or

(iii) it is maintained as a county school in pursuance of an order under section 50.

(2) A primary or secondary school which is maintained by a local education authority is a voluntary school if it is not within paragraph (a) or (b) of subsection (1).

(3) Nothing in this section applies to—

(a) a nursery school;

(b) a special school; or

(c) a pupil referral unit within the meaning of section 19.

Categories of voluntary schools: controlled, aided and special agreement schools

32.—(1) There are three categories of voluntary school—

(a) controlled schools,

(b) aided schools, and

(c) special agreement schools.

(2) A voluntary school is a controlled school if no order such as is mentioned in subsection (3) or (4) is in force in respect of it.

(3) A voluntary school is an aided school if there is in force an order to that effect made under section 48, 51, 54 or 58 of this Act (or under section 15 of the Education Act 1944, section 2 of the Education Act 1946 or section 54 of the Education (No. 2) Act 1986).

(4) A voluntary school is a special agreement school if there is in force an order to that effect made under section 15 of the Education Act 1944 (which provided for the making of such an order where a special agreement had been made in respect of a school).

(5) In this Act "special agreement" means an agreement made under Schedule 3 to the Education Act 1944 or deemed to have been so made by virtue of paragraph 11 of that Schedule (agreement providing for the making of a grant by a local education authority to persons specified in the agreement in consideration of their execution of proposals for the establishment of a school or the alteration of the premises of a school).

(6) Schedule 5 to this Act (which reproduces certain of the provisions of Schedule 3 to that Act) has effect in relation to special agreements.

Maintained nursery schools and maintained special schools

33.—(1) In this Act—

"maintained nursery school" means a nursery school which is maintained by a local education authority; and

"maintained special school" means (in accordance with section 337(3)) a special school which is maintained by a local education authority.

(2) Chapter II of Part IV (special educational needs) has effect in relation to the establishment and approval of schools as maintained special schools.

Meaning of "maintain" etc.

34.—(1) In this Act—

(a) in relation to a school maintained (or proposed to be maintained) by a local education authority, "the local education authority" means that authority; and

(b) in relation to schools falling within subsections (2) to (5), "maintain" shall be read in accordance with those subsections.

(2) In the case of a county school, a maintained nursery school or a maintained special school, the local education authority's duty to maintain the school includes the duty of defraying all the expenses of maintaining it.

(3) In the case of a controlled school, the local education authority's duty to maintain the school includes—

(a) the duty of defraying all the expenses of maintaining it, and

(b) the duty under section 60 of providing new premises for the school under and in accordance with that section.

(4) In the case of an aided or special agreement school, the local education authority's duty to maintain the school includes—

(a) the duty of defraying all the expenses of maintaining it, except any

expenses that by virtue of section 59 or a special agreement are payable by the governing body, and
(b) the duty under section 61 of providing new premises for the school under and in accordance with that section.

(5) It is hereby declared that for the purposes of this Act the expenses of maintaining a voluntary school include the payment of rates.

CHAPTER II

ESTABLISHMENT, ALTERATION ETC. OF COUNTY AND VOLUNTARY SCHOOLS

County schools: establishment, alteration, or change of site

County school: proposals for establishment, alteration or new site

35.—(1) Where a local education authority intend—
(a) to establish a new county school,
(b) to maintain as a county school a school which is not for the time being a county school,
(c) to make any significant change in the character, or any significant enlargement of the premises, of a county school, or
(d) to transfer a county school to a new site in the area,
then (subject to subsections (2) and (8)) they shall publish their proposals for that purpose in such manner as may be required by regulations and submit a copy of the published proposals to the Secretary of State.

(2) The requirement to publish proposals under subsection (1)(d) does not apply in relation to the transfer of a county school to a new site if—
(a) the school is intended to return to its existing site within three years of the time of the transfer; or
(b) the local education authority are satisfied that it is expedient that the school should be transferred to the new site either—
(i) because it is not reasonably practicable to make to the existing premises of the school the alterations necessary for securing that they conform to the standards prescribed under section 542, or
(ii) in consequence of any movement of population or of any action taken or proposed to be taken under the enactments relating to housing or to town and country planning; or
(c) the transfer is authorised by an order made under section 16(1) of the Education Act 1944 (transfer of county schools etc. to new sites).

(3) Proposals published under this section shall include particulars—
(a) of the time or times at which it is intended to implement the proposals, and
(b) of the number of pupils intended to be admitted to the school in each relevant age group in the first school year in relation to which the proposals have been wholly implemented,
and shall be accompanied by a statement of the effect of section 36.

(4) For the purposes of subsection (3)(b) pupils intended to be admitted to the school for nursery education shall be disregarded, and pupils—
(a) already admitted to the school for nursery education, and
(b) intended to be transferred to a reception class at the school,
shall be treated as intended to be admitted to the school on their transfer.

(5) Before publishing any proposals under this section a local education authority shall consult such persons as appear to them to be appropriate; and in discharging their duty under this subsection the authority shall have regard to any guidance given from time to time by the Secretary of State.

(6) Before publishing any proposals under subsection (1)(c) which (if implemented) would affect the facilities for full-time education suitable to the requirements of persons over compulsory school age who have not attained the age of 19, the local education authority shall consult the appro-

priate further education funding council.

(7) Before formulating any proposals under subsection (1)(c) or (d) in respect of a school which is (within the meaning of Part III) eligible for grant-maintained status, the local education authority shall consult the school's governing body.

(8) No proposals shall be published under this section in respect of any school in respect of which proposals for acquisition of grant-maintained status have been approved under section 194.

Objections to proposals under section 35

36.—(1) Objections to any proposals published by a local education authority under section 35 may be submitted to the authority by any of the following—

(a) any ten or more local government electors for the authority's area,

(b) the governing body of any school affected by the proposals,

(c) the appropriate further education funding council (if the proposals affect the provision of education to which section 2(1) of the Further and Higher Education Act 1992 applies), and

(d) any other local education authority concerned.

(2) Objections may be so submitted within the period of two months after the first publication of the proposals.

(3) Where—

(a) an order under section 27 (allocation of responsibility for providing sufficient school places) applies to the area of a local education authority, and

(b) the authority publish proposals under section 35 which affect the provision of relevant education in that area,

the funding authority shall be included among the persons who may submit objections under subsection (1) to the proposals.

(4) Within one month after the end of the period mentioned in subsection (2), the local education authority by whom the proposals were published shall transmit to the Secretary of State copies of all objections made (and not withdrawn in writing) within that period, together with the authority's observations on them.

(5) For the purposes of this section proposals under section 35 shall be taken to have been first published—

(a) on the day on which the requirements of regulations with respect to the publication of the proposals are satisfied; or

(b) where different such requirements are satisfied on different days, on the last of those days.

(6) Where any such requirement imposes a continuing obligation with respect to the publication of any proposals, the requirement shall for the purposes of subsection (5) be taken to be satisfied on the first day in respect of which it is satisfied.

Approval or rejection by Secretary of State of proposals under section 35

37.—(1) Proposals published by a local education authority under section 35 require the approval of the Secretary of State if subsection (2), (3) or (4) applies.

(2) This subsection applies if the proposals are for the maintenance as a county school of a school which is for the time being a voluntary school.

(3) This subsection applies if either—

(a) the Secretary of State, within two months after the submission to him of the published proposals, gives notice to the local education authority that the proposals require his approval, or

(b) objections have been made under section 36 and any of them have not been withdrawn in writing within the period specified in subsection (2) of that section.

(4) This subsection applies if either—

(a) the proposals are first published after proposals for acquisition of grant-maintained status for the school have been published under section 193 but before those proposals are determined or withdrawn, or

(b) after the proposals have first been published but before they are determined or withdrawn, proposals for acquisition of grant-maintained status for the school are published under section 193;

and references in this subsection to proposals being first published shall be construed in accordance with section 36(5) and (6).

(5) Where any proposals require the approval of the Secretary of State under this section, he may (subject to subsections (6) to (8))—

(a) reject them,

(b) approve them without modification, or

(c) after consultation with the local education authority, approve them with such modifications as he thinks desirable.

(6) In a case where subsection (2) applies, the Secretary of State shall not approve the proposals unless he has, in accordance with Schedule 6, approved an agreement under that Schedule between the local education authority and the school's governing body for the transfer to the authority of all necessary interests in the school premises.

(7) In a case where subsection (4) applies, the Secretary of State—

(a) shall consider both sets of proposals together, but

(b) shall not determine the proposals published under section 35 until he has made his determination with respect to the proposals published under section 193.

(8) If the Secretary of State approves the proposals published under section 193, he shall approve the proposals published under section 35 if—

(a) they are proposals under subsection (1)(c) or (d) of that section, and

(b) the governing body incorporated under section 195 give their consent,

but otherwise he shall reject the proposals published under section 35.

(9) Any proposals under section 35(1)(c) or (d) which are approved under subsection (8) shall be treated for the purposes of Part III (grant-maintained schools) as if they had been—

(a) published under section 259 (change of character etc. of grant-maintained school), and

(b) approved under section 261,

and section 262 (approval of school premises) shall apply accordingly.

Determination by LEA whether to implement proposals under section 35

38.—(1) Where any proposals published by a local education authority under section 35 do not require the approval of the Secretary of State under section 37, the authority shall determine whether the proposals should be implemented.

(2) The determination must be made not later than four months after the submission of the proposals to the Secretary of State under section 35.

(3) A local education authority shall notify the Secretary of State of any determination made by them under this section.

Approval of school premises

39.—(1) Where a local education authority publish proposals under section 35, they shall submit to the Secretary of State for his approval such particulars with respect to the premises or proposed premises of the school as he may require.

(2) The particulars shall be so submitted at such time, and in such form and manner, as the Secretary of State may direct.

(3) Schedule 6 has effect in relation to agreements for the transfer of prem-

ises in pursuance of proposals for a voluntary school to become a county school, and the approval of such agreements by the Secretary of State.

Implementation of proposals under section 35, etc.

40.—(1) Subject to subsection (3), a local education authority shall implement any proposals of theirs—

(a) which have been approved by the Secretary of State under section 37, or

(b) which they have determined under section 38 to implement.

(2) Where any particulars have been submitted under section 39 in connection with the proposals, the proposals shall be implemented in accordance with the particulars as approved by the Secretary of State.

(3) The Secretary of State may, at the request of a local education authority, modify any proposals which the authority are required to implement by virtue of this section.

(4) Subject to subsection (5), neither a local education authority nor any other person shall do or undertake to do anything for which proposals are required to be published and submitted under section 35 until the requirements of that section and section 39 have been complied with and any approval necessary under section 37 or 39 has been given.

(5) The Secretary of State may in any case allow such steps to be taken pending compliance with any such requirements and the giving of any such approval as he considers reasonable in the circumstances.

Voluntary schools: establishment, alteration or change of site

Voluntary school: proposals for establishment, alteration or new site

41.—(1) Where any persons propose—

(a) that a school which they or persons whom they represent propose to establish should be maintained by a local education authority as a voluntary school, or

(b) that a school established by them or by persons whom they represent which is not a voluntary school should be so maintained as a voluntary school,

then (subject to subsection (9)) they shall publish proposals for that purpose in such manner as may be required by regulations and submit a copy of the published proposals to the Secretary of State.

(2) Where the governing body of a school which is maintained by a local education authority as a voluntary school intend—

(a) to make a significant change in the character, or a significant enlargement of the premises, of the school, or

(b) to transfer the school to a new site,

then (subject to subsections (3) and (9)) they shall publish proposals for that purpose in such manner as may be required by regulations and submit a copy of the published proposals to the Secretary of State.

(3) The requirement to publish proposals under subsection (2)(b) does not apply in relation to the transfer of a voluntary school to a new site if—

(a) the transfer is authorised by an order made under section 47(1) of this Act (or under section 16(1) of the Education Act 1944); or

(b) the school is intended to return to its existing site within three years of the time of the transfer.

(4) No proposals under subsection (1) shall be approved by the Secretary of State under section 43 if the school or proposed school is to provide—

(a) part-time education suitable to the requirements of persons of any age over compulsory school age, or

(b) full-time education suitable to the requirements of persons who have attained the age of 19 years;

and the reference in subsection (2)(a) to a change in the character of a school does not include a change in character resulting only from persons beginning or ceasing to be provided with education falling within paragraph (a) or (b) above.

(5) Proposals published under this section shall include particulars—

(a) of the time or times at which it is intended to implement the proposals, and

(b) of the number of pupils intended to be admitted to the school in each relevant age group in the first school year in relation to which the proposals have been wholly implemented;

and shall be accompanied by a statement of the effect of section 42.

(6) For the purposes of subsection (5)(b) pupils intended to be admitted to the school for nursery education shall be disregarded, and pupils—

(a) already admitted to the school for nursery education, and

(b) intended to be transferred to a reception class at the school,

shall be treated as intended to be admitted to the school on their transfer.

(7) Before publishing any proposals under this section, the persons concerned shall—

(a) in the case of proposals under subsection (1), consult the local education authority, and

(b) in the case of proposals under either subsection (1) or subsection (2), consult such other persons as appear to them to be appropriate;

and in discharging their duty under this subsection they shall have regard to any guidance given from time to time by the Secretary of State.

(8) Before publishing any proposals under subsection (2)(a) which (if implemented) would affect the facilities for full-time education suitable to the requirements of persons over compulsory school age who have not attained the age of 19, the governing body shall consult the appropriate further education funding council.

(9) No proposals shall be published under this section in respect of any school in respect of which proposals for acquisition of grant-maintained status have been approved under section 194.

Objections to proposals under section 41

42.—(1) Objections to any proposals published under section 41 may be submitted to the Secretary of State by any of the following—

(a) any ten or more local government electors for the area of the local education authority referred to in subsection (1) or (as the case may be) subsection (2) of that section,

(b) the governing body of any school affected by the proposals,

(c) the appropriate further education funding council (if the proposals affect the provision of education to which section 2(1) of the Further and Higher Education Act 1992 applies), and

(d) any local education authority concerned.

(2) Objections may be so submitted within the period of two months after the first publication of the proposals.

(3) Where the proposals are to transfer a school to a site in a different area, objections under subsection (1) to the proposals may also be so submitted by any ten or more local government electors for that area.

(4) Where—

(a) an order under section 27 applies to the area of a local education authority, and

(b) any persons publish proposals under section 41 which affect the provision of relevant education in the area,

the funding authority shall be included among the persons who may submit objections under subsection (1) above to the proposals.

(5) For the purposes of this section proposals under section 41 shall be

taken to have been first published—

(a) on the day on which the requirements of regulations with respect to the publication of the proposals are satisfied; or

(b) where different such requirements are satisfied on different days, on the last of those days.

(6) Where any such requirement imposes a continuing obligation with respect to the publication of any proposals, the requirement shall for the purposes of subsection (5) be taken to be satisfied on the first day in respect of which it is satisfied.

Approval of rejection by Secretary of State of proposals under section 41

43.—(1) Proposals published under section 41 require the approval of the Secretary of State.

(2) The Secretary of State may (subject to subsections (3) to (6))—

(a) reject such proposals,

(b) approve them without modification, or

(c) after consultation with the persons making the proposals and the local education authority by whom the school is, or is to be, maintained, approve them with such modifications as he thinks desirable.

(3) This subsection applies if either—

(a) the proposals are first published after proposals for acquisition of grant-maintained status for the school have been published under section 193 but before those proposals are determined or withdrawn, or

(b) after the proposals have first been published but before they are determined or withdrawn, proposals for acquisition of grant-maintained status for the school are published under section 193;

and references in this subsection to proposals being first published shall be construed in accordance with section 42(5) and (6).

(4) In a case where subsection (3) applies, the Secretary of State—

(a) shall consider both sets of proposals together, but

(b) shall not determine the proposals published under section 41 until he has made his determination with respect to the proposals published under section 193.

(5) If the Secretary of State approves the proposals published under section 193, he—

(a) shall approve the proposals published under section 41 if they were made for the purpose of ensuring consistency in the provision of education made in the area of the local education authority, but

(b) shall otherwise reject the proposals published under that section.

(6) Any proposals under section 41 which are approved under subsection (5) shall be treated for the purposes of Part III as if they had been—

(a) published under section 259 (change of character etc. of grant-maintained school), and

(b) approved under section 261,

and section 262 (approval of school premises) shall apply accordingly.

(7) Where the proposals published under section 41 are to transfer the school to a site in a different area, subsection (2)(c) above requires consultation with the local education authority by whom the school is maintained as well as with the authority by whom it is to be maintained.

Approval of school premises

44.—(1) Where any proposals are published under section 41, the persons making the proposals shall submit to the Secretary of State for his approval such particulars in respect of the premises or proposed premises of the school as he may require.

(2) The particulars shall be so submitted at such time, and in such form and manner, as the Secretary of State may direct.

(3) Before submitting any particulars under this section, the persons making the proposals shall consult the local education authority by whom the school is, or is to be, maintained.

(4) Where the proposals published under section 41 are to transfer the school to a site in a different area, subsection (3) requires consultation with the local education authority by whom the school is to be maintained.

Implementation of proposals under section 41, etc.

45.—(1) Subject to subsections (2) and (4), where any proposals are approved under section 43, they shall be implemented—

(a) in the case of proposals published under section 41(1), by the persons making them or the persons whom they represent (as the case may require) and by the local education authority referred to in that subsection, or

(b) in the case of proposals published under section 41(2), by the school's governing body.

(2) Subject to subsection (4), it shall be the duty of the local education authority—

(a) in the case of any proposals so approved for the transfer of a controlled school to a new site, to implement the proposals (and any associated proposals for a change in the character of the school) so far as they involve the provision of premises or the removal or provision of equipment; and

(b) in any other case, to implement so much of any proposals so approved as relates to the provision of—

(i) playing fields, or

(ii) buildings which are to form part of the school premises but are not to be school buildings.

(3) Where any particulars have been submitted under section 44 in connection with the proposals, the proposals shall be implemented in accordance with the particulars as approved by the Secretary of State.

(4) The Secretary of State may modify any proposals required to be implemented by virtue of this section, but shall do so—

(a) in the case of proposals published under section 41(1), only at the request of the local education authority referred to in that subsection, and

(b) in the case of proposals published under section 41(2), only at the request of the governing body of the school.

(5) Subject to subsection (6), no person shall do or undertake to do anything for which proposals are required to be published and submitted under section 41 until the requirements of that section and section 44 have been complied with and any approval necessary under section 43 or 44 has been given.

(6) The Secretary of State may in any case allow such steps to be taken pending compliance with any such requirements and the giving of any such approval as he considers reasonable in the circumstances.

(7) Where proposals for the transfer of a school to a site in a different area are approved under section 43, then—

(a) in the case of any voluntary school—

(i) the reference in subsection (2) above to the local education authority is to be read as referring to the authority for the new area, and

(ii) upon the transfer the duty to maintain the school shall transfer to that authority; and

(b) in the case of any controlled school, section 60 (together with section 62) shall apply as if the duty to maintain the school had been transferred to the local education authority for the new area.

Establishment of a new voluntary school in substitution for an old one

46.—(1) This section applies where—

(a) proposals for the establishment of any school or schools are submitted to the Secretary of State under section 41(1); and

(b) in connection with those proposals it is claimed that the school or schools should be maintained by the local education authority as a voluntary school or voluntary schools in substitution for any other voluntary school or schools (whether maintained by that or another local education authority) which is or are to be discontinued.

(2) If the Secretary of State—

(a) approves the proposals under section 43, and

(b) is satisfied that the new school or schools will be maintained as mentioned in subsection (1)(b) above,

he may by order direct that the new school or schools shall be established in substitution for the school or schools which is or are to be discontinued.

(3) Where an order is made under this section, section 173 shall not apply with respect to the discontinuance of that school or those schools.

(4) Before making an order under this section, the Secretary of State shall consult—

(a) any local education authority who in his opinion will be affected by the making of the order; and

(b) the governing body of any voluntary school which in his opinion will be so affected.

(5) An order under this section may—

(a) impose such conditions on any such local education authority or governing body, and

(b) contain such incidental and consequential provisions,

as the Secretary of State thinks fit.

Order authorising transfer of voluntary school to new site

47.—(1) Where the Secretary of State is satisfied that the transfer of a voluntary school to a new site is expedient—

(a) because it is not reasonably practicable to make to the existing premises of the school any alterations necessary to secure that they conform to the standards prescribed under section 542, or

(b) in consequence of any movement of population or of any action taken or proposed to be taken under the enactments relating to housing or to town and country planning,

he may by order authorise the transfer of the school to the new site.

(2) The Secretary of State shall not, however, make any such order in the case of an aided or special agreement school unless he is satisfied that the school's governing body will be able and willing, with the assistance of any grant made under section 65, to defray the expenses mentioned in section 59(5).

(3) Before making an order under this section the Secretary of State shall consult—

(a) any local education authority who in his opinion will be affected by the making of the order; and

(b) the governing body of any voluntary school which in his opinion will be so affected.

(4) An order under this section may—

(a) impose such conditions on any such local education authority or governing body, and

(b) contain such incidental and consequential provisions,

as the Secretary of State thinks fit.

Status of new voluntary school

Order that school is to be controlled or aided school

48.—(1) Where, at or before the time when any proposals are submitted to the Secretary of State under section 41(1), an application is duly made to the Secretary of State with respect to the school to which the proposals relate, he may (subject to the following provisions of this section) by order direct—

(a) that the school shall be a controlled school; or

(b) that the school shall be an aided school.

(2) Where on an application for an order under subsection (1)(b) the Secretary of State is satisfied that the governing body of the school will be able and willing, with the assistance of grants under section 65, to defray the expenses that would fall to be borne by them by virtue of section 59(2) and (3) as the governing body of an aided school, he shall make an order directing that the school shall be an aided school.

(3) Where on an application for an order under subsection (1)(b)—

(a) the Secretary of State is not satisfied that the governing body will be able to defray those expenses without the assistance of both—

(i) grants under section 65, and

(ii) a loan under section 67, and

(b) it appears to him that the area to be served by the school will not be also served by a county or controlled school,

he shall comply with subsection (4) before determining the application.

(4) The Secretary of State—

(a) shall consult such persons or bodies of persons as appear to him to be representative of any religion or religious denomination which, in his opinion having regard to the circumstances of the area, is likely to be concerned, and

(b) unless he is satisfied after that consultation that the holding of a local inquiry is unnecessary, cause such an inquiry to be held.

Proposals for a middle school

Proposals under section 35 or 41 for a middle school

49. Proposals published under section 35 or 41 with respect to a school maintained or to be maintained by a local education authority may, if the authority or persons making them think fit—

(a) specify an age below 10 years and six months and an age above 12 years, and

(b) provide that the school is to be a school for providing full-time education suitable to the requirements of pupils whose ages are between the ages so specified.

Division of a single school into two or more schools

Division of a county school

50.—(1) Where—

(a) a county school is organised in two or more departments, and

(b) the local education authority submit to the Secretary of State proposals that the school should be divided into two or more separate schools,

the Secretary of State may by order direct that the school shall be divided into two or more separate county schools.

(2) Any such order shall come into operation on such date as may be specified in the order; and as from that date the local education authority shall maintain as a county school each of the separate schools constituted in pursuance of the order.

(3) An order under this section may contain such incidental, consequential and supplemental provisions as the Secretary of State thinks fit, and may, in particular, include provision for defining the premises of each of the separate schools to be constituted in pursuance of the order.

(4) The constitution of a separate school in pursuance of an order under this section does not amount to the establishment of a new school for the purposes of section 35(1).

(5) In this section "department", in relation to a school, means a part of the school organised under a separate head teacher.

Division of a voluntary school

51.—(1) Where—

(a) a controlled or aided school is organised in two or more separate departments, and

(b) the governing body, after consulting the local education authority, submit to the Secretary of State proposals that the school should be divided into two or more separate schools,

the Secretary of State may by order direct that the school shall be divided into two or more separate voluntary schools.

(2) Where the school is a controlled school, the order shall direct that each of the schools into which it is to be divided shall be a controlled school.

(3) Where the school is an aided school, the order shall direct that each of the schools into which it is to be divided shall be an aided school; except that, if the governing body request the Secretary of State to direct that all or any of those schools shall be controlled schools, the order shall direct accordingly.

(4) An order under this section shall come into operation on such date as may be specified in the order; and as from that date the local education authority shall maintain as a voluntary school each of the separate schools constituted in pursuance of the order.

(5) An order under this section may contain such incidental, consequential and supplemental provisions as the Secretary of State thinks fit, and may, in particular, include provision for defining the premises of each of the separate schools to be constituted in pursuance of the order.

(6) The constitution of a separate school in pursuance of an order under this section does not amount to the establishment of a new school for the purposes of section 41(1).

(7) No order shall be made under this section for the division of a school in respect of which a special agreement is in force.

(8) In this section "department", in relation to a school, means a part of the school organised under a separate head teacher.

Change of status from controlled school to aided school

Proposals for changing a controlled school to an aided school

52.—(1) Where the governing body of a controlled school propose to apply for an order under section 54 directing that the school should become an aided school, they shall, after consultation with the local education authority—

(a) publish their proposals in such manner as may be required by regulations, and

(b) submit a copy of the published proposals to the Secretary of State.

(2) Proposals published under this section shall be accompanied by a statement which—

(a) explains the effect of section 53; and

(b) specifies the date on which the proposals are intended to be implemented.

(3) A governing body who submit proposals to the Secretary of State

under this section shall provide him with such information as he may reasonably require in order to be able to give proper consideration to them.

Objections to proposals

53.—(1) Objections to any proposals published under section 52 may be submitted to the Secretary of State by any of the following—

(a) any ten or more local government electors for the area of the local education authority by whom the school is maintained;

(b) the governing body of any voluntary school affected by the proposals; and

(c) any local education authority concerned.

(2) Objections may be so submitted within the period of two months beginning with the date on which the proposals are first published.

(3) For the purposes of this section proposals under section 52 shall be taken to have been first published—

(a) on the day on which the requirements of regulations under that section with respect to the publication of the proposals are satisfied; or

(b) where different such requirements are satisfied on different days, on the last of those days.

(4) Where any such requirement imposes a continuing obligation with respect to the publication of any proposals, the requirement shall for the purposes of subsection (3) be taken to be satisfied on the first day in respect of which it is satisfied.

Order by Secretary of State

54.—(1) On an application duly made to him by the governing body of any controlled school the Secretary of State may by order direct that, as from such date as is specified in the order, the school shall be an aided school.

(2) The Secretary of State shall not make an order under this section unless he is satisfied that the governing body will be able and willing—

(a) with the assistance of grants under section 65, to defray the expenses mentioned in section 59(2) and (3), and

(b) to pay to the local education authority any compensation payable by the governing body under section 56.

(3) Where the Secretary of State proposes, in making an order under this section, to specify under subsection (1) a date which is different from that specified in pursuance of section 52(2)(b), he shall first consult the governing body and the local education authority as to the date which it would be appropriate to specify in the order.

(4) Where, in consequence of an order made under this section, an amount will be payable by a governing body by way of compensation under section 56, the order—

(a) shall specify the amount of the compensation so payable and the date by which it must be paid; and

(b) may impose such conditions in relation to its payment as the Secretary of State thinks fit.

(5) An order under this section may make such provision (including provision modifying any provision made by or under this Act) as the Secretary of State considers appropriate in connection with the transition of the school in question from controlled to aided status.

(6) In particular, an order under this section may make provision—

(a) as to the circumstances in which, and purposes for which, the school is to be treated before the date specified under subsection (1) as if it were an aided school;

(b) as to the time by which the new instrument of government and articles of government (appropriate for an aided school) are to be made for the school, and the consent and consultation required before they are made;

(c) where the local education authority propose to pass a resolution under section 89 to group the school when it becomes an aided school, as to the consent required before that resolution is passed;

(d) as to the appointment and dismissal of staff for the school;

(e) as to the arrangements to be made in relation to the admission of pupils to the school; and

(f) as to functions exercisable by, or in relation to, the governing body or the governors of any category specified in the order.

Variation of order under section 54

55.—(1) Where the Secretary of State has made an order under section 54, he may, on the application of the local education authority or the foundation governors of the school, by order vary the order under that section so as to specify—

(a) a different date from that specified under subsection (1) of that section, or

(b) a different amount from that specified under subsection (4) of that section.

(2) The foundation governors of a school shall consult the other governors before applying to the Secretary of State under this section.

(3) Before making an order under this section the Secretary of State shall consult—

(a) the local education authority, where the application is by the foundation governors, and

(b) the foundation governors, where the application is by the local education authority.

(4) Where foundation governors are consulted by the Secretary of State under subsection (3), they shall, before giving him their views, consult the other governors of the school.

Compensation payable by governing body to local education authority

56.—(1) Where a controlled school becomes an aided school by virtue of an order under section 54, the governing body shall pay to the local education authority, in accordance with the order, an amount by way of compensation for relevant capital expenditure incurred in respect of the school by the authority or a predecessor of theirs.

(2) In subsection (1) "relevant capital expenditure" means—

(a) expenditure incurred under section 60 (or under paragraph 1 of Schedule 1 to the Education Act 1946) in providing buildings which form part of the school premises;

(b) expenditure incurred under section 63 (or under section 2 of the Education (Miscellaneous Provisions) Act 1953) in defraying expenses of establishing the school; or

(c) expenditure incurred under section 64 (or under section 1 of the Education Act 1946) in defraying expenses of enlarging the school.

(3) The amount payable by way of compensation under this section shall be—

(a) such as may be agreed by the governing body and the local education authority, or

(b) failing such agreement, such as the Secretary of State thinks fit, having regard to the current value of the property in question.

(4) The Secretary of State may, for the purpose of assisting him in any determination which he is required to make under subsection (3), appoint such person as he thinks competent to advise him on the valuation of property.

(5) No contribution, grant or loan shall be paid, or other payment made, by

the Secretary of State to the governing body of a controlled school in respect of any compensation payable by them under this section.

Change of status from aided or special agreement school to controlled or aided school

Change to controlled school where governing body unable or unwilling to carry out financial obligations

57.—(1) If at any time the governing body of an aided school are unable or unwilling to carry out all their obligations under section 59, they shall apply to the Secretary of State for an order revoking—

(a) the order made under section 48, 54 or 58 (or under section 15 of the Education Act 1944 or section 54 of the Education (No. 2) Act 1986), or

(b) the direction in an order made under section 51 (or under section 2 of the Education Act 1946),

by virtue of which the school is an aided school.

(2) If at any time the governing body of a special agreement school are unable or unwilling to carry out all their obligations under section 59, they shall apply to the Secretary of State for an order revoking the order made under section 15 of the Education Act 1944 by virtue of which the school is a special agreement school.

(3) For the purposes of this section the governing body of an aided school or a special agreement school shall not be regarded as unable to carry out any of their obligations under section 59 if they are able to carry them out with the benefit of assistance under section 68 of this Act.

(4) Where an application is made to him under this section, the Secretary of State shall by order revoke the order or direction in question, and the school in question shall thereupon become a controlled school in accordance with section 32(2).

Change to controlled or aided school on repayment of grant under special agreement

58.—(1) Where the Secretary of State is satisfied that the grant made in respect of a school in pursuance of a special agreement has been repaid as mentioned in paragraph 5 of Schedule 5, he shall, on an application made for the purpose by the school's governing body, by order revoke the order under section 15 of the Education Act 1944 by virtue of which the school is a special agreement school.

(2) Where the Secretary of State—

(a) makes an order under this section, and

(b) is satisfied that the governing body of the school will be able and willing, with the assistance of grants under section 65, to defray the expenses that would fall to be borne by them by virtue of section 59(2) and (3) as the governing body of an aided school,

he shall by order direct that the school shall be an aided school.

(3) Where in any other case the Secretary of State makes an order under this section, the school in question shall thereupon become a controlled school in accordance with section 32(2).

CHAPTER III

FUNDING OF VOLUNTARY SCHOOLS

Obligations of governing bodies

Obligations of governing bodies of voluntary schools

59.—(1) The governing body of a controlled school are (in accordance with section 34(3)) not responsible for any of the expenses of maintaining the school.

(2) In the case of an aided or special agreement school, the expenses of discharging any liability incurred by or on behalf of—

(a) the governing body of the school,
(b) any former governors of the school, or
(c) any trustees of the school,

in connection with the provision of premises or equipment for the purposes of the school are payable by the governing body of the school.

(3) In addition, any expenses incurred—

(a) in making to the school buildings of an aided or special agreement school such alterations as may be required by the local education authority for the purpose of securing that the school premises conform to the standards prescribed under section 542, or
(b) in effecting repairs to the school buildings, other than repairs falling within subsection (4),

are payable by the governing body of the school.

(4) The governing body of an aided or special agreement school are not responsible—

(a) for repairs to the interior of the school buildings, or
(b) for repairs to those buildings necessary in consequence of the use of the school premises, in pursuance of a direction or requirement of the local education authority, for purposes other than those of the school.

(5) Where an order is made under section 47 authorising the transfer of an aided or special agreement school to a new site, the expenses of providing any school buildings to be provided on the new site are payable by the governing body of the school.

Obligations of LEAs as regards new sites and buildings

Obligation of LEAs to provide new sites and buildings for controlled schools

60.—(1) In the case of a controlled school, the local education authority shall provide—

(a) any new site which is to be provided in addition to, or instead of, the school's existing site (or part of its existing site), and
(b) any buildings which are to form part of the school premises,

other than any site or buildings that persons other than the authority are under a duty to provide by virtue of proposals required to be implemented under section 45 (or, where a special agreement is in force in respect of the school, under that agreement).

(2) Where a new site is provided for a school under this section, the local education authority shall convey their interest in the site, and in any buildings on the site which are to form part of the school premises, to the trustees of the school to be held on trust for the purposes of the school.

(3) If any doubt or dispute arises as to the persons to whom the authority are required to make the conveyance, it shall be made to such persons as the Secretary of State thinks proper.

(4) Where—

(a) an interest in premises which are to be used for the purposes of a school is conveyed under this section, and
(b) the conveyance is made to persons who possess, or are or may become entitled to, any sum representing proceeds of the sale of other premises which have been used for the purposes of the school,

those persons or their successors shall pay to the local education authority so much of that sum as the Secretary of State may determine to be just having regard to the value of the interest conveyed.

(5) In subsection (4)(b) the reference to proceeds of the sale of other premises includes a reference to consideration for the creation or disposition of

any kind of interest in other premises.

(6) Any sum paid under subsection (4) shall be treated for the purposes of section 14 of the Schools Sites Act 1841 (which relates to the sale or exchange of land held on trust for the purposes of a school) as a sum applied in the purchase of a site for the school.

(7) The Secretary of State shall not make a determination under subsection (4) in respect of any property subject to a trust which has arisen under section 1 of the Reverter of Sites Act 1987 (right of reverter replaced by trust for sale) unless he is satisfied that steps have been taken to protect the interests of the beneficiaries under the trust.

Obligation of LEAs to provide new sites for aided and special agreement schools

61.—(1) In the case of an aided or special agreement school, the local education authority shall provide any new site—

(a) which is to be provided in addition to or instead of the school's existing site (or part of its existing site), and

(b) which is not a site that persons other than the authority are under a duty to provide by virtue of proposals required to be implemented under section 45 or under a special agreement.

(2) Where a new site is provided for a school under this section, the local education authority shall convey their interest in the site, and in any buildings on the site which are to form part of the school premises, to the trustees of the school to be held on trust for the purposes of the school.

(3) If any doubt or dispute arises as to the persons to whom the authority are required to make the conveyance, it shall be made to such persons as the Secretary of State thinks proper.

(4) Where—

(a) a new site is provided for a school under this section, and

(b) work is required to be done to the site for the purpose of clearing it or making it suitable for building purposes,

the local education authority and the governing body of the school may make an agreement providing for the making of such payments, or of such other adjustments of their respective rights and liabilities, as will secure that the cost of the work is borne by the authority.

(5) Where—

(a) a new site is provided for a school under this section, and

(b) there are buildings on the site which are of value for the purposes of the school,

the local education authority and the governing body of the school may make an agreement providing for the making of such payments, or of such other adjustments of their respective rights and liabilities, as appear to be desirable having regard to the governing body's duties under section 59 with respect to the school buildings.

(6) Where it appears to the Secretary of State that provision for any payment or other adjustment ought to have been made under subsection (4) or (5) but has not been made, he may give directions providing for the making of such payment or other adjustment as he thinks proper.

Provisions supplementary to sections 60 and 61

62.—(1) In sections 60(1) and (2) and 61 "site" does not include playing fields but otherwise includes any site which is to form part of the premises of the school in question.

(2) Where, after premises have been conveyed to the trustees of a school under section 60 or 61, a person acquires the premises or part of them from the trustees (whether compulsorily or otherwise), the Secretary of State may require the trustees or their successors to pay to the local education authority

by whom the premises were conveyed so much of the compensation or purchase money paid in respect of the acquisition as he thinks just having regard—

(a) to the value of the premises conveyed by the authority, and
(b) to any sums received by the authority in respect of the premises under section 60 or 61.

(3) In subsection (2) "premises" includes any interest in premises.

(4) Subsection (2) does not apply in the case of an institution which is, or has at any time been, within the further education sector.

Financial assistance for controlled schools

Payment by LEA of expenses of establishing controlled school

63.—(1) Where—

(a) proposals for the establishment of a school are submitted to the Secretary of State under section 41(1),
(b) no application is made under section 48 for an order directing that the school shall be an aided school, and
(c) the persons submitting the proposals and the local education authority satisfy the Secretary of State that subsection (3) below applies,

the Secretary of State may by order direct that the whole or a specified part of the promoters' expenses of establishment shall be defrayed by the local education authority.

(2) In subsection (1) "the promoters' expenses of establishment" means so much of the cost incurred in establishing the school as would, but for the order, fall to be defrayed by the persons who establish it.

(3) This subsection applies if the establishment of the school is required for the purpose of providing accommodation for pupils for whom, or for a substantial proportion of whom, accommodation would have been provided in some other school—

(a) which is or was a voluntary school, or
(b) which is or was a grant-maintained school, having been a voluntary school immediately before it became grant maintained,

if that other school had not been discontinued or had not otherwise ceased to be available for the purpose.

Payment by LEA of expenses of enlarging controlled school

64.—(1) Where the Secretary of State—

(a) is satisfied, on an application made to him by the governing body of a controlled school and the local education authority—
    (i) that there should be a significant enlargement of the school premises, and
    (ii) that subsection (2) or subsection (3) applies, and
(b) approves proposals for the enlargement under section 43,

he may by order direct that the cost of implementing the proposals shall be defrayed by the local education authority.

(2) This subsection applies if the enlargement is wholly or mainly required for the purpose of providing accommodation for pupils for whom accommodation would have been provided in another voluntary school if that other school had not been discontinued or had not otherwise ceased to be available for the purpose.

(3) This subsection applies if the enlargement is desirable for either or both of the following reasons—

(a) for the better provision of primary or secondary education at the premises to be enlarged;
(b) for securing that enough suitable primary or secondary schools are available for the area of the authority.

Financial assistance by Secretary of State for aided and special agreement schools

Grants in respect of expenditure on premises or equipment

65.—(1) The Secretary of State may—

(a) in the case of any aided school or special agreement school, or

(b) where proposals have been approved under section 43 for a school or proposed school to be maintained as a voluntary school and the Secretary of State has made an order under section 48 directing that the school is to be an aided school,

make grants to the governing body in respect of qualifying expenditure incurred by them.

(2) In subsection (1) "qualifying expenditure" means expenditure in respect of the provision, alteration or repair of premises or equipment for the school or proposed school.

(3) The amount of any grant paid under this section to the governing body in respect of any such expenditure—

(a) shall not exceed 85 per cent. of the expenditure, and

(b) in the case of any prescribed class or description of such expenditure, shall be such as may be determined in accordance with regulations.

(4) The times at which, and the manner in which, payments are made in respect of grant under this section shall be such as may be determined from time to time by the Secretary of State.

(5) Without prejudice to any other duty of his, the Secretary of State shall, in performing functions relating to the exercise of the power under this section to make grants in respect of expenditure on—

(a) such alterations to school buildings as are referred to in section 59(3)(a), or

(b) the repair of school buildings,

give priority to paying grant in respect of expenditure which is necessary for the performance by governing bodies of their duties; and the amount of any grant paid in the exercise of that power in respect of such expenditure on the repair of school buildings shall be 85 per cent. of the expenditure.

(6) A governing body to whom any payment is made in respect of grant under this section shall comply with such requirements determined by the Secretary of State as he may from time to time impose.

(7) Such requirements—

(a) may be imposed on, or at any time after, the making of any payment by reference to which they are imposed, and

(b) may at any time be waived, removed or varied by the Secretary of State.

(8) Such requirements may, in particular, if any conditions specified in the requirements are satisfied, require the payment to the Secretary of State of the whole or any part of the following amount.

(9) That amount is—

(a) the amount of the payments made in respect of the grant under this section, or

(b) so much of the value of any premises or equipment in respect of which grant was paid under this section as is determined in accordance with the requirements to be properly attributable to the payment of such grant,

whichever is the greater.

(10) No such requirement as is referred to in subsection (8) may be imposed where any payment is made in respect of grant under this section if—

(a) the grant is made in respect of the provision, alteration or repair of premises for a school or proposed school, and

(b) any freehold interest in the premises in respect of which the grant is made is, or is to be, held on trust for the purposes of the school.

(11) No grant may be paid under this section—

(a) in respect of any expenses incurred in the provision of any premises which it is the duty of the local education authority to provide, or

(b) in the case of a special agreement school, in respect of expenses incurred in the execution of proposals to which the special agreement relates or of repairs or alterations for the execution of which provision is made by the agreement.

(12) In relation to a proposed school, the references in this section to the governing body, in relation to any time before such a body are constituted, are to the persons who propose to establish the school; and where requirements are imposed in relation to grant paid under this section to such persons, the requirements shall be complied with by the governing body, when they are constituted, as well as by those persons.

(13) In this section "repair" does not include repair falling within section 59(4).

Grants in respect of preliminary expenditure

66.—(1) The Secretary of State may pay grants to the governing body of an aided or special agreement school in respect of any preliminary expenditure incurred by them for the purposes of a scheme for the transfer of the school to a new site or the enlargement or alteration of the school premises.

(2) Where any persons propose or are considering whether to propose—

(a) that a school established by them, or by persons whom they represent, should be maintained by a local education authority as an aided school, or

(b) that a school which may be so established should be so maintained,

the Secretary of State may pay grants to them in respect of any preliminary expenditure incurred by them for the purposes of a scheme for the provision of a site for the school or of any buildings which would be school buildings.

(3) Grants under subsection (1) or (2) may be paid in respect of a scheme such as is mentioned in that subsection whether or not—

(a) the details of such a scheme had been formulated at the time when the expenditure was incurred,

(b) where such details were not formulated at that time, they are subsequently formulated,

(c) the governing body or persons in question had determined to proceed with such a scheme at that time, or

(d) where they had not determined to proceed with such a scheme at that time, they subsequently determine to proceed with such a scheme.

(4) Expenditure in respect of which such grants are payable includes, in particular, costs incurred in connection with—

(a) the preparation of plans and specifications for any proposed construction, enlargement or alteration of buildings which are or would be school buildings, and

(b) estimating the sums which would be expended if any such works were carried out,

but does not include any sums expended in carrying out any such works.

(5) A grant under subsection (1) or (2) shall not exceed 85 per cent. of the expenditure in respect of which it is paid.

(6) Where—

(a) a grant is paid under subsection (1) in the case of any school, or

(b) a grant is paid under subsection (2) in the case of any school which becomes, or is established as, a voluntary school,

the grant shall for the purposes of section 173 be treated as expenditure incurred by the Secretary of State (otherwise than in connection with repairs) in respect of the school premises.

Loans in respect of initial expenses

67.—(1) Where, on the application of the governing body of an aided or special agreement school and after consulting persons representing the governing body, the Secretary of State—

(a) is satisfied that the governing body's share of any initial expenses required in connection with the school premises will involve capital expenditure, and

(b) having regard to all the circumstances of the case, considers that that expenditure ought properly to be met by borrowing,

he may make a loan to the governing body for the purpose of helping them meet that expenditure.

(2) The amount, rate of interest and other terms and conditions applicable to the loan shall be such as may be specified in an agreement made between the Secretary of State and the governing body with the consent of the Treasury.

(3) For the purposes of this section "initial expenses" are expenses of any of the following categories—

(a) expenses to be incurred in pursuance of a special agreement;

(b) expenses to be incurred in providing school buildings on a site to which the school is to be transferred pursuant to an order under section 47;

(c) expenses to be incurred in providing a site or school buildings on a significant enlargement of the school premises or on the transfer of the school to a new site, being expenses in respect of which grants may be paid under section 65;

(d) expenses to be incurred in providing a site or school buildings for a new school, being expenses in respect of which grants may be paid under section 65.

(4) For the purposes of this section the governing body's share of any initial expenses shall be taken to be so much of the expenses as remains to be borne by the governing body after taking into account the amount of any grant under section 65 or under a special agreement that may be paid or payable in respect of them.

Assistance by LEAs for governing bodies of aided and special agreement schools

Assistance in respect of maintenance and other obligations of governing body

68. A local education authority may give to the governing body of an aided or special agreement school such assistance as the authority think fit in relation to the carrying out by the governing body of any obligation under—

(a) section 45(1), or

(b) section 59.

Assistance by LEAs for promoters of new voluntary schools

Assistance for promoters of new voluntary school

69. A local education authority may give to persons required under section 45(1) to implement proposals involving the establishment of a school such assistance as the authority think fit in relation to the carrying out by those persons of their obligations under that provision.

Miscellaneous and supplemental

Duty to convey interest in premises provided under section 68 or 69

70.—(1) Where assistance under section 68 or 69 consists of the provision of any premises for use for the purposes of a school, the local education authority shall convey their interest in the premises to the trustees of the school to be held on trust for the purposes of the school.

(2) If any doubt or dispute arises as to the persons to whom the authority are required to make the conveyance, it shall be made to such persons as the Secretary of State thinks proper.

(3) Where trustees make a disposal of an interest conveyed to them by a local education authority under subsection (1), they shall be liable to pay to that authority an amount equal to the net proceeds of the disposal.

(4) In subsection (3)—

"disposal" includes part disposal; and

"net proceeds", in relation to a disposal, means the amount accruing on the disposal less any expenditure reasonably incurred for the purposes of making it.

Powers of Secretary of State where LEA make default in maintaining voluntary school

71.—(1) Where it appears to the Secretary of State that a local education authority have made default in the discharge of their duties relating to the maintenance of a voluntary school, he may—

(a) direct that any act done by or on behalf of the school's governing body for the purpose of securing the proper maintenance of the school shall be taken to have been done by or on behalf of the authority, and

(b) reimburse to the governing body any sums which in his opinion they have properly expended for that purpose.

(2) The amount of any sum reimbursed under subsection (1) shall be recoverable by the Secretary of State as a debt due to him from the authority; and without prejudice to any other method of recovery the whole or any part of any such sum may be deducted from any sums payable to the authority by the Secretary of State in pursuance of any regulations relating to the payment of grants.

Endowments for maintenance of voluntary schools

72. Where any sums accruing in respect of the income of an endowment are required by virtue of the provisions of a trust deed to be applied towards the maintenance of a voluntary school, those sums shall not be payable to the local education authority but shall be applied by the governing body of the school—

(a) towards the discharge of their obligations, if any, under section 59, or

(b) in such other manner, if any, as may be determined by a scheme for the administration of the endowment made after 1st April 1945.

Sums paid for letting or hiring of premises of voluntary schools

73. Any sum which is paid to the governing body or trustees of a voluntary school in respect of the letting or hiring of any part of the school premises other than school buildings shall be paid over to the local education authority.

Execution by LEA of certain works in case of controlled schools

74.—(1) Where a local education authority are liable to defray the cost of carrying out any building work, repair work or work of a similar character which is required for the purposes of a controlled school, the work shall, if the authority so determine, be carried out by employees of theirs.

(2) If the authority make such a determination, the governing body and any trustees of the school shall provide the authority and the authority's employees with all such facilities as they may reasonably require for the purpose of securing that the work is carried out properly.

Disapplication of restriction on local authority disposals

75. Subsection (2) of section 123 of the Local Government Act 1972 (local authority prohibited from making disposal of land under that section below market value without consent of the Secretary of State) shall not apply in the case of a disposal—

(a) to the governors of an aided or special agreement school, or
(b) to persons proposing to establish a school which is proposed to be maintained by a local education authority as a voluntary school and to be an aided school.

CHAPTER IV

GOVERNMENT OF COUNTY, VOLUNTARY AND MAINTAINED SPECIAL SCHOOLS

Instruments of government

Instruments of government

76.—(1) For every county, voluntary and maintained special school there shall be an instrument (known as the instrument of government) providing for the constitution of the school's governing body.

(2) The instrument of government shall be made by order of the local education authority.

(3) The instrument of government—

(a) shall contain such provisions as are required by this Chapter or by any other enactment; and
(b) shall not contain any provision which is inconsistent with any provision made by or under this Act or any other enactment.

(4) The instrument of government shall comply with any trust deed relating to the school.

(5) This section has effect subject to section 89 (grouping of two or more schools under a single governing body) and sections 96 and 97 (temporary governing body for new school pending constitution of its governing body).

Procedure for making and altering instruments of government

77.—(1) Before making an order under section 76, a local education authority shall consult the governing body and the head teacher of the school concerned.

(2) Before making an order under section 76 in respect of a voluntary school, a local education authority shall also—

(a) secure the agreement of the governing body to the terms of the proposed order;
(b) secure the agreement of the foundation governors to any provisions which are of particular concern to those governors; and
(c) have regard to the way in which the school has been conducted.

(3) Where the governing body of a county, voluntary or maintained special school make a proposal to the local education authority for the alteration of the provision made by the instrument of government for the school, the authority shall consider their proposal.

(4) Where—

(a) the foundation governors of a voluntary school make a proposal to the local education authority for the alteration of the provision made by the instrument of government for the school, and

(b) the proposal relates solely to one or more matters which are of particular concern to those governors,

the authority shall consider their proposal.

(5) Where a local education authority—

(a) propose to make an order under section 76 but cannot secure any agreement required by subsection (2), or

(b) refuse, in the case of a voluntary school, to make such an order in response to a proposal of a kind mentioned in subsection (3) or (4),

the authority or (as the case may be) the governing body or foundation governors may refer the matter to the Secretary of State.

(6) On a reference to him under subsection (5), the Secretary of State shall give such direction as he thinks fit having regard, in particular, to the status of the school as a controlled, aided or (as the case may be) special agreement school.

(7) Where it appears to the Secretary of State—

(a) that an order, or proposed order, under section 76 is in any respect inconsistent with the provisions of any trust deed relating to the school concerned, and

(b) that it is expedient in the interests of the school that the provisions of the trust deed should be modified for the purpose of removing the inconsistency,

he may by order make such modifications in the trust deed as appear to him to be just and expedient for that purpose.

(8) References in this section to an order, or proposed order, under section 76 are references to an order, or proposed order, under that section embodying or varying an instrument of government.

Categories of governor

Categories of governor

78.—(1) In this Act "co-opted governor", in relation to a county, voluntary or maintained special school, means a person appointed to be a member of the school's governing body by being co-opted by those governors of the school who have not themselves been so appointed (and accordingly does not include a governor of the school appointed in accordance with any provision made by virtue of section 81 (appointment of parent governors by governing body as a whole)).

(2) In this Act "foundation governor", in relation to a voluntary school, means a person appointed to be a member of the school's governing body, otherwise than by a local education authority or a minor authority, for the purpose of securing (so far as is practicable)—

(a) that the character of the school as a voluntary school is preserved and developed, and

(b) in particular, that the school is conducted in accordance with the provisions of any trust deed relating to it.

(3) In this Act "parent governor", in relation to a county, voluntary or maintained special school, means—

(a) a person who is elected as a member of the school's governing body by parents of registered pupils at the school and is himself such a parent at the time when he is elected, or

(b) (in the case of a county, controlled or maintained special school) a person who is appointed as a member of the governing body in accordance with any provision made by virtue of section 81.

(4) In this Act "teacher governor", in relation to a county, voluntary or maintained special school, means a person who is elected as a member of the school's governing body by teachers at the school and who is himself such a teacher at the time when he is elected.

(5) In relation to any group of schools under section 89 for which the instrument of government makes by virtue of section 93 provision with respect to the election of parent or teacher governors, any reference in subsection (3) or (4) to a person being elected as there mentioned is a reference to his being so elected in accordance with any such provision made by virtue of section 93.

Governing bodies of county, controlled and maintained special schools

Constitution of the governing body of a county, controlled or maintained special school

79.—(1) Subject to section 80 (representative governors for certain schools), the instrument of government for a county or maintained special school shall provide for the governing body to consist of the following (and no others)—

(a) the head teacher, unless he chooses not to be a governor, and
(b) governors of each of the categories specified in the first column of the following table, in the numbers specified in whichever of the other columns relates to the size of the school.

Category of governor	School with less than 100 registered pupils	School with 100 or more but less than 300 registered pupils	School with 300 or more but less than 600 registered pupils	School with 600 or more registered pupils
Parent governors	2	3	4	5
Governors appointed by the local education authority	2	3	4	5
Teacher governors	1	1	2	2
Co-opted governors	3	4	5	6

(2) Subject to section 80, the instrument of government for a controlled school shall provide for the governing body to consist of the following (and no others)—

(a) the head teacher, unless he chooses not to be a governor, and
(b) governors of each of the categories specified in the first column of the following table, in the numbers specified in whichever of the other columns relates to the size of the school.

Category of governor	School with less than 100 registered pupils	School with 100 or more but less than 300 registered pupils	School with 300 or more but less than 600 registered pupils	School with 600 or more registered pupils
Parent governors	2	3	4	5
Governors appointed by the local education authority	2	3	4	5
Teacher governors	1	1	2	2
Foundation governors	2	3	4	4
Co-opted governors	1	1	1	2

(3) Where the instrument of government so provides, a county, controlled or maintained special school with 600 or more registered pupils shall be treated for the purposes of this section as one with 300 or more but less than 600 registered pupils.

(4) Where the head teacher of a county, controlled or maintained special school is a governor he shall be treated for all purposes as being an ex officio governor.

Appointment of representative governors in place of co-opted governors

80.—(1) The instrument of government for a primary school which is a county or controlled school serving an area for which there is a minor authority shall provide for one governor to be appointed by that authority.

(2) The instrument of government for a maintained special school which is established in a hospital shall provide—

(a) (if the hospital is vested in the Secretary of State) for one governor to be appointed by the Health Authority; or

(b) (if the hospital is vested in a National Health Service trust) for one governor to be appointed by that trust.

(3) The instrument of government for a maintained special school which is not established in a hospital shall, if the school has less than 100 registered pupils, provide for one governor to be appointed—

(a) by a voluntary organisation designated by the local education authority, in relation to the school, as the appropriate voluntary organisation concerned with matters in respect of which the school is specially organised; or

(b) jointly by two or more voluntary organisations so designated as appropriate voluntary organisations concerned with such matters;

or, if the school has 100 or more registered pupils, shall provide for two governors to be appointed as mentioned in paragraph (a) or (b).

(4) Where, by virtue of subsection (3) above, an instrument of government is required to provide for the appointment of two governors, it may make different provision in relation to the appointment of one governor from that made in relation to the appointment of the other.

(5) Where a local education authority are satisfied, in relation to any special school, that there is no voluntary organisation which it would be appropriate to designate for the purposes of subsection (3), that subsection shall not apply to the instrument of government for the school.

(6) An instrument of government which is required by this section to provide for the appointment of a governor shall name the person or persons by whom the governor is to be appointed.

(7) Subject to subsection (8), an instrument of government which is required by this section to provide for the appointment of one or (as the case may be) two governors shall in consequence provide for the appointment of one or two fewer co-opted governors than would otherwise be provided for.

(8) If that instrument of government is for a controlled school which—

(a) has less than 600 registered pupils, or

(b) is, by virtue of subsection (3) of section 79, to be treated for the purposes of that section as having less than 600 such pupils,

the instrument shall not provide for the appointment of any co-opted governor.

(9) In subsections (7) and (8) references to co-opted governors are references to governors required to be co-opted by virtue of section 79 but do not include co-opted foundation governors.

Appointment of parent governors by governing bodies

81.—(1) The instrument of government for a county or controlled school, or for a maintained special school which is not established in a hospital, may provide that if at the time when the instrument is made, or at any later time when there is a vacancy for a parent governor—

(a) at least 50 per cent. of the registered pupils at the school are boarders, and

(b) it would, in the opinion of the local education authority, be impracticable for there to be an election of parent governors,

the parent governors, or (as the case may be) the parent governor required to fill that vacancy, shall be appointed by the other members of the governing body.

(2) Where, in the opinion of the local education authority, it is likely to be impracticable for there to be elections of parent governors at a maintained special school which is established in a hospital, the instrument of government for the school may provide for the parent governors to be appointed by the other members of the governing body.

(3) The instrument of government for a county, controlled or maintained special school at which parent governors are to be, or may be, elected shall provide for the required number of parent governors to be made up by parent governors appointed by the other members of the governing body if—

(a) one or more vacancies for parent governors are required to be filled by election; and

(b) the number of parents standing for election as parent governors is less than the number of vacancies.

(4) The instrument of government for a county, controlled or maintained special school shall require governors, in appointing a parent governor under a provision made by virtue of this section—

(a) to appoint a person who is the parent of a registered pupil at the school, where it is reasonably practicable to do so, and

(b) where it is not, to appoint a person who is the parent of one or more children of compulsory school age.

(5) Such an instrument shall also provide that governors shall not appoint as a parent governor under such a provision any person who is—

(a) an elected member of the local education authority, or

(b) an employee of the authority or of the governing body of any aided school maintained by the authority.

Review of the constitution of governing bodies

82.—(1) The constitution of the governing body of a county, controlled or maintained special school shall be reviewed in accordance with this section on, or as soon as is reasonably practicable after, the occurrence of any event which is a relevant event in relation to the school.

(2) For the purposes of this section any of the following is a "relevant event" in relation to a school—

(a) the implementation of any proposals falling within subsection (3);

(b) where no such proposals have been implemented in relation to the school before the fourth anniversary of the date on which the current instrument of government for the school was made, that anniversary; and

(c) where a relevant event has previously occurred in relation to the school, the fourth anniversary of the latest such event.

(3) Proposals fall within this subsection if they provide for an increase in the number of registered pupils at the school and are—

(a) proposals under section 35(1)(c) or (d) (alteration of character or premises of a county school or transfer to a new site) or proposals which would fall to be published under section 35(1)(d) but for section 35(2)(b);

(b) proposals under section 41(2)(a) or (b) (alteration of character or premises of a voluntary school or transfer to a new site);

(c) proposals that the Secretary of State should make an order under section 47 (transfer of voluntary school to a new site); or

(d) proposals under section 339(1)(b) (prescribed alteration to maintained special school).

(4) Any review which is required by virtue of the implementation of proposals falling within subsection (3)(a) or (d) shall be carried out by the local education authority; and any other review which is required by this section shall be carried out by the governing body.

(5) Whenever a local education authority or governing body are required to carry out a review under this section, they shall consider—

(a) whether the governing body are properly constituted; and

(b) whether the provision made by the instrument of government for the school is in any respect different from that which a new instrument of government would be required to make.

(6) Where a governing body have carried out a review under this section and have established that the provision made by the instrument of government is in one or more respects different from that which a new instrument of government would be required to make, they shall report the fact to the local education authority.

(7) Where proposals falling within subsection (3)(a) or (d) have been implemented in relation to a school, the local education authority shall determine the date on which, for the purposes of this section, they are to be taken to have been implemented and shall notify the governing body accordingly.

Adjustment in number of governors

83.—(1) Where—

(a) a county, controlled or maintained special school has more governors of a particular category than are provided for by the instrument of government for the school, and

(b) the excess is not eliminated by the required number of governors of that category resigning,

such number of governors of that category as is required to eliminate the excess shall cease to hold office.

(2) The governors who are to cease to hold office shall be selected on the basis of seniority, the longest-serving governor being the first to be selected, and so on.

(3) Where it is necessary for the purposes of subsection (2) to select one or more governors from a group of equal seniority, it shall be done by drawing lots.

(4) Subsections (2) and (3) do not apply in relation to foundation governors.

(5) The instrument of government for a controlled school shall make provision for the procedure to be adopted whenever subsection (1) requires a foundation governor to cease to hold office.

Governing bodies of aided and special agreement schools

Constitution of the governing body of an aided or special agreement school

84.—(1) The instrument of government for an aided or special agreement school shall provide for the governing body to include—

(a) the head teacher, unless he chooses not to be a governor,

(b) at least one parent governor,

(c) at least one governor appointed by the local education authority,

(d) at least one teacher governor if the school has less than 300 registered pupils, and at least two teacher governors if it has 300 or more registered pupils, and

(e) foundation governors.

(2) The instrument shall provide for such number of foundation governors as will lead to their outnumbering the other governors—

(a) by two, if the governing body will consist of not more than 18 governors; or

(b) by three, if it will consist of more than 18 governors,

and shall provide for at least one of the foundation governors to be (at the time of his appointment) a parent of a registered pupil at the school.

(3) If the school is a primary school serving an area for which there is a minor authority, the instrument shall provide for the governing body to include also at least one governor appointed by that authority.

(4) Where the head teacher of an aided or special agreement school has chosen not to be a governor, he shall nevertheless be counted as one for the purposes of calculating the required number of foundation governors.

(5) Subject to subsection (2), nothing in this section shall be taken to prevent the instrument of government for such a school from providing for the governing body to include governors in addition to those required by virtue of this section.

(6) Where the head teacher of such a school is a governor he shall be treated for all purposes as being an ex officio governor.

Sponsor governors for aided secondary schools

85.—(1) The instrument of government for any secondary school which is an aided school shall, if a direction given by the Secretary of State under this section so requires—

(a) name as a sponsor of the school a person specified in the direction, and

(b) provide for the governing body of the school to include such number of governors appointed by the sponsor, not exceeding four, as is so specified.

(2) A direction under this section in respect of a school, other than one under subsection (4) or (5)—

(a) may only be given at the request, or with the consent, of the governing body, and

(b) may make provision (including the modification of any provision made by or under this Chapter) as to the time by which a new instrument of government is to be made and the consent and consultation which is to be required before it is made.

(3) A direction under this section varying or revoking a previous direction—

(a) may only be made after consulting the governing body, and

(b) may make provision (including the modification of any provision made by or under this Chapter) as to the time by which a new instrument of government is to be made and the consent and consultation which is to be required before it is made.

(4) Where proposals approved under section 43—

(a) provide for a secondary school to be maintained by the local education authority as a voluntary school, and

(b) name a person as a sponsor of the school, and

(c) provide for the governing body of the school to include a specified number of governors, not exceeding four, appointed by the sponsor, the Secretary of State shall, if he makes an order under section 48 directing that the school shall be an aided school, give a direction under this section for the purpose of implementing the proposals.

(5) Where an order under section 54 directs that a secondary school shall be an aided school and the proposals published by the governing body under section 52—

(a) name a person as a sponsor of the school, and

(b) provide for the governing body of the school to include a specified number of governors, not exceeding four, appointed by the sponsor,

the Secretary of State shall give a direction under this section for the purpose of implementing the proposals.

(6) Where the instrument of government for any secondary school which is an aided school names two or more persons as sponsors of the school—

(a) the number of governors appointed under the instrument by virtue of this section may not exceed four, and

(b) the instrument may not provide for any of those governors to be appointed by two or more sponsors acting jointly.

(7) Where in pursuance of this section the instrument of government for a school names a person as a sponsor of the school, section 84(2) shall have effect as if it required the instrument to provide for such number of foundation governors as will lead to their outnumbering the other governors by two.

(8) In this section "direction" means a direction contained in an order made by the Secretary of State.

Governing bodies: general

Instrument of government to reflect current circumstances of school

86.—(1) Subject to subsection (2) and paragraph 5(2) of Schedule 10 (which makes in relation to new schools provision similar to that made by subsection (2) in relation to existing schools), the instrument of government for a county, voluntary or maintained special school shall make such provision as is appropriate having regard to all the circumstances of the school as at the date on which the instrument is made.

(2) Where proposals falling within section 82(3) have been implemented in relation to a school, then for the purposes of subsection (1) the number of registered pupils at the school shall, until the actual number of registered pupils at the school reaches the maximum number of pupils provided for by the proposals, be deemed to be that maximum number.

(3) Where subsection (2) applies in relation to a school—

(a) the local education authority, or

(b) if the proposals fall within section 82(3)(b), the governing body,

may determine that it shall cease to apply (but without prejudice to its operation in relation to the implementation of any further proposals).

Effect of change in circumstances of school

87.—(1) Where the effect of any subsequent change in the circumstances of a county, voluntary or maintained special school is that the provision made by the instrument of government for the school differs in any respect from the provision which a new instrument of government would be required to make, the local education authority shall (subject to subsection (2))—

(a) vary the instrument of government in such manner as is necessary to remove any such difference, or

(b) make a new instrument of government.

(2) For the purposes of subsection (1) any change in the number of registered pupils at a county, controlled or maintained special school occurring after the instrument of government for the school is made, or (as the case may be) varied, may be disregarded until a review under section 82 establishes that the provision made by the instrument differs in any respect from the provision which a new instrument of government for the school would be required to make.

(3) Where section 86(2) has applied in relation to a school but the local education authority or (as the case may be) governing body have subsequently determined that it should cease to apply, subsections (1) and (2) above shall have effect as if a change in the number of registered pupils at the school had occurred at the time when that determination was made.

(4) The instrument of government for a county, voluntary or maintained special school may make provision which would be appropriate in the event of such a change in the circumstances of the school as is anticipated by that provision (including in particular a change in the number of registered pupils at the school).

(5) No provision made by the instrument of government for a county, controlled or maintained special school in anticipation of a change in the number of registered pupils at the school shall have effect before it is established, by a review under section 82, that a new instrument of government would be required to make that provision.

Incorporation, membership and proceedings etc. of governing bodies

88.—(1) Any governing body of a county, voluntary or maintained special school constituted in pursuance of this Chapter shall be constituted as a body corporate; and Schedule 7 has effect in relation to the incorporation of any such governing body.

(2) Schedule 8 has effect in relation to the membership and proceedings of, and other matters relating to, any such governing body.

Grouping of schools under a single governing body

Grouping of schools under a single governing body

89.—(1) Subject to subsection (2), a local education authority may resolve that any two or more schools maintained by them shall be grouped for the purposes of this Chapter.

(2) If the instrument of government of any of the schools names a person as a sponsor of the school, a local education authority may only pass a resolution under subsection (1) if all the schools are secondary schools.

(3) Where any schools are grouped under this section, they shall—

(a) be treated for the purposes of this Chapter as a single school; and

(b) have a single governing body constituted under a single instrument of government.

(4) A group shall be treated for the purposes of this Chapter—

(a) as an aided school, if it contains at least one aided school;

(b) as a special agreement school, if it contains at least one special agreement school and paragraph (a) does not apply;

(c) as a controlled school, if it contains at least one controlled school and neither paragraph (a) nor paragraph (b) applies;

(d) as a maintained special school, if it consists only of maintained special schools; and

(e) as a county school, if none of paragraphs (a) to (d) applies.

(5) In this Part—

"group" means two or more schools grouped under this section; and

"grouped school" means a school which forms a part of a group.

(6) Any reference in any enactment to the governing body or governors of a school shall be construed, in relation to any grouped school, as a reference to the governing body or governors of the group.

Consent of Secretary of State as to grouping

90.—(1) Subject to subsection (2), a local education authority shall, before resolving to group any schools under section 89, obtain the consent of the Secretary of State to the proposed grouping.

(2) The Secretary of State's consent is not required if—

(a) the group will consist only of two primary schools;
(b) both of the schools serve substantially the same area;
(c) neither of the schools is a special school; and
(d) where they are in Wales, there is no significant difference between them in their use of the Welsh language.

(3) Where—

(a) two primary schools have been grouped in circumstances in which, by virtue of subsection (2), the Secretary of State's consent to the grouping was not required, and
(b) a change of circumstances occurs such that a proposal to group those schools made after that change would require his consent,

the local education authority shall obtain his consent to their continuing to be grouped.

(4) The Secretary of State may give his consent to any grouping (or continued grouping) of schools subject to such conditions as to the duration of the grouping as he sees fit to impose.

(5) Where the Secretary of State's consent is required to the grouping or continued grouping of any schools, sections 79 to 81, 84 and 85 and paragraph 2(2) of Schedule 8 (representation of local business community on governing body) shall apply in relation to the group subject to such modifications (if any) as he may direct.

(6) Any dispute as to whether, for the purposes of this section—

(a) two primary schools are to be regarded as serving substantially the same area, or
(b) there is any significant difference between two primary schools in their use of the Welsh language,

shall be determined by the Secretary of State.

Consent of, or consultation with, governing body as to grouping

91.—(1) A local education authority shall not pass a resolution under section 89 applying to a voluntary school without first obtaining the consent of the school's governing body.

(2) A local education authority shall not pass a resolution under section 89 applying to a county or maintained special school without first consulting the school's governing body.

Procedure for making or altering the instrument of government for a group

92.—(1) Before making an order under section 76 embodying the first instrument of government for a group, the local education authority shall consult the governing body and head teacher of each school within the group.

(2) Before making such an order in respect of a group which contains one or more voluntary schools, the local education authority shall also—

(a) secure the agreement of the governing body of each of those schools to the terms of the proposed order,
(b) secure the agreement of the foundation governors of each of those schools to any provision which will be of particular concern to the foundation governors of the group, and
(c) have regard to the way in which those schools have been conducted.

(3) Where an order such as is mentioned in subsection (1) has been made, section 77 shall apply in relation to any subsequent order embodying or varying the instrument of government for the group, or any proposal for the making of such an order, as if the group—

(a) (where it contains one or more voluntary schools) were a single voluntary school; or
(b) (in any other case) were a single county school.

(4) Any agreement required by subsection (2) shall be treated for the purposes of section 77(5) as having been required by section 77(2).

Election of parent and teacher governors for a group

93. The instrument of government for a group—
(a) may provide for the local education authority to have power to determine, in relation to every election of parent or teacher governors, the school or schools within the group—
  (i) the parents of registered pupils at which are entitled to stand and vote at the election, or
  (ii) the teachers at which are entitled to stand and vote at the election,
as the case may be; and
(b) where it so provides, shall require the authority to ensure that the position after any such election will be that there is no school within the group which will not have had an opportunity to participate in accordance with paragraph (a) in the election of at least one of the parent or (as the case may be) teacher governors of the group.

Review of grouping

94.—(1) Where subsection (2) applies in relation to a school which is grouped with one or more other schools under section 89, the local education authority shall review the grouping of those schools and consider whether or not it should be brought to an end.

(2) This subsection applies in relation to a school if—
(a) proposals relating to it are made under—
  (i) section 35 (establishment, alteration etc. of county schools),
  (ii) section 41 (establishment, alteration etc. of voluntary schools),
  (iii) section 52 (controlled schools becoming aided schools),
  (iv) section 167 (discontinuance of county, voluntary and nursery schools), or
  (v) section 339 (establishment etc. of special schools); or
(b) it is proposed that the Secretary of State should make an order relating to it under section 46 (establishment of new voluntary schools in substitution for old ones) or section 47 (transfer of voluntary schools to new sites); or
(c) the Secretary of State makes an order relating to it—
  (i) under section 50 or section 51 (division of county or voluntary school), or
  (ii) under section 57 or 58(1) (revocation of orders by virtue of which schools are aided or special agreement schools); or
(d) it is transferred to a new site in circumstances falling within section 35(2)(b).

(3) Where on a review under this section a local education authority consider that any grouping of schools should be continued, and the Secretary of State's consent to the grouping, or to the continued grouping, of the schools was at any time required by section 90, the authority shall—
(a) report to the Secretary of State on the results of their review; and
(b) provide him with such information as he may reasonably require with a view to enabling him to consider whether or not the grouping should be brought to an end.

Termination of grouping

95.—(1) The Secretary of State may by order bring to an end any grouping under section 89 in respect of which his consent was at any time required by section 90.

(2) Any grouping under section 89 may, if the group does not contain a voluntary school, be brought to an end by resolution of the local education authority.

(3) Any such grouping may, if the group contains a voluntary school but not one whose instrument of government names any person as a sponsor of the school, be brought to an end—

(a) by resolution of the local education authority made with the agreement of the governing body, or

(b) by one year's notice given either by the authority to the governing body or by the governing body to the authority.

(4) Any order under section 76 embodying an instrument of government for two or more schools which are grouped under section 89 shall be taken to have been revoked—

(a) in the case of a group which was established for a specified period, at the end of that period, or

(b) at the time when the grouping is brought to an end in accordance with subsection (1), (2) or (3).

Government of new schools

Temporary governing bodies for new county or maintained special schools

96.—(1) Where—

(a) the Secretary of State has approved under section 37 or section 340 proposals of a kind mentioned in subsection (2), or

(b) a local education authority have determined under section 38 to implement any proposals made by them under section 35,

the local education authority shall (unless they have already exercised their power to do so under subsection (3)) make an arrangement for the constitution of a temporary governing body for the school in question pending the constitution of its governing body under an instrument of government.

(2) The proposals referred to in subsection (1) are any proposals made by a local education authority—

(a) to establish a new county school;

(b) to maintain as a county school a school which is neither a county school nor a voluntary school; or

(c) to establish a new school which is specially organised to make special educational provision for pupils with special educational needs.

(3) Where any such proposals have been duly published under section 35 or (as the case may be) notice of them has been duly served under section 339, the local education authority may make an arrangement such as is mentioned in subsection (1) in anticipation of the Secretary of State's approval of the proposals or (as the case may be) the determination by the authority that they should be implemented.

(4) An arrangement made under subsection (3) shall come to an end if—

(a) the proposals are withdrawn, or

(b) the Secretary of State rejects them under section 37 or (as the case may be) section 340, or

(c) (in the case of proposals made under section 35), the local education authority determine under section 38 not to implement them.

(5) An arrangement made under this section shall, unless it has been brought to an end under subsection (4), come to an end when the requirement for there to be an instrument of government for the school takes effect under section 99.

Temporary governing bodies for new voluntary schools

97.—(1) Where the Secretary of State has approved under section 43 any proposals that a school—

(a) which was established by those making the proposals, or by the persons whom they represent, and is not a voluntary school, or

(b) which is proposed to be so established,

should be maintained by a local education authority as a voluntary school, the local education authority shall (unless they have already exercised their power to do so under subsection (2)) make an arrangement for the constitution of a temporary governing body for the school pending the constitution of its governing body under an instrument of government.

(2) Where any such proposals have been duly published under section 41, the local education authority may make an arrangement such as is mentioned in subsection (1) in anticipation of the Secretary of State's approval of the proposals.

(3) If the proposals so published are for the school in question to be maintained as a controlled school, the authority shall consult the persons making the proposals—

(a) as to whether the power given to the authority by subsection (2) should be exercised, and

(b) if the authority propose to exercise it, as to the date on which the arrangement should be made.

(4) If the proposals so published are for the school in question to be maintained as an aided school, the authority and the persons making the proposals shall consider—

(a) whether the power given to the authority by subsection (2) should be exercised, and

(b) where they agree that it should, on what date the arrangement should be made.

(5) Where, in a case within subsection (4), the authority and the persons making the proposals fail to agree on the question mentioned in paragraph (a) or on that mentioned in paragraph (b), either of them may refer the matter to the Secretary of State.

(6) On a reference under subsection (5), the Secretary of State shall give such direction as he thinks fit.

(7) An arrangement made under subsection (2) shall come to an end if—

(a) the proposals are withdrawn, or

(b) the Secretary of State rejects them under section 43.

(8) An arrangement made under this section, other than one which has been brought to an end under subsection (7), shall come to an end when the requirement for there to be an instrument of government for the school takes effect under section 99.

Constitution, membership and proceedings etc. of temporary governing bodies

98. Schedule 9 has effect in relation to the constitution, membership and proceedings of, and other matters relating to, temporary governing bodies.

Transition from temporary governing body to governing body constituted under an instrument of government

99.—(1) The requirement for there to be an instrument of government for a school (imposed by section 76) shall take effect in relation to a new school from the date on which the relevant proposals are implemented.

(2) Where a question arises as to which date is to be taken for the purposes of this section to be the date on which the relevant proposals are implemented, it shall be determined by the Secretary of State.

(3) Schedule 10 has effect in relation to the transition from a temporary

governing body to a governing body constituted under an instrument of government.

Grouping of new schools

Grouping of new schools

100.—(1) This section applies for the purposes of grouping a new school under section 89 with effect from the relevant time.

(2) Any provision of sections 89 to 91 which operates by reference to the existence or absence of any particular circumstances in the case of a school, or to the status of a school, shall be treated (so far as necessary for the purposes mentioned in subsection (1) above) as so operating by reference to the position as it will be at the relevant time.

(3) In addition section 91 shall have effect for those purposes as if any reference to a school's governing body were a reference to its temporary governing body.

(4) In this section "the relevant time", in relation to a new school, means the time when the requirement for there to be an instrument of government for the school takes effect under section 99.

CHAPTER V

FINANCIAL DELEGATION TO GOVERNING BODIES OF COUNTY, VOLUNTARY AND MAINTAINED SPECIAL SCHOOLS

Introductory

Local education authority schemes for financing schools

101.—(1) In this Part "scheme" means a scheme made by a local education authority under section 103 (including one that is to be treated as so made by virtue of section 104(6)) as from time to time revised under sections 111 to 114.

(2) In this Part "the local education authority", in relation to a scheme, means the local education authority who made (or are to be treated as having made) the scheme.

(3) For the purposes of this Part—

(a) a local education authority's "general schools budget" for a financial year is the amount appropriated by the authority for meeting expenditure in the year in respect of all schools required to be covered in the year by any scheme made by the authority (other than non-qualifying expenditure);

(b) a local education authority's "aggregated budget" for a financial year under a scheme is the part (determined as mentioned in section 105) of the authority's general schools budget for the year which is available for allocation to individual schools under the scheme; and

(c) a school's "budget share" for a financial year under a scheme is the share of the local education authority's aggregated budget for the year which is to be appropriated for the school under the scheme.

(4) In subsection (3)(a) "non-qualifying expenditure" means expenditure in respect of the provision of—

(a) part-time education suitable to the requirements of persons of any age over compulsory school age, or

(b) full-time education suitable to the requirements of persons who have attained the age of 19.

(5) In relation to any scheme any reference in subsection (3) to an amount is a reference to an amount determined (and from time to time revised) in accordance with the scheme.

(6) In this Part references to a school's budget share for a financial year include references to that share as from time to time revised in accordance with the scheme under which it is determined.

Schools required to be covered by a scheme

102. For the purposes of this Part a school is required to be covered by a scheme in any financial year if either—

(a) immediately before the beginning of that year it is maintained by the local education authority as a county or voluntary school, or

(b) at any time during that year it becomes so maintained (whether by virtue of being newly established as a county or voluntary school or by virtue of becoming a county or voluntary school where it was not, immediately before it became so, a school of either description).

Schemes for purposes of Chapter V

Local education authority required to have scheme for purposes of Chapter V

103.—(1) Each local education authority shall have a scheme prepared in accordance with this Chapter and submitted for the approval of the Secretary of State in accordance with section 104.

(2) The scheme shall provide for—

(a) the determination, in respect of each financial year of the local education authority, of the budget share of each school required to be covered by the scheme in the year, and

(b) the delegation by the authority of the management of a school's budget share for a financial year to the school's governing body, where such delegation is required or permitted by or under the scheme.

Preparation and imposition of schemes

104.—(1) A scheme prepared by a local education authority under section 103 shall be submitted to the Secretary of State on or before such date as he may by order direct, either—

(a) generally; or

(b) in relation to any local education authority, or any class or description of such authorities, specified in the order.

(2) In preparing a scheme under that section a local education authority shall take into account any guidance given by the Secretary of State, whether—

(a) generally, or

(b) in relation to that authority or to any class or description of local education authorities to which that authority belongs,

as to the provisions he regards as appropriate for inclusion in the scheme.

(3) Before preparing such a scheme the local education authority shall consult—

(a) the governing body and the head teacher of every county, voluntary or special school maintained by the authority;

(b) the governing body of every grant-maintained school in the area of the authority; and

(c) the governing body of every grant-maintained special school which—

(i) is established under section 339 in the authority's area, or

(ii) before becoming a grant-maintained school was a special school maintained by the authority;

but the Secretary of State may, by notice in writing to the authority, dispense with the duty imposed by paragraphs (b) and (c) above in respect of such schools, or such class or description of schools, as are specified in the notice.

(4) Such a scheme shall not come into force until it has been approved by

the Secretary of State or until such date as he may, in giving his approval, specify; and the Secretary of State may approve such a scheme—

(a) either without modifications or with such modifications as he thinks fit after consulting the authority concerned; and

(b) subject to such conditions as he may specify in giving his approval.

(5) If in the case of any local education authority either—

(a) the authority fail to submit a scheme as required by subsection (1), or

(b) it appears to the Secretary of State that a scheme submitted by the authority as required by that subsection does not accord with any guidance given by him for the purposes of this section and cannot be made to do so merely by modifying it,

he may, after consulting the authority and such other persons as he thinks fit, impose a scheme making such provision of a description required to be made by a scheme under section 103 in relation to the financing by the authority of county and voluntary schools as he considers appropriate.

(6) A scheme imposed by the Secretary of State by virtue of subsection (5)—

(a) shall be treated as if made under 103 by the local education authority concerned; and

(b) shall come into force on such date as may be specified by the scheme.

Provision by a scheme for determination of budget shares

Calculation of local education authority's aggregated budget

105.—(1) The part of a local education authority's general schools budget for a financial year which is available for allocation to individual schools under a scheme (and as such constitutes the authority's "aggregated budget" for the year under the scheme) is the amount remaining after deducting from the amount of the authority's general schools budget for the year—

(a) the amount of any expenditure of the authority in the year on excepted heads or items of expenditure; and

(b) any other amounts which fall in accordance with the scheme to be deducted in determining the authority's aggregated budget for the year.

(2) In subsection (1) "amount" means an amount determined (and from time to time revised) in accordance with the scheme.

(3) In subsection (1) "excepted heads or items of expenditure" means the following heads or items of expenditure (so far as taken into account in determining the authority's general schools budget for the year)—

(a) all expenditure treated by the authority as expenditure of a capital nature;

(b) all expenditure in respect of the repayment of the principal of, the payment of interest on and the discharge of any other financial obligation in connection with any loan raised to meet expenditure falling within paragraph (a);

(c) expenditure falling to be taken into account in determining central government grants of any prescribed description; and

(d) such other items of expenditure as may be prescribed.

Application of the allocation formula

106.—(1) The provision to be included in a scheme for determining the budget share for a financial year of each school required to be covered by the scheme in that year shall require that share to be determined (and from time to time revised) by the application of the allocation formula under the scheme.

(2) For the purposes of this Part the "allocation formula" under a scheme is a formula laid down by the scheme for the purpose of dividing among all

schools required to be covered by the scheme in any financial year the local education authority's aggregated budget for the year.

(3) In subsection (2) "formula" includes methods, principles and rules of any description, however expressed.

(4) The allocation formula under a scheme—

(a) shall include provision for taking into account, in the case of each school required to be covered by the scheme in any financial year, the number and ages of registered pupils at that school on such date or dates as may be determined by or under the scheme in relation to that year, and

(b) may include provision for taking into account any other factors affecting the needs of individual schools which are subject to variation from school to school (including, in particular, the number of registered pupils at a school who have special educational needs and the nature of the special educational provision required to be made for them).

(5) The allocation formula shall, however, not include provision for taking into account persons provided with—

(a) part-time education suitable to the requirements of persons of any age over compulsory school age, or

(b) full-time education suitable to the requirements of persons who have attained the age of 19.

(6) A scheme shall provide for all amounts relevant to the determination of a school's budget share under the scheme for a financial year to be determined initially before the beginning of that year.

Provision by a scheme for financial delegation

The delegation requirement

107.—(1) A scheme shall include provision for requiring, in the case of each school required to be covered by the scheme in any financial year, the delegation by the local education authority to the governing body of the management of the school's budget share for that year.

(2) Any provision included in a scheme by virtue of subsection (1) is referred to in this Part as the "delegation requirement" under the scheme.

Optional delegation

108. A scheme may provide for the management of a school's budget share for any financial year to be delegated by the local education authority to the governing body of the school in a case where the delegation requirement under the scheme does not apply to the school in respect of that year.

Conditions as to delegation

109.—(1) Any delegation under a scheme of the management of a school's budget share shall be subject to such conditions as may be imposed by or under the scheme.

(2) Conditions so imposed may, in particular, relate to—

(a) the arrangements to be made for management of the expenditure of any sum made available to a school's governing body in accordance with the scheme (and in particular for authorising expenditure, or transactions involving commitments to expenditure, to be met from any such sum);

(b) the keeping and audit of accounts and records with respect to such expenditure, and the keeping of records with respect to such transactions;

(c) the provision to the local education authority by the governing body of copies of accounts and records required to be kept by any condition imposed under paragraph (b); and

(d) the provision to the local education authority by the governing body of such other documents and information relating to the application of any sum falling within paragraph (a) as the authority may from time to time require.

(3) In subsection (1) "delegation" means delegation under any provision made by virtue of section 107 or 108.

Initial implementation of the delegation requirement

110.—(1) If a school comes within a scheme in a financial year falling within the scheme's initial period, the delegation requirement under the scheme shall not apply to the school until a date specified in the scheme.

(2) For the purposes of this section a scheme's "initial period" (subject to any order made under subsection (4)) is the period of three years beginning with the date of the coming into force of the scheme.

(3) Different dates may be specified under subsection (1) in relation to different schools or categories of school and in relation to schools coming within the scheme in different financial years or at different times within the same financial year; but—

(a) each date specified must coincide with the beginning of a financial year, and

(b) no date may be specified which falls after the beginning of the financial year next following the end of the scheme's initial period.

(4) The Secretary of State may by order—

(a) substitute a date specified in the order for any date specified in a scheme under subsection (1) (including one specified by virtue of a previous order under this subsection), and

(b) extend any scheme's initial period until a date specified in the order.

(5) For the purposes of this section a school—

(a) comes within a scheme in any financial year if that financial year is the first financial year in which the school is required to be covered by the scheme, and

(b) comes within the scheme—

(i) at the beginning of that year, if it is then a school required to be so covered, and

(ii) otherwise at the time falling within that year when it first becomes such a school.

Revision of schemes

Revision of scheme by LEA: general

111.—(1) Subject to subsection (2) and to sections 112 and 113, the local education authority may revise the whole or any part of a scheme.

(2) Section 104(2) shall apply in relation to the preparation by the authority of any revision under this section as it applies in relation to the preparation by the authority of a scheme.

Revision of scheme by LEA: significant variations

112.—(1) This section applies where the local education authority propose, in revising a scheme under section 111, to make a significant variation of the scheme.

(2) In such a case the authority—

(a) shall first consult every governing body and head teacher whom they are obliged to consult under section 104(3), and

(b) shall then submit a copy of their proposals to the Secretary of State for his approval.

(3) Where the proposals are so submitted, section 104(4) shall apply to the scheme as revised as it applies to a scheme prepared under section 103.

(4) The Secretary of State may by order specify what descriptions of variation are to be regarded as significant for the purposes of this section.

Revision of scheme by LEA: minor revisions

113.—(1) This section applies where the local education authority propose to revise a scheme under section 111 and the revision is in their opinion a minor revision.

(2) In such a case the authority shall give the Secretary of State notice in writing of their proposal, giving brief particulars of the nature of the revision proposed to be made.

(3) If so required by the Secretary of State before the end of the period of two months beginning with the date on which he receives notice under subsection (2) of the authority's proposal, the authority shall send to him a copy of the scheme as proposed to be revised.

(4) It shall be for the Secretary of State to determine whether or not any revision is a minor revision.

(5) In this section "minor revision" means a revision which does not make what would be a significant variation for the purposes of section 112.

Revision of schemes by Secretary of State

114.—(1) The Secretary of State may by a direction revise the whole or any part of any scheme as from such date as may be specified in the direction.

(2) Before giving such a direction the Secretary of State shall consult the local education authority and such other persons as he thinks fit.

Financial delegation under a scheme

Financial delegation: introductory

115. In the following provisions of this Part—

(a) references to a school in respect of which financial delegation is required for a financial year under a scheme are to a school conducted by a governing body to whom the local education authority are for the time being required by or under the scheme to delegate the management of the school's budget share for the year (and the governing body of such a school are said to have a right to a delegated budget for the year), and

(b) references to a school which has a delegated budget are to a school conducted by a governing body to whom a local education authority have for the time being delegated the management of the school's budget share for a financial year in pursuance of a scheme (whether that delegation is required by the scheme or not).

Effect of financial delegation

116.—(1) This section applies where a local education authority's financial provision for county and voluntary schools is subject to regulation by a scheme.

(2) In the case of any county or voluntary school maintained by the authority in respect of which financial delegation is required for a financial year under the scheme, the authority shall put at the disposal of the governing body in respect of the year a sum equal to the school's budget share for the year, to be spent for the purposes of the school.

(3) The times at which, and the manner in which, any such sum is put at the disposal of the governing body shall be such as may be provided by or under the scheme.

(4) Subject to section 125 (financial delegation apart from schemes) and section 489(2) (grants for education support and training), the authority may not delegate to the governing body of any school required to be covered by

the scheme in a financial year the power to spend any appropriated amount otherwise than as required or permitted under the scheme; and for this purpose "appropriated amount" means a sum appropriated by the authority for the purposes of the school in that year.

(5) The governing body of a school which has a delegated budget—

(a) shall be entitled, subject to any provision made by or under the scheme, to spend any sum made available to them in respect of the school's budget share for a financial year as they think fit for the purposes of the school, and

(b) may delegate to the head teacher, to such extent as may be permitted by or under the scheme, their power under paragraph (a) in relation to any part of that sum.

(6) In subsection (5) "the purposes of the school" does not include purposes wholly referable to the provision of—

(a) part-time education suitable to the requirements of persons of any age over compulsory school age, or

(b) full-time education suitable to the requirements of persons who have attained the age of 19.

(7) The governing body of a school which has a delegated budget shall not exercise their powers under subsection (5) to pay to governors any allowances other than travelling and subsistence allowances.

(8) The governors of a school shall not incur any personal liability in respect of anything done in good faith in the exercise or purported exercise of their powers under subsection (5).

Suspension of financial delegation

Suspension of financial delegation for mismanagement etc.

117.—(1) Where it appears to the local education authority that the governing body of a school in respect of which financial delegation is required for the current financial year under a scheme—

(a) have been guilty of a substantial or persistent failure to comply with any requirements applicable under the scheme, or

(b) are not managing the appropriation or expenditure of the sum put at their disposal for the purposes of the school in a satisfactory manner,

the authority may suspend the governing body's right to a delegated budget by giving them not less than one month's notice of the suspension.

(2) The notice shall specify the grounds for the proposed suspension, giving particulars—

(a) of any alleged failure on the part of the governing body to comply with any requirements applicable under the scheme; and

(b) of any alleged mismanagement on their part.

(3) A copy of the notice shall be given to the head teacher of the school at the same time as the notice is given to the governing body.

(4) Where the authority have given a notice under subsection (1) to a governing body, they may suspend the governing body's right to a delegated budget before the expiry of the period of notice if it appears to them to be necessary to do so by reason of any gross incompetence or mismanagement on the part of the governing body or other emergency.

(5) If the authority exercise their power under subsection (4), they shall immediately give to the Secretary of State written notification of their action and the reasons for it.

(6) During any period when a governing body's right to a delegated budget is suspended under this section, the authority's duty under section 116(2) shall not apply in relation to that governing body.

Review of suspension

118.—(1) The local education authority concerned shall review before the beginning of every financial year any suspension under section 117 which is for the time being in force.

(2) For the purposes of the review the authority—

(a) shall give the governing body and the head teacher of the school an opportunity of making representations with respect to the suspension, and

(b) shall have regard to any representations made by the governing body or head teacher.

(3) If on the review the authority consider it appropriate to do so, they shall revoke the suspension.

(4) The authority shall give the governing body and the head teacher written notification of their decision on the review.

(5) The revocation of a suspension on a review under this section shall take effect from the beginning of the financial year next following the review.

Appeal against suspension or refusal to revoke it

119.—(1) A governing body may appeal to the Secretary of State against—

(a) the imposition of any suspension under section 117; or

(b) any refusal of a local education authority to revoke any such suspension on a review under section 118.

(2) On an appeal under this section, the Secretary of State—

(a) may allow or reject the appeal; and

(b) shall have regard, in making his determination, to the gravity of the default on the part of the governing body and the likelihood of its continuing or recurring.

Extension of schemes

Application of schemes to maintained special schools

120.—(1) The Secretary of State may by regulations require or authorise schemes to cover maintained special schools.

(2) Sections 107(1), 108 and 110 shall not apply to schools required to be covered by a scheme by virtue of regulations under subsection (1).

(3) Regulations under subsection (1) may require or authorise schemes to include provision for requiring the local education authority concerned to delegate to the governing body of a maintained special school the management of the school's budget share for the year—

(a) in the case of all schools required to be covered by a scheme in any financial year by virtue of the regulations; or

(b) in the case of such schools required to be covered by a scheme in any financial year by virtue of the regulations as the Secretary of State may direct.

(4) The Secretary of State may by regulations—

(a) make in any of the following, namely—

(i) any provisions of this Chapter, and

(ii) sections 136 to 141, Schedule 14 and paragraphs 2 and 18 to 24 of Schedule 19 (which make provision in relation to the staffing of schools with delegated budgets etc.),

such amendments as appear to him to be required in consequence of any provision made in regulations under subsection (1); and

(b) provide that any scheme shall have effect with such modifications as appear to him to be appropriate in consequence of any provision so made.

Information

Publication of schemes

121. A scheme shall be published in such manner as may be prescribed—

(a) on its coming into force, and
(b) on such subsequent occasions as may be prescribed.

Financial statements

122.—(1) This section applies where a local education authority's financial provision for county and voluntary schools is subject to regulation by a scheme.

(2) Before the beginning of each financial year, the authority shall prepare a statement of the financial provision they plan to make in that year for county and voluntary schools maintained by them.

(3) Part I of Schedule 11 has effect in relation to the contents of a statement under subsection (2).

(4) After the end of each financial year, the authority shall prepare a statement containing such information with respect to the following matters as may be prescribed—

(a) the planned financial provision in that year specified in the statement prepared by the authority under subsection (2);
(b) expenditure actually incurred in the year for the purposes of all schools required to be covered by the scheme; and
(c) expenditure actually incurred in the year which was incurred, or is treated by the authority as having been incurred, for the purposes of each such school.

(5) A statement under this section shall be prepared in such form, and published in such manner and at such times, as may be prescribed.

(6) The authority shall furnish—

(a) the governing body of each school required to be covered by the scheme in any financial year, and
(b) the governing bodies of—
    (i) such grant-maintained schools in the authority's area, and
    (ii) such grant-maintained special schools mentioned in section 104(3)(c),

as may be prescribed,

with a copy of each statement prepared by the authority under this section in relation to that year or, in such circumstances as may be prescribed, with such part or parts of it as may be prescribed.

(7) A governing body provided with a statement under subsection (6) shall secure that a copy of it is available for inspection (at all reasonable times and free of charge) at the school.

Certification of statements by Audit Commission

123.—(1) This section applies where a local education authority's financial provision for county and voluntary schools is subject to regulation by a scheme.

(2) The authority shall, if directed to do so by the Secretary of State, require the Audit Commission for Local Authorities and the National Health Service in England and Wales to make arrangements in accordance with section 29(1)(d) of the Local Government Finance Act 1982 for certifying such statement or statements prepared by the authority under section 122 of this Act as may be specified in the directions; and for the purposes of section 29(1)(d) of that Act any statement under section 122 of this Act shall be treated as a return by the authority.

(3) The arrangements made by the Audit Commission in pursuance of subsection (2) shall include arrangements for sending a copy of any such statement or statements as so certified to the Secretary of State.

(4) Directions given under subsection (2) may relate to any local education authority or to local education authorities generally or to any class or description of such authorities.

Financial statements in respect of special schools not covered by statements under section 122

124.—(1) A local education authority shall prepare, in respect of each financial year during the whole or any part of which they maintain one or more relevant special schools, a statement of the financial provision initially planned by them in respect of the year for that school or those schools.

(2) For the purposes of this section a "relevant special school" is any special school other than one in relation to which (by, virtue of any provision made by regulations having effect under section 120) information is required to be included in a statement prepared by the authority in respect of the year under section 122.

(3) Part II of Schedule 11 has effect in relation to the contents of a statement under subsection (1).

(4) After the end of each financial year in respect of which a local education authority are required to prepare a statement under subsection (1), they shall prepare a statement containing such information in respect of—

(a) expenditure actually incurred in the year for the purposes of all the schools required to be covered by the statement under subsection (1), and

(b) expenditure actually incurred in the year which was incurred, or is treated by the authority as having been incurred, for the purposes of each such school,

as may be prescribed.

(5) Where only one school is required to be covered by the statement under subsection (1), the reference in subsection (4)(a) to all the schools is a reference to that school and subsection (4)(b) does not apply.

(6) A statement prepared under this section shall be prepared in such form, and published in such manner and at such times, as may be prescribed.

(7) The authority shall provide the governing body of any school required to be covered by a statement under subsection (1) in respect of a financial year with a copy of each statement prepared by the authority under this section in relation to that year.

(8) A governing body provided with a statement under subsection (7) shall secure that a copy of it is available for inspection (at all reasonable times and free of charge) at the school.

Financial delegation apart from schemes

Required financial delegation apart from schemes

125.—(1) In respect of any period during which a county, voluntary or maintained special school does not have a delegated budget, the local education authority shall make available a sum of money which (subject to subsection (2)) the governing body of the school are to be entitled to spend at their discretion during that period—

(a) on books, equipment and stationery; and

(b) on such other heads of expenditure (if any) as the authority may specify or as may be prescribed.

(2) In spending that sum the governing body shall comply with such reasonable conditions as the authority think fit to impose.

(3) The governing body may, to such extent as they may specify, delegate their powers in relation to that sum to the head teacher.

(4) Before making any regulations for the purposes of subsection (1), the Secretary of State shall consult—

(a) such associations of local authorities as appear to him to be concerned; and

(b) any local authority with whom consultation appears to him to be desirable.

Financial delegation and new schools

Financial delegation and new schools

126. Schedule 12 has effect for the purpose of applying the other provisions of this Chapter in relation to new schools.

CHAPTER VI

CONDUCT AND STAFFING OF COUNTY, VOLUNTARY AND MAINTAINED SPECIAL SCHOOLS

Articles of government

Articles of government

127.—(1) For every county, voluntary and maintained special school there shall be an instrument (known as the articles of government) in accordance with which the school is to be conducted.

(2) The articles of government shall be made by order of the local education authority.

(3) The articles of government—

(a) shall contain such provisions as are required by this Chapter or by any other enactment; and

(b) shall not contain any provision which is inconsistent with any provision made by or under this Act or any other enactment.

(4) The articles of government shall comply with any trust deed relating to the school.

Procedure for making and altering articles of government

128.—(1) Before making an order under section 127, a local education authority shall consult the governing body and the head teacher of the school concerned.

(2) Before making an order under section 127 in respect of a voluntary school, a local education authority shall also—

(a) secure the agreement of the governing body to the terms of the proposed order; and

(b) have regard to the way in which the school has been conducted.

(3) Where the governing body of a county, voluntary or maintained special school make a proposal to the local education authority for the alteration of the provision made by the articles of government for the school, the authority shall consider their proposal.

(4) Where a local education authority—

(a) propose to make an order under section 127 but cannot secure any agreement required by subsection (2), or

(b) refuse, in the case of a voluntary school, to make such an order in response to a proposal of a kind mentioned in subsection (3),

the authority or (as the case may be) the governing body may refer the matter to the Secretary of State.

(5) On a reference to him under subsection (4), the Secretary of State shall give such direction as he thinks fit having regard, in particular, to the status of the school as a controlled, aided or (as the case may be) special agreement school.

(6) Where it appears to the Secretary of State—

(a) that an order, or proposed order, under section 127 is in any respect inconsistent with the provisions of any trust deed relating to the school, and

(b) that it is expedient in the interests of the school that the provisions of the trust deed should be modified for the purpose of removing the inconsistency,

he may by order make such modifications in the trust deed as appear to him to be just and expedient for that purpose.

(7) References in this section to an order, or proposed order, under section 127 are references to an order, or proposed order, under that section embodying or varying the articles of government for a school.

Overriding, and amendment, of articles where school has a delegated budget

129.—(1) During any period when a school has a delegated budget under such a scheme as is mentioned in section 101(1), any provisions of the articles of government of the school which are inconsistent with the operation during that period of any provisions of Chapter V or of the scheme shall be of no effect to the extent of the inconsistency.

(2) If a school's articles of government contain any provisions to which subsection (1) applies ("inconsistent provisions"), the local education authority shall amend the articles so as to include in relation to each inconsistent provision the statement required by subsection (3).

(3) The statement shall specify—

(a) the inconsistent provision,

(b) the provision of Chapter V or of the scheme with the operation of which it is inconsistent (the "overriding provision"), and

(c) the extent of the inconsistency,

and shall indicate that, during any period when the school has a delegated budget, the inconsistent provision is superseded by the overriding provision to the extent of the inconsistency.

(4) Any amendment required by subsection (2) shall be made within the period of five years beginning with the date on which begins the financial year in which the school first has a delegated budget under the scheme.

(5) Any such amendment shall be made by order under section 127; but section 128 shall not apply in relation to an order made under section 127 by virtue of this subsection.

Conduct of schools: general

Governing body to have general responsibility for conduct of school

130. The articles of government for a county, voluntary or maintained special school shall provide for the conduct of the school to be under the direction of the governing body, but subject—

(a) to any provision of the articles conferring specific functions on a person other than the governing body, and

(b) to any provision (other than a provision of the articles) made by or under this Act or any other enactment.

Consultation with governing body not required in urgent cases

131. Regulations may make provision as to the circumstances in which, in any case where—

(a) any provision made by or under Chapter IV or this Chapter requires the governing body of a county, voluntary or maintained special school to be consulted before a particular step is taken by the local education authority or the head teacher, and

(b) the authority or head teacher require to take that step as a matter of urgency but are unable to contact the chairman or vice-chairman of the governing body,

the authority or (as the case may be) the head teacher may proceed without consulting the governing body.

Separate departments of school to be treated as separate schools

132.—(1) Where a county, voluntary or maintained special school is organised in two or more separate departments, each with a head teacher, any provision made by or under this Act which confers functions on or in relation to the head teacher of the school shall have effect as if each department were a separate school.

(2) Subsection (1) does not apply where the school's articles of government provide otherwise.

Staffing of schools without delegated budgets

Staffing of county, controlled, special agreement and maintained special schools without delegated budgets

133.—(1) A county, controlled, special agreement or maintained special school shall have a complement of teaching and non-teaching posts determined by the local education authority.

(2) The complement shall include—

(a) all full-time teaching posts, and

(b) all part-time teaching posts which are to be filled by persons whose only employment with the authority will be at the school.

(3) The complement shall not include any staff employed by the authority solely in connection with either or both of the following—

(a) the provision of meals;

(b) the supervision of pupils at midday.

(4) Schedule 13 has effect in relation to the staffing of county, controlled, special agreement and maintained special schools.

(5) The appointment and dismissal of staff (including teachers) at a county, controlled, special agreement or maintained special school shall be under the control of the local education authority, subject to—

(a) any provision made by the articles of government for the school in accordance with Schedule 13,

(b) section 135 and any provision made by the articles of government in accordance with that section (appointment and dismissal of clerk to governing body),

(c) sections 143 and 144 (appointment and dismissal of teachers of religious education), and

(d) in the case of a school for which there is a temporary governing body, Schedule 19 (conduct and staffing of new schools).

(6) This section is subject to section 136 (staffing of county, controlled and special agreement schools with delegated budgets).

Staffing of aided schools without delegated budgets

134.—(1) In the case of an aided school the functions of the local education authority and of the governing body with respect to—

(a) the appointment of teachers, and

(b) subject to section 145 (dismissal of teachers of religious education), the dismissal of teachers,

shall be regulated by the articles of government.

(2) The articles of government shall make provision—

(a) for the appointment of the teachers by the governing body, and

(b) for enabling the local education authority to determine the number of teachers to be employed.

(3) The articles of government shall make provision for enabling the local education authority—

(a) to prohibit the dismissal of teachers without the authority's consent, except for reasons for which under section 145 the governing body may dismiss a teacher without the authority's consent; and

(b) to require the dismissal of any teacher.

(4) The articles of government may make such provision as may be agreed between the local education authority and the governing body or, in default of such agreement, as may be determined by the Secretary of State, for enabling the authority—

(a) to prohibit the appointment, without the authority's consent, of teachers to be employed for giving secular education; and

(b) to give directions as to the educational qualifications of the teachers to be employed for giving secular education.

(5) The local education authority may give directions to the governing body of an aided school as to the number and conditions of service of persons employed at the school for the purposes of the care and maintenance of the school premises.

(6) Where the trust deed relating to the school provides for a person other than the governing body to be entitled to control the occupation and use of the school premises to any extent, then, if and to the extent that (disregarding any transfer of control agreement under section 151) the use of those premises is or would be under the control of any such person, the reference in subsection (5) to the governing body shall be read as a reference to that person.

(7) This section is subject to section 137 (staffing of aided schools with delegated budgets).

Appointment etc. of clerk to governing body of school other than aided school

135.—(1) The articles of government for a county or maintained special school shall provide for the clerk to the governing body to be appointed by the local education authority in accordance with arrangements determined by them in consultation with the governing body.

(2) The clerk to the governing body of a controlled or special agreement school shall be appointed—

(a) where the articles of government make provision in relation to his appointment, in accordance with that provision, or

(b) where paragraph (a) does not apply by the local education authority in accordance with arrangements determined by them in consultation with the governing body.

(3) Arrangements determined in respect of a school by virtue of subsection (1) or under subsection (2)(b) may be varied by the authority in consultation with the governing body.

(4) The articles of government for a county or maintained special school shall require the local education authority not to dismiss the clerk except in accordance with arrangements determined by them in consultation with the governing body.

(5) The clerk to the governing body of a controlled or special agreement school may not be dismissed except—

(a) where the articles of government make provision in relation to his dismissal, in accordance with that provision, or

(b) where paragraph (a) does not apply, in accordance with arrangements determined by the local education authority in consultation with the governing body.

(6) The articles of government for a county, controlled, special agreement or maintained special school shall require the local education authority to consider any representations made to them by the governing body as to the dismissal of their clerk.

(7) Subsections (1) to (6) are subject to section 136 (staffing of county,

controlled, and special agreement schools with delegated budgets).

(8) The articles of government for a county, controlled, special agreement or maintained special school shall enable the governing body, where the clerk fails to attend a meeting of theirs, to appoint one of their number to act as clerk for the purposes of that meeting (but without prejudice to his position as a governor).

Staffing of schools with delegated budgets

Staffing of county, controlled and special agreement schools with delegated budgets

136.—(1) This section applies to a county, controlled or special agreement school at any time when it has a delegated budget.

(2) None of the following shall apply in relation to the school—

(a) section 133 and Schedule 13,

(b) section 135(1) to (6), and

(c) any provision made by the articles of government for the school in accordance with Schedule 13 or section 135(1) to (6).

(3) Instead Schedule 14 has effect in relation to the staffing of the school, subject, however, to the provisions of sections 143 and 144 (appointment and dismissal of teachers of religious education).

Staffing of aided schools with delegated budgets

137.—(1) This section applies to an aided school at any time when it has a delegated budget.

(2) None of the following shall apply in relation to the school—

(a) any provision of the articles of government for the school conferring any functions on a local education authority with respect to the number, appointment or dismissal of teachers or other staff to be employed at the school (including any such provision which is required by section 134), and

(b) section 134(5).

(3) If, apart from any provision of the articles of government excluded by subsection (2)(a) they would not otherwise have power to do so, the governing body may appoint, suspend and dismiss staff as they think fit.

(4) Subsection (3) has effect subject to any provision of the articles of government (other than one excluded by subsection (2)(a)).

(5) The governing body shall, on dismissing any member of the staff of the school employed by them, notify the local education authority in writing of the reasons for the dismissal.

(6) Paragraphs 23 to 28 of Schedule 14 apply in relation to the dismissal or withdrawal from the school of any member of the staff who is employed by the local education authority as they apply in relation to the dismissal or withdrawal from a county, controlled or special agreement school which has a delegated budget of a person employed to work at the school.

Staffing of aided schools with delegated budgets: advisory rights of chief education officer

138.—(1) Subsection (2) applies if, in the case of an aided school which has a delegated budget—

(a) the governing body of the school have agreed with the local education authority to accord to the authority's chief education officer advisory rights in relation to the appointment or dismissal of teachers at the school, or

(b) in default of such agreement, the Secretary of State has determined that it would be appropriate that such advisory rights should be accorded to the chief education officer.

(2) During any period when the agreement or determination under subsection (1) is effective, the chief education officer, or an officer of the authority nominated by him, shall be entitled to attend all relevant proceedings of the governing body for the purpose of giving advice to the governing body.

For this purpose "relevant proceedings" means proceedings (including interviews) relating to any action to which the advisory rights accorded to the chief education officer extend.

(3) Advisory rights accorded by an agreement or determination under subsection (1) may relate to the appointment or dismissal, or both to the appointment and to the dismissal, either—

(a) of head teachers and deputy head teachers alone, or

(b) of all teachers at the school.

(4) The agreement of a governing body for the purposes of subsection (1)(a) must be given in writing and may only be withdrawn by notice in writing to the local education authority.

(5) A determination by the Secretary of State for the purposes of subsection (1)(b) may be withdrawn at any time (without prejudice to a further determination for those purposes).

Staffing of schools with delegated budgets: payments in respect of dismissal, etc.

139.—(1) This section applies to a county or voluntary school at any time when it has a delegated budget.

(2) It shall be for the governing body to determine—

(a) whether any payment should be made by the local education authority in respect of the dismissal, or for the purpose of securing the resignation, of any member of the staff of the school, and

(b) the amount of any such payment.

(3) Subsection (2) does not, however, apply in relation to a payment which the authority are required to make—

(a) by virtue of any contract other than one made in contemplation of the impending dismissal or resignation of the member of staff concerned, or

(b) under any statutory provision.

(4) The local education authority—

(a) shall take such steps as may be required for giving effect to any determination of the governing body under subsection (2), and

(b) shall not make, or agree to make, a payment in relation to which that subsection applies except in accordance with such a determination.

(5) Costs incurred by the local education authority in respect of the dismissal or premature retirement, or for the purpose of securing the resignation, of any member of the staff of the school shall not be met from the school's budget share for any financial year except in so far as the authority have good reason for deducting those costs, or any part of those costs, from that share.

(6) The fact that the authority have a policy precluding dismissal of their employees by reason of redundancy is not to be regarded as a good reason for the purposes of subsection (5).

(7) In subsection (6) the reference to dismissal by reason of redundancy shall be read in accordance with section 139 of the Employment Rights Act 1996.

Staffing for non-school activities in community schools

140.—(1) This section applies to a county or voluntary school which has a delegated budget and is a community school.

(2) For the purposes of this section a school is a "community school" if—

(a) activities other than school activities ("non-school activities") are carried on on the school premises, and

(b) all non-school activities which are so carried on are carried on under the management or control of the school's governing body.

(3) A scheme such as is mentioned in section 101(1) may provide for applying sections 136(2), 137(6) and 139 and Schedule 14 in relation to persons employed to work—

(a) partly for the purposes of school activities and partly for the purposes of non-school activities carried on on the premises of a school to which this section applies, or

(b) solely for the purposes of non-school activities so carried on,

as if all activities so carried on were school activities.

Amendment of articles of government relating to staffing

141.—(1) Within the period of five years beginning with the date on which begins the financial year in which a county or voluntary school first has a delegated budget under a scheme, the local education authority shall amend the school's articles of government in accordance with this section.

(2) If the school is a county, controlled or special agreement school, the articles of government shall be amended so as to include a statement—

(a) specifying the provisions made by the articles in accordance with Schedule 13 or section 135(1) to (6), and

(b) indicating that those provisions are superseded by section 136 and Schedule 14 during any period when the school has a delegated budget.

(3) If the school is an aided school the articles of government shall be amended so as to include a statement—

(a) specifying the provisions of the articles which are within section 137(2)(a), and

(b) indicating that those provisions are superseded by sections 137 and 138 during any period when the school has a delegated budget.

(4) An amendment under this section shall be made by order under section 127; but section 128 shall not apply in relation to an order made under section 127 by virtue of this section.

Application of provisions to maintained special schools

142. Section 120(4) confers power on the Secretary of State to make in any of the following, namely—

(a) sections 136 to 141,

(b) Schedule 14, and

(c) paragraphs 2 and 18 to 24 of Schedule 19,

amendments appearing to him to be required in consequence of any provision made in regulations under section 120(1) (application of schemes to maintained special schools).

Appointment and dismissal of teachers of religious education

Appointment etc. of reserved teachers in controlled schools

143.—(1) Where the number of the teaching staff of a controlled school is more than two, the teaching staff shall include persons who—

(a) are selected for their fitness and competence to give such religious education as is required in accordance with arrangements under section 377(2) (arrangements for religious education in accordance with the school's trust deed or with the practice observed before the school became a controlled school), and

(b) are specifically appointed to do so.

(2) In this Chapter "reserved teacher", in relation to a controlled school, means a person employed at the school in pursuance of subsection (1).

(3) The number of reserved teachers in a controlled school shall not exceed one-fifth of the number of the teaching staff, including the head teacher (and for this purpose, where the number of the teaching staff is not a multiple of five, it shall be treated as if it were the next higher multiple of five).

(4) The head teacher of a controlled school shall not, while holding the post of head teacher of such a school, be a reserved teacher.

(5) Where the local education authority propose to appoint a person to be a reserved teacher in a controlled school, the authority—

(a) shall consult the foundation governors, and

(b) shall not so appoint that person unless the foundation governors are satisfied as to his fitness and competence to give such religious education as is mentioned in subsection (1)(a).

(6) If the foundation governors of a controlled school consider that a reserved teacher has failed to give such religious education efficiently and suitably, they may require the local education authority to dismiss him from employment as a reserved teacher in the school.

(7) In subsection (5) "foundation governor" includes a temporary foundation governor.

Appointment etc. of reserved teachers in special agreement schools

144.—(1) In this Chapter "reserved teacher", in relation to a special agreement school, means a person who in pursuance of provision made in the special agreement is employed to give religious education—

(a) in accordance with any provisions of the trust deed relating to the school, or

(b) (where provision for that purpose is not made by any such deed) in accordance with the practice observed in the school before it became a voluntary school.

(2) Where the special agreement made with respect to a special agreement school provides for the employment of reserved teachers and the local education authority propose to appoint a person to be a reserved teacher in the school, the authority—

(a) shall consult the foundation governors, and

(b) shall not appoint that person unless the foundation governors are satisfied as to his fitness and competence to give such religious education as is mentioned in subsection (1).

(3) If the foundation governors of a special agreement school consider that a reserved teacher has failed to give such religious education efficiently and suitably, they may require the local education authority to dismiss him from employment as a reserved teacher in the school.

(4) In subsection (2) "foundation governor" includes a temporary foundation governor.

Dismissal of teachers of religious education in aided schools

145. If a teacher appointed to give religious education in an aided school (other than education in accordance with an agreed syllabus) fails to give such education efficiently and suitably, he may be dismissed on that ground by the governing body without the consent of the local education authority.

Religious opinions of staff etc.

Religious opinions of staff etc.

146.—(1) No person shall be disqualified by reason of his religious opinions, or of his attending or omitting to attend religious worship—

(a) from being a teacher in a county school or from being a teacher (other than a reserved teacher) in a controlled or special agreement school, or

(b) from being employed (otherwise than as a teacher) for the purposes of a county or voluntary school.

(2) No teacher in a county school, and no teacher (other than a reserved teacher) in a controlled or special agreement school, shall be required to give religious education.

(3) No teacher in a county school, and no teacher (other than a reserved teacher) in a controlled or special agreement school, shall receive any less emolument or be deprived of, or disqualified for, any promotion or other advantage—

(a) by reason of the fact that he does or does not give religious education, or

(b) by reason of his religious opinions or of his attending or omitting to attend religious worship.

(4) No teacher in an aided school, and no reserved teacher in a controlled or special agreement school, shall receive any less emolument or be deprived of, or disqualified for, any promotion or other advantage—

(a) by reason of the fact that he gives religious education, or

(b) by reason of his religious opinions or of his attending religious worship.

School terms, holidays and sessions

Responsibility for determining dates of terms and holidays and times of sessions

147.—(1) In the case of a county, controlled or maintained special school—

(a) the articles of government shall require the local education authority to determine the dates when the school terms and holidays are to begin and end; and

(b) the governing body shall determine the times of the school sessions.

(2) In the case of an aided or a special agreement school the articles of government shall require the governing body to determine—

(a) the dates and times when the school terms and holidays are to begin and end, and

(b) the times of the school sessions.

(3) In this section and section 148 "the times of the school sessions" means the times at which each of the school sessions (or, if there is only one, the school session) is to begin and end on any day.

Procedure for changing times of sessions at a county, controlled or maintained special school

148.—(1) Where the governing body of a county, controlled or maintained special school propose to make any change in the times of the school sessions, they shall—

(a) before taking any of the actions mentioned in paragraphs (b) to (h), consult the local education authority and the head teacher;

(b) prepare a statement—

(i) indicating that they propose to make a change in those times,

(ii) specifying the proposed change and when they propose that it should take effect,

(iii) drawing attention to any comment on the proposal included as an annex to the statement by virtue of paragraph (c) and including such response to the comment as they may consider appropriate, and

(iv) giving details of the date, time and place of the meeting which they are required to hold by virtue of paragraph (f);

(c) if so required by the local education authority, include as an annex to that statement such written comment on the proposal as the authority may provide for that purpose;

(d) produce that statement and any annex in such language or languages (in addition to English), if any, as they consider appropriate or as the local education authority may direct;

(e) take such steps as are reasonably practicable to secure—

(i) that the parents of all registered pupils at the school are given (free of charge) a copy of the statement and any annex not less than two weeks before the meeting which the governing body are required to hold by virtue of paragraph (f) and

(ii) that copies of the statement and any annex are available for inspection (at all reasonable times and free of charge) at the school during the two-week period immediately preceding that meeting;

(f) provide an opportunity for discussion of the proposal at a meeting which is open to—

(i) all parents of registered pupils at the school,

(ii) the head teacher, and

(iii) such other persons as the governing body may invite;

(g) consider any comments made at the meeting on the proposal before determining whether any change in those times should be made and (if so) whether the proposal should be implemented with or without any modification; and

(h) not less than three months before any change in those times is to take effect—

(i) inform the local education authority of the change and of when it is to take effect, and

(ii) take such steps as are reasonably practicable to secure that the parents of all registered pupils at the school are so informed.

(2) No change in the times of a school session shall be made under this section so as to take effect otherwise than at the beginning of a school year.

(3) The proceedings at any meeting required to be held by virtue of subsection (1)(f) shall be under the control of the governing body.

(4) Any question whether any person is to be treated for the purposes of this section as the parent of a registered pupil at the school shall be determined by the local education authority.

(5) Section 147(3) applies for the purposes of this section.

Control of school premises

County and maintained special schools: control of use of premises outside school hours

149.—(1) The articles of government for every county and maintained special school shall provide—

(a) for the use of the school premises outside school hours to be under the control of the governing body except to the extent provided by any transfer of control agreement into which they may enter by virtue of paragraph (c);

(b) for the governing body in exercising control of the use of the school premises outside school hours—

(i) to comply with any directions given to them by the local education authority by virtue of this sub-paragraph; and

(ii) to have regard to the desirability of the premises being made available for community use;

(c) for the governing body to have power to enter into a transfer of control agreement if their purpose, or one of their purposes, in doing so is to promote community use of the school premises outside school hours; and

(d) for the governing body, where they enter into a transfer of control agreement, to secure so far as reasonably practicable that the controlling body exercises control in accordance with any directions given to the governing body by virtue of paragraph (b)(i).

(2) A transfer of control agreement shall be taken to include the following terms, namely—

(a) that the governing body shall notify the controlling body of any directions given to the governing body by virtue of subsection (1)(b)(i);

(b) that the controlling body, in exercising control of the use of any premises subject to the agreement—

(i) shall do so in accordance with any directions from time to time notified to that body in pursuance of paragraph (a) above; and

(ii) shall have regard to the desirability of the premises being made available for community use outside school hours; and

(c) that, if reasonable notice is given in writing by the governing body to the controlling body that such of the premises subject to the agreement as may be specified in the notice are reasonably required for use by or in connection with the school at such times as may be so specified, then—

(i) the use of the specified premises at those times shall be under the control of the governing body, and

(ii) accordingly, those premises may be used at those times by or in connection with the school for such purposes as may be specified in the notice,

even though their use at those times would, apart from this paragraph, be under the control of the controlling body.

(3) Subsection (4) applies where a transfer of control agreement makes express provision for the use of any school premises which are subject to the agreement to be occasionally under the control of the governing body, instead of the controlling body, in such circumstances, at such times or for such purposes as may be provided by or under the agreement.

(4) In such a case paragraph (c) of subsection (2) shall not have effect in relation to the transfer of control agreement if, at the time of entering into it, the governing body were of the opinion that the express provision would be more favourable to the interests of the school than the term that would otherwise be included by virtue of that paragraph.

(5) In this section—

"community use" means the use of school premises (when not required by or in connection with the school) by members of the local community;

"the controlling body" means the body or person (other than the governing body) which has control of the use of the whole or any part of the school premises under the transfer of control agreement in question;

"school hours" means any time during a school session or during a break between sessions on the same day, and "outside school hours" shall be construed accordingly;

"school session", in relation to any school, means a school session beginning and ending at such times as may from time to time be determined for that school in accordance with sections 147 and 148; and

"transfer of control agreement" means an agreement which (subject to subsection (2) above) provides for the use of so much of the school premises as may be specified in the agreement to be under the control, at such times outside school hours as may be so specified, of such body or person as may be so specified.

Voluntary schools: control of use of premises

150.—(1) The occupation and use of the premises of a voluntary school shall be under the control of the governing body, subject to—

(a) any directions given by the local education authority under subsection (2) (in the case of a controlled school) or section 152(3) (in the case of an aided or special agreement school);

(b) any transfer of control agreement entered into by the governing body under section 151; and

(c) any requirements of an enactment other than this Act or regulations made under it.

(2) The local education authority may give such directions as to the occupation and use of the premises of a controlled school as they think fit, subject to section 152(1) and (2).

(3) Where the trust deed for a voluntary school provides for any person other than the governing body to be entitled to control the occupation and use of the school premises to any extent, then, if and to the extent that (disregarding any transfer of control agreement made under section 151) the use of those premises is or would be under the control of such a person—

(a) this section, and

(b) sections 151 and 152,

shall have effect in relation to the school with the substitution of references to that person for references to the governing body.

Voluntary schools: transfer of control agreements

151.—(1) Subject to subsection (2), the governing body of any voluntary school shall have power to enter into a transfer of control agreement with any body or person if their purpose, or one of their purposes, in doing so is to promote community use of the whole or any part of the school premises; and—

(a) they may do so even though the trust deed for the school would, apart from this subsection, expressly or impliedly preclude them from entering into such an agreement with that body or person or from conferring control on the controlling body in question; but

(b) they shall not enter into a transfer of control agreement unless the use to which the premises may be put under the agreement is in all other respects in conformity with any such requirements, prohibitions or restrictions imposed by the trust deed as would apply if control were being exercised by the governing body.

(2) The governing body shall not enter into any transfer of control agreement which makes or includes provision for the use of the whole or any part of the school premises during school hours unless they have first obtained the local education authority's consent to the agreement in so far as it makes such provision.

(3) A transfer of control agreement shall be taken to include the following terms, namely—

(a) that the governing body shall notify the controlling body of—

(i) any directions given to the governing body under section 150(2) (in the case of a controlled school) or section 152(3) (in the case of an aided or special agreement school); and

(ii) any determination made by the foundation governors under section 152(2) (in the case of a controlled school);

(b) that the controlling body, in exercising control of the use of any premises subject to the agreement—

(i) shall do so in accordance with any directions or determinations from time to time notified to that body in pursuance of paragraph (a); and

(ii) shall have regard to the desirability of the premises being made available for community use; and

(c) that, if reasonable notice is given in writing by the governing body to the controlling body that such of the premises subject to the agreement as may be specified in the notice are reasonably required for use by or in connection with the school at such times as may be so specified, then—

(i) the use of the specified premises at those times shall be under the control of the governing body, and

(ii) accordingly, those premises may be used at those times by or in connection with the school for such purposes as may be specified in the notice,

even though their use at those times would, apart from this paragraph, be under the control of the controlling body.

(4) Subsection (5) applies where a transfer of control agreement makes express provision for the use of any school premises which are subject to the agreement to be occasionally under the control of the governing body, instead of the controlling body, in such circumstances, at such times or for such purposes as may be provided by or under the agreement.

(5) In such a case paragraph (c) of subsection (3) shall not have effect in relation to the transfer of control agreement if, at the time of entering into it, the governing body were of the opinion that the express provision would be more favourable to the interests of the school than the term that would otherwise be included by virtue of that paragraph.

(6) Where the governing body enter into a transfer of control agreement, they shall so far as reasonably practicable secure that the controlling body exercises control in accordance with any such directions or determinations as are notified to that body in pursuance of subsection (3)(a).

(7) In this section—

"community use" means the use of school premises (when not required by or in connection with the school) by members of the local community;

"the controlling body" means the body or person (other than the governing body) which has control of the use of the whole or any part of the school premises under the transfer of control agreement in question;

"school hours" means any time during a school session or during a break between sessions on the same day;

"school session", in relation to any school, means a school session beginning and ending at such times as may from time to time be determined for that school in accordance with sections 147 and 148; and

"transfer of control agreement" means an agreement which (subject to subsection (3) above) provides for the use of so much of the school premises as may be specified in the agreement to be under the control, at such times as may be so specified, of such body or person as may be so specified.

(8) Section 150(3) applies for the purposes of this section.

Voluntary schools: use of premises outside school hours

152.—(1) The governing body may determine the use to which the premises of a controlled school (or any part of them) are put on Saturdays when not required—

(a) for the purposes of the school, or

(b) for any purpose connected with education or with the welfare of the young for which the local education authority desire to provide accommodation on the premises (or on the part in question).

(2) The foundation governors may determine the use to which the premises of a controlled school (or any part of them) are put on Sundays.

(3) If the local education authority—

(a) desire to provide accommodation for any purpose connected with education or with the welfare of the young, and

(b) are satisfied that there is no suitable alternative accommodation in their area for that purpose,

they may direct the governing body of an aided or special agreement school to provide accommodation free of charge for that purpose on the school premises (or any part of them) on any weekday when not needed for the purposes of the school.

(4) The local education authority shall not exercise their power under subsection (3) so as to direct the governing body to provide accommodation on more than three days in any week.

(5) Section 150(3) applies for the purposes of this section.

Instruction or training outside school premises

Instruction or training outside school premises

153. The articles of government for a county, voluntary or maintained special school shall enable the governing body to require pupils in attendance at the school to attend at any place outside the school premises for the purpose of receiving any instruction or training included in the secular curriculum for the school.

Discipline: general

Responsibility of governing body and head teacher for discipline

154.—(1) The articles of government for a county, voluntary or maintained special school shall make provision for the matters set out in subsections (2) to (6).

(2) The standard of behaviour which is to be regarded as acceptable at the school shall be determined by the head teacher, so far as it is not determined by the governing body.

(3) The head teacher shall determine measures (which may include the making of rules and provision for enforcing them) to be taken with a view to—

(a) promoting, among pupils, self-discipline and proper regard for authority,

(b) encouraging good behaviour and respect for others on the part of pupils,

(c) securing that the standard of behaviour of pupils is acceptable, and

(d) otherwise regulating the conduct of pupils.

(4) The head teacher shall, in determining any such measures—

(a) act in accordance with any written statement of general principles provided for him by the governing body, and

(b) have regard to any guidance that they may offer in relation to particular matters.

(5) The head teacher shall make any such measures generally known within the school.

(6) The governing body and the head teacher shall, before any such measures are determined, consult the local education authority on any matter arising from the proposed measures which can reasonably be expected—

(a) to lead to increased expenditure by the authority, or

(b) to affect the responsibilities of the authority as an employer.

LEA's reserve power to prevent a breakdown of discipline

155.—(1) The local education authority may, in the circumstances mentioned in subsection (3), take such steps in relation to a county, controlled or maintained special school as they consider are required to prevent the breakdown, or continuing breakdown, of discipline at the school.

(2) The governing body and the head teacher of an aided or a special agreement school shall, in the circumstances mentioned in subsection (3), consider any representations made to them by the local education authority.

(3) The circumstances are that—

(a) in the opinion of the authority—

(i) the behaviour of registered pupils at the school, or

(ii) any action taken by such pupils or their parents,

is such that the education of any registered pupils at the school is (or is likely in the immediate future to become) severely prejudiced; and

(b) the governing body have been informed in writing of the authority's opinion.

(4) Steps taken by a local education authority under subsection (1) may include the giving of any direction to the governing body or head teacher.

Power of head teacher to exclude pupils

156.—(1) The articles of government for a county, voluntary or maintained special school shall provide for the power to exclude a pupil from the school (whether by suspension, expulsion or otherwise) to be exercisable only by the head teacher.

(2) The head teacher of any such school may not—

(a) so exercise the power to exclude a pupil from the school for one or more fixed periods that the pupil is so excluded for more than 15 school days in any one term, or

(b) exclude a pupil from the school for an indefinite period;

but this subsection is without prejudice to the power to exclude a pupil from the school permanently.

(3) Subsection (2) has effect, in the case of a school having articles of government, despite anything in the articles.

Exclusion of pupils: duty to inform parents etc.

157.—(1) The head teacher of a county, voluntary or maintained special school shall have the following duties in relation to the exclusion of pupils from the school.

(2) Where the head teacher excludes any pupil, the head teacher shall (without delay) take reasonable steps to inform the relevant person—

(a) of the period of the exclusion (or, if the pupil is being permanently excluded, that he is being so excluded); and

(b) of the reasons for the exclusion; and

(c) that the relevant person may make representations about the exclusion to the governing body and the local education authority.

(3) Where the head teacher excludes any pupil in circumstances in which the pupil would, as a result of the exclusion—

(a) be excluded from the school for a total of more than five school days in any one term, or

(b) lose an opportunity to take any public examination,

the head teacher shall (without delay) inform the local education authority and the governing body of the period of the exclusion (or, if the pupil is being permanently excluded, that he is being so excluded) and of the reasons for it.

(4) Where the head teacher decides that any exclusion of a pupil for a fixed period should be made permanent, he shall (without delay)—

(a) inform the local education authority and the governing body of his decision and of the reasons for it, and

(b) take reasonable steps to inform the relevant person—

(i) of his decision and of the reasons for it, and

(ii) that that person may make representations about the

decision to the governing body and the local education authority.

(5) In this section "the relevant person" means—

(a) in relation to a pupil under the age of 18, a parent of his;

(b) in relation to a pupil who has attained that age, the pupil himself.

Reinstatement of excluded pupils

158. Schedule 15 has effect in relation to the reinstatement of pupils excluded from county, voluntary or maintained special schools.

Appeals against exclusion or reinstatement of pupils

159.—(1) A local education authority shall make arrangements—

(a) for enabling the relevant person to appeal against any decision not to reinstate a registered pupil who has been permanently excluded from a county, controlled or special school maintained by the authority, and

(b) for enabling the governing body of the school to appeal against any direction for the reinstatement of any such pupil which has been given to the head teacher of the school by the authority.

(2) The governing body of an aided or a special agreement school shall make arrangements for enabling the relevant person to appeal against any decision not to reinstate a registered pupil who has been permanently excluded from the school.

(3) Joint arrangements may be made under subsection (2) by the governing bodies of two or more aided or special agreement schools maintained by the same local education authority.

(4) Schedule 16 has effect in relation to the making and hearing of appeals pursuant to arrangements made under subsection (1) or (2); and in subsections (5) and (6) "appeal committee" means an appeal committee constituted in accordance with Part I of Schedule 33 (school admission appeals), as it applies in accordance with paragraph 4 of Schedule 16.

(5) The decision of an appeal committee on an appeal pursuant to arrangements made under subsection (1) or (2) shall be binding on the persons concerned.

(6) Where on such an appeal the appeal committee determines that the pupil in question should be reinstated, the committee shall either direct that he is to be reinstated immediately or direct that he is to be reinstated by a date specified in the direction.

(7) In this section "the relevant person" means—

(a) in relation to a pupil who is under the age of 18, a parent of his;

(b) in relation to a pupil who has attained that age, the pupil himself.

Additional provision for appeals against exclusion of pupils

160.—(1) Where the articles of government for a county, voluntary or maintained special school provide—

(a) for the parents of an excluded pupil to have the right to appeal against his exclusion to a person specified by the articles, and

(b) for the procedure to be followed on such an appeal,

any decision on such an appeal that the pupil should be reinstated, or that he should be reinstated earlier than would otherwise be the case, shall be binding on the head teacher.

(2) In subsection (1) "excluded pupil" means a pupil who is excluded from the school in circumstances in which no right of appeal is given by virtue of section 159.

Reports, meetings and information

Governors' annual reports

161.—(1) The articles of government for a county, voluntary or maintained special school shall require the governing body to prepare once in every school year a report (referred to in this Chapter as "the governors' report") containing—

(a) a summary of the steps taken by the governing body in the discharge of their functions during the period since their last governors' report, and

(b) such other information as the articles may require.

(2) Schedule 17 has effect in relation to governors' reports.

(3) The articles of government shall—

(a) enable the governing body to produce the governors' report in such language or languages (in addition to English) as they consider appropriate, and

(b) require them to produce it in such language or languages (in addition to English and any other language in which they propose to produce it) as the local education authority may direct.

(4) The articles of government shall require the governing body to take such steps as are reasonably practicable to secure—

(a) that the parents of all registered pupils at the school and all persons employed at the school are given (free of charge) a copy of the governors' report;

(b) that copies of the report are available for inspection (at all reasonable times and free of charge) at the school; and

(c) that, where (by virtue of section 162) there is an obligation on the governing body to hold an annual parents' meeting, copies of the report to be considered at that meeting are given to parents not less than two weeks before that meeting.

Annual parents' meetings

162.—(1) Subject to section 163 (special schools in hospitals and boarding schools), the articles of government for a county, voluntary or maintained special school shall require the governing body to hold a meeting once in every school year (referred to in this Chapter as an "annual parents' meeting") which is open to—

(a) all parents of registered pupils at the school;

(b) the head teacher; and

(c) such other persons as the governing body may invite.

(2) The purpose of the meeting shall be to provide an opportunity for discussion of—

(a) the governors' report; and

(b) the discharge by the governing body, the head teacher and the local education authority of their functions in relation to the school.

(3) Schedule 18 has effect in relation to annual parents' meetings.

No annual parents' meeting required in case of certain special and boarding schools

163.—(1) The articles of government for a maintained special school which is established in a hospital shall provide that, where the governing body are of the opinion that it would be impracticable to hold an annual parents' meeting in a particular school year, they may refrain from holding such a meeting in that year.

(2) Where, in the case of a county, voluntary school or maintained special school (other than a special school established in a hospital), the proportion of registered pupils at the school who are boarders is, or is likely to be, at least 50 per cent., the articles of government for the school shall provide that, where—

(a) the governing body are of the opinion that it would be impracticable to hold an annual parents' meeting in a particular school year, and

(b) at least 50 per cent. of the registered pupils at the school are boarders at the time when they form that opinion,

they may refrain from holding such a meeting in that year.

Governors' reports and annual parents' meetings for grouped schools

164.—(1) This section applies where two or more schools are grouped under section 89.

(2) In discharging their duty (by virtue of section 161) to prepare governors' reports, the governing body for the group shall prepare separate reports in relation to each of the schools within the group, except that if they decide to hold a joint annual parents' meeting under subsection (4) they may prepare a single report covering all the schools within the group.

(3) If the governing body prepare a single report covering all the schools within the group, they shall secure that any matters which they propose to report on and which are likely to be mainly of interest to the parents of registered pupils at a particular school within the group are treated separately in the report.

(4) In discharging their duty (by virtue of section 162) to hold an annual parents' meeting for any grouped school, the governing body may, if they think fit, hold a joint annual parents' meeting for all of the schools within the group.

(5) Where—

(a) a joint annual parents' meeting is held, and

(b) the governing body have prepared a separate governors' report in relation to each of the schools within the group,

the governing body shall, when discharging the duty imposed on them by virtue of section 161(4), attach to the report prepared in relation to a particular school within the group copies of the reports prepared for each of the other schools within it.

(6) Where at a joint annual parents' meeting the question is put on any proposed resolution which concerns one or more, but not all, of the schools within the group—

(a) only parents of registered pupils at the school or schools which the proposed resolution concerns may vote on the question; and

(b) the registered pupils at the other schools shall be disregarded for the purposes of any provision made by virtue of paragraph 2 of Schedule 18 (resolution may be passed by simple majority where required number of parents of registered pupils present) as it applies in relation to the proposed resolution.

(7) Where at a joint annual parents' meeting there is any disagreement as to which schools within the group a proposed resolution concerns, the matter shall be decided by the chairman of the governing body.

Provision of information by governing body and head teacher

165.—(1) The articles of government for a county, voluntary or maintained special school shall provide—

(a) for the governing body to provide the local education authority with such reports in connection with the discharge of their functions as the authority may require (either on a regular basis or from time to time); and

(b) for the head teacher to provide the governing body or (as the case may be) the local education authority with such reports in connection with the discharge of his functions as the governing body or the authority may so require.

(2) The articles of government for an aided school shall provide—

(a) for the local education authority to notify the governing body of any requirement of a kind mentioned in subsection (1)(b) which is imposed by them on the head teacher; and

(b) for the head teacher to provide the governing body with a copy of any report which he makes in complying with such a requirement.

New schools

Conduct and staffing of new schools

166. Schedule 19 has effect in relation to the conduct and staffing of new schools.

CHAPTER VII

DISCONTINUANCE OF LOCAL EDUCATION AUTHORITY SCHOOLS

Procedure for discontinuance of county, voluntary or maintained nursery school by local education authority

Proposals for discontinuance of a county, voluntary or nursery school

167.—(1) Where a local education authority intend to cease to maintain—

(a) a county school,

(b) a voluntary school (except in accordance with section 173(7)), or

(c) a nursery school,

then (subject to subsection (6)) they shall publish proposals for that purpose in such manner as may be required by regulations and submit a copy of the published proposals to the Secretary of State.

(2) Proposals published under this section—

(a) shall include particulars of the time or times at which it is intended to implement the proposals; and

(b) shall be accompanied by a statement of the effect of section 168.

(3) Before formulating any such proposals in respect of a county or voluntary school, a local education authority shall consult the school's governing body.

(4) Before publishing any proposals under this section the local education authority shall consult such persons as appear to them to be appropriate; and in discharging their duty under this subsection the authority shall have regard to any guidance given from time to time by the Secretary of State.

(5) Before publishing any proposals under subsection (1)(a) or (b) which (if implemented) would affect the facilities for full-time education suitable to the requirements of persons over compulsory school age who have not attained the age of 19, the local education authority shall consult the appropriate further education funding council.

(6) No proposals shall be published under this section in respect of a school in respect of which proposals for acquisition of grant-maintained status have been approved under section 194.

Objections to proposals

168.—(1) Objections to any proposals published by a local education authority under section 167 may be submitted to the authority by any of the following—

(a) any ten or more local government electors for the authority's area,

(b) the governing body of any school affected by the proposals,

(c) the appropriate further education funding council (if the proposals affect the provision of education to which section 2(1) of the Further and Higher Education Act 1992 applies), and

(d) any other local education authority concerned.

(2) Objections may be so submitted within the period of two months after the first publication of the proposals.

(3) Where—

(a) an order under section 27 applies to the area of a local education authority, and

(b) the authority publish proposals under section 167 which affect the provision of relevant education in that area,

the funding authority shall be included among the persons who may submit objections under subsection (1) to the proposals.

(4) Within one month after the end of the period mentioned in subsection (2), the local education authority by whom the proposals were published shall transmit to the Secretary of State copies of all objections made (and not withdrawn in writing) in that period, together with the authority s observations on them.

(5) For the purposes of this section proposals under section 167 shall be taken to have been first published—

(a) on the day on which the requirements of regulations with respect to the publication of the proposals are satisfied; or

(b) where different such requirements are satisfied on different days, on the last of those days.

(6) Where any such requirement imposes a continuing obligation with respect to the publication of any proposals, the requirement shall for the purposes of subsection (5) be taken to be satisfied on the first day in respect of which it is satisfied.

Approval or rejection by Secretary of State of proposals under section 167

169.—(1) Proposals published by a local education authority under section 167 require the approval of the Secretary of State if subsection (2), (3) or (4) applies.

(2) This subsection applies if the proposals are for ceasing to maintain a voluntary school.

(3) This subsection applies if either—

(a) the Secretary of State, within the period of two months after the submission to him of the published proposals, gives notice to the authority that the proposals require his approval, or

(b) objections have been made under section 168 and any of them have not been withdrawn in writing within the period specified in section 168(2).

(4) This subsection applies if either—

(a) the proposals are first published after proposals for acquisition of grant-maintained status for the school have been published under section 193 but before those proposals are withdrawn or determined, or

(b) after the proposals have first been published but before they are withdrawn or determined, proposals for acquisition of grant-maintained status for the school are published under section 193;

and references in this subsection to proposals being first published shall be construed in accordance with section 168(5) and (6).

(5) Where any proposals require the approval of the Secretary of State under this section, he may (subject to subsection (6))—

(a) reject them,

(b) approve them without modification, or

(c) after consulting the local education authority, approve them with such modifications as he thinks desirable.

(6) In a case where subsection (4) applies, the Secretary of State—

(a) shall consider both sets of proposals together, but

(b) shall not determine the proposals published under section 167 until he has made his determination with respect to the proposals published under section 193,

and, if he approves the proposals published under section 193, he shall reject the proposals published under section 167.

Determination by local education authority whether to implement proposals

170.—(1) Where any proposals published by a local education authority under section 167 do not require the approval of the Secretary of State under section 169, the authority shall determine whether they should be implemented.

(2) The determination must be made not later than four months after the submission of the proposals to the Secretary of State under section 167.

(3) A local education authority shall notify the Secretary of State of any determination made by them under this section.

Duty to implement proposals

171.—(1) Subject to subsection (2), a local education authority shall implement any proposals of theirs—

(a) which have been approved by the Secretary of State under section 169, or

(b) which they have determined under section 170 to implement.

(2) The Secretary of State may, at the request of a local education authority, modify any proposals which the authority are required to implement by virtue of this section.

Restriction on taking steps before sections 167 and 169 have been complied with

172.—(1) Subject to subsection (2), a local education authority shall not—

(a) cease to maintain a county school, a voluntary school (except in accordance with section 173(7)) or a nursery school, or

(b) undertake to do anything towards that end,

until the requirements of section 167 have been complied with and any approval necessary under section 169 has been given.

(2) The Secretary of State may in any case allow such steps to be taken pending compliance with any such requirements and the giving of any such approval as he considers reasonable in the circumstances.

Discontinuance of voluntary school by governing body

Discontinuance of a voluntary school by its governing body

173.—(1) The governing body of a voluntary school shall not discontinue the school unless they have served on the Secretary of State and the local education authority at least two years' notice of their intention to do so.

(2) If expenditure has been incurred on the school premises (otherwise than in connection with repairs)—

(a) by the Secretary of State,

(b) by any local education authority, or

(c) by an authority which was a local education authority within the meaning of any enactment repealed by the Education Act 1944 or an earlier Act,

no notice may be served without leave of the Secretary of State.

(3) If the Secretary of State gives such leave, he may impose any requirements that he thinks just—

(a) in respect of the repayment of all or part of any expenditure so incurred by him;

(b) in respect of the conveyance to the local education authority of any premises used for the purposes of the school which he is satisfied the authority will need for any purpose connected with education;

(c) (where any premises are to be so conveyed) in respect of the payment by the authority of so much of the value of those premises as is just having regard to the extent to which the premises were provided otherwise than at the expense of the authority or of an authority within subsection (2)(c);

(d) (where any premises used for the purposes of the school are not to be so conveyed) in respect of the payment by the governing body to the authority of so much of the value of those premises as is just having regard to the extent to which they were provided at the expense of the authority or of an authority within subsection (2)(c).

(4) If discontinuing the school would affect the facilities for full-time education suitable to the requirements of persons over compulsory school age who have not attained the age of 19, the governing body shall, before serving notice under this section, consult the appropriate further education funding council.

(5) No notice may be served under this section in respect of any school in respect of which the procedure for acquisition of grant-maintained status is pending (within the meaning of Chapter III of Part III).

(6) A notice served under this section may not be withdrawn without the consent of the local education authority.

(7) Where a school is discontinued in accordance with this section, the duty of the local education authority to maintain it as a voluntary school shall cease.

(8) This section and section 174 have effect subject to section 175(2).

Conduct by local education authority of a voluntary school which is subject to notice of discontinuance

174.—(1) If, while a notice under section 173 is in force in respect of a voluntary school, the governing body inform the local education authority that they are unable or unwilling to carry on the school until the notice expires, the authority—

(a) may conduct the school for all or part of the unexpired period of the notice as if it were a county school, and

(b) shall be entitled to use the school premises free of charge for that purpose.

(2) While the school is being so conducted—

(a) the authority shall keep the school premises in good repair, and

(b) any interest in the premises which is held for the purposes of the school shall be deemed, for all purposes relating to the condition, occupation or use of the premises, or the making of alterations to them, to be vested in the authority.

(3) Despite the provisions of subsection (2), the governing body may use the premises, or any part of them, when not required for the purposes of the school to the same extent as if they had continued to carry on the school during the unexpired period of the notice.

Discontinuance of voluntary school in consequence of proposal to establish a further education corporation

175.—(1) This section applies where—

(a) the governing body of a voluntary school intend to discontinue the school; and

(b) the intention arises in connection with a proposal by—

(i) a further education funding council, or

(ii) the Secretary of State,

for the establishment under section 16 of the Further and Higher Education Act 1992 of a further education corporation to conduct an educational institution in the same area.

(2) Where this section applies—

(a) sections 173 and 174 shall not apply;

(b) sections 41, 42, 43 and 45(1) and (4) to (6) shall apply as they would if the intention of the governing body were to make a significant change in the character of the school; and

(c) if the school is discontinued the duty of the local education authority to maintain the school as a voluntary school shall cease.

CHAPTER VIII

MISCELLANEOUS AND SUPPLEMENTARY PROVISIONS

Further education

Provision of further education

176.—(1) The governing body of any county, voluntary or maintained special school shall be responsible for determining whether or not to provide—

(a) part-time education suitable to the requirements of persons of any age over compulsory school age; or

(b) full-time education suitable to the requirements of persons who have attained the age of 19;

but the governing body of a maintained special school shall not determine to provide, or to cease to provide, such education without the consent of the local education authority.

(2) It shall be the duty of the governing body of any such school which provides such education to secure that, except in such circumstances as may be prescribed, such education is not provided at any time in a room where pupils are at that time being taught.

Teacher training

Provision of courses of initial teacher training

177.—(1) Section 12 of the Education Act 1994 confers power on the governing body of a county, voluntary or maintained special school—

(a) to provide courses of initial training for school teachers, or

(b) to join in a partnership or association with other eligible institutions, or (whether alone or jointly with other eligible institutions) to establish a body, for the purpose of providing such courses.

(2) In subsection (1) "eligible institution" has the meaning given by section 4(2) of that Act.

Modification of employment law

Application of employment law during financial delegation

178.—(1) The Secretary of State may by order make such modifications in any enactment relating to employment, and in particular in any enactment—

(a) conferring powers or imposing duties on employers,

(b) conferring rights on employees, or

(c) otherwise regulating the relations between employers and employees,

as he considers necessary or expedient in consequence of the operation of any of the following provisions, namely, sections 136(2) and (3), 137(6) and 139(2) to (4), Schedule 14 and paragraphs 19 to 24 of Schedule 19.

(2) Before making any order under this section the Secretary of State shall consult—

(a) such associations of local authorities,

(b) such bodies representing the interests of governors of voluntary schools, and

(c) such organisations representing staff in schools required to be covered by schemes under section 103 (local education authority schemes for financing schools),

as appear to him to be concerned.

Modification of trust deeds and other instruments

Variation of trust deeds etc. by order

179.—(1) The Secretary of State may by order make such modifications of any trust deed or other instrument relating to a school as, after consultation with the governing body or other proprietor of the school, appear to him to be requisite in consequence of—

(a) any proposals falling to be implemented under section 40 or section 45 (establishment or alteration of a county or voluntary school);
(b) a transfer of the school to a new site in circumstances falling with section 35(2) or section 41(3);
(c) any order made by him under section 46 (establishment of a new voluntary school in substitution for an old one);
(d) any order made by him under section 47 (transfer of voluntary school to a new site); or
(e) any proposals falling to be implemented under section 171 (discontinuance of a county or voluntary school or maintained nursery school).

(2) Any modification made by an order under this section may be made so as to have permanent effect or to have effect for such period as may be specified in the order.

Modification of provisions whereby governors of voluntary schools are ex officio trustees

180.—(1) Where a trust deed or other instrument made before 1st July 1981 contains a provision whereby the persons who are for the time being governors of a voluntary school are by virtue of their office trustees of any property held for the purposes of or in connection with the school, that provision shall have effect as if the only governors of the school were the foundation governors and the governors appointed by the local education authority and any minor authority.

(2) Subsection (1) is without prejudice to any power to amend any such provision as is mentioned in that subsection.

Interpretation of Part II

Meaning of expressions relating to new schools

181.—(1) In this Part "new schools" (without more) means a school or proposed school—

(a) which by virtue of section 96(1) or 97(1) is required to have a temporary governing body, or
(b) in respect of which the local education authority have power under section 96(3) or 97(2) to make an arrangement for the constitution of a temporary governing body.

(2) In this Part "relevant proposals"—

(a) in relation to a new school that will be a county or voluntary school, means the proposals falling within section 96(2) or 97(1) by reference to which it is a new school, and
(b) in relation to a new school that will be a maintained special school, means the proposals falling within section 96(2) by reference to which it is a new school.

(3) In this Part—

(a) "temporary governing body" means a temporary governing body constituted for a new school under an arrangement made under section 96 or 97, and

(b) "temporary governor" means a member of a temporary governing body (and references to a temporary governor of a particular category are to a member of a temporary governing body appointed to it as a member of that category).

Meaning of "governing body" and "governor" in Chapters IV to VI

182. In Chapters IV to VI, except where otherwise provided—

"governing body" does not include a temporary governing body, and

"governor" does not include a temporary governor.

PART III

GRANT-MAINTAINED SCHOOLS

CHAPTER I

PRELIMINARY

"Grant-maintained schools"

183.—(1) A school conducted by a governing body incorporated under this Part, Part II of the Education Act 1993 or Chapter IV of Part I of the Education Reform Act 1988 for the purpose of conducting the school shall be known as a grant-maintained school.

(2) A governing body may be incorporated under this Part—

(a) in pursuance of proposals for the purpose published under section 193 in relation to an existing school (referred to in this Part as "proposals for acquisition of grant-maintained status"),

(b) in pursuance of proposals for the purpose published under section 211 or 212 in connection with the establishment of a school (referred to in this Part as "proposals for the establishment of a new grant-maintained school"), or

(c) in pursuance of proposals for the purpose published under Chapter IX for two or more existing schools to be conducted as a group by a single governing body.

(3) A grant-maintained school must be either a secondary school or a primary school.

(4) Subject to the provisions of this Part, the funding authority shall pay to the governing body of each grant-maintained school such annual grants as may be required to be paid under Chapter VI.

CHAPTER II

PROCEDURE FOR ACQUISITION OF GRANT-MAINTAINED STATUS

Eligibility

Schools eligible for grant-maintained status

184.—(1) Subject to subsections (2) and (3) below, any county or voluntary school is for the purposes of this Part eligible for grant-maintained status.

(2) A county or voluntary school is not eligible for grant-maintained status if proposals by the local education authority to cease to maintain the school have been published under section 167 and either—

(a) the proposals have been approved by the Secretary of State under section 169, or

(b) where the proposals do not require the approval of the Secretary of State, the local education authority have determined to implement the proposals and notified the Secretary of State of their determination in accordance with section 170(3).

(3) A voluntary school is not eligible for grant-maintained status if—

(a) notice of the governing body's intention to discontinue the school has been served under section 173 and has not been withdrawn, or

(b) proposals by the governing body to discontinue the school have been published under section 41 (as applied by section 175(2)(b)) and approved by the Secretary of State under section 43 (as so applied).

Duty of governing body to consider ballot on grant-maintained status

185.—(1) The Secretary of State may by order provide for this section to apply to the governing bodies of all schools, or all schools in England or Wales, which are eligible for grant-maintained status.

(2) Where this section applies to a governing body of a school, they shall, at least once in every school year, consider whether to hold a ballot of parents on the question whether grant-maintained status should be sought for the school.

(3) Subsection (2) does not apply in respect of any school year if a ballot has been held in accordance with section 189 in the school year which precedes it.

(4) The annual report of any governing body to which this section applies shall include—

(a) a statement indicating that in the period since their last report the governing body have considered whether to hold a ballot of parents in pursuance of subsection (2) and giving—

(i) particulars of any decisions made by the governing body following such consideration and the date or dates on which they were made, and

(ii) if the governing body decided not to hold a ballot, an explanation of the reasons for that decision, or

(b) a statement indicating that in that period the governing body have not, for the reasons given in the statement, considered whether to hold a ballot of parents on the question of whether grant-maintained status should be sought for the school.

(5) In this section "annual report" means the report prepared under the articles of government for the school in accordance with section 161.

Initiation of procedure

Initiation of procedure by governing body

186.—(1) Where the governing body of a school which is eligible for grant-maintained status decide by a resolution passed at a meeting of that body to hold a ballot of parents on the question whether grant-maintained status should be sought for the school, they shall—

(a) secure that the ballot is held in accordance with section 189 within the period of 10 weeks beginning with the date of the resolution, and

(b) give notice in writing that the ballot is to be held—

(i) to the local education authority, and

(ii) if the school is a voluntary school, to any person holding property on trust for the purposes of the school.

(2) Notice under subsection (1)(b) must be given within the period of five days beginning with the date of the resolution; but in determining that period no account shall be taken of—

(a) Saturday, Sunday, Good Friday and Christmas Day, or

(b) any day which is a bank holiday in England and Wales.

(3) This section does not apply if in the case of the school in question a ballot has been held in accordance with section 189 within the period of 12

months ending with the date immediately preceding the date of the resolution, unless the Secretary of State gives consent in writing for a new ballot to be held.

Initiation of procedure by parents

187.—(1) This section applies where the governing body of a school which is eligible for grant-maintained status receive a written request to hold a ballot of parents on the question whether grant-maintained status should be sought for the school.

(2) A request under subsection (1) must be signed (or otherwise endorsed in such manner as the governing body may require) by a number of registered parents of registered pupils at the school equal to at least 20 per cent. of the number of registered pupils at the school; and in this subsection "registered" means shown in the register kept under section 434 as that register has effect on the date on which the request is received.

(3) The governing body shall—

(a) secure that the ballot is held in accordance with section 189 within the period of 10 weeks beginning with the date on which the request was received, and

(b) give notice in writing that the ballot is to be held—

(i) to the local education authority, and

(ii) if the school is a voluntary school, to any person holding property on trust for the purposes of the school.

(4) Notice under subsection (3)(b) must be given within the period of five days beginning with the date on which the request was received; but in determining that period no account shall be taken of—

(a) Saturday, Sunday, Good Friday and Christmas Day, or

(b) any day which is a bank holiday in England and Wales.

(5) Subsection (3) does not apply if in the case of the school in question a ballot has been held in accordance with section 189 within the period of 12 months ending with the date immediately preceding the date on which the request is received, unless the Secretary of State gives consent in writing for a new ballot to be held.

(6) A request under subsection (1) shall be taken to have been received by a governing body if given or sent to the chairman of the governing body or to the clerk to the governing body.

Information

Information as to parents of registered pupils

188.—(1) Where any registered parent of a registered pupil at a school which is eligible for grant-maintained status so requests and subsection (2) applies, the governing body shall—

(a) make available to the parent for inspection at the school (at all reasonable times and free of charge) a list containing the name and address of every registered parent of a registered pupil at the school, and

(b) supply the parent with a copy of the list.

(2) This subsection applies if the request is made—

(a) in connection with any proposal that a ballot should be held in accordance with section 189, or

(b) where the governing body are under a duty by virtue of section 186, 187 or 191 to secure that a ballot is held, in connection with the holding of the ballot.

(3) A governing body shall not disclose to a parent under subsection (1) the name and address of any person who has requested the governing body in writing not to disclose that information under that subsection; and accordingly the name and address of that person shall be excluded from the list

there mentioned.

(4) A governing body who in pursuance of subsection (1) supply copies of the list there mentioned may charge such fee as they think fit (not exceeding the cost of supply) in respect of each copy so supplied.

Ballot of parents

Ballot of parents

189.—(1) Where the governing body of a school are under a duty by virtue of section 186 or 187 to secure that a ballot is held, they shall secure that all necessary arrangements for the ballot are made by such body as may be prescribed.

(2) The arrangements shall provide for a secret postal ballot.

(3) The governing body shall secure that the prescribed body take such steps as are reasonably practicable to secure that every person who is eligible to vote in the ballot is—

(a) given the prescribed information,
(b) informed that he is entitled to vote in the ballot, and
(c) given an opportunity to do so.

(4) The governing body shall make available to every person employed to work at the school for inspection at the school (at all reasonable times and free of charge) a document containing the information required by subsection (3)(a) to be given to persons eligible to vote in the ballot.

(5) In determining the arrangements they require to be made by the prescribed body, the governing body shall take into account any guidance given by the Secretary of State from time to time as to the arrangements he considers appropriate for ballots held in accordance with this section.

(6) The governing body may promote (otherwise than as part of the arrangements made for the ballot) the case for seeking grant-maintained status for the school and, in doing so, they shall take into account any guidance given by the Secretary of State as to the action he considers appropriate for the purpose.

Persons eligible to vote in ballot

190.—(1) For the purposes of this Chapter, a person is eligible to vote in a ballot held in respect of a school in accordance with section 189 if he is a registered parent of a registered pupil at the school.

(2) In subsection (1) "registered" means shown in the register kept under section 434 as that register has effect on the date immediately following the end of the period of 14 days beginning with—

(a) the date on which the relevant resolution or request was passed or received by the governing body, or
(b) where the Secretary of State gives his consent for the purposes of section 186(3) or 187(5), the date on which he gives that consent.

(3) In subsection (2) "the relevant resolution or request" means the resolution under section 186, or request under section 187, by reference to which the ballot is required to be held (or, where the ballot is a second ballot held by virtue of section 191, by reference to which the first ballot was required to be held).

Second ballot to be held if insufficient votes cast

191.—(1) Where in any ballot held in accordance with section 189 (other than one held by virtue of this section)—

(a) the total number of votes cast by persons eligible to vote is less than 50 per cent. of the number of persons eligible to vote, or
(b) the number of votes cast in favour is the same as the number of votes cast against,

the governing body shall secure that a second ballot is held within the period of 14 days beginning with the day after that on which the result of the first ballot is determined.

(2) In such a case—

(a) the result of the first ballot shall be disregarded for the purposes of section 193(1), and

(b) subject to the modifications mentioned in subsection (3), section 189 shall apply as it applies in a case where the governing body of a school are under a duty by virtue of section 186 or 187 to secure that a ballot is held.

(3) The modifications are—

(a) that section 189(3)(a) shall be omitted, and

(b) that section 189(4) shall be read as if the information there referred to were the information given for the purposes of the first ballot.

Power to declare ballot void for irregularity

192.—(1) Subsection (2) applies where it appears to the Secretary of State—

(a) that any requirements of section 189 or 191 have been contravened in the case of a ballot held in purported compliance with section 189,

(b) that the arrangements for a ballot so held did not accord with any guidance given by him for the purposes of section 189,

(c) that a governing body have acted unreasonably in the discharge of their duties under section 189 or 191,

(d) that persons other than those eligible to do so have purported to vote in a ballot so held,

(e) that ballot papers returned for the purposes of a ballot so held have been marked by persons other than those to whom they were issued or those duly authorised to act on their behalf,

(f) that persons who were eligible to vote in a ballot so held have been prevented or hindered from doing so, or from doing so freely in accordance with their own opinions, by any other person, or

(g) that voting in a ballot so held is likely to have been influenced to a significant extent by the dissemination of information appearing to the Secretary of State to be to a material extent false or misleading.

(2) The Secretary of State may by notice in writing given to the governing body—

(a) declare the ballot void, and

(b) require that a fresh ballot be held in accordance with section 189 before such date as he may specify in the notice.

(3) Where—

(a) by a notice under subsection (2) the Secretary of State requires the fresh ballot to be held in the school year following that in which fell the date which was the effective date for the register used for the ballot he declares void, and

(b) the notice specifies a date for the purposes of this subsection,

section 190(1) shall have effect in relation to the fresh ballot as if "registered" meant shown in the register kept under section 434 as that register has effect on the date specified for the purposes of this subsection.

Publication of proposals

193.—(1) Subsection (2) applies where the result of a ballot held in accordance with section 189 shows a simple majority of votes cast (by persons eligible to vote in the ballot) in favour of seeking grant-maintained status for the school.

(2) Before the end of the period of four months beginning with the date on which the result of the ballot is determined, the governing body shall—

(a) publish proposals for acquisition of grant-maintained status for the school in accordance with any provisions made by or under paragraph 1 of Schedule 20,

(b) publish any notice in respect of the proposals for the time being required by any such provisions, and

(c) submit to the Secretary of State a copy of the published proposals.

(3) References in this Part to proposals published under this section are, in any case where the Secretary of State has modified such proposals in pursuance of this Part, references to the proposals as so modified.

(4) For the purposes of this Part, proposals published under this section shall be regarded as pending in respect of a school until either the proposals are withdrawn or the Secretary of State makes his determination in respect of them.

(5) Part I of Schedule 20 has effect for the purpose of supplementing this section.

Approval and implementation of proposals

Withdrawal, approval or rejection of proposals

194.—(1) Proposals published under section 193 may not be withdrawn except with the consent of the Secretary of State and subject to such conditions as he may impose (which may, in particular, require further proposals to be published under that section within such period as the Secretary of State may specify).

(2) The Secretary of State—

(a) may reject any proposals published under section 193, or

(b) where a school in respect of which such proposals are made is eligible for grant-maintained status on the date of publication of the proposals, may—

(i) approve them without modification, or

(ii) after consultation with the existing governing body, approve them with such modifications as he thinks desirable.

(3) Where the Secretary of State rejects any proposals published under section 193 in respect of a school which is eligible for grant-maintained status on the date of his determination, he may require the governing body to publish further proposals under section 193 within such period as he may specify.

(4) Where the Secretary of State imposes a requirement under subsection (1) or (3) for the publication of further proposals, section 193(2) and Schedule 20 shall apply as they apply in the case mentioned in section 193(1), but with the following modifications—

(a) the reference in section 193(2) to the period of four months beginning with the date on which the result of the ballot is determined shall be taken as a reference to the period specified by the Secretary of State for submission of the further proposals required, and

(b) the reference in paragraph 2(1)(a) of Schedule 20 to the ballot shall be read as referring to the last ballot held in accordance with section 189 in relation to the school before the requirement in question was imposed.

Incorporation of governing body

195.—(1) Where any proposals are approved under section 194, then—

(a) the persons who, immediately before the proposals are approved, are named in them as initial governors, and

(b) the existing head teacher (as a governor ex officio),

shall on that date be incorporated as the governing body of the school under the name given in pursuance of paragraph 4(1)(g) of Schedule 20.

(2) Where any proposals are approved under section 194, then, in relation

to the period beginning with the incorporation date and ending immediately before the date of implementation of the proposals—

(a) the governing body incorporated under this section are referred to in this Part as the "new governing body", and

(b) any reference in any enactment or instrument or document to the governing body of the school, other than—

(i) an express reference to the new governing body or the governing body incorporated under this section, or

(ii) a reference in Chapter V,

shall be read as a reference to the existing governing body, not the new governing body.

(3) On the date of implementation of the proposals—

(a) the local education authority whose duty it was immediately before that date to maintain the school as a county or voluntary school shall cease to have that duty, and

(b) any special agreement relating to the school shall cease to have effect.

Exercise of powers before proposed date of implementation

196. Schedule 21 (which makes provision in relation to the period after approval and before the date of implementation) has effect in relation to a school once proposals are approved under section 194.

Expenses in connection with proposals

Expenses in connection with proposals for acquisition of grant-maintained status

197.—(1) The Secretary of State may make payments in respect of any expenses incurred by the governing body of a school in exercising, or in connection with the exercise of, their functions under the preceding provisions of this Chapter.

(2) Payments under subsection (1) may be made on such terms as the Secretary of State may determine.

(3) A local education authority shall not incur any expenditure attributable to any period for the purpose of influencing the outcome of ballots held under section 189 if the aggregate of the amounts of expenditure for that purpose attributable to the period exceeds (or, if that expenditure were incurred, would exceed) the limit for that period.

(4) Regulations may make provision for determining for the purposes of this section—

(a) whether expenditure is incurred for the purpose referred to in subsection (3),

(b) the amount of any expenditure,

(c) the period to which expenditure is to be attributed, and

(d) the limit for any period.

(5) Regulations may require each local education authority—

(a) to keep in accordance with regulations, and any directions contained in an order made by the Secretary of State, a separate account of the expenditure incurred for the purpose referred to in subsection (3), and

(b) to prepare in respect of such periods as may be prescribed a statement of account and, if the Secretary of State so requests, send each statement to him before the end of such period as may be prescribed.

Alteration of county school proposed for grant-maintained status

Proposals by governing body for alteration of county school proposed for grant-maintained status

198.—(1) This section applies where—

(a) the governing body of a county school ("the school proposed for grant-maintained status") have published proposals for acquisition of grant-maintained status which have not been withdrawn or determined,

(b) the local education authority have published proposals for any of the purposes mentioned in section 35(1)(c) or (d) (alteration, etc. of county school) in respect of one or more schools in the area, and

(c) the governing body of the school proposed for grant-maintained status intend to make a significant change in the character, or a significant enlargement of the premises, of the school, being a change or enlargement to be made for the purpose of ensuring consistency in the provision of education in the area of the local education authority if the proposals made by the authority are implemented.

(2) The governing body of the school proposed for grant-maintained status may publish in such manner as may be required by regulations proposals for a significant change in the character, or significant enlargement of the premises, of the school for the purpose mentioned in subsection (1)(c).

(3) Chapter VII (alteration etc. of grant-maintained school) shall apply in relation to proposals published under this section as it applies in relation to proposals published under section 259 (proposals for change of character etc. by governing body) but—

(a) as if the governing body of the school proposed for grant-maintained status were the governing body of a grant-maintained school, and

(b) with the modifications in subsections (4) and (5) below.

(4) The particulars of the proposals shall not give as the time or any of the times of implementation of the proposals a time earlier than the date of implementation of the proposals for acquisition of grant-maintained status.

(5) The statement accompanying the proposals shall (in addition to complying with section 259(5))—

(a) state that the proposals are published in connection with the proposed acquisition of grant-maintained status,

(b) state the circumstances in which the governing body are authorised under this section to publish such proposals, and

(c) describe the proposals published by the local education authority in connection with which the proposals under this section are published.

(6) Proposals published under this section may, if the governing body think fit—

(a) specify an age below 10 years and six months and an age above 12 years, and

(b) provide that the school is to be a school for providing full-time education suitable to the requirements to pupils whose ages are between the ages so specified.

Approval or rejection by Secretary of State of proposals under section 198

199.—(1) This section applies where, after proposals for acquisition of grant-maintained status have been published in respect of any school which is eligible for grant-maintained status but before those proposals are withdrawn or determined, proposals in respect of the school are published under section 198.

(2) The Secretary of State shall consider both sets of proposals together but shall not determine the proposals under section 198 until he has made his determination with respect to the proposals for acquisition of grant-maintained status.

(3) If the Secretary of State approves the proposals for acquisition of grant-maintained status, he may approve the proposals under section 198.

(4) If the Secretary of State rejects the proposals for acquisition of grant-maintained status, he shall reject the proposals under section 198.

Supplementary

Chapter II: interpretation, etc.

200.—(1) This section applies in relation to proposals for acquisition of grant-maintained status and to the school to which they relate.

(2) References to the date of implementation of the proposals—

(a) in relation to a school in respect of which proposals for acquisition of grant-maintained status are required to be published under section 193, are to the date specified (in accordance with regulations under section 189(3)(a)) as the proposed date of implementation in the information given to persons eligible to vote in the originating ballot, and

(b) in any other case, are to the date specified in the proposals as the proposed date of implementation.

(3) In subsection (2)(a) "the originating ballot"—

(a) where section 193(2) applies, means the ballot by reference to which it applies, and

(b) where the proposals are required to be published by virtue of a requirement imposed by the Secretary of State under section 194(1) or (3), means the last ballot held in accordance with section 189 in relation to the school before that requirement was imposed.

(4) "The relevant particulars", in relation to a proposed initial governor, means—

(a) his name and address,

(b) whether he is to be a parent, teacher, first, foundation or sponsor governor,

(c) if he is to be a parent or teacher governor, the term of office that applies in his case under paragraph 10 of Schedule 22, and

(d) if he is to be a first, foundation or sponsor governor, the term of office proposed for him in accordance with that paragraph or, in the case of a foundation governor who is to hold office ex officio, the fact that he is to do so.

(5) "The incorporation date" means the date on which the governing body are incorporated.

Chapter III

Property, staff and contracts

Transfer of property and staff, etc.

Transfer of property etc.

201.—(1) Subject to subsection (3), where in relation to any school proposals for acquisition of grant-maintained status are approved—

(a) the property, rights and liabilities mentioned in subsection (2) of any local authority, and

(b) any property, rights and liabilities of the existing governing body,

shall on the date of implementation of the proposals be transferred to, and by virtue of this Act vest in, the governing body incorporated under Chapter II.

(2) The property, rights and liabilities referred to in subsection (1)(a) are—

(a) all land or other property which, immediately before the date of implementation of the proposals, was property used or held by the authority for the purposes of the school, and

(b) all rights and liabilities subsisting immediately before the date of implementation of the proposals which were acquired or incurred by the authority for those purposes.

(3) Subsection (1) shall not apply to rights and liabilities under any contract of employment; and subsection (1)(a) shall not apply to—

(a) any land or other property vested in a local authority as trustees,
(b) any property, rights or liabilities excluded under subsection (5) or (6),
(c) any liability of a local authority in respect of the principal of, or any interest on, any loan, or
(d) any liability of a local authority in respect of compensation for premature retirement of any person formerly employed by them or by any governing body of the school.

(4) Any land or other property of a local authority excluded by virtue of subsection (3)(a) from transfer to the governing body shall, on the date of implementation of the proposals, be transferred to, and by virtue of this Act vest in, the first governors of the school on the trusts applicable immediately before that date under any trust deed regulating the use of that land or other property for the purposes of the school.

(5) If before the date of implementation of the proposals—

(a) the new governing body and the local authority have agreed in writing to exclude any property, and
(b) the Secretary of State has given his written approval of the agreement,

the property, and any rights or liabilities relating to it, shall be excluded.

(6) If in default of agreement under subsection (5)—

(a) the new governing body or the local authority have applied to the Secretary of State to exclude any property, and
(b) the Secretary of State has by order directed its exclusion,

the property, and any rights or liabilities relating to it, shall be excluded.

(7) An agreement under subsection (5) may provide for the property to be used for the purposes of the school acquiring grant-maintained status on such terms as may be specified in or determined in accordance with the agreement; and directions under subsection (6)—

(a) may confer any rights or impose any liabilities that could have been conferred or imposed by such an agreement, and
(b) shall have effect as if contained in such an agreement.

(8) For the purposes of this section, any interest in a dwelling-house which, immediately before the date of implementation of the proposals, is used or held by a local authority for occupation by a person employed to work at the school shall be treated as an interest used or held for the purposes of the school.

(9) References in this section to liabilities incurred by a local authority shall not be read as including liabilities of such an authority to make payments to or in respect of any person in pursuance of any duty imposed on the authority under any statutory provision.

(10) This section is subject to section 198 of the Education Reform Act 1988 (which with Schedule 10 to that Act makes further provision in relation to transfers of property, rights and liabilities), and references in that Schedule as applied by virtue of this subsection to the transfer date are to the date of implementation of the proposals.

Transfer of staff

202.—(1) This section applies to any school where proposals for acquisition of grant-maintained status have been approved in relation to the school; and, subject to subsection (3), applies to any person who—

(a) if the school is an aided school, is immediately before the date of implementation of the proposals employed by the governing body, or
(b) immediately before the date of implementation of the proposals—
    (i) is employed by the local education authority to work solely at the school, or
    (ii) is employed by the local education authority to work at the

school and is designated for the purposes of this section by an order made by the Secretary of State.

(2) A person employed by a local education authority in connection with the provision of meals shall not be regarded for the purposes of subsection (1)(b) as employed to work solely at a school unless the meals are provided solely for consumption by persons at the school.

(3) This section does not apply to—

(a) any person employed as mentioned in subsection (1) whose contract of employment terminates on the day immediately preceding the date of implementation of the proposals, or

(b) any person employed as mentioned in subsection (1)(b) who before that date—

(i) has been appointed or assigned by the local education authority to work solely at another school as from that date, or

(ii) has been withdrawn from work at the school with effect as from that date.

(4) A person who before the date of implementation of the proposals has been appointed or assigned by the local education authority to work at the school as from that date shall be treated for the purposes of this section as if he had been employed by the authority immediately before that date to do such work at the school as he would have been required to do on or after that date under his contract of employment with the authority.

(5) In subsections (6) and (7) "former employer"—

(a) in relation to a person to whom this section applies by virtue of subsection (1)(a), means the governing body of the school immediately before the date of implementation of the proposals, and

(b) in relation to a person to whom this section applies by virtue of subsection (1)(b), means the local education authority.

(6) The contract of employment between a person to whom this section applies and his former employer shall have effect from the date of implementation of the proposals as if originally made between him and the governing body of the grant-maintained school.

(7) Without prejudice to subsection (6)—

(a) all the former employer's rights, powers, duties and liabilities under or in connection with the contract of employment shall by virtue of this section be transferred to the governing body of the grant-maintained school on the date of implementation of the proposals, and

(b) anything done before that date by or in relation to the former employer in respect of that contract or the employee shall be deemed from that date to have been done by or in relation to that governing body.

(8) Subsections (6) and (7) are without prejudice to any right of an employee to terminate his contract of employment if a substantial change is made to his detriment in his working conditions, but no such right shall arise by reason only of the change in employer effected by this section.

(9) An order under this section may designate a person either individually or as a member of a class or description of employees.

Effect of pending procedure for acquisition of grant-maintained status on property disposals, etc.

"Pending" procedure for acquisition of grant-maintained status

203.—(1) For the purposes of this Chapter the procedure for acquisition of grant-maintained status is pending in relation to a school when it has been initiated in relation to the school on any occasion and not terminated (as initiated on that occasion).

(2) For those purposes, that procedure is to be regarded as initiated in relation to a school on any occasion—

(a) on receipt by the local education authority of notice of a meeting of the governing body at which a motion for a resolution to hold a ballot of parents on the question whether grant-maintained status should be sought for the school is to be considered (not being a case falling within section 186(3)), or

(b) where the governing body have received a request under subsection (1) of section 187, on receipt by the local education authority of notice under subsection (3)(b) of that section.

(3) For those purposes, that procedure, as initiated on any occasion, is to be regarded as terminated—

(a) (when initiated as mentioned in subsection (2)(a)) if—

(i) the meeting is not held,

(ii) the meeting is held but the motion is not moved or, though the motion is moved, the resolution is not passed, or

(iii) the resolution is passed but the result of the ballot to which the notice under section 186(1)(b) relates does not show a majority in favour of seeking grant-maintained status for the school;

(b) (when initiated as mentioned in subsection (2)(b)) if the result of the ballot to which the notice under section 187(3)(b) relates does not show a majority in favour of seeking grant-maintained status for the school;

(c) if—

(i) proposals which by reference to the result of a ballot to which a notice under section 186(1)(b) or 187(3)(b) relates are required to be published under section 193, or

(ii) any proposals required in substitution for those proposals,

are rejected by the Secretary of State or withdrawn; or

(d) on the date of implementation of such proposals.

(4) Where section 191 applies in the case of such a ballot, the references in subsection (3) above to the result of that ballot shall be read as references to the result of the second ballot required by that section.

(5) The reference in subsection (3) above to proposals required in substitution for any proposals ("the original proposals") required to be published by reference to the result of a ballot is to any proposals required to be published by virtue of section 194(1) or (3) on withdrawal or (as the case may be) rejection of—

(a) the original proposals, or

(b) any further proposals required to be published by virtue of section 194(1) or (3) in respect of the school without a further ballot.

(6) Proposals published under section 193 shall not be treated for the purposes of subsection (3)(c) as rejected in any case where the Secretary of State imposes a requirement under section 194(3) or as withdrawn in any case where he imposes a requirement under section 194(1) for the publication of further proposals.

Control of disposals of land

204.—(1) During any period when the procedure for acquisition of grant-maintained status is pending in relation to a school, a local authority shall not—

(a) dispose of any land used wholly or partly for the purposes of the school, or

(b) enter into a contract to dispose of any such land,

except with the required consent.

(2) Subsection (1) does not apply in relation to a disposal which is made in pursuance of a contract entered into, or an option granted, before the procedure for acquisition of grant-maintained status was initiated in relation to the school.

(3) Where proposals for acquisition of grant-maintained status are approved, the procedure for acquisition of grant-maintained status is not to be treated as terminated for the purposes of this section and section 205 in relation to any land, where agreement is required to be reached under paragraph 2(1) of Schedule 10 to the Education Reform Act 1988 (identification of property, etc.) on any matter relating to that land, until the date on which that matter is finally determined.

(4) In the case of a disposal made or contract entered into after proposals for acquisition of grant-maintained status have been approved, "the required consent"—

(a) (if it is agreed between the local authority and the new governing body that the value of the land in question does not exceed £6,000) is the consent of the new governing body, and

(b) (if paragraph (a) does not apply) is the consent of both the new governing body and the Secretary of State.

(5) In any other case "the required consent" for any proposed disposal (and for any contract to make it) is the consent of both the existing governing body and the Secretary of State.

(6) A disposal or contract shall not be invalid or void by reason only that it has been made or entered into in contravention of this section; and (subject to section 205) a person acquiring land, or entering into a contract to acquire land, from a local authority shall not be concerned to enquire whether any consent required by this section has been given.

(7) This section has effect notwithstanding anything in section 123 of the Local Government Act 1972 (general power to dispose of land) or in any other enactment; and the consent required by this section shall be in addition to any consent required by subsection (2) of that section or by any other enactment.

(8) In this section and section 205—

(a) references to disposing of land include granting or disposing of any interest in land, and

(b) references to entering into a contract to dispose of land include granting an option to acquire land or such an interest.

(9) Where a proposed disposal forms part of a proposed series of transactions, all disposals forming part of that series shall be treated as one disposal for the purposes of this section.

(10) The Secretary of State may by order substitute for the sum specified in subsection (4) (whether as originally enacted or as previously amended by an order under this subsection) such sum as may be specified in the order.

Wrongful disposals of land

205.—(1) This section applies where—

(a) proposals for acquisition of grant-maintained status in respect of a school have been approved, and

(b) a local authority have made a disposal, or have entered into a contract, in contravention of section 204(1).

(2) In the case of a contract which consists of granting an option to acquire any land or interest in land, the Education Assets Board may by notice in writing served on the option holder repudiate the option at any time before it is exercised.

(3) In the case of a contract to dispose of any land or to grant or dispose of any interest in land, the Education Assets Board may by notice in writing served on the other party to the contract, at any time before the conveyance or grant of the land or any interest in land to which it relates is completed or executed, repudiate the contract.

(4) A repudiation under subsection (2) or (3) shall have effect—

(a) where it is made after the date of implementation of the proposals, as if the local authority (and not the governing body) were party to the contract, and

(b) as if the repudiation were made by the local authority.

(5) In the case of a disposal which consists in granting or disposing of any interest in land (whether or not in pursuance of any earlier contract falling within subsection (2) or (3)) the Education Assets Board may be authorised by the Secretary of State to purchase compulsorily the interest in land which was the subject of the disposal.

(6) The Acquisition of Land Act 1981 shall apply in relation to the compulsory purchase of land under subsection (5) as if references in sections 12 and 13 of that Act to every owner of the land included references to the local authority concerned.

(7) On completion of a compulsory purchase under that subsection of any interest in land, the Education Assets Board shall convey that interest to the governing body incorporated under Chapter II.

(8) Where the Education Assets Board acquire any interest in land by a compulsory purchase under subsection (5) the Board shall be entitled to recover from the local authority concerned an amount equal to the aggregate of—

(a) the amount of compensation agreed or awarded in respect of that purchase, together with any interest payable by the Board in respect of that compensation in accordance with section 11 of the Compulsory Purchase Act 1965 or section 52A of the Land Compensation Act 1973, and

(b) the amount of the costs and expenses incurred by the Board in connection with the making of the compulsory purchase order.

(9) Section 204(8) applies for the purposes of this section.

Control of contracts

206.—(1) Where the procedure for acquisition of grant-maintained status is pending in relation to any school, this section applies to any contract which, if the proposals for acquisition of grant-maintained status were implemented, would or might bind the governing body incorporated under Chapter II.

(2) Except with the appropriate consent, a local authority shall not enter into a contract to which this section applies.

(3) In the case of a contract entered into after the proposals have been approved by the Secretary of State, "the appropriate consent" is that of the new governing body.

(4) In relation to any other contract, "the appropriate consent" is—

(a) the consent of the existing governing body, and

(b) if (on the assumption set out in subsection (1)) the contract will require the governing body incorporated under Chapter II to make payments amounting in aggregate to £15,000 or more, the consent of the Secretary of State.

(5) Any consent for the purposes of this section may be given either in respect of a particular contract or in respect of contracts of any class or description and either unconditionally or subject to conditions.

(6) A contract shall not be void by reason only that it has been entered into in contravention of this section and (subject to section 207) a person entering into a contract with a local authority or governing body shall not be concerned to enquire whether any consent required by this section has been given or any conditions of such a consent have been complied with.

(7) Where there is an obligation under a contract to which this section applies to provide any benefit other than money, subsection (4)(b) shall apply as if the obligation were to pay a sum of money corresponding to the value of the benefit to the recipient.

(8) This section does not apply to—

(a) a works contract (within the meaning of Part III of the Local Government, Planning and Land Act 1980) which is entered into in accordance with section 7 of that Act,

(b) a works contract (within the meaning of Part I of the Local Government Act 1988) which is entered into in accordance with section 4 of that Act,

(c) a contract to dispose of land (within the meaning of section 204) or to grant an option to acquire land or an interest in land, or

(d) a contract of employment.

(9) The Secretary of State may by order substitute for the sum specified in subsection (4) (whether as originally enacted or as previously amended by an order under this subsection) such sum as may be specified in the order.

Wrongful contracts

207.—(1) This section applies where—

(a) proposals for acquisition of grant-maintained status in respect of a school have been approved, and

(b) a local authority have entered into a contract to which section 206 applies in contravention of that section.

(2) The Education Assets Board may by notice in writing served on the other party to the contract repudiate the contract at any time before it is performed.

(3) A repudiation under subsection (2) shall have effect—

(a) where it is made after the date of implementation of the proposals, as if the local authority (and not the governing body) were party to the contract, and

(b) as if the repudiation were made by the local authority.

Restriction on change of purpose for which property used or held

208.—(1) During any period when the procedure for acquisition of grant-maintained status is pending in relation to a school, a local authority shall not, in relation to any land or other property of the authority used or held for the purposes of the school, take without the required consent any action by which the land or other property ceases to any extent to be so used or held.

(2) In the case of anything done after proposals for acquisition of grant-maintained status have been approved, "the required consent" is that of the new governing body.

(3) In any other case "the required consent" is that of both the existing governing body and the Secretary of State.

(4) If in the case of any school—

(a) proposals for acquisition of grant-maintained status are approved, and

(b) a local authority have, in relation to any property, taken any action in contravention of subsection (1),

the provisions relating to the transfer of property shall have effect as if, immediately before the date of implementation of the proposals in relation to the school, the property were used or held by the authority for the purposes for which it was used or held when the procedure for acquisition of grant-maintained status was initiated.

(5) In this section—

(a) "the provisions relating to the transfer of property" means section 201 above and section 198 of, and Schedule 10 to, the Education Reform Act 1988, and

(b) the references to taking action include appropriating property for any purpose.

Restriction on staff changes

209.—(1) During any period when the procedure for acquisition of grant-maintained status is pending in relation to a school, the local education authority shall not do any of the things mentioned in subsection (2) without the required consent.

(2) Those things are—

(a) the appointment of a person to fill a vacancy in a post which is part of the complement of the school or to work solely at the school in any other post,

(b) the dismissal (otherwise than under section 143(6) or 144(3) (special provisions as to religious education in voluntary schools)) of a person to whom subsection (3) applies, and

(c) the withdrawal of such a person from work at the school (otherwise than by dismissing him).

(3) This subsection applies to any person who is employed—

(a) in a post which is part of the complement of the school, or

(b) to work solely at the school in any other post.

(4) The references in this section to the complement of the school are to the complement of teaching and non-teaching posts determined by the local education authority for the school under section 133(1) to (3) (determination of staff complement for schools).

(5) In the case of anything done after proposals for acquisition of grant-maintained status have been approved, "the required consent" is that of the new governing body.

(6) In any other case "the required consent" is that of both the existing governing body and the Secretary of State.

Supplementary

Supplementary provisions about transfers

210.—(1) No duty of a local education authority under section 60(2) or (as the case may be) 61(2) to convey their interest in any site or buildings to the trustees of a voluntary school shall be affected by the school subsequently becoming a grant-maintained school.

(2) Where such a duty is continued by virtue of subsection (1), then, in connection with the site in question, sections 60(2) to (7), 61(2) and (3) and 62 shall continue to apply after the school becomes a grant-maintained school as if it were a controlled school or, as the case may be, an aided or special agreement school.

(3) Where any such duty as is referred to in subsection (1), or imposed by section 70(1), applies in relation to a school, then—

(a) if it applies immediately before the date of implementation of proposals for acquisition of grant-maintained status, section 201(1)(a) shall not apply to, or to any interest in, the site or buildings or, as the case may be, the premises to be conveyed, and

(b) if it applies at a time when the procedure for acquisition of grant-maintained status is pending, section 204 shall not apply to disposing, or entering into a contract to dispose, of the site or buildings or, as the case may be, the premises to be conveyed.

(4) Where immediately before the date of implementation of proposals for acquisition of grant-maintained status there is an agreement relating to any site or buildings made under section 61(4) or (5), section 201(1)(a) shall not apply to any rights or liabilities of any local authority under the agreement; and any directions given before that date under section 61(6), so far as they relate to the governing body of the school, shall have effect on or after that date as if they related to the governing body incorporated under section 195.

Chapter IV

Establishing new grant-maintained schools

Proposals for establishment of new grant-maintained school

Proposals by funding authority

211.—(1) This section has effect in respect of the area of a local education authority if an order under section 27(1) applies to the area.

(2) The funding authority may establish grant-maintained schools for the purpose of providing relevant education.

(3) Where the funding authority intend to establish a grant-maintained school, they shall—

(a) publish proposals for that purpose in such manner as may be prescribed, and

(b) submit a copy of the published proposals to the Secretary of State.

(4) Before publishing any proposals under this section the funding authority shall consult such persons as appear to them to be appropriate; and in discharging their duty under this subsection the funding authority shall have regard to any guidance given to them from time to time by the Secretary of State.

Proposals by promoters

212.—(1) Where any persons (referred to in this Part as "promoters") propose to establish a grant-maintained school, they shall—

(a) publish proposals for that purpose in such manner as may be prescribed, and

(b) submit a copy of the published proposals to the Secretary of State.

(2) Before publishing any proposals under this section the promoters shall consult—

(a) the funding authority, and

(b) such other persons as appear to them to be appropriate;

and in discharging their duty under this subsection the promoters shall have regard to any guidance given from time to time by the Secretary of State.

(3) A local education authority may not establish any grant-maintained school.

Provisions supplementary to sections 211 and 212

213.—(1) Part II of Schedule 20 has effect for the purpose of supplementing sections 211 and 212.

(2) Subsection (3) applies where promoters propose to establish a grant-maintained school in place of an existing independent school which it is proposed to discontinue on or before the date of implementation of the proposals.

(3) Where this subsection applies, the proposals published by the promoters under section 212 shall, in addition to the matters required to be specified by virtue of paragraph 7 of Schedule 20—

(a) specify any arrangements proposed to be made by the promoters for land and other property held for the purposes of the existing independent school to be held for the purposes of the grant-maintained school, and

(b) state whether there is a trust deed or other instrument relating to the existing independent school.

(4) References in this Part to proposals published under section 211 or 212 are, in any case where the Secretary of State has modified such proposals in pursuance of this Part, references to the proposals as so modified.

(5) No proposals may be published under section 211 or 212 for a school

which may provide any education which is neither primary nor secondary education unless it is—

(a) part-time education suitable to the requirements of persons of any age over compulsory school age, or full-time education suitable to the requirements of persons who have attained the age of 19, or

(b) part-time education suitable to the requirements of junior pupils.

Approval and implementation of proposals

Approval, adoption or rejection of proposals

214.—(1) Proposals published under section 211 require the approval of the Secretary of State if—

(a) he gives notice to that effect to the funding authority within two months after the submission to him of the published proposals,

(b) objections have been made under paragraph 10 of Schedule 20 within the period allowed under that paragraph (unless all objections so made have been withdrawn in writing within that period), or

(c) the proposals name a sponsor of the school.

(2) Proposals published under section 212 require the approval of the Secretary of State.

(3) Where under subsection (1) or (2) any proposals require the approval of the Secretary of State, he may—

(a) reject them,

(b) approve them without modification, or

(c) after consulting the funding authority (and, in the case of proposals under section 212, the promoters) approve them with such modifications as he thinks desirable.

(4) In relation to Wales, subsection (3) shall have effect before the Schools Funding Council for Wales begin to exercise their functions with the omission of the reference to consulting the funding authority.

(5) In the case of proposals published under section 211, particulars in respect of the proposed premises of the school prepared under paragraph 12 of Schedule 20 must be adopted by the funding authority.

(6) In the case of proposals published under section 212, particulars in respect of the proposed premises of the school submitted under paragraph 12 of Schedule 20 require the approval of the funding authority.

(7) Where proposals published under section 211 do not require the approval of the Secretary of State, the funding authority shall determine whether to adopt the proposals.

(8) The funding authority shall—

(a) make any determination under subsection (7) not later than four months after the publication of the proposals, and

(b) give notice in writing to the Secretary of State of their determination.

Implementation of proposals

215.—(1) Where any proposals are approved or adopted under section 214, the persons who are appointed in accordance with regulations to be the initial first or (as the case may be) foundation governors shall on the incorporation date be incorporated as the governing body of the school under the name given in pursuance of paragraph 7(1)(f) of Schedule 20.

(2) Where any proposals published under section 211 are so approved or adopted, the funding authority shall implement the proposals or, in a case where, under this subsection, the Secretary of State modifies the proposals at their request, shall implement the proposals as so modified.

(3) Where any proposals published under section 212 are so approved, the promoters shall implement the proposals or, in a case where, under this subsection, the Secretary of State modifies the proposals at their request, shall

implement the proposals as modified.

(4) Proposals required to be implemented under this section shall be implemented in accordance with any particulars adopted or approved under section 214(5) or (6).

Exercise of powers before proposed date of implementation, and payment of grant

216.—(1) Where proposals have been approved or adopted under section 214, the powers conferred on the governing body by or under this Part shall, until the date of implementation of the proposals, be exercised only for the purpose of or in connection with the conduct of the school on or after that date.

(2) In the case of proposals under section 212, the funding authority may at any time after the incorporation date make grants to the governing body in respect of the provision of premises for the school.

(3) So far as the amount of any grant under subsection (2) relates to the provision of a site for the school or of school buildings, it shall not exceed 85 per cent. of the sums expended by the governing body in respect of the provision of the site and buildings in question.

(4) Where proposals have been approved or adopted under section 214, then, in respect of the period beginning with the incorporation date and ending immediately before the date of implementation of the proposals—

(a) Chapter VI (funding of grant-maintained schools) shall not apply, but

(b) the funding authority may make grants to the governing body (other than grants in respect of the provision of premises for the school) in respect of expenditure incurred or to be incurred by that body.

(5) The funding authority may impose on a governing body to whom a grant is made under subsection (2) or (4) such requirements as they may from time to time determine (whether before, at or after the time when the grant is made).

(6) Such requirements may, in particular, if any conditions specified in the requirements are satisfied, require the payment to the funding authority of the whole or any part of the following amount.

(7) That amount is—

(a) the amount of the payments made in respect of the grant, or

(b) so much of the value of any premises or equipment in respect of which the grant was paid as is determined in accordance with the requirements to be properly attributable to the payment of such grant,

whichever is the greater.

(8) No such requirement as is referred to in subsection (6) may be imposed where any grant is made under subsection (2) in respect of the provision of premises for the school if any freehold interest in the premises in respect of which the grant is paid is, or is to be, held on trust for the purposes of the school.

(9) In this section "site" does not include playing fields.

Supplementary

Chapter IV: interpretation

217. In relation to proposals for the establishment of a new grant-maintained school or to a school established in pursuance of such proposals—

(a) the date specified in the proposals as the proposed incorporation date is referred to in this Part as the "incorporation date", and

(b) the date specified in the proposals as the proposed date of implementation is referred to in this Part as the "date of implementation of the proposals".

CHAPTER V

GOVERNMENT, CONDUCT ETC. OF GRANT-MAINTAINED SCHOOLS

The governing instruments

Constitution of governing body and conduct of school

218.—(1) For every governing body of a grant-maintained school there shall be—

(a) an instrument (known as the instrument of government) providing for the constitution of the governing body, and

(b) an instrument (known as the articles of government) in accordance with which the school is to be conducted.

(2) The instrument and articles of government—

(a) shall comply with any requirements imposed by or under this Chapter, and

(b) may make any provision authorised by or under this Chapter to be made and such other provision as may be necessary or desirable.

(3) Subject to any express provision of the instrument or articles of government, the school shall be conducted in accordance with any trust deed relating to it.

(4) Schedule 22 (membership and proceedings etc. of governing bodies) shall have effect.

(5) Schedule 23 (content of articles of government) shall also have effect.

Initial instruments and articles of government

219.—(1) The initial instrument of government for the governing body of a grant-maintained school, and the initial articles of government for such a school, shall be such as are prescribed.

(2) The initial instrument of government shall have effect as from the incorporation date.

(3) The initial articles of government shall have effect as from the date of implementation of the proposals but, in the case of a governing body incorporated in pursuance of proposals for the establishment of a new grant-maintained school, such of the articles as may be prescribed shall have effect as from the incorporation date.

(4) Before making any regulations under this section the Secretary of State shall consult—

(a) a body appearing to him to be representative of the Church of England,

(b) a body appearing to him to be representative of the Church in Wales, and

(c) a body appearing to him to be representative of the Roman Catholic Church,

in matters relating to the provision of education in grant-maintained schools having foundation governors.

Subsequent instruments of government

220.—(1) The Secretary of State may—

(a) if the governing body of a grant-maintained school submit a draft of an instrument of government to have effect in place of their existing instrument, by order make a new instrument of government in terms of the draft or in such terms as he thinks fit, and

(b) if such a governing body submit draft modifications—

(i) of an instrument made under paragraph (a), or

(ii) of an instrument of government made under section 57(1)(a) of the Education Act 1993 or Chapter IV of Part I of the Education Reform Act 1988 which has effect (by virtue of Schedule 39 to this Act) as if made under paragraph (a),

by order modify the instrument concerned in terms of the draft or in such terms as he thinks fit;

but he shall not make a new instrument otherwise than in terms of the draft, or modify the instrument otherwise than in terms of the draft, unless he has consulted the governing body.

(2) No order may be made under subsection (1) in respect of a school having foundation governors unless the governing body have consulted—

(a) the person who appoints the foundation governors, and

(b) in the case of a Church of England, Church in Wales or Roman Catholic Church school, the appropriate diocesan authority (if different).

(3) The Secretary of State may by order modify the instrument of government for the governing body of any grant-maintained school.

(4) An order under subsection (3)—

(a) may relate to all grant-maintained schools, to any category of such schools specified in the order or to any such school so specified, but

(b) shall not be made unless the Secretary of State has consulted—

(i) the governing body of each grant-maintained school to which the order relates,

(ii) (if the order relates only to a school having foundation governors) the person who appoints them and, if it is a Church of England, Church in Wales or Roman Catholic Church school, the appropriate diocesan authority (if different), and

(iii) (if the order relates to two or more schools and any of the schools are Church of England, Church in Wales or Roman Catholic Church schools having foundation governors) a body appearing to the Secretary of State to be representative of the church in question in matters relating to the provision of education in grant-maintained schools having foundation governors.

(5) Where, by reason of the making of a new instrument, or the modification of an instrument, under this section the number of governors of any category will (unless the required number of governors of that category resign) exceed the number provided for in the instrument, the new instrument or, as the case may be, the instrument as modified shall provide—

(a) for such number of governors of that category as is required to eliminate the excess to cease to hold office, and

(b) for the selection of those who are to cease to hold office.

Subsequent articles of government

221.—(1) The governing body of a grant-maintained school may, with the consent of the Secretary of State—

(a) make new articles of government in place of the existing articles for the school, or

(b) modify any articles made under paragraph (a) or, where articles made under section 58(1)(a) of the Education Act 1993 or Chapter IV of Part I of the Education Reform Act 1988 have effect (by virtue of Schedule 39 to this Act) as if made in accordance with this Part, those articles.

(2) Before exercising that power, the governing body of a school having foundation governors shall consult—

(a) the person who appoints the foundation governors, and

(b) in the case of a Church of England, Church in Wales or Roman Catholic Church school, the appropriate diocesan authority (if different).

(3) The Secretary of State may by a direction under this section require the

governing bodies of grant-maintained schools or any class of such schools specified in the direction or the governing body of any particular grant-maintained school so specified to modify their articles of government in any manner so specified.

(4) Before giving a direction under this section, the Secretary of State shall consult—

(a) the governing body or (as the case may be) each governing body to which the direction applies,

(b) (if the direction relates only to a school having foundation governors) the person who appoints them and, if it is a Church of England, Church in Wales or Roman Catholic Church school, the appropriate diocesan authority (if different), and

(c) (if the direction relates to two or more schools and any of the schools are Church of England, Church in Wales or Roman Catholic Church schools having foundation governors) a body appearing to the Secretary of State to be representative of the church in question in matters relating to the provision of education in grant-maintained schools having foundation governors.

Governors

Categories of governors

222. Schedule 24 (expressions used in connection with categories of governors) shall have effect.

Parent governors

223.—(1) Subject to subsection (6), the instrument of government for the governing body of a grant-maintained school shall provide for the governing body to include parent governors.

(2) Subject to subsection (7), the instrument shall provide for the number of parent governors to be—

(a) in the case of a primary school, not less than three nor more than five, and

(b) in the case of a secondary school, five.

(3) The instrument shall provide that if—

(a) one or more vacancies for parent governors are required to be filled by election, and

(b) the number of parents standing for election as parent governors is less than the number of vacancies,

the required number of parent governors shall be made up by persons appointed by the other members of the governing body.

(4) The instrument shall require governors, in appointing a person under a provision made by virtue of subsection (3)—

(a) to appoint a person who is the registered parent of a registered pupil at the school, where it is reasonably practicable to do so, and

(b) where it is not, to appoint a person who is the parent of one or more children of compulsory school age.

(5) In the case of a governing body incorporated in pursuance of proposals for acquisition of grant-maintained status, in relation to the election of a person as a parent governor to the new governing body—

(a) paragraph 7 of Schedule 8 (qualifications and arrangements for election of parent or teacher governors) shall apply as it applies in relation to the election of a parent governor to the existing governing body, and

(b) the new governing body shall inform the authority responsible for election arrangements of any vacancy arising for a parent governor,

and the instrument shall have effect accordingly.

(6) In the case of a governing body incorporated in pursuance of proposals for the establishment of a new grant-maintained school, the instrument shall have effect as if—

(a) before the date of implementation of the proposals, the governing body had power to appoint as parent governors persons who satisfy the prescribed requirements, and

(b) the first appointments were to be made before that date.

(7) In the case of a primary school, the initial instrument shall provide for the number of parent governors to be such number (being not less than three nor more than five) as is specified in the proposals for acquisition of grant-maintained status or, as the case may be, the proposals for the establishment of a new grant-maintained school.

(8) Subsection (3) does not apply, in the case of a governing body incorporated in pursuance of proposals for the establishment of a new grant-maintained school, to vacancies arising before the date of implementation of the proposals.

Teacher governors

224.—(1) Subject to subsection (4), the instrument of government for the governing body of a grant-maintained school shall provide for the governing body to include teacher governors.

(2) Subject to subsection (5), the instrument shall provide for the number of teacher governors to be either one or two.

(3) In the case of a governing body incorporated in pursuance of proposals for acquisition of grant-maintained status, in relation to the election of a person as a teacher governor to the new governing body—

(a) paragraph 7 of Schedule 8 shall apply as it applies in relation to the election of a teacher governor to the existing governing body, and

(b) the new governing body shall inform the authority responsible for election arrangements of any vacancy arising for a teacher governor,

and the instrument shall have effect accordingly.

(4) In the case of a governing body incorporated in pursuance of proposals for the establishment of a new grant-maintained school, the instrument shall have effect as if—

(a) before the date of implementation of the proposals, the governing body had power to appoint as teacher governors persons who satisfy the prescribed requirements, and

(b) the first appointments were to be made before that date.

(5) The initial instrument shall provide for the number of teacher governors to be such number (being either one or two) as is specified in the proposals for acquisition of grant-maintained status or, as the case may be, the proposals for the establishment of a new grant-maintained school.

Head teacher

225.—(1) Subject to subsection (3), the instrument of government for the governing body of a grant-maintained school shall provide for the governing body to include (as a governor ex officio) the person who is for the time being the head teacher.

(2) In the case of a governing body incorporated in pursuance of proposals for acquisition of grant-maintained status, the reference in subsection (1) to the head teacher is, in relation to any time before the date of implementation of the proposals, a reference to the existing head teacher.

(3) In the case of a governing body incorporated in pursuance of proposals for the establishment of a new grant-maintained school, the initial instrument of government for the school shall provide, in relation to any time before the date of implementation of the proposals when a person has been appointed to be the head teacher, for the governing body to include (as a

governor ex officio) that person.

First governors

226.—(1) The instrument of government for the governing body of a grant-maintained school which—

(a) is a county school immediately before it becomes grant-maintained, or

(b) is established in pursuance of proposals published under section 211,

shall provide for the governing body to include first governors.

(2) The instrument shall provide for such number of first governors as will secure that they outnumber the other governors.

(3) Subject to subsections (5) and (6), the instrument—

(a) shall require—

(i) at least two of the first governors to be (on the date or dates on which they respectively take office) parents of registered pupils at the school, and

(ii) at least two of the first governors to be (on the date or dates on which they respectively take office) members of the local community,

but one person may satisfy both requirements, and

(b) shall require the governing body, in appointing first governors, to secure that those governors include persons appearing to them to be members of the local business community (and such persons may also satisfy one or both of the requirements of paragraph (a)(i) and (ii)).

(4) The initial instrument shall provide for the number of first governors to be such number (being a number which will secure that they will outnumber the other governors) as is specified in the proposals for acquisition of grant-maintained status or, as the case may be, the proposals for the establishment of a new grant-maintained school.

(5) In the case of a grant-maintained school which is a county school immediately before it becomes grant-maintained, the instrument shall, despite subsection (3), have effect in relation to the determination of initial first governors—

(a) as if—

(i) it required the first governors to include at least two persons who on the date of their selection or nomination are parents of registered pupils at the school, and

(ii) it required the first governors to include at least two persons who appear to those selecting or nominating them to be members of the local community,

but provided that one person might satisfy both requirements, and

(b) as if it required the first governors to include persons who appear to those selecting or nominating them to be members of the local business community (and provided that such persons might also satisfy one or both of the requirements of paragraph (a)(i) and (ii) above).

(6) In the case of a grant-maintained school established in pursuance of proposals published under section 211—

(a) any provision of the instrument made by virtue of subsection (3)(a)(i) shall not apply in relation to the appointment before the date of implementation of the proposals of any first governor, and

(b) any provision of the instrument made by virtue of subsection (3)(b) shall apply as if references to the governing body were references to the funding authority.

(7) References in this section to governors other than first governors do not include sponsor governors.

Power of the Secretary of State to replace first governors

227.—(1) The instrument of government for the governing body of a grant-maintained school which—

(a) is a county school immediately before it becomes grant-maintained, or

(b) is established in pursuance of proposals published under section 211,

shall provide for the Secretary of State to have power, where any of subsections (2) to (4) apply, to replace all or any of the first governors.

(2) This subsection applies where the governing body have been guilty of substantial or persistent failure to comply or secure compliance with any requirement imposed by or under any enactment.

(3) This subsection applies where—

(a) there is a report of an inspection of the school in which the person who made it expressed the opinion that special measures were required to be taken in relation to the school,

(b) either that person was a member of the Inspectorate or the report stated that the Chief Inspector agreed with his opinion,

(c) if any registered inspector or member of the Inspectorate has made a later report of an inspection of the school under Part I of the School Inspections Act 1996, he did not express the opinion in the report that special measures were not required to be taken in relation to the school, and

(d) the Secretary of State has received a statement prepared under section 17 of that Act or the period allowed by subsection (2) of that section for the preparation of such a statement has expired;

and expressions used in this subsection and in that Act have the same meaning as in that Act.

(4) This subsection applies where in the opinion of the Secretary of State any action taken or proposed by the governing body of the school, or any failure of the governing body to act, is prejudicial to the provision of education by the school.

(5) The instrument of government for a grant-maintained school which—

(a) is a county school immediately before it becomes grant-maintained, or

(b) is established in pursuance of proposals published under section 211,

shall enable the Secretary of State to make such provision as he thinks fit for filling vacancies for first governors if it appears to him that the governing body are unable or unwilling to fill the vacancies.

(6) Any provision made by the instrument of government in pursuance of section 226(3) shall not apply for the purposes of the appointment by virtue of this section of any first governor.

Foundation governors

228.—(1) The instrument of government for the governing body of a grant-maintained school which—

(a) is a voluntary school immediately before it becomes grant-maintained, or

(b) is established in pursuance of proposals published under section 212,

shall provide for the governing body to include foundation governors.

(2) The instrument shall provide for such number of foundation governors as will secure that they outnumber the other governors.

(3) Subject to subsection (5), the instrument may provide for any foundation governorship to be held ex officio.

(4) Subject to subsection (7), the instrument—

(a) where it provides for a foundation governorship to be held ex officio, shall specify the office the holder of which is to be a foundation governor, and

(b) shall name the person or persons (if any) who are entitled to appoint any foundation governor.

(5) An additional foundation governor appointed by virtue of provision made in the instrument of government in pursuance of section 230(2) may

not be appointed to hold office ex officio.

(6) Subject to subsections (8) and (9), the instrument shall provide for at least two of the foundation governors to be (on the date or dates on which they respectively take office) parents of registered pupils at the school.

(7) The initial instrument shall—

(a) provide for the number of foundation governors to be such number (being a number which will secure that they will outnumber the other governors) as is specified;

(b) (in the case of a grant-maintained school which is a voluntary school immediately before it becomes grant-maintained) provide for the person or persons who, immediately before the incorporation date, were named in the school's instrument of government as being entitled to appoint foundation governors (as defined by section 78(2)) to the existing governing body to be entitled to appoint the foundation governors for the governing body of the grant-maintained school;

(c) (in the case of a grant-maintained school established in pursuance of proposals under section 212) provide for the promoters to be entitled to appoint the foundation governors;

(d) (where the instrument provides for a foundation governorship to be held ex officio) provide for it to be held by the holder of a specified office;

and in this subsection "specified" means specified in the proposals for acquisition of grant-maintained status or, as the case may be, the proposals for the establishment of a new grant-maintained school.

(8) In the case of a grant-maintained school which is a voluntary school immediately before it becomes grant-maintained, the instrument shall (despite anything in subsection (6)) have effect in relation to the determination of initial foundation governors as if it provided for the foundation governors to include at least two persons who on the date of their selection or appointment are parents of registered pupils at the school.

(9) In the case of a grant-maintained school established in pursuance of proposals published under section 212, subsection (6) above shall not apply in relation to the appointment of any foundation governor before the date of implementation of the proposals.

Sponsor governors

229.—(1) The instrument of government for the governing body of a grant-maintained secondary school may—

(a) name a person as a sponsor of the school, and

(b) provide for the governing body to include such number of sponsor governors, not exceeding four, as is specified in the instrument.

(2) Where a governing body of a school are to be incorporated in pursuance of proposals for acquisition of grant-maintained status, or proposals for the establishment of a new grant-maintained school, which name a person as a sponsor of the school, and the school is to be a secondary school, the initial instrument of government shall provide—

(a) for the person so named to be a sponsor of the school, and

(b) for the governing body to include such number of sponsor governors, not exceeding four, as is specified in the proposals.

(3) Where the instrument of government provides for two or more persons named as sponsors of the school in such proposals, or (as the case may be) in the instrument, to appoint governors—

(a) it shall provide for each sponsor to appoint such number of governors as is specified in relation to him in the proposals or (as the case may be) instrument, and

(b) it may not provide for any of those governors to be appointed by two or more sponsors acting jointly.

(4) In the case of a governing body incorporated in pursuance of proposals for the establishment of a new grant-maintained school which name a person as a sponsor of the school, the instrument of government shall have effect as if it required the first appointments of sponsor governors to be made before the date of implementation of the proposals.

Additional governors

230.—(1) The instrument of government for the governing body of a grant-maintained school shall enable the Secretary of State to appoint not more than two additional governors if it appears to him that the governing body are not adequately carrying out their responsibilities in respect of the conduct or management of the school.

(2) The instrument shall enable the appointing authority, during any period when any additional governors appointed by the Secretary of State by virtue of subsection (1) are in office, to appoint a number of additional first or, as the case may be, foundation governors not greater than the number of additional governors appointed by the Secretary of State who are then in office.

(3) In subsection (2) "the appointing authority" means the person entitled to appoint the first or, as the case may be, foundation governors on the governing body or, if more than one person is so entitled, the persons so entitled acting jointly.

Powers

Powers of governing body

231.—(1) The governing body of a grant-maintained school incorporated in pursuance of proposals for acquisition of grant-maintained status may conduct a school of the same description as the school immediately before the date of implementation of the proposals.

(2) The governing body of a grant-maintained school incorporated in pursuance of proposals for the establishment of a new grant-maintained school may conduct a school of the description in the proposals.

(3) The school conducted by the governing body of a grant-maintained school shall not, where changes have been made in the character or premises of the school since the date of implementation of the proposals, be regarded as of a different description to that immediately before that date or, as the case may be, to that in the proposals if the changes—

(a) did not require authorisation under Chapter VII (alteration etc. of grant-maintained schools), or

(b) were authorised under that Chapter.

(4) Subject to subsections (6) and (7) and to any provision made by the instrument or articles of government, the governing body of a grant-maintained school may do anything which appears to them to be necessary or expedient for the purpose of or in connection with the conduct of the school as for the time being constituted.

(5) The power conferred by subsection (4) includes in particular power—

(a) in the case of a grant-maintained school established in pursuance of proposals for acquisition of grant-maintained status, to assume the conduct, as from the date of implementation of the proposals, of the school as constituted immediately before that date;

(b) in the case of a grant-maintained school established in pursuance of proposals for the establishment of a new grant-maintained school, to conduct, as from the date of implementation of the proposals, a school of the description in the proposals;

(c) power to borrow such sums as the governing body think fit and, in connection with such borrowing, to grant any mortgage, charge or

other security over any land or other property of the governing body;
(d) to acquire and dispose of land and other property;
(e) to enter into contracts, including, in particular, contracts for the employment of teachers and other staff;
(f) to invest any sums not immediately required for the purposes of meeting the expenses of conducting the school or any liability transferred to the governing body under section 201; and
(g) to accept gifts of money, land or other property and apply it, or hold and administer it on trust, for such purposes.

(6) The power to borrow sums and grant security mentioned in subsection (5)(c) may only be exercised with the written consent of the Secretary of State (which may be given for particular borrowing or for borrowing of a particular class); but this subsection does not apply in relation to loans under section 255.

(7) The power to dispose of land mentioned in subsection (5)(d) may only be exercised with the written consent of the Secretary of State.

(8) Without prejudice to subsection (4), but subject to any provision made by the instrument or articles of government, the governing body of a grant-maintained school may provide education at the school which is neither primary nor secondary education if—
(a) it is part-time education suitable to the requirements of persons of any age over compulsory school age, or full-time education suitable to the requirements of persons who have attained the age of 19,
(b) it is part-time education suitable to the requirements of junior pupils who have not attained the age of five and the school provides full-time education for junior pupils of the same age, or
(c) they do so as agents for a local education authority under arrangements made with the authority for the purpose.

Joint schemes

232.—(1) Two or more grant-maintained schools may enter into a scheme under this section (referred to in this section and section 233 as a "joint scheme").

(2) A joint scheme may—
(a) authorise or require the governing bodies of the schools to which the scheme applies to establish joint committees constituted in accordance with the scheme,
(b) provide for the meetings and proceedings of any joint committee so constituted, and
(c) authorise or require the governing bodies of the schools to which the scheme applies to delegate, in such circumstances as may be determined in accordance with the scheme, such of their functions as may be so determined to any joint committee so constituted.

(3) A scheme providing for any joint committee must provide for the committee—
(a) to consist only of persons who are governors of the schools to which the scheme applies, and
(b) to include a head teacher of one of those schools, a parent governor of one of those schools and a first or foundation governor of one of those schools.

(4) A joint scheme may authorise or require the governing bodies of the schools to which the scheme applies to exercise jointly, in such circumstances as may be determined in accordance with the scheme, such of their functions as may be so determined; but such a scheme may not provide for the joint exercise of any function relating to the employment of teachers unless it also provides for the establishment of a joint committee to exercise that function.

(5) In relation to any teacher employed in pursuance of a joint scheme, the

School Teachers' Pay and Conditions Act 1991 shall have effect as if he were employed by the joint committee required to be established under subsection (4) and that joint committee were the governing body of a grant-maintained school.

(6) A joint scheme shall provide for any expenses of exercising any functions in pursuance of the scheme.

(7) A joint scheme shall have effect despite anything contained (whether in pursuance of a requirement under this Act or otherwise) in the instrument or articles of government for any of the schools to which the scheme applies.

(8) A joint scheme shall not have effect in relation to any matter dealt with in any co-ordinated arrangements for admissions (within the meaning of section 430) contained in an agreement approved by the Secretary of State under that section or made in pursuance of a scheme under that section.

Making and varying joint schemes

233.—(1) A joint scheme shall not come into force until it has been approved by the Secretary of State.

(2) A joint scheme shall provide for the scheme to cease to have effect where the governing bodies of all the schools to which the scheme applies agree.

(3) A joint scheme—

(a) may be varied by the governing bodies of all the schools to which the scheme applies if the variations are minor variations or the Secretary of State has approved the variations,

(b) if the Secretary of State so directs, shall be varied by the governing bodies in accordance with the direction, and

(c) if the Secretary of State so directs, shall cease to have effect.

(4) The Secretary of State may—

(a) approve a scheme, or variations, with such modifications as he thinks fit, or

(b) give a direction under subsection (3)(b) or (c),

only after proper consultations.

(5) In subsection (4) "proper consultations" means consultations with the governing bodies of every school—

(a) (in the case of a proposed scheme) to which the scheme will apply,

(b) (in the case of a variation) to which the scheme applies, or will apply after the variation, or

(c) (in the case of a direction for a scheme to cease to have effect) to which the scheme applies.

(6) The Secretary of State may by order specify what descriptions of variation are to be regarded as minor for the purposes of this section.

Schools acquiring grant-maintained status: determination etc. of initial governors

Determination of initial parent and teacher governors

234.—(1) Where proposals are required to be published under section 193 in respect of a school, this section applies for the purpose of determining the persons who are to be named in the proposals as proposed initial governors of any elected category.

(2) The authority responsible for election arrangements shall secure that—

(a) any election or appointment required for filling any vacancy on the existing governing body occurring before the date of publication of the proposals (including any vacancy arising by virtue of section 235(1)), and

(b) any election or appointment required by subsection (7),

is held or made if possible before that date, and otherwise as soon as possible afterwards.

(3) Subject to subsection (4), any person who on the date of publication of the proposals is an eligible governor of an elected category on the existing governing body shall be named in the proposals as published as a proposed initial governor of that category.

(4) If the number of governors of any elected category to be specified in the proposals is less than the number which, on the date of publication of the proposals, will be the number of eligible governors of that category on the existing governing body, such of the eligible governors of that category as may before the date of publication of the proposals be determined—

(a) by agreement between them, or

(b) in default of agreement, by drawing lots,

shall be named in the proposals as published as the proposed initial governors of that category.

(5) The existing governing body shall secure that any persons required to be named in the proposals in accordance with subsection (4) are determined before the date of publication of the proposals.

(6) Subsection (7) applies if the number which is, or is to be, specified in the proposals of governors of any elected category is greater than the complement of eligible governors of that category on the existing governing body on the date of publication of the proposals; and for those purposes that complement is—

(a) the number (if any) of eligible governors of that category on the existing governing body, plus

(b) the number (if any) of outstanding vacancies for governors of that category on the existing governing body.

(7) The authority responsible for election arrangements shall secure that such number of persons are elected or appointed, by the procedure applicable under Chapter IV of Part II (government of LEA-maintained schools), to hold office on the proposed governing body as governors of that category as is required to make up the difference between the number specified or to be specified in the proposals and the complement of eligible governors of that category on the existing governing body.

(8) In a case to which subsection (7) applies, the persons to be named in the proposals as published as the proposed initial governors of the category concerned shall be—

(a) any eligible governor of that category, and

(b) any person elected or appointed under subsection (7) as an initial governor of that category before the date of publication of the proposals.

Section 234: supplementary provisions

235.—(1) Subject to subsection (2), where the members of the existing governing body of a school to which section 234 applies include a person—

(a) who holds office as a governor of an elected category, and

(b) whose term of office is due to come to an end before the date of implementation of the proposals or at any time within the period of six months beginning with that date,

the governing body may by notice in writing to that person terminate his term of office on a date specified in the notice.

(2) The governing body may only terminate a person's term of office under subsection (1) if—

(a) his term of office is due to come to an end after the proposed date of publication of the proposals, or

(b) it would not in their view be reasonably practicable, in the time available between the date on which his term of office is due to come to an end and the proposed date of publication of the proposals, to fill the vacancy by the procedure applicable under Chapter IV of Part II.

(3) Without prejudice to paragraph 11(1) of Schedule 8 (instrument of government for county, controlled or maintained special school to provide for four-year term of office for governors other than ex officio governors), the term of office of a person elected or appointed in accordance with the requirements of Chapter IV of Part II, and any requirements of the instrument of government of the school to fill a vacancy arising by virtue of subsection (1), shall be four years.

(4) Where any such election or appointment as is referred to in section 234(2) is held or made on or after the date of publication of the proposals, the existing governing body shall publish, at such time and in such manner as may be prescribed, notice of the election or appointment.

Determination of initial first or foundation governors

236.—(1) Where proposals are required to be published under section 193 in respect of a county school, the existing governing body shall select the persons who are to be the initial first governors.

(2) Where proposals are required to be published under section 193 in respect of a voluntary school, the person or persons named in the school's instrument of government as being entitled to appoint foundation governors (as defined by section 78(2)) to the existing governing body shall select the persons who are to be the initial foundation governors.

(3) The duties under subsections (1) and (2) are to be complied with, if possible, before the date of publication of the proposals and otherwise as soon as possible after that date.

(4) Any person selected under subsection (1) or (2) shall, if possible, be named in the proposals as published as a proposed initial first or, as the case may be, foundation governor.

(5) In the case of any person so selected who is not named in the proposals as published, the existing governing body shall—

(a) give the Secretary of State notice in writing of the relevant particulars in respect of the person selected before such date as may be specified in directions given by the Secretary of State, and

(b) publish at such time and in such manner as may be prescribed notice of his selection.

(6) Where the Secretary of State is notified of any particulars under subsection (5), he shall modify the proposals by including in them the particulars notified to him.

(7) The existing governing body shall secure that any selection required by subsection (2) is carried out in accordance with that subsection.

(8) Where any selection falls in accordance with subsection (2) to be made by two or more persons, it shall be made by those persons acting jointly; and if they fail to agree on the selection it shall be made by the Secretary of State or in accordance with directions given by him.

(9) Before selecting, or giving any direction as to the selection of, an initial foundation governor in a case where religious education in accordance with the tenets of a particular religion or religious denomination is given to pupils at the school in pursuance of section 377 or 378 (religious education at voluntary schools), the Secretary of State shall consult the persons appearing to him to be the appropriate authority of the religion or denomination concerned.

Replacement of proposed initial parent and teacher governors before incorporation

237.—(1) This section applies where proposals published under section 193 are pending in respect of a school.

(2) If a person named in the proposals as a proposed governor of an elected

category who has been elected under section 234 or this section—
(a) dies,
(b) becomes prospectively disqualified for holding office as such a governor on the proposed governing body, or
(c) notifies the existing governing body that he is no longer willing to serve on the proposed governing body,

then, subject to subsection (3), the authority responsible for election arrangements in relation to the school shall secure that a person is elected or appointed by the procedure applicable under Chapter IV of Part II to hold office on the proposed governing body in his place.

(3) Where in a case to which subsection (2) applies the Secretary of State is satisfied that it would not be reasonably practicable to hold an election or make an appointment in accordance with that subsection in the time available, he shall modify the proposals by including in them (in substitution, where appropriate, for any particulars they supersede) the relevant particulars in respect of a person nominated by the existing governing body.

(4) If at any time a person named in the proposals as a proposed governor of an elected category who was so named by virtue of being an eligible governor of that category—
(a) ceases to hold office on the existing governing body,
(b) becomes prospectively disqualified for holding office as such a governor on the proposed governing body, or
(c) notifies the existing governing body that he is no longer willing to serve on the proposed governing body,

the Secretary of State shall modify the proposals by including in them (in substitution, where appropriate, for any particulars they supersede) the relevant particulars in respect of a person nominated by the existing governing body who is at that time an eligible governor of that category and who is neither named in the proposals nor prospectively disqualified as mentioned in paragraph (b).

(5) Where in a case to which subsection (4)(a) applies—
(a) there is no such eligible governor at the time in question, and
(b) the Secretary of State is satisfied that it would not be reasonably practicable in the time available before he determines the proposals to fill the vacancy on the existing governing body by the procedure applicable under Chapter IV of Part II,

the Secretary of State shall modify the proposals by including in them (in substitution, where appropriate, for any particulars they supersede) the relevant particulars in respect of a person nominated by the existing governing body.

(6) Where in a case to which subsection (4)(b) or (c) applies there is no such eligible governor at the time in question, subsection (2) shall apply as if the former proposed governor had been elected under section 234.

(7) If a person named in the proposals as a proposed governor of an elected category who has been nominated by the existing governing body under this section—
(a) dies,
(b) becomes prospectively disqualified for holding office as such a governor on the proposed governing body, or
(c) notifies the existing governing body that he is no longer willing to serve on the proposed governing body,

the Secretary of State shall modify the proposals by including in them (in substitution, where appropriate, for any particulars they supersede) the relevant particulars in respect of a person nominated by the existing governing body.

(8) References in this section to a person named in the proposals include any person required to be so named.

(9) The existing governing body shall—

(a) give the Secretary of State notice in writing of the occurrence of any event within subsection (2), (4) or (7),
(b) make any nomination required for the purposes of this section, and
(c) give the Secretary of State notice in writing of the relevant particulars in respect of any person nominated by them under this section.

Replacement of proposed initial first or foundation governors before incorporation

238.—(1) Where proposals published under section 193 are pending in respect of a county school and a person selected under section 236(1) to be a first governor—
(a) dies,
(b) becomes prospectively disqualified for holding office as such a governor on the proposed governing body, or
(c) notifies the existing governing body that he is no longer willing to serve on the proposed governing body,
the Secretary of State shall modify the proposals by including in them (in substitution, where appropriate, for any particulars they supersede) the relevant particulars in respect of a person nominated by the existing governing body.

(2) Where proposals published under section 193 are pending in respect of a voluntary school and a person selected under section 236(2) to be a foundation governor—
(a) dies,
(b) becomes prospectively disqualified for holding office as such a governor on the proposed governing body, or
(c) notifies the existing governing body that he is no longer willing to serve on the proposed governing body,
the Secretary of State shall modify the proposals by including in them (in substitution, where appropriate, for any particulars they supersede) the relevant particulars in respect of a person nominated by the person or persons named in the school's instrument of government as being entitled to appoint the foundation governors (as defined by section 78(2)) to the existing governing body.

(3) Subsections (8) and (9) of section 236 apply for the purposes of subsection (2) above as they apply for the purposes of that section, but as if references to selection were to nomination.

(4) The existing governing body shall—
(a) give the Secretary of State notice in writing of the occurrence of any event within subsection (1) or (2),
(b) make or secure the making of any nomination required for the purposes of this section, and
(c) give the Secretary of State written notification of the relevant particulars in respect of any person nominated under this section.

Elections and appointments required for determining initial governors of an elected category: supplementary provisions

239.—(1) Paragraph 7 of Schedule 8 shall apply in relation to the election of a person under section 234 or 237 to hold office as an initial parent governor or an initial teacher governor as it applies in relation to the election of a parent governor or teacher governor to the existing governing body.

(2) Where the authority responsible for election arrangements in relation to a school to which section 234 applies is the local education authority, the existing governing body shall give notice in writing to the authority of the proposed date of publication of the proposals for acquisition of grant-maintained status for the school.

(3) Where the authority responsible for election arrangements in relation

to a school to which section 234 or 237 applies is the local education authority, the existing governing body shall notify the authority in writing—

(a) of any election or appointment which appears to them to be required under section 234 or 237 in relation to the proposed governing body, and

(b) (if the number of eligible governors of any category on the existing governing body is for the time being less than the proposed number of initial governors of that category) of any vacancy on the existing governing body for a governor of that category.

(4) Where an election or appointment required for determining a proposed initial governor of any category is held or made at a time when proposals published under section 193 are pending in respect of the school, the existing governing body shall give the Secretary of State notice in writing of the relevant particulars in respect of the person elected or appointed.

(5) Where the Secretary of State is notified of any particulars under subsection (4), he shall modify the proposals by including in them the particulars notified to him (in substitution, where appropriate, for any particulars they supersede).

(6) For the purposes of subsection (4) an election or appointment is required for determining a proposed initial governor of any category if—

(a) it is required under section 234 or 237, or

(b) it is required for filling a vacancy on the existing governing body for a governor of that category and the number of eligible governors of that category on the existing governing body is for the time being less than the proposed number of initial governors of that category.

Initial sponsor governors

240.—(1) In relation to any governing body to be incorporated under Chapter II in pursuance of proposals for acquisition of grant-maintained status which give the name of a sponsor of the school, regulations shall make provision—

(a) for the determination of the persons who are to be the initial sponsor governors, and

(b) for the persons so determined to be named in the proposals, whether as published or as modified in pursuance of the regulations.

(2) The regulations may in particular make provision corresponding to any of the provisions of sections 234 to 239.

New grant-maintained schools: determination etc. of initial governors

Initial governors for new grant-maintained schools

241.—(1) This section applies in relation to any governing body to be incorporated under Chapter IV.

(2) Regulations shall make provision for the appointment of the persons who are to be the initial governors and, in particular, shall require each appointing authority—

(a) to obtain the Secretary of State's consent before making any appointment, and

(b) to notify the Secretary of State before the incorporation date of the appointments to all the initial governorships for which the authority is the appointing authority.

(3) In subsection (2) the "appointing authority", in relation to any appointment, means the person entitled to make the appointment.

General and supplementary

Saving for defects in selection or nomination

242.—(1) The proceedings of the governing body of a grant-maintained school shall not be invalidated by any defect in any procedure required under this Chapter in relation to the determination of any person to hold office as an initial governor.

(2) This section is without prejudice to the generality of paragraph 11 of Schedule 22.

Chapter V: interpretation

243.—(1) This section applies for the purposes of this Chapter.

(2) References to the authority responsible for election arrangements in relation to a school are references to the authority or body by whom all necessary arrangements for any election of parent governors or teacher governors to the governing body of the school fall to be made under paragraph 7(3) of Schedule 8 (such arrangements to be made by the local education authority or the school's governing body depending on the type of school).

(3) References, in relation to a vacancy for a governor of an elected category on the existing governing body of a school in respect of which proposals are required to be or have been published under section 193 and in sections 234(7) and 237(2), to the procedure applicable under Chapter IV of Part II are references—

(a) except where any provision made by virtue of section 81 (appointment of parent governors by governing body) applies, to the holding of an election under that Chapter, and

(b) where any such provision applies, to the making of an appointment in accordance with that provision.

(4) A person named in proposals for acquisition of grant-maintained status in respect of a school as a proposed initial governor of any category shall be treated as becoming prospectively disqualified for holding office as such a governor on the proposed governing body if an event occurs in relation to him which, if—

(a) it had occurred on or after the incorporation date, and

(b) the instrument prescribed under section 219 for the governing bodies of schools of the kind in question had then been in force,

would have caused him to become disqualified for holding such office.

CHAPTER VI

FUNDING OF GRANT-MAINTAINED SCHOOLS

Grants: general

Maintenance grants

244.—(1) Subject to the provisions of this Part, the funding authority shall make annual grants (known as maintenance grants) to the governing body of each grant-maintained school, each such grant being made in respect of expenditure for the purposes of the school incurred or to be incurred by the governing body in the financial year to which the grant relates.

(2) The amount of the maintenance grant payable in respect of a school for a financial year shall be such as may be determined (and from time to time revised) in accordance with regulations (referred to in this Chapter as "grant regulations"); and grant regulations may provide for determinations (and revisions) to be made by reference to amounts determined or redetermined for the purposes of this section by the Secretary of State.

(3) Subject to—

(a) any provision made by virtue of section 232(6),

(b) any requirements imposed by the funding authority under section 247(1), and

(c) any requirements as to the application of maintenance grant contained in the articles of government of the school,

the governing body of a grant-maintained school shall apply any payments made to them in respect of maintenance grant solely for the purposes of the school.

(4) In this Chapter "the purposes of the school" do not include purposes wholly referable to the provision of—

(a) part-time education suitable to the requirements of persons of any age over compulsory school age, or

(b) full-time education suitable to the requirements of persons who have attained the age of 19.

Special purpose grants

245.—(1) Grant regulations may provide for the payment by the funding authority to the governing bodies of grant-maintained schools of grants (known as special purpose grants) in respect of expenditure, of any class or description specified in the regulations, incurred or to be incurred by the governing bodies—

(a) for or in connection with educational purposes of any class or description so specified,

(b) in making any provision (whether of educational services or facilities or otherwise) of any class or description so specified which appears to the funding authority to be required for meeting any special needs of the population of the area served by the schools in question, or

(c) in respect of expenses of any class or description so specified, being expenses which it appears to the funding authority the governing bodies of such schools cannot reasonably be expected to meet from maintenance grant.

(2) Grant regulations may provide for special purpose grants to be payable—

(a) on a regular basis in respect of expenditure of a recurrent kind, or

(b) by reference to expenditure incurred or to be incurred on particular occasions or during any particular period.

Capital grants

246.—(1) Grant regulations may provide for the payment by the funding authority to the governing bodies of grant-maintained schools of grants (known as capital grants) in respect of expenditure of a capital nature, of any class or description specified in the regulations, incurred or to be incurred by the governing bodies.

(2) The descriptions of expenditure which are to be regarded for the purposes of capital grant as expenditure of a capital nature shall be such as may be determined by or in accordance with the regulations.

(3) Where the governing body of a grant-maintained school include sponsor governors, the funding authority shall, if directed to do so by the Secretary of State, pay capital grant of such amount as may be specified in the directions in respect of such expenditure falling within subsection (1) as is incurred, or to be incurred, by the governing body for such purposes as may be specified in the directions.

(4) Before giving a direction under subsection (3), the Secretary of State shall consult the funding authority.

(5) A direction under subsection (3) may not be given after the end of the period of twelve months beginning—

(a) (in the case of a governing body incorporated in pursuance of proposals for acquisition of grant-maintained status which include sponsor governors on the incorporation date) with that date,

(b) (in the case of a governing body incorporated in pursuance of proposals for the establishment of a new grant-maintained school which include sponsor governors on the date of implementation of the proposals) with that date, and

(c) (in any other case) with the date when the instrument of government naming a person as the sponsor of the school came into effect.

Imposition of requirements on governing body in receipt of grant

247.—(1) A governing body to whom any payments in respect of maintenance grant, capital grant or special purpose grant are made shall comply with such requirements of a kind mentioned in subsection (2) as the funding authority may from time to time impose.

(2) The kinds of requirements which may be imposed under subsection (1) are—

(a) requirements specified in grant regulations as requirements which may be imposed by the funding authority on governing bodies to whom such payments are made, and

(b) requirements determined in accordance with grant regulations by the funding authority.

(3) Requirements imposed under subsection (1)—

(a) may be imposed on or at any time after the making of any payment by reference to which they are imposed, and

(b) subject to subsection (4), may at any time be varied by the funding authority.

(4) The power of the funding authority to vary such a requirement—

(a) does not apply to a requirement of the kind mentioned in subsection (2)(a), or a requirement required to be imposed by the regulations (by virtue of subsection (9)) or by directions under section 24, unless the Secretary of State has consented to the variation, and

(b) is subject, in the case of a requirement of the kind mentioned in subsection (2)(b), to the provisions of the regulations relating to the determination of the requirements that may be imposed in the case of payments in respect of the grant in question.

(5) Requirements imposed under subsection (1) may at any time be waived or removed by the funding authority with the consent of the Secretary of State.

(6) The requirements which may be specified in or authorised by grant regulations as requirements which may be imposed on governing bodies to whom payments are made in respect of special purpose grant or capital grant may, in particular, if any conditions specified in the requirements are satisfied, require the payment to the funding authority of the whole or any part of the following amount.

(7) That amount is—

(a) the amount of the payments made in respect of the grant, or

(b) so much of the value of any premises or equipment in respect of which the grant was paid as is determined in accordance with the requirements to be properly attributable to the payment of such grant,

whichever is the greater.

(8) No such requirement as is referred to in subsection (6) may be imposed where any payment is made in respect of capital grant if—

(a) the grant is made in respect of the provision, alteration or repair of premises for a school, and

(b) any freehold interest in the premises in respect of which the grant is made is, or is to be, held on trust for the purposes of the school.

(9) Grant regulations may require the funding authority to impose any such requirements as may be imposed under the preceding provisions of this section.

Grants: further provisions

248.—(1) The times at which, and the manner in which, payments are made in respect of—

(a) maintenance grant for a grant-maintained school in respect of any financial year,
(b) special purpose grant, and
(c) capital grant,

shall be such as may be determined from time to time by the funding authority.

(2) Payments in respect of maintenance grant for a school in respect of any financial year may be made, before any amount has been determined in accordance with grant regulations as the amount of such grant payable for that year in respect of the school, by reference to an estimate of the amount which will be so payable made by the funding authority.

(3) Where in respect of any financial year an over-payment of maintenance grant is made to the governing body of a school, a sum equal to the amount of that over-payment shall be recoverable from the governing body by the funding authority.

(4) Where a sum is payable by the governing body of a school to the funding authority—

(a) in respect of an over-payment of maintenance grant in respect of a financial year, or
(b) by way of repayment of special purpose grant or capital grant (whether by virtue of a requirement such as is mentioned in section 247(6) or otherwise),

the funding authority may (without prejudice to any other mode of recovery) recover the whole or any part of that sum by deducting it from any grant payable by them to the governing body.

(5) In this section references to an over-payment of maintenance grant in respect of a financial year are to any amount by which the aggregate amount of any payments in respect of maintenance grant made to the governing body of the school in question in respect of the year exceeds the amount finally determined in accordance with grant regulations as the amount of maintenance grant payable for that year in respect of the school.

(6) The funding authority shall exercise any power conferred on them by this section, by any of sections 216 and 244 to 247, or by paragraph 6 of Schedule 21 in such manner (if any) as may be specified in or determined in accordance with grant regulations.

Grants: Wales (until establishment of the SFCW)

Application of sections 250 to 254

249. Before the Schools Funding Council for Wales begin to exercise their functions, sections 250 to 254 shall have effect in relation to grant-maintained schools in Wales in place of sections 244(1) and (3), 245(1), 246(1), 247 and 248.

Maintenance grants

250.—(1) Subject to the provisions of this Part, the Secretary of State shall make annual grants (known as maintenance grants) to the governing body of each grant-maintained school, each such grant being made in respect of expenditure for the purposes of the school incurred or to be incurred by the governing body in the financial year to which the grant relates.

(2) Subject to—

(a) any provision made by virtue of section 232(6),

(b) any requirements imposed by the Secretary of State under section 253(1) or (3), and
(c) any requirements as to the application of maintenance grant contained in the articles of government of the school,

the governing body of a grant-maintained school shall apply any payments made to them in respect of maintenance grant solely for the purposes of the school.

Special purpose grants

251. Grant regulations may provide for the payment by the Secretary of State to the governing bodies of grant-maintained schools of grants (known as special purpose grants) in respect of expenditure incurred or to be incurred by them of any class or description specified in the regulations—
(a) for or in connection with educational purposes of any class or description so specified,
(b) in making any provision (whether of educational services or facilities or otherwise) of any class or description so specified which appears to the Secretary of State to be required for meeting any special needs of the population of the area served by the school, or
(c) in respect of expenses of any class or description so specified, being expenses which it appears to the Secretary of State the governing bodies of such schools cannot reasonably be expected to meet from maintenance grant.

Capital grants

252. Grant regulations may provide for the payment by the Secretary of State to the governing bodies of grant-maintained schools of grants (known as capital grants) in respect of expenditure of a capital nature, of any class or description specified in the regulations, incurred or to be incurred by the governing bodies.

Imposition of requirements on governing body in receipt of grant

253.—(1) A governing body to whom any payments in respect of maintenance grant or special purpose grants are made shall comply with such requirements of a kind mentioned in subsection (2) as the Secretary of State may from time to time impose.

(2) The kinds of requirements which may be imposed under subsection (1) are—
(a) requirements specified in grant regulations as requirements which may be imposed by the Secretary of State on governing bodies to whom such payments are made, and
(b) requirements determined in accordance with grant regulations by the Secretary of State.

(3) A governing body to whom any payments in respect of capital grant are made shall comply with such requirements determined by the Secretary of State as he may from time to time impose.

(4) Requirements imposed under subsection (1) or (3)—
(a) may be imposed on or at any time after the making of any payment by reference to which they are imposed, and
(b) may at any time be waived or removed or, subject to subsection (5), varied by the Secretary of State.

(5) The power of the Secretary of State to vary such a requirement—
(a) does not apply to a requirement of the kind mentioned in subsection (2)(a), and
(b) is subject, in the case of a requirement of the kind mentioned in subsection (2)(b), to the provisions of the regulations relating to the determination of the requirements that may be imposed in the case of

payments in respect of the grants in question.

(6) The requirements—

(a) which may be specified in or authorised by grant regulations as requirements which may be imposed on governing bodies to whom payments are made in respect of special purpose grant, or

(b) which may be imposed by the Secretary of State on a governing body to whom payments in respect of capital grant are made,

may, in particular, if any conditions specified in the requirements are satisfied, require the payment to the Secretary of State of the whole or any part of the following amount.

(7) That amount is—

(a) the amount of the payments made in respect of the grant, or

(b) so much of the value of any premises or equipment in respect of which the grant was paid as is determined in accordance with the requirements to be properly attributable to the payment of such grant,

whichever is the greater.

(8) No such requirement as is referred to in subsection (6) may be imposed where any payment is made in respect of capital grant if—

(a) the grant is made in respect of the provision, alteration or repair of premises for a school, and

(b) any freehold interest in the premises in respect of which the grant is made is, or is to be, held on trust for the purposes of the school.

Grants: further provisions

254.—(1) The times at which, and the manner in which, payments are made in respect of—

(a) maintenance grant for a grant-maintained school in respect of any financial year,

(b) special purpose grants, and

(c) capital grants,

shall be such as may be determined from time to time by the Secretary of State.

(2) Payments in respect of maintenance grant for a school in respect of any financial year may be made, before any amount has been determined in accordance with grant regulations as the amount of such grant payable for that year in respect of the school, by reference to an estimate of the amount which will be so payable made by the Secretary of State.

(3) Where in respect of any financial year an over-payment of maintenance grant is made to the governing body of a school, a sum equal to the amount of that over-payment shall be recoverable from the governing body by the Secretary of State.

(4) Where a sum is payable by the governing body of a school to the Secretary of State—

(a) in respect of an over-payment of maintenance grant in respect of a financial year, or

(b) by way of repayment of special purpose grant or capital grant (whether by virtue of a requirement such as is mentioned in section 253(6) or otherwise),

the Secretary of State may (without prejudice to any other mode of recovery) recover the whole or any part of that sum by deducting it from any grant payable by him to the governing body.

(5) In this section references to an over-payment of maintenance grant in respect of a financial year are to any amount by which the aggregate amount of any payments in respect of maintenance grant made to the governing body of the school in question in respect of the year exceeds the amount finally determined in accordance with grant regulations as the amount of maintenance grant payable for that year in respect of the school.

Loans

Loans to governing bodies

255.—(1) The appropriate authority may make loans to the governing bodies of grant-maintained schools in respect of expenditure of any class or description specified in regulations ("loan regulations") incurred or to be incurred by the governing bodies for or in connection with such purposes as may be so specified.

(2) Any loan under this section shall be made on such terms as loan regulations may require, being terms specified in or determined in accordance with the regulations.

(3) Where any sum is payable by the governing body of a grant-maintained school to the appropriate authority in respect of the principal of, or interest on, any loan under this section, the appropriate authority may (without prejudice to any other mode of recovery) recover the whole or any part of that sum by deducting it from any grant payable by them to the governing body.

(4) In this section "the appropriate authority"—

(a) in relation to Wales before the Schools Funding Council for Wales begin to exercise their functions, means the Secretary of State, and

(b) in any other case, means the funding authority.

(5) The funding authority shall exercise any power conferred on them by this section in such manner (if any) as may be specified in or determined in accordance with loan regulations.

Recovery from local funds

Recovery from local funds of sums in respect of maintenance grant

256.—(1) Where the Secretary of State so determines, this section applies to a local education authority in respect of any financial year for which the determination is made; and the determination may apply this section in respect of all grant-maintained schools in the area of the authority or in respect of such grant-maintained schools in that area as may be ascertained by or in accordance with the determination.

(2) The Secretary of State shall, in respect of each financial year for which he makes a determination under subsection (1) in respect of a local education authority, give notice in writing to the authority of the terms of the determination.

(3) The Secretary of State may, in the case of a local education authority to which this section applies in respect of any financial year, recover from the authority sums in respect of the maintenance grant payable for that year to the governing bodies of any grant-maintained schools in respect of which the determination applies.

(4) Subject to subsection (5), sums recoverable by virtue of this section in respect of a school for any financial year—

(a) shall be of such amounts, and

(b) shall fall due on such date or dates,

as may be determined by the Secretary of State.

(5) The amount of any sum so recoverable shall be determined by reference to any amount—

(a) which has previously been determined under section 257 as the total amount recoverable in respect of the school and financial year in question, or

(b) (where no amount has previously been determined as mentioned in paragraph (a)) which is estimated by the Secretary of State as the amount which will initially be determined under section 257 as the total amount recoverable in respect of the school and financial year in question,

and which the Secretary of State considers it appropriate to adopt for the time being as a basis for determining the amounts of sums so recoverable.

(6) The Secretary of State may recover sums due to him under this section in either or both of the following ways—

(a) by requiring the local education authority to pay the whole or any part of any such sum at such time or times as he thinks fit, and

(b) by deducting, at such time or times as he thinks fit, the whole or any part of any such sum from any grant payable by him to the authority under any enactment (whenever passed) or from any amount payable by him to the authority under Part III of Schedule 8 to the Local Government Finance Act 1988 (redistributed non-domestic rates).

Determination of total amount recoverable under section 256

257.—(1) The total amount recoverable by virtue of section 256 in respect of a school for any financial year shall be such as may be determined (and from time to time revised) in accordance with regulations made by the Secretary of State ("recoupment regulations").

(2) Subject to any provision made by such regulations by virtue of subsection (3), recoupment regulations shall provide for the total amount so recoverable to be determined by reference to any amount determined under grant regulations as the amount of the maintenance grant payable in respect of the school and the financial year in question (as from time to time revised).

(3) Recoupment regulations may provide for reducing any amount which would otherwise fall to be determined under the regulations as the total amount recoverable from any local education authority by virtue of section 256 for a financial year by reference to any excess amounts recovered under that section in respect of any previous financial year.

(4) For the purposes of subsection (3) an excess amount is recovered under section 256 in respect of a financial year if the aggregate amount of the sums recovered under that section for that year from the local education authority—

(a) in respect of any school in respect of which sums are recoverable from the authority under that section, or

(b) (where there is more than one such school) in respect of both or all of those schools,

exceeds the total amount recoverable in accordance with recoupment regulations in respect of that school or (as the case may be) in respect of both or all of those schools for that year.

Provisions consequential on section 256

258.—(1) For the purposes of sections 492 and 493 (recoupment for provision for education of pupils belonging to, or having connection with, area of another authority), the provision for education made in any financial year in respect of a registered pupil at a grant-maintained school which is not made by the local education authority shall, if sums are recoverable under section 256 in respect of the school and that year from the authority, be taken to have been made by them.

(2) The reference in subsection (1) to provision for education includes a reference to provision of any benefits or services for which provision is made by or under this Act or any other enactment relating to education.

(3) The governing body of a grant-maintained school shall, if sums are recoverable under section 256 in respect of the school from a local education authority, provide the authority with such information relating to the registered pupils at the school as the authority may require for the purpose of claiming any amount in respect of such a pupil from another authority by virtue of regulations under section 492 or 493.

Chapter VII

Alteration etc. of grant-maintained schools

Proposals for change of character etc. by governing body

259.—(1) Subject to subsection (2), where the governing body of a grant-maintained school intend to make a significant change in the character, or a significant enlargement of the premises, of the school or to transfer the school to a new site they shall—

(a) publish proposals for that purpose in such manner as may be prescribed, and

(b) submit to the Secretary of State a copy of the published proposals.

(2) No proposals shall be published under this section for the purpose of making a significant change in the religious character of a school unless the trustees under any trust deed relating to the school have given their consent in writing to the change in question; and the requirement to publish proposals under subsection (1) does not apply in relation to a transfer of a school to a new site if it is intended to return to the existing site within three years of the time of the transfer.

(3) Before publishing any proposals under this section, the governing body shall consult such persons as appear to them to be appropriate; and in discharging their duty under this subsection, the governing body shall have regard to any guidance given to them from time to time by the Secretary of State.

(4) Proposals published under this section shall include particulars—

(a) of the proposed time or times of implementation of the proposals, and

(b) of the number of pupils proposed to be admitted to the school in each relevant age group in the first school year in relation to which the proposals have been wholly implemented,

and, if pupils are proposed to be admitted for nursery education, shall give the prescribed information.

(5) Proposals published under this section shall be accompanied by a statement which—

(a) describes any effect the implementation of the proposals would have on provision at the school for pupils who have special educational needs, and

(b) explains the effect of subsection (6).

(6) Within the period of two months beginning with the date of publication of the proposals, objections to the proposals may be submitted to the Secretary of State by any of the following—

(a) any ten or more local government electors for the area,

(b) the governing body of any school affected by the proposals,

(c) the appropriate further education funding council (if the proposals affect the provision of education to which section 2(1) of the Further and Higher Education Act 1992 applies), and

(d) any local education authority concerned.

(7) Where the proposals are to transfer a school to a site in a different area, objections under subsection (6) to the proposals may also be submitted by any ten or more local government electors for that area.

(8) No decision taken at a meeting of the governing body of a grant-maintained school that would result in the publication of proposals under this section shall have effect unless it is confirmed at a second meeting of the governing body held not less than 28 days after the first.

Proposals for change of character etc. by funding authority

260.—(1) This section has effect in respect of the area of a local education authority if an order under section 27(1) applies to the area.

(2) Where the funding authority are of the opinion that—

(a) a significant change should be made in the character of a grant-maintained school,

(b) a significant enlargement of the premises of such a school should be made, or

(c) such a school should be transferred to a new site in the area or in another area to which an order under section 27(1) applies,

they may publish proposals for that purpose in such manner as may be prescribed and submit a copy of the published proposals to the Secretary of State.

(3) No proposals shall be published under this section for the purpose of making a significant change in the religious character of a school; and subsection (2) does not apply in relation to a transfer of a school to a new site if it is intended to return to the existing site within three years of the time of the transfer.

(4) Before publishing any proposals under this section the funding authority shall consult—

(a) such persons as appear to them to be appropriate, and

(b) (in the case of a Church of England, Church in Wales or Roman Catholic Church school having any foundation governor who is appointed by the appropriate diocesan authority) that authority;

and in discharging their duty under paragraph (a) the funding authority shall have regard to any guidance given to them from time to time by the Secretary of State.

(5) Proposals published under this section shall include particulars—

(a) of the proposed time or times of implementation of the proposals, and

(b) of the number of pupils proposed to be admitted to the school in each relevant age group in the first school year in relation to which the proposals have been wholly implemented,

and, if pupils are proposed to be admitted for nursery education, shall give the prescribed information.

(6) Proposals published under this section shall be accompanied by a statement which—

(a) describes any effect the implementation of the proposals would have on provision at the school for pupils who have special educational needs, and

(b) explains the effect of subsection (7).

(7) Within the period of two months beginning with the date of publication of the proposals, objections to the proposals may be submitted to the funding authority by any of the following—

(a) any ten or more local government electors for the area,

(b) the governing body of the school to which the proposals relate,

(c) the governing body of any other school affected by the proposals,

(d) the appropriate further education funding council (if the proposals affect the provision of education to which section 2(1) of the Further and Higher Education Act 1992 applies), and

(e) any local education authority concerned.

(8) Where the proposals are to transfer a school to a site in a different area, objections under subsection (7) to the proposals may also be submitted by any ten or more local government electors for that area.

(9) Not later than one month after the end of that period, the funding authority shall send to the Secretary of State copies of all such objections made (and not withdrawn in writing) together with their observations on them.

Approval, adoption or rejection of proposals

261.—(1) Proposals published under section 259 require the approval of the Secretary of State.

(2) Proposals published under section 260 require the approval of the Secretary of State if—

(a) he gives notice to that effect to the funding authority within two months after the submission to him of the published proposals, or

(b) objections have been made under subsection (7) of that section within the period allowed under that subsection (unless all objections so made have been withdrawn in writing within that period).

(3) Where under subsection (1) or (2) any proposals require the approval of the Secretary of State, he may—

(a) reject them,

(b) approve them without modification, or

(c) after consulting the governing body (and, in the case of proposals published under section 260, the funding authority) approve them with such modifications as he thinks desirable.

(4) Where proposals published under section 260 do not require the approval of the Secretary of State, the funding authority shall determine whether to adopt the proposals.

(5) The funding authority shall—

(a) make any determination under subsection (4) not later than four months after the publication of the proposals, and

(b) give notice in writing to the Secretary of State and the governing body of their determination.

Approval of school premises

262.—(1) Where the governing body of a grant-maintained school publish proposals under section 259, they shall, if the funding authority so direct, submit to the authority, at such time and in such form and manner as the authority may direct, the particulars mentioned in subsection (3); and particulars so submitted require the approval of the funding authority under this section.

(2) Where the funding authority publish proposals under section 260, they shall, if in their opinion the circumstances so require, prepare the particulars mentioned in subsection (3); and particulars so prepared require adoption by the funding authority under this section.

(3) The particulars are—

(a) particulars of the provision made or to be made in respect of the means of access to and within the premises or proposed premises of the school, and

(b) such other particulars in respect of the premises or proposed premises of the school as the funding authority may require or, in the case of proposals published under section 260, as may be required.

(4) The particulars prepared or submitted under subsection (3)(a) shall indicate the extent to which the provision referred to conforms with the minimum requirements, so far as they are relevant to school premises, of—

(a) Design Note 18 "Access for Disabled People to Educational Buildings" published in 1984 on behalf of the Secretary of State, or

(b) (if that Note has been replaced by a document prescribed by regulations made or having effect as if made under the Town and Country Planning Act 1990) that document.

Implementation of proposals, etc.

263.—(1) Where any proposals are approved or adopted under section 261, it shall be the duty of the governing body of the school to which the proposals relate to implement them.

(2) Proposals required to be implemented under this section shall be implemented in accordance with any particulars approved or adopted under section 262.

(3) The Secretary of State may, at the request of a governing body, modify any proposals published under section 259 which the governing body are required to implement under this section.

(4) The Secretary of State may—

(a) at the request of a governing body, or

(b) at the request of the funding authority and after consulting the governing body,

modify any proposals published under section 260 which the governing body are required to implement under this section.

(5) Neither the governing body of a grant-maintained school nor any other person shall make any significant change in the character, or significant enlargement of the premises, of the school or transfer the school to a new site, or undertake to do any of those things, unless proposals have been published under section 259 or 260 and any requirements of section 261 have been complied with.

(6) Subsection (5) does not—

(a) prevent the Secretary of State allowing such steps to be taken by the governing body of a grant-maintained school, pending compliance with those requirements and the giving or making of the approval or adoption, as the Secretary of State considers reasonable in the circumstances, or

(b) apply to any transfer of a school to a new site falling within section 259(2) or 260(3).

Power to transfer functions under preceding provisions etc.

264.—(1) The Secretary of State may by order provide for this Part to have effect with the modifications in subsections (2) to (7) in relation to any proposals published by the governing body of a grant-maintained school under section 259 after the coming into force of the order.

(2) The governing body shall submit a copy of the proposals to the funding authority as well as to the Secretary of State.

(3) Any objections under subsection (6) of that section to the proposals shall be submitted to the funding authority instead of to the Secretary of State.

(4) If any objection is made under subsection (6) of that section within the period allowed under that subsection and not withdrawn in writing within that period, then, not later than one month after the end of that period—

(a) the funding authority shall send to the Secretary of State copies of all such objections made (and not withdrawn in writing) together with their observations on them, and

(b) may themselves submit to the Secretary of State an objection to the proposals.

(5) Sections 261(1) and 263(3) shall not apply to the proposals unless—

(a) the Secretary of State gives notice to the funding authority within two months after the submission to him of the published proposals that the proposals require his approval, or

(b) objections have been made under subsection (6) of section 259 within the period allowed under that subsection (unless all objections so made have been withdrawn in writing within that period).

(6) Where sections 261(1) and 263(3) do not apply to the proposals—

(a) the proposals shall require the approval of the funding authority,

(b) the funding authority may reject them, approve them without modification or, after consulting the governing body, approve them with such modifications as they think desirable, and

(c) where the governing body are required to implement the proposals under section 263, the funding authority may at their request modify the proposals.

(7) Paragraph 20 of Schedule 4 shall not apply in relation to the proposals.

(8) In this Part—

(a) references to approval under, or the requirements of, section 261 include approval under, or the requirements of, this section, and

(b) references to the modification of proposals under section 263(3) include the modification of proposals under subsection (6)(c).

(9) This section does not apply to proposals published under section 198 (to which this Chapter is applied by subsection (3) of that section); and section 263(3) is not disapplied by this section in the case of proposals treated for the purposes of this Part (by virtue of section 37(9) or 43(6)) as if they had been approved under section 261.

Proposals for change of character approved before school becomes grant-maintained

265.—(1) This section applies where—

(a) proposals for a change in the character or an enlargement of the premises of a county or voluntary school, or for the transfer of a county or voluntary school to a new site, have been approved under section 35 or 41, and

(b) the school becomes a grant-maintained school before the proposals are implemented.

(2) The proposals—

(a) shall be treated for the purposes of this Part as if they had been published under section 260 and approved under section 261, and

(b) shall be implemented in accordance with any particulars approved under section 39 or (as the case may be) 44.

(3) Subsection (2) is subject to section 210.

Chapter VII: interpretation

266.—(1) References in this Part to a change in the character of a school do not include any change resulting only from persons beginning or ceasing to be provided with—

(a) part-time education suitable to the requirements of persons of any age over compulsory school age,

(b) part-time education suitable to the requirements of junior pupils who have not attained the age of five where the school provides full-time education for junior pupils of the same age, or

(c) full-time education suitable to the requirements of persons who have attained the age of 19.

(2) Where proposals for a significant change in the character, or significant enlargement of the premises, of a school or for the transfer of a school to a new site have been approved or adopted under section 261, references in this Chapter to the proposals are references to the proposals as approved or adopted, subject to any modifications of the proposals under section 263(3) or (4).

CHAPTER VIII

DISCONTINUANCE OF GRANT-MAINTAINED SCHOOLS

Proposals for discontinuance

Proposals by governing body for discontinuance

267.—(1) The governing body of a grant-maintained school may publish proposals under this section for the discontinuance of the school if they—

(a) decide by a resolution passed at a meeting of that body to publish such proposals, and

(b) confirm that decision by a resolution passed at a subsequent meeting of the governing body held not less than 28 days after that at which the first resolution was passed.

(2) Before passing such a resolution as is mentioned in subsection (1)(a), the governing body shall consult such persons as appear to them to be appropriate; and in discharging their duty under this subsection the governing body shall have regard to any guidance given to them from time to time by the Secretary of State.

(3) The governing body shall, as soon as practicable after the passing of the second resolution, give notice in writing of the second resolution to the local education authority.

(4) The governing body may, within the period of six months beginning with the date of the second resolution, publish proposals for the discontinuance of the school in such manner as may be prescribed and, where they do so, shall submit to the Secretary of State a copy of the published proposals.

(5) The published proposals shall specify the proposed date of discontinuance of the school.

(6) The published proposals shall be accompanied by a statement—

(a) indicating whether or not there are any proposals for the premises of the school to be used by any new or existing school, and

(b) explaining the effect of subsection (7).

(7) Within the period of two months beginning with the date of publication of the proposals, objections to the proposals may be submitted to the Secretary of State by any of the following—

(a) any ten or more local government electors,

(b) the governing body of any school affected by the proposals,

(c) the appropriate further education funding council (if the proposals affect the provision of education to which section 2(1) of the Further and Higher Education Act 1992 applies), and

(d) any local education authority concerned.

Proposals by funding authority for discontinuance

268.—(1) This section has effect in respect of the area of a local education authority if an order under section 27(1) applies to the area.

(2) The funding authority may publish, in such manner as may be prescribed, proposals for the discontinuance of any grant-maintained school and, where they do so, shall submit to the Secretary of State a copy of the published proposals.

(3) The published proposals shall specify the proposed date of discontinuance of the school.

(4) Before publishing any proposals under this section the funding authority shall consult—

(a) such persons as appear to them to be appropriate, and

(b) (in the case of a Church of England, Church in Wales or Roman Catholic Church school having any foundation governor who is appointed by the appropriate diocesan authority) that authority;

and in discharging their duty under paragraph (a) the funding authority shall have regard to any guidance given to them from time to time by the Secretary of State.

(5) The published proposals shall be accompanied by a statement—

(a) indicating whether or not there are any proposals for the premises of the school to be used by any new or existing school, and

(b) explaining the effect of subsection (6).

(6) Within the period of two months beginning with the date of publication of the proposals, objections to the proposals may be submitted to the funding authority by any of the following—

(a) any ten or more local government electors,

(b) the governing body of the school to which the proposals relate,
(c) the governing body of any school affected by the proposals,
(d) the appropriate further education funding council (if the proposals affect the provision of education to which section 2(1) of the Further and Higher Education Act 1992 applies), and
(e) any local education authority concerned.

(7) Not later than one month after the end of that period, the funding authority shall send to the Secretary of State copies of all such objections made (and not withdrawn in writing) together with their observations on them.

Approval, adoption or rejection of proposals

269.—(1) Proposals published under section 267 require the approval of the Secretary of State.

(2) Proposals published under section 268 require the approval of the Secretary of State if—
(a) he gives notice to that effect to the funding authority within two months after the submission to him of the published proposals, or
(b) objections have been made under subsection (6) of that section within the period allowed under that subsection (unless all objections so made have been withdrawn in writing within that period).

(3) Where under subsection (1) or (2) any proposals require the approval of the Secretary of State, he may—
(a) reject them,
(b) approve them without modification, or
(c) after consulting the governing body (and, in the case of proposals published under section 268, the funding authority) approve them with the substitution of a different date for the date of discontinuance proposed.

(4) Where the Secretary of State approves any such proposals he shall give notice in writing of that fact and of the discontinuance date to the governing body and (except where the school is in Wales and the Schools Funding Council for Wales have not begun to exercise their functions) the funding authority.

(5) Where proposals published under section 268 do not require the approval of the Secretary of State, the funding authority shall determine whether to adopt the proposals.

(6) The funding authority shall—
(a) make any determination under subsection (5) not later than four months after the publication of the proposals, and
(b) give notice in writing to the Secretary of State and the governing body of their determination and, if they adopt the proposals, of the discontinuance date.

Implementation of proposals

270.—(1) Where any proposals are approved under section 269, the governing body shall cease to conduct the school on the discontinuance date.

(2) In this section "the discontinuance date" means—
(a) the date of discontinuance specified in the proposals as approved, or
(b) if—

(i) at the request of the governing body, or
(ii) in the case of proposals published under section 268, at the request of the funding authority and after consulting the governing body,

the Secretary of State subsequently fixes another date (whether in substitution for the date specified in the proposals as approved or in substitution for a date previously fixed under this subsection), that date.

(3) The governing body of a grant-maintained school shall not discontinue the school except in pursuance of proposals published under section 267 or 268 and approved or adopted under section 269.

Power to transfer functions under preceding provisions

271.—(1) The Secretary of State may by order provide for this Part to have effect with the modifications in subsections (2) to (7) in relation to any proposals published by the governing body of a grant-maintained school under section 267 after the coming into force of the order.

(2) The governing body shall submit a copy of the proposals to the funding authority as well as to the Secretary of State.

(3) Any objections under subsection (7) of that section to the proposals shall be submitted to the funding authority instead of to the Secretary of State.

(4) If any objection is made under subsection (7) of that section within the period allowed under that subsection and not withdrawn in writing within that period, then, not later than one month after the end of that period—

(a) the funding authority shall send to the Secretary of State copies of all such objections made (and not withdrawn in writing) together with their observations on them, and

(b) may themselves submit to the Secretary of State an objection to the proposals.

(5) Section 269(1) shall not apply to the proposals unless—

(a) the Secretary of State gives notice to the funding authority within two months after the submission to him of the published proposals that the proposals require his approval, or

(b) objections have been made under subsection (7) of section 267 within the period allowed under that subsection (unless all objections so made have been withdrawn in writing within that period).

(6) Where section 269(1) does not apply to the proposals—

(a) the proposals shall require the approval of the funding authority,

(b) the funding authority may reject them, approve them without modification or, after consulting the governing body, approve them with the substitution of a different date for the date of discontinuance proposed,

(c) where the funding authority approve them, they shall give notice in writing of that fact and of the discontinuance date to the governing body, and

(d) the reference in section 270(2)(b) to the Secretary of State shall be read as a reference to the funding authority.

(7) Paragraph 21(b) of Schedule 4 shall not apply in relation to the proposals.

(8) References in this Part to approval under section 269 include approval under this section.

Withdrawal of grant

Withdrawal of grant where school is unsuitable to continue as grant-maintained school

272.—(1) This section applies where the Secretary of State is satisfied that a grant-maintained school as currently constituted or conducted is unsuitable to continue as a grant-maintained school on either or both of the following grounds—

(a) that the number of registered pupils at the school is too small for sufficient and suitable instruction to be provided for them at reasonable cost, and

(b) that the governing body have been guilty of substantial or persistent failure to comply or secure compliance with any other requirement imposed by or under this Act or any other enactment.

(2) The Secretary of State may give to the governing body a notice in writing stating the grounds on which he considers that the school as currently constituted or conducted is unsuitable to continue as a grant-maintained school together with full particulars of the matters relevant to each such ground.

(3) Where any of those matters are stated in the notice to be in the opinion of the Secretary of State irremediable, the notice shall also state that the funding authority's duty to maintain the school will cease on a date specified in the notice.

(4) Where subsection (3) does not apply, the notice shall—

(a) state that the funding authority's duty to maintain the school will cease unless the matters of which particulars are given in the notice are remedied,

(b) specify the measures necessary in the opinion of the Secretary of State to remedy those matters, and

(c) specify the time, not being less than six months after the date on which the notice is given to the governing body, within which the governing body are required to take those measures.

(5) Where the governing body fail to take the measures required under subsection (4)(b) by the notice within the time specified in the notice (or allowed by any previous notice under this subsection), the Secretary of State shall, within the period of two months beginning with the date next following the end of the time so specified (or allowed), either—

(a) give notice in writing to the governing body extending the period within which those measures are required to be taken, or

(b) after consulting the local education authority (and, if the school provides education to which section 2(1) of the Further and Higher Education Act 1992 applies, the appropriate further education funding council) give notice in writing to the governing body that the funding authority's duty to maintain the school will cease on a specified date.

(6) Where the Secretary of State gives a notice under subsection (2) or (5) which states that the funding authority's duty to maintain the school will cease on a specified date—

(a) he shall give a copy of the notice to the funding authority, and

(b) the funding authority shall cease to be under a duty to make maintenance grants to the governing body of the school in respect of any period beginning on or after that date, and shall cease on that date to have the power to pay capital or special purpose grant to the governing body.

(7) In relation to a school in Wales before the Schools Funding Council for Wales have begun to exercise their functions, this section and section 273 shall have effect as if subsection (6)(a) above and section 273(4) and (5) were omitted.

Withdrawal or variation of notice under section 272

273.—(1) The Secretary of State may by giving notice in writing to the governing body—

(a) withdraw a notice under section 272(2) or (5)(b),

(b) vary a notice under section 272(2) in relation to which section 272(3) applies or a notice under section 272(5)(b) by substituting another date for the date for the time being specified in the notice as the date on which the funding authority's duty to maintain the school will cease, or

(c) vary a notice under section 272(2), so far as relating to any measures specified in it by virtue of section 272(4)(b).

(2) If by virtue of subsection (1)(c) the Secretary of State varies a notice so as to require different measures to be taken, he shall also substitute for the time specified in the notice by virtue of section 272(4)(c) a time which is not earlier than that time or, where the time so specified has been extended under section 272(5)(a), than that time as so extended.

(3) Any variation under subsection (2) of the time specified in a notice is without prejudice to any further extension of that time under section 272(5)(a).

(4) Where the Secretary of State withdraws a notice by virtue of subsection (1)(a), he shall give notice in writing of that fact to the funding authority.

(5) Where the Secretary of State varies a notice by virtue of subsection (1)(b), he shall give a copy of the notice as varied to the funding authority.

Winding up and disposal of property

Power to provide by order for winding-up and disposal of property

274.—(1) Where—

(a) proposals for the discontinuance of a grant-maintained school have been approved or adopted under section 269, or

(b) the Secretary of State has given notice to the governing body of a grant-maintained school under section 272 specifying a date on which the funding authority's duty to maintain the school will cease,

the Secretary of State may by order make provision for the winding up of the governing body and the disposal of the school property.

(2) Subsections (3) to (7) apply for the purposes of this section and sections 275 to 279.

(3) "Governing body in liquidation" means a governing body in respect of which any order has been made under this section.

(4) "School property", in relation to a grant-maintained school conducted or formerly conducted by a governing body in liquidation, means—

(a) the premises used or formerly used for the purposes of the school,

(b) any interest belonging to the governing body, or held by any trustees on trust for the purposes of the school, in a dwelling-house used or held or formerly used or held for occupation by a person employed to work at the school, and

(c) all other equipment and property used or held or formerly used or held for the purposes of the school (including any right to such property), except money and any investments to which section 279 applies.

(5) References to a grant-maintained school formerly conducted by a governing body in liquidation apply in circumstances where the school has been discontinued before the dissolution date and refer to the school as conducted immediately before discontinuance (and "formerly" in subsection (4)(a) to (c) applies in the same circumstances and refers to the time immediately before the discontinuance of the school concerned).

(6) "Dissolution date", in relation to a governing body in liquidation or the grant-maintained school conducted or formerly conducted by such a body, means the date appointed in relation to that body by virtue of section 275(5).

(7) "Section 67 loan liabilities", in relation to a governing body in liquidation, means any liabilities in respect of any loans made under section 67 (or section 105 of the Education Act 1944) which were transferred to the governing body under section 201.

Winding up

275.—(1) An order under section 274 may set out a proposed timetable for the winding up of the governing body and, in particular, for—

(a) securing that all property belonging to the governing body or held by any trustees on trust for the purposes of the school is brought into the custody or control of that body or those trustees (as the case may require),

(b) discharging any liabilities of the governing body,

(c) making any provision mentioned in subsection (2), and

(d) the preparation and audit of the governing body's final accounts.

(2) The provision referred to in subsection (1)(c) is provision authorised to be made—

(a) by section 277 (for or in connection with the transfer of the school property), or

(b) by section 278 (in respect of the discharge of the liabilities of the governing body).

(3) An order under section 274 may make provision as to the exercise of the governing body's functions in relation to the school including, in particular—

(a) provision requiring the governing body in the exercise of those functions to comply with any directions given by the Secretary of State,

(b) provision authorising any of those functions to be exercised by a member of the governing body specified in the order, and

(c) provision for the application of the seal of the governing body to be authenticated by the signature of a person specified in the order.

(4) An order under section 274—

(a) may make provision for conferring or imposing functions on the governing body in relation to the winding up and the management and disposal of the school property, and

(b) may require the governing body to give to persons employed by them notice terminating their contracts of employment as from a date specified in the order.

(5) Subject to subsection (6), an order under section 274 may appoint a date on which the governing body are to be dissolved.

(6) The Secretary of State shall not appoint a dissolution date unless he is satisfied that—

(a) all liabilities of the governing body (other than any section 67 loan liabilities which fall to be transferred or terminated under section 278) have been discharged,

(b) all costs of the winding up have been met,

(c) any provision authorised by any of sections 277 to 279 which is possible and expedient in the circumstances of the case has been made, and

(d) anything required to be done by the governing body for the purposes of or in connection with any such provision has been done.

Grants to governing body in liquidation

276.—(1) The funding authority may make grants to a governing body in liquidation for the purpose of—

(a) discharging any liabilities of that governing body (other than section 67 loan liabilities), and

(b) meeting any costs incurred by that governing body for the purposes of the winding up in pursuance of an order under section 274.

(2) The funding authority may impose on a governing body to whom such a payment is made such requirements as they may from time to time determine (whether before, at or after the time when the payment in question is made).

Disposal of school property

277.—(1) Subject to the provisions of any order under section 274, any school property held by the governing body in liquidation immediately before the dissolution date, other than property held by them on trust for the purposes of the school, shall—

(a) in the case of a governing body incorporated in pursuance of proposals for acquisition of grant-maintained status, vest on that date in the local education authority, and

(b) in the case of a governing body incorporated in pursuance of proposals for the establishment of a new grant-maintained school, vest on that date in the funding authority.

(2) Such an order may, on such date as may be specified in the order as the transfer date, vest the school property or any part of it in any person specified in the order and, where the order does so, it may provide for any property so vested to be held beneficially or on such trusts as may be specified in the order.

(3) Where any school property is—

(a) vested under subsection (1) in any person other than the funding authority, or

(b) vested in pursuance of an order under section 274,

such an order may require the person in whom any property is so vested to pay in respect of the property to the Secretary of State or to such other person as may be so specified such consideration (not exceeding the maximum consideration) as may be so specified.

(4) Subsection (3) does not apply to property held on trust for the purposes of the school otherwise than by the governing body; but, where an order under section 274 vests in any person property so held otherwise than by the governing body, the order shall require that person to pay to the trustees the maximum consideration in respect of the property.

(5) The maximum consideration that may be specified in such an order in respect of any school property is—

(a) so far as the property consists of premises (including any interest in a dwelling-house such as is mentioned in section 274(4)(b)), such an amount as the Secretary of State determines to be the market value of the premises as at, or as at a date no earlier than six months before, the dissolution date or, as the case may be, the transfer date, and

(b) so far as it consists of other property, such an amount as the Secretary of State determines to be a fair consideration for the transfer of that property.

(6) Where such an order requires any person in whom any premises are vested to pay any consideration in respect of the premises, the order shall specify the amount determined by the Secretary of State under subsection (5)(a); and any dispute as to that amount may be referred to the Lands Tribunal by—

(a) the person in whom the premises are vested,

(b) the person from whom they are transferred, or

(c) the person to whom the consideration is to be paid,

and shall then be determined by the Tribunal.

(7) Where—

(a) by virtue of subsection (3) or (4) such an order requires any person in whom any premises are vested to pay any consideration in respect of the premises, and

(b) on a reference under subsection (6) the Lands Tribunal determine a different amount from that determined by the Secretary of State,

the Secretary of State shall consider whether the amount of the consideration specified in the order requires alteration in the light of the determination of the Tribunal and, if it does, he shall vary the order accordingly.

(8) Where—

(a) any school property has been vested in the funding authority, or a local education authority, under subsection (1) and, in the case of property vested in the local education authority, no order under section 274 required them to pay any consideration in respect of the property, and

(b) the funding authority or local education authority subsequently dispose of the property so vested, or any part of it, the Secretary of State may require the authority concerned to pay to him or to such person as he may specify the whole or any part of the proceeds of the disposal.

(9) Nothing in subsection (1) or in any provision included in an order under section 274 by virtue of this section shall affect any interest or right of a person in, to or over any school property, being an interest or right which is held by that person otherwise than for the purposes of the school.

Disposal of school property: supplementary

278.—(1) Where by virtue of an order under section 274 the premises used or formerly used for the purposes of the school, or any part of those premises, are vested in persons proposing to establish a new independent school on the premises—

(a) such an order may require those persons to discharge any liabilities of the governing body in liquidation in respect of redundancy payments, and

(b) where the order does so, those liabilities shall be taken into account in determining the amount of consideration (if any) which those persons are required to pay by virtue of section 277(3).

(2) Subsection (1) does not apply to any property held on trust for the purposes of the school otherwise than by the governing body.

(3) Where the premises used or formerly used for the purposes of the school, or any part of those premises, are to be used for the purposes of a new or existing grant-maintained school, an order under section 274 may provide for the transfer to the governing body of the new or existing school of such rights or liabilities of the governing body in liquidation as were acquired or incurred in connection with the premises which are to be so used.

(4) If—

(a) the school was an aided or special agreement school immediately before it became grant-maintained,

(b) proposals have been approved under section 43 (approval of proposals for establishment or alteration of voluntary schools) for the maintenance as a voluntary school of a school which is proposed to be established on the school premises, and

(c) the Secretary of State has directed that the proposed school shall be an aided school,

any section 67 loan liabilities of the governing body in liquidation shall on the dissolution date be transferred to and become liabilities of the temporary governing body of the new school (subject to any variation of the terms applicable in relation to the loans in question immediately before that date that may be agreed between the Secretary of State and that governing body).

(5) If—

(a) subsection (4)(a) and (b) apply, but

(b) no direction that the proposed school shall be an aided school has been given before the dissolution date,

any section 67 loan liabilities of the governing body shall be terminated on that date.

(6) If—

(a) any liabilities of the governing body have been terminated by virtue of subsection (5), and

(b) a new voluntary school is established on the school premises in pursuance of any proposals approved under section 43,

the amount of those liabilities shall be treated for the purposes of section 173 (restrictions on discontinuance of voluntary schools by governors) as expenditure incurred by the Secretary of State (otherwise than in connection with repairs) in respect of the premises of the new school.

Surplus money and investments

279.—(1) Subject to the following provisions of this section—

(a) any money held by or for a governing body in liquidation (whether held in cash or to their account at or on deposit with any bank or other institution), and

(b) any investments to which this section applies held by or for such a governing body,

shall, after discharge of the liabilities and costs mentioned in subsection (2), be paid or (as the case may be) transferred by the governing body to the Secretary of State.

(2) The liabilities and costs referred to in subsection (1) are—

(a) all the liabilities of the governing body in liquidation (other than any not required to be discharged before the dissolution date is appointed), and

(b) all costs of the winding up.

(3) Where the Secretary of State is satisfied as to the whole or any part of any such money or as to any such investments—

(a) that the money or that part of it was derived, or (as the case may be) those investments were acquired, otherwise than from grants paid by him or the funding authority under this Part, and

(b) that it ought to be paid, or the investments ought to be transferred, to a local education authority or to some other person,

he may require the governing body to pay the money or (as the case may be) an amount equal to the part in question, or to transfer those investments, to such local education authority or other person as he may specify, either beneficially or to be held on trust for such purposes as he may specify.

(4) Where the premises of the school are to be used for the purposes of a new or existing grant-maintained school, the Secretary of State may require the governing body in liquidation, after discharge of the liabilities mentioned in subsection (2)—

(a) to pay any money held by or for them, and

(b) to transfer any investments to which this section applies held by or for them,

to the governing body of the new or existing grant-maintained school, either beneficially or to be held on trust for such purposes as he may specify.

(5) Without prejudice to the powers of the Secretary of State under subsections (3) and (4), any payment of money or transfer of investments under this section shall be free of any trusts on which the money or investments are held by the governing body before the payment or transfer is made.

(6) This section applies to any investment within the meaning of the Financial Services Act 1986 which falls within—

(a) any of paragraphs 1 to 6 of Schedule 1 to that Act (investments and investment business), or

(b) paragraph 11 of that Schedule, so far as referring to investments falling within any of paragraphs 1 to 6.

(7) References in subsection (6) to any paragraphs of Schedule 1 to the Financial Services Act 1986 include references to those paragraphs as amended by any order under section 2 of that Act (power to extend or restrict scope of Act) which amends those paragraphs for the purposes of all the provisions of that Act.

CHAPTER IX

GROUPS OF GRANT-MAINTAINED SCHOOLS

Nature of group

280.—(1) Subject to the provisions of this Chapter, two or more grant-maintained schools may be conducted as a group by a single governing body.

(2) In the case of such a group—

(a) there shall be an instrument (known as the instrument of government) providing for the constitution of the governing body, and

(b) for each school in the group there shall be an instrument (known as the articles of government) in accordance with which the school is to be conducted.

(3) The instrument and articles of government—

(a) shall comply with any requirements imposed by or under this Chapter, and

(b) may make any provision authorised by or under this Chapter to be made and such other provision as may be necessary or desirable.

(4) Subject to any express provision of the instrument or articles of government, each school in such a group shall be conducted in accordance with any trust deed relating to it.

(5) The provisions of Schedules 22 and 23 (other than paragraph 14 of Schedule 22) shall have effect in relation to groups of grant-maintained schools with such modifications as may be prescribed.

(6) Subject to any provision made by or under this Chapter, where there is a group of grant-maintained schools any provision of an enactment which applies to such schools shall apply separately in relation to each of the schools.

(7) References in this Chapter to a group are to a group of grant-maintained schools conducted, or to be conducted, by a single governing body.

Instruments and articles of government for group

281.—(1) The initial instrument of government for the governing body of a group and the initial articles of government for each school in the group shall be such as are prescribed.

(2) The initial instrument of government shall have effect as from the date on which the governing body are incorporated.

(3) The initial articles of government shall have effect as from the date of implementation of the proposals in pursuance of which the school became a member of the group.

(4) Section 220 shall apply in relation to the governing body of a group as it applies in relation to the governing body of a grant-maintained school.

(5) Section 221 shall apply in relation to a school in a group as it applies in relation to other grant-maintained schools.

Parent governors

282.—(1) The instrument of government for the governing body of a group shall provide for the governing body to include parent governors.

(2) The number of parent governors shall not be—

(a) less than three, or

(b) (subject to paragraph (a)) more than the number of schools in the group.

(3) Subject to subsection (6), the parent governors shall be elected by persons who are registered parents of registered pupils at schools in the group; but, if any of the schools in the group is established in a hospital, the instrument may provide for any of the parent governors to be appointed by the other members of the governing body.

(4) To qualify for such election a person must when he is elected be a registered parent of a registered pupil at one of the schools in the group and, to qualify for such appointment, a person must when he is appointed be such a parent or, if that is not reasonably practicable, a parent of one or more children of compulsory school age.

(5) The instrument shall provide for each parent governor to hold office for a term of four years.

(6) The instrument shall provide that if—

(a) one or more vacancies for parent governors are required to be filled by election, and

(b) the number of parents standing for election as parent governors is less than the number of vacancies,

the required number of parent governors shall be made up by persons appointed by the other members of the governing body.

(7) The instrument shall require governors, in appointing a person under a provision made by virtue of subsection (6)—

(a) to appoint a person who is the registered parent of a registered pupil at one of the schools in the group, where it is reasonably practicable to do so, and

(b) where it is not, to appoint a person who is the parent of one or more children of compulsory school age.

Teacher governors

283.—(1) The instrument of government for the governing body of a group shall provide for the governing body to include either one or two teacher governors.

(2) Each teacher governor shall be elected by persons who are teachers at schools in the group.

(3) To qualify for such election, a person must when he is elected be a teacher at one of the schools in the group.

(4) The instrument shall provide for each teacher governor to hold office for a term of four years.

Head teacher governors

284. The instrument of government for the governing body of a group shall provide for the head teacher of each school in the group to be an ex officio governor, unless he chooses not to be.

Core governors

285.—(1) The instrument of government for the governing body of a group shall provide for the governing body to include core governors.

(2) Schedule 25 (which makes provision in relation to core governors for groups) shall have effect.

(3) The instrument shall provide for core governors to hold office for such term (not being less than five nor more than seven years) as may be specified in the instrument.

Power of the Secretary of State to replace core governors

286.—(1) The instrument of government for the governing body of a group shall provide for the Secretary of State to have power, where any of subsections (2) to (4) apply, to replace all or any of the core governors, other than any externally appointed core governor appointed in respect of a particular school.

(2) This subsection applies where the governing body have been guilty of substantial or persistent failure to comply or secure compliance with any requirement imposed by or under any enactment.

(3) This subsection applies where—

(a) there is a report of an inspection of any of the schools in which the person who made it expressed the opinion that special measures were required to be taken in relation to the school,

(b) either that person was a member of the Inspectorate or the report stated that the Chief Inspector agreed with his opinion,

(c) if any registered inspector or member of the Inspectorate has made a later report of an inspection of the school under Part I of the School Inspections Act 1996, he did not express the opinion in the report that special measures were not required to be taken in relation to the school, and

(d) the Secretary of State has received a statement prepared under section 17 of that Act or the period allowed by subsection (2) of that section for the preparation of such a statement has expired;

and expressions used in this subsection and in that Act have the same meaning as in that Act.

(4) This subsection applies where in the opinion of the Secretary of State any action taken or proposed by the governing body, or any failure of the governing body to act, is prejudicial to the provision of education by any of the schools.

(5) The instrument of government shall enable the Secretary of State to make such provision as he thinks fit for filling vacancies for core governors other than externally appointed governors if it appears to him that the governing body are unable or unwilling to fill the vacancies.

(6) Any provision made by the instrument of government in pursuance of Schedule 25 shall not apply for the purposes of the appointment by virtue of this section of any core governor.

Additional governors

287.—(1) The instrument of government for the governing body of a group shall enable the Secretary of State to appoint not more than two additional governors if it appears to him that the governing body are not adequately carrying out their responsibilities in respect of the conduct or management of any of the schools in the group.

(2) The instrument shall enable the governing body, during any period when any additional governors appointed by the Secretary of State by virtue of subsection (1) are in office, to appoint a number of additional core governors not greater than the number of additional governors appointed by the Secretary of State who are then in office.

(3) Section 285(3) and Schedule 25 do not apply to additional core governors.

Powers

288. In the case of a group of grant-maintained schools conducted by a single governing body, that body shall have in relation to each of the schools the powers conferred by section 231 on the governing body of a grant-maintained school.

Application of maintenance grants in the case of groups

289.—(1) For each financial year the governing body of a group shall apply for the purposes of each school in the group the share of maintenance grant which is attributable to that school.

(2) For the purposes of subsection (1), in each financial year the share of maintenance grant which is attributable to each school in a group is the amount which in the case of that school is the prescribed percentage of the maintenance grant payable in respect of the school.

(3) The governing body of a group shall not apply otherwise than for the purposes of schools in the group any payments made to them in respect of maintenance grant.

(4) This section is subject to—

(a) any requirements imposed under section 247(1) or, as the case may be, 253(1), and

(b) any requirements as to the application of maintenance grant contained in the articles of government for any of the schools.

(5) In relation to groups of grant-maintained schools, this section has effect in place of section 244(3) or, as the case may be, 250(2).

School acquiring grant-maintained status as a member of a group, etc.

290.—(1) Regulations may make provision—

(a) for two or more schools, each of which is eligible for grant-maintained status and satisfies the prescribed requirements, to become grant-maintained schools conducted by a single governing body,

(b) for two or more grant-maintained schools, each of which is not a member of a group and satisfies the prescribed requirements, to become a new group conducted by a single governing body,

(c) for a school which is eligible for grant-maintained status, or is a grant-maintained school, and satisfies the prescribed requirements to become a member of an existing group,

(d) for the schools in two or more existing groups, where each of the schools satisfies the prescribed requirements, to become one group, and

(e) for a school in a group, where the school satisfies the prescribed requirements, to leave the group but continue to be a grant-maintained school (whether as a member of a group or not).

(2) Regulations shall require in the case of each school which is not a grant-maintained school but is to acquire grant-maintained status as a member of a group—

(a) a resolution of the existing governing body to hold a ballot of parents on the question of whether grant-maintained status as a member of a group should be sought for the school,

(b) a ballot of parents at the school,

(c) the publication by the existing governing body (together with the existing governing bodies of any other schools which are to acquire grant-maintained status as members of the same group) of proposals for the schools to acquire grant-maintained status and be conducted by a single governing body, and

(d) the approval of such proposals, as originally published or as modified by the Secretary of State (whether before or after they are approved).

(3) Regulations shall require in the case of each grant-maintained school which is not a member of a group but is to become a member of a new group—

(a) a resolution for the purpose of the existing governing body,

(b) the publication by the existing governing body (together with the governing bodies of any other schools which are to become members of the group) of proposals for the schools to become a new group conducted by a single governing body, and

(c) the approval of such proposals, as originally published or as modified by the Secretary of State (whether before or after they are approved).

(4) Regulations made by virtue of subsection (2) or (3) shall not enable the Secretary of State to modify any proposals after approving them so as to exclude any school to which they relate; and where under such regulations the Secretary of State modifies any proposals so as to exclude any school to which they relate—

(a) he may not approve them without the consent of the existing governing bodies of the schools to which the proposals as modified relate, and

(b) if he approves them, the regulations shall have effect as if the proposals as published had related only to those schools.

(5) Where proposals for the purposes of subsection (1)(a) or (b) are approved, regulations shall provide—

(a) for the determination of the persons who are to be the initial members of the governing body,
(b) for their incorporation, and
(c) for sections 282 to 286, Schedule 25 and the instrument of government to have effect in relation to any person who becomes a member of the governing body—
(i) before the date of implementation of the proposals, or
(ii) before the date on which the first instrument under section 220(1) for the governing body comes into effect,
with such modifications as may be prescribed.

(6) Where proposals for the purposes of subsection (1)(a) in relation to any schools, or proposals for the purposes of subsection (1)(c) in relation to a school which is eligible for grant-maintained status, are approved, regulations shall provide in relation to each of the schools—
(a) for the local education authority to cease to be under a duty to maintain the school,
(b) for any special agreement relating to the school to cease to have effect, and
(c) for the functions, during the period beginning with the approval of the proposals and ending with their implementation, of the governing body incorporated under the regulations.

(7) Where proposals for the purposes of subsection (1)(b) are approved, regulations shall provide for the functions, during the period beginning with the approval of the proposals and ending with their implementation, of the governing body incorporated under the regulations.

(8) In relation to—
(a) any schools seeking to acquire grant-maintained status as a group or grant-maintained schools seeking to become a new group,
(b) any school seeking to become a member of an existing group, and
(c) schools in a group,
regulations may provide for any relevant provision of this Act to apply with such modifications as may be prescribed.

(9) For the purposes of subsection (8) "relevant provision of this Act" means—
(a) any provision of this Part other than—
(i) section 198, 199, 291, 292, 294, 307 or 308, or
(ii) a provision of this Chapter, or
(b) any provision of this Act not contained in this Part which reproduces a provision of Part II of the Education Act 1993 (other than Chapter IX of that Part of that Act).

(10) Regulations may make provision for the governing body of a group to be reconstituted where any change occurs in the membership of the group.

(11) The Secretary of State may instead of, or in addition to, prescribing requirements for the purposes of subsection (1) issue guidance as to the requirements he would expect to be satisfied for any application—
(a) for any maintained schools, or grant-maintained schools, to become a new group,
(b) to join or leave a group, or
(c) for the merger of groups,
to be approved.

(12) In subsection (11) "maintained school" means any county school or voluntary school and any maintained special school not established in a hospital.

(13) This section does not apply to nursery schools.

Chapter X

General and Miscellaneous

Middle schools

Grant-maintained middle schools

291. Proposals published under section 211, 212, 259 or 260 may, if the authority, persons or body making them think fit—

(a) specify an age below 10 years and six months and an age above 12 years, and

(b) provide that the school to which the proposals relate is to be a school for providing full-time education suitable to the requirements of pupils whose ages are between the ages so specified.

Nursery education

Nursery education in grant-maintained schools

292.—(1) No proposals may be published—

(a) under section 211 or 212 for the establishment of any nursery school, or

(b) under section 259 or 260 for a school to become a nursery school;

and nothing in Chapter II applies to a nursery school.

(2) Subject to subsection (1) above, proposals under section 211, 212, 259 or 260 may, in particular, be made for the purpose of securing the provision of education for junior pupils who have not attained the age of five.

Further education

Provision of further education in grant-maintained schools

293. It shall be the duty of the governing body of any grant-maintained school which provides—

(a) part-time education suitable to the requirements of persons of any age over compulsory school age, or

(b) full-time education suitable to the requirements of persons who have attained the age of 19,

to secure that, except in such circumstances as may be prescribed, it is not provided at any time in a room where pupils are at that time being taught.

Teacher training

Provision of courses of initial teacher training

294.—(1) Section 12 of the Education Act 1994 confers power on the governing body of a grant-maintained school—

(a) to provide courses of initial training for school teachers, or

(b) to join in a partnership or association with other eligible institutions, or (whether alone or jointly with other eligible institutions) to establish a body, for the purpose of providing such courses.

(2) In subsection (1) "eligible institution" has the meaning given by section 4(2) of that Act.

Provision of benefits and services by local education authority

Provision of benefits and services for pupils etc. by local education authority

295.—(1) Where—

(a) a local education authority are under a duty, or have power, to provide any benefits or services for pupils, and

(b) the duty is to be performed, or the power may be exercised, both in relation to pupils at schools maintained by a local education authority and in relation to pupils at grant-maintained schools,

the authority shall in performing the duty, or exercising the power, treat pupils at grant-maintained schools no less favourably (whether as to the benefits or services provided or as to the terms on which they are provided) than pupils at schools maintained by a local education authority.

(2) Where—

(a) a local education authority are under a duty, or have power, to provide any benefits or services for persons, other than pupils, receiving education at a school, and

(b) the duty is to be performed, or the power may be exercised, both in relation to such persons at schools maintained by a local education authority and in relation to such persons at grant-maintained schools,

the authority shall in performing the duty, or in exercising the power, treat such persons at grant-maintained schools no less favourably (whether as to the benefits or services provided or as to the terms on which they are provided) than such persons at schools maintained by a local education authority.

Transfer and disposal of premises

Transfer of premises to trustees

296.—(1) Where grant under section 216(2) or capital grant is paid to the governing body of a grant-maintained school established in pursuance of proposals published under section 212 in respect of the provision of a site for the school or of school buildings, a requirement shall be imposed under section 216 or, as the case may be, Chapter VI for the purpose of securing that the site or buildings in question are held on trust by trustees of the school.

(2) Where buildings are to be provided for any grant-maintained school which are—

(a) to form part of the school premises, and

(b) to be constructed partly on land held by the governing body and partly on land held on trust for the purposes of the school by persons other than the governing body,

the governing body shall transfer to those persons the land held by the governing body on which the buildings are to be constructed; and section 231(7) does not apply to a transfer required by this subsection.

(3) In this section "site" does not include playing fields.

Disposal of premises on transfer of school to new site

297.—(1) Where—

(a) the funding authority pay capital grant in respect of a transfer of a grant-maintained school to a new site authorised under Chapter VII, and

(b) the governing body or any trustees of the school possess, or are or may become entitled to, a sum representing the proceeds of disposal of other premises which have been used for the purposes of the school,

the governing body or (as the case may be) the trustees or their successors shall pay to the Secretary of State the whole of that sum, if it is equal to or less than the amount of the capital grant, and otherwise so much of it as is required to repay that amount.

(2) Any sum paid under subsection (1) shall, in a case where any interest in the new site has vested in any trustees of the school, be treated for the purposes of section 14 of the Schools Sites Act 1841 (which relates to the sale or exchange of land held on trust for the purposes of a school) as a sum applied

in the purchase of a site for the school.

(3) Where trustees of a grant-maintained school are required to pay any sum to the Secretary of State under subsection (1) in a case where any interest in the new site is or is to be held by the governing body, then—

(a) if the interest or, as the case may be, all the interests held by any persons for the purposes of the school in the previous site were freehold interests held by the trustees, the governing body shall transfer their interest in the new site to the trustees, and

(b) if in any other case the trustees held any interest in the previous site, the governing body shall, if directed to do so by the Secretary of State, transfer to the trustees their interest in the whole of the new site or such part of it as may be specified in the direction.

(4) Where trustees of a grant-maintained school are required to pay any sum to the Secretary of State under subsection (1) in a case in which they may also be required to pay any sum to a local education authority under section 62(2) in respect of the disposal of the same premises, section 62(2) shall have effect as if—

(a) in relation to that disposal, the reference to the purchase money paid in respect of the acquisition of the premises were a reference to so much of the amount of that purchase money as remains after deducting the amount of the payment under subsection (1) above, and

(b) any premises transferred to the trustees in pursuance of subsection (3) above were premises conveyed by the authority as mentioned in section 62(2).

(5) In subsection (3)(a) "site" does not include playing fields.

Disposal of premises transferred under section 201

298.—(1) This section applies where the governing body of a grant-maintained school apply to the Secretary of State for his consent to the disposal of—

(a) any premises transferred to the governing body under section 201(1)(a), or

(b) any premises acquired wholly or partly with the proceeds of the disposal of any premises so transferred or of any premises so acquired.

(2) Subject to subsection (3), the Secretary of State may—

(a) require the premises or any part of the premises to be transferred to such local authority as the Secretary of State may specify, subject to the payment by that authority of such sum by way of consideration (if any) as he determines to be appropriate, or

(b) where he does not impose a requirement under paragraph (a), require the governing body, when the premises are disposed of, to pay to such local authority as the Secretary of State may specify the whole or any part of the proceeds of disposal.

(3) Where the occasion of the disposal is a transfer of the school to a new site in respect of which the funding authority have paid capital grant—

(a) no requirement shall be imposed under subsection (2)(a), and

(b) the reference in subsection (2)(b) to the proceeds of disposal shall be read as a reference to such part (if any) of those proceeds as remains after repayment of the amount of that capital grant in accordance with section 297.

Disposal of premises held by trustees

299.—(1) This section applies where any premises—

(a) transferred to the governing body of a grant-maintained school under section 201(1)(a), or

(b) acquired by such a governing body wholly or partly with the proceeds of the disposal of any premises so transferred or of any premises so acquired,

have been transferred by them to be held on trust by the trustees of the school.

(2) If at any time the trustees dispose of the premises the Secretary of State may require them to pay to such local authority as he may specify the whole or any part of the proceeds of the disposal.

Disposal of premises provided, etc. by the funding authority

300.—(1) Where the governing body of a grant-maintained school apply to the Secretary of State for his consent to the disposal of—

(a) any premises provided by the funding authority, or

(b) any premises acquired wholly or partly with the proceeds of the disposal of any premises so provided or of any premises so acquired,

the Secretary of State may require the governing body, when the premises are disposed of, to pay to him or to the funding authority the whole or any part of the proceeds of disposal.

(2) Where—

(a) any premises falling within subsection (1)(a) or (b) are transferred by the governing body to be held on trust by the trustees of the school, or

(b) any premises in respect of which capital grant was paid are transferred by the governing body (otherwise than in pursuance of a requirement imposed in accordance with section 296 or in pursuance of section 297(3)) to be held on trust by the trustees of the school,

then, if at any time the trustees dispose of the premises, the Secretary of State may require them to pay to him or to the funding authority the whole or any part of the proceeds of the disposal.

Interpretation of sections 296 to 300

301.—(1) For the purposes of sections 297 and 298, the funding authority are to be regarded as paying capital grant in respect of the transfer of a school to a new site if they pay capital grant in respect of the acquisition of the new site or the provision on that site of the school buildings or of any other buildings forming part of the new school premises.

(2) In sections 296 to 300 "trustees of the school" means any person (other than the governing body) holding property on trust for the purposes of the school.

(3) For the purposes of sections 297 to 300—

(a) a governing body or trustees are to be regarded as disposing of any premises if those premises are acquired from them, whether compulsorily or otherwise, and

(b) "proceeds of disposal", in relation to a disposal of premises by a governing body or trustees, means the compensation or purchase money paid in respect of the acquisition from them of those premises.

(4) In subsection (3)—

(a) references to the acquisition of premises from a governing body or trustees include, in the case of any premises held under a tenancy to which Part II of the Landlord and Tenant Act 1954 ("the 1954 Act") applies, the termination of that tenancy under that Part of that Act, and

(b) the reference to the purchase money paid in respect of such an acquisition includes any compensation paid by the landlord on the quitting of any such premises by the governing body or trustees (whether or not the compensation is required to be paid by section 37 of that Act (compensation where order for new tenancy precluded on certain grounds)).

(5) In subsection (4) expressions to which a meaning is given for the purposes of the 1954 Act have the same meaning as in that Act.

Modification of instruments

Variation of trust deeds etc. by order

302.—(1) The Secretary of State may by order make such modifications of any trust deed or other instrument relating to a school as, after consultation with the governing body of the school and the trustees (if any), appear to him to be requisite—

(a) in consequence of the approval of proposals for acquisition of grant-maintained status for the school,

(b) for removing any inconsistency between the provisions of that trust deed or other instrument and any provisions included or proposed to be included in any instrument or articles of government made for the school under Chapter V, or in any scheme under section 232, which it appears to him to be expedient to remove in the interests of the school, or

(c) in consequence of any proposals as to a change in the character or an enlargement of the premises of the school or a transfer of the school to a new site which fall to be implemented under section 263.

(2) The Secretary of State may by order make such modifications of any trust deed or other instrument relating to an independent school where proposals have been approved for the establishment of a grant-maintained school in its place as, after consultation with the promoters and the trustees (if any), appear to him to be requisite—

(a) in consequence of the approval of the proposals, or

(b) for removing any inconsistency between the provisions of that trust deed or other instrument and any provisions included or proposed to be included in any instrument or articles of government made for the grant-maintained school under Chapter V which it appears to him to be expedient to remove in the interests of the school.

(3) Any modification made by an order under this section may be made to have permanent effect or to have effect for such period as may be specified in the order.

Modification of instruments relating to land held for purposes of voluntary schools

303. Any provision of an instrument relating to any land held for the purposes of a voluntary school which—

(a) confers on any person an option to acquire an interest in that land, or

(b) provides (in whatever terms) for the determination or forfeiture of any such interest,

in the event of the school's ceasing to be a voluntary school or (as the case may be) ceasing to be maintained by a specified local education authority shall, if the school becomes a grant-maintained school, have effect as if the event referred to were the school's ceasing to be a school which is either a grant-maintained school or a voluntary school.

Religious opinions etc. of staff

Former county schools and certain schools established as grant-maintained schools

304.—(1) Subject to section 306, subsections (2) to (4) apply in relation to a grant-maintained school if—

(a) it was a county school immediately before it became grant-maintained,

(b) it was established in pursuance of proposals published under section 211, or

(c) it was established in pursuance of proposals published under section

212 and neither any trust deed relating to the school nor the statement required by paragraph 8 of Schedule 20 makes provision as to the religious education for pupils at the school.

(2) No person shall be disqualified by reason of his religious opinions, or of his attending or omitting to attend religious worship—

(a) for being a teacher at the school, or

(b) for being employed (otherwise than as a teacher) for the purposes of the school.

(3) No teacher at the school shall be required to give religious education.

(4) No teacher at the school shall receive any less emolument or be deprived of, or disqualified for, any promotion or other advantage—

(a) by reason of the fact that he does or does not give religious education, or

(b) by reason of his religious opinions or of his attending or omitting to attend religious worship.

Former voluntary schools and certain schools established as grant-maintained schools

305.—(1) Subject to section 306, subsections (2) and (3) apply in relation to a grant-maintained school if—

(a) it was a voluntary school immediately before it became grant-maintained, or

(b) it was established in pursuance of proposals published under section 212 and either any trust deed relating to the school or the statement required by paragraph 8 of Schedule 20 makes provision as to the religious education for pupils at the school.

(2) No person shall be disqualified by reason of his religious opinions, or of his attending or omitting to attend religious worship, for being employed (otherwise than as a teacher) for the purposes of the school.

(3) No teacher at the school shall receive any less emolument or be deprived of, or disqualified for, any promotion or other advantage—

(a) by reason of the fact that he gives religious education, or

(b) by reason of his religious opinions or of his attending religious worship.

(4) Without prejudice to subsections (2) and (3), in the case of a school which was a voluntary school immediately before it became grant-maintained, any of the provisions of section 146 (saving as to position of teachers) which, immediately before the school became grant-maintained, applied in relation to a teacher in the school shall continue to apply in relation to him until he ceases to be employed as a teacher in the school.

Changes in religious character of schools

306.—(1) Where, in the case of a school in relation to which section 304(2) to (4) for the time being applies, proposals that the required provision for religious education should be provision for religious education in accordance with the tenets of a particular religion or religious denomination are approved under section 261—

(a) section 305(2) and (3) shall apply in relation to the school from the time at which the proposals fall to be implemented, and

(b) subject to subsection (2), section 304(2) to (4) shall cease to apply in relation to the school from that time.

(2) Without prejudice to section 305(2) and (3), section 304(2) to (4) shall continue to apply in relation to any teacher who was employed at the school immediately before the proposals referred to in subsection (1) above fell to be implemented until he ceases to be employed as a teacher at the school.

(3) Where, in the case of any grant-maintained school, proposals that the required provision for religious education should be provision for religious

education otherwise than in accordance with the tenets of a particular religion or religious denomination are approved under section 261—

(a) section 304(2) to (4) shall apply in relation to the school from the time at which the proposals fall to be implemented, and

(b) section 305(2) and (3) shall cease to apply in relation to the school from that time.

(4) In this section "the required provision for religious education", in relation to a school, means the provision for religious education for pupils at the school which is required by section 352(1)(a) to be included in the school's basic curriculum.

Exclusion of pupils

Restrictions on power to exclude pupils

307.—(1) The head teacher of any grant-maintained school may not—

(a) so exercise the power to exclude a pupil from the school for one or more fixed periods that the pupil is so excluded for more than 15 school days in any one term, or

(b) exclude a pupil from the school for an indefinite period;

but this subsection is without prejudice to the power to exclude a pupil from the school permanently.

(2) Subsection (1) has effect, in the case of a school having articles of government, despite anything in the articles.

Appeal committees

Duties of governing body in relation to appeal committees

308.—(1) This section applies to any governing body of a grant-maintained school who are required by the articles of government for the school to make arrangements for appeals to such an appeal committee as is mentioned in paragraph 6(1) of Schedule 23 (appeals against decisions on admissions or exclusions).

(2) The Secretary of State may by regulations require any governing body to which this section applies—

(a) to advertise, in such manner and at such times as may be prescribed, for persons eligible to be lay members of any appeal committee required to be constituted for the purposes of arrangements made by that body to apply to the body for appointment as such members; and

(b) in appointing persons as such members, to consider any persons eligible to be so appointed who have applied to the body in response to an advertisement placed in pursuance of paragraph (a).

(3) A governing body to which this section applies shall indemnify the members of any appeal committee required to be constituted for the purposes of arrangements made by that body against any reasonable legal costs and expenses reasonably incurred by those members in connection with any decision or action taken by them in good faith in pursuance of their functions as members of that committee.

Supplementary

Manner of giving notification to governing body

309. Any notification to the governing body of a school for the purposes of any provision of this Part may be given, and withdrawn, in such manner as the governing body may require.

Inspection of accounts and reports to Parliament

310.—(1) The accounts of the governing body of any grant-maintained school shall be open to the inspection of the Comptroller and Auditor General.

(2) The Comptroller and Auditor General shall, in each session of Parliament, report to the House of Commons—

(a) whether he has carried out under section 6 of the National Audit Act 1983 any examinations in respect of grant-maintained schools, and

(b) if he has, the results of such examinations.

(3) Each report under subsection (2) shall cover a period beginning at the end of the period covered by the preceding report under that subsection.

(4) In determining whether to carry out any examination under that section in respect of grant-maintained schools and, if he determines to do so, the nature of the examination, the Comptroller and Auditor General shall have regard to any relevant published report of any study promoted or undertaken by the Audit Commission for Local Authorities and the National Health Service in England and Wales under section 220 of the Education Reform Act 1988.

Interpretation

Interpretation of Part III

311.—(1) In this Part—

"Church in Wales school" means a school in the Province of Wales in which the religious education provided is provided in accordance with the faith and practice of the Church in Wales and "appropriate diocesan authority", in relation to such a school, means the Diocesan Board of Finance for the diocese of the Church in Wales in which the school is situated or such other person as the Secretary of State may by order designate in respect of that diocese;

"Church of England school" means a school in the Province of Canterbury or York in which the religious education provided is provided in accordance with the faith and practice of the Church of England and "appropriate diocesan authority", in relation to such a school, means the Diocesan Board of Education for the diocese of the Church of England in which the school is situated;

"premises" includes any interest in or easement, right or charge in, to or over premises;

"Roman Catholic Church school" means a school in which the religious education provided is provided in accordance with the faith and practice of the Roman Catholic Church and "appropriate diocesan authority", in relation to such a school, means the bishop of the Roman Catholic diocese in which the school is situated.

(2) Before making an order in respect of any diocese in Wales in exercise of the power conferred by the definition of "appropriate diocesan authority" the Secretary of State shall consult the bishop for the diocese.

(3) The following provisions apply for the purposes of this Part.

(4) References to the character of a school are to the kind of school it is, determined by any matter relating to—

(a) the provision of education at the school, or

(b) the arrangements for admission of pupils to the school,

the alteration of which would amount to a change in the character of the school.

(5) The transfer to a reception class of pupils who have been admitted to a school for nursery education shall be treated as admission to the school.

(6) References, in relation to proposals under this Part, to the date of publication of the proposals are—

(a) to the date on which the requirements of this Part, or of regulations made by virtue of this Part, with respect to the publication of the proposals (or of any notice relating to the proposals) are satisfied, or

(b) where different requirements are satisfied on different dates, to the last of those dates,

and references to the time at which such proposals are published shall be construed accordingly.

(7) In this Part references to "local government electors for the area" are references to such electors for the local education authority area in which the school in question is, or is to be, situated.

(8) Nothing in this Part, or in any order made under it, relating to the trusts subject to which any land or other property or rights transferred under this Part are to be held by the transferee shall be taken as prejudicing any modification of those trusts after that transfer under any provision of this Part or otherwise.

PART IV

SPECIAL EDUCATIONAL NEEDS

CHAPTER I

CHILDREN WITH SPECIAL EDUCATIONAL NEEDS

Introductory

Meaning of "special educational needs" and "special educational provision" etc.

312.—(1) A child has "special educational needs" for the purposes of this Act if he has a learning difficulty which calls for special educational provision to be made for him.

(2) Subject to subsection (3) (and except for the purposes of section 15(5)) a child has a "learning difficulty" for the purposes of this Act if—

(a) he has a significantly greater difficulty in learning than the majority of children of his age,

(b) he has a disability which either prevents or hinders him from making use of educational facilities of a kind generally provided for children of his age in schools within the area of the local education authority, or

(c) he is under the age of five and is, or would be if special educational provision were not made for him, likely to fall within paragraph (a) or (b) when of or over that age.

(3) A child is not to be taken as having a learning difficulty solely because the language (or form of the language) in which he is, or will be, taught is different from a language (or form of a language) which has at any time been spoken in his home.

(4) In this Act "special educational provision" means—

(a) in relation to a child who has attained the age of two, educational provision which is additional to, or otherwise different from, the educational provision made generally for children of his age in schools maintained by the local education authority (other than special schools) or grant-maintained schools in their area, and

(b) in relation to a child under that age, educational provision of any kind.

(5) In this Part—

"child" includes any person who has not attained the age of 19 and is a registered pupil at a school;

"maintained school" means any county or voluntary school or any maintained special school not established in a hospital.

Code of Practice

Code of Practice

313.—(1) The Secretary of State shall issue, and may from time to time revise, a code of practice giving practical guidance in respect of the discharge by local education authorities and the governing bodies of maintained or grant-maintained schools, or grant-maintained special schools, of their functions under this Part.

(2) It shall be the duty of—

(a) local education authorities, and such governing bodies, exercising functions under this Part, and

(b) any other person exercising any function for the purpose of the discharge by local education authorities, and such governing bodies, of functions under this Part,

to have regard to the provisions of the code.

(3) On any appeal under this Part to the Tribunal, the Tribunal shall have regard to any provision of the code which appears to the Tribunal to be relevant to any question arising on the appeal.

(4) The Secretary of State shall publish the code as for the time being in force.

(5) In this Part "the Tribunal" means the Special Educational Needs Tribunal.

Making and approval of code

314.—(1) Where the Secretary of State proposes to issue or revise a code of practice, he shall prepare a draft of the code (or revised code).

(2) The Secretary of State shall consult such persons about the draft as he thinks fit and shall consider any representations made by them.

(3) If he determines to proceed with the draft (either in its original form or with such modifications as he thinks fit) he shall lay it before both Houses of Parliament.

(4) If the draft is approved by resolution of each House, the Secretary of State shall issue the code in the form of the draft, and the code shall come into effect on such day as the Secretary of State may by order appoint.

Special educational provision: general

Review of arrangements

315.—(1) A local education authority shall keep under review the arrangements made by them for special educational provision.

(2) In doing so the authority shall, to the extent that it appears necessary or desirable for the purpose of co-ordinating provision for children with special educational needs, consult the funding authority and the governing bodies of county, voluntary, maintained special and grant-maintained schools in their area.

Children with special educational needs normally to be educated in mainstream schools

316.—(1) Any person exercising any functions under this Part in respect of a child with special educational needs who should be educated in a school shall secure that, if the conditions mentioned in subsection (2) are satisfied, the child is educated in a school which is not a special school unless that is incompatible with the wishes of his parent.

(2) The conditions are that educating the child in a school which is not a special school is compatible with—

(a) his receiving the special educational provision which his learning difficulty calls for,

(b) the provision of efficient education for the children with whom he will be educated, and

(c) the efficient use of resources.

Duties of governing body or LEA in relation to pupils with special educational needs

317.—(1) The governing body, in the case of a county, voluntary or grant-maintained school, and the local education authority, in the case of a maintained nursery school, shall—

(a) use their best endeavours, in exercising their functions in relation to the school, to secure that, if any registered pupil has special educational needs, the special educational provision which his learning difficulty calls for is made,

(b) secure that, where the responsible person has been informed by the local education authority that a registered pupil has special educational needs, those needs are made known to all who are likely to teach him, and

(c) secure that the teachers in the school are aware of the importance of identifying, and providing for, those registered pupils who have special educational needs.

(2) In subsection (1)(b) "the responsible person" means—

(a) in the case of a county, voluntary or grant-maintained school, the head teacher or the appropriate governor (that is, the chairman of the governing body or, where the governing body have designated another governor for the purposes of this paragraph, that other governor), and

(b) in the case of a nursery school, the head teacher.

(3) To the extent that it appears necessary or desirable for the purpose of co-ordinating provision for children with special educational needs—

(a) the governing bodies of county, voluntary and grant-maintained schools shall, in exercising functions relating to the provision for such children, consult the local education authority, the funding authority and the governing bodies of other such schools, and

(b) in relation to maintained nursery schools, the local education authority shall, in exercising those functions, consult the funding authority and the governing bodies of county, voluntary and grant-maintained schools.

(4) Where a child who has special educational needs is being educated in a county, voluntary or grant-maintained school or a maintained nursery school, those concerned with making special educational provision for the child shall secure, so far as is reasonably practicable and is compatible with—

(a) the child receiving the special educational provision which his learning difficulty calls for,

(b) the provision of efficient education for the children with whom he will be educated, and

(c) the efficient use of resources,

that the child engages in the activities of the school together with children who do not have special educational needs.

(5) The annual report for each county, voluntary, maintained special or grant-maintained school shall include a report containing such information as may be prescribed about the implementation of the governing body's policy for pupils with special educational needs.

(6) The annual report for each county, voluntary or grant-maintained school shall also include a report containing information as to—

(a) the arrangements for the admission of disabled pupils;

(b) the steps taken to prevent disabled pupils from being treated less favourably than other pupils; and

(c) the facilities provided to assist access to the school by disabled pupils;

and for this purpose "disabled pupils" means pupils who are disabled persons for the purposes of the Disability Discrimination Act 1995.

(7) In this section "annual report" means the report prepared under the articles of government for the school in accordance with section 161 or, as the case may be, paragraph 7 of Schedule 23.

Provision of goods and services in connection with special educational needs

318.—(1) A local education authority may, for the purpose only of assisting—

(a) the governing bodies of county, voluntary or grant-maintained schools (in their or any other area) in the performance of the governing bodies' duties under section 317(1)(a), or

(b) the governing bodies of maintained or grant-maintained special schools (in their or any other area) in the performance of the governing bodies' duties,

supply goods or services to those bodies.

(2) The terms on which goods or services are supplied by local education authorities under this section—

(a) to the governing bodies of grant-maintained schools or grant-maintained special schools, or

(b) to the governing bodies of county, voluntary or maintained special schools,

in any other area may, in such circumstances as may be prescribed, include such terms as to payment as may be prescribed.

(3) A local education authority may supply goods or services to any authority or other person (other than a governing body within subsection (1)) for the purpose only of assisting them in making for any child in respect of whose education grants are (or are to be) made under arrangements under section 1 of the Nursery Education and Grant-Maintained Schools Act 1996 any special educational provision which any learning difficulty of the child calls for.

(4) This section is without prejudice to the generality of any other power of local education authorities to supply goods or services.

Special educational provision otherwise than in schools

319.—(1) Where a local education authority are satisfied that it would be inappropriate for—

(a) the special educational provision which a learning difficulty of a child in their area calls for, or

(b) any part of any such provision,

to be made in a school, they may arrange for the provision (or, as the case may be, for that part of it) to be made otherwise than in a school.

(2) Before making an arrangement under this section, a local education authority shall consult the child's parent.

Provision outside England and Wales for certain children

320.—(1) A local education authority may make such arrangements as they think fit to enable a child for whom they maintain a statement under section 324 to attend an institution outside England and Wales which specialises in providing for children with special needs.

(2) In subsection (1) "children with special needs" means children who have particular needs which would be special educational needs if those children were in England and Wales.

(3) Where a local education authority make arrangements under this section in respect of a child, those arrangements may in particular include contributing to or paying—

(a) fees charged by the institution,

(b) expenses reasonably incurred in maintaining him while he is at the institution or travelling to or from it,

(c) his travelling expenses, and

(d) expenses reasonably incurred by any person accompanying him while he is travelling or staying at the institution.

(4) This section is without prejudice to any other powers of a local education authority.

Identification and assessment of children with special educational needs

General duty of local education authority towards children for whom they are responsible

321.—(1) A local education authority shall exercise their powers with a view to securing that, of the children for whom they are responsible, they identify those to whom subsection (2) below applies.

(2) This subsection applies to a child if—

(a) he has special educational needs, and

(b) it is necessary for the authority to determine the special educational provision which any learning difficulty he may have calls for.

(3) For the purposes of this Part a local education authority are responsible for a child if he is in their area and—

(a) he is a registered pupil at a maintained, grant-maintained or grant-maintained special school,

(b) education is provided for him at a school which is not a maintained, grant-maintained or grant-maintained special school but is so provided at the expense of the authority or the funding authority,

(c) he does not come within paragraph (a) or (b) above but is a registered pupil at a school and has been brought to the authority's attention as having (or probably having) special educational needs, or

(d) he is not a registered pupil at a school but is not under the age of two or over compulsory school age and has been brought to their attention as having (or probably having) special educational needs.

Duty of Health Authority or local authority to help local education authority

322.—(1) Where it appears to a local education authority that any Health Authority or local authority could, by taking any specified action, help in the exercise of any of their functions under this Part, they may request the help of the authority, specifying the action in question.

(2) An authority whose help is so requested shall comply with the request unless—

(a) they consider that the help requested is not necessary for the purpose of the exercise by the local education authority of those functions, or

(b) subsection (3) applies.

(3) This subsection applies—

(a) in the case of a Health Authority, if that authority consider that, having regard to the resources available to them for the purpose of the exercise of their functions under the National Health Service Act 1977, it is not reasonable for them to comply with the request, or

(b) in the case of a local authority, if that authority consider that the request is not compatible with their own statutory or other duties and obligations or unduly prejudices the discharge of any of their functions.

(4) Regulations may provide that, where an authority are under a duty by virtue of subsection (2) to comply with a request to help a local education authority in the making of an assessment under section 323 or a statement under section 324 of this Act, they must, subject to prescribed exceptions, comply with the request within the prescribed period.

(5) In this section "local authority" means a county council, a county borough council, a district council (other than one for an area for which there is a

county council), a London borough council or the Common Council of the City of London.

Assessment of educational needs

323.—(1) Where a local education authority are of the opinion that a child for whom they are responsible falls, or probably falls, within subsection (2), they shall serve a notice on the child's parent informing him—

(a) that they propose to make an assessment of the child's educational needs,

(b) of the procedure to be followed in making the assessment,

(c) of the name of the officer of the authority from whom further information may be obtained, and

(d) of the parent's right to make representations, and submit written evidence, to the authority within such period (which must not be less than 29 days beginning with the date on which the notice is served) as may be specified in the notice.

(2) A child falls within this subsection if—

(a) he has special educational needs, and

(b) it is necessary for the authority to determine the special educational provision which any learning difficulty he may have calls for.

(3) Where—

(a) a local education authority have served a notice under subsection (1) and the period specified in the notice in accordance with subsection (1)(d) has expired, and

(b) the authority remain of the opinion, after taking into account any representations made and any evidence submitted to them in response to the notice, that the child falls, or probably falls, within subsection (2),

they shall make an assessment of his educational needs.

(4) Where a local education authority decide to make an assessment under this section, they shall give notice in writing to the child's parent of that decision and of their reasons for making it.

(5) Schedule 26 has effect in relation to the making of assessments under this section.

(6) Where, at any time after serving a notice under subsection (1), a local education authority decide not to assess the educational needs of the child concerned they shall give notice in writing to the child's parent of their decision.

Statement of special educational needs

324.—(1) If, in the light of an assessment under section 323 of any child's educational needs and of any representations made by the child's parent in pursuance of Schedule 27, it is necessary for the local education authority to determine the special educational provision which any learning difficulty he may have calls for, the authority shall make and maintain a statement of his special educational needs.

(2) The statement shall be in such form and contain such information as may be prescribed.

(3) In particular, the statement shall—

(a) give details of the authority's assessment of the child's special educational needs, and

(b) specify the special educational provision to be made for the purpose of meeting those needs, including the particulars required by subsection (4).

(4) The statement shall—

(a) specify the type of school or other institution which the local education authority consider would be appropriate for the child,

(b) if they are not required under Schedule 27 to specify the name of any school in the statement, specify the name of any school or institution (whether in the United Kingdom or elsewhere) which they consider would be appropriate for the child and should be specified in the statement, and

(c) specify any provision for the child for which they make arrangements under section 319 and which they consider should be specified in the statement.

(5) Where a local education authority maintain a statement under this section, then—

(a) unless the child's parent has made suitable arrangements, the authority—

(i) shall arrange that the special educational provision specified in the statement is made for the child, and

(ii) may arrange that any non-educational provision specified in the statement is made for him in such manner as they consider appropriate, and

(b) if the name of a maintained, grant-maintained or grant-maintained special school is specified in the statement, the governing body of the school shall admit the child to the school.

(6) Subsection (5)(b) does not affect any power to exclude from a school a pupil who is already a registered pupil there.

(7) Schedule 27 has effect in relation to the making and maintenance of statements under this section.

Appeal against decision not to make statement

325.—(1) If, after making an assessment under section 323 of the educational needs of any child for whom no statement is maintained under section 324, the local education authority do not propose to make such a statement, they shall give notice in writing of their decision, and of the effect of subsection (2) below, to the child's parent.

(2) In such a case, the child's parent may appeal to the Tribunal against the decision.

(3) On an appeal under this section, the Tribunal may—

(a) dismiss the appeal,

(b) order the local education authority to make and maintain such a statement, or

(c) remit the case to the authority for them to reconsider whether, having regard to any observations made by the Tribunal, it is necessary for the authority to determine the special educational provision which any learning difficulty the child may have calls for.

Appeal against contents of statement

326.—(1) The parent of a child for whom a local education authority maintain a statement under section 324 may—

(a) when the statement is first made,

(b) where the description in the statement of the authority's assessment of the child's special educational needs, or the special educational provision specified in the statement, is amended, or

(c) where, after conducting an assessment of the educational needs of the child under section 323, the local education authority determine not to amend the statement,

appeal to the Tribunal against the description in the statement of the authority's assessment of the child's special educational needs, the special educational provision specified in the statement or, if no school is named in the statement, that fact.

(2) Subsection (1)(b) does not apply where the amendment is made in pursuance of—

(a) paragraph 8 (change of named school) or 11(3)(b) (amendment ordered by Tribunal) of Schedule 27, or

(b) directions under section 442 (revocation of school attendance order);

and subsection (1)(c) does not apply to a determination made following the service of notice under paragraph 10 (amendment by LEA) of Schedule 27 of a proposal to amend the statement.

(3) On an appeal under this section, the Tribunal may—

(a) dismiss the appeal,

(b) order the authority to amend the statement, so far as it describes the authority's assessment of the child's special educational needs or specifies the special educational provision, and make such other consequential amendments to the statement as the Tribunal think fit, or

(c) order the authority to cease to maintain the statement.

(4) On an appeal under this section the Tribunal shall not order the local education authority to specify the name of any school in the statement (either in substitution for an existing name or in a case where no school is named) unless—

(a) the parent has expressed a preference for the school in pursuance of arrangements under paragraph 3 (choice of school) of Schedule 27, or

(b) in the proceedings the parent, the local education authority, or both have proposed the school.

(5) Before determining any appeal under this section the Tribunal may, with the agreement of the parties, correct any deficiency in the statement.

Access for local education authority to certain schools

327.—(1) This section applies where—

(a) a local education authority maintain a statement for a child under section 324, and

(b) in pursuance of the statement education is provided for the child at—

(i) a school maintained by another local education authority,

(ii) a grant-maintained school, or

(iii) a grant-maintained special school.

(2) Any person authorised by the local education authority shall be entitled to have access at any reasonable time to the premises of any such school for the purpose of monitoring the special educational provision made in pursuance of the statement for the child at the school.

Reviews of educational needs

328.—(1) Regulations may prescribe the frequency with which assessments under section 323 are to be repeated in respect of children for whom statements are maintained under section 324.

(2) Where—

(a) the parent of a child for whom a statement is maintained under section 324 asks the local education authority to arrange for an assessment to be made in respect of the child under section 323,

(b) no such assessment has been made within the period of six months ending with the date on which the request is made, and

(c) it is necessary for the authority to make a further assessment under section 323,

the authority shall comply with the request.

(3) If in any case where subsection (2)(a) and (b) applies the authority determine not to comply with the request—

(a) they shall give notice of that fact and of the effect of paragraph (b) below to the child's parent, and

(b) the parent may appeal to the Tribunal against the determination.

(4) On an appeal under subsection (3) the Tribunal may—

(a) dismiss the appeal, or

(b) order the authority to arrange for an assessment to be made in respect of the child under section 323.

(5) A statement under section 324 shall be reviewed by the local education authority—

(a) on the making of an assessment in respect of the child concerned under section 323, and

(b) in any event, within the period of 12 months beginning with the making of the statement or, as the case may be, with the previous review.

(6) Regulations may make provision—

(a) as to the manner in which reviews of such statements are to be conducted,

(b) as to the participation in such reviews of such persons as may be prescribed, and

(c) in connection with such other matters relating to such reviews as the Secretary of State considers appropriate.

Assessment of educational needs at request of child's parent

329.—(1) Whereas—

(a) the parent of a child for whom a local education authority are responsible but for whom no statement is maintained under section 324 asks the authority to arrange for an assessment to be made in respect of the child under section 323,

(b) no such assessment has been made within the period of six months ending with the date on which the request is made, and

(c) it is necessary for the authority to make an assessment under that section,

the authority shall comply with the request.

(2) If in any case where subsection (1)(a) and (b) applies the authority determine not to comply with the request—

(a) they shall give notice of that fact and of the effect of paragraph (b) below to the child's parent, and

(b) the parent may appeal to the Tribunal against the determination.

(3) On an appeal under subsection (2) the Tribunal may—

(a) dismiss the appeal, or

(b) order the authority to arrange for an assessment to be made in respect of the child under section 323.

Assessment of educational needs at request of governing body of grant-maintained school

330.—(1) Where in the case of a child for whom a local education authority are responsible but for whom no statement is maintained under section 324—

(a) a grant-maintained school is specified in a direction in respect of the child under section 431 (direction to admit child to specified school),

(b) the governing body of the school ask the authority to arrange for an assessment to be made in respect of the child under section 323, and

(c) no such assessment has been made within the period of six months ending with the date on which the request is made,

the local education authority shall serve a notice under subsection (2) on the child's parent.

(2) The notice shall inform the child's parent—

(a) that the local education authority propose to make an assessment of the child's educational needs,

(b) of the procedure to be followed in making the assessment,

(c) of the name of the officer of the authority from whom further information may be obtained, and

(d) of the parent's right to make representations, and submit written evidence, to the authority within such period (which must not be less than 29 days beginning with the date on which the notice is served) as may be specified in the notice.

(3) Where—

(a) a local education authority have served a notice under subsection (2) and the period specified in the notice in accordance with subsection (2)(d) has expired, and

(b) the authority are of the opinion, after taking into account any representations made and any evidence submitted to them in response to the notice, that the child falls, or probably falls, within subsection (4),

they shall make an assessment of his educational needs under section 323.

(4) A child falls within this subsection if—

(a) he has special educational needs, and

(b) it is necessary to determine the special educational provision which any learning difficulty he may have calls for.

(5) Where a local education authority decide in pursuance of this section to make an assessment under section 323, they shall give notice in writing to the child's parent, and to the governing body of the grant-maintained school, of that decision and of their reasons for making it.

(6) Where, at any time after serving a notice under subsection (2), a local education authority decide not to assess the educational needs of the child concerned, they shall give notice in writing to the child's parent and to the governing body of the grant-maintained school of their decision.

Assessment of educational needs of children under two

331.—(1) Where a local education authority are of the opinion that a child in their area who is under the age of two falls, or probably falls, within subsection (2)—

(a) they may, with the consent of his parent, make an assessment of the child's educational needs, and

(b) they shall make such an assessment if requested to do so by his parent.

(2) A child falls within this subsection if—

(a) he has special educational needs, and

(b) it is necessary for the authority to determine the special educational provision which any learning difficulty he may have calls for.

(3) An assessment under this section shall be made in such manner as the authority consider appropriate.

(4) After making an assessment under this section, the authority—

(a) may make a statement of the child's special educational needs, and

(b) may maintain that statement,

in such manner as they consider appropriate.

Duty of Health Authority or National Health Service trust to notify parent etc.

332.—(1) This section applies where a Health Authority or a National Health Service trust, in the course of exercising any of their functions in relation to a child who is under the age of five, form the opinion that he has (or probably has) special educational needs.

(2) The Authority or trust—

(a) shall inform the child's parent of their opinion and of their duty under paragraph (b), and

(b) after giving the parent an opportunity to discuss that opinion with an officer of the Authority or trust, shall bring it to the attention of the appropriate local education authority.

(3) If the Authority or trust are of the opinion that a particular voluntary organisation is likely to be able to give the parent advice or assistance in connection with any special educational needs that the child may have, they

shall inform the parent accordingly.

Special Educational Needs Tribunal

Constitution of Tribunal

333.—(1) There shall continue to be a tribunal known as the Special Educational Needs Tribunal which shall exercise the jurisdiction conferred on it by this Part.

(2) There shall be appointed—

(a) a President of the Tribunal (referred to in this Part as "the President"),

(b) a panel of persons (referred to in this Part as "the chairmen's panel") who may serve as chairman of the Tribunal, and

(c) a panel of persons (referred to in this Part as "the lay panel") who may serve as the other two members of the Tribunal apart from the chairman.

(3) The President and the members of the chairmen's panel shall each be appointed by the Lord Chancellor.

(4) The members of the lay panel shall each be appointed by the Secretary of State.

(5) Regulations may—

(a) provide for the jurisdiction of the Tribunal to be exercised by such number of tribunals as may be determined from time to time by the President, and

(b) make such other provision in connection with the establishment and continuation of the Tribunal as the Secretary of State considers necessary or desirable.

(6) The Secretary of State may, with the consent of the Treasury, provide such staff and accommodation as the Tribunal may require.

The President and members of the panels

334.—(1) No person may be appointed President or member of the chairmen's panel unless he has a seven year general qualification (within the meaning of section 71 of the Courts and Legal Services Act 1990).

(2) No person may be appointed member of the lay panel unless he satisfies such requirements as may be prescribed.

(3) If, in the opinion of the Lord Chancellor, the President is unfit to continue in office or is incapable of performing his duties, the Lord Chancellor may revoke his appointment.

(4) Each member of the chairmen's panel or lay panel shall hold and vacate office under the terms of the instrument under which he is appointed.

(5) The President or a member of the chairmen's panel or lay panel—

(a) may resign office by notice in writing to the Lord Chancellor or (as the case may be) the Secretary of State, and

(b) is eligible for re-appointment if he ceases to hold office.

Remuneration and expenses

335.—(1) The Secretary of State may pay to the President, and to any other person in respect of his service as a member of the Tribunal, such remuneration and allowances as the Secretary of State may, with the consent of the Treasury, determine.

(2) The Secretary of State may defray the expenses of the Tribunal to such amount as he may, with the consent of the Treasury, determine.

Tribunal procedure

336.—(1) Regulations may make provision about the proceedings of the Tribunal on an appeal under this Part and the initiation of such an appeal.

(2) The regulations may, in particular, include provision—

(a) as to the period within which, and the manner in which, appeals are to be instituted,

(b) where the jurisdiction of the Tribunal is being exercised by more than one tribunal—

(i) for determining by which tribunal any appeal is to be heard, and

(ii) for the transfer of proceedings from one tribunal to another,

(c) for enabling any functions which relate to matters preliminary or incidental to an appeal to be performed by the President, or by the chairman,

(d) for the holding of hearings in private in prescribed circumstances,

(e) for hearings to be conducted in the absence of any member other than the chairman,

(f) as to the persons who may appear on behalf of the parties,

(g) for granting any person such discovery or inspection of documents or right to further particulars as might be granted by a county court,

(h) requiring persons to attend to give evidence and produce documents,

(i) for authorising the administration of oaths to witnesses,

(j) for the determination of appeals without a hearing in prescribed circumstances,

(k) as to the withdrawal of appeals,

(l) for the award of costs or expenses,

(m) for taxing or otherwise settling any such costs or expenses (and, in particular, for enabling such costs to be taxed in the county court),

(n) for the registration and proof of decisions and orders, and

(o) for enabling the Tribunal to review its decisions, or revoke or vary its orders, in such circumstances as may be determined in accordance with the regulations.

(3) The Secretary of State may pay such allowances for the purpose of or in connection with the attendance of persons at the Tribunal as he may, with the consent of the Treasury, determine.

(4) Part I of the Arbitration Act 1996 shall not apply to any proceedings before the Tribunal but regulations may make provision corresponding to any provision of that Act.

(5) Any person who without reasonable excuse fails to comply with—

(a) any requirement in respect of the discovery or inspection of documents imposed by the regulations by virtue of subsection (2)(g), or

(b) any requirement imposed by the regulations by virtue of subsection (2)(h),

is guilty of an offence.

(6) A person guilty of an offence under subsection (5) is liable on summary conviction to a fine not exceeding level 3 on the standard scale.

Chapter II

Schools providing for special educational needs

Special schools

Special schools

337.—(1) A school which is specially organised to make special educational provision for pupils with special educational needs and is for the time being approved by the Secretary of State under section 342 shall be known as a special school.

(2) There are three categories of special school—

(a) maintained special schools;

(b) grant-maintained special schools; and

(c) special schools which are neither maintained nor grant-maintained schools.

(3) A special school is a maintained special school if it is maintained by a local education authority.

(4) A special school is a grant-maintained special school if it is conducted by a governing body incorporated in pursuance of proposals for the purpose—

(a) made by the funding authority under section 339 of this Act (or section 183 of the Education Act 1993), or

(b) made under section 345 of this Act (or section 186 of that Act).

Establishment etc. of special schools

Power of funding authority to establish grant-maintained special school

338.—(1) The funding authority may establish in the area of any local education authority a school which is specially organised to make special educational provision for pupils with special educational needs if—

(a) an order under section 27(1) (allocation of responsibility for providing sufficient school places) applies to the area, and

(b) the school is intended to provide relevant education for pupils in the area, whether or not it also provides other education or education for pupils from outside the area.

(2) Subsection (1) has effect subject to section 339(4).

Establishment, etc. of maintained or grant-maintained special schools

339.—(1) Where a local education authority intend—

(a) to establish a school which is specially organised to make special educational provision for pupils with special educational needs, or

(b) to make any prescribed alteration to a maintained special school, or

(c) to discontinue such a school,

they shall serve under subsection (5) notice of their proposals.

(2) Where the funding authority—

(a) intend to establish a school which is specially organised to make special educational provision for pupils with special educational needs, or

(b) are of the opinion that any prescribed alteration should be made to a grant-maintained special school, or

(c) are of the opinion that such a school should be discontinued,

and an order under section 27(1) applies to the area concerned, they shall serve under subsection (5) notice of their proposals.

(3) Where the governing body of a grant-maintained special school intend—

(a) to make any prescribed alteration to the school, or

(b) to discontinue the school,

they shall serve under subsection (5) notice of their proposals.

(4) Except in pursuance of proposals under this section approved under section 340—

(a) a local education authority or the funding authority may not establish a school which is specially organised to make special educational provision for pupils with special educational needs,

(b) no prescribed alteration may be made to a maintained or grant-maintained special school, and

(c) a maintained or grant-maintained special school may not be discontinued.

(5) Notice for the purposes of subsections (1) to (3) above shall be served on—

(a) the Secretary of State, and

(b) such other persons as may be prescribed,
and shall give such information as may be prescribed.

(6) If the proposals are approved under section 340—

(a) the body which served the notice, or

(b) in the case of proposals under subsection (2)(b) or (c) above, the governing body of the school,

shall implement them.

(7) If proposals under subsection (2)(a) above are so approved, a governing body of the school shall be incorporated on such date as may be specified in the proposals (referred to in this Part as the "incorporation date").

(8) In relation to the establishment of a school in pursuance of proposals under subsection (2)(a) above, regulations may apply any provision of Chapter IV or V of Part III of this Act with or without modification.

(9) In this Part—

(a) references to the discontinuance of a maintained special school are to the local education authority ceasing to maintain it, and

(b) references to an alteration to a school include the transfer of the school to a new site.

Procedure for dealing with proposals

340.—(1) Before a body serve notice of any proposals under section 339 they shall consult such persons as appear to them to be appropriate; and in discharging their duty under this subsection the body shall have regard to any guidance given from time to time by the Secretary of State.

(2) Within such period as may be specified in the notice under that section (which must not be less than two months beginning with the date on which the notice is served), any person may submit objections to the proposals to the body which served the notice.

(3) Within one month after the end of the period for making objections specified in the last notice to be served under that section, the body which served the notice shall transmit to the Secretary of State copies of all objections which have been duly made (and not withdrawn in writing), together with their observations on them.

(4) The Secretary of State may, after considering the proposals, any objections to the proposals and any observations on the objections—

(a) reject the proposals,

(b) approve them without modification, or

(c) after consulting the body which served notice of them (and, in the case of proposals under section 339(2)(b) or (c), the governing body) approve them with such modifications as he thinks desirable.

(5) The Secretary of State may modify any proposals required under section 339 to be implemented—

(a) in the case of proposals under section 339(2)(b) or (c)—

(i) at the request of the governing body, or

(ii) at the request of the funding authority and after consulting the governing body, or

(b) in any other case, at the request of the body which served notice of the proposals.

(6) References in this Part to proposals under section 339, in any case where the Secretary of State has modified such proposals in pursuance of this section, are to the proposals as so modified.

(7) Service of a notice under that section which is sent by post in accordance with section 572 (service of notices) shall be taken to have been effected on the second day after the day on which the notice is posted.

Approval of premises of maintained or grant-maintained special schools

341.—(1) Where a body serve under section 339(5) notice of proposals for the establishment of a school which is specially organised to make special educational provision for pupils with special educational needs, they shall submit to the Secretary of State the particulars in respect of the proposed premises of the school mentioned in subsection (3).

(2) Where a body serve under section 339(5) notice of proposals for making a prescribed alteration to a special school, they shall, if the Secretary of State so directs, submit to him the particulars in respect of the premises or proposed premises of the school mentioned in subsection (3).

(3) The particulars are—

(a) particulars of the provision made or to be made in respect of the means of access to and within the premises or proposed premises of the school, and

(b) such other particulars in respect of the premises or proposed premises of the school as the Secretary of State may require,

and they shall be submitted at such time and in such form and manner as the Secretary of State may direct.

(4) The particulars submitted under subsection (3)(a) shall indicate the extent to which the provision referred to conforms with the minimum requirements, so far as they are relevant to school premises, of—

(a) Design Note 18 "Access for Disabled People to Educational Buildings" published in 1984 on behalf of the Secretary of State, or

(b) (if that Note has been replaced by a document prescribed by regulations made or having effect as if made under the Town and Country Planning Act 1990) that document.

(5) Particulars submitted under this section in respect of the premises or proposed premises of the school require the approval of the Secretary of State.

(6) Where any proposals falling within subsection (1) or (2) are required to be implemented, they shall be implemented in accordance with any particulars approved under this section.

Approval of special schools

342.—(1) The Secretary of State may approve under this section any school which is specially organised to make special educational provision for pupils with special educational needs (and which is not a maintained or grant-maintained school), and may give his approval before or after the school is established.

(2) Regulations may make provision as to the requirements which are to be complied with as a condition of approval under subsection (1) above.

(3) Any school which—

(a) is established in pursuance of proposals approved under section 340 (or section 184 of the Education Act 1993), or

(b) was a special school immediately before 1st April 1994 (the date when section 184 of that Act came into force),

shall be treated, subject to subsection (4) below, as approved under this section.

(4) Regulations may make provision as to—

(a) the requirements which are to be complied with by a school while approved under this section, and

(b) the withdrawal of approval from a school (including approval treated as given under subsection (3)) at the request of the proprietor or on the ground that there has been a failure to comply with any prescribed requirement.

(5) Without prejudice to the generality of subsections (2) and (4), the requirements which may be imposed by the regulations include requirements—

(a) which call for arrangements to be approved by the Secretary of State,

or
(b) as to the organisation of any special school as a primary school or as a secondary school.

(6) Regulations shall make provision for securing that, so far as practicable, every pupil attending a special school—
(a) receives religious education and attends religious worship, or
(b) is withdrawn from receiving such education or from attendance at such worship in accordance with the wishes of his parent.

(7) Where approval is withdrawn from a maintained special school or grant-maintained special school, the local education authority or, as the case may be, the governing body shall serve under section 339 notice of their proposals to discontinue the school.

(8) For the purposes of proposals made under subsection (7)—
(a) section 339 shall have effect as if the school had not ceased to be a special school on the withdrawal of the approval, and
(b) section 340 shall have effect as if subsections (1) to (3), and the reference in subsection (4) to the rejection of proposals, were omitted.

Nursery education in grant-maintained special schools

343.—(1) No notice of proposals for a school to become a nursery school may be given under section 339(2) or (3).

(2) Subject to subsection (1) above, proposals under section 339(2) or (3) may, in particular, be made for the purpose of securing the provision of education for junior pupils who have not attained the age of five.

Government etc. of special schools

Government etc. of special schools

344.—(1) Chapters IV and VI of Part II have effect in relation to the government and conduct of maintained special schools and other matters relating to such schools; and section 120 provides for schemes under Chapter V of that Part (financial delegation) to apply to such schools.

(2) Schedule 28 has effect in relation to the government and conduct of grant-maintained special schools and other matters relating to such schools.

Maintained special school becoming grant-maintained

Maintained special school becoming grant-maintained special school

345.—(1) Regulations may make provision for maintained special schools, or any class or description of such schools, to cease to be maintained by the local education authority and become grant-maintained special schools.

(2) Regulations shall require, before a maintained special school becomes a grant-maintained special school in pursuance of the regulations—
(a) the submission to the Secretary of State of proposals for the purpose by the governing body of the school, and
(b) the approval of such proposals, as originally submitted or as modified by the Secretary of State (whether before or after they are approved).

(3) If the proposals are so approved, a governing body of the school shall be incorporated in accordance with Schedule 28 on the date of approval (referred to in this Part as the "incorporation date").

(4) Regulations made for the purposes of this section may apply any provision of—
(a) Chapter II (apart from section 198) or Chapter III or V of Part III,
(b) section 340, or
(c) section 35(7) or (8), section 37(1), (4), (7), (8) or (9), section 167(3) or (6) or section 169(1), (4) or (6),
with or without modification.

Grouping of grant-maintained special schools

Groups including grant-maintained special schools

346.—(1) Regulations may modify the provisions of Chapter IX of Part III (groups of grant-maintained schools) for the purpose of securing that—

(a) two or more grant-maintained special schools, or one or more grant-maintained special schools together with one or more grant-maintained schools, may be conducted as a group by a single governing body,

(b) a special school maintained by a local education authority may cease to be so maintained and may be conducted by a governing body incorporated under that Chapter, and

(c) a grant-maintained special school may become a member of a group of schools conducted by such a governing body,

and that, where a group of schools including one or more special schools is conducted by such a governing body, the governing body are appropriately constituted.

(2) Regulations made for the purpose mentioned in subsection (1) may modify sections 338 to 342 and Schedule 28.

(3) Where that Chapter applies to special schools by virtue of regulations—

(a) section 183(1) shall not be read as applying to such schools,

(b) a special school conducted by a governing body incorporated under that Chapter shall be known as a grant-maintained special school, and

(c) in Chapter II of Part I of the School Inspections Act 1996 (procedure for school inspections) references to a group of grant-maintained schools include a group of one or more grant-maintained special schools together with one or more grant-maintained schools.

Independent schools providing special education

Approval of independent schools

347.—(1) The Secretary of State may approve an independent school as suitable for the admission of children for whom statements are maintained under section 324.

(2) Regulations may make provision as to—

(a) the requirements which are to be complied with by a school as a condition of its approval under this section,

(b) the requirements which are to be complied with by a school while an approval under this section is in force in respect of it, and

(c) the withdrawal of approval from a school at the request of the proprietor or on the ground that there has been a failure to comply with any prescribed requirement.

(3) An approval under this section may be given subject to such conditions (in addition to those prescribed) as the Secretary of State sees fit to impose.

(4) In any case where there is a failure to comply with such a condition imposed under subsection (3), the Secretary of State may withdraw his approval.

(5) No person shall so exercise his functions under this Part that a child with special educational needs is educated in an independent school unless—

(a) the school is for the time being approved by the Secretary of State as suitable for the admission of children for whom statements are maintained under section 324, or

(b) the Secretary of State consents to the child being educated there.

Provision of special education at non-maintained schools

348.—(1) This section applies where—

(a) special educational provision in respect of a child with special educational needs is made at a school which is not a maintained school, and

(b) either the name of the school is specified in a statement in respect of the child under section 324 or the local education authority are satisfied—

(i) that his interests require the necessary special educational provision to be made for him at a school which is not a maintained school, and

(ii) that it is appropriate for the child to be provided with education at the particular school.

(2) Where this section applies, the local education authority shall pay the whole of the fees payable in respect of the education provided for the child at the school, and if—

(a) board and lodging are provided for him at the school, and

(b) the authority are satisfied that the necessary special educational provision cannot be provided for him at the school unless the board and lodging are also provided,

the authority shall pay the whole of the fees payable in respect of the board and lodging.

(3) In this section "maintained school" means—

(a) a school maintained by a local education authority,

(b) a grant-maintained school, and

(c) a grant-maintained special school.

Variation of deeds

Variation of trust deeds etc. by order

349.—(1) The Secretary of State may by order make such modifications of any trust deed or other instrument relating to a school as, after consultation with the governing body or other proprietor of the school, appear to him to be necessary to enable the governing body or proprietor to meet any requirement imposed by regulations under section 342 or 347.

(2) Any modification made by an order under this section may be made to have permanent effect or to have effect for such period as may be specified in the order.

PART V

THE CURRICULUM

CHAPTER I

PRELIMINARY

Meaning of "maintained school" etc. in Part V

350.—(1) In this Part "maintained school" means—

(a) any county or voluntary school,

(b) except where otherwise stated, any maintained special school which is not established in a hospital, and

(c) except so far as that expression has effect in relation to a local education authority, any grant-maintained school.

(2) In this Part "assess" includes examine and test, and related expressions shall be construed accordingly.

General duties in respect of the curriculum

351.—(1) The curriculum for a school satisfies the requirements of this section if it is a balanced and broadly based curriculum which—

(a) promotes the spiritual, moral, cultural, mental and physical development of pupils at the school and of society, and

(b) prepares pupils at the school for the opportunities, responsibilities and experiences of adult life.

(2) The Secretary of State shall exercise his functions with a view to securing that the curriculum for every maintained school satisfies the requirements of this section.

(3) Every local education authority shall exercise their functions with a view to securing that the curriculum for every maintained school which they maintain satisfies the requirements of this section.

(4) The governing body and head teacher of every maintained school shall exercise their functions with a view to securing that the curriculum for the school satisfies the requirements of this section.

(5) The functions referred to in subsections (2) to (4) include in particular functions conferred by this Part in relation to religious education, religious worship and the National Curriculum.

Basic curriculum for every maintained school

352.—(1) The curriculum for every maintained school shall comprise a basic curriculum which includes—

(a) provision for religious education for all registered pupils at the school (in accordance with such of the provisions of sections 376 to 381 as apply in relation to the school),

(b) a curriculum for all registered pupils at the school of compulsory school age (known as "the National Curriculum") which meets the requirements of section 353,

(c) in the case of a secondary school, provision for sex education for all registered pupils at the school, and

(d) in the case of a special school, provision for sex education for all registered pupils at the school who are provided with secondary education.

(2) Subsection (1)(a) does not apply in the case of a maintained special school (provision as to religious education in special schools being made by regulations under section 342(6)).

(3) In this Act "sex education" includes education about—

(a) Acquired Immune Deficiency Syndrome and Human Immunodeficiency Virus, and

(b) any other sexually transmitted disease.

CHAPTER II

SECULAR EDUCATION

The National Curriculum: general

The National Curriculum

353. The National Curriculum shall comprise the core and other foundation subjects and specify in relation to each of them—

(a) the knowledge, skills and understanding which pupils of different abilities and maturities are expected to have by the end of each key stage (referred to in this Part as "attainment targets"),

(b) the matters, skills and processes which are required to be taught to pupils of different abilities and maturities during each key stage (referred to in this Part as "programmes of study"), and

(c) the arrangements for assessing pupils in respect of each key stage for the purpose of ascertaining what they have achieved in relation to the attainment targets for that stage (referred to in this Part as "assessment arrangements").

The core subjects and other foundation subjects

354.—(1) The core subjects are—
(a) mathematics, English and science, and
(b) in relation to schools in Wales which are Welsh-speaking schools, Welsh.

(2) The other foundation subjects are—
(a) technology and physical education,
(b) in relation to the first, second and third key stages, history, geography, art and music,
(c) in relation to the third and fourth key stages, a modern foreign language specified in an order of the Secretary of State, and
(d) in relation to schools in Wales which are not Welsh-speaking schools, Welsh.

(3) In relation to schools in England—
(a) a modern foreign language is not a foundation subject in relation to the fourth key stage until the relevant date; and
(b) technology is a foundation subject in relation to pupils who entered the first year of the fourth key stage in 1993 but otherwise is not a foundation subject in relation to that key stage until the relevant date.

(4) In subsection (3) "the relevant date" means—
(a) 1st August 1996, in the case of pupils entering the first year of the fourth key stage in 1996; and
(b) 1st August 1997, in the case of all other pupils.

(5) In relation to schools in Wales—
(a) a modern foreign language is not a foundation subject in relation to the fourth key stage; and
(b) technology is a foundation subject in relation to pupils who entered the first year of the fourth key stage in 1993 but otherwise is not a foundation subject in relation to that key stage.

(6) The Secretary of State may by order amend subsections (1) to (5).

(7) In this section "school" includes part of a school.

(8) For the purposes of this section a school is Welsh-speaking if more than one half of the following subjects are taught (wholly or partly) in Welsh—
(a) religious education, and
(b) the subjects other than English and Welsh which are foundation subjects in relation to pupils at the school.

The key stages

355.—(1) The key stages in relation to a pupil are—
(a) the period beginning with his becoming of compulsory school age and ending at the same time as the school year in which the majority of pupils in his class attain the age of seven ("the first key stage"),
(b) the period beginning at the same time as the school year in which the majority of pupils in his class attain the age of eight and ending at the same time as the school year in which the majority of pupils in his class attain the age of 11 ("the second key stage"),
(c) the period beginning at the same time as the school year in which the majority of pupils in his class attain the age of 12 and ending at the same time as the school year in which the majority of pupils in his class attain the age of 14 ("the third key stage"), and
(d) the period beginning at the same time as the school year in which the majority of pupils in his class attain the age of 15 and ending with the expiry of the school year in which the majority of pupils in his class cease to be of compulsory school age ("the fourth key stage").

(2) The Secretary of State may by order—

(a) amend subsection (1), or
(b) provide that, in relation to any subject specified in the order, subsection (1) shall have effect as if for the ages of seven and eight there mentioned there were substituted such other ages (less than 11 and 12 respectively) as may be specified in the order.

(3) The head teacher of a school may elect, in relation to a particular pupil and a particular subject, that subsection (1) shall have effect as if any reference to the school year in which the majority of pupils in that pupil's class attain a particular age were a reference to the school year in which that pupil attains that age.

(4) If at any time, in the case of a pupil of compulsory school age, subsection (1) does not, apart from this subsection, apply to determine the period within which that time falls, that subsection shall have effect as if—
(a) in the case of paragraphs (a) to (c), any reference to the school year in which the majority of pupils in that pupil's class attain a particular age were a reference to the school year in which that pupil attains that age, and
(b) in the case of paragraph (d), the period were a period beginning at the same time as the school year in which he attains the age of 15 and ending when he ceases to be of compulsory school age.

(5) In this section—

"class", in relation to a particular pupil and a particular subject, means—
(a) the teaching group in which he is regularly taught that subject, or
(b) where there are two or more such groups, such one of them as may be designated by the head teacher of the school; and

"school year" means the period beginning with the first school term to begin after July and ending with the beginning of the next school year.

Establishment of the National Curriculum by order

356.—(1) The Secretary of State shall so exercise the powers conferred by subsection (2) as to—
(a) establish a complete National Curriculum as soon as is reasonably practicable (taking first the core subjects and then the other foundation subjects), and
(b) revise the National Curriculum whenever he considers it necessary or expedient to do so.

(2) The Secretary of State may by order specify in relation to each of the foundation subjects—
(a) such attainment targets,
(b) such programmes of study, and
(c) such assessment arrangements,

as he considers appropriate for that subject.

(3) An order made under subsection (2) may not require—
(a) the allocation of any particular period or periods of time during any key stage to the teaching of any programme of study or any matter, skill or process forming part of it, or
(b) the making in school timetables of provision of any particular kind for the periods to be allocated to such teaching during any such stage.

(4) An order under subsection (2) may, instead of containing the provisions to be made, refer to provisions in a document published by Her Majesty's Stationery Office and direct that those provisions are to have effect or, as the case may be, are to have effect as amended by the order.

(5) An order under subsection (2)(c)—
(a) may confer or impose such functions on—
(i) the governing body and the head teacher, and

(ii) (except in the case of grant-maintained schools) on the local education authority,

as appear to the Secretary of State to be required, and

(b) may specify any such assessment arrangements as may for the time being be made by a person specified in the order.

(6) Provision shall be made for determining the extent to which any assessment arrangements, and the implementation of the arrangements, achieve the purpose for which the arrangements are made; and such provision may be made by or under the order specifying the arrangements or (where the order specifies the person making the arrangements) in the arrangements themselves.

(7) The duties that may be imposed by virtue of subsection (5)(a) include, in relation to persons exercising any power in pursuance of provision made by virtue of subsection (6), the duty to permit them—

(a) to enter the premises of the school,

(b) to observe the implementation of the arrangements, and

(c) to inspect, and take copies of, documents and other articles.

(8) An order under subsection (2)(c) may authorise the making of such provisions giving full effect to or otherwise supplementing the provisions made by the order (other than provision conferring or imposing functions as mentioned in subsection (5)(a)) as appear to the Secretary of State to be expedient; and any provisions made under such an order shall, on being published by Her Majesty's Stationery Office, have effect for the purposes of this Part as if made by the order.

(9) The Secretary of State shall, in exercising his power under subsection (2), ensure that the subject of science does not include—

(a) Acquired Immune Deficiency Syndrome and Human Immunodeficiency Virus,

(b) any other sexually transmitted disease, or

(c) aspects of human sexual behaviour, other than biological aspects.

Implementation of the National Curriculum in schools

357.—(1) In relation to any maintained school and any school year—

(a) the local education authority and the governing body shall exercise their functions with a view to securing, and

(b) the head teacher shall secure,

that the National Curriculum as subsisting at the beginning of that year is Implemented.

(2) In relation to any time before the beginning of the school year following the establishment of the National Curriculum so far as relating to a particular subject and a particular key stage, subsection (1) shall have effect as if the Curriculum required that subject to be taught for a reasonable time during that stage.

The School Curriculum and Assessment Authority

The School Curriculum and Assessment Authority

358.—(1) There shall continue to be a body corporate known as the School Curriculum and Assessment Authority.

(2) The Authority shall consist of not less than 10 nor more than 15 members appointed by the Secretary of State.

(3) Of the members of the Authority, the Secretary of State—

(a) shall appoint one as chairman, and

(b) may appoint another as deputy chairman.

(4) The Secretary of State shall include among the members of the Authority persons who appear to him—

(a) to have experience of, and to have shown capacity in, the provision of education, or

(b) to have held, and to have shown capacity in, any position carrying responsibility for the provision of education.

(5) Where, in carrying out his functions under subsection (4), the Secretary of State proposes to appoint a person who appears to him to have experience of, and to have shown capacity in, the provision of education, he shall have regard to the desirability of including persons engaged in the provision of primary or secondary education.

(6) Schedule 29 has effect in relation to the Authority.

Functions

359.—(1) The School Curriculum and Assessment Authority shall have, in relation to England, the following general functions so far as relevant for the purpose of advancing education—

(a) to keep under review all aspects of the curriculum for maintained schools and all aspects of school examinations and assessment;

(b) to advise the Secretary of State on such matters concerned with the curriculum for maintained schools or with school examinations and assessment as he may refer to them or as they may see fit;

(c) to advise the Secretary of State on, and if so requested by him assist him to carry out, programmes of research and development for purposes connected with the curriculum for schools or with school examinations and assessment;

(d) to publish and disseminate, and assist in the publication and dissemination of, information relating to the curriculum for maintained schools or to school examinations and assessment;

(e) to make arrangements with appropriate bodies for auditing the quality of assessments made in pursuance of assessment arrangements;

(f) to advise the Secretary of State on the exercise of his powers under section 400 (approval of external qualifications);

(g) to advise the Secretary of State on such other matters connected with the provision of education in maintained schools, or in non-maintained special schools, as the Secretary of State may specify by order; and

(h) to carry out such ancillary activities as the Secretary of State may direct.

(2) For the purposes of paragraph (h) of subsection (1), activities are ancillary activities in relation to the Authority if the Secretary of State considers it is appropriate for the Authority to carry out those activities for the purposes of or in connection with the carrying out by the Authority of any of their other functions under that subsection.

(3) In carrying out their functions, the Authority shall—

(a) comply with any directions given by the Secretary of State,

(b) act in accordance with any plans approved by him, and

(c) so far as relevant, have regard to the requirements of section 351.

(4) The Authority shall supply the Secretary of State with such reports and other information with respect to the carrying out of their functions as he may require.

(5) In this section "non-maintained special school" means a special school not maintained by a local education authority.

The Curriculum and Assessment Authority for Wales

The Curriculum and Assessment Authority for Wales

360.—(1) There shall continue to be a body corporate known as Awdurdod Cwricwlwm ac Asesu Cymru or the Curriculum and Assessment Authority for Wales.

(2) The Authority shall consist of not less than 10 nor more than 15 members appointed by the Secretary of State.

(3) Of the members of the Authority, the Secretary of State—

(a) shall appoint one as chairman, and

(b) may appoint another as deputy chairman.

(4) The Secretary of State shall include among the members of the Authority persons having relevant knowledge or experience in education.

(5) Schedule 30 has effect in relation to the Authority.

Functions

361.—(1) The Curriculum and Assessment Authority for Wales shall have, in relation to Wales, the following general functions so far as relevant for the purpose of advancing education—

(a) to keep under review all aspects of the curriculum for maintained schools and all aspects of school examinations and assessment;

(b) to advise the Secretary of State on such matters concerned with the curriculum for maintained schools or with school examinations and assessment as he may refer to them or as they may see fit;

(c) to advise the Secretary of State on, and if so requested by him assist him to carry out, programmes of research and development for purposes connected with the curriculum for schools or with school examinations and assessment;

(d) to publish and disseminate, and assist in the publication and dissemination of, information relating to the curriculum for maintained schools or to school examinations and assessment;

(e) to make arrangements with appropriate bodies for auditing the quality of assessments made in pursuance of assessment arrangements;

(f) to advise the Secretary of State on the exercise of his powers under section 400 (approval of external qualifications);

(g) to advise the Secretary of State on such other matters connected with the provision of education in maintained schools, or in non-maintained special schools, as the Secretary of State may specify by order;

(h) to carry out such ancillary activities as the Secretary of State may direct.

(2) For the purposes of paragraph (h) of subsection (1), activities are ancillary activities in relation to the Authority if the Secretary of State considers it is appropriate for the Authority to carry out those activities for the purposes of or in connection with the carrying out by the Authority of any of their other functions under that subsection.

(3) In carrying out their functions, the Authority shall—

(a) comply with any directions given by the Secretary of State,

(b) act in accordance with any plans approved by him, and

(c) so far as relevant, have regard to the requirements of section 351.

(4) The Authority shall supply the Secretary of State with such reports and other information with respect to the carrying out of their functions as he may require.

(5) In this section "non-maintained special school" means a special school not maintained by a local education authority.

The National Curriculum: special cases

Development work and experiments

362.—(1) For the purpose of enabling development work or experiments to be carried out, the Secretary of State may direct in respect of a particular maintained school that, for such period as may be specified in the direction, the National Curriculum—

(a) shall not apply, or
(b) shall apply with such modifications as may be specified in the direction.

(2) A direction under subsection (1) may apply either generally or in such cases as may be specified in the direction.

(3) In the case of a county, controlled or maintained special school, a direction shall not be given under subsection (1) except on an application—

(a) by the governing body with the agreement of the local education authority,
(b) by the local education authority with the agreement of the governing body, or
(c) by the appropriate curriculum authority with the agreement of both the local education authority and the governing body.

(4) In the case of a grant-maintained, aided or special agreement school, a direction shall not be given under subsection (1) except on an application by the governing body or by the appropriate curriculum authority with the agreement of the governing body.

(5) The Secretary of State may make it a condition of a direction under subsection (1) that any person by whom or with whose agreement the request for the direction was made should, when so directed or at specified intervals, report to the Secretary of State on any matters specified by him.

(6) The Secretary of State may by a direction under this subsection vary or revoke a direction under subsection (1).

(7) In this section "the appropriate curriculum authority" means—

(a) in relation to England, the School Curriculum and Assessment Authority, and
(b) in relation to Wales, the Curriculum and Assessment Authority for Wales.

Exceptions by regulations

363. Regulations may provide that the National Curriculum, or such of the provisions of the National Curriculum as may be specified in the regulations—

(a) shall not apply, or
(b) shall apply with such modifications as may be specified in the regulations,

in such cases or circumstances as may be specified in the regulations.

Pupils with statements of special educational needs

364. The special educational provision for any pupil specified in a statement under section 324 of his special educational needs may include provision—

(a) excluding the application of the National Curriculum, or
(b) applying the National Curriculum with such modifications as may be specified in the statement.

Temporary exceptions for individual pupils

365.—(1) Regulations may enable the head teacher of a maintained school, in such cases or circumstances and subject to such conditions as may be prescribed, to direct in respect of a registered pupil at the school that, for such period as may be specified in the direction (the "operative period" of the direction), the National Curriculum—

(a) shall not apply, or
(b) shall apply with such modifications as may be specified in the direction.

(2) The conditions prescribed by the regulations shall, in particular, limit the operative period that may be specified in a direction to a maximum

period specified in the regulations.

(3) Any maximum period specified (whether in relation to directions given under the regulations or in relation to directions given under the regulations in circumstances specified in the regulations) shall be either—

(a) a fixed period not exceeding six months, or

(b) a period determinable (in such manner as may be specified in the regulations) not later than six months from its beginning.

(4) Any maximum period so specified may, without prejudice to the generality of section 569(4) (which provides that regulations under this Act may make different provision for different cases or circumstances etc.), differ according to whether or not the direction in question is given in respect of a period beginning—

(a) immediately after the end of the operative period of a previous direction, or

(b) within such period after the end of the operative period of a previous direction as may be specified in the regulations.

(5) The regulations may enable the head teacher of a maintained school, in such cases or circumstances and subject to such conditions as may be prescribed—

(a) to revoke any direction given by him under the regulations, and

(b) to vary such a direction, except so as to extend its operative period.

(6) Before making any regulations under this section, the Secretary of State shall consult with any persons with whom consultation appears to him to be desirable.

Information concerning directions under section 365

366.—(1) Where a head teacher gives or varies a direction under regulations made under section 365, he shall, in such manner as may be prescribed, give the information mentioned in subsection (2)—

(a) to the governing body, and

(b) where the school is a county, voluntary or maintained special school, to the local education authority by whom the school is maintained,

and shall take such steps as may be prescribed to give that information also to a parent of the pupil concerned.

(2) That information is—

(a) the fact that he has taken the action in question, its effect and his reasons for taking it;

(b) the provision that is being or is to be made for the pupil's education during the operative period of the direction; and

(c) either a description of the manner in which he proposes to secure the full implementation of the National Curriculum in relation to the pupil after the end of that period, or an indication that he has the opinion mentioned in subsection (3).

(3) That opinion is that the pupil has or probably has special educational needs by virtue of which the responsible authority would be required to determine the special educational provision that should be made for him (whether initially or on a review of any statement of his special educational needs which the authority are for the time being required under section 324 to maintain).

(4) Where—

(a) the head teacher of a county, voluntary or maintained special school includes an indication of any such opinion in information given under subsection (1), and

(b) the local education authority by whom the school is maintained are not the responsible authority in relation to pupil in question,

the head teacher shall also give that information, in such manner as may be prescribed, to the responsible authority.

(5) Where the head teacher of a grant-maintained school includes an indication of any such opinion in information given to the governing body under subsection (1), he shall also give that information, in such manner as may be prescribed, to the responsible authority.

(6) Where the responsible authority receive information given to them under subsection (1), (4) or (5) which includes an indication that the head teacher has the opinion mentioned in subsection (3), they shall consider whether any action on their part is required in the case of the pupil concerned under section 323 (assessment of special educational needs).

(7) In this section "the responsible authority", in relation to a pupil, means the local education authority responsible for him for the purposes of Part IV.

Appeals against directions under section 365 etc.

367.—(1) Where a head teacher—

(a) gives, revokes or varies a direction under regulations made under section 365,

(b) refuses to give, revoke or vary such a direction in response to a request made, in such manner and circumstances as may be prescribed by the regulations, by the parent of a registered pupil at the school, or

(c) following the making of such a request, fails within such period as may be prescribed by the regulations to give, revoke or vary such a direction in accordance with the request,

the parent of the pupil concerned may appeal to the governing body.

(2) On such an appeal, the governing body may—

(a) confirm the head teacher's action, or

(b) direct the head teacher to take such action authorised by the regulations as they consider appropriate in the circumstances.

(3) The head teacher shall comply with any directions of the governing body given under subsection (2)(b).

(4) The governing body shall notify the appellant and the head teacher in writing of their decision on such an appeal.

The National Curriculum: supplementary provisions

Procedure for making certain orders and regulations

368.—(1) Subject to subsection (9), this section applies where the Secretary of State proposes to make—

(a) an order under section 354(6), 355(2) or 356(2)(a) or (b), or

(b) regulations under section 363.

(2) The Secretary of State shall refer the proposal to the appropriate curriculum authority and shall give them directions as to the time within which they are to report to him.

(3) The authority shall give notice of the proposal—

(a) to such associations of local education authorities, bodies representing the interests of school governing bodies and organisations representing school teachers as appear to the authority to be concerned, and

(b) to any other persons with whom consultation appears to the authority to be desirable,

and shall give them a reasonable opportunity of submitting evidence and representations as to the issues arising.

(4) The report of the authority to the Secretary of State shall contain—

(a) a summary of the views expressed during the consultations,

(b) the authority's recommendations as to the proposal, and

(c) such other advice relating to the proposal as the authority think fit.

(5) The authority shall, after submitting their report to the Secretary of State, arrange for the report to be published.

(6) Where the authority have reported to the Secretary of State, he shall publish in such manner as, in his opinion, is likely to bring them to the notice of persons having a special interest in education—

(a) a draft of the proposed order or regulations and any associated document, and

(b) a statement explaining his reasons for any failure to give effect to the recommendations of the authority,

and shall send copies of the documents mentioned in paragraphs (a) and (b) to the authority and to each of the persons consulted by the authority.

(7) The Secretary of State shall allow a period of not less than one month for the submission of evidence and representations as to the issues arising.

(8) When the period so allowed has expired, the Secretary of State may make the order or regulations, with or without modifications.

(9) This section does not apply where—

(a) the Secretary of State proposes to make such an order as is, or such regulations as are, referred to in subsection (1), and

(b) arrangements for consultation about the proposed order or regulations were made before 1st September 1996 under section 242 of the Education Act 1993,

(and accordingly, the arrangements for consultation applicable in the case of the proposed order or regulations shall be those mentioned in paragraph (b) above).

(10) In subsection (2) "the appropriate curriculum authority" means—

(a) in relation to an order or regulations relating to maintained schools in England or pupils at such schools, the School Curriculum and Assessment Authority, and

(b) in relation to an order or regulations relating to maintained schools in Wales or pupils at such schools, the Curriculum and Assessment Authority for Wales.

Programmes of research etc. in relation to Wales

369. The Secretary of State may incur expenses in connection with the commissioning by him of such work, including programmes of research, development and dissemination, as he may require to be carried out for the purpose of facilitating the discharge, in relation to Wales, of any of his functions under sections 354 to 356.

General functions of LEA, governing body and head teacher in relation to curriculum

Duty of local education authority to state policy

370.—(1) A local education authority shall—

(a) determine, and keep under review, their policy in, relation to the secular curriculum for the county, voluntary and special schools maintained by them, and

(b) make, and keep up to date, a written statement of that policy.

(2) In discharging their duty under subsection (1), the authority shall consider, in particular—

(a) the range of the secular curriculum, and

(b) the balance between its different components.

(3) In carrying out their functions under this Act or any other enactment, the authority shall have regard to their policy as expressed in their statement.

Functions of governing body: county, controlled and maintained special schools

371.—(1) This section applies to the articles of government for a county, controlled or maintained special school.

(2) The articles shall require the governing body to consider—

(a) the policy of the local education authority as expressed in the statement made by the authority under section 370,

(b) what, in the governing body's opinion, should be the aims of the secular curriculum for the school, and

(c) how (if at all) the authority's policy with regard to matters other than sex education should in their opinion be modified in relation to the school,

and to make, and keep up to date, a written statement of their conclusions.

(3) The articles shall require the governing body—

(a) to consider separately (while having regard to the local education authority's statement under section 370) the question whether sex education should form part of the secular curriculum for the school, and

(b) to make, and keep up to date, a separate written statement—

(i) of their policy with regard to the content and organisation of the relevant part of the curriculum, or

(ii) where they conclude that sex education should not form part of the secular curriculum, of that conclusion.

(4) The articles shall require the governing body—

(a) when considering the matters mentioned in subsections (2) and (3), to do so in consultation with the head teacher and to have regard to any representations—

(i) which are made to them by any persons connected with the community served by the school, or

(ii) which are made to them by the chief officer of police and are connected with his responsibilities; and

(b) to consult the local education authority before making or varying any statement under subsection (2).

(5) The articles shall provide that the governing body may review their conclusions about the matters mentioned in subsection (2) or (3) whenever they think fit, and that they shall do so immediately following—

(a) the implementation of any proposals of a kind mentioned in subsection (7) which materially affect the school, or

(b) the implementation of any proposal under section 339 (establishment, alteration and discontinuance of maintained special school).

(6) The articles shall require the governing body, where they have completed such a review and consider it appropriate to make a fresh statement, to do so.

(7) The kinds of proposals referred to in subsection (5) are—

(a) proposals under section 35 (establishment, alteration etc. of a county school) or section 41 (establishment, alteration etc. of a voluntary school); and

(b) proposals for a voluntary school to be transferred to a new site in pursuance of an order under section 47;

and the reference above to proposals under section 35 includes a reference to proposals which would fall to be published by virtue of that section but for subsection (2)(b) of that section.

(8) In relation to sex education, this section has effect subject to section 404(3).

Functions of head teacher: county, controlled and maintained special schools

372.—(1) The articles of government for a county, controlled or maintained special school shall—

(a) provide for the determination and organisation of the secular curriculum for the school to be the responsibility of the head teacher, and

(b) require the head teacher to secure that that curriculum is followed within the school.

(2) The articles shall provide that, in discharging his duties in relation to the secular curriculum for the school, the head teacher shall consider the statement made by the local education authority under section 370 and those made by the governing body by virtue of section 371.

(3) The articles shall also provide that, in discharging those duties, the head teacher shall have regard to any representations with regard to the determination or organisation of the secular curriculum—

(a) which are made to him by any persons connected with the community served by the school, or

(b) which are made to him by the chief officer of police and are connected with that officer's responsibilities.

(4) The articles shall also provide that, in discharging those duties, the head teacher shall ensure that the secular curriculum—

(a) so far as it relates to sex education, is compatible with the governing body's policy (as expressed in the statement made by them by virtue of section 371(3)) except where that policy is incompatible with any part of the syllabus for a course which forms part of that curriculum and leads to a public examination;

(b) so far as it relates to other matters, is compatible with the policy of the local education authority (as expressed in the statement made by them under section 370) as modified by the statement made by the governing body by virtue of section 371(2), and

(c) is compatible with the provisions of this Act and any other enactments relating to education (including, in particular, provisions relating to children with special educational needs).

(5) In relation to sex education subsection (4) has effect subject to section 404(3).

Functions of governing body and head teacher: aided and special agreement schools

373.—(1) The articles of government for an aided or special agreement school shall provide—

(a) for the content of the secular curriculum for the school to be under the control of the governing body,

(b) for the governing body to have regard to the policy of the local education authority as expressed in the statement made by the authority under section 370, and

(c) for the head teacher to be allocated by the governing body such functions as will, subject to the resources available, enable him to determine and organise the curriculum and secure that it is followed within the school.

(2) The articles shall require the governing body, when considering the content of the secular curriculum for the school, to have regard to any representations with regard to that curriculum—

(a) which are made to them by any persons connected with the community served by the school, or

(b) which are made to them by the chief officer of police and are connected with his responsibilities.

Functions of governing body and head teacher: grant-maintained schools

374. Paragraph 4 of Schedule 23 has effect for securing the discharge by the governing body and the head teacher of a grant-maintained school of duties imposed on them under the provisions of this Part mentioned in paragraph 4(1).

Chapter III

Religious education and worship

Agreed syllabuses

Agreed syllabuses of religious education

375.—(1) Subject to the provisions of Schedule 31, any agreed syllabus in force immediately before the commencement of this Act shall continue to have effect.

(2) In this Act "agreed syllabus" means a syllabus of religious education—

(a) prepared before the commencement of this Act in accordance with Schedule 5 to the Education Act 1944 or after commencement in accordance with Schedule 31, and

(b) adopted by a local education authority under that Schedule,

whether it is for use in all the schools maintained by them or for use in particular such schools or in relation to any particular class or description of pupils in such schools.

(3) Every agreed syllabus shall reflect the fact that the religious traditions in Great Britain are in the main Christian whilst taking account of the teaching and practices of the other principal religions represented in Great Britain.

(4) Any reference in this Act to an agreed syllabus adopted by a local education authority includes a reference to an agreed syllabus deemed to be adopted by such an authority by virtue of paragraph 11 of Schedule 5 to the Education Act 1944 or paragraph 14 of Schedule 31; and accordingly, in relation to an agreed syllabus deemed to be so adopted, any reference to the date on which an agreed syllabus was adopted is a reference to the date of deemed adoption specified by the Secretary of State in a direction under that paragraph.

(5) Subsection (3) does not apply to any agreed syllabus adopted before 29th September 1988.

Required provision for religious education

Religious education: county schools

376.—(1) In the case of a county school, the provision for religious education for pupils at the school which is required by section 352(1)(a) to be included in the school's basic curriculum is provision for religious education in accordance with an agreed syllabus adopted for the school or for those pupils.

(2) No agreed syllabus shall provide for religious education to be given to pupils at a county school by means of any catechism or formulary which is distinctive of a particular religious denomination (but this is not to be taken as prohibiting provision in such a syllabus for the study of such catechisms or formularies).

(3) If, in the case of a county secondary school so situated that arrangements cannot conveniently be made for the withdrawal of pupils from it in accordance with section 389 to receive religious education elsewhere, the local education authority are satisfied—

(a) that the parents of any pupils at the school desire them to receive religious education in the school in accordance with the tenets of a particular religion or religious denomination, and

(b) that satisfactory arrangements have been made for the provision of such education to those pupils in the school, and for securing that the cost of providing such education to those pupils in the school will not fall upon the authority, the authority shall (unless they are satisfied that because of any special circumstances it would be unreasonable to do so) provide facilities for the carrying out of those arrangements.

Religious education: controlled schools

377.—(1) In the case of a controlled school, the provision for religious education for pupils at the school which is required by section 352(1)(a) to be included in the school's basic curriculum shall be provision for religious education—

(a) in accordance with any arrangements made under subsection (2), or
(b) subject to any such arrangements, in accordance with an agreed syllabus adopted for the school or for those pupils.

(2) Where the parents of any pupils at a controlled school request that they may receive religious education—

(a) in accordance with any provisions of the trust deed relating to the school, or
(b) where provision for that purpose is not made by such a deed, in accordance with the practice observed in the school before it became a controlled school,

the foundation governors shall (unless they are satisfied that because of any special circumstances it would be unreasonable to do so) make arrangements for securing that such religious education is given to those pupils in the school during not more than two periods in each week.

Religious education: aided and special agreement schools

378.—(1) In the case of an aided or special agreement school, the provision for religious education for pupils at the school which is required by section 352(1)(a) to be included in the school's basic curriculum is provision for religious education—

(a) in accordance with any provisions of the trust deed relating to the school, or
(b) where provision for that purpose is not made by such a deed, in accordance with the practice observed in the school before it became a voluntary school, or
(c) in accordance with any arrangements made under subsection (2).

(2) Where the parents of any pupils at an aided or special agreement school—

(a) desire them to receive religious education in accordance with any agreed syllabus adopted by the local education authority, and
(b) cannot with reasonable convenience cause those pupils to attend a school at which that syllabus is in use,

arrangements shall be made (unless the authority are satisfied that because of any special circumstances it would be unreasonable to do so) for religious education in accordance with that syllabus to be given to those pupils in the school.

(3) Religious education under any such arrangements shall be given during the times set apart for the giving of religious education in the school in accordance with the provision for that purpose included in the school's basic curriculum by virtue of section 352(1)(a).

(4) Any arrangements under subsection (2) shall be made by the governing body, unless the local education authority are satisfied that the governing body are unwilling to make them, in which case they shall be made by the authority.

(5) Subject to subsection (4), the religious education given to pupils at an aided or special agreement school shall be under the control of the governing body.

Religious education: grant-maintained schools (former county schools and certain new schools)

379.—(1) Subject to section 383, this section applies in relation to a grant-maintained school if—

(a) it was a county school immediately before it became grant-maintained,

(b) it was established in pursuance of proposals published under section 211, or

(c) it was established in pursuance of proposals published under section 212 and neither any trust deed relating to the school nor the statement required by paragraph 8 of Schedule 20 makes provision as to the religious education for pupils at the school.

(2) The provision for religious education for pupils at the school which is required by section 352(1)(a) to be included in the school's basic curriculum is provision for religious education in accordance with the appropriate agreed syllabus.

(3) That syllabus shall not provide for religious education to be given to pupils at the school by means of any catechism or formulary which is distinctive of a particular religious denomination (but this is not to be taken as prohibiting provision in the syllabus for the study of such catechisms or formularies).

(4) If, in the case of a secondary school so situated that arrangements cannot conveniently be made for the withdrawal of pupils from it in accordance with section 389 to receive religious education elsewhere, the governing body are satisfied—

(a) that the parents of any pupils at the school desire them to receive religious education in the school in accordance with the tenets of a particular religion or religious denomination, and

(b) that satisfactory arrangements have been made for the provision of such education to those pupils in the school, and for securing that the cost of providing such education to those pupils in the school will not fall upon the governing body,

the governing body shall (unless they are satisfied that because of any special circumstances it would be unreasonable to do so) provide facilities for the carrying out of those arrangements.

Religious education: grant-maintained schools (former controlled schools)

380.—(1) Subject to section 383, this section applies in relation to a grant-maintained school which was a controlled school immediately before it became grant-maintained.

(2) The provision for religious education for pupils at the school which is required by section 352(1)(a) to be included in the school's basic curriculum is provision for religious education—

(a) in accordance with any arrangements made under subsection (3), or

(b) subject to any such arrangements, in accordance with the appropriate agreed syllabus.

(3) Where the parents of any pupils at the school have requested (whether before or after the school became grant-maintained) that the pupils may receive religious education—

(a) in accordance with any provisions of the trust deed relating to the school, or

(b) where provision for that purpose is not made by such a deed, in accordance with the practice observed in the school before it became a grant-maintained school,

the foundation governors shall (unless they are satisfied that because of any special circumstances it would be unreasonable to do so) make arrangements for securing that such religious education is given to those pupils in the school during not more than two periods in each week.

Religious education: grant-maintained schools (former aided or special agreement schools and certain new schools)

381.—(1) Subject to section 383, this section applies in relation to a grant-maintained school if—

(a) it was an aided or special agreement school immediately before it became grant-maintained, or

(b) it was established in pursuance of proposals published under section 212 and either any trust deed relating to the school or the statement required by paragraph 8 of Schedule 20 makes provision as to the religious education for pupils at the school.

(2) The provision for religious education for pupils at the school which is required by section 352(1)(a) to be included in the school's basic curriculum is provision for religious education—

(a) in accordance with any provisions of any trust deed relating to the school, or

(b) where provision for that purpose is not made by such a deed, in accordance with—

(i) the practice observed in the school before it became a grant-maintained school, if it is a former aided or special agreement school, or

(ii) the statement required by paragraph 8 of Schedule 20, if it is a school established in pursuance of proposals published under section 212, or

(c) in accordance with any arrangements made under subsection (3).

(3) Where the parents of any pupils at the school—

(a) desire them to receive religious education in accordance with any agreed syllabus adopted by the local education authority for the area in which the school is situated for use in schools maintained by the authority, and

(b) cannot with reasonable convenience cause those pupils to attend a school at which that syllabus is in use,

the governing body shall (unless they are satisfied that because of any special circumstances it would be unreasonable to do so) make arrangements for religious education in accordance with that syllabus to be given to those pupils in the school.

(4) Religious education under any such arrangements shall be given during the times set apart for the giving of religious education in the school in accordance with the provision for that purpose included in the school's basic curriculum by virtue of section 352(1)(a).

(5) The head teacher of a school to which this section applies shall give notice in writing of any agreed syllabus which is in use at the school in accordance with subsection (3) to the standing advisory council on religious education constituted by the local education authority in whose area the school is situated.

Meaning of "the appropriate agreed syllabus" in sections 379 and 380

382.—(1) For the purposes of sections 379(2) and 380(2) "the appropriate agreed syllabus", in relation to a grant-maintained school or to any pupils at it, is—

(a) the agreed syllabus adopted for the time being by the local education authority for the area in which the school is situated for use in the schools maintained by the authority;

(b) if there is more than one such syllabus, such one of them as the governing body shall determine; or

(c) if the governing body select for the school or those pupils an agreed syllabus which—

(i) was adopted on or after 29th September 1988 by a local education authority other than the authority in whose area the school is situated, and

(ii) has not been replaced by a new agreed syllabus,

that syllabus.

(2) In relation to a school in Wales, in subsection (1)(c) "local education authority" means a local education authority in Wales.

Changes in religious education and worship

383.—(1) Subsection (2) applies where, in the case of a grant-maintained school in relation to which section 379 or 380 for the time being applies, proposals that the required provision for religious education should be provision for religious education in accordance with the tenets of a particular religion or religious denomination are approved under section 261.

(2) From the time at which the proposals fall to be implemented—

(a) the required provision for religious education shall (subject to subsection (3)) be provision for religious education either in accordance with the tenets of that religion or religious denomination or in accordance with any arrangements made under section 381(3) (as applied by paragraph (b)),

(b) section 381(3) to (5) shall apply in relation to the school, and

(c) any provisions of section 379, 380, 385(4), 386 or 387 which apply in relation to the school shall cease to apply in relation to it.

(3) Where, in the case of any grant-maintained school, proposals that the required provision for religious education should be provision for religious education otherwise than in accordance with the tenets of a particular religion or religious denomination are approved under section 261—

(a) sections 379 and 386 shall apply in relation to the school from the time at which the proposals fall to be implemented, and

(b) any provisions of section 380 or 381 which apply in relation to the school shall cease to apply in relation to it from that time.

(4) In this section "the required provision for religious education", in relation to a school, means the provision for religious education for pupils at the school which is required by section 352(1)(a) to be included in the school's basic curriculum.

Duty to secure religious education is given in accordance with required provision in curriculum

384. Subject to section 389, in relation to any maintained school (other than a maintained special school)

(a) the local education authority and the governing body shall exercise their functions with a view to securing, and

(b) the head teacher shall secure,

that religious education is given in accordance with the provision for such education included in the school's basic curriculum by virtue of section 352(1)(a).

Religious worship

Collective worship

385.—(1) Subject to section 389, all pupils in attendance at a maintained school other than a maintained special school shall on each school day take part in an act of collective worship.

(2) The arrangements for the collective worship in a school required by

this section may, in respect of each school day, provide for a single act of worship for all pupils or for separate acts of worship for pupils in different age groups or in different school groups.

(3) For the purposes of subsection (2) a "school group" is any group in which pupils are taught or take part in other school activities.

(4) Subject to subsection (6), the arrangements for the collective worship required by this section shall be made—

(a) in the case of a county school or a grant-maintained school in relation to which section 379 applies, by the head teacher after consultation with the governing body; and

(b) in the case of a voluntary school or a grant-maintained school other than one in relation to which section 379 applies, by the governing body after consultation with the head teacher.

(5) Subject to subsection (6), the collective worship in a school required by this section shall take place on the school premises.

(6) If the governing body of an aided, special agreement or grant-maintained school are of the opinion that it is desirable that any act of collective worship in the school required by this section should, on a special occasion, take place elsewhere than on the school premises, they may, after consultation with the head teacher, make such arrangements for that purpose as they think appropriate.

(7) The powers of a governing body under subsection (6) shall not be exercised so as to derogate from the rule that the collective worship in the school required by this section must normally take place on the school premises.

Collective worship in county schools and certain grant-maintained schools to be broadly Christian

386.—(1) Subsections (2) to (6) apply—

(a) (subject to section 387) in relation to a county school, and

(b) (subject to sections 383 and 387) in relation to a grant-maintained school in relation to which section 379 applies,

(2) The collective worship required in the school by section 385 shall be wholly or mainly of a broadly Christian character.

(3) For the purposes of subsection (2), collective worship is of a broadly Christian character if it reflects the broad traditions of Christian belief without being distinctive of any particular Christian denomination.

(4) Not every act of collective worship in the school required by section 385 need comply with subsection (2) provided that, taking any school term as a whole, most such acts which take place in the school do comply with that subsection.

(5) Subject to subsections (2) and (4)—

(a) the extent to which (if at all) any acts of collective worship required by section 385 which do not comply with subsection (2) take place in the school,

(b) the extent to which any act of collective worship in the school which complies with subsection (2) reflects the broad traditions of Christian belief, and

(c) the ways in which those traditions are reflected in any such act of collective worship,

shall be such as may be appropriate having regard to any relevant considerations relating to the pupils concerned which fall to be taken into account in accordance with subsection (6).

(6) Those considerations are—

(a) any circumstances relating to the family backgrounds of the pupils which are relevant for determining the character of the collective worship which is appropriate in their case, and

(b) their ages and aptitudes.

(7) In subsections (2) to (6) as they apply in relation to a grant-maintained school, references to acts of collective worship in the school include such acts which by virtue of section 385(6) take place otherwise than on the school premises.

Disapplication of requirement for Christian collective worship

387.—(1) Subsection (2) applies where—

(a) a standing advisory council on religious education determine (under section 394) that it is not appropriate for the requirement imposed by section 386(2) to apply in the case of a school or in the case of any class or description of pupils at a school, or

(b) such a council had so determined in the case of a grant-maintained school, or pupils at such a school, before the school became grant-maintained.

(2) While the determination has effect—

(a) section 386 shall not apply in relation to the school or (as the case may be) pupils in question, and

(b) the collective worship required by section 385 in the case of the school or pupils shall not be distinctive of any particular Christian or other religious denomination;

but paragraph (b) shall not be taken as preventing that worship from being distinctive of any particular faith.

(3) In this section references to a school are references to a county school or to a grant-maintained school in relation to which section 379 applies.

Duty to secure participation in collective worship

388. Subject to section 389, in relation to any maintained school (other than a maintained special school)—

(a) the local education authority and the governing body shall exercise their functions with a view to securing, and

(b) the head teacher shall secure,

that all pupils in attendance at the school take part in the daily collective worship required by section 385.

Exceptions and special arrangements

Exceptions and special arrangements

389.—(1) If the parent of a pupil at a maintained school requests that he may be wholly or partly excused—

(a) from receiving religious education given in the school in accordance with the school's basic curriculum,

(b) from attendance at religious worship in the school, or

(c) both from receiving such education and from such attendance,

the pupil shall be so excused until the request is withdrawn.

(2) In subsection (1)—

(a) the reference to religious education given in accordance with the school's basic curriculum is to such education given in accordance with the provision included in the school's basic curriculum by virtue of section 352(1)(a), and

(b) the reference to religious worship in the school includes religious worship which by virtue of section 385(6) takes place otherwise than on the school premises.

(3) Where in accordance with subsection (1) a pupil has been wholly or partly excused from receiving religious education or from attendance at religious worship and the responsible authority are satisfied—

(a) that the parent of the pupil desires him to receive religious education of a kind which is not provided in the school during the periods of time during which he is so excused,

(b) that the pupil cannot with reasonable convenience be sent to another maintained school where religious education of the kind desired by the parent is provided, and

(c) that arrangements have been made for him to receive religious education of that kind during school hours elsewhere,

the pupil may be withdrawn from the school during such periods of time as are reasonably necessary for the purpose of enabling him to receive religious education in accordance with the arrangements.

(4) A pupil may not be withdrawn from school under subsection (3) unless the responsible authority are satisfied that the arrangements there mentioned are such as will not interfere with the attendance of the pupil at school on any day except at the beginning or end of a school session (or, if there is only one, the school session) on that day.

(5) Where the parent of a pupil who is a boarder at a maintained school requests that the pupil be permitted—

(a) to receive religious education in accordance with the tenets of a particular religion or religious denomination outside school hours, or

(b) to attend worship in accordance with such tenets on Sundays or other days exclusively set apart for religious observance by the religious body to which his parent belongs,

the governing body shall make arrangements for giving the pupil reasonable opportunities for doing so.

(6) Arrangements under subsection (5) may provide for making facilities for such education or worship available on the school premises, but the arrangements shall not entail expenditure by the responsible authority.

(7) In this section—

"maintained school" does not include a maintained special school, and

"the responsible authority", in relation to a county or voluntary school, means the local education authority, and, in relation to a grant-maintained school, means the governing body.

Constitution of standing advisory councils on religious education

Constitution of advisory councils

390.—(1) A local education authority shall constitute a standing advisory council on religious education for the purposes mentioned in section 391(1).

(2) The council shall consist of—

(a) such groups of persons appointed by the authority as representative members ("representative groups") as are required by subsection (4), and

(b) a person appointed as a member by the governing bodies of the grant-maintained schools within the area of the authority in relation to which section 379 or 380 applies.

(3) The council may also include co-opted members (that is, persons co-opted as members of the council by members of the council who have not themselves been so co-opted).

(4) The representative groups required by this subsection are—

(a) a group of persons to represent such Christian denominations and other religions and denominations of such religions as, in the opinion of the authority, will appropriately reflect the principal religious traditions in the area;

(b) except in the case of an area in Wales, a group of persons to represent the Church of England;

(c) a group of persons to represent such associations representing teachers as, in the opinion of the authority, ought to be represented, having regard to the circumstances of the area; and

(d) a group of persons to represent the authority.

(5) Where a representative group is required by subsection (4)(b), the representative group required by subsection (4)(a) shall not include persons appointed to represent the Church of England.

(6) The number of representative members appointed to any representative group under subsection (4)(a) to represent each denomination or religion required to be represented shall, so far as consistent with the efficient discharge of the group's functions, reflect broadly the proportionate strength of that denomination or religion in the area.

(7) On any question to be decided by the council only the representative groups on the council shall be entitled to vote, and each representative group shall have a single vote.

Functions of advisory councils

391.—(1) The purposes referred to in section 390(1) are—

(a) to advise the local education authority upon such matters connected with religious worship in county schools and the religious education to be given in accordance with an agreed syllabus as the authority may refer to the council or as the council may see fit, and

(b) to carry out the functions conferred on them by section 394.

(2) The matters referred to in subsection (1)(a) include, in particular, methods of teaching, the choice of materials and the provision of training for teachers.

(3) The representative groups on the council required by section 390(4), other than the group consisting of persons appointed to represent the authority, may at any time require a review of any agreed syllabus for the time being adopted by the authority.

(4) Each representative group concerned shall have a single vote on the question of whether to require such a review.

(5) Paragraph 3 of Schedule 31 has effect to require the authority, on receiving written notification of any such requirement, to cause a conference constituted in accordance with that Schedule to be convened for the purpose of reconsidering any agreed syllabus to which the requirement relates.

(6) The council shall in each year publish a report as to the exercise of their functions and any action taken by representative groups on the council under subsection (3) during the last preceding year.

(7) The council's report shall in particular—

(a) specify any matters in respect of which the council have given advice to the authority,

(b) broadly describe the nature of the advice given, and

(c) where any such matter was not referred to the council by the authority, give the council's reasons for offering advice on that matter.

(8) The council shall send to the head teacher of any grant-maintained school to which section 379 applies and which is in the area of the authority a copy of advice which they give to the authority upon matters connected with religious worship.

(9) The council shall send a copy of advice which they give to the authority on the religious education to be given in accordance with an agreed syllabus to the head teacher of any grant-maintained school which is in the area of the authority and which—

(a) is required, by virtue of section 379 or 381, to provide religious education in accordance with an agreed syllabus, or

(b) was a controlled school immediately before it became grant-maintained.

(10) The council shall send a copy of each report published by them under subsection (6)—

(a) in the case of a council for an area in England, to the School Curriculum and Assessment Authority, and

(b) in the case of a council for an area in Wales, to the Curriculum and Assessment Authority for Wales.

Advisory councils: supplementary provisions

392.—(1) In this section "the council" means the standing advisory council on religious education constituted by a local education authority under section 390.

(2) Before appointing a person to represent any religion, denomination or associations as a member of the council, the authority shall take all reasonable steps to assure themselves that he is representative of the religion, denomination or associations in question.

(3) A member of the council who was appointed by the authority may be removed from membership by the authority if, in their opinion, he ceases to be representative of the religion, denomination or associations which he was appointed to represent or (as the case may be) he ceases to be representative of the authority.

(4) A member of the council required by section 390(2)(b) may at any time be removed from membership by the governing body or (as the case may be) by the governing bodies of the grant-maintained school or schools concerned.

(5) A person co-opted as a member of the council shall hold office on such terms as may be determined by the members co-opting him.

(6) A member of the council may at any time resign his office.

(7) Subject to section 390(7), the council and, in relation to any question falling to be decided by members of the council of any particular category, the members of that category, may regulate their own proceedings.

(8) The validity of proceedings of the council or of the members of the council of any particular category shall not be affected—

(a) by a vacancy in the office of any member of the council required by section 390(2), or

(b) on the ground that a member of the council appointed to represent any religion, denomination or associations does not at the time of the proceedings represent the religion, denomination or associations in question.

Duty to constitute new standing advisory council

393.—(1) This section has effect in respect of the area of a local education authority if an order under section 27(1)(b) (allocation to funding authority of responsibility for providing school places) applies to the area.

(2) Within six months of the date of the first such order the local education authority shall constitute a new standing advisory council on religious education under section 390.

(3) For the purposes of the constitution required by subsection (2) (and of any subsequent constitution)—

(a) section 390 shall have effect as if—

(i) subsection (2)(b) were omitted, and

(ii) subsection (4) required the appointment of a representative group, in addition to those listed in paragraphs (a) to (d) of that subsection, comprising persons representing relevant grant-maintained schools, and

(b) section 391 shall have effect as if, in subsection (3), for "the group consisting of persons appointed to represent the authority" there were substituted "the groups consisting of persons appointed to represent the authority or relevant grant-maintained schools".

(4) For this purpose "relevant grant-maintained schools" means the grant-maintained schools within the area of the local education authority in relation to which section 379 or 380 applies.

(5) Before appointing a person to represent relevant grant-maintained schools in accordance with subsection (3) the local education authority shall take all reasonable steps to assure themselves that he is acceptable as such to the governing bodies of the majority of such schools; but the validity of the council's proceedings shall not be affected because the person was not so acceptable unless it is shown that the local education authority failed to take such steps.

(6) A person appointed to represent relevant grant-maintained schools in accordance with subsection (3) may be removed from membership of the council if in the opinion of the local education authority he ceases to be acceptable as such to the governing bodies of the majority of such schools.

Determinations by standing advisory councils

Determination of cases in which requirement for Christian collective worship is not to apply

394.—(1) The council constituted by a local education authority under section 390 shall, on an application made by the head teacher of—

(a) any county school maintained by the authority, or

(b) any grant-maintained school which is in the authority's area and in relation to which section 379 applies,

consider whether it is appropriate for the requirement imposed by section 386(2) to apply in the case of the school or in the case of any class or description of pupils at the school.

(2) In determining whether it is appropriate for that requirement to apply as mentioned in subsection (1), the council shall have regard to any circumstances relating to the family backgrounds of the pupils at the school, or of the pupils of the particular class or description in question, which are relevant for determining the character of the collective worship appropriate in their case.

(3) The council shall give the head teacher written notification of their decision on the application.

(4) Where the council determine that it is not appropriate for the requirement to apply as mentioned in subsection (1), the determination shall take effect for the purposes of section 387 on such date as may be specified in the notification of the council's decision under subsection (3).

(5) Before making an application under subsection (1), the head teacher of a school shall consult the governing body.

(6) On being consulted by the head teacher, the governing body may if they think fit take such steps as they consider appropriate for consulting all persons appearing to them to be parents of registered pupils at the school.

(7) An application under subsection (1) shall be made in such manner and form as the council may require.

(8) Where an application is made under subsection (1)(a) in respect of a school which becomes a grant-maintained school before the application is determined, it shall, unless withdrawn by the head teacher, continue as if made under subsection (1)(b).

Review of determinations under section 394

395.—(1) Any determination by a council under section 394 by virtue of which the requirement imposed by section 386(2) does not for the time being apply in the case of a school or a class or description of pupils at a school shall be reviewed by the council—

(a) at any time on an application made by the head teacher, and

(b) in any event not later than the end of the period of five years beginning with the date on which the determination first took effect or (where it has since been reviewed under this section) with the effective date of the decision on the last review.

(2) On any review under subsection (1)(b) the council shall give the head teacher an opportunity of making representations as to the determination under review.

(3) On a review under this section, the council may—

(a) confirm the determination, with or without variation, or

(b) revoke it (without prejudice to any further determination under section 394).

(4) The council shall give the head teacher written notification of their decision, specifying the effective date of that decision for the purposes of subsection (1)(b).

(5) Any determination which is required to be reviewed under subsection (1)(b) shall cease to have effect, if not confirmed on such a review, at the end of the period there mentioned.

(6) The head teacher of a school shall consult the governing body before making an application under subsection (1)(a) or any representations under subsection (2).

(7) On being consulted by the head teacher, the governing body may if they think fit take such steps as they consider appropriate for consulting all persons appearing to them to be parents of registered pupils at the school.

(8) An application under subsection (1)(a) shall be made in such manner and form as the council may require.

Power of Secretary of State to direct advisory council to revoke determination or discharge duty

396.—(1) Where the Secretary of State is satisfied, either on complaint by any person or otherwise, that any standing advisory council on religious education constituted by a local education authority under section 390—

(a) have acted, or are proposing to act, unreasonably in determining for the purposes of section 394 or 395 whether it is appropriate for the requirement imposed by section 386(2) to apply in the case of any school or any class or description of pupils at a school, or

(b) have failed to discharge any duty imposed under section 394 or 395,

he may give the council such directions as to the revocation of the determination, or the withdrawal of the proposed determination or (as the case may be) the discharge of the duty as appear to him to be expedient; and the council shall comply with the directions.

(2) Directions under subsection (1) may provide for the making by the council of a new determination to take effect in place of the determination or proposed determination to be revoked or withdrawn by them.

Access to meetings and documents

Religious education: access to meetings and documents

397.—(1) This section applies to—

(a) any conference convened under any of paragraphs 1 to 3 of Schedule 31, and

(b) any standing advisory council on religious education constituted under section 390.

(2) Regulations may make provision—

(a) for meetings of conferences or councils to be, subject to prescribed exceptions, open to members of the public,

(b) requiring conferences or councils to give notice, in such manner as may be prescribed, of the time and place of such meetings, and

(c) requiring conferences or councils, at such time or times as may be prescribed—

(i) to make available for inspection, or

(ii) to provide on payment of such fee as they think fit (not exceeding the cost of supply),

copies of the agendas and reports for such meetings to members of the public.

(3) Regulations made under subsection (2) may apply to—

(a) committees appointed by local education authorities under paragraph 4 of Schedule 31,

(b) sub-committees appointed by conferences under that Schedule, and

(c) representative groups on councils appointed under section 390(4),

as they apply to conferences and councils.

Miscellaneous

No requirement of attendance at Sunday school etc.

398. It shall not be required, as a condition of—

(a) a pupil attending a maintained school, or

(b) a person attending such a school to receive further education or teacher training,

that he must attend or abstain from attending a Sunday school or a place of religious worship.

Determination of question whether religious education in accordance with trust deed

399. Where any trust deed relating to a voluntary or grant-maintained school makes provision whereby a bishop or any other ecclesiastical or denominational authority has power to decide whether the religious education given in the school which purports to be in accordance with the provisions of the trust deed does or does not accord with those provisions, that question shall be determined in accordance with the provisions of the trust deed.

CHAPTER IV

MISCELLANEOUS AND SUPPLEMENTARY PROVISIONS

Courses leading to external qualifications

Courses leading to external qualifications

400.—(1) No course of study leading to a qualification authenticated by an outside person shall be provided for pupils of compulsory school age by or on behalf of a maintained school unless—

(a) the qualification is for the time being approved by the Secretary of State or by a designated body, and

(b) subsection (2) is satisfied.

(2) This subsection is satisfied if either—

(a) a syllabus provided by the outside person for the purposes of the course is for the time being approved by a designated body, or

(b) criteria provided by the outside person for determining a syllabus for the purposes of the course are for the time being so approved.

(3) An approval under this section may be given either generally or in relation to particular cases.

(4) In relation to any maintained school—

(a) the local education authority and the governing body shall exercise their functions with a view to securing, and

(b) the head teacher shall secure,

that subsection (1) is not contravened.

(5) In this section—

"designated" means designated by the Secretary of State, and
"outside person", in relation to a school, means a person other than a member of staff of the school.

Power to extend section 400 to senior pupils and FE students

401.—(1) The Secretary of State may by order direct that the provisions of section 400 shall have effect as if—

(a) any reference to pupils of compulsory school age included a reference to—

(i) senior pupils who are of or over that age, and

(ii) persons in full-time further education who are of or over that age but have not attained the age of 19 (referred to in this section as "FE students");

(b) any reference to a maintained school (except in relation to a local education authority) included a reference to—

(i) any institution (other than a university or an institution within the higher education sector) which provides further education and is a grant-aided institution, and

(ii) any institution within the further education sector; and

(c) any reference to the head teacher of such a school included a reference to the principal or other head of such an institution.

(2) An order under this section may make such consequential modifications of section 359(1) as appear to the Secretary of State to be necessary or expedient.

(3) In relation to FE students in relation to whom section 400 has effect by virtue of an order under this section, section 408 shall have effect—

(a) with the modifications mentioned in subsection (1)(b) and (c) above;

(b) as if the information referred to in subsection (1)(a) of that section were information with respect to the following matters—

(i) the qualifications authenticated by outside persons (within the meaning of section 400) for which courses of study are to be provided by or on behalf of the institution concerned for such students;

(ii) the courses of study leading to such qualifications which are to be so provided;

(iii) the syllabuses which have been provided or determined for the purposes of those courses, and

(iv) the results of the assessments of such students for the purposes of those qualifications;

(c) as if in subsection (6)—

(i) the reference to the results of an individual pupil's assessment (whether under this Part or otherwise) included a reference to the results of an individual student's assessment for the purposes of any such qualification, and

(ii) any reference to the pupil concerned included a reference to the student concerned; and

(d) with the omission of subsections (1)(b), (2) and (3).

(4) Before making an order under this section the Secretary of State shall consult any persons with whom consultation appears to him to be desirable.

(5) For the purposes of this section an institution is at any time a grant-aided institution if it is maintained by persons who have received any grants under regulations made under section 485 in respect of expenditure incurred or to be incurred for the academic year of the institution current at that time.

Obligation to enter pupils for public examinations

Obligation to enter pupils for public examinations

402.—(1) Subject to subsections (2) and (3), the governing body of a maintained school shall secure that each registered pupil at the school is entered, at such time as they consider appropriate, for each prescribed public examination for which he is being prepared at the school at the time in question in each syllabus for that examination for which he is being so prepared.

(2) The governing body are not required to secure that a pupil is entered for any examination, or for an examination in any syllabus for that examination, if either—

(a) they consider that there are educational reasons in the case of that particular pupil for not entering him for that examination or (as the case may be) for not entering him for that examination in that syllabus, or

(b) the parent of the pupil requests in writing that the pupil should not be entered for that examination or (as the case may be) for that examination in that syllabus;

but this subsection does not apply to an examination which is part of the assessment arrangements for the fourth key stage and applies in the case of that pupil.

(3) The governing body are not required to secure that a pupil is entered for any examination in any syllabus for that examination if they have secured his entry for another prescribed public examination in a corresponding syllabus.

(4) For the purposes of subsection (3) a syllabus for a prescribed public examination shall be regarded as corresponding to a syllabus for another prescribed public examination if the same course of study is provided at the school in preparation for both syllabuses.

(5) As soon as practicable after determining whether or not to secure the entry of any pupil for a prescribed public examination in any syllabus for which he is being prepared at the school, the governing body shall notify the pupil's parent in writing of their determination in relation to each such syllabus.

(6) In this section—

(a) "maintained school" includes a maintained special school established in a hospital; and

(b) references to a prescribed public examination shall be construed in accordance with section 462.

Sex education

Sex education: manner of provision

403.—(1) The local education authority, governing body and head teacher shall take such steps as are reasonably practicable to secure that where sex education is given to any registered pupils at a maintained school, it is given in such a manner as to encourage those pupils to have due regard to moral considerations and the value of family life.

(2) In subsection (1) "maintained school" includes a maintained special school established in a hospital.

Sex education: statements of policy

404.—(1) The governing body of a maintained school shall—

(a) make, and keep up to date, a separate written statement of their policy with regard to the provision of sex education, and

(b) make copies of the statement available for inspection (at all reasonable times) by parents of registered pupils at the school and provide a copy of the statement free of charge to any such parent who asks for one.

(2) In subsection (1) "maintained school" includes, in relation to pupils who are provided with secondary education, a maintained special school

established in a hospital.

(3) In relation to—

(a) a county, or controlled, secondary school, and

(b) pupils who are provided with secondary education in a maintained special school,

section 371 shall have effect with the omission of subsection (3) of that section and of the references to the matters mentioned in that subsection, and section 372 shall have effect with the omission of subsection (4)(a) of that section.

Exemption from sex education

405. If the parent of any pupil in attendance at a maintained school requests that he may be wholly or partly excused from receiving sex education at the school, the pupil shall, except so far as such education is comprised in the National Curriculum, be so excused accordingly until the request is withdrawn.

Politics

Political indoctrination

406.—(1) The local education authority, governing body and head teacher shall forbid—

(a) the pursuit of partisan political activities by any of those registered pupils at a maintained school who are junior pupils, and

(b) the promotion of partisan political views in the teaching of any subject in the school.

(2) In the case of activities which take place otherwise than on the school premises, subsection (1)(a) applies only where arrangements for junior pupils to take part in the activities are made by—

(a) any member of the school's staff (in his capacity as such), or

(b) anyone acting on behalf of the school or of a member of the school's staff (in his capacity as such).

(3) In this section "maintained school" includes a maintained special school established in a hospital.

Duty to secure balanced treatment of political issues

407.—(1) The local education authority, governing body and head teacher shall take such steps as are reasonably practicable to secure that where political issues are brought to the attention of pupils while they are—

(a) in attendance at a maintained school, or

(b) taking part in extra-curricular activities which are provided or organised for registered pupils at the school by or on behalf of the school,

they are offered a balanced presentation of opposing views.

(2) In this section "maintained school" includes a maintained special school established in a hospital.

Information

Provision of information

408.—(1) Regulations may require, in relation to every maintained school, the local education authority, the governing body or the head teacher to make available either generally or to prescribed persons, in such form and manner and at such times as may be prescribed—

(a) such information (including information as to the matters mentioned in subsection (2)) relevant for the purposes of any of the relevant provisions of this Part, and

(b) such copies of the documents mentioned in subsection (3),

as may be prescribed.

(2) The matters referred to in subsection (1)(a) are—

(a) the curriculum for maintained schools,

(b) the educational provision made by the school for pupils at the school and any syllabuses to be followed by those pupils,

(c) the educational achievements of pupils at the school (including the results of any assessments of those pupils, whether under this Part or otherwise, for the purpose of ascertaining those achievements), and

(d) the educational achievements of pupils at such categories of school as may be prescribed (including results of the kind mentioned in paragraph (c)).

(3) The documents referred to in subsection (1)(b) are—

(a) any written statement made by the local education authority under section 370,

(b) any written statement made by the governing body in pursuance of provision made under section 371,

(c) any written statement made by the governing body of their policy as to the curriculum for the school, and

(d) any report prepared by the governing body under section 161 or paragraph 7 of Schedule 23 (governors' annual reports).

(4) For the purposes of subsection (1) the relevant provisions of this Part are—

(a) sections 350 to 368;

(b) sections 375(3) and 384;

(c) sections 385 and 388 and, so far as relating to county schools, sections 386 and 387;

(d) sections 389 to 392;

(e) sections 394 to 396;

(f) sections 398, 400, 401 and 405; and

(g) section 409.

(5) Before making any regulations under this section, the Secretary of State shall consult any persons with whom consultation appears to him to be desirable.

(6) Regulations under this section shall not require information as to the results of an individual pupil's assessment (whether under this Part or otherwise) to be made available to any persons other than—

(a) the parents of the pupil concerned,

(b) the pupil concerned,

(c) in the case of a pupil who has transferred to a different school, the head teacher of that school,

(d) the governing body of the school, or

(e) the local education authority;

and shall not require such information to be made available to the governing body, the head teacher or the local education authority except where relevant for the purposes of the performance of any of their functions.

(7) Regulations under this section may authorise local education authorities, governing bodies and head teachers to make a charge (not exceeding the cost of supply) for any documents supplied by them in pursuance of the regulations.

(8) In relation to any maintained school, the local education authority and the governing body shall exercise their functions with a view to securing that the head teacher complies with any regulations made under this section.

Complaints and enforcement

Complaints and enforcement: county, voluntary and maintained special schools

409.—(1) A local education authority shall, with the approval of the Secretary of State and after consultation with governing bodies of aided schools and of special agreement schools, make arrangements for the consideration and disposal of any complaint to which subsection (2) applies.

(2) This subsection applies to any complaint which is to the effect that the authority, or the governing body of any county or voluntary school maintained by the authority or of any special school so maintained which is not established in a hospital—

(a) have acted or are proposing to act unreasonably in relation to the exercise of a power conferred on them by or under a relevant enactment, or

(b) have acted or are proposing to act unreasonably in relation to the performance of, or have failed to discharge, a duty imposed on them by or under a relevant enactment.

(3) In subsection (2) "relevant enactment" means—

(a) any provision which by virtue of section 408(4) is a relevant provision of this Part for the purposes of section 408(1), and

(b) any other enactment (whether contained in this Part or otherwise) so far as relating to the curriculum for, or religious worship in, maintained schools other than grant-maintained schools.

(4) The Secretary of State shall not entertain under section 496 (power to prevent unreasonable exercise of functions) or 497 (powers where a local education authority or governing body fail to discharge their duties) any complaint to which subsection (2) applies, unless a complaint concerning the same matter has been made and disposed of in accordance with arrangements made under subsection (1).

Nursery education

Application of Part V in relation to nursery education

410. Nothing in this Part applies in relation to a nursery school or in relation to a nursery class in a primary school.

PART VI

SCHOOL ADMISSIONS, ATTENDANCE AND CHARGES

CHAPTER I

SCHOOL ADMISSIONS

Parental preferences

Parental preferences

411.—(1) A local education authority shall make arrangements for enabling the parent of a child in the area of the authority—

(a) to express a preference as to the school at which he wishes education to be provided for his child in the exercise of the authority's functions, and

(b) to give reasons for his preference.

(2) Subject to subsection (3) and section 430(2) (co-ordinated admission arrangements), a local education authority and the governing body of a county or voluntary school shall comply with any preference expressed in accordance with arrangements made under subsection (1).

(3) The duty imposed by subsection (2) does not apply—

(a) if compliance with the preference would prejudice the provision of efficient education or the efficient use of resources;

(b) if the preferred school is an aided or a special agreement school and compliance with the preference would be incompatible with any arrangements between the governing body and the local education authority made under section 413; or

(c) if the arrangements for admission to the preferred school are based wholly or partly on selection by reference to ability or aptitude and compliance with the preference would be incompatible with selection under the arrangements.

(4) Where the arrangements for the admission of pupils to a school maintained by a local education authority provide for applications for admission to be made to (or to a person acting on behalf of) the governing body of the school, a parent who makes such an application shall be regarded for the purposes of subsection (2) as having expressed a preference for that school in accordance with arrangements made under subsection (1).

(5) The duty imposed by subsection (2) in relation to a preference expressed in accordance with arrangements made under subsection (1) shall apply also in relation to—

(a) any application for the admission to a school maintained by a local education authority of a child who is not in the area of the authority, and

(b) any application made by a parent as mentioned in section 438(4) or 440(2) (application for a particular school to be specified in a school attendance order);

and references in subsection (3) to a preference and a preferred school shall be construed accordingly.

(6) No prejudice shall be taken to arise for the purposes of subsection (3)(a) from the admission to a county or voluntary school in a school year of a number of pupils in a relevant age group which does not exceed—

(a) the relevant standard number, or

(b) the admission number fixed in accordance with section 416,

whichever is the greater.

(7) In this Chapter "the relevant standard number", in relation to a county or voluntary school, a relevant age group and a school year, means the standard number applying under sections 417 to 420 to the school in relation to that age group and year.

(8) In this section "child" includes a person who has not attained the age of 19.

Admission arrangements for county and voluntary schools

Consultation as to admission arrangements

412.—(1) Where the governing body of a county or voluntary school are responsible for determining the arrangements for the admission of pupils to the school, they shall—

(a) consult the local education authority before determining, or varying, any of those arrangements, and

(b) at least once in every school year, consult the local education authority as to whether those arrangements are satisfactory.

(2) Where the local education authority are responsible for determining the arrangements for the admission of pupils to a county or voluntary school, they shall—

(a) consult the governing body before determining, or varying, any of those arrangements, and

(b) at least once in every school year, consult the governing body as to whether those arrangements are satisfactory.

Admission arrangements to preserve character of aided or special agreement school

413.—(1) If the governing body of an aided or special agreement school so request, the local education authority shall make with the governing body arrangements in respect of the admission of pupils to the school for preserving the character of the school; and, in default of agreement between the authority and the governing body, the terms of any such arrangements shall be determined by the Secretary of State.

(2) If one of the parties to arrangements under subsection (1) proposes that the arrangements should be modified or replaced by substitute arrangements but the other party does not agree, the party making the proposal may refer the matter to the Secretary of State.

(3) On a reference under subsection (2), the Secretary of State may direct—

(a) that the arrangements shall remain as they are;
(b) that they shall be modified or replaced as proposed; or
(c) that they shall be modified in such other manner, or replaced by such other substitute arrangements, as may be specified in the direction.

(4) Where the Secretary of State directs as mentioned in subsection (3)(b) or (c), the modification or, as the case may be, the substitute arrangements shall have effect, from such date as may be specified in the direction, as if agreed between the parties.

Information as to schools and admission arrangements

414.—(1) A local education authority shall, for each school year, publish particulars of—

(a) the arrangements for the admission of pupils to schools maintained by the authority other than aided or special agreement schools,
(b) the authority's arrangements for the provision of education at schools maintained by another local education authority or not maintained by a local education authority, and
(c) the arrangements made by the authority under sections 411(1) and 423(1) (admission appeals).

(2) The governing body of an aided or a special agreement school shall, for each school year, publish particulars of—

(a) the arrangements for the admission of pupils to the school, and
(b) the arrangements made by them under section 423(2) (admission appeals).

(3) The particulars to be published under subsections (1)(a) and (2)(a) shall Include particulars of—

(a) in the case of each school to which the arrangements relate, the admission number applicable in each school year in relation to the age group in which pupils are normally admitted (or, if there is more than one such group, the admission number so applicable in relation to each such group),
(b) the respective admission functions of the local education authority and the governing body,
(c) the policy followed in deciding admissions, and
(d) the arrangements made in respect of pupils not belonging to the area of the local education authority.

(4) In subsection (3)(a) references to the admission number applicable in a school year in relation to an age group are to—

(a) the standard number applying under sections 417 to 420 to the school in question in relation to that age group and year, or
(b) the admission number fixed in relation to the school in accordance with section 416 for that age group and year,

whichever is the greater.

(5) The particulars to be published under subsection (1)(b) shall include particulars of—

(a) the criteria for offering places at schools not maintained by a local education authority, and

(b) the names of, and number of places at, any such schools in respect of which the authority have standing arrangements.

(6) The governing body of a school maintained by a local education authority—

(a) shall publish such information as respects that school as may be required by regulations; and

(b) may publish such other information with respect to the school as they think fit.

(7) For the purposes of this section information about the continuing education of pupils leaving a school, or the employment or training taken up by such pupils on leaving, is to be treated as information about the school.

(8) A local education authority may, with the agreement of the governing body of any school maintained by the authority, publish on behalf of the governing body the particulars or information referred to in subsection (2) or (6) above.

(9) References in this section to publication are references to publication at such time or times and in such manner as may be required by regulations.

Admission numbers for county and voluntary schools

Meaning of "the admission authority"

415. In this Chapter "the admission authority", in relation to a county or voluntary school, means—

(a) the local education authority, where they are responsible for determining the arrangements for the admission of pupils to the school, or

(b) the governing body, where they are responsible for determining those arrangements.

Fixing admission numbers

416.—(1) The admission authority for a county or voluntary school shall not fix as the admission number for any relevant age group and any school year a number which is less than the relevant standard number.

(2) Despite any provision of the articles of government of the school (but subject to section 412), the admission authority may fix as the admission number for any relevant age group and any school year a number which exceeds the relevant standard number.

(3) A proposal may be made to the admission authority in accordance with subsections (4) and (5) for fixing as the admission number for any relevant age group and any school year a number which exceeds both—

(a) the relevant standard number, and

(b) any admission number fixed, or proposed to be fixed, for that age group and year by the admission authority.

(4) The proposal may be made—

(a) where the local education authority are the admission authority, by the governing body, or

(b) where the governing body are the admission authority, by the local education authority.

(5) Any such proposal—

(a) shall be made in writing,

(b) may relate to one or more relevant age groups, and

(c) may relate to a particular school year or to each school year falling within any period specified in the proposal.

(6) If the admission authority do not give the authority making the pro-

posal notice in writing rejecting the proposal within the period of two months beginning with the day after that on which the proposal was received by the admission authority, the admission authority shall give effect to the proposal.

(7) Where the admission authority give such notice within that period, the authority making the proposal may, within 28 days of receiving the notice, make an application to the Secretary of State for an order under section 420(2) increasing the relevant standard number.

(8) In this section references, in relation to a school, to the "admission number" for any relevant age group and any school year are references to the number of pupils in that age group it is intended to admit to the school in that school year.

Standard numbers for admissions to secondary schools

417.—(1) Subject to subsection (2), if pupils in any age group were admitted to a county or voluntary secondary school in the school year beginning in 1989, the standard number applying to the school for that age group in any subsequent school year shall be—

(a) the standard number applying to the school under section 15 of the Education Act 1980 ("the 1980 Act") for that age group in the school year beginning in 1989, or

(b) the number of pupils in that age group admitted in the school year beginning in 1989,

whichever is the greater.

(2) If proposals under section 35 or 41 above or section 12 or 13 of the 1980 Act (proposals for the establishment or alteration of a school) have fallen to be implemented in relation to a county or voluntary secondary school, the number stated in the proposals for any school year and age group shall constitute the standard number applying to the school for that age group—

(a) in any school year beginning after 1989 in relation to which the proposals have been wholly implemented, and

(b) subject to any variation made by the Secretary of State, in any school year beginning after 1989 in relation to which they have been partly implemented.

(3) In subsection (2) "the number stated in the proposals" means the number so stated in accordance with section 35(3)(b) or 41(5)(b) above (or, as the case may be, section 12(2) of the 1980 Act or section 12(2) as applied by section 13(2) of that Act).

(4) Any standard number applying under subsection (2) is without prejudice to the application under that subsection of a new standard number if further proposals under section 35 or 41 above fall to be implemented.

(5) References in this section to proposals under section 35 or 41 above or section 12 or 13 of the 1980 Act are to the proposals with any modifications made by the Secretary of State under section 37, 40, 43 or 45 above or, as the case may be, under section 12 or 13 of the 1980 Act.

Standard numbers for admissions to primary schools

418.—(1) Subject to subsection (2), if pupils in any age group were admitted to a county or voluntary primary school in the school year beginning in 1991, the standard number applying to the school for that age group in any subsequent year shall be—

(a) the number applicable in relation to the school and in relation to that age group in accordance with section 419, or

(b) the number of pupils in that age group admitted in the school year beginning in 1991,

whichever is the greater.

(2) If proposals published under section 35 or 41 above or section 12 or 13 of the Education Act 1980 (proposals for the establishment or alteration of a

school) have fallen to be implemented in relation to a county or voluntary primary school, the number stated in the proposals for any school year and age group shall constitute the standard number applying to the school for that age group—

(a) in any school year beginning after 1991 in relation to which the proposals have been wholly implemented, and

(b) subject to any variation made by the Secretary of State, in any school year beginning after 1991 in relation to which they have been partly implemented.

(3) Section 417(3) to (5) shall apply for the purposes of subsection (2) of this section as they apply for the purposes of section 417(2).

Special provisions supplementary to section 418

419.—(1) In this section "the 1980 standard number", in relation to any school and age group, means the standard number applying to the school under section 15 of the Education Act 1980 ("the 1980 Act") in relation to that age group in the school year beginning in 1991.

(2) In the case of a primary school to which section 418(1) applies, the number applicable in relation to the school and in relation to any age group there mentioned is—

(a) if the 1980 standard number for that age group is a number determined under section 15(5) of the 1980 Act by reference to the number of pupils in that age group admitted to the school in the school year beginning in 1979, the recalculated 1979 admission number;

(b) if the 1980 standard number for that age group is a number determined under section 15(6) of that Act by reference to the number of pupils in that age group admitted to the school in any school year beginning after 1979 (and not varied by the Secretary of State under that provision), the recalculated post 1979 admission number; and

(c) if the 1980 standard number for that age group is a number applicable by virtue of section 15(7) of that Act which has not been varied by the Secretary of State, the aggregate of the number so applicable and the additional admission number.

(3) In subsection (2)(a) "the recalculated 1979 admission number", in relation to any school and age group, means the number of pupils admitted to the school in that age group in the school year beginning in 1979 (as determined in accordance with section 436, which relates to children admitted for nursery education).

(4) In subsection (2)(b) "the recalculated post–1979 admission number", in relation to any school and age group, means the number of pupils admitted to the school in that age group in the school year by reference to which the 1980 standard number for that school and age group was determined (as determined in accordance with section 436).

(5) In subsection (2)(c) "the additional admission number", in relation to any school and age group, means the aggregate of—

(a) the number of pupils admitted to the school in that age group in the first school year in relation to which the proposals in question had been wholly implemented who were admitted otherwise than for nursery education and were under the age of four years and six months on the date of their admission, and

(b) the number of pupils already admitted to the school for nursery education transferred in that year to a reception class at the school.

Variation of standard numbers

420.—(1) The Secretary of State may by order applying to county or voluntary schools of any class or description vary any standard number that would otherwise apply by virtue of section 417 or 418.

(2) Subject to subsections (3) to (5), the Secretary of State may by order vary any standard number that would otherwise apply to an individual school by virtue of section 417 or 418 or by virtue of any order made under subsection (1).

(3) An order under subsection (2) reducing a standard number may only be made on the application of the admission authority for the school, and is subject to the procedure provided for in Schedule 32.

(4) An order under subsection (2) increasing a standard number may be made on the application of the admission authority for the school or on an application made by the governing body or local education authority in accordance with section 416(7).

(5) On an application for an order under subsection (2) increasing a standard number, the Secretary of State may—

(a) make an order under subsection (2) increasing the standard number to the number proposed,
(b) after consultation with both the local education authority and the governing body of the school, make an order under subsection (2) increasing the standard number to such number (less than the number proposed) as he thinks desirable, or
(c) refuse to make an order increasing the standard number.

Review of standard numbers

421.—(1) The admission authority for a county or voluntary school shall keep under review any standard numbers applying to the school under sections 417 to 420, having regard to any change in the school's capacity to accommodate pupils as compared with its capacity at the beginning of the school year in which those standard numbers first applied (whether by virtue of section 15 of the Education Act 1980, section 27 of the Education Reform Act 1988 or sections 417 to 420 above).

(2) For the purposes of this section a school's capacity to accommodate pupils is changed if—

(a) as a result of changes in the availability or use of accommodation at the school, there is any change in the amount of accommodation available for use by pupils at the school; or
(b) as a result of changes in the requirements applicable to the school under regulations made under section 542 there is any change in the number of pupils for whom accommodation may lawfully be provided at the school;

and a school's capacity to accommodate pupils is reduced if the result of the changes is, in a case within paragraph (a), less accommodation or, in a case within paragraph (b), a reduction in the number there mentioned.

New county and voluntary schools

Admission of pupils to new schools

422.—(1) The initial arrangements for the admission of pupils to a new school shall be made—

(a) where the school will be a county or controlled school, by the local education authority; or
(b) where it will be an aided school, by the temporary governing body or by the promoters if
    (i) that body have not been constituted, and
    (ii) the promoters consider that it is expedient for the arrangements to be determined without delay.

(2) Any body or persons making any initial arrangements under this section shall have regard to the arrangements in force for the admission of pupils to comparable schools in the area of the local education authority.

(3) Before making any such initial arrangements for a new school which will be a county school, the authority shall consult the temporary governing body unless—

(a) that body have not been constituted, and

(b) the authority consider that it is expedient for the initial arrangements to be determined without delay.

(4) Before making any such arrangements for a new school which will be a controlled school the authority shall consult—

(a) the temporary governing body; or

(b) where that body have not been constituted, the promoters.

(5) Before making any such initial arrangements for a new school which will be an aided school the temporary governing body or (as the case may be) the promoters shall consult the authority.

(6) Sections 411, 413, 414 and 423 shall have effect in relation to a new school as if the references to the governing body included references to the person responsible for the admission of pupils under the initial arrangements for the school.

(7) In this section "new school" and "temporary governing body" have the meaning given by section 181(1) and (3) respectively; and "the promoters" means the persons making the relevant proposals (as defined by section 181(2)).

Admissions appeals relating to county and voluntary schools

Appeal arrangements

423.—(1) A local education authority shall make arrangements for enabling the parent of a child to appeal against—

(a) any decision made by or on behalf of the authority as to the school at which education is to be provided for the child in the exercise of the authority's functions, other than a decision leading to or embodied in a direction under section 431 (directions for admission), and

(b) any decision made by or on behalf of the governing body of a county or controlled school maintained by the authority refusing the child admission to the school.

(2) The governing body of an aided or a special agreement school shall make arrangements for enabling the parent of a child to appeal against any decision made by or on behalf of the governing body refusing the child admission to the school.

(3) Joint arrangements may be made under subsection (2) by the governing bodies of two or more aided or special agreement schools maintained by the same local education authority.

(4) Schedule 33 has effect in relation to the making and hearing of appeals pursuant to arrangements made under this section.

(5) The decision of an appeal committee on such an appeal shall be binding—

(a) on the local education authority or governing body by or on whose behalf the decision under appeal was made, and

(b) in the case of a decision made by or on behalf of a local education authority, on the governing body of any county or controlled school at which the appeal committee determines that a place should be offered to the child in question.

(6) In this section and Schedule 33 "child" includes a person who has not attained the age of 19.

Nursery and special schools, etc.

Admission of pupils to nursery schools and special schools, etc.

424.—(1) Subject to subsection (2), nothing in section 411,413,414 or 423

applies in relation to—
(a) nursery schools, or
(b) children who will be under the age of five at the time of their proposed admission.

(2) Where the arrangements for the admission of pupils to a school maintained by a local education authority provide for the admission to the school of children who will be under the age of five at the time of their proposed admission, those sections shall apply in relation to the admission of such pupils to the school otherwise than for nursery education

(3) None of the provisions of sections 411, 413, 414 and 423, apart from section 414(6) to (9), apply in relation to—
(a) special schools, or
(b) children for whom statements of special educational needs are maintained under section 324.

Admission arrangements for grant-maintained schools

Admission arrangements and information about them

425. Paragraph 5 of Schedule 23 has effect—
(a) for making the governing body of a grant-maintained school responsible for determining the arrangements for admitting pupils to the school; and
(b) for requiring the governing body of such a school to publish particulars of such arrangements and of the procedures applicable in relation to the admission of pupils to the school.

Admission numbers for grant-maintained schools

Minimum number for admission

426.—(1) The governing body of a grant-maintained school shall not fix as the number of pupils in any relevant age group it is intended to admit to the school in any school year a number which is less than the approved admission number for that age group.

(2) Subject to subsections (3) and (4) and sections 427 and 428, the approved admission number for any relevant age group is the number specified in the relevant proposals as the number of pupils intended to be admitted to the school in that age group in the first school year beginning on or after the date of implementation of the proposals.

For this purpose "the relevant proposals" means the proposals published under section 193, 211 or 212 above (or, as the case may be, under section 32, 48 or 49 of the Education Act 1993 or section 62 of the Education Reform Act 1988).

(3) Where proposals for a significant change in the character, or significant enlargement of the premises, of a grant-maintained school or for the transfer of such a school to a new site have been approved or adopted under section 261 above (or, as the case may be, under section 98 of the Education Act 1993 or section 89 of the Education Reform Act 1988), the approved admission number for any relevant age group for any school year for which the proposals have been wholly or partly implemented is—
(a) the number specified in the proposals as the number of pupils proposed to be admitted to the school in that age group in the first school year in relation to which the proposals have been wholly implemented, or
(b) if for any school year in relation to which the proposals have been partly implemented the Secretary of State directs the substitution of a different number, that number.

(4) The approved admission number in relation to any relevant age group

may be varied in the case of any such school with the approval of the Secretary of State.

Alteration of minimum number by Secretary of State

427.—(1) This section applies in relation to any grant-maintained school unless the funding authority have the function under section 428 in relation to that school.

(2) The Secretary of State may by order increase the approved admission number for any relevant age group to such number as may be specified in the order for any school year specified in the order beginning after the date of the order.

(3) No order may be made under subsection (2) which would have the effect of requiring such an increase in the number of pupils to be admitted to the school as would—

(a) constitute a significant change in the character of the school, or

(b) involve any alteration of the premises of the school.

Section 311(4) shall apply for the purposes of this subsection.

Alteration of minimum number by funding authority

428.—(1) If an order under section 27(1) (allocation of responsibility for providing sufficient school places) applies to the area of a local education authority, the funding authority may give a direction under subsection (2) to the governing body of a grant-maintained school in the area.

(2) A direction under this subsection—

(a) may increase the approved admission number for any relevant age group to such number as may be specified in the direction for any school year specified in the direction beginning after the date of the direction, and

(b) if any alteration would be required to the premises of the school in consequence of any increase in any approved admission number made by the direction, shall give particulars of the alteration.

(3) No direction may be given under subsection (2) which would have the effect of requiring such an increase in the number of pupils to be admitted to the school as would—

(a) constitute a significant change in the character of the school, or

(b) involve a significant enlargement of the premises of the school.

Section 311(4) shall apply for the purposes of this subsection.

(4) Before deciding to give a direction under subsection (2) the funding authority shall consult the governing body about the proposed content of the direction.

(5) Before giving a direction under subsection (2) the funding authority shall serve a draft of the proposed direction on the governing body.

(6) A governing body on which a draft is served under subsection (5) may, within the period of 15 days beginning with the day on which it was served, refer the matter to the Secretary of State and, if they do so, shall inform the funding authority.

(7) On a reference under subsection (6) the Secretary of State may—

(a) require the funding authority not to give any direction in the terms of the draft, or

(b) authorise the funding authority to give a direction in those terms, or in those terms as required to be modified by the Secretary of State;

and any direction given by the funding authority shall be in the terms authorised under paragraph (b).

(8) Where the funding authority give a direction under this section, then—

(a) if any particulars are specified in pursuance of subsection (2)(b), the governing body shall secure the alteration of the school premises in accordance with the particulars, and

(b) the funding authority shall make to them a grant of an amount equal to the reasonable expenses incurred or to be incurred in doing so.

Admissions appeals relating to grant-maintained schools

Appeal arrangements

429. Paragraph 6 of Schedule 23 has effect for requiring the governing body of a grant-maintained school—

(a) to make arrangements for appeals to an appeal committee against decisions or action taken in relation to admissions of pupils to the school; and

(b) to publish particulars of such arrangements.

Co-ordinated arrangements for admissions

Co-ordinated arrangements for admissions

430.—(1) In this section "co-ordinated arrangements for admissions", in relation to any two or more maintained or grant-maintained schools, means arrangements under an agreement to which this section applies for the purpose of co-ordinating arrangements for admitting pupils to the schools concerned.

(2) Co-ordinated arrangements for admissions, if—

(a) contained in an agreement approved by the Secretary of State under this section, or

(b) made in pursuance of a scheme under this section,

and any provision contained in any other arrangements for admitting pupils to any maintained or grant-maintained school in pursuance of a scheme under this section, shall have effect in the case of any school to which they relate despite anything in section 411(2) or in the instrument or articles of government for the school.

(3) This section applies to an agreement made in relation to any two or more maintained or grant-maintained schools to which each authority responsible for determining the arrangements for admitting pupils to any of the schools is a party, whether or not any local education authority for any area in which any of the schools is situated is also a party.

(4) The Secretary of State may make a scheme under this section for the purpose of co-ordinating arrangements, or assisting in the co-ordination of arrangements, for admitting pupils to any maintained or grant-maintained schools to which the scheme applies.

(5) A scheme under this section may in particular require each authority responsible for determining the arrangements for admitting pupils to any of the schools to which the scheme applies—

(a) to include in their arrangements for admitting pupils such provisions as may be required by the scheme;

(b) to secure the making in accordance with the scheme of an agreement for the purpose of co-ordinating arrangements for admitting pupils to the schools to which the scheme applies; or

(c) to secure the modification in accordance with the scheme of any such agreement to which they are a party.

(6) Before making a scheme under this section the Secretary of State shall, in respect of each school which appears to him to be a school to which the scheme will apply, consult—

(a) the governing body, and

(b) in the case of a maintained school, the local education authority.

(7) A scheme under this section may apply—

(a) to all schools which for the time being are maintained or grant-maintained schools;

(b) to all schools which for the time being are maintained or grant-maintained schools falling within any category of such schools specified in the scheme; or

(c) to any maintained or grant-maintained school so specified.

(8) Section 570 (revocation and variation) applies to a scheme under this section as it applies to an order made by the Secretary of State.

(9) In this section "maintained school" means a county or voluntary school or a maintained special school which is not established in a hospital.

Power to direct admission of child to school

Direction to admit child to specified school

431.—(1) The appropriate authority may give a direction under this section if, in the case of any child in the area of a local education authority, either (or both) of the following conditions is satisfied in relation to each school which is a reasonable distance from his home and provides suitable education, that is—

(a) he has been refused admission to the school, or

(b) he is permanently excluded from the school.

(2) A direction under this section shall specify a school—

(a) which is a reasonable distance from the child's home, and

(b) from which the child is not permanently excluded.

(3) A direction under this section shall, unless it is given on the determination of the Secretary of State under section 432(4) or by the funding authority, specify a school in the area referred to in subsection (1).

(4) Where a school is specified in a direction under this section, the governing body (and, if the school is a county or voluntary school and the local education authority are not the appropriate authority, the local education authority) shall admit the child to the school.

(5) Subsection (4) does not affect any power to exclude from a school a pupil who is already a registered pupil there.

(6) In this section "suitable education", in relation to a child, means efficient full-time education suitable to his age, ability and aptitude and to any special educational needs he may have.

(7) In this section and section 432—

(a) references to the appropriate authority are (subject to subsection (8)) references to the local education authority; and

(b) references to schools are references to county, voluntary and grant-maintained schools.

(8) Where the education which is suitable education for the child is also education of a kind to which there relates an order made under section 27(1)(b) in respect of the area referred to in subsection (1) above, references in this section and section 432 to the appropriate authority are to be read in relation to—

(a) that child, and

(b) any county, voluntary or grant-maintained school in that area, and any such school in any other area to which an order under section 27(1)(b) applies which provides education which is relevant education in relation to that order,

as references to the funding authority.

Procedure for giving direction under section 431

432.—(1) Before deciding to give a direction under section 431, the appropriate authority shall consult—

(a) the parent of the child,

(b) the governing body of the school they propose to specify in the direction, and

(c) (if different) the authority which have a duty to maintain the school or to pay maintenance grant to the governing body ("the maintaining authority").

(2) Where the appropriate authority decide to give such a direction specifying any school they shall, before doing so, serve a notice in writing of their decision on—

(a) the governing body and head teacher of the school, and

(b) (if subsection (1)(c) applies) the maintaining authority,

and shall not give the direction until the period for referring the matter to the Secretary of State under subsection (3) has expired and, if it is so referred, the Secretary of State has made his determination.

(3) Any body or authority on whom a notice is served under subsection (2) may, within the period of 15 days beginning with the day on which the notice was served, refer the matter to the Secretary of State and, if they do so, shall inform the appropriate authority.

(4) On a reference under subsection (3) the Secretary of State may determine which school is to be required to admit the child and, if he does so, that school shall be specified in the direction.

(5) Where the appropriate authority give such a direction specifying a school, they shall give notice in writing of that fact to—

(a) the governing body and head teacher of the school, and

(b) (if subsection (1)(c) applies) the maintaining authority.

Time for admission of pupils

Time for admission of pupils

433.—(1) Section 14 (which requires a local education authority to secure that sufficient schools for providing primary and secondary education are available for their area) shall not be construed as imposing any obligation on the proprietor of a school to admit children as pupils otherwise than at the beginning of a school term.

(2) Where, however, a child was prevented from entering a school at the beginning of a term—

(a) by his being ill or by other circumstances beyond his parent's control, or

(b) by his parent's having been then resident at a place from which the school was not accessible with reasonable facility,

the school's proprietor is not entitled by virtue of subsection (1) to refuse to admit him as a pupil during the currency of the term.

(3) In cases where subsection (2) does not apply, the governing body of a school maintained by a local education authority shall comply with any general directions given by the authority as to the time of admission of children as pupils.

(4) General directions given by a local education authority as respects the time of admission of children as pupils shall not prevent the admission to a school of children in respect of whose education grants may be made under arrangements which have been made under section 1 of the Nursery Education and Grant-Maintained Schools Act 1996.

(5) Despite section 7 (duty of parent of child of compulsory school age to cause him to receive full-time education), a parent is not under a duty to cause a child to receive full-time education during any period during which, having regard to subsections (1) and (2), it is not practicable for the parent to arrange for him to be admitted as a pupil at a school.

Registration of pupils

Registration of pupils

434.—(1) The proprietor of a school shall cause to be kept, in accordance with regulations, a register containing the prescribed particulars in respect of all persons who are pupils at the school.

(2) Without prejudice to the generality of subsection (1), the prescribed particulars shall include particulars of the name and address of every person known to the proprietor to be a parent of a pupil at the school.

(3) The regulations shall prescribe the grounds on which names are to be deleted from a register kept under this section; and the name of a person entered in such a register as a pupil at a school—

(a) shall, when any of the prescribed grounds is applicable, be deleted from the register on that ground; and

(b) shall not be deleted from the register otherwise than on any such ground.

(4) The regulations may make provision—

(a) for enabling registers kept under this section to be inspected;

(b) for enabling extracts from such registers to be taken for the purposes of this Act by persons authorised to do so under the regulations; and

(c) for requiring the person by whom any such register is required to be kept to make to—

(i) the Secretary of State,

(ii) the funding authorities, and

(iii) local education authorities,

such periodical or other returns as to the contents of the register as may be prescribed.

(5) In this Act—

"registered pupil", in relation to a school, means a person registered as a pupil at the school in the register kept under this section; and

"registered", in relation to the parents of pupils at a school or in relation to the names or addresses of such parents or pupils, means shown in that register.

(6) A person who contravenes or fails to comply with any requirement imposed on him by regulations under this section is guilty of an offence and liable on summary conviction to a fine not exceeding level 1 on the standard scale.

Withdrawal of pupils from primary school for secondary education

Withdrawal of pupils from a primary school for secondary education

435. A local education authority may make arrangements in respect of a primary school maintained by them (other than one that is for the time being organised for the provision of both primary and secondary education) under which any registered pupils who are under the age of 12 but have attained the age of 10 years and six months may be required to be withdrawn from the school for the purpose of receiving secondary education.

Supplementary

Effect of admission for nursery education

436.—(1) Children admitted to a school for nursery education and subsequently transferred to a reception class at the school shall be regarded for the purposes of this Chapter as admitted to the school (otherwise than for nursery education) on being so transferred.

(2) The admission of children to a school for nursery education shall be disregarded for the purpose of—

(a) applying in relation to a primary school any provision of sections 416 to 421 (apart from section 419) which refers to the number of pupils admitted or intended to be admitted to a school in any school year, or

(b) applying section 419(3) or (4) in relation to a primary school, or

(c) determining for the purposes of any provision of sections 416 to 421 what is a relevant age group in relation to a primary school,

and for the purposes of sections 426 to 428.

CHAPTER II

SCHOOL ATTENDANCE

School attendance orders

School attendance orders

437.—(1) If it appears to a local education authority that a child of compulsory school age in their area is not receiving suitable education, either by regular attendance at school or otherwise, they shall serve a notice in writing on the parent requiring him to satisfy them within the period specified in the notice that the child is receiving such education.

(2) That period shall not be less than 15 days beginning with the day on which the notice is served.

(3) If—

(a) a parent on whom a notice has been served under subsection (1) fails to satisfy the local education authority, within the period specified in the notice, that the child is receiving suitable education, and

(b) in the opinion of the authority it is expedient that the child should attend school,

the authority shall serve on the parent an order (referred to in this Act as a "school attendance order"), in such form as may be prescribed, requiring him to cause the child to become a registered pupil at a school named in the order.

(4) A school attendance order shall (subject to any amendment made by the local education authority) continue in force for so long as the child is of compulsory school age, unless—

(a) it is revoked by the authority, or

(b) a direction is made in respect of it under section 443(2) or 447(5).

(5) Where a maintained or grant-maintained school is named in a school attendance order, the local education authority shall inform the governing body and the head teacher.

(6) Where a maintained or grant-maintained school is named in a school attendance order, the governing body (and, in the case of a maintained school, the local education authority) shall admit the child to the school.

(7) Subsection (6) does not affect any power to exclude from a school a pupil who is already a registered pupil there.

(8) In this Chapter—

"maintained school" means any county or voluntary school or any maintained special school which is not established in a hospital; and

"suitable education", in relation to a child, means efficient full-time education suitable to his age, ability and aptitude and to any special educational needs he may have.

Choice of school: child without statement of special educational needs

438.—(1) This section applies where a local education authority are required by virtue of section 437(3) to serve a school attendance order in respect of a child, other than a child for whom they maintain a statement under section 324.

(2) Before serving the order, the authority shall serve on the parent a notice in writing—

(a) informing him of their intention to serve the order,

(b) specifying the school which the authority intend to name in the order and, if they think fit, one or more other schools which they regard as

suitable alternatives, and
(c) stating the effect of subsections (3) to (6).

(3) If the notice specifies one or more alternative schools and the parent selects one of them within the period of 15 days beginning with the day on which the notice is served, the school selected by him shall be named in the order.

(4) If—
(a) within the period mentioned in subsection (3)—
(i) the parent applies for the child to be admitted to a school maintained by a local education authority and, where that authority are not the authority by whom the notice was served, notifies the latter authority of the application, or
(ii) the parent applies for the child to be admitted to a grant-maintained school and notifies the authority by whom the notice was served of the application, and
(b) the child is offered a place at the school as a result of the application,

that school shall be named in the order.

(5) If—
(a) within the period mentioned in subsection (3), the parent applies to the local education authority by whom the notice was served for education to be provided for the child at a school which is not maintained by a local education authority and is not a grant-maintained school, and
(b) the child is offered a place at the school under arrangements made by the authority under which the fees payable in respect of the education provided at the school are to be paid by them under section 517,

that school shall be named in the order.

(6) If, within the period mentioned in subsection (3)—
(a) the parent—
(i) applies for the child to be admitted to a school which is not maintained by a local education authority and is not a grant-maintained school, and in respect of which no application is made under subsection (5), and
(ii) notifies the local education authority by whom the notice was served of the application,
(b) the child is offered a place at the school as a result of the application, and
(c) the school is suitable to his age, ability and aptitude and to any special educational needs he may have,

that school shall be named in the order.

Specification of schools in notices under section 438(2)

439.—(1) Subject to subsection (3), a local education authority shall not, if it appears to them that subsection (2) applies in relation to any school, specify the school in a notice under section 438(2) unless they are responsible for determining the arrangements for the admission of pupils to the school.

(2) This subsection applies where, if the child concerned were admitted to the school in accordance with a school attendance order resulting from the notice, the number of pupils at the school in the child's age group would exceed the number fixed—
(a) in the case of a maintained school, in accordance with section 416, or
(b) in the case of a grant-maintained school, in accordance with sections 426 to 428,

as the number of pupils in that age group which it is intended to admit to the school in the school year in which he would be admitted.

(3) Subsection (1) does not prevent a local education authority specifying in a notice under section 438(2) any maintained or grant-maintained school

if—

(a) there is no maintained or grant-maintained school in their area which—

(i) the authority are not (apart from this subsection) prevented by subsection (1) from specifying, and

(ii) is, in the opinion of the authority, a reasonable distance from the home of the child concerned, and

(b) in the opinion of the authority, the school in question is a reasonable distance from the home of the child concerned.

(4) A local education authority shall not specify in a notice under section 438(2) a school from which the child concerned is permanently excluded.

(5) Before deciding to specify a particular maintained or grant-maintained school in a notice under section 438(2) a local education authority shall consult—

(a) the governing body, and

(b) if another local education authority are responsible for determining the arrangements for the admission of pupils to the school, that authority.

(6) Where a local education authority decide to specify a particular maintained or grant-maintained school in a notice under section 438(2) they shall, before serving the notice, serve notice in writing of their decision on—

(a) the governing body and head teacher of the school, and

(b) if another local education authority are responsible for determining the arrangements for the admission of pupils to the school, that authority.

(7) A governing body or local education authority on whom notice is served under subsection (6) may, within the period of 15 days beginning with the day on which the notice was received, apply to the Secretary of State for a direction under this section and, if they do so, shall inform the local education authority which served the notice.

(8) Where the Secretary of State gives a direction under this section, the school or schools to be specified in the notice under section 438(2) shall be determined in accordance with the direction.

Amendment of order at request of parent: child without statement of special educational needs

440.—(1) This section applies where a school attendance order is in force in respect of a child, other than a child for whom the local education authority maintain a statement under section 324.

(2) If at any time—

(a) the parent applies for the child to be admitted to a school maintained by a local education authority or grant-maintained school which is different from the school named in the order,

(b) the child is offered a place at the school as a result of the application, and

(c) the parent requests the local education authority by whom the order was served to amend it by substituting that school for the one currently named,

the authority shall comply with the request.

(3) If at any time—

(a) the parent applies to the authority for education to be provided for the child at a school which is not maintained by a local education authority or a grant-maintained school and which is different from the school named in the order,

(b) the child is offered a place at the school under arrangements made by the authority under which the fees payable in respect of the education provided at the school are to be paid by them under section 517, and

(c) the parent requests the authority to amend the order by substituting that school for the one currently named,

the authority shall comply with the request.

(4) If at any time—

(a) the parent applies for the child to be admitted to a school which is not maintained by a local education authority and is not a grant-maintained school, which is different from the school named in the order and in respect of which no application is made under subsection (3),

(b) as a result of the application, the child is offered a place at the school, being a school which is suitable to his age, ability and aptitude and to any special educational needs he may have, and

(c) the parent requests the authority to amend the order by substituting that school for the one currently named,

the authority shall comply with the request.

Choice of school: child with statement of special educational needs

441.—(1) Subsections (2) and (3) apply where a local education authority are required by virtue of section 437(3) to serve a school attendance order in respect of a child for whom they maintain a statement under section 324.

(2) Where the statement specifies the name of a school, that school shall be named in the order.

(3) Where the statement does not specify the name of a school—

(a) the authority shall, in accordance with paragraph 10 of Schedule 27, amend the statement so that it specifies the name of a school, and

(b) that school shall then be named in the order.

(4) Where—

(a) a school attendance order is in force in respect of a child for whom the local education authority maintain a statement under section 324, and

(b) the name of the school specified in the statement is changed,

the local education authority shall amend the order accordingly.

Revocation of order at request of parent

442.—(1) This section applies where a school attendance order is in force in respect of a child.

(2) If at any time the parent applies to the local education authority requesting that the order be revoked on the ground that arrangements have been made for the child to receive suitable education otherwise than at school, the authority shall comply with the request, unless they are of the opinion that no satisfactory arrangements have been made for the education of the child otherwise than at school.

(3) If a parent is aggrieved by a refusal of the local education authority to comply with a request under subsection (2), he may refer the question to the Secretary of State.

(4) Where a question is referred to the Secretary of State under subsection (3), he shall give such direction determining the question as he thinks fit.

(5) Where the child in question is one for whom the authority maintain a statement under section 324—

(a) subsections (2) to (4) do not apply if the name of a school or other institution is specified in the statement, and

(b) in any other case a direction under subsection (4) may require the authority to make such amendments in the statement as the Secretary of State considers necessary or expedient in consequence of his determination.

School attendance: offences and education supervision orders

Offence: failure to comply with school attendance order

443.—(1) If a parent on whom a school attendance order is served fails to comply with the requirements of the order, he is guilty of an offence, unless he proves that he is causing the child to receive suitable education otherwise than at school.

(2) If, in proceedings for an offence under this section, the parent is acquitted, the court may direct that the school attendance order shall cease to be in force.

(3) A direction under subsection (2) does not affect the duty of the local education authority to take further action under section 437 if at any time the authority are of the opinion that, having regard to any change of circumstances, it is expedient to do so.

(4) A person guilty of an offence under this section is liable on summary conviction to a fine not exceeding level 3 on the standard scale.

Offence: failure to secure regular attendance at school of registered pupil

444.—(1) If a child of compulsory school age who is a registered pupil at a school fails to attend regularly at the school, his parent is guilty of an offence.

(2) Subsections (3) to (6) below apply in proceedings for an offence under this section in respect of a child who is not a boarder at the school at which he is a registered pupil.

(3) The child shall not be taken to have failed to attend regularly at the school by reason of his absence from the school—

(a) with leave,

(b) at any time when he was prevented from attending by reason of sickness or any unavoidable cause, or

(c) on any day exclusively set apart for religious observance by the religious body to which his parent belongs.

(4) The child shall not be taken to have failed to attend regularly at the school if the parent proves—

(a) that the school at which the child is a registered pupil is not within walking distance of the child's home, and

(b) that no suitable arrangements have been made by the local education authority or the funding authority for any of the following—

(i) his transport to and from the school,

(ii) boarding accommodation for him at or near the school, or

(iii) enabling him to become a registered pupil at a school nearer to his home.

(5) In subsection (4) "walking distance"—

(a) in relation to a child who is under the age of eight, means 3.218688 kilometres (two miles), and

(b) in relation to a child who has attained the age of eight, means 4.828032 kilometres (three miles),

in each case measured by the nearest available route.

(6) If it is proved that the child has no fixed abode, subsection (4) shall not apply, but the parent shall be acquitted if he proves—

(a) that he is engaged in a trade or business of such a nature as to require him to travel from place to place,

(b) that the child has attended at a school as a registered pupil as regularly as the nature of that trade or business permits, and

(c) if the child has attained the age of six, that he has made at least 200 attendances during the period of 12 months ending with the date on which the proceedings were instituted.

(7) In proceedings for an offence under this section in respect of a child who is a boarder at the school at which he is a registered pupil, the child shall

be taken to have failed to attend regularly at the school if he is absent from it without leave during any part of the school term at a time when he was not prevented from being present by reason of sickness or any unavoidable cause.

(8) A person guilty of an offence under this section is liable on summary conviction to a fine not exceeding level 3 on the standard scale.

(9) In this section "leave", in relation to a school, means leave granted by any person authorised to do so by the governing body or proprietor of the school.

Presumption of age

445.—(1) This section applies for the purposes of any proceedings for an offence under section 443 or 444.

(2) In so far as it is material, the child in question shall be presumed to have been of compulsory school age at any time unless the parent proves the contrary.

(3) Where a court is obliged by virtue of subsection (2) to presume a child to have been of compulsory school age, section 565(1) (provisions as to evidence) does not apply.

Institution of proceedings

446. Proceedings for an offence under section 443 or 444 shall not be instituted except by a local education authority.

Education supervision orders

447.—(1) Before instituting proceedings for an offence under section 443 or 444, a local education authority shall consider whether it would be appropriate (instead of or as well as instituting the proceedings) to apply for an education supervision order with respect to the child.

(2) The court—

(a) by which a person is convicted of an offence under section 443, or

(b) before which a person is charged with an offence under section 444,

may direct the local education authority instituting the proceedings to apply for an education supervision order with respect to the child unless the authority, having consulted the appropriate local authority, decide that the child's welfare will be satisfactorily safeguarded even though no education supervision order is made.

(3) Where, following such a direction, a local education authority decide not to apply for an education supervision order, they shall inform the court of the reasons for their decision.

(4) Unless the court has directed otherwise, the information required under subsection (3) shall be given to the court before the end of the period of eight weeks beginning with the date on which the direction was given.

(5) Where—

(a) a local education authority apply for an education supervision order with respect to a child who is the subject of a school attendance order, and

(b) the court decides that section 36(3) of the Children Act 1989 (education supervision orders) prevents it from making the order,

the court may direct that the school attendance order shall cease to be in force.

(6) In this section—

"the appropriate local authority" has the same meaning as in section 36(9) of the Children Act 1989, and

"education supervision order" means an education supervision order under that Act.

Exemption

Exemption where child becomes five during term

448. Where—

(a) a child attains the age of five during the school term of a grant-maintained school, and

(b) arrangements have been made for the admission of the child to that school at the start of the next school term,

then, during the period beginning with his attaining that age and ending with the start of that next school term, section 7 (duty of parents to secure the education of their children) and section 437 shall not apply to the child.

Chapter III

Charges in connection with education at LEA or grant-maintained schools

Preliminary

Meaning of "maintained school" in Chapter III

449. In this Chapter "maintained school" means—

(a) any school maintained by a local education authority, and

(b) any grant-maintained school.

Prohibition of charges

Prohibition of charges for admission

450.—(1) No charge shall be made in respect of admission to a maintained school.

(2) Subsection (1) does not apply to the admission of any person to any maintained school for the purpose of—

(a) part-time education suitable to the requirements of persons of any age over compulsory school age;

(b) full-time education suitable to the requirements of persons who have attained the age of 19; or

(c) teacher training.

Prohibition of charges for provision of education

451.—(1) Subject to subsection (5), this section applies in relation to education provided at any maintained school for a registered pupil at the school.

(2) Where the education is provided for the pupil during school hours no charge shall be made in respect of it.

(3) Subsection (2) does not apply in relation to tuition in playing a musical instrument where the tuition is provided either individually or to a group of not more than four pupils, unless the tuition is—

(a) required as part of a syllabus for a prescribed public examination which is a syllabus for which the pupil is being prepared at the school, or

(b) provided in pursuance of a duty imposed by section 357(1) or 384 (implementation of National Curriculum or of provision for religious education in school's basic curriculum).

(4) Where the education is provided for the pupil outside school hours no charge shall be made in respect of it if it is—

(a) required as part of a syllabus for a prescribed public examination which is a syllabus for which the pupil is being prepared at the school, or

(b) provided in pursuance of a duty imposed by section 357(1) or 384.

(5) Nothing in this section applies in relation to education provided at a grant-maintained school in pursuance of arrangements made under section 231(8).

Application of section 451 where education is provided partly during and partly outside school hours etc.

452.—(1) Where a period allowed for any educational activity at a maintained school falls partly during school hours and partly outside school hours, then—

(a) if 50 per cent. or more of the time occupied by that period together with any connected school travelling time falls during school hours, so much of the education provided during that period as is provided outside school hours shall be treated for the purposes of section 451 as provided during school hours, and

(b) in any other case, so much of the education provided during that period as is provided during school hours shall be treated for those purposes as provided outside school hours.

(2) In subsection (1) "connected school travelling time" means time spent during school hours by the pupils taking part in the educational activity concerned in getting to or from the place where the activity takes place.

(3) Where any education provided at a maintained school is provided on a residential trip, then—

(a) if the number of school sessions taken up by the trip is equal to or greater than 50 per cent. of the number of half days spent on the trip, any education provided on the trip which is provided outside school hours shall be treated for the purposes of section 451 as provided during school hours, and

(b) in any other case, any education provided on the trip which is provided during school hours shall be treated for those purposes as provided outside school hours.

(4) In this section "half day" means any period of 12 hours ending with noon or midnight on any day.

(5) For the purposes of subsection (3)—

(a) where 50 per cent. or more of a half day is spent on a residential trip, the whole of that half day shall be treated as spent on the trip, and

(b) a school session on any day on which such a session takes place at the school concerned shall be treated as taken up by a residential trip if the time spent on the trip occupies 50 per cent. or more of the time allowed for that session at the school.

(6) Nothing in section 451 shall be read as prohibiting the making of a charge in respect of board and lodging provided for a registered pupil at a maintained school on a residential trip.

Examinations: prohibition of charges and recovery of wasted fees

453.—(1) No charge shall be made in respect of the entry of a registered pupil at a maintained school for a prescribed public examination in any syllabus for that examination for which the pupil has been prepared at the school.

(2) Despite subsection (1), where—

(a) the governing body of a maintained school or the local education authority have paid or are liable to pay a fee in respect of the entry of a registered pupil at the school for a public examination in any syllabus for that examination, and

(b) the pupil fails without good reason to meet any examination requirement for that syllabus,

that body or authority may recover the amount of the fee from the pupil's parent.

(3) It shall be for the body or authority who have paid or are liable to pay the fee in question to determine for the purposes of this section any question whether a pupil who has failed to meet an examination requirement had good reason for the failure.

Prohibition of incidental charges

454.—(1) Neither the parent of a registered pupil at a maintained school nor the pupil himself shall be required to pay for or supply any materials, books, instruments or other equipment for use for the purposes of or in connection with—

(a) education provided for the pupil at the school in respect of which, by virtue of section 451, no charge may be made, or

(b) a syllabus for a prescribed public examination which is a syllabus for which the pupil has been prepared at the school.

(2) Nothing in subsection (1) shall prevent the parent of a pupil from being required to pay for or supply any materials for use for the purposes of the production, in the course of the provision of education for the pupil at the school, of any article incorporating those materials, where the parent has indicated before that requirement is made that he wishes the article to be owned by him or by the pupil.

(3) No charge shall be made in respect of transport provided for a registered pupil at a maintained school where the transport is either—

(a) incidental to education provided for the pupil at the school in respect of which, by virtue of section 451, no charge may be made, or

(b) provided for the purpose of enabling him to meet any examination requirement for any syllabus for a prescribed public examination which is a syllabus for which he has been prepared at the school.

(4) For the purposes of subsection (3)(a) transport is incidental to education provided for registered pupils at a school if it is provided for the purpose of carrying such pupils—

(a) to or from any part of the school premises in which education is provided for those pupils, from or to any other part of those premises, or

(b) to or from any place outside the school premises in which education is provided for those pupils under arrangements made by or on behalf of the governing body or the local education authority, from or to the school premises or any other such place.

Permitted charges

Permitted charges

455.—(1) Subject to subsection (2), a charge may be made in respect—

(a) education provided for a registered pupil at a maintained school other than education in respect of which, by virtue of section 451, no charge may be made,

(b) the entry of a registered pupil at a maintained school for a public examination in any syllabus for that examination otherwise than in circumstances in which, by virtue of section 453(1), no charge may be made,

(c) transport provided for a registered pupil at a maintained school other than transport in respect of which, by virtue of section 454(3) or 509(2), no charge may be made, and

(d) board and lodging provided for a registered pupil at a maintained school on a residential trip.

(2) A charge may not be made—

(a) by virtue of subsection (1)(a) in respect of the provision for a pupil of education,
(b) by virtue of subsection (1)(b) in respect of the entry of a pupil for an examination in any syllabus for that examination, or
(c) by virtue of subsection (1)(c) in respect of the provision for a pupil of transport,

unless the education is provided, the pupil is entered for the examination in that syllabus, or the transport is provided, by agreement with the pupil's parent.

(3) Any education, examination entry or transport in respect of which a charge may be made by virtue of subsection (1) is referred to in this Chapter as an "optional extra".

Regulation of permitted charges

456.—(1) This section applies in relation to any charge permitted under section 455, other than a charge in respect of education provided at a grant-maintained school in pursuance of arrangements made under section 231(8); and a charge to which this section applies is referred to in this section as a "regulated charge".

(2) The amount of any regulated charge shall be payable by the parent of the pupil concerned.

(3) A regulated charge shall not exceed the cost of the provision of the optional extra or the board and lodging in question.

(4) Without prejudice to the generality of subsection (3), the cost of the provision of an optional extra includes costs, or an appropriate proportion of the costs—

(a) incurred in respect of the provision of any materials, books, instruments or other equipment used for the purposes of or in connection with the provision of the optional extra, or
(b) attributable to the provision of non-teaching staff for any purpose connected with the provision of the optional extra, or
(c) attributable to the provision of teaching staff engaged under contracts for services for the purpose of providing it.

(5) Subject to subsection (6), the cost of the provision of an optional extra shall not be taken to include any costs attributable to the provision of teaching staff other than staff engaged as mentioned in subsection (4)(c).

(6) Where the optional extra in question consists of tuition in playing a musical instrument, the cost of its provision shall include costs, or an appropriate proportion of the costs, attributable to the provision of teaching staff employed for the purpose of providing the tuition.

(7) Where charging is permitted under section 455 and the charge would be a regulated charge, the question whether any charge should be made, and the amount of any charge to be made, shall be determined—

(a) in a case where the cost of the provision of the optional extra or board and lodging in question is met by or from funds at the disposal of the governing body, by the governing body, and
(b) in any other case, by the local education authority.

(8) The whole or any part of the amount of any charge which the local education authority determine under subsection (7)(b) to make—

(a) shall, if the governing body so determine, be met by or from funds at the disposal of the governing body, and
(b) to the extent that it is so met, shall not be payable by the parent of the pupil concerned.

Charges and remissions policies

457.—(1) Every governing body of a maintained school and every local education authority shall determine and keep under review a policy with respect to—

(a) the provision of, and

(b) the classes or descriptions of case in which they propose to make charges for,

any optional extra or board and lodging in respect of which charges are permitted by section 455.

This subsection does not apply in relation to education provided at a grant-maintained school in pursuance of arrangements made under section 231(8).

(2) No such body or authority shall make such a charge unless they have both—

(a) determined a policy under subsection (1)(b) (their "charging policy"), and

(b) determined a policy (their "remissions policy") setting out any circumstances in which they propose to remit (in whole or in part) any charge which would otherwise be payable to them in accordance with their charging policy.

(3) A remissions policy determined by the governing body of a school other than a grant-maintained school shall set out any circumstances in which the governing body propose to meet (in whole or in part) any charge payable to the local education authority, in accordance with the authority's charging policy, for an optional extra or board and lodging provided for a registered pupil at the school.

(4) A remissions policy shall provide for complete remission of any charges otherwise payable in respect of board and lodging provided for a pupil on a residential trip if—

(a) the education provided on the trip is education in respect of which, by virtue of section 451, no charge may be made, and

(b) the pupil's parents are in receipt of

(i) income support,

(ii) family credit,

(iii) an income-based jobseeker's allowance (payable under the Jobseekers Act 1995), or

(iv) disability working allowance,

in respect of any period wholly or partly comprised in the time spent on the trip.

(5) A remissions policy shall be kept under review by the governing body or local education authority by whom it was determined.

Charges for board and lodging at boarding schools

458.—(1) Subject to subsections (2) to (5), where a registered pupil at a maintained school is provided at the school with board and lodging, there shall be payable in respect of the board and lodging by the parent of the pupil concerned—

(a) to the local education authority, in the case of a school maintained by such an authority, or

(b) to the governing body, in the case of a grant-maintained school,

charges not exceeding the cost to the authority or governing body of providing the board and lodging.

(2) Where—

(a) the board and lodging are provided for the pupil at a school maintained by a local education authority, and

(b) the local education authority for his area are of the opinion that education suitable to his age, ability and aptitude and to any special educational needs he may have cannot otherwise be provided for him,

then, where the school is maintained by the local education authority for his area, that authority shall remit the whole of the charges payable under this section and, in any other case, that authority shall pay the whole of the charges payable under this section to the authority which maintain the school.

(3) Where—

(a) the board and lodging are provided for the pupil at a grant-maintained school, and

(b) the local education authority for his area are of the opinion that education suitable to his age, ability and aptitude and to any special educational needs he may have cannot otherwise be provided for him,

the whole of the charges payable under this section shall be payable by the authority instead of by the pupil's parent.

(4) Where the local education authority for the pupil's area are satisfied that payment of the full charges payable under this section would involve financial hardship to the parent of the pupil concerned, the authority—

(a) in the case of charges payable to the authority; shall remit so much of those charges as falls in accordance with subsection (5) to be so remitted, and

(b) in the case of charges payable to another local education authority or to the governing body of a grant-maintained school in respect of board and lodging, shall pay so much of those charges as falls in accordance with subsection (5) to be so paid.

(5) The amount that falls to be remitted or paid by a local education authority by virtue of subsection (4)(a) or (b) is—

(a) such part of the charges in question as the authority consider ought not to be paid by the pupil's parent in order to avoid such hardship as is mentioned in subsection (4), or

(b) the whole of those charges if, in their opinion, such hardship cannot otherwise be avoided.

Supplementary

Provision of information

459. Regulations may require, in relation to every maintained school, the local education authority, the governing body or the head teacher to make available either generally or to prescribed persons, in such form and manner and at such times as may be prescribed—

(a) such information relevant for the purposes of this Chapter as to the school hours at the school, and

(b) such information as to the policies determined under section 457 which apply in relation to the school,

as may be prescribed.

Contributions and charges unaffected by Chapter III

460.—(1) Nothing in this Chapter shall be read as prohibiting or in any way restricting or regulating any request or invitation by or on behalf of the governing body of a maintained school or a local education authority for voluntary contributions for the benefit of the school or any school activities.

(2) Any request or invitation made by or on behalf of such a body or authority for contributions for the benefit of a school or school activities shall not be regarded for the purposes of subsection (1) as a request or invitation for voluntary contributions unless it is clear from the terms in which it is made—

(a) that there is no obligation to make any contribution, and

(b) that registered pupils at the school will not be treated differently according to whether or not their parents have made any contribution in response to the request or invitation.

(3) Nothing in this Chapter relating to charges in respect of a registered pupil at a maintained school shall be read as relating to—

(a) charges made by persons other than the governing body or the local education authority, or

(b) charges to be paid by persons other than the parent of the pupil or the pupil himself.

Recovery of sums as civil debt

461. Any sum payable under section 453(2), 455 or 458 by the parent of a registered pupil at a maintained school shall be recoverable summarily as a civil debt.

Interpretation of Chapter III

462.—(1) In this Chapter—

"equipment" does not include clothing;

"examination requirement", in relation to a syllabus for an examination, means a requirement which a pupil must meet in order to qualify for assessment for the purposes of determining his achievements in that examination in that syllabus.

(2) In this Chapter "residential trip" means any trip—

(a) which is arranged for registered pupils at a maintained school by or on behalf of the governing body or the local education authority, and

(b) which requires the pupils taking part to spend one or more nights away from their usual overnight accommodation.

(3) For the purposes of this Chapter, a pupil shall be regarded as having been prepared at a school for a syllabus for a prescribed public examination if any part of the education provided with a view to preparing him for that examination in that syllabus has been provided for him at that school.

(4) In this Chapter references to a public examination (or a prescribed public examination) are references to such an examination as it applies in relation to persons who are entered for a syllabus for that examination with a view to meeting the examination requirements for that syllabus so as to qualify for assessment for the purposes of determining their achievements in that examination on any particular occasion in any year when an assessment takes place.

(5) For the purposes of subsection (4)—

(a) "an assessment" means an assessment for the purposes of determining the achievements of persons entered for the examination in question; and

(b) such an assessment is to be regarded as taking place on any occasion on which it is determined in relation to each person entered for any syllabus in that examination who has met the examination requirements for that syllabus—

(i) whether he has passed or failed, and

(ii) if grades are assigned for the purposes of the examination, the grade to be assigned in his case.

PART VII

INDEPENDENT SCHOOLS

CHAPTER I

PRELIMINARY

Meaning of "independent school"

463. In this Act "independent school" means any school at which full-time education is provided for five or more pupils of compulsory school age (whether or not such education is also provided at it for pupils under or over that age) and which is not—

(a) a school maintained by a local education authority,
(b) a special school not so maintained, or
(c) a grant-maintained school.

CHAPTER II

REGISTRATION OF INDEPENDENT SCHOOLS

Registration

Separate registration for England and for Wales

464.—(1) A register of all independent schools in England shall be kept by an officer of the Secretary of State who is appointed by the Secretary of State to be Registrar of Independent Schools for England.

(2) A register of all independent schools in Wales shall be kept by an officer of the Secretary of State who is appointed by the Secretary of State to be Registrar of Independent Schools for Wales.

(3) Each register shall be open to public inspection at all reasonable times.

(4) In this Part "the Registrar of Independent Schools" (or "the Registrar") means—

(a) in relation to a school in England, the Registrar of Independent Schools for England, and
(b) in relation to a school in Wales, the Registrar of Independent Schools for Wales,

and references, in relation to a school, to the register or to registration are to the register kept by the relevant Registrar or to registration in that register.

Provisional and final registration of a school

465.—(1) Subject to subsection (2), the Registrar of Independent Schools shall enter in the register the name of any independent school whose proprietor—

(a) makes an application for registration in such manner as may be prescribed, and
(b) provides such particulars as may be prescribed.

(2) A school shall not be registered if—

(a) by virtue of an order made under section 470 or 471, the proprietor is disqualified from being the proprietor of an independent school or the school premises are disqualified from being used as a school, or
(b) the school premises are used or proposed to be used for any purpose for which they are disqualified by virtue of such an order.

(3) The registration of a school shall initially be provisional only, and shall remain so until such time as the Secretary of State, after the school has been inspected on his behalf under Part I of the School Inspections Act 1996, gives notice to the proprietor that the registration is final.

(4) In this Part—

"provisionally registered school" means an independent school whose registration is provisional only, and

"registered school" means an independent school whose registration is final.

(5) In this section "proprietor", in relation to a school, includes any person or body of persons proposing to be the proprietor.

Enforcement of registration: offences

466.—(1) Subject to subsection (2), a person is guilty of an offence if he conducts an independent school which is not a registered school or a provisionally registered school.

(2) A person is not guilty of an offence under subsection (1) by reason of

conducting a school at any time within the period of one month from the date on which it was first conducted (whether by that person or another) if an application for the registration of the school has been duly made under section 465 within that period.

(3) The proprietor of an independent school is guilty of an offence if, while it is a provisionally registered school, he does any act calculated to lead to the belief that it is a registered school.

Provision of information about registered and provisionally registered schools

467.—(1) Regulations may make provision for requiring the proprietor of a registered or provisionally registered school to provide the Registrar of Independent Schools from time to time with such particulars relating to the school as may be prescribed.

(2) Regulations made under this section may in particular require the proprietor of a school to furnish the Registrar with such information as is required by the local authority for the purpose of determining whether the school is a children's home (within the meaning of the Children Act 1989).

(3) Regulations may make provision for enabling the Secretary of State to order the deletion from the register of the name of any school in respect of which any requirement imposed by or under regulations made under this section is not complied with.

(4) Subsection (9) of section 537 (general power of Secretary of State to require information from governing bodies etc.) confers power on the Secretary of State to make similar provision in relation to noncompliance with any requirement imposed by or under regulations under that section.

School may be struck off for contravention of regulations about employment of teachers

468. Where the Secretary of State is satisfied that a person whose employment is prohibited or restricted by virtue of regulations under section 218(6) of the Education Reform Act 1988 (employment prohibited or restricted on medical grounds or for misconduct etc.)—

(a) is employed in a registered or provisionally registered school in contravention of those regulations, or

(b) is the proprietor of such a school,

he may order that the school be struck off the register or (as the case may be) that the Registrar is not to register the school.

Complaints about registered and provisionally registered schools

Notice of complaint by Secretary of State

469.—(1) This section applies where the Secretary of State is satisfied that one or more of the following grounds of complaint apply in relation to a registered or provisionally registered school—

(a) the school premises or any parts of them are unsuitable for a school;

(b) the accommodation provided at the school premises is inadequate or unsuitable having regard to the number, ages, and sex of the pupils attending the school;

(c) efficient and suitable instruction is not being provided at the school having regard to the ages and sex of the pupils attending it;

(d) the proprietor of the school or any teacher or other employee employed in the school is not a proper person to be the proprietor of an independent school or (as the case may be) to be a teacher or other employee in any school;

(e) there has been a failure, in relation to a child provided with accommodation by the school, to comply with the duty imposed by section 87 of the Children Act 1989 (welfare of children accommodated in independent schools).

(2) The Secretary of State shall serve on the proprietor of the school a notice of complaint stating the grounds of complaint which apply together with full particulars of the matters complained of.

(3) Unless any of those matters are stated in the notice to be in the opinion of the Secretary of State irremediable, the notice shall specify—

(a) the measures necessary in the opinion of the Secretary of State to remedy those matters, and

(b) the time, not being less than six months after the service of the notice, within which those measures are required to be taken.

(4) If it is alleged by the notice that a person employed as a teacher or other employee at the school is not a proper person to be a teacher or other employee in any school—

(a) that person shall be named in the notice,

(b) the particulars given in the notice shall specify the grounds of the allegation, and

(c) a copy of the notice shall be served on him.

(5) Any notice of complaint, or copy of a notice of complaint, served under this section shall limit the time, not being less than one month after the service of the notice or copy, within which the complaint may be referred to an Independent Schools Tribunal under section 470.

(6) In this section and sections 470 to 473 "employee" means a person employed in work which brings him regularly into contact with persons who have not attained the age of 19.

Determination of complaint by an Independent Schools Tribunal

470.—(1) Any person on whom a notice of complaint or copy of a notice of complaint is served under section 469 may, within the time limited by the notice or copy, appeal against the notice by referring the complaint to an Independent Schools Tribunal.

(2) On the complaint being so referred, the tribunal, after giving all parties concerned an opportunity of being heard and after considering such evidence as may be tendered by them or on their behalf, may—

(a) order that the complaint be annulled;

(b) order that the school to which the complaint relates be struck off the register;

(c) order that the school be so struck off unless the requirements of the notice (subject to such modifications, if any, as may be specified in the order) are complied with to the satisfaction of the Secretary of State before the expiry of such time as may be specified in the order;

(d) if satisfied—

(i) that any premises alleged by the notice to be unsuitable for use as a school are in fact unsuitable for such use, or

(ii) that any part of such premises is in fact unsuitable for such use,

by order disqualify the premises, or that part, from being so used;

(e) if satisfied that the accommodation provided at the school premises is inadequate or unsuitable having regard to the number, ages and sex of the pupils attending the school, by order disqualify the premises from being used as a school for pupils exceeding such number or of such age or sex as may be specified in the order;

(f) if satisfied that any person alleged by the notice of complaint to be a person who is not proper to be the proprietor of an independent school or to be a teacher or other employee in any school is in fact such a person, by order disqualify that person from being the proprietor of any independent school or (as the case may be) from being a teacher or other employee in any school.

Determination of complaint by Secretary of State

471.—(1) Where—

(a) a notice of complaint has been served on the proprietor of a school under section 469, and

(b) the complaint is not referred by him to an Independent Schools Tribunal under section 470 within the time limited by the notice,

the Secretary of State may (subject to subsection (2)) make any order which such a tribunal would have had power to make if the complaint had been so referred.

(2) If—

(a) it is alleged by the notice that a person employed as a teacher or other employee at the school is not a proper person to be a teacher or other employee in any school, and

(b) that person has, within the time limited by the copy of the notice served on him, referred the complaint to an Independent Schools Tribunal under section 470,

the Secretary of State may not make an order disqualifying him from being a teacher or other employee in any school.

Effect of personal disqualification

472. Where, by virtue of an order made—

(a) by an Independent Schools Tribunal under section 470, or

(b) by the Secretary of State under section 471,

a person is disqualified either from being the proprietor of an independent school or from being a teacher or other employee in any school, then (unless the order otherwise directs) he shall by virtue of the order be disqualified both from being the proprietor of an independent school and from being a teacher or other employee in any school.

Enforcement of disqualification

473.—(1) A person is guilty of an offence if he uses any premises for purposes for which they are disqualified by virtue of an order made under section 470 or 471.

(2) A person is guilty of an offence if he—

(a) acts as the proprietor of an independent school, or

(b) accepts or endeavours to obtain employment as a teacher or other employee in any school,

while he is disqualified from so acting or from being so employed by virtue of an order made under section 470 or 471.

Removal of disqualification

474.—(1) If on the application of any person the Secretary of State is satisfied that any disqualification imposed by an order made under section 470 or 471 is, by reason of any change of circumstances, no longer necessary, he may by order remove the disqualification.

(2) Any person who is aggrieved by the refusal of the Secretary of State to remove any such disqualification may appeal to an Independent Schools Tribunal within such time after the refusal has been communicated to him as may be limited by rules made under section 476.

Duty of Registrar to comply with order for the deletion of a school from the register

475. Where an order directing that a school be struck off the register is made—

(a) by the Secretary of State under section 468 or 471, or
(b) by an Independent Schools Tribunal under section 470,
the Registrar of Independent Schools shall strike the school off the register as from the date on which the direction takes effect.

Independent Schools Tribunals

Constitution and proceedings of Independent Schools Tribunals

476.—(1) Schedule 34 has effect in relation to the constitution of Independent Schools Tribunals and the remuneration of their members.

(2) The Lord Chancellor may, with the concurrence of the Lord President of the Council, make rules as to—

(a) the practice and procedure to be followed with respect to the constitution of Independent Schools Tribunals;
(b) the manner of making appeals to such tribunals; and
(c) proceedings before such tribunals and matters incidental to or consequential on such proceedings.

(3) The rules may, in particular, make provision—

(a) requiring such a tribunal to sit at such places as may be directed in accordance with the rules; and
(b) as to appearance before such tribunals by counsel or a solicitor.

(4) Part I of the Arbitration Act 1996 shall not apply to any proceedings before an Independent Schools Tribunal, except so far as any provisions of that Act may be applied, with or without modifications, to such proceedings by the rules.

(5) Every order of an Independent Schools Tribunal shall be registered by the Registrar of Independent Schools and shall be open to public inspection at all reasonable times.

Supplementary

Disqualification in Scotland

477. For the purposes of this Part, except section 474, a person who is disqualified by an order made (or having effect as if made) under section 100 of the Education (Scotland) Act 1980—

(a) from being the proprietor of an independent school within the meaning of that Act, or
(b) from being a teacher in any school,

shall be taken to be disqualified from being the proprietor of an independent school within the meaning of this Act, or (as the case may be) from being a teacher in any school, by virtue of an order made under section 470 or 471.

Offences: institution of proceedings and punishment

478.—(1) No proceedings shall be instituted for an offence under section 466 or 473 except by or on behalf of the Secretary of State.

(2) A person guilty of an offence under section 466 or 473 is liable on summary conviction—

(a) to a fine not exceeding level 4 on the standard scale, or
(b) to imprisonment for a term not exceeding three months,

or both.

CHAPTER III

ASSISTED PLACES AT INDEPENDENT SCHOOLS

The assisted places scheme

479.—(1) For the purpose of enabling pupils who might otherwise not be able to do so to benefit from education at independent schools, the Secretary of State shall continue to operate a scheme (referred to in this Part as "the assisted places scheme") whereby—

(a) participating schools remit fees that would otherwise be chargeable in respect of pupils selected for assisted places under the scheme, and

(b) the Secretary of State reimburses the schools for the fees that are remitted.

(2) In this Part "participating school" means an independent school providing secondary education with which the Secretary of State makes an agreement (referred to in this Part as a "participation agreement") for the purposes of the assisted places scheme.

(3) The fees in relation to which the assisted places scheme has effect are—

(a) tuition and other fees the payment of which is a condition of attendance at a participating school but excluding boarding fees and such other fees, if any, as may be excluded by the participation agreement, and

(b) entrance fees for public examinations paid by a participating school in respect of candidates from the school.

(4) In determining whether to make a participation agreement with any school, the Secretary of State shall have regard to the desirability of securing an equitable distribution of assisted places throughout England and Wales and between boys and girls.

(5) A participation agreement—

(a) shall contain provisions as to the number of assisted places to be available at the school, and

(b) may contain conditions to be complied with by the school in addition to those prescribed under section 480;

and Schedule 35 has effect with respect to the termination of a participation agreement.

(6) In this section "independent school" means a registered school that is conducted for charitable purposes only.

(7) Except where the context otherwise requires, references in this section and sections 480 and 481 to a school include the proprietors of the school and persons acting with their authority.

Assisted places: further provision by regulations

480.—(1) Regulations shall prescribe—

(a) the requirements as to age, residence or otherwise which are to be the conditions of eligibility for selection for an assisted place under the assisted places scheme;

(b) the conditions subject to which, the extent to which, and the arrangements in accordance with which, fees are to be remitted by participating schools;

(c) the time and manner in which participating schools are to claim and receive reimbursements from the Secretary of State;

(d) conditions to be complied with by participating schools with respect to the selection of pupils for assisted places, the admission of pupils, the fees to be charged, the keeping and auditing of accounts and the provision of information to the Secretary of State; and

(e) such other matters as appear to the Secretary of State to be requisite for the purposes of the scheme.

(2) Regulations under this section may authorise the Secretary of State to make provision for any purpose specified in the regulations.

(3) Regulations made under subsection (1)(b) shall be reviewed by the Secretary of State at intervals of not more than two years.

(4) The Secretary of State shall—

(a) before making regulations under this section, or

(b) when conducting any review under subsection (3),

consult such bodies as appear to him to be appropriate and to be representative of participating schools.

Incidental expenses of pupils holding assisted places

481.—(1) Regulations may require or enable participating schools to make grants in respect of such incidental expenses, and to remit such incidental charges, as may be specified in the regulations.

For this purpose expenses or charges are "incidental" if they are in respect of matters incidental to or arising out of the attendance at the schools of pupils holding assisted places under the assisted places scheme.

(2) Any regulations made under this section shall require any amounts granted or remitted by a school in accordance with the regulations to be reimbursed to the school by the Secretary of State.

(3) Regulations under this section may in particular prescribe—

(a) the conditions subject to which, the extent to which, and the arrangements in accordance with which, grants and remissions are to be made, and

(b) the time and manner in which schools are to claim and receive reimbursements from the Secretary of State.

(4) Regulations under this section may authorise the Secretary of State to make provision for any purpose specified in the regulations.

Chapter IV

City colleges

City technology colleges and city colleges for the technology of the arts

482.—(1) The Secretary of State may enter into an agreement with any person under which—

(a) that person undertakes to establish and maintain, and to carry on or provide for the carrying on of, an independent school with such characteristics as are specified in the agreement and in subsection (2), and

(b) the Secretary of State agrees to make payments to that person in consideration of those undertakings.

(2) The characteristics mentioned above are that the school—

(a) is situated in an urban area,

(b) provides education for pupils of different abilities who have attained the age of 11 and who are wholly or mainly drawn from the area in which the school is situated, and

(c) has a broad curriculum with an emphasis either on science and technology or on technology in its application to the performing and creative arts.

(3) A school to which an agreement under this section relates shall be known—

(a) as a city technology college, if the emphasis of its curriculum is on science and technology, or

(b) as a city college for the technology of the arts, if the emphasis of its curriculum is on technology in its application to the performing and creative arts.

(4) An agreement under this section shall make any payments by the Secretary of State dependent on the fulfilment of—

(a) conditions and requirements imposed for the purpose of securing that no charge is made in respect of admission to the school or, subject to such exceptions as may be specified in the agreement, in respect of education provided at, the school, and

(b) such other conditions and requirements in relation to the school as are specified in the agreement.

(5) Any requirements having effect in relation to the school by virtue of section 218(2B) of the Education Reform Act 1988 (requirements as to the training and teaching experience of teachers at city colleges who seek to become qualified teachers) shall have effect for the purposes of this section and section 483 as requirements falling within subsection (4).

City colleges: financial provisions

483.—(1) Payments under an agreement under section 482 may be in respect of capital or current expenditure.

(2) In so far as such payments relate to current expenditure, the agreement shall provide for their continuance (subject to the fulfilment of the conditions and requirements falling within section 482(4))—

(a) for a period of not less than seven years, or
(b) for an indefinite period terminable by the Secretary of State by not less than seven years' written notice.

(3) Where such payments relate to capital expenditure, the agreement shall provide for the repayment to the Secretary of State, in the event of the school at any time discontinuing or ceasing to have the characteristics specified in the agreement and in section 482(2), of sums determined by reference to—

(a) the value at that time of the school premises and other assets held for the purposes of the school, and
(b) the extent to which expenditure incurred in providing those assets was met by payments under the agreement.

(4) Without prejudice to subsection (1), an agreement under section 482 may provide for indemnifying a person, in the event of the agreement being terminated by the Secretary of State, for expenditure—

(a) incurred by that person in carrying out the undertakings mentioned in section 482(1), or
(b) incurred by that person (otherwise than by virtue of subsection (3)) in consequence of the termination of the agreement.

PART VIII

GRANTS AND OTHER FINANCIAL MATTERS

Grants

Grants for education support and training

484.—(1) The Secretary of State may pay grants, known as grants for education support and training, to local education authorities in respect of eligible expenditure incurred or to be incurred by them.

(2) In this section "eligible expenditure" means expenditure of any class or description for the time being specified in regulations, being expenditure for or in connection with educational purposes which it appears to the Secretary of State that local education authorities should be encouraged to incur in the interests of education in England and Wales.

(3) The regulations shall provide that any grant for education support and training payable in pursuance of the regulations—

(a) shall only be payable in respect of eligible expenditure incurred or to be incurred by a local education authority in a financial year to the extent to which that expenditure is approved for that year by the Secretary of State for the purposes of the regulations, and
(b) shall be payable at such rate as may be specified in the regulations.

(4) The regulations may provide for the time and manner of payment of

any grant for education support and training.

(5) The regulations may provide for expenditure incurred or to be incurred by any local education authority in making payments, whether by way of maintenance, assistance or otherwise, to any body or persons who incur expenditure for or in connection with educational purposes (including another local education authority) to be treated, in such circumstances as may be specified in the regulations, as eligible expenditure.

(6) The Secretary of State may exercise his power under subsection (1) separately and differently in relation to local education authorities in England and local education authorities in Wales, and "education in England and Wales" in subsection (2) shall be construed accordingly.

(7) Nothing in section 29(1) or 507 applies in relation to any function of the Secretary of State under this section or under section 489 so far as it relates to regulations under this section; and nothing in sections 495 to 497 applies in relation to any function arising by virtue of section 489 so far as it relates to such regulations.

Grants in aid of educational services or research

485. Regulations shall make provision for the payment by the Secretary of State to persons other than local education authorities of grants in respect of expenditure incurred or to be incurred by them—

(a) for the purposes of, or in connection with, the provision (or proposed provision) of educational services, or
(b) for the purposes of educational research.

Grants to bodies whose objects are promotion of learning or research

486. Regulations may provide for the payment of grants to bodies other than local education authorities whose object or main object is, in the opinion of the Secretary of State, the promotion of learning or research.

Grants for education in Welsh

487. Regulations shall make provision for the payment by the Secretary of State to local education authorities and other persons of grants in respect of expenditure incurred or to be incurred in, or in connection with, the teaching of the Welsh language or the teaching in that language of other subjects.

Grants for education of travellers and displaced persons

488.—(1) Regulations may make provision for the payment to local education authorities of grants in respect of expenditure incurred or to be incurred by them in making provision the purpose (or main purpose) of which is to promote and facilitate the education of persons to whom this section applies.

(2) This section applies to a person if—

(a) by reason of his way of life (or, in the case of a child, his parent's way of life) he either has no fixed abode or leaves his main abode to live elsewhere for significant periods in each year;
(b) he fell within paragraph (a) within a prescribed period immediately preceding the making of the provision in question; or
(c) he is for the time being resident in a camp or other accommodation or establishment provided for refugees or for displaced or similar persons.

(3) The regulations may—

(a) prescribe classes or descriptions of expenditure in respect of which

grants are payable under the regulations, and
(b) provide for the determination of the amount of any grant so payable.

Conditions as to payment of grants under sections 484 and 488

489.—(1) Regulations made under any of sections 484 to 488 may provide—

(a) for the payment of grant under the regulations to be dependent on the fulfilment of such conditions as may be determined by or in accordance with the regulations, and
(b) for requiring persons to whom payments have been made under the regulations to comply with such requirements as may be so determined.

(2) Conditions and requirements determined under subsection (1)(a) and (b) by or in accordance with regulations made under section 484 may include conditions and requirements obliging the local education authority in question to delegate decisions about the spending of—

(a) grant for education support and training, and
(b) amounts allocated by the authority to meet eligible expenditure (within the meaning of that section) which is approved by the Secretary of State,

to such persons as may be determined by or in accordance with the regulations.

(3) The Secretary of State may by order make such modifications of any trust deed or other instrument relating to or regulating any institution that—

(a) provides or is concerned in the provision of educational services, or
(b) is concerned in educational research,

as, after consultation with the persons responsible for the management of the institution, appear to him to be requisite to enable them to fulfil any condition or meet any requirement imposed by regulations under section 485.

(4) Any modification made by an order under subsection (3) may be made to have permanent effect or to have effect for such period as may be specified in the order.

Grants in respect of special provision for ethnic minorities

490.—(1) Where subsection (2) applies, the power conferred by section 11 of the Local Government Act 1966 (grants in respect of ethnic minority population) shall apply in relation to the payment of grants by the Secretary of State to—

(a) the governing body of a grant-maintained school, or
(b) a person who in pursuance of undertakings under an agreement under section 482 maintains and carries on, or provides for the carrying on of, a city technology college or a city college for the technology of the arts,

as it applies in relation to the payment of grants to a local authority who in his opinion are required to make special provision in exercise of any of their functions in consequence of the presence within their area of such persons as are referred to in section 11 of that Act.

(2) This subsection applies if, in the Secretary of State's opinion, special provision is made by the governing body or person in question in consequence of the presence within the locality of the school or college of such persons as are referred to in section 11 of that Act.

Payment of fees etc.

Payment of school fees and expenses

491.—(1) Regulations shall make provision for the payment by the Secretary of State, for the purpose of enabling pupils to take advantage without hardship to themselves or their parents of any educational facilities available to them, of the whole or any part of the fees and expenses payable in respect of children attending schools at which fees are payable.

(2) Regulations under this section may provide—

(a) for the making of payments under the regulations to be dependent on the fulfilment of such conditions as may be determined by or in accordance with the regulations, and

(b) for requiring persons to whom payments have been made under the regulations to comply with such requirements as may be so determined.

Recoupment

Recoupment: adjustment between local education authorities

492.—(1) Regulations may provide, in relation to cases where any provision for education to which this section applies is made by a local education authority in respect of a person who belongs to the area of another local education authority, for requiring or authorising the other authority to pay to the providing authority—

(a) such amount as the authorities may agree, or

(b) failing agreement, such amount as may be determined by or under the regulations.

(2) This section applies to primary education, secondary education and further education and to part-time education for those who have not attained the age of five.

(3) The regulations may provide for the amounts payable by one authority to another—

(a) to reflect the whole or any part of the average costs incurred by local education authorities in the provision of education (whether in England and Wales as a whole or in any particular area or areas); and

(b) to be based on figures for average costs determined by such body or bodies representing local education authorities, or on such other figures relating to costs so incurred, as the Secretary of State considers appropriate.

(4) The regulations may provide for the amounts so payable, in such cases as may be specified in or determined in accordance with the regulations, to be such amounts as may be determined by the Secretary of State.

(5) Any dispute between local education authorities as to whether one of them is entitled to be paid any amount by another under the regulations shall be determined by the Secretary of State.

(6) In this section—

(a) references to provision for education include provision of any benefits or services for which provision is made by or under this Act or any other enactment relating to education; and

(b) "further education" does not include further education of a kind such that expenditure on its provision would fall within paragraph 6 of Schedule 10 to the Local Government, Planning and Land Act 1980.

Recoupment: cross-border provisions

493.—(1) Regulations may make provision requiring or authorising payments of amounts determined by or under the regulations to be made by one authority to another where—

(a) the authority receiving the payment makes, in such cases or circumstances as may be specified in the regulations, provision for education in respect of a person having such connection with the area of the paying authority as may be so specified, and

(b) one of the authorities is a local education authority and the other an education authority in Scotland.

(2) Subsections (3) and (4) of section 492 shall apply for the purposes of this section as they apply for the purposes of that section.

(3) Any question concerning the connection of any person with the area of a particular local education authority or education authority shall be decided in accordance with the regulations.

(4) In subsection (1) "provision for education" includes provision of any benefits or services for which provision is made by or under this Act or any other enactment relating to education.

Recoupment: excluded pupils

494.—(1) Subsection (2) applies where a pupil is permanently excluded from any school maintained by a local education authority or any grant-maintained school and, in the financial year in which the exclusion first takes effect—

(a) he is subsequently provided with—

(i) education at a school maintained by a local education authority,

(ii) education provided by such an authority otherwise than at school, or

(iii) education at a grant-maintained school, and

(b) the person accountable for that education ("the new provider") is not the same as the person accountable for the education provided for him immediately before his exclusion ("the former provider").

(2) The former provider shall pay to the new provider an amount determined in accordance with regulations as the appropriate amount of funding to be transferred to the new provider in respect of that pupil for that financial year.

(3) Every local education authority shall, where any scheme made (or treated as made) by them as mentioned in section 101(1) does not make the provision required by subsection (4) below, exercise their powers to revise the scheme so that it makes such provision.

(4) The provision required by this subsection, in relation to a local education authority, is—

(a) provision requiring the authority, where a pupil is permanently excluded from a school and the exclusion first takes effect in a financial year in which the school is required to be covered by the scheme, to reduce the school's budget share for that year by an amount determined in accordance with regulations as the appropriate amount of funding in respect of that pupil for that year to be subtracted from the school's budget share; and

(b) provision requiring the authority, where a pupil admitted to a school in a financial year in which the school is required to be covered by the scheme has been permanently excluded—

(i) from a school maintained by them or any other local education authority, or

(ii) from any grant-maintained school,

and the exclusion (as well as the admission) first took effect in that year, to allocate for the purposes of the school in that year an amount determined in accordance with regulations as the appropriate amount of funding in respect of that pupil for that year to be allocated for those purposes.

(5) Expressions used in subsection (4) and in Chapter V of Part II have the same meaning as in that Chapter.

(6) Subject to subsection (7), for the purposes of this section—

(a) the local education authority are accountable for education provided at any school maintained by them or education provided by them otherwise than at school; and

(b) the governing body are accountable for education provided at a grant-maintained school.

(7) Where a pupil is permanently excluded from any school maintained by a local education authority or from any grant-maintained school and, in the financial year in which the exclusion first takes effect, the following events subsequently occur—

(a) he is first provided with education for which a different local education authority or, in the case of exclusion from a grant-maintained school, any local education authority are accountable ("the first new provider") and which is provided in a pupil referral unit or otherwise than at school, and

(b) at any time afterwards he is provided with education at a grant-maintained school or with education for which a local education authority other than the first new provider are accountable,

then, in relation to the education mentioned in paragraph (b), the first new provider is to be treated as accountable for the education provided for the pupil immediately before the exclusion first took effect.

(8) Any dispute as to whether any local education authority or governing body of a grant-maintained school are entitled to be paid any amount under this section by any other such authority or body shall be determined by the Secretary of State.

(9) For the purposes of this section the permanent exclusion of a pupil does not take effect until—

(a) any review under the articles of government of the decision to exclude him has been completed, and

(b) either any time for appealing under section 159 or those articles has expired without such an appeal being made or such an appeal has been finally concluded.

(10) In this section "grant-maintained school" includes a grant-maintained special school.

PART IX

ANCILLARY FUNCTIONS

CHAPTER I

ANCILLARY FUNCTIONS OF SECRETARY OF STATE

General functions

Determination of disputes

495.—(1) Except where this Act expressly provides otherwise, any dispute between a local education authority and the governing body of a school as to the exercise of any power conferred or the performance of any duty imposed by or under this Act may be referred to the Secretary of State (despite any enactment which makes the exercise of the power or the performance of the duty contingent upon the opinion of the authority or of the governing body).

(2) The Secretary of State shall determine any dispute referred to him under subsection (1).

(3) Any dispute between two or more local education authorities as to which of them is responsible for the provision of education for any pupil shall be determined by the Secretary of State.

Power to prevent unreasonable exercise of functions

496.—(1) If the Secretary of State is satisfied (either on a complaint by any person or otherwise) that a body to which this section applies have acted or are proposing to act unreasonably with respect to the exercise of any power conferred or the performance of any duty imposed by or under this Act, he may give such directions as to the exercise of the power or the performance of the duty as appear to him to be expedient (and may do so despite any enactment which makes the exercise of the power or the performance of the duty contingent upon the opinion of the body).

(2) The bodies to which this section applies are—

(a) any local education authority,

(b) the governing body of any county, voluntary or maintained special school, and

(c) the governing body of any grant-maintained school.

General default powers

497.—(1) If the Secretary of State is satisfied (either on a complaint by any person interested or otherwise) that a body to which this section applies have failed to discharge any duty imposed on them by or for the purposes of this Act, he may make an order—

(a) declaring the body to be in default in respect of that duty, and

(b) giving such directions for the purpose of enforcing the performance of the duty as appear to him to be expedient.

(2) The bodies to which this section applies are—

(a) any local education authority,

(b) the governing body of any county, voluntary or maintained special school, and

(c) the governing body of any grant-maintained school.

(3) Any directions given under subsection (1)(b) shall be enforceable, on an application made on behalf of the Secretary of State, by an order of mandamus.

Appointment of governors, etc.

Powers where no properly constituted governing body

498.—(1) Where it appears to the Secretary of State that, by reason of the default of any person, there is no properly constituted governing body of a school to which this section applies, the Secretary of State—

(a) may make such appointments and give such directions as he thinks desirable for the purpose of securing that there is a properly constituted governing body of that school, and

(b) may give directions rendering valid any acts or proceedings which in his opinion are invalid or otherwise defective by reason of the default.

(2) This section applies to—

(a) any county, voluntary or maintained special school, and

(b) any grant-maintained school.

Membership of education committees

Power to direct appointment of members of education committees

499.—(1) Subsection (2) applies to any local authorities which in accordance with section 102(1) of the Local Government Act 1972 have appointed any committees wholly or partly for the purpose of discharging any functions with respect to education which are conferred on them in their capacity as local education authorities.

(2) The Secretary of State may by directions to any local authorities to which this subsection applies require—

(a) every such committee, or

(b) any such committee of a description specified in the direction,

to include persons appointed, in accordance with the directions, for securing the representation on the committee of persons who appoint foundation governors for voluntary schools in the area for which the committee acts.

(3) Subsection (4) applies to any two or more local authorities which in accordance with section 102(1) of the Local Government Act 1972 have appointed any committees wholly or partly for the purpose of discharging any functions with respect to education which are conferred on them in their capacity as local education authorities.

(4) The Secretary of State may by directions to any local authorities to which this subsection applies require—

(a) every such committee, or

(b) any such committee of a description specified in the direction,

to include persons appointed, in accordance with the directions, for securing the representation on the committee of persons who appoint foundation governors for voluntary schools in the area for which the committee acts or in such area as may be specified in the direction.

(5) The power of the Secretary of State to give directions under subsection (2) or (4) shall be exercisable in relation to any sub-committees which—

(a) are appointed by the authorities concerned or any such committee as is mentioned in that subsection, and

(b) are so appointed wholly or partly for the purpose of discharging the authorities' functions as mentioned in subsection (1) or (3) or the committee's functions with respect to education,

as it is exercisable in relation to the committees themselves.

Rationalisation of school places

Directions to bring forward proposals to remedy excessive provision

500.—(1) Where the Secretary of State is of the opinion that the provision for primary or secondary education in maintained schools in the area of any local education authority is excessive, then, for the purpose of remedying the excess—

(a) he may by an order under this paragraph direct the local education authority to exercise their powers to make proposals for the establishment, alteration or discontinuance of schools, and

(b) in the case of any voluntary school in the area, he may by an order under this paragraph direct the governing body to exercise their powers to make proposals for the alteration of their school.

(2) Where—

(a) the Secretary of State is of the opinion that the provision for primary or secondary education in grant-maintained schools in the area of any local education authority is excessive, and

(b) an order under section 27(1) (allocation of responsibility for providing sufficient school places) applies to the area,

he may by an order under this subsection direct the funding authority to exercise their powers to make proposals for the establishment, alteration or discontinuance of schools for the purpose of remedying the excess.

(3) An order under subsection (1) or (2) shall—

(a) require the proposals to be published, or (as the case may be) notice of the proposals to be served, not later than such date as may be specified in the order, and

(b) require the proposals to apply such principles in giving effect to the direction as may be specified in the order.

(4) An order under subsection (1)(a) or (2) may not require the proposals to relate to any named school.

Directions to bring forward proposals for additional provision in maintained schools

501.—(1) The powers conferred by subsection (2) are exercisable where—

(a) an order under section 27(1)(b) applies to the area of a local education authority, and

(b) the Secretary of State is of the opinion that the schools providing relevant education which are available for the area are not sufficient for the purposes of section 14 and that additional provision for relevant education should be made in maintained schools in the area.

(2) The Secretary of State may—

(a) by an order under this paragraph direct the local education authority to exercise their powers to make proposals for the establishment, alteration or discontinuance of schools, and

(b) in the case of any voluntary school in the area, by an order under this paragraph direct the governing body to exercise their powers to make proposals for the alteration of their school,

with a view (in each case) to securing that provision is made for such additional number of pupils in the area as may be specified in the order.

(3) An order under subsection (2) shall—

(a) require the proposals to be published, or (as the case may be) notice of the proposals to be served, not later than such date as may be specified in the order, and

(b) require the proposals to apply such principles in giving effect to the direction as may be specified in the order.

(4) An order under subsection (2)(a) may not require the proposals to relate to any named school.

(5) Paragraph 7 of Schedule 4 does not apply in relation to the implementation of any proposals under section 35 where the Secretary of State has made an order under subsection (2) above.

Publication of proposals by Secretary of State

502.—(1) Where—

(a) the Secretary of State has, in relation to the area of any local education authority, made an order under section 500(1) or (2) directing the local education authority, the funding authority or the governing body of a voluntary school to make proposals for the establishment, alteration or discontinuance of schools or (as the case may be) for the alteration of their school, and

(b) the time allowed under the order, and under any other order under that section relating to that area, for the publication of the proposals or (as the case may be) the service of notice of the proposals has expired,

he may make in such manner as may be prescribed any such proposals as might have been made in accordance with the order or orders relating to that area by the person or persons to whom the directions were given.

(2) Proposals made under this section shall—

(a) include particulars of the proposed time or times of implementation of the proposals, and

(b) except where they are proposals to cease to maintain or discontinue any school or relate to a special school—

(i) include particulars of the number of pupils proposed to be admitted to the school to which the proposals relate in each relevant age group in the first school year in relation to which the proposals have been wholly implemented, and

(ii) if, in the case of a grant-maintained school, pupils are proposed to be admitted for nursery education, give the prescribed information.

(3) For the purposes of subsection (2)(b)—

(a) admission to a maintained school for nursery education shall be disregarded; and

(b) the transfer to a reception class of pupils admitted to a school for nursery education shall be treated as admission to the school.

(4) Proposals made under this section shall be accompanied by a statement which—

(a) describes any effect the implementation of the proposals would have on provision at the school for pupils who have special educational needs, and

(b) explains the effect of subsection (5).

(5) Within the period of one month beginning with the date on which the proposals are made, objections to the proposals may be made by any of the following—

(a) any ten or more local government electors for the area,

(b) the governing body of any school affected by the proposals and, in the case of a voluntary school, the person or persons who are named in the school's instrument of government as being entitled to appoint foundation governors,

(c) the appropriate further education funding council (if the proposals affect the provision of education to which section 2(1) of the Further and Higher Education Act 1992 applies), and

(d) any local education authority concerned.

(6) Where—

(a) an order under section 27 applies to the area of a local education authority, and

(b) the Secretary of State makes proposals under this section which affect the provision of relevant education in the area,

the funding authority shall be included among the persons who may submit objections to the proposals.

(7) The reference in subsection (5) to the date on which the proposals are made is to the date on which the prescribed requirements in respect of the proposals are satisfied.

Public inquiry into proposals

503.—(1) This section applies where in relation to the area of any local education authority the Secretary of State has made proposals under section 502 (otherwise than in pursuance of section 504(1)) which he has not withdrawn.

(2) If objections have been made under section 502(5) within the period allowed under that subsection, then, unless all objections so made have been withdrawn in writing within that period, the Secretary of State shall cause a local inquiry to be held to consider his proposals, any proposals he refers to the inquiry and any objections.

(3) Any proposals referred to a local inquiry under this section require the approval of the Secretary of State (if they would not require such approval apart from this subsection).

(4) Where the Secretary of State has a duty to cause a local inquiry to be held under this section, he shall refer to the inquiry—

(a) any proposals made by him in relation to the area of the local education authority (and not withdrawn) but in respect of which he is not required under this section to cause a local inquiry to be held,

(b) any proposals made by the local education authority, or made in relation to the area by the funding authority, in the exercise of their powers to make proposals for the establishment, alteration or discontinuance of schools (and not withdrawn), and

(c) any proposals made by the governing body of any voluntary school in the area in exercise of their powers to make proposals for the alteration of their school (and not withdrawn),

where those proposals are not determined before he causes the inquiry to be held and appear to him to be related to the proposals made under section 502 in respect of which he is required under this section to cause the inquiry to be held.

(5) If, before the Secretary of State causes the inquiry to be held, he forms the opinion that any proposals ought to be implemented, subsection (4) does not require him to refer those proposals to the inquiry unless—

(a) before the proceedings on the inquiry are concluded, or

(b) (if earlier) the proposals are determined,

he subsequently forms a different opinion.

(6) It shall not be open to the inquiry to question the principles specified in the order under section 500 or 501.

(7) References in this section to the determination of any proposals are to any determination whether or not to approve, adopt or implement the proposals under section 37, 38, 43, 169 or 170, under Part III or under section 340.

Adoption of proposals and approval of related proposals

504.—(1) Where the Secretary of State has made proposals under section 502 in respect of which he is required to cause a local inquiry to be held, he may when he has considered the report of the person appointed to hold the inquiry do one or more of the following—

(a) adopt, with or without modifications, or determine not to adopt the proposals or any other proposals made by him under that section which he referred to the inquiry;

(b) approve, with or without modifications, or reject any other proposals which he referred to the inquiry; and

(c) make any such further proposals under section 502 as might have been made in accordance with the order or orders relating to the area of the local education authority concerned by the person or persons to whom the directions were given.

(2) Where the Secretary of State has made proposals under section 502 in respect of which he is not required to cause a local inquiry to be held and which he is not required to refer to such an inquiry, he may, after considering any objections made under subsection (5) of that section (and not withdrawn) within the period allowed under that subsection—

(a) adopt the proposals with or without modifications; or

(b) determine not to adopt the proposals.

(3) Proposals adopted by the Secretary of State under this section shall have effect—

(a) if they relate to a maintained school, as if they—

(i) had been made by the local education authority under their powers to make proposals for the establishment, alteration or discontinuance of schools, or

(ii) in the case of a voluntary school, had been made by the governing body under their powers to make proposals for the alteration of their school,

and had been approved by the Secretary of State under section 37, 43 or 169 or, as the case may be, section 340; and

(b) if they relate to a grant-maintained school, as if they had been made by the funding authority under those powers and approved by the Secretary of State under Part III or, as the case may be, section 340;

and the provisions of section 39 or 44 or Part III or, as the case may be, section 341 as to the approval of particulars of premises or proposed premises of schools shall have effect accordingly.

Supplementary provisions

505.—(1) An order under section 500 or 501 may not require any significant change to be made in the religious character of a voluntary school.

(2) Where the governing body of a voluntary school make any proposals in pursuance of an order under section 500 or 501—

(a) the person or persons who are named in the school's instrument of government as being entitled to appoint foundation governors shall be included among the persons who may submit objections to the proposals, and

(b) the local education authority shall reimburse any expenditure reasonably incurred by the governing body in making the proposals.

(3) Proposals made in pursuance of an order under section 500 may not be withdrawn without the consent of the Secretary of State and such consent may be given on such conditions (if any) as the Secretary of State considers appropriate.

(4) Where—

(a) proposals made by the governing body of a voluntary school in pursuance of an order under section 500 or 501 are approved, or

(b) proposals adopted by the Secretary of State under section 504 have effect as mentioned in subsection (3)(a)(ii) of that section,

then, despite anything in section 45(1), the local education authority shall defray the cost of implementing the proposals.

(5) Despite anything in section 184, a county or voluntary school is not eligible for grant-maintained status—

(a) if the local education authority have made any proposals in pursuance of an order under section 500 to cease to maintain the school which have not been withdrawn and no determination whether or not to approve or implement the proposals has been made under section 169 or 170 or section 504, or

(b) if the Secretary of State has made any proposals under section 502 for the local education authority to cease to maintain the school which have not been withdrawn and no determination whether or not to adopt the proposals has been made under section 504.

(6) Section 37(4), (7) and (8) or, as the case may be, section 43(3), (4) and (5) do not apply in relation to any proposals under section 35(1)(c) or (d) or 41(2) made in pursuance of an order under section 500.

(7) In sections 500 to 504 "powers to make proposals for the alteration of their school", in relation to the governing body of a voluntary school, means their powers to publish proposals under section 41(2).

(8) In sections 500 to 504—

(a) "powers to make proposals for the establishment, alteration or discontinuance of schools" means—

(i) in relation to the local education authority, all or any of the powers to publish proposals under section 35 or 167,

(ii) in relation to the funding authority, all or any of the powers to publish proposals under sections 211, 260 or 268, and

(iii) in relation to either authority, the power to serve notice of proposals under section 339;

(b) references to maintained schools are references to county, voluntary and maintained special schools; and

(c) references to grant-maintained schools include grant-maintained special schools.

Medical examinations

Power to require medical examination of pupils

506.—(1) Where—

(a) a question is referred to the Secretary of State under section 442(3) or 495, and

(b) in his opinion the examination of any pupil by a registered medical practitioner appointed by him for the purpose would assist in determining the question,

he may serve a notice on the parent of that pupil requiring the parent to present the pupil for examination by such a practitioner.

(2) Any parent who without reasonable excuse fails to comply with any requirements of a notice served on him under subsection (1) is guilty of an offence.

(3) A person guilty of an offence under this section is liable on summary conviction to a fine not exceeding level 1 on the standard scale.

Local inquiries

Power to direct local inquiries

507.—(1) The Secretary of State may cause a local inquiry to be held for the purpose of the exercise of any of his functions under this Act.

(2) Subsections (2) to (5) of section 250 of the Local Government Act 1972 (giving evidence at and defraying costs of local inquiries) shall have effect with respect to any such inquiry as they have effect with respect to an inquiry held under that section.

CHAPTER II

ANCILLARY FUNCTIONS OF LOCAL EDUCATION AUTHORITIES

Provision of services

Functions in respect of facilities for recreation and social and physical training

508.—(1) A local education authority shall secure that the facilities for primary, secondary and further education provided for their area include adequate facilities for recreation and social and physical training.

(2) For that purpose a local education authority—

(a) may establish, maintain and manage, or assist the establishment, maintenance and management of,—

(i) camps, holiday classes, playing fields, play centres, and

(ii) other places, including playgrounds, gymnasiums and swimming baths not appropriated to any school or other educational institution,

at which facilities for recreation and social and physical training are available for persons receiving primary, secondary or further education;

(b) may organise games, expeditions and other activities for such persons; and

(c) may defray, or contribute towards, the expenses of such games, expeditions and other activities.

(3) When making arrangements for the provision of facilities or the organisation of activities in the exercise of their powers under subsection (2), a local education authority shall, in particular, have regard to the expediency of co-operating with any voluntary societies or bodies whose objects include the provision of facilities or the organisation of activities of a similar character.

Provision of transport etc.

509.—(1) A local education authority shall make such arrangements for the provision of transport and otherwise as they consider necessary, or as the Secretary of State may direct, for the purpose of facilitating the attendance of persons receiving education—

(a) at schools,

(b) at any institution maintained or assisted by the authority which provides further education or higher education (or both),
(c) at any institution within the further education sector, or
(d) at any institution outside both the further and the higher education sectors, where a further education funding council has secured provision for those persons at the institution under section 4(3) or (5) of the Further and Higher Education Act 1992.

(2) Any transport provided in pursuance of arrangements under subsection (1) shall be provided free of charge.

(3) A local education authority may pay the whole or any part, as they think fit, of the reasonable travelling expenses of any person receiving education—
(a) at a school, or
(b) at any such institution as is mentioned in subsection (1),
for whose transport no arrangements are made under that subsection.

(4) In considering whether or not they are required by subsection (1) to make arrangements in relation to a particular person, a local education authority shall have regard (amongst other things)—
(a) to the age of the person and the nature of the route, or alternative routes, which he could reasonably be expected to take; and
(b) to any wish of his parent for him to be provided with education at a school or institution in which the religious education provided is that of the religion or denomination to which his parent adheres.

(5) Arrangements made by a local education authority under subsection (1) shall—
(a) make provision for pupils at grant-maintained schools which is no less favourable than the provision made in pursuance of the arrangements for pupils at schools maintained by a local education authority;
(b) make provision for persons receiving full-time education at any institution within the further education sector which is no less favourable than the provision made in pursuance of the arrangements for pupils of the same age at schools maintained by a local education authority; and
(c) make provision for persons receiving full-time education at institutions mentioned in subsection (1)(d) which is no less favourable than—
(i) the provision made in pursuance of the arrangements for persons of the same age with learning difficulties (within the meaning of section 15(5)) at schools maintained by a local education authority, or
(ii) where there are no such arrangements, the provision made in pursuance of the arrangements for such persons for whom the authority secures the provision of education at any other institution.

(6) Regulations under section 414(6) may require publication (within the meaning of that section) by every local education authority of such information as may be required by the regulations with respect to the authority's policy and arrangements for provision under this section for persons attending institutions mentioned in subsection (1)(c) or (d) who are over compulsory school age and who have not attained the age of 19.

Provision of clothing

510.—(1) A local education authority may provide clothing for—
(a) any pupil who is a boarder at an educational institution maintained by the authority or at a grant-maintained school,
(b) any pupil at a nursery school maintained by the authority, and
(c) any pupil in a nursery class at a school maintained by the authority or at a grant-maintained school.

(2) A local education authority may also provide clothing for any pupil—

(a) for whom they are providing board and lodging elsewhere than at an educational institution maintained by them, and

(b) for whom special education provision is made in pursuance of arrangements made by them.

(3) Where it appears to a local education authority, in a case where neither subsection (1) nor subsection (2) applies, that a pupil at—

(a) a school maintained by them or a grant-maintained school, or

(b) a special school (whether maintained by them or not),

is unable by reason of the inadequacy or unsuitability of his clothing to take full advantage of the education provided at the school, the authority may provide him with such clothing as in their opinion is necessary for the purpose of ensuring that he is sufficiently and suitably clad while he remains a pupil at the school.

(4) A local education authority may provide—

(a) for pupils at a school maintained by them, at a grant-maintained school or at an institution maintained by them which provides further education or higher education (or both),

(b) for persons who have not attained the age of 19 and who are receiving education at an institution within the further education sector, and

(c) for persons who make use of facilities for physical training made available for them by the authority under section 508(2),

such articles of clothing as the authority may determine suitable for the physical training provided at that school or institution or under those facilities.

(5) A local education authority may—

(a) with the consent of the proprietor of a school not maintained by the authority, other than a grant-maintained school or special school, and

(b) on such financial and other terms, if any, as may be determined by agreement between the authority and the proprietor,

make arrangements, in the case of any pupil at the school who is unable by reason of the inadequacy or unsuitability of his clothing to take full advantage of the education provided at the school, for securing for the pupil the provision of such clothing as is necessary for the purpose of ensuring that he is sufficiently and suitably clad while he remains a pupil at the school.

(6) Any arrangements made under subsection (5) shall be such as to secure, so far as is practicable, that the expense incurred by the authority in connection with the provision of any article under the arrangements does not exceed the expense which would have been incurred by them in the provision of it if the pupil had been a pupil at a school maintained by them.

Provisions supplementary to section 510

511.—(1) Provision of clothing under section 510 may be made in such way as to confer either a right of property in the clothing or a right of user only (at the option of the providing authority), except in any circumstances for which the adoption of one or other of those ways of making such provision is prescribed.

(2) Where a local education authority have provided a person with clothing under section 510, then, in such circumstances respectively as may be prescribed—

(a) the authority shall require his parent to pay to them in respect of its provision such sum (if any) as in their opinion he is able to pay without financial hardship, not exceeding the cost to the authority of its provision;

(b) the authority may require his parent to pay to them in respect of its provision such sum as is mentioned in paragraph (a) or any lesser sum; or

(c) his parent shall not be required to pay any sum in respect of its provision.

(3) Any sum which a parent is duly required to pay by virtue of subsection (2)(a) or (b) may be recovered summarily as a civil debt.

(4) Where a person who has attained the age of 18 (other than a registered pupil at a school) is provided with clothing under section 510, any reference in subsection (2) or (3) to his parent shall be read as a reference to him.

Provision of meals etc. at schools maintained by local education authorities

512.—(1) A local education authority may provide registered pupils at any school maintained by them with milk, meals and other refreshment, either on the school premises or at any place other than the school premises where education is being provided.

(2) Subject to subsection (3), a local education authority shall—

(a) charge for anything provided by them under subsection (1), and

(b) charge every pupil the same price for the same quantity of the same item.

(3) In relation to a pupil whose parents are in receipt of income support or of an income-based jobseeker's allowance (payable under the Jobseekers Act 1995) or who is himself in receipt of that benefit, a local education authority—

(a) shall so exercise their power under subsection (1) as to ensure that such provision is made for him in the middle of the day as appears to them to be requisite, and

(b) shall make that provision for him free of charge.

(4) A local education authority shall provide at any school maintained by them such facilities as they consider appropriate for the consumption of any meals or other refreshment brought to the school by registered pupils.

(5) Subsections (1) and (4) shall apply in relation to—

(a) persons, other than pupils, who receive education at a school maintained by a local education authority, and

(b) the authority maintaining the school,

as they apply in relation to pupils at any such school and the authority maintaining the school; and a local education authority shall charge for anything provided under subsection (1) as it so applies, and shall charge every such person the same price for the same quantity of the same item.

Provision of meals etc. at schools not maintained by local education authorities

513.—(1) A local education authority may, with the consent of the proprietor of a school in their area which is not maintained by them, make arrangements for securing the provision of milk, meals and other refreshment for pupils in attendance at the school.

(2) Any arrangements under this section—

(a) shall be on such financial and other terms, if any, as may be determined by agreement between the authority and the proprietor of the school; and

(b) shall be such as to secure, so far as is practicable, that the expense incurred by the authority in connection with the provision of any service or item under the arrangements shall not exceed the expense which would have been incurred by them in providing it if the pupil had been a pupil at a school maintained by them.

Provision of board and lodging otherwise than at school

514.—(1) Where a local education authority are satisfied with respect to any pupil—

(a) that primary or secondary education suitable to his age, ability and aptitude and to any special educational needs he may have can best be provided for him at a particular county, voluntary, grant-maintained or special school, but

(b) that such education cannot be so provided unless boarding accommodation is provided for him otherwise than at the school,

they may provide such board and lodging for him under such arrangements as they think fit.

(2) Where a local education authority are satisfied with respect to a pupil with special educational needs that provision of board and lodging for him is necessary for enabling him to receive the required special educational provision, they may provide such board and lodging for him under such arrangements as they think fit.

(3) In making any arrangements under this section, a local education authority shall, so far as practicable, give effect to the wishes of the pupil's parent as to the religion or religious denomination of the person with whom the pupil will reside.

(4) Subject to subsection (5), where a local education authority have provided a pupil with board and lodging under arrangements under this section, they shall require the pupil's parent to pay them such sums, if any, in respect of the board and lodging as in their opinion he is able to pay without financial hardship.

(5) No sum is recoverable under subsection (4) if the arrangements were made by the authority on the ground that in their opinion education suitable to the pupil's age, ability and aptitude or special educational needs could not otherwise be provided for him.

(6) The sums recoverable under subsection (4) shall not exceed the cost to the authority of providing the board and lodging.

(7) Any sum payable under subsection (4) may be recovered summarily as a civil debt.

Provision of teaching services for day nurseries

515.—(1) Subject to subsection (2), a local education authority may, in accordance with arrangements made by them for that purpose, make available to a day nursery the services of any teacher who—

(a) is employed by them in a nursery school or in a primary school having one or more nursery classes, and

(b) has agreed to provide his services for the purposes of the arrangements.

(2) Arrangements under subsection (1) in respect of a teacher in a voluntary school require the concurrence of the governing body of the school.

(3) Arrangements under this section may make provision—

(a) for the supply of equipment for use in connection with the teaching services made available under the arrangements;

(b) for regulating the respective functions of any teacher whose services are made available under the arrangements, the head teacher of his school and the person in charge of the day nursery; and

(c) for any supplementary or incidental matters connected with the arrangements, including, where the teacher's school and the day nursery are in the areas of different local education authorities, financial adjustments between those authorities.

(4) In this section "day nursery" means a day nursery provided under section 18 of the Children Act 1989 (provision by local authorities of day care for pre-school and other children).

(5) A teacher shall not be regarded as ceasing to be a member of the teaching staff of his school and subject to the general directions of his head teacher by reason only of his services being made available in pursuance of arrangements under this section.

Supply by LEA of goods and services to grant-maintained and grant-maintained special schools

516.—(1) Where the Secretary of State by order provides for this section to apply to a local education authority, the functions of the authority shall include the supply by the authority of such goods or services as may be specified in the order to the governing bodies of grant-maintained schools or grant-maintained special schools in such area as may be so specified.

(2) The area specified in the order may not extend beyond the area which comprises—

(a) the area of the authority, and

(b) the area of any other local education authority which shares any boundary with the authority.

(3) The terms on which goods and services are supplied by a local education authority in the exercise of a function exercisable by virtue of this section shall be such as can reasonably be expected to secure that the full cost of exercising the function is recovered by the authority.

(4) This section shall not apply to a local education authority after the end of the period of two years beginning with the time when it first applies to the authority.

(5) This section is without prejudice to the generality of any other enactment conferring functions on local education authorities.

Payment of fees

Payment of fees at schools not maintained by a local education authority

517.—(1) Where, in pursuance of arrangements made under section 18 or Part IV (special educational needs), primary or secondary education is provided for a pupil at a school not maintained by them or another local education authority, the local education authority by whom the arrangements are made shall—

(a) if subsection (2), (3) or (4) applies, pay the whole of the fees payable in respect of the education provided in pursuance of the arrangements; and

(b) if board and lodging are provided for the pupil at the school and subsection (5) applies, pay the whole of the fees payable in respect of the board and lodging.

(2) This subsection applies where—

(a) the pupil fills a place in the school which the proprietor of the school has put at the disposal of the authority; and

(b) the school is one in respect of which grants are made by the Secretary of State under section 485.

(3) This subsection applies where the authority are satisfied that, by reason of a shortage of places in every school maintained by them or another local education authority to which the pupil could be sent with reasonable convenience, education suitable—

(a) to his age, ability and aptitude, and

(b) to any special educational needs he may have,

cannot be provided by them for him except at a school not maintained by them or another local education authority.

(4) This subsection applies where (in a case in which neither subsection (2) nor subsection (3) applies) the authority are satisfied—

(a) that the pupil has special educational needs, and

(b) that it is expedient in his interests that the required special educational provision should be made for him at a school not maintained by them or another local education authority.

(5) This subsection applies where the authority are satisfied that education suitable—

(a) to the pupil's age, ability and aptitude, and
(b) to any special educational needs he may have,

cannot be provided by them for him at any school unless board and lodging are also provided for him (either at school or elsewhere).

(6) As from such day as the Secretary of State may by order appoint this section shall have effect with the following modifications—

(a) in subsections (1) and (3), for "not maintained by them or another local education authority" substitute "which is neither a maintained nor a grant-maintained school";
(b) in subsection (3), for "every school maintained by them or another local education authority" substitute "every maintained or grant-maintained school";
(c) in subsections (3) and (5), for "provided by them" substitute "provided";
(d) omit subsection (4) and the reference to it in subsection (1); and
(e) at the end add—

"(7) In this section "grant-maintained school" includes a grant-maintained special school, and subsection (5) does not apply where section 348(2) applies."

(7) An order under subsection (6) may appoint different days for different provisions and for different purposes.

Payment of school fees and expenses; grant of scholarships etc.

518. Regulations shall empower local education authorities, for the purpose of enabling persons to take advantage without hardship to themselves or their parents of any educational facilities available to them—

(a) to defray such expenses of children attending county, voluntary, grant-maintained or special schools as may be necessary to enable them to take part in any school activities, and
(b) to pay the whole or any part of the fees and expenses payable in respect of children attending schools at which fees are payable, and
(c) to grant scholarships, exhibitions, bursaries and other allowances in respect of persons over compulsory school age.

Allowances for governors

Travelling and subsistence allowances for governors of schools and further or higher education institutions

519.—(1) A local education authority may, in accordance with the provisions of a scheme made by them for the purposes of this section, pay travelling and subsistence allowances to governors of—

(a) any county, voluntary or maintained special school which does not have a delegated budget (construed in accordance with section 115); and
(b) any institution providing higher education or further education (or both) which is maintained by a local education authority.

(2) Such a scheme may make different provision in relation to schools or other institutions of different categories (including provision for allowances not to be paid in respect of certain categories) but shall not make different provision in relation to different categories of governor of the same school or institution.

(3) Subject to subsections (4) and (5), a local education authority may pay travelling and subsistence allowances to any person appointed to represent them on the governing body of—

(a) any institution providing higher education or further education (or both) which is not maintained by them; or
(b) any independent school or special school which is not maintained by them.

(4) A local education authority shall not pay any allowance under subsection (3) for expenses in respect of which the person incurring them is entitled to reimbursement by any person other than the authority.

(5) A local education authority shall not pay any allowance under subsection (3) if they have not made any scheme under subsection (1) or if the arrangements under which the allowance would otherwise be payable—

(a) provide for allowances which are to any extent more generous than the most generous payable by the authority under any such scheme; or

(b) contain any provision which the authority would not have power to include in any such scheme.

(6) No allowance may be paid to any governor of a school or institution of a kind mentioned in subsection (1), in respect of the discharge of his functions as such a governor, otherwise than under this section.

Medical arrangements

Medical inspection and treatment of pupils

520.—(1) A local education authority shall make arrangements for encouraging and assisting pupils to take advantage of the provision for medical and dental inspection and treatment made for them in pursuance of section 5(1) or (1A) of the National Health Service Act 1977 or paragraph 1(a)(i) of Schedule 1 to that Act.

(2) If the parent of a pupil gives notice to the authority that he objects to the pupil availing himself of any of the provision so made, the pupil shall not be encouraged or assisted to do so.

(3) A local education authority's duty under subsection (1) does not apply in relation to pupils at a grant-maintained school (in relation to whom the school's governing body have a similar duty under section 536(1)).

Cleanliness of pupils

Examination of pupils for cleanliness

521.—(1) A local education authority may by directions in writing authorise a medical officer of theirs to have the persons and clothing of pupils in attendance at relevant schools examined whenever in his opinion such examinations are necessary in the interests of cleanliness.

(2) Directions under subsection (1) may be given with respect to—

(a) all relevant schools, or

(b) any relevant schools named in the directions.

(3) An examination under this section shall be made by a person authorised by the authority to make such examinations; and, if the examination is of a girl, it shall not be made by a man unless he is a registered medical practitioner.

(4) For the purposes of this section "relevant schools" are—

(a) schools maintained by the authority; and

(b) grant-maintained schools within the authority's area.

Compulsory cleansing of a pupil

522.—(1) If, on an examination under section 521, the person or clothing of a pupil is found to be infested with vermin or in a foul condition, any officer of the local education authority may serve a notice on the pupil's parent requiring him to cause the pupil's person and clothing to be cleansed.

(2) The notice shall inform the parent that, unless within the period specified in the notice the pupil's person and clothing are cleansed to the satisfaction of such person as is specified in the notice, the cleansing will be carried out under arrangements made by the authority.

(3) The period so specified shall not be less than 24 hours from the service of the notice.

(4) If, on a report being made to him by the specified person at the end of the specified period, a medical officer of the authority is not satisfied that the pupil's person and clothing have been properly cleansed, he may by order direct that they shall be cleansed under arrangements made by the authority under section 523.

(5) An order made under subsection (4) shall be sufficient to authorise any officer of the authority—

(a) to cause the pupil's person and clothing to be cleansed in accordance with arrangements made by the authority under section 523, and

(b) for that purpose to convey the pupil to, and detain him at, any premises provided in accordance with such arrangements.

Arrangements for cleansing of pupils

523.—(1) A local education authority shall make arrangements for securing that the person or clothing of any pupil required to be cleansed under section 522 may be cleansed (whether at the request of a parent or in pursuance of an order under section 522(4)) at suitable premises, by suitable persons and with suitable appliances.

(2) Where the council of a district in the area of the authority are entitled to the use of any premises or appliances for cleansing the person or clothing of persons infested with vermin, the authority may require the council to permit the authority to use those premises or appliances for such purposes upon such terms as may be determined—

(a) by agreement between the authority and the council, or

(b) in default of such agreement, by the Secretary of State.

(3) Subsection (2) does not apply in relation to Wales.

(4) A girl may be cleansed under arrangements under this section only by a registered medical practitioner or by a woman authorised for the purpose by the authority.

Exclusion of a pupil pending examination or cleansing

524.—(1) Where—

(a) a medical officer of a local education authority suspects that the person or clothing of a pupil in attendance at a relevant school is infested with vermin or in a foul condition, but

(b) action for the examination or cleansing of the pupil's person and clothing cannot be taken immediately,

the medical officer may direct that the pupil is to be excluded from the school until such action has been taken, if he considers it necessary to do so in the interests either of the pupil or of other pupils in attendance at the school.

(2) A direction under subsection (1) is a defence to any proceedings under Chapter II of Part VI in respect of the failure of the pupil to attend school on any day on which he is excluded in pursuance of the direction, unless it is proved that the giving of the direction was necessitated by the wilful default of the pupil or his parent.

(3) For the purposes of this section a "relevant school" is—

(a) a school maintained by the local education authority, or

(b) a grant-maintained school within the authority's area.

Offence of neglecting the cleanliness of a pupil

525.—(1) If, after the person or clothing of a pupil has been cleansed under section 522—

(a) his person or clothing is again infested with vermin, or in a foul condition, at any time while he is in attendance at a relevant school, and

(b) the condition of his person or clothing is due to neglect on the part of his parent,

the parent is guilty of an offence.

(2) A person guilty of an offence under this section is liable on summary conviction to a fine not exceeding level 1 on the standard scale.

(3) For the purposes of this section a "relevant school" is a school maintained by a local education authority or a grant-maintained school.

Educational research and conferences

Powers as to educational research

526. A local education authority may make such provision for conducting, or assisting the conduct of, research as appears to them to be desirable for the purpose of improving the educational facilities provided for their area.

Powers as to educational conferences

527. A local education authority may—

(a) organise, or participate in the organisation of, conferences for the discussion of questions relating to education, and

(b) expend such sums as may be reasonable in paying, or contributing towards, any expenditure incurred in connection with conferences for the discussion of such questions, including the expenses of any person authorised by them to attend such a conference.

Disability statements relating to further education

Duty of LEA to publish disability statements relating to further education

528.—(1) Every local education authority shall publish disability statements at such intervals as may be prescribed.

(2) In subsection (1) "disability statement" means a statement containing information of a prescribed description about the provision of facilities for further education made by the local education authority in respect of persons who are disabled persons for the purposes of the Disability Discrimination Act 1995.

Acquisition and holding of property

Power to accept gifts on trust for educational purposes

529.—(1) A local education authority may accept, hold and administer any property on trust for purposes connected with education.

(2) Any intention on the part of a local education authority that a school (other than a nursery school or a special school) should be vested in the authority as trustees shall be treated for the purposes of section 35(1) as an intention to maintain the school as a county school (so that proposals for that purpose shall be published and submitted as required by that subsection); and the other provisions of section 35 and sections 36 to 40 shall apply accordingly.

(3) Any school which in accordance with subsection (2) is vested in a local education authority as trustees shall be a county school.

Compulsory purchase of land

530.—(1) The Secretary of State may authorise a local education authority to purchase compulsorily any land (whether within or outside their area) which—

(a) is required for the purposes of any school or institution which is, or is to be, maintained by them or which they have power to assist, or

(b) is otherwise required for the purposes of their functions under this Act.

(2) The Secretary of State shall not authorise the compulsory purchase of any land required for the purposes of a voluntary school unless he is satisfied that the arrangements made—

(a) as to the vesting of the land to be purchased, and

(b) as to the appropriation of that land for the purposes of the school,

are such as to secure that the expenditure ultimately borne by the local education authority will not include any expenditure which, if the land had been purchased by the governing body of the school, would have fallen to be borne by the governing body.

(3) Subsection (2) shall not, however, apply where the local education authority propose that expenditure to be incurred in connection with the purchase should ultimately be borne by them under section 68 (power to give assistance).

(4) In this section "land" includes buildings and other structures and land covered with water.

Acquisition of land by agreement

531.—(1) For the removal of doubt, it is declared that making land available for the purposes of a school or institution—

(a) which is, or is to be, maintained by a local education authority, or

(b) which such an authority have power to assist,

is a function of the authority within the meaning of section 120 of the Local Government Act 1972 (which relates to the acquisition by a local authority by agreement of land for the purpose of any of their functions), even though the land will not be held by the authority.

(2) A local education authority shall not acquire by agreement any land required for the purposes of a voluntary school unless they are satisfied that the arrangements made—

(a) as to the vesting of the land to be acquired, and

(b) as to the appropriation of that land for the purposes of the school,

are such as to secure that the expenditure ultimately borne by them will not include any expenditure which, if the land had been acquired by the governing body of the school, would have fallen to be borne by the governing body.

Appointment of chief education officer

Appointment of chief education officer

532. A local education authority's duties under the Local Government Act 1972 with respect to the appointment of officers shall (without prejudice to the generality of the provisions of that Act) include the duty of appointing a fit person to be the chief education officer of the authority.

CHAPTER III

ANCILLARY FUNCTIONS OF GOVERNING BODIES

Provision of services

Duties of governing bodies of maintained schools with respect to provision of school meals etc.

533.—(1) The governing body of any school maintained by a local education authority shall—

(a) afford the authority such facilities as they require to enable them to perform their functions under section 512, and

(b) allow the authority to make such use of the premises and equipment of the school, and such alterations to the school buildings, as the authority consider necessary for that purpose.

(2) Nothing in subsection (1) shall require the governing body of a voluntary school to incur any expenditure.

(3) Where the governing body of a school which has a delegated budget (within the meaning of Part II) provide pupils or other persons who receive education at the school with milk, meals or other refreshment, they shall—

(a) charge for everything so provided,

(b) charge every such pupil the same price for the same quantity of the same item, and

(c) charge every person other than a pupil the same price for the same quantity of the same item.

Duties of governing bodies of grant-maintained schools with respect to provision of school meals etc.

534.—(1) The governing body of a grant-maintained school may provide registered pupils at the school with milk, meals and other refreshment, either on the school premises or at any place other than the school premises where education is being provided.

(2) Subject to subsection (3), a governing body shall—

(a) charge for anything provided by them under subsection (1), and

(b) charge every pupil the same price for the same quantity of the same item.

(3) In relation to a pupil whose parents are in receipt of income support or of an income-based jobseeker's allowance (payable under the Jobseekers Act 1995) or who is himself in receipt of that benefit, a governing body—

(a) shall so exercise their power under subsection (1) as to ensure that such provision is made for him in the middle of the day as appears to them to be requisite, and

(b) shall make that provision for him free of charge.

(4) A governing body of a grant-maintained school shall provide at the school such facilities as they consider appropriate for the consumption of any meals or other refreshment brought to the school by registered pupils.

(5) Subsections (1) and (4) shall apply in relation to—

(a) persons, other than pupils, who receive education at a grant-maintained school, and

(b) the governing body of the school,

as they apply in relation to pupils at any such school and its governing body; and a governing body shall charge for anything provided under subsection (1) as it so applies, and shall charge every such person the same price for the same quantity of the same item.

Provision of teaching services for day nurseries

535.—(1) Subject to subsection (2), the governing body of a county or voluntary primary school having one or more nursery classes may, in accordance with arrangements made by them for that purpose, make available to a day nursery the services of any teacher who is employed by them in the school and has agreed to provide his services for the purposes of the arrangements.

(2) No arrangements shall be made under subsection (1) except at the request of the local education authority and on terms approved by them.

(3) Arrangements under this section may make provision—

(a) for the supply of equipment for use in connection with the teaching services made available under the arrangements,

(b) for regulating the respective functions of any teacher whose services are made available under the arrangements, the head teacher of his school and the person in charge of the day nursery, and

(c) for any supplementary or incidental matters connected with the arrangements, including, where the teacher's school and the day nursery are in the areas of different local education authorities, financial adjustments between those authorities.

(4) In this section "day nursery" means a day nursery provided under section 18 of the Children Act 1989 (provision by local authorities of day care for pre-school and other children).

(5) A teacher shall not be regarded as ceasing to be a member of the teaching staff of his school and subject to the general directions of his head teacher by reason only of his services being made available in pursuance of arrangements under this section.

Medical arrangements

Medical inspection and treatment of pupils at grant-maintained schools

536.—(1) The governing body of a grant-maintained school shall make arrangements for encouraging and assisting pupils at the school to take advantage of the provision for medical and dental inspection and treatment made for them in pursuance of section 5(1) or (1A) of the National Health Service Act 1977 or paragraph 1(a)(i) of Schedule 1 to that Act.

(2) If the parent of a pupil gives notice to the governing body that he objects to the pupil availing himself of any of the provision so made, the pupil shall not be encouraged or assisted to do so.

CHAPTER IV

PROVISION OF INFORMATION BY GOVERNING BODIES ETC.

Power of Secretary of State to require information from governing bodies etc.

537.—(1) The Secretary of State may by regulations make provision requiring—

(a) the governing body of every school which is—

(i) maintained by a local education authority, or

(ii) a grant-maintained school, or

(iii) a special school which is not maintained by a local education authority, and

(b) the proprietor of each independent school,

to provide such information about the school as may be prescribed.

(2) For the purposes of this section information about the continuing education of pupils leaving a school, or the employment or training taken up by such pupils on leaving, is to be treated as information about the school.

(3) Where the Secretary of State exercises his power to make regulations under this section he shall do so with a view to making available information which is likely to—

(a) assist parents in choosing schools for their children;

(b) increase public awareness of the quality of the education provided by the schools concerned and of the educational standards achieved in those schools; or

(c) assist in assessing the degree of efficiency with which the financial resources of those schools are managed.

(4) Information which is required by virtue of regulations under this section shall be provided—

(a) in such form and manner,

(b) on such occasions, and

(c) to such person or persons, in addition to or in place of the Secretary of State,

as may be prescribed.

(5) No information provided in accordance with regulations under this section shall name any pupil to whom it relates.

(6) The Secretary of State may—

(a) publish information provided in accordance with regulations under this section in such form and manner as he considers appropriate;

(b) make arrangements for such information to be published in such form and manner, and by such persons, as he may specify for the purposes of this section;

(c) make regulations requiring local education authorities to publish prescribed categories of such information, together with such supplementary information as may be prescribed, in such form and manner as may be prescribed.

(7) The Secretary of State may make regulations requiring—

(a) the governing body of any school which is maintained by a local education authority or which is a grant-maintained school,

(b) the proprietor of any city technology college or city college for the technology of the arts, or

(c) any local education authority,

to provide prescribed persons with prescribed categories of information published under subsection (6).

(8) Information provided under subsection (7) shall be provided in such form and manner as may be prescribed.

(9) Regulations under this section may make provision enabling the Secretary of State, in such circumstances as may be prescribed, to order the deletion from the register of independent schools of the name of any independent school the proprietor of which fails to comply with any requirement imposed by or under the regulations.

(10) In subsection (9) "the register of independent schools" means—

(a) in relation to any school in England, the register of independent schools kept under section 464 by the Registrar of Independent Schools for England; and

(b) in relation to any school in Wales, the equivalent register kept by the Registrar of Independent Schools for Wales.

(11) Without prejudice to the generality of section 569(4), regulations under this section may make provision for the designation by the Secretary of State, in accordance with the regulations, of particular schools or classes of schools for the purposes of the application of particular provisions of the regulations in relation to such schools.

(12) This section is not to be taken as restricting, or otherwise affecting, any other powers that the Secretary of State may have to make regulations with respect to, or otherwise to require, the provision of information by any person.

(13) This section does not apply to nursery schools.

Provision of information to Secretary of State by governing bodies of maintained schools

538. The governing body or temporary governing body of a county, voluntary or maintained special school shall make such reports and returns, and give such information, to the Secretary of State as he may require for the purpose of the exercise of his functions in relation to education.

Provision of information by governing body of grant-maintained schools

539.—(1) The governing body of a grant-maintained school shall publish, at such times and in such manner as may be required by regulations made by the Secretary of State, such information in respect of the school as may be so required.

(2) The governing body shall make such reports and returns, and give such information, to the Secretary of State as he may require for the purpose of his functions in relation to education.

(3) The governing body shall make such reports and returns, and give such information, to the funding authority as they may require for the purpose of the exercise of their functions.

(4) The governing body shall make such reports and returns, and give such information, to any local education authority by whom any functions are exercisable—

(a) in relation to the school, or
(b) in relation to registered pupils at the school,

as the authority may require for the purpose of the exercise of those functions.

(5) The governing body shall make such reports and returns, and give such information, in relation to registered pupils at the school aged five or under as any local education authority may require for the purpose of exercising their functions under section 19(1)(a) of the Children Act 1989 (review of provision for day care).

Distribution of information about schools providing secondary education

540.—(1) Where the governing body of any school providing primary education receive a request which—

(a) is made by the governing body of any school providing secondary education, and
(b) relates to the distribution of information about the school providing secondary education to parents of pupils at the school providing primary education without charge to those parents,

the governing body of that school shall secure that the request is treated no less favourably (whether as to services provided or as to the terms on which they are provided) than any such request made by the governing body of any other school providing secondary education.

(2) In this section "school" means—

(a) any county or voluntary school or any maintained special school which is not established in a hospital, or
(b) any grant-maintained school or any grant-maintained special school.

Distribution of information about further education institutions

541.—(1) The Secretary of State may by regulations require—

(a) the governing body of any school providing secondary education, and
(b) the proprietor of any city technology college or city college for the technology of the arts,

to provide such persons as may be prescribed with such categories of information falling within subsection (2) as may be prescribed.

(2) Information falls within this subsection if it is—

(a) published under section 50 of the Further and Higher Education Act 1992 (information with respect to institutions within the further education sector), and
(b) made available to governing bodies and proprietors for distribution.

(3) Information provided under subsection (1) shall be provided in such form and manner as may be prescribed.

(4) In this section "school" means—

(a) any county or voluntary school or any maintained special school which is not established in a hospital, or
(b) any grant-maintained school or any grant-maintained special school.

PART X

MISCELLANEOUS AND GENERAL

CHAPTER I

EDUCATIONAL PREMISES

Required standards for educational premises

Prescribed standards for school premises

542.—(1) Regulations shall prescribe the standards to which the premises of schools maintained by local education authorities and of grant-maintained schools are to conform; and without prejudice to the generality of section 569(4) different standards may be prescribed for such descriptions of schools as are specified in the regulations.

(2) Where a school is maintained by a local education authority, the authority shall secure that the school premises conform to the prescribed standards.

(3) Where a school is a grant-maintained school, the governing body shall secure that the school premises conform to the prescribed standards.

(4) Subsections (2) and (3) have effect subject to section 543.

Relaxation of prescribed standards in special cases

543.—(1) Where subsection (2), (3) or (4) applies in relation to a school, the Secretary of State may direct that, despite the fact that the prescribed requirement referred to in that subsection is not satisfied, the school premises shall be taken, as respects the matters specified in the direction, to conform to the standards prescribed under section 542 so long as—

(a) the direction remains in force, and

(b) any conditions specified in the direction as respects those matters are observed.

(2) This subsection applies if the Secretary of State is satisfied, having regard—

(a) to the nature of the school's existing site,

(b) to any existing buildings on the site, or

(c) to other special circumstances affecting the school premises,

that it would be unreasonable to require conformity with any prescribed requirement as to any matter.

(3) This subsection applies if—

(a) the school is to have an additional or new site, and

(b) the Secretary of State is satisfied, having regard to the shortage of suitable sites, that it would be unreasonable to require conformity with any prescribed requirement relating to sites.

(4) This subsection applies if—

(a) the school is to have additional buildings, or is to be transferred to a new site,

(b) existing buildings not previously part of the school premises, or temporary buildings, are to be used for that purpose, and

(c) the Secretary of State is satisfied, having regard to the need to control public expenditure in the interests of the national economy, that it would be unreasonable to require conformity with any prescribed requirement relating to buildings.

(5) In this section "prescribed requirement" means a requirement of regulations under section 542.

Approval etc. of school premises and boarding hostels

544.—(1) Regulations may make provision requiring the Secretary of

State's approval (or, in such cases as may be prescribed, the approval of the funding authority) to be obtained for the provision of new premises for, or the alteration of the premises of—

(a) any school to which this section applies, or

(b) any boarding hostel provided by a local education authority for persons receiving education at any such school.

(2) Regulations may make provision for the inspection of any such hostel.

(3) The schools to which this section applies are—

(a) any school maintained by a local education authority,

(b) any grant-maintained school, and

(c) any special school not maintained by a local education authority.

Exemption from building byelaws of approved buildings

545.—(1) Where plans for, or particulars in respect of, a building required for the purposes of any school or other educational institution are approved by the Secretary of State, he may by order direct that any provision of a local Act or of a byelaw made under such an Act—

(a) shall not apply in relation to the building, or

(b) shall apply in relation to it with such modifications as may be specified in the order.

(2) The reference in subsection (1) to plans or particulars approved by the Secretary of State includes a reference to—

(a) particulars submitted to and approved by him under regulations under section 544 or section 218(7) of the Education Reform Act 1988, or

(b) particulars given in pursuance of section 428(2)(b).

Control of potentially harmful materials and apparatus

Control of potentially harmful materials and apparatus in schools

546.—(1) Regulations may make provision for requiring the Secretary of State's approval to be obtained for the use in schools to which this section applies of such materials or apparatus as may be specified in the regulations, being materials or apparatus which could or might involve a serious risk to health.

(2) The schools to which this section applies are—

(a) any school maintained by a local education authority,

(b) any grant-maintained school, and

(c) any special school not maintained by a local education authority.

Nuisance or disturbance on school premises

Nuisance or disturbance on school premises

547.—(1) Any person who without lawful authority is present on premises to which this section applies and causes or permits nuisance or disturbance to the annoyance of persons who lawfully use those premises (whether or not any such persons are present at the time) is guilty of an offence and liable on summary conviction to a fine not exceeding level 2 on the standard scale.

(2) This section applies to premises, including playgrounds, playing fields and other premises for outdoor recreation, of—

(a) any school maintained by a local education authority, or

(b) any grant-maintained school.

(3) If—

(a) a police constable, or

(b) (subject to subsection (5)) a person whom a local education authority have authorised to exercise the power conferred by this subsection,

has reasonable cause to suspect that any person is committing or has committed an offence under this section, he may remove him from the premises in question.

(4) The power conferred by subsection (3) may also be exercised, in relation to premises of an aided, special agreement or grant-maintained school, by a person whom the governing body have authorised to exercise it.

(5) A local education authority may not authorise a person to exercise the power conferred by subsection (3) in relation to premises of a voluntary or grant-maintained school without first obtaining the consent of the governing body.

(6) Subject to subsection (7), no proceedings for an offence under this section shall be brought by any person other than—

(a) a police constable, or

(b) a local education authority.

(7) Proceedings for an offence under this section committed on premises of an aided, special agreement or grant-maintained school may be brought by a person whom the governing body have authorised to bring such proceedings.

(8) A local education authority may not bring proceedings for an offence under this section committed on premises of a voluntary or grant-maintained school without first obtaining the consent of the governing body.

CHAPTER II

CORPORAL PUNISHMENT

No right to give corporal punishment

548.—(1) Where, in any proceedings, it is shown that corporal punishment has been given to any pupil to whom this subsection applies by or on the authority of a member of the staff, giving the punishment cannot be justified on the ground that it was done in pursuance of a right exercisable by the member of the staff by virtue of his position as such.

(2) Where, in any proceedings, it is shown that corporal punishment has been given to any pupil by or on the authority of a member of the staff, giving the punishment cannot be justified if it was inhuman or degrading.

(3) Subsection (1) applies to—

(a) any pupil for whom education is provided—

(i) at a school maintained by a local education authority,

(ii) at a special school not so maintained, or

(iii) at a grant-maintained school;

(b) any pupil for whom education is provided at an independent school—

(i) which is maintained or assisted by a Minister of the Crown (including a school of which a government department is a proprietor) or is assisted by a local education authority, and

(ii) which falls within a prescribed class;

(c) any pupil for whom education is provided by a local education authority otherwise than at a school; and

(d) any pupil who is an assisted person for the purposes of this paragraph and for whom education is provided at an independent school not falling within paragraph (b) above.

(4) A pupil is an assisted person for the purposes of subsection (3)(d) if—

(a) he holds an assisted place under the scheme operated by the Secretary of State under section 479;

(b) any of the fees or expenses payable in respect of his attendance at school are paid by—

(i) the Secretary of State under section 491, or

(ii) a local education authority under section 517, or

(iii) the funding authority or a local education authority under paragraph 9 or 10 of Schedule 4;

(c) any of the fees payable in respect of his attendance at school are paid

by a local education authority under section 518; or
(d) he falls within a prescribed category of persons.

(5) The Secretary of State may prescribe, for the purposes of subsection (4)(d), one or more categories of persons who appear to him to be persons in respect of whom any fees are paid out of public funds.

(6) A person does not commit an offence by reason of any conduct relating to a pupil which would, apart from this section, be justified on the ground that it is done in pursuance of a right exercisable by a member of the staff by virtue of his position as such.

Interpretation of section 548

549.—(1) Subject to subsection (2), references in section 548 to giving corporal punishment are to doing anything for the purpose of punishing the pupil concerned (whether or not there are also other reasons for doing it) which, apart from any justification, would constitute battery.

(2) A person is not to be taken for the purposes of section 548 as giving corporal punishment by virtue of anything done for reasons that include averting an immediate danger of personal injury to, or an immediate danger to the property of, any person (including the pupil concerned).

(3) In determining for the purposes of section 548(2) whether punishment is inhuman or degrading regard shall be had to all the circumstances of the case, including the reason for giving it, how soon after the event it is given, its nature, the manner and circumstances in which it is given, the persons involved and its mental and physical effects.

(4) In section 548 "member of the staff" means—
(a) in relation to a person who is a pupil by reason of the provision of education for him at a school, any teacher who works at the school and any other person who has lawful control or charge of the pupil and works there; and
(b) in relation to a person who is a pupil by reason of the provision of education for him by a local education authority at a place other than a school, any teacher employed by the authority who works at that place and any other person employed by the authority who has lawful control or charge of the pupil and works there.

(5) In section 548 and this section "pupil" does not include any person who has attained the age of 18.

No avoidance of section 548 by refusing admission to school etc.

550. A person shall not be debarred from receiving education (whether by refusing him admission to a school, suspending his attendance or otherwise) by reason of the fact that any provision of section 548 applies in relation to him or, if he were admitted, might so apply.

CHAPTER III

OTHER PROVISIONS ABOUT SCHOOLS

Duration of school day etc.

Regulations as to duration of school day etc.

551.—(1) Regulations may make provision with respect to the duration of the school day and school year at, and the granting of leave of absence from, any schools to which this section applies.

(2) The schools to which this section applies are—
(a) any school maintained by a local education authority;
(b) any grant-maintained school; and
(c) any special school not maintained by a local education authority.

Single-sex schools

Transitional exemption orders for purposes of Sex Discrimination Act 1975

552.—(1) Where—

(a) by reason of section 37(7)(b), 43(4)(b), 169(6)(b) or 199(2) any proposals for a school to cease to be an establishment which admits pupils of one sex only may not be determined until the Secretary of State has made his determination with respect to any proposals for acquisition of grant-maintained status, and

(b) the proposals for acquisition of grant-maintained status and the proposals for the school to cease to be such an establishment are approved (with or without modification),

paragraph 1 of Schedule 2 to the 1975 Act shall not apply but the new governing body shall be treated as having applied for the making by the Secretary of State of a transitional exemption order, and he may make such an order accordingly.

(2) Where the governing body of a grant-maintained school publish under section 259 proposals for the school to cease to be an establishment which admits pupils of one sex only and (by virtue of section 264(1)) Part III of this Act has effect with the modifications in section 264(2) to (7) in relation to the proposals, then—

(a) paragraph 1 of Schedule 2 to the 1975 Act shall not apply unless the proposals require the approval of the Secretary of State, and

(b) in any other case, the governing body shall be treated as having applied for the making by the funding authority of a transitional exemption order, and the funding authority may make such an order accordingly.

(3) Where under section 260 the funding authority submit to the Secretary of State a copy of proposals for a school to cease to be an establishment which admits pupils of one sex only, then—

(a) if the proposals require the approval of the Secretary of State, the governing body shall be treated as having applied for the making by him of a transitional exemption order, and

(b) in any other case, the governing body shall be treated as having applied for the making by the funding authority of such an order,

and the Secretary of State or, as the case may be, the funding authority may make such an order accordingly.

(4) Where in pursuance of section 339(1)(b) a local education authority serve notice of proposals for a maintained special school to cease to be an establishment which admits pupils of one sex only, the responsible body shall be treated as having applied for the making by the Secretary of State of a transitional exemption order, and the Secretary of State may make such an order accordingly.

(5) Where proposals made by the Secretary of State under section 502—

(a) are for a school to cease to be an establishment which admits pupils of one sex only, and

(b) have effect as mentioned in section 504(3),

the responsible body shall be treated as having applied for the making by the Secretary of State of a transitional exemption order, and the Secretary of State may make such an order accordingly.

(6) In this section—

"the 1975 Act" means the Sex Discrimination Act 1975,

"responsible body" has the same meaning as in section 22 of the 1975 Act, and

"transitional exemption order" has the same meaning as in section 27 of the 1975 Act,

and references to proposals for a school to cease to be an establishment which admits pupils of one sex only are references to proposals which are or include proposals for such an alteration in a school's admissions arrangements as is mentioned in section 27(1) of the 1975 Act (single-sex establishments becoming co-educational).

Educational trusts

Schemes under the Endowed Schools Acts

553.—(1) Where under any provision (however expressed) of a scheme made under the Endowed Schools Acts 1869 to 1948 the power of the trustees under the scheme to apply any property to which the scheme relates for purposes authorised by the scheme is subject to the approval or order of any other person, the scheme shall have effect as if no such approval or order was required.

(2) The Secretary of State may, on the application of any person whose approval or order would apart from this section be required under such a scheme, direct that the requirement shall continue to have effect despite subsection (1); but no liability shall be taken to have been incurred in respect of any failure before the making of such a direction to obtain any such approval or order.

Religious educational trusts

Power to make new provision as to use of endowments

554.—(1) This section applies where—

(a) the premises of a voluntary or grant-maintained school have ceased to be used for a voluntary or (as the case may be) grant-maintained school; or

(b) in the opinion of the Secretary of State it is likely such premises will cease to be so used.

(2) In such a case the Secretary of State may (subject to sections 555 and 556(1) and (2)) by order make new provision as to the use of any endowment if it is shown either—

(a) that the endowment is or has been held wholly or partly for or in connection with the provision at the school of religious education in accordance with the tenets of a particular religion or religious denomination; or

(b) that the endowment is or has been used wholly or partly for or in connection with the provision at the school of such religious education and that (subject to subsection (4)) the requirements of subsection (3) are fulfilled.

(3) The requirements of this subsection are—

(a) that the school was or has been maintained as a voluntary school since 1st April 1945 (the date when Part II of the Education Act 1944 came into force) or, in the case of a grant-maintained school, was so maintained from that date until immediately before it became a grant-maintained school; and

(b) that religious education in accordance with the tenets of the religion or denomination concerned—

(i) is, and has been from that date, provided at the school, or

(ii) where the premises have ceased to be used for the purposes of the school, was provided at the school from that date until immediately before the premises ceased to be so used,

in pursuance of section 377 or 378 or section 380 or 381 (or any corresponding earlier enactment).

(4) For the purposes of this section—

(a) where in the case of any school falling within subsection (3)(a) it is shown—

(i) that religious education in accordance with the tenets of a particular religion or denomination is provided at the school, or

(ii) if the premises have ceased to be used for the purposes of the school, such religious education was so provided immediately before the premises ceased to be so used,

such religious education shall be taken to have been provided at the school from 1st April 1945, unless the contrary is shown; and

(b) where religious education in accordance with such tenets is shown to have been given to any pupils at a controlled school or a grant-maintained school which was a controlled school immediately before it became a grant-maintained school, the religious education shall be taken to have been given to them at the request of their parents, unless the contrary is shown.

(5) For the purposes of this section—

"endowment" includes property not subject to any restriction on the expenditure of capital; and

"shown" means shown to the satisfaction of the Secretary of State.

(6) This section applies where the premises of a non-provided public elementary school ceased before 1st April 1945 to be used for such a school as it applies where the premises of a voluntary school have ceased to be used for such a school.

Procedure applicable to orders under section 554

555.—(1) No order shall be made under section 554 except on the application of the persons appearing to the Secretary of State to be the appropriate authority of the religion or denomination concerned.

(2) The Secretary of State shall, not less than one month before making an order under section 554, give notice of the proposed order and of the right of persons interested to make representations on it.

(3) Such notice shall be given—

(a) by giving to any persons appearing to the Secretary of State to be trustees of an endowment affected by the proposed order a notice of the proposal to make it, together with a draft or summary of the provisions proposed to be included; and

(b) by publishing, in such manner as the Secretary of State thinks sufficient for informing any other persons interested, a notice of the proposal to make the order and of the place where any person interested may (during a period of not less than a month) inspect such a draft or summary, and by keeping a draft or summary available for inspection in accordance with the notice.

(4) The Secretary of State shall take into account any representations made to him by any person interested before the order is made.

(5) In this section "endowment" has the same meaning as in section 554.

Content of orders under section 554

556.—(1) An order under section 554—

(a) may require or authorise the disposal by sale or otherwise of any land or other property forming part of an endowment affected by the order, including the premises of the school and any teacher's dwelling-house; and

(b) may consolidate any endowments to be dealt with by the scheme.

(2) Subject to subsection (1), and to any provision affecting the endowments which is a provision of a public general Act of Parliament, an order under section 554 shall establish and give effect, with a view to enabling the religion or denomination concerned to participate more effectively in the administration of the statutory system of public education, to a scheme or

schemes for the endowments dealt with by the order to be used for appropriate educational purposes either—

(a) in connection with schools which are voluntary schools or grant-maintained schools; or

(b) partly in connection with such schools (or either description of such schools) and partly in other ways related to the locality served by the voluntary or grant-maintained school at the premises that have gone or are to go out of use for such a school.

(3) In subsection (2) "use for appropriate educational purposes" means use for educational purposes in connection with the provision of religious education in accordance with the tenets of the religion or denomination concerned (including in particular, but without prejudice to the generality of the foregoing, use for any purpose specified in Schedule 36).

(4) A scheme given effect under section 554—

(a) may provide for the retention of the capital of any endowment and application of the accruing income; or

(b) may authorise the application or expenditure of capital to such extent and subject to such conditions as may be determined by or in accordance with the scheme;

and any such scheme may provide for the endowments dealt with by the scheme or any part of them to be added to any existing endowment applicable for any such purpose as is authorised for the scheme by subsection (2).

(5) Where a scheme given effect under section 554 provides for the endowments dealt with by the order or any part of them to be used for the purposes specified in Schedule 36, any such scheme may provide for the endowments thereby dealt with or any part of them to be added to any existing endowment applicable for those purposes (whether it is so applicable by virtue of a scheme given effect to under that section or otherwise).

(6) Section 568(5) does not apply to an order under section 554, but such an order may include such incidental or supplementary provisions as appear to the Secretary of State to be necessary or expedient either for the bringing into force or for the operation of any scheme established by it, including in particular provisions—

(a) for the appointment and powers of trustees of the property comprised in the scheme or, if the property is not all applicable for the same purposes, of any part of that property; and

(b) for the property or any part of it to vest by virtue of the scheme in the first trustees under the scheme or trustees of any endowment to which it is to be added or, if not so vested, to be transferred to them.

(7) Any order under section 554 shall have effect despite any Act of Parliament (other than a public general Act), letters patent or other instrument relating to, or trust affecting, the endowments dealt with by the order.

(8) In this section "endowment" has the same meaning as in section 554.

Adoption of statutory trusts

557.—(1) This section applies to endowments which are—

(a) regulated by a qualifying scheme under the Endowed Schools Acts 1869 to 1948 as applied by section 86(1) of the Education Act 1944 or by an order under section 554 of this Act or section 2 of the Education Act 1973; and

(b) held under any such scheme or order on trusts which provide for capital or income or both to be applicable for or in connection with—

(i) the provision of religious education at relevant schools, or relevant schools of any description (but not only at a particular school or schools) in a diocese or other geographical area; or

(ii) the provision of premises for relevant schools, or relevant schools of any description (but not only at a particular school or schools) at which religious education is or is to be provided in a diocese or other geographical area;

but this section does not apply to an endowment if or in so far as it constitutes a religious education fund.

(2) The trustees of any endowments to which this section applies may, by resolution complying with subsection (6), adopt the uniform statutory trusts as the trusts on which those endowments are to be held.

(3) The uniform statutory trusts are those set out in Schedule 36.

(4) On the adoption by trustees of the uniform statutory trusts in respect of any endowments the scheme or order which regulates the endowments shall have effect as if the uniform statutory trusts are incorporated in the scheme or order to the exclusion of the corresponding provisions of the scheme or order.

(5) The trustees of two or more endowments which are held on the uniform statutory trusts may, by resolution complying with subsection (6), consolidate all or any of those endowments and, where they do so, the endowments shall be treated, for all purposes, as held for the purposes of a single charity.

(6) For a resolution to comply with this subsection—

(a) it must be passed by a simple majority of the trustees or, if the trustees are a body corporate or a company, by a simple majority of the members of the body corporate or an ordinary resolution of the company; and

(b) it must be recorded in the records of the decisions of the trustees affecting the endowments of the trust.

(7) Where trustees pass a resolution under subsection (2), it shall be their duty to send a copy of the resolution to the Secretary of State.

(8) The uniform statutory trusts applicable to endowments to which this section applies shall not affect—

(a) the rights of any person under the third proviso to section 2 of the School Sites Act 1841, under section 86(3) of the Education Act 1944 or under section 1 of the Reverter of Sites Act 1987 (rights replacing certain reversionary interests in land), or

(b) the rights of any local education authority which have arisen under paragraph 7 or 8 of the First Schedule to the Education Act 1946 (rights in relation to school sites provided by such authorities) or which may arise under section 60(4) or 62(2),

except in so far as any right falling within paragraph (a) above is or has been extinguished by an order under section 554 of this Act or section 2 of the Education Act 1973 made by virtue of section 5 of the Reverter of Sites Act 1987.

(9) In this section—

"company" means a company formed under the Companies Acts;

"the Companies Acts" means the Companies Act 1985, the Companies Act 1948 or any Act repealed by that Act of 1948;

"endowment" has the same meaning as in section 554;

"provision", in relation to premises, means provision by the purchase of a site, the erection of premises or the maintenance, improvement or enlargement of premises;

"qualifying scheme" means a scheme in force on 1st January 1994 (the date when section 287 of the Education Act 1993 came into force);

"relevant school" means a voluntary school or a grant-maintained school;

"religious education" means religious education in accordance with the tenets of a particular religion or religious denomination; and

"religious education fund" includes a Sunday school fund.

(10) In Schedule 36 as incorporated in any scheme or order—

"the area" means the diocese or other geographical area within which the trust assets may be applied under the scheme or order, as the case may be;

"relevant school" means a relevant school at which the religious education provided for in the scheme or order, as the case may be, is or is to be provided; and

"the relevant trust assets" means the endowments in respect of which the trustees have adopted the uniform statutory trusts, including the income derived therefrom.

CHAPTER IV

EMPLOYMENT OF CHILDREN AND YOUNG PERSONS

Meaning of "child" for purposes of enactments relating to employment of children or young persons

558. For the purposes of any enactment relating to the prohibition or regulation of the employment of children or young persons, any person who is not over compulsory school age shall be deemed to be a child within the meaning of that enactment.

Power of local education authorities to prohibit or restrict employment of children

559.—(1) If it appears to a local education authority that a child who is a registered pupil at a county, voluntary or special school is being employed in such a manner as to be prejudicial to his health, or otherwise to render him unfit to obtain the full benefit of the education provided for him, the authority may serve a notice in writing on the employer—

(a) prohibiting him from employing the child, or

(b) imposing such restrictions upon his employment of the child as appear to them to be expedient in the interests of the child.

(2) A local education authority may serve a notice in writing on the parent or employer of a child who is a registered pupil at a county, voluntary or special school requiring the parent or employer to provide the authority, within such period as may be specified in the notice, with such information as appears to the authority to be necessary for the purpose of enabling them to ascertain whether the child is being employed in such a manner as to render him unfit to obtain the full benefit of the education provided for him.

(3) A person who—

(a) employs a child in contravention of any prohibition or restriction imposed under subsection (1), or

(b) fails to comply with the requirements of a notice served under subsection (2),

shall be guilty of an offence.

(4) A person guilty of an offence under this section shall be liable on summary conviction—

(a) to a fine not exceeding level 1 on the standard scale, or

(b) to imprisonment for a term not exceeding one month,

or both.

(5) Section 28(1) and (3) of the Children and Young Persons Act 1933 (powers of entry for the enforcement of the provisions of Part II of that Act as to the employment of children) shall apply with respect to the provisions of any notice served under this section as they apply with respect to the provisions of Part II of that Act.

(6) This section shall cease to have effect on the coming into force of section 2 of the Employment of Children Act 1973.

Work experience in last year of compulsory schooling

560.—(1) The enactments relating to the prohibition or regulation of the employment of children shall not apply to the employment of a child in his last year of compulsory schooling if the employment is in pursuance of arrangements made or approved—

(a) by the local education authority, or
(b) in the case of a child at a grant-maintained school, by the governing body of the school,

with a view to providing him with work experience as a part of his education.

(2) For the purposes of subsection (1) a child shall be taken to be in his last year of compulsory schooling from the beginning of the term at his school which precedes the beginning of the school year in which he would cease to be of compulsory school age.

(3) Subsection (1) shall not be taken to permit the employment of a person in any way contrary to—

(a) an enactment which in terms applies to persons of less than, or not over, a specified age expressed as a number of years, or
(b) section 1(2) of the Employment of Women, Young Persons and Children Act 1920 or section 55(1) of the Merchant Shipping Act 1995 (which prohibit the employment of children in ships).

(4) No arrangements shall be made under subsection (1) for a child to be employed in any way which would be contrary to an enactment prohibiting or regulating the employment of young persons if he were a young person (within the meaning of the enactment) and not a child.

(5) Where a child is employed in pursuance of arrangements made under subsection (1), so much of any enactment as—

(a) regulates the employment of young persons (whether by excluding them from any description of work, prescribing the conditions under which they may be permitted to do it or in any other way), and
(b) would apply in relation to him if he were of an age to be treated as a young person for the purposes of that enactment,

shall apply in relation to him, in and in respect of the employment arranged for him, in all respects as if he were of an age to be so treated.

(6) Nothing in section 495 or 496 applies in relation to any power conferred on a local education authority or the governing body of a grant-maintained school by subsection (1).

(7) In this section "enactment" includes any byelaw, regulation or other provision having effect under an enactment.

CHAPTER V

PERSONS NOT COVERED BY ACT

Act not to apply to persons in service of the Crown

561. No power or duty conferred or imposed by this Act on—

(a) the Secretary of State,
(b) local education authorities, or
(c) parents,

shall be construed as relating to any person who is employed by or under the Crown in any service or capacity with respect to which the Secretary of State certifies that, by reason of the arrangements made for the education of children and young persons so employed, the exercise and performance of those powers and duties with respect to such children and young persons is unnecessary.

Act not to apply to persons detained under order of a court

562.—(1) No power or duty conferred or imposed by or under this Act on—

(a) the Secretary of State,

(b) local education authorities, or
(c) parents,

shall be construed as relating to any person who is detained in pursuance of an order made by a court or of an order of recall made by the Secretary of State, but a local education authority may make arrangements for a person who is detained in pursuance of such an order to receive the benefit of educational facilities provided by the authority.

(2) A child or young person who is being educated as a boarder at a school shall not be regarded for the purposes of subsection (1) as detained in pursuance of an order made by a court by reason of the fact that he is required to be at the school—

(a) by virtue of an order made by a court under the Children and Young Persons Act 1933 or by virtue of anything done under such an order; or
(b) by virtue of a requirement of a probation order or by virtue of anything done under such a requirement.

CHAPTER VI

GENERAL

Documents and evidence

Educational records

563.—(1) Regulations may make provision as to—

(a) the keeping, disclosure and transfer of educational records about persons receiving education at schools to which this section applies; and
(b) the supply of copies of such records to such persons, and in such circumstances, as may be determined by or under the regulations.

(2) The regulations may authorise persons who supply copies of such records in pursuance of the regulations to charge such fee as they think fit (not exceeding the cost of supply) in respect of each copy so supplied.

(3) The schools to which this section applies are—

(a) any school maintained by a local education authority;
(b) any grant-maintained school; and
(c) any special school not maintained by a local education authority.

Certificates of birth and registrars' returns

564.—(1) Where the age of any person is required to be proved for the purposes of this Act or of any enactment relating to the employment of children or young persons, the registrar having the custody of the register of birth and deaths containing the entry relating to the birth of that person shall—

(a) on being presented by any person ("the applicant") with a written requisition in such form and containing such particulars as may be determined by regulations, and
(b) on payment of a fee of £2.00,

supply the applicant with a copy of the entry certified under his hand.

(2) A registrar shall, on being requested so to do, supply free of charge a form of requisition for the purposes of subsection (1).

(3) A registrar shall supply to a local education authority such particulars of the entries contained in any register of births and deaths in his custody, and in such form, as (subject to regulations) the authority may from time to time require.

(4) In this section—

"register of births and deaths" means a register of births and deaths kept under the Births and Deaths Registration Act 1953, and

"registrar" includes a registrar of births and deaths and a superintendent registrar.

Evidence: presumption as to age

565.—(1) Where in any proceedings under this Act the person by whom the proceedings are brought—

(a) alleges that any person whose age is material to the proceedings is under, of, or over, any age, and

(b) satisfies the court that, having used all reasonable diligence to obtain evidence as to the age of that person, he has been unable to do so,

the court may, unless the contrary is proved, presume that person to be under, of, or (as the case may be) over, the age alleged.

(2) This section has effect subject to section 445(3).

Evidence: documents

566.—(1) In any legal proceedings, any of the following documents, namely—

(a) a document purporting to be a document issued by a local education authority, and to be signed by the clerk of that authority or by the chief education officer of that authority or by any other officer of the authority authorised to sign it,

(b) a document purporting to be an extract from the minutes of the proceedings of the governing body of a county or voluntary school, and to be signed by the chairman of the governing body or by their clerk,

(c) a document purporting to be a certificate giving particulars of the attendance of a child or young person at a school, and to be signed by the head teacher of the school, and

(d) a document purporting to be a certificate issued by a medical officer of a local education authority, and to be signed by such an officer,

shall be received in evidence and shall be treated, without further proof, as the document which it purports to be and as having been signed by the person by whom it purports to have been signed, unless the contrary is proved.

(2) In any legal proceedings, any such extract or certificate as is mentioned in subsection (1)(b), (c) or (d) shall be evidence of the matters stated in it.

Stamp duty

Stamp duty

567.—(1) Subject to subsection (5), stamp duty shall not be chargeable in respect of any transfer effected under—

(a) section 201 (taken with section 198 of, and Schedule 10 to, the Education Reform Act 1988), or

(b) section 279(3) or (4).

(2) Subject to subsection (5), stamp duty shall not be chargeable in respect of any transfer to a funding authority under section 277.

(3) Subject to subsection (5), stamp duty shall not be chargeable in respect of any transfer to a local education authority—

(a) under or by virtue of section 277(1)(a) or 298(2) of property which immediately after the transfer is held by the authority for the purposes of a county or voluntary school or a maintained special school not established in a hospital, or

(b) by virtue of section 277(2) of property which immediately after the transfer is held by the authority for the purposes of a new county school.

(4) Subject to subsection (5), stamp duty shall not be chargeable in respect of any transfer to the governing body of a grant-maintained school—

(a) by virtue of section 277(2), or

(b) in the case of a school established under section 211(2) or 212, from the funding authority.

(5) No instrument (other than a statutory instrument) made or executed

under or in pursuance of any of the provisions mentioned in subsections (1) to (4) above shall be treated as duly stamped unless it is stamped with the duty to which it would, but for this section (and, if applicable, section 129 of the Finance Act 1982), be liable or it has, in accordance with the provisions of section 12 of the Stamp Act 1891, been stamped with a particular stamp denoting that it is not chargeable with any duty or that it has been duly stamped.

Orders, regulations and directions

Orders

568.—(1) Any power of the Secretary of State to make orders under this Act (other than an order under any of the excepted provisions) shall be exercised by statutory instrument.

(2) For the purposes of subsection (1) "the excepted provisions" are—
sections 24 and 27;
sections 46 to 48, 50, 51, 54, 55, 57, 58, 63, 64, 77(7), 85, 95(1), 104(1), 110(4), 112(4), 128(6) and 179;
sections 202, 220, 233, 274 and 302 and the definition of "Church in Wales school" in section 311(1);
section 349;
sections 420(2) and 427;
sections 468, 471(1) and 474;
section 489(3),
sections 497, 500, 501 and 516;
section 545; and
paragraph 5 of Schedule 21 and paragraph 3 of Schedule 28.

(3) A statutory instrument containing any order made by the Secretary of State under this Act, other than an order under—
section 354(6), 355(2)(a), 356(2)(c) or 401,
section 517(6),
section 554,
section 583(3) or (4), or
Schedule 40,
shall be subject to annulment in pursuance of a resolution of either House of Parliament.

(4) No order shall be made under section 354(6), 355(2)(a) or 401 unless a draft of the instrument containing the order has been laid before, and approved by a resolution of, each House of Parliament.

(5) Any order made—
(a) by the Secretary of State under this Act by statutory instrument, or
(b) by the funding authority under section 220, 233 or 302 or paragraph 5 of Schedule 21,
may make different provision for different cases, circumstances or areas and may contain such incidental, supplemental, saving or transitional provisions as the Secretary of State thinks fit.

(6) Without prejudice to the generality of subsection (5), an order made by the Secretary of State under this Act by statutory instrument may make in relation to Wales provision different from that made in relation to England.

Regulations

569.—(1) Any power of the Secretary of State to make regulations under this Act shall be exercised by statutory instrument.

(2) A statutory instrument containing regulations under this Act, other than regulations under section 480 or 492 or paragraph 1(4) of Schedule 20, shall be subject to annulment in pursuance of a resolution of either House of Parliament.

(3) No regulations shall be made under section 480 or 492 or paragraph 1(4) of Schedule 20 unless a draft of the instrument containing the regulations has been laid before, and approved by a resolution of, each House of Parliament.

(4) Regulations under this Act may make different provision for different cases, circumstances or areas and may contain such incidental, supplemental, saving or transitional provisions as the Secretary of State thinks fit.

(5) Without prejudice to the generality of subsection (4), regulations under this Act may make in relation to Wales provision different from that made in relation to England.

(6) Subsection (5) does not apply to regulations under section 579(4).

Revocation and variation of certain orders and directions

570.—(1) This section applies to any order or directions made or given under this Act by—

(a) the Secretary of State,
(b) the funding authority, or
(c) a local education authority,

other than an order to which section 568(1) applies.

(2) Subject to subsection (3), any such order or directions may be varied or revoked by a further order or directions made or given by the Secretary of State, the funding authority or the local education authority, as the case may be.

(3) Where the power to make or give any such order or directions is only exercisable—

(a) on the application or with the consent of any person or body of persons, or
(b) after consultation with any person or body of persons, or
(c) subject to any other conditions,

no order or directions made or given under that power may be varied or revoked under subsection (2) unless the same conditions are complied with.

Guidance

Publication of guidance

571.—(1) The Secretary of State shall publish any guidance given by him for the purposes of any of the provisions mentioned in subsection (2) below in such manner as he thinks fit.

(2) Those provisions are—

(a) sections 35(5), 41(7), 104 and 167(4);
(b) sections 189, 211, 212, 259(3), 260(4), 267(2) and 268(4); and
(c) section 340(1).

Service of documents

Service of notices and other documents

572. Any order, notice or other document required or authorised by this Act to be served on any person may be served—

(a) by delivering it to that person, or
(b) by leaving it at his usual or last known place of residence, or
(c) by sending it in a prepaid letter addressed to him at that place.

Construction

Meaning of expressions relating to alteration etc. of premises or character of schools

573.—(1) The following provisions apply for the purposes of this Act except where the context otherwise requires.

(2) References to the alteration of school premises include making improvements, extensions or additions to the premises; and "alterations", in relation to any school premises, shall be construed similarly except that it does not include a significant enlargement of the premises.

(3) References to the enlargement of any school premises include any modification of the school's existing premises which has the effect of increasing the number of pupils for whom accommodation can be provided.

(4) Subject to section 41(4) and section 266(1), references to a change in the character of a school include, in particular, changes in character resulting from—

(a) education beginning or ceasing to be provided for pupils above or below a particular age, for boys as well as girls or for girls as well as boys, or
(b) the making or alteration of arrangements for the admission of pupils by reference to ability or aptitude.

(5) In relation to a change in the character of a school or an enlargement of school premises, "significant" implies that there is a substantial change in the function or size of the school.

(6) If a question arises whether a change in the character of a county, voluntary or grant-maintained school or an enlargement of its premises would be a significant change or enlargement, that question shall be determined by the Secretary of State.

Changes to school not amounting to discontinuance etc.

574.—(1) For the purposes of this Act and any other enactment relating to the duties of a local education authority neither—

(a) references in whatever terms to discontinuing a school (including those to a local authority ceasing to maintain a school), nor
(b) references in whatever terms to establishing a new school,

shall be read as applying by reason only of a change such as is mentioned in subsection (2) being made to an existing school (so that, where such a change is made to an existing school, the school shall be regarded as continuing despite the change and as being the same school before and after it, unless for other reasons it is to be regarded as discontinued).

(2) The changes are—

(a) education beginning or ceasing to be provided for pupils above or below a particular age, for boys as well as girls or for girls as well as boys;
(b) an enlargement or alteration of the school premises; and
(c) the transfer of the school to a new site.

Meaning, for certain purposes, of expressions relating to employment

575.—(1) In the provisions to which this section applies—

(a) "contract of employment", "employee" and "employer" have the same meaning as in the Employment Rights Act 1996, and
(b) "employed" means employed under a contract of employment.

(2) This section applies to—

(a) the provisions of Chapter VI of Part II relating to schools with delegated budgets;
(b) Parts III and V; and
(c) Schedule 7.

(3) For the purposes of the provisions to which this section applies—

(a) a person employed by a local education authority is to be regarded as employed to work at a school if his employment with the authority for the time being involves work at that school, and
(b) a person employed by a local education authority is to be regarded as

employed to work solely at a school if his only employment with the authority (disregarding any employment under a separate contract with the authority) is for the time being at that school.

(4) Subsection (1) also applies for construing references to "employed" in subsection (3).

(5) Nothing in this section affects the construction of any of the expressions defined by this section where they occur in provisions of this Act other than those to which this section applies.

Meaning of "parent"

576.—(1) In this Act, unless the context otherwise requires, "parent", in relation to a child or young person, includes any person—

(a) who is not a parent of his but who has parental responsibility for him, or

(b) who has care of him,

except that in the provisions mentioned in subsection (2) it only includes such a person if he is an individual.

(2) Those provisions are—

(a) sections 78(3), 81(4), 162, 186 to 188, 190, 200, 223, 226 and 228; and

(b) paragraph 7(2) and (7) of Schedule 8, paragraph 7(1) of Schedule 9, Schedule 18, paragraph 8 of Schedule 23 and Schedule 24.

(3) In subsection (1) "parental responsibility" has the same meaning as in the Children Act 1989.

(4) In determining for the purposes of subsection (1) whether an individual has care of a child or young person, any absence of the child or young person at a hospital or boarding school and any other temporary absence shall be disregarded.

Minor authorities

577.—(1) For the purposes of this Act a school maintained by a local education authority serves an area for which there is a minor authority if the area served by the school is—

(a) a parish or community;

(b) an area in England which is not within a parish and is not situated in—

(i) a county for which there is no council, or

(ii) a county in which there are no district councils; or

(c) an area comprising two or more areas each of which falls within paragraph (a) or (b).

(2) Where the area served by the school is a parish, the minor authority in relation to the school is—

(a) the parish council (if there is one), or

(b) the parish meeting (if there is no parish council).

(3) Where the area served by the school is a community, the minor authority in relation to the school is the community council.

(4) Where the area served by the school is an area falling within subsection (1)(b), the minor authority in relation to the school is the district council for the area.

(5) Where the area served by the school is an area falling within subsection (1)(c), the relevant authorities acting jointly are the minor authority in relation to the school.

(6) In subsection (5) "the relevant authorities" means the bodies which, if the two or more constituent areas referred to in subsection (1)(c) were taken separately, would be the minor authorities for those areas.

(7) References in this section to the area served by a school are references to the area appearing to the local education authority to be served by the school.

Meaning of "the Education Acts"

578. In this Act "the Education Acts" means this Act together with the following Acts—

the Education Act 1962;
the Education Act 1967;
the Education Act 1973;
the Education Act 1980;
the Education (Fees and Awards) Act 1983;
the Further Education Act 1985 (except sections 4 and 5);
the Education Act 1986;
the Education (No. 2) Act 1986;
the Education Reform Act 1988;
the Education (Student Loans) Act 1990;
the School Teachers' Pay and Conditions Act 1991;
the Further and Higher Education Act 1992;
the Education Act 1994;
the Education (Student Loans) Act 1996;
the Nursery Education and Grant-Maintained Schools Act 1996;
the School Inspections Act 1996.

General interpretation

579.—(1) In this Act, unless the context otherwise requires—

"the appropriate further education funding council" has the meaning given by section 1(6) of the Further and Higher Education Act 1992;

"boarder" includes a pupil who boards during the week but not at weekends;

"child" means a person who is not over compulsory school age;

"clothing" includes footwear;

"exclude", in relation to the exclusion of a pupil from a school (otherwise than under section 524), means exclude on disciplinary grounds (and "exclusion" shall be construed accordingly);

"financial year" means a period of twelve months ending with 31st March;

"functions" includes powers and duties;

"governing body" or "governors" (without more), in relation to a voluntary school and any function conferred or imposed by this Act exclusively on the foundation governors of such a school, means the foundation governors of the school;

"head teacher" includes acting head teacher;

"higher education" means education provided by means of a course of any description mentioned in Schedule 6 to the Education Reform Act 1988;

"land" includes buildings and other structures, land covered with water, and any interest in land;

"liability" includes obligation;

"local authority" means a county council, a county borough council, a district council, a London borough council or the Common Council of the City of London;

"the local education authority"—

(a) in relation to a school maintained (or proposed to be maintained) by a local authority, means (in accordance with section 34(1)) that authority; and

(b) in relation to a grant-maintained school, means the local education authority for the area in which the school is situated;

"local government elector" has the meaning given by section 270(1) of the Local Government Act 1972;

"medical officer", in relation to a local education authority, means a registered medical practitioner who is employed or engaged (whether regularly or for the purposes of any particular case) by the authority or whose services are made available to the authority by the Secretary of State;

"modifications" includes additions, alterations and omissions and "modify" shall be construed accordingly;

"premises", in relation to a school, includes any detached playing fields but, except where otherwise expressly provided, does not include a teacher's dwelling-house;

"prescribed" means prescribed by regulations;

"proprietor", in relation to a school, means the person or body of persons responsible for the management of the school (so that, in relation to a county, voluntary or grant-maintained school, it means the governing body);

"reception class" means a class in which education is provided which is suitable to the requirements of pupils aged five and any pupils under or over that age whom it is expedient to educate with pupils of that age;

"regulations" means regulations made by the Secretary of State;

"relevant age group", in relation to a school, means an age group in which pupils are normally admitted (or, as the case may be, will normally be admitted) to the school;

"school buildings", in relation to a school, means any building or part of a building forming part of the school premises, other than a building or part required only—

(a) as a caretaker's dwelling,

(b) for use in connection with playing fields,

(c) to afford facilities for enabling the Secretary of State facilities to carry out his functions under section 5(1) or (1A) of, and Schedule 1 to, the National Health Service Act 1977 (which relate to the provision of medical and dental services for pupils), or

(d) to afford facilities for providing milk, meals or other refreshment for pupils in attendance at the school;

"school day", in relation to a school, means any day on which at that school there is a school session;

"trust deed", in relation to a voluntary school, includes any instrument (other than an instrument of government or articles of government made under this Act) regulating the constitution of the school's governing body or the maintenance, management or conduct of the school;

"young person" means a person over compulsory school age but under the age of 18.

(2) References in this Act to an interest in land include any easement, right or charge in, to or over land.

(3) For the purposes of this Act children are to be regarded as admitted to a school for nursery education if they are or are to be placed on admission in a nursery class.

(4) For the purposes of this Act a person shall be treated as belonging, or as not belonging, to the area of a particular local education authority in accordance with regulations; and any question under the regulations shall, in the case of a dispute, be determined by the Secretary of State.

(5) For the purposes of this Act a school shall be regarded as "assisted" by a local education authority who do not maintain it if the authority make to its proprietor any grant in respect of the school or any payment in consideration of the provision of educational facilities there.

(6) Subject to subsection (7), an institution other than a school shall be regarded for the purposes of this Act as "assisted" by a local education auth-

ority if the authority make to the persons responsible for its maintenance any grant in respect of the institution or any payment in consideration of the provision of educational facilities there.

(7) Neither—

(a) a university, nor

(b) any institution within the further education sector or within the higher education sector other than a university,

shall be regarded for the purposes of this Act as "assisted" by a local education authority by virtue of the making by the authority to the persons responsible for the maintenance of the university or institution of any grant or payment such as is mentioned in subsection (6).

Index

580. The expressions listed in the left-hand column below are defined by, or (as the case may be) are to be interpreted in accordance with, the provisions of this Act listed in the right-hand column in relation to those expressions.

Expression	*Relevant provision*
admission authority (in Chapter I of Part VI)	section 415
admitted to a school for nursery education	section 579(3)
aggregated budget (in Part II)	section 101(3) and 105
agreed syllabus	section 375(2) and (4)
aided school	section 32(1) and (3)
allocation formula (in Part II)	section 106(2)
alteration (of school premises) and alterations (in relation to such premises)	section 573(2)
annual parents' meeeting (in Chapter VI of Part II)	section 162(1)
appropriate diocesan authority (in Part III in relation to a Church of England, Church in Wales or Roman Catholic Church school)	section 311(1)
appropriate further education funding council	section 579(1)
area (of a local education authority)	section 12(6)
articles of government	
(in relation to a county, voluntary or maintained special school)	section 127(1)
(in relation to a grant-maintained school)	section section 218(1)
(in relation to a grant-maintained special school)	paragraph 1 of Schedule 28
(in relation to a group of grant-maintained schools)	section 280(2)
assess (in Part V)	section 350(2)
assessment arrangement (in Part V)	section 353
assisted (in relation to a school or other institution)	section 579(5) to (7)
assisted places scheme (in Part VII)	section 479(1)
attainment targets (in Part V)	section 353
authority responsible for election arrangements (in Chapter V or Part III)	section 243(2)
belonging to the area of a local education authority (in relation to a person)	section 579(4)
boarder	section 579(1)
budget share (in Part II)	section 101(3) and (6)
capital grant (in relation to grant-maintained schools)	section 246(1) (or section 252)
cease to maintain (in relation to a school)	section 574
the chairmen's panel (in Part IV)	section 333(2)
change in character (in relation to a school)	section 573(4)
character (of a school) (in Part III)	section 311(4)

child	
(generally)	section 579(1)
(in Part IV)	section 312(5)
child for whom a local education authority are responsible (in Part IV)	section 321(3)
Church in Wales school	section 311(1)
Church of England school	section 311(1)
city college of the technology of the arts	section 482(3)
city technology college	section 482(3)
clothing	section 579(1)
commencement of this Act	section 583(2)
compulsory school age	section 8 (or paragraph 1 of Schedule 40)
contract of employment (in relation to provisions specified in section 575(2)	section 575(1)
controlled school	section 32(1) and (2)
co-opted governor (in relation to a county, voluntary or maintained special school)	section 78(1)
core governor	section 285 and Schedule 25
county school	section 31(1)
date of implementation	
(in Part III in relation to proposals for acquisition of grant-maintained status)	section 200(2)
(in Part III in relation to a new grant-maintained school)	section 217
date of publication of proposals (in Part III in relation to proposals under that Part)	section 311(6)
delegation requirement (in Part II)	section 107(2)
discontinue (in relation to a school)	section 574
disposal of premises (in sections 297 to 300)	section 301(3)
dissolution date (in sections 274 to 279)	section 274(6)
the Education Acts	section 578
eligible for grant-maintained status (in Part III)	section 184
eligible governor (in Part III)	paragraph 4 of Schedule 24
eligible to vote in a ballot held in accordance with section 189 (in Chapter II of Part III)	section 190(1)
employed, employee, employer (in relation to provisions specified in section 575(2))	section 575(1)
employed to work, or to work solely, at a school (in relation to provisions specified in section 575(2))	section 575(3)
employee (in sections 469 to 473)	section 469(6)
enlargement (in relation to school premises)	section 573(3)
establish (in relation to a new school)	section 574
examination requirement (in Chapter III of Part VI	section 462(1)
exclude, exclusion (except in section 524)	section 579(1)
financial year	section 579(1)
first governor (in relation to a grant-maintained school)	paragraphs 7 and 12 of Schedule 24
foundation governor	
(in relation to a voluntary school)	section 78(2)
(in relation to a grant-maintained school)	paragraphs 8 and 13 of Schedule 24
foundation subjects	section 354(1) and (2)
functions	section 579(1)

funding authority	section 26
further education	section 2(3) to (5)
general schools budget (in Part II)	section 101(3)
governing body, governor	
(in Chapters IV to VI of Part II)	section 182
(in relation to a school grouped for purposes of Chapter IV of Part II)	section 89(6)
(in relation to a voluntary school and functions of foundation governors)	section 579(1)
governing body in liquidation (in sections 274 to 279)	section 274(3)
governor of an elected category (in Part III)	paragraph 3 of Schedule 24
governors' report (in Chapter VI of Part II)	section 161(1)
grant-maintained school	
(generally)	section 183(1)
(in sections 500 to 504)	section 505(8)
grant-maintained school formerly conducted by a governing body in liquidation (in sections 274 to 279)	section 274(5)
grant-maintained special school	sections 337(4) and 346(3)
grant regulations (in Chapter VI of Part III)	section 244(2)
grants for education support and training	section 484(1)
group (of schools)	
(in Part II)	section 89(5)
(in Chapter IX of Part III)	section 280(7)
head teacher	
(generally)	section 579(1)
(in relation to a county, voluntary or maintained special school organised into separate departments)	section 132
higher education	section 579(1)
incorporation date	
(in Chapter II of Part III)	section 200(5)
(in Chapter IV of Part III)	section 217
(in Part IV)	section 345(3)
independent school	section 463
initial governor (in Part III)	paragraph 2 of Schedule 24
institution outside (or within) the further education sector	section 4(3)
institution outside (or within) the higher education sector	section 4(4)
instrument of government	
(in relation to a county, voluntary or maintained special school)	section 76(1)
(in relation to a grant-maintained school)	section 218(1)
(in relation to a grant-maintained special school)	paragraph 1 of Schedule 28
(in relation to a group of grant-maintained schools)	section 280(2)
interest in land	section 579(2)
junior pupil	section 3(2)
key stage	section 355(1)
land	section 579(1)
the lay panel (in Part IV)	section 333(2)
learning difficulty	section 312(2) and (3)

liability	section 579(1)
local authority	section 579(1)
local education authority	section 12(1) to (5)
the local education authority	
(generally)	section 579(1)
(in relation to a scheme under Part II)	section 101(2)
local government elector	
(generally)	section 579(1)
(in Part III in relation to an area)	section 311(7)
maintain (in relation to a school maintained by a local education authority)	section 34
maintained school	
(in Part IV)	section 312(5)
(in Part V)	section 350(1)
(in Chapter II of Part VI)	section 437(8)
(in Chapter III of Part VI)	section 449
(in sections 500 to 504)	section 505(8)
maintained nursery school	sections 6(1) and 33(1)
maintained special school	sections 6(2), 33(1) and 337(3)
maintenance grant (in relation to grant-maintained schools)	section 244(1) (or section 250(1))
medical officer (in relation to a local education authority)	section 579(1)
minor authority	section 577
middle school	section 5(3)
modifications, modify	section 579(1)
the National Curriculum	sections 352(1) and 353
new governing body (in Part III)	section 195(2)
new school (in Part II)	section 181(1)
nursery school	section 6(1)
optional extra (in Chapter III of Part VI)	section 455(3)
parent	section 576
parent governor	
(in relation to a county, voluntary or maintained special school)	section 78(3)
(in relation to a grant-maintained school)	paragraphs 5 and 10 of Schedule 24
participating school (in Part VII)	section 479(2)
participating agreement (in Part VII)	section 479(2)
pending	
(in Part III in relation to proposals published under section 193)	section 193(4)
(in Chapter III of Part III in relation to the procedure for acquisition of grant-maintained status)	section 203(1)
powers to make proposals for the alteration of their school (in sections 500 to 504 in relation to the governing body of a voluntary school	section 505(7)
powers to make proposals for the establishment, alteration or discontinuance of schools (in sections 500 to 504)	section 505(8)
premises	
(in relation to a school)	section 579(1)
(in Part III)	section 311(1)
prescribed	section 579(1)

the President (in Part IV)	section 333(2)
primary education	section 2(1)
primary school	section 5(1)
programmes of study (in Part V)	section 353
proceeds of disposal (in sections 297 to 300)	section 301(3)
procedure applicable under Chapter IV of Part II (in Chapter V of Part III)	section 243(3)
promoters (in Part III)	section 212(1)
proposals (in Chapter VII of Part III)	section 266(2)
proposals for acquisition of grant-maintained status (in Part III)	section 183(2)
proposals for the establishment of a new grant-maintained school (in Part III)	section 183(2)
proprietor (in relation to a school)	section 579(1)
prospectively disqualified (in Chapter V of Part III)	section 243(4)
provisionally registered school (in Part VII)	section 465(4)
pupil	sections 3(1) and 19(5)
reception class	section 579(1)
register, registration (in Part VII in relation to independent schools)	section 464(4)
registered (in relation to parents or pupils)	section 434(5)
registered school (in Part VII)	section 465(4)
Registrar of Independent Schools (or the Registrar in Part VII)	section 464(4)
regulations	section 579(1)
relevant age group	section 579(1)
relevant education (in relation to an order under section 27(1))	section 27(7)
relevant particulars (in relation to a proposed initial governor of a grant-maintained school)	section 200(4)
relevant proposals (in Part II)	section 181(2)
relevant standard number (in Chapter I of Part VI)	section 411(7)
required to be covered by a scheme (in Part II in relation to a school)	section 102
reserved teacher (in Chapter VI of Part II in relation to a controlled school)	section 143(2)
reserved teacher (in Chapter VI of Part II in relation to a special agreement school)	section 144(1)
residential trip (in Chapter III of Part VI)	section 462(2)
responsible for a child (in Part IV in relation to a local education authority)	section 321(3)
right to a delegated budget (in Part II)	section 115(a)
Roman Catholic Church school	section 311(1)
scheme (in Part II)	section 101(1)
school	section 4(1) and (2)
school in respect of which financial delegation is required (in Part II)	section 115
school which has a delegated budget (in Part II)	section 115
school attendance order	section 437(3)
school buildings	section 579(1)
school day	section 579(1)
school property (in sections 274 to 279)	section 274(4)
secondary education	section 2(2) and (5)
secondary school	section 5(2)
section 67 loan liabilities (in sections 274 to 279)	section 274(7)
senior pupil	section 3(2)
sex education	section 352(3)

significant (in relation to a change in character or enlargement of premises of a school)	section 573(5)
special agreement	section 32(5)
special agreement school	section 32(1) and (4)
special educational needs	section 312(1)
special educational provision	section 312(4)
special purpose grant (in relation to grant-maintained schools)	section 245(1) (or section 251)
special school	section 6(2) and 337
sponsor governor (in Part III)	paragraphs 9 and 14 of Schedule 24
suitable education (in Chapter II of Part VI)	section 437(8)
teacher governor	
(in relation to a county, voluntary or maintained special school)	section 78(4)
(in relation to a grant-maintained school)	paragraphs 6 and 11 of Schedule 24
temporary governing body, temporary governor (in Part II)	section 181(3)
time of publication of proposals (in Part III in relation to proposals under that Part)	section 311(6)
the Tribunal (in Part IV)	section 313(5)
trust deed (in relation to a voluntary school)	section 579(1)
trustees of the school (in sections 296 to 300)	section 301(2)
voluntary school	sections 31(2) and 32
young person	section 579(1)

Final provisions

Application to Isles of Scilly

581. This Act shall apply to the Isles of Scilly—

(a) as if the Isles were a separate non-metropolitan county (and the Council of the Isles of Scilly were accordingly a county council), and

(b) subject to such other modifications as are specified in an order made by the Secretary of State.

Consequential amendments, repeals, transitional provisions etc.

582.—(1) The enactments specified in Schedule 37 are amended in accordance with that Schedule, the amendments being consequential on the provisions of this Act.

(2) The enactments and instruments specified in Schedule 38 are repealed or revoked to the extent specified.

(3) The transitional and saving provisions contained in Schedule 39 shall have effect.

(4) The transitory provisions contained in Schedule 40 shall have effect.

Short title, commencement and extent

583.—(1) This Act may be cited as the Education Act 1996.

(2) Subject to subsection (3), this Act shall come into force on 1st November 1996 (and references to the commencement of this Act are to its coming into force on that date).

(3) The following provisions—

section 8,
section 317(6),
section 348,
section 528,
Part II of Schedule 37 and section 582(1) so far as relating thereto, and

Part II of Schedule 38 and section 582(2) so far as relating thereto, shall come into force on such day as the Secretary of State may by order appoint; and different days may be appointed for different provisions and for different purposes.

(4) The Secretary of State may by order make such incidental, supplemental, saving or transitional provision as he thinks fit in connection with the coming into force in accordance with subsection (2) of any provision of this Act reproducing the effect of a provision of the Education Act 1993 which has not previously been brought into force by an order under section 308(3) of that Act (commencement).

(5) Where an order under subsection (3) brings into force any provision of section 317(6) or 528, then in relation to the coming into force of that provision—

(a) section 568(5) and (6) shall not apply to the order, but

(b) the order may make such provision as is authorised to be made, by virtue of section 67(2) and (3) of the Disability Discrimination Act 1995 (regulations and orders), by an order under section 70(3) of that Act (commencement).

(6) Subject to subsections (7) and (8), this Act extends to England and Wales only.

(7) This section, section 493 and section 569 so far as relating to regulations under section 493 extend also to Scotland; and this section extends also to Northern Ireland.

(8) Section 582 and Schedules 37 to 40 have the same extent as the enactments to which they relate.

SCHEDULES

Section 19

SCHEDULE 1

Pupil referral units

General adaptations of enactments

1. References in any enactment to the proprietor or governing body of a school shall be read, in relation to a pupil referral unit, as references to the local education authority.

2. References in any enactment to the head teacher of a school shall be read, in relation to a pupil referral unit, as references to the teacher in charge of the unit (whether known as the head teacher or not).

Modifications of enactments by regulations

3. Regulations may provide for any enactments relating to schools maintained by local education authorities (or schools including such schools)—

(a) to apply in relation to pupil referral units,

(b) to apply in relation to such units with such modifications as may be prescribed, or

(c) not to apply in relation to such units.

Registration

4.—(1) A person who is registered as a pupil at a school other than a pupil referral unit shall not, by reason only of being registered also as a pupil at such a unit, cease for the purposes of the Education Acts to be treated as a registered pupil at that school.

(2) In this Schedule "registered" means shown in the register kept under section 434.

Application of Local Government Act 1986

5. A pupil referral unit is a maintained school for the purposes of section 2A(1)(b) of the Local Government Act 1986 (prohibition on promoting homosexuality).

Curriculum

6.—(1) Section 370(1) (duty of LEA to state policy) applies in relation to pupil referral units as it applies in relation to county schools.

(2) In relation to every pupil referral unit, the Secretary of State, the local education authority and the teacher in charge shall exercise their functions with a view to securing that the curriculum for the unit satisfies the requirements of section 351 (balanced and broadly based curriculum) and of any other enactment which applies to the curriculum for pupil referral units.

(3) Each local education authority shall, with the approval of the Secretary of State, make arrangements for the consideration and disposal of any complaint to the effect that the authority, or the teacher in charge of any pupil referral unit—

(a) have acted or are proposing to act unreasonably with respect to the exercise of any power conferred, or the performance of any duty imposed, on them by or under any enactment referred to in subparagraph (2) above, or

(b) have failed to discharge any such duty.

(4) The Secretary of State shall not entertain under section 496 or 497 (power to prevent unreasonable exercise of functions; general default powers) any complaint in respect of any local education authority if it is a complaint—

(a) for which arrangements are required to be made under sub-paragraph (3) above, or

(b) that a local education authority have failed to exercise their powers to secure compliance by the teacher in charge of a pupil referral unit with any such duty as is referred to in that sub-paragraph,

unless a complaint in respect of the local education authority or, as the case may be, the teacher in charge of the unit has been made in respect of the same matter and disposed of in accordance with arrangements under that sub-paragraph.

Discipline

7. The teacher in charge of a pupil referral unit may exclude a pupil from the unit on disciplinary grounds.

Sex education, political indoctrination and political issues

8. Sections 403, 406 and 407 (sex education, political indoctrination, and treatment of political issues) apply in relation to pupil referral units as they apply in relation to county schools.

Charges

9.—(1) Chapter III of Part VI applies in relation to pupil referral units as if the references to governing bodies were omitted.

(2) Section 458(2)(b) (charges for board and lodging) shall have effect in relation to a pupil provided with board and lodging at a unit as if after "that" there were inserted "for the time being".

Application of Environmental Protection Act 1990

10. A pupil referral unit is an educational institution for the purposes of Part IV of the Environmental Protection Act 1990 (litter).

Information

11. Each local education authority shall—

(a) on such occasions, and

(b) in such form and manner,

as may be prescribed, make available to registered parents of registered pupils at any pupil referral unit such information about the unit as may be prescribed.

Disapplication of Schedule 4

12. Schedule 4 (distribution of functions where order made under section 27) does not apply in relation to pupil referral units or the provision for pupils at such units of board and lodging (whether at units or elsewhere).

Children with special educational needs

13. Sections 317(1) to (4), 318 and 324(5)(b), and paragraph 3(4) of Schedule 27, apply in relation to pupil referral units as they apply in relation to maintained schools.

School attendance orders

14.—(1) Where a pupil referral unit is named in a school attendance order—

(a) the local education authority shall inform the teacher in charge of the unit, and

(b) if another local education authority are responsible for determining the arrangements for the admission of pupils to the unit, that authority shall admit the child to the unit;

but paragraph (b) above does not affect any power to exclude from a unit a pupil who is already a registered pupil there.

(2) Section 438(4) does not apply in relation to a pupil referral unit.

(3) A local education authority—

(a) shall, before deciding to specify a particular pupil referral unit in a notice under section 438(2) where another local education authority are responsible for determining the arrangements for the admission of pupils to the unit, consult that authority; and

(b) if they decide to specify the unit in the notice, shall serve notice in writing of their decision on that authority.

(4) Section 439(7) and (8) apply where a notice is served on a local education authority under sub-paragraph (3) above as they apply where notice is served under section 439(6).

(5) The parent of a child in respect of whom a school attendance order is in force may not under section 440 request the local education authority to amend the order by substituting a pupil referral unit for the school named in the order.

(6) Where a child is a registered pupil at both a pupil referral unit and at a school other than a unit, the references in section 444 to the school at which he is a registered pupil shall be read as references to the unit.

Sections 20 and 21

SCHEDULE 2

The Funding Authorities

Status

1. A funding authority shall not be regarded as the servant or agent of the Crown or as enjoying any status, immunity or privilege of the Crown; and the property of the authority shall not be regarded as property of, or property held on behalf of, the Crown.

Powers

2.—(1) Subject to sub-paragraph (2) below, a funding authority may do anything which appears to them to be necessary or expedient for the purpose of or in connection with the discharge of their functions, including in particular—

(a) acquiring and disposing of land and other property,

(b) entering into contracts,

(c) investing sums not immediately required for the purpose of the discharge of their functions, and

(d) accepting gifts of money, land or other property.

(2) A funding authority shall not borrow money.

3.—(1) The Secretary of State may authorise a funding authority to purchase compulsorily any land required for the purpose of implementing any proposals under section 211, 212 or 260 (establishment or change in character of grant-maintained school) which are required to be implemented.

(2) The Acquisition of Land Act 1981 shall apply to compulsory purchase under this paragraph.

Tenure of members

4.—(1) A person shall hold and vacate office as a member of a funding authority in accordance with the terms of his appointment and, on ceasing to be a member, shall be eligible for re-appointment.

(2) A member of a funding authority may at any time resign his office by notice in writing to the Secretary of State.

5. If the Secretary of State is satisfied that a member of a funding authority—

(a) has been absent from meetings of the authority for a period longer than six consecutive months without the permission of the authority, or

(b) is unable or unfit to discharge the functions of a member,

the Secretary of State may, by notice in writing to that member, remove him from office and thereupon the office shall become vacant.

Salaries, allowances and pensions

6.—(1) A funding authority—

(a) shall pay to their members such salaries or fees, and such travelling, subsistence or other allowances, as the Secretary of State may determine, and

(b) shall, as regards any member in whose case the Secretary of State may so determine, pay or make provision for the payment of such sums by way of pension, allowances and gratuities to or in respect of him as the Secretary of State may determine.

(2) If a person ceases to be a member of a funding authority and it appears to the Secretary of State that there are special circumstances which make it right that he should receive compensation, the Secretary of State may direct the authority to make to that person a payment of such amount as the Secretary of State may determine.

(3) A funding authority shall pay to the members of any of their committees who are not members of the authority such travelling, subsistence and other allowances as the Secretary of State may determine.

(4) A determination or direction of the Secretary of State under this paragraph requires the approval of the Treasury.

Staff

7.—(1) A funding authority may, with the approval of the Secretary of State as to numbers, appoint such employees as they think fit on such terms and conditions as to remuneration and other matters as the authority may determine.

(2) A determination under sub-paragraph (1) above requires the approval of the Secretary of State given with the consent of the Treasury.

(3) An employee of a funding authority may not be appointed as a member of the authority, and a member of a funding authority may not be appointed as an employee of the authority.

Chief officer

8.—(1) One of the employees of a funding authority shall be the chief officer.

(2) The first chief officer shall be appointed by the Secretary of State on such terms and conditions as to remuneration and other matters as the Secretary of State may with the consent of the Treasury determine.

(3) Each subsequent chief officer shall be appointed by the authority with the approval of the Secretary of State.

Superannuation of employees

9.—(1) Employment with a funding authority shall continue to be included among the kinds of employment to which a scheme under section 1 of the Superannuation Act 1972 can apply.

(2) A funding authority shall pay to the Treasury, at such times as the Treasury may direct, such sums as the Treasury may determine in respect of the increase attributable to sub-paragraph (1) in the sums payable out of money provided by Parliament under the Superannuation Act 1972.

(3) Where an employee of a funding authority ceases to be such an employee and becomes a member of the authority and was by reference to his employment by the authority a participant in a scheme under section 1 of that Act, the Treasury may determine that his service as a member shall be treated for the purposes of the scheme as service as an employee of the authority (whether or not any benefits are payable to him by virtue of paragraph 6 above).

Committees

10.—(1) A funding authority may establish a committee for any purpose.

(2) The authority shall fix the number of the members which a committee established under this paragraph may have, and the terms on which they are to hold and vacate office.

(3) A committee may include persons who are not members of the authority.

(4) The authority shall keep under review the structure of committees established by them under this paragraph and the scope of each committee's activities.

Delegation of functions

11. A funding authority may authorise the chairman, the chief officer or any committee established by them under paragraph 10 above to exercise such of their functions as they may determine.

Proceedings

12. Without prejudice to any other rights the Secretary of State may require to be accorded to him as a condition of any grants made to a funding authority under section 25—

(a) a representative of the Secretary of State shall be entitled to attend and take part in any deliberations (but not in decisions) at meetings of the authority or of any of their committees, and

(b) the authority shall provide the Secretary of State with such copies of any documents distributed to members of the authority or of any of their committees as he may require.

13. The validity of any proceedings of a funding authority or of any of their committees shall not be affected by a vacancy amongst the members or by any defect in the appointment of a member.

14. Subject to the preceding provisions of this Schedule, a funding authority may regulate their own procedure and that of any of their committees.

Accounts

15.—(1) A funding authority shall—

(a) keep proper accounts and proper records in relation to the accounts;
(b) prepare a statement of accounts in respect of each financial year of the authority; and
(c) send copies of the statement to the Secretary of State and to the Comptroller and Auditor General before the end of the month of August next following the financial year to which the statement relates.

(2) The statement of accounts shall comply with any directions given by the Secretary of State with the approval of the Treasury as to—

(a) the information to be contained in it,
(b) the manner in which the information contained in it is to be presented, or
(c) the methods and principles according to which the statement is to be prepared,

and shall contain such additional information as the Secretary of State may with the approval of the Treasury require to be provided for the information of Parliament.

(3) The Comptroller and Auditor General shall examine, certify and report on each statement received by him in pursuance of this paragraph and shall lay copies of each statement and of his report before each House of Parliament.

(4) In this paragraph "financial year" means the period beginning with the date on which the authority is established and ending with the next following 31st March, and each successive period of twelve months.

Application of seal and proof of instruments

16. The application of the seal of a funding authority shall be authenticated by the signature—

(a) of the chairman or of some other person authorised either generally or specifically by the authority to act for that purpose, and
(b) of one other member.

17. Any document purporting to be an instrument made or issued by or on behalf of a funding authority and to be—

(a) duly executed under their seal, or
(b) signed or executed by a person authorised by the authority to act in that behalf,

shall be received in evidence and be treated, without further proof, as being so made or issued unless the contrary is shown.

Section 22

SCHEDULE 3

TRANSFER TO FUNDING AUTHORITY OF FUNCTIONS OF SECRETARY OF STATE

Functions relating to grant-maintained schools

1.—(1) The Secretary of State may by order provide for any of his functions under the provisions of this Act mentioned in sub-paragraph (2) to be exercisable instead by a funding authority, either generally or in such circumstances as may be specified in the order.

(2) Those provisions are—

(a) sections 220 and 221 (alterations to instruments and articles of government);
(b) section 231(6) (consent to borrowing);
(c) section 233 (making and varying joint schemes);
(d) section 302 (variation of trust deeds);
(e) paragraph 5 of Schedule 21 (transitional powers of governing bodies); and
(f) paragraph 15 of Schedule 22 (approval of schemes for payment of allowances to governors).

(3) An order under this paragraph may—

(a) confer or impose such related functions on the funding authority, and

(b) provide for Part III of this Act to have effect with such modifications,

as the Secretary of State considers necessary or desirable in connection with any transfer of any functions under the provisions of this Act mentioned in sub-paragraph (2).

Functions under agreements relating to CTCs and CCTAs

2.—(1) The Secretary of State may by order provide—

(a) for a funding authority to exercise the function of making and receiving payments under all or any of the agreements which he has entered into or may enter into under section 482 (CTCs and CCTAs); and

(b) for any such agreement to have effect accordingly.

(2) Any sums received by a funding authority in the exercise of those functions shall be paid to the Secretary of State.

Functions in respect of grants for certain expenditure due to ethnic minority population

3.—(1) The Secretary of State may by order impose on a funding authority the function of paying on his behalf grants under section 11 of the Local Government Act 1966 (grants in respect of ethnic minority population) so far as payable by him by virtue of section 490 (grants to grant-maintained schools, CTCs and CCTAs).

(2) The payments shall be of such amounts and be paid to such persons as the Secretary of State may, in accordance with section 11 of the Local Government Act 1966, determine.

Section 27

SCHEDULE 4

Distribution of functions where order made under section 27

Part I

Introductory

1.—(1) Where an order under section 27 is in force, the Education Acts shall have effect subject to—

(a) this Schedule, and

(b) the provisions of this Act which modify the effect of any provision of those Acts, or confer new functions, in respect of any area to which such an order applies.

(2) In particular, to the extent that this Schedule governs the payments to be made to any local education authority or the governing body of any grant-maintained school in respect of charges by that authority or body for the provision of board and lodging (at a boarding school or otherwise than at school), section 458(2) to (5) and section 514(5) (charges) shall not apply.

(3) In this Schedule—

(a) sections 458(1) and 514(4) are referred to as the "existing charging provisions"; and

(b) "maintained school" means any county or voluntary school or any maintained special school not established in a hospital.

Part II

Functions where responsibility for providing sufficient school places is shared

Introductory

2. If an order under section 27(1)(a) applies to the area of a local education authority, this Part of this Schedule has effect in respect of that area in relation to relevant education.

Responsibility for providing sufficient school places

3.—(1) If the schools providing relevant education which are available for the area are not sufficient, the funding authority shall, for the purpose of securing the availability of sufficient schools providing such education for the area, exercise their powers to make proposals for the establishment, alteration and discontinuance of schools.

(2) In performing that duty, the funding authority shall have regard to the need for securing that special educational provision is made for pupils who have special educational needs.

(3) The schools available for any area shall not be treated as sufficient for the purposes of this paragraph unless they are sufficient for the purposes of section 14(1) (duty of local education authority to secure availability of schools).

(4) Nothing in this paragraph requires a funding authority to take any action where to do so would not be an effective use of their resources.

(5) In this paragraph "powers to make proposals for the establishment, alteration and discontinuance of schools" means all or any of the powers to publish proposals under sections 211, 260 or 268 or give notice of proposals under section 339.

PART III

FUNCTIONS WHERE RESPONSIBILITY FOR PROVIDING SUFFICIENT SCHOOL PLACES IS TRANSFERRED

Introductory

4. If an order under section 27(1)(b) applies to the area of a local education authority, this Part of this Schedule has effect in respect of that area in relation to relevant education.

Responsibility for providing sufficient school places

5.—(1) The duty under section 14(1) shall be discharged by the funding authority instead of the local education authority.

(2) In discharging that duty the funding authority shall, in particular, have regard to the matters referred to in section 14(6)(b) (provision for pupils who have special educational needs).

(3) The funding authority may provide board and lodging otherwise than at school for pupils at maintained or grant-maintained schools; and, where the authority do so, the parents of the pupils concerned shall, subject to the following provisions of this Schedule, pay charges to the authority not exceeding the cost to the authority of the provision.

(4) Where the governing body of a grant-maintained school provide board and lodging at the school for pupils there, the parents of the pupils concerned shall, subject to the following provisions of this Schedule, pay charges to the governing body not exceeding the cost to the governing body of the provision.

6.—(1) The local education authority may continue to secure the provision of relevant education falling within section 14(1) and (subject to paragraph 7) to secure the provision of schools for that purpose.

(2) In exercising those powers the local education authority shall, in particular, have regard to the matters referred to in section 14(6) (which include the separation of primary and secondary education, and the provision of boarding accommodation for those for whom boarding is desirable).

(3) Where the local education authority—

(a) provide board and lodging at a maintained school for pupils there, or

(b) provide board and lodging otherwise than at school for pupils at maintained or grant-maintained schools,

the parents of the pupils concerned shall, subject to the following provisions of this Schedule, pay charges to the authority not exceeding the cost to the authority of the provision.

Powers to establish, maintain and alter schools

7.—(1) The local education authority may not exercise the power under section 16 to establish any school, or to begin to maintain as a county school any school which is not such a school, (in both cases referred to in this paragraph as "the school in question") unless—

(a) under sections 167 to 171 or section 173 their duty to maintain one or more other schools ceases; and

(b) the school in question is intended to provide education for pupils in the area which was served by the other school or (as the case may be) the other schools.

(2) This paragraph does not apply—

(a) to special schools;

(b) to nursery schools;

(c) where relevant education is only primary education, if the school in question is or will be a secondary school which also provides primary education; or

(d) where relevant education is only secondary education, if the school in question is or will be a primary school which also provides secondary education.

8.—(1) No proposals in respect of any school (referred to in this paragraph as "the school in question") published under section 41(1) (proposal that existing or proposed school should be maintained as a voluntary school) may be implemented unless—

(a) under sections 167 to 171 or section 173 the duty of the local education authority to maintain one or more other schools ceases; and

(b) the school in question is intended to provide education for pupils in the area which was served by the other school or (as the case may be) the other schools.

(2) This paragraph does not apply—

(a) where relevant education is only primary education, if the school in question is or will be a secondary school which also provides primary education; or

(b) where relevant education is only secondary education, if the school in question is or will be a primary school which also provides secondary education.

Charges for board and lodging or independent education

9.—(1) Sub-paragraph (3) below applies where—

(a) any pupil of compulsory school age ordinarily resident in the area is being provided with board and lodging (at a boarding school or otherwise than at school) or with education at a school which is not a maintained or grant-maintained school;

(b) the funding authority are of the opinion that it is not practicable for the pupil to obtain admission to any maintained or grant-maintained school which is a reasonable distance from his home and provides efficient full-time education suitable to his age, ability and aptitude and to any special educational needs he may have; and

(c) the authority are of the opinion that it is appropriate for the pupil to be provided with the particular board and lodging or, as the case may be, education.

(2) Sub-paragraph (3) below also applies where—

(a) any pupil ordinarily resident in the area is being provided with board and lodging (at a boarding school or otherwise than at school) or with education at a school which is not a maintained or grant-maintained school; and

(b) the funding authority are of the opinion that—

(i) the conditions in sub-paragraph (1) above have been, but are no longer, met by reason only of the pupil having ceased to be of compulsory school age or sub-paragraph (1)(b) above having ceased to apply, and

(ii) it would not be desirable for the pupil to cease to be provided with the particular board and lodging or, as the case may be, education.

(3) Where this sub-paragraph applies—

(a) if board and lodging is provided by the funding authority, no charge shall be payable to the authority under this Schedule in respect of the board and lodging;

(b) if board and lodging is provided at a maintained or grant-maintained school or by a local education authority, the funding authority shall pay the whole of the charges payable to any local education authority or governing body under this Schedule or the existing charging provisions in respect of the board and lodging; and

(c) in any other case the funding authority shall pay the whole of the fees payable in respect of the board and lodging or, as the case may be, the education.

(4) This paragraph does not apply in the case of a pupil for whom a statement is maintained under section 324.

10.—(1) This paragraph applies where any pupil ordinarily resident in the area is being provided—

(a) with board and lodging (at a boarding school or otherwise than at school), or

(b) with education at a school which is not a maintained or grant-maintained school,

but does not apply in any case where paragraph 9(3) applies.

(2) If board and lodging is provided at a school maintained by the responsible education authority and the authority are of the opinion that it is desirable for the pupil to be provided with board and lodging, or board and lodging otherwise than at school is provided by the authority, then—

(a) the authority may remit the whole or any part of the charges payable to them under this Schedule in respect of the board and lodging; and

(b) if they are of the opinion that, in order to avoid financial hardship to the pupil's parent, the parent should not pay the whole or any part of those charges, the authority shall remit the whole or, as the case may be, that part of those charges.

(3) If board and lodging otherwise than at school is provided by the funding authority, or board and lodging is provided at a grant-maintained school or a school maintained by another local education authority, then—

(a) the responsible education authority may pay the charges payable to the funding authority, or any local education authority or governing body, under this Schedule or the existing charging provisions in respect of the board and lodging; and

(b) if they are of the opinion that it is desirable for the pupil to be provided with board and lodging, they shall pay so much (if any) of those charges as in their opinion is required to be paid by them in order to avoid financial hardship to the parent.

(4) In any other case to which this paragraph applies—

(a) the local education authority may pay the whole of the fees payable in respect of the board and lodging or, as the case may be, the education; and

(b) if they are of the opinion that it is—

(i) desirable for the pupil to be provided with board and lodging, and

(ii) appropriate for him to be provided with the particular board and lodging, they shall pay so much (if any) of the fees payable in respect of board and lodging as in their opinion is required to be paid by them in order to avoid financial hardship to the parent; and

(c) if they are of the opinion that it is—

(i) desirable for the pupil to be provided with education otherwise than in a maintained or grant-maintained school, and

(ii) appropriate for him to be provided with the particular education,

they shall pay so much (if any) of the fees payable in respect of the education as in their opinion is required to be paid by them in order to avoid financial hardship to the parent.

(5) In this paragraph "the responsible education authority", in relation to a pupil ordinarily resident in any area, means the local education authority for the area.

(6) This paragraph does not apply in the case of a pupil for whom a statement is maintained under section 324.

11.—(1) Where a pupil in the area for whom a statement is maintained under section 324 is attending a maintained or grant-maintained school, this paragraph applies if he is provided with board and lodging at the school or otherwise than at school and either—

(a) the school is named in the statement and—

(i) the responsible education authority are satisfied that the necessary special educational provision cannot be provided for him at the school unless the particular board and lodging are also provided, or

(ii) the responsible education authority are satisfied that the necessary special educational provision cannot be provided for him at the school unless board and lodging are also provided and that it is appropriate for him to be provided with the particular board and lodging; or

(b) the school is not named in the statement but the responsible education authority are satisfied that the necessary special educational provision cannot be provided for him unless board and lodging are also provided and that it is appropriate for him to be provided with the particular board and lodging.

(2) Where the board and lodging is provided by the responsible education authority, no charge shall be payable to the authority under this Schedule in respect of the board and lodging.

(3) Where the board and lodging is provided—

(a) by the funding authority or another local education authority, or

(b) at a grant-maintained school or a school maintained by another local education authority,

the responsible education authority shall pay the charges payable to the funding authority or any local education authority or governing body under this Schedule or the existing charging provisions in respect of the board and lodging.

(4) In any other case to which this paragraph applies, the responsible education authority shall pay to the person providing the boat and lodging the whole of the fees in respect of the board and lodging.

(5) In this paragraph "the responsible education authority" in relation to a pupil means the local education authority responsible for the pupil for the purposes of Part IV (special educational needs).

12.—(1) Where a pupil in the area for whom a statement is maintained under section 324 is attending a maintained or grant-maintained school and is provided with board and lodging at the school or otherwise than at school, then—

(a) where the board and lodging is provided by the responsible education authority, the authority may remit the whole or any part of the charges payable to them under this Schedule in respect of the board and lodging;

(b) where the board and lodging is provided—

(i) by the funding authority or another local education authority, or

(ii) at a grant-maintained school or a school maintained by another local education authority,

the responsible education authority may pay the whole or any part of the charges payable to the funding authority or any local education authority or governing body under this Schedule or the existing charging provisions in respect of the board and lodging; and

(c) in any other case, the responsible education authority may pay to the person providing the board and lodging the whole or any part of the fees in respect of the board and lodging.

(2) In this paragraph "the responsible education authority", in relation to a pupil, means the local education authority responsible for the pupil for the purposes of Part IV.

General

13.—(1) The following provisions shall not apply—

(a) section 458 (charges and remission of charges for board and lodging in maintained and grant-maintained schools);

(b) section 514 (power of LEA to provide board and lodging otherwise than at school and recovery of charges from parents); and

(c) section 517(3) (payment by LEA of fees where pupil attends non-maintained school because of shortage of places in maintained and grant-maintained schools).

(2) Any charges payable to the local education authority, the funding authority or the governing body of a grant-maintained school under this Schedule may be recovered summarily as a civil debt.

14.—(1) Section 438 shall have effect as if for subsection (5) there were substituted—

"(5) If—

(a) within the period mentioned in subsection (3), the parent—

(i) applies to the funding authority, or the local education authority by whom the notice was served, for education to be provided for the child at a school which is not a school maintained by a local education authority or a grant-maintained school, and

(ii) in the case of an application to the funding authority, notifies the local education authority by whom the notice was served of the application,

(b) the child is offered a place at the school, and

(c) either the funding authority are required under paragraph 9 of Schedule 4 to pay the fees payable in respect of the education provided at the school or the local education authority agree to pay the whole of those fees under paragraph 10 of that Schedule,

that school shall be named in the order.

(2) Section 440 shall have effect as if for subsection (3) there were substituted—

"(3) If at any time—

(a) the parent applies to the funding authority or the local education authority by whom the notice was served for education to be provided for the child at a school which is not a school maintained by a local education authority or a grant-maintained school and is different from the school named in the order,

(b) the child is offered a place at the school,

(c) either the funding authority are required under paragraph 9 of Schedule 4 to pay the fees payable in respect of the education provided at the school or the local education authority agree to pay the whole of those fees under paragraph 10 of that Schedule, and

(d) the parent requests the local education authority to amend the order by substituting that school for the one currently named,

the authority shall comply with the request."

PART IV

FUNCTIONS WHERE RESPONSIBILITY EITHER SHARED OR TRANSFERRED

Introductory

15. If an order under section 27(1)(a) or (b) applies to the area of a local education authority, this Part of this Schedule has effect in respect of that area in relation to relevant education.

Responsibility for providing sufficient school places

16. In relation to any power under section 211 to publish proposals for the establishment of a grant-maintained school—

(a) references to establishing a school for the purpose of providing primary education include establishing a primary school which also provides secondary education; and

(b) references to establishing a school for the purpose of providing secondary education include establishing a secondary school which also provides primary education.

17.—(1) Where relevant education is only primary education—

(a) no proposals may be published under section 260 in respect of any grant-maintained school which is a secondary school or if the implementation of the proposals would cause the school to become a secondary school;

(b) no proposals may be published under section 268 in respect of any grant-maintained secondary school; and

(c) no direction may be given under section 428(2) to the governing body of any grant-maintained secondary school.

(2) Where relevant education is only secondary education—

(a) no proposals may be published under section 260 in respect of any grant-maintained school which is a primary school or if the implementation of the proposals would cause the school to become a primary school;

(b) no proposals may be published under section 268 in respect of any grant-maintained primary school; and
(c) no direction may be given under section 428(2) to the governing body of any grant-maintained primary school.

18. The funding authority shall not by virtue of paragraph 3 or 5 be under any duty in respect of junior pupils who have not attained the age of five.

Boarding schools

19. The powers of the funding authority to publish proposals under sections 211 and 260 or to give notice of proposals under section 339 may, in particular, be so exercised as to secure the provision of boarding accommodation at boarding schools.

Other modifications of this Act

20. Section 259 shall have effect as if the funding authority were among the persons who may submit objections under subsection (6) of that section to proposals under that section.

21. Section 267 shall have effect as if—
(a) the reference in subsection (3) to the local education authority included the funding authority; and
(b) the funding authority were among the persons who may submit objections under subsection (7) of that section to proposals under that section.

22. Section 272 shall have effect as if—
(a) paragraph (a) of subsection (1) were omitted, and
(b) the funding authority were among the persons required to be consulted under subsection (5)(b).

23. Section 426(4) shall have effect as if the reference to the Secretary of State were to the funding authority.

Section 32

SCHEDULE 5

Special agreements

Preservation of special agreements

1. Any special agreement in force immediately before the commencement of this Act shall continue in force despite the repeal by this Act of Schedule 3 to the Education Act 1944.

Variation of special agreements

2.—(1) A special agreement may be varied by a further agreement between the local education authority and the governors of the school to which it relates, or in such other manner (if any) as may be specified in the agreement.

(2) Sub-paragraph (1) has effect subject to the requirements of paragraph 3.

The grant requirements

3.—(1) A special agreement shall provide for the making of a grant by the local education authority to persons specified in the agreement in consideration of the execution by those persons of the proposals to which the agreement relates.

(2) Subject to sub-paragraph (3), the amount of any such grant shall be not less than half, and not more than three-quarters, of the cost of executing the proposals to which the agreement relates.

(3) Where the proposals include proposals for establishing a playing field or any buildings of a kind which it is, under section 45(2)(b), the duty of the local education authority to provide, then—
(a) if the proposals as respects the playing field or buildings are to be executed by the persons specified in the agreement, the amount of the grant (so far as attributable to the cost thereof) shall be equal to the whole of the cost; and
(b) if those proposals are to be executed by the local education authority the cost thereof shall be borne by them and excluded in computing the amount of the grant.

Religious education

4.—(1) A special agreement may provide—
(a) for the giving of religious education in the school in accordance with the provisions of the trust deed relating to it, or (where provision for that purpose is not made by such a deed)

in accordance with the practice observed in the school before it became a voluntary school; and

(b) for the employment in the school, for the purpose of giving such religious education, of such number of reserved teachers as may be specified in the agreement.

(2) Sub-paragraph (1)(a) has effect subject to section 378(1)(c) and any arrangements made under section 378(2).

Repayment of grants

5. Any grant made in respect of a school in pursuance of a special agreement may, at any time while the school is a special agreement school, be repaid by the governing body to the local education authority by whom the school is maintained.

Modification of obligations with respect to repairs and alterations

6. Where a special agreement is in force in relation to a school, then, until the proposals to which the agreement relates have been carried out—

(a) the provisions of Part II relating to the respective obligations of the governing bodies of voluntary schools and the local education authority in respect of repairs and alterations to the premises of the school shall not have effect in relation to the school; and

(b) the respective obligations of the governing body of the school and the local education authority in relation to those matters shall instead be such as may be determined by agreement between the governing body and the authority or, in default of agreement, by the Secretary of State.

Section 39

SCHEDULE 6

TRANSFER OF PREMISES WHERE VOLUNTARY SCHOOL CHANGES TO COUNTY SCHOOL

1. In connection with proposals by a local education authority under section 35(1)(b) for the maintenance as a county school of a school which is for the time being maintained by them as a voluntary school, they and the school's governing body may make an agreement for the transfer to the authority of any interest in the school premises which is held by any persons for the purposes of any trust deed relating to the school.

2. Such an agreement shall not take effect unless it has been approved by the Secretary of State.

3. The Secretary of State shall not approve such an agreement unless—

(a) he is satisfied that due notice of the agreement has been given to—

(i) any persons (other than the governing body) who have an interest in the school by virtue of a trust deed relating to it, and

(ii) any other persons who appear to him to be concerned; and

(b) he is satisfied that the execution of the agreement will effect the transfer of all interests necessary for the purpose of enabling the authority to maintain the school as a county school.

4. Before approving an agreement under this Schedule, the Secretary of State shall consider any representations made to him by or on behalf of any persons appearing to him to be concerned with the proposed transfer.

5. An agreement under this Schedule—

(a) may provide for the transfer to the authority, subject to any conditions, reservations and restrictions specified in the agreement, either of the whole of any such interest as is referred to in paragraph 1 or of a lesser interest in the premises, and

(b) may include such other provisions (whether relating to the consideration for the transfer or otherwise) as may be agreed upon between the authority and the governing body.

6. Where an agreement under this Schedule has been approved by the Secretary of State, the governing body may, whether or not the interest to be transferred under the agreement is vested in them, convey that interest to the authority.

7. Where a person other than the governing body has a right to the occupation or use of the school premises or any part of them for a particular purpose, no provision of an agreement under this Schedule shall affect that right unless he has consented to it.

8. In this Schedule "premises" includes a teacher's dwelling-house.

Section 88(1) SCHEDULE 7

INCORPORATION OF GOVERNING BODIES OF COUNTY, VOLUNTARY AND MAINTAINED SPECIAL SCHOOLS

Name and seal of incorporated body

1.—(1) A governing body incorporated under section 88(1) shall be known as "The governing body of ..." with the addition of the name of the school.

(2) The application of the seal of any such governing body must be authenticated by the signature—

(a) of the chairman of the governing body, or

(b) of some other member authorised either generally or specially by the governing body to act for that purpose, together with the signature of any other member.

(3) Every document purporting to be an instrument made or issued by or on behalf of any such governing body and—

(a) to be duly executed under the seal of the governing body, or

(b) to be signed or executed by a person authorised by the governing body to act in that behalf,

shall be received in evidence and be treated, without further proof, as being so made or issued unless the contrary is shown.

Powers of incorporated body

2.—(1) A governing body incorporated under section 88(1) may do anything (including in particular the things referred to in the following sub-paragraphs) which appears to them to be necessary or expedient for the purpose of or in connection with the exercise of any of the functions conferred on them under or in pursuance of any enactment.

(2) A governing body so incorporated may—

(a) acquire and dispose of land and other property;

(b) enter into contracts, other than contracts of employment;

(c) invest any sums not immediately required for the purposes of carrying on any activities they have power to carry on;

(d) accept gifts of money, land and other property and apply it, or hold and administer it on trust, for any of those purposes; and

(e) do anything incidental to the conduct of the school.

(3) Sub-paragraphs (1) and (2) have effect subject to—

(a) any provisions of the instrument of government or articles of government for the school, and

(b) if the school has a delegated budget (as defined in section 115(b)) any provisions of the scheme falling within section 101(1) which covers the school.

(4) The governing body so incorporated of an aided school may enter into contracts for the employment of teachers and other staff, subject to any provisions of the articles of government for the school other than any provisions for the time being excluded by section 137(2) (aided schools having delegated budgets) from applying to the school.

Property, rights and liabilities

3. On the incorporation under section 88(1) of a governing body ("the new governing body") for a school which, immediately before the incorporation date, was conducted by a temporary governing body constituted under arrangements made under section 96 or 97—

(a) all land and other property which, immediately before the date of incorporation, was property of the temporary governing body used or held for the purposes of the school, and

(b) all rights and liabilities of the temporary governing body subsisting immediately before that date which were acquired or incurred for those purposes,

shall be transferred to and, by virtue of this Act, vest in the new governing body.

4. On the incorporation under section 88(1) of a governing body ("the new governing body") constituted under an instrument of government for two or more schools grouped in pursuance of a resolution under section 89—

(a) all land and other property which, immediately before the date of incorporation, was property of the governing body of any of those schools used or held for the purposes of the school in question, and

(b) all rights and liabilities of the governing body of any of those schools subsisting immediately before that date which were acquired or incurred for those purposes, shall be transferred to and, by virtue of this Act, vest in the new governing body.

Contracts of employment

5. Without prejudice to the generality of paragraphs 3 and 4, where those provisions effect a transfer of rights and liabilities under a contract of employment—

(a) the contract shall have effect from the date of incorporation as if originally made between the employee and the incorporated governing body, and

(b) without prejudice to sub-paragraph (a) above, anything done before that date by or in relation to the former employer in respect of that contract or the employee shall be deemed from that date to have been done by or in relation to the incorporated governing body,

but no right of the employee to terminate his contract of employment if a substantial change is made to his detriment in his working conditions shall arise by reason only of the change of employer effected by those provisions.

Dissolution and discontinuance

6.—(1) A governing body incorporated under section 88(1) are dissolved by virtue of this paragraph—

(a) if the school they conduct is discontinued;

(b) where the school becomes a grant-maintained school or grant-maintained special school, when the local education authority cease to maintain the school; or

(c) if a new governing body of the school are constituted under Chapter IV of Part II.

(2) Where such a governing body conduct two or more schools, sub-paragraph (1) applies when, in relation to each of the schools, paragraph (a), (b) or (c) is satisfied.

7.—(1) Where such a governing body are to be dissolved by reason of—

(a) the discontinuance of the county, voluntary or maintained special school which they conduct, or

(b) in the case of a governing body conducting two or more such schools, the discontinuance of each such school conducted by them,

they shall have power to transfer any land or other property of theirs which is used or held for the purposes of the school to any person who provides education.

(2) Where such a governing body are so dissolved—

(a) any such land or property for which no provision has been made under sub-paragraph (1) for transfer, and

(b) all rights and liabilities of the governing body subsisting immediately before the date of dissolution which were acquired or incurred for the purposes of the school in question,

shall be transferred to and, by virtue of this Act, vest in the local education authority.

(3) Sub-paragraphs (1) and (2) do not apply to any land or other property held by the governing body on trust for the purposes of a voluntary school; and any such land or other property so held shall be transferred to and, by virtue of this Act, vest in the trustees of the school.

8.—(1) This paragraph applies where such a governing body dissolved by virtue of paragraph 6 are the governing body of two or more schools grouped in pursuance of a resolution under section 89.

(2) Where none of the schools in the group are discontinued, then in the case of each school formerly a member of the group—

(a) all land and other property which, immediately before the date of dissolution, was property of the governing body used or held for the purposes of that school, and

(b) all rights and liabilities of the governing body subsisting immediately before that date which were acquired or incurred for those purposes,

shall be transferred to and, by virtue of this Act, vest in the new governing body of the school in accordance with the order providing for the instrument of government for the school.

(3) An order made by virtue of sub-paragraph (2) may provide that—

(a) the whole or any part of any such land and other property which was property of the governing body used or held for the purposes of the schools in the group, and

(b) any such rights and liabilities of the governing body which were acquired or incurred for those purposes,

shall be transferred to and, by virtue of this Act, vest in the new governing body of the school.

(4) Where not all of the schools in the group are discontinued, then in the case of each school formerly a member of the group which is not discontinued—

(a) all land and other property which, immediately before the date of dissolution, was property of the governing body used or held for the purposes of that school, and

(b) all rights and liabilities of the governing body subsisting immediately before that date which were acquired or incurred for those purposes, shall be transferred to and, by virtue of this Act, vest in the new governing body of the school in accordance with the order providing for the instrument of government for the school.

(5) An order made by virtue of sub-paragraph (4) may provide that—

(a) the whole or any part of any such land and other property which was property of the governing body used or held for the purposes of any school which is to be discontinued or the schools in the group, and

(b) any such rights and liabilities of the governing body which were acquired or incurred for those purposes,

shall be transferred to and, by virtue of this Act, vest in the new governing body of the school.

(6) Sub-paragraph (5) does not apply to any land or other property held by the governing body on trust for the purposes of a voluntary school; and any such land or other property so held shall be transferred to and, by virtue of this Act, vest in the trustees of the school.

9.—(1) This paragraph applies in relation to the governing body of two or more schools grouped in pursuance of a resolution under section 89.

(2) Where one or more schools conducted by the governing body are discontinued but the governing body are not dissolved by reason of the discontinuance, then in the case of each school formerly a member of the group which is discontinued—

(a) all land and other property which, immediately before the date of dissolution, was property of the governing body used or held for the purposes of that school, and

(b) all rights and liabilities of the governing body subsisting immediately before that date which were acquired or incurred for those purposes,

shall be held by the governing body for the purposes of the schools in the group.

(3) Sub-paragraph (2) does not apply to any land or other property held by the governing body on trust for the purposes of a voluntary school; and any such land or other property so held shall be transferred to and, by virtue of this Act, vest in the trustees of the school.

(4) Where, in the case of one or more schools conducted by the governing body, new governing bodies are constituted under Chapter IV of Part II to conduct those schools but the governing body are not dissolved by reason of the constitution of such bodies, then in the case of each school formerly a member of the group—

(a) all land and other property which, immediately before the date of dissolution, was property of the governing body used or held for the purposes of that school, and

(b) all rights and liabilities of the governing body subsisting immediately before that date which were acquired or incurred for those purposes,

shall be transferred to and, by virtue of this Act, vest in the new governing body of the school in accordance with the order providing for the instrument of government for the school.

10. For the purposes of this Schedule, references to the discontinuance of a school are—

(a) to the local education authority ceasing to maintain it in accordance with proposals under section 167 (discontinuance of county or voluntary schools) or section 339 (discontinuance of special schools), or

(b) to its discontinuance under section 173 (discontinuance by governors of voluntary schools).

Supplementary provisions about transfers

11. Where a transfer under this Schedule relates to registered land, it shall be the duty of the transferor—

(a) to execute any such instrument under the Land Registration Acts 1925 to 1986,

(b) to deliver any such certificate under those Acts, and

(c) to do such other things under those Acts,

as he would be required to execute, deliver or do in the case of a transfer by agreement between the transferor and the transferee.

12. Paragraphs 6 to 8 of Schedule 10 to the Education Reform Act 1988 (construction of agreements) shall apply in relation to transfers effected by this Schedule as they apply to transfers to which that Schedule applies.

Section 88(2)

SCHEDULE 8

MEMBERSHIP AND PROCEEDINGS ETC. OF GOVERNING BODIES OF COUNTY, VOLUNTARY AND MAINTAINED SPECIAL SCHOOLS

Introductory

1. In this Schedule, except where a school of a particular category is referred to—

"governing body" means the governing body of a county, voluntary or maintained special school, and "school" means a county, voluntary or maintained special school.

Co-option or other appointment of governors

2.—(1) Subject to sub-paragraph (2), where the instrument of government for a county, controlled or maintained special school provides for one or more persons to be co-opted by governors as members of the governing body, it shall not make any provision which has the effect of restricting those governors in their choice of person to co-opt.

(2) The instrument of government for a county, controlled or maintained special school shall require the governors concerned, in co-opting a person to be a member of the governing body—

(a) to have regard—

(i) to the extent to which they and the other governors are members of the local business community, and

(ii) to any representations made to the governing body as to the desirability of increasing the connection between the governing body and that community, and

(b) where it appears to them that no governor of the school is a member of the local business community or that it is desirable to increase the number of governors who are, to co-opt a person who appears to them to be a member of that community.

(3) In this paragraph references to the co-option of governors—

(a) are to the co-option of governors required to be co-opted by virtue of section 79; but

(b) do not include the co-option of foundation governors.

3. If—

(a) the instrument of government for a school provides for one or more governors to be appointed by persons acting jointly, and

(b) those persons fail to make an agreed appointment,

the appointment shall be made by, or in accordance with a direction given by, the Secretary of State.

4. The instrument of government for a voluntary school shall name the person or persons (if any) who are entitled to appoint any foundation governor.

Ex officio governors

5. If a school has more than one head teacher (whether or not as a result of two or more schools being grouped under section 89), each of them shall be a governor (ex officio) unless he chooses not to be.

6. The instrument of government for a voluntary school may provide for any foundation governorship to be held ex officio by the holder of an office named in the instrument.

Election of governors

7.—(1) In this paragraph "the appropriate authority"—

(a) in relation to a county, controlled or maintained special school, means the local education authority, and

(b) in relation to an aided or special agreement school, means the governing body.

(2) The appropriate authority in relation to a school shall determine—

(a) for the purposes of an election of parent governors, any question whether a person is a parent of a registered pupil at the school, and

(b) for the purposes of an election of teacher governors, any question whether a person is a teacher at the school.

(3) The appropriate authority shall make all necessary arrangements for, and determine all other matters relating to, an election of parent governors or teacher governors.

(4) The power conferred by sub-paragraph (3)—

(a) includes power to make provision as to qualifying dates, but

(b) does not include power to impose any requirement as to the minimum number of votes required to be cast for a candidate to be elected.

(5) Any election of parent governors or teacher governors which is contested shall be held by secret ballot.

(6) The arrangements made under sub-paragraph (3) shall, in the case of any election of a parent governor, provide for every person who is entitled to vote in the election to have an opportunity to do so by post or, if he prefers, by having his ballot paper returned to the school by a registered pupil at the school.

(7) Where a vacancy for a parent governor is required to be filled by election, the appropriate authority shall take such steps as are reasonably practicable to secure that every person who is known to them to be a parent of a registered pupil at the school is—

(a) informed of the vacancy and that it is required to be filled by election;

(b) informed that he is entitled to stand as a candidate, and vote, at the election; and

(c) given an opportunity to do so.

Qualifications of governors and tenure of office

8. No person shall be qualified for membership of a governing body unless he is aged 18 or over at the date of his election or appointment.

9. No person shall at any time hold more than one governorship of the same school.

10.—(1) Regulations may make provision as to the circumstances in which persons are to be disqualified for holding office as governors of schools.

(2) The instrument of government for a school may make provision as to circumstances in which persons are to be disqualified for holding office as governors of the school.

(3) The fact that a person is qualified to be elected or appointed as a governor of a particular category of a school does not disqualify him for election or appointment as a governor of any other category of that school.

11.—(1) The instrument of government for a county, controlled or maintained special school shall provide for each governor, other than one who is a governor ex officio, to hold office for a term of four years.

(2) The instrument of government for an aided secondary school shall provide for each governor appointed by a person named in the instrument as a sponsor of the school to hold office for such term (not being less than five nor more than seven years) as may be specified in the instrument.

(3) This paragraph shall not be taken to prevent a governor—

(a) from being elected or appointed for a further term, or

(b) from being disqualified, by virtue of provision made under paragraph 10, for continuing to hold office.

12. Any governor of a school may at any time resign his office.

13.—(1) Any governor of a school who was appointed otherwise than by being co-opted, or any foundation governor of a voluntary school, may be removed from office by the person or persons who appointed him.

(2) For the purposes of this paragraph, a parent governor appointed in accordance with any provision made by virtue of section 81 shall be treated as having been co-opted.

Meetings and proceedings

14. The proceedings of a governing body of a school shall not be invalidated by—

(a) any vacancy among their number, or

(b) any defect in the election or appointment of any governor.

15.—(1) Regulations may make provision (including provision modifying the effect of paragraph 14) as to the meetings and proceedings of governing bodies.

(2) The instrument of government for a school may make provision as to the meetings and proceedings of the school's governing body.

(3) The provision that may be made under sub-paragraph (1) or (2) includes, in particular, provision—

(a) for the election by the governors of a school of one of their number to be chairman, and one to be vice-chairman, of the governing body;

(b) for the period for which the chairman and vice-chairman are to be elected;

(c) for the establishment by the governing body of committees (which may include persons who are not members of the governing body) and for the constitution, meetings and proceedings of committees so established;

(d) for the delegation of functions of the governing body, in such circumstances as may be specified, to committees established by that body, to any member of that body or to the head teacher;

(e) for the chairman, or such other member of a governing body as may be specified, to have power in specified circumstances to discharge any of the governing body's functions as a matter of urgency; and

(f) as to the quorum required for the purposes of making appointments of parent governors in accordance with any provision made by virtue of section 81 or when business is transacted by governors of a particular category.

(4) In sub-paragraph (3) "specified" means specified in regulations or the instrument of government (as the case may be).

16.—(1) No decision of a kind mentioned in sub-paragraph (2) which is taken at a meeting of the governing body of an aided or special agreement school shall have effect unless it is confirmed at a second meeting of the governing body held not less than 28 days after the first.

(2) The decisions in question are—

(a) any decision that would result in—

(i) the submission of any proposals under section 41 (alteration etc. of school), or

(ii) a transfer of the school to a new site in circumstances falling within section 41(3), or

(iii) the submission of any proposals under section 51 (division of school into two or more schools);

(b) any decision—

(i) to request the making of an order under section 46 (establishment of new school in substitution for old) or section 47 (transfer to new site), or

(ii) as to the submissions to be made to the Secretary of State in any consultations under section 46(4) or section 47(3) (transfer to new site);

(c) any decision that would result in an application under section 57 or 58(1) (revocation of order by virtue of which school is aided or special agreement school);

(d) any decision to serve a notice under section 173 (discontinuance of school); and

(e) any decision to make an agreement under Schedule 6 (transfer to local education authority of interests in school premises on school changing to county school).

Information as to meetings and proceedings

17. The minutes of the proceedings of the governing body of a school shall be open to inspection by the local education authority.

18.—(1) Regulations may require the governing body of a school to make available, to such persons or classes of person as may be prescribed, such documents and information relating to the meetings and proceedings of the governing body as may be prescribed.

(2) Documents and information required by the regulations to be made available shall be made available in such form and manner, and at such times, as may be prescribed.

Travelling and subsistence allowances

19. Section 519 makes provision for a local education authority to pay travelling and subsistence allowances to governors of a school where it does not have a delegated budget.

Information and training for governors

20.—(1) The local education authority shall secure that every governor of a school is provided (free of charge) with—

(a) a copy of the school's instrument of government and articles of government, and

(b) such other information as they consider appropriate in connection with the discharge of his functions as a governor.

(2) The local education authority shall also secure that there is made available to every governor of a school (free of charge) such training as the authority consider necessary for the effective discharge of those functions.

Conflict between instrument of government and regulations

21. Any provision made by an instrument of government by virtue of paragraph 10(2), 11 or 15(2) which relates to a matter dealt with by regulations under paragraph 10(1) or 15(1) shall have effect subject to the regulations.

Section 98

SCHEDULE 9

TEMPORARY GOVERNING BODIES OF COUNTY, VOLUNTARY AND MAINTAINED SPECIAL SCHOOLS

Preliminary

1. In this Schedule—

"arrangement" means an arrangement made under section 96 or 97 for the constitution of a temporary governing body; and

"promoters", in relation to a new school which will be a voluntary school, means the persons making the relevant proposals.

Constitution of temporary governing bodies

2.—(1) Subject to the following provisions of this Schedule, a temporary governing body of a new school shall be constituted—

(a) in accordance with sections 79 and 80 (so far as applicable), where the school will be a county, controlled or maintained special school, and

(b) in accordance with sections 84 and 85 (so far as applicable), where the school will be an aided school.

(2) For the purposes of the application of section 79, 80, 84 or 85 in relation to the constitution of the temporary governing body of a new school, the new school shall be treated as having as registered pupils the maximum number of pupils referred to in the relevant proposals.

3.—(1) A local education authority shall not make an arrangement in respect of a new school which will be a controlled school without the agreement of the promoters as to the provision which will be made in relation to the temporary foundation governors; and in the event of any disagreement between the authority and the promoters in respect of that provision, either of them may refer the matter to the Secretary of State.

(2) A local education authority shall not make an arrangement in respect of a new school which will be an aided school without the agreement of the promoters as to the composition of the temporary governing body; and in the event of any disagreement between the authority and the promoters as to the composition of that body, either of them may refer the matter to the Secretary of State.

(3) On a reference under this paragraph, the Secretary of State shall give such direction as he thinks fit.

Appointment of temporary governors

4. The temporary parent governors of a new school shall, subject to paragraph 6, be appointed—

(a) where the school will be a county, controlled or maintained special school, by the local education authority, and

(b) where it will be an aided school, by the promoters.

5. The temporary teacher governors of a new school shall, subject to paragraph 6, be co-opted by a resolution passed at a meeting of those temporary governors who have not themselves been co-opted.

6.—(1) Where—

(a) two or more schools have been, or are to be, discontinued, and

(b) the registered pupils at those schools, or a substantial number of those pupils, are expected to transfer to a new school,

the local education authority may provide for any of the governing bodies of the discontinued schools to appoint some or all of the temporary parent or teacher governors of the new school.

(2) No provision may be made under sub-paragraph (1) for the appointment of temporary parent or teacher governors of a new school which will be an aided school without the agreement of the promoters; and in the event of any disagreement between the authority and the promoters as to whether any such provision should be made, either of them may refer the matter to the Secretary of State.

(3) On a reference under sub-paragraph (2), the Secretary of State shall give such direction as he thinks fit.

(4) Before making any provision under sub-paragraph (1) for the appointment of temporary parent or teacher governors of a new school which will be a controlled school, the local education authority shall consult the promoters.

7.—(1) No person shall be appointed under paragraph 4 or 6 as a temporary parent governor of a new school unless—

(a) he is the parent of a child who is likely to become a registered pupil at the school, or

(b) where it is not reasonably practicable to appoint such a person, he is the parent of a child of compulsory school age.

(2) No person shall be appointed under paragraph 4 as a temporary parent governor of a new school if he is—

(a) an elected member of the local education authority; or

(b) an employee of the authority or of the governing body of any aided school maintained by the authority.

(3) No person shall be appointed under paragraph 5 or 6 as a temporary teacher governor of a new school unless he is employed as a teacher in a school maintained by a local education authority.

8.—(1) Where any person, other than a prospective sponsor, appoints a person as a temporary governor of a new school, he shall have regard to the desirability of that person being suitably experienced.

(2) For the purposes of this paragraph a person is suitably experienced—

(a) if he has served as a governor or temporary governor of a school, and

(b) in particular, in a case where registered pupils at another school which has been, or is to be, discontinued are expected to transfer to the new school, if he has served as a governor or temporary governor of that other school.

(3) In sub-paragraph (1) "prospective sponsor" means a person who is to be named in the instrument of government as a sponsor of the school in question.

9.—(1) Subject to sub-paragraph (2), where temporary governors are required to co-opt one or more persons to be members of the temporary governing body, the arrangement under which the temporary governing body are constituted shall not make any provision which has the effect of restricting those temporary governors in their choice of person to co-opt.

(2) In co-opting a person to be a member of a temporary governing body of a new school which will be a county, controlled or maintained special school, the temporary governors concerned shall have regard—

(a) to the extent to which they and the other temporary governors are members of the local business community, and

(b) to any representations made to the temporary governing body as to the desirability of increasing the connection between the temporary governing body and that community,

and, where it appears to them that no temporary governor of the new school is a member of the local business community or that it is desirable to increase the number of temporary governors who are, shall co-opt a person who appears to them to be a member of that community.

(3) This paragraph does not apply in relation to the co-option of temporary foundation governors, and sub-paragraph (2) does not apply in relation to the co-option of temporary teacher governors.

10. If—

(a) a temporary governor is to be appointed by persons acting jointly, and

(b) those persons fail to make an agreed appointment,

the appointment shall be made by, or in accordance with a direction given by, the Secretary of State.

Qualifications of temporary governors and tenure of office

11. No person shall be qualified for membership of a temporary governing body unless he is aged 18 or over at the date of his appointment.

12.—(1) No person shall at any time hold more than one temporary governorship of the same school.

(2) The fact that a person is qualified to be appointed as a temporary governor of a particular category of a new school does not disqualify him for appointment as a temporary governor of any other category of that school.

13. Regulations may make provision as to the circumstances in which persons are to be disqualified for holding office as temporary governors.

14. A member of a temporary governing body may at any time resign his office, or be removed from office, in the same way as a member of a governing body constituted under an instrument of government.

Meetings and proceedings

15.—(1) The proceedings of a temporary governing body shall not be invalidated by—

(a) any vacancy among their number, or

(b) any defect in the appointment of any temporary governor.

(2) If the clerk to a temporary governing body fails to attend any meeting of theirs, they may appoint one of their number to act as clerk for the purposes of that meeting (but without prejudice to his position as a temporary governor).

16. Regulations may make provision in relation to temporary governing bodies similar to that which may be made in relation to governing bodies by regulations under paragraph 15(1) of Schedule 8.

17.—(1) Subject to sub-paragraph (2), the first meeting of a temporary governing body shall be called by their clerk.

(2) Where the clerk fails to call the first meeting within such period as the local education authority consider reasonable, the authority shall call it.

Information as to meetings and proceedings

18. The minutes of the proceedings of a temporary governing body shall be open to inspection by the local education authority.

Travelling and subsistence allowances

19. Section 519 (allowances for governors) shall apply in relation to the members of a temporary governing body as it applies in relation to the members of a governing body of a school falling within subsection (1)(a) of that section.

Expenses of temporary governing bodies

20. Where a temporary governing body are constituted for a new school, the local education authority shall be under the same duty to defray the expenses incurred in relation to the temporary governing body as they would be if the relevant proposals had been implemented and the temporary governing body were the governing body of the school.

Information for temporary governing bodies

21. A local education authority shall secure that the temporary governing body of a new school which will be maintained by them are, on being constituted, provided (free of charge) with such explanatory and other information as the authority consider is required to enable the temporary governing body to discharge their functions effectively.

Powers of the Secretary of State

22. For the purposes of the following provisions—

(a) section 495(1) (determination of disputes),

(b) section 496 (prevention of unreasonable exercise of functions), and

(c) sections 497 and 498 (default powers),

a temporary governing body shall be treated as if they were the governing body of the school in question.

Section 99

SCHEDULE 10

Transition from Temporary Governing Body to Governing Body Constituted under an Instrument of Government

Time limit for constitution of governing body

1. The local education authority shall secure that the governing body of a new school are constituted—

(a) as soon as is reasonably practicable after the requirement for there to be an instrument of government for the school takes effect under section 99, and

(b) in any event not later than the last day of the term in which pupils first attend the new school or (as the case may be) first attend the school after it becomes maintained by the authority.

Status of temporary governing body pending constitution of governing body

2. Where the requirement for there to be an instrument of government for a new school has taken effect under section 99, the temporary governing body shall, until such time as the governing body are constituted—

(a) continue in existence (despite the fact that the arrangement under which they were constituted has come to an end under section 96 or 97); and

(b) be treated as if they were the governing body.

Role of temporary governing body as regards constitution of governing body

3.—(1) Before making an order under section 76 as to the instrument of government for a new school, the local education authority shall consult the temporary governing body and the head teacher.

(2) Before making such an order in respect of a new school which will be a voluntary school, the authority shall—

(a) secure the agreement of the temporary governing body to the terms of the proposed order; and

(b) secure the agreement of the temporary foundation governors to any provisions which are of particular concern to those governors.

(3) Where a local education authority propose to make an order under section 76 as to the instrument of government for a new school but cannot secure any agreement required by this paragraph, they or (as the case may be) the temporary governing body or temporary foundation governors may refer the matter to the Secretary of State.

(4) On a reference under sub-paragraph (3), the Secretary of State shall give such direction as he thinks fit.

4.—(1) A temporary governing body shall recommend (with reasons) persons who belong to the community served by the new school and who are, in their opinion, suitable for appointment as co-opted members of the governing body who will succeed them.

(2) Before making any recommendations under this paragraph, a temporary governing body shall consult representatives of the local business community.

Initial constitution of governing body

5.—(1) When the requirement for there to be an instrument of government for a new school takes effect under section 99, sub-paragraph (2) shall apply for the purposes of the application of section 79, 80, 84 or 85 in relation to the constitution of the school's governing body.

(2) Where this sub-paragraph applies, the school shall be treated as having as registered pupils the maximum number of pupils referred to in the relevant proposals.

(3) Subject to sub-paragraph (4), sub-paragraph (2) shall, as from the time when the governing body is first constituted, continue to apply for the purposes of determining what provision would be required to be made by a new instrument of government for the school.

(4) Sub-paragraph (2) shall cease so to apply in relation to the school at such time as—

(a) the number of registered pupils at the school reaches the maximum referred to in that sub-paragraph; or

(b) the local education authority give any direction by virtue of subparagraph (5).

(5) The instrument of government for a school in relation to which subparagraph (2) applies when the instrument is made shall provide for the local education authority to have power to direct that sub-paragraph (2) shall cease to apply in relation to the school.

Information about temporary governing body for successors

6.—(1) Immediately before the arrangement under which a temporary governing body are constituted comes to an end under section 96 or 97, they shall prepare, for the purpose of assisting the governing body who will succeed them, a brief report of the action which they have taken in the discharge of their functions.

(2) All minutes and papers of a temporary governing body, including the report prepared under sub-paragraph (1), shall be made available to their successors.

Sections 122 and 124

SCHEDULE 11

Contents of statements under section 122(2) and section 124(1)

Part I

Statements under section 122(2)

1.—(1) This Part of this Schedule applies to any statement prepared by a local education authority under section 122(2).

(2) In this Part of this Schedule "the scheme" means the scheme referred to in section 122(1).

2. The statement shall contain the following particulars in respect of the financial year to which it relates—

(a) the amount of the authority's general schools budget for the year (as initially determined for the purposes of the scheme),

(b) the amount of the authority's aggregated budget for the year under the scheme (as so determined),

(c) such particulars as may be prescribed of amounts deducted in respect of excepted heads or items of expenditure (as defined in section 105(3)) in arriving at the amount specified in the statement by virtue of subparagraph (b),

(d) such particulars as may be prescribed of amounts deducted by virtue of section 105(1)(b) in arriving at the amount so specified, and

(e) such particulars of the allocation formula under the scheme as may be prescribed.

3.—(1) The statement shall also contain, with respect to each school required to be covered by the scheme in the year in question, particulars in relation to that year of the planned expenditure per pupil arising from the division of the school's budget share (as initially determined for the purposes of the scheme) by the initial pupil number.

(2) In sub-paragraph (1) "the initial pupil number" means the number of registered pupils at the school in question which is required under the scheme to be used in applying the allocation formula under the scheme for initial determination of the school's budget share for the year.

4. The statement shall contain such further information in respect of the financial provision the authority plan to make in the year in question for county and voluntary schools maintained by them as may be prescribed.

PART II

STATEMENTS UNDER SECTION 124(1)

5.—(1) A statement prepared by a local education authority under section 124(1) shall give the following particulars in respect of the financial year to which it relates—

(a) the initial amount appropriated for meeting expenditure in the year in respect of all the schools required to be covered by the statement,
(b) the amount remaining after deducting from that initial amount the aggregate of the amounts referred to in sub-paragraph (2), and
(c) such particulars as may be prescribed of the amounts referred to in subparagraph (2).

(2) Those amounts are the initial amounts appropriated for meeting the following descriptions of expenditure in the year in respect of all the schools required to be covered by the statement—

(a) expenditure treated by the authority as expenditure of a capital nature,
(b) expenditure in respect of the repayment of the principal of, the payment of interest on and the discharge of any other financial obligation in connection with any loan used to meet expenditure falling within paragraph (a), and
(c) expenditure of such other descriptions as may be prescribed.

6.—(1) The statement shall also give, in relation to each school required to be covered by it, the following particulars in respect of the year—

(a) the share of the general expenditure amount which is appropriated by the authority for meeting expenditure for the purposes of the school,
(b) the share which is so appropriated of such of the amounts referred to in paragraph 5(2)(c) as may be prescribed,
(c) the amount of any expenditure initially planned for the purposes of the school and treated by the authority as expenditure of a capital nature, and
(d) such particulars as may be prescribed of the basis on which the authority determine the shares specified in the statement by virtue of paragraphs (a) and (b).

(2) In sub-paragraph (1) "the general expenditure amount" means the amount of which particulars are required to be given by paragraph 5(1)(b).

7. The statement shall contain such further information in respect of the financial provision initially planned by the authority for the schools required to be covered by the statement as may be prescribed.

8. Where only one school is required to be covered by the statement, the references in paragraph 5 to all the schools are references to that school and paragraph 6 does not apply.

Section 126

SCHEDULE 12

FINANCIAL DELEGATION AND NEW SCHOOLS

Preliminary

1. In this Schedule "temporary governing body" does not include a temporary governing body who by virtue of paragraph 2 of Schedule 10 fall to be treated as a governing body.

New county and voluntary schools

2.—(1) For the purposes of applying (in accordance with this Schedule) sections 101 to 122 and Part I of Schedule 11 in relation to new schools which will be county or voluntary schools—

(a) references to a school conducted by a governing body shall be read as including a new school which has a temporary governing body, and
(b) other references to the governing body of a school shall be read as including the temporary governing body of a new school.

(2) For those purposes—

(b) references to a county or voluntary school maintained by a local education authority, and
(b) references, in a context referring to a local education authority, to county and voluntary schools,

shall be read as including a new school which on implementation of the relevant proposals will be a county or voluntary school maintained by the authority.

3.—(1) A new school which will be a county or voluntary school is required to be covered by a scheme in any financial year if it has a temporary governing body during the whole or any part of that year.

(2) In the case of such a school, sections 101 to 122 and Part I of Schedule 11 apply subject to the modifications set out in paragraphs 4 to 7.

4.—(1) Where a school required to be covered by a scheme in a financial year is a new school during the whole or any part of that year, the provision required by section 106(4)(a) shall not apply in relation to the determination of the school's budget share for the year, so far as that share falls in accordance with the scheme to be treated as referable to planned expenditure by the local education authority for the purposes of the school in respect of any period before the implementation of the relevant proposals.

(2) Accordingly—

(a) paragraph 3(1) of Schedule 11 shall apply in relation to the school as if it referred to such part (if any) of the school's budget share for the year as falls to be determined in accordance with the provision required by section 106(4)(a); and

(b) the statement under section 122(2) shall include in relation to the school the additional particulars mentioned in sub-paragraph (3).

(3) Those particulars are the amount of such part (if any) of the school's budget share for the year (as initially determined for the purposes of the scheme) as falls in accordance with the scheme to be treated as referable to planned expenditure such as is mentioned in sub-paragraph (1).

(4) Sub-paragraph (1) shall not be taken as prejudicing the inclusion in the allocation formula under a scheme, by virtue of section 106(4)(b), of provision taking into account in relation to a new school any forecast made in accordance with the scheme of the number of pupils it will have on implementation of the relevant proposals.

5. The delegation requirement under a scheme shall not apply in relation to a new school (where it is not a school to which section 110 applies) until such date as may be determined by or under the scheme.

6. Section 110 shall have effect, in relation to a new school to which it applies, with the omission of subsection (3)(a).

7. Section 122(7) shall not apply in relation to the temporary governing body of a new school.

New special schools

8.—(1) Any reference—

(a) in section 120, to maintained special schools or to a maintained special school, or

(b) in section 124, to special schools or to a special school,

shall be read as including a new school proposed to be established by a local education authority which will be a maintained special school and which has a temporary governing body.

(2) Any reference in section 120 or 124 to a school's governing body shall be read, in relation to such a new school, as a reference to its temporary governing body.

(3) The reference in section 124(1) to a local education authority maintaining a special school or special schools shall be read, in relation to such a new school, as a reference to the authority being under a duty by virtue of paragraph 20 of Schedule 9 to defray expenses in relation to its temporary governing body.

9. Section 124(8) shall not apply in relation to the temporary governing body of a new school.

Financial delegation apart from schemes

10. Section 125 shall not apply in relation to a new school.

Section 133

SCHEDULE 13

STAFFING OF COUNTY, CONTROLLED, SPECIAL AGREEMENT AND MAINTAINED SPECIAL SCHOOLS

The selection panel

1.—(1) The articles of government for a county, controlled, special agreement or maintained special school shall provide—

(a) for the constitution of a selection panel whenever such a panel is required by virtue of this Schedule in relation to the appointment of a head teacher or deputy head teacher, and

(b) for a selection panel to consist of a specified number of persons appointed to it by the local education authority and a specified number of governors appointed to it by the governing body.

(2) Neither of the numbers specified by virtue of sub-paragraph (1)(b) shall be less than three; and the number specified in relation to appointments made by the governing body shall not be less than the number specified in relation to appointments made by the authority.

(3) The articles shall provide for the governing body and the authority to have power to replace, at any time, any member of a selection panel whom they have appointed.

2. Regulations may make provision as to the meetings and proceedings of selection panels.

Appointment of head teacher

3.—(1) The articles of government for a county, controlled, special agreement or maintained special school shall, in relation to the appointment of a head teacher for the school, make provision for the matters set out in sub-paragraphs (2) to (11).

(2) If the post of head teacher is vacant, the local education authority shall appoint an acting head teacher after consulting the governing body.

(3) Before appointing a head teacher, the local education authority shall advertise the vacancy in such publications circulating throughout England and Wales as they consider appropriate.

(4) The local education authority shall not appoint a person to be head teacher unless his appointment has been recommended by a selection panel constituted in accordance with the articles.

(5) The selection panel shall interview such applicants for the post as they think fit.

(6) If the panel fail to agree on the applicants whom they wish to interview—

(a) the members of the panel appointed by the governing body are to have the right to nominate not more than two applicants to be interviewed by the panel, and

(b) the other members of the panel are to have the right to nominate not more than two other applicants to be interviewed.

(7) Where the panel consider it appropriate to do so, they shall recommend to the authority for appointment as head teacher one of the applicants interviewed by them.

(8) If the panel are unable to agree on a person to recommend to the authority, they shall—

(a) repeat (with a view to reaching agreement) such of the steps mentioned in sub-paragraphs (5) to (7) as they think fit,

(b) where—

(i) they have repeated any of those steps in pursuance of paragraph (a) and remain unable to agree, or

(ii) they have decided that it is not appropriate to repeat any of those steps,

require the authority to re-advertise the vacancy, and

(c) where the vacancy is re-advertised, repeat all of the steps mentioned in sub-paragraphs (5) to (7).

(9) If the authority decline to appoint a person recommended by the panel, the panel shall—

(a) where there are applicants for the post whom they have not interviewed, interview such of those applicants (if any) as they think fit,

(b) recommend another of the applicants interviewed by them, if they think fit,

(c) ask the authority to re-advertise the vacancy, if they consider that it should be re-advertised, and

(d) where the vacancy is re-advertised, repeat the steps mentioned in subparagraphs (5) to (7).

(10) The authority shall re-advertise the vacancy where they are required to do so by the panel, and may do so where—

(a) it has been duly advertised,

(b) the panel have failed either to make a recommendation which is acceptable to the authority or to request that the vacancy be re-advertised, and

(c) the authority are of the opinion that the panel have had sufficient time in which to carry out their functions.

(11) The chief education officer of the authority, or a member of his department nominated by him, shall have the right to attend all proceedings of the panel (including interviews) for the purpose of giving advice to members of the panel.

(12) In this paragraph "head teacher" does not include an acting head teacher.

Appointment of deputy head teacher

4.—(1) The articles of government for a county, controlled, special agreement or maintained special school shall, in relation to the appointment of a deputy head teacher for the school, make either—

(a) the same provision, modified as mentioned in sub-paragraphs (2) and (3), as that made (in accordance with paragraph 3) in relation to the appointment of a head teacher for the school, or

(b) the same provision as that made (in accordance with paragraph 5) in relation to the appointment of other teachers at the school.

(2) If the articles (in accordance with sub-paragraph (1)(a)) provide for the appointment of a deputy head teacher to be on the recommendation of a selection panel, they shall provide that where the head teacher is not a member of the panel—

(a) he may be present, for the purpose of giving advice, at any proceedings of the panel (including interviews), and
(b) whether or not he attends any such proceedings, he shall be consulted by the panel before they make any recommendation to the local education authority.

(3) No provision similar to that set out in paragraph 3(2) is required in the articles in relation to the appointment of a deputy head teacher.

Appointment of other staff: general

5.—(1) The articles of government for a county, controlled, special agreement or maintained special school shall make provision for the matters set out in sub-paragraphs (2) and (3).

(2) Where there is a vacancy in a post (other than that of head teacher or deputy head teacher) which is part of the complement of the school, the local education authority shall decide whether, if the post is not a new one, it should be retained.

(3) If the authority decide that the post should be retained or it is a new post, they shall—
(a) advertise the vacancy and fill it in accordance with the procedure laid down by virtue of paragraph 6, unless they have the intention mentioned in paragraph (b) below;
(b) fill the vacancy in accordance with the procedure laid down by virtue of paragraph 7, if they intend to appoint a person who, at the time when they form that intention, is an employee of theirs or has been appointed to take up employment with them at a future date.

(4) Nothing in this paragraph (or in any of paragraphs 6 to 9) applies in relation to any temporary appointment pending—
(a) the return to work of the holder of the post in question, or
(b) the taking of any steps required by the articles in relation to the vacancy in question.

Appointment of other staff: vacancy advertised

6.—(1) The articles of government for any school to which paragraph 5(1) applies shall make provision for the matters set out in sub-paragraphs (2) to (7).

(2) Where the local education authority decide to advertise the vacancy, they shall do so in a manner likely in their opinion to bring it to the notice of persons (including employees of theirs) who are qualified to fill the post.

(3) Where the vacancy is advertised, the governing body shall—
(a) interview such applicants for the post as they think fit, and
(b) where they consider it appropriate to do so, recommend to the authority for appointment to the post one of the applicants interviewed by them.

(4) If the governing body are unable to agree on a person to recommend to the authority, they shall—
(a) repeat the steps mentioned in sub-paragraph (3), if they consider that to do so might lead to their reaching agreement,
(b) where they have repeated those steps and remain unable to agree, or decide that it is not appropriate to repeat them, ask the authority to readvertise the vacancy, and
(c) where the vacancy is re-advertised, repeat those steps.

(5) If the authority decline to appoint a person recommended by the governing body, the governing body shall—
(a) where there are applicants for the post whom they have not interviewed, interview such of those applicants (if any) as they think fit,
(b) recommend another of the applicants interviewed by them, if they think fit,
(c) ask the authority to re-advertise the vacancy, if they consider that it should be re-advertised, and
(d) where the vacancy is re-advertised, repeat the steps mentioned in sub-paragraph (3).

(6) Where the authority are asked to re-advertise the vacancy by the governing body, they shall do so unless—
(a) they decide that the post is to be removed from the complement of the school, or
(b) they decide to appoint a person who, at the time when that decision is made, is an employee of theirs or has been appointed to take up employment with them at a future date.

(7) Whenever governors meet to discuss the appointment or an applicant is interviewed—
(a) the head teacher (if he would not otherwise be entitled to be present), and
(b) such person (if any) as the authority appoint to represent them,
shall be entitled to be present for the purpose of giving advice.

Appointment of other staff: vacancy not advertised

7.—(1) The articles of government for any school to which paragraph 5(1) applies shall make provision for the matters set out in sub-paragraphs (2) and (3).

(2) Where the vacancy is not advertised, the governing body—

(a) shall be entitled to determine a specification for the post in consultation with the head teacher, and

(b) if they do so, shall send a copy of it to the local education authority.

(3) When considering whom to appoint to the post, the authority shall—

(a) have regard to any such specification, and

(b) consult the governing body and the head teacher.

Delegation of functions under paragraph 6 or 7

8.—(1) The articles of government for any school to which paragraph 5(1) applies shall make provision for the matters set out in sub-paragraphs (2) and (3).

(2) The governing body shall have power, in relation to the filling of a particular vacancy or a vacancy of a kind specified by them, to delegate any of the functions which are theirs by virtue of paragraph 6 or 7—

(a) to one or more governors,

(b) to the head teacher, or

(c) to one or more governors and the head teacher acting together.

(3) In such a case, the provision made by virtue of paragraph 6(6) shall apply with the substitution of references to the person or persons to whom the functions are delegated for references to the governing body.

Restriction on making appointment where vacancy advertised

9. Where a local education authority have advertised a vacancy in accordance with the provision made by the articles of government for a school by virtue of paragraph 6(2), they shall not appoint a person to the post unless—

(a) his appointment has been recommended in accordance with the provision made by the articles by virtue of paragraph 6(3) to (5), or

(b) they decide to appoint a person who, at the time when that decision is made, is an employee of theirs or has been appointed to take up employment with them at a future date.

Consultation by LEA before appointing certain non-teaching staff

10. The articles of government for a county, controlled, special agreement or maintained special school shall require the local education authority to consult the governing body and the head teacher before appointing any person to work solely at the school otherwise than—

(a) in a teaching post,

(b) in a non-teaching post which is part of the complement of the school, or

(c) solely in connection with either or both of the following—

(i) the provision of meals;

(ii) the supervision of pupils at midday.

Dismissal etc. of staff

11.—(1) The articles of government for a county, controlled, special agreement or maintained special school shall make provision for the matters set out in sub-paragraphs (2) to (7).

(2) The local education authority shall consult the governing body and (except where he is the person concerned) the head teacher before—

(a) dismissing a person to whom sub-paragraph (3) applies, or

(b) otherwise requiring such a person to cease to work at the school, or

(c) permitting such a person to retire in circumstances in which he would be entitled to compensation for premature retirement.

(3) This sub-paragraph applies to any person who is—

(a) employed in a post which is part of the complement of the school, or

(b) employed to work solely at the school in any other post, otherwise than solely in connection with either or both of the following

(i) the provision of meals;

(ii) the supervision of pupils at midday.

(4) Where a teacher at the school is required to complete an initial period of probation, the local education authority shall consult the governing body and the head teacher before—

(a) extending his period of probation, or

(b) deciding whether he has completed it successfully.

(5) Where the governing body recommend to the local education authority that a person should cease to work at the school, the authority shall consider their recommendation.

(6) Both the governing body and the head teacher shall have power to suspend a person employed to work at the school where, in the opinion of the governing body or (as the case may be) the head teacher, his exclusion from the school is required.

(7) The governing body or head teacher shall—

(a) when exercising that power, immediately inform the local education authority and the head teacher or (as the case may be) governing body, and

(b) end the suspension if directed to do so by the authority.

(8) In this paragraph "suspend" means suspend without loss of emoluments; and in sub-paragraph (2) the reference to dismissing a person does not include a dismissal under section 143(6) or 144(3) (dismissal of teachers of religious education).

Section 136

SCHEDULE 14

STAFFING OF COUNTY, CONTROLLED AND SPECIAL AGREEMENT SCHOOLS WITH DELEGATED BUDGETS

Introductory

1.—(1) In this Schedule "the school" means a county, controlled or special agreement school at any time when it has a delegated budget.

(2) References in this Schedule to a vacancy in any post include a prospective vacancy in the post.

(3) References in this Schedule to staff qualification requirements are to any requirements with respect to—

(a) qualifications,

(b) health and physical capacity, or

(c) fitness on educational grounds or in any other respect,

of teachers and other persons employed in work that brings them regularly into contact with persons who have not attained the age of 19 which for the time being apply under regulations under section 218 of the Education Reform Act 1988.

(4) References in this Schedule to the chief education officer of a local education authority include any officer of the authority nominated by the chief education officer.

Appointment of head teacher and deputy head teacher

2. Paragraphs 3 to 7 apply in relation to an appointment to fill a vacancy in the post of head teacher or deputy head teacher of the school.

3. The governing body shall notify the local education authority of the vacancy in writing before taking any of the steps mentioned below.

4.—(1) Where the vacancy is in the post of head teacher and either the post has not been filled, or it appears to the governing body that the post will not be filled, by an appointment made in accordance with paragraphs 5 to 7 before the date on which it falls vacant—

(a) the governing body shall recommend a person for appointment as acting head teacher, and

(b) the local education authority shall appoint the person recommended unless he does not meet any staff qualification requirements which are applicable in relation to his appointment.

(2) Where the vacancy is in the post of deputy head teacher and either the post has not been filled, or it appears to the governing body that the post will not be filled, by an appointment made in accordance with paragraphs 5 to 7 before the date on which it falls vacant—

(a) the governing body may recommend a person for appointment as acting deputy head teacher, and

(b) if they do recommend a person, the local education authority shall appoint him unless he does not meet any staff qualification requirements which are applicable in relation to his appointment.

(3) If the authority decline to appoint a person recommended by the governing body for appointment as acting head teacher, the governing body shall recommend another person for appointment.

5. Before recommending a person for appointment as head teacher or deputy head teacher, the governing body shall advertise the vacancy in such publications circulating throughout England and Wales as they consider appropriate.

6.—(1) The governing body shall appoint a selection panel consisting of at least three of their members to perform the functions conferred on them by this paragraph.

(2) The selection panel shall—

(a) interview such applicants for the post as they think fit,

(b) where they consider it appropriate to do so, recommend to the governing body for appointment one of the applicants interviewed by them, and

(c) if their recommendation is approved by the governing body, recommend the applicant in question to the local education authority for appointment.

(3) If the panel are unable to agree on a person to recommend to the governing body, or the governing body do not approve their recommendation, the governing body—

(a) may, if they think fit, re-advertise the vacancy in the manner required by paragraph 5, and

(b) whether or not they re-advertise the vacancy, may require the panel to repeat the steps mentioned in sub-paragraph (2).

7.—(1) The local education authority shall appoint the person recommended by the selection panel unless he does not meet any staff qualification requirements which are applicable in relation to his appointment.

(2) If the authority decline to appoint the person recommended by the panel, the governing body—

(a) may, if they think fit, re-advertise the vacancy in the manner required by paragraph 5, and

(b) whether or not they re-advertise the vacancy, may require the panel to repeat the steps mentioned in paragraph 6(2).

Appointment of other teachers

8. Subject to paragraph 9, paragraphs 10 to 14 apply in relation to an appointment to fill a vacancy in any teaching post (whether full-time or part-time) at the school, other than the post of head teacher or deputy head teacher.

9.—(1) Paragraphs 10 to 14 do not apply in relation to a temporary appointment to fill such a vacancy—

(a) for a period not exceeding four months, or

(b) where it appears to the governing body that the period for which the person appointed will hold the post in question will not exceed four months.

(2) Where it appears to the governing body in the case of any post that it would be appropriate to make an appointment such as is mentioned in sub-paragraph (1)—

(a) they may recommend a person for appointment to the post on such terms as to the duration of the appointment as they may specify, and

(b) the local education authority shall appoint the person recommended on the terms specified unless he does not meet any staff qualification requirements which are applicable in relation to his appointment.

10. Before taking any of the steps mentioned below, the governing body shall—

(a) determine a specification for the post in consultation with the head teacher, and

(b) send a copy of the specification to the local education authority.

11.—(1) The local education authority may nominate for consideration for appointment to the post any person who appears to them to be qualified to fill it and who at the time of his nomination either—

(a) is an employee of theirs or has been appointed to take up employment with them at a future date, or

(b) is employed by the governing body of an aided school maintained by them.

(2) The authority shall not nominate a person within sub-paragraph (1)(b) without the consent of the governing body of the aided school.

12.—(1) The governing body may advertise the vacancy at any time after they have sent a copy of the specification for the post to the local education authority in accordance with paragraph 10, and shall do so unless either—

(a) they accept for appointment to the post a person nominated by the local education authority under paragraph 11, or

(b) they decide to recommend to the authority for appointment to the post a person who is already employed to work at the school.

(2) Where the governing body advertise the vacancy, they shall do so in a manner likely in their opinion to bring it to the notice of persons (including employees of the authority) who are qualified to fill it.

13.—(1) Where the governing body advertise the vacancy, they shall—

(a) interview such applicants for the post and such of the persons (if any) nominated by the local education authority under paragraph 11 as they think fit, and

(b) where they consider it appropriate to do so, either recommend to the authority for appointment one of the applicants interviewed by them or notify the authority that they accept for appointment any person nominated by the authority under paragraph 11.

(2) If the governing body are unable to agree on a person to recommend or accept for appointment, they may repeat the steps mentioned in sub-paragraph (1)(a) and (b), with or without first re-advertising the vacancy in accordance with paragraph 12(2).

14.—(1) The local education authority shall appoint the person recommended or accepted for appointment by the governing body unless (in the case of a person other than one nominated by the authority) he does not meet any staff qualification requirements which are applicable in relation to his appointment.

(2) If the authority decline to appoint a person recommended by the governing body, the governing body shall repeat such of the steps mentioned in paragraph 13(1)(a) and (b) as they think fit, with or without first re-advertising the vacancy in accordance with paragraph 12(2).

15. The governing body may, in relation to the filling of a particular vacancy or a vacancy of a kind specified by them, delegate any of their functions under paragraphs 9 to 14—

(a) to one or more governors,

(b) to the head teacher, or

(c) to one or more governors and the head teacher acting together.

Advice of chief education officer on appointments of teachers

16.—(1) The chief education officer of the local education authority shall be entitled to attend, for the purpose of giving advice—

(a) all proceedings (including interviews) of the governing body, and of any selection panel appointed under paragraph 6, relating to appointments to which paragraphs 3 to 7 apply, and

(b) all proceedings (including interviews) of the governing body, and of any persons to whom any functions of the governing body under paragraphs 9 to 14 are delegated, relating to appointments to which paragraph 9 applies or to which paragraphs 10 to 14 apply.

(2) The chief education officer shall offer such advice as he considers appropriate with respect to—

(a) the appointment of a head teacher, a deputy head teacher, an acting head teacher or an acting deputy head teacher, or

(b) any matter arising in connection with such an appointment.

(3) If requested to do so by the governing body, the chief education officer shall give such advice as he considers appropriate in relation to any appointment to which paragraph 9 applies or to which paragraphs 10 to 14 apply.

(4) Any advice given by the chief education officer to—

(a) the governing body,

(b) any selection panel appointed under paragraph 6, or

(c) any persons to whom any functions of the governing body under paragraphs 9 to 14 are delegated,

with respect to any matter which relates to an appointment and falls to be determined by them shall be considered by them before determining that matter, whether or not the advice was given at their request.

Advice of head teacher on appointments of teachers

17. Except in relation to the appointment of a head teacher—

(a) paragraph 16(1) applies in relation to the head teacher (if not otherwise entitled to be present at the proceedings there mentioned) as it applies in relation to the chief education officer, and

(b) paragraph 16(4) applies in relation to advice given by the head teacher as it applies in relation to advice given by the chief education officer.

Appointment of non-teaching staff

18.—(1) Where the governing body wish to appoint a person to work in a non-teaching post at the school, they may recommend a person to the local education authority for appointment to the post.

(2) A recommendation under this paragraph shall be in writing and shall specify—

(a) the duties to be performed by the person appointed (including, where the post is part-time, his hours of work);

(b) the grade (on the scale of grades currently applicable in relation to employment with the authority) which the governing body consider appropriate for the post; and

(c) where the authority have a discretion with respect to the remuneration to be paid to a person appointed to the post, the determination of any matter to which that discretion applies and which the governing body consider appropriate in the case of the person recommended for appointment.

(3) Before selecting a person to recommend under this paragraph and determining in relation to such a recommendation any matters mentioned in sub-paragraph (2), the governing body shall consult—

(a) the head teacher (where he would not otherwise be involved in the decision), and

(b) if the post involves (or in the case of a new post, it is proposed that it should involve) work at the school for 16 hours a week or more, the chief education officer of the authority.

(4) For the purposes of sub-paragraph (2)(c), the authority are to be regarded as having a discretion with respect to the remuneration to be paid to a person appointed to a post if any provisions regulating the rates of remuneration or allowances payable to persons in the authority's employment either—

(a) do not apply in relation to that appointment, or

(b) leave to the authority any degree of discretion as to rate of remuneration or allowances in the case of that appointment.

19.—(1) The local education authority shall appoint a person recommended to them under paragraph 18 unless he does not meet any staff qualification requirements which are applicable in relation to his appointment.

(2) Any such appointment shall be on such terms as to give effect, so far as they relate to any matter mentioned in paragraph 18(2), to the governing body's recommendation in respect of that matter.

The clerk to the governing body

20.—(1) Where there is a vacancy in the office of clerk to the governing body of the school, the local education authority shall appoint a person selected by the governing body.

(2) Before selecting a person to recommend for such appointment, the governing body shall consult the chief education officer of the authority.

Discipline

21.—(1) The regulation of conduct and discipline in relation to the staff of the school, and any procedures for giving members of the staff opportunities for seeking redress of any grievances relating to their employment, shall be under the control of the governing body.

(2) The governing body shall establish—

(a) disciplinary rules and procedures, and

(b) procedures such as are mentioned in sub-paragraph (1),

and shall take such steps as appear to them to be appropriate for making them known to the staff at the school.

(3) Where the implementation of any determination made by the governing body in the exercise of their control over the conduct and discipline of the staff requires any action which—

(a) is not within the functions exercisable by the governing body by virtue of this Act, but

(b) is within the power of the local education authority,

the authority shall take that action at the request of the governing body.

Suspension

22.—(1) Both the governing body and the head teacher shall have power to suspend any person employed to work at the school where, in the opinion of the governing body or (as the case may be) the head teacher, his exclusion from the school is required.

(2) The governing body or head teacher shall, when exercising that power, immediately inform the local education authority and the head teacher or (as the case may be) governing body.

(3) A suspension under this paragraph may only be ended by the governing body.

(4) The governing body shall, on ending such a suspension, immediately inform the authority and the head teacher.

(5) In this paragraph "suspend" means suspend without loss of emoluments.

Dismissal, etc.

23.—(1) Where the governing body determine—

(a) that any person employed to work at the school should cease to work there, or

(b) that the clerk to the governing body should be dismissed,

they shall notify the local education authority in writing of their determination and the reasons for it.

(2) If in a case within sub-paragraph (1)(a) the person concerned is employed to work solely at the school (and he does not resign), the authority shall, before the end of the period of 14 days beginning with the date on which the notification under sub-paragraph (1) is given, either—

(a) give him such notice terminating his contract of employment with the authority as is required under that contract, or
(b) terminate that contract without notice if the circumstances are such that they are entitled to do so by reason of his conduct.

(3) If in a case within sub-paragraph (1)(a) the person concerned is not employed to work solely at the school, the authority shall require him to cease to work at the school.

(4) In a case within sub-paragraph (1)(b), the authority shall dismiss the clerk to the governing body on receipt of the notification from the governing body.

24.—(1) Where paragraph 23(3) applies, no part of the costs incurred by the local education authority in respect of the emoluments of the person concerned, so far as they relate to any period falling after the expiration of his contractual notice period, shall be met from the school's budget share.

(2) The reference in sub-paragraph (1) to the person's contractual notice period is to the period of notice that would have been required under his contract of employment with the authority for termination of that contract if such notice had been given on the date on which the notification under paragraph 23(1) was given.

25.—(1) The governing body shall—
(a) make arrangements for giving any person in respect of whom they propose to make a determination under paragraph 23(1) an opportunity of making representations as to the action they propose to take (including, if he so wishes, oral representations to such person or persons as the governing body may appoint for the purpose), and
(b) have regard to any representations made by him.

(2) The governing body shall also make arrangements for giving any person in respect of whom they have made a determination under paragraph 23(1) an opportunity of appealing against it before they notify the local education authority of the determination.

26.—(1) The head teacher (except where he is the person concerned) and the chief education officer of the local education authority shall be entitled to attend, for the purpose of giving advice, all proceedings of the governing body relating to a determination under paragraph 23(1).

(2) The governing body shall consider any advice given by a person who is entitled to attend such proceedings under this paragraph before making a determination under paragraph 23(1).

27.—(1) The local education authority shall not dismiss a person employed by them to work solely at the school except as provided by paragraph 23.

(2) Sub-paragraph (1) does not apply in a case where the dismissal of the person in question is required under regulations under section 218(6) of the Education Reform Act 1988 (regulations prohibiting or restricting employment or further employment of teachers etc. in cases of misconduct or on medical or educational grounds).

School meals staff

28. Nothing in paragraphs 18, 19 and 21 to 27 applies in relation to the appointment of a person to work at the school, or in relation to a person so employed, where—
(a) the person concerned is to be, or is, employed to work solely in connection with the provision of meals, and
(b) less than 50 per cent. of the person's remuneration will be, or is, met from the school's delegated budget.

Section 158

SCHEDULE 15

Reinstatement of pupils excluded from county, voluntary or maintained special Schools

Part I

County, Controlled and Maintained Special Schools

Preliminary

1. The articles of government for a county, controlled or maintained special school shall make provision for the matters set out in paragraphs 2 to 7.

Reinstatement of permanently excluded pupils

2.—(1) Where the local education authority have been informed of the permanent exclusion of a pupil from the school, they shall—
(a) after giving the governing body an opportunity to express their views, and
(b) after considering any views expressed within the prescribed period by the governing body,

consider whether the pupil should be reinstated immediately, reinstated by a particular date or not reinstated.

(2) If the authority decide that the pupil should be reinstated, they shall—

(a) give the appropriate direction to the head teacher, and

(b) inform the relevant person and the governing body of the direction.

(3) If the authority decide that the pupil should not be reinstated, they shall inform the relevant person of their decision.

3.—(1) The head teacher shall comply with any direction for the reinstatement of a pupil who has been permanently excluded from the school—

(a) which is given by the local education authority by virtue of paragraph 2, or

(b) which is given by the governing body.

(2) If conflicting directions are given by the authority and the governing body, the head teacher shall comply with the direction which will lead to the earlier reinstatement of the pupil.

4. Where the governing body direct the head teacher to reinstate a pupil who has been permanently excluded from the school, they shall inform the relevant person and the local education authority of the direction.

Reinstatement of pupils excluded for a fixed period

5.—(1) Where a pupil is excluded from the school for a fixed period in circumstances in which he would, as a result of the exclusion—

(a) be excluded from the school for a total of more than five school days in any one term, or

(b) lose an opportunity to take a public examination,

the head teacher shall comply with any direction given by the local education authority or the governing body for the pupil's reinstatement.

(2) If conflicting directions are given by the authority and the governing body, the head teacher shall comply with the direction which will lead to the earlier reinstatement of the pupil.

6.—(1) Where the local education authority—

(a) have been informed of the exclusion of a pupil from the school for a fixed period, and

(b) propose to give any such direction as is mentioned in paragraph 5(1),

they shall consult the governing body before giving such a direction.

(2) Where they give such a direction, the authority shall inform the relevant person and the governing body of the direction.

7. Where the governing body give any such direction as is mentioned in paragraph 5(1), they shall inform the relevant person and the local education authority of the direction.

PART II

AIDED AND SPECIAL AGREEMENT SCHOOLS

Preliminary

8. The articles of government for an aided or a special agreement school shall make provision for the matters set out in paragraphs 9 to 13.

Reinstatement of permanently excluded pupils

9.—(1) Where the governing body have been informed of the permanent exclusion of a pupil from the school, they shall consider whether he should be reinstated immediately, reinstated by a particular date or not reinstated.

(2) If the governing body decide that the pupil should be reinstated, they shall—

(a) give the appropriate direction to the head teacher, and

(b) inform the relevant person and the local education authority of the direction.

(3) If the governing body decide that the pupil should not be reinstated, they shall (without delay) inform the relevant person and the local education authority of their decision.

10. The head teacher shall comply with any direction for the reinstatement of the pupil given by the governing body by virtue of paragraph 9.

Reinstatement of pupils excluded for a fixed period

11.—(1) Where a pupil is excluded from the school for a fixed period in circumstances in which he would, as a result of the exclusion—

(a) be excluded from the school for a total of more than five school days in any one term, or

(b) lose an opportunity to take a public examination,

the head teacher shall comply with any direction given by the governing body or the local education authority for the pupil's reinstatement.

(2) If conflicting directions are given by the authority and the governing body, the head teacher shall comply with the direction which will lead to the earlier reinstatement of the pupil.

12.—(1) Before giving any such direction as is mentioned in paragraph 11(1) the local education authority shall—

(a) give the governing body an opportunity to express their views; and
(b) consider any views expressed within the prescribed period by the governing body.

(2) Where the authority give any such direction, they shall inform the relevant person and the governing body of the direction.

13. Where the governing body give any such direction as is mentioned in paragraph 11(1), they shall inform the relevant person and the local education authority of the direction.

PART III

GENERAL

Power to prescribe periods for the taking of any required steps

14. Regulations may provide that, where a local education authority or governing body of a school are required under the preceding provisions of this Schedule to take any step, the duty must, subject to prescribed exceptions, be performed within the prescribed period; but such a provision shall not relieve the authority or body of the duty to take any step which has not been taken within that period.

Meaning of "the relevant person"

15. In this Schedule "the relevant person" means—

(a) in relation to a pupil under the age of 18, a parent of his;
(b) in relation to a pupil who has attained that age, the pupil himself.

Section 159

SCHEDULE 16

APPEALS AGAINST EXCLUSION OR REINSTATEMENT OF PUPILS

Duty to inform parent or pupil of right of appeal

1.—(1) The articles of government for a county, controlled or maintained special school shall require the local education authority, where by virtue of paragraph 2(3) of Schedule 15 they inform the relevant person of their decision that a pupil should not be reinstated, to give him notice in writing—

(a) of his right to appeal against the decision;
(b) of the last date on which an appeal may be made (calculated in accordance with paragraph 3(1) below);
(c) of his right to give notice under paragraph 3(2) below stating that he does not intend to appeal;
(d) that no appeal may be made after notice under that provision is given.

(2) The articles of government for an aided or a special agreement school shall require the governing body, where by virtue of paragraph 9(3) of Schedule 15 they inform the relevant person of their decision that a pupil should not be reinstated, to give him notice in writing—

(a) of his right to appeal against the decision;
(b) of the last date on which an appeal may be made (calculated in accordance with paragraph 3(1) below);
(c) of his right to give notice under paragraph 3(2) below stating that he does not intend to appeal;
(d) that no appeal may be made after notice under that provision is given.

Suspension of direction for reinstatement pending appeal etc.

2.—(1) A direction for the reinstatement of a pupil given by virtue of paragraph 2 of Schedule 15 shall not have effect for a period ending with the fifth school day ending after the governing body are informed of the direction by the local education authority unless, within that period, the governing body inform the authority that they do not intend to appeal against the direction.

(2) Where, within that period, the governing body lodge an appeal against the direction in accordance with the arrangements made by the local education authority under section 159(1)—

(a) the authority shall, before the end of the fourth school day after the day on which the appeal is lodged, inform the relevant person of his right to make representations to the appeal committee, and

(b) the direction shall not have effect unless it is confirmed by the appeal committee or the appeal is withdrawn.

(3) No appeal against such a direction may be made by the governing body after the direction has taken effect.

Time limits and notices waiving right to appeal

3.—(1) No appeal under section 159(1)(a) or (2) against a decision not to reinstate a pupil may be made after the 15th school day after the day on which the relevant person is given notice in writing under paragraph 1(1) or (2).

(2) Any notice in writing given by the relevant person to the body responsible for making any arrangements under section 159(1) or (2) which states that he does not intend to appeal against a decision not to reinstate the pupil shall be final.

(3) The time limit for appealing under section 159 shall be treated as having expired on the day on which notice is given under sub-paragraph (2) (if earlier than the last day on which an appeal may be made in accordance with sub-paragraph (1)).

Appeal committees

4.—(1) Part I of Schedule 33 (school admission appeals) shall have effect in relation to appeals under section 159 with the necessary modifications.

(2) Accordingly, in the application of that Part of that Schedule in relation to any such appeals—

(a) any reference to section 423(1) shall be read as a reference to section 159(1);

(b) any reference to section 423(2) shall be read as a reference to section 159(2); and

(c) any reference to section 423(3) shall be read as a reference to section 159(3).

Procedure on an appeal

5. In the following provisions of this Schedule—

"appeal" means an appeal under section 159;

"appeal committee" means an appeal committee constituted in accordance with Part I of Schedule 33, as it applies in accordance with paragraph 4 above.

6. An appeal shall be by notice in writing setting out the grounds on which it is made.

7. The appeal committee shall meet to consider an appeal—

(a) within the period ending with the 15th school day after the day on which the appeal is lodged, or

(b) if the body responsible for making any arrangements under section 159 has determined a shorter period, within that period.

8.—(1) On an appeal by a pupil or parent the appeal committee shall give the appellant an opportunity of appearing and making oral representations, and may allow him to be accompanied by a friend or to be represented.

(2) On such an appeal the committee shall allow—

(a) the local education authority and the governing body to make written representations, and

(b) an officer of the authority nominated by the authority, and a governor nominated by the governing body, to appear and make oral representations.

9.—(1) On an appeal by a governing body the appeal committee shall give a governor nominated by the governing body an opportunity of appearing and making oral representations, and shall allow the governing body to be represented.

(2) On such an appeal the committee shall allow—

(a) the relevant person to make written representations and to appear and make oral representations,

(b) the local education authority to make written representations, and

(c) an officer of the authority nominated by the authority to appear and make oral representations.

10.—(1) The body responsible for making any arrangements under section 159 shall, in setting any time limits in connection with appeals, have regard to the desirability of securing that appeals are disposed of without delay.

(2) If the relevant person making an appeal under section 159(1)(a) or (2) requests that body to do so, it may in exceptional circumstances extend the period in which an appeal committee is to hear the appeal and communicate its decision.

11.—(1) Appeals shall be heard in private except when the local education authority or governing body by whom the arrangements under section 159 are made direct otherwise.

(2) Without prejudice to any of the provisions of this Schedule—

(a) a member of the local education authority may attend, as an observer, any hearing of an appeal by an appeal committee; and

(b) any member of the Council on Tribunals may attend, as an observer, any meeting of an appeal committee at which an appeal is considered.

12. Two or more appeals may be combined and dealt with in the same proceedings if the appeal committee consider that it is expedient to do so because the issues raised by the appeals are the same or connected.

13. In the event of a disagreement between the members of an appeal committee, the appeal under consideration shall be decided by a simple majority of the votes cast and, in the case of an equality of votes, the chairman of the committee shall have a second or casting vote.

14. The decision of an appeal committee and the grounds on which it is made shall be communicated by the committee in writing to the relevant person, the local education authority and the governing body, and shall be so communicated—

(a) within the period ending with the 17th school day after the day on which the appeal is lodged, or

(b) if the body responsible for making any arrangements under section 159 has determined a shorter period, within that period.

15.—(1) Subject to paragraphs 6 to 14, all matters relating to the procedure on appeals, including the time within which they are to be brought, shall be determined by the local education authority or governing body by whom the arrangements under section 159 are made.

(2) Neither section 106 of the Local Government Act 1972 nor paragraph 44 of Schedule 12 to that Act (procedure of committees of local authorities) shall apply to an appeal committee.

Notices

16.—(1) Where in accordance with paragraph 1(1) or (2) notice in writing is required to be given to a person, the notice may be given either—

(a) by delivering it to the person's last-known address, or

(b) by properly addressing, pre-paying and sending by first class post to the person's last-known address a letter containing the notice.

(2) For the purposes of calculating the period referred to in paragraph 3(1), a notice shall be taken to have been given—

(a) where first class post is used, on the second school day after the date of posting, or

(b) where the notice is delivered, on the date of delivery,

unless (in either case) the contrary is shown.

Meaning of "the relevant person"

17. In this Schedule "the relevant person" means—

(a) in relation to a pupil under the age of 18, a parent of his;

(b) in relation to a pupil who has attained that age, the pupil himself.

Power of Secretary of State to make amendments

18. The Secretary of State may by order amend the preceding provisions of this Schedule.

Section 161

SCHEDULE 17

Governors' annual reports

General

1.—(1) The articles of government for a county, voluntary or maintained special school shall impose the requirements set out in paragraphs 2 to 9.

(2) In those paragraphs "the report" means a governors' report prepared under section 161.

2. The report shall be as brief as is reasonably consistent with the requirements as to its contents.

Requirements as to contents

3. Where there is an obligation on the governing body (by virtue of section 162) to hold an annual parents' meeting, the report shall—

(a) give details of the date, time and place for the next annual parents' meeting and its agenda;

(b) indicate that the purpose of that meeting will be to discuss both the governors' report and the discharge by the governing body, the head teacher and the local education authority of their functions in relation to the school; and

(c) report on the consideration which has been given to any resolutions passed at the previous annual parents' meeting.

4. The report shall—

(a) give the name of each governor and indicate whether he—
   (i) is a parent, teacher or foundation governor,
   (ii) was co-opted or otherwise appointed as a governor, or
   (iii) is an ex officio governor;
(b) in the case of an appointed governor, say by whom he was appointed;
(c) in relation to each governor who is not an ex officio governor, give the date on which his term of office comes to an end; and
(d) name, and give the address of, the chairman of the governing body and their clerk.

5. The report shall give such information as is available to the governing body about arrangements for the next election of parent governors.

6. The report shall contain a financial statement—

(a) reproducing or summarising any financial statement of which a copy has been provided to the governing body by the local education authority under section 122 or 124 since the last governors' report was prepared under section 161;
(b) indicating, in general terms, how any sum made available to the governing body by the authority—
   (i) in respect of the school's budget share, or
   (ii) under section 125,

   in the period covered by the report was used;
(c) giving details of the application of any gifts made to the school in that period; and
(d) stating the total amount of any travelling and subsistence allowances paid to members of the governing body in that period.

7. The report shall give such information about—

(a) public examinations and other assessments of pupils' achievements,
(b) pupils' absences from the school,
(c) the continuing education of pupils leaving the school, and
(d) the employment or training taken up by such pupils,

as is required to be published by virtue of section 414(6) and (7).

8. The report shall describe what steps have been taken by the governing body to develop or strengthen the school's links with the community (including links with the police).

9. The report shall draw attention to the information made available by the governing body in accordance with regulations made under section 408 so far as relating to the matters mentioned in subsection (2)(b) of that section (information as to educational provision made for pupils at the school and syllabuses followed by them).

Power of Secretary of State to make amendments

10. The Secretary of State may by order amend the preceding provisions of this Schedule.

Section 162

SCHEDULE 18

Annual parents' meetings

Proceedings at an annual parents' meeting

1. The articles of government for a county, voluntary or maintained special school shall provide for the proceedings at an annual parents' meeting to be under the control of the governing body.

2.—(1) The articles of government for a county, voluntary or maintained special school shall provide for any annual parents' meeting at which the required number of parents of registered pupils at the school are present to be entitled to pass (by a simple majority) resolutions on any matters which may properly be discussed at the meeting.

(2) In sub-paragraph (1) "the required number", in relation to a school, means any number equal to or greater than 20 per cent. of the number of registered pupils at the school.

3. No person who is not a parent of a registered pupil at the school may vote on any question put to an annual parents' meeting.

Consideration of resolutions passed at an annual parents' meeting

4.—(1) The articles of government for a county, voluntary or maintained special school shall require the governing body—

(a) to consider any resolution which is duly passed at an annual parents' meeting and which they consider is a matter for them;

(b) to send to the head teacher a copy of any resolution which is so passed and which they consider is a matter for him; and
(c) to send to the local education authority a copy of any resolution which is so passed and which they consider is a matter for the authority.

(2) The articles of government shall in addition—
(a) require the head teacher to consider any resolution a copy of which has been sent to him by virtue of sub-paragraph (1)(b) and to provide the governing body with a brief comment on it (in writing) for inclusion in their next governors' report; and
(b) require the local education authority to do likewise in relation to any resolution a copy of which has been sent to them by virtue of sub-paragraph (1)(c).

Determination of question whether person is to be treated as pupil's parent

5.—(1) The articles of government for a county, controlled or maintained special school shall provide for any question whether any person is to be treated, for the purposes of any provision of the articles relating to the annual parents' meeting, as the parent of a registered pupil at the school to be determined by the local education authority.

(2) The articles of government for an aided or a special agreement school shall provide for any such question to be determined by the governing body.

Section 166

SCHEDULE 19

Conduct and staffing of new county, voluntary and maintained special schools

Part I

General

Articles of government for new schools

1.—(1) The requirement for there to be articles of government for a school (imposed by section 127) shall not apply in relation to a new school until the requirement for there to be an instrument of government for the school takes effect under section 99.

(2) Before making an order under section 127 as to the articles of government for a new school, the local education authority shall consult the temporary governing body and the head teacher.

(3) Before making such an order in respect of a new school which will be a voluntary school, the authority shall—
(a) secure the agreement of the temporary governing body to the terms of the proposed order, and
(b) secure the agreement of the temporary foundation governors to any provisions which are of particular concern to those governors.

(4) Where a local education authority propose to make an order under section 127 in respect of a new school but cannot secure any agreement required by this paragraph, they or (as the case may be) the temporary governing body or temporary foundation governors may refer the matter to the Secretary of State.

(5) On a reference to him under this paragraph, the Secretary of State shall give such direction as he thinks fit.

2. Section 129(2) (amendment of articles) shall not apply in relation to a new school, but if the articles of government for a new county or voluntary school contain any provisions to which section 129(1) would apply during any period when the school had a delegated budget ("inconsistent provisions") they shall also include in relation to each inconsistent provision the statement required by section 129(3).

Conduct of new schools: general

3. The determination of those matters relating to the conduct of a new school which require to be determined before a governing body is constituted for the school under an instrument of government shall be under the direction of the temporary governing body, but subject to any provision made by or under this Act (including, in particular, this Schedule) or any other enactment.

4. Regulations may make in relation to consultation with temporary governing bodies provision similar to the provision that may be made in relation to consultation with governing bodies by regulations under section 131 (consultation not required in urgent cases).

PART II

STAFFING OF NEW SCHOOLS: FINANCIAL DELEGATION NOT PROPOSED

Staffing of new county, controlled or maintained special schools

5. Subject to paragraph 19(4), paragraphs 6 to 11 apply in relation to any new school for which a temporary governing body have been constituted and which will be a county, controlled or maintained special school.

6.—(1) The complement of teaching and non-teaching posts for the school shall be determined by the local education authority.

(2) Section 133(2) and (3) (staff complements) shall apply in relation to a complement determined under this paragraph.

7.—(1) Whenever a selection panel is required by virtue of paragraph 8 or 9, it shall be constituted in accordance with this paragraph.

(2) A selection panel shall consist of—

(a) such number of persons appointed to it by the local education authority, and

(b) such number of temporary governors appointed to it by the temporary governing body, as the authority shall determine.

(3) Neither of the numbers so determined shall be less than three; and the number determined in relation to appointments made by the temporary governing body shall not be less than the number determined in relation to appointments made by the authority.

(4) The temporary governing body and the authority may replace, at any time, any member of a selection panel whom they have appointed.

(5) Regulations may make provision, for the purposes of this paragraph, as to the meetings and proceedings of selection panels.

8.—(1) Subject to sub-paragraph (2) below, sub-paragraphs (3) to (11) of paragraph 3 of Schedule 13 (appointment of head teacher) shall apply in relation to the appointment of a head teacher for the school—

(a) as if they had effect as independent enactments (rather than for the purposes of the provision to be made by articles of government); and

(b) subject to any necessary modifications.

(2) Where—

(a) two or more schools are to be discontinued ("the discontinued schools"), and

(b) the registered pupils at those schools, or a substantial number of those pupils, are expected to transfer to the new school,

the local education authority may, in consultation with the temporary governing body, appoint one of the head teachers of the discontinued schools as the first head teacher for the new school, instead of following the procedure set out in sub-paragraphs (3) to (11) of paragraph 3 of Schedule 13 (as applied by sub-paragraph (1) above).

(3) If the post of head teacher is vacant, the authority may, if they think fit, appoint an acting head teacher after consulting the temporary governing body.

9.—(1) Subject to sub-paragraph (2) below, sub-paragraphs (3) to (11) of paragraph 3 of Schedule 13 shall apply in relation to the appointment of a deputy head teacher for the school—

(a) as if they had effect as independent enactments (rather than for the purposes of the provision to be made by articles of government); and

(b) subject to any necessary modifications.

(2) If the local education authority so decide, those provisions of Schedule 13 shall not so apply and instead the general staff appointment provisions shall apply in relation to the appointment of a deputy head teacher for the school—

(a) as if they had effect as independent enactments (rather than for the purposes of the provision to be made by articles of government); and

(b) subject to any necessary modifications.

(3) Where (in accordance with sub-paragraph (1)) the appointment of a deputy head teacher is on the recommendation of a selection panel and the head teacher is not a member of the panel, the head teacher—

(a) shall be entitled to be present, for the purpose of giving advice, at any proceedings of the panel (including interviews), and

(b) whether or not he attends any such proceedings, shall be consulted by the panel before they make any recommendation to the local education authority.

(4) In this paragraph and paragraph 10 "the general staff appointment provisions" means the following provisions of Schedule 13—
(a) paragraph 5(3);
(b) paragraph 6(2) to (7);
(c) paragraph 7(2) and (3); and
(d) paragraph 8(2) and (3).

10.—(1) The general staff appointment provisions shall apply in relation to the appointment of a person to a post (other than that of head teacher or deputy head teacher) which is part of the complement of the school as if they had effect as independent enactments (rather than for the purposes of the provision to be made by articles of government).

(2) The local education authority shall consult the temporary governing body and the head teacher before appointing any person to work solely at the school otherwise than—
(a) in a teaching post,
(b) in a non-teaching post which is part of the complement of the school, or
(c) solely in connection with either or both of the following—
(i) the provision of meals;
(ii) the supervision of pupils at midday.

(3) This paragraph does not apply in relation to a temporary appointment pending—
(a) the return to work of the holder of the post in question, or
(b) the taking of any steps required by virtue of this Schedule in relation to the vacancy in question.

(4) Paragraph 9(4) applies for the purposes of this paragraph.

11.—(1) The clerk to the temporary governing body shall be appointed by the local education authority.

(2) When the arrangement for the constitution of the temporary governing body comes to an end under section 96 or 97, the person who was the clerk to that body shall act as clerk to the governing body who succeed them, pending the appointment of a clerk under section 135.

12. Subject to paragraph 19(4), a local education authority shall, in discharging their duty under paragraph 21 of Schedule 9 (temporary governing bodies) to provide information to the temporary governing body of a new school which will be a county, controlled or maintained special school, inform the temporary governing body, in particular—
(a) of the number of members of any selection panel required by virtue of paragraph 8 or 9 above who are to be appointed by the authority and the number who are to be appointed by the temporary governing body;
(b) where the authority intend to exercise the power conferred on them by paragraph 8(2) above, of their intention to do so;
(c) of the provision which is to apply in relation to the appointment of the deputy head teacher of the school;
(d) of the complement of staff for the school; and
(e) of the authority's proposals with regard to the appointment of staff for the school and the timing of appointments.

Staffing of new aided schools

13. Subject to paragraph 19(5), paragraphs 14 to 16 apply in relation to a new school which will be an aided school.

14. Subject to paragraph 15(1), the local education authority and the temporary governing body shall have the same powers, and be under the same duties, for the purposes of the appointment and dismissal of staff at the school as would the authority and the governing body for an aided school whose articles of government provided for—
(a) staff employed solely in connection with the provision of school meals to be appointed by the authority, and
(b) other staff employed at the school to be appointed by the governing body.

15.—(1) The first appointment of a clerk to the temporary governing body shall be made by the promoters of the school (that is, the persons making the relevant proposals).

(2) When the arrangement for the constitution of the temporary governing body comes to an end under section 97, the person who was the clerk to that body shall act as clerk to the governing body who succeed them, pending the appointment of their clerk.

16.—(1) The local education authority shall, with a view to enabling staff to be appointed in good time, notify the temporary governing body of any determination, prohibition or direction they intend to make or give pursuant to subsection (2)(b), (4)(a) or (b) or (5) of section 134 (staffing of aided schools).

(2) The authority shall, in discharging their duty under paragraph 21 of Schedule 9 to provide information to the temporary governing body of a new school which will be an aided school,

inform the temporary governing body, in particular, of the authority's proposals with regard to the appointment of staff for the school and the timing of appointments.

Expenditure on staff for new schools

17. Where a temporary governing body are constituted for a new school, the local education authority shall be under the same duty to defray the expenses incurred in relation to the staff appointed in accordance with paragraphs 6 to 11 or (as the case may be) 14 and 15, as they would be if the relevant proposals had been implemented and the temporary governing body were the governing body of the school.

PART III

STAFFING OF NEW SCHOOLS: FINANCIAL DELEGATION PROPOSED

Adaptation of references

18. For the purposes of the application (in accordance with paragraphs 19 to 24) of sections 136 to 141 and Schedule 14 in relation to new schools which will be county or voluntary schools—
(a) references to the governing body of a school shall be read as including the temporary governing body of a new school;
(b) references to a county school shall be read as including a new school which on implementation of the relevant proposals will be a county school; and
(c) references to a voluntary school of a particular category, or maintained by a particular local education authority, shall be read as including a new school which on implementation of the relevant proposals will be a voluntary school of that category, or maintained by that authority.

Application or otherwise of provisions about staffing

19.—(1) Subject to paragraphs 20 to 24, section 136 or (as the case may be) section 137 (staffing of county or voluntary schools with delegated budgets) shall apply to a new school which on implementation of the relevant proposals will be a school of a category to which that section applies not only at any time when (by virtue of Schedule 12) the new school has a delegated budget but also at any time when it has a temporary governing body and sub-paragraph (2) or (3) is satisfied.

(2) This sub-paragraph is satisfied if the delegation requirement under the scheme will apply to the school on or before the implementation of the relevant proposals.

(3) This sub-paragraph is satisfied if the local education authority propose to exercise any power under the scheme to delegate the management of the school's budget share for a financial year by making such a delegation—
(a) to the temporary governing body before the implementation of the relevant proposals, or
(b) to the governing body of the school on implementation of those proposals.

(4) Paragraphs 6 to 12 of this Schedule shall not apply in relation to a new school to which section 136 for the time being applies.

(5) Paragraphs 14 to 16 of this Schedule shall not apply in relation to a new school to which section 137 for the time being applies.

20. Sections 136, 137 and 138 and Schedule 14 (staffing of schools with delegated budgets) shall apply, in the case of a new school, for the purposes only of—
(a) the appointment of staff at the school, and
(b) the taking of such steps with respect to any other matters referred to in those provisions as may be appropriate in preparation for the conduct of the school following implementation of the relevant proposals.

21. In the case of a new school which is a proposed county, controlled, aided or special school, no appointments of staff for the school shall be made by the local education authority before the constitution of a temporary governing body for the school.

22. Section 139(2) and (5) (payments in respect of dismissal) shall not apply in relation to a new school.

23. Any provision included in a scheme by virtue of subsection (3) of section 140 (community schools), so far as it relates to the appointment of staff at a school to which that section applies, shall apply in relation to a new school which on implementation of the relevant proposals will be a school to which that section applies.

24.—(1) Section 141 (amendment of articles) shall not apply in relation to a new school.

(2) The local education authority shall, however, incorporate—
(a) the statement mentioned in section 141(2) in the articles of government for a new school which will be a county or controlled school and to which section 136 applies, or

(b) the statement mentioned in section 141(3) in the articles of government for a new school which will be an aided school and to which section 137 applies.

PART IV

OTHER MATTERS RELATING TO CONDUCT ETC. OF NEW SCHOOLS

Preparation of curriculum

25.—(1) The head teacher of a new school for which a temporary governing body have been constituted shall, in preparing to discharge his functions under Part V in relation to the curriculum for the school, consult that body and the local education authority.

(2) Any authority who have been consulted under this paragraph shall inform the head teacher of the resources which are likely to be made available to the school; and the head teacher shall have regard to any information so given to him.

School terms, holidays and sessions

26.—(1) Pending the coming into force of the articles of government for a new school which will be a county or controlled school—

(a) the dates when the school terms and holidays are to begin and end shall be determined by the local education authority, and

(b) the times of the school sessions shall be determined by the temporary governing body after consultation with the authority.

(2) Pending the coming into force of the articles of government for a new school which will be an aided school—

(a) the dates and times when the school terms and holidays are to begin and end, and

(b) the times of the school sessions,

shall be determined by the temporary governing body.

(3) In this paragraph "the times of the school sessions" means the times at which each of the school sessions (or, if there is only one, the school session) is to begin and end on any day.

Discipline

27. Pending the coming into force of the articles of government for a new school, section 154(2) to (6) (responsibility for discipline) shall apply—

(a) in relation to the head teacher, and

(b) subject to any necessary modifications, in relation to the temporary governing body,

as if they had effect as independent enactments (rather than for the purposes of the provision to be made by articles of government).

Reports and information

28.—(1) A temporary governing body shall provide the local education authority with such reports in connection with the discharge of their functions as the authority may require (either on a regular basis or from time to time).

(2) The head teacher of a new school for which a temporary governing body have been constituted shall provide that body or (as the case may be) the local education authority with such reports in connection with the discharge of his functions as that body or the authority may require (either on a regular basis or from time to time).

(3) In the case of a new school which will be an aided school—

(a) the local education authority shall notify the temporary governing body of any requirement imposed by them on the head teacher under sub-paragraph (2), and

(b) the head teacher shall provide the temporary governing body with a copy of any report which he makes in complying with any such requirement.

Consultation on expenditure by local education authority

29.—(1) Where a temporary governing body have been constituted for a new school, the local education authority shall consult that body and the head teacher on their proposed expenditure on books, equipment and stationery for the school.

(2) Sub-paragraph (1) does not apply in relation to a new school which has a delegated budget.

Sections 193 and 213 SCHEDULE 20

PROPOSALS FOR SCHOOLS TO BECOME, OR BE ESTABLISHED AS, GRANT-MAINTAINED SCHOOLS

PART I

PROPOSALS FOR ACQUISITION OF GRANT-MAINTAINED STATUS

Publication of proposals and notice

1.—(1) Where proposals are required to be published under section 193, they shall be published by being—

(a) posted at or near the main entrance to the school, or (if there is more than one main entrance) all of them,

(b) posted in at least one conspicuous place within the area served by the school, and

(c) made available for inspection at all reasonable times at the school or at any other place within that area to which members of the public may conveniently have access.

(2) Within the period of 10 days beginning with the date of publication of the proposals there shall be published in at least one newspaper circulating in that area a notice in respect of the proposals containing such summary of the proposals as the governing body may think appropriate (including, in particular, the information required by sub-paragraph (3)).

(3) The notice shall—

(a) state that proposals for acquisition of grant-maintained status have been published and submitted to the Secretary of State for approval,

(b) specify the proposed date of implementation of the proposals,

(c) state that, if the proposals are approved, the school will on that date cease to be maintained by the local education authority,

(d) state that, if the proposals are approved, the school will on and after that date be conducted by a governing body incorporated under Part III and receive annual grants from the funding authority,

(e) give the information required to be specified in the proposals by paragraph 4(1)(a) and (2)(a),

(f) state where the proposals may be inspected, and

(g) explain the effect of paragraph 5.

(4) The Secretary of State may by regulations make such provision (whether by way of modification of, or substitution for, the provisions of sub-paragraphs (1) to (3)) as he considers appropriate in relation to—

(a) the publication of proposals for acquisition of grant-maintained status, and

(b) the publication of such notice (if any) in respect of proposals for acquisition of grant-maintained status as may be prescribed.

(5) For the purposes of the application of section 311(6) in relation to sub-paragraph (2) above the requirement to publish a notice under that sub-paragraph shall not be regarded as a requirement with respect to the publication of the proposals in question.

Statement to be annexed to proposals

2.—(1) There shall be annexed to any proposals published under section 193 a statement which shall—

(a) state the result of the ballot, giving the number of votes cast in favour of seeking grant-maintained status for the school, the percentage of those eligible to vote who voted, and the number of votes cast against,

(b) state whether the school is a county, controlled, aided or special agreement school,

(c) briefly describe the existing character of the school including, in the case of a school which has a particular religious character, that character and the religion or religious denomination (if any) in accordance with whose tenets religious education is provided,

(d) state the number of pupils for whom accommodation can be provided at the school, and

(e) give such other information as may be prescribed.

(2) The statement so annexed shall be treated for the purposes of section 193 and of paragraph 1 as forming part of the proposals.

Statement to accompany published proposals

3. Any proposals published under section 193 shall be accompanied by a statement which shall—

(a) describe the requirements of Part III as to the membership of the governing body of a grant-maintained school,
(b) state that the head teacher will be a governor of the school ex officio if the school becomes a grant-maintained school,
(c) explain the circumstances in which a person named in the proposals in accordance with section 234 or 236, or regulations made by virtue of section 240, as a proposed initial governor may be replaced under section 237 or 238 or the regulations,
(d) explain the procedure applicable under Part III in each case in which such a replacement is required,
(e) if the determination of an initial governor of an elected category is pending on the date of publication of the proposals, explain the requirements applicable under Part III in any such case,
(f) explain the effect of paragraph 5, and
(g) give such other information as may be prescribed.

Details of proposals

4.—(1) Any proposals published under section 193 shall—
(a) where any person is proposed as a sponsor of the school, state the name of that person and the number of initial sponsor governors to be appointed by him (in accordance with section 229),
(b) specify the number of initial parent, teacher and first or, as the case may be, foundation governors proposed for the governing body (in accordance with sections 223 to 228),
(c) give the name of the person who is the head teacher of the school on the date of publication of the proposals,
(d) give the relevant particulars in respect of each person required by section 234 or 236, or regulations made by virtue of section 240, to be named in the proposals as published as a proposed initial governor,
(e) where it is proposed that any foundation governorship be held ex officio, specify the relevant office,
(f) if the determination of an initial governor of an elected category is pending on the date of publication of the proposals, state that fact and refer to the explanation given in the statement accompanying the proposals in accordance with paragraph 3(e),
(g) give the name under which it is proposed that the governing body should be incorporated under section 195, and
(h) specify the proposed date of implementation of the proposals.

(2) The proposals shall describe the arrangements it is proposed to adopt, if the school becomes a grant-maintained school, in respect of—
(a) the admission of pupils to the school,
(b) the provision to be made at the school for pupils who have special educational needs, and
(c) the induction of newly-qualified teachers at the school and the in-service training and professional development of teachers at the school.

(3) In giving the information required by sub-paragraph (2)(a), the proposals shall in particular specify the number of pupils proposed to be admitted to the school in each relevant age group in the first school year beginning on or after the proposed date of implementation of the proposals and, if pupils are proposed to be admitted for nursery education, give the prescribed information.

Objections to proposals

5. Within the period of two months beginning with the date of publication of any proposals under section 193, objections to the proposals may be submitted to the Secretary of State by any of the following—
(a) any ten or more local government electors for the area,
(b) any persons holding property on trust for the purposes of the school,
(c) the governing body of any school affected by the proposals, and
(d) any local education authority concerned.

Interpretation

6.—(1) For the purposes of this Part of this Schedule, the determination of an initial governor of an elected category is pending on the date of publication of any proposals under section 193 if sub-paragraph (2) or (3) applies.

(2) This sub-paragraph applies if an election or appointment required by section 234(7) has not been held or made by the date of publication.

(3) This sub-paragraph applies if—

(a) an election or appointment required for filling an outstanding vacancy for a governor of an elected category on the existing governing body has not been held or made by the date of publication, and
(b) the vacancy falls to be taken into account in determining whether an election or appointment is required by section 234(7).

PART II

PROPOSALS FOR ESTABLISHMENT OF NEW GRANT-MAINTAINED SCHOOL

Content of proposals

7.—(1) Proposals published under section 211 or 212 shall—
(a) where any person is proposed as a sponsor of the school, state the name of that person and the number of sponsor governors to be appointed by him (in accordance with section 229),
(b) specify the number of initial first or, as the case may be, foundation governors proposed for the governing body (in accordance with sections 226 to 228),
(c) specify the number of parent and teacher governors proposed for the governing body (in accordance with sections 223 and 224),
(d) specify in the case of initial first, initial foundation or sponsor governors their proposed term of office (not being less than five nor more than seven years),
(e) where it is proposed that any foundation governorship be held ex officio, specify the relevant office,
(f) give the name under which it is proposed that the governing body should be incorporated under section 215, and
(g) specify the proposed incorporation date and the proposed date of implementation of the proposals.

(2) The proposals shall describe the arrangements it is proposed to adopt in respect of the admission of pupils to the school and, in particular, shall specify the number of pupils proposed to be admitted to the school in each relevant age group in the first school year beginning on or after the date of implementation of the proposals and, if pupils are proposed to be admitted for nursery education, give the prescribed information.

Statement to be annexed to proposals

8. There shall be annexed to any proposals published under section 211 or 212 a statement briefly describing the intended character of the proposed school including, in the case of proposals published under section 212 for a school which is intended to have a particular religious character, that character and the religion or religious denomination (if any) in accordance with whose tenets religious education is to be provided.

Statement to accompany published proposals

9. Any proposals published under section 211 or 212 shall be accompanied by a statement explaining the effect of paragraph 10 or (as the case may be) paragraph 11.

Objections

10.—(1) Within the period of two months beginning with the date of publication of any proposals under section 211, objections to the proposals may be submitted to the funding authority by any of the following—
(a) any ten or more local government electors for the area,
(b) the governing body of any school affected by the proposals,
(c) the appropriate further education funding council (if the proposals are for a school which may provide education to which section 2(1) of the Further and Higher Education Act 1992 applies), and
(d) any local education authority concerned.

(2) Within one month after the end of the period mentioned in sub-paragraph (1), the funding authority shall send to the Secretary of State copies of any objections made under that sub-paragraph (and not withdrawn in writing) within that period, together with their observations on them.

11. Within the period of two months beginning with the date of publication of any proposals under section 212, objections to the proposals may be submitted to the Secretary of State by any of the following—
(a) any ten or more local government electors for the area,
(b) the governing body of any school affected by the proposals,

(c) the appropriate further education funding council (if the proposals affect the provision of education to which section 2(1) of the Further and Higher Education Act 1992 applies),

(d) the funding authority (except, in relation to Wales, before the Schools Funding Council for Wales begin to exercise their functions), and

(e) any local education authority concerned.

Approval of school premises

12.—(1) Where proposals for the establishment of a new grant-maintained school are published under section 211, the funding authority shall prepare the particulars in respect of the proposed premises of the school mentioned in sub-paragraph (3).

(2) Where proposals for the establishment of a new grant-maintained school are published under section 212, the particulars in respect of the proposed premises of the school mentioned in sub-paragraph (3) shall be submitted to the funding authority, at such time and in such form and manner as the authority may direct, by the promoters.

(3) The particulars are—

(a) particulars of the provision made or to be made in respect of the means of access to and within the proposed premises of the school, and

(b) such other particulars in respect of the proposed premises of the school as may be required or, in the case of proposals published under section 212, as the funding authority may require.

(4) The particulars prepared or submitted under sub-paragraph (3)(a) shall indicate the extent to which the provision referred to conforms with the minimum requirements, so far as they are relevant to school premises, of—

(a) Design Note 18 "Access for Disabled People to Educational Buildings" published in 1984 on behalf of the Secretary of State, or

(b) (if that Note has been replaced by a document prescribed by regulations made or having effect as if made under the Town and Country Planning Act 1990) that document.

Section 196

SCHEDULE 21

Acquisition of grant-maintained status: exercise of powers before date of implementation

Introductory

1. The functions conferred by or under paragraphs 2 to 5 on the new governing body or any members of the body—

(a) may be exercised by them at any time during the period beginning with the incorporation date and ending immediately before the date of implementation of the proposals, but

(b) may be exercised only for the purpose of or in connection with the conduct of the school on or after the date of implementation of the proposals,

and those functions shall be exercised in accordance with any requirements of regulations (or, in the case of paragraph 3 or 5, of the directions or order in question) as to the circumstances, manner and conditions of their exercise.

Powers to contract, etc.

2. The new governing body may—

(a) enter into contracts including, in particular, contracts for the employment of teachers and other staff, and

(b) acquire and dispose of land and other property.

Access to school

3. Any member of, or person authorised by, the new governing body shall, if the Secretary of State directs that this paragraph applies in relation to the school, be entitled to have access to and use the premises of the school.

Information

4.—(1) If the new governing body request the existing governing body or the local education authority in writing to provide them with such information falling within sub-paragraph (2) as may be prescribed, the existing governing body or, as the case may be, the authority shall comply with the request.

(2) Information falls within this sub-paragraph if—

(a) it is held by the existing governing body or, as the case may be, the local education authority, and
(b) it relates to the school, including persons employed to work at the school and pupils at the school.

General powers of Secretary of State

5.—(1) The Secretary of State may by order make such provision as he considers appropriate in connection with the school's transition to grant-maintained status and the impending transfer of responsibility for the conduct of the school.

(2) An order under sub-paragraph (1) may in particular provide for any provision of this Act specified in the order to have effect as if references to the governing body included the new governing body.

(3) Such an order may in particular—
(a) exclude or modify any powers of the local education authority or of the existing governing body in relation to any matter to which any power exercisable by the new governing body in accordance with any provision made by virtue of sub-paragraph (2) applies,
(b) require the new governing body to be consulted before the local education authority or the existing governing body exercise in relation to the school any function of a description specified in the order or take in relation to the school any action of a description so specified, and
(c) require or enable the new governing body to participate in the exercise in relation to the school of any such function or the taking in relation to the school of any such action.

Grants to new governing body

6.—(1) The funding authority may make grants to the new governing body of a school in respect of expenditure incurred or to be incurred by that body in pursuance of any provision made by or under paragraphs 2 to 5 in respect of the period beginning with the incorporation date and ending immediately before the date of implementation of the proposals.

(2) The funding authority may impose on a new governing body to whom such a grant is made such requirements as they may from time to time determine (whether before, at or after the time when the grant is made).

(3) Such requirements may, in particular, if any conditions specified in the requirements are satisfied, require the payment to the funding authority of the whole or any part of the following amount.

(4) That amount is—
(a) the amount of the payments made in respect of the grant, or
(b) so much of the value of any premises or equipment in respect of which the grant was paid as is determined in accordance with the requirements to be properly attributable to the payment of such grant,

whichever is the greater.

Liability for expenses of new governing body

7. The duty of a local education authority to maintain any school shall not apply in relation to any expenses incurred by the new governing body of the school.

Section 218(4) SCHEDULE 22

GOVERNING BODIES OF GRANT-MAINTAINED SCHOOLS

Introductory

1. In this Schedule—
"school" means a grant-maintained school, and
"instrument", in relation to a school, means the instrument of government for the school.

Election of governors

2. The instrument for a school may make provision—
(a) as to the procedure for the election of members of the governing body, and
(b) for the determination of any questions arising in connection with, or matters relating to, such elections.

Disqualification for, tenure of and removal from office

3. A person who is a member of the teaching or other staff at a school which is required to have first governors shall be disqualified for holding office as such a governor on the governing body.

4. The instrument for a school may make provision as to the circumstances in which persons are to be disqualified for holding office as members of the governing body.

5. Subject to paragraph 10, the instrument for a school must provide for each governor of an elected category to hold office for a term of four years.

6.—(1) Subject to paragraph 10, the instrument for a school must make the following provision for the term of office of—

(a) first or, as the case may be, foundation governors, other than a foundation governor who is a governor ex officio, and

(b) where there are sponsor governors, those governors.

(2) Except where sub-paragraph (3), (4) or (5) applies, such a governor is to hold office for such term (not being less than five nor more than seven years) as may be specified in the instrument.

(3) The initial instrument must provide, except where sub-paragraph (4) or (5) applies—

(a) subject to paragraph (b), for such a governor to hold office for such term as was specified in the proposals for acquisition of grant-maintained status or, as the case may be, the proposals for the establishment of a new grant-maintained school as the proposed term of office for initial governors of the category in question, and

(b) in the case of a governing body incorporated in pursuance of proposals for the establishment of a new grant-maintained school which name a person as a sponsor of the school, for any sponsor governor to hold office for such term as was specified as the proposed term of office for such governors in those proposals.

(4) Any additional first or foundation governor appointed in pursuance of provision made in the instrument by virtue of section 230(2) is to hold office for such term (not being more than five years) as may be specified in the terms of that governor's appointment.

(5) Any first governor appointed in pursuance of provision made in the instrument by virtue of section 227 is to hold office for such term (not being less than five nor more than seven years) as may be specified in the terms of his appointment.

7. No provision made in the instrument by virtue of paragraph 5, 6 or 10 shall be taken to prevent a governor—

(a) from being elected or appointed for a further term, or

(b) from being disqualified, by virtue of paragraph 3 or any provision made by virtue of paragraph 4, for continuing to hold office.

8. The instrument for a school must provide that any member of the governing body may at any time resign his office.

9.—(1) The instrument for a school must provide that any foundation governor (other than one holding office ex officio) and any sponsor governor may be removed from office by the person or persons who appointed him.

(2) For the purposes of this paragraph, an initial foundation governor shall be treated as having been appointed by the person or persons entitled to appoint foundation governors under provision included in the instrument in accordance with section 228(7)(b).

Initial appointments: terms of office

10.—(1) The instrument for a school must, until every initial governor has ceased to hold office, make the provision required by sub-paragraphs (2) and (3).

(2) In the case of a governing body incorporated under Chapter II of Part III—

(a) an initial governor of an elected category who was a governor of that category on the governing body of the school immediately before the incorporation date shall hold office for the remainder of his term of office on the former governing body, and

(b) an initial governor of an elected category who was elected under section 234, or elected or nominated under section 237 to hold office as such. shall hold office for a term of four years.

(3) An initial first governor, initial foundation governor (other than a foundation governor who is a governor ex officio) or initial sponsor governor shall hold office for such term (not being less than five nor more than seven years) beginning with the incorporation date as may be specified as his proposed term of office in the proposals for acquisition of grant-maintained status or, as the case may be, the proposals for the establishment of a new grant-maintained school.

(4) In the case of a governing body incorporated under Chapter IV of Part III, the instrument for a school must, until every governor of an elected category appointed before the date of implementation of the proposals has ceased to hold office, provide for any such governor to hold office for the prescribed term.

Meetings and proceedings

11. The proceedings of the governing body of a school shall not be invalidated by—

(a) any vacancy among their number, or
(b) any defect in the election or appointment of any governor.

12. Subject to the provisions of Chapter V of Part III and any instrument of government or articles of government made under that Chapter, the governing body of a school may regulate their own procedure.

13.—(1) The instrument for a school may make provision as to the meetings and proceedings of the governing body.

(2) The provision that may be made in pursuance of this paragraph includes, in particular, provision—

(a) as to the election of a chairman and vice-chairman,
(b) as to the establishment, constitution, meetings and proceedings of committees,
(c) for the delegation of the governing body's functions, in such circumstances as may be specified in the instrument, to committees established by that body or to any member of that body, and
(d) as to the procedure (including any quorum) when business is transacted by members of the governing body of a particular category.

(3) The provision mentioned in sub-paragraph (2)(b) may provide for a committee to include persons who are not members of the governing body.

(4) The instrument shall make provision for an appeal committee for the purposes of paragraph 6(1) of Schedule 23 to include among its members (with full voting powers) a person nominated by the governing body from among persons who are eligible to be lay members.

(5) A person is eligible to be a lay member for the purposes of sub-paragraph (4) if—

(a) he is a person without personal experience in the management of any school or the provision of education in any school (disregarding any such experience as a governor or in any other voluntary capacity), and
(b) he does not have, and has not at any time had, any connection with—
    (i) the school, or
    (ii) any person who is a member of, or employed by, the governing body of the school,

of a kind which might reasonably be taken to raise doubts about his ability to act impartially in relation to the school.

Information as to meetings and proceedings

14.—(1) Regulations may require the governing body of a school to make available, to such persons or classes of person as may be prescribed, such documents and information relating to the meetings and proceedings of the governing body as may be prescribed.

(2) Documents and information required by the regulations to be made available shall be made available in such form and manner, and at such times, as may be prescribed.

Allowances for governors

15.—(1) The governing body of a school may pay to their members such travelling, subsistence or other allowances as may be determined in accordance with a scheme made by the governing body and approved by the Secretary of State.

(2) A scheme under this paragraph may be varied or revoked by a subsequent scheme made under this paragraph.

Seal etc.

16.—(1) The application of the seal of the governing body of a school must be authenticated by the signature—

(a) of the chairman of the governing body, or
(b) of some other member authorised either generally or specially by the governing body to act for that purpose,

together with the signature of any other member.

(2) Every document purporting to be an instrument made or issued by or on behalf of the governing body of a school and—

(a) to be duly executed under the seal of the governing body, or
(b) to be signed or executed by a person authorised by the governing body to act in that behalf,

shall be received in evidence and be treated, without further proof, as being so made or issued unless the contrary is shown.

Section 218(5)

SCHEDULE 23

CONTENT OF ARTICLES OF GOVERNMENT FOR GRANT-MAINTAINED SCHOOLS

Introductory

1. In this Schedule—
"school" means a grant-maintained school, and
"articles", in relation to a school, means the articles of government for the school.

Performance and delegation of functions

2.—(1) The articles must make provision as to the functions to be exercised in relation to the school by—
(a) the Secretary of State,
(b) the funding authority,
(c) the governing body,
(d) any committee or other body established by the governing body,
(e) the head teacher, and
(f) any other persons specified in or determined under the articles.

(2) The articles must also include provision as to the, delegation of such functions by those on whom they are imposed or conferred by or under the articles.

(3) The articles may include provision as to the establishment by the governing body of committees or other bodies of persons for the purposes of or in connection with the performance in relation to the school of such functions as may be determined by or under the articles.

Staff

3.—(1) The articles must include provision as to—
(a) disciplinary rules and procedures applicable to members of the staff of the school, and
(b) procedures for giving them opportunities for seeking redress of any grievances relating to their employment.

(2) The articles must also include provision as to arrangements—
(a) for giving any member of the staff an opportunity of making representations as to any proposal to dismiss him by the governing body or any persons authorised under the articles to dismiss him, including (if he so wishes) oral representations to such person or persons as may be appointed for the purpose,
(b) for requiring the governing body or any persons authorised under the articles to dismiss him to have regard to any representations made by him before taking any decision to dismiss him, and
(c) for giving any member of staff whom it has been decided to dismiss an opportunity of appealing against that decision before any action is taken to implement it.

Curriculum

4.—(1) The articles must include provision for securing the discharge by the governing body and the head teacher of duties imposed on them under Chapters I and II of Part V and sections 384, 388, 389, 400 and 408.

(2) The articles must include provision as to arrangements for the consideration and disposal of complaints relating to any matter concerning the curriculum followed within the school including, in particular, the discharge by the governing body of those duties.

(3) The articles must require the governing body, when considering the content of the secular curriculum for the school, to have regard to any representations with regard to that curriculum—
(a) which are made to them by any persons connected with the community served by the school, or
(b) which are made to them by the chief officer of police and are connected with his responsibilities.

Admission arrangements

5.—(1) The articles must—
(a) provide for the governing body to be responsible for determining the arrangements for admitting pupils to the school; and
(b) include provision as to the policy to be followed in deciding admissions.

(2) The articles must also require the governing body to publish, for each school year, particulars of—

(a) the arrangements for admission of pupils to the school; and
(b) the procedures applicable under the articles in relation to the admission of pupils to the school.

Appeals relating to admission and exclusion of pupils

6.—(1) The articles must include provision as to the arrangements for appeals (in such circumstances as may be provided by the articles) to an appeal committee constituted in accordance with the instrument of government against any decision or action taken—
(a) by the governing body, or
(b) by any persons authorised under the articles to take any decision or action of the kind in question,
in relation to admissions of pupils to the school or the permanent exclusion of a pupil from the school.

(2) The articles must enable the governing body to make such arrangements jointly with the governing body of one or more other grant-maintained schools.

(3) The articles must require the governing body to publish, for each school year, particulars of any arrangements made by them in respect of appeals by parents against any such decision or action in relation to admissions of pupils to the school as is mentioned in sub-paragraph (1) above.

Annual reports

7.—(1) The articles must require the governing body to prepare once in every school year a report in such form and containing such information as the articles may require.

(2) The articles must require the governing body to take such steps as are reasonably practicable to secure that—
(a) the registered parents of all registered pupils at the school and all persons employed at the school are given (free of charge) a copy of the report, and
(b) copies of the report are available for inspection (at all reasonable times and free of charge) at the school.

Annual parents' meetings

8.—(1) The articles must require the governing body, subject to any exceptions provided for in the articles, to hold a meeting once in every school year which is open to—
(a) all parents of registered pupils at the school, and
(b) such other persons as the governing body may invite.

(2) The articles must include provision as to—
(a) the procedure to be followed and the matters to be considered at such a meeting,
(b) the determination of any questions arising in connection with such a meeting, and
(c) the taking by the governing body or any other persons of such action as may be required by the articles for the purposes of, or in connection with, such a meeting or any resolutions passed at it.

Section 222

SCHEDULE 24

CATEGORIES OF GOVERNORS

PART I

INTRODUCTORY

Application

1.—(1) This Schedule applies, in relation to the governing body of a grant-maintained school, for the purposes of Part III.

(2) Part II of this Schedule applies for the purpose of determining who are to be the initial governors of a grant-maintained school.

(3) Part III of this Schedule applies for the purpose of determining who are to be the governors of a grant-maintained school on and after the incorporation date.

General interpretation

2. References to an initial governor are to any person who becomes a member of the governing body on the incorporation date.

3. References to a governor of an elected category are to a person who is a parent or teacher governor as defined by section 78(3) or (4) or is such a governor within the meaning of this Schedule.

4. In relation to any proposals for acquisition of grant-maintained status in respect of a school, a person who is a governor of an elected category on the existing governing body of the school is an eligible governor of that category if—

(a) his term of office as a governor is due to end after the date of implementation of the proposals, and

(b) he has notified the existing governing body that he is willing to serve on the proposed governing body and has not withdrawn that notification.

PART II

INITIAL GOVERNORS

Parent governors

5.—(1) In relation to a governing body to be incorporated under Chapter II of Part III, "parent governor" means—

(a) a person who, immediately before the incorporation date in relation to the school, is a parent governor (as defined by section 78(3)) in relation to the school, or

(b) a person elected or appointed under section 234, or elected, appointed or nominated under section 237, to hold office as an initial parent governor on the governing body.

(2) A person elected under section 234 to hold office as an initial parent governor must be elected by registered parents of registered pupils at the school and a person elected or appointed under that section to hold such office must when he is elected or appointed be such a parent.

(3) A person elected, appointed or nominated under section 237 to hold office as an initial parent governor—

(a) in the case of an election, must be elected by registered parents of registered pupils at the school and must when he is elected be such a parent, and

(b) in the case of an appointment or nomination, must be a registered parent of a registered pupil at the school at the time of his appointment or nomination.

Teacher governors

6.—(1) In relation to a governing body to be incorporated under Chapter II of Part III, "teacher governor" means—

(a) a person who, immediately before the incorporation date in relation to the school, is a teacher governor (as defined by section 78(4)) in relation to the school, or

(b) a person elected under section 234, or elected or nominated under section 237, to hold office as an initial teacher governor on the governing body.

(2) A person elected under section 234 to hold office as an initial teacher governor must be elected by teachers at the school and must when he is elected be such a teacher.

(3) A person elected or nominated under section 237 to hold office as an initial teacher governor—

(a) in the case of an election, must be elected by teachers at the school and must when he is elected be such a teacher, and

(b) in the case of a nomination, must be a teacher at the school at the time of his nomination.

First governors

7.—(1) In relation to a governing body to be incorporated under Chapter II of Part III, "first governor" means a person who is selected under section 236(1), or nominated under section 238(1), and appears to the persons selecting or nominating him to be committed to the good government and continuing viability of the school.

(2) In relation to a governing body to be incorporated under Chapter IV of Part III, "first governor" means a person appointed by the funding authority who appears to them to be committed to the good government and continuing viability of the proposed school.

Foundation governors

8.—(1) In relation to a governing body to be incorporated under Chapter II of Part III, "foundation governor" means—

(a) a person who is selected under section 236(2) or nominated under section 238(2),

(b) where the statement annexed (under paragraph 2 of Schedule 20) to the proposals for acquisition of grant-maintained status describes the religious character of the school, a person who is appointed for the purpose of securing that (subject to the approval or adoption under section 261 of any proposals) the religious character of the school is such as is indicated in the statement, and

(c) where there is a trust deed relating to the school, a person who is appointed for the purpose of securing that the school is conducted in accordance with the deed.

(2) In relation to a governing body to be incorporated under Chapter IV of Part III, "foundation governor" means—

(a) a person who is appointed by the promoters,

(b) where the statement annexed under paragraph 8 of Schedule 20 to the proposals for the establishment of a new grant-maintained school describes the religious character of the school, a person who is appointed for the purpose of securing that (subject to the approval or adoption under section 261 of any proposals) the religious character of the proposed school is such as is indicated in the statement, and

(c) where there is a trust deed relating to the proposed school, a person who is appointed for the purpose of securing that the proposed school is conducted in accordance with that deed.

Sponsor governors

9. In relation to a governing body to be incorporated under Chapter II of Part III, "sponsor governor" means a person appointed by a person named as a sponsor of the school in the proposals for acquisition of grant-maintained status.

PART III

GOVERNORS OTHER THAN INITIAL GOVERNORS

Parent governors

10.—(1) "Parent governor" means a person who—

(a) is elected by registered parents of registered pupils at the school,

(b) is appointed under a provision of the instrument of government made by virtue of section 223(3),

(c) is appointed by virtue of section 223(6), or

(d) is an initial parent governor.

(2) To qualify for such election, the person must when he is elected be a registered parent of a registered pupil at the school.

Teacher governors

11.—(1) "Teacher governor" means a person who—

(a) is elected by teachers at the school,

(b) is appointed by virtue of section 224(4), or

(c) is an initial teacher governor.

(2) To qualify for such election, the person must when he is elected be a teacher at the school.

First governors

12. "First governor" means—

(a) a person appointed by the governing body who appears to them to be committed to the good government and continuing viability of the school,

(b) a person appointed under a provision of the instrument of government made by virtue of section 227 who appears to the person appointing him to be committed to the good government and continuing viability of the school, or

(c) an initial first governor.

Foundation governors

13. "Foundation governor" means a person who—

(a) is appointed otherwise than by a local education authority or the funding authority,

(b) where paragraph 8(1)(b) or (2)(b) applies, is appointed for the purpose there referred to, and

(c) where there is a trust deed relating to the school, is appointed for the purpose of securing that the school is conducted in accordance with that deed.

Sponsor governors

14. "Sponsor governor" means—

(a) a person appointed by a person named in the instrument of government as a sponsor of the school,

(b) while the instrument of government is the initial instrument, a person appointed by a person named as a sponsor of the school in the proposals for acquisition of grant-maintained status or, as the case may be, the proposals for the establishment of a new grant-maintained school, or

(c) an initial sponsor governor.

Section 285

SCHEDULE 25

CORE GOVERNORS FOR GROUPS

Introductory

1. The provision made for core governors in the instrument of government for the governing body of a group must be in accordance with this Schedule.

Kinds of core governor

2.—(1) Core governors may be either—

(a) appointed by the governing body, or

(b) externally appointed.

(2) Externally appointed core governors may be either—

(a) appointed in respect of a particular school in the group, being a school—

(i) which was a voluntary school immediately before it became grant-maintained, or

(ii) which was established in pursuance of proposals published under section 212, or

(b) where the group consists only of such schools, appointed in respect of the group otherwise than by the governing body.

(3) A person appointed as mentioned in sub-paragraph (2)(a) must be appointed by the persons named in the instrument of government for the group as being entitled to appoint externally appointed core governors in respect of the school.

(4) A person appointed as mentioned in sub-paragraph (2)(a) must be appointed—

(a) (where any statement annexed to the proposals in pursuance of which the school became a grant-maintained school described the religious character of the school) for the purpose of securing that, subject to any change in the character of the school which may be authorised by or under Part III, the religious character of the school is such as was indicated in the statement, and

(b) (where there is a trust deed relating to the school) for the purpose of securing that the school is conducted in accordance with the deed.

(5) Core governors, other than externally appointed core governors appointed in respect of particular schools in the group, must be appointed from among persons who appear to the person making the appointment to be committed to the good government and continuing viability of all the schools in the group.

(6) A person who is a member of the teaching or other staff at any of the schools in the group is disqualified from holding office as a core governor, other than an externally appointed core governor.

Groups consisting only of former voluntary schools or section 212 schools

3.—(1) This paragraph applies in the case of such a group as is mentioned in paragraph 2(2)(b).

(2) The minimum number of externally appointed core governors (referred to in this paragraph as "MN") is one greater than the number of governors other than externally appointed core governors.

(3) Any head teacher of a school in the group who has chosen not to be a governor shall be counted as one for the purposes of sub-paragraph (2).

(4) In respect of each school in the group there must be the same number of externally appointed core governors.

(5) The total number of externally appointed core governors in respect of schools in the group must not be less than the highest number, not exceeding MN, that is consistent with sub-paragraph (4).

Other groups

4.—(1) This paragraph applies in the case of a group other than such a group as is mentioned in paragraph 2(2)(b).

(2) If any school in the group falls within paragraph 2(2)(a), one externally appointed governor must be appointed in respect of that school.

(3) The appropriate number of the core governors must (on the date or dates on which they respectively take office) be parents of registered pupils at schools in the group, and the appropriate number of the core governors must (on the date or dates on which they respectively take office) be members of the local community; but one person may satisfy both requirements.

(4) In sub-paragraph (3) "the appropriate number" means not less than two or, if all but one of the schools in the group fall within paragraph 2(2)(a), at least one.

(5) In appointing core governors, the governing body must secure that those governors include persons appearing to the governing body to be members of the local business community (and such persons may also satisfy one or both of the requirements of sub-paragraph (3)).

(6) The number of core governors must be such number, not being—

(a) less than five, or

(b) (subject to paragraph (a)) more than the number of schools in the group,

as will secure that they and the parent governors outnumber the other governors.

(7) Any head teacher of a school in the group who has chosen not to be a governor shall be counted as one for the purposes of sub-paragraph (6).

Section 323 SCHEDULE 26

MAKING OF ASSESSMENTS UNDER SECTION 323

Introductory

1. In this Schedule "assessment" means an assessment of a child's educational needs under section 323.

Medical and other advice

2.—(1) Regulations shall make provision as to the advice which a local education authority are to seek in making assessments.

(2) Without prejudice to the generality of sub-paragraph (1), the regulations shall require the authority, except in such circumstances as may be prescribed, to seek medical, psychological and educational advice and such other advice as may be prescribed.

Manner, and timing, of assessments, etc.

3.—(1) Regulations may make provision—

(a) as to the manner in which assessments are to be conducted,

(b) requiring the local education authority, where, after conducting an assessment under section 323 of the educational needs of a child for whom a statement is maintained under section 324, they determine not to amend the statement, to serve on the parent of the child a notice giving the prescribed information, and

(c) in connection with such other matters relating to the making of assessments as the Secretary of State considers appropriate.

(2) Sub-paragraph (1)(b) does not apply to a determination made following the service of notice under paragraph 10 of Schedule 27 (amendment of statement by LEA) of a proposal to amend the statement.

(3) Regulations may provide that, where a local education authority are under a duty to make an assessment, the duty must, subject to prescribed exceptions, be performed within the prescribed period.

(4) Such provision shall not relieve the authority of the duty to make an assessment which has not been performed within that period.

Attendance at examinations

4.—(1) Where a local education authority propose to make an assessment, they may serve a notice on the parent of the child concerned requiring the child's attendance for examination in accordance with the provisions of the notice.

(2) The parent of a child examined under this paragraph may be present at the examination if he so desires.

(3) A notice under this paragraph shall—

(a) state the purpose of the examination,
(b) state the time and place at which the examination will be held,
(c) name an officer of the authority from whom further information may be obtained,
(d) inform the parent that he may submit such information to the authority as he may wish, and
(e) inform the parent of his right to be present at the examination.

Offence

5.—(1) Any parent who fails without reasonable excuse to comply with any requirements of a notice served on him under paragraph 4 commits an offence if the notice relates to a child who is not over compulsory school age at the time stated in it as the time for holding the examination.

(2) A person guilty of an offence under this paragraph is liable on summary conviction to a fine not exceeding level 2 on the standard scale.

Section 324

SCHEDULE 27

MAKING AND MAINTENANCE OF STATEMENTS UNDER SECTION 324

Introductory

1. In this Schedule "statement" means a statement of a child's special educational needs under section 324.

Copy of proposed statement

2. Before making a statement, a local education authority shall serve on the parent of the child concerned—
(a) a copy of the proposed statement, and
(b) a written notice explaining the arrangements under paragraph 3, the effect of paragraph 4 and the right to appeal under section 326 and containing such other information as may be prescribed,

but the copy of the proposed statement shall not specify any matter in pursuance of section 324(4) or any prescribed matter.

Choice of school

3.—(1) Every local education authority shall make arrangements for enabling a parent on whom a copy of a proposed statement has been served under paragraph 2 to express a preference as to the maintained, grant-maintained or grant-maintained special school at which he wishes education to be provided for his child and to give reasons for his preference.

(2) Any such preference must be expressed or made within the period of 15 days beginning—
(a) with the date on which the written notice mentioned in paragraph 2(b) was served on the parent, or
(b) if a meeting has (or meetings have) been arranged under paragraph 4(1)(b) or (2), with the date fixed for that meeting (or the last of those meetings).

(3) Where a local education authority make a statement in a case where the parent of the child concerned has expressed a preference in pursuance of such arrangements as to the school at which he wishes education to be provided for his child, they shall specify the name of that school in the statement unless—
(a) the school is unsuitable to the child's age, ability or aptitude or to his special educational needs, or
(b) the attendance of the child at the school would be incompatible with the provision of efficient education for the children with whom he would be educated or the efficient use of resources.

(4) A local education authority shall, before specifying the name of any maintained, grant-maintained or grant-maintained special school in a statement, consult the governing body of the school and, if the school is maintained by another local education authority, that authority.

Representations

4.—(1) A parent on whom a copy of a proposed statement has been served under paragraph 2 may—
(a) make representations (or further representations) to the local education authority about the content of the statement, and
(b) require the authority to arrange a meeting between him and an officer of the authority at which the statement can be discussed.

(2) Where a parent, having attended a meeting arranged by a local education authority under sub-paragraph (1)(b), disagrees with any part of the assessment in question, he may require the authority to arrange such meeting or meetings as they consider will enable him to discuss the relevant advice with the appropriate person or persons.

(3) In this paragraph—

"relevant advice" means such of the advice given to the authority in connection with the assessment as they consider to be relevant to that part of the assessment with which the parent disagrees, and

"appropriate person" means the person who gave the relevant advice or any other person who, in the opinion of the authority, is the appropriate person to discuss it with the parent.

(4) Any representations under sub-paragraph (1)(a) must be made within the period of 15 days beginning—

(a) with the date on which the written notice mentioned in paragraph 2(b) was served on the parent, or

(b) if a meeting has (or meetings have) been arranged under sub-paragraph (1)(b) or (2), with the date fixed for that meeting (or the last of those meetings).

(5) A requirement under sub-paragraph (1)(b) must be made within the period of 15 days beginning with the date on which the written notice mentioned in paragraph 2(b) was served on the parent.

(6) A requirement under sub-paragraph (2) must be made within the period of 15 days beginning with the date fixed for the meeting arranged under sub-paragraph (1)(b).

Making the statement

5.—(1) Where representations are made to a local education authority under paragraph 4(1)(a), the authority shall not make the statement until they have considered the representations and the period or the last of the periods allowed by paragraph 4 for making requirements or further representations has expired.

(2) The statement may be in the form originally proposed (except as to the matters required to be excluded from the copy of the proposed statement) or in a form modified in the light of the representations.

(3) Regulations may provide that, where a local education authority are under a duty (subject to compliance with the preceding requirements of this Schedule) to make a statement, the duty, or any step required to be taken for performance of the duty, must, subject to prescribed exceptions, be performed within the prescribed period.

(4) Such provision shall not relieve the authority of the duty to make a statement, or take any step, which has not been performed or taken within that period.

Service of statement

6. Where a local education authority make a statement they shall serve a copy of the statement on the parent of the child concerned and shall give notice in writing to him—

(a) of his right under section 326(1) to appeal against—

(i) the description in the statement of the authority's assessment of the child's special educational needs,

(ii) the special educational provision specified in the statement, or

(iii) if no school is named in the statement, that fact, and

(b) of the name of the person to whom he may apply for information and advice about the child's special educational needs.

Keeping, disclosure and transfer of statements

7.—(1) Regulations may make provision as to the keeping and disclosure of statements.

(2) Regulations may make provision, where a local education authority become responsible for a child for whom a statement is maintained by another authority, for the transfer of the statement to them and for Part IV to have effect as if the duty to maintain the transferred statement were their duty.

Change of named school

8.—(1) Sub-paragraph (2) applies where—

(a) the parent of a child for whom a statement is maintained which specifies the name of a school or institution asks the local education authority to substitute for that name the name of a maintained, grant-maintained or grant-maintained special school specified by the parent, and

(b) the request is not made less than 12 months after—

(i) an earlier request under this paragraph,

(ii) the service of a copy of the statement under paragraph 6,

(iii) if the statement has been amended, the date when notice of the amendment is given under paragraph 10(3)(b), or

(iv) if the parent has appealed to the Tribunal under section 326 or this paragraph, the date when the appeal is concluded,

whichever is the later.

(2) The local education authority shall comply with the request unless—

(a) the school is unsuitable to the child's age, ability or aptitude or to his special educational needs, or

(b) the attendance of the child at the school would be incompatible with the provision of efficient education for the children with whom he would be educated or the efficient use of resources.

(3) Where the local education authority determine not to comply with the request—

(a) they shall give notice of that fact and of the effect of paragraph (b) below to the parent of the child, and

(b) the parent of the child may appeal to the Tribunal against the determination.

(4) On the appeal the Tribunal may—

(a) dismiss the appeal, or

(b) order the local education authority to substitute for the name of the school or other institution specified in the statement the name of the school specified by the parent.

(5) Regulations may provide that, where a local education authority are under a duty to comply with a request under this paragraph, the duty must, subject to prescribed exceptions, be performed within the prescribed period.

(6) Such provision shall not relieve the authority of the duty to comply with such a request which has not been complied with within that period.

Procedure for amending or ceasing to maintain a statement

9.—(1) A local education authority may not amend, or cease to maintain, a statement except in accordance with paragraph 10 or 11.

(2) Sub-paragraph (1) does not apply where the local education authority—

(a) cease to maintain a statement for a child who has ceased to be a child for whom they are responsible,

(b) amend a statement in pursuance of paragraph 8,

(c) are ordered to cease to maintain a statement under section 326(3)(c), or

(d) amend a statement in pursuance of directions under section 442 (revocation of school attendance order).

10.—(1) Before amending a statement, a local education authority shall serve on the parent of the child concerned a notice informing him—

(a) of their proposal, and

(b) of his right to make representations under sub-paragraph (2).

(2) A parent on whom a notice has been served under sub-paragraph (1) may, within the period of 15 days beginning with the date on which the notice is served, make representations to the local education authority about their proposal.

(3) The local education authority—

(a) shall consider any representations made to them under sub-paragraph (2), and

(b) on taking a decision on the proposal to which the representations relate, shall give notice in writing to the parent of their decision.

(4) Where a local education authority make an amendment under this paragraph to the description in a statement of the authority's assessment of a child's special educational needs or to the special educational provision specified in a statement, they shall give notice in writing to the parent of his right under section 326(1) to appeal against—

(a) the description in the statement of the authority's assessment of the child's special educational needs,

(b) the special educational provision specified in the statement, or

(c) if no school is named in the statement, that fact.

(5) A local education authority may only amend a statement under this paragraph within the prescribed period beginning with the service of the notice under sub-paragraph (1).

11.—(1) A local education authority may cease to maintain a statement only if it is no longer necessary to maintain it.

(2) Where the local education authority determine to cease to maintain a statement—

(a) they shall give notice of that fact and of the effect of paragraph (b) below to the parent of the child, and

(b) the parent of the child may appeal to the Tribunal against the determination.

(3) On an appeal under this paragraph the Tribunal may—

(a) dismiss the appeal, or

(b) order the local education authority to continue to maintain the statement in its existing form or with such amendments of—

(i) the description in the statement of the authority's assessment of the child's special educational needs, or

(ii) the special educational provision specified in the statement, and such other consequential amendments, as the Tribunal may determine.

(4) Except where the parent of the child appeals to the Tribunal under this paragraph, a local education authority may only cease to maintain a statement under this paragraph within the prescribed period beginning with the service of the notice under sub-paragraph (2).

Section 344(2)

SCHEDULE 28

GOVERNMENT AND CONDUCT OF GRANT-MAINTAINED SPECIAL SCHOOLS

Constitution of governing body and conduct of school

1.—(1) For every governing body of a grant-maintained special school there shall be—

(a) an instrument (known as the instrument of government) providing for the constitution of the governing body, and

(b) an instrument (known as the articles of government) in accordance with which the school is to be conducted.

(2) The instrument and articles of government—

(a) shall comply with any requirements imposed by or under Part IV, and

(b) may make any provision authorised by or under Part IV to be made and such other provision as may be necessary or desirable.

(3) Subject to any express provision of the instrument or articles of government, the school shall be conducted in accordance with any trust deed relating to it.

Initial instruments and articles of government

2.—(1) The initial instrument of government for the governing body of a grant-maintained special school, and the initial articles of government for such a school, shall be such as are prescribed.

(2) The initial instrument of government shall have effect as from the incorporation date.

(3) The initial articles of government shall have effect as from the date of implementation of the proposals made under section 339(2)(a) or 345 but, in the case of a governing body incorporated in pursuance of proposals made under section 339(2)(a), such of the articles as may be prescribed shall have effect as from the incorporation date.

Subsequent instruments of government

3.—(1) The Secretary of State may—

(a) if the governing body of a grant-maintained special school submit a draft of an instrument of government to have effect in place of their existing instrument, by order make a new instrument of government in terms of the draft or in such terms as he thinks fit, and

(b) if such a governing body submit draft modifications of an instrument made under paragraph (a) above, by order modify the instrument concerned in terms of the draft or in such terms as he thinks fit,

but shall not make a new instrument otherwise than in the terms of the draft, or modify the instrument otherwise than in terms of the draft, unless he has consulted the governing body.

(2) The Secretary of State may by order modify the instrument of government for the governing body of any grant-maintained special school.

(3) An order under sub-paragraph (2)—

(a) may relate to all grant-maintained special schools, to any category of such schools specified in the order or to any such school so specified, but

(b) shall not be made unless the Secretary of State has consulted the governing body of each grant-maintained special school to which the order relates.

(4) Where, by reason of the making of a new instrument, or the modification of an instrument, under this paragraph, the number of governors of any category will (unless the required number of governors of that category resign) exceed the number provided for in the instrument, the new instrument or, as the case may be, the instrument as modified shall provide—

(a) for such number of governors of that category as is required to eliminate the excess to cease to hold office, and

(b) for the selection of those who are to cease to hold office.

Subsequent articles of government

4.—(1) The governing body of a grant-maintained special school may, with the consent of the Secretary of State—

(a) make new articles of government in place of the existing articles for the school, or

(b) modify the existing articles for the school.

(2) The Secretary of State may by a direction under this paragraph require—

(a) the governing bodies of grant-maintained special schools or any class of such schools specified in the direction, or

(b) the governing body of any particular grant-maintained special school so specified,

to modify their articles of government in any manner so specified.

(3) Before giving a direction under this paragraph, the Secretary of State shall consult the governing body or (as the case may be) each governing body to which the direction applies.

Parent governors

5.—(1) The instrument of government for the governing body of a grant-maintained special school shall provide for the governing body to include not less than three nor more than five parent governors.

(2) Subject to sub-paragraph (5), the parent governors—

(a) in the case of a school not established in a hospital, shall be elected by persons who are registered parents of registered pupils at the school, and

(b) in the case of a school so established, shall be appointed by the other members of the governing body.

(3) To qualify for such election a person must when he is elected be a registered parent of a registered pupil at the school; and to qualify for appointment under sub-paragraph (2)(b) a person must when he is appointed be such a parent or, if that is not reasonably practicable, a parent of one or more children of compulsory school age.

(4) The instrument shall provide for each parent governor to hold office for a term of four years.

(5) In the case of a school not established in a hospital, the instrument shall provide that if—

(a) one or more vacancies for parent governors are required to be filled by election, and

(b) the number of parents standing for election as parent governors is less than the number of vacancies,

the required number of parent governors shall be made up by persons appointed by the other members of the governing body.

(6) The instrument shall require governors, in appointing a person under a provision made by virtue of sub-paragraph (5)—

(a) to appoint a person who is the registered parent of a registered pupil at the school, where it is reasonably practicable to do so, and

(b) where it is not, to appoint a person who is the parent of one or more children of compulsory school age with special educational needs or, if that also is not reasonably practicable, a person who is the parent of a person of any age with special educational needs.

Teacher governors

6.—(1) The instrument of government for the governing body of a grant-maintained special school shall provide for the governing body to include either one or two teacher governors.

(2) Each teacher governor shall be elected by persons who are teachers at the school.

(3) To qualify for such election, a person must when he is elected be a teacher at the school.

(4) The instrument shall provide for each teacher governor to hold office for a term of four years.

Head teacher

7. The instrument of government for the governing body of a grant-maintained special school shall provide for the governing body to include (as a governor ex officio) the person who is for the time being the head teacher.

First governors

8.—(1) The instrument of government for the governing body of a grant-maintained special school shall provide for the governing body to include first governors.

(2) The instrument shall provide for such number of first governors as will secure that they outnumber the other governors.

(3) The instrument—

(a) shall require

(i) that, where it is reasonably practicable, at least two of the first governors shall be (on the date or dates on which they respectively take office) parents of registered pupils at the school, and

(ii) that at least two of the first governors shall be persons with experience of education for those with special educational needs,

but one person may satisfy both requirements, and

(b) shall require the governing body, in appointing first governors, to secure that those governors include a person appearing to them to be a member of the local business community (and such a person may also satisfy one or both of the requirements of paragraph (a)(i) and (ii) above).

(4) The instrument shall provide for the first governors to be appointed by the governing body from among persons who appear to the governing body to be committed to the good government and continuing viability of the school.

(5) The instrument shall provide for first governors to hold office for such term (not being less than five nor more than seven years) as may be specified in the instrument.

(6) A person who is a member of the teaching or other staff at the school shall be disqualified for holding office as a first governor.

(7) References in this paragraph to governors other than first governors do not include sponsor governors.

Power of Secretary of State to replace first governors

9.—(1) The instrument of government for the governing body of a grant-maintained special school shall provide for the Secretary of State to have power, where any of sub-paragraphs (2) to (4) apply, to replace all or any of the first governors.

(2) This sub-paragraph applies where the governing body have been guilty of substantial or persistent failure to comply or secure compliance with any requirement imposed by or under any enactment.

(3) This sub-paragraph applies where—

(a) there is a report of an inspection of the school in which the person who made it expressed the opinion that special measures were required to be taken in relation to the school,

(b) either that person was a member of the Inspectorate or the report stated that the Chief Inspector agreed with his opinion,

(c) if any registered inspector or member of the Inspectorate has made a later report of an inspection of the school under Part I of the School Inspections Act 1996, he did not express the opinion in the report that special measures were not required to be taken in relation to the school, and

(d) the Secretary of State has received a statement prepared under section 17 of that Act or the period allowed by subsection (2) of that section for the preparation of such a statement has expired;

and expressions used in this sub-paragraph and in that Act have the same meaning as in that Act.

(4) This sub-paragraph applies where in the opinion of the Secretary of State any action taken or proposed by the governing body of the school, or any failure of the governing body to act, is prejudicial to the provision of education by the school.

(5) The instrument of government for a grant-maintained special school shall enable the Secretary of State to make such provision as he thinks fit for filling vacancies for first governors if it appears to him that the governing body are unable or unwilling to fill the vacancies.

(6) Any provision made by the instrument of government in pursuance of paragraph 8(3) shall not apply for the purposes of the appointment by virtue of this paragraph of any first governor.

Sponsor governors

10. The instrument of government for the governing body of a grant-maintained special school which provides secondary education may—

(a) name a person as a sponsor of the school, and

(b) provide for the governing body to include such number of sponsor governors, not exceeding four, as is specified in the instrument.

Additional governors

11.—(1) The instrument of government for the governing body of a grant-maintained special school shall enable the Secretary of State to appoint not more than two additional governors if it appears to him that the governing body are not adequately carrying out their responsibilities in respect of the conduct or management of the school.

(2) The instrument shall enable the governing body, during any period when any additional governors appointed by the Secretary of State by virtue of sub-paragraph (1) are in office, to appoint a number of additional first governors not greater than the number of additional governors appointed by the Secretary of State who are then in office.

(3) Any additional first governor appointed in pursuance of such a provision is to hold office for such term (not being more than five years) as may be specified in the terms of his appointment.

Powers

12. Section 231 of this Act shall have effect in relation to the governing body of a grant-maintained special school with such modifications as may be prescribed.

Transitory provisions

13. Regulations may modify the provisions of paragraphs 5 to 12 in relation to—

(a) the initial instrument of government, or

(b) governors holding office, elected or appointed, before the date of implementation of the proposals in pursuance of which the governing body are constituted.

General application of enactments

14. In relation to any governing body incorporated in pursuance of proposals under section 339(2)(a) or 345 or any school conducted or formerly conducted by such a governing body, regulations may provide for any provision of—

(a) Schedules 22 and 23 (governing bodies; articles),

(b) Chapters VI, VII, VIII and X of Part III (funding; alteration; discontinuance, etc.), and

(c) any other enactment (not contained in Part III) relating to grant-maintained schools or maintained special schools (or schools including such schools),

to have effect with or without modification.

15. Section 307 (exclusion of pupils) applies to a grant-maintained special school as it applies to a grant-maintained school.

Section 358

SCHEDULE 29

THE SCHOOL CURRICULUM AND ASSESSMENT AUTHORITY

Status

1. The Authority shall not be regarded as a servant or agent of the Crown or as enjoying any status, immunity or privilege of the Crown; and the Authority's property shall not be regarded as property of, or property held on behalf of, the Crown.

Powers

2.—(1) The Authority may do anything which is calculated to facilitate, or is incidental or conducive to, the carrying out of any of their functions.

(2) In particular, the Authority may—

(a) acquire or dispose of land or other property,

(b) enter into contracts,

(c) form bodies corporate or subscribe for shares or stock,

(d) invest any sums not immediately required for the purpose of carrying out their functions,

(e) accept gifts of money, land or other property, and

(f) borrow money.

3.—(1) The Authority may also give to any person or body (whether or not in the United Kingdom) such assistance, other than financial assistance, as they may determine.

(2) Assistance may be provided on such terms and subject to such conditions (if any) as the Authority may determine.

(3) In particular, assistance may be provided free of charge or on such terms as to payment as the Authority may determine.

(4) The consent of the Secretary of State is required for the exercise of any power conferred by this paragraph.

Chief officer

4. The Authority shall have a chief officer who shall be appointed by the Authority with the approval of the Secretary of State on such terms and conditions as the Authority may with the approval of the Secretary of State determine.

Chairman and chief officer: division of functions

5.—(1) The Secretary of State may, on appointing a person to be the chairman of the Authority, confer on him such additional functions in relation to the Authority as may be specified in the appointment.

(2) The functions for the time being conferred by virtue of appointment as chief officer of the Authority shall not include any function for the time being conferred under sub-paragraph (1) on the chairman of the Authority.

Tenure of office

6.—(1) A person shall hold and vacate office as a member or as chairman or deputy chairman of the Authority in accordance with the terms of his appointment and shall, on ceasing to be a member, be eligible for reappointment.

(2) A person may at any time by notice in writing to the Secretary of State resign his office as a member or as chairman or deputy chairman of the Authority.

7. The Secretary of State may, if satisfied that a member of the Authority—

(a) has been absent from meetings of the Authority for a continuous period of more than six months without the permission of the Authority, or

(b) is unable or unfit to discharge the functions of a member,

remove him from office by giving him notice in writing and thereupon the office shall become vacant.

8. If the chairman or deputy chairman of the Authority ceases to be a member of the Authority, he shall also cease to be chairman or deputy chairman.

Payments to members

9.—(1) The Authority shall pay to their members such salaries or fees, and such travelling, subsistence or other allowances, as the Secretary of State may determine.

(2) The Authority shall, as regards any member in whose case the Secretary of State may so determine, pay, or make provision for the payment of, such sums by way of pension, allowances and gratuities to or in respect of him as the Secretary of State may determine.

(3) If a person ceases to be a member of the Authority and it appears to the Secretary of State that there are special circumstances which make it right that he should receive compensation, the Secretary of State may direct the Authority to make to that person a payment of such amount as the Secretary of State may determine.

(4) A determination or direction of the Secretary of State under this paragraph requires the approval of the Treasury.

Staff

10. Subject to the approval of the Secretary of State, given with the consent of the Treasury, the Authority—

(a) may appoint such number of employees, on such terms and conditions, as they may determine; and

(b) shall pay to their employees such remuneration and allowances as they may determine.

11.—(1) Employment with the Authority shall continue to be included among the kinds of employment to which a scheme under section 1 of the Superannuation Act 1972 can apply.

(2) The Authority shall pay to the Treasury, at such times as the Treasury may direct, such sums as the Treasury may determine in respect of the increase attributable to this paragraph in the sums payable under the Superannuation Act 1972 out of money provided by Parliament.

(3) Where an employee of the Authority is (by reference to that employment) a participant in a scheme under section 1 of that Act and is also a member of the Authority, the Treasury may determine that his service as such a member shall be treated for the purposes of the scheme as service as an employee of the Authority (whether or not any benefits are payable to or in respect of him by virtue of paragraph 9).

Finance

12.—(1) The Secretary of State may make grants to the Authority of such amount as he thinks fit in respect of expenses incurred or to be incurred by the Authority in carrying out their functions.

(2) The payment of grant under this paragraph shall be subject to the fulfilment of such conditions as the Secretary of State may determine.

(3) The Secretary of State may also impose such requirements as he thinks fit in connection with the payment of grant under this paragraph.

Committees

13.—(1) The Authority may establish a committee for any purpose.

(2) The Authority shall determine the number of members which a committee established under this paragraph shall have, and the terms on which they are to hold and vacate office.

(3) A committee may include persons who are not members of the Authority.

(4) The Authority shall keep under review the structure of committees established under this paragraph and the scope of each committee's activities.

Delegation of functions

14. The Authority may authorise the chairman, the deputy chairman, the chief officer or any committee established under paragraph 13 to carry out such of the Authority's functions as the Authority may determine.

Proceedings

15.—(1) A representative of the Secretary of State shall be entitled to attend and take part in deliberations (but not in decisions) at meetings of the Authority or of any committee of the Authority.

(2) The Authority shall provide the Secretary of State with such copies of any documents distributed to members of the Authority or of any such committee as he may require.

16.—(1) Her Majesty's Chief Inspector of Schools in England, or a representative of his, shall be entitled to attend and take part in deliberations (but not in decisions) at meetings of the Authority or of any committee of the Authority.

(2) The Authority shall provide Her Majesty's Chief Inspector of Schools in England with such copies of any documents distributed to members of the Authority or of any such committee as he may require.

17.—(1) The chairman of the Curriculum and Assessment Authority for Wales, or a representative of his, shall be entitled to attend and take part in deliberations (but not in decisions) at meetings of the Authority or of any committee of the Authority.

(2) The Authority shall provide the chairman of the Curriculum and Assessment Authority for Wales with such copies of any documents distributed to members of the Authority or of any such committee as he may require.

18. The validity of the Authority's proceedings shall not be affected by a vacancy among the members or any defect in the appointment of a member.

19. Subject to the preceding provisions of this Schedule, the Authority may regulate their own procedure and that of any of their committees.

Accounts

20.—(1) The Authority shall—

(a) keep proper accounts and proper records in relation to the accounts;

(b) prepare a statement of accounts in respect of each financial year of the Authority; and

(c) send copies of the statement to the Secretary of State and to the Comptroller and Auditor General before the end of the month of August next following the financial year to which the statement relates.

(2) The statement of accounts shall comply with any directions given by the Secretary of State with the approval of the Treasury as to—

(a) the information to be contained in it;

(b) the manner in which the information contained in it is to be presented; or

(c) the methods and principles according to which the statement is to be prepared.

(3) The Comptroller and Auditor General shall examine, certify and report on each statement received by him in pursuance of this paragraph and shall lay copies of each statement and of his report before each House of Parliament.

Documents

21. The application of the seal of the Authority shall be authenticated by the signature—

(a) of the chairman or some other person authorised either generally or specially by the Authority to act for that purpose, and

(b) of one other member.

22. Any document purporting to be an instrument made or issued by or on behalf of the Authority and to be duly executed by a person authorised by the Authority in that behalf, shall

be received in evidence and be treated, without further proof, as being so made or issued unless the contrary is shown.

Section 360

SCHEDULE 30

THE CURRICULUM AND ASSESSMENT AUTHORITY FOR WALES

Status

1. The Authority shall not be regarded as a servant or agent of the Crown or as enjoying any status, immunity or privilege of the Crown; and the Authority's property shall not be regarded as property of, or property held on behalf of, the Crown.

Powers

2.—(1) The Authority may do anything which is calculated to facilitate, or is incidental or conducive to, the carrying out of any of their functions.

(2) In particular, the Authority may—

(a) acquire or dispose of land or other property,
(b) enter into contracts,
(c) form bodies corporate or subscribe for shares or stock,
(d) invest any sums not immediately required for the purpose of carrying out their functions,
(e) accept gifts of money, land or other property, and
(f) borrow money.

3.—(1) The Authority may also give to any person or body (whether or not in the United Kingdom) such assistance, other than financial assistance, as they may determine.

(2) Assistance may be provided on such terms and subject to such conditions (if any) as the Authority may determine.

(3) In particular, assistance may be provided free of charge or on such terms as to payment as the Authority may determine.

(4) The consent of the Secretary of State is required for the exercise of any power conferred by this paragraph.

Chief officer

4.—(1) The Authority shall have a chief officer who shall be appointed—

(a) in the case of a person who is also chairman of the Authority, by the Secretary of State, and
(b) in any other case, by the Authority with the approval of the Secretary of State.

(2) The appointment of the chief officer shall be on such terms and conditions as the Secretary of State, or (as the case may be) the Authority with the approval of the Secretary of State, may determine.

(3) No member of the Authority other than the chairman shall be appointed as chief officer.

Tenure of office

5.—(1) A person shall hold and vacate office as a member or as chairman or deputy chairman of the Authority in accordance with the terms of his appointment and shall, on ceasing to be a member, be eligible for reappointment.

(2) A person may at any time by notice in writing to the Secretary of State resign his office as a member or as chairman or deputy chairman of the Authority.

6. The Secretary of State may, if satisfied that a member of the Authority—

(a) has been absent from meetings of the Authority for a continuous period of more than six months without the permission of the Authority, or
(b) is unable or unfit to discharge the functions of a member,

remove him from office by giving him notice in writing and thereupon the office shall become vacant.

7. If the chairman or deputy chairman of the Authority ceases to be a member of the Authority, he shall also cease to be chairman or deputy chairman.

Payments to members

8.—(1) The Authority shall pay to their members such salaries or fees, and such travelling, subsistence or other allowances, as the Secretary of State may determine.

(2) The Authority shall, as regards any member in whose case the Secretary of State may so determine, pay, or make provision for the payment of, such sums by way of pension, allowances and gratuities to or in respect of him as the Secretary of State may determine.

(3) If a person ceases to be a member of the Authority and it appears to the Secretary of State that there are special circumstances which make it right that he should receive compensation, the Secretary of State may direct the Authority to make to that person a payment of such amount as the Secretary of State may determine.

(4) A determination or direction of the Secretary of State under this paragraph requires the approval of the Treasury.

Staff

9. Subject to the approval of the Secretary of State, given with the consent of the Treasury, the Authority—

(a) may appoint such number of employees, on such terms and conditions, as they may determine; and

(b) shall pay to their employees such remuneration and allowances as they may determine.

10.—(1) Employment with the Authority shall continue to be included among the kinds of employment to which a scheme under section 1 of the Superannuation Act 1972 can apply.

(2) The Authority shall pay to the Treasury, at such times as the Treasury may direct, such sums as the Treasury may determine in respect of the increase attributable to this paragraph in the sums payable under the Superannuation Act 1972 out of money provided by Parliament.

(3) Where an employee of the Authority is (by reference to that employment) a participant in a scheme under section 1 of that Act and is also a member of the Authority, the Treasury may determine that his service as such a member shall be treated for the purposes of the scheme as service as an employee of the Authority (whether or not any benefits are payable to or in respect of him by virtue of paragraph 8).

Finance

11.—(1) The Secretary of State may make grants to the Authority of such amount as he thinks fit in respect of expenses incurred or to be incurred by the Authority in carrying out their functions.

(2) The payment of grant under this paragraph shall be subject to the fulfilment of such conditions as the Secretary of State may determine.

(3) The Secretary of State may also impose such requirements as he thinks fit in connection with the payment of grant under this paragraph.

Committees

12.—(1) The Authority may establish a committee for any purpose.

(2) The Authority shall determine the number of members which a committee established under this paragraph shall have, and the terms on which they are to hold and vacate office.

(3) A committee may include persons who are not members of the Authority.

(4) The Authority shall keep under review the structure of committees established under this paragraph and the scope of each committee's activities.

Delegation of functions

13. The Authority may authorise the chairman, the deputy chairman, the chief officer or any committee established under paragraph 12 to carry out such of the Authority's functions as the Authority may determine.

Proceedings

14.—(1) The chairman of the School Curriculum and Assessment Authority, or a representative of his, shall be entitled to attend and take part in deliberations (but not in decisions) at meetings of the Authority or of any committee of the Authority.

(2) The Authority shall provide the chairman of the School Curriculum and Assessment Authority with such copies of any documents distributed to members of the Authority or of any such committee as he may require.

15. The validity of the Authority's proceedings shall not be affected by a vacancy among the members or any defect in the appointment of a member.

16. Subject to the preceding provisions of this Schedule, the Authority may regulate their own procedure and that of any of their committees.

Accounts

17.—(1) The Authority shall—

(a) keep proper accounts and proper records in relation to the accounts;

(b) prepare a statement of accounts in respect of each financial year of the Authority; and
(c) send copies of the statement to the Secretary of State and to the Comptroller and Auditor General before the end of the month of August next following the financial year to which the statement relates.

(2) The statement of accounts shall comply with any directions given by the Secretary of State with the approval of the Treasury as to—
(a) the information to be contained in it;
(b) the manner in which the information contained in it is to be presented; or
(c) the methods and principles according to which the statement is to be prepared.

(3) The Comptroller and Auditor General shall examine, certify and report on each statement received by him in pursuance of this paragraph and shall lay copies of each statement and of his report before each House of Parliament.

Documents

18. The application of the Authority's seal shall be authenticated by the signature of the chairman or deputy chairman and that of one other member.

19. Any document purporting to be an instrument made or issued by or on behalf of the Authority and to be—
(a) duly executed under the Authority's seal, or
(b) signed or executed by a person authorised by the Authority to act in that behalf,
shall be received in evidence and be treated, without further proof, as being so made or issued unless the contrary is shown.

Section 375

SCHEDULE 31

Agreed syllabuses of religious education

Duty to convene conference to reconsider agreed syllabus

1.—(1) Where the agreed syllabus for the time being adopted by a local education authority was adopted by them on or after 29th September 1988 but before 1st April 1994, they shall, within the period of five years beginning with the date on which they adopted the syllabus, convene a conference for the purpose of reconsidering the syllabus.

(2) Sub-paragraph (1) does not apply where the authority have already convened such a conference on or after 1st April 1994 in pursuance of paragraph 12(3) of Schedule 5 to the Education Act 1944.

2.—(1) A local education authority shall from time to time cause further conferences to be convened for the purpose of reconsidering any agreed syllabus for the time being adopted by them (whether adopted before, on or after 1st April 1994).

(2) No such conference shall be convened later than the end of the period of five years beginning with the date (falling after 31st March 1994) on which—
(a) the authority adopted the syllabus, or
(b) the authority gave effect to a recommendation under paragraph 10(2) below (or under paragraph 13 of Schedule 5 to the Education Act 1944) that the syllabus should continue to be the agreed syllabus.

3. On receipt by a local education authority of written notification of any such requirement as is mentioned in section 391(3), the authority shall cause a conference to be convened for the purpose of reconsidering any agreed syllabus to which the requirement relates.

Constitution of conference

4.—(1) A conference convened under this Schedule shall consist of such groups of persons ("committees") appointed by the local education authority which convenes the conference as are required by sub-paragraph (2).

(2) Those committees are—
(a) a committee of persons representing such Christian denominations and other religions and denominations of such religions as, in the opinion of the authority, will appropriately reflect the principal religious traditions in the area;
(b) except in the case of an area in Wales, a committee of persons representing the Church of England;
(c) a committee of persons representing such associations representing teachers as, in the opinion of the authority, ought to be represented, having regard to the circumstances of the area; and

(d) a committee of persons representing the authority.

(3) Where a committee is required to be appointed by virtue of sub-paragraph (2)(b), the committee required to be appointed by virtue of sub-paragraph (2)(a) shall not include persons appointed to represent the Church of England.

(4) The number of persons appointed under sub-paragraph (2)(a) to represent each denomination or religion required to be represented shall, so far as is consistent with the efficient discharge of the committee's functions, reflect broadly the proportionate strength of that denomination or religion in the area.

5. Any sub-committees appointed by the conference shall each include at least one member of each of the committees constituting the conference.

6. On any question to be decided by the conference or by any sub-committee of the conference, a single vote shall be given for each of the committees constituting the conference.

7.—(1) Before appointing a person to represent any religion, denomination or associations as a member of a committee, the local education authority shall take all reasonable steps to assure themselves that he is representative of the religion, denomination or associations in question.

(2) No proceedings under this Schedule shall be invalidated on the ground that a member of a committee did not represent the religion, denomination or associations which he was appointed to represent, unless it is shown that the authority failed to take the steps required by sub-paragraph (1).

8. A person appointed as a member of a committee—

(a) may resign his membership, or

(b) may be withdrawn from membership by the local education authority if, in their opinion, he ceases to be representative of the religion, denomination or associations which he was appointed to represent or (as the case may be) of the authority.

9. Where a person resigns or is withdrawn from a committee, the local education authority shall appoint someone in his place in the same manner as that in which they made the original appointment.

Reconsideration of agreed syllabus

10.—(1) This paragraph applies where a local education authority cause a conference to be convened for the purpose of reconsidering any agreed syllabus under any of paragraphs 1 to 3.

(2) If—

(a) the conference—

(i) unanimously recommend that the existing syllabus should continue to be the agreed syllabus, or

(ii) unanimously recommend a new syllabus to be adopted in substitution for the existing syllabus, and

(b) it appears to the local education authority that the syllabus or, as the case may be, the new syllabus, reflects the fact that the religious traditions in Great Britain are in the main Christian while taking account of the teaching and practices of the other principal religions represented in Great Britain,

the authority may give effect to the recommendation.

(3) If—

(a) the authority report to the Secretary of State that the conference are unable to reach unanimous agreement, or

(b) the conference unanimously recommend that the existing syllabus should continue to be the agreed syllabus but the local education authority consider that sub-paragraph (2)(b) prevents them from giving effect to the recommendation, or

(c) it appears to the Secretary of State that the authority have failed to exercise their power under sub-paragraph (2) to give effect to the unanimous recommendation of the conference,

the Secretary of State shall proceed in accordance with paragraph 12.

11. Where any agreed syllabus for the time being adopted by a local education authority which is in use at a grant-maintained school within the area of the authority (or for any pupils at such a school) falls to be reconsidered under this Schedule, the conference shall consult the governing body of the grant-maintained school before making any recommendation.

Preparation of new syllabus by appointed body

12.—(1) Where required by paragraph 10 to proceed in accordance with this paragraph, the Secretary of State shall appoint a body of persons having experience in religious education to prepare a syllabus of religious education.

(2) The appointed body shall, so far as is practicable, be of a representative character which is the same as that required by paragraph 4 in the case of a conference.

13.—(1) The appointed body shall—

(a) give the local education authority, the conference and every committee constituting the conference an opportunity of making representations to it;

(b) after considering any such representations made to it, prepare a syllabus of religious education; and

(c) transmit a copy of that syllabus to the authority and to the Secretary of State.

(2) Subject to sub-paragraph (1)(a), the appointed body may conduct its proceedings in such manner as it thinks fit.

14. The syllabus prepared by the appointed body shall be deemed to be the agreed syllabus adopted for use in the schools for which, or for the class or description of pupils for which, it was prepared—

(a) as from such date as the Secretary of State may direct, and

(b) until a new syllabus is adopted for use in those schools, or for pupils of that class or description, in accordance with this Schedule.

Special provisions applicable where order under section 27(1)(b) applies

15.—(1) This paragraph has effect in respect of the area of a local education authority if an order under section 27(1)(b) (allocation of responsibility for providing sufficient school places to funding authority) applies to the area.

(2) Within six months of the date of the first such order the authority shall reconvene any conference—

(a) which they have convened under any of paragraphs 1 to 3 above (or for the purpose set out in paragraph 1 or 12 of Schedule 5 to the Education Act 1944 (preparation and reconsideration of agreed syllabuses) or section 11(8) of the Education Reform Act 1988 (standing advisory councils on religious education)), and

(b) which has not made a recommendation under paragraph 10(2)(a) above (or under paragraph 9 or 13(2) of that Schedule), and

(c) in respect of which the authority have not made a report under paragraph 10(3)(a) above (or under paragraph 10 or 13(4) of that Schedule).

(3) Where a conference is convened (or reconvened) after the date of the order—

(a) paragraph 4 shall have effect as if it required the appointment of a committee, in addition to those listed in sub-paragraph (2)(a) to (d) of that paragraph, consisting of persons representing relevant grant-maintained schools, and

(b) paragraph 11 shall have effect only in relation to grant-maintained schools, or pupils at such schools, at which the syllabus is in use in accordance with section 381(3);

and paragraph 4(4) shall apply in relation to a conference reconvened by virtue of this paragraph (whether or not it applied when the conference was originally convened).

(4) Before appointing a person to represent relevant grant-maintained schools in accordance with sub-paragraph (3)(a), the local education authority shall take all reasonable steps to assure themselves that he is acceptable as such to the governing bodies of the majority of such schools.

(5) No proceedings under this Schedule shall be invalidated on the ground that any such person was not so acceptable unless it is shown that the local education authority failed to take those steps.

(6) A person so appointed—

(a) may resign his membership of the committee, or

(b) may be withdrawn from the committee by the local education authority if, in their opinion, he ceases to be acceptable as a representative of relevant grant-maintained schools to the governing bodies of the majority of such schools.

(7) Where any such person resigns or is withdrawn from the committee, the local education authority shall appoint someone in his place in the same manner as that in which they made the original appointment.

(8) For the purposes of this paragraph "relevant grant-maintained schools" means those grant-maintained schools within the area of the local education authority in relation to which section 379 or 380 applies.

Section 420

SCHEDULE 32

Reduction of standard number for admission of pupils

Proposals for reduction of standard number

1. Where the admission authority for a county or voluntary school intend to apply for an order under section 420(2) reducing any standard number applying to the school under sections 417 to 420 for any age group in any year, they shall—

(a) publish their proposals relating to the reduction in such manner as may be required by regulations, and

(b) submit a copy of the published proposals to the Secretary of State together with their application.

2. The published proposals shall be accompanied by a statement explaining the effect of—

(a) paragraph 3, where the local education authority are the admission authority, or

(b) paragraph 4, where the governing body are the admission authority.

3.—(1) Where the local education authority are the admission authority objections to the proposals may, within the period of two months beginning with the date of publication of the proposals, be submitted to the authority by any of the following—

(a) any ten or more local government electors for the authority's area,

(b) the governing body of any school affected by the proposals, and

(c) any other local education authority concerned.

(2) Within one month after the end of the period mentioned in sub-paragraph (1), the authority shall transmit to the Secretary of State copies of all objections made (and not withdrawn in writing) within that period, together with their observations on them.

4. Where the governing body are the admission authority, objections to the proposals may, within the period of two months beginning with the date of publication of the proposals, be submitted to the Secretary of State by any of the following—

(a) any ten or more local government electors for the local education authority's area,

(b) the governing body of any school affected by the proposals, and

(c) any local education authority concerned.

Order of Secretary of State

5.—(1) Subject to sub-paragraph (2), where an application is made to the Secretary of State for any such order reducing a standard number as is mentioned in paragraph 1, he may—

(a) make an order reducing the standard number to the number proposed;

(b) after consultation with both the local education authority and the governing body, make an order reducing the standard number to such number (greater than the number proposed) as he thinks desirable; or

(c) refuse to make any order reducing the standard number.

(2) The Secretary of State shall not make an order reducing the standard number unless he is satisfied that the reduction is necessary, having regard to any reduction in the school's capacity to accommodate pupils as compared with its capacity at the beginning of the school year in which the current standard number first applied in relation to the age group in question (whether by virtue of section 15 of the Education Act 1980, section 27 of the Education Reform Act 1988 or sections 417 to 420 of this Act).

(3) For the purposes of sub-paragraph (2) a school's capacity to accommodate pupils is changed if—

(a) as a result of changes in the availability or use of accommodation at the school, there is any change in the amount of accommodation available for use by pupils at the school; or

(b) as a result of changes in the requirements applicable to the school under regulations made under section 542 there is any change in the number of pupils for whom accommodation may lawfully be provided at the school;

and a school's capacity to accommodate pupils is reduced if the result of the changes is, in a case within paragraph (a), less accommodation or, in a case within paragraph (b), a reduction in the number there mentioned.

Consultation before making application

6.—(1) Where the local education authority are the admission authority for a county or voluntary school, they shall not make an application for an order under section 420(2) reducing any standard number applying to the school without first consulting the governing body.

(2) Where the governing body are the admission authority for such a school, they shall not make such an application without first consulting the local education authority.

References to date of publication of proposals

7.—(1) References in this Schedule, in relation to proposals under paragraph 1, to the date of publication of the proposals are references—

(a) to the date on which the requirements of regulations with respect to the publication of the proposals are satisfied; or

(b) where different such requirements are satisfied on different dates, to the last of those dates.

(2) Where any such requirement imposes a continuing obligation with respect to the publication of any such proposals, the requirement shall for the purposes of sub-paragraph (1) be taken to be satisfied on the first date in respect of which it is satisfied.

Section 423

SCHEDULE 33

ADMISSION APPEALS

PART I

CONSTITUTION OF APPEAL COMMITTEES

Appeal arrangements made by local education authorities

1.—(1) An appeal pursuant to arrangements made by a local education authority under section 423(1) shall be to an appeal committee constituted in accordance with this paragraph.

(2) An appeal committee shall consist of—

(a) one person nominated by the authority from among persons who are eligible to be lay members; and

(b) two, four or six other members nominated by the authority from among persons appointed by the authority under sub-paragraph (3).

(3) The persons appointed by the authority under this sub-paragraph shall comprise—

(a) members of the authority, and

(b) persons who are not members of the authority but who have experience in education, are acquainted with the educational conditions in the area of the authority or are parents of registered pupils at a school,

but shall not include any person employed by the authority otherwise than as a teacher.

(4) Sufficient persons may be appointed by the authority under sub-paragraph (3) to enable two or more appeal committees to sit at the same time.

(5) The authority shall not nominate a person under sub-paragraph (2)(a) if he is a member of the authority or is employed by them.

(6) The members of an appeal committee who are members of the authority shall not outnumber the others.

(7) A person who is a member of the authority or employed by the authority shall not be chairman of an appeal committee.

(8) A person shall not be a member of an appeal committee for the consideration of an appeal against a decision if he was among those who made the decision or took part in discussions as to whether the decision should be made.

(9) A person who is a teacher at a school shall not be a member of an appeal committee for the consideration of an appeal involving a question whether a child is to be admitted to that school.

Appeal arrangements made by governing bodies

2.—(1) An appeal pursuant to arrangements made by the governing body of an aided or a special agreement school under section 423(2) shall be to an appeal committee constituted in accordance with this paragraph.

(2) An appeal committee shall consist of—

(a) one person nominated by the governing body from among persons who are eligible to be lay members; and

(b) two, four or six other members nominated by the governing body from among persons appointed by them under sub-paragraph (3).

(3) The persons appointed by the governing body under this sub-paragraph—

(a) may include one or more of the governors,

(b) shall include persons appointed from a list drawn up by the local education authority by whom the school is maintained, and

(c) shall not include any person employed by the authority otherwise than as a teacher.

(4) Sufficient persons may be appointed by the governing body under subparagraph (3) to enable two or more appeal committees to sit at the same time.

(5) Of the members of an appeal committee—

(a) three shall be nominated from among those mentioned in subparagraph (3)(b) in the case of a committee consisting of seven members;

(b) two shall be so nominated in the case of a committee consisting of five members; and

(c) one shall be so nominated in the case of a committee consisting of three members.

(6) The governing body shall not nominate under sub-paragraph (2)(a) a person who falls within sub-paragraph (3)(a) or (b) or is employed by the local education authority by whom the school is maintained.

(7) None of the governors shall be chairman of an appeal committee.

(8) A person shall not be a member of an appeal committee for the consideration of an appeal against a decision if he was among those who made the decision or took part in discussions as to whether the decision should be made.

(9) A person who is a teacher at a school shall not be a member of an appeal committee for the consideration of an appeal involving a question whether a child is to be admitted to that school.

3. Where (by virtue of section 423(3)) joint arrangements are made under section 423(2) by the governing bodies of two or more schools, paragraph 2 shall apply as if any reference to the governing body or to the governors were a reference to the governing bodies or (as the case may be) the governors of both or all the schools; and an appeal pursuant to such joint arrangements shall be to an appeal committee constituted in accordance with paragraph 2 as it so applies.

4. An appeal committee constituted in accordance with paragraph 2 (or in accordance with that paragraph as it applies by virtue of paragraph 3)—

(a) shall be included in the bodies to which section 174 of the Local Government Act 1972 (travelling and subsistence allowances) applies; and

(b) for the purpose of the payment of financial loss allowance under section 173(4) of that Act to members of the committee, shall be included among the bodies to which section 173 applies.

Lay members

5.—(1) A person is eligible to be a lay member for the purposes of paragraphs 1(2)(a) and 2(2)(a) if—

(a) he is a person without personal experience in the management of any school or the provision of education in any school (disregarding any such experience as a governor or in any other voluntary capacity), and

(b) he satisfies the conditions specified in sub-paragraph (2).

(2) Those conditions are—

(a) in the case of a person to be nominated as a lay member for the purposes of paragraph 1(2)(a), that he does not have, and has not at any time had, any connection with—

(i) the local education authority in question, or

(ii) any person who is a member of, or employed by, that authority,

of a kind which might reasonably be taken to raise doubts about his ability to act impartially in relation to the authority, and

(b) in the case of a person to be nominated as a lay member for the purposes of paragraph 2(2)(a), that he does not have, and has not at any time had, any connection with—

(i) the school in question, or

(ii) any person who is a member of, or employed by, the governing body of that school,

of a kind which might reasonably be taken to raise doubts about his ability to act impartially in relation to the school.

6. The Secretary of State may by regulations require any local education authority or governing body who are required by section 423(1) or (2) to make arrangements under that provision—

(a) to advertise, in such manner and at such times as may be prescribed, for persons eligible to be lay members of any appeal committee required to be constituted for the purposes of such arrangements to apply to the authority or body for appointment as such members, and

(b) in appointing persons as such members, to consider any persons eligible to be so appointed who have applied to the authority or body in response to an advertisement placed in pursuance of sub-paragraph (a) above.

Indemnity

7. Any local education authority or governing body required to make arrangements under section 423(1) or (2) shall indemnify the members of any appeal committee required to be constituted for the purposes of those arrangements against any reasonable legal costs and expenses reasonably incurred by those members in connection with any decision or action taken by them in good faith in pursuance of their functions as members of that committee.

Part II

Procedure

8. In this Part "appeal" means an appeal pursuant to any arrangements made under section 423.

9. An appeal shall be by notice in writing setting out the grounds on which it is made.

10. An appeal committee shall give the appellant an opportunity of appearing and making oral representations, and may allow him to be accompanied by a friend or to be represented.

11. The matters to be taken into account by an appeal committee in considering an appeal shall include—

(a) any preference expressed by the appellant in respect of the child as mentioned in section 411, and

(b) the arrangements for the admission of pupils published by the local education authority or the governing body under section 414.

12.—(1) Appeals shall be heard in private except when the local education authority or governing body (or bodies) by whom the arrangements under section 423 are made direct otherwise.

(2) Without prejudice to any of the other provisions of this Schedule—

(a) a member of the local education authority may attend, as an observer, any hearing of an appeal by an appeal committee constituted in accordance with paragraph 1; and

(b) a member of the Council on Tribunals may attend as an observer any meeting of any appeal committee at which an appeal is considered.

13. In the event of a disagreement between the members of an appeal committee, the appeal under consideration shall be decided by a simple majority of the votes cast and, in the case of an equality of votes, the chairman of the committee shall have a second or casting vote.

14. The decision of an appeal committee and the grounds on which it is made shall be communicated by the committee in writing to—

(a) the appellant and the local education authority, and

(b) in the case of an appeal to an appeal committee constituted in accordance with paragraph 2 (or in accordance with that paragraph as it applies by virtue of paragraph 3), to the governing body by whom or on whose behalf the decision appealed against was made.

15.—(1) Subject to paragraphs 9 to 14, all matters relating to the procedure on appeals, including the time within which they are to be brought, shall be determined by the local education authority or governing body (or bodies) by whom the arrangements under section 423 are made.

(2) Neither section 106 of the Local Government Act 1972 nor paragraph 44 of Schedule 12 to that Act (procedure of committees of local authorities) shall apply to an appeal committee constituted in accordance with paragraph 1.

Section 476

SCHEDULE 34

Independent Schools Tribunals

Appointment of legal and educational panels

1.—(1) For the purpose of enabling Independent Schools Tribunals to be constituted as occasion may require there shall be two panels.

(2) One of the panels (the "legal panel") shall consist of persons who will be available to act when required as chairmen of such tribunals and shall be appointed by the Lord Chancellor.

(3) The other panel (the "educational panel") shall consist of persons who will be available to act when required as members of such tribunals and shall be appointed by the Lord President of the Council.

Qualifications for appointment

2.—(1) A person is not qualified to be appointed to the legal panel unless he possesses such legal qualifications as the Lord Chancellor considers suitable.

(2) A person is not qualified to be appointed to the educational panel unless he has had such experience in teaching or in the conduct, management or administration of schools as the Lord President of the Council considers suitable.

(3) A person who is—

(a) an officer of a government department, or

(b) employed by a local education authority otherwise than as a teacher,

is disqualified from being appointed to either panel.

Terms and conditions of appointment

3.—(1) Subject (in the case of a member of the legal panel) to sub-paragraph (2), a person appointed to be a member of a panel shall hold office as such subject to such conditions as to the period of his membership and otherwise as may be determined by the Lord Chancellor or the Lord President of the Council, as the case may be.

(2) No appointment of a person to be a member of the legal panel shall be such as to extend beyond the day on which he attains the age of 70; but this sub-paragraph has effect subject to section 26(4) to (6) of the Judicial Pensions and Retirement Act 1993 (power to authorise continuance in office up to the age of 75).

Constitution of tribunal

4.—(1) Where an appeal is required to be determined by an Independent Schools Tribunal, the tribunal shall consist of—

(a) a chairman who is a member of the legal panel, and

(b) two other members who are members of the educational panel.

(2) The chairman and other members of the tribunal shall be impartial persons appointed from those panels by the Lord Chancellor and the Lord President of the Council respectively.

Remuneration

5. The Secretary of State may pay to the members of an Independent Schools Tribunal such remuneration and allowances as he may determine with the consent of the Treasury.

Section 479

SCHEDULE 35

Termination of participation agreements

1.—(1) A participation agreement shall provide that it may be terminated in accordance with this Schedule.

(2) A participation agreement shall not be capable of being terminated by either party otherwise than in accordance with this Schedule.

2. The proprietors of the school may terminate a participation agreement by giving three years' written notice to the Secretary of State or such shorter notice as he may in any particular case accept.

3. Subject to paragraph 4, the Secretary of State may terminate a participation agreement by giving three years' written notice to the proprietors of the school.

4.—(1) If in the case of a participation agreement the Secretary of State—

(a) is satisfied that any condition applying to the school under the agreement or by virtue of regulations made under section 480 has been contravened, or

(b) is not satisfied that appropriate educational standards are being maintained at the school, or

(c) is not satisfied that section 550 (which provides that a person is not to be refused education at a school because section 548 would prevent his being given corporal punishment) is being complied with in relation to the school,

he may at any time terminate the agreement by written notice to the proprietors of the school.

(2) A notice of termination given under this paragraph may provide that it shall be treated as of no effect if the proprietors of the school satisfy the Secretary of State within such time as may be specified in the notice that they have complied with any condition so specified.

5. A notice of termination given under paragraph 3 or 4 shall contain a statement of the reason for which it is given.

6. The termination of a participation agreement shall not affect the operation of the agreement or of the assisted places scheme (including any regulations made under section 480) in relation to any pupil holding an assisted place at the school on the date of the termination.

Section 557

SCHEDULE 36

Uniform statutory trusts for educational endowments

1. The trustees may, after payment of any expenses incurred in connection with the administration of the trust, apply the capital and income of the relevant trust assets for any of the following purposes—

(a) in or towards the purchase of a site for, or the erection, improvement or enlargement of, the premises of any relevant school in the area,
(b) for the maintenance of any relevant school in the area;
(c) in or towards the purchase of a site for, or the erection, improvement or enlargement of, the premises of a teacher's house for use in connection with any relevant school in the area; and
(d) for the maintenance of a teacher's house for use in connection with any relevant school in the area.

2. The trustees may also, after payment of any expenses incurred in connection with the administration of the trust, apply the income of the relevant trust assets for any of the following purposes—
(a) in or towards the provision of advice, guidance and resources (including materials) in connection with any matter related to the management of, or education provided at, any relevant school in the area;
(b) the provision of services for the carrying out of any inspection of any relevant school in the area required by Part I of the School Inspections Act 1996; and
(c) to defray the cost of employing or engaging staff in connection with—
(i) the application of income of the relevant trust assets for either of the purposes referred to in sub-paragraphs (a) and (b) above, or
(ii) the application of capital or income of the relevant trust assets for any of the purposes referred to in paragraph 1 above.

Section 582(1)

SCHEDULE 37

CONSEQUENTIAL AMENDMENTS

PART I

AMENDMENTS COMING INTO FORCE ON 1ST NOVEMBER 1996

Children and Young Persons Act 1933 (c. 12)

1. Section 96 of the Children and Young Persons Act 1933 (provisions as to local authorities) shall continue to have effect with the following amendments (originally made by Schedule 8 to the Education Act 1944)—
(a) in subsection (3), for the words from "for elementary education" onwards there is substituted "shall be defrayed as expenses under the enactments relating to education"; and
(b) in subsection (4), for the second "under" there is substituted "in accordance with".

Public Records Act 1958 (c. 51)

2. In Schedule 1 to the Public Records Act 1958 (definition of public records) Part II of the Table at the end of paragraph 3 (organisations whose records are public records) shall continue to include the following entries (originally inserted by Schedule 19 to the Education Act 1993, taken with Schedule 15 to that Act)—
"Curriculum and Assessment Authority for Wales",
"Funding Agency for Schools",
"School Curriculum and Assessment Authority", and
"Schools Funding Council for Wales".

Church Schools (Assistance by Church Commissioners) Measure 1958 (1958 No. 2)

3. In section 2(1) of the Church Schools (Assistance by Church Commissioners) Measure 1958 (interpretation) for "the Education Acts, 1944 to 1993" there is substituted "the Education Act 1996".

Education Act 1962 (c. (12)

4.—(1) Section 1 of the Education Act 1962 (local education authority awards for designated courses) shall continue to have effect with the following amendment (originally made by section 4 of the Education (Grants and Awards) Act 1984).

(2) In subsection (3)(d), for the words from "for the higher diploma" onwards there is substituted "or for the higher national diploma of the body corporate known at the passing of the Education (Grants and Awards) Act 1984 as the Business & Technician Education Council.".

5. In section 3(c)(i) of that Act (awards by Secretary of State) for "section 100 of the Education Act 1944" there is substituted "section 485 of the Education Act 1996".

6. For section 14(4) of that Act there is substituted—
"(4) This Act shall be construed as one with the Education Act 1996.".

7. In paragraph 2 of Schedule 1 to that Act (ordinary residence) for "section 31(3) of the Education Act 1980" there is substituted "the Education Act 1996 in accordance with regulations made under section 579(4) of that Act.".

London Government Act 1963 (c. 33)

8. In section 30(1) of the London Government Act 1963 (local education authorities) for "the Education Acts 1944 to 1962 or in any other Act" there is substituted "any Act".

9. In section 31(5) of that Act (primary, secondary and further education in Greater London) for "except in accordance with the Education Acts 1944 to 1980" there is substituted "except in accordance with the Education Act 1996".

Children and Young Persons Act 1963 (c. 37)

10. In section 37(3) of the Children and Young Persons Act 1963 (exceptions to restriction on persons under 16 taking part in public performances etc.) for "the Education Act 1944" there is substituted "the Education Act 1996".

11. In section 38 of that Act (restriction on licences for performances by children under 13—
(a) in subsection (1) for "thirteen" there is substituted "fourteen";
(b) subsection (2) is omitted; and
(c) in the sidenote, for "13" there is substituted "14".

Veterinary Surgeons Act 1966 (c. 36)

12. In Schedule 3 to the Veterinary Surgeons Act 1966 (exemptions from restrictions on practice of veterinary surgery), in the definition of "recognised institution" following paragraph 5, for "the Education Act 1944" there is substituted "the Education Act 1996".

Education Act 1967 (c. 3)

13. In section 6(2) of the Education Act 1967 (construction as one) for "the Education Acts 1944 to 1965" there is substituted "the Education Act 1996".

Public Expenditure and Receipts Act 1968 (c. 14)

14. In Schedule 3 to the Public Expenditure and Receipts Act 1968 (variation of fees, etc.) for "The Education Act 1944 (c. 31) section 94" there is substituted "The Education Act 1996 (c. 56) section 564".

Children and Young Persons Act 1969 (c. 54)

15. In section 12C(3) of the Children and Young Persons Act 1969 (requirements as to education) for "the Education Act 1944" there is substituted "the Education Act 1996".

16. In section 19(17) of that Act (facilities for the carrying out of supervisor's directions etc.) for "the Education Act 1944" there is substituted "the Education Act 1996".

Local Authorities (Goods and Services) Act 1970 (c. 39)

17.—(1) Subject to sub-paragraph (2), in the Local Authorities (Goods and Services) Act 1970 (supply of goods and services by local authorities to public bodies) "public body" shall include the School Curriculum and Assessment Authority and the Curriculum and Assessment Authority for Wales.

(2) The provision in sub-paragraph (1) shall have effect as if made by an order under section 1(5) of that Act (power to provide that a person shall be a public body for the purposes of the Act).

Local Authority Social Services Act 1970 (c. 42)

18. In Schedule 1 to the Local Authority Social Services Act 1970 (enactments conferring functions assigned to social services committee) the entry relating to the Education Act 1993 is omitted and at the end there is added—

"Education Act 1996.	
Section 322	Help for local education authority in exercising functions under Part IV of the Act."

Chronically Sick and Disabled Persons Act 1970 (c. 44)

19. In section 8(2) of the Chronically Sick and Disabled Persons Act 1970 (access to and facilities at university and school buildings) for the words from "and expressions used" onwards there is substituted "and expressions used in paragraph (b) above and in the Education Act 1996 have the same meanings as in that Act".

Pensions (Increase) Act 1971 (c. 56)

20. In Part II of Schedule 2 to the Pensions (Increase) Act 1971 (official pensions payable out of local funds), in paragraph 57, for "the Education Act 1944" there is substituted "the Education Act 1996".

Superannuation Act 1972 (c. 11)

21.—(1) Schedule 1 to the Superannuation Act 1972 shall continue—

(a) to include the entry relating to the School Curriculum and Assessment Authority (originally inserted by Schedule 14 to the Education Act 1993) and the entries relating to the Funding Agency for Schools and the Schools Funding Council for Wales (originally inserted by Schedule 19 to that Act); and

(b) to have effect with the amendment set out in sub-paragraph (2) (originally made by Schedule 15 to that Act).

(2) In the list of Other Bodies, for "Curriculum Council for Wales" there is substituted "Curriculum and Assessment Authority for Wales".

Local Government Act 1972 (c. 70)

22.—(1) Section 104(2)(a) of the Local Government Act 1972 (teachers not disqualified for being members of committees) shall continue to have effect with the following amendment (originally made by Schedule 19 to the Education Act 1993).

(2) For "for the purposes of the enactments relating to education" there is substituted "wholly or partly for the purpose of discharging any functions with respect to education conferred on them in their capacity as local education authorities".

23. In section 112(4)(b) of that Act (appointment of staff) for "section 88 of the Education Act 1944" there is substituted "section 532 of the Education Act 1996".

24. In section 139(4) of that Act (acceptance of gifts of property) for "the Education Acts 1944 to 1971" there is substituted "the Education Act 1996".

25. In section 177(1) of that Act (supplementary provisions as to allowances) for "paragraph 4 of Schedule 2 to the Education Act 1980" there is substituted "paragraph 4 of Schedule 33 to the Education Act 1996".

Fair Trading Act 1973 (c. 41)

26. In Schedule 4 to the Fair Trading Act 1973 (services excluded from sections 14 and 109), in paragraph 14, for "the Education Act 1944," there is substituted "the Education Act 1996,".

Local Government Act 1974 (c. 7)

27. In section 25 of the Local Government Act 1974 (authorities subject to investigation by Local Commissioner) for subsection (5) there is substituted—

"(5) Any reference to an authority to which this Part of this Act applies also includes a reference to any appeal committee constituted—

(a) for the purposes of paragraph 6 of Schedule 23 to the Education Act 1996, or

(b) in accordance with paragraph 1 or 2 of Schedule 33 to that Act."

28. In section 31A(2) of that Act (consideration of adverse reports) for "paragraph 1 of Schedule 2 to the Education Act 1980" there is substituted "paragraph 1 of Schedule 33 to the Education Act 1996".

29. In paragraph 5(1) of Schedule 5 to that Act (matters not subject to investigation) for the words from "section 23" to "1986" there is substituted "section 370 of the Education Act 1996 or section 17 of the Education (No.2) Act 1986".

House of Commons Disqualification Act 1975 (c. 24)

30.—(1) Part III of Schedule 1 to the House of Commons Disqualification Act 1975 (disqualifying offices)—

(a) shall be amended as provided in sub-paragraphs (2) and (3); and

(b) shall continue to include the entries set out in sub-paragraph (4) (originally inserted by Schedule 19 to the Education Act 1993).

(2) For the entry relating to the Curriculum and Assessment Authority for Wales there is substituted—

"Any member of the Curriculum and Assessment Authority for Wales constituted under section 360 of the Education Act 1996 in receipt of remuneration".

(3) For the entry relating to the School Curriculum and Assessment Authority there is substituted—

"Any member of the School Curriculum and Assessment Authority constituted under section 358 of the Education Act 1996 in receipt of remuneration".

(4) The entries referred to in sub-paragraph (1)(b) are—

"Any member of an education association in receipt of remuneration",

"Any member of the Funding Agency for Schools in receipt of remuneration", and

"Any member of the Schools Funding Council for Wales in receipt of remuneration".

Sex Discrimination Act 1975 (c. 65)

31. In section 23(1) of the Sex Discrimination Act 1975 (other discrimination by local education authorities) for "the Education Acts 1944 to 1996" there is substituted "the Education Acts".

32. In section 23A of that Act (discrimination by Further Education and Higher Education Funding Councils) for "the Education Acts 1944 to 1994" there is substituted "the Education Acts".

33. For the section 23C inserted in that Act by Schedule 19 to the Education Act 1993 there is substituted—

"**Discrimination by Funding Agency for Schools or Schools Funding Council for Wales**

23C. It is unlawful for the Funding Agency for Schools or the Schools Funding Council for Wales in carrying out their functions imposed by or under the Education Acts to do any act which constitutes sex discrimination."

34. In section 24(2)(c) of that Act (designated establishments) for "the Education Act 1944" there is substituted "the Education Act 1996".

35.—(1) Section 25 of that Act (general duty in public sector of education)—

(a) shall be amended in accordance with sub-paragraphs (2)(a) to (c), (3)(b), and (4)(a); and

(b) shall continue to have effect with the amendments set out in sub-paragraphs (2)(d), (3)(a) and (4)(b) (originally made by Schedule 19 to the Education Act 1993 and subsequently amended by the Education Act 1994).

(2) In subsection (2)—

(a) for "the Education Act 1944" there is substituted "the Education Act 1996";

(b) in paragraph (a), for "section 68" there is substituted "section 496";

(c) in paragraph (b), for "section 99" there is substituted "section 497"; and

(d) for "and 23" there is substituted "23, 23A, 23C and 23D".

(3) In subsection (4)—

(a) for "and 23" there is substituted "23, 23A, 23C and 23D"; and

(b) for "either" there is substituted "any".

(4) In subsection (6)—

(a) in paragraph (c)(iii), for "section 100 of the Education Act 1944" there is substituted "section 485 of the Education Act 1996"; and

(b) after paragraph (d) there is added—

"(e) the Funding Agency for Schools and the Schools Funding Council for Wales."

36. In section 82 of that Act (general interpretation), in subsection (1)—

(a) after the definition of "education" there is inserted—

" "the Education Acts" has the meaning given by section 578 of the Education Act 1996;";

(b) in the definition of "further education", for "section 41(3) of the Education Act 1944 as read with section 14 of the Further and Higher Education Act 1992" there is substituted "section 2 of the Education Act 1996";

(c) in the definition of "independent school", for "section 114(1) of the Education Act 1944" there is substituted "section 463 of the Education Act 1996";

(d) in the definition of "proprietor", for "section 114(1) of the Education Act 1944" there is substituted "section 579 of the Education Act 1996"; and

(e) in the definition of "school", for "section 114(1) of the Education Act 1944" there is substituted "section 4 of the Education Act 1996".

37. In Schedule 2 to that Act (transitional exemption orders for educational admissions)—

(a) in paragraph 1, for the words from "under the provisions" to "that section," there is substituted "under section 35, 41 or 259 of the Education Act 1996 a responsible body submits to the Secretary of State"; and

(b) in paragraph 3—

(i) for "section 100 of the Education Act 1944" there is substituted "section 485 of the Education Act 1996"; and

(ii) for "subsection (1)(b) of the said section 100" there is substituted "the said section 485".

Restrictive Trade Practices Act 1976 (c. 34)

38. In Schedule 1 to the Restrictive Trade Practices Act 1976 (services excluded from section 13), in paragraph 14, for "the Education Act 1944," there is substituted "the Education Act 1996,".

Race Relations Act 1976 (c. 74)

39. In section 18(1) of the Race Relations Act 1976 (other discrimination by local education authorities) for "the Education Acts 1944 to 1996" there is substituted "the Education Acts".

40. In section 18A of that Act (discrimination by Further Education and Higher Education Funding Councils) for "the Education Acts 1944 to 1994" there is substituted "the Education Acts".

41. For the section 18C inserted in that Act by Schedule 19 to the Education Act 1993 there is substituted—

"**Discrimination by Funding Agency for Schools or Schools Funding Council for Wales**

18C. It is unlawful for the Funding Agency for Schools or the Schools Funding Council for Wales in carrying out their functions imposed by or under the Education Acts to do any act which constitutes racial discrimination."

42.—(1) Section 19 of that Act (general duty in public sector of education)—

(a) shall be amended in accordance with sub-paragraphs (2)(a) to (c), (3)(b) and (4)(a); and

(b) shall continue to have effect with the amendments set out in subparagraphs (2)(d), (3)(a) and (4)(b) (originally made by Schedule 19 to the Education Act 1993 and subsequently amended by the Education Act 1994).

(2) In subsection (2)—

(a) for "the Education Act 1944" there is substituted "the Education Act 1996";

(b) in paragraph (a), for "section 68" there is substituted "section 496";

(c) in paragraph (b), for "section 99" there is substituted "section 497"; and

(d) for "and 18" there is substituted "18, 18A, 18C and 18D".

(3) In subsection (4)—

(a) for "and 18" there is substituted "18, 18A, 18C and 18D"; and

(b) for "either" there is substituted "any".

(4) In subsection (6)—

(a) in paragraph (c)(iii), for "section 100 of the Education Act 1944" there is substituted "section 485 of the Education Act 1996"; and

(b) after paragraph (d) there is added—

"(e) the Funding Agency for Schools and the Schools Funding Council for Wales."

43. In section 78 of that Act (general interpretation), in subsection (1)—

(a) after the definition of "education" there is inserted—

""the Education Acts" has the meaning given by section 578 of the Education Act 1996;";

(b) in the definition of "independent school", for "section 114(1) of the Education Act 1944" there is substituted "section 463 of the Education Act 1996";

(c) in the definition of "proprietor", for "section 114(1) of the Education Act 1944" there is substituted "section 579 of the Education Act 1996"; and

(d) in the definition of "school", for "section 114(1) of the Education Act 1944" there is substituted "section 4 of the Education Act 1996".

National Health Service Act 1977 (c. 49)

44. In section 28A(2)(c) of the National Health Service Act 1977 (power to make payments to local education authority)—

(a) for "the Education Acts 1944 to 1996" there is substituted "the Education Act 1996"; and

(b) for "those Acts" there is substituted "the Education Acts (within the meaning of that Act)".

45. In section 128(1) of that Act (interpretation), in the definition of "local education authority", for "the Education Act 1944" there is substituted "the Education Act 1996".

46. In Schedule 1 to that Act (medical and dental inspection and treatment of pupils etc.)—

(a) in paragraph 1(a)(ii), for "section 163 or 298 of the Education Act 1993" there is substituted "section 19 or 319 of the Education Act 1996"; and

(b) in paragraph 4, for "by section 114(1) of the Education Act 1944" there is substituted "for the purposes of the Education Act 1996".

Education Act 1980 (c. 20)

47.—(1) Section 38 of the Education Act 1980 (citation etc.) shall be amended as follows.

(2) Subsections (2) and (4) to (6) are omitted.

(3) For subsection (3) there is substituted—

"(3) This Act shall, in its application to England and Wales, be construed as one with the Education Act 1996."

(4) In subsection (7), for the words from the beginning to "Northern Ireland;" there is substituted "In this Act section 20 and this section extend to Northern Ireland,".

Education (Scotland) Act 1980 (c. 44)

48.—(1) Section 48A of the Education (Scotland) Act 1980 (corporal punishment) shall continue to have effect with the following amendments (originally made by section 294 of the Education Act 1993).

(2) In subsection (1), after "pupil" there is inserted "to whom this subsection applies", and after that subsection there is inserted—

"(1A) Where, in any proceedings, it is shown that corporal punishment has been given to a pupil by or on the authority of a member of the staff, giving the punishment cannot be justified if the punishment was inhuman or degrading.

(1B) In determining whether punishment is inhuman or degrading regard shall be had to all the circumstances of the case, including the reason for giving it, how soon after the event it is given, its nature, the manner and circumstances in which it is given, the persons involved and its mental and physical effects.".

(3) In subsection (5) for the words preceding paragraph (a) there is substituted "In this section "pupil" means a person for whom education is provided at a school or for whom school education is provided by an education authority otherwise than at a school.

(5A) Subsection (1) above applies to a pupil—".

(4) In subsection (8)(a) for "(5)(a)(iii)" there is substituted "(5A)(a)(iii)".

Local Government, Planning and Land Act 1980 (c. 65)

49. In paragraph 10 of Schedule 10 to the Local Government, Planning and Land Act 1980 (adjustment of block grant in connection with education etc.: interpretation) for "Section 38(5) of the Education Act 1980" there is substituted "Section 579(4) of the Education Act 1996".

Acquisition of Land Act 1981 (c. 67)

50. In section 1(2) of the Acquisition of Land Act 1981 (application of Act) for "section 90(1) of the Education Act 1944" there is substituted "section 530(1) of the Education Act 1996".

51.—(1) Section 17(4) of that Act (statutory undertakers) shall have effect with the following amendment instead of that made by section 11 of the Education Act 1993.

(2) After paragraph (aa) of the definition of "statutory undertakers" there is inserted—

"(ab) the Funding Agency for Schools,

(ac) the Schools Funding Council for Wales,".

Greater London Council (General Powers) Act 1981 (c. xvii)

52. In section 16 of the Greater London Council (General Powers) Act 1981 (exemptions from Part IV)—

(a) in paragraph (b) for "the Education Act 1944" there is substituted "the Education Act 1996"; and

(b) in paragraph (k) for "section 100(1)(b) of the said Act of 1944" there is substituted "section 485 of the Education Act 1996".

Agricultural Training Board Act 1982 (c. 9)

53. In section 4(5) of the Agricultural Training Board Act 1982 (meaning of "post-school education"), for paragraph (a) there is substituted—

"(a) in England and Wales, "higher education" as defined by section 120(1) of the Education Reform Act 1988 or "further education" as defined by section 2(3) to (5) of the Education Act 1996; and".

Industrial Training Act 1982 (c. 10)

54. In section 5 of the Industrial Training Act 1982 (functions of boards) for the subsection (7) inserted by the Education Reform Act 1988 there is substituted—

"(8) In this section "post-school education" means—

(a) in England and Wales, "higher education" as defined by section 120(1) of the Education Reform Act 1988 or "further education" as defined by section 2(3) to (5) of the Education Act 1996; and

(b) in Scotland, "further education" within the meaning of the Education (Scotland) Act 1980.".

Local Government (Miscellaneous Provisions) Act 1982 (c. 30)

55. In section 40 of the Local Government (Miscellaneous Provisions) Act 1982 (nuisance and disturbance on educational premises) for subsections (2) to (10) there is substituted—

"(2) This section applies to premises, including playing fields and other premises for outdoor recreation, of an institution (other than a school) which—

(a) is maintained by a local education authority; and

(b) provides further education or higher education (or both).

(3) If—

(a) a police constable; or

(b) a person whom a local education authority have authorised to exercise the power conferred by this subsection,

has reasonable cause to suspect that any person is committing or has committed an offence under this section, he may remove him from the premises in question.

(4) No proceedings under this section shall be brought by any person other than—

(a) a police constable; or

(b) a local education authority.

(5) Expressions used in this section and in the Education Act 1996 have the same meaning as in that Act.".

Representation of the People Act 1983 (c. 2)

56.—(1) Paragraph 22 of Schedule 1 to the Representation of the People Act 1983 (use of schools for the purpose of taking a poll) shall continue to have effect with the following amendment (originally made by Schedule 19 to the Education Act 1993).

(2) In sub-paragraph (l)(i), after "authority" there is inserted "a grant-maintained school".

Education (Fees and Awards) Act 1983 (c. 40)

57. In section 1(4) of the Education (Fees and Awards) Act 1983 (fees at universities and further education establishments)—

(a) for "section 100(1)(b) of the Education Act 1944" there is substituted "section 485 of the Education Act 1996"; and

(b) for "the Education Act 1944" there is substituted "the 1996 Act".

Registered Homes Act 1984 (c. 23)

58.—(1) Section 1 of the Registered Homes Act 1984 (requirement of registration: independent schools) shall be amended as follows.

(2) In subsection (5)—

(a) in paragraph (f), for "section 114 of the Education Act 1944" there is substituted "section 4 of the Education Act 1996"; and

(b) in paragraph (g), for "section 100(1)(b) of the Education Act 1944" there is substituted "section 485 of the Education Act 1996".

(3) In subsection (6)—

(a) for "the Education Act 1944" there is substituted "the Education Act 1996"; and

(b) for "section 189(1) of the Education Act 1993" there is substituted "section 347 of the Education Act 1996".

(4) In subsection (7), for "section 100(1)(b) of the Education Act 1944" there is substituted "section 485 of the Education Act 1996".

Building Act 1984 (c. 55)

59. In section 4(1)(a) of the Building Act 1984 (exemption of educational buildings etc) for sub-paragraphs (i) to (iv) substitute—

"(i) plans that have been approved by the Secretary of State,

(ii) particulars submitted and approved under section 39 or 44 of the Education Act 1996 or under regulations made under section 544 of that Act or section 218(7) of the Education Reform Act 1988,

(iii) particulars approved or adopted under section 214, 262 or 341 of the Education Act 1996, or

(iv) particulars given in a direction under section 428 of that Act.".

Greater London Council (General Powers) Act 1984 (c. xxvii)

60. In section 10(2)(g) of the Greater London Council (General Powers) Act 1984 (buildings excepted from Part IV) for "section 100(1)(b) of the Education Act 1944" there is substituted "section 485 of the Education Act 1996".

Further Education Act 1985 (c. 47)

61. In section 8(3) (short title etc.) for "the Education Act 1944" there is substituted "the Education Act 1996".

Housing Act 1985 (c. 68)

62. In Schedule 1 (tenancies which are not secure tenancies), in paragraph 10(4), for "the Education Act 1944" there is substituted "the Education Act 1996".

Local Government Act 1986 (c. 10)

63. In section 2A(4)(a) of the Local Government Act 1986 (prohibition on promoting homosexuality) for "the Education Act 1944" there is substituted "the Education Act 1996".

Disabled Persons (Services, Consultation and Representation) Act 1986 (c. 33)

64.—(1) Section 5 of the Disabled Persons (Services, Consultation and Representation) Act 1986 (disabled persons leaving special education) shall be amended as follows.

(2) In subsection (1)(a) for "or 168 of the Education Act 1993" there is substituted "section 168 of the Education Act 1993 or section 324 of the Education Act 1996".

(3) In subsection (8)—

(a) for "paragraph 7 of Schedule 10 to the Education Act 1993" there is substituted "paragraph 7 of Schedule 27 to the Education Act 1996", and

(b) for "maintained under section 168" there is substituted "maintained under section 324".

(4) In subsection (9)—

(a) for "Part III of the Education Act 1993" there is substituted "Part IV of the Education Act 1996"; and

(b) for "the Education Act 1944" there is substituted "the Education Act 1996".

Education (No. 2) Act 1986 (c. 61)

65.—(1) Section 50 of the Education (No. 2) Act 1986 (grants for teacher training etc.) shall continue to have effect with the following amendments (originally made by section 278 of and Schedule 19 to the Education Act 1993).

(2) In subsection (1)—

(a) for "local authorities and other persons" there is substituted "persons other than local education authorities"; and

(b) for the words from the end of paragraph (a) onwards there is substituted—

"and

(b) such other classes of persons as may be prescribed."

(3) In subsection (2)(b), for "capacity as an employee of the kind in question" there is substituted "employment".

66.—(1) Section 67 of that Act (short title etc.) shall be amended as follows.

(2) Subsections (2), (5) and (6) are omitted.

(3) In subsection (3), for "the 1944 Act" there is substituted "the Education Act 1996".

(4) In subsection (7), for the words from the beginning to "Northern Ireland;" there is substituted "In this Act section 48 and this section extend to Scotland,".

Reverter of Sites Act 1987 (c. 15)

67.—(1) The Reverter of Sites Act 1987 shall be amended as follows.

(2) In section 1(5) (right of reverter replaced by trust for sale) for "section 2 of the Education Act 1973" there is substituted "section 554 of the Education Act 1996".

(2) In section 5 (orders under Education Act 1973—

(a) in subsection (1), for "section 2 of the Education Act 1973" there is substituted "section 554 of the Education Act 1996"; and

(b) for "section 2 of the said Act of 1973", wherever occurring, there is substituted "section 554 of the 1996 Act".

Local Government Act 1988 (c. 9)

68. In paragraph 8(3)(a) of Schedule 1 to the Local Government Act 1988 (competition) for "section 53 of the Education Act 1944 (whether or not also provided under section 41 of that Act)" there is substituted "section 508 of the Education Act 1996 (whether or not also provided under section 15 of that Act)".

Criminal Justice Act 1988 (c. 33)

69. In section 139A(6) and (7) of the Criminal Justice Act 1988 (as amended by the Offensive Weapons Act 1996), for "section 14(5) of the Further and Higher Education Act 1992" there is substituted "section 4 of the Education Act 1996".

Education Reform Act 1988 (c. 40)

70. In section 124(2)(b) of the Education Reform Act 1988 (powers of a higher education corporation) for "within the meaning of section 41(9) of the Education Act 1944)" there is substituted ", as defined by section 15(6) and (7) of the Education Act 1996)".

71. In section 161(1)(b)(i) of that Act (interpretation of Part II) for "section 41 of the 1944 Act" there is substituted "section 15 of the Education Act 1996".

72. In section 163(1) of that Act (new education authorities for London) for "the Education Acts 1944 to 1996" there is substituted "the Education Act 1996".

73. In section 166(5) of that Act (responsibility for schools) for "the Education Acts 1944 to 1993" there is substituted "the Education Act 1996".

74.—(1) Section 197 of that Act (Education Assets Board) shall be amended as follows.

(2) In subsection (6), for "the Education Acts 1944 to 1993" there is substituted "the Education Acts".

(3) Subsection (7) shall continue to have effect with the insertion of the words "and any governing body of a maintained or grant-maintained school" (originally inserted by section 47(5) of the Education Act 1993); and in that subsection for "the Education Acts 1944 to 1993" there is substituted "the Education Acts".

(4) In subsection (7B), for "the Education Acts 1944 to 1992" there is substituted "the Education Acts".

(5) At the end of the section there is added—

"(10) In this section "the Education Acts" has the meaning given by section 578 of the Education Act 1996."

75. In section 198 of that Act (transfers under Parts I and II)—

(a) in subsection (1), for "or section 38 of the Education Act 1993" there is substituted "or section 201 of the Education Act 1996"; and

(b) in subsection (4), for "or under the Education Act 1993", in both places, there is substituted "or under the Education Act 1996".

76.—(1) Section 218 of that Act (school and further and higher regulations)—

(a) shall be amended as provided in sub-paragraphs (2) to (5); and

(b) shall continue to have effect with the amendments set out in sub-paragraph (6) (originally made by section 290 of the Education Act 1993).

(2) In subsection (1) the following are omitted—

(a) in paragraphs (e) and (f), the words "schools and"; and

(b) paragraph (g).

(3) For subsection (2B) (renumbered by paragraph 8(4) of Schedule 2 to the Education Act 1994) there is substituted—

"(2B) Regulations under subsection (2) above may impose requirements on persons carrying on city technology colleges or city colleges for the technology of the arts as to the training and teaching experience of persons employed as teachers at such colleges who seek to become (in relation to schools) qualified teachers."

(4) In subsection (7), the following are omitted—

(a) the words from "or, in such cases" to "the funding authority"; and

(b) the words "school or" (where first occurring) and "any school or".

(5) Subsections (8) and (13) are omitted.

(6) The amendments referred to in sub-paragraph (1)(b) are—

(a) after subsection (6)(c) there is added "or

(d) by the proprietors of independent schools or at such schools as teachers or in any such work,"; and

(b) in subsection (12) after "section" there is inserted "other than in subsection (6)(d) above".

77. For section 219 of that Act there is substituted—

"Powers of the Secretary of State in relation to certain educational institutions

219.—(1) This section applies to any institution which is maintained by a local education authority and provides higher education or further education (or both).

(2) Section 495(1) of the Education Act 1996 (determination of disputes by the Secretary of State) shall apply in relation to the governing body of an institution to which this section applies as it applies in relation to the governing body of a school.

(3) Each of sections 496 and 497 of that Act (power of Secretary of State to prevent unreasonable exercise of functions and Secretary of State's general default powers) shall have effect as if any reference to a body to which that section applies included a reference to the governing body of an institution to which this section applies.

(4) Section 498 of that Act (powers of Secretary of State where there is no properly constituted governing body) shall have effect as if any reference to a school to which that section applies included a reference to an institution to which this section applies."

78.—(1) Section 220 of that Act (extension of functions of Audit Commission) shall continue to have effect with the following amendments (originally made by section 10 of the Education Act 1993).

(2) At the beginning of subsection (1)(c) there is inserted "the Funding Agency for Schools, the Schools Funding Council for Wales or".

(3) After subsection (2)(bb) there is inserted—

"(bc) with respect to studies relating to the Funding Agency for Schools, the agency;

(bd) with respect to studies relating to the Schools Funding Council for Wales, the council;".

(4) In subsection (2)(c) after "school," there is inserted "the funding authority or".

79. In section 228 of that Act (transfer of property to grant-aided institutions in Wales), in subsection (2)(a), for "section 100(1)(b) of the 1944 Act" there is substituted "section 485 of the Education Act 1996".

80. In section 232 of that Act (orders and regulations)—

(a) in subsection (2), for the words from "sections" to "Schedule 5" there is substituted "section 157";

(b) subsection (3) is omitted; and

(c) in subsection (4), "3(4)(a), 4(2)(c), 24," is omitted.

81.—(1) Section 235 of that Act (general interpretation) shall be amended as follows.

(2) In subsection (1) the definition of "the 1980 Act" is omitted.

(3) In subsection (2)(c), after "1944 Act" there is inserted "or section 485 of the Education Act 1996".

(4) In subsections (7) and (8), for "the 1944 Act" in each place there is substituted "the Education Act 1996".

82.—(1) Schedule 10 to that Act (supplementary provisions with respect to transfers)—

(a) shall continue to have effect with the amendments set out in sub-paragraph (2) (originally made by section 47 of the Education Act 1993); and

(b) shall be amended as provided in sub-paragraph (3).

(2) The amendments mentioned in sub-paragraph (1)(a) are as follows—

(a) in paragraph 1(1) of the Schedule, after "held" there is inserted "or used";

(b) in paragraph 4(1) of the Schedule, for "by virtue of section 126 or 130" there is substituted "to which this Schedule applies"; and

(c) for "local education authority", wherever occurring in the Schedule, there is substituted "local authority".

(3) In the Schedule—

(a) in paragraph 1(4)(a)(i), for "or under the Education Act 1993" there is substituted "or under the Education Act 1996";

(b) in paragraph 2(1)(b), for "or of the Education Act 1993" there is substituted "or of the Education Act 1996";
(c) in paragraph 5, for "or of the Education Act 1993" there is substituted "or of the Education Act 1996";
(d) in paragraph 7, for "or of the Education Act 1993" there is substituted "or of the Education Act 1996"; and
(e) in paragraph 9(6)(b), for "or of the Education Act 1993" there is substituted "or of the Education Act 1996".

Copyright, Designs and Patents Act 1988 (c. 48)

83. In section 174(3) of the Copyright, Patents and Designs Act 1988 (meaning of "school") for "the Education Act 1944" there is substituted "the Education Act 1996".

Children Act 1989 (c. 41)

84. In section 28(4) of the Children Act 1989 (local authority support for children and families: consultation with local education authorities) for "Part III of the Education Act 1993" there is substituted "Part IV of the Education Act 1996".

85. In section 36(5) of that Act (education supervision orders: presumption that child is not being properly educated)—
(a) for "section 37 of the Education Act 1944" there is substituted "section 437 of the Education Act 1996"; and
(b) for "section 39" there is substituted "section 444".

86.—(1) Section 63 of that Act (children not to be cared for and accommodated in unregistered children's homes) shall be amended as follows.

(2) For subsection (6) there is substituted—

"(6) An independent school is a children's home at any time if at that time accommodation is provided for children at the school and either—
(a) in each year that fell within the period of two years ending at that time accommodation was provided for more than three of the children at the school or under arrangements made by the proprietor of the school, for more than 295 days in that year, or
(b) it is intended to provide accommodation for more than three of the children at the school, or under arrangements made by the proprietor of the school, for more than 295 days in any year,

unless the school is approved by the Secretary of State under section 347(1) of the Education Act 1996 (approval of independent schools for children with statements); and in this subsection "year" means a period of twelve months and "proprietor" has the same meaning as in that Act."

87. In section 87(10) of that Act (welfare of children accommodated in independent schools) for "the Education Act 1944" there is substituted "the Education Act 1996".

88. In section 87A(6) of that Act (inspection of independent schools), in paragraph (a), for "the Education Act 1944" there is substituted "the Education Act 1996".

89. In section 87B(4) of that Act (duties of inspectors of independent schools), in paragraph (a), for "the Education Act 1944" there is substituted "the Education Act 1996".

90. In section 91(5) of that Act (effect and duration of orders: school attendance orders) for "section 37 of the Education Act 1944" there is substituted "section 437 of the Education Act 1996".

91. In section 105(1) of that Act (interpretation) for "the Education Act 1944" in each place where it occurs, and for "the Education Act 1993", there is substituted "the Education Act 1996".

92. In paragraph 3(b) of Schedule 2 to that Act (local authority support for children and families: assessment of children's needs) for "Part III of the Education Act 1993" there is substituted "Part IV of the Education Act 1996".

93.—(1) Part III of Schedule 3 to that Act (education supervision orders) shall be amended as follows.

(2) In paragraph 13—
(a) in sub-paragraph (1) for "section 36 of the Education Act 1944 (duty to secure education of children) and section 199 of the Education Act 1993 (duty" there is substituted "sections 7 and 444 of the Education Act 1996 (duties to secure education of children and"; and
(b) in sub-paragraph (2)—

(i) in paragraph (a)(i) for "section 192 of that Act" there is substituted "section 437 of the Education Act 1996",

(ii) in paragraph (b)(i) for "section 192" there is substituted "section 437",

(iii) in paragraph (b)(ii) for "section 76 of the Education Act 1944" there is substituted "section 9 of that Act", and

(iv) in paragraph (b)(iii) for "sections 6 and 7 of the Education Act 1980" there is substituted "sections 411 and 423 of that Act".

(3) In paragraph 21 for "the Education Act 1944 (as amended by Schedule 13)" there is substituted "the Education Act 1996."

94.—(1) Paragraph 3 of Schedule 9 to that Act (child minding and day care: exemption of certain schools) shall be amended as follows.

(2) In sub-paragraph (1)—

(a) for "section 100 of the Education Act 1944" there is substituted "section 485 of the Education Act 1996", and

(b) for "section 53 of the Act of 1944" there is substituted "section 508 of that Act".

(3) In sub-paragraph (3)—

(a) for "the Education Act 1944" there is substituted "the Education Act 1996", and

(b) for "the Education Act 1993" there is substituted "that Act".

Local Government and Housing Act 1989 (c. 42)

95. In section 2(6)(a) of the Local Government and Housing Act 1989 (politically restricted posts) for "section 88 of the Education Act 1944" there is substituted "section 532 of the Education Act 1996".

96.—(1) Section 13 of that Act (voting rights of members of committees)—

(a) shall be amended as provided in sub-paragraphs (2), (3) and (5); and

(b) shall continue to have effect with the amendment set out in sub-paragraph (4) (originally made by Schedule 19 to the Education Act 1993).

(2) In subsection (4)(f) for "Part I of Schedule 2 to the Education Act 1980 (appeal committees for hearing school admissions appeals)" there is substituted "Part I of Schedule 33 to the Education Act 1996 (constitution of appeal committees for admission appeals etc.)".

(3) For subsection (5) there is substituted—

"(5) Nothing in this section shall prevent the appointment of a person who is not a member of a local education authority as a voting member of—

(a) any committee or sub-committee appointed by the local authority wholly or partly for the purpose of discharging any functions with respect to education conferred on them in their capacity as a local education authority,

(b) any joint committee appointed by two or more local authorities wholly or partly for the purpose of discharging any functions with respect to education conferred on them in their capacity as local education authorities, or

(c) any sub-committee appointed by any such committee or joint committee wholly or partly for the purpose of discharging any of that committee's functions with respect to education,

where that appointment is required by directions given by the Secretary of State under section 499 of the Education Act 1996 (power of Secretary of State to direct appointment of members of committees)."

(4) In subsection (7) for "education committee or sub-committee of an education committee" there is substituted "committee, joint committee or sub-committee appointed for the purpose mentioned in that subsection".

(5) In subsection (9) the definition of "foundation governors" and the "and" immediately following it are omitted.

97. In section 18(5)(c) of that Act (schemes for allowances for local authority members) for "paragraph 2 or 3 of Schedule 2 to the Education Act 1980" there is substituted "paragraph 2 or 3 of Schedule 33 to the Education Act 1996".

Education (Student Loans) Act 1990 (c. 6)

98. In section 1(3)(a) of the Education (Student Loans) Act 1990 (meaning of "institutions receiving support from public funds") for "section 100(1)(b) of the Education Act 1944" there is substituted "section 485 of the Education Act 1996".

Town and Country Planning Act 1990 (c. 8)

99. In section 76 of the Town and Country Planning Act 1990 (duty to draw attention to certain provisions for benefit of disabled) for subsection (3) there is substituted—

"(3) Expressions used in subsection (1)(e) and in the Education Act 1996 have the same meanings as in that Act."

Environmental Protection Act 1990 (c. 43)

100. In section 98(2) of the Environmental Protection Act 1990 (definitions)—
(a) in paragraph (c)(i) for "section 100(1)(b) of the Education Act 1944" there is substituted "section 485 of the Education Act 1996"; and
(b) in paragraph (e) for "section 105 of the Education Reform Act 1988)" there is substituted "section 482 of the Education Act 1996)".

School Teachers' Pay and Conditions Act 1991 (c. 49)

101.—(1) The School Teachers' Pay and Conditions Act 1991—
(a) shall continue to have effect with the amendment set out in sub-paragraph (2) (originally made by Schedule 19 to the Education Act 1993); and
(b) shall be amended as provided in sub-paragraphs (3) and (4).

(2) In section 2 (orders relating to statutory conditions of employment), in subsections (6) and (7) for "section 3" there is substituted "sections 3 and 3A".

(3) For the section 3A inserted by section 289 of the Education Act 1993 there is substituted—

"**Special provisions for teachers on transfer of employment**

3A.—(1) This section applies where a school teacher employed to teach at an independent school—
(a) which becomes a county or voluntary school in pursuance of proposals published under section 35(1)(b) or, as the case may be, 41(1) of the Education Act 1996, or
(b) in place of which a grant-maintained school is established in pursuance of proposals published under section 212 of that Act,

becomes employed (in the case of a county or voluntary school) by the local education authority or the governing body or (in the case of a grant-maintained school) by the governing body in accordance with the Transfer of Undertakings (Protection of Employment) Regulations 1981.

(2) A pay and conditions order shall not apply to the statutory conditions of employment of such a teacher unless he gives notice in writing to the new employer that the order is to so apply.

(3) Where the governing body of an aided school receive notice given under subsection (2) above, they shall inform the local education authority."

(4) In section 5 (interpretation etc.)—
(a) in subsection (1)—
(i) in the definition of "school which has a delegated budget" for "Chapter III of Part I of the Education Reform Act 1988" there is substituted "Part II of the Education Act 1996", and
(ii) for "the Education Act 1944" there is substituted "that Act"; and
(b) in subsection (5), for "sections 68 and 99(1) of the Education Act 1944" there is substituted "sections 496 and 497 of the Education Act 1996".

Diocesan Boards of Education Measure 1991 (1991 No. 2)

102.—(1) Section 3 of the Diocesan Boards of Education Measure 1991 (transactions for which advice or consent of Diocesan Board required)—
(a) shall continue to have effect with the amendment set out in sub-paragraph (2) (originally made by Schedule 19 to the Education Act 1993); and
(b) shall be amended as provided in sub-paragraph (3).

(2) In subsection (4) for the words from "by a resolution" to the end there is substituted "to hold a meeting to consider whether to hold a ballot of parents on the question of whether grant-maintained status should be sought for the school, it shall—
(a) give to the secretary of the Board for the diocese in which the school is situated at least seven days' notice that such a meeting is to be held at such time and place as is specified in the notice, and
(b) have regard to any relevant advice given by the Board, when considering at the meeting whether to hold a ballot of parents on that question,

and in paragraph (b) above "relevant advice" means advice given in connection with the acquisition of grant-maintained status for the school whether given for the purposes of that school or for Church of England voluntary schools generally".

(3) In subsection (5) for "section 96 of the Education Act 1993" there is substituted "section 259 of the Education Act 1996".

103.—(1) Section 5 of that Measure (proposals for acquisition of grant-maintained status)—

(a) shall be amended as provided in sub-paragraph (2); and

(b) shall continue to have effect with the amendment set out in sub-paragraph (3) (originally made by Schedule 19 to the Education Act 1993).

(2) For "paragraph 2 of Schedule 3 to the Education Act 1993" there is substituted "paragraph 2 of Schedule 20 to the Education Act 1996".

(3) For "the advice given by the Board under section 3(4) above" there is substituted "any relevant advice (defined in section 3(4) above) given by the Board".

104.—(1) Section 6 of that Measure (Board to be consulted in certain cases) shall be amended as follows.

(2) In subsection (1)—

(a) for "section 13(1) of the 1988 Act" there is substituted "section 392(2) of the Education Act 1996"; and

(b) for "section 11" there is substituted "section 390".

(3) In subsection (2), for "section 136 of the Education Act 1993" there is substituted "section 302 of the Education Act 1996".

105. In section 7(3) of that Measure (powers of Board to give directions to governing bodies of aided church schools)—

(a) for "section 15(4) of the Education Act 1944" there is substituted "section 57(1) of the Education Act 1996";

(b) for "section 13(1)(b) of the Education Act 1980" there is substituted "section 41(2) of that Act"; and

(c) for "the Education Acts 1944 to 1993" there is substituted "that Act".

106. In section 9 of that Measure (attendance of diocesan director of education at governing bodies' proceedings) for "section 45(6) of the 1988 Act" there is substituted "section 138(2) of the Education Act 1996".

107. In section 10 (interpretation)—

(a) in subsection (1) the definition of "the 1988 Act" is omitted;

(b) for the definition of "church school" in that subsection there is substituted—

" "church school" means—

(a) a Church of England voluntary school,

(b) a grant-maintained school which was such a voluntary school immediately before it became grant-maintained,

(c) a grant-maintained school established in pursuance of proposals published under section 212 of the Education Act 1996 where either any trust deed relating to the school or the statement required by paragraph 8 of Schedule 20 to that Act provides for religious education at the school to accord with the faith and practice of the Church of England, or

(d) a grant-maintained school in respect of which proposals for the required provision for religious education to be provision for religious education in accordance with the faith and practice of the Church of England are approved under section 261 of that Act"; and

(c) in subsection (3)—

(i) for "the 1988 Act or the Education Act 1993" there is substituted "the Education Act 1996", and

(ii) for "those Acts" there is substituted "that Act".

Further and Higher Education Act 1992 (c. 13)

108. In section 21(3) of the Further and Higher Education Act 1992 (initial instruments and articles) for "Chapter IV of Part I of the Education Reform Act 1988" there is substituted "Chapter V of Part III of the Education Act 1996 (or any corresponding earlier enactment)".

109. In section 28(3)(a) of that Act (institutions which are grant-aided or eligible to receive aid by way of grant) for "section 100(1)(b) of the Education Act 1944" there is substituted "section 485 of the Education Act 1996".

110.—(1) Section 37 of that Act (attribution of surpluses and deficits) shall be amended as follows.

(2) In subsection (1), for the words from "section 33" to "higher education)" there is substituted "section 103 of the Education Act 1996 (schemes for financing schools)".

(3) In subsection (7)—

(a) in the definition of "budget share", for "Chapter III of Part I or Chapter III of Part II of the Education Reform Act 1988" there is substituted "Part II of the Education Act 1996"; and

(b) in the definition of "financial year", for "the Education Reform Act 1988" there is substituted "the Education Act 1996".

111. In section 54(2) of that Act (duty to give information) for the words from "section 51" to "section 52 of that Act" there is substituted "regulations under section 492 or 493 of the Education Act 1996".

112. At the end of section 56 of that Act (directions) there is added—

"(3) Section 496 of the Education Act 1996 (power to prevent unreasonable exercise of functions) applies in relation to a council as it applies in relation to a body falling within subsection (2) of that section."

113. For section 57(6) of that Act (intervention in event of mismanagement etc.) there is substituted—

"(6) In the Education Act 1996—

(a) section 496 (power to prevent unreasonable exercise of functions) applies in relation to the governing body of an institution within the further education sector as it applies in relation to a body falling within subsection (2) of that section; and

(b) section 507 (power to direct local inquiries) applies for the purposes of the Secretary of State's functions under this section as it applies for the purposes of his functions under that Act."

114. In section 89(5) of that Act (orders, regulations and directions) for "Section 111 of the Education Act 1944" there is substituted "Section 570 of the Education Act 1996".

115.—(1) Section 90 of that Act (interpretation) shall be amended as follows.

(2) In subsection (1)—

(a) in the definition of "the Education Acts", for "means the Education Acts 1944 to 1996" there is substituted "has the meaning given by section 578 of the Education Act 1996"; and

(b) after that definition there is inserted—

" "further education" has the meaning given by section 2(3) to (5) of that Act;".

(3) In subsection (5), for "the Education Act 1944" there is substituted "the Education Act 1996".

116. In section 92 of that Act (Index)—

(a) in the entry for "further education", for "section 14(1) to (4)" there is substituted "section 90(1)"; and

(b) the entries for "pupil", "secondary education" and "school" are omitted.

117.—(1) Schedule 8 to that Act—

(a) shall continue to have effect with the amendment set out in sub-paragraph (2) (originally made by section 47(6) of the Education Act 1993); and

(b) shall be amended as provided in sub-paragraphs (3) and (4).

(2) In paragraph 61, for "by virtue of section 126 or 130 and in such a case" there is substituted "and".

(3) In paragraph 62(3), for "or (as the case may be) the Education Act 1993" there is substituted "or (as the case may be) the Education Act 1996".

(4) In—

(a) paragraph 79(2) (which provides that, in relation to a further education corporation or a Further Education Funding Council, the reference in section 25(2) of the Sex Discrimination Act 1975 to section 99 of the Education Act 1944 is to be read as a reference to section 57(3) of the 1992 Act), and

(b) paragraph 88(2) (which makes similar provision in relation to section 19(2) of the Race Relations Act 1976),

for "section 99 of the Education Act 1944" there is substituted "section 497 of the Education Act 1996".

Tribunals and Inquiries Act 1992 (c. 53)

118.—(1) The Tribunals and Inquiries Act 1992 shall be amended as follows.

(2) Section 11(1) (appeals from certain tribunals) shall continue to have effect with the substitution for "15(a) or (d)" of "15(a), (d) or (e)" (originally made by section 181 of the Education Act 1993).

(3) In paragraph 15 of Schedule 1 (tribunals under general supervision of Council on Tribunals)—

(a) in sub-paragraph (a), for "section 72 of, and Schedule 6 to, the Education Act 1944 (c. 31)" there is substituted "section 476 of, and Schedule 34 to, the Education Act 1996 (c. 56)";

(b) in sub-paragraph (b), for "Part I of Schedule 2 to the Education Act 1980 (c. 20)" there is substituted "Part I of Schedule 33 to that Act";

(c) in sub-paragraph (c), for "paragraph 5(1) of Schedule 6 to the Education Act 1993" there is substituted "paragraph 6(1) of Schedule 23 to that Act"; and

(d) for sub-paragraph (e) there is substituted—

"(e) the Special Educational Needs Tribunal constituted under section 333 of that Act".

Charities Act 1993 (c. 10)

119. For section 79(9) of the Charities Act 1993 (parochial charities) there is substituted—

"(9) This section shall not affect the trusteeship, control or management of any voluntary or grant-maintained school within the meaning of the Education Act 1996."

120.—(1) Schedule 2 to that Act (exempt charities) shall continue to have effect with the following amendments (originally made by Schedules 15 and 19 to the Education Act 1993).

(2) After paragraph (d) there is inserted—

"(da) the School Curriculum and Assessment Authority;".

(3) For paragraph (f) there is substituted—

"(f) the Curriculum and Assessment Authority for Wales;".

121. At the end of paragraph 1(b) of Schedule 4 to that Act (charities over which the court has jurisdiction) there is added "or section 554 of the Education Act 1996".

Welsh Language Act 1993 (c. 38)

122. In section 6(1)(1) of the Welsh Language Act 1993 (meaning of "public body") for "the Education Acts 1944 to 1992" there is substituted "the Education Act 1996".

Local Government (Wales) Act 1994 (c. 19)

123.—(1) Section 30 of the Local Government (Wales) Act 1994 (area committees) shall be amended as follows.

(2) In subsection (7) for "section 297 of the Education Act 1993" there is substituted "section 499 of the Education Act 1996".

(3) In subsections (9) and (14) for "section 297 of the Act of 1993" there is substituted "section 499 of the Act of 1996".

124.—(1) Section 31 of that Act (sub-committees of area committees) shall be amended as follows.

(2) In subsection (6) for "section 297 of the Education Act 1993" there is substituted "section 499 of the Education Act 1996".

(3) In subsections (8) and (12) for "section 297 of the Act of 1993" there is substituted "section 499 of the Act of 1996".

Value Added Tax Act 1994 (c. 23)

125. In Schedule 9 to the Value Added Tax Act 1994 (exemptions), in paragraph (a) of Note (1) to Group 6 (education)—

(a) for "the Education Acts 1944 to 1996" there is substituted "the Education Act 1996";
(b) in sub-paragraph (iii), for "a maintained school within the meaning of the Education Act 1993 or" there is substituted "a county school, voluntary school or maintained special school (other than one established in a hospital) within the meaning of the Education Act 1996 or a maintained school within the meaning of";
(c) in sub-paragraph (v), for "section 22 of the Education Act 1993" there is substituted "the Education Act 1996"; and
(d) in sub-paragraph (vii), for "section 182(3) of the Education Act 1993" there is substituted "the Education Act 1996".

Education Act 1994 (c. 30)

126. After section 11 of the Education Act 1994 there is inserted—

"*General duty of Secretary of State*

General duty of Secretary of State with respect to teacher training

11A. In carrying out his duties under sections 10 and 11 of the Education Act 1996 the Secretary of State shall, in particular, make such arrangements as he considers expedient for securing that sufficient facilities are available for the training of teachers to serve in schools maintained by local education authorities, grant-maintained schools, institutions within the further education sector and institutions which are maintained by such authorities and provide higher education or further education (or both)."

127.—(1) Section 12 of that Act (power of schools to provide courses of initial teacher training) shall be amended as follows.

(2) In subsection (5), for "section 12 or 13 of the Education Act 1980 or section 96 of the Education Act 1993" there is substituted "section 35, 41 or 259 of the Education Act 1996".

(3) In subsection (6)—

(a) for "sections 33 to 43 of the Education Reform Act 1988" there is substituted "sections 101 to 123 of the Education Act 1996", and

(b) for "Chapter VI of Part II of the Education Act 1993" there is substituted "Chapter VI of Part III of that Act".

128. In section 19 of that Act (interpretation)—

(a) in subsection (3), for "section 156 of the Education Act 1993" there is substituted "section 312 of the Education Act 1996"; and

(b) in subsection (5), for "the Education Act 1944" there is substituted "the Education Act 1996".

Disability Discrimination Act 1995 (c. 50)

129. In section 19(5)(a)(ii) of the Disability Discrimination Act 1995 (discrimination in relation to goods, facilities and services) for "section 14(5) of the Further and Higher Education Act 1992" there is substituted "section 4(1) and (2) of the Education Act 1996".

Employment Rights Act 1996 (c. 18)

130. In section 134(1) of the Employment Rights Act 1996 (dismissal of teachers in aided schools) for "paragraph (a) of the proviso to section 24(2) of the Education Act 1944" there is substituted "section 134(3) of the Education Act 1996".

Nursery Education and Grant-Maintained Schools Act 1996 (c. 57)

131.—(1) Section 4 of the Nursery Education and Grant-Maintained Schools Act 1996 (children with special educational needs) shall be amended as follows.

(2) In subsection (1)—

(a) for "section 157 of the Education Act 1993)" there is substituted "section 313 of the Education Act 1996)"; and

(b) for "Part III" there is substituted "Part IV".

(3) In each of subsections (2) and (3), for "Part III of the Education Act 1993" there is substituted "Part IV of the Education Act 1996".

132. In section 11 of that Act (citation etc.) for subsection (2) there is substituted—

"(2) This Act shall be construed as one with the Education Act 1996."

Part II

Amendments coming into force on appointed day

Children and Young Persons Act 1933 (c. 12)

133. In section 30(1)(a) of the Children and Young Persons Act 1933 (interpretation) for the words from "for the purposes" to the end of paragraph (a) there is substituted "over compulsory school age (construed in accordance with section 8 of the Education Act 1996)".

Agriculture (Safety, Health and Welfare Provisions) Act 1956 (c. 49)

134. In section 24(1) of the Agriculture (Safety, Health and Welfare Provisions) Act 1956 (interpretation) in the definition of "young person", for "for the purposes of the Education Act 1944" there is substituted "(construed in accordance with section 8 of the Education Act 1996)".

Factories Act 1961 (c. 34)

135. In section 176(1) of the Factories Act 1961 (general interpretation) for the definition of "child" there is substituted—

" "child" means any person who is not over—

(a) compulsory school age (construed in accordance with section 8 of the Education Act 1996), or

(b) school age (construed in accordance with section 31 of the Education (Scotland) Act 1980);".

Matrimonial Causes Act 1973 (c. 18)

136. In section 29(2)(a) of the Matrimonial Causes Act 1973 (age limit on making certain orders in favour of children) for the words from "(that is to say" to "that section)" there is substituted "(construed in accordance with section 8 of the Education Act 1996)".

Sex Discrimination Act 1975 (c. 65)

137. In section 24(2)(d) of the Sex Discrimination Act 1975 (designated establishments) after "school age" there is inserted "(construed in accordance with section 8 of the Education Act 1996)".

Domestic Proceedings and Magistrates' Courts Act 1978 (c. 22)

138. In section 5(2)(a) of the Domestic Proceedings and Magistrates' Courts Act 1978 (age limit on making certain orders in favour of children) for the words from "(that is to say" to "that section)" there is substituted "(construed in accordance with section 8 of the Education Act 1996)".

Employment Act 1989 (c. 38)

139. In section 10 of the Employment Act 1989 (removal of restrictions relating to employment of young persons), in subsection (6), for "for the purposes of the Education Act 1944" there is substituted "(construed in accordance with section 8 of the Education Act 1996)".

Section 582(2)

SCHEDULE 38

REPEALS AND REVOCATIONS

PART I

REPEALS COMING INTO FORCE ON 1ST NOVEMBER 1996

Chapter	Short Title	Extent of repeal
1944 c.31.	Education Act 1944.	The whole Act.
1946 c.49.	Acquisition of Land (Authorisation Procedure) Act 1946.	In Schedule 4, the entry relating to the Education Act 1944.
1946 c.50.	Education Act 1946.	The whole Act.
1948 c.40.	Education (Miscellaneous Provisions) Act 1948.	The whole Act.
1953 c.33.	Education (Miscellaneous Provisions) Act 1953.	The whole Act.
1959 c.53.	Town and Country Planning Act 1959.	In Schedule 4, paragraph 4.
1959 c.60.	Education Act 1959.	The whole Act.
1961 c.45.	Rating and Valuation Act 1961.	The whole Act.
1962 c.12.	Education Act 1962.	Section 9. Section 13(4). Section 14(2).
1963 c.37.	Children and Young Persons Act 1963.	Section 38(2).
1964 c.82.	Education Act 1964.	The whole Act.
1967 c.3.	Education Act 1967.	Section 2. In section 6(1), the words from "and this Act" onwards.
1967 c.80.	Criminal Justice Act 1967.	In Part I of Schedule 3, the entry relating to the Education Act 1944.
1968 c.17.	Education Act 1968.	The whole Act.
1968 c.xxxix.	Greater London Council (General Powers) Act 1968.	Section 56.
1970 c.42.	Local Authority Social Services Act 1970.	In Schedule 1, the entry relating to the Education Act 1993.
1970 c.52.	Education (Handicapped Children) Act 1970.	The whole Act.
1972 c.70.	Local Government Act 1972.	Section 192.
1973 c.16.	Education Act 1973.	Section 1(2). Section 2. In section 5(1), the words from ", and the Education Acts" onwards. In Schedule 1, paragraph 3.

Chapter	Short Title	Extent of repeal
1973 c.23.	Education (Work Experience) Act 1973.	The whole Act.
1975 c.2.	Education Act 1975.	The whole Act.
1976 c.5.	Education (School-leaving Dates) Act 1976.	The whole Act.
1976 c.81.	Education Act 1976.	The whole Act.
1977 c.49.	National Health Service Act 1977.	In Schedule 14, in paragraph 13(1)(b) "7 to 9". In Schedule 15, paragraphs 2 and 3.
1979 c.49.	Education Act 1979.	The whole Act.
1980 c.20.	Education Act 1980.	Sections 1 to 18. Sections 21 and 22. Section 24. Section 26. Sections 28 to 30. Section 33(3). Sections 34 and 35. Section 37. In section 38, subsections (2) and (4) to (6). Schedules 1 to 4. Schedule 7.
1980 c.65.	Local Government, Planning and Land Act 1980.	Section 2(3).
1981 c.60.	Education Act 1981.	The whole Act.
1982 c.48.	Criminal Justice Act 1982.	In Schedule 3, the entries relating to the Education Act 1944.
1984 c.11.	Education (Grants and Awards) Act 1984.	The whole Act.
1985 c.47.	Further Education Act 1985.	Section 8(2).
1986 c.50.	Social Security Act 1986.	Section 77 so far as relating to section 22 of the Education Act 1980.
1986 c.61.	Education (No.2) Act 1986.	Sections 1 to 42. Sections 44 to 47. Sections 51 to 60. In section 62(1), paragraph (a) and the "(b)" immediately following it. In section 63, in subsection (1) the words "(other than under section 2(7), 9(6) or 54)", in subsection (2) "51 or", and subsection (2A). In section 65(1), all the definitions except that of "establishment of higher or further education". In section 66, in subsection (1) "60 and" and "to (3)", and in subsection (2) "and 59". In section 67, subsections (2), (5) and (6). Schedules 1 to 3. In Schedule 4, paragraphs 1, 2 and 5. Schedules 5 and 6.
1987 c.15.	Reverter of Sites Act 1987.	Section 8(1).
1988 c.40.	Education Reform Act 1988.	Part I. Section 120(5) and (9). In section 210, in each of subsections (1) and (3)(d) the words "local education authorities or". In section 211, paragraphs (a) and (b) and the words "the school or". Sections 212 and 213.

Chapter	Short Title	Extent of repeal
		In section 218, in subsection (1) in each of paragraphs (e) and (f) the words "schools and" and paragraph (g), in subsection (7) the words from "or, in such cases" to "the funding authority" and the words "school or" (where first occurring) and "any school or", and subsections (8) and (13).
		Section 222.
		Sections 225 and 227.
		Section 229(1).
		In section 230(1), "section 15(2)".
		In section 232, subsection (3) and, in subsection 4(b), "3(4)(a), 4(2)(c), 24".
		Section 234.
		In section 235, in subsection (1) the definition of "the 1980 Act".
		In section 236, in subsection (1) the words from "section 1" to "section 119" and "sections 212 and 213", and subsections (2) and (3).
		Section 238(2).
		Schedules 1 to 4.
		In Schedule 12, paragraphs 1 to 8, 14, 17, 24, 25, 34, 35, 37, 54 to 62, 69(4), 76, 77, 81, 82, 87(3), 99, 102, 103 and 106.
1989 c.41.	Children Act 1989.	In Schedule 13, paragraphs 9 and 10.
1989 c.42.	Local Government and Housing Act 1989.	In section 13(9), the definition of "foundation governors" and the "and" immediately following it.
		Section 188.
1990 c.6.	Education (Student Loans) Act 1990.	Section 4(2).
1990 c.19.	National Health Service and Community Care Act 1990.	In Schedule 9, paragraph 31.
1990 c.38.	Employment Act 1990.	Section 14.
		In section 18(2), the words from "section 14" to "experience)".
1991 c.21.	Disability Living Allowance and Disability Working Allowance Act 1991.	In Schedule 3, paragraph 12.
1991 c.49.	School Teachers' Pay and Conditions Act 1991.	Section 6(2).
1991 No.2.	Diocesan Boards of Education Measure 1991.	In section 10(1), the definition of "the 1988 Act".
1992 c.13.	Further and Higher Education Act 1992.	Sections 10 to 14.
		Section 59.
		In section 92, the entries for "pupil", "secondary education" and "school".
		Section 94(2).
		In Schedule 8, paragraphs 1 to 17, 24 to 26, 28, 43(b), 50, 53, 54, 56, 57 and 82.
1992 c.38.	Education (Schools) Act 1992.	Section 16.
		In Schedule 4, paragraphs 1 and 4 to 6.
1993 c.8.	Judicial Pensions and Retirement Act 1993.	In Schedule 6, paragraph 51.

Chapter	Short Title	Extent of repeal
1993 c.10.	Charities Act 1993.	In Schedule 2, paragraphs (e) and (g).
1993 c.35.	Education Act 1993.	The whole Act.
1994 c.19.	Local Government (Wales) Act 1994.	Section 21. In Schedule 16, paragraphs 8 and 105.
1994 c.30.	Education Act 1994.	Section 27(2). In Schedule 2, paragraphs 5(2) and (4)(a), 6(2) and (4)(a) and 8(2) to (4).
1995 c.17.	Health Authorities Act 1995.	In Schedule 1, paragraphs 112 and 124.
1995 c.18.	Jobseekers Act 1995.	In Schedule 2, paragraphs 3 and 17.
1995 c.21.	Merchant Shipping Act 1995.	In Schedule 13, paragraph 48.
1995 c.50.	Disability Discrimination Act 1995.	Section 29(1) and (2). Section 30(7) to (9).
1996 c.9.	Education (Student Loans) Act 1996.	Section 4(2).
1996 c.18.	Employment Rights Act 1996.	In Schedule 1, paragraph 59.
1996 c.23.	Arbitration Act 1996.	In Schedule 3, paragraphs 4 and 59.
1996 c.50.	Nursery Education and Grant-Maintained Schools Act 1996.	Section 7. In Schedule 3, paragraphs 1 to 8 and 10 to 15.

Part II

Repeals coming into force on appointed day

Chapter	Short Title	Extent of repeal
1975 c.65.	Sex Discrimination Act 1975.	In section 82(1), the definition of "upper limit of compulsory school age".
1976 c.74.	Race Relations Act 1976.	In section 78(1), the definition of "upper limit of compulsory school age".
1995 c.36.	Children (Scotland) Act 1995.	In Schedule 4, paragraph 10(a).

PART III

REVOCATIONS

S.I. Number	Title	Extent of revocation
S.I. 1977/293.	Local Authorities etc. (Miscellaneous Provision) Order 1977.	Article 4(1) and (5).
S.I. 1991/1890.	Education (Financial Delegation for Primary Schools) Regulations 1991.	The whole Regulations.
S.I. 1992/110.	Education (Financial Delegation for Primary Schools) (Amendment) Regulations 1992.	The whole Regulations.
S.I. 1992/1548.	Education (National Curriculum) (Foundation Subjects at Key Stage 4) Order 1992.	The whole Order.
S.I. 1993/2709.	Education (No. 2) Act 1986 (Amendment) Order 1993.	The whole Order.
S.I. 1993/2827.	Education (No. 2) Act 1986 (Amendment) (No. 2) Order 1993.	The whole Order.
S.I. 1994/692.	Education (No. 2) Act 1986 (Amendment) Order 1994.	The whole Order.
S.I. 1994/1814.	Education (National Curriculum) (Foundation Subjects at Key Stage 4) Order 1994.	The whole Order.
S.I. 1994/2092.	Education (No. 2) Act 1986 (Amendment) (No. 2) Order 1994.	The whole Order.
S.I. 1994/2732.	Education (No. 2) Act 1986 (Amendment) (No. 3) Order 1994.	The whole Order.
S.I. 1996/710.	Local Government Changes for England (Education) (Miscellaneous Provisions) Regulations 1996.	Regulation 19.
S.I. 1996/951.	Deregulation (Length of the School Day) Order 1996.	The whole Order.

Section 582(3)

SCHEDULE 39

TRANSITIONAL PROVISIONS AND SAVINGS

PART I

GENERAL

General transitional provisions

1.—(1) The repeal and re-enactment of provisions by this Act does not affect the continuity of the law.

(2) Any subordinate legislation made or other thing done, or having effect as if made or done, under or for the purposes of any provision repealed and re-enacted by this Act shall, if in force or effective immediately before the commencement of the corresponding provision of this Act, have effect thereafter as if made or done under or for the purposes of that corresponding provision.

(3) Any reference (express or implied) in this Act or any other enactment or in any instrument or document—

(a) to any provision of this Act, or

(b) to things done or falling to be done under or for the purposes of any provision of this Act,

shall (so far as the context permits) be construed as including, in relation to times, circumstances or purposes in relation to which the corresponding provision repealed by this Act had effect, a reference—

(i) to that corresponding provision, or

(ii) to things done or falling to be done under or for the purposes of that corresponding provision,

as the case may be.

(4) Any reference (express or implied) in any enactment or in any instrument or document—

(a) to any provision repealed and re-enacted by this Act, or

(b) to things done or falling to be done under or for the purposes of any such provision,

shall (so far as the context permits) be construed as including, in relation to times, circumstances or purposes in relation to which the corresponding provision of this Act has effect, a reference—

(i) to that corresponding provision, or

(ii) to things done or falling to be done under or for the purposes of that corresponding provision,

as the case may be.

(5) Without prejudice to the generality of sub-paragraph (4), where a power conferred by an Act is expressed to be exercisable in relation to enactments contained in Acts passed before or in the same Session as the Act conferring the power, the power is also exercisable in relation to provisions of this Act which reproduce such enactments.

(6) Sub-paragraphs (1) to (5) have effect instead of section 17(2) of the Interpretation Act 1978 (but are without prejudice to any other provision of that Act); and sub-paragraph (1) has effect subject to any amendments of the law which give effect to recommendations of the Law Commission.

(7) Sub-paragraph (2) does not apply to any subordinate legislation in so far as it is reproduced in this Act.

Extension of references to provisions repealed by Education Act 1993

2.—(1) Paragraph 1(3) above shall have effect, for the purpose of extending references so as to include references to (or to things done or falling to be done under) the pre-1993 Act enactments, as if any reference in paragraph 1(3) to the corresponding provision repealed by this Act were a reference to the corresponding provision of those enactments.

(2) Paragraph 1(4) above shall have effect, for the purpose of extending references to (or to things done or falling to be done under) the pre-1993 Act enactments, as if any reference in paragraph 1(4) to any provision repealed and re-enacted by this Act were a reference to a provision of those enactments.

(3) Any reference in any provision of the Education Acts to a funding authority, in relation to any function which, under a corresponding provision of the pre-1993 Act enactments, was exercisable by the Secretary of State shall (so far as the context permits) be construed, in relation to times, circumstances or purposes in relation to which the corresponding provision of those enactments had effect, as a reference to the Secretary of State.

(4) In this paragraph "the pre-1993 Act enactments" means the enactments specified in Part I of Schedule 21 to the Education Act 1993 (repeals).

Construction of pre-1944 Act references

3. Where immediately before the commencement of this Act any reference in any enactment, instrument or document had effect as if it were a reference to the Secretary of State or the Department for Education and Employment by virtue of the operation of section 2(1) of the Education Act 1944 and any order made under the Ministers of the Crown Act 1975, it shall continue to do so despite the repeal of that provision by this Act.

4.—(1) This paragraph applies to enactments passed before 1st April 1945.

(2) Unless the context otherwise requires any such enactment shall be construed as if—

(a) any reference to an elementary school or to a public elementary school (whether or not any reference is made there to the payment of parliamentary grants in respect of the school) were a reference to a county school or voluntary school, as the context may require;

(b) any reference to a school certified by the Board of Education, in accordance with the provisions of Part V of the Education Act 1921, as suitable for providing education for blind, deaf, defective or epileptic children were a reference to a special school;

(c) any reference to the managers of a school, in relation to a county school or voluntary school, were a reference to the governors (or, if the context so requires, the governing body) of the school;

(d) any reference to elementary education or to higher education were a reference to such education as may be provided by a local education authority in the exercise of their functions under sections 13 to 15 of this Act; and

(e) any reference to a local education authority, to a local education authority for elementary education or to a local education authority for higher education were a reference to a local education authority within the meaning of this Act.

Effect of old transitional provisions and savings

5. The repeals made by this Act shall not affect the operation of any transitional provision or saving relating to the coming into force of a provision reproduced in this Act in so far as the transitional provision or saving is not specifically reproduced in this Act but remains capable of having effect in relation to the corresponding provision of this Act or otherwise.

6.—(1) The repeal by this Act of an enactment previously repealed subject to savings does not affect the continued operation of those savings.

(2) The repeal by this Act of a saving on the previous repeal of an enactment does not affect the saving so far as it is not specifically reproduced in this Act but remains capable of having effect.

Use of existing forms etc.

7. Any reference to an enactment repealed by this Act which is contained in a document made, served or issued after the commencement of that repeal shall be construed, except so far as a contrary intention appears, as a reference or (as the context may require) including a reference to the corresponding provision of this Act.

Pre-commencement offences

8. Nothing in this Act affects the enactments repealed by this Act in their operation in relation to offences committed before the commencement of this Act.

PART II

SPECIFIC PROVISIONS

Governing bodies of LEA-maintained schools

9.—(1) Any governing body which immediately before the commencement of this Act was incorporated by virtue of section 238 of the Education Act 1993 (incorporation of governing bodies of county, voluntary and maintained special schools) shall continue in existence as a body corporate despite the repeal of that section by this Act.

(2) In Schedule 7 to this Act any reference to a governing body incorporated under section 88(1) of this Act includes a reference to a governing body falling within sub-paragraph (1).

(3) Despite the repeal by this Act of Schedule 13 to the Education Act 1993 (incorporated governing bodies for county, voluntary and maintained special schools)—

(a) paragraph 3 of that Schedule (contracts of employment) shall continue to apply to, or in relation to, any contract of employment to which it applied immediately before the commencement of this Act; and

(b) to the extent that any provision of paragraphs 13 to 15 (general provisions about transfers) applied in relation to any transfer immediately before the commencement of this Act, it shall continue so to apply.

10.—(1) The reproduction by this Act of any reference, in an enactment repealed by this Act, to the governors of a school of any description as a reference to the governing body of a school of that description shall not be taken to affect the construction or operation of that enactment in relation to any times, circumstances or purposes in relation to which it had effect.

(2) Where by virtue of section 1(4) of the Education Act 1980 any enactment or document referred immediately before the commencement of this Act to the governors, foundation gover-

nors, instrument of government or articles of government of a primary school to which section 1(2) and (3) of that Act applied, it shall continue to do so despite the repeal of section 1(4) by this Act.

11. Where any instrument under which the governing body of an aided or special agreement school is constituted was in force immediately before the commencement of this Act by virtue of paragraph 1 of Schedule 5 to the Education (No. 2) Act 1986, the instrument shall have effect thereafter as if made by order under section 76 of this Act; but this paragraph shall cease to apply to any such school if it is grouped with any other school or schools under section 89 of this Act.

Special agreement schools

12.—(1) Any order under section 15(2) of the Education Act 1944 directing that a school is to be a special agreement school shall, if in force immediately before the commencement of this Act, continue in force despite the repeal by this Act of section 15(2) of that Act.

(2) Sub-paragraph (1) does not prejudice the operation of paragraph 1(2) above in relation to other orders in force under section 15(2) of that Act immediately before the commencement of this Act.

Proposals to establish etc. maintained or grant-maintained schools

13.—(1) Nothing in sections 35 to 45 or in sections 259 to 263 of this Act applies in relation to any proposals published before the commencement of this Act; and the corresponding provisions of the Education Act 1980 and the Education Act 1993 shall continue to apply in relation to any proposals duly published under section 12(1)(a) to (d) or 13 of the 1980 Act or section 96 or 97 of the 1993 Act as if this Act had not been passed.

(2) Sub-paragraph (1) does not prevent references in other provisions of this Act to proposals published or implemented under any of those sections of this Act from applying, by virtue of paragraph 1(3) above, to any proposals falling within sub-paragraph (1).

Review of constitution of governing bodies

14.—(1) Subject to sub-paragraph (2), nothing in section 82 of this Act applies in relation to the implementation of any proposal made before the commencement of this Act, and section 11 of the Education (No. 2) Act 1986 shall continue to apply in relation to the implementation of any such proposal falling within subsection (2)(a) of that section as if this Act had not been passed.

(2) In section 82(2) of this Act—

(a) in paragraph (b), the reference to proposals falling within subsection (3) of that section includes a reference to proposals falling within section 11(2) of the 1986 Act; and

(b) in paragraph (c) the reference to a relevant event for the purposes of section 82 includes a reference to a relevant event for the purposes of section 11 of the 1986 Act;

and any date determined by the local authority under section 11(6) of the 1986 Act shall be taken, for the purposes of section 82(2) of this Act, to be the date on which the proposals in question were implemented.

Confirmation of certain decisions of governing body

15. Paragraph 16(1) of Schedule 8 to this Act does not apply to any decision taken before the commencement of this Act, and section 8(11) of the Education (No. 2) Act 1986 shall continue to apply to any such decision falling within section 8(12) as if this Act had not been passed.

Review of grouping

16. The reference in section 94(2)(c) of this Act to an order under section 50 or 51 or 58(1) of this Act does not, by virtue of paragraph 1(3) above, include a reference to an order made before the commencement of this Act under section 2 of the Education Act 1946 or section 15(5) of the Education Act 1944.

Financial delegation

17.—(1) Without prejudice to paragraph 1(3) above—

(a) the reference in section 101(1) of this Act to a scheme made by a local education authority under section 103 of this Act includes a reference to a scheme in force immediately before the commencement of this Act which was made under section 33 of the Education Reform Act 1988 (including one made by way of variation or replacement of such a scheme under section 35 of that Act); and

(b) the reference in section 104(6) of this Act to section 104(5) includes a reference to section 34(6) of that Act.

(2) In relation to any such scheme made (or treated as if made) under section 33 of that Act, the reference in section 110(2) of this Act to the date of the coming into force of the scheme is (subject to sub-paragraph (3) below) a reference to the date of its coming into force as first made under section 33 (or 34(6)) of that Act.

(3) Where the initial period of any such scheme made before 1st January 1994 (the date on which section 274 of the Education Act 1993 came into force) was before 1st January 1994 determined by reference to a date later than that referred to in sub-paragraph (2) above, section 110(2) of this Act shall have effect in relation to the scheme as if it instead referred to that later date.

18. Nothing in section 141 of this Act requires a local education authority to amend the articles of government of a school if, before the commencement of this Act, they have already amended those articles in accordance with section 44(4) of the Education Reform Act 1988.

School sessions

19. For the purposes of section 147(1)(b) of this Act as it applies to a county, controlled or maintained special school, any determination as to the times of the school sessions (within the meaning of section 147) which had effect immediately before the commencement of this Act, whether made—

(a) by the governing body, or
(b) by the local education authority before 1st May 1989 (the date on which section 115 of the Education Reform Act 1988 came into force),

shall continue to have effect, as if made for those purposes, subject to any new determination under section 148 of this Act.

Exclusion of pupils

20. Nothing in section 157 of this Act applies in relation to any pupil excluded from a school before the commencement of this Act, and section 23 of the Education (No. 2) Act 1986 shall continue to apply to any such pupil as if this Act had not been passed.

School premises: pre-1993 Act transfer of control agreements

21.—(1) This paragraph applies to any agreement to which paragraph 6 or 7 of Schedule 13 to the Education Act 1993 (pre-existing transfer of control agreements) applied immediately before the commencement of this Act.

(2) The provisions of paragraph 6 or (as the case may be) paragraph 7 shall continue to apply in relation to any such agreement as if this Act had not been passed.

Variation of trust deeds etc.

22. In section 179(1) of this Act—

(a) paragraph (b) does not apply to a transfer made before the commencement of this Act unless it was made in pursuance of proposals that fell to be implemented under section 12 or 13 of the Education Act 1980; but
(b) in paragraph (d) the reference to any order made by the Secretary of State under section 47 of this Act includes a reference to any order made under section 16(1) of the Education Act 1944 (whether made in relation to a county school or a voluntary school).

Ballots relating to acquisition of grant-maintained status

23. Section 190(2)(b) of this Act applies where after the commencement of this Act the Secretary of State has given his consent for the purposes of section 186(3) or section 187(5) of this Act.

Instruments and articles for grant-maintained schools incorporated under pre-1993 Act law

24.—(1) This paragraph applies in relation to a grant-maintained school where—

(a) the governing body of the school were incorporated under Chapter IV of Part I of the Education Reform Act 1988;
(b) an instrument and articles of government were made for the school under that Chapter before 1st January 1994; and
(c) immediately before the commencement of this Act those instruments had effect (in accordance with paragraph 1(2) of Schedule 20 to the Education Act 1993 (transitional provisions and savings)) subject to the modifications specified in either or both of paragraphs 8 and 9 of the Education Act 1993 (Commencement No. 2 and Transitional Provisions) Order 1993.

(2) The instrument and articles of government for the school shall continue to have effect, subject to those modifications, as if made under section 220 of this Act and in accordance with Part III of this Act.

25.—(1) This paragraph applies in relation to a grant-maintained school where—

(a) the governing body of the school were incorporated under Chapter IV of Part I of the Education Reform Act 1988;

(b) paragraph 24(1)(b) above does not apply; and

(c) immediately before the commencement of this Act the instrument and articles of government prescribed by virtue of section 56 of the Education Act 1993 had effect in relation to the school (in accordance with paragraph 1(3) of Schedule 20 to that Act).

(2) The instrument and articles of government for the school shall continue to have effect as if made under section 219 of this Act; and while they remain in force Schedule 24 to this Act shall apply in relation to the school with the following modifications.

(3) In paragraph 10(1) there shall be inserted at the end of paragraph (d) "or

(e) in the case of a governing body incorporated under Chapter IV of Part I of the Education Reform Act 1988, became a member of the governing body on the incorporation date in relation to the school (as defined by section 104(3) of that Act) and—

(i) immediately before that date, was a parent governor (within the meaning of the Education (No. 2) Act 1986) in relation to the school, or

(ii) was elected under section 66, or elected or nominated under section 68, of the Education Reform Act 1988 to hold office as a parent governor on the governing body."

(4) In paragraph 11(1) there shall be inserted at the end of paragraph (c) "or

(d) in the case of a governing body incorporated under Chapter IV of Part I of the Education Reform Act 1988, became a member of the governing body on the incorporation date in relation to the school (as defined by section 104(3) of that Act) and—

(i) immediately before that date, was a teacher governor (within the meaning of the Education (No. 2) Act 1986) in relation to the school, or

(ii) was elected under section 66, or elected or nominated under section 68, of the Education Reform Act 1988 to hold office as a teacher governor on the governing body."

(5) In paragraph 12(1) there shall be inserted at the end of paragraph (c) "or

(d) in the case of a governing body incorporated under Chapter IV of Part I of the Education Reform Act 1988—

(i) became a member of the governing body on the incorporation date in relation to the school (as defined by section 104(3) of that Act), and

(ii) was selected under section 66, or nominated under section 68, of that Act as being a person appearing to be a member of the local community committed to the good government and continuing viability of the school."

26.—(1) This paragraph applies in relation to a grant-maintained school where—

(a) the governing body of the school were incorporated under Chapter IV of Part I of the Education Reform Act 1988; and

(b) the school was a voluntary school before it became grant-maintained.

(2) Schedule 24 to this Act shall apply in relation to the school with the substitution of the following paragraph for paragraph 13—

"13. "Foundation governor" means—

(a) a person appointed otherwise than by a local education authority for the purpose of securing, so far as is practicable, that the established character of the school at the time when it became grant-maintained is preserved and developed and, in particular, that the school is conducted in accordance with the provisions of any trust deed relating to it; or

(b) a person selected under section 66, or nominated under section 68, of the Education Reform Act 1988 for the purpose referred to in sub-paragraph (a) above."

Appeal committees

27. Nothing in—

(a) section 308(3) of this Act, or

(b) paragraph 7 of Schedule 33 to this Act,

applies in relation to any decision or action taken by the members of an appeal committee before 1st January 1994.

28. Paragraph 13(4) of Schedule 22 to this Act does not apply to any appeal committee constituted before 1st January 1994 in accordance with the instrument of government for any grant-maintained school for the purposes referred to in section 58(5)(d) of the Education Reform Act

1988 (articles of government—admission appeal committees) while all the members of the committee are persons who were nominated before that date.

29. Where immediately before the commencement of this Act an appeal committee was constituted in accordance with the provisions of Part I of Schedule 2 to the Education (No. 2) Act 1986 as they had effect by virtue of paragraph 6 of Schedule 20 to the Education Act 1993 (namely without the amendments made by Schedule 16 to that Act), those provisions shall continue to apply to the committee (in place of the corresponding provisions of Part I of Schedule 33 to this Act) while all the members of the committee are persons nominated before 1st January 1994.

30. Nothing in this Act affects the restriction imposed by paragraph 4(2) of Schedule 2 to the Education Act 1993 (Commencement No. 1 and Transitional Provisions) Order 1993 on the jurisdiction exercisable by a Local Commissioner, by virtue of section 25(5) of the Local Government Act 1974, in relation to cases where notice of appeal was served before 1st October 1993.

Maintenance etc. grants

31.—(1) The former grants code shall continue to have effect in relation to—

(a) any payments of maintenance grant under section 79(1) of the Education Reform Act 1988 in respect of any financial year ending before 1st April 1994; and

(b) any payments of capital and special purpose grants under section 79(3) of that Act made before that date.

(2) The functions conferred on the Secretary of State by or under the former grants code (as it has effect by virtue of sub-paragraph (1) above) shall, so far as relating to any amounts which—

(a) fall or may fall to be paid in any financial year beginning on or after 1st April 1994 in respect of any grant under that code, or

(b) have been paid by the Secretary of State before that date in respect of any such grant,

be exercisable by the funding authority.

(3) In this paragraph "the former grants code" means sections 79 and 80 of the Education Reform Act 1988 (maintenance, special purpose and capital grants) in their application to England.

32. Section 81 of the Education Reform Act 1988 (recovery from local funds of sums in respect of maintenance grant) shall continue to have effect in relation to any sums recoverable by the Secretary of State under section 81(1) of that Act for any financial year ending before 1st April 1994.

33. The Education (Grant-maintained Schools) (Finance) Regulations 1990, so far as in force immediately before the commencement of this Act, shall continue in force despite the repeals made by this Act.

Assessments and statements of special educational needs

34. Any assessment or statement of special educational needs which—

(a) was made pursuant to a notice or copy of a proposed statement served before 1st September 1994, and

(b) immediately before the commencement of this Act was treated, by virtue of paragraph 2(7) or 4(3) of Schedule 4 to the Education Act 1993 (Commencement No.5 and Transitional Provisions) Order 1994, as if it had been made under section 167 or 168 of the Education Act 1993,

shall have effect as if made under section 323 or 324 of this Act (as the case may be).

Applications relating to special schools

35. Any application which—

(a) was made to the Secretary of State before 1st April 1994, and

(b) immediately before the commencement of this Act was treated, by virtue of paragraph 5 of Schedule 3 to the Education Act 1993 (Commencement No. 3 and Transitional Provisions) Order 1994, as if it had been made in accordance with—

(i) paragraph (a) or paragraph (b) of subsection (2), and subsection (6), of section 183 of the Education Act 1993, and

(ii) section 184(1) to (3) of that Act,

shall have effect as if made in accordance with paragraph (a) or (as the case may be) paragraph (b) of subsection (1), and subsection (5), of section 339 of this Act and section 340(1) to (3) of this Act.

Contracts of staff transferred to School Curriculum and Assessment Authority or Curriculum and Assessment Authority for Wales

36.—(1) The repeal by this Act of—

(a) section 15 of the Education Reform Act 1988 (transfer of staff of School Curriculum Development Committee or Secondary Examinations Council), or

(b) section 248 of the Education Act 1993 (transfer of staff of National Curriculum Council and School Examinations and Assessment Council),

shall not affect the continued operation of section 15(3) to (5) or (as the case may be) section 248(2) and (3) in relation to any contract of employment in relation to which those provisions applied immediately before the commencement of this Act.

(2) Nothing in this Act shall affect the continued operation of Article 4 of the Education (School Curriculum and Assessment Authority) (Transfer of Functions) Order 1995 in relation to the person mentioned in that Article.

Information about directions under section 365

37. Nothing in section 366 of this Act applies, by virtue of paragraph 1 above, to any direction given before the commencement of this Act under regulations made under section 19 of the Education Reform Act 1988, and that section shall continue to apply in relation to any such direction as if this Act had not been passed.

Review of conclusions about policy relating to curriculum

38. Any articles of government of a county, controlled or maintained special school made under section 18(7) of the Education (No. 2) Act 1986 shall, in their operation after the commencement of this Act in accordance with paragraph 1 above, have effect as if the events requiring the governing body to review their conclusions about the matters mentioned in section 371(2) and (3) of this Act included the implementation of any proposals made after that time which—

(a) would fall to be published by virtue of section 35 of this Act but for subsection (2)(b) of that section, and

(b) materially affect the school.

Agreed syllabuses of religious education

39.—(1) Nothing in this Act affects the constitution of, or the operation of Schedule 5 to the Education Act 1944 in relation to, any conference convened (or reconvened) before the commencement of this Act.

(2) Any regulations made under section 258(2) of the Education Act 1993 and having effect immediately before the commencement of this Act in relation to any conference or other body falling within section 258(1) or (3) shall continue to have effect in relation to any such conference or body, subject to the provisions of any regulations made under section 397(2) of this Act.

Arrangements for collective worship

40. In section 385 of this Act—

(a) subsection (4)(b) does not affect any arrangements for collective worship in the case of a grant-maintained school that was formerly a voluntary school which were made before the commencement of this Act for the purposes of section 6 of the Education Reform Act 1988; and

(b) subsection (6) does not affect any arrangements made for the purposes of section 6(5) of that Act before the commencement of this Act.

Disqualification for purposes of Part VII

41. Sections 472 and 473 of this Act shall apply to a person who is disqualified—

(a) from being the proprietor of an independent school, or

(b) from being a teacher in any school,

by virtue of an order under Part III of the Education Act 1944 made before 1st January 1994 as if the words "or other employee" were omitted, wherever occurring.

Chairmen of Independent Schools Tribunals

42. In its application to a person who, immediately before 31st March 1995, was a member of the legal panel appointed under paragraph 1 of Schedule 6 to the Education Act 1944, paragraph 3(2) of Schedule 34 to this Act has effect subject to Schedule 7 to the Judicial Pensions and Retirement Act 1993 (transitional provisions), as well as to section 26(4) to (6) of that Act.

Training grants

43. The Education (Training Grants) Regulations 1993 shall continue to have effect in so far as they relate to the payment of grant on and after 1st April 1994, or to grant paid before that date, in respect of expenditure incurred before that date.

Education committees etc. and members of those committees

44.—(1) Sub-paragraph (2) below applies to—

(a) any education committee established in accordance with paragraph 1 of Part II of Schedule 1 to the Education Act 1944, and

(b) any sub-committee of any such committee appointed in accordance with paragraph 10 of that Part,

which was in existence immediately before 1st April 1994.

(2) Any committee or sub-committee to which this sub-paragraph applies shall, for the purposes of any enactment, be treated as if it had been—

(a) appointed on that date—

(i) in the case of a committee, by the local authority, or

(ii) in the case of a sub-committee, by the committee appointed by the authority,

in accordance with section 102(1) of the Local Government Act 1972, and

(b) so appointed wholly or partly for the purpose of discharging any functions with respect to education conferred on them in their capacity as a local education authority or, as the case may be, the committee's functions with respect to education.

(3) Sub-paragraph (4) below applies to any person who was immediately before 1st April 1994 a member of an education committee or sub-committee of such a committee appointed for a term of office.

(4) Any person to whom this sub-paragraph applies shall, for the purposes of any enactment, be treated—

(a) as if he had been appointed on that date as a member of a committee or sub-committee appointed as mentioned in sub-paragraph (2) above for the residue of that term, and

(b) if he was a member of an education committee or sub-committee by virtue of directions given by the Secretary of State under paragraph 5A of Part II of Schedule 1 to the Education Act 1944, as if he had been appointed on that date as a member of a committee or sub-committee appointed as mentioned in sub-paragraph (2) above by virtue of directions given by the Secretary of State under section 297 of the Education Act 1993 or, in relation to any time after the commencement of this Act, under section 499 of this Act.

Documents issued by divisional executives

45. Section 566(1) of this Act applies to a document purporting—

(a) to be a document issued by a divisional executive (within the meaning of Part III of Schedule 1 to the Education Act 1944), and

(b) to be signed by the person authorised by the executive to sign it,

as it applies to a document falling within paragraph (a) of that provision.

PART III

MISCELLANEOUS SAVINGS ETC.

Handicapped children

46. The repeal by this Act of the Education (Handicapped Children) Act 1970 shall not affect the operation of any order made under section 1 of that Act so far as in force immediately before the commencement of this Act or of any statement of terms and conditions of employment given in connection with any such order.

Byelaws under Children and Young Persons Act 1933

47. Despite the repeal by this Act of section 120(5) of the Education Act 1944—

(a) references to a "child" in any byelaws made under Part II of the Children and Young Persons Act 1933 (employment of children) shall continue to be construed as references to a child within the meaning of that Part of that Act; and

(b) any such byelaws made before 1st April 1945 which were continued in force by section 120(5) shall, if in force immediately before the commencement of this Act, continue in force as if made by the local education authority for the area in question and may be varied or revoked accordingly.

Disputes as to property transferred by virtue of 1944 Act

48. Any question which, if it had arisen before the commencement of this Act, would have fallen to be determined by the Secretary of State in accordance with section 96(2) of the Education Act 1944 (questions relating to property etc. transferred to LEAs) shall be determined by him despite the repeal of that provision by this Act.

Modifications of deeds made prior to Education Act 1973

49. Without prejudice to the generality of paragraph 6(2) above, any order to which paragraph 3 of Schedule 1 to the Education Act 1973 (saving on repeals made by that Act) applied immediately before the commencement of this Act shall continue in force despite the repeal by this Act of that paragraph; and section 570 of this Act shall apply to any such order as if it had been made under this Act.

Instruments made prior to Local Government Act 1972

50. The repeal by this Act of section 192(5) and (6) of the Local Government Act 1972 (transitional provisions about instruments made by old LEAs) shall not affect the continued operation of those provisions in relation to any instrument in relation to which they applied or were applicable immediately before the commencement of this Act.

PART IV

INTERPRETATION

51. In this Schedule "repeal" includes (so far as the context permits) revoke or revocation.

Section 582(4)

SCHEDULE 40

TRANSITORY PROVISIONS

Compulsory school age: general

1.—(1) Until the day appointed under section 583(3) for the coming into force of section 8—
(a) this paragraph shall have effect for defining "compulsory school age" for the purposes of this Act; and
(b) in the enactments to which Part II of Schedule 37 relates or any other enactment, or in any instrument or document—
(i) any reference (however expressed) to compulsory school age within the meaning of the Education Act 1944 shall be construed as a reference to compulsory school age as defined by this paragraph, and
(ii) any reference to section 9 of the Education Act 1962 shall be construed as reference to sub-paragraphs (3) to (7) of this paragraph.

(2) "Compulsory school age" means any age between five and 16, so that—
(a) a person is of compulsory school age if he has attained the age of five and is under the age of 16, and
(b) a person is over compulsory school age if he has attained the age of 16.

(3) The following provisions apply in relation to a person who attains the age of 16 on a day when either—
(a) he is a registered pupil at a school, or
(b) not being such a pupil, he has been a registered pupil at a school within the preceding period of 12 months.

(4) If he attains that age within the period from the beginning of September to the end of January, he shall be treated for the purposes of this paragraph as not having attained it until the end of the following spring term at his school (that is, the last term at his school to end before the following May).

(5) If he attains that age after the end of January but before the May school-leaving date (that is, the Friday before the last Monday in May), he shall be treated for the purposes of this paragraph as not having attained it until the May school-leaving date.

(6) If he attains that age after the May school-leaving date but before the beginning of September, he shall be treated for the purposes of this paragraph as having attained it on the May school-leaving date.

(7) In sub-paragraph (4) the references to a person's school are to the last school at which he is a registered pupil for a term ending before the May referred to in that sub-paragraph or for part of such a term.

Section 231: powers of governing body of grant-maintained school

2.—(1) If section 7 of the Nursery Education and Grant-Maintained Schools Act 1996 has not come into force before the commencement of this Act, this Act shall have effect with the following modifications until the relevant commencement date.

(2) Section 231 shall have effect as if—

(a) subsection (5)(c) were omitted; and

(b) the following subsections were substituted for subsections (6) and (7)—

"(6) Subsection (4) does not confer power to borrow money, except money lent under section 255.

(7) The power to dispose of land mentioned in subsection (5)(d) above—

(a) does not include power to grant any mortgage, charge or other security in respect of any land, and

(b) may only be exercised with the written consent of the Secretary of State."

(3) Section 296(2) shall have effect as if "section 231(7)(b)" were substituted for "section 231(7)".

(4) Paragraph 1 of Schedule 3 shall have effect as if sub-paragraph (2)(b) were omitted.

Section 318: provision by LEAs of goods and services

3. If paragraph 12 of Schedule 3 to the Nursery Education and Grant-Maintained Schools Act 1996 has not come into force before the commencement of this Act, section 318 shall have effect until the relevant commencement date as if subsection (3) were omitted.

Sections 336 and 476: Misapplication of arbitration legislation

4. If paragraphs 4 and 59 of Schedule 3 to the Arbitration Act 1996 have not come into force before the commencement of this Act, sections 336(4) and 476(4) shall have effect until the relevant commencement date as if in each case "The Arbitration Act 1950" were substituted for "Part I of the Arbitration Act 1996".

Section 355: the "key stages"

5. Until the day appointed under section 583(3) for the coming into force of section 8, section 355(1)(d) shall have effect as if for the words from "the expiry of" to the end there were substituted "the majority of pupils in his class ceasing to be of compulsory school age."

Section 357: implementation of National Curriculum

6. Until the relevant commencement date, section 357(2) shall not apply, in relation to pupils in the fourth key stage, to any of the foundation subjects other than the core subjects.

Section 433: time for admission of pupils

7. If paragraph 2 of Schedule 3 to the Nursery Education and Grant-Maintained Schools Act 1996 has not come into force before the commencement of this Act, section 433 shall have effect until the relevant commencement date as if subsection (4) were omitted.

Sections 457, 512 and 534: jobseeker's allowances

8.—(1) If paragraph 17 of Schedule 2 to the Jobseekers Act 1995 has not come into force before the commencement of this Act, section 457(4)(b) shall have effect until the relevant commencement date with the omission of sub-paragraph (iii).

(2) If paragraph 3 of Schedule 2 to that Act has not come into force before the commencement of this Act, sections 512(3) and 534(3) shall each have effect until the relevant commencement date with the omission of "or of an income-based jobseeker's allowance (payable under the Jobseekers Act 1995)".

Section 560: work experience

9. Until the day appointed under section 583(3) for the coming into force of section 8, section 560(2) shall have effect as if "by virtue of paragraph 1 of Schedule 40 he would be entitled to leave school" were substituted for "he would cease to be of compulsory school age".

Section 578 and Schedule 37: "the Education Acts"; consequential amendments

10. If the provisions of Schedule 3 to the Nursery Education and Grant-Maintained Schools Act 1996 (other than paragraph 2 and paragraphs 9 to 12) have not come into force before the commencement of this Act—

(a) section 578 shall have effect until the relevant commencement date as if the following Acts were omitted—
the Education Act 1994;
the Education (Student Loans) Act 1996; and
the Nursery Education and Grant-Maintained Schools Act 1996; and
(b) the amendments made by Schedule 37 to this Act in such of the enactments amended by those provisions of Schedule 3 to that Act as are not reproduced in this Act shall be construed as operating instead on the statutory references in those enactments as they have effect without the amendments made by those provisions.

Meaning of "the relevant commencement date"

11.—(1) Subject to sub-paragraph (2), in any of the preceding paragraphs "the relevant commencement date" means such day as the Secretary of State may by order appoint in relation to that paragraph; and different days may be so appointed for different purposes.

(2) If, in the case of any provision or provisions referred to in any of paragraphs 2, 3, 4, 7, 8 and 10 above which has or have not come into force before the commencement of this Act, an order under the Act in question has been made before that time appointing a day for the coming into force of that provision or those provisions, "the relevant commencement date", in relation to that provision or those provisions, means the day so appointed.

TABLE OF DERIVATIONS

Notes:

1. This Table shows the derivation of the provisions of the Bill.

2. The following abbreviations are used in the Table:—

Acts of Parliament

1944	=	Education Act 1944 (c.31)
1946	=	Education Act 1946 (c.50)
1948	=	Education (Miscellaneous Provisions) Act 1948 (c.40)
1953	=	Education (Miscellaneous Provisions) Act 1953 (c.33)
1962	=	Education Act 1962 (c.12)
1964	=	Education Act 1964 (c.82)
1967	=	Education Act 1967 (c.3)
1968	=	Education Act 1968 (c.17)
1972LG	=	Local Government Act 1972 (c.70)
1973EWE	=	Education (Work Experience) Act 1973 (c.23)
1973NHSR	=	National Health Service Reorganisation Act 1973 (c.32)
1976	=	Education Act 1976 (c.81)
1978IA	=	Interpretation Act 1978 (c.30)
1980	=	Education Act 1980 (c.20)
1981	=	Education Act 1981 (c.60)
1982LG(MP)	=	Local Government (Miscellaneous Provisions) Act 1982 (c.30)
1984	=	Education (Grants and Awards) Act 1984 (c.11)
1986	=	Education (No. 2) Act 1986 (c.61)
1988	=	Education Reform Act 1988 (c.40)
1992FHE	=	Further and Higher Education Act 1992 (c.13)
1992(S)	=	Education (Schools) Act 1992 (c.38)
1993	=	Education Act 1993 (c.35)
1994LG(W)	=	Local Government (Wales) Act 1994 (c.19)
1994	=	Education Act 1994 (c.30)
1995HA	=	Health Authorities Act 1995 (c.17)
1996ER	=	Employment Rights Act 1996 (c.18)
1996N	=	Nursery Education and Grant-Maintained Schools Act 1996 (c.50)

Subordinate legislation

S.I. 1968/1699	=	Secretary of State for Social Services Order 1968
S.I. 1977/293	=	Local Authorities etc. (Miscellaneous Provision) Order 1977
S.I. 1991/1890	=	Education (Financial Delegation for Primary Schools) Regulations 1991
S.I. 1992/110	=	Education (Financial Delegation for Primary Schools) (Amendment) Regulations 1992
S.I. 1992/1548	=	Education (National Curriculum) (Foundation Subjects at Key Stage 4) Order 1992
S.I. 1993/1975	=	Education Act 1993 (Commencement No. 1 and Transitional Provisions) Order 1993
S.I. 1993/3106	=	Education Act 1993 (Commencement No. 2 and Transitional Provisions) 1993
S.I. 1994/507	=	Education Act 1993 (Commencement No. 3 and Transitional Provisions) Order 1994
S.I. 1994/1814	=	Education (National Curriculum) (Foundation Subjects at Key Stage 4) Order 1994
S.I. 1994/2038	=	Education Act 1993 (Commencement No. 5 and Transitional Provisions) Order 1994
S.I. 1994/2092	=	Education (No. 2) Act 1986 (Amendment) (No. 2) Order 1994
S.I. 1996/951	=	Deregulation (Length of the School Day) Order 1996.

3. The abbreviation "Law Com. Rec. No." followed by a number refers to a recommendation set out in the paragraph of that number in Appendix 1 to the Report of the Law Commission (Cm. 3251).

4. By virtue of the Secretary of State for Education and Science Order 1964 (S.I. 1964/490) all the functions of the Minister of Education were transferred to the Secretary of State for Education and Science. By virtue of further Transfer of Functions Orders (S.Is. 1970/1536, 1978/274 and 1995/2986) all the functions so transferred are now exercisable by the Secretary of State at large. The effect of these Orders is not separately acknowledged in the Table against each of the provisions affected.

5. The Table also does not separately acknowledge the provisions of general effect contained in the Criminal Law Act 1977 and the Criminal Justice Act 1982 which secure that, where the maximum fine that may be imposed on the commission of a summary offence was originally expressed as a particular amount (or one particular amount on a first conviction and another on subsequent convictions), the amount of the maximum fine is now a particular level on the standard scale.

Provision	Derivation
1(1)	1944 s.7.
(2) to (4)	Drafting.
2(1)	1944 ss.8(1)(a), 114(1) ("primary education"); 1948 s.3(2).
(2)	1944 ss.8(1)(b), 114(1) ("secondary education"); 1992FHE ss.10(1), 14(2), Sch. 8 para. 13(2).
(3)	1944 ss.41(3), (4), 114(1) ("further education"); 1992FHE s.11, Sch. 8 para. 13(2).
(4)	1992FHE s.14(1).
(5)	1992FHE s.14(3).
(6)	1944 s.41(5); 1992FHE s.11.
(7)	1992FHE s.14(4).
3(1)	1944 s.114(1) ("pupil"); 1992FHE s.14(6), Sch. 8 para. 13(2).
(2)	1944 s.114(1) ("junior pupil"; "senior pupil").
(3)	1992FHE s.14(6).
4(1)	1944 s.114(1) ("school"); 1992FHE s.14(5); 1993 s.304(1).
(2)	Law Com. Rec. No. 2.
(3)	1992FHE s.91(3).
(4)	1992FHE s.91(5).
5(1)	1944 s.114(1) ("primary school"); 1992FHE Sch. 8 para. 13(2); 1993 s.304(2).
(2)	1944 s.114(1) ("secondary school"); 1992FHE Sch. 8 para. 13(2); 1993 Sch. 19 para. 24(1).
(3)	Drafting.

Provision	Derivation
(4)	1964 s.1(2); 1980 Sch. 3 para. 12.
(5)	1964 s.1(3); 1993 Sch. 19 para. 38(3).
6(1)	1944 s.9(4).
(2)	1993 s.182(1).
7	1944 s.36; 1981 s.17.
8	1993 s.277.
9	1944 s.76; 1993 Sch. 19 para. 20; 1996N Sch. 3 para. 1.
10	1993 s.1.
11	1993 s.2.
12(1)	1944 ss.6(1), 114(1) ("county"; "local education authority"); 1972LG ss.179(2), 192(1); S.I. 1977/293; 1994LG(W) s.21(2).
(2)	1944 s.114(1) ("local education authority"); 1972LG s.192(1); S.I. 1977/293 art. 4; Local Government Changes for England Regulations 1994 (S.I. 1994/867) reg. 5(6); Local Government Changes for England (Amendment) Regulations 1996 (S.I. 1996/611) reg. 2.
(3)	London Government Act 1963 (c.33) s.30(1)(a); 1988 s.163.
(4)	1988 ss.163, 235(4).
(5)	1944 ss.6(1), 114(1) ("local education authority"); 1972LG s.192(1); S.I. 1977/293; 1994LG(W) s.21(1), (2).
(6)	Drafting.
13(1)	1944 s.7.
(2)	1992FHE s.91(2), (4), Sch. 8 para. 2.
14(1)	1944 s.8(1); 1992FHE s.10(1).
(2), (3)	1944 s.8(1).
(4)	1980 s.24(2).
(5)	1944 s.8(1A); 1992FHE s.10(2).
(6)	1944 s.8(2); 1981 s.2(1); 1992FHE s.10(3).
(7)	1944 s.8(2) proviso; 1964 s.1(3).
15(1) to (3)	1944 s.41(1), (2); 1992FHE s.11.
(4)	1944 s.41(6); 1992FHE s.11.
(5)	1944 s.41(7), (8); 1992FHE s.11.
(6), (7)	1944 s.41(9), (10); 1992FHE s.11.
(8)	1944 s.41(2), (11); 1992FHE s.11.
16(1)	1944 s.9(1); 1992FHE Sch. 8 para. 4.
(2)	1944 s.9(6).
(3)	1944 s.9(7); 1992FHE s.12(1).
17(1)	1980 s.24(1).
(2)	1980 s.24(2).
18	1953 s.6(1).
19(1) to (4)	1993 s.298(1) to (4).
(5) to (7)	1993 s.298(6) to (8).
20	1993 s.3.
21	1993 s.4.
22	Drafting.
23	1993 s.8.
24	1993 s.9.
25	1993 s.6.
26	1993 s.5.
27	1993 s.12.
28	1993 s.20.
29(1)	1944 s.92.
(2)	1993 s.7(3).
(3), (4)	1993 s.21(2), (3).
(5)	1980 s.8(5B), (7); 1992(S) Sch. 4 para. 4.
(6)	1980 s.9(1).
30(1), (2)	1993 s.7(1), (2).
(3)	1993 s.7(4).
(4)	1993 s.21(1).
(5)	1993 s.21(3).

Provision	Derivation
31(1), (2)	1944 s.9(2).
(3)	1944 s.9(2); 1993 s.298(5).
32(1)	1944 s.15(1).
(2)	1944 s.15(2); 1986 Sch. 4 para. 1.
(3), (4)	Drafting.
(5)	1944 s.114(1), Sch. 3 para. 11.
(6)	Drafting.
33	Drafting.
34(1)	1944 s.114(1) ("maintain"), (2); 1993 s.305(1) ("local education authority"); drafting.
(2)	1944 s.114(2).
(3)	1944 s.114(2); 1946 Sch. 1 para. 1.
(4)	1944 sd.114(2); 1946 Sch. 1 para. 1.
(5)	Rating and Valuation Act 1961 (c.45) s.12(6).
35(1)	1980 s.12(1); 1993 s.229(1).
(2)	1980 s.16(1A); 1993 Sch. 19 para. 78; Law Com. Rec. No. 3.
(3)	1980 s.12(2).
(4)	1980 s.12(2A); 1988 s.31(4).
(5)	1980 s.12(1A); 1993 s.229(1).
(6)	1992FHE s.59(3), (4).
(7)	1993 ss.272(6), 273(1).
(8)	1993 s.273(2).
36(1)	1980 s.12(3); 1993 s.229(2).
(2)	1980 s.12(3).
(3)	1993 s.229(3).
(4)	1980 s.12(3).
(5), (6)	1980 s.16(3A), (3B); 1988 Sch. 12 para. 81.
37(1)	1980 s.12(4), (5); 1993 s.273(4).
(2)	1980 s.12(4).
(3)	1980 s.12(5).
(4)	1993 s.273(3).
(5)	1980 s.12(6).
(6)	1980 s.12(4).
(7)	1993 s.273(4).
(8)	1993 s.273(5).
(9)	1993 s.273(6).
38(1), (2)	1980 s.12(7).
(3)	1980 s.12(8)
39(1), (2)	1980 s.14(1).
(3)	Drafting.
40(1)	1980 s.12(9).
(2)	1980 s.14(3).
(3)	1980 s.12(9).
(4), (5)	1980 s.16(1).
41(1)	1980 s.13(1).
(2)	1980 s.13(1); 1993 s.230(1).
(3)	1980 s.16(1A); 1993 Sch. 19 para. 78; Law Com. Rec. No. 3.
(4)	1980 s.13(1A); 1992FHE s.12(2).
(5), (6)	1980 s.13(2); 1988 s.31(5).
(7)	1980 s.13(1B); 1993 s.230(1).
(8)	1992FHE s.59(3), (4).
(9)	1993 s.273(2).
42(1)	1980 s.13(3); 1993 s.230(2).
(2)	1980 s.13(3).
(3)	1980 s.13(3A); 1993 s.230(3).
(4)	1993 s.230(6).
(5), (6)	1980 s.16(3A), (3B); 1988 Sch. 12 para. 81.
43(1), (2)	1980 s.13(4).
(3) to (6)	1993 s.273(3) to (6).

Provision	Derivation
(7)	Law Com. Rec. No. 4.
44(1)	1980 s.14(1); 1993 Sch. 19 para. 77.
(2)	1980 s.14(1).
(3), (4)	1980 s.14(2); Law Com. Rec. No. 4.
45(1)	1980 s.13(5); Law Com. Rec. No. 4.
(2)	1980 s.13(6); 1993 s.230(4).
(3)	1980 s.14(3).
(4)	1980 s.13(7).
(5), (6)	1980 s.16(1).
(7)	1980 s.13(8); 1993 s.230(5).
46(1)	1944 s.16(2); 1980 Sch. 3 para. 1.
(2)	1944 s.16(2).
(3)	1944 s.16(2).
(4)	1944 s.16(3).
(5)	1944 s.16(3).
47(1)	1944 s.16(1).
(2)	1946 Sch. 1 para. 2(1); Law Com. Rec. No. 5.
(3), (4)	1944 s.16(3).
48(1)	1944 s.15(2); 1986 Sch. 4 para. 1.
(2)	1944 s.15(2); 1993 Sch. 19 para. 7.
(3)	1944 s.105(3).
(4)	1944 s.105(3); 1993 Sch. 19 para. 23(b).
49	1964 s.1(1); 1968 s.2; 1980 Sch. 3 para. 11.
50(1)	1946 s.2(1).
(2)	1946 s.2(1), (7).
(3)	1946 s.2(7).
(4)	1946 s.2(2); 1980 Sch. 3 para. 7.
(5)	1946 s.16(1) ("department").
51(1)	1946 s.2(1).
(2), (3)	1946 s.2(3), (4)
(4)	1946 s.2(1), (7).
(5)	1946 s.2(7).
(6)	1946 s.2(2); 1980 Sch. 3 para. 7.
(7)	1946 s.2(8).
(8)	1946 s.16(1) ("department").
52(1)	1986 s.54(3).
(2)	1986 s.54(4).
(3)	1986 s.54(3).
53(1), (2)	1986 s.54(5).
(3), (4)	1986 s.54(13), (14); 1988 Sch. 12 para. 102.
54(1)	1986 s.54(1).
(2)	1986 s.54(2); Law Com. Rec. No. 6.
(3)	1986 s.54(7).
(4)	1986 s.54(6).
(5), (6)	1986 s.54(12).
55	1986 s.54(8) to (11).
56(1)	1986 s.55(1), (2).
(2)	1986 s.55(2).
(3)	1986 s.55(1).
(4), (5)	1986 s.55(3), (4).
57(1)	1944 s.15(4); 1946 s.2(5), Sch. 1 para. 2(1).
(2)	1944 s.15(4); 1946 Sch. 1 para. 2(1).
(3)	1944 s.15(4A); 1946 Sch. 1 para. 2(2); 1993 s.282(2), (4).
(4)	1944 s.15(4); 1946 s.2(5), Sch. 1 para. 2(1); drafting.
58(1)	1944 s.15(5).
(2)	1944 s.15(5); 1993 Sch. 19 para. 7.
(3)	Drafting.
59(1)	1944 s.15(3).
(2)	1944 s.15(3); 1946 Sch. 2 Pt. II.

Provision	Derivation
(3)	1944 s.15(3); 1946 Sch. 2 Pt. II.
(4)	1944 s.15(3); 1946 Sch. 2 Pt. II.
(5)	1946 Sch. 1 para. 2(1).
60(1)	1946 Sch. 1 para. 1; 1980 Sch. 3 para. 8.
(2), (3)	1946 Sch. 1 para. 6.
(4) to (6)	1946 Sch. 1 para. 7.
(7)	Reverter of Sites Act 1987 (c.15) s. 8(1).
61(1)	1946 Sch. 1 para. 1; 1980 Sch. 3 para. 8.
(2), (3)	1946 Sch. 1 para. 6.
(4)	1946 Sch. 1 para. 3.
(5)	1946 Sch. 1 para. 4.
(6)	1946 Sch. 1 para. 5.
62(1)	1946 s.16(1) ("site").
(2), (3)	1946 Sch. 1 para. 8.
(4)	1946 Sch. 1 para. 9; 1992FHE Sch. 8 para. 14.
63(1)	1953 s.2; 1980 Sch. 3 para. 9.
(2)	1953 s.2.
(3)	1953 s.2; 1988 s.114, Sch. 12 para. 8.
64(1)	1946 s.1(1); 1953 s.3; 1968 Sch. 1 para. 6; 1980 Sch. 3 para. 6.
(2)	1946 s.1(1).
(3)	1946 s.1(1); 1953 s.3; 1967 s.2.
65	1993 s.281.
66	1988 s.212.
67(1), (2)	1944 s.105(1).
(3)	1944 s.105(2); 1968 Sch. 1 para. 4(2); 1993 Sch. 19 para. 23(a).
(4)	1944 s.105(2); 1993 Sch. 19 para. 23(a).
68	1993 s.282(1).
69	1993 s.283.
70	1993 s.284.
71	1944 s.99(3).
72	1944 s.65.
73	1946 s.4(1).
74	1946 s.6.
75	1993 s.285.
76(1)	1986 s.1(1).
(2)	1986 s.1(2).
(3), (4)	1986 s.1(3), (5).
(5)	1986 s.1(6).
77(1) to (7)	1986 s.2.
(8)	Drafting.
78(1)	1986 s.65(1) ("co-opted governor").
(2)	1944 s.114(1) ("foundation governors"); 1980 Sch. 1 para. 13(a).
(3)	1986 s.65(1) ("parent governor").
(4)	1986 s.65(1) ("teacher governor").
(5)	1986 s.65(1) ("parent governor"; "teacher governor").
79(1), (2)	1986 s.3(1) to (5).
(3), (4)	1986 s.3(6), (7).
80(1)	1986 s.7(1).
(2)	1986 s.7(2); National Health Service and Community Care Act 1990 (c.19) Sch. 9 para. 31; 1995HA Sch. 1 para. 112.
(3) to (5)	1986 s.7(3) to (5).
(6)	1986 s.7(6).
(7)	1986 s.7(6).
(8)	1986 s.7(6).
(9)	1986 s.7(7).
81(1)	1986 s.5(1).
(2)	1986 s.5(3).
(3)	1986 s.5(2).
(4), (5)	1986 s.5(4).

Provision	Derivation
82(1)	1986 s.11(1).
(2)	1986 s.11(2).
(3)	1986 s.11(2); 1993 Sch. 19 para. 91(a); Law Com. Rec. No. 3.
(4)	1986 s.11(3); 1993 Sch. 19 para. 91(d); Law Com. Rec. No. 7.
(5), (6)	1986 s.11(4), (5).
(7)	1986 s.11(6); 1993 Sch. 19 para. 91(d); Law Com. Rec. No. 7.
83	1986 s.14.
84(1)	1986 s.4(1), (2).
(2)	1986 s.4(3).
(3)	1986 s.4(2).
(4) to (6)	1986 s.4(4) to (6).
85	1986 s.4A; 1993 s.271(1).
86	1986 s.13(1) to (3).
87(1)	1986 s.13(4).
(2)	1986 s.13(7), (9).
(3)	1986 s.13(8).
(4)	1986 s.13(5).
(5)	1986 s.13(6), (9).
88(1)	1993 s.238(1), (8); drafting.
(2)	Drafting.
89(1)	1986 s.9(1).
(2)	1986 s.9(1A); 1993 s.271(3)(a).
(3)	1986 s.9(2).
(4)	1986 s.9(3).
(5), (6)	1986 Sch. 1 para. 1(1), (2).
90(1), (2)	1986 s.10(1).
(3)	1986 s.10(3).
(4)	1986 s.10(2).
(5)	1986 s.10(4).
(6)	1986 s.10(7).
91(1)	1986 s.10(5).
(2)	1986 s.10(6).
92(1)	1986 Sch. 1 para. 2(1).
(2)	1986 Sch. 1 para. 2(1).
(3)	1986 Sch. 1 para. 2(2).
(4)	1986 Sch. 1 para. 2(3).
93	1986 Sch. 1 para. 3.
94(1)	1986 s.9(4).
(2)	1986 s.9(5); 1993 Sch. 19 para. 90; Law Com. Rec. No. 8.
(3)	1986 s.9(4).
95(1)	1986 s.9(6).
(2)	1986 s.9(7).
(3)	1986 s.9(7); 1993 s.271(3)(b).
(4)	1986 s.9(8).
96(1)	1986 s.12(1); 1993 Sch. 19 para. 92(a).
(2)	1986 s.12(2); 1993 Sch. 19 para. 92(b).
(3)	1986 s.12(4); 1993 Sch. 19 para. 92(d).
(4)	1986 Sch. 2 para. 5(2); 1993 Sch. 19 para. 109(c).
(5)	1986 Sch. 2 para. 5(1).
97(1)	1986 s.12(1), (2), (9).
(2)	1986 s.12(4).
(3)	1986 ss.12(5), (9), 65(1) ("promoters"); Law Com. Rec. No. 9.
(4)	1986 ss.12(6), (9), 65(1) ("promoters"); Law Com. Rec. No. 9.
(5)	1986 ss.12(7), 65(1) ("promoters"); Law Com. Rec. No. 9.
(6)	1986 s.12(8).
(7)	1986 Sch. 2 para. 5(2).
(8)	1986 Sch. 2 para. 5(1).
98	Drafting.
99(1)	1986 Sch. 2 para. 3(1).

Provision	Derivation
(2)	1986 Sch. 2 para. 3(7).
(3)	Drafting.
100(1), (2)	Law Com. Rec. No. 10.
(3)	1986 Sch. 2 para. 3(6).
(4)	1986 Sch. 2 para. 3(6); drafting.
101(1)	1988 s.51(2)(a)(i); 1993 s.274(4).
(2)	1988 s.51(2)(a)(ii).
(3)	1988 s.33(2), (4); 1992FHE s.12(5).
(4)	1988 s.33(4); 1992FHE s.12(5).
(5)	1988 s.33(5).
(6)	1988 s.51(2)(b).
102	1988 s.33(3).
103	1988 s.33(1), (2).
104(1), (2)	1988 s.34(1), (2).
(3)	1988 s.34(4); 1993 s.274(1).
(4) to (6)	1988 s.34(5) to (7).
105(1)	1988 s.33(4).
(2)	1988 s.33(5).
(3)	1988 ss.33(4), 38(4), 51(1) ("expenditure of a capital nature").
106(1)	1988 s.38(1).
(2)	1988 s.38(1), (2).
(3)	1988 s.38(2).
(4)	1988 s.38(3).
(5)	1988 s.38(3A); 1992FHE s.12(7).
(6)	1988 s.33(5).
107(1)	1988 s.39(1); S.I. 1991/1890; S.I. 1992/110.
(2)	1988 s.39(4); S.I. 1991/1890; S.I. 1992/110.
108	1988 s.39(10).
109(1)	1988 s.39(11).
(2)	1988 s.39(12).
(3)	1988 s.39(11).
110(1)	1988 s.40(1).
(2)	1988 s.40(2); 1993 s.274(3).
(3) to (5)	1988 s.40(3) to (5).
111	1988 s.35(1), (2); 1993 s.274(2).
112(1) to (3)	1988 s.35(3); 1993 s.274(2).
(4)	1988 s.35(4); 1993 s.274(2).
113(1), (2)	1988 s.35(5); 1993 s.274(2).
(3), (4)	1988 s.35(6); 1993 s.274(2).
(5)	1988 s.35(4); 1993 s.274(2).
114	1988 s.35(7), (8); 1993 s.274(2).
115	1988 s.33(6)(a), (b).
116(1) to (3)	1988 s.36(1) to (3).
(4)	1988 s.36(4); 1993 Sch. 19 para. 125(a).
(5)	1988 s.36(5).
(6)	1988 s.36(5A); 1992FHE s.12(6).
(7)	1988 s.36(5B); 1993 Sch. 19 para. 125(b).
(8)	1988 s.36(6).
117(1)	1988 s.37(1).
(2), (3)	1988 s.37(2).
(4), (5)	1988 s.37(3).
(6)	1988 s.37(4).
118(1) to (3)	1988 s.37(5).
(4), (5)	1988 s.37(6), (7).
119	1988 s.37(8), (9).
120	1988 s.43; 1993 s.276.
121	1988 s.42(1).
122(1), (2)	1988 s.42(2), (3).
(3)	Drafting.

Provision	Derivation
(4)	1988 s.42(4); 1993 s.275(1)(c).
(5)	1988 s.42(7).
(6)	1988 s.42(8); 1993 s.275(1)(d).
(7)	1988 s.42(9).
123	1988 s.42A; 1993 s.275(2).
124(1)	1988 s.50(2), (5).
(2)	1988 s.50(3).
(3)	Drafting.
(4)	1988 s.50(6).
(5)	1988 s.50(10).
(6) to (8)	1988 s.50(7) to (9).
125(1)	1988 s.49(1).
(2), (3)	1988 s.49(2).
(4)	1988 s.49(3).
126	Drafting.
127(1), (2)	1986 s.1(1), (2).
(3), (4)	1986 s.1(4), (5).
128(1) to (3)	1986 s.2(1) to (3).
(4) to (6)	1986 s.2(5) to (7).
(7)	Drafting.
129(1)	1988 s.51(3).
(2), (3)	1988 s.51(4), (5).
(4)	1988 s.51(4).
(5)	1988 s.51(6).
130	1986 s.16(1).
131	1986 s.16(2).
132	1986 s.16(3); Law Com. Rec. No. 11.
133(1) to (3)	1986 s.34.
(4)	Drafting.
(5)	1986 s.35(1).
(6)	Drafting.
134(1)	1944 s.24(2).
(2), (3)	1944 s.24(2), proviso (a).
(4)	1944 s.24(2), proviso (b).
(5)	1944 s.22(4); 1986 Sch. 4 para. 2; 1993 Sch. 13 para. 4(6).
(6)	1944 s.22(5); 1993 Sch. 13 para. 4(4).
(7)	Drafting.
135(1) to (4)	1986 s.40(1) to (4).
(5), (6)	1986 s.40(6), (7).
(7)	Drafting.
(8)	1986 s.40(5).
136(1), (2)	1988 s.44(1), (2); Law Com. Rec. No. 12.
(3)	1988 s.44(3), (5).
137(1), (2)	1988 s.45(1), (2).
(3), (4)	1988 s.45(3).
(5)	1988 s.45(9).
(6)	1988 s.45(10).
138(1)	1988 s.45(1), (4).
(2)	1988 s.45(6).
(3)	1988 s.45(5).
(4)	1988 s.45(7).
(5)	1988 s.45(8).
139(1), (2)	1988 s.46(2).
(3) to (6)	1988 s.46(3) to (6).
(7)	1988 s.235(2)(f); 1996ER Sch. 1 para. 37(5).
140	1988 s.47.
141(1)	1988 ss.44(4), 45(11).
(2)	1988 s.44(4); Law Com. Rec. No. 12.
(3)	1988 s.45(11).

Provision	Derivation
(4)	1988 s.51(6).
142	Drafting.
143(1), (2)	1944 s.27(2).
(3)	1944 s.27(2) proviso.
(4) to (6)	1944 s.27(3) to (5); 1988 Sch. 1 para. 2(1).
(7)	Drafting.
144(1), (2)	1944 s.28(3), Sch. 3 para. 7; 1988 Sch. 1 para. 3(2).
(3)	1944 s.28(4); 1988 Sch. 1 para. 3(2).
(4)	Drafting.
145	1944 s.28(2); 1988 Sch. 1 para. 3(2).
146(1)	1944 s.30.
(2) to (4)	1944 s.30; 1988 Sch. 1 para. 4(b).
147(1)	1986 s.21(1); 1988 s.115; S.I. 1996/951 art. 3(1).
(2)	1986 s.21(4); 1988 s.115.
(3)	1986 s.21(4); 1988 s.115; S.I. 1996/951 art. 3(1).
148(1) to (4)	S.I. 1996/951 art. 3(2) to (5).
(5)	Drafting.
149(1), (2)	1986 s.42(1), (2); 1993 Sch. 13 para. 5.
(3). (4)	1986 s.42(3); 1993 Sch. 13 para. 5.
(5)	1986 s.42(4); 1993 Sch. 13 para. 5; S.I. 1996/951 art. 5.
150(1)	1944 s.22(3); 1993 Sch. 13 para. 4(2), (6).
(2)	1944 s.22(1).
(3)	1944 s.22(5); 1993 Sch. 13 para. 4(4).
151(1) to (3)	1944 s.22(3A) to (3C); 1993 Sch. 13 para. 4(3).
(4), (5)	1944 s.22(3D); 1993 Sch. 13 para. 4(3).
(6)	1944 s.22(3E); 1993 Sch. 13 para. 4(3).
(7)	1944 s.22(6); 1978IA s.17(2)(a); 1993 Sch. 13 para. 4(5).
(8)	Drafting.
152(1), (2)	1944 s.22(1); 1993 Sch. 13 para. 4(6).
(3), (4)	1944 s.22(2); 1993 Sch. 13 para. 4(6).
(5)	Drafting.
153	1986 s.21(5); 1988 s.115.
154(1)	1986 s.22.
(2)	1986 s.22(d).
(3)	1986 s.22(a); 1993 Sch. 19 para. 95.
(4)	1986 s.22(b).
(5)	1986 s.22(c).
(6)	1986 s.22(e).
155	1986 s.28.
156(1)	1986 s.22(f).
(2), (3)	1993 s.261(1), (2).
157(1)	Law Com. Rec. No. 13.
(2)	1986 s.23(a); Law Com. Rec. No. 13.
(3)	1986 s.23(b).
(4)	1986 s.23(a), (b); Law Com. Rec. No. 13.
(5)	1986 s.23(a); Law Com. Rec. No. 13.
158	Drafting.
159(1) to (4)	1986 s.26(1) to (4).
(5), (6)	1986 s.26(5).
(7)	1986 s.26(1), (2).
160	1986 s.27.
161(1)	1986 s.30(1).
(2)	Drafting.
(3)	1986 s.30(3).
(4)	1986 s.30(4).
162(1), (2)	1986 s.31(1), (2).
(3)	Drafting.
163	1986 s.31(7), (8).
164(1)	1986 Sch. 1 paras. 4, 5.

Provision	Derivation
(2)	1986 Sch. 1 para. 4(1).
(3)	1986 Sch. 1 para. 4(2).
(4) to (7)	1986 Sch. 1 para. 5.
165	1986 s.32.
166	Drafting.
167(1)	1980 s.12(1).
(2)	1980 s.12(2).
(3)	1993 s.273(1).
(4)	1980 s.12(1A); 1993 s.229(1).
(5)	1992FHE s.59(3), (4).
(6)	1993 s.273(2).
168(1)	1980 s.12(3); 1993 s.229(2).
(2)	1980 s.12(3).
(3)	1993 s.229(3).
(4)	1980 s.12(3).
(5), (6)	1980 s.16(3A), (3B); 1988 Sch. 12 para. 81.
169(1)	1980 s.12(4), (5); 1993 s.273(4).
(2)	1980 s.12(4).
(3)	1980 s.12(5).
(4)	1993 s.273(3).
(5)	1980 s.12(6).
(6)	1993 s.273(4), (5)(a).
170(1), (2)	1980 s.12(7).
(3)	1980 s.12(8).
171	1980 s.12(9).
172	1980 s.16(1).
173(1)	1944 s.14(1).
(2)	1944 s.14(1), 114(1) ("former authority"); 1946 Sch. 2 Pt. II.
(3)	1944 s.14(1); 1946 Sch. 2 Pt. II.
(4)	1992FHE s.59(3), (4).
(5)	1993 s.273(2).
(6)	1944 s.14(2).
(7)	1944 s.14(5).
(8)	Drafting.
174(1)	1944 s.14(3).
(2), (3)	1944 s.14(4).
175	1992FHE s.59(1), (2).
176	1986 s.16A; FHE 1992 s.12(3).
177	Drafting.
178	1988 s.222.
179(1)	1973 s.1(2); 1980 Sch. 3 para. 17; Law Com. Rec. No. 3.
(2)	1973 s.1(2).
180	1980 s.5.
181(1)	1986 Sch. 2 para. 1 ("new school"); 1988 s.48(2).
(2)	1986 Sch. 2 para. 1 ("relevant proposal"); 1988 s.48(2).
(3)	1988 s.48(2) ("temporary governing body"); drafting.
182	1986 s.65(2).
183	1993 s.22.
184	1993 s.23.
185	1993 s.24.
186	1993 s.25.
187	1993 s.26.
188	1993 s.27.
189	1993 s.28.
190(1)	1993 s.29(1).
(2)	1993 s.29(2); Law Com. Rec. No. 14.
(3)	1993 s.29(3).
191	1993 s.30.
192	1993 s.31.

Provision	Derivation
193	1993 s.32.
194	1993 s.33.
195	1993 s.34.
196	1993 s.35.
197	1993 s.36.
198(1) to (5)	1993 s.272(1) to (5).
(6)	1964 s.1(1); 1993 Sch. 19 para. 38.
199(1) to (3)	1993 s.273(3) to (5).
(4)	1993 s.273(7).
200	1993 s.37.
201(1) to (8)	1993 s.38(1) to (8).
(9)	1993 s.155(8).
(10)	1993 s.38(9).
202	1993 s.39.
203.	1993 s.40.
204	1993 s.41.
205	1993 s.42.
206	1993 s.43.
207	1993 s.44.
208	1993 s.45.
209	1993 s.46.
210	1993 s.47(1) to (4).
211	1993 s.48.
212	1993 s.49(1) to (3).
213	1993 s.50.
214	1993 s.51.
215	1993 s.52.
216	1993 s.53.
217	1993 s.54.
218	1993 s.55.
219(1) to (3)	1993 s.56.
(4)	1993 s.301(5).
220	1993 s.57.
221	1993 s.58.
222	1993 s.59.
223	1993 s.60.
224	1993 s.61.
225	1993 s.62.
226	1993 s.63.
227	1993 s.64.
228	1993 s.65.
229	1993 s.66.
230	1993 s.67.
231(1) to (4)	1993 s.68(1) to (4).
(5) to (7)	1993 s.68(5) to (7); 1996N s.7(2) to (4).
(8)	1993 s.68(8).
232	1993 s.69.
233	1993 s.70.
234	1993 s.71.
235	1993 s.72.
236	1993 s.73.
237	1993 s.74.
238	1993 s.75.
239	1993 s.76.
240	1993 s.77.
241	1993 s.78.
242	1993 s.79.
243	1993 s.80.
244	1993 s.81.

Provision	Derivation
245	1993 s.82.
246	1993 s.83.
247	1993 s.84.
248	1993 s.85.
249	1993 s.86.
250	1993 s.87.
251	1993 s.88.
252	1993 s.89.
253	1993 s.90.
254	1993 s.91.
255	1993 s.92.
256	1993 s.93(1) to (6).
257	1993 s.94.
258	1993 s.95.
259	1993 s.96; Law Com. Rec. No. 3.
260	1993 s.97; Law Com. Rec. No. 3.
261	1993 s.98.
262	1993 s.99.
263	1993 s.100; Law Com. Rec. No. 3.
264	1993 s.101.
265	1993 s.102.
266	1993 s.103(2), (3).
267	1993 s.104.
268	1993 s.105.
269	1993 s.106.
270	1993 s.107.
271	1993 s.108.
272	1993 s.109.
273	1993 s.110.
274	1993 s.111.
275	1993 s.112.
276	1993 s.113.
277	1993 s.114.
278	1993 s.115.
279	1993 s.116.
280	1993 s.117.
281	1993 s.118.
282	1993 s.119.
283	1993 s.120.
284	1993 s.121.
285	1993 s.122.
286	1993 s.123.
287	1993 s.124.
288	1993 s.125.
289	1993 s.126.
290(1) to (7)	1993 s.127(1) to (7).
(8), (9)	1993 s.127(8).
(10), (11)	1993 s.127(9), (10).
(12)	1993 s.305(1).
(13)	1993 s.127(11).
291	1964 s.1(1); 1993 Sch. 19 para. 38.
292(1)	1993 s.231(1); drafting.
(2)	1993 s.232(2).
293	1993 s.128.
294	Drafting.
295	1993 s.129.
296(1)	1993 s.130(1).
(2)	1993 s.130(2); 1996N Sch. 3 para. 11.
297	1993 s.131.

Provision	Derivation
298	1993 s.132.
299	1993 s.133.
300	1993 s.134.
301	1993 s.135.
302	1993 s.136.
303	1993 s.137.
304	1993 s.143.
305	1993 s.144.
306	1993 s.145.
307(1), (2)	1993 s.261(1), (2).
308(1)	1993 ss.267(1), 268(1).
(2)	1993 s.267(2).
(3)	1993 s.268(2).
309	1993 s.152.
310	1993 s.154.
311(1)	1993 ss.155(1) ("premises"), 305(1) ("Church in Wales school"; "Church of England school"; "Roman Catholic Church school").
(2)	1993 s.305(4).
(3)	1993 s.155(2).
(4)	1993 s.155(3).
(5)	1993 s.155(6).
(6)	1993 s.155(7).
(7)	Drafting.
(8)	1993 s.155(11).
312(1) to (4)	1993 s.156(1) to (4).
(5)	1993 ss.156(5), 305(1) ("maintained school").
313(1) to (4)	1993 s.157.
(5)	Drafting.
314	1993 s.158.
315	1993 s.159.
316	1993 s.160.
317(1) to (5)	1993 s.161(1) to (5).
(6), (7)	1993 s.161(6), (7); Disability Discrimination Act 1995 (c.50) s.29(2).
318(1), (2)	1993 s.162(1), (2).
(3)	1993 s.162(2A); 1996N Sch. 3 para. 12.
(4)	1993 s.162(3).
319	1993 s.163.
320	1993 s.164.
321	1993 s.165.
322(1)	1993 s.166(1); 1995HA Sch. 1 para. 124(2).
(2)	1993 s.166(2).
(3)	1993 s.166(3); 1995HA Sch. 1 para. 124(2).
(4)	1993 s.166(4).
(5)	1993 s.166(5); 1994LG(W) Sch. 16 para. 105(1); Local Government Changes for England Regulations 1994 (S.I. 1994/867) reg. 5(6); Local Government Changes for England (Amendment) Regulations 1996 (S.I. 1996/611) reg. 2.
323	1993 s.167.
324	1993 s.168.
325	1993 s.169.
326	1993 s.170.
327	1993 s.171.
328	1993 s.172.
329	1993 s.173.
330	1993 s.174.
331	1993 s.175.
332	1993 s.176; 1995HA Sch. 1 para. 124(3).
333	1993 s.177.
334	1993 s.178.

Provision	Derivation
335	1993 s.179.
336	1993 s.180; Arbitration Act 1996 (c.23) Sch. 3 para. 59.
337(1)	1993 s.182(1).
(2)	Drafting.
(3), (4)	1993 s.182(2), (3).
338(1)	1993 s.183(1).
(2)	Drafting.
339	1993 s.183(2) to (10).
340	1993 s.184.
341	1993 s.185.
342	1993 s.188.
343	1993 s.231.
344(1)	Drafting.
(2)	1993 s.182(4).
345	1993 s.186.
346	1993 s.187.
347	1993 s.189.
348	1993 s.190.
349	1993 s.191.
350(1)	1988 s.25(1) ("maintained school"); 1993 s.245(5).
(2)	1988 s.25(1) ("assess").
351(1)	1988 s.1(2).
(2) to (5)	1988 s.1(1).
352(1)	1988 ss.2(1), 8(2); 1993 s.241(1), Sch. 19 para. 114.
(2)	1988 s.2(3).
(3)	1944 s.114(1) ("sex education"); 1993 s.241(2).
353	1988 s.2(2); 1993 ss.240(1), 245(5).
354(1)	1988 s.3(1).
(2)	1988 s.3(2); S.I. 1992/1548 art. 2; S.I. 1994/1814 art. 2(2) to (4).
(3) to (5)	1988 s.3(2A), (2B); S.I. 1994/1814 art. 2(5).
(6)	1988 s.3(4).
(7)	1988 s.3(6) ("school").
(8)	1988 s.3(7).
355(1)	1988 s.3(3); 1993 Sch. 19 para. 113.
(2)	1988 s.3(4).
(3)	1988 s.3(5).
(4)	1988 s.3(5A); 1993 s.240(2).
(5)	1988 s.3(6) ("class"; "school year"); 1993 s.240(3).
356(1) to (4)	1988 s.4(1) to (4).
(5) to (8)	1988 s.4(5) to (8); 1993 s.240(4).
(9)	1993 s.241(4).
357(1)	1988 s.10(2).
(2)	1988 s.10(3).
358	1993 s.244.
359(1)	1993 s.245(1).
(2)	1993 s.245(4).
(3)	1993 s.245(3).
(4)	1993 s.245(2).
(5)	1993 s.245(5).
360(1)	1988 s.14(1); 1993 s.253(1).
(2) to (4)	1988 s.14(2); 1993 Sch. 15 para. 4(3), Sch. 19 para. 118(a).
(5)	1988 s.14(7).
361(1)	1988 s.14(3); 1993 Sch. 15 para. 4(3), Sch. 19 para. 118(b); Education (School Curriculum and Assessment Authority) (Transfer of Functions) Order 1994 (S.I. 1994/645); Education (School Curriculum and Assessment Authority) (Transfer of Functions) Order 1995 (S.I. 1995/903).
(2)	1988 s.14(5); 1993 Sch. 15 para. 4(3), Sch. 19 para. 118(c).
(3), (4)	1988 s.14(6); 1993 Sch. 15 para. 4(3), Sch. 19 para. 118(d).

Provision	Derivation
(5)	Drafting.
362(1), (2)	1988 s.16(1), (2).
(3), (4)	1988 s.16(3); 1993 Sch. 19 para. 119(a).
(5), (6)	1988 s.16(4), (5).
(7)	1988 s.16(6); 1993 Sch. 15 para. 4(4), Sch. 19 para. 119(b).
363	1988 s.17.
364	1988 s.18; 1993 Sch. 19 para. 120.
365(1)	1988 s.19(1).
(2) to (4)	1988 s.19(2).
(5)	1988 s.19(1).
(6)	1988 s.19(10).
366(1)	1988 s.19(3).
(2)	1988 s.19(4).
(3)	1988 s.19(4); 1993 Sch. 19 para. 121(a); Law Com. Rec. No. 15.
(4)	Law Com. Rec. No. 15.
(5)	1988 s.19(5); Law Com. Rec. No. 15.
(6)	1988 s.19(6); 1993 Sch. 19 para. 121(b); Law Com. Rec. No. 15.
(7)	Law Com. Rec. No. 15.
367(1)	1988 s.19(7).
(2), (3)	1988 s.19(8).
(4)	1988 s.19(9).
368(1)	1988 ss.20(1), 21(1).
(2)	1988 ss.20(2), 21(2); 1993 s.243.
(3)	1988 ss.20(3), 21(3); 1993 s.243.
(4), (5)	1988 ss.20(4), 21(3A); 1993 s.243.
(6), (7)	1988 ss.20(5), 21(3B); 1993 s.243.
(8)	1988 ss.20(6), 21(4).
(9)	1993 s.242(1), (3).
(10)	1988 ss.20(2), 21(2); 1993 Sch. 15 para. 4(5), Sch. 19 para. 122; drafting.
369	1988 s.227(1).
370(1)	1986 s.17(1).
(2), (3)	1986 s.17(2), (3).
371(1), (2)	1986 s.18(1).
(3)	1986 s.18(2).
(4)	1986 s.18(3).
(5)	1986 s.18(7); 1993 Sch. 19 para. 94.
(6)	1986 s.18(8).
(7)	1986 s.18(7); Law Com. Rec. No. 3.
(8)	Drafting.
372(1)	1986 s.18(5).
(2) to (4)	1986 s.18(6).
(5)	Drafting.
373(1), (2)	1986 s.19.
374	Drafting.
375(1)	Drafting.
(2)	1944 s.114(1) ("agreed syllabus"); 1988 Sch. 1 para. 6.
(3)	1988 s.8(3).
(4)	1944 s.114(1) ("agreed syllabus"), Sch. 5 para. 11; 1988 Sch. 1 para. 6.
(5)	1988 s.8(3).
376(1)	1944 s.26(1); 1988 Sch. 1 para. 1.
(2)	1944 s.26(2); 1988 Sch. 1 para. 1.
(3)	1944 s.26(3), (4); 1988 Sch. 1 para. 1; 1993 Sch. 19 para. 9.
377(1)	1944 s.27(6); 1988 Sch. 1 para. 2(2).
(2)	1944 s.27(1); 1988 Sch. 1 para. 2(1).
378(1)	1944 s.28(1); 1988 Sch. 1 para. 3(1).
(2), (3)	1944 s.28(1B); 1988 Sch. 1 para. 3(1).
(4)	1944 s.28(1C); 1988 Sch. 1 para. 3(1).
(5)	1944 s.28(1A); 1988 Sch. 1 para. 3(1).
379(1)	1993 s.138(1).

Provision	Derivation
(2) to (4)	1993 s.138(9) to (11).
380	1993 s.139.
381	1993 s.140.
382	1993 s.142.
383	1993 s.141.
384	1988 s.10(1).
385(1)	1988 s.6(1), (7).
(2)	1988 s.6(2).
(3)	1988 s.6(7).
(4)	1988 s.6(3); 1993 s.138(8); Law Com. Rec. No. 16.
(5)	1988 s.6(4).
(6)	1988 s.6(5); Law Com. Rec. No. 16.
(7)	1988 s.6(6).
386(1)	1988 s.7(1); 1993 s.138(1).
(2)	1988 s.7(1); 1993 s.138(2).
(3)	1988 s.7(2); 1993 s.138(3).
(4)	1988 s.7(3); 1993 s.138(4).
(5)	1988 s.7(4); 1993 s.138(5).
(6)	1988 s.7(5); 1993 s.138(6).
(7)	1993 s.138(12).
387	1988 s.7(6); 1993 s.138(7).
388	1988 s.10(1).
389(1)	1988 s.9(3).
(2)	1988 s.9(9).
(3)	1988 s.9(4).
(4)	1988 s.9(6).
(5)	1988 s.9(7); 1993 Sch. 19 para. 115.
(6)	1988 s.9(8).
(7)	1988 s.9(2), (5).
390(1)	1988 s.11(1).
(2)	1988 s.11(3), (4); 1993 s.147(1).
(3)	1988 ss.11(3), 13(4).
(4)	1988 s.11(4); 1993 Sch. 19 para. 116(a).
(5)	1988 s.11(5).
(6)	1988 s.11(5); 1993 s.255(2).
(7)	1988 s.11(6).
391(1)	1988 s.11(1).
(2)	1988 s.11(2).
(3)	1988 s.11(7).
(4)	1988 s.11(7).
(5)	1988 s.11(8).
(6)	1988 s.11(9).
(7)	1988 s.11(10).
(8), (9)	1988 s.11(11), (12); 1993 s.147(2).
(10)	1988 s.11(13); 1993 Sch. 15 para. 4(2), Sch. 19 para. 116(b).
392(1)	1988 s.11(1).
(2)	1988 s.13(1); 1993 Sch. 19 para. 117.
(3)	1988 s.13(2); 1993 Sch. 19 para. 117.
(4)	1988 s.13(3).
(5)	1988 s.13(4).
(6)	1988 s.13(5).
(7)	1988 s.13(6).
(8)	1988 s.13(7); 1993 Sch. 19 para. 117.
393	1993 s.16.
394(1)	1988 ss.11(1), 12(1); 1993 s.148(a).
(2), (3)	1988 s.12(2), (3).
(4)	1988 s.12(4); 1993 s.148(b).
(5)	1988 s.12(1).
(6)	1988 s.12(9); 1993 s.148(c).

Provision	Derivation
(7)	1988 s.12(10).
(8)	1988 s.12(11); 1993 s.148(d).
395(1)	1988 s.12(5).
(2)	1988 s.12(6).
(3), (4)	1988 s.12(7).
(5)	1988 s.12(8).
(6)	1988 s.12(5), (6).
(7)	1988 s.12(9); 1993 s.148(c).
(8)	1988 s.12(10).
396(1)	1988 s.12A(1), (3); 1993 s.257.
(2)	1988 s.12A(2); 1993 s.257.
397	1993 s.258.
398	1988 s.9(1), 9(1A); 1992FHE s.12(4); 1994 Sch. 2 para. 8(2).
399	1944 s.67(3); 1988 Sch. 1 para. 4, Sch. 12 para. 4.
400(1), (2)	1988 s.5(1).
(3)	1988 s.5(2).
(4)	1988 s.10(2).
(5)	1988 s.5(3).
401(1)	1988 s.24(1); 1992FHE Sch. 8 para. 28.
(2)	1988 s.24(2); 1993 Sch. 19 para. 124.
(3), (4)	1988 s.24(3), (4).
(5)	1988 s.235(2)(c).
402(1)	1988 s.117(1).
(2)	1988 s.117(2); 1993 s.240(5).
(3) to (5)	1988 s.117(3) to (5).
(6)	1988 s.118(7), (8).
403(1)	1986 ss.46, 46A; 1988 Sch. 12 para. 34.
(2)	1986 s.46.
404(1), (2)	1993 s.241(5).
(3)	1993 s.241(6).
405	1988 s.17A; 1993 s.241(3).
406(1), (2)	1986 ss.44(1), (2), 46A; 1988 Sch. 12 para. 34.
(3)	1986 s.44(1).
407(1)	1986 ss.45, 46A; 1988 Sch. 12 para. 34.
(2)	1986 s.45.
408(1)	1988 s.22(1).
(2)	1988 s.22(2); 1992(S) Sch. 4 para. 6(2).
(3)	1988 s.22(3); 1993 Sch. 19 para. 123.
(4)	1988 s.22(1); Law Com. Rec. No. 17.
(5)	1988 s.22(4).
(6)	1988 s.22(5); 1992(S) Sch. 4 para. 6(3), (4).
(7), (8)	1988 s.22(6), (7).
409(1) to (3)	1988 s.23(1).
(4)	1988 s.23(2).
410	1988 s.25(2); Law Com. Rec. No. 17.
411(1), (2)	1980 s.6(1), (2).
(3)	1980 s.6(3); 1988 s.30(2).
(4)	1980 s.6(4).
(5)	1980 s.6(5); 1978IA s.17(2)(a).
(6)	1988 s.26(9).
(7)	1988 s.26(10).
(8)	1980 s.38(4).
412	1986 s.33.
413(1)	1980 s.6(6); 1988 s.30(3).
(2) to (4)	1980 s.6(7) to (9); 1993 s.270.
414(1), (2)	1980 s.8(1), (2).
(3), (4)	1980 s.8(3); 1988 s.31(2).
(5)	1980 s.8(4).
(6) to (8)	1980 s.8(5), (5A), (6); 1992(S) Sch. 4 para. 4(1).

Provision	Derivation
(9)	1980 s.8(7).
415	Drafting.
416(1)	1988 s.26(1).
(2) to (7)	1988 s.26(3) to (8).
(8)	1988 s.26(1), (3), (4).
417(1)	1988 ss.27(1), (2), 32(4).
(2), (3)	1988 s.27(3).
(4), (5)	1988 s.27(9).
418(1)	1988 ss.27(1), (2), 32(4); Education Reform Act 1988 (Commencement No. 9) Order 1991 (S.I. 1991/409).
(2)	1988 s.27(3).
(3)	1988 s.27(3), (9).
419(1)	1988 s.29(7).
(2) to (5)	1988 s.29(1) to (4).
420(1) to (3)	1988 s.27(4) to (6).
(4), (5)	1988 s.27(7).
421(1)	1988 s.27(8).
(2)	1988 s.32(1).
422(1) to (6)	1986 Sch. 2 para. 19.
(7)	1986 s.65(1) ("promoters"), Sch. 2 para. 1; drafting; Law Com. Rec. No. 9.
423(1)	1980 s.7(1); 1993 Sch. 19 para. 73.
(2), (3)	1980 s.7(2), (3).
(4)	1980 s.7(4).
(5)	1980 s.7(5).
(6)	1980 s.38(4).
424(1)	1980 s.9(1); 1988 s.31(3).
(2)	1980 s.9(1A); 1988 s.31(3).
(3)	1980 s.9(2); 1981 Sch. 3 para. 14; 1992(S) Sch. 4 para. 4(2); 1993 Sch. 19 para. 74.
425	Drafting.
426	1993 s.149(1) to (4).
427	1993 s.150.
428	1993 s.151.
429	Drafting.
430(1) to (8)	1993 s.260.
(9)	1993 s.305(1) ("maintained school").
431(1) to (6)	1993 s.13(1) to (6).
(7), (8)	1993 ss.13(7), (8), 305(1) ("maintained school").
432	1993 s.14.
433(1), (2)	1948 s.4(2).
(3)	1948 s.4(3).
(4)	1948 s.4(3A); 1996N Sch. 3 para. 2.
(5)	1948 s.4(2).
434(1)	1944 s.80(1).
(2)	1944 s.80(1A); 1988 Sch. 12 para. 58.
(3)	1948 s.4(6).
(4)	1944 s.80(1); 1993 Sch. 19 para. 21.
(5)	1944 s.114(1); 1993 s.155(1), Sch. 19 para. 24(a)(ii).
(6)	1944 s.80(2).
435	1948 s.4(1).
436(1)	1980 s.9(1A); 1988 ss.29(5), 31(3); 1993 s.155(6).
(2)	1988 s.29(5), (6); 1993 s.149(5).
437(1) to (7)	1993 s.192(1) to (7).
(8)	1993 ss.192(8), 197(6), 198(4), 305(1) ("maintained school").
438	1993 s.193.
439	1993 s.194.
440	1993 s.195.
441	1993 s.196.
442	1993 s.197(1) to (5).

Provision	Derivation
443(1) to (3)	1993 s.198(1) to (3).
(4)	1993 s.201(2).
444(1) to (4)	1993 s.199(1) to (4).
(5)	1993 s.199(5); Units of Measurement Regulations 1995 (S.I. 1995/1804) Reg. 3.
(6), (7)	1993 s.199(6), (7).
(8)	1993 s.201(2).
(9)	1993 s.199(8).
445	1993 s.200.
446	1993 s.201(1).
447	1993 s.202.
448	1993 s.203.
449	1988 s.118(7).
450(1)	1988 s.106(1).
(2)	1988 s.106(1A); 1992FHE s.12(9); 1994 Sch. 2 para. 8(3).
451(1), (2)	1988 s.106(2).
(3)	1988 s.106(3), (4); 1993 s.280.
(4)	1988 s.106(4).
(5)	1988 s.106(3), (4); 1993 Sch. 19 para. 127.
452(1) to (4)	1988 s.107(1) to (4).
(5)	1988 s.107(5), (6).
(6)	1988 s.106(9).
453(1)	1988 s.106(5).
(2), (3)	1988 s.108.
454(1)	1988 s.106(6).
(2)	1988 s.118(3).
(3), (4)	1988 s.106(7), (8).
455(1)	1988 s.109(1).
(2)	1988 s.109(2).
(3)	1988 ss.109(2), 110(5).
456(1)	1988 s.109(3); 1978IA s.17(2)(a).
(2) to (8)	1988 s.109(4) to (10).
457(1)	1988 s.110(1); 1993 Sch. 19 para. 128.
(2), (3)	1988 s.110(2).
(4)	1988 s.110(3); Disability Living Allowance and Disability Working Allowance Act 1991 (c.21) Sch. 3 para. 12; Jobseekers Act 1995 (c.18) Sch. 2 para. 17.
(5)	1988 s.110(4).
458(1) to (4)	1988 s.111(1) to (3) and (5); 1993 Sch. 19 para. 129.
(5)	1988 s.111(6).
459	1988 s.118(5).
460(1), (2)	1988 s.118(1), (2).
(3)	1988 s.118(4).
461	1988 s.118(6).
462(1)	1988 s.118(7)(a), (e).
(2)	1988 s.106(10).
(3)	1988 s.106(11).
(4)	1988 s.118(7)(d).
(5)	1988 s.118(7)(d), (8).
463	1944 s.114(1) ("independent school"); 1980 s.34(1); 1988 Sch. 12 para. 7.
464(1) to (3)	1944 s.70(1); Transfer of Functions (Education and Employment) Order 1995 (S.I. 1995/2986) art. 11(2).
(4)	Drafting.
465(1)	1944 s.70(1).
(2)	1944 s.70(1) proviso (a).
(3)	1944 s.70(1) proviso (b).
(4)	1944 s.114(1) ("provisionally registered school"; "registered school").
466(1)	1944 s.70(3).
(2)	1944 s.70(3A); 1980 s.34(6).

Provision	Derivation
(3)	1944 s.70(3).
467(1)	1944 s.70(4); 1980 s.34(7).
(2)	1944 s.70(4A); 1993 s.292(2).
(3)	1944 s.70(4); 1980 s.34(7).
(4)	Drafting.
468	1944 s.71(4); 1993 s.290(1).
469(1)	1944 s.71(1); Children Act 1989 (c.41) Sch. 13 para. 9; 1993 s.290(2).
(2), (3)	1944 s.71(1).
(4)	1944 s.71(2); 1993 s.290(2).
(5)	1944 s.71(3).
(6)	1944 s.71(5); 1993 s.290(1).
470(1)	1944 s.72(1).
(2)	1944 s.72(2); 1993 s.290(2).
471(1)	1944 s.72(3).
(2)	1944 s.72(3) proviso; 1993 s.290(2).
472	1944 s.72(4); 1993 s.290(2).
473(1)	1944 s.73(2).
(2)	1944 s.73(3); 1993 s.290(2).
474	1944 s.74.
475	1944 s.73(1).
476(1)	Drafting.
(2), (3)	1944 s.75(1).
(4)	1944 s.75(2); Arbitration Act 1996 (c.23) Sch. 3 para. 4.
(5)	1944 s.75(3).
477	1944 s.73(5); 1946 Sch. 2 Pt. I; 1978IA s.17(2)(a).
478(1)	1944 s.73(4).
(2)	1944 ss.70(3), 73(2), (3); Criminal Justice Act 1982 (c.48) Sch. 3.
479(1) to (3)	1980 s.17(1) to (3).
(4)	1980 s.17(2).
(5)	1980 s.17(4), (5).
(6), (7)	1980 s.17(10).
480(1), (2)	1980 s.17(6), (7).
(3)	1980 s.17(9).
(4)	1980 s.17(8), (9).
481	1980 s.18.
482(1)	1988 s.105(1).
(2)	1988 s.105(2).
(3)	1988 s.105(1), (2).
(4)	1988 s.105(3).
(5)	1988 s.218(2B); 1993 s.291; 1994 Sch. 2 para. 8(4).
483(1), (2)	1988 s.105(4).
(3), (4)	1988 s.105(5), (6).
484(1)	1984 s.1(1), (2); 1993 s.278(2).
(2)	1984 s.1(2), (6).
(3), (4)	1984 s.1(3), (4); 1993 s.278(2).
(5)	1984 s.1(5).
(6)	1984 s.1(7).
(7)	Drafting.
485	1944 s.100(1)(b); 1988 s.213(3).
486	1988 s.213(1); Transfer of Functions (Science) Order 1995 (S.I. 1995/2985) Sch. para. 5.
487	1980 s.21(1).
488	1988 s.210.
489(1)	1944 s.100(3); 1980 s.21(2); 1984 s.1(4); 1988 ss.210(3), 213(2).
(2)	1984 s.1(4A); 1993 s.278(4).
(3), (4)	1973 s.1(2).
490	1988 s.211; 1978IA s.17(2)(a).
491(1)	1944 s.100(1)(c).
(2)	1944 s.100(3).

Provision	Derivation
492(1) to (4)	1986 s.51(1) to (4); 1993 s.279(1).
(5)	1986 s.51(11); 1993 Sch. 19 para. 103(d).
(6)	1986 s.51(7), (8); 1993 Sch. 19 para. 103(a).
493(1)	1986 s.52(1); 1992FHE Sch. 8 para. 25.
(2)	1986 s.52(2); 1993 Sch. 19 para. 104.
(3)	1986 s.52(3); 1992FHE Sch. 8 para. 25.
(4)	1986 s.52(4).
494	1993 s.262.
495(1), (2)	1944 s.67(1).
(3)	1944 s.67(2).
496(1)	1944 s.68.
(2)	1944 s.68; 1988 s.219(2).
497(1)	1944 s.99(1).
(2)	1944 s.99(1); 1988 s.219(3).
(3)	1944 s.99(1).
498(1)	1944 s.99(2)
(2)	1944 s.99(2); 1988 s.219(3).
499	1993 s.297.
500	1993 s.232.
501	1993 s.233.
502	1993 s.234.
503(1) to (6)	1993 s.235(1) to (6).
(7)	1993 s.235(8).
504	1993 s.236.
505(1) to (7)	1993 s.237(1) to (7).
(8)	1993 ss.237(8), 305((1) ("maintained school").
506	1944 s.69(2); Criminal Justice Act 1967 (c.80) Sch. 3; 1978IA s.17(2)(a); Medical Act 1983 (c.54) Sch. 6 para. 11.
507(1)	1944 s.93.
(2)	1944 s.93; 1972LG s.272(2); 1993 s.235(7).
508(1)	1944 s.53(1).
(2)	1944 s.53(1); 1948 Sch. 1 Pt. I; 1988 Sch. 12 para. 54.
(3)	1944 s.53(2).
509(1), (2)	1944 s.55(1); 1992FHE Sch. 8 para. 5.
(3)	1944 s.55(2); 1948 Sch. 1 Pt. I; 1988 Sch. 12 para. 55; 1992FHE Sch. 8 para. 5.
(4)	1944 s.55(3); 1986 s.53; 1992FHE Sch. 8 para. 5; 1993 Sch. 19 para. 15.
(5)	1944 s.55(4); 1992FHE Sch. 8 para. 5.
(6)	1944 s.55(5); 1992FHE Sch. 8 para. 5.
510(1)	1948 s.5(1); 1988 s.100(4).
(2)	1948 s.5(1); 1953 Sch. 1; 1981 Sch. 3 para. 7.
(3)	1948 s.5(2); 1988 s.100(4).
(4)	1948 s.5(3); 1980 s.29(1); 1988 s.100(4), Sch. 12 para. 61; 1992FHE Sch. 8 para. 16.
(5)	1948 s.5(4); 1988 s.100(4).
(6)	1948 s.5(4).
511(1)	1948 s.5(5).
(2), (3)	1948 s.5(6).
(4)	1948 s.5(6A); 1980 s.29(2).
512(1)	1980 s.22(1); Social Security Act 1986 (c.50) s.77(1).
(2)	1980 s.22(2); Social Security Act 1986 (c.50) s.77(2).
(3)	1980 s.22(3); Social Security Act 1986 (c.50) s.77(2); Jobseekers Act 1995 (c.18) Sch. 2 para. 3.
(4)	1980 s.22(1).
(5)	1980 s.22(3B); 1992FHE Sch. 8 para. 17.
513	1944 s.78(2).
514(1)	1944 s.50(1); 1946 Sch. 2 Pt. I; 1981 Sch. 3 para. 3; 1988 s.100(2).
(2)	1944 s.50(1); 1948 Sch. 1 Pt. I; 1981 Sch. 3 para. 3.
(3)	1944 s.50(2); 1946 Sch. 2 Pt. I; 1993 Sch. 19 para. 12.
(4)	1944 s.52(1).

Provision	Derivation
(5)	1944 s.52(1) proviso; 1981 Sch. 3 para. 4.
(6)	1944 s.52(2).
(7)	1944 s.52(3).
515(1)	1980 s.26(1).
(2)	1980 s.26(3).
(3)	1980 s.26(4).
(4)	1980 s.26(5); 1978IA s.17(2)(a).
(5)	1980 s.26(6).
516	1993 s.295.
517(1)	1953 s.6(2); 1993 Sch. 19 para. 31(a).
(2)	1953 s.6(2)(a)(i).
(3)	1953 s.6(2)(a)(ii); 1981 Sch. 3 para. 8.
(4)	1953 s.6(2)(a)(iii).
(5)	1953 s.6(2)(b); 1981 Sch. 3 para. 8.
(6)	1993 Sch. 19 para. 31(b) to (f).
(7)	1993 s.308(3).
518	1944 s.81; 1988 Sch. 12 para. 6; 1992FHE Sch. 8 para. 11.
519(1)	1986 s.58(1); 1988 Sch. 12 para. 103; 1993 Sch. 19 para. 106.
(2)	1986 s.58(2).
(3)	1986 s.58(5); 1988 Sch. 12 para. 103.
(4), (5)	1986 s.58(6).
(6)	1986 s.58(7).
520(1), (2)	1944 s.48(4); 1973NHSR Sch. 4 para. 7; National Health Service Act 1977 (c.49) Sch. 15 para. 2; 1978IA s.17(2)(a).
(3)	Drafting.
521(1), (2)	1944 s.54(1).
(3)	1944 s.54(2), (8); Medical Act 1983 (c.54) Sch. 6 para. 11.
(4)	1944 s.54(1); 1993 Sch. 19 para. 14(a).
522(1)	1944 s.54(2).
(2) to (4)	1944 s.54(3).
(5)	1944 s.54(5).
523(1), (2)	1944 s.54(4); S.I. 1968/1699 art. 5; 1972LG s.179(3).
(3)	1944 s.54(9); 1994LG(W) Sch. 16 para. 8.
(4)	1944 s.54(8); Medical Act 1983 (c.54) Sch. 6 para. 11.
524(1), (2)	1944 s.54(7).
(3)	1944 s.54(7); 1993 Sch. 19 para. 14(c).
525(1)	1944 s.54(6).
(2)	1944 s.54(6).
(3)	1944 s.54(6); 1993 Sch. 19 para. 14(b).
526	1944 s.82.
527	1944 s.83.
528	1944 s.41(2A), (2B); Disability Discrimination Act 1995 (c.50) s.30(8).
529(1)	1944 s.85(1).
(2), (3)	1944 s.85(2), (3); 1980 Sch. 3 para. 3.
530(1)	1944 s.90(1); Acquisition of Land (Authorisation Procedure) Act 1946 (c.49) Sch. 4; 1948 s.10(1); 1988 Sch. 12 para. 59.
(2)	1944 s.90(1) proviso; Acquisition of Land (Authorisation Procedure) Act 1946 (c.49) Sch. 4.
(3)	1944 s.90(1A); 1993 s.282(3).
531(1)	1948 s.10(2); 1972LG s.272(2); 1988 Sch. 12 para. 62.
(2)	1948 s.10(3).
532	1944 s.88; 1978IA s.17(2)(a).
533(1), (2)	1980 s.22(4).
(3)	1980 s.22(4A); 1993 Sch. 19 para. 79.
534(1) to (4)	1980 s.22(3A); 1988 Sch. 12 para. 24.
(5)	1980 s.22(3B); 1992FHE Sch. 8 para. 17.
535(1)	1980 s.26(2).
(2)	1980 s.26(3).
(3)	1980 s.26(4).

Provision	Derivation
(4)	1980 s.26(5); 1978IA s.17(2)(a).
(5)	1980 s.26(6).
536(1), (2)	1944 s.48(4); 1973NHSR Sch. 4 para. 7; National Health Service Act 1977 (c.49) Sch. 15 para. 2; 1978IA s.17(2)(a); 1988 Sch. 12 para. 2.
537(1) to (6)	1992(S) s.16(1) to (6).
(7)	1992(S) s.16(7); 1993 s.263.
(8) to (10)	1992(S) s.16(8) to (10).
(11)	1992(S) s.19(2).
(12), (13)	1992(S) s.16(11), (12).
538	1986 s.56, Sch. 2 para. 13(2).
539	1993 s.153.
540(1)	1993 s.264(1).
(2)	1993 ss.264(2), 305(1) ("maintained school").
541(1) to (3)	1993 s.265.
(4)	1993 ss.265(1), 305(1) ("maintained school").
542(1)	1944 s.10(1); 1988 Sch. 12 para. 1.
(2) to (4)	1944 s.10(2); 1988 Sch. 12 para. 1.
543	1944 s.10(2) proviso; 1948 s.7(1); 1968 s.3(3).
544(1)	1988 s.218(7); 1992FHE Sch. 8 para. 49; 1993 Sch. 19 para. 136.
(2)	1988 s.218(7).
(3)	1988 s.218(12).
545(1)	1944 s.63(2); 1993 Sch. 19 para. 18.
(2)	1988 s.218(8); 1993 Sch. 19 para. 19.
546(1)	1988 s.218(1)(e).
(2)	1988 s.218(12).
547(1)	1982LG(MP) s.40(1).
(2)	1982LG(MP) s.40(2); 1988 Sch. 12 para. 29.
(3)	1982LG(MP) s.40(3).
(4), (5)	1982LG(MP) s.40(4), (5); 1988 Sch. 12 para. 29.
(6)	1982LG(MP) s.40(6).
(7), (8)	1982LG(MP) s.40(7), (8); Sch. 12 para. 29.
548(1)	1986 s.47(1); 1993 s.293(2).
(2)	1986 s.47(1A); 1993 s.293(2).
(3)	1986 s.47(5); 1988 Sch. 12 para. 35; 1993 s.293(3), Sch. 19 para. 101(a).
(4)	1986 s.47(6); 1993 Sch. 19 para. 101(b).
(5)	1986 s.47(7).
(6)	1986 s.47(4).
549(1), (2)	1986 s.47(2), (3).
(3)	1986 s.47(1B); 1993 s.293(2).
(4)	1986 s.47(10).
(5)	1986 s.47(5); 1993 s.293(3).
550	1986 s.47(8).
551(1)	1988 s.218(1)(g).
(2)	1988 s.218(12).
552(1)	1993 Sch. 19 para. 62(5).
(2), (3)	1993 Sch. 19 para. 62(2), (3).
(4)	1993 Sch. 19 para. 62(1).
(5)	1993 Sch. 19 para. 62(4).
(6)	1993 Sch. 19 para. 62(6).
553	1988 s.113.
554(1)	1973 s.2(1); 1988 s.112(2).
(2)	1973 s.2(1); 1988 s.112(2); 1993 Sch. 19 para. 52(a).
(3)	1973 s.2(1A); 1988 s.112(2); 1993 Sch. 19 para. 52(b).
(4)	1973 s.2(1C); 1988 s.112(2); 1993 Sch. 19 para. 52(c).
(5)	1973 s.2(1B); 1988 s.112(2).
(6)	1973 s.2(8).
555(1)	1973 s.2(2); 1993 Sch. 19 para. 52(c).
(2) to (4)	1973 s.2(2).
(5)	1973 s.2(1B); 1988 s.112(2).

Provision	Derivation
556(1)	1973 s.2(3); 1993 s.288(3).
(2)	1973 s.2(4); 1988 s.112(3); 1993 Sch. 19 para. 52(c).
(3)	1973 s.2(4); 1993 s.288(2), Sch. 19 para. 52(c).
(4)	1973 s.2(5).
(5)	1973 s.2(5A); 1993 s.288(4).
(6), (7)	1973 s.2(6), (7).
(8)	1973 s.2(1B); 1988 s.112(2).
557	1993 s.287.
558	1944 s.58.
559(1), (2)	1944 s.59(1), (2).
(3), (4)	1944 s.59(3).
(5)	1944 s.59(4).
(6)	Employment of Children Act 1973 (c.24) s.3(4).
560(1)	1973EWE s.1(1); 1988 Sch. 12 para. 14.
(2)	1973EWE s.1(4); Employment Act 1990 (c.38) s.14.
(3)	1973EWE s.1(2); Merchant Shipping Act 1995 (c.21) Sch. 13 para. 48.
(4), (5)	1973EWE s.1(3).
(6)	Drafting.
(7)	1973EWE s.1(4).
561	1944 s.115.
562	1944 s.116; 1948 Sch. 1 Pt. I; 1993 Sch. 19 para. 25.
563(1)	1988 s.218(1)(f); 1992FHE Sch. 8 para. 49.
(2)	1988 s.218(4).
(3)	1988 s.218(12).
564(1)	1944 s.94(1); S.I. 1968/1699 art. 5; Registration of Births, Deaths and Marriages (Fees) Order 1995 (S.I. 1995/3162) Sch.
(2)	1944 s.94(1).
(3)	1944 s.94(2); S.I. 1968/1699 art. 5.
(4)	1944 s.94(3); 1978IA s.17(2)(a).
565(1)	1944 s.95(1).
(2)	1993 s.200(3).
566	1944 s.95(2).
567(1), (2)	1993 s.299(1), (2).
(3)	1993 ss.299(3), 305(1) ("maintained school").
(4), (5)	1993 s.299(4), (5).
568(1)	1973 s.2(1); 1986 s.63(1); 1988 s.232(1); 1993 s.301(1); Law Com. Rec. No. 19.
(2)	1986 ss.4A(8), 63(1); 1988 s.232(2); 1993 ss.271(1), 301(2).
(3)	1986 s.63(2); 1988 s.232(4); 1993 s.301(3).
(4)	1988 s.232(3).
(5)	1986 s.63(3); 1988 s.232(5); 1993 s.301(6); Law Com. Rec. No. 18.
(6)	1988 s.232(6); Law Com. Rec. No. 18.
569(1)	Statutory Instruments Act 1946 (c.36) s.1(2); 1948 s.12; 1980 s.35(1); 1984 s.3(1); 1986 s.63(1); 1988 s.232(1); 1992(S) s.19(1); 1993 s.301(1); Law Com. Rec. No. 18.
(2)	1944 s.112; Statutory Instruments Act 1946 (c.36) s.5(2); 1948 s.12; 1980 s.35(3); 1984 s.3(3); 1986 s.63(2); 1988 s.232(4); 1992(S) s.19(2); 1993 ss.279(2)(a), 301(3).
(3)	1980 s.35(2); 1986 s.63(2A); 1993 ss.279(2)(b), 301(4).
(4)	1980 s.35(4); 1984 s.3(4); 1986 s.63(3); 1988 s.232(5); 1992(S) s.19(3); 1993 s.301(6), Sch. 19 para. 107(a); Law Com. Rec. No. 18.
(5)	1944 s.111A; 1980 s.35(5); 1988 ss.229(1), 232(6); Law Com. Rec. No. 18.
(6)	1980 s.35(5).
570(1), (2)	1944 s.111; S.I. 1968/1699 art. 5; 1993 s.301(7).
(3)	1944 s.111 proviso.
571	1980 ss.12(1B), 13(1C); 1988 s.34(3); 1993 ss.229(1), 230(1), 300.
572	1944 s.113; 1946 Sch. 2 Pt. I.
573(1)	Drafting.

Provision	Derivation
(2)	1944 s.114(1) ("alterations"); 1968 Sch. 1 para. 5(a); 1993 s.305(1).
(3)	1944 s.114(1) ("enlargement"); 1968 Sch. 1 para. 5(b).
(4)	1980 s.16(2); 1993 s.103(1).
(5)	1944 s.114(1) ("significant"); 1968 Sch. 1 para. 5(c).
(6)	1944 s.67(4); 1968 Sch. 1 para. 3; 1988 Sch. 12 para. 4.
574	1968 s.1(1); 1980 Sch. 3 para. 15; 1993 Sch. 19 para. 41.
575(1), (2)	1988 s.235(1); 1993 s.305(1); 1996ER Sch. 1 paras. 37(5), 59.
(3)	1988 s.235(3); 1933 s.155(9), (10).
(4)	1988 s.235(1); 1993 s.305(1) 1996ER Sch. 1 paras. 37(5), 59.
576(1)	1944 s.114(1D); Children Act 1989 (c.41) Sch. 13 para. 10.
(2)	1944 s.114(1E); Children Act 1989 (c.41) Sch. 13 para. 10; 1993 Sch. 19 para. 24(b).
(3), (4)	1944 s.114(1F); Children Act 1989 (c.41) Sch. 13 para. 10.
577	1944 s.114 ("minor authority"); 1972LG s.192(4); Local Government Changes for England (Education) (Miscellaneous Provisions) Regulations 1996 (S.I. 1996/710) reg. 19.
578	1992FHE s.90(1) ("the Education Acts"); 1993 s.305(1) ("the Education Acts"); 1996N Sch. 3 para. 8.
579(1)	"boarder": 1986 s.65(1). "child": 1944 s.114(1). "clothing": 1944 s.114(1). "exclude": 1986 s.65(1). "financial year": 1984 s.1(6); 1988 s.235(1), Sch. 2 para. 18; 1993 s.305(1), Sch. 14 para. 20. "functions": 1988 s.235(1); 1993 s.305(1). "governing body"; "governor": 1944 s.114(1); 1980 Sch. 1 para. 13. "higher education": 1944 s.114(1); 1988 s.120(9). "land": 1988 s.235(1); 1993 s.306(1). "liability": 1988 s.235(1); 1993 s.305(1). "local authority": 1988 s.235; 1993 s.305(1); 1994LG(W) Sch. 16 paras. 83, 105(2). "the local education authority": 1944 s.114(1); 1988 s.118(7)(b); 1993 s.305(1). "local government elector": 1944 s.114(1); 1972LG s.272(2). "medical officer": 1944 s.114(1); 1973NHSR Sch. 4 para. 8; Medical Act 1983 (c.54) Sch. 6 para. 11. "modifications": 1988 s.235(1); 1993 s.305(1). "premises": 1944 s.114(1). "prescribed": 1944 s.114(1); 1993 s.305(1). "proprietor": 1944 ss.80(1), 114(1); 1988 Sch. 12 para. 5. "reception class": 1980 s.38(5A)(b); 1988 ss.31(6), 119(1)(b); 1993 s.155(1). "relevant age group": 1980 s.16(3); 1988 s.32(2); 1993 s.155(4). "school buildings": 1946 s.4(2); 1973NHSR Sch. 4 para. 9; National Health Service Act 1977 (c.49) Sch. 15 para. 3; 1978IA s.17(2)(a). "school day": 1986 s.65(1). "trust deed": 1944 s.114(1). "young person": 1944 s.114(1).
(2)	1988 s.235(3)(g); 1993 s.305(2).
(3)	1980 s.38(5A); 1988 ss.31(6), 119(1)(a); 1993 s.155(5).
(4)	1980 s.38(5); 1986 s.51(10); 1993 Sch. 19 para. 103.
(5)	1944 s.114(2)(b).
(6)	1944 s.114(2)(b); 1988 s.234(2)(a), (3)(a).
(7)	1944 s.114(2A); 1988 s.234(2)(b); 1992FHE Sch. 8 para. 13(4).
580	—
581	1944 s.118; S.I. 1977/293 art. 4; Law Com. Rec. No. 19.
582	—
583	—
Sch. 1	1993 Sch. 18.
Sch. 2	
para. 1	1993 Sch. 1 para. 16.

Provision	Derivation
paras. 2 to 8	1993 Sch. 1 paras. 1 to 7.
para. 9	1993 Sch. 19 para. 46 to 48.
paras. 10 to 14	1993 Sch. 1 paras. 8 to 12.
para. 15	1993 Sch. 1 para. 15.
paras. 16, 17	1993 Sch. 1 paras. 13, 14.
Sch. 3	
para. 1	1993 s.17; 1996N Sch. 3 para. 10.
para. 2	1993 s.18.
para. 3	1993 s.19.
Sch. 4	
para. 1	1993 Sch. 2 para. 1, s.305(1) ("maintained school").
paras. 2 to 23	1993 Sch. 2 paras. 2 to 23.
Sch. 5	
para. 1	—
para. 2	1944 Sch. 3 para. 8.
para. 3	1944 Sch. 3 paras. 4, 5; 1948 Sch. 1, Pt. I; 1980 Sch. 3 para. 5.
para. 4	1944 Sch. 3 para. 7; drafting.
para. 5	1944 Sch. 3 para. 9.
para. 6	1944 Sch. 3 para. 10.
Sch. 6	1944 Sch. 2.
Sch. 7	
para. 1	1993 s.238(5) to (7).
para. 2	1993 s.239.
para. 3	1993 Sch. 13 para. 2.
para. 4	1993 Sch. 13 para. 1.
para. 5	1993 Sch. 13 para. 3.
paras. 6 to 10	1993 Sch. 3 paras. 8 to 12.
paras. 11, 12	1993 Sch. 13 paras. 14, 15.
Sch. 8	
para. 1	Drafting.
para. 2	1986 ss.6, 15(12), (13); drafting.
para. 3	1986 s.15(11).
para. 4	1986 s.15(7).
para. 5	1986 s.15(1).
para. 6	1986 s.15(8).
para. 7	Drafting; 1986 s.15(2) to (6), (15).
para. 8	1986 s.15(14).
para. 9	1986 s.15(10).
para. 10	1986 ss.8(6), (9), 15(9).
para. 11	1986 s.8(2), (3); 1993 s.271(2).
para. 12	1986 s.8(4).
para. 13	1986 s.8(5).
para. 14	1986 s.8(1).
para. 15	1986 s.8(6), (7), (9); 1988 s.116; drafting.
para. 16	1986 s.8(11), (12); Law Com. Rec. Nos. 3, 20.
para. 17	1986 s.8(8).
para. 18	1986 s.62.
para. 19	Drafting.
para. 20	1986 s.57.
para. 21	1986 s.8(10).
Sch. 9	
para. 1	1986 s.65(1) ("promoters"), Sch. 2 para. 1; Law Com. Rec. No. 9.
para. 2	1986 Sch. 2 para. 2(1), (2); 1993 Sch. 19 para. 109(a), (b)(i).
para. 3	1986 Sch. 2 para. 6.
para. 4	1986 Sch. 2 para. 7(1).
para. 5	1986 Sch. 2 para. 8(1).
para. 6	1986 Sch. 2 para. 7(2) to (5).
para. 7	1986 Sch. 2 paras. 7(6), (7), 8(2).
para. 8	1986 Sch. 2 para. 9(1), (2); 1993 Sch. 19 para. 109(e).

Provision	Derivation
para. 9	1986 Sch. 2 paras. 2(3), 11(4), (5).
para. 10	1986 Sch. 2 para. 11(3).
para. 11	1986 Sch. 2 para. 11(6).
para. 12	1986 Sch. 2 para. 11(1), (2).
para. 13	1986 Sch. 2 para. 10(4).
para. 14	1986 Sch. 2 para. 10(2).
para. 15	1986 Sch. 2 paras. 10(1), 26(3).
para. 16	1986 Sch. 2 para. 10(4).
para. 17	1986 Sch. 2 para. 2(4).
para. 18	1986 Sch. 2 para. 10(3).
para. 19	1986 Sch. 2 para. 27.
para. 20	1986 Sch. 2 para. 28.
para. 21	1986 Sch. 2 para. 30(1).
para. 22	1986 Sch. 2 para. 29.
Sch. 10	
para. 1	1986 Sch. 2 para. 3(4).
para. 2	1986 Sch. 2 para. 3(5).
para. 3	1986 Sch. 2 para. 4.
para. 4	1986 Sch. 2 para. 13(3), (4).
para. 5	1986 Sch. 2 paras. 2(2), 3(2), (3); 1993 Sch. 19 para. 109(b)(i).
para. 6	1986 Sch. 2 para. 13(3), (5).
Sch. 11	
para. 1	Drafting.
para. 2	1988 ss.33(6), 42(4)(a) to (d).
para. 3	1988 s.42(4)(e), (5)(a).
para. 4	1988 s.42(4)(j).
paras. 5 to 7	1988 s.50(5); 51(1) ("expenditure of a capital nature").
para. 8	1988 s.50(10).
Sch. 12	
para. 1	1988 s.48(2) ("temporary governing body").
para. 2	1988 Sch. 4 para. 1(2)(a), (b).
para. 3	1988 Sch. 4 paras. 1(1), 2(1).
para. 4	1988 Sch. 4 para. 2(2) to (5).
para. 5	1988 Sch. 4 para. 2(6); S.I. 1991/1890; S.I. 1992/110.
para. 6	1988 Sch. 4 para. 2(8).
para. 7	1988 Sch. 4 para. 2(9).
para. 8	1988 Sch. 4 para. 3.
para. 9	1988 Sch. 4 para. 6.
para. 10	1988 Sch. 4 para. 5.
Sch. 13	
para. 1	1986 s.36(1).
para. 2	1986 s.36(2).
para. 3	1986 s.37.
para. 4	1986 s.39.
para. 5	1986 s.38(1), (2).
para. 6	1986 s.38(3).
para. 7	1986 s.38(4).
para. 8	1986 s.38(6).
para. 9	1986 s.38(5).
para. 10	1986 s.35(2).
para. 11(1), (2)	1986 s.41(1)(a).
(3)	1986 s.41(3).
(4) to (7)	1986 s.41(1)(b) to (e).
(8)	1986 s.41(3).
Sch. 14	
para. 1	1988 Sch. 3 paras. 1(1), (2), (6), 2(1), 4(1), 5(1), 6(1), 7(1), 8(1), 10(1), 11(3); 1978IA s.17(2)(a).
para. 2	1988 Sch. 3 para. 1(1).

Provision	Derivation
para. 3	1988 Sch. 3 para. 1(3).
para. 4	1988 Sch. 3 para. 1(4), (5), (12).
para. 5	1988 Sch. 3 para. 1(7).
para. 6	1988 Sch. 3 para. 1(8) to (10).
para. 7	1988 Sch. 3 para. 1(11), (13).
para. 8	1988 Sch. 3 para. 2(1).
para. 9	1988 Sch. 3 para. 2(2), (3).
para. 10	1988 Sch. 3 para. 2(4).
para. 11	1988 Sch. 3 para. 2(5).
para. 12	1988 Sch. 3 para. 2(6), (7).
para. 13	1988 Sch. 3 para. 2(8), (9).
para. 14	1988 Sch. 3 para. 2(10), (11).
para. 15	1988 Sch. 3 para. 2(12).
para. 16	1988 Sch. 3 para. 3(1) to (3).
para. 17	1988 Sch. 3 para. 3(4).
para. 18	1988 Sch. 3 para. 4(1) to (3), (5).
para. 19	1988 Sch. 3 para. 4(4).
para. 20	1988 Sch. 3 para. 5.
para. 21	1988 Sch. 3 para. 6.
para. 22	1988 Sch. 3 para. 7 .
para. 23	1988 Sch. 3 para. 8(1) to (3), (6).
para. 24	1988 Sch. 3 para. 8(4), (5).
para. 25	1988 Sch. 3 para. 8(7), (8).
para. 26	1988 Sch. 3 para. 8(9).
para. 27	1988 Sch. 3 para. 9; 1978IA s.17(2)(a).
para. 28	1988 Sch. 3 para. 10; 1993 Sch. 19 para. 142.
Sch. 15	
para. 1	1986 s.24.
para. 2	1986 s.24(a), (h); 1993 Sch. 13 para. 97.
para. 3	1986 s.24(b), (f), (g).
para. 4	1986 s.24(h).
para. 5	1986 s.24(b), (g).
para. 6	1986 s.24(d), (h).
para. 7	1986 s.24(h).
para. 8	1986 s.25.
para. 9	1986 s.25(a), (h).
para. 10	1986 s.25(b).
para. 11	1986 s.25(b), (g).
para. 12	1986 s.25(c), (h); 1993 Sch. 19 para. 98.
para. 13	1986 s.25(h).
para. 14	1993 Sch. 19 para. 99.
para. 15	Drafting.
Sch. 16	
para. 1	1986 Sch. 3 paras. 1, 2; S.I. 1994/2092.
para. 2	1986 Sch. 3 para. 3; S.I. 1994/2092.
para. 3	1986 Sch. 3 para. 3A; S.I. 1994/2092.
para. 4	1986 Sch. 3 para. 4; drafting.
para. 5	1986 Sch. 3 para. 16.
para. 6	1986 Sch. 3 para. 6.
para. 7	1986 Sch. 3 para. 6A; S.I. 1994/2092.
para. 8	1986 Sch. 3 para. 7; Education (No. 2) Act 1986 (Amendment) (No. 2) Order 1993 (S.I. 1993/2827) art. 2.
para. 9	1986 Sch. 3 para. 8; Education (No. 2) Act 1986 (Amendment) Order 1993 (S.I. 1993/2709) art. 2.
para. 10	1986 Sch. 3 para. 9; S.I. 1994/2092 art. 8.
para. 11	1986 Sch. 3 para. 13.
para. 12	1986 Sch. 3 para. 14.
para. 13	1986 Sch. 3 para. 11.
para. 14	1986 Sch. 3 para. 12; S.I. 1994/2092 art. 9.

Provision	Derivation
para. 15	1986 Sch. 3 para. 15.
para. 16	1986 Sch. 3 para. 17; S.I. 1994/2092 art. 10.
para. 17	Drafting.
para. 18	1986 Sch. 3 para. 5.
Sch. 17	
para. 1	1986 s.30(2).
para. 2	1986 s.30(2)(a).
para. 3	1986 s.30(2)(b).
para. 4	1986 s.30(2)(c) to (e).
para. 5	1986 s.30(2)(g).
para. 6	1986 s.30(2)(h); 1988 s.51(9); Education (No. 2) Act 1986 (Amendment) Order 1994 (S.I. 1994/692) art. 2.
para. 7	1986 s.30(2)(i); Education (No. 2) Act 1986 (Amendment) (No. 3) Order 1994 (S.I. 1994/2732).
para. 8	1986 s.30(2)(j).
para. 9	1986 s.30(2)(k); 1978IA s.17(2)(a).
para. 10	1986 s.30(5); 1992(S) Sch. 4 para. 5.
Sch. 18	
para. 1	1986 s.31(4)(a).
para. 2	1986 s.31(4)(b), (9).
para. 3	1986 s.31(3).
para. 4	1986 s.31(4)(c), (d).
para. 5	1986 s.31(5), (6).
Sch. 19	
para. 1	1986 Sch. 2 paras. 4, 12(1).
para. 2	1988 Sch. 4 para. 7.
para. 3	1986 Sch. 2 para. 12(2).
para. 4	1986 Sch. 2 para. 12(3).
para. 5	1986 Sch. 2 para. 20(5).
para. 6	1986 Sch. 2 para. 21.
para. 7	1986 Sch. 2 para. 22.
para. 8	1986 Sch. 2 para. 23.
para. 9	1986 Sch. 2 para. 25.
para. 10	1986 Sch. 2 para. 24.
para. 11	1986 Sch. 2 para. 26(1), (2).
para. 12	1986 Sch. 2 para. 30(2).
para. 13	Drafting.
para. 14	1986 Sch. 2 para. 20(1).
para. 15	1986 Sch. 2 para. 20(2), (3); Law Com. Rec. No. 9.
para. 16	1986 Sch. 2 paras. 20(4), 30(3).
para. 17	1986 Sch. 2 para. 28.
para. 18	1988 Sch. 4 para. 1.
para. 19	1988 Sch. 4 para. 4(1), (4), (5).
para. 20	1988 Sch. 4 para. 4(2).
para. 21	1988 Sch. 4 para. 4(3); Education (Application of Financing Schemes to Special Schools) Regulations 1992 (S.I. 1992/164).
para. 22	1988 Sch. 4 para. 4(7).
para. 23	1988 Sch. 4 para. 4(8).
para. 24	1988 Sch. 4 para. 4(6).
para. 25	1986 Sch. 2 para. 15.
para. 26	1986 Sch. 2 para. 16; 1988 Sch. 12 para. 106.
para. 27	1986 Sch. 2 para. 17.
para. 28	1986 Sch. 2 paras. 13(1), 14.
para. 29	1986 Sch. 2 para. 18; 1988 Sch. 4 para. 2(10).
Sch. 20	
para. 1	1993 Sch. 3 para. 1(1) to (4); drafting.
paras. 2 to 12	1993 Sch. 3 paras. 2 to 12.
Sch. 21	1993 Sch. 4.

Provision	Derivation
Sch. 22	
paras. 1 to 13	1993 Sch. 5 paras. 1 to 13.
para. 14	1986 s.62; 1988 Sch. 12 para. 37.
paras. 15, 16	1993 Sch. 5 paras. 14, 15.
Sch. 23	
paras. 1 to 3	1993 Sch. 6 paras. 1 to 3.
para. 4	1993 Sch. 6 para. 7.
para. 5	1993 Sch. 6 paras. 4, 6.
para. 6	1993 Sch. 6 paras. 5, 6.
paras. 7, 8	1993 Sch. 6 paras. 8, 9.
Sch. 24	1993 Sch. 7.
Sch. 25	1993 Sch. 8.
Sch. 26	1993 Sch. 9.
Sch. 27	1993 Sch. 10.
Sch. 28	
paras. 1 to 14	1993 Sch. 11, paras. 1 to 14.
para. 15	1993 s.261(1), (2), (5).
Sch. 29	
paras. 1 to 16	1993 Sch. 14 paras. 1 to 16.
para. 17	1993 Sch. 14 para. 17; 1993 Sch. 15 para. 6(2).
paras. 18 to 22	1993 Sch. 14 paras. 18 to 22.
Sch. 30	
paras. 1 to 5	1988 Sch. 2 paras. 2 to 6; 1993 Sch. 15 para. 4(6).
paras. 6, 7	1988 Sch. 2 para. 7; 1993 Sch. 15 para. 4(6).
para. 8	1988 Sch. 2 para. 8; 1993 Sch. 15 para. 4(6), Sch. 19 para. 141.
paras. 9, 10	1988 Sch. 2 para. 10; 1993 Sch. 15 para. 4(6).
para. 11	1988 Sch. 2 para. 11; 1993 s.249, Sch. 15 para. 4(6).
paras. 12, 13	1988 Sch. 2 paras. 12, 13; 1993 Sch. 15 para. 4(6).
para. 14	1988 Sch. 2 para. 13A; 1993 s.250, Sch. 15 para. 4(6).
paras. 15, 16	1988 Sch. 2 paras. 14, 15; 1993 Sch. 15 para. 4(6).
para. 17	1988 Sch. 2 para. 18; 1993 s.251(3), Sch. 15 para. 4(6).
paras. 18, 19	1988 Sch. 2 paras. 16, 17; 1993 Sch. 15 para. 4(6).
Sch. 31	
para. 1	1944 Sch. 5 para. 12(1), (3); 1993 s.256(1).
para. 2	1944 Sch. 5 para. 12(4); 1993 s.256(1).
para. 3	1988 s.11(8).
para. 4	1944 Sch. 5 paras. 2, 5; 1988 Sch. 1 para. 7; 1993 s.254(3), Sch. 19 para. 27.
paras. 5, 6	1944 Sch. 5 paras. 7, 8.
para. 7	1944 Sch. 5 para. 3; 1988 Sch. 1 para. 7; 1993 Sch. 19 para. 27.
paras. 8, 9	1944 Sch. 5 para. 4; 1993 Sch. 19 para. 27.
para. 10	1944 Sch. 5 para. 13; 1988 Sch. 1 para. 7; 1993 s.256(2).
para. 11	1993 s.146.
para. 12	1944 Sch. 5 paras. 10, 13(4); 1988 Sch. 1 para. 7.
para. 13	1944 Sch. 5 para. 11; 1988 Sch. 1 para. 7.
para. 14	1944 Sch. 5 para. 11.
para. 15	1993 s.15.
Sch. 32	
para. 1	1988 s.28(1).
para. 2	1988 s.28(2).
para. 3	1988 s.28(3), (4).
para. 4	1988 s.28(5).
para. 5	1988 ss.28(6), (7), 32(1).
para. 6	1988 s.28(8).
para. 7	1988 s.119(2), (3).
Sch. 33	
para. 1	1980 Sch. 2 para. 1; 1993 Sch. 16 para. 2.
para. 2	1980 Sch. 2 para. 2; 1993 Sch. 16 para. 3.
para. 3	1980 Sch. 2 para. 3.
para. 4	1980 Sch. 2 para. 4; Local Government and Housing Act 1989 (Commencement No. 11 and Savings) Order 1991 (S.I. 1991/344) Sch. para. 1.

Provision	Derivation
para. 5	1980 Sch. 2 para. 4A; 1993 Sch. 16 para. 4.
para. 6	1993 s.267.
para. 7	1993 s.268.
para. 8	Drafting.
paras. 9 to 11	1980 Sch. 2 paras. 5 to 7.
para. 12	1980 Sch. 2 para. 10.
para. 13	1980 Sch. 2 para. 8.
para. 14	1980 Sch. 2 para. 9.
para. 15	1980 Sch. 2 para. 11.
Sch. 34	
para. 1	1944 Sch. 6 para. 1.
para. 2	1944 Sch. 6 para. 2.
para. 3	1944 Sch. 6 paras. 3, 3A; Judicial Pensions and Retirement Act 1993 (c.8) Sch. 6 para. 51.
para. 4	1944 Sch. 6 para. 4.
para. 5	1976 s.6(1).
Sch. 35	
paras. 1 to 3	1980 Sch. 4 paras. 1 to 3.
para. 4	1980 Sch. 4 para. 4; 1986 s.47(9).
paras. 5, 6	1980 Sch. 4 paras. 5, 6.
Sch. 36	1993 Sch. 17.
Schs. 37, 38	—
Sch. 39	
para. 1	—
para. 2	1993 s.303.
para. 3	1944 s.2(1).
para. 4	1944 s.120(1).
paras. 5 to 9	—
para. 10(1)	—
(2)	1980 s.1(4).
para. 11	1986 Sch. 5 para. 1.
paras. 12 to 16	—
para. 17(1)	—
(2)	1993 s.274(3).
(3)	1993 s.274(5).
para. 18	Law Com. Rec. No. 12.
para. 19	S.I. 1996/951 art. 4.
paras. 20 to 23	—
para. 24	1993 Sch. 20 para. 1; S.I. 1993/3106 Sch. 2 paras. 8, 9.
para. 25	1993 Sch. 20 para. 1; S.I. 1993/3106 Sch. 2 para. 10.
para. 26	S.I. 1993/3106 para. 11.
para. 27	S.I. 1993/3106 Sch. 2 para. 14.
para. 28	1993 Sch. 20 para. 5.
para. 29	1993 Sch. 20 para. 6.
para. 30	S.I. 1993/1975 Sch. 2 para. 4(2).
para. 31	1993 Sch. 20 para. 2; S.I. 1994/507 Sch. 3 para. 10.
para. 32	S.I. 1994/507 Sch. 3 para. 11.
para. 33	S.I. 1994/507 Sch. 3 para. 12.
para. 34	S.I. 1994/2038 Sch. 4 paras. 2(7), 4(3).
para. 35	S.I. 1994/507 Sch. 3 para. 5.
paras. 36 to 42	—
para. 43	S.I. 1993/507 Sch. 3 para. 7.
para. 44	1993 Sch. 20 para. 4.
para. 45	1946 s.13(1).
para. 46	—
para. 47	1944 s.120(5).
para. 48	—
para. 49	1973 Sch. 1 para. 3.
para. 50	—
Sch. 40	—

TABLE OF DESTINATIONS

Education Act 1944
(c.31)

1944	1996
s.2(1)	Sched. 39, para. 3
6(1)	s.12(1), (5)
7	ss.1(1), 13(1)
8(1)	s.14(1), (2), (3)
(a)	2(1)
(b)	2(2)
(1A)	14(5)
8(2)	14(6)
(2) proviso	14(7)
9(1)	16(1)
(2)	31(1), (2), (3)
(4)	6(1)
(6)	16(2)
(7)	16(3)
10(1)	542(1)
(2)	542(2)
(2) proviso	543
14(1)	173(1), (2), (3)
(2)	173(6)
(3)	174(1)
(4)	174(2), (3)
(5)	173(7)
15(1)	32(1)
(2)	ss.32(2), 48(1), (2)
(3)	s.59(1), (2), (3), (4)
(4)	57(1), (2), (4)
(4A)	57(3)
(5)	58(1), (2)
16(1)	47(1)
(2)	46(1), (2), (3)
(3)	ss.46(4), (5), 47(3), (4)
22(1)	150(2), 152(1), (2)
(2)	s.152(3), (4)
(3)	150(1)
(3A)	151(1) to (3)
(3B)	151(1) to (3)
(3C)	151(1) to (3)
(3D)	151(4), (5)
(3E)	151(6)
(4)	134(5)
(5)	ss.134(6), 150(3)
(6)	s.151(7)
24(2)	134(1), (2), (3), (4)
(a) proviso	134(2), (3)
(b) proviso	134(4)
26(1)	376(1)
(2)	376(2)
(3)	376(3)
(4)	376(3)
27(1)	377(2)
(2)	143(1), (2)
(2) proviso	143(3)
(3)	143(4) to (6)
(4)	143(4) to (6)
(5)	143(4) to (6)
(6)	377(1)
28(1)	378(1)
s.28(1A)	s.378(5)
(1B)	378(2), (3)
(1C)	378(4)
(2)	145
(3)	144(1), (2)
(4)	144(3)
30	146(1), (2) to (4)
36	7
41(1)	15(1) to (3)
(2)	15(1) to (3), (8)
(2A)	528
(2B)	528
(3)	2(3)
(4)	2(3)
(5)	(6)
(7)	15(5)
(8)	15(5)
(9)	15(6), (7)
(10)	15(6), (7)
(11)	15(8)
48(4)	ss.520(1), (2), 536(1), (2)
50(1)	514(1), (2)
(2)	514(3)
52(1)	514(4)
(1) proviso	514(5)
(2)	514(6)
(3)	514(7)
53(1)	508(1), (2)
(2)	508(3)
54(1)	521(1), (2), (4)
(2)	ss.521(3), 522(1)
(3)	522(2) to (4)
(4)	523(1), (2)
(5)	522(5)
(6)	525(1), (2), (3)
(7)	524(1), (2), (3)
(8)	ss.521(3), 523(3)
(9)	s.523(3)
55(1)	509(1), (2)
(2)	509(3)
(3)	509(4)
(4)	509(5)
(5)	509(6)
58	558
59(1)	559(1), (2)
(2)	559(1), (2)
(3)	559(3), (4)
(4)	559(5)
63(2)	545(1)
65	72
67(1)	495(1), (2)
(2)	495(3)
(3)	399
(4)	573(6)
68	496(1), (2)
69(2)	506
70(1)	ss.464(1) to (3), 465(1), (2)
s.70(1) proviso (a)	s.465(2)
(1) proviso (b)	465(3)
(3)	ss.466(1), (3), 478(2)
(3A)	s.466(2)
(4)	467(1), (3)
(4A)	467(2)
71(1)	469(1), (2), (3)
(2)	469(4)
(3)	469(5)
(4)	468
(5)	469(6)
72(1)	470(1)
(2)	470(2)
(3)	471(1)
(3) proviso	471(2)
(4)	472
73(1)	475
(2)	ss.473(1), 478(2)
(3)	473(2), 478(2)
(4)	s.478(1)
(5)	477
74	474
75(1)	476(2), (3)
(2)	476(4)
(3)	476(5)
76	9
78(2)	513
80(1)	434(1), (4)
80(1A)	434(2)
(2)	434(6)
81	518
82	526
83	527
85(1)	529(1)
(2)	529(2), (3)
(3)	529(2), (3)
88	532
90(1)	530(1)
(1) proviso	530(2)
(1A)	530(3)
92	29(1)
93	507(1), (2)
94(1)	564(1), (2)
(2)	564(3)
(3)	564(4)
95(1)	565(1)
(2)	566
99(1)	497(1), (2), (3)
(2)	498(1), (2)
(3)	71
100(1)(b)	485
(c)	491(1)
(3)	ss.489(1), 491(2)
105(1)	s.67(1), (2)
(2)	67(3), (4)
(3)	48(3), (4)
111	570(1), (2)
111 proviso	570(3)
111A	569(5)

1944	1996
s.112	s.569(2)
113	572
114, "minor authority"	577
114(1),	ss.32(5), 434(5)
"agreed syllabus"	s.375(2), (4)
"alterations"	573(2)
"county"	12(1)
"enlargement"	573(3)
"former authority"	173(2)
"foundation governors"	78(2)
"further education"	2(3)
"independent school"	463
"junior pupil"	3(2)
"local education authority"	12(1), (2), (5)
"maintain"	34(1)
"primary education"	2(1)
"primary school"	5(1)
"provisionally registered school"	465(4)
"pupil"	3(1)
"registered school"	465(4)
"school"	4(1)
"secondary education"	2(2)
s.114—*cont.*	
"secondary school"	s.5(2)
"senior pupil"	3(2)
"sex education"	352(3)
"significant"	573(5)
114(1D)	576(1)
(1E)	576(2)
(1F)	576(3), (4)
(2)	34(1), (2), (3), (4)
(b)	579(5), (6)
(2A)	(7)
115	561
116	562
118	581
120(1)	Sched. 39, para. 4
120(5)	Sched. 39, para. 47
Sched. 2	Sched. 6
Sched. 3,	
para. 4	Sched. 5, para. 3
para. 5	Sched. 5, para. 3
para. 7	s.144(1), (2), Sched. 5, para. 4
para. 8	Sched. 5, para. 2
para. 9	Sched. 5, para. 5
para. 10	Sched. 5, para. 6
para. 11	s.32(5)
Sched. 5,	
para. 2	Sched. 31, para. 4
para. 3	Sched. 31, para. 7
para. 4	Sched. 31, paras. 8, 9
para. 5	Sched. 31, para. 4
para. 7	Sched. 31, paras. 5, 6
para. 8	Sched. 31, paras. 5, 6
para. 10	Sched. 31, para. 12
para. 11	s.375(4), Sched. 31, paras. 13, 14
para. 12(1)	Sched. 31, para. 1
para. 12(3)	Sched. 31, para. 1
para. 12(4)	Sched. 31, para. 2
para. 13	Sched. 31, para. 10
para. 13(4)	Sched. 31, para. 12
Sched. 6,	
para. 1	Sched. 34, para. 1
para. 2	Sched. 34, para. 2
para. 3	Sched. 34, para. 3
para. 3A	Sched. 34, para. 3
para. 4	Sched. 34, para. 4

STATUTORY INSTRUMENTS ACT 1946
(c.36)

1946	1996
s.1(2)	s.569(1)
5(2)	569(2)

ACQUISITION OF LAND (AUTHORISATION PROCEDURE) ACT 1946
(c.49)

1946	1996
Sched. 4	s.530(1), (2)

EDUCATION ACT 1946
(c.50)

1946	1996
s.1(1)	s.64(1), (2), (3)
2(1)	ss.50(1), (2), 51(1), (4)
2(2)	s.50(4)
2(3)	51(2), (3)
2(4)	51(2), (3)
2(5)	57(1), (4)
2(7)	ss.50(2), (3), 51(4), (5)
2(8)	s.51(7)
4(1)	73
6	74
s.13(1)	Sched. 39, para. 45
16(1), "department"	ss.50(5), 51(8)
"site"	s.62(1)
Sched. 1,	
para. 1	ss.34(3), (4), 60(1), 61(1)
para. 2(1)	47(2), 57(1), (2), (4), 59(5)
para. 2(2)	s.57(3)
para. 3	61(4)
Sched. 1—*cont.*	
para. 4	s.61(5)
para. 5	61(6)
para. 6	ss.60(2), (3), 61(2), (3)
para. 7	s.60(4) to (6)
para. 8	62(2), (3)
para. 9	62(4)
Sched. 2,	
Pt.I	ss.477, 514(1), (3), 572
Pt.II	59(2), (3), (4), 173(2), (3)

Table of Destinations

Education (Miscellaneous Provisions) Act 1948
(c.40)

1948	1996
s.3(2)	s.2(1)
4(1)	435
(2)	433(1), (2), (5)
(3)	433(3)
(3A)	433(4)
(6)	434(3)
5(1)	510(1), (2)
(2)	510(3)
(3)	510(4)
(4)	510(5), (6)
(5)	511(1)
(6)	511(2), (3)
(6A)	511(4)
7(1)	543
10(1)	530(1)
(2)	531(1)
(3)	531(2)
12	569(1), (2)
Sched. 1, Pt.I	ss.508(2), 509(3), 514(2), 562, Sched. 5, para. 3

Education (Miscellaneous Provisions) Act 1953
(c.33)

1953	1996
s.2	s.63(1), (2), (3)
3	64(1), (3)
6(1)	18
(2)	517(1)
(a)(i)	517(2)
(ii)	517(3)
(iii)	517(4)
(b)	517(5)
Sched. 1	510(2)

Rating and Valuation Act 1961
(c.45)

1961	1996
s.12(6)	s.34(5)

London Government Act 1963
(c.33)

1963	1996
s.30(1)(a)	s.12(3)

Table of Destinations

Education Act 1964
(c.82)

1964	1996
s.1(1)	ss.49, 198(6), 291
1(2)	s.5(4)
(3)	ss.5(5), 14(7)

Education Act 1967
(c.3)

1967	1996
s.2	64(3)

Criminal Justice Act 1967
(c.80)

1967	1996
Sched. 3	s.506

Education Act 1968
(c.17)

1968	1996
s.1(1)	s.574
2	49
3(3)	543
Sched. 1,	
para. 3	573(6)
para. 4(2)	67(3)
para. 5(b)	573(3)
para. 5(c)	573(5)
para. 5(a)	573(2)
para. 6	64(1)

Local Government Act 1972
(c.70)

1972	1996
s.179(2)	s.12(1)
(3)	523(1), (2)
192(1)	12(1), (2), (5)
(4)	577
272(2)	ss.507(2), 531(1)

Education Act 1973
(c.16)

1973	1996
s.1(2)	ss.179(1), (2), 489(3), (4)
2(1)	ss.554(1), (2), 568(1)
2(1A)	554(3)
(1B)	ss.554(5), 555(5), 556(8)
(1C)	s.554(4)
(2)	555(1), (2) to (4)
(3)	556(1)
(4)	556(2), (3)
(5)	556(4)
(5A)	556(5)
(6)	556(6), (7)
(7)	556(6), (7)
(8)	554(6)
Sched. 1,	
para. 3	Sched. 39, para. 49

Table of Destinations

Education (Work Experience) Act 1973
(c.23)

1973	1996
s.1(1)	s.560(1)
(2)	560(3)
(3)	560(4), (5)
(4)	560(2), (7)

Employment of Children Act 1973
(c.24)

1973	1996
s.3(4)	s.559(6)

National Health Service Reorganisation Act 1973
(c.32)

1973	1996
Sched. 4, para. 7	ss.520(1), (2), 536(1), (2)

Education Act 1976
(c.81)

1976	1996
s.6(1)	Sched. 34, para. 5

National Health Service Act 1977
(c.49)

1977	1996
Sched. 15, para. 2	ss.520(1), (2), 536(1), (2)

Interpretation Act 1978
(c.30)

1978	1996
s.17(2)(a)	ss.151(7), 411(5), 456(1), 477, 490, 506, 515(4), 520(1), (2), 532, 535(4), 536(1), (2), 564(4), Sched. 14, paras. 1, 27, Sched. 17, para. 9

Table of Destinations

Education Act 1980
(c.20)

1980	1996
s.1(4)	Sched. 39, para. 10(2)
5	s.180
6(1)	411(1), (2)
(2)	411(1), (2)
(3)	411(3)
(4)	411(4)
(5)	411(5)
(6)	413(1)
(7)	413(2) to (4)
(8)	413(2) to (4)
(9)	413(2) to (4)
7(1)	423(1)
(2)	423(2), (3)
(3)	423(2), (3)
(4)	423(4)
(5)	423(5)
8(1)	414(1), (2)
(2)	414(1), (2)
(3)	414(3), (4)
(4)	414(5)
(5)	414(6) to (8)
(5A)	414(6) to (8)
(5B)	29(5)
(6)	414(6) to (8)
(7)	ss.29(5), 414(9)
9(1)	29(6), 424(1)
(1A)	424(2), 436(1)
(2)	s.424(3)
12(1)	ss.35(1), 167(1)
(1A)	35(5), 167(4)
(1B)	571
(2)	ss.35(3), 167(2)
(2A)	s.35(4)
(3)	ss.36(1), (2), (4), 168(1), (2), (4)
(4)	37(1), (2), (6), 169(1), (2)
(5)	37(1), (3), 169(1), (3)
(6)	37(5), 169(5)
(7)	38(1), (2), 170(1), (2)
(8)	38(3), 170(3)
12(9)	40(1), (3), 171
13(1)	s.41(1), (2)
(1A)	41(4)
(1B)	41(7)
(1C)	571
(2)	41(5), (6)
(3)	42(1), (2)
(3A)	42(3)
(4)	43(1), (2)
(5)	45(1)
(6)	45(2)
(7)	45(4)
(8)	45(7)
s.14(1)	ss.39(1), (2), 44(1), (2)
14(2)	s.44(3), (4)
(3)	ss.40(2), 45(3)
16(1)	ss.40(4), (5), 45(5), (6), 172
(1A)	35(2), 41(3)
(2)	s.573(4)
(3A)	ss.35(5), (6), 42(5), (6), 168(5), (6)
(3B)	35(5), (6), 42(5), (6), 168(5), (6)
17(1)	s.479(1) to (3)
(2)	479(1) to (3), (4)
(3)	479(1) to (3)
(4)	479(5)
(5)	479(5)
(6)	480(1), (2)
(7)	480(1), (2)
(8)	480(4)
(9)	480(3), (4)
(10)	479(6), (7)
18	481
21(1)	487
(2)	489(1)
22(1)	512(1), (4)
(2)	512(2)
(3)	512(3)
(3A)	534(1) to (4)
(3B)	ss.512(5), 534(5)
(4)	s.533(1), (2)
(4A)	533(3)
24(1)	17(1)
(2)	ss.14(4), 17(2)
26(1)	s.515(1)
(2)	535(1)
26(3)	ss.515(2), 535(2)
(4)	ss.515(3), 535(3)
(5)	ss.515(4), 535(4)
(6)	ss.515(5), 535(5)
29(1)	s.510(4)
(2)	511(4)
34(1)	463
(6)	466(2)
(7)	467(1), (3)
35(1)	569(1)
(2)	569(3)
(3)	569(2)
(4)	569(4)
(5)	569(5), (6)
s.38(4)	ss.411(8), 423(6)
(5)	s.579(4)
(5A)	579(3)
Sched. 1, para. 13(a)	78(2)
Sched. 2, para. 1	Sched. 33, para. 1
2	Sched. 33, para. 2
3	Sched. 33, para. 3
4	Sched. 33, para. 4
4A	Sched. 33, para. 5
5	Sched. 33, paras. 9 to 11
6	Sched. 33, paras. 9 to 11
7	Sched. 33, paras. 9 to 11
8	Sched. 33, para. 13
9	Sched. 33, para. 14
10	Sched. 33, para. 12
11	Sched. 33, para. 15
Sched. 3, para. 1	s.46(1)
3	529(2), (3)
5	Sched. 5, para. 3
6	s.64(1)
7	ss.50(4), 51(6)
8	60(1), 61(1)
9	s.63(1)
11	49
12	5(4)
15	574
17	179(1)
Sched. 4, para. 1	Sched. 35, paras. 1 to 3
2	Sched. 35, paras. 1 to 3
3	Sched. 35, paras. 1 to 3
4	Sched. 35, para. 4
5	Sched. 35, paras. 5, 6
6	Sched. 35, paras. 5, 6

EDUCATION ACT 1981
(c.60)

1981	1996
s.2(1)	s.14(6)
17	7
Sched. 3,	
para. 3	514(1), (2)
para. 4	514(5)
para. 7	510(2)
para. 8	517(3), (5)
para. 14	424(3)

LOCAL GOVERNMENT (MISCELLANEOUS PROVISIONS) ACT 1982
(c.30)

1982	1996
s.40(1)	s.547(1)
(2)	547(2)
(3)	547(3)
(4)	547(4), (5)
(5)	547(4), (5)
(6)	547(6)
(7)	547(7), (8)
(8)	547(7), (8)

CRIMINAL JUSTICE ACT 1982
(c.48)

1982	1996
Sched. 3	s.478(2)

MEDICAL ACT 1983
(c.54)

1983	1996
Sched. 6,	
para. 11	ss.506, 521(3), 523(4)

EDUCATION (GRANTS AND AWARDS) ACT 1984
(c.11)

1984	1996
s.1(1)	s.484(1)
(2)	484(1), (2)
(3)	484(3), (4)
(4)	ss.484(3), (4), 489(1)
(4A)	s.489(2)
(5)	484(5)
(6)	484(2)
(7)	484(6)
3(1)	569(1)
(3)	569(2)
(4)	569(4)

SOCIAL SECURITY ACT 1986
(c.50)

1986	1996
s.77(1)	s.512(1)
(2)	512(2), (3)

Table of Destinations

Education (No.2) Act 1986 (c.61)

1986	1996
s.1(1)	ss.76(1), 127(1), (2)
(2)	76(2), 127(1), (2)
(3)	s.76(3), (4)
(4)	127(3), (4)
(5)	ss.76(3), (4), 127(3), (4)
(6)	s.76(5)
2	77(1)–(7)
(1)–(3)	128(1)–(3)
(5)–(7)	128(4)–(6)
3(1)–(5)	79(1), (2)
(6), (7)	79(3), (4)
4(1)	84(1)
(2)	84(1), (3)
(3)	84(2)
(4)–(6)	84(4)–(6)
4A	85
(8)	568(2)
5(1)	81(1)
(2)	81(3)
(3)	81(2)
(4)	81(4), (5)
6	Sched. 8, para. 2
7(1)	s.80(1)
(2)	80(2)
(3)–(5)	80(3)–(5)
(6)	80(6), (7), (8)
(7)	80(9)
8(1)	Sched. 8, para. 14
(2)	Sched. 8, para. 11
(3)	Sched. 8, para. 11
(4)	Sched. 8, para. 12
(5)	Sched. 8, para. 13
(6)	Sched. 8, paras. 10, 15
(7)	Sched. 8, para. 15
(8)	Sched. 8, para. 17
(9)	Sched. 8, paras. 10, 15
(10)	Sched. 8, para. 21
(11)	Sched. 8, para. 16
(12)	Sched. 8, para. 16
9(1)	s.89(1)
(1A)	89(2)
(2)	89(3)
(3)	89(4)
(4)	94(1), (3)
(5)	94(2)
(6)	95(1)
(7)	95(2), (3)
(8)	95(4)
10(1)	90(1), (2)
(2)	90(4)
(3)	90(3)
(5)	91(1)
s.10(6)	s.91(2)
(7)	90(6)
s.11(1)	82(1)
(2)	82(2), (3)
(3)	82(4)
(4), (5)	82(5), (6)
(6)	82(7)
12(1)	ss.96(1), 97(1)
(2)	96(2), 97(1)
(4)	96(3), 97(2)
(5)	s.97(3)
(6)	97(4)
(7)	97(5)
(8)	97(6)
(9)	97(1), (3), (4)
13(1)–(3)	86
(4)	87(1)
(5)	87(4)
(6)	87(5)
(7)	87(2)
(8)	87(3)
(9)	87(2), (5)
14	83
15(1)	Sched. 8, para. 5
(2)	Sched. 8, para. 7
(3)	Sched. 8, para. 7
(4)	Sched. 8, para. 7
(5)	Sched. 8, para. 7
(6)	Sched. 8, para. 7
(7)	Sched. 8, para. 4
(8)	Sched. 8, para. 6
(9)	Sched. 8, para. 10
(10)	Sched. 8, para. 9
(11)	Sched. 8, para. 3
(12)	Sched. 8, para. 2
(13)	Sched. 8, para. 2
(14)	Sched. 8, para. 8
(15)	Sched. 8, para. 7
16(1)	s.130
(2)	131
(3)	132
16A	176
17(1)	370(1)
(2), (3)	370(2), (3)
18(1)	371(1), (2)
(2)	371(3)
(3)	371(4)
(5)	372(1)
(6)	372(2)–(4)
(7)	371(5), (7)
(8)	371(6)
19	373(1), (2)
21(1)	147(1)
s.21(4)	s.147(2), (3)
(5)	153
22	154(1)
(a)	154(3)
(b)	154(4)
(c)	154(5)
(d)	154(2)
(e)	154(6)
(f)	156(1)
23(a)	157(2), (4), (5)
(b)	157(3), (4)
24	Sched. 15, para. 1
(a)	Sched. 15, para. 2
(b)	Sched. 15, paras. 3, 5
(d)	Sched. 15, para. 6
(f)	Sched. 15, para. 3
(g)	Sched. 15, paras. 3, 5
24(h)	Sched. 15, paras. 2, 4, 6, 7
25	Sched. 15, para. 8
(a)	Sched. 15, para. 9
(b)	Sched. 15, paras. 10, 11
(c)	Sched. 15, para. 12
(g)	Sched. 15, para. 11
(h)	Sched. 15, paras. 9, 12, 13
26(1), (2)	s.159(1)–(4), (7)
(3), (4)	159(1)–(4)
(5)	159(5), (6)
27	160
28	155
30(1)	161(1)
(2)	Sched. 17, para. 1
(a)	Sched. 17, para. 2
(b)	Sched. 17, para. 3
(c)	Sched. 17, para. 4
(d)	Sched. 17, para. 4
(e)	Sched. 17, para. 4
(g)	Sched. 17, para. 5
(h)	Sched. 17, para. 6
(i)	Sched. 17, para. 7
(j)	Sched. 17, para. 8
(k)	Sched. 17, para. 9

1986	1996
s.30(3)	s.161(3)
(4)	161(4)
(5)	Sched. 17, para. 10
31(1), (2)	s.162(1), (2)
(3)	Sched. 18, para. 3
(4)(a)	Sched. 18, para. 1
(b)	Sched. 18, para. 2
(c)	Sched. 18, para. 4
(d)	Sched. 18, para. 4
(5)	Sched. 18, para. 5
(6)	Sched. 18, para. 5
(7)–(8)	s.163
31(9)	Sched. 18, para. 2
32	s.165
33	412
34	133(1)–(3)
35(1)	133(5)
(2)	Sched. 13, para. 10
36(1)	Sched. 13, para. 1
(2)	Sched. 13, para. 2
37	Sched. 13, para. 3
38(1)	Sched. 13, para. 5
(2)	Sched. 13, para. 5
(3)	Sched. 13, para. 6
(4)	Sched. 13, para. 7
(5)	Sched. 13, para. 9
(6)	Sched. 13, para. 8
39	Sched. 13, para. 4
40(1)–(4)	s.135(1)–(4)
(5)	135(8)
(6)–(7)	135(5), (6)
41(1)(a)	Sched. 13, para. 11(1), (2)
(b)–(e)	Sched. 13, paras. 11(4)–(7)
(3)	Sched. 13, para. 11(3), (8)
42(1), (2)	s.149(1), (2)
(3)	149(3), (4)
(4)	149(5)
44(1)	406(1), (2), (3)
(2)	406(1), (2)
45	407(1), (2)
46	403(1), (2)
46A	ss.403(1), 406(1), (2), 407(1)

1986	1996
s.47(1)	s.548(1)
(1A)	548(2)
(1B)	549(3)
(2)–(3)	549(1), (2)
(4)	548(6)
(5)	ss.548(3), 549(5)
(6)	s.548(4)
(7)	548(5)
(8)	550
(9)	Sched. 35, para. 4
(10)	s.549(4)
51(1)–(4)	492(1)–(4)
(7), (8)	492(6)
(10)	579(4)
(11)	492(5)
52(1)	493(1)
(2)	493(2)
(3)	493(3)
(4)	493(4)
53	509(4)
54(1)	54(1)
(2)	54(2)
(3)	52(1), (3)
(4)	52(2)
(5)	53(1), (2)
(6)	54(4)
(7)	54(3)
(8)–11	55
(12)	54(5), (6)
(13)	53(3), (4)
(14)	53(3), (4)
55(1)	56(1), (3)
(2)	56(1), (2)
(3)	56(4), (5)
(4)	56(4), (5)
56	538
57	Sched. 8, para. 20
58(1)	s.519(1)
(2)	519(2)
(5)	519(3)
(6)	519(4), (5)
(7)	519(6)
62	Sched. 8, para. 18 Sched. 22, para. 14
63(1)	ss.568(1), (2), 569(1)
(2)	568(3), 569(2)
(2A)	s.569(3)
(3)	ss.568(5), 569(4)
65(1), "co-opted governor"	s.78(1)
"parent governor"	78(3), (5)
"promoters"	ss.97(3), (4), (5), 422(7), Sched. 9, para. 1
"teacher governor"	s.78(4), (5)
65(2)	812

1986	1996
Sched. 1, para. 1(1), (2)	s.89(5), (6)
2(1)	92(1), (2)
(2)	92(3)
(3)	92(4)
3	93
4	164(1)
(1)	164(2)
(2)	164(3)
5	164(1), (4)–(7)
Sched. 2, para. 1	422(7), Sched. 9, para. 1
"new school"	s.181(1)
"relevant proposal"	181(2)
para. 2(1)	Sched. 9, para. 2
(2)	Sched. 9, para. 2 Sched. 10, para. 5
(3)	Sched. 9, para. 9
(4)	Sched. 9, para. 17
para. 3(1)	s.99(1)
(2)	Sched. 10, para. 5
(3)	Sched. 10, para. 5
(4)	Sched. 10, para. 1
(5)	Sched. 10, para. 2
(6)	s.100(3), (4)
(7)	99(2)
para. 4	Sched. 10, para. 3 Sched. 19, para. 1
para. 5(1)	ss.96(5), 97(8)
(2)	96(4), 97(7)
para. 6	Sched. 9, para. 3
para. 7(1)	Sched. 9, para. 4
(2)	Sched. 9, para. 6
(3)	Sched. 9, para. 6
(4)	Sched. 9, para. 6
(5)	Sched. 9, para. 6
(6)	Sched. 9, para. 7
(7)	Sched. 9, para. 7
para. 8(1)	Sched. 9, para. 5
(2)	Sched. 9, para. 7
para. 9(1)	Sched. 9, para. 8
(2)	Sched. 9, para. 8
para. 10(1)	Sched. 9, para. 15

1986	1996
Sched. 2—*cont.*	
para. 10(2)	Sched. 9, para. 14
(3)	Sched. 9, para. 18
(4)	Sched. 9, paras. 13, 16
para. 11(1)	Sched. 9, para. 12
(2)	Sched. 9, para. 12
(3)	Sched. 9, para. 10
(4)	Sched. 9, para. 9
(5)	Sched. 9, para. 9
(6)	Sched. 9, para. 11
para. 12(1)	Sched. 19, para. 1
(2)	Sched. 19, para. 3
(3)	Sched. 19, para. 4
para. 13(1)	Sched. 19, para. 28
(2)	s.538
(3)	Sched. 10, paras. 4, 6
(4)	Sched. 10, para. 4
(5)	Sched. 10, para. 6
para. 14	Sched. 19, para. 28
para. 15	Sched. 19, para. 25
para. 16	Sched. 19, para. 26
para. 17	Sched. 19, para. 27
Sched. 2—*cont.*	
para. 18	Sched. 19, para. 29
para. 19	s.422(1)–(6)
para. 20(1)	Sched. 19, para. 14
(2)	Sched. 19, para. 15
(3)	Sched. 19, para. 15
(4)	Sched. 19, para. 16
(5)	Sched. 19, para. 5
para. 21	Sched. 19, para. 6
para. 22	Sched. 19, para. 7
para. 23	Sched. 19, para. 8
para. 24	Sched. 19, para. 10
para. 25	Sched. 19, para. 9
para. 26(1)	Sched. 19, para. 11
(2)	Sched. 19, para. 11
para. 27	Sched. 9, para. 19
para. 28	Sched. 9, para. 20 Sched. 19, para. 17
para. 29	Sched. 9, para. 22
para. 30(1)	Sched. 9, para. 21
(2)	Sched. 19, para. 12
(3)	Sched. 19, para. 16
Sched. 3,	
para. 1	Sched. 16, para. 1
para. 2	Sched. 16, para. 1
para. 3	Sched. 16, para. 2
para. 3A	Sched. 16, para. 3
para. 4	Sched. 16, para. 4
para. 5	Sched. 16, para. 18
para. 6	Sched. 16, para. 6
para. 6A	Sched. 16, para. 7
para. 7	Sched. 16, para. 8
para. 8	Sched. 16, para. 9
para. 9	Sched. 16, para. 10
para. 11	Sched. 16, para. 13
para. 12	Sched. 16, para. 14
para. 13	Sched. 16, para. 11
para. 14	Sched. 16, para. 12
para. 15	Sched. 16, para. 15
para. 16	Sched. 16, para. 5
para. 17	Sched. 16, para. 16
Sched. 4,	
para. 1	ss.32(2), 48(1)
para. 2	s.134(5)
Sched. 5,	
para. 1	Sched. 39, para. 11

REVERTER OF SITES ACT 1987 (c.15)

1987	1996
s.8(1)	s.60(7)

EDUCATION REFORM ACT 1988 (c.40)

1988	1996
s.1(1)	s.351(2)–(5)
(2)	351(1)
2(1)	352(1)
(2)	353
(3)	352(2)
3(1)	354(1)
(2)	354(2)
(2A), (2B)	354(3)–(5)
(3)	355(1)
(4)	ss.354(6), 355(2)
(5)	s.355(3)
(5A)	355(4)
s.3(6),	
"class"	s.355(5)
"school"	354(7)
"school year"	355(5)
(7)	354(8)
4(1)–(4)	356(1)–(4)
4(5)–(8)	356(5)–(8)
5(1)	400(1), (2)
(2)	400(3)
(3)	400(5)
6(1)	385(1)
(2)	385(2)
(3)	385(4)
(4)	385(5)
s.6(5)	s.385(6)
(6)	385(7)
(7)	385(1), (3)
7(1)	386(1), (2)
(2)	386(3)
(3)	386(4)
(4)	386(5)
(5)	386(6)
(6)	387
8(2)	352(1)
(3)	375(3), (5)
9(1), (1A)	398
(2)	389(7)
(3)	389(1)

Table of Destinations

1988	1996
s.9(4)	s.389(3)
(5)	389(7)
(6)	389(4)
(7)	389(5)
(8)	389(6)
(9)	389(2)
10(1)	ss.384, 388
(2)	357(1), 400(4)
(3)	s.357(2)
11(1)	ss.390(1), 391(1), 392(1), 394(1)
(2)	s.391(2)
(3)	390(2), (3)
(4)	390(2), (3), (4)
(5)	390(5), (6)
(6)	390(7)
(7)	391(3), (4)
(8)	391(5), Sched. 31, para. 3
(9)	391(6)
(10)	391(7)
(11), (12)	391(8), (9)
(13)	391(10)
12(1)	394(1)
(2)	394(2), (3), (5)
(3)	394(2), (3)
(4)	394(4)
(5)	395(1), (6)
(6)	395(2), (6)
(7)	395(3), (4)
(8)	395(5)
(9)	ss.394(6), 395(7)
(10)	394(7), 395(8)
(11)	s.394(8)
12A(1)	396(1)
(2)	396(2)
(3)	396(1)
13(1)	392(2)
(2)	392(3)
(3)	392(4)
(4)	392(5)
(5)	392(6)
(6)	392(7)
(7)	392(8)
14(1)	360(1)
(2)	360(2)–(4)
(3)	361(1)
(5)	361(2)
(6)	361(3), (4)
(7)	360(5)
16(1), (2)	362(1), (2)
(3)	362(3), (4)
(4), (5)	362(5), (6)
(6)	362(7)
17	363
17A	405
18	364
19(1)	365(1), (5)
(2)	365(2)–(4)
(3)	366(1)
(4)	366(2), (3)
(5)	366(5)
(6)	366(6)
(7)	367(1)

1988	1996
s.19(8)	s.367(2), (3)
(9)	367(4)
(10)	365(6)
20(1)	368(1)
(2)	368(2), (10)
(3)	368(3)
(4)	368(4), (5)
(5)	369(6), (7)
(6)	368(8)
21(1)	368(1)
(2)	368(2), (10)
(3)	368(3)
(3A)	368(4), (5)
(3B)	368(6), (7)
(4)	368(8)
22(1)	408(1), (4)
(2)	408(2)
(3)	408(3)
(4)	408(5)
(5)	408(6)
(6), (7)	408(7), (8)
23(1)	409(1)–(3)
(2)	409(4)
24(1)	401(1)
(2)	401(2)
(3), (4)	401(3), (4)
25(1), "assess"	350(2)
"maintained school"	350(1)
25(2)	410
26(1)	416(1), (8)
(3), (4)	416(2)–(7), (8)
(5)–(8)	416(2)–(7)
(9)	411(6)
(10)	411(3)
27(1), (2)	ss.417(1), 418(1)
(3)	417(2), (3), 418(2), (3)
(4)–(6)	s.420(1)–(3)
(7)	420(4), (5)
(8)	421(1)
(9)	ss.417(3), 418(3)
28(1), (2)	Sched. 32, para. 1
(3), (4)	Sched. 32, para. 3
(5)	Sched. 32, para. 4
(6), (7)	Sched. 32, para. 5
(8)	Sched. 32, para. 6
29(1)–(4)	s.419(2)–(5)
(5)	436(1), (2)
(6)	436(2)
(7)	419(1)
30(2)	411(3)
(3)	413(1)
31(2)	414(3), (4)
(3)	ss.424(1), (2), 436(1)
(4)	s.35(4)
(5)	41(5), (6)
(6)	579(3)
32(1)	421(2), Sched. 32, para. 5

1988	1996
s.32(4)	ss.417(1), 418(1)
33(1)	s.103
(2)	ss.101(3), 103
(3)	s.102
(4)	ss.101(3), (4), 105(1), (3)
(5)	ss.101(5), 105(1)
(6)	Sched. 11, para. 2
(a), (b)	s.115
34(1), (2)	104(1), (2)
(3)	571
(4)	104(3)
(5)–(7)	104(4)–(6)
35(1), (2)	111
(3)	112(1)–(3)
(4)	ss.112(4), 113(5)
(5)	s.113(1), (2)
(6)	113(3), (4)
(7), (8)	114
36(1)–(3)	116(1)–(3)
(4)	116(4)
(5)	116(5)
(5A)	116(6)
(5B)	116(7)
(6)	116(8)
37(1)	117(1)
(2)	117(2), (3)
(3)	117(4), (5)
(4)	117(6)
(5)	118(1)–(3)
(6), (7)	118(4), (5)
(8), (9)	119
38(1)	106(1), (2)
(2)	106(2), (3)
(3)	106(4)
(3A)	106(5)
(4)	105(3)
(5)	106(6)
39(1)	107(1)
(4)	107(2)
(10)	108
(11)	109(1), (3)
(12)	109(2)
40(1)	110(1)
(2)	110(2)
(3)–(5)	110(3)–(5)
42(1)	121
(2), (3)	122(1), (2)
(4)	122(4)
(a)–(d)	Sched. 11, para. 2
(e)	Sched. 11, para. 3
(j)	Sched. 11, para. 4
(5)(a)	Sched. 11, para. 3
(7)	122(5)
(8)	122(6)
(9)	122(7)
42A	123
43	120
44(1), (2)	136(1), (2)
(3)	136(3)
(4)	141(1), (2)
(5)	136(3)

1988	1996
s.45(1)	ss.137(1), (2), 138(1)
(2)	s.137(1), (2)
(3)	137(3), (4)
(4)	138(1)
(5)	138(3)
(6)	138(2)
(7)	138(4)
(8)	138(5)
(9)	137(5)
(10)	137(6)
(11)	141(1), (3)
46(2)	139(1), (2)
(3)–(6)	139(3)–(6)
47	140
48(2),	181(1), (2)
"temporary governing body"	181(3), Sched. 12, para. 1
49(1)	125(1)
(2)	125(2), (3)
(4)	125(4)
50(2)	124(1)
(3)	124(2)
(5)	124(1), Sched. 11, paras. 5–7
(6)	124(4)
(7)–(9)	124(6)–(8)
(10)	124(5), Sched. 11, para. 8
51(1), "expenditure of a capital nature"	s.105(3), Sched. 11, paras. 5–7
(a)(i)	101(1)
(ii)	101(2)
(b)	101(6)
(3)	129(1)
(4)	129(2), (3), (4)
(5)	129(2), (3)
(6)	ss.129(5), 141(4)
(9)	Sched. 17, para. 6
100(2)	514(1)
(4)	510(1), (3), (4), (5)
105(1)	482(1), (3)
(2)	482(2), (3)
(3)	482(4)
(4)	483(1), (2)
(5), (6)	483(3), (4)
106(1)	450(1)
(1A)	450(2)
(2)	451(1), (2)
(3)	451(3), (5)
(4)	451(3), (4), (5)
(5)	453(1)
(6)	454(1)
(7), (8)	454(3), (4)
(9)	452(6)
(10)	462(2)
(11)	462(3)

1988	1996
s.107(1)–(4)	s.452(1)–(4)
(5), (6)	452(5)
108	453(2), (3)
109(1)	455(1)
(2)	455(2), (3)
(3)	456(1)
(4)–(10)	456(2)–(8)
110(1)	457(1)
(2)	457(2), (3)
(3)	457(4)
(4)	457(5)
(5)	455(3)
111(1)–(3)	458(1)–(4)
(5)	458(1)–(4)
(6)	458(5)
112(2)	ss.554(1), (2), (3), (4), (5), 555(5), 556(8)
(3)	s.556(2)
113	553
114	63(3)
115	ss.147(1), (2), (3), 153
116	Sched. 8, para. 15
117(1)	s.402(1)
(2)	402(2)
(3)–(5)	402(3)–(5)
118(1), (2)	460(1), (2)
(3)	454(2)
(4)	460(3)
(5)	459
(6)	461
(7)	ss.402(6), 449
(a)	s.462(1)
(d)	462(4), (5)
(e)	462(1)
(8)	ss.402(6), 462(5)
119(1)(a)	s.579(3)
(2), (3)	Sched. 32, para. 7
163	s.12(3), (4)
210	488
(3)	489(1)
211	490
212	66
213(1)	486
(2)	489(1)
(3)	485
218(1)(e)	546(1)
(f)	563(1)
(g)	551(1)
(2B)	482(5)
(4)	563(2)
(7)	544(1), (2)
(8)	545(2)
(12)	ss.544(3), 546(2), 551(2), 563(3)
219(2)	s.496(2)
(3)	ss.497(2), 498(2)
222	s.178
227(1)	369
229(1)	569(5)
232(1)	ss.568(1), 569(1)
(2)	s.568(2)
(3)	568(4)
(4)	ss.568(3), 569(2)

1988	1996
s.232(5)	ss.568(5), 569(4)
(6)	568(6), 569(5)
234(2)(a)	s.579(6)
(b)	579(7)
(3)(a)	579(6)
235(1)	575(1), (2), (4)
(2)(c)	401(5)
(f)	139(7)
(3)	575(3)
(g)	570(2)
(4)	12(4)
Sched. 1, para. 1	376(1), (2), (3)
para. 2(1)	ss.143(4)–(6), 377(2)
(2)	s.377(1)
para. 3(1)	378(1), (2), (3), (4), (5)
(2)	ss.144(1), (2), (3), 145
para. 4	s.399
(b)	146(2)–(4)
para. 6	375(2), (4)
para. 7	Sched. 31, paras. 4, 7, 10, 12, 13
Sched. 2, para. 2	Sched. 30, paras. 1–5
para. 3	Sched. 30, paras. 1–5
para. 4	Sched. 30, paras. 1–5
para. 5	Sched. 30, paras. 1–5
para. 6	Sched. 30, paras. 1–5
para. 7	Sched. 30, paras. 6, 7
para. 8	Sched. 30, para. 8
para. 10	Sched. 30, paras. 9, 10
para. 11	Sched. 30, para. 11
para. 12	Sched. 30, paras. 12, 13
para. 13	Sched. 30, paras. 12, 13
para. 13A	Sched. 30, para. 14
para. 14	Sched. 30, paras. 15, 16
para. 15	Sched. 30, paras. 15, 16
para. 16	Sched. 30, paras. 18, 19
para. 17	Sched. 30, paras. 18, 19
para. 18	Sched. 30, para. 17
Sched. 3, para. 1(1)	Sched. 14, paras. 1, 2
(2)	Sched. 14, para. 1

1988	1996
Sched. 3—*cont.*	
para. 1(3)	Sched. 14, para. 3
(4)	Sched. 14, para. 4
(5)	Sched. 14, para. 4
(6)	Sched. 14, para. 1
(7)	Sched. 14, para. 5
(8)	Sched. 14, para. 6
(9)	Sched. 14, para. 6
(10)	Sched. 14, para. 6
(11)	Sched. 14, para. 7
(12)	Sched. 14, para. 4
(13)	Sched. 14, para. 7
para. 2(1)	Sched. 14, paras. 1, 8
(2)	Sched. 14, para. 9
(3)	Sched. 14, para. 9
(4)	Sched. 14, para. 10
(5)	Sched. 14, para. 11
(6)	Sched. 14, para. 12
(7)	Sched. 14, para. 12
(8)	Sched. 14, para. 13
(9)	Sched. 14, para. 13
(10)	Sched. 14, para. 14
(11)	Sched. 14, para. 14
(12)	Sched. 14, para. 15
para. 3(1)	Sched. 14, para. 16
(2)	Sched. 14, para. 16
(3)	Sched. 14, para. 16
(4)	Sched. 14, para. 17
para. 4(1)	Sched. 14, paras. 1, 18
(2)	Sched. 14, para. 18
(3)	Sched. 14, para. 18
(4)	Sched. 14, para. 19

1988	1996
Sched. 3—*cont.*	
para. 4(5)	Sched. 14, para. 18
para. 5	Sched. 14, para. 20
(1)	Sched. 14, para. 1
para. 6	Sched. 14, para. 21
(1)	Sched. 14, para. 1
para. 7	Sched. 14, para. 22
(1)	Sched. 14, para. 1
para. 8(1)	Sched. 14, paras. 1, 23
(2)	Sched. 14, para. 23
(3)	Sched. 14, para. 23
(4)	Sched. 14, para. 24
(5)	Sched. 14, para. 24
(6)	Sched. 14, para. 23
(7)	Sched. 14, para. 25
(8)	Sched. 14, para. 25
(9)	Sched. 14, para. 26
para. 9	Sched. 14, para. 27
para. 10	Sched. 14, para. 28
(1)	Sched. 14, para. 1
para. 11(3)	Sched. 14, para. 1
Sched. 4,	
para. 1	Sched. 19, para. 18
para. 1(1)	Sched. 12, para. 3
(2)(a)	Sched. 12, para. 2
(b)	Sched. 12, para. 2
para. 2(1)	Sched. 12, para. 3
(2)	Sched. 12, para. 4
(3)	Sched. 12, para. 4
(4)	Sched. 12, para. 4
(5)	Sched. 12, para. 4
(6)	Sched. 12, para. 5

1988	1996
Sched. 4—*cont.*	
para. 2(8)	Sched. 12, para. 6
(9)	Sched. 12, para. 7
(10)	Sched. 19, para. 29
para. 3	Sched. 12, para. 8
para. 4(1)	Sched. 19, para. 19
(2)	Sched. 19, para. 20
(3)	Sched. 19, para. 21
(4)	Sched. 19, para. 19
(5)	Sched. 19, para. 19
(6)	Sched. 19, para. 24
(7)	Sched. 19, para. 22
(8)	Sched. 19, para. 23
para. 5	Sched. 12, para. 10
para. 6	Sched. 12, para. 9
para. 7	Sched. 19, para. 2
Sched. 12,	
para. 1	s.542(1), (2)–(4)
para. 2	536(1), (2)
para. 4	ss.399, 573(6)
para. 6	s.518
para. 7	463
para. 8	63(3)
para. 14	560(1)
para. 24	534(1)–(4)
para. 29	547(2), (4), (5), (7), (8)
para. 34	ss.403(1), 406(1), (2), 407(1)
para. 35	s.548(3)
para. 37	Sched. 22, para. 14
para. 54	508(2)
para. 55	509(3)
para. 58	434(2)
para. 59	530(1)
para. 61	510(4)
para. 62	531(1)
para. 81	ss.36(5), (6), 42(5), (6), 168(5), (6)
para. 102	s.53(3), (4)
para. 103	519(1), (3)
para. 106	Sched. 19, para. 26

CHILDREN ACT 1989
(c.41)

1989	1996
Sched. 13,	
para. 9	s.469(1)
para. 10	576(1), (2), (3), (4)

NATIONAL HEALTH SERVICE AND COMMUNITY CARE ACT 1990
(c.19)

1990	1996
Sched. 9,	
para. 31	s.80(2)

EMPLOYMENT ACT 1990
(c.38)

1990	1996
s.14	s.560(2)

DISABILITY LIVING ALLOWANCE AND DISABILITY WORKING ALLOWANCE ACT 1991
(c.21)

1991	1996
Sched. 3,	
para. 12	s.457(4)

FURTHER AND HIGHER EDUCATION ACT 1992
(c.13)

1992	1996
s.10(1)	ss.2(2), 14(1)
(2)	s.14(5)
(3)	14(6)
11	ss.2(6), 15(1)–(3), (4), (5), (6), (7), (8)
12(1)	16(3)
(2)	41(4)
(3)	176
(4)	398
(5)	101(3), (4)
(6)	116(6)
(7)	106(5)
(9)	450(2)
14(1)	2(4)
(2)	2(2)
(3)	2(5)
s.14(4)	s.2(7)
(5)	4(1)
(6)	3(1), (3)
59(1), (2)	175
(3), (4)	ss.35(6), 41(8), 167(5), 173(4)
90(1), "the Education Acts"	s.578
91(2)	13(2)
(3)	4(3)
(4)	13(2)
(5)	4(4)
Sched. 8,	
para. 2	13(2)
Sched. 8—*cont.*	
para. 4	s.16(1)
para. 5	509(1), (2), (3), (4), (5), (6)
para. 11	518
para. 13(2)	ss.2(2), (3), 3(1), 5(1), (2)
(4)	s.579(7)
para. 14	62(4)
para. 16	510(4)
para. 17	ss.512(5), 534(5)
para. 25	493(1), (3)
para. 28	401(1)
para. 49	ss.544(1), 563(1)

Table of Destinations

Education (Schools) Act 1992
(c.38)

1992	1996
s.16(1)–(6)	s.537(1)–(6)
(7)	537(7)
(8)–(10)	537(8)–(10)
(11), (12)	537(12), (13)
19(1)	569(1)
(2)	ss.537(11), 569(2)
s.19(3)	s.569(4)
Sched. 4, para. 4	29(5)
(1)	414(6)–(8)
(2)	424(3)
Sched. 4—*cont.* para. 5	Sched. 17, para. 10
para. 6(2)	s.408(2)
(3)	408(6)
(4)	408(6)

Judicial Pensions and Retirement Act 1993
(c.8)

1993	1996
Sched. 6, para. 51	Sched. 34, para. 3

Education Act 1993
(c.35)

1993	1996
s.1	s.10
2	11
3	20
4	21
5	26
6	25
7(1), (2)	30(1), (2)
(3)	29(2)
(4)	30(3)
8	23
9	24
12	27
13(1)–(6)	431(1)–(6)
13(7), (8)	431(7), (8)
14	432
15	Sched. 31, para. 15
16	393
17	Sched. 3, para. 1
18	Sched. 3, para. 2
19	Sched. 3, para. 3
20	28
21(1)	30(4)
(2)	29(3), (4)
(3)	ss.29(3), (4), 30(5)
22	s.183
23	184
24	185
25	186
26	187
27	188
28	189
29(1)	190(1)
(2)	190(2)
(3)	190(3)
30	191
31	192
s.32	s.193
33	194
34	195
35	196
36	197
37	200
38(1)–(8)	201(1)–(8)
(9)	201(10)
39	202
40	203
41	204
42	205
43	206
44	207
45	208
46	209
47(1)–(4)	210
48	211
49(1)–(3)	212
50	213
51	214
52	215
53	216
54	217
55	218
56	219(1)–(3)
57	220
58	221
59	222
60	223
61	224
62	225
63	226
64	227
65	228
66	229
67	230
68(1)–(4)	231(1)–(4)
(5)–(7)	231(5)–(7)
(8)	231(8)
69	232
70	233
s.71	s.234
72	235
73	236
74	237
75	238
76	239
77	240
78	241
79	242
80	243
81	244
82	245
83	246
84	247
85	248
86	249
87	250
88	251
89	252
90	253
91	254
92	255
93(1)–(6)	256
94	257
95	258
96	259
97	260
98	261
99	262
100	263
101	264
102	265
103(1)	573(4)
103(2), (3)	266
104	267
105	268
106	269
107	270
108	271
109	272
110	273
111	274

1993	1996
s.112	s.275
113	276
114	277
115	278
116	279
117	280
118	281
119	282
120	283
121	284
122	285
123	286
124	287
125	288
126	289
127(1)–(7)	290(1)–(7)
(8)	290(8), (9)
(9), (10)	290(10), (11)
(11)	290(13)
128	293
129	295
130(1)	296(1)
(2)	296(2)
131	297
132	298
133	299
134	300
135	301
136	302
137	303
138(1)	ss.379(1), 386(1)
(2)	s.386(2)
(3)	386(3)
(4)	386(4)
(5)	386(5)
(6)	386(6)
(7)	387
(8)	385(4)
(9)–(11)	379(2)–(4)
(12)	386(7)
139	380
140	381
141	383
142	382
143	304
144	305
146	Sched. 31, para. 11
147(1)	390(2)
(2)	391(8), (9)
148(a)	394(1)
(b)	394(4)
(c)	ss.394(6), 395(7)
(d)	s.394(8)
149(1)–(4)	426
(5)	436(2)
150	427
151	428
152	309
153	539
154	310
155(1)	434(5)
"premises"	311(1)
(2)	311(3)
(3)	311(4)
(5)	579(3)

1993	1996
s.155(6)	ss.311(5), 436(1)
(7)	s.311(6)
(8)	201(9)
(9)	575(3)
(10)	575(3)
(11)	311(8)
156(1)–(4)	312(1)–(4)
(5)	312(5)
157	313(1)–(4)
158	314
159	315
160	316
161(1)–(5)	317(1)–(5)
(6), (7)	317(6), (7)
162(1), (2)	318(1), (2)
(2A)	318(3)
(3)	318(4)
163	319
164	320
165	321
166(1)	322(1)
(2)	322(2)
(3)	322(3)
(4)	322(4)
(5)	322(5)
167	323
168	324
169	325
170	326
171	327
172	328
173	329
174	330
175	331
176	332
177	333
178	334
179	335
180	336
182(1)	ss.6(2), 337(1)
(2), (3)	337(3), (4)
(4)	344(2)
183(1)	338(1)
(2)–(10)	339
184	340
185	341
186	345
187	346
188	342
189	347
190	348
191	349
192(1)–(7)	437(1)–(7)
(8)	437(8)
193	438
194	439
195	440
196	441
197(1)–(5)	442
(6)	437(8)
198(1)–(3)	443(1)–(3)
(4)	437(8)
199(1)–(4)	444(1)–(4)
(5)	444(5)
(6), (7)	444(6), (7)
(8)	444(9)
200	445

1993	1996
s.200(3)	s.565(2)
201(1)	446
(2)	ss.443(4), 444(8)
202	s.447
203	448
229(1)	ss.35(1), (4), 167(4), 571
(2)	36(1), 168(1)
(3)	36(3), 168(3)
230(1)	41(2), (7), 571
(2)	s.42(1)
(3)	42(3)
(4)	45(2)
(5)	45(7)
(6)	42(4)
231	343
(1)	292(1)
(2)	292(2)
232	500
233	501
234	502
235(1)–(6)	503(1)–(6)
(7)	507(2)
(8)	503(7)
236	504
237(1)–(7)	505(1)–(7)
(8)	505(8)
238(1)	88(1)
(5)–(7)	Sched. 7, para. 1
(8)	88(1)
239	Sched. 7, para. 2
240(1)	s.353
(2)	355(4)
(3)	355(5)
(4)	356(5)–(8)
(5)	402(2)
241(1)	352(1)
(2)	352(3)
(3)	405
(4)	356(9)
(5)	404(1), (2)
(6)	404(3)
242(1), (3)	368(9)
243	368(2), (3), (4), (5), (6), (7)
244	358
245(1)	359(1)
(2)	359(4)
(3)	359(3)
(4)	359(2)
(5)	ss.350(1), 353, 359(5)
249	Sched. 30, para. 11
250	Sched. 30, para. 14
251(3)	Sched. 30, para. 17
253(1)	s.360(1)
254(3)	Sched. 31, para. 4
255(2)	s.390(6)
256(1)	Sched. 31, paras. 1, 2

1993	1996
s.256(2)	Sched. 31, para. 10
257	s.396(1), (2)
258	397
260	430(1)–(8)
261(1)	ss.156(2), (3), 307(1), (2), Sched. 28, para. 15
(2)	ss.156(2), (3), 307(1), (2), Sched. 28, para. 15
(5)	Sched. 28, para. 15
262	s.494
263	537(7)
264(1)	540(1)
(2)	540(2)
265	541(1)–(3)
(1)	541(4)
267	Sched. 33, para. 6
(1)	s.308(1)
(2)	308(2)
268	Sched. 33, para. 7
(1)	s.308(1)
(2)	308(3)
270	413(2)–(4)
271(1)	ss.85, 568(2)
(2)	Sched. 8, para. 11
(3)(a)	s.89(2)
(b)	95(3)
272(1)–(5)	198(1)–(5)
(6)	35(6)
273(1)	ss.35(7), 167(3)
(2)	35(8), 41(9), 167(6), 173(5)
(3)	37(4), 43(3)–(6), 169(4), 199(1)–(3)
(4)	37(1), (7), 43(3)–(6), 169(1), (6), 199(1)–(3)
(5)	37(8), 43(3)–(6), 199(1)–(3)
(a)	s.169(6)
(6)	ss.37(9), 43(3)–(6)
(7)	s.199(4)
274(1)	104(3)
(2)	ss.111, 112(1)–(3), (4), 113(1), (2), (3), (4), (5), 114
(3)	s.110(2), Sched. 39, para. 17(2)
(4)	s.101(1)
(5)	Sched. 39, para. 17(3)
275(1)(c)	s.122(4)
(d)	122(6)
(2)	123

1993	1996
s.276	s.120
277	8
278(2)	484(1), (3), (4)
(4)	489(2)
279(1)	492(1)–(4)
(2)(a)	569(2)
(b)	569(3)
280	451(3)
281	65
282(1)	68
(2)	57(3)
(3)	530(3)
(4)	57(3)
283	69
284	70
285	75
287	557
288(2)	556(3)
(3)	556(1)
(4)	556(4)
290(1)	ss.468, 469(6)
(2)	469(1), (4), 470(2), 471(2), 472, 473(2)
291	s.482(5)
292(2)	467(2)
293(2)	ss.548(1), (2), 549(3)
(3)	548(3), 549(5)
295	s.516
297	499
298(1)–(4)	19(1)–(4)
(5)	31(3)
(6)–(8)	19(5)–(7)
299(1), (2)	567(1), (2)
(3)	567(3)
(4), (5)	567(4), (5)
300	571
301(1)	ss.568(1), 569(1)
(2)	s.568(2)
(3)	ss.568(3), 569(2)
(4)	s.569(3)
(5)	219(4)
(6)	ss.568(5), 569(4)
(7)	s.570(1), (2)
303	Sched. 39, para. 2
304(1)	s.4(1)
(2)	5(1)
305(1)	ss.290(12), 573(2), 575(1), (2), (4)
"Church of England school"	s.311(1)
"Church in Wales school"	311(1)
"local education authority"	34(1)

1993	1996
s.305(1)—*cont.*	
"maintained school"	ss.312(5), 430(9), 431(7), (8), 437(8), 505(8), 540(2), 541(4), 567(3), Sched. 4, para. 1
"Roman Catholic Church school"	s.311(1)
"the Education Acts"	578
(2)	579(2)
(4)	311(2)
308(3)	517(7)
Sched. 1,	
para. 1	Sched. 2, paras. 2–8
para. 2	Sched. 2, paras. 2–8
para. 3	Sched. 2, paras. 2–8
para. 4	Sched. 2, paras. 2–8
para. 5	Sched. 2, paras. 2–8
para. 6	Sched. 2, paras. 2–8
para. 7	Sched. 2, paras. 2–8
para. 8	Sched. 2, paras. 10–14
para. 9	Sched. 2, paras. 10–14
para. 10	Sched. 2, paras. 10–14
para. 11	Sched. 2, paras. 10–14
para. 12	Sched. 2, paras. 10–14
para. 13	Sched. 2, paras. 16, 17
para. 14	Sched. 2, paras. 16, 17
para. 15	Sched. 2, para. 15
para. 16	Sched. 2, para. 1
Sched. 2,	
para. 1	Sched. 4, para. 1
para. 2	Sched. 4, paras. 2–23
para. 3	Sched. 4, paras. 2–23
para. 4	Sched. 4, paras. 2–23
para. 5	Sched. 4, paras. 2–23
para. 6	Sched. 4, paras. 2–23
para. 7	Sched. 4, paras. 2–23

1993	1996
Sched. 2—*cont.*	
para. 8	Sched. 4, paras. 2–23
para. 9	Sched. 4, paras. 2–23
para. 10	Sched. 4, paras. 2–23
para. 11	Sched. 4, paras. 2–23
para. 12	Sched. 4, paras. 2–23
para. 13	Sched. 4, paras. 2–23
para. 14	Sched. 4, paras. 2–23
para. 15	Sched. 4, paras. 2–23
para. 16	Sched. 4, paras. 2–23
para. 17	Sched. 4, paras. 2–23
para. 18	Sched. 4, paras. 2–23
para. 19	Sched. 4, paras. 2–23
para. 20	Sched. 4, paras. 2–23
para. 21	Sched. 4, paras. 2–23
para. 22	Sched. 4, paras. 2–23
para. 23	Sched. 4, paras. 2–23
Sched. 3,	
para. 1(1)	Sched. 20, para. 1
(2)	Sched. 20, para. 1
(3)	Sched. 20, para. 1
(4)	Sched. 20, para. 1
para. 2	Sched. 20, paras. 2–12
para. 3	Sched. 20, paras. 2–12
para. 4	Sched. 20, paras. 2–12
para. 5	Sched. 20, paras. 2–12
para. 6	Sched. 20, paras. 2–12
para. 7	Sched. 20, paras. 2–12
para. 8	Sched. 20, paras. 2–12
para. 9	Sched. 20, paras. 2–12
para. 10	Sched. 20, paras. 2–12
para. 11	Sched. 20, paras. 2–12
para. 12	Sched. 20, paras. 2–12
Sched. 4	Sched. 21
Sched. 5,	
para. 1	Sched. 22, paras. 1–13
para. 2	Sched. 22, paras. 1–13

1993	1996
Sched. 5—*cont.*	
para. 3	Sched. 22, paras. 1–13
para. 4	Sched. 22, paras. 1–13
para. 5	Sched. 22, paras. 1–13
para. 6	Sched. 22, paras. 1–13
para. 7	Sched. 22, paras. 1–13
para. 8	Sched. 22, paras. 1–13
para. 9	Sched. 22, paras. 1–13
para. 10	Sched. 22, paras. 1–13
para. 11	Sched. 22, paras. 1–13
para. 12	Sched. 22, paras. 1–13
para. 13	Sched. 22, paras. 1–13
para. 14	Sched. 22, paras. 14, 15
para. 15	Sched. 22, paras. 14, 15
Sched. 6,	
para. 1	Sched. 23, paras. 1–3
para. 2	Sched. 23, paras. 1–3
para. 3	Sched. 23, paras. 1–3
para. 4	Sched. 23, para. 5
para. 5	Sched. 23, para. 6
para. 6	Sched. 23, paras. 5, 6
para. 7	Sched. 23, para. 4
para. 8	Sched. 23, paras. 7, 8
para. 9	Sched. 23, paras. 7, 8
Sched. 7	Sched. 24
Sched. 8	Sched. 25
Sched. 9	Sched. 26
Sched. 10	Sched. 27
Sched. 11,	
para. 1	Sched. 28, paras. 1–14
para. 2	Sched. 28, paras. 1–14
para. 3	Sched. 28, paras. 1–14
para. 4	Sched. 28, paras. 1–14
para. 5	Sched. 28, paras. 1–14
para. 6	Sched. 28, paras. 1–14
para. 7	Sched. 28, paras. 1–14
para. 8	Sched. 28, paras. 1–14
para. 9	Sched. 28, paras. 1–14

1993	1996
Sched. 11—*cont.*	
para. 10	Sched. 28, paras. 1–14
para. 11	Sched. 28, paras. 1–14
para. 12	Sched. 28, paras. 1–14
para. 13	Sched. 28, paras. 1–14
para. 14	Sched. 28, paras. 1–14
Sched. 13,	
para. 1	Sched. 7, para. 4
para. 2	Sched. 7, para. 3
para. 3	Sched. 7, para. 5
para. 4(2)	s.150(1)
(3)	151(1)–(3), (4), (5), (6)
(4)	ss.134(6), 150(3)
(5)	s.151(7)
(6)	ss.134(5), 150(1), 152(1), (2), (3), (4)
para. 5	s.149(1), (2), (3), (4), (5)
para. 8	Sched. 7, paras. 6–10
para. 9	Sched. 7, paras. 6–10
para. 10	Sched. 7, paras. 6–10
para. 11	Sched. 7, paras. 6–10
para. 12	Sched. 7, paras. 6–10
para. 14	Sched. 7, paras. 11, 12
para. 15	Sched. 7, paras. 11, 12
Sched. 14,	
para. 1	Sched. 29, paras. 1–16
para. 2	Sched. 29, paras. 1–16
para. 3	Sched. 29, paras. 1–16
para. 4	Sched. 29, paras. 1–16
para. 5	Sched. 29, paras. 1–16
para. 6	Sched. 29, paras. 1–16
para. 7	Sched. 29, paras. 1–16
para. 8	Sched. 29, paras. 1–16
para. 9	Sched. 29, paras. 1–16
para. 10	Sched. 29, paras. 1–16
para. 11	Sched. 29, paras. 1–16
para. 12	Sched. 29, paras. 1–16
para. 13	Sched. 29, paras. 1–16

1993	1995
Sched. 14—*cont.*	
para. 14	Sched. 29, paras. 1–16
para. 15	Sched. 29, paras. 1–16
para. 16	Sched. 29, paras. 1–16
para. 17	Sched. 29, para. 17
para. 18	Sched. 29, paras. 18–22
para. 19	Sched. 29, paras. 18–22
para. 20	Sched. 29, paras. 18–22
para. 21	Sched. 29, paras. 18–22
para. 22	Sched. 29, paras. 18–22
Sched. 15,	
para. 4(2)	s.391(10)
(3)	ss.360(2)–(4), 361(1), (2), (3), (4)
(4)	s.362(7)
(5)	368(10)
(6)	Sched. 30, paras. 1–5, 6, 7, 8, 9, 10, 11, 12, 13, 14, 15, 16, 17, 18, 19
para. 6(2)	Sched. 29, para. 17
Sched. 16,	
para. 2	Sched. 33, para. 1
para. 3	Sched. 33, para. 2
para. 4	Sched. 33, para. 5
Sched. 17	Sched. 36
Sched. 18	Sched. 1
Sched. 19,	
para. 7	ss.48(2), 58(2)
para. 9	s.376(3)
para. 12	514(3)
para. 14(a)	521(4)
(b)	525(3)
(c)	524(3)
para. 15	509(4)
para. 18	545(1)
para. 19	545(2)
para. 20	9
para. 21	434(4)

1993	1996
Sched. 19—*cont.*	
para. 23(a)	s.67(3), (4)
(b)	48(4)
para. 24(1)	5(2)
(a)(ii)	434(5)
(b)	576(2)
para. 25	562
para. 27	Sched. 31, paras. 4, 7, 8
para. 31(a)	s.517(1)
(b)–(f)	517(6)
para. 38	ss.198(6), 291
(3)	s.5(5)
para. 41	574
para. 46	Sched. 2, para. 9
para. 47	Sched. 2, para. 9
para. 48	Sched. 2, para. 9
para. 52(a)	s.554(2)
(b)	554(3)
(c)	ss.554(4), 555(1), 556(2), (3)
para. 62(2), (3)	s.552(2), (3)
(2), (3)	552(2)
(4)	552(5)
(5)	552(1)
(6)	552(6)
para. 73	423(1)
para. 74	424(3)
para. 77	44(1)
para. 78	ss.35(2), 41(3)
para. 79	533(3)
para. 90	94(2)
para. 91(a)	82(3)
(d)	82(4), (7)
para. 92(a)	96(1)
(b)	96(2)
(d)	96(3)
para. 94	371(5)
para. 95	154(3)
para. 97	Sched. 15, para. 2
para. 98	Sched. 15, para. 12
para. 99	Sched. 15, para. 14
para. 101(a)	548(3)
(b)	548(4)
para. 103	579(4)

1993	1996
Sched. 19—*cont.*	
para. 103(a)	s.492(6)
(d)	492(5)
para. 104	493(2)
para. 106	519(1)
para. 107(a)	569(4)
para. 109(a)	Sched. 9, para. 2
(b)(i)	Sched. 9, para. 2 Sched. 10, para. 5
(c)	96(4)
(e)	Sched. 9, para. 8
para. 113	s.355(1)
para. 114	352(1)
para. 115	389(5)
para. 116(a)	390(4)
(b)	391(10)
para. 117	392(2), (3), (8)
para. 118(a)	360(2)–(4)
(b)	361(1)
(c)	361(2)
(d)	361(3), (4)
para. 119(a)	362(3), (4)
(b)	362(7)
para. 120	364
para. 121(a)	366(3)
(b)	366(6)
para. 122	368(10)
para. 123	408(3)
para. 124	401(2)
para. 125(a)	116(4)
(b)	116(7)
para. 127	451(5)
para. 128	457(1)
para. 129	458(1)–(4)
para. 136	544(1)
para. 141	Sched. 30, para. 8
para. 142	Sched. 14, para. 28
Sched. 20,	
para. 1	Sched. 39, paras. 24, 25
para. 2	Sched. 39, para. 31
para. 4	Sched. 39, para. 44
para. 5	Sched. 39, para. 28
para. 6	Sched. 39, para. 29

LOCAL GOVERNMENT (WALES) ACT 1994 (c.19)

1994	1996
s.21(1)	s.12(5)
(2)	12(1), (5)
Sched. 16, para. 8	523(3)
para. 105(1)	322(5)

Table of Destinations

Education Act 1994
(c.30)

1994	1996
Sched. 2,	
para. 8(2)....	s.398
para. 8(3)....	450(2)
para. 8(4)....	482(5)

Health Authorities Act 1995
(c.17)

1995	1996
Sched. 1,	
para. 112	s.80(2)
para. 124(2) .	322(1), (3)
para. 124(3) .	332

Jobseekers Act 1995
(c.18)

1995	1996
Sched. 2,	
para. 3	s.512(3)
para. 17	457(4)

Merchant Shipping Act 1995
(c.21)

1995	1996
Sched. 13,	
para. 48	s.560(3)

Disability Discrimination Act 1995
(c.50)

1995	1996
s.29(2)........	s.317(6), (7)
30(8)........	528

Employment Rights Act 1996
(c.18)

1996	1996
Sched. 1,	
para. 37(5)...	ss.139(7), 575(1), (2), (4)
para. 59	s.575(1), (2), (4)

Arbitration Act 1996
(c.23)

1996	1996
Sched. 3,	
para. 4	s.476(4)
para. 59	336

NURSERY EDUCATION AND GRANT-MAINTAINED SCHOOLS ACT 1996 (c.50)

1996	1996
s.7(2)–(4)	s.231(5)–(7)
Sched. 3,	
para. 1	9
para. 2	433(4)
para. 8	578
para. 10	Sched. 3, para. 1
para. 11	s.296(2)
para. 12	318(3)

SECRETARY OF STATE FOR SOCIAL SERVICES ORDER 1968 (S.I.1968 No.1699)

1968	1996
art.5	ss.523(1), (2), 564(1), (3), 570(1), (2)

LOCAL AUTHORITIES ETC. (MISCELLANEOUS PROVISION) ORDER (S.I.1977 No.293)

1977	1996
S.I. 1977 No. 293	s.12(1), (5)
art.4	ss.12(2), 581

LOCAL GOVERNMENT AND HOUSING ACT 1989 (COMMENCEMENT NO.11 AND SAVINGS) ORDER 1991 (S.I.1991 No.344)

1991	1996
Sched.,	
para. 1	Sched. 33, para. 4

EDUCATION REFORM ACT 1988 (COMMENCEMENT NO.9) ORDER 1991 (S.I.1991 No.409)

1991	1996
S.I. 1991 No. 409	s.418(1)

EDUCATION (FINANCIAL DELEGATION FOR PRIMARY SCHOOLS) REGULATIONS 1991 (S.I.1991 No.1890)

1991	1996
S.I. 1991 No. 1890	s.107(1), (2), Sched. 12, para. 5

Table of Destinations

Education (Financial Delegation for Primary Schools) (Amendment) Regulations 1992 (S.I.1992 No.110)

1992	1996
S.I. 1992 No. 110	s.107(1), (2), Sched. 12, para. 5

Education (Application of Financing Schemes to Special Schools) Regulations 1992 (S.I.1992 No.164)

1992	1996
S.I. 1992 No. 164	Sched. 19, para. 21

Education (National Curriculum) (Foundation Subjects at Key Stage 4) Order 1992 (S.I.1992 No.1548)

1992	1996
art.2	s.354(2)

Education Act 1993 (Commencement No.1 and Transitional Provisions) Order 1993 (S.I.1993 No.1975)

1993	1996
Sched. 2, para. 4(2)	Sched. 39, para. 30

Education (No.2) Act 1986 (Amendment) (No.2) Order 1993 (S.I.1993 No.2827)

1993	1996
art.2	Sched. 16, paras. 8, 9

Education Act 1993 (Commencement No.2 and Transitional Provisions) Order 1993 (S.I.1993 No.3106)

1993	1996
Sched. 2, para. 8	Sched. 39, para. 24
para. 9	Sched. 39, para. 24
para. 10	Sched. 39, para. 25
para. 11	Sched. 39, para. 26
para. 14	Sched. 39, para. 27

EDUCATION ACT 1993 (COMMENCEMENT NO.3 AND TRANSITIONAL PROVISIONS) ORDER 1994 (S.I.1994 NO.507)

1994	1996
Sched. 3,	
para. 5	Sched. 39, para. 35
para. 7	Sched. 39, para. 43
para. 10	Sched. 39, para. 31
para. 11	Sched. 39, para. 32
para. 12	Sched. 39, para. 33

EDUCATION (SCHOOL CURRICULUM AND ASSESSMENT AUTHORITY) (TRANSFER OF FUNCTIONS) ORDER 1994 (S.I.1994 NO.645)

1994	1996
S.I. 1994 No. 645	s.361(1)

EDUCATION (NO.2) ACT 1986 (AMENDMENT) ORDER 1994 (S.I.1994 NO.692)

1994	1996
art.2	Sched. 17, para. 6

LOCAL GOVERNMENT CHANGES FOR ENGLAND REGULATIONS 1994 (S.I.1994 NO.867)

1994	1996
reg.5(6)	ss.12(2), 322(5)

EDUCATION (NATIONAL CURRICULUM) (FOUNDATION SUBJECTS AT KEY STAGE 4) ORDER 1994 (S.I.1994 NO.1814)

1994	1996
art.2(2)	s.354(2)
(3)	354(2)
(4)	354(2)
(5)	354(3)–(5)

EDUCATION ACT 1993 (COMMENCEMENT NO.5 AND TRANSITIONAL PROVISIONS) ORDER 1994 (S.I.1994 NO.2038)

1994	1996
Sched. 4,	
para. 2(7)	Sched. 39, para. 34
para. 4(3)	Sched. 39, para. 34

EDUCATION (NO.2) ACT 1986 (AMENDMENT) (NO.2) ORDER 1994
(S.I.1994 No.2092)

1994	1996
S.I. 1994 No.	
2092	Sched. 16, paras. 1, 2, 3, 7
art.8..........	Sched. 16, para. 10
art.9..........	Sched. 16, para. 14
art.10	Sched. 16, para. 16

EDUCATION (NO.2) ACT 1986 (AMENDMENT) (NO.3) ORDER 1994
(S.I.1994 No.2732)

1994	1996
S.I. 1994 No.	
2732	Sched. 17, para. 7

EDUCATION (SCHOOL CURRICULUM AND ASSESSMENT AUTHORITY) (TRANSFER OF FUNCTIONS) ORDER 1995
(S.I.1995 No.903)

1995	1996
S.I. 1995 No.	
903	s.361(1)

UNITS OF MEASUREMENT REGULATIONS 1995
(S.I.1995 No.1804)

1995	1996
reg.3	s.444(5)

TRANSFER OF FUNCTIONS (EDUCATION AND EMPLOYMENT) ORDER 1995
(S.I.1995 No.2986)

1995	1996
art.11(2)......	s.464(1)–(3)
Sched., para. 5	486

REGISTRATION OF BIRTHS, DEATHS AND MARRIAGES (FEES) ORDER 1995
(S.I.1995 No.3162)

1995	1996
Sched.	s.564(1)

LOCAL GOVERNMENT CHANGES FOR ENGLAND (AMENDMENT) REGULATIONS 1996
(S.I.1996 No.611)

1996	1996
reg.2	ss.12(2), 322(5)

LOCAL GOVERNMENT CHANGES FOR ENGLAND (EDUCATION) (MISCELLANEOUS PROVISIONS) REGULATIONS 1996
(S.I.1996 No.710)

1996	1996
reg.19	s.577

DEREGULATION (LENGTH OF THE SCHOOL DAY) ORDER 1996
(S.I.1996 No.951)

1996	1996
art.3(1)	s.147(1), (3)
art.3(2)–(5)	148(1)–(4)
art.4	Sched. 39, para. 19
art.5	149(5)

APPENDIX 1 TO THE REPORT OF THE LAW COMMISSION
(CM.3251)

Cm.3251	1996
No.3	ss.35(1), 41(3), 82(3), 179(1), 259, 260, 263, 371(7), Sched. 8, para. 16
No.4	ss.43(7), 44(3), (4), 45(1)
No.5	s.47(2)
No.6	54(2)
No.7	82(4), (7)
No.8	94(2)
No.9	ss.97(3), (4), (5), 422(7), Sched. 9, para. 1 Sched. 19, para. 15
No.10	s.100(1), (2)
No.11	132
No.12	ss.136(1), (2), 141(2), Sched. 39, para. 18
No.13	s.157(1), (2), (4), (5)
No.14	190(2)
No.15	366(3), (4), (5), (6), (7)
No.16	385(4), (6)
No.17	410
No.18	ss.568(5), (6), 569(1), (4), (5)
No.19	568(1), 581
No.20	Sched. 8, para. 16

INDEX

References are to sections and Schedules

SCHOOL INSPECTIONS ACT 1996*

(1996 c. 57)

[A Table showing the derivation of the provisions of this Consolidation Act will be found at the end of the Act. The Table has no official status.]

ARRANGEMENT OF SECTIONS

PART I

SCHOOL INSPECTIONS

CHAPTER I

SCHOOL INSPECTORS AND INSPECTIONS CARRIED OUT BY THEM

Her Majesty's Inspectorate for England

Her Majesty's Inspectorate for Wales

Registered inspectors

Inspections by registered inspectors

CHAPTER II

PROCEDURE FOR INSPECTIONS UNDER CHAPTER I

Introductory

Inspections and reports: all schools

Destination of reports and special measures: schools within s.11(2)

* Annotations by Neville S. Harris, LL.M., Ph.D., Barrister, Professor of Law, Liverpool John Moores University

SCHEDULES:

An Act to consolidate provisions of the Education (Schools) Act 1992 and Part V of the Education Act 1993, with amendments to give effect to recommendations of the Law Commission. [24th July 1996]

PARLIAMENTARY DEBATES

Hansard, H.L. Vol. 572, cols. 209, 658; Vol. 573, col. 1024; Vol. 574, col. 836. H.C. Vol. 282, col. 368.

INTRODUCTION AND GENERAL NOTE

This Act consolidates the Education (Schools) Act 1992 (c. 38) and Pt. V of the Education Act 1993 (c. 35). It comprises the statutory framework for quality assurance in the schools sector (apart from publication of school performance information, which was dealt with by the 1992 Act but is now consolidated in the Education Act 1996 (c. 56)). The Act covers, *inter alia*, the appointment and functions of the Chief Inspectors of Schools, the inspection of schools by registered inspectors and the "special measures" which may be taken in respect of schools which are considered to be failing to provide an acceptable standard of education. In the course of consolidating the legislation, the opportunity was taken to effect some minor amendments recommended by the Law Commission in its report accompanying the Bill (Cm 3251, HMSO, 1996); these were "intended to rectify a number of inconsistencies and omissions in the present law" (*Hansard*, H.L., Vol. 572, col. 657, May 20, 1996, *per* Lord Mackay of Clashfern, L.C.). Note that the Office for Standards in Education (OfSTED), which currently operates the school inspections system and assists the Chief Inspector in respect of other functions, including monitoring of standards, is not referred to in the legislation and was created by government.

The Act does not cover inspections of nursery education funded via grants made under the Nursery Education and Grant-Maintained Schools Act 1996 (c. 50); that Act provides for a separate inspection regime (see Sched. 1 to that Act and the Nursery Education Regulations 1996, S.I. 1996 No. 2086). Inspections of other forms of nursery education will be conducted under the School Inspections Act 1996.

Various statutory instruments made under the 1992 and 1993 Acts prescribe the intervals at which inspections are to take place and other matters as to the carrying out of inspections: see, in particular, the Education (School Inspection) (No. 2) Regulations 1993 (S.I. 1993 No. 1986), as amended and the Education (School Inspection) (Wales) (No. 2) Regulations 1993 (S.I. 1993 No. 1982), as amended. Schedule 8 to this Act makes provision for any such subordinate legislation which is in force immediately before the commencement of the Act, to continue to have effect and be treated as if made under the Act.

The School Inspections Act is one of the two major consolidation Acts covering education enacted at the end of the 1995–96 Parliamentary session, the other being the much lengthier and wide-ranging Education Act 1996.

Arrangement of the Act

The Act is in three parts.

Part I is concerned with school inspections and provides for: the appointment and functions of the Chief Inspectors; the registration of inspectors of schools; duties concerning the inspection of specified categories of schools and reporting on inspections; inspections of religious education; and local education authority inspection of schools. Part I replicates the main parts of the Education (Schools) Act 1992.

Part II sets out the powers concerning schools requiring special measures, including the power to establish education associations to take over the stewardship of schools which are failing to provide an acceptable standard of education.

Part III deals with miscellaneous matters, including inspection of computer records for the purposes of school inspections, authorised by Pt. I.

Part I: School Inspections

Chap. I (ss.1–10)

Sections 1–3 and Sched. 1 provide for the appointment of a Chief Inspector for England; prescribe the functions of the Chief Inspector; and empower the Chief Inspector to arrange for inspections of schools.

Sections 4–6 and Sched. 1 make equivalent provision for Wales to that in England (in ss.1–3).

Section 7 deals with registration of inspectors for schools in England and Wales.

Section 8 prescribes the circumstances in which the name of a registered inspector may be removed from the register maintained by the Chief Inspector.

Section 9 and Sched. 2 provide for a right of appeal to a tribunal against a refusal of registration as an inspector, removal from the register or the imposition or variation of a condition of registration.

Section 10 and Sched. 3 impose duties on the Chief Inspectors for England and Wales to ensure that prescribed categories of schools are inspected at prescribed intervals, specify the general duties of inspectors when conducting inspections, make provision for the selection of inspectors and inspection teams, and exclude religious education and collective worship at denominational schools from the scope of inspections under its provisions.

Chap. II (ss.11–22)

Section 11 makes provision as to the application of various sections within Chap. II, particularly as regards reports of inspections and on schools requiring "special measures".

Section 12 provides for inspections of schools by a member of the Inspectorate and modifies certain provisions in the case of such inspections.

Sections 13 and 14 require a registered inspector to make a report of his inspection and a summary and prescribes the procedure whereby reports of a registered inspector or a member of the Inspectorate indicating a need for special measures should be dealt with.

Section 15 makes provision as to the timing of reports of inspections and extensions of time.

Sections 16 and 20 make provision as to the destination of reports of inspections.

Sections 17, 18 and 21 impose duties where schools have been found to require special measures, particularly with regard to the preparation of statements.

Sections 19 and 22 provide for monitoring of special measures and further inspections of schools.

Chap. III (ss.23–25)

Section 23 and Sched. 4 require the governing bodies of prescribed categories of school to secure that denominational education is inspected at regular intervals and makes similar provision in respect of inspection of collective worship at prescribed categories of school.

Section 24 empowers a local education authority to provide a school inspection service for schools within its area.

Section 25 empowers local education authorities to carry out inspections of schools for a specific purpose.

Part II: Powers over schools requiring special measures

Sections 26–30 make provision, *inter alia*, as to the special measures that may be taken in respect of schools failing to provide an acceptable standard of education.

Section 31 and Sched. 5 provide a power to establish education associations and make provision as to their constitution and certain other matters.

Sections 32–36 make provision as to the transfer of responsibility to an education association, the effect of such a transfer and the functions of such an association once established.

Sections 37 and 38 make provision for the acquisition of grant-maintained status by, or the discontinuance of, a school conducted by an education association.

Section 40 prescribes certain duties following an inspection, by a member of the Inspectorate, of a school conducted by an education association, who has concluded that the school no longer requires special measures.

Section 41 enables regulations to be made for the purpose of making relevant enactments applicable to various prescribed situations arising under or by virtue of Pt. II.

Part III: General

Section 42 deals with inspection of computer records for the purposes of school inspection.

Section 43 provides for payment of fees into the Consolidated Fund.

Section 44 deals with payment of stamp duty.

Section 45 makes provision regarding orders and regulations.

Section 46 is an interpretation section.

Section 47 and Scheds. 6–8 make provision for amendment and repeal of enactments and prescribe transitional arrangements.

Section 48 specifies the short title, commencement and extent.

ABBREVIATIONS

1992 Act	:	the Education (Schools) Act 1992 (c. 38)
1993 Act	:	the Education Act 1993 (c. 35)
1993 Regulations	:	the Education (School Inspection) (No. 2) Regulations 1993 (S.I. 1993 No. 1986), as amended and the Education (School Inspection) (Wales) (No. 2) Regulations 1993 (S.I. 1993 No. 1982), as amended.
1996 Act	:	the Education Act 1996 (c. 56)
C.I.	:	the Chief Inspector
GM	:	grant-maintained
OfSTED	:	Office for Standards in Education
HMI	:	Her Majesty's Inspectorate (of Schools)

PART I

SCHOOL INSPECTIONS

CHAPTER I

SCHOOL INSPECTORS AND INSPECTIONS CARRIED OUT BY THEM

Her Majesty's Inspectorate for England

Her Majesty's Inspectorate of Schools in England

1.—(1) Her Majesty may by Order in Council appoint a person to the office of Her Majesty's Chief Inspector of Schools in England ("the Chief Inspector for England").

(2) Her Majesty may by Order in Council appoint persons as Her Majesty's Inspectors of Schools in England.

(3) Any person appointed as one of Her Majesty's Inspectors of Schools in England shall serve, in accordance with the terms and conditions on which he is appointed, as a member of the staff of the Chief Inspector for England.

(4) The Chief Inspector for England shall hold and vacate office in accordance with the terms of his appointment, but—

(a) shall not be appointed for a term of more than five years;

(b) may at any time resign by giving written notice to the Secretary of State;

(c) may be removed from office by Her Majesty on the ground of incapacity or misconduct.

(5) The previous appointment of a person as Chief Inspector for England shall not affect his eligibility for re-appointment.

(6) Schedule 1 to this Act makes further provision with respect to the Chief Inspector for England and his staff.

GENERAL NOTE

This section was previously s.1 of the 1992 Act. It provides for the appointment of Her Majesty's Chief Inspector of Schools in England ("the Chief Inspector for England"). The main statutory duties of the C.I. for England are set out in ss.2, 3 and 10.

Subs. (2)

The present Chief Inspector is Christopher Woodhead: the Education (Chief Inspector of Schools in England) Order 1994 (S.I. 1994 No. 1633).

Subss. (4)(a) and (5)

The Chief Inspector may be appointed for a term of up to five years, but may be eligible for re-appointment. Prior to the 1992 Act the two most recent Chiefs of Her Majesty's Inspectorate of Schools had each served for eight years (*Hansard*, H.C. Standing Committee F, col. 58, November 28, 1991).

Subs. (6)

Schedule 1 replaces, with some variation in paragraph numbering and some tidying-up, the corresponding Schedule in the 1992 Act.

Paragraph 2 makes provision for additional inspectors to assist the Chief Inspector. Prior to the 1992 Act such inspectors were appointed by the Secretary of State (under s.77(2) of the Education Act 1944 (c. 31)) "for short or long periods—to provide specific expertise that the existing complement of H.M.I. lacked; to widen the experience of inspectors; to bring an outside perspective to the inspectorate or even, on occasions, to fill gaps caused by extended illness" (*Hansard*, H.C. Standing Committee F, col. 79, November 1991, Mr Fallon, M.P., Under-Secretary of State).

Functions of the Chief Inspector for England

2.—(1) The Chief Inspector for England shall have the general duty of keeping the Secretary of State informed about—

(a) the quality of the education provided by schools in England;
(b) the educational standards achieved in those schools;
(c) whether the financial resources made available to those schools are managed efficiently; and
(d) the spiritual, moral, social and cultural development of pupils at those schools.

(2) When asked to do so by the Secretary of State, the Chief Inspector for England shall—

(a) give advice to the Secretary of State on such matters as may be specified in the Secretary of State's request;
(b) inspect and report on such school, or class of school, in England as may be so specified.

(3) The Chief Inspector for England shall, in addition, have the following specific duties—

(a) establishing and maintaining the register mentioned in section 7(1);
(b) giving guidance to inspectors registered in that register, and such other persons as he considers appropriate, in connection with inspections of schools in England under section 10 and the making of reports of such inspections;
(c) keeping under review the system of inspecting schools under that section (so far as it relates to schools in England) and, in particular, the standard of such inspections and of the reports made by registered inspectors;
(d) keeping under review the extent to which any requirement imposed by or under this Act, or any other enactment, on any registered inspector, local education authority, proprietor of a school or governing body in relation to inspections of schools in England is complied with;
(e) promoting efficiency in the conduct and reporting of inspections of schools in England by encouraging competition in the provision of services by registered inspectors.

(4) The Chief Inspector for England may at any time give advice to the Secretary of State on any matter connected with schools, or a particular school, in England.

(5) The Chief Inspector for England shall have such other functions in connection with schools in England, including functions with respect to the training of teachers for such schools, as may be assigned to him by the Secretary of State.

(6) In exercising his functions the Chief Inspector for England shall have regard to such aspects of government policy as the Secretary of State may direct.

(7) The Chief Inspector for England—

(a) shall make an annual report to the Secretary of State, who shall lay a copy of it before each House of Parliament;

(b) may make such other reports to the Secretary of State, with respect to matters which fall within the scope of his functions, as he considers appropriate; and

(c) may arrange for any report made by him under this subsection to be published in such manner as he considers appropriate.

(8) The Chief Inspector for England, when inspecting a school for the purposes of subsection (2)(b), shall have at all reasonable times—

(a) a right of entry to the premises of the school; and

(b) a right to inspect, and take copies of, any records kept by the school, and any other documents containing information relating to the school, which he requires for the purposes of the inspection.

(9) It shall be an offence wilfully to obstruct the Chief Inspector for England in the exercise of his functions in relation to the inspection of a school for the purposes of subsection (2)(b).

(10) A person guilty of an offence under subsection (9) shall be liable on summary conviction to a fine not exceeding level 4 on the standard scale.

DEFINITIONS

"registered inspector": s.46(1).

GENERAL NOTE

This section replaces ss.2 and 4 of the 1992 Act, in specifying the principal duties of the C.I. for England, and also (in subss. (8)–(10)) clarifies the powers of the C.I. as regards entry and taking of documents and establishes a penalty for wilfully obstructing the C.I. when exercising his functions as regards the inspection of a school under this section.

Subss. (2)(a) and (4)

Prior to the 1992 Act, it was accepted practice for unsolicited advice to be proffered to the Secretary of State by Her Majesty's Chief Inspector (H.M.C.I.). Although subs. (2)(a) refers only to advice requested by the Secretary of State, the minister explained during the passage of the 1992 Act that "there was absolutely nothing in the Bill that would prevent H.M.C.I. providing his advice... when and on what subjects and in what way [he] feels is most appropriate" (*Hansard*, H.C. Standing Committee F, col. 85, December 3, 1991, *per* Mr T. Eggar M.P., Minister of State for Education). Subsection (4) in any event permits the C.I. to give advice to the Secretary of State on any matter connected with schools or a particular school.

Subs. (2)(b)

Note that in the White Paper which preceded the 1992 Act (*Choice and Diversity: A new framework for schools*, Cm 2021, HMSO) the Government emphasised that "... the Secretary of State may ask [Her Majesty's Chief Inspector] to inspect any school—irrespective of its place in the normal four year cycle—about which he receives particularly disturbing reports" (para. 11.4).

Subs. (2)(d)

The inclusion of "social" development was intended "to ensure that matters of discipline and behaviour, and relationships between pupils and staff are fully covered" (*Hansard*, H.L. Vol. 536, col. 1224, March 10, 1992, *per* Baroness Blatch, Minister of State).

Subs. (6)

During the passage of the 1992 Act, the minister said that this provision was intended to enable the Secretary of State to direct the C.I.'s attention to specific policies so that account is taken of them in order to maximise the usefulness of the advice given by the C.I. (see *Hansard*, H.C. Standing Committee F, col. 176, December 5, 1991, *per* Mr T. Eggar, M.P., Minister of State for Education).

Subs. (7)

In addition to being required to make an annual report to the Secretary of State, who must lay it before both Houses of Parliament, the C.I. is empowered to make other reports and arrange for them to be published.

Subss. (8)–(10)
See General Note above.

Power of Chief Inspector for England to arrange for inspections

3.—(1) The Chief Inspector for England may cause any school in England to be inspected by one or more of Her Majesty's Inspectors of Schools in England (in this section referred to as "Inspectors").

(2) Where an inspection of a school in England is being conducted by a registered inspector under section 10 of this Act, the Chief Inspector for England may arrange for that inspection to be monitored by one or more Inspectors.

(3) Any Inspector inspecting a school, or monitoring an inspection, under this section shall have at all reasonable times—

(a) a right of entry to the premises of the school; and
(b) a right to inspect, and take copies of, any records kept by the school, and any other documents containing information relating to the school, which he considers relevant to the discharge of his functions.

(4) It shall be an offence wilfully to obstruct any Inspector in the exercise of any of his functions under this section.

(5) A person guilty of an offence under subsection (4) shall be liable on summary conviction to a fine not exceeding level 4 on the standard scale.

DEFINITIONS
"Inspector": subs. (1).
"registered inspector": s.46(1).

GENERAL NOTE
This section replaces s.3 of the 1992 Act. It empowers the C.I. to cause any school in England to be inspected by a member of H.M.I. (subs. (1)) and to arrange for H.M.I. to monitor any inspection carried out by a registered inspector under s.10; it also provides for the member of the Inspectorate to have a power of entry and inspection and to take copies of documents.

Her Majesty's Inspectorate for Wales

Her Majesty's Inspectorate of Schools in Wales

4.—(1) Her Majesty may by Order in Council appoint a person to the office of Her Majesty's Chief Inspector of Schools in Wales ("the Chief Inspector for Wales").

(2) Her Majesty may by Order in Council appoint persons as Her Majesty's Inspectors of Schools in Wales.

(3) Any person appointed as one of Her Majesty's Inspectors of Schools in Wales shall serve, in accordance with the terms and conditions on which he is appointed, as a member of the staff of the Chief Inspector for Wales.

(4) The Chief Inspector for Wales shall hold and vacate office in accordance with the terms of his appointment, but—

(a) shall not be appointed for a term of more than five years;
(b) may at any time resign by giving written notice to the Secretary of State;
(c) may be removed from office by Her Majesty on the ground of incapacity or misconduct.

(5) The previous appointment of a person as Chief Inspector for Wales shall not affect his eligibility for re-appointment.

(6) Schedule 1 to this Act makes further provision with respect to the Chief Inspector for Wales and his staff.

GENERAL NOTE
This section replicates s.5 of the 1992 Act and makes parallel provision for a Chief Inspector for Wales to that contained in s.1 in the case of the Chief Inspector for England.

Subs. (2)

This subsection provides for the specific appointment of Her Majesty's Inspectors of Schools for Wales. Prior to the 1992 Act, Wales was not covered by separate provision.

Subs. (5)

Mr R.L. James was re-appointed C.I. for Wales from March 1, 1997 to May 31, 1997 by virtue of the Education (Chief Inspector of Schools in Wales) Order 1996 (S.I. 1996 No. 3172).

Subs. (6)

Schedule 1 provides for the appointment of additional inspectors and authorises Her Majesty's Inspectors to carry out functions under the Act for or on behalf of the Chief Inspector for Wales. See further the note to s.1(6).

Functions of the Chief Inspector for Wales

5.—(1) The Chief Inspector for Wales shall have the general duty of keeping the Secretary of State informed about—

(a) the quality of the education provided by schools in Wales;
(b) the educational standards achieved in those schools;
(c) whether the financial resources made available to those schools are managed efficiently; and
(d) the spiritual, moral, social and cultural development of pupils at those schools.

(2) When asked to do so by the Secretary of State, the Chief Inspector for Wales shall—

(a) give advice to the Secretary of State on such matters as may be specified in the Secretary of State's request;
(b) inspect and report on such school, or class of school, in Wales as may be so specified.

(3) The Chief Inspector for Wales shall, in addition, have the following specific duties—

(a) establishing and maintaining the register mentioned in section 7(2);
(b) giving guidance to inspectors registered in that register, and such other persons as he considers appropriate, in connection with inspections of schools in Wales under section 10 and the making of reports of such inspections;
(c) keeping under review the system of inspecting schools under that section (so far as it relates to schools in Wales) and, in particular, the standard of such inspections and of the reports made by registered inspectors;
(d) keeping under review the extent to which any requirement imposed by or under this Act, or any other enactment, on any registered inspector, local education authority, proprietor of a school or governing body in relation to inspections of schools in Wales is complied with;
(e) promoting efficiency in the conduct and reporting of inspections of schools in Wales by encouraging competition in the provision of services by registered inspectors.

(4) The Chief Inspector for Wales may at any time give advice to the Secretary of State on any matter connected with schools, or a particular school, in Wales.

(5) The Chief Inspector for Wales shall have such other functions in connection with schools in Wales, including functions with respect to the training of teachers for such schools, as may be assigned to him by the Secretary of State.

(6) In exercising his functions the Chief Inspector for Wales shall have regard to such aspects of government policy as the Secretary of State may direct.

(7) The Chief Inspector for Wales—

(a) shall make an annual report to the Secretary of State, who shall lay a copy of it before each House of Parliament;

(b) may make such other reports to the Secretary of State, with respect to matters which fall within the scope of his functions, as he considers appropriate; and

(c) may arrange for any report made by him under this subsection to be published in such manner as he considers appropriate.

(8) The Chief Inspector for Wales, when inspecting a school for the purposes of subsection (2)(b), shall have at all reasonable times—

(a) a right of entry to the premises of the school; and

(b) a right to inspect, and take copies of, any records kept by the school, and any other documents containing information relating to the school, which he requires for the purposes of the inspection.

(9) It shall be an offence wilfully to obstruct the Chief Inspector for Wales in the exercise of his functions in relation to the inspection of a school for the purposes of subsection (2)(b).

(10) A person guilty of an offence under subsection (9) shall be liable on summary conviction to a fine not exceeding level 4 on the standard scale.

DEFINITIONS

"registered inspector": s.46(1).

GENERAL NOTE

Section 5 replicates ss.6 and 8 of the 1992 Act as well as clarifying various powers (subss.(8)–(10)). It makes corresponding provision for Wales to that made by s.2 for England (see the note to that section).

Power of Chief Inspector for Wales to arrange for inspections

6.—(1) The Chief Inspector for Wales may cause any school in Wales to be inspected by one or more of Her Majesty's Inspectors of Schools in Wales (in this section referred to as "Inspectors").

(2) Where an inspection of a school in Wales is being conducted by a registered inspector under section 10, the Chief Inspector for Wales may arrange for that inspection to be monitored by one or more Inspectors.

(3) Any Inspector inspecting a school, or monitoring an inspection, under this section shall have at all reasonable times—

(a) a right of entry to the premises of the school; and

(b) a right to inspect, and take copies of, any records kept by the school, and any other documents containing information relating to the school, which he considers relevant to the discharge of his functions.

(4) It shall be an offence wilfully to obstruct any Inspector in the exercise of any of his functions under this section.

(5) A person guilty of an offence under subsection (4) shall be liable on summary conviction to a fine not exceeding level 4 on the standard scale.

DEFINITIONS

"Inspector": subs. (1).

"registered inspector": s.46(1).

GENERAL NOTE

This section makes corresponding provision for Wales to that made for England by s.3 (see note to that section).

Registered inspectors

Registration of inspectors

7.—(1) No person shall conduct an inspection of any school in England under section 10(1) unless he is registered as an inspector in a register kept by the Chief Inspector for England for the purposes of this Part.

(2) No person shall conduct an inspection of any school in Wales under section 10(2) unless he is registered as an inspector in a register kept by the Chief Inspector for Wales for the purposes of this Part.

(3) The Chief Inspector shall not register a person under this section unless, having regard to any conditions that he proposes to impose under subsection (5)(c), it appears to him that that person—

(a) is a fit and proper person for discharging the functions of a registered inspector; and

(b) will be capable of conducting inspections under this Part competently and effectively.

(4) An application for registration under this section—

(a) shall be made in such manner, and be accompanied by such particulars, as the Chief Inspector may direct; and

(b) shall be accompanied by the prescribed fee.

(5) On an application duly made under this section the Chief Inspector may—

(a) register the applicant;

(b) refuse to register him; or

(c) register him subject to such conditions as the Chief Inspector considers it appropriate to impose.

(6) Conditions imposed under subsection (5)(c) may be conditions applying generally in relation to all cases, or particular classes of case, or such conditions together with specific conditions applying in the particular case.

(7) Where a person is registered subject to conditions imposed under subsection (5)(c), he shall be taken to be authorised to act as a registered inspector only so far as those conditions permit.

(8) The period for which any registration is to have effect shall be determined by the Chief Inspector and shall be entered in the register kept by him.

(9) Nothing in subsection (8) is to be taken as preventing a registered inspector from applying for a fresh registration to take effect immediately on the expiry of his current registration.

(10) Subsections (1) and (2) have effect subject to section 12.

DEFINITIONS

"Chief Inspector": s.46(1).
"Chief Inspector for England": s.46(1).
"Chief Inspector for Wales": s.46(1).
"prescribed": s.46(1).
"registered inspector": s.46(1).

GENERAL NOTE

Apart from minor drafting amendments, s.7 replicates s.10 of the 1992 Act. It provides for registration of inspectors.

Subss. (1), (2) and (10)

Only persons registered as inspectors in the register maintained by the C.I. (see ss.2(3)(a) and 5(3)(a)) may conduct an inspection of a school under s.10, apart from members of H.M.I., who may conduct such inspections where it is not reasonably practicable to arrange for an inspection by an inspector registered under s.7: subs.(10) and s.12.

It is, in fact, only necessary for one of the persons engaged in the inspection to be a registered inspector, because Sched. 3, para. 3(1) provides for s.10 inspections to be conducted "by a registered inspector with the assistance of a team (an 'inspection team')".

Subs. (3)

A person may only be registered as an inspector if, having regard to any condition of registration imposed under subs.(5)(a), he or she is regarded by the C.I. as being a "fit and proper person" for carrying out the required responsibilities and as "capable of conducting inspections. . . competently and effectively". He or she will also have to undergo training before being able to inspect a school under the Act: see Sched. 3, paras. 4 and 5.

Note that the right of appeal in relation to registration, provided by s.9, does not apply to the C.I.'s refusal to register but only to, *inter alia*, refusal to renew a registration and the removal of a person's name from the register.

Subss. (5)–(7)

These subsections relate to the imposition of conditions of registration as an inspector. There is a right of appeal against the imposition or variation of any such condition: s.9(1)(b).

Removal from register and imposition or variation of conditions

8.—(1) If the Chief Inspector is satisfied that any of the conditions mentioned in subsection (2) is satisfied with respect to an inspector registered in his register, he may remove the name of that inspector from that register.

(2) The conditions are that—

(a) he is no longer a fit and proper person for discharging the functions of a registered inspector under this Part;

(b) he is no longer capable of conducting inspections under this Part competently and effectively;

(c) there has been a significant failure on his part to comply with any condition imposed under section 7(5)(c) and subject to which his registration has effect;

(d) he has knowingly or recklessly produced a report of an inspection which is, in whole or in part, seriously misleading.

(3) If the Chief Inspector is satisfied—

(a) that he is authorised by subsection (2) to remove the name of an inspector from his register, or

(b) that it would otherwise be in the public interest to act under this subsection,

he may vary any condition subject to which the registration of that inspector has effect or vary that registration by imposing a condition subject to which it will have effect.

(4) Either Chief Inspector may, in exercising his functions under this section with respect to a registered inspector, have regard to any action taken by the other Chief Inspector with respect to that registered inspector.

Definitions

"Chief Inspector": s.46(1).

"registered inspector": s.46(1).

General Note

This replaces s.11 of the 1992 Act. It empowers the C.I. to remove from the register the name of any inspector on the grounds set out in subs. (2), and to vary any conditions of registration, or vary a registration by imposing a condition, on either of the grounds in subs. (3).

Subs. (2)(d)

The inclusion of the words "in whole or in part" was the result of an amendment to the 1992 Act as it progressed through the House of Lords. It was promoted by Lord Elton but had the minister's support: "[I]f a registered inspector knowingly or recklessly produces an inspection report which is seriously misleading, even in part, the chief inspector should be able to remove that inspector from the register without further ado" (*Hansard*, H.L., Vol. 536, col. 1288, March 10, 1992, *per* Baroness Denton).

Subs. (4)

There are separate registers of inspectors for England and Wales, although a person may be registered in both or may seek registration in one, having been refused registration in the other jurisdiction. This subsection empowers the relevant C.I. to take account of any action, such as the imposition of a particular condition of registration or a refusal to register, taken by the other C.I.

Appeals in relation to registration

9.—(1) Any person who is aggrieved by—

(a) the refusal of the Chief Inspector to renew his registration under section 7,

(b) the imposition or variation of any condition subject to which he is registered under that section,

(c) the removal of his name from the relevant register under section 8, may appeal against the Chief Inspector's decision to a tribunal constituted in accordance with Schedule 2 to this Act.

(2) No such decision of the Chief Inspector shall have effect until—

(a) the disposal of any appeal against it which is duly made under this section; or

(b) the period within which an appeal may be made has expired without an appeal having been made.

(3) Subsection (2) shall not apply where the Chief Inspector—

(a) is satisfied that the circumstances of the case are exceptional and justify the decision in question taking effect immediately, or earlier than would otherwise be the case; and

(b) notifies the person concerned to that effect.

(4) On determining any appeal under this section, the tribunal may—

(a) confirm, reverse or vary the decision appealed against; or

(b) remit the case to the Chief Inspector with directions as to the action to be taken by him.

(5) Schedule 2 to this Act makes further provision with respect to tribunals constituted to hear appeals under this section.

DEFINITIONS

"Chief Inspector": s.46(1).

GENERAL NOTE

Section 9 replicates s.12 of the 1992 Act. It makes provision for appeal to a tribunal against a decision concerning registration, but only on the specific grounds set out in subs.(1).

Subs. (1)

This sets out the grounds of appeal under this section.

Subss. (2) and (3)

Normally (subs. (3) prescribes the exception) the decision of the C.I. will not take effect until an appeal has been disposed of or the time allowed for the lodging of an appeal (which may be prescribed by the Secretary of State under Sched. 2, para. 2: see note to subs. (5)) has expired without an appeal being made (subs. (2)).

Subs. (4)

This prescribes the powers of the tribunal.

Subs. (5)

The tribunal is to comprise a legally qualified chairman appointed by the Lord Chancellor and two other members appointed by the Secretary of State (Sched. 2, para. 1) and it falls under the supervision of the Council on Tribunals (Sched. 1, Pt. I, para. 15 of the Tribunals and Inquiries Act 1992 (c. 53), as amended by Sched. 6, para. 5 to this Act). Procedure relating to appeals is to be determined by regulations made by the Secretary of State (para. 2): see the Education (Registered Inspectors of Schools Appeal Tribunal) (Procedure) Regulations 1994 (S.I. 1994 No. 717), which have continuing effect by virtue of Sched. 8 to this Act.

Inspections by registered inspectors

Inspection of certain schools by registered inspectors

10.—(1) It shall be the duty of the Chief Inspector for England to secure that every school in England to which this section applies is inspected, at such intervals as may be prescribed, by an inspector registered under section 7(1).

(2) It shall be the duty of the Chief Inspector for Wales to secure that every school in Wales to which this section applies is inspected, at such intervals as may be prescribed, by an inspector registered under section 7(2).

(3) Subject to subsection (4), the schools to which this section applies are—

(a) county schools;

(b) voluntary schools;

(c) special schools;

(d) grant-maintained schools;
(e) independent schools approved by the Secretary of State under section 347(1) of the Education Act 1996 (approval of independent schools as suitable for admitting children with statements);
(f) city technology colleges;
(g) city colleges for the technology of the arts; and
(h) maintained nursery schools.

(4) This section does not apply to any school conducted by an education association in accordance with Part II.

(5) It shall be the general duty of any registered inspector conducting an inspection under this section to report on—

(a) the quality of the education provided by the school;
(b) the educational standards achieved in the school;
(c) whether the financial resources made available to the school are managed efficiently; and
(d) the spiritual, moral, social and cultural development of pupils at the school.

(6) In prescribing the intervals mentioned in subsections (1) and (2) the Secretary of State may make provision as to the period within which the first inspection of a school under this section is to begin.

(7) Subsections (1) and (2) have effect subject to section 12.

(8) An inspection which is required under this section shall not extend to—

(a) denominational education, or
(b) the content of collective worship which falls to be inspected under section 23.

(9) Schedule 3 to this Act makes further provision with respect to inspections under this section.

Definitions

"city college for the technology of the arts": 1996 Act, s.580.
"city technology college": 1996 Act, s.580.
"county school": 1996 Act, s.580.
"denominational education": s.46(1).
"grant-maintained school": 1996 Act, s.580.
"independent school": 1996 Act, s.580.
"maintained nursery school": 1996 Act, s.580.
"prescribed": s.46(1).
"registered inspector": s.46(1).
"special school": 1996 Act, s.580.
"voluntary school": 1996 Act, s.580.

General Note

Section 10 replicates s.9 of the 1992 Act, as amended by para. 173(1) of Sched. 19 to the 1993 Act, with a minor technical improvement (in subs. (7)). In combination with Sched. 3 it makes provision for the inspection of schools in England and Wales by registered inspectors. The section requires each C.I. to arrange for the schools in their areas and which are covered by the section (see subs. (3)) to be inspected "at such intervals as may be prescribed" (subss. (1) and (2)), defines the general remit of such inspections (subs. (4)) and excludes denominational education and (in the case of the schools referred to in s.23(2)) collective worship from its scope (subs. (8)). Schedule 3 makes more specific provision in relation to the carrying out of inspections.

Subss. (1) and (2)

The Secretary of State is to prescribe the intervals between school inspections for the purposes of subss. (1) and (2) by statutory instrument: see the Education (School Inspection) (No. 2) Regulations 1993 (S.I. 1993 No. 1986), as amended and the Education (School Inspection) (Wales) (No. 2) Regulations 1993 (S.I. 1993 No. 1982), as amended.

Subss. (3) and (4)

These specify the categories of school which may be inspected by registered inspectors under s.10. Most independent schools are not covered by these subsections. Subsection (4) excludes from the scope of the section any school which is under the control of an education association (see generally ss.31–41).

Subs. (5)

This subsection imposes a general duty on registered inspectors to report on the matters set out in paras. (a)–(d).

Subs. (6)

The regulations (see the note to subss. (1) and (2)) specify the dates concerned.

Subs. (8)

See the introduction to this general note above.

Subs. (9)

Schedule 3 sets out various matters relating to inspections under s.10: the selection of a registered school inspector for a particular inspection, following a tendering process (para. 2); the membership of the "inspection team" for the inspection concerned (para. 3); requirements as to training for inspections (paras. 4 and 5); a duty on the "appropriate authority" (as defined in para. 1) to notify parents of a forthcoming inspection of the school and to arrange a meeting between the inspector and the parents in accordance with the prescribed provisions (para. 6; and see the Education (School Inspection) (No. 2) Regulations 1993 (S.I. 1993 No. 1986), as amended and the Education (School Inspection) (Wales) (No. 2) Regulations 1993 (S.I. 1993 No. 1982), as amended); rights of entry and of inspecting and taking copies of document (para. 7); and the offence of wilfully obstructing an inspector or a member of the inspection team (para. 8).

Paragraph 3(2) and (4) of Sched. 3 requires the inspector to ensure that at least one member of the inspection team is a person without personal experience of school management or educational provision (other than as a school governor or in a voluntary capacity) and whose primary function is not that of providing financial or business expertise. The rationale behind what some might regard as a rather illogical qualification for a role in school inspection was explained by the Minister of State, Baroness Blatch as the need for "a fresh perspective... the intelligent outside view applied to all aspects of a school... a valid and valuable addition to the professional view" (*Hansard*, H.L., Vol. 536, col. 697, March 2, 1992). In any event, no-one may become engaged in the inspection of a school unless he or she has, in the opinion of the C.I., satisfactorily completed a course of training provide or approved by the C.I. (paras. 4 and 5).

CHAPTER II

PROCEDURE FOR INSPECTIONS UNDER CHAPTER I

Introductory

Application of provisions of Chapter II

11.—(1) Except as is otherwise provided in section 15, sections 13 to 15, in their application to—

(a) inspections under section 2(2)(b), 3(1), 5(2)(b) or 6(1) by a member of the Inspectorate, or

(b) inspections under section 10,

apply irrespective of the nature of the schools inspected.

(2) Except as is otherwise provided in section 18, sections 16 to 19, in their application to such inspections, apply with respect to county, voluntary, maintained special, grant-maintained or grant-maintained special schools.

(3) Sections 20 to 22, in their application to such inspections, apply with respect to schools not falling within subsection (2) above.

(4) In this Chapter, in its application to an inspection of a school falling within subsection (2)—

"appropriate appointing authority" means, in relation to any aided or special agreement school—

(a) the appropriate diocesan authority, if it is a Church of England school, Church in Wales school or Roman Catholic Church school, and

(b) in any other case, the person who appoints the foundation governors; and "appropriate authority"—

(a) in relation to any county, voluntary or maintained special school, means the school's governing body or, if the governing body do not have a delegated budget, the local education authority, and

(b) in relation to a grant-maintained or grant-maintained special school, means the school's governing body.

(5) In this Chapter, in its application to an inspection of a school falling within subsection (3), "appropriate authority" means—

(a) in the case of a school falling within paragraph (e), (f) or (g) of section 10(3), the proprietor of the school;

(b) in the case of a maintained nursery school whose governing body does not have a delegated budget, the local education authority; and

(c) in any other case, the school's governing body.

(6) In this Chapter "section 10 inspection" means an inspection under section 10.

DEFINITIONS

"aided school": 1996 Act, s.580.
"Church in Wales school": s.46(1).
"Church of England school": s.46(1).
"county school": 1996 Act, s.580.
"delegated budget": s.46(1).
"foundation governor": 1996 Act, s.580.
"grant-maintained school": 1996 Act, s.580.
"grant-maintained special school": 1996 Act, s.580.
"maintained special school": 1996 Act, s.580.
"Roman Catholic Church school": s.46(1).

GENERAL NOTE

This section specifies which categories of school are covered by particular statutory arrangements concerning inspections and reports, monitoring special measures and further inspections, laid down in Chap. II (ss.11–22). It also defines particular terms used in that Chapter.

Inspections by members of the Inspectorate

12.—(1) Where an inspection of a school is required under section 10 but the Chief Inspector is satisfied that it is not reasonably practicable to secure that the school is inspected by a suitable registered inspector, he shall secure that it is inspected by a member of the Inspectorate.

(2) Where such an inspection is conducted by a member of the Inspectorate by virtue of this section, the following provisions, namely—

(a) section 10(1), (2) and (5) and Schedule 3, and

(b) section 13(1),

shall (unless the context otherwise requires) have effect in relation to the inspection as if the member of the Inspectorate were a registered inspector.

(3) If the Chief Inspector so elects in the case of any inspection of a school by a member of the Inspectorate under section 2(2)(b), 3(1), 5(2)(b) or 6(1), that inspection shall be treated for the purposes of the relevant provisions—

(a) as if it were an inspection under section 10, and

(b) in the case of sections 10(1) and (2) and 13(1), as if the member of the Inspectorate were a registered inspector.

(4) In subsection (3) "the relevant provisions" means sections 10(1) and (2), 13(1) and 14 and—

(a) (in the case of an inspection of a school falling within section 11(2)) sections 16 to 19; and

(b) (in the case of an inspection of a school falling within section 11(3)) sections 20 to 22.

DEFINITIONS

"Chief Inspector": s.46(1).
"member of the Inspectorate": s.46(1).
"registered inspector": s.46(1).
"the relevant provisions": subs. (4).

GENERAL NOTE

Section 12 requires the C.I. to arrange for schools to be inspected by a member of H.M.I. if it is not reasonably practicable for them to be inspected by a suitable registered inspector; and applies certain provisions relating to the conduct of the inspections (including the whole of Sched. 3) to such inspections by H.M.I (subss. (1) and (2)). It also (in subs. (3)) treats, for the purposes of certain provisions of the Act (specified in subs. (4)), inspections by H.M.I. carried out by request of the Secretary of State or under the C.I.'s general power to cause a school to be inspected as inspections under s.10.

Inspections and reports: all schools

Section 10 inspections by registered inspectors

13.—(1) Where a section 10 inspection by a registered inspector has been completed, the inspector shall make in writing a report of the inspection and a summary of the report.

(2) Where the inspector is of the opinion that special measures are required to be taken in relation to the school he shall submit a draft of the report of the inspection to the Chief Inspector.

(3) If the Chief Inspector so requests, an inspector who has submitted a draft under subsection (2) shall provide the Chief Inspector with such further information as the Chief Inspector may specify.

(4) The Chief Inspector shall inform an inspector who has submitted a draft under subsection (2) whether he agrees or disagrees with the inspector's opinion.

(5) Where—

(a) the Chief Inspector informs the inspector that he disagrees with the inspector's opinion, but

(b) the inspector remains of the opinion that special measures are required to be taken in relation to the school,

the inspector may not make a report stating that opinion unless the terms in which he makes the report are substantially the same (except as to the statement required by subsection (7)(b)) as the draft or as a subsequent draft submitted to the Chief Inspector under this subsection.

(6) Where a subsequent draft is submitted under subsection (5), the Chief Inspector shall inform the inspector whether he agrees or disagrees with the inspector's opinion.

(7) A report made by a registered inspector who is of the opinion that special measures are required to be taken in relation to the school shall—

(a) state his opinion, and

(b) state whether the Chief Inspector agrees or disagrees with his opinion.

(8) If a report of an inspection of a school by a registered inspector is made in circumstances where—

(a) he is of the opinion that special measures are not required to be taken in relation to the school, but

(b) in the latest report of an inspection of the school, the person making the report stated that in his opinion such measures were required to be taken and either—

(i) that person was a member of the Inspectorate, or

(ii) the report stated that the Chief Inspector agreed with his opinion, the registered inspector shall state his opinion in the report.

(9) For the purposes of this Act special measures are required to be taken in relation to a school if the school is failing or likely to fail to give its pupils an acceptable standard of education.

DEFINITIONS

"Chief Inspector": s.46(1).
"registered Inspector": s.46(1).
"special measures": s.46(2).
"section 10 inspection": s.11(6).

GENERAL NOTE

This replicates (with the exception of subs. (9), which was previously covered by other provisions: see the destination table), Sched. 2 para. 9 to the 1992 Act and s.206 of the 1993 Act. The section is concerned with the reporting of the inspector's findings and the C.I.'s role on receiving a report that special measures are needed in respect of the school.

Subss. (1)–(4)

If the inspector considers that special measures are needed, he must submit a draft of his report to the C.I. and may be required by the C.I. to submit further information to him. The C.I. is required to indicate to the inspector whether or not he agrees with the inspector's opinion on whether special measures are needed.

Subs. (5)

This applies when the inspector has stated in his/her draft report that special measures are needed, the C.I. disagrees with that opinion, but the inspector continues to hold his/her original opinion. The inspector may not express in his report his opinion that special measures are needed unless the report is couched in substantially the same terms as the draft (or subsequent draft) submitted to the C.I. under subs. (2).

Subs. (8)

Normally the inspector would not make any reference to "special measures" if the school was operating satisfactorily. What this subsection says is that where the latest inspection report (*i.e.* the report of the previous inspection) indicated that special measures were needed and, in the case of an inspection by a registered inspector, the C.I. had agreed, the inspector in the current inspection must state in his report, if he or she considers that special measures are not needed. The intention seems to be to indicate that the school has been given the "all clear" after previously being considered to be an "at risk" school.

Subs. (9)

This replicates s.204(3) of the 1993 Act in defining the circumstances in which "special measures" would be required to be taken in the case of a school.

Reports of inspections by members of the Inspectorate

14.—(1) Where on the completion of any inspection of a school under section 2(2)(b), 3(1), 5(2)(b) or 6(1) by a member of the Inspectorate, that person is of the opinion that special measures are required to be taken in relation to the school, he shall—

(a) prepare in writing a report of the inspection and a summary of the report, and

(b) state his opinion in the report.

(2) If on the completion of any such inspection of a school by a member of the Inspectorate in circumstances where—

(a) he is of the opinion that special measures are not required to be taken in relation to the school, but

(b) in the latest report of an inspection of the school, the person making the report stated that in his opinion such measures were required to be taken and either—

(i) that person was a member of the Inspectorate, or

(ii) the report stated that the Chief Inspector agreed with his opinion, the member of the Inspectorate shall prepare in writing a report of the inspection and a summary of the report and state his opinion in the report.

(3) A report of a section 10 inspection of a school by a member of the Inspectorate shall, if he is of the opinion that special measures are required to be taken in relation to the school, state his opinion.

(4) If a report of a section 10 inspection of a school by a member of the Inspectorate is made in circumstances where—

(a) he is of the opinion that special measures are not required to be taken in relation to the school, but

(b) in the latest report of an inspection of the school, the person making the report stated that in his opinion such measures were required to be taken and either—

(i) that person was a member of the Inspectorate, or

(ii) the report stated that the Chief Inspector agreed with his opinion,

the member of the Inspectorate shall state his opinion in the report.

DEFINITIONS

"Chief Inspector": s.46(1).
"member of the Inspectorate": s.46(1).
"section 10 inspection": s.11(6).
"special measures": s.46(2).

GENERAL NOTE

This replicates s.207 of the 1993 Act and para. 9A of Sched. 2 to the 1992 Act. It specifies the steps which must be taken by a member of H.M.I. after his or her inspection of a school under the provisions specified in subs. (1).

Subss. (1) and (2)

If the Inspector carrying out the inspection considers that special measures (see s.13(9)) are needed, he or she must say so in the report. If the previous report on the school concluded that special measures were needed, but the H.M.I. Inspector now considers that they are not, he must, in specified circumstances, prepare a written report and state his opinion in it.

Subss. (3) and (4)

Section 12(1) empowers the C.I. to arrange for a member of H.M.I. to carry out a periodical inspection (a s.10 inspection) of a school in certain circumstances. These subsections make similar provision to that in subss. (1) and (2) for the purposes of such inspections.

Timing of section 10 inspections by registered inspectors

15.—(1) The carrying out of a section 10 inspection shall be completed by the time allowed under subsection (2) below, and the making of the report required by section 13 shall be completed within the period allowed under that subsection.

(2) The time, and the period, allowed shall be such as may be prescribed, subject to any such extension of the period as the Chief Inspector may consider necessary to make; but the total period allowed must not exceed the prescribed period extended by three months.

(3) In the case of an inspection of a school falling within section 11(2) the Chief Inspector shall give notice in writing of any extension under subsection (2) above to—

(a) the inspector;

(b) the local education authority in the case of a county, voluntary or maintained special school; and

(c) the governing body.

(4) In the case of an inspection of a school falling within section 11(3) the Chief Inspector shall give notice in writing of any extension under subsection (2) above to—

(a) the inspector;

(b) the appropriate authority; and

(c) the Secretary of State, except where the school is a maintained nursery school.

(5) This section does not apply to a section 10 inspection carried out by a member of the Inspectorate.

DEFINITIONS

"appropriate authority": s.11(4).
"Chief Inspector": s.46(1).
"county school": 1996 Act, s.580.
"maintained nursery school": 1996 Act, s.580.
"member of the Inspectorate": s.46(1).
"special school": 1996 Act, s.580.
"voluntary school": 1996 Act, s.580.

GENERAL NOTE

This provides for time limits for the completion and preparation of reports in respect of s.10 inspections other than those carried out by members of H.M.I.

Destination of reports and special measures: schools within s.11(2)

Destination of reports

16.—(1) In the case of a report of a section 10 inspection of a school falling within section 11(2), the person making the report shall without delay—

(a) send a copy of the report together with the summary of it to the appropriate authority for the school and, if it is a grant-maintained or grant-maintained special school, to the Secretary of State; and

(b) if in the case of a county, voluntary or maintained special school the report states that the person making it is of the opinion that special measures are required to be taken in relation to the school, and either—

(i) that person is a member of the Inspectorate, or

(ii) the report states that the Chief Inspector agrees with his opinion,

send a copy of the report and summary to the Secretary of State.

(2) In a case where—

(a) a report of an inspection of a school falling within section 11(2) is made by a member of the Inspectorate, and

(b) he is required by section 14(1)(b) to state in the report that he is of the opinion that special measures are required to be taken in relation to the school,

the member of the Inspectorate shall send a copy of the report together with the summary of it to the appropriate authority for the school and the Secretary of State.

(3) In any case, copies of the report and summary referred to in subsection (1) or (2) shall be sent by the person who made the report—

(a) to the Chief Inspector (unless the report was made by a member of the Inspectorate);

(b) to the head teacher of the school;

(c) in the case of a county, voluntary or maintained special school, to whichever of the local education authority and the governing body are not the appropriate authority;

(d) in the case of a school having foundation governors, to the person who appoints them and (if different) to the appropriate appointing authority;

(e) to any person named as a sponsor of the school in the instrument of government; and

(f) in the case of any school in a group of grant-maintained schools in respect of which any person has power to appoint an externally appointed core governor under a provision of the instrument of government made in pursuance of Schedule 25 to the Education Act 1996 (core governors for groups), to that person.

(4) The appropriate authority shall—

(a) make a copy of any report and summary sent to the authority under subsection (1) or (2) available for inspection by members of the public at such times and at such place as may be reasonable;

(b) provide a copy of the report and summary, free of charge or in prescribed cases on payment of such fee as they think fit (not exceeding the cost of supply), to any person who asks for one; and

(c) take such steps as are reasonably practicable to secure that every registered parent of a registered pupil at the school receives a copy of the summary as soon as is reasonably practicable.

DEFINITIONS

"appropriate appointing authority": s.11(4).
"appropriate authority": s.11(4).
"Chief Inspector": s.46(1).
"core governor": 1996 Act, s.580.
"county school": 1996 Act, s.580.
"foundation governor": 1996 Act, s.580.
"grant-maintained school": 1996 Act, s.580.
"grant-maintained special school": 1996 Act, s.580.
"instrument of government": 1996 Act, s.580.
"maintained special school": 1996 Act, s.580.
"member of the Inspectorate": s.46(1).
"prescribed": s.46(1).
"registered": 1996 Act, s.580.
"section 10 inspection": s.11(6).
"special measures": s.46(2).
"voluntary school": 1996 Act, s.580.

GENERAL NOTE

This section makes provision as to the destination of reports of inspections of those categories of school prescribed by s.11(2) carried out by registered inspectors or members of H.M.I. The Secretary of State is to be sent, without delay, a copy of a report on any grant-maintained or grant-maintained special school and other schools where the report indicates that special measures are needed and, in the case of inspections by registered inspectors, the C.I. agrees. Reports, plus summaries, must also be sent to those listed in subs. (3). Copies of a report and summary are to be made available to the public; and parents of registered pupils at the school must be sent a copy of the summary (subs. (4)).

Special measures by appropriate authority

17.—(1) Where there is sent to the appropriate authority for a school falling within section 11(2) either—

(a) a report of a section 10 inspection of the school, or

(b) a report of an inspection of the school by a member of the Inspectorate in which that person is required by section 14(1)(b) to state that he is of the opinion that special measures are required to be taken in relation to the school,

the appropriate authority shall prepare a written statement of the action which they propose to take in the light of the report and the period within which they propose to take it.

(2) It is the duty of the appropriate authority to prepare the statement within the period allowed by this subsection, that is—

(a) such period as may be prescribed, or

(b) if—

(i) the report states that the person making it is of the opinion that special measures are required to be taken in relation to the school, and

(ii) either that person is a member of the Inspectorate or the report states that the Chief Inspector agrees with his opinion, and

(iii) the Secretary of State is of the opinion that the urgency of the case requires a shorter period,

such shorter period as the Secretary of State may direct;

but this subsection does not relieve the appropriate authority of any duty to prepare a statement which has not been performed within that period.

(3) Where such a statement has been prepared by the appropriate authority they shall, before the end of the prescribed period, send copies of it—

(a) to the Chief Inspector;

(b) in the case of a county, voluntary or maintained special school, to whichever of the governing body and the local education authority are not the appropriate authority;

(c) in the case of a grant-maintained or grant-maintained special school, to the Secretary of State; and

(d) in such circumstances as may be prescribed, to such other persons (if any) as may be prescribed.

(4) If in the case of a county, voluntary or maintained special school—

(a) the statement is prepared in response to a report of an inspection of the school in which the person who made the report states that in his opinion special measures are required to be taken in relation to the school, and

(b) either that person is a member of the Inspectorate or the report states that the Chief Inspector agrees with his opinion,

the appropriate authority shall, before the end of the prescribed period, send a copy of the statement to the Secretary of State.

(5) The appropriate authority shall also send a copy of the statement—

(a) in the case of a school having foundation governors, to the person who appoints them and (if different) to the appropriate appointing authority;

(b) to any person named as a sponsor of the school in the instrument of government; and

(c) in the case of any school in a group of grant-maintained schools in respect of which any person has power to appoint an externally appointed core governor under a provision of the instrument of government made in pursuance of Schedule 25 to the Education Act 1996 (core governors for groups), to that person.

(6) The appropriate authority shall—

(a) make any statement prepared by them under this section available for inspection by members of the public, at such times and at such place as may be reasonable;

(b) provide a copy of the statement, free of charge or in prescribed cases on payment of such fee as they think fit (not exceeding the cost of supply); and

(c) take such steps as are reasonably practicable to secure that every registered parent of a registered pupil at the school receives a copy of the statement as soon as is reasonably practicable.

(7) Where the governing body of a school have prepared a statement under this section, they shall in the report referred to in—

(a) section 161 of the Education Act 1996 (governors' report in case of county, voluntary or maintained special school), or

(b) paragraph 7 of Schedule 23 to that Act (governors' report for grant-maintained school),

as the case may be, state the extent to which the proposals set out in the statement (or if there is more than one, the most recent statement) have been carried into effect.

DEFINITIONS

"appropriate appointing authority": s.11(4).
"appropriate authority": s.11(4).
"Chief Inspector": s.46(1).
"core governor": 1996 Act, s.580.
"county school": 1996 Act, s.580.
"foundation governor": 1996 Act, s.580.
"grant-maintained school": 1996 Act, s.580.
"grant-maintained special school": 1996 Act, s.580.
"instrument of government": 1996 Act, s.580.
"maintained special school": 1996 Act, s.580.
"member of the Inspectorate": s.46(1).
"prescribed": s.46(1).
"registered": 1996 Act, s.580.
"section 10 inspection": s.11(6).
"special measures": s.46(2).
"voluntary school": 1996 Act, s.580.

GENERAL NOTE

Section 17 applies to schools listed in s.11(2) and replicates s.210 of the 1993 Act.

Subs. (1)

The governing body must prepare a written statement of the action it proposes to take in the light of a section 10 inspection of a school or of an inspection by a member of H.M.I. who considers that special measures (see s.13(9)) are needed. The statement must specify the period within which it is proposed that the action will be taken.

Subs. (2)

The preparation of the statement under subs. (1) must be completed within a prescribed period (see the Education (School Inspection) (No. 2) Regulations 1993 (S.I. 1993 No. 1986), as amended and the Education (School Inspection) (Wales) (No. 2) Regulations 1993 (S.I. 1993 No. 1982), as amended) or within such shorter period as is directed by the Secretary of State in cases of urgency in certain circumstances. If the statement is not prepared within the set time limit, the duty to prepare it will nevertheless continue.

Subss. (3)–(5) and (6)(c)

These prescribe the destination of copies of the statement of action prepared under subs. (1). Note that there is no time limit for the destination of statements to those persons specified in subs. (5).

Subs. (4)

This specifies the circumstances in which a statement should be sent to the Secretary of State.

Subs. (7)

The annual report of the governing body must state the extent to which the statement prepared under subs. (1) has been carried into effect.

Additional special measures by local education authority

18.—(1) This section applies in circumstances where—

(a) in a report of an inspection of a county, voluntary or maintained special school the governing body of which have a delegated budget, the person who made the report stated that in his opinion special measures were required to be taken in relation to the school; and

(b) either that person was a member of the Inspectorate or the report stated that the Chief Inspector agreed with his opinion; and

(c) either—

(i) the local education authority have received a copy of a statement prepared under section 17 in response to the report, or

(ii) the period prescribed for the purposes of subsection (3) of that section has expired.

(2) The local education authority shall—

(a) prepare a written statement of any action they propose to take in the light of the report, and the period within which they propose to take such action, or, if they do not propose to take any such action, of their reasons for not doing so, and

(b) send a copy of the statement prepared under paragraph (a) above, together with their comments on any statement prepared under section 17 of which they have received a copy, to the Secretary of State and the Chief Inspector and, in the case of an aided or special agreement school—

(i) to the person who appoints the foundation governors, and

(ii) (if different) to the appropriate appointing authority.

(3) It is the duty of the local education authority to prepare the statement within the period allowed by this subsection, that is—

(a) such period as may be prescribed, or

(b) if the Secretary of State is of the opinion that the urgency of the case requires a shorter period, such shorter period as the Secretary of State may direct;

but this subsection does not relieve the local education authority of any duty to prepare a statement which has not been performed within that period.

DEFINITIONS

"aided school": 1996 Act, s.580.
"appropriate appointing authority": s.11(4).
"Chief Inspector": s.46(1).
"county school": 1996 Act, s.580.
"delegated budget": s.46(1).
"foundation governor": 1996 Act, s.580.
"maintained special school": 1996 Act, s.580.
"member of the Inspectorate": s.46(1).
"prescribed": s.46(1).
"special agreement school": 1996 Act, s.580.
"special measures": s.46(2).
"voluntary school": 1996 Act, s.580.

GENERAL NOTE

Local education authorities have a power, first introduced under the 1993 Act, to appoint additional governors (see s.27 of this Act). The 1993 Act also gave them enhanced powers to suspend delegated budgets (see s.28 of this Act). They are required by s.18 to indicate (via a statement which is to be sent to prescribed persons/bodies: subs. (2)): (i) the action, if any, that they propose to take once they have received a report that special measures are needed in relation to a school which has a delegated budget (not a grant-maintained or grant-maintained special school); and (ii) their reasons for non-intervention if that is their decision.

It is clear from subs. (1)(c) that the LEA must consider whether to take any action, and, if it decides to act, what action to take, not later than the date by which the governing body of the school should have prepared a statement of its proposed action under s.17(1).

Subs. (3)

This prescribes or provides for time limits for the preparation of a statement by the LEA under the section. Non-compliance with the time limit does not extinguish the LEA's duty to prepare the required statement.

Monitoring special measures and further inspections

19.—(1) This section applies in circumstances where—

(a) in a report of an inspection of a school falling within section 11(2) the person who made it stated that in his opinion special measures were required to be taken in relation to the school; and

(b) either that person was a member of the Inspectorate or the report stated that the Chief Inspector agreed with his opinion; and

(c) either—

(i) a statement has been prepared under section 17, or

(ii) the period prescribed for the purposes of subsection (3) of that section has expired; and

(d) if any registered inspector or member of the Inspectorate has made a later report of an inspection of the school, he did not state in the report that in his opinion special measures were not required to be taken in relation to the school.

(2) Regulations may make provision with a view to securing that any measures taken by—

(a) the appropriate authority, and

(b) in the case of a school which has a delegated budget, the local education authority,

for improving the standard of education at the school are monitored in accordance with the regulations by such persons as may be prescribed.

(3) The regulations may, in particular, provide for reports to be made by such persons and at such intervals as may be prescribed.

(4) The regulations may authorise the Secretary of State to require the Chief Inspector to conduct further inspections of the school and prepare further reports of such inspections.

(5) In respect of cases where—

(a) any report prepared in pursuance of a requirement imposed by virtue of subsection (4) states that, in the opinion of the person who prepared it, special measures are required to be taken in relation to the school concerned, but the grounds for that opinion are substantially different from the grounds for the opinion in any preceding report by a registered inspector or member of the Inspectorate, or

(b) any report prepared in pursuance of any such requirement states that, in the opinion of the person who prepared it, special measures are not required to be taken in relation to the school concerned,

the regulations may make provision corresponding to any of the provisions of this Chapter so far as it has effect in relation to schools falling within section 11(2).

DEFINITIONS

"Chief Inspector": s.46(1).
"member of the Inspectorate": s.46(1).
"prescribed": s.46(1).
"registered inspector": s.46(1).
"regulations": s.46(1).
"special measures": s.46(2).

GENERAL NOTE

Section 19 replicates s.212 of the 1993 Act. It provides for monitoring, in prescribed circumstances, of measures taken for improving standards of education at a section 11(2) school which is failing, or which is likely to fail, to provide an acceptable standard of education (see s.13(9)). It also provides for reports on such monitoring and for further inspections.

Destination of reports and special measures: schools within s.11(3)

Destination of reports

20.—(1) In the case of a report of a section 10 inspection of a school falling within section 11(3), the person making the report shall without delay—

(a) send a copy of the report together with the summary of it—

(i) to the appropriate authority for the school, and

(ii) (unless the person making it is a member of the Inspectorate) to the Chief Inspector, and

(b) if the report states that the person making it is of the opinion that special measures are required to be taken in relation to the school, and either—

(i) that person is a member of the Inspectorate, or

(ii) the report states that the Chief Inspector agrees with his opinion, send a copy of the report and summary to the Secretary of State.

(2) In a case where—

(a) a report of an inspection of a school falling within section 11(3) is made by a member of the Inspectorate, and

(b) he is required by section 14(1)(b) to state in the report that he is of the opinion that special measures are required to be taken in relation to the school,

the member of the Inspectorate shall send a copy of the report together with the summary of it to the appropriate authority for the school and to the Secretary of State.

(3) In the case of—

(a) a special school which is not a maintained or grant-maintained special school, or

(b) an independent school approved by the Secretary of State under section 347(1) of the Education Act 1996 (approval of independent schools as suitable for admitting children with statements),

the appropriate authority shall without delay send a copy of any report and summary sent to them under subsection (1) or (2) to the funding authority, or any local education authority, if the authority are paying fees in respect of the attendance of a registered pupil at the school.

(4) The appropriate authority shall—

(a) make any report and summary sent to the authority under subsection (1) or (2) available for inspection by members of the public at such times and at such place as may be reasonable;

(b) provide a copy of the report and summary, free of charge or in prescribed cases on payment of such fee as they think fit (not exceeding the cost of supply), to any person who asks for one; and

(c) take such steps as are reasonably practicable to secure that every registered parent of a registered pupil at the school receives a copy of the summary as soon as is reasonably practicable.

DEFINITIONS

"appropriate authority": s.11(5).
"Chief Inspector": s.46(1).
"funding authority": 1996 Act, s.580.
"grant-maintained school": 1996 Act, s.580.
"grant-maintained special school": 1996 Act, s.580.
"independent school": 1996 Act, s.580.
"member of the Inspectorate": s.46(1).
"prescribed": s.46(1).
"registered": 1996 Act, s.580.
"section 10 inspection": s.11(6).
"special measures": s.46(2).
"special school": 1996 Act, s.580.

GENERAL NOTE

By virtue of subs. (1) and s.11(3), this section applies only to schools covered by s.10 (see s.10(3) and (4)) which are not county, voluntary, maintained special, grant-maintained and grant-maintained special schools. It makes corresponding, although different, provision for the destination of reports of inspections to that made by s.16 in the case of these other types of school.

Special measures by appropriate authority

21.—(1) Where there is sent to the appropriate authority for a school falling within section 11(3) either—

(a) a report of a section 10 inspection of the school, or

(b) a report of an inspection of the school made by a member of the Inspectorate in which that person is required by section 14(1)(b) to state that he is of the opinion that special measures are required to be taken in relation to the school, the appropriate authority shall prepare a written statement of the action which they propose to take in the light of the report and the period within which they propose to take it.

(2) It is the duty of the appropriate authority to prepare the statement within the period allowed by this subsection, that is—

(a) such period as may be prescribed, or

(b) if—

(i) the report states that the person making it is of the opinion that special measures are required to be taken in relation to the school, and

(ii) either that person is a member of the Inspectorate or the report states that the Chief Inspector agrees with his opinion, and

(iii) the Secretary of State is of the opinion that the urgency of the case requires a shorter period,

such shorter period as the Secretary of State may direct;

but this subsection does not relieve the appropriate authority of any duty to prepare a statement which has not been performed within that period.

(3) Where such a statement has been prepared by the appropriate authority they shall, before the end of the prescribed period, send copies of it—

(a) to the Chief Inspector;

(b) to the Secretary of State, except in the case of a maintained nursery school; and

(c) in such circumstances as may be prescribed, to such other persons (if any) as may be prescribed.

(4) In the case of—

(a) a special school which is not a maintained or grant-maintained special school, or

(b) an independent school approved by the Secretary of State under section 347(1) of the Education Act 1996 (approval of independent schools as suitable for admitting children with statements),

the appropriate authority shall, before the end of the prescribed period, send a copy of any such statement prepared by them to the funding authority, or any local education authority, if the authority are paying fees in respect of the attendance of a registered pupil at the school.

(5) The appropriate authority shall—

(a) make any statement prepared by them under this section available for inspection by members of the public, at such times and at such place as may be reasonable;

(b) provide a copy of the statement, free of charge or in prescribed cases on payment of such fee as they think fit (not exceeding the cost of supply); and

(c) take such steps as are reasonably practicable to secure that every registered parent of a registered pupil at the school receives a copy of the statement as soon as is reasonably practicable.

DEFINITIONS

"appropriate authority": s.11(5).
"Chief Inspector": s.46(1).
"funding authority": 1996 Act, s.580.
"grant-maintained school": 1996 Act, s.580.
"grant-maintained special school": 1996 Act, s.580.
"independent school": 1996 Act, s.580.
"maintained nursery school": 1996 Act, s.580.
"member of the Inspectorate": s.46(1).
"prescribed": s.46(1).
"registered": 1996 Act, s.580.
"section 10 inspection": s.11(6).
"special measures": s.46(2).
"special school": 1996 Act, s.580.

GENERAL NOTE

This section covers the same schools as s.20 (see note to that section) and makes equivalent, although different, provision to that made by s.17 in respect of other schools.

Subss. (1) and (2)

Subsection (1) imposes a duty on the appropriate authority, in specified circumstances, to prepare a written statement of the action they propose to take in the light of an inspection and the time within which the action will be taken. The appropriate authority must prepare the report within the period of time prescribed by subs. (2).

Subss. (3) and (4)

This imposes a duty on the appropriate authority, in specified circumstances, to send copies of the statement to prescribed persons/bodies within a prescribed period.

Subs. (5)

This imposes a duty on the appropriate authority to make a copy of its statement which has been prepared under subs. (1) available in prescribed ways to prescribed persons.

Monitoring special measures

22.—(1) This section applies in circumstances where—

(a) in a report of an inspection of a school falling within section 11(3) the person who made it stated that in his opinion special measures were required to be taken in relation to the school; and

(b) either that person was a member of the Inspectorate or the report stated that the Chief Inspector agreed with his opinion; and

(c) either—

(i) a statement has been prepared under section 21 of this Act, or

(ii) the period prescribed for the purposes of subsection (3) of that section has expired; and

(d) if any registered inspector or member of the Inspectorate has made a later report of an inspection of the school, he did not in the report state that, in his opinion, special measures were not required to be taken in relation to the school.

(2) Regulations may make provision with a view to securing that any measures taken by the appropriate authority for improving the standard of education at the school are monitored in accordance with the regulations by such persons as may be prescribed.

(3) The regulations may, in particular, provide for reports to be made by such persons and at such intervals as may be prescribed.

(4) The regulations may authorise the Secretary of State to require the Chief Inspector to conduct further inspections of the school and prepare further reports of such inspections.

(5) In respect of cases where—

(a) any report prepared in pursuance of a requirement imposed by virtue of subsection (4) states that, in the opinion of the person who prepared it, special measures are required to be taken in relation to the school concerned, but the grounds for that opinion are substantially different from the grounds for the opinion in any preceding report by a registered inspector or member of the Inspectorate, or

(b) any report prepared in pursuance of any such requirement states that, in the opinion of the person who prepared it, special measures are not required to be taken in relation to the school concerned,

the regulations may make provision corresponding to any of the provisions of this Chapter so far as it has effect in relation to schools falling within section 11(3).

DEFINITIONS

"Chief Inspector": s.46(1).
"prescribed": s.46(1).
"registered inspector": s.46(1).
"regulations": s.46(1).
"special measures": s.46(2).

General Note

This section applies to the same schools as s.20 (see note to that section) and makes equivalent, but slightly different provision in respect of these schools to that made by s.19 in the case of other schools. It provides for monitoring, in prescribed circumstances, of measures taken for improving standards of education at a section 11(3) school which is failing, or which is likely to fail, to provide an acceptable standard of education (see s.13(9)). It also provides for reports on such monitoring and for further inspections. Despite the almost identical content to s.19, the marginal note is, for no clear reason, different.

Chapter III

Other inspections

Religious education

Inspection of religious education

23.—(1) It shall be the duty of the governing body of—

(a) any voluntary school, or

(b) any grant-maintained school,

in which denominational education is given to any pupils to secure that that education is inspected under this section.

(2) It shall be the duty of the governing body of—

(a) any voluntary school, or

(b) any grant-maintained school falling within subsection (3),

to secure that the content of the school's collective worship is inspected under this section.

(3) A grant-maintained school falls within this subsection if—

(a) it was a voluntary school immediately before it became grant-maintained, or

(b) it was established in pursuance of proposals published under section 212 of the Education Act 1996 (proposals by promoters) and either—

(i) any trust deed relating to the school, or

(ii) the statement required by paragraph 8 of Schedule 20 to that Act,

makes provision as to religious education for pupils at the school, or

(c) it is a school in respect of which there are approved under section 261 of that Act (approval of proposed alterations etc.) proposals for the required provision for religious education to be provision for religious education in accordance with the tenets of a particular religion or religious denomination.

(4) In this Act "denominational education", in relation to a school, means any religious education which—

(a) is required by section 352(1)(a) of the Education Act 1996 to be included in the school's basic curriculum, but

(b) is not required by any enactment to be given in accordance with an agreed syllabus;

and in this section—

(i) "the required provision for religious education" means the provision for religious education for pupils at the school which is required as mentioned in paragraph (a) above, and

(ii) references to collective worship are references to collective worship required by section 385 of that Act.

(5) An inspection under this section shall be conducted by a person chosen by—

(a) the foundation governors, in the case of a controlled school; and

(b) the governing body, in any other case.

(6) The person chosen need not be a registered inspector.

(7) Inspections under this section shall be carried out at such intervals as may be prescribed; and in prescribing the intervals the Secretary of State may make provision as to the period within which the first inspection under this section with respect to a school is to begin.

(8) It shall be the general duty of a person conducting an inspection under this section—

(a) if the inspection is conducted by virtue of subsection (1), to report on the quality of the denominational education provided by the school for pupils to whom denominational education is given by the school, or

(b) if the inspection is conducted by virtue of subsection (2), to report on the content of the school's collective worship,

and any such person may report on the spiritual, moral, social and cultural development of pupils at the school.

(9) A person conducting an inspection under this section may do so with the assistance of such other persons chosen by him as are in his opinion fit and proper persons for carrying out the inspection.

(10) Schedule 4 to this Act makes further provision with respect to inspections under this section.

DEFINITIONS

"action plan": Sched. 4, para. 3(1).
"agreed syllabus": 1996 Act, s.580.
"controlled school": 1996 Act, s.580.
"denominational education": subs. (4) and s.46(1).
"foundation governors": 1996 Act, s.580.
"governors' report": Sched. 4, para. 3(5).
"grant-maintained school": 1996 Act, s.580.
"prescribed": s.46(1).
"registered inspector": s.46(1).
"the required provision for religious education": s.23(4)(i).
"voluntary school": 1996 Act, s.580.

GENERAL NOTE

Section 23 replaces s.13 of the 1992 Act, as amended by s.259 of the 1993 Act. Schedule 4 (see subs. (10)) replaces the relevant parts of Sched. 2 to the 1992 Act.

The section provides for the inspection of denominational education in voluntary and grant-maintained schools. It also provides for inspection of collective worship in voluntary schools and prescribed categories (see subs. (3)) of grant-maintained school.

The section is very specific as to the coverage of the inspection regime it provides for. County schools are outside the scope of the section (subs. (1)); in any event their religious education is given in accordance with an agreed syllabus drawn up by a local conference (see the 1996 Act, ss.375 and 376) which is specifically excluded from the definition of "denominational education" by subs. (4). A former county school which has become grant-maintained would only be covered by the section if there had been an approved change to the religious character of the school (see 1996 Act, ss.259(2) and 261). New schools which are established as G.M. schools will be covered by the section if the conditions in subs. (3)(b) apply.

When separate arrangements for inspection of denominational education were first introduced under the 1992 Act, the Minister explained that:

"Religious education in Church schools has been subject to different arrangements for over 150 years... It would have been a very great break with that long-standing agreement to have required Church schools to use secular registered inspectors for the inspection of their own denominational provision" (*Hansard*, H.L., Vol. 536, col. 684, March 2, 1992, *per* Baroness Blatch).

Subss. (5), (6) and (9)

The inspector, who need not be a registered inspector and may select his/her own assistants for the inspection, is to be chosen by the governing body or, in the case of a controlled school, the foundation governors.

Subs. (7)

"*... at such intervals as may be prescribed*": see the 1993 Regulations.

Subs. (10)

Schedule 4 makes provision for the writing of an inspection report and summary and prescribes the duty of the governing body (i) to distribute and make available copies of the inspection report and/or summary; and (ii) to prepare, distribute and make available copies of their action plan in response to the inspector's report.

Local authority inspection services

Provision of inspection services by local education authorities

24.—(1) Any local education authority may provide a school inspection service for schools within their area.

(2) In this section "school inspection service", in relation to any local education authority, means a service providing for the inspection of schools under section 10 or 23 by officers of the authority.

(3) Any school inspection service provided by a local education authority may, in addition to providing for the inspection of schools which are maintained by them, provide for the inspection of schools which are not maintained by them.

(4) Any school inspection service provided by a local education authority shall be operated by the authority in such a way as can reasonably be expected to secure that the full cost of providing the service is recovered by way of charges made by the authority to those using the service.

(5) The Secretary of State may by regulations—

(a) make provision as to the making of tenders by local education authorities (as required by paragraph 2 of Schedule 3 to this Act);

(b) make provision with respect to the accounts to be kept by local education authorities in connection with any school inspection services provided by them; and

(c) make such incidental and supplemental provision with respect to school inspection services provided by local education authorities as the Secretary of State considers appropriate.

DEFINITIONS

"regulations": s.46(1).

"school inspection service": subs. (2).

GENERAL NOTE

This section replicates s.14 of the 1992 Act. The section permits local education authorities to carry out inspections, including inspections of denominational education (see the scope of subs. (2)), by providing a "school inspection service" on a full cost basis (see subs. (4)) and subject to competitive tendering (see subs. (5)(a)). This service may be offered to "schools in the area", including schools which are not maintained by the LEA (subss. (1) and (3)).

Power of local education authority to inspect maintained school for specific purpose

25.—(1) Where—

(a) for the purpose of enabling them to exercise any function of theirs, a local education authority require information about any matter in connection with a school which is maintained by them, and

(b) it is not reasonably practicable for them to obtain the information in any other manner,

they may cause an inspection of the school to be made by one or more of their officers for the purpose of obtaining the information.

(2) Any officer of a local education authority inspecting a school under this section shall have at all reasonable times a right of entry to the premises of the school.

General Note

This replicates s.15 of the 1992 Act, which empowered LEAs to inspect schools which they maintain but which limited the power from its previously wide scope in s.77(3) of the Education Act 1944. The section seems to be intended to permit inspections by local education authorities outside the framework for formal, periodical inspection provided for by Chap. II (see *Hansard*, H.L., Vol. 536, cols. 665–674, March 2, 1992).

Part II

Powers over schools requiring special measures

Miscellaneous powers and restrictions

Schools to which sections 27 to 30 apply

26. Sections 27 to 30 apply only to county, voluntary and maintained special schools and do not apply to a school at any time unless, at that time—

(a) there is a report of an inspection of the school in which the person who made it stated that in his opinion special measures were required to be taken in relation to the school,

(b) either that person was a member of the Inspectorate or the report stated that the Chief Inspector agreed with his opinion,

(c) if any registered inspector or member of the Inspectorate has made a later report of an inspection of the school under Part I, he did not state in the report that in his opinion special measures were not required to be taken in relation to the school, and

(d) the Secretary of State has not exercised his powers under section 33 in relation to the school.

Definitions

"Chief Inspector": s.46(1).
"county school": 1996 Act, s.580.
"maintained special school": 1996 Act, s.580.
"member of the Inspectorate": 1996 Act, s.580.
"special measures": s.46(2).
"voluntary school": 1996 Act, s.580.

General Note

This section, previously comprising s.213 of the 1993 Act, applies provisions (ss.27–30) specifying powers in respect of schools requiring special measures (see s.13(9)) to county, voluntary and maintained special schools. The conditions in paras. (a)–(d) must be satisfied.

Has not exercised his powers under section 33. This relates to the power to transfer overall responsibility for the running of a school to an education association (see ss.31 *et seq.*).

Appointment of additional governors

27.—(1) If at any time—

(a) this section applies in relation to any county, controlled or maintained special school, and

(b) the conditions in subsection (2) are satisfied,

the local education authority may appoint such number of additional governors as they think fit.

(2) Those conditions are that—

(a) a copy of a statement prepared—

(i) (in the case of a school not having a delegated budget) under section 17, and

(ii) (in any other case) under section 18,

has been sent to the Secretary of State;

(b) the local education authority have received a notice in writing in which the Secretary of State acknowledges receipt of the copy; and

(c) a period of not less than ten days has elapsed since the date of the notice.

(3) The Secretary of State may in respect of any particular school determine that subsection (2)(c) above shall have effect as if the reference to ten days were to such shorter period as he may determine.

(4) In relation to any appointment made by the local education authority by virtue of subsection (1) to the governing body of a school—

(a) the instrument of government for the school, or

(b) if the governing body of the school are constituted in accordance with arrangements under section 96 or 97 of the Education Act 1996 (temporary governing bodies for new schools), those arrangements,

shall have effect as if, notwithstanding subsection (1) or (2) of section 79 of that Act (governing bodies for county schools, etc.), the instrument or, as the case may be, arrangements authorised the local education authority to appoint such number of additional governors as they think fit.

(5) If at any time—

(a) this section applies in relation to an aided or special agreement school, and

(b) the conditions in subsection (6) are satisfied,

the appropriate appointing authority may appoint such number of additional foundation governors as they think fit.

(6) Those conditions are—

(a) that a period of not less than ten days has elapsed since the expiry of—

(i) (in the case of a school not having a delegated budget) the period prescribed for the purposes of section 17(3), or

(ii) (in any other case) the period allowed under section 18(3) for preparing a statement under section 18, and

(b) that the Secretary of State has received a copy of a statement prepared—

(i) (in the case of a school not having a delegated budget) under section 17, or

(ii) (in any other case) under section 18,

and has served notice in writing on the appropriate appointing authority stating that the power conferred by subsection (5) is exercisable.

(7) The Secretary of State may by notice in writing served on the appropriate appointing authority determine that subsection (6)(a) shall have effect as if the reference to ten days were to such shorter period as he may determine.

(8) In the case of any appointment made by virtue of subsection (5) to the governing body of a school—

(a) the instrument of government for the school, or

(b) if the governing body are constituted in accordance with arrangements under section 97 of the Education Act 1996, those arrangements,

shall have effect as if, notwithstanding section 84(2) of that Act (foundation governors for aided and special agreement schools), the instrument or, as the case may be, arrangements authorised the appropriate appointing authority to appoint such number of additional foundation governors as they think fit.

(9) Subject to subsection (10), references in this section to the appropriate appointing authority in relation to any aided or special agreement school are references—

(a) to the appropriate diocesan authority, if it is a Church of England School, Church in Wales school or Roman Catholic Church school; or

(b) in any other case, to the person who appoints the foundation governors.

(10) Where, in the case of any aided or special agreement school not falling within subsection (9)(a) there are different powers to appoint foundation

governors, references in this section (excluding subsections (6) and (7)) to the appropriate appointing authority are references—

(a) to all those persons who have any such power acting jointly, or

(b) if they are unable to agree, to such of them acting jointly, or such one of them, as the Secretary of State may, after consulting all those persons, determine.

DEFINITIONS

"aided school": 1996 Act, s.580.
"appropriate appointing authority": subs. (9).
"appropriate diocesan authority": s.46(1).
"Church in Wales school": s.46(1).
"Church of England School": s.46(1).
"foundation governor": 1996 Act, s.580.
"instrument of government": 1996 Act, s.580.
"Roman Catholic Church school": s.46(1).
"special agreement school": 1996 Act, s.580.

GENERAL NOTE

Section 27 replicates s.214 of the 1993 Act, with one addition (subs. (9), which replicates s.204(2) of that Act). The section empowers a local education authority or, in the case of aided or special agreement school, "the appropriate appointing authority", to appoint additional governors to the governing body of a school (as prescribed by s.26) continuing to require special measures, if certain conditions are met.

Subss. (1)–(4)

These apply only to the categories of school prescribed in subs. (1). Note that the local education authority has a discretion as to the number of additional governors to be appointed. Under subs. (4), the relevant provisions of the 1996 Act relating to the constitution of the governing body of the school under the instrument of government must be read as including the appointment of additional governors by the local education authority under this section.

Subss. (5)–(8)

These apply, in prescribed circumstances, only to aided or special agreement schools. Note that the additional governors to be appointed by the appropriate appointing authority (see subss. (9) and (10)) will be additional *foundation* governors.

Note: Sections 96 and 97 of the 1996 Act, one or both of which are referred to in subss. (4)(b) and 8(b), make provision for temporary governing bodies of new LEA-maintained schools. Additional governors may be appointed to these schools under s.27.

Suspension of right to delegated budget

28.—(1) If at any time—

(a) this section applies in relation to a county, controlled or maintained special school in respect of which financial delegation is required, and

(b) the conditions in subsection (2) are satisfied,

the local education authority may by giving the governing body of the school notice of suspension suspend the right to a delegated budget with effect from the receipt by the governing body of the notice; and a copy of the notice shall be given to the head teacher of the school at the same time as the notice is given to the governing body.

(2) Those conditions are that—

(a) a copy of a statement prepared under section 18 has been sent to the Secretary of State;

(b) the local education authority have received a notice in writing in which the Secretary of State acknowledges receipt of the copy; and

(c) a period of not less than ten days has elapsed since the date of the notice.

(3) The Secretary of State may in respect of any particular school determine that subsection (2)(c) shall have effect as if the reference to ten days were to such shorter period as he may determine.

(4) A suspension by virtue of this section shall have effect for the purposes of Chapter V of Part II of the Education Act 1996 as if made under section 117 of that Act, but section 119(1)(a) of that Act (right to appeal against imposition of suspension) does not apply in relation to a suspension by virtue of this section.

(5) Expressions used in this section and that Chapter have the same meaning as in that Chapter.

DEFINITIONS

"controlled school": 1996 Act, s.580.
"county school": 1996 Act, s.580.
"delegated budget": s.46(1).
"maintained special school": 1996 Act, s.580.

GENERAL NOTE

This section replicates s.215 of the 1993 Act. It empowers local education authorities in prescribed circumstances to suspend the governing body's right to a delegated budget.

Subss. (2) and (3)

These lay down the conditions which must be satisfied before a notice of suspension can be served on the governing body. Note that the Secretary of State can give permission for, or order, an earlier implementation of the suspension, in the case of a particular school, than would normally occur.

Subss. (4) and (5)

The effect of this provision is that the power of suspension under this section is subject to, *inter alia*, the 1996 Act relating to review and revocation of suspension. It would mean that the governing body could appeal to the Secretary of State over the refusal of the authority to revoke a suspension following its review of it (although the right to appeal against the imposition of the suspension itself is excluded).

Grouping and de-grouping

29.—(1) If at any time—

(a) this section applies in relation to a county, voluntary or maintained special school, and
(b) the local education authority have received a copy of the report referred to in section 26(a),

they may not pass a resolution under section 89 of the Education Act 1996 (grouping of schools under single governing body) for two or more schools to be grouped if those schools would include the school to which this section applies.

(2) If at any time—

(a) this section applies in relation to a county, voluntary or maintained special school, and
(b) the Secretary of State has received a copy of the report referred to in section 26(a),

he may by order under section 95(1) of the Education Act 1996 bring to an end any grouping of schools under that section which includes the school to which this section applies, whether or not the grouping is one in respect of which his consent was at any time required under section 90 of that Act.

DEFINITIONS

"controlled school": 1996 Act, s.580.
"county school": 1996 Act, s.580.
"maintained special school": 1996 Act, s.580.

GENERAL NOTE

This section replicates s.216 of the 1993 Act. It applies only to county, voluntary or maintained special schools. It states that if there is a report under s.26(a), stating that special measures are required to be taken in respect of the school: (i) the local education authority is prohibited from authorising the grouping of two or more schools under one governing body (under s.89 of the 1996 Act); and (ii) the Secretary of State is empowered to bring an existing grouping to an end.

Prohibition on ballot under Part III of Education Act 1996

30.—(1) If at any time—

(a) this section applies in relation to a county or voluntary school, and

(b) the governing body have received a copy of the report referred to in section 26(a),

then, notwithstanding anything in section 186 or 187 of the Education Act 1996 (initiation of ballot procedure), the governing body of the school may not secure that any ballot is held under Chapter II of Part III of that Act.

(2) If at any time—

(a) this section applies in relation to a maintained special school, and

(b) the governing body have received a copy of the report referred to in section 26(a),

regulations under section 345 of that Act (maintained special school becoming grant-maintained special school) shall not apply in relation to the school.

DEFINITIONS

"county school": 1996 Act, s.580.
"grant-maintained special school": 1996 Act, s.580.
"maintained special school": 1996 Act, s.580.
"regulations": s.46(1).
"voluntary school": 1996 Act, s.580.

GENERAL NOTE

Where there has been an inspection report indicating the conclusion that the school requires special measures to be taken (s.26(a)), the governing body of the school may not hold a ballot on whether the school should acquire (in the case of a county or voluntary school) grant-maintained status or (in the case of a maintained special school) grant-maintained special school status.

Subs. (2)

Regulations under section 345 of that Act (*i.e.* the 1996 Act). See the Education (Grant-Maintained Special Schools) Regulations 1994 (S.I. 1994 No. 653).

Education associations

Power to establish education associations

31.—(1) Where—

(a) the powers conferred by section 33 are exercisable by the Secretary of State in relation to a county or voluntary school, and

(b) he is of the opinion that the school should be conducted by a body corporate established under this section and that no suitable body corporate has been so established,

he may by order provide for the establishment of a body corporate under the name given in the order.

(2) Bodies corporate established under this section shall be known as "education associations".

(3) An education association shall consist of not less than five members appointed by the Secretary of State, one of whom shall be so appointed as chairman.

(4) Before making an order under this section in the case of a voluntary school, the Secretary of State shall consult—

(a) if it is a Church of England school, Church in Wales school or Roman Catholic Church school, the appropriate diocesan authority; and

(b) in any other case, the person who appoints the foundation governors.

(5) An education association—

(a) must include at least one member who appears to the Secretary of State—

(i) to have experience of, and to have shown capacity in, the provision of primary or secondary education, or

(ii) to have held, and shown capacity in, any position carrying responsibility for the provision of such education; and

(b) if the association conduct a school which was a voluntary school, must include at least one member who appears to the Secretary of State to have experience of, and to have shown capacity in, the provision of education in voluntary schools; and

(c) if the association conduct a special school, must include at least one member who appears to the Secretary of State to have experience of, and to have shown capacity in, providing for children with special educational needs;

but one person may satisfy the requirement in paragraph (a) as well as that in paragraph (b) or (c).

(6) Schedule 5 to this Act makes further provision with respect to education associations.

(7) Subject to the following provisions of this Part—

(a) references in any enactment to the governing body of any school, or to the foundation governors of any school, are to be read, in relation to a school conducted by an education association, as references to that association; and

(b) references in any enactment to the governors of any school are to be read, in relation to a school conducted by an education association, as references to the members of the association.

(8) Where an education association conduct more than one school, then, subject to the following provisions of this Part, any provision of an enactment which applies to schools shall apply separately in relation to each of the schools.

DEFINITIONS

"Church in Wales school": s.46(1).
"Church of England school": s.46(1).
"education association": subs. (2).
"foundation governor": 1996 Act, s.580.
"Roman Catholic Church School": s.46(1).
"special educational needs": 1996 Act, s.580.

GENERAL NOTE

This section was formerly s.218 of the 1993 Act. It empowers the Secretary of State to establish an "education association" which would be responsible for ensuring the effective running of a school which has been found to require special measures (and for ensuring that other conditions set out in s.33 are met). As the 1992 White Paper put it, the effect would be "to put the school under new management until its performance has reached a satisfactory level" (*Choice and Diversity* Cm 2021, 1992, para. 11.7.). It was also explained that once taking over the stewardship of one school in a particular area, the association "could subsequently take in as many schools in the area, including neighbouring LEAs, as were found to be failing" (*ibid*., para. 11.9).

Subs. (1)

This specifies the circumstances in which an education association may be established, by order (see, for example, the North-East London Education Association Order 1995 (S.I. 1995 No. 2037)).

Subs. (3)

Although the subsection prescribed five persons as the minimum size of an education association, the Government's intention is that an association would be a "small and cohesive body" with a "chairman and typically some five other part-time members". The first association to be established, the North East London Education Association (NELEA), had precisely such a constitution.

Subs. (5)

This makes provision as to the persons who may be appointed to an education association. When this provision was before Parliament prior to becoming law in the 1993 Act, the Minister explained that an association's members would be drawn mainly from the local community, including "businessmen, professionals and, possibly, parents", "heads or former heads who have been successful in similar schools" and persons with specific skills relevant to the problems at the school, such as "personnel skills, or accountancy skills" (Official Report, Standing Committee E, cols. 1245–1246, *per* Mr T. Boswell, M.P., Under-Secretary of State). For the constitution of the NELEA (referred to in the note to subs. (3)), see *R. v. Secretary of State for Education and Employment and the North East London Education Association ex p. M and Others* [1996] E.L.R. 162, at 167G–168B.

Subs. (6)

Schedule 5 makes provision for supplementary powers of an education association and other matters. Note the powers of an association to establish committees (para. 5) and to delegate functions (para. 6).

Subss. (7) and (8)

The effect of subs. (7) is that all the powers and duties imposed by relevant legislation on governing bodies of schools, and all references to school governors in legislation, are imposed on education associations. Those collective powers and duties apply, so far as a single education association conducting more than one school is concerned, separately in relation to individual schools (subs. (8)).

Supervision of education associations by the Secretary of State

32.—(1) An education association shall, in exercising their functions, comply with any directions given by the Secretary of State.

(2) Before giving a direction under this section, the Secretary of State shall consult the education association or (as the case may be) each education association to which the direction applies unless, for reasons of urgency, it is not in his opinion reasonably practicable for him to do so.

(3) The Secretary of State shall publish any directions given by him under this section in such manner as he thinks fit.

DEFINITIONS

"education association": s.31(2).

GENERAL NOTE

This replicates s.219 of the 1993 Act. It requires an education association to comply with any directions given by the Secretary of State (subs. (1)) and requires the Secretary of State to consult with an education association to which a direction will apply, before making a direction (subs. (2)), and to publish any directions given by him (subs. (3)).

Transfer of responsibility for conducting school to an education association

33.—(1) The powers conferred by this section are exercisable by the Secretary of State in relation to a county school or voluntary school at any time if, at that time—

(a) there is a report of an inspection of the school in which the person who made it stated that in his opinion special measures were required to be taken in relation to the school;

(b) either that person was a member of the Inspectorate or the report stated that the Chief Inspector agreed with his opinion;

(c) the Secretary of State has received a statement prepared under section 17 or the period allowed by subsection (2) of that section for the preparation of such a statement has expired; and

(d) if any registered inspector or member of the Inspectorate has made a later report of an inspection of the school, he did not state in the report that in his opinion special measures were not required to be taken in relation to the school.

(2) Where—

(a) the powers conferred by this section are exercisable by the Secretary of State in relation to a school,

(b) he is of the opinion that the school should be conducted by an education association, and

(c) if the school is a voluntary school, he has consulted the person who appoints the school's foundation governors and such other persons as he thinks appropriate,

he may by order provide for the school to be conducted by an education association named in the order as from such date as may be specified in the order (referred to in this Act as the "transfer date").

(3) On making an order under this section the Secretary of State shall give notice in writing of the order to the governing body and head teacher of the school, to the local education authority and (except in the case of a school in Wales before the Schools Funding Council for Wales begin to exercise their functions) the funding authority.

(4) On the transfer date—

(a) the local education authority whose duty it was immediately before that date to maintain the school as a county or voluntary school shall cease to have that duty, and

(b) any special agreement relating to the school shall cease to have effect.

DEFINITIONS

"Chief Inspector": s.46(1).
"county school": 1996 Act, s.580.
"education association": s.31(2).
"foundation governor": 1996 Act, s.580.
"funding authority": 1996 Act, s.580.
"registered inspector": s.46(1).
"special measures": s.46(2).
"transfer date": subs. (2).
"voluntary school": 1996 Act, s.580.

GENERAL NOTE

This was formerly s.220 of the 1993 Act. It empowers the Secrètary of State, in prescribed circumstances, to make an order providing for a school which has been found to require special measures to be conducted by an education association from a particular date.

Subs. (1)

This prescribes the circumstances in which the power to put an education association in control of a school is exercisable. However, this must be read subject to the requirements of subs. (2).

Subs. (2)

The Secretary of State has a wide discretion as regards the exercise of the power under the section, as he merely has to be "of the opinion that the school should be conducted by an education association" (para. (b)). When the power was first considered by Parliament (in the Bill which became the 1993 Act), the Minister explained that if the action plans prepared in respect of the school "were carried out diligently and the school was clearly on the road to recovery, there would be little need to impose an education association" (*Hansard*, Vol. 545, col. 651, *per* Baroness Blatch, Minister of State).

In the case of a voluntary school, there must be prior consultation with those who appoint the foundation governors (para. (c)).

Subs. (3)

This requires the Secretary of State to give notice to the prescribed bodies of an order made under subs. (2).

Subs. (4)

On the transfer date, the local education authority's duty to maintain the school ceases (para. (a)). Paragraph (b) presumably applies exclusively to a special agreement school: the agreement under which the local education authority will pay a contribution grant of part of the cost of building a school or enlarging an existing one, will terminate on the transfer date.

Effect of order under section 33

34.—(1) This section applies in relation to a school where an order under section 33 has been made.

(2) A school conducted by an education association may not cease to be so conducted unless—

(a) it becomes a grant-maintained school, or

(b) the school is discontinued.

(3) The following subsections have effect subject to the following provisions of this Part.

(4) Subject to section 10(4) and subsection (7) below, references in any enactment to grant-maintained schools include schools conducted by education associations.

(5) References in any enactment to schools the governing bodies of which are incorporated under Chapter II of Part III of the Education Act 1996 (however expressed) include schools conducted by education associations.

(6) Subject to subsection (7) below, references in any enactment—

(a) to any school becoming grant-maintained (whether the reference is to its acquiring grant-maintained status or is expressed in any other form), or

(b) to the date of implementation of the proposals under which it becomes grant-maintained,

are in the case of schools conducted by education associations references to the school beginning to be conducted by the association or, as the case may be, to the transfer date.

(7) References in any enactment to schools the governing bodies of which are incorporated under Chapter IV of Part III of the Education Act 1996 (however expressed) do not include schools conducted by education associations.

DEFINITIONS

"date of implementation": 1996 Act, s.580.

"education association": s.31(2).

GENERAL NOTE

This section replicates s.221 of the 1993 Act.

Subs. (2)

This provides that a school may only cease to be conducted by an education association if it either becomes grant-maintained (see further, s.37) or is discontinued (see further, s.38). According to the White Paper in 1992 (*Choice and Diversity*, Cm 2021, para. 11.13) the "normal expectation is that the school will ... become grant-maintained". See also Department for Education Circular 17/93.

Subss. (3)–(7)

These provisions specify the status of school which is being conducted by an education association for the purposes of various statutory provisions. In effect, the school is, by virtue of subss. (4)–(6), to be treated as a grant-maintained school. But when reference is made in any enactment to a governing body of a new grant-maintained school established by a funding authority or by promoters under Chap. IV of Pt. III of the 1996 Act, it cannot be taken to refer to an education association (subs. (7)).

Functions of education associations

35.—(1) Where an order under section 33 provides for an education association to conduct a school, the association may as from the transfer date conduct the school; and their power under this subsection is to conduct a school of the same description as the school as it was immediately before that date.

(2) An education association shall conduct any school for which they are the governing body so as to secure, so far as it is practicable to do so, the elimination of any deficiencies in the conduct of the school identified in any report made by a registered inspector or member of the Inspectorate.

(3) A school conducted by an education association shall not, where changes have been made in the character or premises of the school since the

transfer date, be regarded as being of a different description from the school as it was immediately before that date if the changes—

(a) did not require authorisation under Chapter VII of Part III of the Education Act 1996, or

(b) were authorised under that Chapter.

(4) Subject to any provision made by the articles of government for the school, an education association may provide education at any school conducted by them which is neither primary nor secondary education if—

(a) it is part-time education suitable to the requirements of persons of any age over compulsory school age, or full-time education suitable to the requirements of persons who have attained the age of 19;

(b) it is part-time education suitable to the requirements of junior pupils who have not attained the age of 5 and the school provides full-time education for junior pupils of the same age; or

(c) they do so as agents for a local education authority under arrangements made with the authority for the purpose.

DEFINITIONS

"articles of government": 1996 Act, s.580.
"education association": s.31(2).
"member of the Inspectorate": s.46(1).
"registered inspector": s.46(1).
"transfer date": s.33(2).

GENERAL NOTE

Subs. (1)

The function of the education is to conduct a school, with the description of the school (presumably "county" or "voluntary"—the classification used in s.33(1)—although it could also refer to "primary" or "secondary") for this purpose being the same as before the association was put in control.

Subs. (2)

The education association must aim, so far as is practicable, to remove deficiencies in the conduct of the school which were identified by the inspectors. According to the White Paper (*Choice and Diversity*, Cm 2021, (HMSO, 1992) para. 11.11), the Secretary of State will "set the [education association] a remit to improve each identified school within a defined period, with an option to review the position and extend the period as necessary".

Subs. (3)

The effect of s.34 seems to be, *inter alia*, that a school which is under the control of an education association is run as though a grant-maintained school and thus may undergo a change of character or other alteration as provided for by Chap. VII of Pt. III of the 1996 Act. This subsection states that such changes, made after the education association is put in control of the school, should not, for the purposes of s.35, be regarded as altering the description of the school.

Subs. (4)

This gives an education association equivalent powers to provide further education and part-time education for junior pupils to that which grant-maintained schools enjoy under s.231(8) of the 1996 Act.

Conduct of school

36.—(1) Each school conducted by an education association shall be conducted in accordance with an instrument to be known as the articles of government.

(2) Subject to any express provision of the articles of government, the school shall be conducted in accordance with any trust deed relating to it.

(3) The initial articles of government for such a school shall be such as are prescribed and, subject to subsection (4), shall have effect as from the transfer date.

(4) Such of the articles as may be prescribed shall have effect as from such date prior to the transfer date as may be prescribed.

(5) The education association may, with the consent of the Secretary of State—

(a) make new articles of government in place of the existing articles for the school, or

(b) modify the existing articles for the school.

(6) The Secretary of State may by a direction under this section, in the case of—

(a) schools conducted by education associations,

(b) any class of such schools specified in the direction, or

(c) any particular school conducted by an education association so specified,

require each education association conducting any school to which the direction applies to modify its articles of government in any manner so specified.

(7) Before giving a direction under this section, the Secretary of State shall consult each education association conducting any school to which the direction applies.

DEFINITIONS

"articles of government": subs. (1).
"education association": s.31(2).
"prescribed": s.46(1).
"transfer date": s.33(2).

GENERAL NOTE

This section, which replicates s.223 of the 1993 Act, provides for a school under the control of an education association to be conducted in accordance with prescribed articles of government and any trust deed relating to the school; and it enables articles to be replaced with the consent of the Secretary of State, or modified with his consent (after prescribed consultation and in relation to any school or class of school) or under his direction. The articles are prescribed by the Education (Schools Conducted by Education Associations) (Initial Articles of Government) Regulations 1994 (S.I. 1994 No. 2849).

School conducted by education association acquiring grant-maintained status

37.—(1) Where the Secretary of State—

(a) has received a copy of a report under section 40(2) in respect of a school conducted by an education association, and

(b) is of the opinion that the school should become a grant-maintained school,

he may give notice in writing of his opinion to the head teacher of the school, the education association, the local education authority and (except in the case of a school in Wales before the Schools Funding Council for Wales have begun to exercise their functions) the funding authority.

(2) An education association which receive a notice under subsection (1) above in respect of a school shall, within the period of three months beginning with the receipt of the notice, publish proposals under section 193 of the Education Act 1996 (proposals to seek grant-maintained status).

(3) In relation to proposals published under that section by virtue of this section and the incorporation of a governing body in pursuance of such proposals, Chapters II and V of Part III of that Act shall have effect—

(a) as if the school to which the proposals relate had continued, after the transfer date, to be a county or, as the case may be, voluntary school, and

(b) with such other modifications as may be prescribed.

DEFINITIONS

"education association": s.31(2).
"funding authority": 1996 Act, s.580.
"grant-maintained school": 1996 Act, s.580.
"prescribed": s.46(1).
"Schools Funding Council for Wales": 1996 Act, s.21(1).

GENERAL NOTE

This section, which replicates s.224 of the 1993 Act, empowers the Secretary of State to communicate his opinion that a school which is under the control of an education association but which has been found, following an inspection, not to require special measures (see s.40), should become grant-maintained; and, it requires an education association, in such a case, to publish proposals (under s.193 of the 1996 Act) for the school to acquire such status and prescribes the relevant arrangements. See further the note to s.34(2).

Subs. (3)

The position vis-a-vis the process of acquiring grant-maintained status, incorporation and the arrangements for the government of the school will be as though the school continued to be a county or voluntary school whose governing body had published proposals for the acquisition of grant-maintained status for the school.

Discontinuance of school conducted by education association

38.—(1) Where the Secretary of State is of the opinion that a school conducted by an education association should be discontinued, he shall give notice in writing of his opinion and of the discontinuance date to—

(a) the education association;

(b) the local education authority;

(c) the funding authority (except in the case of a school in Wales before the Schools Funding Council for Wales have begun to exercise their functions); and

(d) if the school provides education to which section 2(1) of the Further and Higher Education Act 1992 applies, the appropriate further education funding council.

(2) The education association shall cease to conduct the school—

(a) on the date specified in the notice; or

(b) if at the request of the education association the Secretary of State subsequently fixes another date (whether in substitution for the date specified in the notice or in substitution for a date previously fixed under this subsection), on that date.

(3) Where the Secretary of State has given notice under this section, he may by order make provision for the disposal of the school property and the discharge of any liabilities of the education association in respect of the school.

(4) An order under subsection (3) may make any such provision (except provision for the dissolution of the education association) as is made by, or may be made by an order under, sections 274 to 279 of the Education Act 1996 (winding up and disposal of property) where proposals for the discontinuance of a grant-maintained school have been approved under section 269 of that Act.

DEFINITIONS

"education association": s.31(2).
"funding authority": 1996 Act, s.580.
"further education funding council": Further and Higher Education Act 1992 (c. 13), s.1(1).
"grant-maintained school": 1996 Act, s.580.
"liability": 1996 Act, s.580.
"Schools Funding Council for Wales": 1996 Act, s.21(1).

GENERAL NOTE

An education association's stewardship of a school comes to an end by the school either becoming grant-maintained or being discontinued (see s.34(2)). Although the Government's normal expectation would be that the first of these two outcomes would occur (see note to s.34(2)), closures are possible and a small number have occurred since this provision, originally comprising s.225 of the 1993 Act, was first introduced. Under this section, the Secretary of State has the power to give notice to the bodies specified in subs. (1) of the discontinuance of the school as from the date determined with reference to subs. (2) and to order the disposal of the school property and other assets and the discharge of any liabilities of the association in respect of the school (subss. (3) and (4)). See further s.41. As to the effect of the absence of a statutory duty to consult on a closure under this section (and s.225 before it), see *R. v. Secretary of State for Education and Employment and the North East London Education Association ex p. M and Others* [1996] E.L.R. 162, at 206A–210D.

Winding-up of education association

39.—(1) Where this section applies to the school or, as the case may be, each of the schools conducted or formerly conducted by an education association, the Secretary of State may by order provide for the dissolution of the association and the transfer to him of the property, rights and liabilities of the association.

(2) This section applies where—

(a) the Secretary of State has approved proposals for the school to become a grant-maintained school, or

(b) the Secretary of State has given notice under section 38 of his opinion that the school should be discontinued.

DEFINITIONS

"education association": s.31(2).
"grant-maintained school": 1996 Act, s.580.
"liability": 1996 Act, s.580.

GENERAL NOTE

Once the school, or all of the schools, under its control become grant-maintained or closed under ss.37 and 38, respectively, the education association's work is in effect complete. Section 39, which replicates s.226 of the 1993 Act, makes provision as to the winding-up of an education association and the transfer to the Secretary of State of the property, rights and liabilities of the association.

Reports showing school no longer requires special measures

40.—(1) Where, on the completion of any inspection of a school conducted by an education association which is carried out under section 2(2)(b), 3(1), 5(2)(b) or 6(1) by a member of the Inspectorate, that person is of the opinion that special measures are not required to be taken in relation to the school, he shall prepare in writing a report of the inspection and a summary of the report and state his opinion in the report.

(2) The member of the Inspectorate shall send a copy of the report, together with a summary of it, to the head teacher of the school, the education association and the Secretary of State.

(3) The education association shall—

(a) make any copy report and summary sent to them under subsection (2) available for inspection by members of the public at such times and at such place as may be reasonable;

(b) provide a copy of the report and summary, free of charge or in prescribed cases on payment of such fee as they think fit (not exceeding the cost of supply), to any person who asks for one; and

(c) take such steps as are reasonably practicable to secure that every registered parent of a registered pupil at the school receives a copy of the summary as soon as is reasonably practicable.

DEFINITIONS

"education association": s.31(2).
"member of the Inspectorate": s.46(1).
"prescribed": s.46(1).
"registered pupil": 1996 Act, s.580.
"special measures": s.46(2).

GENERAL NOTE

This section, which replicates s.227 of the 1993 Act, makes provision for the preparation, dissemination and availability of a report of an inspection of a school which has been found no longer to require special measures. Specific duties are imposed on the member of H.M.I. and the education association.

Regulations for the purposes of Part II

41.—(1) Regulations may provide for any relevant enactments to have effect in relation to—

(a) the transfer to an education association under section 33 of responsibility for the conduct of any school and the subsequent conduct of the school by the association,

(b) the transfer to a governing body incorporated in pursuance of proposals published by virtue of section 37 of responsibility for the conduct of any school conducted by an education association, and

(c) the discontinuance under section 38 of any school conducted by an education association,

with such modifications as seem to the Secretary of State to be necessary or desirable.

(2) In subsection (1) "relevant enactment" means any enactment relating to grant-maintained schools (or schools including grant-maintained schools), including an enactment relating to the acquisition of grant-maintained status.

(3) Subsection (1) does not apply in relation to schools which are or were maintained special schools; but regulations may provide for sections 33 to 40 to have effect in relation to any such schools as they have effect in relation to county schools but with such modifications as seem to the Secretary of State to be necessary or desirable.

(4) Regulations may make such provision as the Secretary of State considers necessary or desirable in relation to—

(a) the transfer to an education association under section 33 of responsibility for the conduct of any maintained special school and the subsequent conduct of the school by the association, and

(b) where a former maintained special school is being conducted by an education association, the discontinuance of the school under section 38.

(5) In relation to any former maintained special school being conducted by an education association—

(a) section 345 of the Education Act 1996 (maintained special school becoming grant-maintained school) shall apply as it applies to any maintained special school, but as if the reference in subsection (1) to the school ceasing to be maintained by the local education authority were to its ceasing to be conducted by an education association, and

(b) section 37 above shall apply—

(i) as if the reference in subsection (1) to a grant-maintained school were to a grant-maintained special school,

(ii) as if the reference in subsection (2) to section 193 of that Act were to section 345 of that Act, and

(iii) with the omission of subsection (3).

DEFINITIONS

"county school": 1996 Act, s.580.
"education association": s.31(2).
"grant-maintained school": 1996 Act, s.580.
"grant-maintained special school": 1996 Act, s.580.
"maintained special school": 1996 Act, s.580.
"regulations": s.46(1).
"relevant enactment": subs. (2).
"special school": 1996 Act, s.580.

GENERAL NOTE

This section replicates, apart from some technical improvements, s.228 of the 1993 Act.

Subss. (1)–(3)

Subsections (1) and (2) enable regulations to apply provisions relating to grant-maintained schools (save as modified by the Secretary of State) in order to regulate the matters referred to in paras. (a)–(c) of subs. (1). Thus, for example, so far as para.(b) is concerned, parts of Chap. VIII of Pt. III of the 1996 Act on discontinuance may be applied (see *Hansard*, H.L., Vol. 545, col. 690 and the Education (Schools Conducted by Education Associations) Regulations 1993 (S.I. 1993 No. 3103), as amended.

Subsection (1) must be read in conjunction with subs. (3) in the case of maintained special schools.

Subss. (3) and (4)

County and voluntary schools can be put under the control of an education association (see s.33(1)), and these subsections enable regulations to bring maintained special schools within the possible remit of an association (and then to be discontinued). See the Education (Special Schools Conducted by Education Associations) Regulations 1994 (S.I. 1994 No. 1084).

Subs. (5)

This enables former maintained special schools being conducted by an education association to acquire grant-maintained special school status under s.345 of the 1996 Act via the arrangements made by s.37 of this Act (as modified).

PART III

GENERAL

Inspection of computer records

Inspection of computer records for purposes of Part I

42. Any person authorised by Part I to inspect records—

(a) shall be entitled at any reasonable time to have access to, and inspect and check the operation of, any computer and any associated apparatus or material which is or has been in use in connection with the records in question; and

(b) may require—

(i) the person by whom or on whose behalf the computer is or has been so used; or

(ii) any person having charge of, or otherwise concerned with the operation of, the computer, apparatus or material,

to afford him such assistance as he may reasonably require.

Financial provisions

Payment of fees into Consolidated Fund

43. Any sums received by the Chief Inspector under—

(a) section 7(4)(b), or

(b) paragraph 4(2) or 5(2) of Schedule 3,

shall be paid into the Consolidated Fund.

Stamp duty

44.—(1) Subject to subsection (2) below, stamp duty shall not be chargeable in respect of—

(a) any transfer effected under section 39;

(b) any transfer—

(i) to a funding authority, or
(ii) to the governing body of a grant-maintained school,
by virtue of section 38(3); or

(c) any transfer to a local education authority by virtue of section 38(3) of property which immediately after the transfer is held by the authority for the purposes of—
(i) a county or voluntary school or maintained special school not established in a hospital, or
(ii) a new county school.

(2) No instrument (other than a statutory instrument) made or executed under or in pursuance of any of the provisions mentioned in subsection (1) shall be treated as duly stamped unless—

(a) it is stamped with the duty to which it would, but for this section (and, if applicable, section 129 of the Finance Act 1982), be liable, or
(b) it has, in accordance with the provisions of section 12 of the Stamp Duty Act 1891, been stamped with a particular stamp denoting that it is not chargeable with any duty or that it has been duly stamped.

Orders and regulations

Orders and regulations

45.—(1) Any power conferred by this Act to make an order or regulations (except an order under section 38) shall be exercisable by statutory instrument.

(2) Any statutory instrument containing any such order or regulations (except an order under section 31, 33 or 39) shall be subject to annulment in pursuance of a resolution of either House of Parliament.

(3) Any order or regulations made under this Act may make different provision for different cases, circumstances or areas and may contain such incidental, supplemental, saving or transitional provisions as the Secretary of State thinks fit.

(4) Without prejudice to the generality of subsection (3), any such regulations may include provision for the designation by the Secretary of State, in accordance with the regulations, of particular schools or classes of school for the purposes of the application of particular provisions of the regulations in relation to such schools.

Construction

Interpretation

46.—(1) In this Act—

"Chief Inspector" (without more) shall be read—
(a) in relation to any school in England or registration under section 7(1), as a reference to the Chief Inspector for England; and
(b) in relation to any school in Wales or registration under section 7(2), as a reference to the Chief Inspector for Wales;

"Chief Inspector for England" means the person referred to in section 1(1);

"Chief Inspector for Wales" means the person referred to in section 4(1);

"Church in Wales school", "Church of England school" and "Roman Catholic Church school", and "appropriate diocesan authority" in each case, have the meaning given by section 311(1) of the Education Act 1996;

"delegated budget" has the same meaning as in section 116 of the Education Act 1996;

"denominational education" has the meaning given in section 23(4);
"member of the Inspectorate" means the Chief Inspector, any of Her Majesty's Inspectors of Schools in England or, as the case may be, Wales and any additional inspector authorised under paragraph 2 of Schedule 1;
"prescribed" means prescribed by regulations;
"registered inspector" means a person registered under section 7(1) or (2);
"regulations" means regulations made by the Secretary of State under this Act;
"the transfer date" shall be construed by reference to section 33(2).

(2) References in this Act to special measures being, or not being, required to be taken in relation to a school shall be construed in accordance with section 13(9).

(3) For the purposes of this Act any reference to a condition imposed under section 7(5)(c) includes a reference to a condition imposed under section 8(3).

(4) This Act and the Education Act 1996 shall be construed as one.

Final provisions

Consequential amendments, repeals and transitional provisions

47.—(1) The enactments specified in Schedule 6 are amended in accordance with that Schedule, the amendments being consequential on the provisions of this Act.

(2) The enactments specified in Schedule 7 are repealed to the extent specified.

(3) The transitional provisions contained in Schedule 8 shall have effect.

Short title, commencement and extent

48.—(1) This Act may be cited as the School Inspections Act 1996.

(2) This Act shall come into force on 1st November 1996.

(3) Subject to subsections (4) and (5), this Act extends to England and Wales only.

(4) This section and paragraph 6 of Schedule 1 also extend to Scotland and Northern Ireland.

(5) The amendments in Schedule 6 and the repeals in Schedule 7 have the same extent as the enactments to which they refer.

SCHEDULES

Sections 1 and 4

SCHEDULE 1

HER MAJESTY'S CHIEF INSPECTORS

Chief Inspector's other staff

1. The Chief Inspector may, with the approval of the Treasury as to numbers and terms and conditions of service, appoint such staff, in addition to Inspectors who are members of his staff by virtue of section 1(3) or (as the case may be) 4(3) of this Act, as he thinks fit.

Additional inspectors

2.—(1) The Chief Inspector may arrange for such persons as he thinks fit to assist him in the discharge of any of his functions in relation to a particular case or class of case.

(2) Any person assisting the Chief Inspector under any such arrangements shall be known as an additional inspector.

(3) Any arrangements which provide for assistance by persons who are not members of the Chief Inspector's staff shall be made on terms agreed by him with the Treasury.

(4) An additional inspector acting within the authority conferred on him by the Chief Inspector shall have all the powers of an Inspector.

Remuneration, pensions etc.

3.—(1) There shall be paid to the Chief Inspector such remuneration, and such travelling and other allowances, as the Secretary of State may determine.

(2) In the case of any such Chief Inspector as may be determined by the Secretary of State, there shall be paid—

(a) such pension, allowance or gratuity to or in respect of him, or

(b) such contributions or payments towards provision for such a pension, allowance or gratuity,

as may be so determined.

(3) If, when any person ceases to hold office as Chief Inspector, the Secretary of State determines that there are special circumstances which make it right that he should receive compensation, there may be paid to him such sum by way of compensation as may be determined by the Secretary of State.

(4) Any determination of the Secretary of State under this paragraph requires the approval of the Minister for the Civil Service.

(5) Any determination made under this paragraph with respect to one Chief Inspector may be different from any corresponding determination made with respect to the other Chief Inspector.

Official seal

4. The Chief Inspector shall have an official seal for the authentication of documents required for the purposes of his functions.

Performance of functions

5.—(1) Anything authorised or required by or under this Part of this Act or any other enactment to be done by the Chief Inspector for England may be done by—

(a) any of Her Majesty's Inspectors of Schools in England,

(b) any other member of his staff, or

(c) any additional inspector,

who is authorised generally or specially in that behalf by the Chief Inspector for England.

(2) Anything authorised or required by or under this Part of this Act or any other enactment to be done by the Chief Inspector for Wales may be done by—

(a) any of Her Majesty's Inspectors of Schools in Wales,

(b) any other member of his staff, or

(c) any additional inspector,

who is authorised generally or specially in that behalf by the Chief Inspector for Wales.

(3) Without prejudice to the generality of sub-paragraph (1) or (2), the references to the Chief Inspector in—

(a) section 2(8) or (9), or

(b) section 5(8) or (9),

include references to any person authorised to act on his behalf in conducting an inspection under section 2(2)(b) or section 5(2)(b) (as the case may be).

Documentary evidence

6. The Documentary Evidence Act 1868 shall have effect, in relation to the Chief Inspector for England and in relation to the Chief Inspector for Wales, as if—

(a) he were included in the first column of the Schedule to that Act;

(b) he and any person authorised to act on his behalf were mentioned in the second column of that Schedule, and

(c) the regulations referred to in that Act included any document issued by him or by any such person.

DEFINITIONS

"Chief Inspector": s.46(1).

"regulations": s.46(1).

GENERAL NOTE
See the note to s.1(6).

Section 9

SCHEDULE 2

TRIBUNALS HEARING APPEALS UNDER SECTION 9

Constitution of tribunals

1.—(1) A tribunal constituted to hear an appeal under section 9 of this Act ("a tribunal") shall consist of—
(a) a Chairman appointed by the Lord Chancellor; and
(b) two other members appointed by the Secretary of State.

(2) To be qualified for appointment as Chairman of a tribunal, a person must have a 7 year general qualification (within the meaning of section 71 of the Courts and Legal Services Act 1990).

(3) A person shall not be appointed after the day on which he attains the age of 70 to be the Chairman of a tribunal.

Procedure of tribunals

2.—(1) The Secretary of State may by regulations make provision with respect to the making of appeals to, and the procedure to be followed by, tribunals.

(2) The regulations may, in particular, make provision—
(a) as to the period within which, and manner in which, appeals must be brought;
(b) for the holding of hearings in private in prescribed circumstances;
(c) as to the persons who may appear on behalf of the parties;
(d) for enabling hearings to be conducted even though a member of the tribunal, other than the Chairman, is absent;
(e) as to the disclosure by the appellant, and others, of documents and the inspection of documents;
(f) requiring persons to attend the proceedings and give evidence;
(g) as to the payment of expenses incurred by persons compelled to attend proceedings by regulations made by virtue of paragraph (f);
(h) authorising the administration of oaths to witnesses;
(i) as to the withdrawal of appeals;
(j) as to costs and expenses incurred by any party to the proceedings; and
(k) authorising preliminary or incidental matters in relation to an appeal to be dealt with by the Chairman of the tribunal hearing that appeal.

Staff

3. The Secretary of State may, with the consent of the Treasury, make such provision as he thinks fit for—
(a) the allocation of staff for any tribunal;
(b) the remuneration of members of tribunals and the reimbursement of their expenses;
(c) defraying any reasonable expenses incurred by any tribunal.

DEFINITIONS
"a tribunal": para. 1(1).
"prescribed": s.46(1).
"regulations": s.46(1).

GENERAL NOTE
See the note to s.9(5).

Section 10

SCHEDULE 3

INSPECTIONS UNDER SECTION 10

1. In this Schedule—
"appropriate authority" means—
(a) in the case of a county, voluntary, maintained special or maintained nursery school whose governing body does not have a delegated budget, the local education authority;
(b) in the case of a school falling within paragraph (e), (f) or (g) of section 10(3), the proprietor of the school;

(c) in any other case, the school's governing body;

"inspection" means an inspection under section 10.

Selection of registered inspectors

2. Before entering into any arrangement for an inspection, the Chief Inspector shall, after consulting the appropriate authority for the school concerned as to the tender specification, invite tenders from at least two registered inspectors who can reasonably be expected—

(a) to wish to tender for the proposed inspection; and
(b) to tender at arm's length from each other.

Inspection teams

3.—(1) Every inspection shall be conducted by a registered inspector with the assistance of a team (an "inspection team") consisting of persons who are fit and proper persons for carrying out the inspection.

(2) It shall be the duty of the registered inspector to ensure that—

(a) at least one member of the inspection team is a person—
  (i) without personal experience in the management of any school or the provision of education in any school (otherwise than as a governor or in any other voluntary capacity); and
  (ii) whose primary function on the team is not that of providing financial or business expertise; and
(b) no member of the inspection team falls within a category of person prescribed for the purposes of this sub-paragraph.

(3) Otherwise, the composition of the inspection team shall be determined by the registered inspector, subject to his complying with any condition imposed under section 7(5)(c).

(4) Any experience of a kind mentioned in sub-paragraph (2)(a) which it is reasonable to regard as insignificant, having regard to the purposes of sub-paragraph (2), may be ignored by the registered inspector.

(5) It shall be the duty of the registered inspector to ensure that no person takes any part in an inspection if he has, or has at any time had, any connection with—

(a) the school in question,
(b) any person who is employed at the school,
(c) any person who is a member of the school's governing body, or
(d) the proprietor of the school,

of a kind which might reasonably be taken to raise doubts about his ability to act impartially in relation to that school.

Training for inspections

4.—(1) No person shall conduct an inspection of a school in England, or act as a member of an inspection team for such a school, unless he has, in the opinion of the Chief Inspector for England, satisfactorily completed a course of training provided by, or complying with arrangements approved by, that Chief Inspector.

(2) Where the Chief Inspector for England provides such training he may charge such fees as are reasonable for the purpose of recovering the whole, or part, of the cost of providing it.

(3) Sub-paragraph (1) shall not apply in such circumstances as may be specified, either generally or in relation to a particular case or class of case, by the Chief Inspector for England.

5.—(1) No person shall conduct an inspection of a school in Wales, or act as a member of an inspection team for such a school, unless he has, in the opinion of the Chief Inspector for Wales, satisfactorily completed a course of training provided by, or complying with arrangements approved by, that Chief Inspector.

(2) Where the Chief Inspector for Wales provides such training he may charge such fees as are reasonable for the purpose of recovering the whole, or part, of the cost of providing it.

(3) Sub-paragraph (1) shall not apply in such circumstances as may be specified, either generally or in relation to a particular case or class of case, by the Chief Inspector for Wales.

Meeting with parents

6. Where an inspection is arranged, the appropriate authority for the school concerned shall—

(a) take such steps as are reasonably practicable to notify—
  (i) the parents of registered pupils at the school, and

(ii) such other persons as may be prescribed,

of the time when the inspection is to take place; and

(b) arrange a meeting, in accordance with such provisions as may be prescribed, between the inspector conducting the inspection and those parents of registered pupils at the school who wish to attend.

Rights of entry etc.

7. A registered inspector conducting an inspection, and the members of his inspection team, shall have at all reasonable times—

(a) a right of entry to the premises of the school concerned; and

(b) a right to inspect, and take copies of, any records kept by the school, and any other documents containing information relating to the school, which he requires for the purposes of the inspection.

Offence of obstructing inspector or inspection team

8.—(1) It shall be an offence wilfully to obstruct—

(a) a registered inspector, or

(b) a member of an inspection team,

in the exercise of his functions in relation to an inspection of a school.

(2) Any person guilty of an offence under sub-paragraph (1) shall be liable on summary conviction to a fine not exceeding level 4 on the standard scale.

DEFINITIONS

"appropriate authority": para. 1.
"Chief Inspector": s.46(1).
"inspection": para. 1.
"inspection team": para. 3(1).
"prescribed": s.46(1).
"registered inspector": s.46(1).

GENERAL NOTE

See the note to s.10(9).

Section 23 SCHEDULE 4

INSPECTIONS OF DENOMINATIONAL EDUCATION

Construction

1. In this Schedule—

"inspection" means an inspection of a school under section 23; and
"inspector" means the person conducting the inspection.

Inspectors' reports

2.—(1) An inspection shall be carried out within such period as may be prescribed.

(2) When an inspection has been completed, the inspector shall, before the end of the prescribed period, prepare in writing a report of the inspection and a summary of the report.

(3) The inspector shall, without delay, send the report and summary to the governing body for the school concerned.

(4) The governing body shall—

(a) make any such report and its accompanying summary available for inspection by members of the public, at such times and at such a place as may be reasonable;

(b) provide a copy of the report and summary, free of charge or in prescribed cases on payment of such fee as they think fit (not exceeding the cost of supply), to any person who asks for one; and

(c) take such steps as are reasonably practicable to secure that every parent of a registered pupil at the school—

(i) for whom the school provides denominational education, or

(ii) who takes part in acts of collective worship the content of which falls to be inspected under section 23,

as the case may be, receives a copy of the summary as soon as is reasonably practicable.

Action plans

3.—(1) The governing body to whom an inspector has reported under this Schedule shall, before the end of the prescribed period, prepare a written statement ("the action plan") of the action which they propose to take in the light of his report and the period within which they propose to take it.

(2) Where an action plan has been prepared by a governing body, they shall, before the end of the prescribed period, send copies of it to the person who appoints the school's foundation governors and—

(a) in the case of a voluntary school, to the local education authority, or

(b) in the case of a grant-maintained school, to the Secretary of State,

and to such other persons (if any), in such circumstances, as may be prescribed.

(3) The governing body shall—

(a) make any action plan prepared by them available for inspection by members of the public, at such times and at such a place as may be reasonable;

(b) provide a copy of the plan, free of charge or in prescribed cases on payment of such fee as they think fit (not exceeding the cost of supply), to any person who asks for one; and

(c) take such steps as are reasonably practicable to secure that every parent of a registered pupil at the school—

(i) for whom the school provides denominational education, or

(ii) who takes part in acts of collective worship the content of which falls to be inspected under section 23,

as the case may be, receives a copy of the plan as soon as is reasonably practicable.

(4) Where the governing body of a school have prepared an action plan, they shall include in their governors' report a statement of the extent to which the proposals set out in the plan have been carried into effect.

(5) In sub-paragraph (4) "governors' report" means—

(a) in the case of a voluntary school, the report referred to in section 161 of the Education Act 1996; and

(b) in the case of a grant-maintained school, the report referred to in paragraph 7(1) of Schedule 23 to that Act.

(6) Sub-paragraph (4) applies only in relation to the most recent action plan for the school in question.

DEFINITIONS

"the action plan": para. 3(1).
"denominational education": s.23(4).
"governors' report": para. 3(5).
"grant-maintained school": 1996 Act, s.580.
"inspection": para. 1.
"inspector": para. 1.
"prescribed": s.46(1).
"voluntary school": 1996 Act, s.580.

GENERAL NOTE

See the note to s.23(10).

Section 31 SCHEDULE 5

EDUCATION ASSOCIATIONS

Supplementary powers

1.—(1) Subject to sub-paragraph (2) and to the articles of government of any school they conduct, an education association may do anything which appears to them to be necessary or expedient for the purpose of or in connection with the discharge of their functions, including in particular—

(a) acquiring and disposing of land and other property,

(b) entering into contracts,

(c) investing sums not immediately required for the purpose of the discharge of their functions, and

(d) accepting gifts of money, land or other property.

(2) An education association shall not borrow money except money lent under section 255 of the Education Act 1996.

(3) The power to dispose of land mentioned in sub-paragraph (1)(a) above—

(a) does not include power to grant any mortgage, charge or other security in respect of any land, and

(b) may only be exercised with the written consent of the Secretary of State.

Tenure of members

2.—(1) A person shall hold and vacate office as a member of an education association in accordance with the terms of his appointment and shall, on ceasing to be a member, be eligible for re-appointment.

(2) A person may at any time by notice in writing to the Secretary of State resign his office as a member of an education association.

3. If the Secretary of State is satisfied that a member of an education association—

(a) has been absent from meetings of the association for a period longer than six consecutive months without the permission of the association, or

(b) is unable or unfit to discharge the functions of a member,

the Secretary of State may by notice in writing to that member remove him from office and thereupon the office shall become vacant.

Salaries, allowances and pensions

4.—(1) The Secretary of State may—

(a) pay to the members of an education association such salaries or fees, and such travelling, subsistence or other allowances, as he may determine, and

(b) may, as regards any member of the association in whose case the Secretary of State may so determine, pay or make provision for the payment of such sums by way of pension, allowances and gratuities to or in respect of him as the Secretary of State may determine.

(2) If a person ceases to be a member of an education association and it appears to the Secretary of State that there are special circumstances which make it right that he should receive compensation, the Secretary of State may make to that person a payment of such amount as the Secretary of State may determine.

(3) Any determination of the Secretary of State under this paragraph requires the approval of the Treasury.

Committees

5.—(1) An education association may establish a committee for any purpose.

(2) The number of the members of a committee established under this paragraph, and the terms on which they are to hold and vacate office, shall be fixed by the association.

(3) Such a committee may include persons who are not members of the association.

(4) The association shall keep under review the structure of committees established by them under this paragraph and the scope of each such committee's activities.

Delegation of functions

6. An education association may authorise the chairman or any committee established by them under paragraph 5 to exercise such of their functions as they may determine.

Proceedings

7. The validity of any proceedings of an education association or of any of their committees shall not be affected by a vacancy amongst the members or by any defect in the appointment of a member.

8. Subject to the preceding provisions of this Schedule, an education association may regulate their own procedure and that of any of their committees.

Application of seal and proof of instruments

9. The application of the seal of an education association shall be authenticated by the signature—

(a) of the chairman or of some other person authorised either generally or specifically by the association to act for that purpose, and

(b) of one other member.

10. Every document purporting to be an instrument made or issued by or on behalf of an education association and to be duly executed under their seal, or to be signed or executed by a

person authorised by the association to act in that behalf, shall be received in evidence and be treated, without further proof, as being so made or issued unless the contrary is shown.

DEFINITIONS
"education association": s.31(2).

Section 47(1)

SCHEDULE 6

CONSEQUENTIAL AMENDMENTS

Parliamentary Commissioner Act 1967 (c. 13)

1. Schedule 2 to the Parliamentary Commissioner Act 1967 shall continue to include the following entries (originally inserted by paragraph 8 of Schedule 1 to the Education (Schools) Act 1992)—

"Her Majesty's Chief Inspector of Schools in England."
"Her Majesty's Chief Inspector of Schools in Wales."

House of Commons Disqualification Act 1975 (c. 24)

2. Part III of Schedule 1 to the House of Commons Disqualification Act 1975 shall continue to include the following entries (originally inserted by paragraph 9 of Schedule 1 to the Education (Schools) Act 1992)—

"Her Majesty's Chief Inspector of Schools in England."
"Her Majesty's Chief Inspector of Schools in Wales."

Northern Ireland Assembly Disqualification Act 1975 (c. 25)

3. Part III of Schedule 1 to the Northern Ireland Assembly Disqualification Act 1975 shall continue to include the same entries as those specified in paragraph 2 above (originally inserted by paragraph 9 of Schedule 1 to the Education (Schools) Act 1992).

Education Reform Act 1988 (c. 40)

4.—(1) Section 226(2)(b) of the Education Reform Act 1988 (inspection of schools in other member States providing education for British children) shall continue to have effect with the following amendment (originally made by paragraph 7 of Schedule 4 to the Education (Schools) Act 1992).

(2) For the words from "school" to the end of the paragraph there is substituted "by, or under the direction of, one or more of Her Majesty's Inspectors of Schools for England".

Tribunals and Inquiries Act 1992 (c. 53)

5. In Schedule 1 to the Tribunals and Inquiries Act 1992, in paragraph 15 of Part I, in sub-paragraph (d) for "Schedule 3 to the Education (Schools) Act 1992" there is substituted "Schedule 2 to the School Inspections Act 1996".

Judicial Pensions and Retirement Act 1993 (c. 8)

6. In section 26(8)(h) of the Judicial Pensions and Retirement Act 1993, for "Schedule 3 to the Education (Schools) Act 1992" there is substituted "Schedule 2 to the School Inspections Act 1996".

Nursery Education and Grant-Maintained Schools Act 1996 (c. 50)

7.—(1) Schedule 1 to the Nursery Education and Grant-Maintained Schools Act 1996 shall be amended in accordance with sub-paragraphs (2) to (5).

(2) In paragraph 2(3)(c) for "the Education (Schools) Act 1992" there is substituted "the School Inspections Act 1996".

(3) In paragraph 6(2) for "section 9 of the Education (Schools) Act 1992" there is substituted "section 10 of the School Inspections Act 1996".

(4) In paragraph 10(2) for "section 12 of the Education (Schools) Act 1992; and paragraph 2 (procedure) and paragraph 3(1) (staff) of Schedule 3 to that Act" there is substituted "section 9 of the School Inspections Act 1996; and paragraph 2 (procedure) and paragraph 3 (staff) of Schedule 2 to that Act".

(5) In paragraph 14—

(a) for "paragraph (a) of sections 4 and 8 of the Education (Schools) Act 1992" there is substituted "subsection (7)(a) of sections 2 and 5 of the School Inspections Act 1996"; and

(b) for "paragraph (b)" there is substituted "subsection (7)(b)".

Section 47(2)

SCHEDULE 7

REPEALS

Chapter	*Short title*	*Extent of repeal*
1992 c. 38.	Education (Schools) Act 1992.	The whole Act except sections 16, 17 and 21(5) and paragraphs 1 and 4 to 6 of Schedule 4.
1993 c. 8.	Judicial Pensions and Retirement Act 1993.	In Schedule 6, paragraph 67.
1993 c. 35.	Education Act 1993.	Part V. Section 259. Section 299 so far as relating to section 225 or 226 of the Act. In section 306, the entries "appropriate appointing authority (in Part V)", "appropriate authority (in Part V)", "inspection by a member of the Inspectorate (in Part V)", "member of the Inspectorate (in Part V)", "section 9 inspection (in Part V)", "special measures (in Part V)" and "transfer date (in Part V)". Schedule 12. In Schedule 19, paragraph 173.

Section 47(3)

SCHEDULE 8

TRANSITIONAL PROVISIONS

Continuity of the law

1.—(1) The repeal (or revocation) and re-enactment of provisions by this Act does not affect the continuity of the law.

(2) Any subordinate legislation made or other thing done, or having effect as if done, under or for the purposes of any provision repealed and re-enacted by this Act shall, if in force or effective immediately before the commencement of the corresponding provision of this Act, have effect thereafter as if made or done under or for the purposes of that corresponding provision.

(3) Any reference (express or implied) in this Act or any other enactment or in any instrument or document—

(a) to any provision of this Act, or

(b) to things done or falling to be done under or for the purposes of any provision of this Act,

shall (so far as the context permits) be construed as including, in relation to times, circumstances or purposes in relation to which the corresponding provision repealed by this Act had effect, a reference—

(i) to that corresponding provision, or

(ii) to things done or falling to be done under or for the purposes of that corresponding provision,

as the case may be.

(4) Any reference (express or implied) in any enactment or in any instrument or document—

(a) to any provision repealed and re-enacted by this Act, or

(b) to things done or falling to be done under or for the purposes of any such provision,

shall (so far as the context permits) be construed as including, in relation to times, circumstances or purposes in relation to which the corresponding provision of this Act has effect, a reference—

(i) to that corresponding provision, or

(ii) to things done or falling to be done under or for the purposes of that corresponding provision,

as the case may be.

(5) Without prejudice to the generality of sub-paragraph (4), where a power conferred by an Act is expressed to be exercisable in relation to enactments contained in Acts passed before or in the same Session as the Act conferring the power, the power is also exercisable in relation to provisions of this Act which reproduce such enactments.

(6) Sub-paragraphs (1) to (5) have effect instead of section 17(2) of the Interpretation Act 1978 (but are without prejudice to any other provision of that Act); and sub-paragraph (1) has effect subject to any amendments of the law which give effect to recommendations of the Law Commission.

New documents referring to repealed enactments

2. Any reference to an enactment repealed by this Act which is contained in a document made, served or issued after the commencement of that repeal shall be construed, except so far as a contrary intention appears, as a reference to or (as the context may require) including a reference to the corresponding provision of this Act.

Application of sections 2(9) and 5(9)

3. Sections 2(9) and 5(9) shall not have effect in relation to anything done before they come into force.

General Note

See the Introduction and General Note to the Act.

TABLE OF DERIVATIONS

Notes:

1. This Table shows the derivation of the provisions of the Bill.

2. The following abbreviations are used in the Table:—

1992 = Education (Schools) Act 1992 (c. 38)
1993 = Education Act 1993 (c. 35)

3. The abbreviation "Law Com. Rec. No." followed by a number refers to a recommendation set out in the paragraph of that number in Appendix 1 to the Report of the Law Commission (Cm.3251).

Provision	Derivation
1	1992 s.1.
2(1) to (6)	1992 s.2.
(7)	1992 s.4.
(8) to (10)	Law Com. Rec. No. 22.
3	1992 s.3.
4	1992 s.5.
5(1) to (6)	1992 s.6.
(7)	1992 s.8.
(8) to (10)	Law Com. Rec. No. 22.
6	1992 s.7.
7(1) to (9)	1992 s.10.
(10)	Drafting.
8	1992 s.11.
9	1992 s.12.
10(1), (2)	1992 s.9(1), (2).
(3)	1992 s.9(3); 1993 Sch. 19 para. 173(1)(a).
(4)	1993 s.227(4).
(5), (6)	1992 s.9(4), (5).
(7)	Drafting.
(8)	1992 s.9(6); 1993 Sch. 19 para. 173(1)(b).
(9)	1992 s.9(7); 1993 Sch. 19 para. 173(1)(c).
11(1)	1992 s.9(7); 1993 s.204(1), (4), Sch. 19 para. 173(1)(c).
(2)	1993 s.204(1).
(3)	1992 s.9(7); 1993 s.204(4), Sch. 19 para. 173(1)(c).
(4)	1993 s.204(2).
(5)	1992 Sch. 2 para. 1.
(6)	1992 Sch. 2 para. 1; 1993 s.204(2), Sch. 19 para. 173(3).
12(1), (2)	1992 Sch. 2 para. 12(1), (2); 1993 s.205(1), (2), Sch. 19 para. 173(7); Law Com. Rec. No. 23.
(3), (4)	1992 Sch. 2 para. 12(3); 1993 s.205(3), Sch. 19 para. 173(7); Law Com. Rec. No. 23.

Provision	Derivation
13(1) to (8)	1992 Sch. 2 para. 9; 1993 s.206, Sch. 19 para. 173(5).
(9)	1992 Sch. 2 para. 1; 1993 s.204(3), Sch. 19 para. 173(3).
14	1992 Sch. 2 para. 9A; 1993 s.207, Sch. 19 para. 173(5).
15(1), (2)	1992 Sch. 2 para. 9B(1), (2); 1993 s.208(1), (2), Sch. 19 para. 173(5).
(3)	1993 s.208(3).
(4)	1992 Sch. 2 para. 9B(3); 1993 Sch. 19 para. 173(5).
(5)	1992 Sch. 2 para. 9B(4); 1993 s.208(4), Sch. 19 para. 173(5).
16	1993 s.209.
17	1993 s.210.
18	1993 s.211.
19	1993 s.212.
20(1)	1992 Sch. 2 para. 9C(1), (3); 1993 Sch. 19 para. 173(5).
(2)	1992 Sch. 2 para. 9C(2); 1993 Sch. 19 para. 173(5).
(3), (4)	1992 Sch. 2 para. 9C(4), (5); 1993 Sch. 19 para. 173(5).
21	1992 Sch. 2 para. 10; 1993 Sch. 19 para. 173(6).
22	1992 Sch. 2 para. 11; 1993 Sch. 19 para. 173(6).
23(1) to (4)	1992 s.13(1) to (3A); 1993 s.259(2).
(5) to (7)	1992 s.13(4) to (6).
(8)	1992 s.13(7); 1993 s.259(3).
(9), (10)	1992 s.13(8), (9).
24	1992 s.14.
25	1992 s.15.
26	1993 s.213.
27(1) to (8)	1993 s.214(1) to (8).
(9)	1993 s.204(2).
(10)	1993 s.214(9).
28	1993 s.215.
29	1993 s.216.
30	1993 s.217.
31	1993 s.218.
32	1993 s.219.
33	1993 s.220.
34	1993 s.221.
35	1993 s.222.
36	1993 s.223.
37	1993 s.224.
38	1993 s.225.
39	1993 s.226.
40	1993 s.227(1) to (3).
41(1), (2)	1993 s.228(1).
(3) to (5)	1993 s.228(2) to (4).
42	1992 s.18(3).
43	1992 s.20(2).
44(1)	1993 s.299(1) to (4).
(2)	1993 s.299(5).
45(1)	1992 s.19(1); 1993 s.301(1), (2).
(2)	1992 s.19(2); 1993 s.301(3).
(3), (4)	1992 s.19(3); 1993 s.301(6); Law Com. Rec. No. 24.
46(1)	1992 s.18(1); Interpretation Act 1978 (c. 30) s.17(2)(a) ("denominational education"); 1992 Sch. 2 para. 1 ("member of the Inspectorate"); 1993 ss.204(2), 305(1), Sch. 19 para. 173(3).
(2)	Drafting.
(3)	1992 s.18(2).
(4)	1992 s.18(4); 1993 s.305(3).
47	Drafting.
48(1), (2)	Drafting.
(3)	1992 s.21(4); 1993 s.308(4); drafting.
(4)	1992 s.21(6); drafting.
(5)	Drafting.

Provision	Derivation
Sch. 1	
paras. 1, 2	1992 Sch. 1 paras. 1, 2.
para. 3	1992 Sch. 1 para. 3; The Transfer of Functions (Treasury and Minister for the Civil Service) Order 1995 (S.I. 995/269) Art. 3, Sch. para. 19.
para. 4	1992 Sch. 1 para. 5.
para. 5	1992 Sch. 1 para. 6; Law Com. Rec. No. 22.
para. 6	1992 Sch. 1 para. 7.
Sch. 2	
para. 1	1992 Sch. 3 para. 1; Judicial Pensions and Retirement Act 1993 (c. 8) Sch. 6 para. 67.
para. 2	1992 Sch. 3 para. 2.
para. 3	1992 Sch. 3 para. 3(1).
Sch. 3	
para. 1	1992 Sch. 2 para. 1; 1993 Sch. 19 para. 173(3).
paras. 2, 3	1992 Sch. 2 paras. 2, 3; 1993 Sch. 19 para. 173(4).
para. 4(1)	1992 Sch. 3 para. 4(1); 1993 Sch. 19 para. 173(4).
(2)	1992 Sch. 3 para. 4(3).
(3)	1992 Sch. 3 para. 4(2).
para. 5(1)	1992 Sch. 3 para. 5(1); 1993 Sch. 19 para. 173(4).
(2)	1992 Sch. 3 para. 5(3).
(3)	1992 Sch. 3 para. 5(2).
paras. 6, 7	1992 Sch. 3 paras. 6, 7; 1993 Sch. 19 para. 173(4).
para. 8	1992 Sch. 3 para. 8.
Sch. 4	
para. 1	1992 Sch. 2 para. 13.
para. 2	1992 Sch. 2 para. 14; 1993 Sch. 19 para. 173(8).
para. 3	1992 Sch. 2 para. 15; Interpretation Act 1978 (c. 30) s.17(2)(a) ("governors' report"); 1993 Sch. 19 para. 173(9).
Sch. 5	1993 Sch. 12.
Sch. 6	
para. 1	1992 Sch. 1 para. 8.
paras. 2, 3	1992 Sch. 1 para. 9.
paras. 4 to 7	Drafting.
Sch. 7	Drafting.
Sch. 8	Drafting.

TABLE OF DESTINATIONS

Interpretation Act 1978
(c. 30)

1978	1996
s.17(2)(a) "denominational education"	s.46(1)
"governors' report"	Sched. 4, para. 3

Education (Schools) Act 1992
(c. 38)

1992	1996
s.1	s.1
2	2(1) to (6)
3	3
4	2(7)
5	4
6	5(1) to (6)
7	6
8	5(7)
9(1)	10(1), (2)
(2)	10(1), (2)
(3)	10(3)
(4)	10(5), (6)
(5)	10(5), (6)
(6)	10(8)
(7)	10(9), 11(1), (3)
10	7(1) to (9)
11	8
12	9
13(1)	23(1) to (4)
(2)	23(1) to (4)
(3)	23(1) to (4)
(3A)	23(1) to (4)
(4)	23(5) to (7)
(5)	23(5) to (7)
(6)	23(5) to (7)
(7)	23(8)
(8)	23(9), (10)
(9)	23(9), (10)
14	24
15	25
18(1)	46(1)
(2)	46(3)
(4)	46(4)
(3)	42
19(1)	45(1)
(2)	45(2)
(3)	45(3), (4)
20(2)	43

1962	1996
s.21(4)	s.48(3)
(6)	48(4)
Sched. 1, para. 1	Sched. 1, paras. 1, 2
2	Sched. 1, paras. 1, 2
3	Sched. 1, para. 3
5	Sched. 1, para. 4
6	Sched. 1, para. 5
7	Sched. 1, para. 6
8	Sched. 6, para. 1
9	Sched. 6, paras. 2, 3
Sched. 2, para. 1	ss.11(5), (6), 13(9), Sched. 3, para. 1
"member of the Inspectorate"	s.46(1)
2	Sched. 3, paras. 2, 3
3	Sched. 3, paras. 2, 3
9	s.13(1) to (8)
para. 9A	14
9B(1)	15 (1), (2)
(2)	15(1), (2)
(3)	15(4)
(4)	15(5)
9C(1)	20(1)
(2)	20(2)

1962	1996
Sched. 2—*cont.*	
para. 9C(3)	s.20(1)
(4)	20(3), (4)
(5)	20(3), (4)
10	21
11	22
12(1)	12(1), (2)
(2)	12(1), (2)
(3)	12(3), (4)
13	Sched. 4, para. 1
14	Sched. 4, para. 2
15	Sched. 4, para. 3
Sched. 3, para. 1	Sched. 2, para. 1
2	Sched. 2, para. 2
3(1)	Sched. 2, para. 3
4(1)	Sched. 3, para. 4(1)
(2)	Sched. 3, para. 4(3)
(3)	Sched. 3, para. 4(2)
5(1)	Sched. 3, para. 5(1)
(2)	Sched. 3, para. 5(3)
(3)	Sched. 3, para. 5(2)
6	Sched. 3, paras. 6, 7
7	Sched. 3, paras. 6, 7
8	Sched. 3, para. 8

Judicial Pensions and Retirement Act 1993
(c. 8)

1993	1996
Sched. 6, para. 67	Sched. 2, para. 1

Table of Destinations

Education Act 1993
(c. 35)

1993	1996
s.204(1)	s.11(1), (2)
(2)	11(4), (6), 27(9), 46(1)
(3)	13(9)
(4)	11(1), (3)
205(1)	12(1), (2)
(2)	12(1), (2)
(3)	12(3), (4)
206	13(1) to (8)
207	14
208(1)	15(1), (2)
(2)	15(1), (2)
(3)	15(3)
(4)	15(5)
209	16
210	17
211	18
212	19
213	26
214(1)	27(1) to (8)
(2)	27(1) to (8)
(3)	27(1) to (8)
(4)	27(1) to (8)
(5)	27(1) to (8)
(6)	27(1) to (8)
(7)	27(1) to (8)
(8)	27(1) to (8)
(9)	27(10)
215	28

1978	1996
s.216	s.29
217	30
218	31
219	32
220	33
221	34
222	35
223	36
224	37
225	38
226	39
227(1)	40
(2)	40
(3)	40
228(1)	41(1), (2)
(2)	41(3) to (5)
(3)	41(3) to (5)
(4)	41(3) to (5)
259(2)	23(1) to (4)
(3)	23(8)
299(1)	44(1)
(2)	44(1)
(3)	44(1)
(4)	44(1)
(5)	44(2)
301(1)	45(1)
(2)	45(1)
(3)	45(2)
(6)	45(3), (4)

1978	1996
s.305(1)	s.46(1)
(3)	46(4)
308(4)	48(3)
Sched. 12	Sched. 5
Sched. 19,	
para. 173(1)(a)	s.10(3)
(1)(b)	10(8)
(1)(c)	10(9), 11(1), (3)
(3)	11(6), 13(9), 46(1), Sched. 3, para. 1
(4)	Sched. 3, para. 2
	3
	4(1)
	5(1)
	6
	7
(5)	ss.13(1) to (8), 14, 15(1), (2), (4), (5), 20(1), (2), (3), (4)
(6)	21, 22
(7)	12(1), (2), (3), (4)
(8)	Sched. 4, para. 2
(9)	Sched. 4, para. 3

The Transfer Of Functions (Treasury And Minister For The Civil Service) Order 1995
(S.I. 1995 No. 269)

1995	1996
art.3	Sched. 1, para. 3
Sched., para. 19	Sched. 1, para. 3

Report of the Law Commission
(cm. 3251)

3251	1996
Appendix 1, No.22	ss.2(8) to (10), 5(8) to (10), Sched. 1, para. 5
No.23	12(1), (2),(3), (4)
No.24	45(3), (4)

INDEX

References are to sections and Schedules

DEER (SCOTLAND) ACT 1996

(1996 c. 58)

PART I

The Deer Commission for Scotland

An Act to consolidate the legislation relating to deer in Scotland.

[24th July 1996]

PARLIAMENTARY DEBATES

Hansard, H.L. Vol. 572, cols. 656, 1839; Vol. 574, cols. 1002, 1176. H.C. Vol. 281, col. 472.

INTRODUCTION

This Act consolidates provisions from the Deer (Scotland) Act 1959 (c. 40), the Deer (Amendment) (Scotland) Act 1967 (c. 37), the Deer (Amendment) (Scotland) Act 1982 (c. 19) and the Deer (Amendment) (Scotland) Act 1996 (c. 43). The Act deals with, *inter alia*, the Deer Commission for Scotland, conservation, control and sustainable management of deer, offences in relation to deer and enforcement and licensing of venison dealing and miscellaneous provisions.

PART I

THE DEER COMMISSION FOR SCOTLAND

The Deer Commission for Scotland

1.—(1) There shall continue to be a commission known as the Deer Commission for Scotland (in this Act referred to as "the Commission") which shall—

(a) in accordance with the provisions of this Act, further the conservation, control and sustainable management of deer in Scotland, and keep under review all matters, including their welfare, relating to deer; and

(b) exercise such other functions as are conferred on them by or under this Act or any other enactment.

(2) It shall be the duty of the Commission, in exercising their functions, to take such account as may be appropriate in the circumstances of—

(a) the size and density of the deer population and its impact on the natural heritage;
(b) the needs of agriculture and forestry; and
(c) the interests of owners and occupiers of land.

(3) The Commission shall carry out their functions in accordance with such directions of a general character as may be given by the Secretary of State.

(4) The Commission shall be appointed by the Secretary of State and shall consist of a chairman and such number of other members, being not less than nine nor more than twelve in total, as the Secretary of State considers appropriate to represent the interests of persons or organisations concerned with each of the matters mentioned in paragraph (a) of subsection (5) below; and subsections (5) and (6) below shall apply to the appointment of the members other than the chairman.

(5) Subject to subsection (4) above and subsection (6) below, the Secretary of State may appoint any person who appears to him—

(a) to have knowledge or experience of one or more of the following matters—
  (i) deer management;
  (ii) agriculture (including crofting);
  (iii) forestry and woodland management; and
  (iv) the natural heritage,

  in so far as that matter may be affected by the Commission's exercise of their functions; and
(b) generally, to be an appropriate person,

to be a member of the Commission; and, subject to subsection (6)(c) below, of the persons so appointed, at least one third shall be persons having knowledge or experience of deer management.

(6) Before making an appointment under subsection (5) above, the Secretary of State shall—

(a) afford to such organisations as appear to him to represent the interests of persons concerned with the matters mentioned in subsection (5)(a) above an opportunity to suggest the name of any person who would in their view be an appropriate person for such an appointment;
(b) consider any such suggestions; and
(c) where names have been suggested by organisations representing the interests of deer managers, select the one third of the Commission referred to in subsection (5) above from among those names.

(7) Schedule 1 to this Act (which makes supplementary provision with respect to the Commission) shall have effect.

Advice and annual reports to Secretary of State

2.—(1) The Commission shall—

(a) advise the Secretary of State on any such matter relating to the purposes of this Act as he may refer to them; and
(b) bring to his attention any matter relating to deer of which in the opinion of the Commission he ought to be apprised.

(2) The Commission shall make an annual report to the Secretary of State on the exercise of their functions under this Act.

(3) The Secretary of State shall lay a copy of the report made under subsection (2) above before each House of Parliament, together with such comments as he may think fit to make.

Power of the Commission to facilitate exercise of functions

3.—(1) The Commission shall have power—

(a) to issue guidance or advice, whether general or particular, to any person or organisation; and

(b) to conduct, or to collaborate with any person or organisation which is conducting—

(i) any research, inquiry or investigation into questions of practical or scientific importance; or

(ii) any experiment, trial or demonstration,

relating to the conservation, control or sustainable management of deer or to any other aspect of the Commission's functions.

(2) For the avoidance of doubt, it is provided that the Commission may exercise the powers conferred by subsection (1) above in relation to the general welfare of deer, in so far as that matter is not otherwise included in their functions under this Act.

Appointment of panels

4.—(1) Subject to the approval of the Secretary of State, the Commission may appoint for any locality a panel for the purposes of this section consisting of such number of persons, not exceeding nine, as they consider appropriate, one of whom shall act as chairman.

(2) Before making an appointment under subsection (1) above, the Commission may afford to such persons or organisations as they think fit an opportunity to suggest the name of any person who would in their view be an appropriate person for such an appointment.

(3) Where the Commission have sought suggestions as mentioned in subsection (2) above, they shall consider any such suggestions before making an apppointment under subsection (1) above.

(4) The Commission may appoint a member of the Commission or a member of the Commission's staff to act as observer to the panel for the purposes of—

(a) sitting with the panel at any meeting;

(b) taking part in their discussions; and

(c) informing the Commission of information arising during and decisions taken at such meetings.

(5) An observer appointed under subsection (4) above shall not be a member of the panel.

(6) The Commission may refer to any such panel any matter relating to the functions of the Commission, and it shall be the duty of the panel to advise the Commission on the matter.

PART II

CONSERVATION, CONTROL AND SUSTAINABLE MANAGEMENT OF DEER

Close seasons

Close seasons

5.—(1) The Secretary of State—

(a) shall, in relation to the female of every species of deer; and

(b) may, in relation to the male of any species of deer,

by order fix a period in each year during which no person shall take or wilfully kill or injure any deer of the sex and species named in the order, and different periods may be so fixed in relation to different species and in relation to the male and female of any species.

(2) Before making an order under subsection (1) above, the Secretary of State may consult such persons or organisations as he thinks fit, or may direct the Commission to carry out such consultation on his behalf.

(3) Where the Secretary of State has directed the Commission to carry out consultation on his behalf under subsection (2) above, they shall—

(a) report the results of that consultation, and

(b) tender such advice as they may wish in relation to the making of an order under subsection (1) above,

to him within such period as he may so direct.

(4) Where the Secretary of State or the Commission have carried out consultation under subsection (2) or (3) above the Secretary of State shall have regard to the results of that consultation, and to any advice tendered by the Commission under subsection (3) above, before making an order under subsection (1) above.

(5) Subject to sections 14 and 25 of this Act and to subsections (6) and (7) below, any person who contravenes an order made under subsection (1) above shall be guilty of an offence.

(6) Without prejudice to section 26, and subject to section 37, of this Act, and notwithstanding anything any agreement between an occupier of land and the owner thereof, the Commission may authorise the owner or the occupier of any land or any person nominated in writing by either of them to take or kill, and to sell or otherwise dispose of, any deer found on that land during the period specified in relation to that sex and species of deer in an order under subsection (1) above, where they are satisfied that—

(a) the taking or killing is necessary—

(i) to prevent serious damage to any unenclosed woodland which forms part of that land, or serious damage, whether direct or indirect, to the natural heritage generally; or

(ii) in the interests of public safety; and

(b) no other means of control which might reasonably be adopted in the circumstances would be adequate.

(7) Subject to section 37 of this Act, the Commission may, for any scientific purpose, authorise any person to take or kill deer during the period specified in relation to that sex and species of deer in an order under subsection (1) above.

Control agreements and control schemes

Control areas

6. In this Act the area to which a control agreement or a control scheme relates is, in relation to that agreement or, as the case may be, scheme, referred to as the "control area".

Control agreements

7.—(1) Subject to the following provisions of this section, where the Commission are satisfied that, on any land, deer—

(a) have caused, are causing, or are likely to cause—

(i) damage to woodland, to agricultural production, including any crops or foodstuffs, or, whether directly or indirectly, to the natural heritage generally; or

(ii) injury to livestock, whether by serious overgrazing of pastures, competing with any such livestock for supplementary feeding, or otherwise; or

(b) have become a danger or a potential danger to public safety,

and that for the prevention of further such damage, injury or, as the case may be, danger or potential danger, the deer in that locality should be reduced in number, they shall form a preliminary view, having due regard to the nature and character of the land in question, as to what measures should be taken for that reduction in number; and, for the purposes of this section and section 8 of this Act, "measures" includes the taking and removal of deer.

(2) For the purposes of subsection (1) above "the natural heritage" includes any alteration or enhancement of the natural heritage which is taking place, or is proposed to take place, either naturally or as a result of a

change of use determined by the owner or occupier of the land in question; and "damage" shall be construed accordingly.

(3) Where it appears to the Commission that the circumstances obtaining in a particular area require the complete exclusion of all deer, or of all deer of any species, from that area, they may form the view that any deer within that area should be taken, removed or killed.

(4) After they have formed—

(a) the preliminary view mentioned in subsection (1) above; or

(b) the view mentioned in subsection (3) above,

the Commission shall consult with such owners or occupiers of land as the Commission consider to be substantially interested, to secure agreement—

(i) that measures require to be taken;

(ii) as to what measures require to be taken, and within what time limit;

(iii) as to who is to carry out such measures; and

(iv) as to any other matters which appear to the Commission to be necessary for the purposes of such an agreement.

(5) Where agreement is reached on the matters mentioned in subsection (4) above the Commission shall draw up an agreement (a "control agreement") specifying the parties to it, and any such control agreement may—

(a) describe the control area by reference to a map and specify the approximate extent of that area;

(b) specify the measures which are to be taken in relation to the deer in that area or any part of it;

(c) specify, where the deer are to be reduced in number, the number and, if necessary in the opinion of the Commission, the species, sex and class, of the deer to be killed in or taken and removed from the control area or any part of it, and the limit on the number of deer of each species, sex or class to be allowed to be established in the control area or any part of it;

(d) specify the measures which are to be taken by the owners or occupiers for the time being of land in the control area or any of them for the purposes of the agreement; and

(e) set out the time limits within which the owners or occupiers are to take any such measures,

and the Commission shall send a copy of the control agreement to all the persons who were involved in the consultation referred to in subsection (4) above.

(6) The Commission and any of the parties to a control agreement may agree at any time to vary its terms.

Control schemes

8.—(1) Where the Commission are satisfied—

(a) that—

(i) it is not possible to secure a control agreement; or

(ii) that a control agreement is not being carried out; and

(b) that—

(i) deer have caused and are causing serious damage to woodland or to agricultural production, including crops and foodstuffs, or serious damage, whether directly or indirectly, to the natural heritage, or serious injury to livestock, however caused, or have become and remain a danger to public safety; and

(ii) action is necessary to prevent such serious damage, serious injury, or danger,

they shall make a scheme (a "control scheme") for the carrying out of such measures as they consider necessary for the purposes mentioned in subsection (1) or, as the case may be, subsection (3) of section 7 of this Act.

(2) Subsection (1) above does not apply in relation to any control agreement proposed or entered into for the purpose of altering or enhancing the natural heritage.

(3) A control scheme shall—

(a) describe the control area by reference to a map and specify the approximate extent of that area;

(b) specify the measures which are to be taken in relation to the deer in that area or any part of it;

(c) specify, where the deer are to be reduced in number, the number and, if necessary in the opinion of the Commission, the species, sex and class, of the deer to be killed in or taken and removed from the control area or any part of it, and the limit on the number of deer of each species, sex or class to be allowed to be established in the control area or any part of it;

(d) specify the measures which are to be taken by the owners or occupiers for the time being of land in the control area or any of them for the purposes of paragraphs (a) to (c) above;

(e) prescribe time limits within which the owners or occupiers are to take any such measures as are mentioned in paragraph (d) above;

(f) include any incidental, consequential or supplemental provisions that may be necessary.

(4) A control scheme may specify different measures to be taken by different owners or occupiers of land in the control area, and may provide for the extension of any time limit prescribed therein.

(5) Nothing in subsection (3) or (4) above shall empower the Commission to impose on any owner or occupier of land a requirement to construct a fence on his land or on any part of it against the movement of deer, and for the purposes of this section "fence" shall include any artificial obstruction.

(6) A control scheme shall require confirmation by the Secretary of State before it comes into operation; and Schedule 2 to this Act (which makes provision in relation to the making, confirmation, variation and revocation of control schemes) shall have effect.

(7) Where any control scheme has been confirmed, every owner or occupier shall take such measures as the scheme may require of him in accordance with its provisions.

(8) Where the Commission are of the opinion that any owner or occupier of land has failed to comply with subsection (7) above, they shall carry out the requirement, if they are satisfied that it is still necessary to do so; and where the carrying out of such a requirement involves the killing or taking of deer, the Commission shall have power to dispose by sale or otherwise of any deer so killed or taken.

Recovery of expenses incurred in fulfilment of control scheme

9.—(1) Where any expenses incurred by the Commission in the performance of their duty under section 8(8) of this Act exceed the amount of the proceeds of the sale of any deer killed or taken in pursuance of that performance, the excess shall be recoverable by them from the owner or occupier concerned.

(2) The Commission shall furnish to any owner or occupier concerned a statement showing—

(a) the expenses incurred in the performance of their duty under the said section 8(8);

(b) the amount received in respect of the sale of deer; and

(c) the amount recoverable from any owner or occupier under this section.

(3) Any owner or occupier who is aggrieved by a statement under subsection (2) above may, within one month of the statement having been furnished to him, appeal to the Scottish Land Court.

(4) On an appeal under subsection (3) above, the Scottish Land Court may, if it appears to them to be equitable to do so, vary the amount recoverable from the appellant.

(5) Subject to the approval of the Secretary of State, the Commission may, in any particular case, waive their right to any expenses recoverable under this section.

Emergency measures

Emergency measures to prevent damage by deer

10.—(1) This subsection applies where the Commission are satisfied—

(a) that deer—

(i) are causing serious damage to woodland or to agricultural production, including any crops or foodstuffs; or

(ii) are causing injury to livestock, whether by serious overgrazing of pastures, competing with any such livestock for supplementary feeding, or otherwise; or

(iii) constitute a danger or a potential danger to public safety;

(b) that none of their other powers is adequate to deal with the situation; and

(c) that the killing of the deer is necessary to prevent further such damage or injury or to remove the danger or potential danger.

(2) Where subsection (1) applies and the Commission are satisfied that—

(a) the deer mentioned in that subsection come from particular land; and

(b) any person having the right to kill deer on that land will forthwith undertake the killing of the deer so mentioned,

the Commission shall make a request in writing to that person to that effect.

(3) Where a request under subsection (2) above has been made to a person, the Commission shall not issue an authorisation under subsection (4) below unless it appears to them that he has become unable or unwilling to comply with the terms of the request.

(4) Subject to subsection (3) above, where subsection (1) above applies the Commission shall authorise in writing, subject to such conditions as may be specified in the authorisation, any person who in their opinion is competent to do so to follow and kill on such land as may be mentioned in the authorisation such deer as appear to that person to be causing the damage or injury or constituting the danger or potential danger.

(5) Where, as mentioned in paragraph (a)(iii) of subsection (1) above, deer constitute a danger or potential danger to public safety, and, in the opinion of the Commission or the person authorised by them under subsection (4) above, the killing of the deer would itself constitute a potential danger to public safety, the person so authorised by the Commission shall instead take and remove the deer from the land in question by such means as are appropriate.

(6) An authorisation under subsection (4) above shall remain in force from the date on which it is issued for such period, not exceeding twenty eight days, as may be specified in the authorisation.

(7) Where the Commission—

(a) intend to issue an authorisation under subsection (4) above; and

(b) are of the opinion that any person is likely to be on any land to be mentioned in that authorisation,

they shall as soon as practicable give to that person such warning of their intention as they consider necessary to prevent danger to him.

(8) The Commission shall give to the owner of any land which is to be mentioned in an authorisation under subsection (4) above such notice of their intention to issue such an authorisation as may be practicable.

(9) Without prejudice to section 16 of this Act, any notice to be served under subsection (7) or (8) above on an owner of land shall, where an agent or employee is responsible for the management or farming of the land, be duly served if it is served on the said agent or employee.

(10) Where any deer has been killed or taken and removed from land under an authorisation granted by the Commission under subsection (4) above, the Commission shall have power to dispose of it by sale or otherwise.

Application of section 10 in relation to the natural heritage

11. Section 10 of this Act shall apply in relation to the natural heritage as it applies to woodland, where the Commission are satisfied that deer are causing serious damage to the natural heritage—

(a) on enclosed land; or

(b) on unenclosed land, but only if the Commission are also satisfied that the damage is being caused by reason of the presence on the land in question of a significantly higher density of deer population than is usual in all the circumstances.

Control agreements, control schemes and emergency measures: supplementary provisions

Power of Commission to provide services and equipment and to make certain payments

12.—(1) The Commission may by agreement with any owner or occupier of land assist in or undertake, whether in pursuance of a control agreement, a control scheme or otherwise—

(a) the taking or killing of deer; and

(b) (the disposal of deer or their carcases.

(2) An agreement under subsection (1) above may make provision for the providing of equipment by the Commission.

(3) An agreement under subsection (1) above shall, unless the Commission with the approval of the Secretary of State otherwise decide, make provision for the payment of any expenses incurred by the Commission under the agreement.

(4) The Commission may make in respect of the services of any person, who is not a member of staff of the Commission, authorised by them under section 10 of this Act such payment as may be agreed.

Offences in relation to Part II

13.—(1) Any person who refuses or wilfully fails to comply with any requirement laid upon him by a control scheme shall be guilty of an offence.

(2) A person who wilfully obstructs any person acting in the execution of this Part of this Act or of any authorisation issued under this Part, other than an authorisation under subsection (6) or (7) of section 5 of this Act, shall be guilty of an offence.

Limitation of criminal liability

14.—(1) Subject to subsections (2) to (4) below, where a person performs an act at the request of or under the authority of the Commission in pursuance of—

(a) a control agreement;

(b) a control scheme; or

(c) section 10 of this Act,

he shall not by reason of that act be liable to be proceeded against under this Act.

(2) Where the act is performed by a member of the staff of the Commission in pursuance of section 10 of this Act, he shall be liable to be proceeded against if the act constitutes an offence under section 17(3) of this Act.

(3) Where the act is performed by—

(a) a member of the staff of the Commission in pursuance of a control agreement or control scheme; or

(b) any other person in pursuance of a control agreement, a control scheme or section 10 of this Act,

he shall be liable to be proceeded against if the act constitutes an offence under either section 17(3) or section 18(1) of this Act.

(4) In subsections (2) and (3)(a) above, "member of the staff of the Commission" includes any person engaged by the Commission under a contract for services.

Power to enter on land

15.—(1) For the purpose of the exercise of any of the functions of the Commission under section 10 of this Act, any person duly authorised in writing by the Commission shall have power at all reasonable times to enter upon any land.

(2) A person authorised in writing by the Commission for the purposes mentioned in subsection (3) below shall have power at all reasonable times to enter upon any land where—

(a) notice has been given to the owner and to the occupier of the land that it is proposed to enter during a period specified in the notice, not exceeding one month beginning a least fourteen days after the giving of the notice; and

(b) the exercise of that power takes place within the period so specified.

(3) The purposes for which a person may be authorised by the Commission are—

(a) the taking of a census of deer in any area in pursuance of their functions under section 1(1) of this Act;

(b) the determination of whether any of their functions under section 7 or 8 of this Act should be exercised;

(c) the exercise of any such function under the said section 7 or 8;

(d) the determination of how far and in what manner any requirement placed on any person by virtue of this Part of this Act has been complied with.

(4) Any person who proposes to exercise any power of entry conferred by this section shall, if so required, produce the written document authorising him for such purpose.

Service of notices

16.—(1) Subject to the provisions of this section, any notice for the purposes of this Act shall be in writing, and any notice or other document required or authorised by or under this Act to be given to or served on any person shall be duly given or served if it is delivered to him or left at his proper address or sent to him by post.

(2) Any such notice or other document required or authorised to be served on any person for the purposes of this Act shall be duly served, if that person is an incorporated company or body, if it is served on the clerk or secretary of that company or body.

(3) For the purposes of this section and section 7 of the Interpretation Act 1978, the proper address of any person on whom any such notice or document is to be served shall, in the case of the clerk or secretary of any incorporated company or body, be that of the registered or principal office of such

company or body, and in any other case be the last known address of the person in question.

(4) Where any notice or other document is to be given to or served on a person as being the person having any interest in land and it is not practicable after reasonable inquiry to ascertain his name or address, the notice or document may be given or served by addressing it to him by the description of the person having that interest in the land (naming it) and delivering the notice or document to some responsible person on the land or by affixing it, or a copy of it, to some conspicuous object on the land.

(5) Nothing in this section shall require the Commission to give written notice of their intention to issue an authorisation in pursuance of section 10 of this Act.

PART III

OFFENCES IN RELATION TO DEER

Unlawful killing, taking and injuring of deer

17.—(1) Subject to section 25 of this Act, any person who, without legal right to take or kill deer or without permission from a person having such right, takes or wilfully kills or injures deer on any land shall be guilty of an offence.

(2) Subject to section 25 of this Act, any person who, without legal right to take or kill deer on any land or without permission from a person having such right, removes any deer carcase from that land shall be guilty of an offence.

(3) Subject to section 25 of this Act, any person who wilfully kills or injures any deer otherwise than by shooting shall be guilty of an offence.

(4) In subsection (3) above "shooting" means discharging a firearm of a class prescribed in an order under section 21(1) of this Act.

Taking or killing at night

18.—(1) Subject to sections 25 and 41(2) of this Act and to subsection (2) below, any person who takes or wilfully kills or injures deer between the expiration of the first hour after sunset and the commencement of the last hour before sunrise shall be guilty of an offence.

(2) Notwithstanding anything contained in any agreement between the occupier of agricultural land or of woodland and the owner thereof, but subject to section 37 of this Act, the Commission may authorise such an occupier or any person nominated in writing by such an occupier to take or kill, and to sell or otherwise dispose of, any deer on any such land or woodland during the period specified in subsection (1) above, where they are satisfied that—

(a) the taking or killing is necessary to prevent serious damage to crops, pasture, human or animal foodstuffs, or to woodland; and

(b) no other means of control which might reasonably be adopted in the circumstances would be adequate.

Use of vehicles to drive deer

19.—(1) Subject to section 41(2) of this Act and to subsection (2) below, any person who uses a vehicle to drive deer on any land with the intention of taking, killing or injuring them shall be guilty of an offence.

(2) Subject to section 37 of this Act, the Commission may authorise the owner of any land which deer are on, or any person nominated in writing by him, to use any vehicle to drive deer in order to take or kill them for the purposes of deer management.

(3) In subsection (2) above—

"deer management" does not include driving deer in the course of any sporting activity; and "vehicle" does not include any aircraft or hovercraft.

Other offences connected with moving vehicles

20.—(1) Subject to sections 25 and 41(2) of this Act and to subsection (2) below, any person who—

(a) discharges any firearm, or discharges or projects any missile, from any moving vehicle at any deer; or

(b) uses any aircraft for the purposes of transporting any live deer other than in the interior of the aircraft,

shall be guilty of an offence.

(2) Nothing in subsection (1)(b) above shall make unlawful anything done by, or under the supervision of, a veterinary surgeon or practitioner.

(3) In subsection (2) above—

"veterinary practitioner" means a person who is for the time being registered in the supplementary register; and

"veterinary surgeon" means a person who is for the time being registered in the register of veterinary surgeons.

Firearms and ammunition

21.—(1) The Secretary of State shall have power to make such order as he thinks fit regarding the classes of firearms, ammunition, sights and other equipment which may lawfully be used in connection with killing or taking deer, and the circumstances in which any class of firearms, ammunition, sights or other equipment may be so used.

(2) Before making an order under subsection (1) above the Secretary of State shall consult any organisations which in his opinion represent persons likely to be interested in or affected by the order.

(3) Any person who fails to comply with an order under subsection (1) above shall be guilty of an offence.

(4) No order shall be made under this section unless a draft of the order has been laid before Parliament and approved by a resolution of each House of Parliament.

(5) Any person who uses any firearm or any ammunition for the purpose of wilfully injuring any deer shall be guilty of an offence.

Offences committed by more than one person

22. Where two or more persons acting together do any act which would constitute an offence under any of sections 17 to 21 of this Act, every such person shall be guilty of an offence.

Illegal possession of deer

23.—(1) A person who is in possession of a deer or of firearms or ammunition in circumstances which make it reasonable to infer that—

(a) he obtained the deer by committing a relevant offence; or

(b) he had used the firearm or ammunition for the purpose of committing a relevant offence; or

(c) he knew that—

(i) a relevant offence had been committed in relation to the deer; or

(ii) the firearm or ammunition had been used for the purpose of committing a relevant offence,

shall be guilty of an offence.

(2) It shall be a defence in proceedings for an offence under subsection (1) above for the accused to show that no relevant offence had been committed, or that he had no reason to believe that such an offence had been committed.

(3) For the purposes of this section a "relevant offence" is an offence under any of sections 5 or 17 to 22 of this Act.

(4) A person shall not be guilty of an offence under subsection (1) above in respect of anything done in good faith, including conduct which would otherwise constitute a relevant offence in relation to any deer, where what is done is done for purposes connected with the prevention or detection of crime or the investigation or treatment of disease.

(5) It shall be lawful to convict a person charged under subsection (1) above on the evidence of one witness.

Attempts to commit offences

24. Without prejudice to the operation of section 294 of, and paragraph 10 of Schedule 3 to, the Criminal Procedure (Scotland) Act 1995, any person who—

(a) attempts to commit; or

(b) does any act preparatory to the commission of,

an offence under section 5(5) or this Part of this Act shall be guilty of an offence.

Exemption for certain acts

Action intended to prevent suffering

25. A person shall not be guilty of an offence against this Act or any order made under this Act in respect of any act done for the purpose of preventing suffering by—

(a) an injured or diseased deer; or

(b) by any deer calf, fawn or kid deprived, or about to be deprived, of its mother.

Right of occupier in respect of deer causing serious damage to crops etc. on certain ground

26.—(1) Notwithstanding anything contained in section 5 of this Act, it shall be lawful for a person to whom this subsection applies to take or kill, and to sell or otherwise dispose of, any deer found, as the case may be, on—

(a) arable land, improved permanent pasture (other than moorland) and land which has been regenerated so as to be able to make a significant contribution to the productivity of a holding which forms part of that agricultural land; or

(b) on enclosed woodland,

where the occupier has reasonable ground for believing that serious damage will be caused to crops, pasture or human or animal foodstuffs on that agricultural land, or to that woodland, if the deer are not taken or killed.

(2) Subsection (1) above applies to the occupier in person and, if duly authorised in writing by the occupier for the purposes of that subsection, to any of—

(a) the owner in person;

(b) the owner's employees;

(c) the occupier's employees, or any other person normally resident, on the land;

(d) any other person approved in writing by the Commission as a fit and competent person for the purpose.

(3) Nothing contained in any agreement between an occupier of agricultural land or enclosed woodland and the owner of that land shall prohibit any act made lawful by subsection (1) above.

(4) Any authority given to a person under subsection (2) above shall expire—

(a) at the end of such period as the occupier may specify in it;
(b) when a person to whom it was given under paragraphs (b) or (c) of that subsection ceases to be in the employment of the owner or, as the case may be, the occupier, or ceases to be normally resident on the land;
(c) when a person to whom it was given under paragraph (d) of that subsection ceases to be so approved;
(d) if the occupier revokes it.

PART IV

ENFORCEMENT, LICENSING OF VENISON DEALING AND MISCELLANEOUS PROVISIONS

Enforcement

Powers of search and seizure

27.—(1) A constable may seize any deer liable to be forfeited on conviction of an offence under this Act.

(2) Where a sheriff or any justice of the peace is satisfied by information on oath that—
(a) there is reasonable ground to suspect a relevant offence to have been committed; and
(b) evidence of the commission of the offence is to be found on any premises or in any vehicle,
he may grant a warrant authorising any constable at any time or times within one week of the date of such warrant to enter, if necessary by force, the said premises and every part thereof or the said vehicle for the purpose of detecting the offence.

(3) A constable authorised by a warrant granted under subsection (2) above may—
(a) search every person who is found in, or whom he has reasonable ground to believe to have recently left or to be about to enter the premises or, as the case may be, vehicle to which the warrant relates; and
(b) seize any article found on the premises, or in the vehicle, or on any such person which he has reasonable grounds for believing to be evidence of the commission of a relevant offence.

(4) Where a constable has reasonable grounds to—
(a) suspect that—
(i) a relevant offence has been committed; and
(ii) evidence of the commission of the offence is to be found in any vehicle; and
(b) believe that by reason of urgency or other good cause it is impracticable to apply for a warrant to search such a vehicle,
he may stop and search that vehicle, and may exercise the same power of search and seizure in relation to it as might be conferred under subsection (2) above by a warrant of the sheriff or of a justice of the peace.

(5) In subsections (2) to (4) above, a "relevant offence" is an offence under Part III, or under section 36(1) or (4), of this Act.

(6) No search of a female person shall be carried out in pursuance of any search authorised by this section except by a female person.

Power of arrest

28. Where any person is found committing an offence under Part III of this Act, any constable may arrest that person.

Offences by bodies corporate

29. Where an offence under this Act has been committed by a body corporate and it is proved to have been committed with the consent or connivance of, or to be attributable to any neglect on the part of, any director, manager, secretary or other similar officer of the body corporate, or any person purporting to act in such capacity, he, as well as the body corporate, shall be deemed to be guilty of that offence and shall be liable to be proceeded against and punished accordingly.

Power of court on trial for one offence to convict of another

30. If, upon a trial for an offence under any of sections 5, 17, 18, 19, 20, 21, 22 or 23 of this Act, or any rule of law relating to reset, the court is—

(a) not satisfied that the accused is guilty of the offence charged, but

(b) satisfied that he is guilty of another of those offences,

it may acquit him of the offence charged but find him guilty of the other offence and he shall then be liable to the same punishment as for that other offence.

Powers of court on conviction for offences

31.—(1) Where a person is convicted of an offence under an enactment specified in column 1 and described in column 2 of the Table set out in Schedule 3 to this Act, he shall be liable—

(a) on summary conviction, to a penalty not exceeding the maximum penalty set out in column 3(a) of that Table in relation to that offence; and

(b) on conviction on indictment, to a penalty not exceeding the maximum set out in column 3(b) of that Table in relation to that offence.

(2) Where a person is convicted of an offence under any of sections 17 to 23 of this Act, the court shall have power (in addition to any other power) to cancel any firearm or shotgun certificate held by him.

(3) Where a court cancels a firearm or shotgun certificate under subsection (2) above—

(a) the court shall cause notice in writing of that fact to be sent to the chief constable by whom the certificate was granted;

(b) the chief constable shall by notice in writing require the holder of the certificate to surrender it; and

(c) if the holder of the certificate fails to surrender the certificate within twenty one days from the date of that requirement, he shall be guilty of an offence.

(4) Where a person is convicted of an offence under any of sections 5(5), 17(1), (2) or (3), 18(1), 20(1), 22 or 23(1) of this Act, he shall be liable to the forfeiture of any deer illegally taken, killed or removed by him or in his possession at the time of the offence.

(5) Where a person is convicted of an offence under Part III or section 36 of this Act, the court shall have power to disqualify him from holding or obtaining a licence under section 33 of this Act.

Disposal of deer liable to forfeiture

32.—(1) Where any deer seized under section 27(1) of this Act is liable to forfeiture the person by whom it is seized may sell it and the net proceeds of the sale shall be liable to forfeiture in the same manner as the deer sold.

(2) A person shall not be subject to any liability on account of his neglect or failure to exercise the power conferred on him by subsection (1) above.

Licensing of dealing in venison

Licences to deal in venison

33.—(1) A council may grant to any person whom they shall think fit a licence to deal in venison (which shall continue to be known as a "venison dealer's licence").

(2) The Secretary of State shall have power by order to regulate—

(a) applications for venison dealers' licences and the manner in which they are to be dealt with (including power to authorise councils to charge fees in respect of such applications); and

(b) the procedure—

(i) by which venison dealers' licences may be surrendered; and

(ii) for handing in of licences where a court has ordered their forfeiture or the holders have ceased to deal in venison.

(3) The Secretary of State may in regulations under subsection (2) above apply any provision of Schedule 1 to the Civic Government (Scotland) Act 1982, as he thinks fit.

(4) A venison dealer's licence shall be valid for three years (unless the dealer has been disqualified from holding a licence by reason of his conviction of an offence under this Act), and may be renewed provided he is not at the time of the application subject to such disqualification.

(5) Every council which grants a venison dealer's licence shall cause to be sent to the Commission as soon as may be a copy of the licence.

(6) Every council by whom venison dealers' licences are granted shall as soon as may be after the first day of January in each year make a return to the Commission of the names and addresses of the persons who on that day held venison dealer's licences issued by the council.

(7) In this section and sections 34 to 36 "venison" means the carcase or any edible part of the carcase of a deer, and "deer" means deer of any species, whether or not deer within the meaning of section 45 of this Act, and includes farmed deer.

(8) In this section and section 36 of this Act "council" means a council constituted under section 2 of the Local Government etc. (Scotland) Act 1994.

Records kept by venison dealers

34.—(1) Every licensed venison dealer shall keep a book in which shall be entered records in the prescribed form of all purchases and receipts of venison by him and shall enter in such book forthwith the prescribed particulars of such purchases and receipts.

(2) Any person authorised in writing in that behalf by the Secretary of State or by the Commission (an "authorised person") or any constable, may inspect any book kept in pursuance of subsection (1) above.

(3) An authorised person shall show his written authority when so requested.

(4) A licensed venison dealer shall produce for inspection by an authorised person or constable—

(a) any book kept in pursuance of subsection (1) above;

(b) all invoices, consignment notes, receipts and other documents (including copies of them where the originals are not available) which may be required to verify any entry in such book; and

(c) all venison in his possession or under his control, or on premises or in vehicles under his control,

and shall allow the authorised person or constable to take copies of such book or document or extracts therefrom.

(5) Every book kept in pursuance of subsection (1) above shall be kept until the end of the period of three years beginning with the day on which the

last entry was made in the book and any such documents as are mentioned in subsection (4)(b) above shall be kept for a period of three years beginning with the date of the entry to which they refer.

(6) In this section "prescribed" means prescribed by order.

Reciprocal arrangements

35. A licensed venison dealer who has purchased or received venison from another licensed venison dealer or from a licensed game dealer within the meaning of section 10(5) of the Deer Act 1991 shall be deemed to have complied with the requirements of section 34 of this Act if he has recorded in his book kept in pursuance of subsection (1) of that section—

(a) that the venison was so purchased or received;

(b) the name and address of the other licensed venison dealer or of the licensed game dealer;

(c) the date when the venison was so purchased or received;

(d) the number of carcases and sex of the venison; and

(e) the species of deer, provided that it is possible to identify it.

Offences in connection with venison dealing

36.—(1) Subject to subsection (2) below, any person who—

(a) sells, offers or exposes for sale; or

(b) has in his possession, transports or causes to be transported for the purpose of sale at any premises,

any venison shall be guilty of an offence.

(2) A person is not guilty of an offence under subsection (1) above if—

(a) he is a licensed venison dealer; or

(b) he does the act constituting the offence for the purpose of selling to a licensed venison dealer; or

(c) he has purchased the venison from a licensed venison dealer.

(3) In subsection (2) above "licensed venison dealer" means the holder of a venison dealer's licence granted by the council within whose area the sale, offer or exposure for sale takes place, or where the premises concerned are situated.

(4) Any person who—

(a) sells, offers or exposes for sale;

(b) has in his possession for the purpose of sale at any premises;

(c) transports for the purpose of sale; or

(d) purchases or offers to purchase or receives,

the carcase of a deer, or any part of such a carcase, which he knows or has reason to believe has been killed unlawfully shall be guilty of an offence.

(5) Any licensed venison dealer who fails to comply with any provision of section 34 of this Act or who knowingly or recklessly makes in any book or document he is required to keep under that section an entry which is false or misleading in any material particular shall be guilty of an offence.

(6) Any person who obstructs an authorised person or a constable making an inspection under section 34 of this Act shall be guilty of an offence.

(7) In this section "sale" includes barter, exchange and other transactions by which venison is disposed of for value.

Further powers of the Commission

Restrictions on granting of certain authorisations

37.—(1) The Commission shall not grant an authorisation under any of sections 5(6) or (7), 18(2) or 19(2) of this Act (in subsections (2) to (5) below referred to as an "authorisation") unless they are satisfied that the person concerned is a fit and competent person to receive an authorisation under that provision.

(2) An authorisation shall—

(a) be in writing; and

(b) specify the duration of its validity.

(3) No authorisation shall be granted under section 18(2) or 19(2) of this Act unless a relevant code of practice has been published under subsection (5) below, and any such authorisation shall contain a condition that the person concerned shall comply with the relevant provisions of any such code.

(4) An authorisation may contain such conditions, other than that mentioned in subsection (3) above, as the Commission think fit.

(5) The Commission shall prepare and publish, and from time to time revise, a code of practice for—

(a) night shooting; and

(b) the use of vehicles for the purposes of deer management, within the meaning of section 19(2) of this Act,

to which they shall have regard when exercising their power under section 18(2) or, as the case may be, section 19(2) of this Act.

Limitation on requirement to obtain game licence

38. Any person authorised or required by the Commission to kill any deer under this Act shall not be required to obtain for that purpose a licence to kill game.

Deer killed under the authority of the Commission

39. Without prejudice to sections 8(8), 9, 10(10) and 12(1) of this Act, the Commission shall have no power to dispose of deer taken or killed under their authority.

Power of Commission to require return of number of deer killed

40.—(1) The Commission may, for the purposes of any of their functions, by notice served on the owner or occupier of any land require him to make a return, in such form as the Commission may require, showing the number of deer of each species and of each sex which to his knowledge have been taken or killed on the land.

(2) A notice served under subsection (1) above shall—

(a) be in writing;

(b) specify a period, immediately preceding the date of service of the notice, for which the return must be completed.

(3) A period specified by virtue of subsection (2)(b) above shall not exceed five years.

(4) Any person on whom a notice under subsection (1) above has been served who—

(a) fails without reasonable cause to make the required return within thirty-six days after the service of the notice; or

(b) in making the return knowingly or recklessly furnishes any information which is false in a material particular,

shall be guilty of an offence.

Miscellaneous and general provisions

Savings for certain rights

41.—(1) Nothing in Parts I or II (except section 5) of this Act or anything done thereunder shall preclude any occupier of any land from recovering any compensation for damage caused by deer which he would have been entitled to recover if this Act had not been passed.

(2) Nothing in sections 18(1), 19(1) or 20(1)(a) of this Act shall be construed as prohibiting—

(a) a person having a legal right to take deer on any land; or

(b) a person having permission in writing from any such person as is mentioned in paragraph (a) above,

from taking a deer on that land in any manner which does not cause it unnecessary suffering.

Information to be supplied to owner of certain land

42. The occupier of any agricultural land or enclosed or unenclosed woodland shall supply, as soon as practicable after being requested to do so by the owner of the land, information to the owner as to the number, sex and species of deer taken or killed by him or by any other person, other than the owner or his employees, authorised or nominated by him under or by virtue of section 5(6), 18(2) or 26(2) of this Act within the period of twelve months immediately preceding the request.

Application of Act to farmed deer

43.—(1) Subject to subsections (2) to (4) below, this Act does not apply in respect of farmed deer.

(2) The following provisions of this Act apply as respects farmed deer—

(a) subsections (3) and (4) of section 17;

(b) section 21;

(c) sections 33 to 36;

(d) section 45.

(3) The provisions of sections 24 and 27 to 32 of this Act shall apply in respect of an offence committed by virtue of subsection (2) above.

(4) In this section "farmed deer" means deer of any species which are on agricultural land enclosed by a deer-proof barrier and are kept on that land by any person as livestock.

Application of Act to the Crown

44.—(1) This Act shall apply, subject to such modifications as may be prescribed, to land an interest in which belongs to Her Majesty in right of the Crown and land an interest in which belongs to a government department or is held in trust for Her Majesty for the purposes of a government department.

(2) In subsection (1) above, "prescribed" means prescribed in regulations made by the Secretary of State under this Act.

Interpretation

45.—(1) In this Act, unless the context otherwise requires—

"agricultural land" has the meaning given by the Agricultural Holdings (Scotland) Act 1991;

"ammunition" and "firearm" have the meanings respectively given in the Firearms Act 1968;

"animal foodstuffs", for the purposes of sections 18(2) and 26 of this Act, includes foodstuffs intended for consumption by farmed deer;

"control agreement" has the meaning given by section 7 of this Act;

"control area" has the meaning given by section 6 of this Act;

"control scheme" has the meaning given by section 8 of this Act;

"deer" means fallow deer, red deer, roe deer and sika deer and any other species of deer specified in an order made under subsection (2) below and includes any hybrid of those species and, where appropriate, the carcase of any deer or any part of it;

"deer management" includes the management of deer for sporting purposes;

"deer proof barrier" means a barrier which will, having regard to the character and nature of the land, prevent the entry of deer on to or, as the case may be, the escape of deer from any land;

"enclosed" means enclosed by a stock-proof fence or other barrier, and "unenclosed" shall be construed accordingly;

"fallow deer" means deer of the species *Dama dama*;

"farmed deer" has the meaning given in section 43 of this Act;

"functions" includes powers and duties;

"land" does not include a dwelling house or any yard, garden, outhouses and pertinents belonging thereto or usually enjoyed therewith;

"livestock" has the meaning given by the Agriculture (Miscellaneous Provisions) Act 1968 and, for the purposes of sections 7, 8 and 10 of this Act, includes farmed deer;

"natural heritage" includes flora and fauna, geological and physiographical features and the natural beauty and amenity of the countryside;

"occupier" in relation to any land includes any tenant or sub-tenant, whether in actual occupation of the land or not;

"owner" in relation to any land includes any person who under the Land Clauses Acts would be enabled to sell and convey the land to promoters of an undertaking;

"red deer" means deer of the species *Cervus elaphus*;

"roe deer" means deer of the species *Capreolus capreolus*;

"sika deer" means deer of the species *Cervus nippon*;

"species" includes any hybrid of different species of deer;

"take", in relation to deer, means take alive, and cognate expressions shall be construed accordingly;

"vehicle" includes an aircraft, hovercraft or boat; and

"woodland" means land on which trees are grown, whether or not commercially, and includes any such trees and any vegetation planted or growing naturally among such trees on that land.

(2) The Secretary of State may, by order, specify other species of deer which are to be "deer" for the purposes of subsection (1) above.

Financial provisions

46. The expenses of the Commission shall be defrayed by the Secretary of State, and any sums received by them shall be paid to the Secretary of State.

Orders, regulations etc.

47.—(1) Subject to section 21(4) of this Act, any order or regulations made under this Act shall be made by statutory instrument which shall be subject to annulment in pursuance of a resolution by either House of Parliament.

(2) Any order made under this Act may be varied or revoked by a subsequent order made in the like manner.

Short title, consequential amendments, repeals, extent and commencement

48.—(1) This Act may be cited as the Deer (Scotland) Act 1996.

(2) Schedule 4 (which makes provisions consequential on this Act) and Schedule 5 (which repeals provisions consolidated by this Act) shall have effect.

(3) Subject to subsection (4) below, this Act shall extend to Scotland only.

(4) The amendments contained in Schedule 4 and the repeals contained in Schedule 5 have the same extent as the enactments therein amended or, as the case may be, repealed.

(5) Schedule 6 (which contains transitional and transitory provisions and a saving) shall have effect.

(6) This Act shall come into force at the expiry of the period of one month beginning with the date on which the Deer (Amendment) (Scotland) Act 1996 comes into force.

SCHEDULES

Section 1(7)

SCHEDULE 1

DEER COMMISSION FOR SCOTLAND: SUPPLEMENTARY PROVISIONS

1. The Commission shall be a body corporate and shall have a common seal.

2.—(1) Every member of the Commission shall hold and vacate office in accordance with the terms of the instrument under which he is appointed.

(2) Notwithstanding anything in an instrument of appointment, any member of the Commission may resign his office by a notice given under his hand to the Secretary of State.

(3) A member of the Commission who has ceased to hold office shall be eligible for re-appointment.

3. If the Secretary of State is satisfied that the chairman or a member of the Commission—

(a) has had his estate sequestrated, has been adjudged bankrupt, has made an arrangement with his creditors, or has granted a trust deed for his creditors or has made a composition contract with his creditors;

(b) is incapacitated by reason of physical or mental illness;

(c) has been absent from meetings of the Commission for a period of more than three consecutive months without the permission of the Commission or of the Secretary of State; or

(d) is otherwise unable or unfit to discharge the functions of a member of the Commission, or is unsuitable to continue as chairman,

the Secretary of State shall have power to remove him from his office.

4. Where a person ceases to be a member of the Commission otherwise than on the expiry of his term of office and it appears to the Secretary of State that there are special circumstances which make it right for that person to receive compensation, the Secretary of State may make to that person a payment of such amount as the Secretary of State may determine.

5. The Secretary of State may make such provision, if any, as he may determine for the payment of pensions to or in respect of members of the Commission.

6. The Secretary of State—

(a) shall pay to—

(i) the chairman of the Commission such remuneration and such allowances; and

(ii) the other members of the Commission such allowances; and

(b) may pay to other member of the Commission such remuneration,

as he may determine.

7. The Commission may pay to the members of any panel appointed in pursuance of section 4 of this Act the like allowances as are payable by the Secretary of State to members of the Commission under paragraph 6 above.

Meetings and proceedings of the Commission

8. The quorum of the Commission shall be five or such larger number as the Commission may from time to time determine.

9. The proceedings of the Commission shall not be invalidated by—

(a) any vacancy in the membership of the Commission; or

(b) any defect in the appoint of any member of the Commission.

10. If at any meeting of the Commission the votes are equally divided on any question, the person acting as chairman of the meeting shall have a second or casting vote.

11. Subject to paragraphs 8 to 10 above, the Commission shall have power to regulate their own procedure and that of any panel appointed by them.

Office and staff of the Commission

12. The Commission shall have an office at which communications and notices will be received.

13. The Secretary of State may provide the services of such staff as the Commission may require.

Section 8(6)

SCHEDULE 2

Provisions as to control schemes

Part I

Procedure for making control schemes

1. Where the Commission decide to make a control scheme they shall—

(a) serve on every owner and every occupier of land on whom the scheme proposes to impose any requirement—

(i) a copy of the said scheme, together with

(ii) a notice stating that any such owner or occupier may, within twenty-eight days of the service of the notice, object to the Secretary of State in such manner as may be specified in the notice to the scheme or to any provision contained in it; and

(b) publish in two successive weeks in the Edinburgh Gazette and in one or more newspapers circulating in the district in which the control area is situated a notice—

(i) stating that a control scheme has been prepared,

(ii) describing the control area,

(iii) naming a place within the district where a copy of the control scheme and of the map referred to in it may be inspected at all reasonable hours, and

(iv) stating that any person may, within twenty-eight days of the first publication of such notice, object to the Secretary of State in such a manner as may be specified in the notice to the control scheme or to any provision contained in it.

2. If no objection is duly made under paragraph 1 above or if all objections so made are withdrawn, the Secretary of State may confirm the control scheme either in the form submitted to him or, subject to paragraph 4 below, with modifications.

3. If any objection duly made under paragraph 1 above is not withdrawn, the Secretary of State shall, before deciding whether to confirm the control scheme, cause a public inquiry to be held, and after considering the objection and the report of the person who held the inquiry may confirm the scheme either in the form submitted to him or, subject to paragraph 4 below, with modifications.

4. A control scheme shall not be confirmed with any modification unless either—

(a) every—

(i) person served with a copy of the scheme by virtue of paragraph 1 above has been served with notice of the proposal to make the modification, and

(ii) other person on whom the modification, if made, would impose a requirement, has been served with a notice of the proposal to make the modification along with a copy of the said scheme,

and either has consented to it or has not, before the expiry of fourteen days from the service of the notice, notified the Secretary of State in writing that he objects to it; or

(b) the modification arises from representations made at an inquiry held under paragraph 3 above or from the findings or recommendations of the person holding that inquiry, and every person in respect of whom the modification, if made, would vary or impose a requirement has been served with a copy of the scheme as mentioned in sub-paragraph (a) above and been afforded an opportunity to appear and be heard at the inquiry.

Part II

Procedure for varying or revoking control schemes

5. On the application of the Commission, the Secretary of State may make a scheme varying a control scheme or may revoke a control scheme.

6. Before making any such variation or revocation the Secretary of State shall—

(a) serve on every owner and every occupier of land on whom the control scheme has imposed any requirement or would, if varied as proposed, impose any requirement—

(i) a draft of the scheme varying the control scheme or, as the case may be, an intimation of the proposed revocation, together with

(ii) a notice stating that any such owner or occupier may, within twenty-eight days of the service of the draft scheme or the intimation, as the case may be, object to the Secretary of State in such a manner as may be specified in the notice to the variation or revocation of the control scheme; and

(b) publish in two successive weeks in the Edinburgh Gazette and in one or more newspapers circulating in the district in which the control area is situated a notice—

(i) stating that the control scheme is to be varied or revoked, and

(ii) stating that any person may, within twenty-eight days of the first publication of such notice, object in such manner as may be specified in the notice to the making of the variation or revocation, and

(iii) naming, in the case of any such variation, a place within the district where a copy of the scheme as proposed to be varied and any map referred to in it may be inspected at all reasonable hours.

7. If no objection is duly made under paragraph 6 above or if all objections so made are withdrawn, the Secretary of State may vary or revoke the control scheme, as the case may be.

8. If any objection duly made under paragraph 6 above is not withdrawn, the Secretary of State shall, before deciding whether to make the variation or revocation as the case may be, cause a public inquiry to be held, and after considering the objection and the report of the person who held the inquiry may make the variation, either in the form of the draft or with modifications, or the revocation, as the case may be.

9. A variation of a control scheme shall not be made with any modification unless either—

(a) every—

(i) person served with a copy of the draft scheme by virtue of paragraph 6 above has been served with notice of the proposal to make the modification, and

(ii) other person on whom the modification, if made, would impose a requirement has been served with a notice of the proposal to make the modification along with a copy of the said draft scheme,

and either has consented to it or has not, before the expiry of fourteen days from the service of the notice, notified the Secretary of State in writing that he objects to it; or

(b) the modification arises from representations made at an inquiry held under paragraph 8 above or from the findings or recommendations of the person holding that inquiry, and every person in respect of whom the modification, if made, would vary or impose a requirement has been served with a copy of the draft scheme as mentioned in sub-paragraph (a) above and been afforded an opportunity to appear and be heard at the inquiry.

Part III

General procedural provisions

10. Notwithstanding anything in paragraphs 3 or 8 above, the Secretary of State may require any person who has made an objection to state in writing the grounds for it, and may disregard the objection for the purposes of this Schedule if he is satisfied that the objection is frivolous.

11. The provisions of subsection (2) to (8) of section 210 of the Local Government (Scotland) Act 1973 (which relate to the holding of local inquiries) shall apply in relation to a public local inquiry held under paragraph 3 or 8 above as they apply in relation to local inquiries held under the said section 210.

Part IV

Provisions as to the validity of control schemes and of variations and revocations of such schemes

12. On confirming a control scheme or on varying or revoking such a scheme the Secretary of State shall forthwith—

(a) serve on every person on whom a notice was required to be served under any of the following provisions—

(i) sub-paragraph (a) of paragraph 1 above;

(ii) sub-paragraph (a) of paragraph 4 above;

(iii) sub-paragraph (a) of paragraph 6 above;

(iv) sub-paragraph (a) of paragraph 9 above,

a notice stating that the scheme has been confirmed or, as the case may be, that a variation or revocation of such a scheme has been made;

(b) publish in the Edinburgh Gazette and in one or more newspapers circulating in the district in which the control area is situated a notice—

(i) stating that the scheme has been confirmed or varied or revoked, as the case may be, and

(ii) naming a place within the district where a copy of the scheme or, as the case may be, the scheme as varied, and of any maps referred to in the scheme, may be inspected at all reasonable hours.

13.—(1) Subject to sub-paragraphs (2) and (3) below, a control scheme or any variation or revocation of such a scheme shall not at any time be questioned in any proceedings whatsoever.

(2) Any person aggrieved by a control scheme or by any variation or revocation of such a scheme may apply, within six weeks from the date of the first publication of the notice referred to in sub-paragraph (b) of paragraph 12 above, to the Court of Session for the purpose of questioning its validity on the ground that—

(a) it is not within the powers of this Act; or

(b) any requirement of this Act has not been complied with.

(3) Where any such application is duly made the Court may, where it is satisfied that—

(a) the scheme or any variation or revocation of such a scheme is not within the powers of this Act; or

(b) the interests of the applicant have been substantially prejudiced by a failure to comply with any requirement of this Act,

quash the scheme or any such variation or revocation, either generally or in so far as it affects the applicant.

SCHEDULE 3

Penalties

Enactment	Offence	Penalty	
		(a) on summary conviction	(b) on conviction on indictment
5(5)	Taking, killing or injuring deer in close season	a fine of level 4 on the standard scale for each deer in respect of which the offence is committed or 3 months' imprisonment or both	
13(1)	Failure to comply with control scheme	a fine of level 4 on the standard scale or 3 months' imprisonment or both	
13(2)	Obstruction of authorised person	a fine of level 3 on the standard scale or 3 months' imprisonment or both	
17(1)	Poaching	a fine of level 4 on the standard scale for each deer in respect of which the offence is committed or 3 months' imprisonment or both	
17(2)	Removal of deer carcase without right or permission	a fine of level 4 on the standard scale for each deer carcase in respect of which the offence is committed or 3 months' imprisonment or both	
18(1)	Taking or killing at night	a fine of level 4 on the standard scale for each deer in respect of which the offence is committed or 3 months' imprisonment or both	

Enactment	Offence	Penalty	
		(a) on summary conviction	(b) on conviction on indictment
19(1)	Use of vehicle to drive deer	a fine of level 4 on the standard scale or 3 months' imprisonment or both	
20(1)	Offences connected with use of vehicles and aircraft	a fine of level 4 on the standard scale for each deer in respect of which the offence is committed or 3 months' imprisonment or both	
21(3), (5)	Offences relating to firearms and ammunition	a fine of level 4 on the standard scale for each deer in respect of which the offence is committed or 3 months' imprisonment or both	
22	Unlawful killing, taking or injuring of deer or breach of firearms order by more than one person	a fine of the statutory maximum in respect of each deer killed, taken or injured or 6 months' imprisonment or both	a fine or imprisonment for a term not exceeding 2 years or both
23(1)	Illegal possession of deer or firearms	a fine of level 4 on the standard scale or 3 months' imprisonment or both	
24(a)	Attempting to commit certain offences	the same penalty as may be imposed in respect of the offence attempted	
24(b)	Acts preparatory to the commission of certain offences	the same penalty as may be imposed for the offence, subject to a maximum of a fine not exceeding level 4 on the standard scale or 3 months' imprisonment or both	
31(3)(c)	Failure to surrender cancelled firearm or shotgun certificate	a fine of level 2 on the standard scale	

36(1)	Unauthorised sale etc. of venison	a fine of level 3 on the standard scale	
36(4)	Sale etc. of unlawfully killed deer	a fine of level 4 on the standard scale or 3 months imprisonment or both	
36(5)	Failure to comply with section 34	a fine of level 2 on the standard scale	
36(6)	Obstruction of person carrying out inspection under section 34	a fine of level 3 on the standard scale	
40(4)	Failure to make, or making false, return of number of deer killed	a fine of level 3 on the standard scale or 3 months imprisonment or both	

Section 48(2)

SCHEDULE 4

Consequential amendments

The Agriculture (Scotland) Act 1948 (c.45)

1.—(1) The Agriculture (Scotland) Act 1948 shall be amended as follows.

(2) In section 39(3A) (exclusion of certain deer from provisions of that section), for the words "section 35A of the Deer (Scotland) Act 1959" there shall be substituted the words "section 45 of the Deer (Scotland) Act 1996".

(3) In section 42A (definition of "animals for the purposes of sections 40 to 42), for the words "section 35A of the Deer (Scotland) Act 1959" there shall be substituted the words "section 45 of the Deer (Scotland) Act 1996".

The Deer Act 1991 (c.54)

2. In section 11(3) of the Deer Act 1991 (details to be recorded where venison bought from a licensed dealer), for the words "Part IIIA of the Deer (Scotland) Act 1959" there shall be substituted the words "section 33 of the Deer (Scotland) Act 1996".

Section 48(2)

SCHEDULE 5

Repeals

Chapter	*Short title*	*Extent of repeal*
1959 c.40	The Deer (Scotland) Act 1959	The whole Act.
1967 c.37	The Deer (Amendment) (Scotland) Act 1967	The whole Act.
1973 c.65	The Local Government (Scotland) Act 1973	In Schedule 27, paragraph 143.
1982 c.19	The Deer (Amendment) (Scotland) Act 1982	The whole Act.
1991 c.54	The Deer Act 1991	Section 17(5).
1996 c.43	The Deer (Amendment) (Scotland) Act 1996	The whole Act.

Section 48(5)

SCHEDULE 6

Transitional, transitory and saving provisions

Transitional provision

1. Where on the commencement of this Act a code has been published or falls to be treated as having been published under section 33A(11)(a) of the Deer (Scotland) Act 1959, that code shall be treated, after that commencement, as if it had been published under section 37(5)(a) of this Act.

Transitory provisions

2. Until an order in relation to red deer stags and hinds is made under section 5(1) of this Act, the period for the purposes of that subsection for—

(a) such stags shall be the period commencing on the twenty first day of October and ending on the thirtieth day of June; and

(b) such hinds shall be the period commencing on the sixteenth day of February and ending on the twentieth day of October.

3. Until a code is published under section 37(5)(b) of this Act, section 19(1) of this Act shall have effect as if for the word "any" in the second place where it occurs, there is substituted the word "unenclosed".

Savings

4. The amendments made by paragraphs 2 to 4 of Schedule 1 to the Deer (Amendment) (Scotland) Act 1996 shall not be affected by the repeal of that Act by this Act.

TABLE OF DERIVATIONS

Notes:

1. This Table shows the derivation of the provisions of the Bill.
2. The following abbreviations are used in the Table:—

Acts of Parliament

1959 = Deer (Scotland) Act 1959 (c.40)
1967 = Deer (Amendment) (Scotland) Act 1967 (c.37)
1982 = Deer (Amendment) (Scotland) Act 1982 (c.19)
1996 = Deer (Amendment) (Scotland) Act 1996 (c.43)

Provision	Derivation
1(1)	1959 s.1(1), substituted 1996 s.1(1).
(2)	1959 s.1(1A), inserted 1996 s.1(1).
(3)	1959 s.1(2).
(4)	1959 s.1(3), amended 1996 s.1(2).
(5)	1959 s.1(3A), inserted 1996 s.1(3).
(6)	1959 s.1(3B), inserted 1996 s.1(3).
(7)	1959 s.1(6).
2	1959 s.3, amended 1982 s.1(1), 1996 s.13(1) and Schedule 1, para. 1(3).
3	1959 s.4, substituted 1996 s.3.
4(1) to (3)	1959 s.2(1) to (1B), inserted 1996 s.2.
(4), (5)	1959 s.2(1), amended 1982 s.2(1).
(6)	1959 s.2(2).
5(1) to (5)	1959 s.21(1) to (4), (5) part, amended 1982 s.6, substituted 1996 s.8.
(6), (7)	1959 s.33A(5) and (6), inserted 1996 s.10(1).
6	1959 s.7(9), substituted 1996 s.6.
7	1959 s.7(1) to (6), substituted 1996 s.6.
8	1959 s.7(7), (8) and (10), substituted 1996 s.6; 1959 s.8, amended 1982 s.1(2), 1996 s.13(1) and Schedule 1, paragraph 1(7); 1959 s.9(1); 1959 s.10, amended 1996 s.13(1) and Schedule 1, paragraph 1(9).
9	1959 s.11(1), amended 1982 s.1(2), substituted 1996 s.13(1) and Schedule 1, paragraph 1(10)(a); 1959 s.11(2), amended 1996 s.13(1) and Schedule 1, paragraph 1(10)(b); 1959 s.11(3).
10	1959 s.6(1) to (7), (9) amended 1982 s.3(b), 1996 s.13(1) and Schedule 1, paragraph 1(5)(a); subsection (1) substituted 1982 s.3(a), 1996 s.4(2); subsection (1A) inserted 1996 s.4(2); subsection (9) inserted 1996 s.4(3).
11	1959 s.6AA, inserted 1996 s.5.
12(1) to (3)	1959 s.12, amended 1982 s.1(2), 1996 s.13(1) and Schedule 1, paragraph 1(11), part repealed 1982 s.15(2) and Schedule 3.
(4)	1959 s.6(8), amended 1996 s.13(1) and Schedule 1, paragraph 1(5)(b).
13	1959 s.9(2) part; 1959 s.17 part.
14(1) to (4)	1959 s.33(2), repealed and replaced 1967 s.2(2), amended 1996, s.13(1) and Schedule 1, paragraph 1(30)(b).
15	1959 s.15, amended 1967 s.1, 1982 s.1(2), part repealed 1996 s.13, Schedule 1, paragraph 1(13) and Schedule 2.
16	1959 s.16, amended 1996 s.13(1) and Schedule 1, paragraph 1(14).
17(1), (2)	1959 s.22, amended 1982 ss.6(c), (d), 14(1) and Schedule 1, 1996 s.13(1) and Schedule 1, paragraph 1(18).
(3), (4)	1959 s.23(2), amended 1982 s.6(a), 1996 s.13(1) and Schedule 1, paragraph 1(19)(b).
18(1)	1959 s.23(1) 1982 s.6(d), 1996 s.13(1) and Schedule 1, paragraph 1(19)(a).
(2)	1959 s.33A(2), inserted 1996 s.10(1).
19(1)	1959 s.23(3A), inserted 1982 s.9, amended 1996 s.13(1) and Schedule 1, paragraph 1(19)(e).
(2) to (3)	1959 s.33A(3), inserted 1996 s.10(1).
20	1959 s.23(2A) to (2C), inserted 1982 s.8(1), amended 1996 s.13(1) and Schedule 1, paragraph 1(19)(c).
21	1959 s.23A(1), (2), (3) part, (4) and (5) part, inserted 1982 s.10(1).
22	1959 s.24 part, amended 1982 s.10(2).
23	1959 s.25, substituted 1996 s.9.

Provision	Derivation
24	1959 s.26, amended 1996 s.13(1) and Schedule 1, paragraph 1(25)(a) and (b).
25	1959 s.33(1), amended 1967 s.2(1), 1982 s.12, 1996 s.13(1) and Schedule 1, paragraph 1(30)(a).
26	1959 s.33(3), (3A), substituted 1967 s.2(2), 1982 s.13(1), amended 1996 s.13(1) and Schedule 1, paragraph 1(30)(c).
27	1959 s.27, amended 1982 ss.14(3), 15(1) and Schedule 2, paragraph 2; part repealed 1996 s.13, Schedule 1, paragraph 1(26) and Schedule 2.
28	1959 s.28.
29	1959 s.31 part.
30	1959 s.25AA, inserted 1996 s.9.
31(1), (2), (3)	1959 s.28A(1), (2)(a), (b) and (c) part, inserted 1982 s.15(1) and Schedule 2, paragraph 1.
(4)	1959 s.21(5), amended 1982 s.14(1) and Schedule 1; 1959 s.22(1) part; 1959 s.22(2) part, inserted 1982 s.6; s.23(3), amended 1982 s.14(1) and Schedule 1; 1959 s.24 part, amended 1982 s.14(1) and Schedule 1; 1959 s.25(1) part, substituted 1996 s.9.
(5)	1959 s.25D(7), inserted 1982 s.11.
32	1959 s.30.
33	1959 s.25A, inserted 1982 s.11, amended Local Government etc. (Scotland) Act 1994 (c.39) s.180 and Schedule 13, paragraph 53(1), (2); 1959 s.25F part, inserted 1982 s.11, amended Local Government etc. (Scotland) Act 1994 (c.39) s.180 and Schedule 13 paragraph 53(1), (4), 1996 s.13(1) and Schedule 1, paragraph 1(24).
34	1959 s.25B, inserted 1982 s.11.
35	1959 s.25C, inserted 1982 s.11, amended Deer Act 1991 (c.54) s.17(5).
36	1959 s.25D part, inserted 1982 s.11, amended Local Government etc. (Scotland) Act 1994 (c.39) s.180 and Schedule 13, paragraph 53(1), (3); 1959 s.25F part, inserted 1982 s.11.
37	1959 s.33A(7) to (11), inserted 1996 s.10(1).
38	1959 s.14, amended 1982 s.1(2), part repealed 1996 s.13, Schedule 1, paragraph 1(12) and Schedule 2.
39	1959 s.13, substituted 1996 s.7.
40	1959 s.5(1), (2) part, amended 1982 ss.1(2), part repealed 1996 s.13, Schedule 1, paragraph 1(4) and Schedule 2.
41(1)	1959 s.19, amended 1982 s.1(2), part repealed 1996 s.13, Schedule 1, paragraph 1(16) and Schedule 2.
(2)	1959 s.23(5), part repealed 1996 s.13, Schedule 1, paragraph 1(19)(f) and Schedule 2.
42	1959 s.33B, inserted 1996 s.13(1) and Schedule 1, paragraph 1(31).
43	1959 s.34A, inserted 1996 s.11.
44	1959 s.34.
45	1959 s.35A, inserted 1996 s.12.
46	1959 s.18(1).
47	1959, s.35, amended 1982 s.15(1) and Schedule 2, paragraph 3.
Schedule 1	1959 Schedule 1, part repealed House of Commons Disqualification Act 1975 s.10 and Schedule 3 and Requirements of Writing (Scotland) Act 1995 s.14(2) and Schedule 5, amended 1982 s.5 and 1996 s.13(1) and Schedule 1, paragraph 1(32).
Schedule 2	1959 Schedule 2, amended Local Government (Scotland) Act 1973 s.214 and Schedule 27, paragraph 143.
Schedule 3	1959 s.5(2) part, amended 1982 s.14(1) and Schedule 1, 1996 s.13(1) and Schedule 1, paragraph 1(4)(b); 1959 s.9(2) part, amended 1982 s.14(1) and Schedule 1, 1996 s.13(1) and Schedule 1, paragraph 1(8); 1959 s.17 part, amended 1982 s.14(1) and Schedule 1, 1996 s.13(1) and Schedule 1, paragraph 1(15); 1959 s.21(5) part, amended 1982 s.14(1) and Schedule 1, substituted 1996 s.7; 1959 22(1) part, (2) part, amended 1982 s.14(1) and Schedule 1, 1996 s.13(1) and Schedule 1, paragraph 1(18)(c); 1959 s.23(3) part, amended 1982 ss.8(2), 14(1) and Schedule 1, 1996 s.13(1) and Schedule 1, paragraph 1(19)(d); 1959 s.23(3A) part, inserted 1982

Provision	Derivation
	s.9, amended 1996 s.13(1) and Schedule 1, paragraph 1(19)(e)(iii); 1959 s.23A(3) part, (5) part, inserted 1982 s.10(1), amended 1996 s.13(1) and Schedule 1, paragraph 1(20); 1959 s.24(a) part, (b) part, amended 1982 s.14(1) and Schedule 1, 1996 s.13(1) and Schedule 1, paragraph 1(21); 1959, s.25(1) part, substituted 1996 s.9; 1959 s.25D part, inserted 1982 s.11, amended 1996 s.13(1) and Schedule 1, paragraph 1(22); 1959 s.26 part, amended 1982 s.14(1) and Schedule 1, 1996 s.13(1) and Schedule 1, paragraph 1(25)(c); 1959 s.28A(2)(c) part, inserted 1982 s.15(1) and Schedule 2, paragraph 1, amended 1996 s.13(1) and Schedule 1, paragraph 1(27).
Schedule 6	
Paragraph 1	1996 s.14(3).
Paragraph 2	1996 s.10(2).
Paragraph 3	1996 s.10(3).

TABLE OF DESTINATIONS

DEER (SCOTLAND) ACT 1959
(c. 40)

1959	1996
s.1(1)	s.1(1)
(1A)	1(2)
(2)	1(3)
(3)	1(4)
(3A)	1(5)
(3B)	1(6)
(6)	1(7)
2(1)	4(1)–(3), (4), (5)
(1A), (1B)	4(1)–(3)
(2)	4(6)
3	2
4	3
5(1)	40
(2) part	40, Sched. 3
6(1)–(7)	10
(8)	12(4)
(9)	10
6AA	11
7(1)–(6)	7
(7), (8)	8
(9)	6
(10)	8
8	8
9(1)	8
(2) part	13, Sched. 3
10	8
11(1)–(3)	9
12	12(1)–(3)
13	39
14	38
15	15
16	16
17 part	13, Sched. 3
18(1)	46
s.19	s.41(1)
21(1)–(4)	5(1)–(5)
(5)	31(4)
(5) part	5(1)–(5), Sched. 3
22	17(1), (2)
(1),(2) part	31(4), Sched. 3
23(1)	18(1)
(2)	17(3), (4)
(2A), (2B), (2C)	20
(3)	31(4), Sched. 3
(3A)	19(1)
(3A) part	Sched. 3
(5)	s.41(2)
23A(1), (2)	21
(3) part	21, Sched. 3
(4)	21
(5) part	21, Sched. 3
24 part	ss.22, 31(4)
(a),(b) part	Sched. 3
25	s.23
(1) part	31(4), Sched. 3
25A	33
B	34
C	35
D part	36, Sched. 3
D(7)	31(5)
F part	ss.33, 36
25AA	s.30
26	24
part	Sched. 3
s.27	s.27
28	28
(2)(c) part	Sched. 3
28A(1)	s.31(2), (3)
(2)(a), (b)	31(2), (3)
(c) part	31(2), (3)
30	32
31 part	29
33(1)	25
(2)	14(1)–(4)
(3)	26
(3A)	26
33A(2)	18(2)
(3)	19(2)–(3)
(5), (6)	5(6), (7)
(7)–(11)	37
33B	42
34	44
34A	43
35	47
35A	45
Sched. 1, (part amended 1982 s.5; subsection (1) substituted 1982 s.3(a), 1996 s.4(2); subsection (1A) inserted 1996 s.4(2); subsection (9) inserted 1996 s.4(3))	Sched. 1
Sched. 2	Sched. 2

DEER (AMENDMENT) (SCOTLAND) ACT 1967
(c. 37)

1967	1996
s.1(2) part	s.15
2(1) (amending 1959, s.33(1))	25
(2) (repealing and replacing 1959, s.33(2))	14(1)–(4)
(substituting 1959, s.33(3), (3A))	26
(7) (substituting 1959, s.13)	39

Table of Destinations

Local Government (Scotland) Act 1973
(c. 65)

1973	1996
s.214 (amending 1959, Sched. 2)	Sched. 2
Sched. 27, para. 143 (amending 1959, Sched. 2)	Sched. 2

House of Commons Disqualification Act 1975
(c. 24)

1975	1996
s.10 (part repealing 1959, Sched. 1)	Sched. 1
Sched. 3, (part repealing 1959, Sched. 1)	Sched. 1

Deer (Amendment) (Scotland) Act 1982
(c. 19)

1982	1996
s.1(1) (amending 1959, s.3)	s.2
(2)	15
(amending 1959, s.5(1), (2) part)	40
(amending 1959, s.8)	8
(amending 1959, s.11(1))	9
(amending 1959, s.12)	12(1)–(3)
(amending 1959, s.14)	38
(amending 1959, s.19)	41(1)
2(1) (amending 1959, s.2(1))	4(4), (5)
3(b) (amending 1959, s.6(1)–(7), (9))	10
6 (amending 1959, 21(1)–(4), (5) part)	5(1)–(5)
(inserted into 1959, s.22(2) part)	31(4)
s.6(a) (amending 1959, s.23(2))	s.17(3), (4)
(c), (d) (amending 1959, s.22)	17(1), (2)
(amending 1959, s.23(1))	17(3), (4)
8(1) (inserted into 1959, s.23(2A) to (2C))	20
(2) (amending 1959, s.23(3) part)	Sched. 3
9 (inserted into 1959, s.23(3A) part)	Sched. 3
(inserted into 1959, s.23 (3A))	s.19(1)
10(1) (inserted into 1959, s.23A (1), (2), (3) part, (4), (5) part)	21
10(1) (inserted into 1959, s.23(3) part, (5) part)	Sched. 3
s.10(2) (amending 1959, s.24 part)	s.22
11 (inserted into 1959, s.25A)	33
(inserted into 1959, s.25C)	35
(inserted into 1959, s.25D and 25D part)	ss.34, 36, Sched. 3
(inserted into 1959, s.25D (7))	s.31(5)
(inserted into 1959, s.25F part)	ss.33, 36
12	s.25
13(1)	26
14(1) (amending 1959, s.5(2) part)	Sched. 3
(amending 1959, s.9(2) part)	Sched. 3
(amending 1959, s.17 part)	Sched. 3

1982	1996
s.14(1)—*cont.*	
(amending 1959, s.21(5) part)	Sched. 3
(amending 1959, s.21(5))	s.31(4)
(amending 1959, s.22(1) part)	Sched. 3
(amending 1959, s.22)	s.17(1), (2)
(amending 1959, s.22(2) part)	Sched. 3
(amending 1959, s.23(3) part)	Sched. 3
(amending 1959, s.23(3))	s.31(4)
(amending 1959, s.24 part)	31(4)
(amending 1959, s.24(a) part, (b) part)	Sched. 3
(amending 1959, s.26 part)	Sched. 3
(3) (amending 1959, s.27)	s.27
15(1) (amending 1959, s.27)	27
s.15(1)—*cont.*	
(inserted into 1959, s.28A (1), (2)(a), (b) and (c) part)	s.31(2), (3)
(inserted into 1959, s.28A(2) (c))	Sched. 3
(amending 1959, s.35)	s.47
15(2) (part repealing 1959, s.12 as amended by 1982, s.1(2), further amended by 1996 s.13(1) and Sched. 1, para. 1(11))	12(1)–(3)
Sched. 1	
(amending 1959, s.5(2) part)	Sched. 3
(amending 1959, s.9(2) part)	Sched. 3
(amending 1959, s.17 part)	Sched. 3
(amending 1959, s.21(5) part)	Sched. 3
(amending 1959, ss.21(5))	s.31(4)
(amending 1959, s.22)	17(1), (2)
Sched. 1—*cont.*	
(amending 1959, s.22(1) part)	Sched. 3
(amending 1959, s.22(2) part)	Sched. 3
(amending 1959, s.22(3) part)	Sched. 3
(amending 1959, s.23(3))	s.31(4)
(amending 1959, s.24 part)	31(4)
(amending 1959, s.24(a) part, (b) part)	Sched. 3
(amending 1959, s.26 part)	Sched. 3
Sched. 2, para. 1 (inserted into 1959, s.28A (1), (2)(a), (b) and (c) part)	s.31(2), (3)
(inserted into 1959, s.28A(2) (c))	Sched. 3
para. 2 (amending 1959, s.22)	s.27
para. 3 (amending 1959, s.35)	47

DEER ACT 1991
(c. 54)

1991	1996
s.17(5) (amending 1959, s.25C as inserted by 1982, s.11)	s.35

LOCAL GOVERNMENT ETC. (SCOTLAND) ACT 1994
(c. 39)

1994	1996
s.180 (amending 1959, s.25A as inserted by 1982, s.11)	s.33
(amending 1959, s.25D as inserted by 1982, s.11)	36
(amending 1959, s.25F part as inserted by 1982, s.11)	33
Sched. 13, para. 53(1) (amending 1959, s25A as	
Sched. 13, para. 53(1)—*cont.* inserted by 1982, s.11)	s.33
(amending 1959, s.25D as inserted by 1982, s.11)	36
(amending 1959, s.25F part as inserted by 1982, s.11)	33
para. 53(2) (amending 1959, s.25A as inserted by 1982, s.11)	33
Sched. 13—*cont.*	
para. 53(3) (amending 1959, s.25D as inserted by 1982, s.11)	36
para. 53(4) (amending 1959, s.25F part as inserted by 1982, s.11)	33

DEER (AMENDMENT) (SCOTLAND) ACT 1996
(c. 43)

1996 (c. 43)	**1996 (c. 58)**
s.1(1) (substituting 1959, s.1(1))	s.1(1)
(inserted into 1959, s.1(1A))	1(2)
(2) (amending 1959, s.1(3))	1(4)
(3) (inserted into 1959, s.1(3A))	1(5)
inserted into 1959, s.1(3B))	1(6)
2 (inserted into 1959, s.2(1)–(1B))	4(1)–(3)
3 (substituting 1959, s.4)	3
5 (inserted into 1959, s.6AA)	11
6 (substituting 1959, s.7(1)–(6))	7
(substituting 1959, s.7(7), (8))	8
(substituting 1959, s.7(9))	6
(substituting 1959, s.7(10))	8
7 (substituting 1959, s.21(5) part as amended by 1982, s.14(1) and Sched. 1)	Sched. 3
8 (substituting 1959, s.21(1)–(4), (5) part as amended by 1982 s.6)	s.5(1)–(5)
9 (substituting 1959, s.25)	23
(inserted into 1959, s.25AA)	30
(substituting 1959, s.25(1) part)	31(4), Sched. 3
10(1) (inserted into 1959, s.33A (2))	s.18(2)
(inserted into 1959, s.33A (3))	19(2)–(3)
s.10(1)—*cont.* (inserted into 1959, s.33A(5) and (6))	s.5(6), (7)
(inserted into 1959, s.33A (7)–(11))	37
(2)	Sched. 6, para. 2
(3)	Sched. 6, para. 3
11 (inserted into 1959, s.34A)	s.43
12 (inserted into 1959, s.35A)	45
13 (part repealing 1959, s.5(1), (2) part as amended by 1982, s.1(2))	40
(part repealing 1959, s.14 as amended by 1982, s.1(2))	38
(part repealing 1959, s.15 as amended by 1967, s.1(2))	15
(part repealing 1959, s.19 as amended by 1982, s.1(2))	41(1)
(part repealing 1959, s.23(5))	41(2)
(part repealing 1959, s.27 as amended by 1982, ss.14(3), 15(1) and Sched. 2, para. 2)	27
13(1)	18(1)
(amending 1959, s.3 as amended by 1982, s.1(1))	2
(amending 1959, s.5(2) part as amended by 1982, s.14(1) and Sched. 1)	Sched. 3
(amending 1959, s.6(1)–(7), (9) as amended by 1982, s.3(b))	s.10
(amending 1959, s.6(8))	12(4)
s.13(1)—*cont.* (amending 1959, s.8 as amended by 1982, s.1(2))	s.8
(amending 1959, s.9(2) part as amended by 1982, s.14(1) and Sched. 1)	Sched. 3
(amending 1959, s.10)	s.8
(substituting 1959, s.11(1) as amended by 1982, s.1(2))	9
(amending 1959, s.11(2))	9
(amending 1959, s.12 as amended by 1982, s.1(2))	12(1)–(3)
(amending 1959, s.16)	16
(amending 1959, s.17 part as amended by 1982, s.14(1) and Sched. 1)	Sched. 3
(amending 1959, s.22 as amended by 1982, ss.6(c), (d), 14(1) and Sched. 1)	s.17(1), (2)
(amending 1959, s.22(1) part, (2) part as amended by 1982, s.14(1) and Sched. 1)	Sched. 3
(amending 1959, s.23(2) as amended by 1982, s.6(a))	s.17(3), (4)
(amending 1959, s.23(2A) to (2C) as inserted by 1982, s.8(1))	20
(amending 1959, s.23(3) part as amended by 1982, ss.8(2), 14(1) and Sched. 1)	Sched. 3
(amending 1959, s.23(3A) as inserted by 1982, s.9)	s.19(1), Sched. 3

1996 (c. 43)	1996 (c. 58)
s.13(1)—*cont.*	
(amending 1959, s.23A(3) part, (5) part as inserted by 1982, s.9)	Sched. 3
(amending 1959, s.24(a) part, (b) part as amended by 1982, s.14(1) and Sched. 1)	Sched. 3
(amending 1959, s.25D part as inserted by 1982, s.11)	Sched. 3
(amending 1959, s.25F part as inserted by 1982, s.11)	s.33
(amending 1959, s.26)	24
(amending 1959, s.26 part as amended by 1982, s.14(1) and Sched. 1)	Sched. 3
(amending 1959, s.28A(2) (c) part as inserted by 1982, s.15(1) and Sched. 2, para. 1)	Sched. 3
(amending 1959, s.33(1) as amended by 1967, s.2(1))	s.25
(amending 1959, s.33(2) as repealed and replaced by 1967, s.2(2))	14(1)–(4)
(amending 1959, s.33(3), (3A) as substituted by 1967, s.2(2))	2
(inserted into 1959, s.33B)	42
14(3)	Sched. 6, para. 1
Sched. 1, para. 1(3) (amending 1959, s.3 as amended by 1982, s.1(1))	s.2
para. 1(4) (part repealing 1959, s.5(1), (2) part as amended by 1982, s.1(2))	40
Sched. 1—*cont.*	
para. 1(4)(b) (amending 1959, s.5(2) part as amended by 1982, s.14(1) and Sched. 1)	Sched. 3
para. 1(5)(a) (amending 1959, s.6(1)–(7), (9) as amended by 1982, s.3(b))	10
para. 1(5)(b) (amending 1959, s.6(8))	12(4)
para. 1(7) (amending 1959, s.8 as amended by 1982, s.1(2))	8
para. 1(8) (amending 1959, s.9(2) part as amended by 1982, s.14(1) and Sched. 1)	Sched. 3
para. 1(11) (amending 1959, s.12 as amended by 1982, s.1(2))	12(1)–(3)
para. (9) (amending 1959, s.10)	8
para. 1(10)(a) (substituting 1959, s.11(1) as amended by 1982, s.1(2))	9
para. 1(10)(b) (amending 1959, s.11(2))	9
para. 1(12) (part repealing 1959, s.14 as amended by 1982, s.1(2))	38
para. 1(13) (part repealing 1959, s.15 as amended by 1967, s.1(2))	15
para. 1(14) (amending 1959, s.16)	16
para. 1(15) (amending 1959, s.17 part as amended by 1982, s.14(1) and Sched. 1)	Sched. 3
Sched. 1—*cont.*	
para. 1(16) (part repealing 1959, s.19 as amended by 1982, s.1(2))	s.41(1)
para. 1(18) (amending 1959, s.22 as amended by 1982, ss.6(c), (d), 14(1) and Sched. 1)	17(1), (2)
para. 1(18)(c) (amending 1959, s.22(1) part, (2) part) as amended by 1982, s.14(1) and Sched. 1)	Sched. 3
para. 1(19)(a)	s.18(1)
para. 1(19)(b) (amending 1959, s.23(2) as amended by 1982, s.6(a))	17(3), (4)
para. 1(19)(c) (amending 1959, s.23(2A) to (2C) as inserted by 1982, s.8(1))	20
para. 1(19)(d) (amending 1959, s.23(3) part as amended by 1982, ss.8(2), 14(1) and Sched. 1)	Sched. 3
para. 1(19)(e) (amending 1959, s.23(3A) as inserted by 1982, s.9)	s.19(1)
para. 1(19)(f) (part repealing 1959, s.23(5))	41(2)
para. 1(19)(iii) (e) (amending 1959, s.23(3A) as inserted by 1982, s.9)	Sched. 3
para. 1(20) (amending 1959, s.23A(3) part (5) part as inserted by 1982, s.9)	Sched. 3
para. 1(21) (amending 1959, s.24(a) part, (b) part as amended by 1982, s.14(1) and Sched. 1)	Sched. 3

1996 (c. 43)	1996 (c. 58)
Sched. 1—*cont.*	
para. 1(22) (amending 1959, s.25D part as inserted by 1982, s.11) ...	Sched. 3
para. 1(24) (amending 1959, s.25F part as inserted by 1982, s.11) ...	s.33
para. 1(25)(a) (amending 1959, s.26) ...	24
para. 1(25)(b) (amending 1959, s.26) ...	24
para. 1(25)(c) (amending 1959 s.26 part as amended by 1982, s.14(1) and Sched. 1)	Sched. 3
para. 1(26) (part repealing 1959, s.27 as amended by 1982, ss.14(3), 15(1) and Sched. 2, para. 2)	s.27
para. 1(27) (amending 1959, s.28A(2) (c) part as inserted by 1982, s.15(1) and Sched. 2, para. 1)	Sched. 3
para. 1(30)(a) (amending 1959, s.33(1) as amended by 1967, s.2(1))	s.25
para. 1(30)(b) (amending 1959, s.33(2) as repealed and replaced by 1967, s.2(2))	14(1)–(4)
para. 1(30)(c) (amending 1959, s.33(3), (3A) as substituted by 1967, s.2(2)) .	26
para. 1(31) (inserted into 1959, s.33B) .	42
Sched. 2	
(part repealing 1959, s.5(1), (2) part as amended by 1982, s.1(2)) .	40
(part repealing 1959, s.14 as amended by 1982, s.1(2)) .	38
(part repealing 1959, s.15 as amended by 1967, s.1(2)) .	15
(part repealing 1959, s.19 as amended by 1982, s.1(2)) .	41(1)
(part repealing 1959, s.23(5))	41(2)
(part repealing 1959, s.27 as amended by 1982, ss.14(3), 15(1) and Sched. 2, para. 2)	27

INDEX

References are to sections and Schedules

PUBLIC ORDER (AMENDMENT) ACT 1996

(1996 c. 59)

An Act to amend the power of arrest of section 5 of the Public Order Act 1986. [17th October 1996]

PARLIAMENTARY DEBATES

Hansard, H.C. Vol. 279, col. 686; Vol. 281, col. 760. H.L. Vol. 574, cols. 620, 1497, 1689.

INTRODUCTION

This short Act amends s.5(4)(a) of the Public Order Act 1986 (c. 64) to widen police powers of arrest. The subsection now reads: "A constable may arrest a person without warrant if he engages in offensive conduct which a [formerly 'the'] constable warns him to stop".

Power of arrest

1. Section 5(4)(a) of the Public Order Act 1986 shall be amended by leaving out the word "the" and inserting the word "a".

Citation

2. This Act may be cited as the Public Order (Amendment) Act 1996.

INDEX

References are to sections

CONSOLIDATED FUND (NO. 2) ACT 1996

(1996 c. 60)

An Act to apply certain sums out of the Consolidated Fund to the service of the years ending on 31st March 1997 and 1998. [18th December 1996]

PARLIAMENTARY DEBATES
Hansard, H.C. Vol. 287, col. 187. H.L. Vol. 576, cols. 1085, 1395.

INTRODUCTION
This Act makes provision for the application of £2,424,973,000 from the Consolidated Fund for the service of the year ending on March 31, 1997 and for the application of £96,861,662,000 for the service of the year ending on March 31, 1998.

Most Gracious Sovereign,

We, Your Majesty's most dutiful and loyal subjects, the Commons of the United Kingdom in Parliament assembled, towards making good the supply which we have cheerfully granted to Your Majesty in this Session of Parliament, have resolved to grant unto Your Majesty the sums hereinafter mentioned; and do therefore most humbly beseech Your Majesty that it may be enacted, and be it enacted by the Queen's most Excellent Majesty, by and with the advice and consent of the Lords Spiritual and Temporal, and Commons, in this present Parliament assembled, and by the authority of the same, as follows:—

Issue out of the Consolidated Fund for the year ending 31st March 1997

1. The Treasury may issue out of the Consolidated Fund of the United Kingdom and apply towards making good the supply granted to Her Majesty for the service of the year ending on 31st March 1997 the sum of £2,424,973,000.

Issue out of the Consolidated Fund for the year ending 31st March 1998

2. The Treasury may issue out of the Consolidated Fund of the United Kingdom and apply towards making good the supply granted to Her Majesty for the service of the year ending on 31st March 1998 the sum of £96,861,662,000.

Short title

3. This Act may be cited as the Consolidated Fund (No. 2) Act 1996.

INDEX

References are to section number